go across (to) [Vp emph, Vpr, Vp.pr] pass from one side (of sth) (to the other). **o:** (**across**) road, bridge; river; Channel; (**to**) shop; other bank; France: [Vpr] Planks were laid so that the villagers could ***go across*** *the marshy area.* ○ [Vp.pr] 'I'm just ***going across to*** *the pub for half an hour.'* = go over (to). ⇨ get across 1, send across (to), take across (to).

make a good etc job of [Vn.pr pass rel] (*informal*) perform (a task) well, badly etc. **adj:** good, excellent, satisfactory; poor, dreadful. **o:** car, cooker; bathroom, kitchen; report, revision: *Many machines wash, rinse, spin-dry — but the new Acme Twin Speed Combination* ***makes a better job of*** *all three.* DM ○ *You can hand over to her any rewriting that needs to be done, knowing that a* ***first-class job*** *will be* ***made of*** *it.*

spray on/onto [Vn.pr pass rel] send (liquid) in a stream of tiny drops (onto sth). **O:** paint, varnish; perfume; disinfectant, weed-killer. **o:** wall; skin; plant: *The gardener* ***sprayed*** *insecticide* ***on*** *the rose-bushes* (or: ***sprayed*** *the rose-bushes* ***with*** *insecticide*). ○ *Insect repellent should be* ***sprayed onto*** *the skin to discourage mosquitoes* (or: *The skin should be* ***sprayed with*** *insect repellent* etc).

spray with [Vn.pr pass rel] ⇨ previous entry

turn in 1 [Vp, Vn.p pass adj] (cause sth to) face or curve inwards. **S** [Vp], **O** [Vn.p]: ⚠one's toes, feet, knees: *His big toe* ***turns in*** (ie towards the other toes on that foot). ○ *His feet* ***turn in*** (ie towards each other).

- optional prep in headphrase – 1.2
- codes preceding each example – 3.1.2
- preps repeated before collocates – 6.2.2
- cross-references to related verbs – 9.3
- reference to set of adjs – 1.4, 7.2.5
- style label – 4.1
- grammatical function of collocates – 6.2
- source of quotation – 7.1
- internal arrangement of collocate lists – 6.4
- transform shown in examples – 7.4
- dummy entry – 9.5
- sense number: order of entries – 2
- restricted set of collocates – 6.5

OXFORD DICTIONARY OF PHRASAL VERBS

A P Cowie

R Mackin

Oxford University Press

Oxford University Press, Walton Street, Oxford OX2 6DP

Oxford New York Toronto Delhi Bombay Calcutta Madras Karachi
Kuala Lumpur Singapore Hong Kong Tokyo Nairobi Dar es Salaam
Cape Town Melbourne Auckland

and associated companies in Berlin Ibadan Madrid

OXFORD and OXFORD ENGLISH are
trade marks of Oxford University Press

New edition. Previous edition published as
Oxford Dictionary of Current Idiomatic English Vol. 1 (1975)

First published 1993
Second impression 1993

ISBN 0 19 431284-4 (hardback)
0 19 431285-2 (paperback)

Phototypeset by Tradespools Ltd., Frome, Somerset.
Printed in Hong Kong.

CONTENTS

Acknowledgements

This new edition has benefited from generous help and expert advice from several sources. We would particularly like to thank Oxford University Press for kindly allowing us to draw on the Oxford Corpus of the English Language for numerous up-to-date items and examples, and for generously allowing us to use quotations collected for the updating of *OED*. We are also indebted to the late Isabel McCaig, co-author of the *Oxford Dictionary of English Idioms*, for the many examples of phrasal verbs which she noted while gathering material for that volume, and which are now gratefully made use of.

The revision and updating of *Phrasal Verbs* has been the responsibility of Tony Cowie. His task was greatly simplified and speeded up by being allowed the use of a computer for continuous on-screen editing of the text. Grateful thanks are due to Oxford University Press for the loan of the equipment and particularly to Bill Coumbe for technical advice and assistance.

We finally wish to express our thanks to members of the editorial staff at OUP and most particularly to Helen Warren, Gary Johns and David Wilson.

Anthony Cowie and Ronald Mackin

Abbreviations and symbols used in the dictionary

(For the initials used to identify the source of quotations ⇨ *List of sources*, pp 488–493; for the coding system used in the grammatical patterns ⇨ inside back cover)

Abbreviations

A	Adjunct (adverbial phrase)	n	noun
adj	adjective, adjectival; participial adjective	neg	negative
		nom	nominalized (noun) form
adv	adverb (phrase, clause)	no, nos	number, numbers
alt	alternative (construction, form, spelling)	**O**	Direct Object
		o	object of a preposition
attrib	attributive(ly)	pass	passive (transform)
cf, cp	compare	pl	plural
e.g.	for example	pp	past participle
emph	emphatic (transform)	prep	preposition
esp	especially	reflex	reflexive
etc	and the rest of these	rel	relative (transform)
fig	figurative(ly)	**S**	Subject
GB	British (usage)	sb	somebody
i.e.	that is	sing	singular
Inf, inf	infinitive	sth	something
-ing form	non-finite verb form in *-ing* (e g *eating, drinking*)	*to*-inf	infinitive preceded by *to* (e g *to eat, to drink*)
interr	interrogative	US	American (usage)
lit	literal(ly)	usu	usually
m	(adverbial) modifier of a particle	v	verb

Symbols

□	marks the beginning of a usage note after example sentences
○	separates individual examples from each other (⇨ 7, *Examples*)
⚠	marks words in the list of collocations (after **S, O, o** etc) that are part of a 'restricted' set (⇨ 6.5, *Collocations*)
⇨	see (the entry for, etc)
=	is equivalent to, means the same thing as
↔	means the opposite of
*	marks an unacceptable phrase, sentence etc
?	marks an unlikely phrase, sentence etc

Alphabetical list of particles and prepositions

The lists below gather together all those particles and propositions that are used to form part of the headphrases in the dictionary.

Particles

aback	down
aboard	downhill
about	downstairs
above	forth
abreast	forward(s)
abroad	home
across	in
adrift	indoors
after	in front
aground	inside
ahead	near
aloft	off
along	on
alongside	on top
apart	out
around	outside
aside	over
astray	overboard
away	past
back	round
backwards	through
before	to
behind	together
below	under
between	underground
beyond	up
by	upstairs
counter	without

Prepositions

aboard	in
about	in front of
above	inside
across	into
after	like
against	near
ahead of	of
along	off
alongside	on
among	onto
around	on top of
as	out of
as far as	outside
astride	over
at	past
before	round
behind	through
below	to
beneath	toward(s)
beside	under
between	underneath
beyond	up
by	upon
down	with
for	within
from	without

Note: **in front** (cf **before**; **behind**) and **on top** (cf **under**) are regarded as the equivalent of *particles* which are written as a single word; **ahead of**, **as far as** (cf **to**), **in front of**, **on top of** and **out of** (cf **from**; **into**) are regarded as the equivalent of *prepositions* which are written as a single word.

PHRASAL VERBS – a brief introduction

This introduction is a brief explanation of the way phrasal verbs and more complex idioms are analysed and presented in the dictionary. For a more detailed explanation of the points dealt with here, see 0.1 *The Scope of the Dictionary* (page 422). For help in finding phrasal verbs in the dictionary and using them correctly, see the *Student's Guide* which follows this introduction.

The vocabulary of English is full of short phrases consisting of a verb and a 'particle' such as *up, down, through*, and *across*. Although they may appear simple, combinations such as ***break down, make up*** and ***take out*** represent one of the most complex and difficult problems for students of the language. There are three major areas of difficulty.

Grammar

The same combination of words may be used in a variety of grammatical structures. Think of ***run up*** as used in *A girl* ***ran up****, The spider* ***ran up*** *the wall, The soldier* ***ran up*** *a flag*, and *Would you mind* ***running*** *me* ***up*** *the road?* Here the sentence patterns are all quite different, even though the meanings are related. In this dictionary, the possible structures for each phrasal verb are shown by means of a series of simple codes in which letters stand for 'verb', 'particle' and so on. (See section 3.4 at the back of the dictionary for a detailed account).

Idiomatic or non-idiomatic

How do we know whether the words ***fall out*** as used in *I was pleased with the way things had* ***fallen out*** form a unit of meaning (an idiom) or not? An idiom can be recognized by a number of simple tests, and these have to do with meaning rather than grammar. One test is to ask whether one word can be substituted for the whole phrase ***fall*** + ***out***. (We can substitute 'happen' and 'occur'.) Another test is to ask whether the second word can be deleted. (It can't.) We can see from these tests alone that ***fall out*** cannot be broken up: its form is fixed. In fact, this information can be found in the entries. If we turn to the entry for ***fall out***, we will see as the definition the words 'happen' and 'occur'. We notice too that the particle cannot be replaced with another particle. (If it could, the replacement would appear alongside ***out***, in dark print). These are clear indications that the combination is a unit of meaning (a phrasal verb). (For a full discussion of idioms and how they are recognized, see 0.1, *The Scope of the Dictionary*, on page 422).

The fact that a particular combination of verb + particle is idiomatic need not affect its grammar. The combination ***make up*** as used in *She* ***made up*** *her face* is quite clearly an idiom (a unit of meaning). Yet the grammar of the idiomatic ***make up*** is similar in many respects to the grammar of the non-idiomatic ***carry away***. For instance, the direct object can be changed around in both cases:

She ***made up*** *her face/ She* ***made*** *her face* ***up***.

Bill ***carried away*** *the rubbish/ Bill* ***carried*** *the rubbish* ***away***.

Similarly, it is equally possible to move the particle to the front and the subject to the end of the sentence whether you use ***come down*** idiomatically (*The prices* ***came down/ Down came*** *the prices*) or non-idiomatically (*The ceiling* ***came down/ Down came*** *the ceiling*).

Complex idioms

Sometimes a pair of words, such as ***make up*** or ***blow off***, seem to have an additional word (or words) attached to them in such a way that the whole phrase forms one complex idiom. Consider in this respect ***make one's mind up*** and ***blow off steam***. It is not always easy for the learner to see that the extra words form part of a larger whole, one that must be learned as a single unit.

How can we be sure that phrases such as ***make one's mind up*** and ***blow off steam*** are units of meaning (like phrasal verbs but more complex still). If ***one's mind*** is a fixed part of ***make one's mind up***, it should not be possible to delete it without making nonsense of the whole phrase. Look at this:

He always takes ages to **make his mind up**.

If we take away ***his mind***, we have this:

He always takes ages to **make up**.

This is either a nonsense phrase or one with a different meaning. (He's perhaps an actor who always takes a long time to put on his greasepaint.) Information about more complex idioms (like this one) is also presented systematically in the dictionary. All the words that form a fixed part of the expression are shown in bold print at the top of the dictionary entry, like this:

make one's mind up **blow off steam** **put the clock back**

Notice that there is no difference in grammatical pattern between the complex idiom ***make one's mind up*** and the phrasal verb ***make*** (*one's face*) ***up***. The position of the direct object can be changed and the verb can be made passive in both cases:

make one's mind up	***make*** *(one's face)* ***up***
make up one's mind	***make up*** *(one's face)*
her mind is made up	*(her face)* ***is made up***

The Student's Guide to the Dictionary

This practical guide has been designed especially for student users of the *Oxford Dictionary of Phrasal Verbs*. It will help you find the kinds of information about phrasal verbs that you need most often. Generally, this information is of two kinds:

You need to be able to find phrasal verbs and their meanings.

You need to be able to use phrasal verbs in their correct grammatical patterns and appropriate contexts.

You will not find here an explanation of all the information that the dictionary contains. This guide is intended to *start* you using the dictionary successfully. If you want fuller information about phrasal verbs and their meanings and uses, you should turn to the back of the book and look at *The Dictionary – a detailed description*.

Finding Phrasal Verbs and Complex Idioms

Phrasal Verbs

1 What is a phrasal verb?

In English, verbs are often put together with short adverbs (or PARTICLES), as in *run back, put (the dish) down, warm (the milk) up*. Verbs often combine with PREPOSITIONS too, as in *come into (the room), drop (the vase) on (the floor), translate (the play) into (French)*. All these combinations are easy to understand, because you can work out their meanings from those of the *individual* verbs and particles or prepositions. (So, *put the dish down* means 'place the dish in a lower position'.)

But sometimes the combinations are more difficult to understand. Look at the combination *break out* (verb + particle) as it is used in this sentence:

Cholera **broke out** *in the north of the country.*

In this example, the verb *break* doesn't have the meaning it has in phrases like *break a window* or *break a stick*. And *out* doesn't mean 'outside in the open'. The combination has to be understood as *one unit*, meaning 'start suddenly or violently'. When a verb + particle (or a verb + preposition) is a unit of meaning like this it is a PHRASAL VERB.

Sometimes you will find a verb, a particle *and* a preposition combining to form one unit of meaning. A well-known example is *put up with* (meaning 'tolerate'). This too is a phrasal verb.

The chief aim of this dictionary is to help you understand and use phrasal verbs. They form the majority of the entries, though the dictionary contains some 'literal' combinations, too – like *get off (my motorbike)* and *put (your knitting) down.*

2 Looking up a phrasal verb in the dictionary

Let us suppose that you meet this sentence while reading a book or newspaper:

The dealer may round down the price to £600.

Here, you have difficulty in understanding *round down*, which you think may be a phrasal verb. There are eight entries in the dictionary beginning with **round**, and they are headed by the word **round** in extra large dark print. First you look for that. Then you look for **round down**. It is the first of the eight entries:

round down ... bring (a price etc) to a round figure by lowering it ....

round off ... make (sth) round and smooth.
round off (with) ... end, complete (sth) suitably or satisfactorily....

3 Phrasal verbs in the past tense, etc

Sometimes the phrasal verb in the text you are reading is in the past tense or past participle form. Look at this example:

The traffic eased off around seven o'clock.

Here the phrasal verb is in the past tense (*eased off*), so you must make the simple change from past to present before looking up the entry, which is **ease off**. Watch for irregular past tense and past participle forms: note for instance that *went off* and *gone off* have to be looked up under **go off**.

4 Phrasal verbs divided by a noun phrase

Often in writing or speech you will meet phrasal verbs with a noun phrase *between* the two parts of the combination, like this:

Engineers let the explosives off safely.

But, as with many phrasal verbs, you can change the order of *the explosives* (the direct object) and *off* (the particle), like this:

Engineers let off the explosives safely.

This shows that *let* and *off* belong together. Now you look up **let off** in the dictionary.

5 Phrasal verbs with several different meanings

You have just been asked to look up the entry **let off**. But when you try to do this, you find there are *six* numbered **let off** entries. Here are the first four:

let off 1 ... allow (sb) to disembark or alight (from sth).
2 ... release (sb) without punishing him.
3 ... allow (sb) not to do (an unpleasant task).
4 ... fire (sth); explode (sth).

This numbered list shows that *let off* is a phrasal verb with several meanings. Which is the meaning used in your example? There are two strategies you can use to find the right meaning: (a) Try to guess the meaning of *let off* from your example sentence; then compare it with the above definitions. Let us suppose your guess is 'explode': you will find this meaning at **let off** ... **4**. (b) Compare the words in your example with those in the examples of the entry you have just chosen. Here is your example:

Engineers let the explosives off safely.

And here are the examples at **let off** ... **4**:

let off ... **4** ... *A brass cannon was* ***let off*** *dangerously with real gunpowder.* ○ *Some small boys* ***let*** *some fireworks* ***off***.

You'll see that *the explosive*, the object off *let off* in your sentence, is related in meaning to *some fireworks*, the object in the second dictionary example, so your guess is correct.

Complex Idioms

1 What is a complex idiom?

In this dictionary, a COMPLEX IDIOM is a verb + particle, or a verb + preposition (or a verb + particle + preposition), but it always contains one or more other words as well. The additional words may be a possessive word and a noun, as in: *snap someone's head off* and *snap one's fingers at someone*. Or they may be an adjective and a noun, as in: *tie up the loose ends, turn a blind eye (on/to)*. Other types of words may be used too. Like ordinary phrasal verbs, these expressions are units of meaning. This is why they are called *complex idioms*.

2 Looking up complex idioms in the dictionary

Suppose that you have just read the following sentence:

She didn't like the arrangements for the holiday at all, but was resigned to making the best of a bad job.

You are puzzled by *making the best of a bad job*, which seems unconnected with work or with being employed. In other words it seems like an idiom. How do you look it up? (a) First, you look for the block of entries headed by the word **make** in large print. (b) Then you search for phrasal verbs consisting simply of **make** + **of**. (There is only one of these.) (c) Now you look at the entries immediately after **make of**. Here are the next four entries:

make the best of ...
make the best of a bad job ...
make the best of both worlds ...
make capital of ...

The idiom you are looking for is the second one. Notice that if you take away **make** and **of** from the idioms, they are arranged *first* in the order of the first significant word (so **best** comes before **capital**), and *then* in the order of the second important word (so **bad** comes before **both**) – and so on.

Nominalized Forms

1 What is a nominalized form?

A nominalized form ('nom form' for short) is a noun formed from a phrasal verb: *make-up*, for instance, is formed from *make up* (ie 'apply cosmetics to one's face') and *take-off* is formed from *take off* (ie 'leave the ground in an aircraft'). Sometimes nom forms have a spelling which includes the letters *-ing*: *tell off* (ie 'reproach, reprimand') has the nom form *telling-off*.

2 Looking up nominalized forms in the dictionary

All the above nom forms can be found by referring to the entries for the phrasal verbs concerned. Suppose that you meet the following sentence:

The director wants to do a walk-through of that scene now.

Here the nom form is *walk-through*. To find it in the dictionary, you look for the entry *walk through*. Here you will find the abbreviation 'nom' in brackets at the top, and an example of the nom form lower down:

walk through [Vn.p nom ...] (*theatre*) show (sb) the movements he must make in a scene etc ... *After lunch I want to do a* **walk-through** *of the ghost scene.*

Some nom forms exist independently: there is no phrasal verb that they can be directly linked to. Look at this example:

Technicians have made a mock-up of the plane's cockpit.

Here the nom form is *mock-up* ('full-size model'), but there is no phrasal verb *mock up*. We can't say:

**Technicians have mocked up the plane's cockpit.*

So you must look up the entry **mock-up**. You will find this listed in its exact alphabetical place, like this:

mix with 1 . . . 2
mock-up
model on/upon
monkey about/around

Using Phrasal Verbs and Complex Idioms

Grammar

1 Phrasal verbs with a choice between particle and preposition

Suppose that you wish to know whether a phrasal verb containing a particle can also be used with a preposition of similar meaning. You may have seen an example like this (where *in* is a particle):

Her train pulled in ten minutes early.

and you want to know whether you can also say this (where *into* is a preposition):

Her train pulled into Bristol ten minutes early.

This is how you can find out: (a) You look for an entry in the dictionary in which the verb **pull** is followed by both **in** and **into**, like this: **pull in/into.** That seems to confirm that the particle *or* the preposition can be used. (b) But there are two entries like this. So check if one has the meaning of the phrasal verb in your examples ('arrive (at)' or 'enter'). The entry **pull in/into 1** does. You are now sure that in your first example you can use the preposition instead of the particle. (c) Lastly, look at the examples in the dictionary entry:

pull in/into 1 . . . *As we* ***pulled in****, an hour late, our connection to Rome was pulling out.* ○ *Our train* ***pulled into*** *Paddington dead on time.*

The first example could be changed to: *As we* ***pulled into*** *Milan Station, an hour late, . . .* How could the second example be changed?

2 Prepositions that can be deleted

Sometimes you need to know whether the preposition at the end of a phrasal verb (or a more complex idiom) can be removed without changing the meaning of the remainder, or making nonsense of it. Look at these two examples (with the idioms specially marked):

Not many students ***make use of*** *this library.*
She'd better ***make a start on*** *the job now.*

It would be nonsensical to say: *Not many students* ***make use****.* Here we can't delete ***of*** *this library*. But we can say: *She'd better* ***make a start*** *now*. Here we can remove ***on*** *the job* without producing nonsense.

How do you find out whether a preposition can be deleted? (a) Look up the entry **make use of** in the dictionary (following the instructions given for looking up complex idioms). (b) The entry you need is **make use of 1**, where the meaning is 'employ and benefit from (sth/sb)'. (c) Notice that there is no bracket around **of** in **make use of**. This means that the preposition *cannot* be taken away. (d) Now look up the entry for **make a start on**. (e) You will find **make a start (on)**, with the preposition in brackets. This shows that **on** can be removed without making nonsense of the rest of the idiom.

3 Changing the order of direct object and particle in a phrasal verb

When you use a phrasal verb with a direct object, you need to know whether the object can be placed either before or after the particle – or whether its position is fixed. Look at this example:

Jane **banged** *the parcel* **down** *on the table.*

Here the object is the noun phrase *the parcel*. What you need to know is whether this phrase can be placed after the particle *down*, like this:

Jane **banged down** *the parcel on the table.*

The dictionary can help you with this problem. (a) Look up the entry for **bang down**. (b) Near the beginning of the entry you will find in square brackets some letters and reversed arrows, like this:

bang down [Vn⇄p . . .] . . .

(c) Here, 'V' means verb, 'n' means noun phrase and 'p'means particle. The arrows show that when you have a *short* noun phrase as object, it can be placed on either side of the particle. (d) Since *the parcel* is a short noun phrase you would be correct to place it after the particle *down*, as in the second example. (All the abbreviations used to indicate the patterns in which phrasal verbs are used are explained, with examples, inside the back cover of the dictionary.)

Collocations

1 What is a collocation?

One of the difficulties facing the learner wishing to write (or speak) acceptable English is the difficulty of knowing exactly which nouns or adjectives can combine with particular phrasal verbs. A native English speaker will know that it is natural and normal to say *carry out an investigation* NOT *carry on an investigation*. On the other hand, we normally say *carry on a conversation* NOT *carry out a conversation*. Combinations of words that are natural and normal to native speakers are called COLLOCATIONS. The actual nouns etc that can combine with a particular phrasal verb are called its COLLOCATES. (So *conversation* is one of the collocates of *carry on*.)

2 Where to find the collocates of phrasal verbs

(a) Start by looking at the entry from which the example *carry out an investigation* has been taken. This is ***carry out*** . . . ***2***. (b) Near the beginning of the entry, after the capital letter **O**, you will see a list of nouns. These are collocates of **carry out**, and they can be used as direct objects of that phrasal verb:

carry out . . . **2** . . . **O:** experiment, test; research, investigation . . .

3 How to use collocates to make up sentences

Suppose you want to make up a sentence with *carry out* and a direct object. (a) You can choose as objects any of the words listed after **O**, above. So you can say *carry out an experiment, carry out a test*, and so on. (b) Now look at this entry:

carry on . . . **4** . . . conduct, hold (sth). **O:** conversation, talk, discussion . . .

Try making up short sentences using *carry on* and the collocates listed at **O**.

4 'Restricted' lists of collocates

When you make up sentences with *carry on*, it is possible to use words which do not actually appear in the list after **O**, but are related in meaning to those that do. Among the words that you can add to the list are *debate* and *negotiations* (both of which are types of discussion). In some entries, though, it is not possible to add words as freely as this. Look at this example:

Police are keeping the suspects under observation.

Here the phrasal verb is *keep under*, and instead of *observation* we could use *scrutiny* or *surveillance*. But it would not seem normal or natural to say *keep under view, examination* or *watch*, even though those words are related in meaning to *observation*, etc.

The dictionary will tell you when the choice of collocates is limited in this way. (a) Look up the entry for **keep under . . . 4**:

keep under . . . 4 . . . O: suspect, patient; premises. **o:** ⚠ observation, surveillance, scrutiny: . . .

(b) Here you will find two lists of collocates, one after **O** (direct object) and one after **o** (object of the preposition *under*). (c) The first list can be added to in the way just explained. We can say:

Police are keeping the suspects, terrorist gang, drug smugglers (etc) under observation.

(d) You'll notice that the second list is preceded by a danger sign ⚠. This tells you that English speakers would not normally add to the words listed (*observation, surveillance, scrutiny*). It is a warning to proceed with caution!

Synonyms

1 What are synonyms?

A phrasal verb may have a SYNONYM, ie another phrasal verb listed in the dictionary with the same meaning. Look at *shell out* as used in this example:

I hate shelling out money on house repairs.

Instead of *shell out* here we could use *fork out*, with no change of meaning or style (both are *informal* phrasal verbs). These two phrasal verbs are very close synonyms.

2 Where do you find synonyms in the dictionary?

Synonyms of a particular phrasal verb are referred to at the end of the entry for the phrasal verb, after an 'equals' sign, like this:

shell out . . . (*informal*) pay (sth), usu unwillingly. . . . = fork out.

Very often a synonym will be referred to at the end of a numbered entry, and the synonym itself will be a numbered entry:

break into . . . 3 . . . suddenly begin to produce (flowers etc). . . . = burst into 2.

3 How do you use this information?

The equals sign tells you that two (or more) entries have the same meaning. But it should also serve as a reminder that those entries may be *different in other ways*, for instance in style or in grammar. To check whether such differences exist, *you should always look up the entry for the synonym before you use it in place of the phrasal verb you already have*. Suppose that you have written the following sentence:

'If we keep calm and stick together we shall be all right.'

(a) You think there is a phrasal verb *stand together* which means the same as *stick together*, and you decide to check the entry **stick together**. (b) You find at the end = stand together, and this confirms that the two entries have the same meaning. However, you suspect that *stick together* is more informal than *stand together*. (c) You compare the two entries: **stick together** has the label (*informal*), but **stand together** has *no* style label. (d) You realize that by using one phrasal verb in place of another you may change the style of a sentence, perhaps making it more formal, even though the meaning may remain the same.

A quick guide to abbreviations used in the dictionary

Three kinds of abbreviations have been mentioned briefly in this Student's Guide:
1 'grammar codes' in square brackets (eg [Vn⇄pl]);
2 letters introducing collocate lists (eg **O** and **o**);
3 a sign directing you to another entry (the '=' pointing to a synonym).
Here, abbreviations of all three types are set out in tables with explanations and examples:

1 Grammar codes

[Vp] Verb + particle (eg **take off**):
The pilot ***took off*** *smoothly.*

[Vpr] Verb + prepositional phrase (eg **glance through**):
He ***glanced through*** *the article quickly.*

[Vp.pr] Verb + particle + prepositional phrase (eg **put up with**):
We ***put up with*** *these interruptions cheerfully enough.*

[Vn⇄p] Verb + object noun phrase + particle (eg **play back**):
We can ***play*** *the recorded programmes* ***back***. (*reversible*).
We can ***play back*** *the recorded programmes.*

[Vn.p] Verb + object noun phrase + particle (eg **move along**):
The police ***moved*** *the spectators* ***along***. (*non-reversible*).

[Vp.n] Verb + particle + object noun phrase (eg **put out**):
The plants ***put out*** *early shoots.* (*non-reversible*).

[Vn.pr] Verb + object noun phrase + prepositional phrase (eg **get through**):
Bill will ***get*** *you* ***through*** *your driving test.*

[Vn.p.pr] Verb + object noun phrase + particle +prep. phrase (eg **bring round to**):
We finally ***brought*** *them* ***round to*** *our point of view.*

(For a key to these codes with 'transforms' included, see inside the back cover. For a detailed explanation of the codes, see 3.4, *Tables of patterns*, on page 448.)

2 Letters introducing collocate lists

S (= subject)
shrivel up . . . **S:** leaf, shoot; blade (of grass); skin; face . . . *In the long drought the leaves* ***shrivelled up*** *and died.*

O (= direct object)
bang in . . . **O:** application, request; form, letter . . . *You'd better* ***bang*** *your application* ***in*** *straight away.*

o (= object of a preposition)
refrain from . . . **o:** bad language, anti-social behaviour; aggression, hostilities; smoking, drinking . . . *Please* ***refrain from*** *smoking during the performance.*

A (= adverbial phrase or clause)
poke about/around . . . **A:** among papers, possessions; in one's study, spare room . . . *'What are you doing* ***poking about*** *among my private papers?'*

(For a more detailed treatment, see 6, *Collocations*, on page 475).

3 Signs directing you to synonyms, opposites and other related entries

'=' directs you to a *synonym* – an entry with the same meaning:
angle for . . . try to obtain (sth) by means of hints . . . = fish for.
fish for . . . try to obtain (sth) by means of hints . . . = angle for.

'↔' directs you to an entry that is *opposite* in meaning:
put back 2 . . . move the hands of a clock back . . . ↔ put forward 3.
put forward 3 . . . move the hands of a clock forward . . . ↔ put back 2.

'⇨' directs you to an entry that is *related in some other way*:
bring about 1 . . . cause (sth) to happen . . . ⇨ come about 1.
come about 1 . . . happen . . . ⇨ bring about 1.

(Here, both entries have the meaning 'happen' but **bring about** has the additional meaning 'cause (sth) to . . .'.)

A

abandon

abandon oneself to [Vn.pr emph rel] (*formal*) allow oneself to be overcome by (sth). **S:** widow, bereaved relative; writer, artist. **o:** grief, despair; one's wildest fantasies: *After his wife's death, George* **abandoned himself** *more and more* **to** *gloom and remorse.* ○ *The author should resist* **abandoning himself to** *such elaborate flights of fancy.* = give way (to).

abide

abide by [Vpr] observe or obey (sth); accept. **S:** contestants, parties, sides, members. **o:** rules, regulations; decision, verdict: *The two players agreed to* **abide by** *the referee's decision.* ○ *Unless they* **abide by** *the rules of the club, they will have to leave.* = comply with, conform (to/with).

abound

abound in/with [Vpr rel] have great numbers or quantities of (sth); be full of (sth). **S:** commerce, industry; subject, discipline; locality, area. **o:** openings, opportunities; difficulties, snags; plants, animals; vermin, lice: *Modern industry* **abounds in** *opportunities for young people with good scientific qualifications.* ○ *This language* **abounds in** *difficulties for the foreign learner* (or: *Difficulties for the foreign learner* **abound in** *this language*). ○ *The region* **abounds in/with** *wild life of every kind* (or: *Wild life . . .* **abounds in** *the region*). ⇨ teem in.

abscond

abscond (from) [Vpr emph rel] (*formal*) go away from, leave (a place) unlawfully. **S:** boy, prisoner. **o:** remand home, detention centre; custody: *After* **absconding** *twice* **from** *an open prison, Jones was sent to a closed prison for the completion of his sentence.*

abscond with [Vpr rel] (*formal*) steal (sth) and carry it away. **o:** family jewels, firm's secret plan: *A junior cashier has* **absconded with** *ten thousand pounds, accompanied by the boss's attractive secretary.* = go off with 2, run away with 1, run off with.

absolve

absolve from [Vn.pr pass emph rel] (*legal* or *formal*) declare (sb) free from (sth). **S:** priest; court, investigating commission, judge. **O:** dying man, repentant woman; accused person, company, jury. **o:** sin, guilt; blame, responsibility, obligation: *Having been* **absolved** *by the court* **from** *all responsibility in the death of the pedestrian, the man went to the nearest pub and got drunk by way of celebration.* ○ *After a trial lasting for three weeks and ending in the conviction of all the accused, the jury were* **absolved from** *further service for the rest of their lives.*

absorb

absorbed in [adj pred (Vn.pr)] have one's attention totally occupied by (sth). **o:** book, story; what was going on outside: *The children were so* **absorbed in** *their game that they did not notice the passage of time.* □ used with *appear* etc. = engrossed (in), wrapped up in.

abstain

abstain (from) [Vpr pass rel] not begin to do (sth), stop doing (sth). **o:** alcohol, sex; criticism; interrupting the speaker, scattering paper about: *Many Catholics still* **abstain from** *eating meat on Fridays.* ○ *Several MPs* **abstained from** *voting at the end of the debate.* □ often followed by an *-ing* form. = refrain from.

abut

abut on [Vpr rel] (*formal*) touch the boundary of (sth): *The residence of the Archbishop* **abuts on** *the medieval walls of the city.*

accede

accede to 1 [Vpr pass emph rel] (*formal*) gain (a vacant title etc). **S:** heir; prince, princess; vice-president. **o:** throne, title, estate; presidency: *George VI* **acceded to** *the throne in 1936.* = succeed (to).

2 [Vpr pass emph rel] (*formal*) give one's approval to (sth). **S:** company; manager, doctor, principal. **o:** request, demand, application: *The Committee regrets that it cannot* **accede to** *your request for a month's unpaid leave.* ○ *My application for a change of department was readily* **acceded to.** = agree (to), assent (to), consent (to).

accord

accord with [Vpr rel] (*formal*) be in agreement with (sth); match. **S:** information, statement, claim, account. **o:** facts, data, our records: *My information does not* **accord with** *the report which has just been presented.* ○ *His behaviour does not* **accord with** *my idea of a gentleman.* □ usu neg or interr. = agree (with) 2, be in accord/harmony/tune (with), correspond (to/with).

account

account for 1 [Vpr pass] give a satisfactory record of (sth). **S:** cashier, accountant. **o:** expenses, payments, outlay: *He was unable to* **account for** *the deficit in the firm's bank balance.* ○ *I'm afraid that you'll have to* **account for** *every penny of the money that was entrusted to you.* = answer for 2. ⇨ unaccounted for 1.

2 [Vpr pass] know the location, and safety or welfare, of (sb/sth). **S:** teacher; guide, rescue team; control tower; RAF. **o:** children; walkers, mountaineers; helicopter; fighter: *Five climbers lost in the Cairngorms are not yet* **accounted for.** ○ *There are still two aircraft we've not been able to* **account for.** ⇨ unaccounted for.

3 [Vpr pass] explain (sth). **S:** he etc; his state of mind; fact. **o:** presence, absence; attitude; surprise, shock; position: *Peter must be ill; it's the only thing that will* **account for** *his strange behaviour.* ○ *'The video's out of order.' 'Oh, that would* **account for** *the strange noise it's making.'*

4 [Vpr pass] compose or constitute (sth). **S:** cars, machinery; the unemployed, pensioners, students. **o:** a large proportion of their exports; the majority, a substantial part: *University flats* **account for** *40% of student accommodation.* ○ *The elderly* **account for** *an increasing proportion of the population.*

5 [Vpr pass] be responsible for killing, destroying, knocking out etc (sth/sb). **S:** gunner; enemy-fire, fighter aircraft; guard, policeman. **o:** raider, bomber, tank; intruder, bandit: *The fighter screen* **accounted for** *three of the enemy aircraft.* ○ *Two masked intruders were* **accounted for** *by security men.* = put out of action.

not account for preferences/taste(s) [Vpr] not be able to explain why sb prefers one thing to another: *One simply can***not account for tastes** (or: *There's simply* **no accounting for tastes**). ○ SONIA: *Sorry, it seems I'm married to this man for better or worse.* JASON: *That man? There's* ***no accounting for taste***. DPM

account to (for) [Vpr pass emph rel] give an explanation to (sb) (about sth); be responsible to (sb) (for sth). **o:** (**to**) superior, manager; parent; (**for**) one's actions; expenditure; behaviour: *You'll have to* ***account to*** *me* (or: *You'll be* ***accountable to*** *me*) *if anything happens to this girl while she is in your care.* ○ *She'll* ***account to*** *me* ***for*** *every penny moving in and out of this office.* □ usu with the implication that failure to explain adequately will be punished; note the variant be accountable to sb (for sth). = answer to (for).

accrue

accrue (to) (from) [Vpr emph rel] (*formal*) come (to sb) as an increase or benefit, esp financial, (from sth). **S:** money, interest; power, wealth. **o:** (**to**) saver, investor; ruler, dictator; (**from**) account, investment; source: *Interest at 8.5%* ***accrues to*** *us annually* ***from*** *a building society account.* ○ *The enormous sums* ***accruing to*** *these traders were not invested in industrial development at home.*

accuse

accuse (of) [Vn.pr pass rel] say (sb) is guilty (of sth). **S:** police, prosecution; mother-in-law. **o:** stealing a car; theft, robbery; treason, perjury: *Fred's teacher* ***accused*** *him* ***of*** *cheating in the exam.* ○ *I've been* ***accused of*** *many things in my life, but never of cowardice.* ○ (ironic) *'You can never* ***accuse*** *Cyril* ***of*** *overwork.'* □ often followed by an -ing form.

accustom

accustom to [Vn.pr pass emph rel] make (sb) learn to expect or accept (sth). **O:** oneself; pupils, staff; elderly people. **o:** (new) conditions, situation; a change of routine; retirement, a different kind of life; doing without luxuries, taking orders. **A:** quickly, slowly, with difficulty, at last: *You'll find it hard to* ***accustom*** *your family* ***to*** *the living conditions here.* ○ *You'll just have to* ***accustom*** *yourself* ***to*** *the new diet and stop complaining.* ○ *She thought she would never* ***accustom*** *herself* ***to*** *eating nothing but fruit and vegetables.* □ often preceded by *find it difficult/easy/hard to.* = habituate to. ⇨ next entry

accustomed to [pass (Vn.pr)] having learned to expect or accept (sth). **o:** conditions, situation; food, weather, light: *Conditions here are not what she's* ***accustomed to***. ○ *You'll soon get* ***accustomed to*** *the change of climate.* ○ *He'd become* ***accustomed to*** *having his meals brought to him.* □ used with *appear* etc. = used to. ⇨ previous entry

ache

ache for [Vpr emph rel] strongly want to have (sth). **S:** traveller; the unemployed; worker. **o:** home; jobs, work; a new challenge: *I'm parched and positively* ***aching for*** *a cup of tea!* = long for, yearn (for).

acquaint

acquaint with [Vn.pr pass rel] (*formal*) (help sb to) learn or discover (sth). **O:** oneself; pupil; colleague, wife. **o:** facts, details, circumstances: *When I was a teacher I always made a point of* ***acquainting*** *myself* ***with*** *the home background of all my pupils.* ○ *You should try to* ***acquaint*** *yourself* (or: *get* ***acquainted***) ***with*** *the facts, before you express an opinion.* ○ *Are you* ***acquainted with*** *the works of Maria Edgeworth?*

acquiesce

acquiesce (in) [Vpr pass emph rel] (*formal*) offer no opposition (to sth). **A:** weakly, feebly, tamely. **o:** arrangement, action, change: *He said he would never* ***acquiesce in*** *his lifelong enemy being made a director of the company.* ○ *I was appalled to find that their proposal to take control had been weakly* ***acquiesced in***. = agree (to).

acquit

acquit (of) [Vn.pr pass rel] (*legal*) find (sb) not guilty (of sth). **S:** magistrate, judge, jury, court. **O:** prisoner, accused. **o:** charge; aiding and abetting, causing grievous bodily harm; murder, manslaughter: *After a trial lasting several days the jury* ***acquitted*** *Stephens (***of*** *the charge of murder).* ○ *The accused was* ***acquitted of*** *manslaughter but found guilty of dangerous driving.*

act

act for [Vpr rel] perform duties etc on behalf of (sb); represent. **S:** solicitor; union, professional organization. **o:** private citizen, member: *Since old Mr Smith fell ill, his son has been* ***acting for*** *him in all his affairs.* ○ *During the sergeant-major's absence on a training course, the senior sergeant* ***acted for*** *him.*

act on/upon 1 [Vpr pass emph rel] be guided by (sth); follow. **o:** advice; (recent, up-to-date) information, news; one's own initiative, intuition: ***Acting on*** *your recommendation, I have decided to emigrate to Australia.* ○ *If my advice had been* ***acted upon***, *the firm would not have gone bankrupt.* ○ *'Yes, there aren't any perfect murders, are there? I dare say there'll be a clue at the post-mortem* ***on*** *which you can persuade Segura to* ***act***.' OMIH = take action (on).

2 [Vpr emph rel] have an effect on (sth); affect. **S:** medicines, pills, drugs. **o:** organ; heart, liver, spleen, gland: *These pills* ***act on*** *the liver.* ○ ***On*** *which part of the brain does this drug* ***act***?

act out [Vn ⇆ p pass] express (feelings) in one's behaviour so as to release tensions etc; imitate (events) in the form of a play; enact. **O:** feelings, emotions; drama, comedy; scenes, events: *She looked at the boy* ***acting out*** *his injured innocence and stared at him until he looked down.* TT ○ *In the enclosed life of this small village, many passions are brought to the surface and* ***acted out***. = play out 2.

act up 1 [Vp] (*informal*) be a nuisance or irritation: *'You look a bit down in the mouth* (= depressed). *Boy friend* ***acting up***?' *'Oh yes, he* ***acts up***.' TGLY = play up 2.

2 [Vp] (*informal*) fail to work properly: *'Sorry I'm late. The car's been* ***acting up***.' ○ *If you don't take care, your leg will start* ***acting up*** *again.* = play up 1.

adapt

adapt (for) [Vn.pr pass rel] rewrite, rearrange or modify (sth) (for sth). **O:** novel, play, story; machine. **o:** stage, radio, TV; children; use in schools; a special purpose. **A:** specially; skilfully: *The author is going to* ***adapt*** *her play* ***for*** *television.* ○ *It's surprising that this novel hasn't yet been* ***adapted for*** *the cinema.* ○ *These tractors have been* ***adapted for*** *use in very cold climates.* □ adapt (for) and adapt (from) (⇨ next entry) may be combined: *He appeared in a series* ***adapted for*** *radio* ***from*** *a French original.*

adapt (from) [Vn.pr pass rel] translate or modify (sth) (from sth). **O:** novel, play, story. **o:** French, Spanish; the original: *This play has been skilfully* ***adapted from*** *the original.* ⇨ previous entry

adapt to [Vn.pr pass rel] modify or rearrange (sth) so as to make it suitable for (sth). **O:** building; ship, bus, plane. **o:** new conditions; the special needs of children; civilian uses; the use of the elderly: *We'll have to* ***adapt*** *the building* ***to*** *the needs of the old people who are going to live in it.* ○ *The ships were found unsuitable for the conditions* ***to*** *which they had supposedly been* ***adapted****.*

adapt (oneself) to [Vpr pass rel, Vn.pr rel] change one's outlook or behaviour to suit (sth). **o:** (new) circumstances, situation, conditions; way of life; environment, climate: *The new teacher was very slow to* ***adapt to*** *the unusual rules of the school.* ○ *I don't think I shall ever* ***adapt myself to*** *this hot climate.* = adjust (oneself) to.

add

add in [Vn ⇆ p pass adj] place or pour (sth) in; include. **O:** flour, butter, egg. **A:** while/before/after mixing, heating, stirring etc: *Should you* ***add in*** *the lemon juice before or after beating the eggs?* □ often used in recipes, in the imperative form.

add on [Vn ⇆ p pass] include or attach (sth). **O:** a few pounds; a bit extra; trimmings, decorations: *'Here's your bill, sir. I've* ***added on*** *the ten per cent service charge.'* ○ *She wrote me rather a cold letter; even the inquiry about my health looked as if it had been* ***added on*** *as an afterthought.*

add to [Vpr pass, Vn.pr pass rel] increase (sth) in extent or quantity; supplement. **S:** discovery, work, research. **O:** much, a good deal, something, nothing. **o:** (store of) knowledge, wealth, enjoyment, understanding, appreciation; difficulties, problems: [Vpr] *The recent excavations have* ***added*** *greatly* ***to*** *our knowledge of life in Britain during the Stone Age.* ○ [Vpr] *The palace had been* ***added to*** *from time to time, and as a result incorporated various styles of architecture.* ○ [Vn.pr] *Nothing has been* ***added to*** *our understanding of this disease by all the cruel experiments on animals.* ○ [Vn.pr] *Will you* ***add*** *your name* ***to*** *a petition against the building of another nuclear power station?*

add together [Vn ⇆ p pass adj] combine or join (elements) to make a total or whole. **O:** figures, numbers; factors; chemicals, ingredients: *When* ***added together****, flour and water make a very strong paste.* ○ *When you* ***add*** *all the elements of her story* ***together*** *it's hardly surprising that she left him.*

add up 1 [Vp] (*informal*) present a reasonable picture; make sense; lead to an obvious conclusion. **S:** facts, evidence; their behaviour; it: *Sometimes she would greet him happily; sometimes he found her in tears. It just didn't* ***add up****.* ○ *The murder had obviously been committed in the house, yet the snow around the house was smooth and undisturbed: it didn't* ***add up****.*

2 [Vp,Vn ⇆ p pass] find the sum (of various amounts); combine, take together. **O:** figures, numbers, score; the effects (of sth): *Try* ***adding up*** *this time instead of subtracting.* ○ *Every time I* ***add*** *these figures* ***up*** *I get a different answer.* ○ *The practical connections of Britain with her fellow-members are numerous and important, and when* ***added up*** *comprise a good part of Britain's external relations.* SC ↔ take away (from) 4.

add up to 1 [Vp.pr] (*informal*) have a certain value; be equal to (sth). **S:** information, news; contribution, discovery, acquisition. **o:** (not) much, (not) a lot; very little: *Their knowledge of how other people live doesn't* ***add up to*** *much.* ○ *Sir Percy said he was surprised that the annual leakage by theft, smuggling and illicit digging did not* ***add up to*** *more than the figures given to him.* DS ○ *The entertainment is most notable for its male dancing, yet in total it* ***adds up to*** *little more than a fiesta of classical dancing.* T □ usu neg or interr. = amount to 1, come to 3.

2 [Vp.pr] mean (sth) overall or in total. **S:** refusal, statement, attitude. **o:** what (in initial position); the fact that: *'What your statement* ***adds up to*** *is that you helped to plan the break-in.'* ○ *'Your evidence, then, really* ***adds up to*** *this — that you were nowhere near the scene of the crime?'* = amount to 2.

addicted

addicted (to) [pass (Vn.pr)] devoted (to sth); having (sth) as a strong, almost unbreakable habit. **o:** smoking, cigarettes; alcohol, drink; drugs, opium, LSD, heroin; women, sex; reading, television. **A:** hopelessly, strongly, desperately: *He became* ***addicted to*** *drugs at quite an early age.* ○ *The two things that Appleby is most* ***addicted to*** *are big cars and big cigars.* □ also used with *seem, become, get.*

address

address oneself to [Vn.pr emph rel] (*formal*) give one's full attention to (sth); tackle. **o:** (urgent) task, job, problem; matter, business in hand. **A:** with vigour, with (some) misgivings; energetically, single-mindedly: *When his father died, Paul had to* ***address himself to*** *the business of earning his own living.* ○ *There are two questions* ***to*** *which I will* ***address myself*** *in this lecture.*

adhere

adhere to 1 [Vpr emph rel] (*formal*) become or remain attached to (sth). **S:** material, preparation; paste, paint. **o:** surface, wall; wood, metal, glass, paper. **A:** firmly, securely: *This paint will* ***adhere to*** *any surface, whether rough or smooth.*

2 [Vpr pass emph rel] (*formal*) not abandon or change (sth); maintain. **o:** plan, original programme; (one's) principles, ideas; promise, offer; demand(s), proposal(s), suggestion(s). **A:** firmly, resolutely; through thick and thin; come what may: *He resolutely* ***adhered to*** *what he had said at the meeting: he had not changed his mind in any* *way.* ○ *We decided to* **adhere to** *our original plan, in spite of the appalling weather.* = hold to 1, keep to 2, stick to 2.

adjourn

adjourn (to) [Vpr rel, Vn.pr pass emph rel] (*formal*) be interrupted, interrupt (sth), with the intention that it will resume (at another place or time). **S** [Vpr], **O** [Vn.pr]**:** meeting, debate; hearing; seminar, conference. **S** [Vn.pr]**:** chairman; judge, magistrate. **o:** another room; next week; the next session: *The debate* **adjourned to** (or: *till*) *the following week.* ○ *The judge decided to* **adjourn** *the hearing* **to** *the scene of the crime.* ○ *'Might I suggest that we* **adjourn** *the meeting* **to** *this time tomorrow* (or: *until this time tomorrow*)*?'*

adjourn to [Vpr] (*formal* or *jocular*) interrupt sth and move off (to another place). **o:** garden, terrace; bar: *Bill immediately proposed that we* **adjourned to** *the bar for drinks.*

adjust

adjust (oneself) to [Vpr rel, Vn.pr pass rel] change one's outlook or behaviour to suit (sth). **o:** new circumstances, environment, situation, condition(s). **A:** quickly, slowly, (im)perfectly, (in)completely, gradually: *I don't think I shall ever be able to* **adjust myself to** *life in this remote place.* ○ *Jenkins was well* **adjusted to** *the community in which he lived.* = adapt (oneself) to.

admit

admit of [Vpr] (*formal*) leave room for (sth). **S:** word(s), statement; facts, evidence. **o:** (only one) meaning, interpretation; no contradiction: *His problems did not really* **admit of** *any solution.* HD ○ *His statement* **admits of** *one interpretation only: that he was fully aware of what he was doing.* ○ *These facts* **admit of** *no contradiction.* = allow of, permit of.

admit (to) 1 [Vn.pr pass rel] allow (sb) to enter or join (sth). **S:** ticket, letter. **O:** the bearer; one, two. **o:** (football) match; tournament; ground, arena; museum, zoo, palace; membership: *This ticket* **will admit** *three (***to** *the concert).* ○ *He was* **admitted to** *the local branch of the Bird Watchers' Association.*

2 [Vn.pr pass rel] allow (sb) to enter (a place) for tuition, care, treatment etc. **S:** doctor, social services; school governors, university. **O:** casualty, elderly patient; child; applicant, candidate. **o:** hospital, clinic, nursing home; school; advanced degree course: *Mary was* **admitted to** *the Infirmary yesterday and kept in overnight for observation.* ○ *Suitably qualified non-graduates can be* **admitted to** *this course.*

admit to [Vpr pass rel] (*formal* or *jocular*) acknowledge, not deny (sth). **o:** weakness, taste, liking for; doing sth; everything, nothing. **A:** willingly, reluctantly, readily: *Mr Pearson* **admitted** *readily* **to** *a great liking for horror films.* ○ *Mrs Cross* **admits to** *being easily annoyed.* ○ *She* **admits to** *earning £100 000; she probably earns about £130 000.* = confess to.

adorn

adorn (with) [Vn.pr pass rel] (*formal*) add beauty to (sb/sth) (with sth). **O:** oneself; maiden; (her) hair, body; building, temple, statue, boat. **o:** garlands, flowers; jewels, gold: *The girls* **adorned** *themselves* **with** *flowers and garlands before entering the banqueting hall.* ○ *The goddess's head was* **adorned with** *a crown of many jewels.* = deck with.

advance

advance on/towards/upon [Vpr rel] move in the direction of (sb/a place), eg in order to attack him/it: *We were ordered to* **advance on** *the enemy's position under cover of darkness.* ○ *As I* **advanced towards** *the trapped animal, it snarled and struck at me with its free paw.* ○ *The villages* **on** *which they now* **advanced** *had been turned into veritable strongholds.*

advertise

advertise (for) [Vpr pass rel] make known one's need (for sth/sb) by means of notices in newspapers etc. **o:** house, bedsitter; daily help, gardener; second-hand bicycle, washing-machine: *When I* **advertised for** *my first articled clerk the women candidates just happened to be better.* G ○ *'I suppose a suitable flat will turn up. It's been* **advertised for** *enough, hasn't it?'*

advise

advise of [Vn.pr pass rel] (*formal*) inform or notify (sb) about (sth). **o:** vacancy, opportunity; deficit, payment: *May I take this opportunity of* **advising** *you* **of** *two further payments by your late father's solicitors?* □ often used in business correspondence.

advise on [Vpr, Vn.pr pass rel] give advice to (sb) about (sth): *John makes a good living* **advising on** *interior decoration and lighting.* ○ *'Have you ever been* **advised on** *the best way of exploiting your talents as a singer?'*

affiliate

affiliate (to/with) [Vn.pr pass rel] connect (sth) (with sth), perhaps as a branch. **O:** group, body; union, association: *This college is* **affiliated to** *the University of London.* ○ *The Committee regrets that it cannot at present* **affiliate** *your group* **to** *our Society.* ○ *Our professional association is not yet* **affiliated with** *the Trades Union Congress.* □ usu passive.

affix

affix (to) [Vn.pr pass emph rel] (*formal*) add or fasten (sth) (to sth); attach (to). **O:** label, sticker, seal. **o:** letter, parcel: *Please* **affix** *a passport-sized photograph* **to** *the enclosed form and return it to us at once.* ○ *Unless stamps to the correct value are* **affixed** *(***to** *your letter), it will be sent by surface mail.*

afflict

afflict with [Vn.pr pass rel] cause (sb) to suffer or be preoccupied with (sth); bother with. **O:** wife, teacher, employer. **o:** (one's) troubles, worries, complaints: *I wish you wouldn't* **afflict** *me* **with** *your complaints. I've enough problems of my own.* ○ *The poor boy was* **afflicted with** *diabetes.* ○ *It's awful to be* **afflicted with** *a sense of inferiority.* □ usu passive.

agitate

agitate (for) [Vpr pass emph rel] demand (sth) in an organized, sometimes disruptive, manner. **S:** movement, party; women, students. **o:** reform, change (in the law etc); freedom, independence; higher wages, lower taxes, better pensions; improved conditions; shorter hours: *Women had to* **agitate for** *the vote for many years before they finally got it.* ○ *These were much-overdue reforms* **for** *which they had* **agitated** *and fought.*

agree

agree (on/upon) [Vpr pass adj emph rel] reach or make an agreement concerning (sth); find (sth) which is mutually acceptable. **o:** price; date; position; cease-fire; terms: *It seemed as though the two sides would never* **agree** *(***on** *an end to hostilities).* ○ *Once the price for the land has been* **agreed upon**, *we can go ahead and build the house.* ○ **On** *this we can* **agree***: no sale before January.*

agree (to) [Vpr pass emph rel] give one's approval (to sth). **o:** terms, suggestions, proposals; plan, arrangement; conditions; what you say: *I find it impossible to* **agree to** *your terms.* ○ *After much argument, his proposal was finally* **agreed to**. = accede to 2, assent (to), consent (to).

agree (with) 1 [Vpr emph rel, Vn.pr pass emph rel] have the same opinion (as sb else). **o:** you; what he says; John's father: *I entirely* **agree with** *you: that road is very dangerous.* ○ *I'm afraid I shall never* **agree with** *you* (or: *we shall never* **agree**) *about the reintroduction of capital punishment.* ○ *Do you* **agree with** *me that fox-hunting is a cruel sport?* □ followed by a that-clause in the [Vn.pr] pattern, as in the last example. = be at one (with). ↔ disagree (with) (about/over).

2 [Vpr emph rel] be equal (to sth); match. **S:** figures; news report, story; her opinion. **o:** previous estimate; official statement; my view: *'This total doesn't* **agree with** *the figures you gave me earlier.'* ○ *What I heard on the radio* **agrees with** *the way the newspapers are presenting the crisis.* = accord with, be in accord/harmony/tune (with), correspond (to/with). ↔ disagree (with).

3 [Vn.pr pass emph rel] win the approval of (sb) about (sth). **O:** agenda, plan, change, strategy. **o:** colleague, partner, team: *The new government will have to* **agree** *all proposals* **with** *its coalition partners before making changes to the law.* ○ *The Tottenham manager confirmed that a fee had been* **agreed with** *an Italian club for the transfer of the England international.*

agree with [Vpr] suit the digestion, health, temperament or character of (sb). **S:** food, fish, meat; climate; conditions, altitude: *I don't feel well. That meat pie hasn't* **agreed with** *me.* ○ *That hot, damp climate didn't* **agree with** *him — he always felt tired or unwell.* ○ *'Does the sea-air* **agree with** *you?' 'Rather! I thrive on it.'* □ usu neg or interr. ↔ disagree with.

aim

aim at 1 [Vpr pass rel, Vn.pr pass emph rel] try to hit (sth/sb), have (sth/sb) as one's target. **O:** rifle, fire, stone, missile; remarks, criticism. **o:** target; man, animal, bird; young people, the privileged few: [Vpr] *Mr Appleby* **aimed at** *a rabbit, but hit a bird.* ○ [Vn.pr] *He* **aimed** *his gun* **at** *a policeman, and fired.* ○ [Vn.pr] *I don't know which particular newspaper the Minister's remarks were* **aimed at**. = direct at.

2 [Vpr rel] have (sth) as one's objective, whether stated or not. **o:** goal, objective; position, job: *It's not just a Cabinet post he's* **aiming at**, *but the Premiership itself!* ○ *I don't understand that girl's behaviour. What's she* **aiming at**? = direct at/to/towards.

alienate

alienate from [Vn.pr pass rel] (*formal*) cause (sb) to be estranged from (others). **o:** society; one's family; former friends, workmates: *The man's unsociable behaviour gradually* **alienated** *him* **from** *all his friends.* ○ *The Secretary of State's views on Britain's role in the European Community* **alienated** *him still further* **from** *Cabinet colleagues.*

alight

alight (from) [Vpr emph rel] get off, out or down (from sth). **o:** horse, train, bus, taxi: *As Caroline was* **alighting from** *her car a child on roller-skates collided with her.* ○ *The carriage* **from** *which the guests were now* **alighting** *had the royal coat-of-arms emblazoned on the doors.*

alight on [Vpr emph rel] descend from the air and come to rest on (sth). **S:** bird, bee, spider. **o:** branch; flower, ledge: *A long-tailed tit* **alighted on** *the window-ledge and began to peck at the nuts we'd put out for it.* ○ *Every evening the seagulls returned from their feeding-grounds,* **alighted on** *the rocks and settled down for the night.*

align

align with [Vn.pr pass rel] make (sth) match or agree with (sth else); (cause sb/oneself to) adopt the same political etc position as (sb else). **S:** he etc; country; (party) leader. **O:** view(s), opinion(s); itself; party, group. **o:** that/those of; the West; the Opposition, the Government: *He was always careful to* **align** *his views* **with** *those of the majority in his party.* ○ *The Communist Party unexpectedly* **aligned** *itself* **with** *the Christian Socialists.*

allocate

allocate (to) [Vn.pr pass emph rel] give (sth) (to sb) to meet a special need or be used for a particular purpose. **S:** government, committee, council, company. **O:** funds, duties, shares. **o:** refugees; famine relief; building, education: *The Government has* **allocated** *ten million pounds* **to** *the stricken area.* ○ *Half of the medical supplies have already been* **allocated** *(***to** *the victims of the earthquake).* = allot (to).

allot

allot (to) [Vn.pr pass emph rel] give (sth) (to sb) to meet a special need or be used for a particular purpose. **S:** government; association; company. **O:** funds; duties, work; time; house, accommodation. **o:** victims; staff; task; the homeless: *There were many needy families* **to** *whom accommodation had still not been* **allotted**. ○ *How much time has been* **allotted to** *this work?* = allocate (to).

allow

allow for [Vpr pass emph rel] include (sth) in one's calculations etc. **S:** he etc; measurement; instructions; estimate. **o:** expansion; (unexpected) difficulty; (any possible) delay, error, miscalculation; factor, eventuality; the fact that: *Don't forget to* **allow for** *a little shrinkage when you're making that material up.* ○ *He missed the target because the wind hadn't been* **allowed for**. = make allowances (for), take into account/consideration, take account of.

allow of [Vpr] (*formal*) leave room for (sth). **S:** situation, position; attitude, behaviour, principles. **o:** no discussion, argument; (only one) interpretation; no relaxation (in, of sth); (no) deviation (from sth): *Mr Pearson's income* ***allows of*** *no extravagance in his way of living.* ○ *The cult of success by which he lived could* ***allow of*** *no tolerance of his parents.* HD □ usu neg. = admit of, permit of.

allude

allude to [Vpr pass emph rel] (*formal*) mention (sth), usu indirectly. **S:** speaker, writer; book, article, letter, paper. **o:** author, scholar, contributor; work, investigation (of others): *In the course of his lecture Sir Basil* ***alluded*** *many times* ***to*** *the work of his predecessors.* ○ *If the question of the legacy must be* ***alluded to****, you will be discreet, won't you?* ○ *This is a matter* ***to*** *which I have often* ***alluded*** *in correspondence.* = refer to 1.

ally

ally (oneself) with [Vn.pr pass rel] have a close political or military link with (sb/sth); combine with (sb/sth) by treaty etc. **S:** country, (political) party. **o:** superpower, neighbour, opposition group: *Britain has been* ***allied with*** *Portugal for many centuries.* ○ *At one time the Social Democrats were on the point of* ***allying themselves with*** *the Green Party.*

allied (to) [pass (Vn.pr)] have a number of the same features (as sth); share certain characteristics (with sth). **S:** organism; disease; humour; insecurity. **o:** bacteria; cancer; creativity; aggression. **A:** closely, clearly, in no way: *This disease seems (to be) closely* ***allied to*** *malaria.* ○ *Love is* ***allied to*** *hatred* (or: *Love and hatred are* ***allied***). □ also used with *appear, seem.*

alternate

alternate (with) [Vpr rel] happen, occur, by turns. **S:** (good) weather, fortune, times; success; tears. **o:** (bad) weather etc; failure; laughter. **A:** over a long period, throughout his career: *While they were on holiday sunshine* ***alternated*** *regularly* ***with*** *wintry conditions* (or: *sunshine and wintry conditions* ***alternated***). ○ *Fortunately, cheerfulness* ***alternates with*** *his bad moods.*

amalgamate

amalgamate (with) [Vpr rel, Vn.pr pass rel] join (sth) (with another) to form one unit. **S** [Vpr], **O** [Vn.pr]**:** group, company, organization, society. **S** [Vn.pr]**:** director, board. **o:** an American company, former rivals: *If the German company* ***amalgamates with*** *the Dutch giant, they will become the biggest electronics conglomerate in Europe.* ○ *We've just been* ***amalgamated with*** *a Birmingham company.* = unite (with).

amount

amount to 1 [Vpr] be equal to or reach (a total). **S:** bill(s), debt(s), liabilities, assets. **o:** sum, total; quantity; very little; (not) much; nothing: *The current trade deficit* ***amounts to*** *several thousands of millions of pounds.* ○ *His total worldly possessions* ***amounted to*** *little more than the clothes he stood up in.* □ often neg. = add up to 1, come to 3.

2 [Vpr] mean (sth). **S:** it; statement, suggestion, proposal, offer, idea(s). **o:** this; (not) much; very little: *He always has a lot to say, but looked at closely it never* ***amounts to*** *much.* ○ *What this* ***amounts to*** *is that she's simply not willing to give us her support.* ○ *Whether I pay or my wife pays* ***amounts to*** *the same thing, because we share all our money.* = add up to 2.

3 [Vpr] become successful or make progress in life. **o:** ⚠ (not) very much, (not) anything: *Jimmy doesn't know where he is or where he's going. He'll never do anything, and he'll never* ***amount to*** *anything.* LBA □ usu neg.

angle

angle for [Vpr pass adj rel] (*informal*) try to obtain (sth) by means of hints. **o:** compliment; promotion; useful information; invitation: *I do wish Liz wouldn't* ***angle for*** *compliments in such an obvious way.* ○ *The promotion* ***for*** *which he had long been* ***angling*** *eventually came his way.* = fish for.

annex

annex (to) [Vn.pr pass] add (sth) to the territory of a country, estate etc. **O:** land, area, region: *In the years leading up to the outbreak of war in 1939, Hitler succeeded in* ***annexing*** *various parts of Europe (****to*** *Germany) without firing a shot.*

answer

answer back 1 [Vp, Vn.p pass] speak or interrupt (sb) rudely when being scolded. **S:** child; servant; private. **O:** mother; employer; officer, NCO: *When your mother scolds you, you shouldn't* ***answer*** *(her)* ***back****.* ○ *'Don't* ***answer*** *(me)* ***back****, or I'll send you to the headmaster!'.* ○ *She longed to assert herself, and found herself being impertinent in small matters, almost* ***answering back****.* PW

2 [Vp, Vn.p pass] defend oneself; speak up for oneself (perhaps impudently): *Cressett complains of an injustice and John criticizes in public a man whose position forbids him to* ***answer back****.* ASA ○ *It's unfair to attack a person in the newspaper when he can't* ***answer*** *(you)* ***back****.*

answer for 1 [Vpr] be responsible for (sth); be blamed for (sth). **o:** actions, behaviour; madness, failure; the consequences: *Don't forget that one day you'll have to* ***answer for*** *your foolish behaviour — perhaps to the police, even.* ○ *If you insist on carrying on with this mad experiment I won't* ***answer for*** *the consequences.* ○ *That poor woman seems to be more neurotic every time I see her: her husband's got a lot to* ***answer for****.*

2 [Vpr pass rel] give a satisfactory record of (sth). **o:** expenditure, receipts; stock: *We keep detailed records, because every single pound has to be* ***answered for****.* = account for 1.

3 [Vpr] speak, or accept responsibility, on behalf of (others). **o:** others, anyone else; (my) brother; our allies: *My opinion is that you are the best man for the job, but I can't* ***answer for*** *the other members of the committee, of course.* ⇨ speak for.

answer (to) [Vpr] be controlled by (sth); obey. **S:** boat, car, aircraft. **o:** rudder, steering-wheel; movement, jerk, tug; wind, breeze: *The horse* ***answers to*** *the slightest pull on the rein.* ○ *The boat seemed very slow to* ***answer to*** *any movement of the helm.* = respond (to).

answer to (for) [Vpr] give an explanation to (sb) (about sth); be responsible to (sb) (for sth). **o:** (**to**) father, employer, police; (**for**) crime, misdeed, mistake: *You'll have to* ***answer to*** *me* (or: *You'll be*

answerable to *me) if any harm comes to this child.* ○ *One day you will have to* ***answer to*** *a higher authority* ***for*** *your sins of omission and commission.* □ the implication is that failure to act responsibly will be punished; note the variant answerable to sb (for sth). = account to (for).

answer to the description (of) [Vpr] fit, match a description of (sth). **S:** (stolen) car, handbag; (wanted) man: *This car exactly* ***answers to the description of*** *the stolen vehicle.* ○ *Pearson was arrested because he seemed to* ***answer to the description of*** *the escaped prisoner.*

answer to the name (of) [Vpr] be called or named (sth); recognize as one's own the name of (sth): *They had an old goat that* ***answered to the name of*** *Smelly.* ○ *There's no one here* ***answering to that name.***

apologize

apologize (to) (for) [Vpr pass rel] express regret (to sb) (for sth); say one is sorry (for sth). **o:** being late, forgetting his name; offence, inconvenience, delay: *She* ***apologized*** *profusely* ***for*** *treading on my toe.* ○ *You'd better* ***apologize to*** *Mary* ***for*** *not writing to her earlier.* ○ *He's not used to being* ***apologized to.*** ○ *That's not something that has to be* ***apologized for.*** □ two passive forms: be apologized to/for.

appeal

appeal (to) (against) [Vpr pass rel] (esp *legal*) ask (a higher body) to reconsider (a judgment). **o:** (**to**) Supreme Court; House of Lords; (**against**) verdict, sentence: *She was sentenced to three years' imprisonment but intends to* ***appeal against*** *the judgment.* ○ *The union is now* ***appealing against*** *the sequestration of its assets.* □ two passive forms: be appealed to/against.

appeal (to) (for) [Vpr pass rel] earnestly request (sb) (to give or grant sth). **S:** prisoner; manager, steward; mountaineer. **o:** (**to**) court, tribunal, crowd; workers, employees; rescue team, Red Cross; (**for**) clemency; quiet; assistance: *The condemned man* ***appealed to*** *the court* ***for*** *mercy.* ○ *The police saw that the two sides might come to blows, and* ***appealed for*** *calm.* □ two passive forms: be appealed to/for. = plead (with) (for).

appear

appear for [Vpr] (*legal*) represent (sb) in court, at an inquiry etc: *Mr Peebles* ***appeared for*** *the defence in a case brought by the Crown against two alleged terrorists.* ○ *Residents have invited a local solicitor to* ***appear for*** *them in the inquiry into the siting of a new airport near the village.*

append

append (to) [Vpr pass emph rel] (*formal*) make (sth) a part of (sth). **O:** rider, codicil. **o:** document; lease, will: ***To*** *the original agreement between the parties an important clause concerning the disposal of assets has now been* ***appended.*** = affix (to).

appertain

appertain to [Vpr] (*formal*) properly concern (sth/sb); rightfully belong to (sth/sb). **S:** right to do sth; conditions. **o:** post; holder (of post): *The duties and privileges* ***appertaining to*** *the post of warden of the students' residence have never been officially stated.*

apply

apply (for) [Vpr pass emph rel] ⇨ apply (to) (for).

apply (to) 1 [Vpr rel] concern or affect (sb). **S:** rules, restrictions, instructions; remarks, criticisms; what I say; taxes: *'Do these regulations* ***apply to*** *me?' 'Yes, they* ***apply to*** *everyone, without exception.'* ○ *The categories* ***to*** *whom the new charges do not* ***apply*** *are: persons under the age of 18 and old age pensioners.* = refer to 2.

2 [Vn.pr pass rel] put (sth) (on sth) as a covering or treatment. **O:** paint, emulsion; cream, ointment, lotion; plaster, poultice. **o:** surface; burns, sore, cut. **A:** evenly, generously; sparingly, promptly: *Do not* ***apply*** *this ointment* ***to*** *the affected parts until all dirt has been removed.* ○ *The lotion should be* ***applied*** *sparingly* ***to*** *the skin.* ○ *The surface* ***to*** *which the paint is* ***applied*** *should be free of grease and dirt.* □ often imperative.

3 [Vn.pr emph rel] put (one's energy etc) fully (into sth/doing sth). **O:** ⚠ oneself; one's mind, energies, thoughts. **o:** work, task, job; business, matter in hand; solving the problem, passing one's exams. **A:** with a will; enthusiastically, wholeheartedly; with zest: *If you really* ***apply*** *your mind* ***to*** *the job, you'll soon finish it.* ○ *Had he* ***applied*** *himself as enthusiastically* ***to*** *work as* ***to*** *pleasure he might have been very successful.*

apply (to) (for) [Vpr pass emph rel] make a request (to sb), usu in writing (for sth). **o:** (**to**) manager, secretary; address; branch, head office; post office, police station; (**for**) position, vacancy, promotion, increase (in salary); visa, permit, permission: *Miss O'Hara has just* ***applied to*** *British Telecom* ***for*** *a job.* ○ ***For*** *further information,* ***apply to*** *the Company Secretary.* ○ *'****To*** *whom should I* ***apply for*** *a licence?'* ○ *Those over fifty need not* ***apply.*** □ often imperative.

appoint

appoint (to) [Vn.pr pass rel] select (sb) (as the person to occupy a post). **S:** employer, selection board. **O:** applicant, candidate. **o:** post; vacancy: *Jeffries was* ***appointed to*** *the Chairmanship of the Finance Committee.*

apprise

apprise of [Vn.pr pass emph rel] (*formal*) make (sb) aware of (sth). **o:** (true, grave) situation, facts; (sb's) feelings, intentions; peril, danger: *Several committee members had not been* ***apprised of*** *the contents of the document.* ○ *A spokesman said that the Minister was fully* ***apprised of*** *the importance of the discovery and would be making a statement later in the day.* POS □ usu passive.

approach

approach (about) [Vn.pr pass emph rel] talk to (sb) (concerning sth); put a request to (sb) (concerning sth). **O:** director, headmaster; Information Department, Inquiries (office). **o:** grievance, complaint, loss. **A:** informally, privately, confidentially: *Have you* ***approached*** *the manager* ***about*** *taking a day off next week?* ○ *The bank will need to be*

approached about *extending our overdraft for another six months.*

appropriate

appropriate (for) [Vn.pr pass emph rel] (*formal*) take and use (funds etc) officially (for a specific purpose). **O:** money, funds; sum, amount. **o:** building, repairs; road improvements; training: *The Council has* ***appropriated*** *£1m* ***for*** *the provision of better sporting facilities in the inner city areas.*

appropriate to oneself/one's own use [Vn.pr pass] (*formal*) take for one's own use or as one's own property: *The army has* ***appropriated*** *a large area of woodland* ***to its own use****.*

approve

approve (of) [Vpr pass rel] like or admire (sb/sth); consider (sb/sth) to be acceptable. **o:** him etc; attitude, behaviour; manner, appearance; him/his getting drunk, them/their making a mess: *'I took him home to meet my parents, but they didn't exactly* ***approve (of*** *him).'* ○ *'I certainly don't* ***approve of*** *you riding your motorbike over the speed limit.'*

approximate

approximate to [Vpr rel] (*formal*) come near to (sth); be nearly or roughly (sth). **S:** account, description (of the event, proposal); cost of the completed building. **o:** facts, truth; (original) version, intention; estimate. **A:** roughly, on the whole, closely: *Your latest design* ***approximates*** *much more closely* ***to*** *what I understood the building to be like.* ○ *His original conception,* ***to*** *which this sketch* ***approximates*** *roughly, was for a five-door saloon car.*

arbitrate

arbitrate (between) [Vpr rel] (*legal*) seek an agreement which is acceptable (to two contending persons etc). **S:** judge, referee, umpire: *An experienced industrial lawyer has been asked to* ***arbitrate between*** *the contending parties.* ○ *There is no statutory body whose duty it is to* ***arbitrate between*** *these workers and their employers.*

arch

arch over [Vpr pass rel] form a sort of cover over (sth); overhang: *Along this part of the river, the trees on both banks* ***arch over*** *the water.* ○ *The drive was* ***arched over*** *with thick foliage.*

argue

argue about/over [Vpr pass rel] discuss (sth) vigorously and with differing views; dispute. **o:** meaning, origin (of); the best way to do sth; who should do it; size, weight, colour (of): *'What are you two* ***arguing about****?'* ○ *While they were* ***arguing over*** *who should cook the dinner, the dog ran off with the meat.* ○ *He's a crook; and that's not something that can be* ***argued about****.*

argue against 1 [Vpr rel] give reasons, evidence etc, for not doing (sth). **o:** (proposed) plan, action; appointment, nomination; award: *The treasurer* ***argued*** *fiercely* ***against*** *any increase in expenditure for the children's annual party.* ○ *The scheme* ***against*** *which I had* ***argued*** *so strongly turned out to be a great success.*

2 [Vpr rel] (*formal*) indicate or suggest the opposite of (sth). **S:** information, evidence; previous experience: *All the evidence* ***argued against*** *the theory that the disease was transmitted by water.*

argue out [Vn.p pass] discuss (sth), esp with feeling, until a conclusion is reached. **O:** ⚠ things, matters; it: *I wanted to bundle the three raincoats up into a pillow . . . for a nice long sleep, while Ned and Robert* ***argued*** *it* ***out****.* CON

argue (with) [Vpr pass rel] try to persuade (sb) to change his mind; protest to (sb) against instructions he has given: *Mrs Burns is a very stubborn woman; not the kind to be* ***argued with****.* ○ *'Don't* ***argue (with*** *me)! Just do as I tell you.'*

arise

arise from [Vpr rel] (*formal*) have its origin in (sth); be due to, be caused by (sth). **S:** problem, misunderstanding, difficulty; (his) poor condition, state of health. **o:** (poor) communications, distance; neglect, isolation, malnutrition: *The company's poor trading record* ***arises*** *almost entirely* ***from*** *the increase in interest rates.* ○ *His condition will not improve until the cause* ***from*** *which it* ***arises*** *has been removed.* = spring from 2, stem from.

arm

arm (against) (with) [Vn.pr pass rel] supply or provide (sb) (with weapons) as a precaution or defence. **O:** oneself; friends, allies; the people. **o:** (**against**) invasion, threat; attack, subversion; (**with**) sword, gun; information, religious faith: *I* ***armed*** *myself* ***with*** *a poker and hid behind the curtain.* ○ *It is not enough to condemn aggression: we must* ***arm*** *our friends* ***against*** *possible attack* ***with*** *the latest weapons.* ○ *The students' leaders arrived at the inquiry* ***armed with*** *an impressive collection of facts and figures to prove that their grants were quite inadequate.*

arouse

arouse (from) [Vn.pr pass rel] (*formal*) make (sb) conscious. **o:** sleep, slumber; stupor, lethargy, apathy, indifference. **A:** gently, roughly, hurriedly: *Mr Murray was* ***aroused from*** *his slumber by his wife whispering urgently in his ear, 'There's a burglar downstairs!'* ○ *The spread of disease among the refugees at last* ***aroused*** *local people* ***from*** *their indifference to the newcomers' welfare.* = awake(n) (from).

arrange

arrange (for) 1 [Vn.pr pass rel] fix (sth), set (sth) in order (on sb's behalf). **S:** secretary, receptionist; (travel) agency. **O:** appointment, meeting; trip, excursion, outing. **o:** employer, visitor, guest: *Ring up, and try to* ***arrange*** *an appointment* ***for*** *me with the dentist.* ○ *You'll find that everything will have been* ***arranged for*** *you when you arrive.*

2 [Vn.pr pass rel] rewrite (music) written for one instrument (or combination) so that it can be played by another. **O:** piece, composition. **o:** string quartet, chamber orchestra: *The composer has* ***arranged*** *Chopin's nocturnes* ***for*** *full orchestra.*

arrange for [Vpr] make plans for (sth to be done/sb to do sth). **o:** fish to be bought, the newspapers to be cancelled; Mary to prepare the food: *I'll* ***arrange for*** *the parcel to be delivered first thing tomorrow.* ○ *We've* ***arranged for*** *a car to pick them up at the station.*

arrive

arrive (at) [Vpr rel] reach (a destination). **o:** station; hotel; finishing point: *We* ***arrived at*** *the station just as the train was leaving.*

arrive at [Vpr pass rel] achieve (sth). **o:** goal; result, conclusion; decision: *The two research teams* ***arrived at*** *the same conclusion quite independently.*

ascribe

ascribe to 1 [Vn.pr pass emph rel] (*formal*) consider (sth) to be the result of (sth). **O:** success, achievement; failure, mistake; illness, recovery. **o:** luck, fortune; tenacity, determination; poor judgement, carelessness; a healthy life, sensible living: *The success of the project can be* ***ascribed to*** *the dogged efforts of ordinary members of the team.* = attribute to 1, put down to 2.

2 [Vn.pr pass emph rel] consider (sth), perhaps wrongly, to be the work of (sb). **O:** painting, sculpture; symphony; play: *For years these poems were wrongly* ***ascribed to*** *Marlowe.* = attribute to 2.

ask

ask (about) [Vpr rel, Vn.pr pass rel] seek information from (sb) (about sth). **O:** travel agent; airline. **o:** train times; holiday flights; suitable hotels: *'We had someone in earlier* ***asking about*** *flights to Corfu.'* ○ *'Has anyone booked a hotel room?' 'I don't know; you'd better* ***ask*** *Jane* ***about*** *that.'* = inquire (about).

ask after [Vpr pass] seek news of (the health of) (sb): *Don't forget to* ***ask after*** *your uncle when you see Mary this afternoon.* ○ *I met John yesterday; he was* ***asking after*** *you.* ○ *Your health was* ***asked after****. They all seemed very concerned.* = inquire after.

ask around [Vp, Vpr] ask various people, possibly in various places, about sth: *'How did you find her?' 'I just* ***asked around****. The locals were quite helpful.'* ○ *I was told, when I* ***asked around****, that this might be because he was a party member.* IND

ask for 1 [Vpr pass rel] request or seek (sth). **o:** food, drink, shelter; help, advice; the gate to be repaired: *If you get into difficulties, don't hesitate to* ***ask for*** *help.* ○ *I only wanted a little equipment for my research, but it was like* ***asking for*** *the moon.* ○ *It's now almost a month since I* ***asked for*** *the clock to be mended.*

2 [Vpr rel] say that one wants to see or speak to (sb). **O:** boss, director; security, the registry: *'Ring Head Office and* ***ask for*** *the Health and Safety Officer.'* ○ *'Get through to the switchboard and* ***ask for*** *Bill Jones.'*

ask for it/trouble [Vpr] (*informal*) invite or provoke punishment, retaliation etc: *'You'd better not disturb the papers on your father's desk; if you do, you're just* ***asking for*** *trouble.'* ○ *'You* ***asked for it****', Mother said as she slapped Fred, 'and now you've got it!'.*

ask (of) [Vn.pr pass emph rel] request (sb) to behave, or hope he will behave, in a certain way. **O:** ⚠ a lot, a great deal, too much. **o:** children, students; staff; old people: *You can't expect the man to work seven days a week: that's too much to* ***ask of*** *anyone.* ○ *'Aren't you* ***asking*** *rather a lot* ***of*** *your son — expecting him to be top in every subject?'* = expect (of).

ask over/round [Vn.p pass] invite (sb) to come to one's house, office etc from another place: *She ... wants to congratulate me. I suppose in exchange for her good wishes the silly bag (=woman) wants to be* ***asked over*** *for some parlour games.* JFTR = invite in/over/round.

ask out (to) [Vn.p pass, Vn.p.pr pass rel] invite (sb) to go out (usu for a treat of some kind, whether stated or not). **O:** girl; neighbour. **o:** dinner; the theatre: *I've been* ***asked out*** *for the evening by the boy next door.* ○ *She's been* ***asked out to*** *lunch by an old school friend.*

aspire

aspire to [Vpr pass emph rel] (*formal*) desire to obtain (sth) or become (sth); be ambitious for (sth). **o:** fame, fortune; eminence, distinction: *My father never* ***aspired to*** *the job of managing director, and was very surprised when it was offered to him.* ○ *The fame* ***to*** *which Mr Hastings* ***aspired*** *was quite beyond his reach.*

assail

assail with [Vn.pr pass rel] (*formal*) trouble, bother (sb) by asking (sth). **o:** questions; accusations, criticisms: *As soon as John returned home, his parents* ***assailed*** *him* ***with*** *questions about the interview.*

assent

assent (to) [Vpr pass rel] (*formal*) give one's approval (to sth). **o:** suggestion, proposal, plan, scheme; my going abroad. **A:** willingly, readily, unhesitatingly: *My father will never* ***assent to*** *my spending a holiday abroad before I'm 16.* ○ *The marriage,* ***to*** *which their parents had so unwillingly* ***assented****, turned out to be extremely happy.* = agree (to).

assess

assess (at) [Vn.pr pass rel] estimate (sth) to be (sth). **S:** judge; Inspector of Taxes; valuer, surveyor. **O:** income, expenditure, value. **o:** sum, figure: *The Inspector of Taxes has* ***assessed*** *your income for the year ending 31 March* ***at*** *£20 000.* ○ *The value of the property has been* ***assessed at*** *£200 000.*

assign

assign to [Vn.pr pass rel] (*formal*) reserve (sth) for the use of (sb); give (sth) to (sb) as a task. **O:** room, building; task, duty, work. **o:** staff, guest; office, department: *The Director* ***assigned*** *a wing of the building* ***to*** *the important visitors.* ○ *The defence of the oil installation had been* ***assigned to*** *my regiment* (or: *My regiment had been* ***assigned to*** *its defence*).

assimilate

assimilate (into/with) [Vpr rel, Vn.pr pass rel] (*formal*) (help sb to) become so much like (others) that he cannot be distinguished from them. **o:** population; tribe, group: *Language was the chief obstacle which prevented immigrants from Eastern Europe* ***assimilating with*** *the German population.* ○ *In less than a century the Huguenot refugees had become fully* ***assimilated into*** *the local community.*

associate

associate with 1 [Vpr rel] (*formal*) keep company with (sb); spend a lot of time with (sb). **o:** thieves, prostitutes, riff-raff; the rich, the successful: *I*

wouldn't trust him any further than I could throw him — he **associates with** *all sorts of undesirable characters.* ○ *The people* **with** *whom Mr Smart* **associates** *are all highly respectable.* = consort with.
2 [Vn.pr pass emph rel] (*formal*) connect (sb/sth) with (sth), often mentally. **O:** him etc; place, experience; sound, smell, feel (of sth). **o:** plan, proposal, activity; childhood, school; failure, success: *I always* **associate** *the smell of jasmine* **with** *Uruguay.* ○ *The doctor was always* **associated** *in the child's mind* **with** *injections and pain.* ○ *'Do you wish your name to be* **associated with** *our fund-raising scheme?' 'No, it's something* **with** *which I'd rather not* **associate** *myself.'*

assure

assure of [Vn.pr pass emph rel] (*formal*) make (sb) feel confident or certain about (sth); promise. **o:** (one's) willingness, readiness; (great, warm, enthusiastic) reception, welcome; (careful, sympathetic) consideration of sth: *I can* **assure** *you* **of** *my full support for your plan.* ○ *Peter* **assured** *me* **of** *his continued interest in my work.* □ note: be assured of meaning 'be certain of': *As soon as they adopted the new procedures, they were* **assured of** *success.*

atone

atone for [Vpr pass rel] (*formal*) repay sb for (sth one has done or failed to do). **o:** offence, injury; rudeness, insensitivity; failing to do sth: *Your son is doing his best to* **atone for** *his bad behaviour last night.* ○ *I think you can now consider your unfortunate mistake to be fully* **atoned for**. = make amends (to) (for), make up for 2.

attach

attach (to) [Vn.pr pass emph rel] fasten, fix (sth) (on or to sth). **O:** handle; buckle. **o:** door; belt: *Is it possible to* **attach** *this bracket (***to** *the wall)?* ○ **To** *the bridegroom's car his friends had* **attached** *a lot of old boots and empty tin cans.* ↔ detach (from).

attach to 1 [Vn.pr pass rel] make (sb) a member of (an organization), esp for a short time. **O:** officer, administrator, scientist. **o:** unit, bureau, laboratory: *Two young trainees will be* **attached to** *the department to gain practical experience of management.* ○ *For the first time, British astronauts are being* **attached to** *a Soviet space programme.* □ esp passive.
2 [Vn.pr pass emph rel] consider (sth) to be (important etc). **O:** ⚠ (too much) importance, credence; significance, meaning. **o:** news; announcement, report; what the papers say; his being there: *Too much importance is being* **attached to** *rumours of impending revolution in these republics.* ○ *You* **attach** *altogether too much significance* **to** *the Prime Minister's words.*
3 [Vn.pr pass emph rel] (*formal*) consider that (sb) can be blamed etc. **S:** court, crown. **O:** blame, suspicion; charge of neglect. **o:** accused, prisoner: *The court decided that it could* **attach** *no possible blame* **to** *the driver of the lorry.* ○ *No suspicion in this case can be* **attached to** *the accountant.*
4 [Vpr] (*formal*) be associated with (sth); be due to (sth). **S:** (great, considerable) importance; credit for doing sth; (no) suspicion, blame. **o:** decision, vote; outcome of the discussions; the Prime Minister, the Union leaders; accountant: *Far-reaching implications* **attach to** *the railwaymen's decision to go on strike.* ○ *The main credit for the party's electoral success* **attaches to** *the prestige and confidence of its leader.*

attach oneself/itself to [Vn.pr rel] join or fasten oneself/itself to (sb/sth), often in an unwelcome manner. **S:** child; dog; thistle, thread, wire: *A stray dog* **attached itself to** *me while I was out walking and would not leave me.* ○ *Leeches* **attached themselves to** *his legs.*

attached to [adj pred (Vn.pr)] (be) strongly tied to (sb/sth) emotionally; (be) fond of (sb/sth). **o:** one's wife, family; heritage, traditions: *She's become* **attached to** *someone she met at university.* ○ *He's always been strongly* **attached to** *the regiment and its traditions.* □ used with *appear, seem, become, get.*

attend

attend (on/upon) [Vpr pass rel] (*formal*) tend (sb). **S:** servant; doctor, physician, nurse. **o:** patient, sick man: *Two nurses* **attended** *night and day* **on** *the dying man.* ○ *He was called out to a patient* **(on)** *whom he had* **attended** *some years previously.*

attend (to) [Vpr rel] listen carefully (to sb/sth). **o:** teacher, parent; advice, counsels; what people say: *If she'd* **attended to** *what her instructor told her, she wouldn't have had an accident.* ○ *If you don't* **attend** *(***to** *your teachers), you'll never learn anything.* = pay attention (to).

attend to 1 [Vpr pass rel] tend or nurse (sb). **o:** invalid, patient, sick child: *If you go out, who will* **attend to** *the baby?* ○ *'I'll get someone in to* **attend to** *father.'* = look after 1, take care (of) 1.
2 [Vpr pass rel] take responsibility for (sth/sb). **o:** shop, business; client, customer: *'Don't worry, everything will be* **attended to** *in good time!'* ○ (in a shop) *'Is someone* **attending to** *you* (or: *Are you being* **attended to**)*?'* = look after 2, take care (of) 2.

attire

attire (oneself) (in) [Vn.pr pass rel] (*formal*) dress (in special clothes), usu for a formal occasion. **S:** judge, official; king, queen; the bride. **o:** crimson, purple; robes of state, office; white. **A:** from head to foot, splendidly: *The Lords were* **attired in** *their ceremonial robes for the opening of Parliament.* □ usu passive.

attract

attract (to) [Vn.pr pass emph rel] cause (sb) to move (towards sth). **S:** activity; noise; light, smell; opportunities, markets. **O:** crowd; onlooker(s), spectator(s); customer(s), investor(s). **o:** market; fight, accident; stall, shop; locality: *The bright lights and noisy music* **attracted** *many children* **to** *the fairground.* ○ *The government is finding it difficult to* **attract** *overseas investment* **to** *the area.* = draw to/towards.

attribute

attribute to 1 [Vn.pr pass emph rel] (*formal*) explain (sth) by means of (sth); give (sth) as the origin, cause or reason for (sth). **O:** good, bad health, longevity; prosperity, success; misfortune, failure. **o:** sound diet, regular exercise; hard work; good, bad, luck: *Mr Dolittle* **attributes** *his good health* **to** *careful living.* ○ **To** *his mother can be* **attributed** *his intelligence, and* **to** *his father his* *rather casual attitude to life and work.* = ascribe to 1, put down to 2.

2 [Vn.pr pass rel] (*formal*) suggest (sb) as the author of (sth). **S:** critic; musicologist. **O:** painting; sonnet; song, symphony. **o:** (minor) artist; poet; composer: *Shakespeare's plays have often been* ***attributed to*** *others, and especially* ***to*** *Bacon.* = ascribe to 2.

attuned

attuned (to) [pass (Vn.pr)] (*formal*) made or shaped so that others can understand and appreciate it: *T S Eliot's poetic language was successfully* ***attuned to*** *the times in which he lived.* ○ *His mind is well* ***attuned to*** *mine* (or: *Our minds are well* ***attuned***). = be in accord/harmony/tune (with). □ also used with *appear* etc, or after a noun.

auction

auction off [Vn ⇆ p pass] sell all of (sth), get rid of (sth), by auction. **S:** Army, Navy, Air Force; Civil Service; store, factory. **O:** surplus; unwanted goods, supplies, stocks, materials: *From time to time the Army* ***auctions off*** *unwanted supplies of various kinds.* ○ *Machinery* ***auctioned off*** *by bankrupt industries could be acquired for next to nothing.*

augur

augur ill/well for [Vpr] (*formal*) suggest or indicate that (sb/sth) will probably develop badly/well. **S:** action, behaviour; (recent) events, (new) taxes; his coming to power. **o:** us etc; our relationship, partnership; the future of industry; our hopes of bringing about change: *John and Mary have started quarrelling already. That doesn't* ***augur well for*** *their future happiness.* ○ *Failure to agree on the composition of the government* ***augurs ill for*** *the stability of the regime.*

avail

avail oneself of [Vn.pr rel] (*formal*) use or exploit (sth); seize. **o:** facilities (provided); chance, opportunity; offer, proposal; every means in one's power. **A:** always, fully; without hesitation, with pleasure: *You should* ***avail yourself of*** *every opportunity to practise your English.* ○ *Those wishing to* ***avail themselves of*** *these facilities should speak to our trained staff.* □ note the form in letters and speeches: *May I* ***avail myself of*** *this opportunity to …; I should like to* ***avail myself of*** *….* = take advantage of 1.

avenge

avenge oneself (on) (for) [Vn.pr rel] (*formal*) act (against sb) in return for some injury one has suffered. **o:** (**on**) rival family; gunman; terrorist gang; (**for**) misfortune, loss; murder, savage killing: *He swore to* ***avenge himself*** *(****on*** *his enemy)* ***for*** *the humiliation he had suffered.* ○ *The man* ***on*** *whom the terrorists* ***avenged themselves*** *had no connection with a paramilitary organization.* □ also: *The young king* ***avenged*** *his father's murder.* = revenge (oneself) on, take revenge (on) (for).

average

average out (at) [Vp, Vp.pr rel, Vn ⇆ p pass, Vn.p.pr pass rel] show an average (of sth); calculate the average (of sth) (at a particular figure). **S** [Vp, Vp.pr], **O** [Vn.p, Vn.p.pr]: revenue, takings; salary, wages; cost; output; score, (number of) goals, runs; (hours of) sunshine, rainfall: [Vp.pr] *The rainfall for the period under review* ***averaged out at*** *about three inches a month.* ○ [Vp.pr] *Our speed* ***averaged out at*** *40 miles an hour (= We* ***averaged*** *40 miles an hour all the way).* ○ [Vn.p.pr] *The tax inspectors* ***averaged*** *his profit* ***out at*** *£10 000 a year for five years.*

avert

avert (from) [Vn.pr pass rel] (*formal*) stop facing, looking at or considering (sb/sth). **O:** eyes, gaze; mind, thoughts. **o:** sight, prospect; problem, idea; (likely) consequences, results; (approaching) examination, trial, test; (his) predicament; poverty, misery, unhappiness: *I did my best to* ***avert*** *my thoughts* ***from*** *the approaching confrontation with my employers.* ○ *It's no use* ***averting*** *your eyes (****from*** *the poverty and suffering which is all around you).* = turn away (from) 1.

awake

awake(n) (from) [Vpr rel, Vn.pr pass rel] wake up (from sth); return to reality (from sth). **o:** (deep, light, profound) sleep; dream. **A** [Vpr]**:** suddenly, gradually, slowly; with a start. [Vn.pr] roughly, gently: *He* ***awoke*** *(****from*** *a restless sleep) to find that all his fears were unfounded.* ○ *He was rudely* ***awakened from*** *his dream of making a quick fortune when his partner made off with £100 000.*

awake(n) to [Vpr rel, Vn.pr pass rel] (*formal*) (make sb) realize or understand (sth). **o:** realities, facts; possibilities, opportunities, potentialities; dangers, risks; urgency. **A:** painfully, slowly, gradually: *It's time you* ***awoke to*** *the realities of the situation.* ○ *We have at last* ***awoken*** *John* ***to*** *the fact that there's no easy way to success.* ○ *During the 1930s Churchill tried to* ***awaken*** *the British people* ***to*** *the urgent need for rearmament.* = wake up to.

award

award (to) [Vn.pr pass emph rel] give or grant (sth) officially (to sb). **S:** judge, committee, jury. **O:** prize; medal, cup, certificate; sum, amount; damages, compensation. **o:** winner, runner-up, loser; plaintiff, widow: *The jury* ***awarded*** *the first prize* ***to*** *Jill* (or: ***awarded*** *Jill the first prize*). ○ *£120 000 was the amount* ***awarded*** *by the court (****to*** *the victim of the accident).*

B

babble

babble on [Vp] chatter continuously in a thoughtless or confused way: *I* ***babbled on*** *continuously about my upbringing, my schooldays and my career.* SU

back

back away (from) [Vp, Vp.pr emph rel] move back (from sb/sth) through fear or dislike. **S:** prisoner, suspect; child, animal. **o:** guard, policeman; noise, fire: *As the men at the bar reached for their guns, the onlookers* ***backed away.*** ○ *George* ***backed away****, but there was no visible escape route.* FL ○ *Even well-disposed people* ***back away from***

Richard when they see that ingratiating smile. = back off 2.

back down [Vp] withdraw charges, claims, accusations etc; retreat. **S:** critic, rival, opponent. **A:** completely, abjectly: *Faced with fresh evidence of their involvement, the other side had to* ***back down****.* ○ *Even those who seemed to have good reason to criticize have* ***backed down****.*

back into [Vpr pass, Vn.pr pass rel] drive (a vehicle) backwards into (sth), esp through carelessness or inexperience. **S** [Vpr], **O** [Vn.pr]**:** car, lorry, tractor. **S** [Vpr, Vn.pr]**:** driver, farmer. **o:** (another) car; tree, gatepost: *I don't exactly enjoy being* ***backed into*** *by learner drivers.* ○ *He succeeded in* ***backing*** *his new car* ***into*** *the only lamp-post in the street.*

back off 1 [Vp] move (a vehicle) back from a position too close to sth else. **S:** driver; car, bus; line of traffic. **A:** a bit, a few yards: *'Do you mind* ***backing off*** *a bit, Sir, while we clear this wreck out of the way?'* ○ *'I don't like that car sitting on my tail. Wave to him to* ***back off****.'*

2 [Vp] move back from sb/sth through fear or dislike. **S:** child, visitor: *Sheila* ***backed off*** *as he extended an oily hand.* ○ *I took one look at those staring eyes and* ***backed off****.* = back away (from).

3 [Vp] withdraw from a course of action one was going to take: *Christian leaders who have been contemplating such a move have* ***backed off****.* G

back on to [Vp.pr] have at its back, face at the back. **S:** house, shop; study, kitchen. **o:** courtyard; lane, alley: *The burglar is unlikely to have got in through the dining-room window — it* ***backs on to*** *several other houses.* ⇨ look onto/out on.

back out/out of 1 [Vp, Vpr, Vn ⇆ p pass, Vn.pr pass] (cause a vehicle to) move backwards (from a place). **S** [Vp, Vpr], **O** [Vn.p, Vn.pr]**:** car, lorry, bus.**o:** garage, drive: *'Can you move your van please? I can't* ***back out****.'* ○ *The car* ***backed*** *noisily* ***out of*** *the double gateway into the lane.* SE

2 [Vp, Vpr pass] retreat (from a place), leave, through shyness, fear etc. **O:** room, hall: *'Excuse me', mouthed Ermyn,* ***backing out*** *as quietly as she could and closing the oak door.* SE

3 [Vp, Vpr pass] withdraw (from an undertaking, promise). **o:** agreement, scheme, arrangement: *Once you've given your word, don't try to* ***back out****.* ○ *It's no good* ***backing out of*** *it now — with my own ears I heard your last words.* HSG

back up 1 [Vn ⇆ p nom pass adj] give physical, military or legislative support to (sb/sth); reinforce. **O:** attack, landing; course, programme; legislation. **A:** fully, amply, adequately: *The lectures and seminars are* ***backed up*** *by a heavy programme of practical work.* ○ ***Back-up*** *materials in the form of videos and cassettes are supplied with the course books.* ○ *If they* (= soldiers on patrol) *have to go alone, the rule is that military* ***back-up*** *is never less than a quarter-of-a-mile away.* ST ○ *He is determined to seek statutory* ***back-up*** *powers to control pay and prices.* T

2 [Vn ⇆ p nom pas adj] give moral support to (sb). **O:** colleague, subordinate. **A:** loyally, unstintingly: *Alexander* ***backed*** *me* ***up*** *enthusiastically, as he always did.* MFM ○ *Ada's been complaining that there's nobody to* ***back*** *her* ***up*** *if anybody gets nasty.* HD

3 [Vn ⇆ p nom pass adj] wind (sth) backwards through a camera, video etc. **O:** film, tape: *Now just* ***back*** *the film* ***up*** *a couple of frames.* ○ *Here's another shot on our* ***back-up*** (device for showing a picture, or series of pictures, that have been shown earlier). ITV

4 [Vp] (*cricket*) (of the non-striking batsman) move down the wicket as the ball is delivered, to support a possible attempt at a run by the striker: *Jameson* ***backed up****, was sent back, struggled for a foothold, and was run out when a fielder hit the stumps.* G ○ *Although Botham made no contribution to Worcestershire's total of 433, he was unlucky to be run out* ***backing up****.* G

bail

bail out 1 [Vn ⇆ p pass adj] (*legal*) free (sb) until trial by paying a cash guarantee. **S:** friend, well-wisher. **O:** prisoner, accused: *An anonymous well-wisher* ***bailed*** *the prisoners* ***out****.*

2 [Vp, Vn ⇆ p pass adj] empty (sth) of water with buckets etc; remove (water) from a boat in this way. **S:** sailor, passenger. **O:** boat; water: *A few survivors clambered aboard the lifeboat and began to* ***bail it out****.* ○ *Clive Vincent says surveyors holed his 90-year-old barge ... He now has to* ***bail out*** *20 gallons of water a week.* G □ alt spelling: bale.

3 [Vn ⇆ p pass adj] (*informal*) help or support (sb/sth) financially, esp when he/it is in extreme difficulty. **O:** relative, friend; firm, company: *Bessie was to live in a state of financial chaos, requiring constantly to be* ***bailed out*** *by family and friends.* HB

balance

balance out [Vp, Vn.p] match, be equal. **S:** debits and credits, weights, teams; advantages, faults. **O:** each other, one another: *At the end of the financial year his accounts* ***balanced out****.* ○ *The experience of our side and the youthful determination of the other* ***balance*** *each other* ***out****.*

balance up [Vp, Vn ⇆ p pass] (cause two quantities, factors etc to) match or equal each other. **S** [Vp], **O** [Vn.p]**:** facts, amounts; merits, advantages: *Now, do the two sets of figures* ***balance up****?* ○ *This record enables me to* ***balance up*** *the facts of my life and decide what to do with it.* LIFE

bale

bale out/out of [Vp, Vpr] (*aviation*) jump by parachute (from a damaged aircraft). **S:** pilot, crew. **o:** plane, balloon; cockpit: *Realizing he could do nothing to save his aircraft, the pilot* ***baled out****.* ○ *You must practise your* ***baling-out*** *drill.* □ alt spelling: bail.

balk

balk at [Vpr pass adj] hesitate or refuse to face or accept (sth). **S:** horse, mount; customer, authorities. **o:** fence, wall; conditions, terms: *His horse* ***balked at*** *the water jump.* ○ *Our accountant* ***balked at*** *the high cost of the new proposals.* □ alt spelling: baulk. = buck at, jib at.

ball

ball up 1 [Vn ⇆ p pass] make (sth) into a ball. **O:** (news)paper; rubbish, waste: *It was too much for one day.... He* ***balled*** *the Guardian* (a newspaper) ***up*** *and threw it into the fire.* NY

2 [Vn ⇆ p pass] (esp *US, taboo*) ruin, spoil (sth). **O:** job, delivery, mission; game: *We'll have one more drink ... Then I'll wander back and see how*

they've ***balled up*** *that new front page* (ie of a newspaper edition). PP = mess up.

balls up [Vn ⇆ p nom pass adj] (*taboo*) ruin, mishandle (sth). **O:** organization, work; game, outing: *The public would laugh fit to burst if someone really* ***ballsed up*** *the Civil Service or the Cabinet.* JFTR ○ *Don't let that firm handle your auditing: they made a complete* ***balls-up*** *of ours.* = mess up.

bamboozle

bamboozle into [Vn.pr pass rel] (*informal*) persuade (sb) to do (sth) by trickery. **O:** shopper, consumer; worker, supporter. **o:** donating money, relinquishing rights: *He* ***bamboozled*** *all four of the occupying powers ...* ***into*** *accepting unity more or less on his terms.* ECON ○ *By Thursday, the moderates* (ie in a workforce) *were claiming that they had been* ***bamboozled into*** *an all-out strike.* OBS

band

band together [Vp, Vn.p] unite, form groups. **S:** workers, employers, townspeople. **O:** themselves, ourselves: *The Pre-Raphaelite Brotherhood was a group of young artists who* ***banded together*** *in 1848.* ○ *The villagers* ***banded*** *themselves* ***together*** *to protect their homes and property from armed marauders.*

bandy

bandy about [Vn.p pass adj, Vn.pr pass] (*informal*) pass (sth) from person to person casually or with disrespect. **O:** story, name, word; it ... that he's been in prison: *Mr Charlton was not used to hearing the word virgin* ***bandied about*** *very much, especially in public.* DBM ○ *I know you'll* ***bandy*** *it* ***about*** *that I'm nothing to reckon with, and I don't like that.* ○ *Responsibility for the environment is a much* ***bandied-about*** *phrase in official circles nowadays.* ○ *I don't think it is helpful for the media to report these rumours that are being* ***bandied about*** *the place.* BBCR

bandy words (with) [Vn.pr emph rel] (*dated*) argue, dispute (with sb), usu in an undignified way: *'I don't propose to waste my time* ***bandying words with*** *you!'* ○ *Palmer's dignity did not allow her to* ***bandy words with*** *her social inferiors.* WDM

bang

bang one's head against a brick wall [Vn.pr] (*informal*) continue trying to achieve sth after painful experience has shown that it cannot be achieved: *'Can't you see that he has no intention of paying you back? You're* ***banging your head against a brick wall****.'* ○ *She hasn't a hope of getting him to change his mind. She's just* ***banging her head against a brick wall****.* □ continuous tenses only. = run one's head against/into a brick wall.

bang down [Vn ⇆ p pass] place (sth) forcibly and loudly on the ground etc. **O:** boot, chair; plate, cup; book, folder: *Fred* ***banged*** *his passport* ***down*** *on the table and challenged the official to examine it.*

bang in [Vn ⇆ p pass] (*informal*) submit (sth) quickly, with urgency. **O:** application, request; form, letter: *The deadline is next Monday, so you'd better* ***bang*** *your application* ***in*** *straight away.*

bang the door in sb's face [Vn.pr pass] shut a door forcibly so that sb cannot enter by it; reject some approach or initiative in a hostile way: *She had no answer and* ***banged the door in my face****.* AH ○ *If I tried to sell the machine to Smithers the door would be banged in my face* (or: *I'd have* ***the door banged in my face***). = slam the door in sb's face.

bang out (on) [Vn ⇆ p pass adj, Vn.p.pr pass rel] produce or play (sth) by striking sth loudly. **O:** tune, rhythm; message. **o:** drum; table; typewriter: *Thenke* ***banged out*** *a big triumphant Amen which shook the piano.* PPLA ○ *Jill was* ***banging*** *a letter* ***out on*** *an ancient typewriter.* = beat out (on), hammer out (on), thump out (on).

bang up [Vn ⇆ p pass] (*slang*) make (sb) pregnant: *He said sex was no fun if you couldn't get a girl* ***banged up****.* ORRF = knock up 6.

bank

bank on 1 [Vpr pass adj rel] confidently expect (an event). **o:** change, success, co-operation; being first, winning the fight: *Stupidly, I had only* ***banked on*** *catching two or three animals, so had not brought a really large cage with me.* BB ○ *Her support for the proposal could not be* ***banked on****.* = depend on/upon 2, reckon on/upon.

2 [Vpr pass] (*informal*) trust (sth) to behave or function well. **o:** food, fabric, car; service, company: *You can* ***bank on*** *this creamy-white wool.* H ○ *Those brakes can't be* ***banked on*** *if we have to pull up suddenly.* □ usu with can/could. = depend on/upon 1, rely on/upon.

bank up 1 [Vp, Vn ⇆ p pass adj] (make sth) form into a heap or ridge. **S** [Vp], **O** [Vn.p]**:** earth, gravel, snow, sand: *Seaweed* ***banks up*** *along the water's edge.* ○ ***Banked-up*** *drifts of snow had made the roads impassable.* = heap up.

2 [Vn ⇆ p pass adj] heap (a fire) with fuel (to ensure that it burns slowly for a long time, eg overnight). **O:** fire, furnace, stove: *'Don't forget to* ***bank up*** *the fire before coming up to bed.'*

bargain

bargain away [Vn ⇆ p pass adj] abandon (sth) in return for sth of less value, often through weakness or imprudence. **O:** rights, freedom; advantage, privilege: *In a few minutes they've* ***bargained away*** *concessions which it's taken months of patient bargaining to secure.* ○ *Our hard-won liberties should not be* ***bargained away*** *so lightly.*

bargain for [Vpr pass] (*informal*) be willing or prepared to accept (sth); expect. **o:** such behaviour, his refusal to cooperate; being cheated, him/his being late: *We didn't exactly* ***bargain for*** *him turning up like that, out of the blue.* ○ *The College ... was run by the Marist Fathers with a strict pettiness that Belloc had not* ***bargained for****.* HB ○ *When he married for a second time, Fred got more than he* ***bargained for****.* □ used in questions and negative sentences, or in the form *get more than one bargains for, give sb more than he bargains for*.

barge

barge in/into [Vp, Vpr pass] (*informal*) enter or interrupt (sth) rudely or clumsily. **o:** house, room; discussion, argument: *Midge doesn't like strangers* ***barging in****.* AITC ○ *'Why must you always come* ***barging into*** *the conversation?'*

bark

bark up the wrong tree [Vpr] (*informal*) direct an inquiry or accusation at the wrong place or person: *If the police think I was mixed up in the bank robbery, they're* ***barking up the wrong tree****.*

barrel

barrel across, along, away etc [Vp, Vpr] (*informal*) move noisily and at speed across etc. **S:** car, truck; plane: *On the main road, as you* ***barrel through****, you will see a filling station and a barber's shop.* OBS

barter

barter away [Vn ⇆ p pass adj] ⇨ bargain away.

base

base on/upon [Vn.pr pass emph rel] obtain or derive (sth) from the evidence etc provided by (sth else). **O:** policy, strategy; appeal, argument. **o:** fear, prejudice; reason, evidence: *His success in business is* ***based on*** *a shrewd assessment of what the customer wants.* ○ *The Chancellor is* ***basing*** *his trading forecast* ***on*** *an incomplete set of figures.* = model on/upon. ⇨ rest on/upon.

bask

bask in [Vpr rel] relax while enjoying (sth). **o:** heat, warmth, sunshine; sb's approval, favour: *Couples were out along the seafront,* ***basking in*** *the warm spring sunshine.* ○ *She wanted only to* ***bask in*** *the sunshine of love.* GJ

bathe

bathed in/with [pass (Vn.pr)] bright or wet all over with (sth). **S:** wall, room; square; face, body. **o:** (sun)light, sunshine; tears, sweat: *The room was* ***bathed in*** *early morning light.* REC ○ *After his exertions in the gym, his body was* ***bathed in*** *sweat.*

batten

batten down the hatches [Vp.n pass] (*nautical*) secure hatches firmly (with battens); prepare a ship generally for a storm at sea. **S:** sailor, crew: *All hands were mustered to* ***batten down the hatches****.*

batten on [Vpr pass emph rel] (*formal*) prosper, live well, at the expense of (others' efforts). **S:** unscrupulous trader, lazy colleague, parasite. **o:** work, achievement, generosity (of others): *He was warning fellow traders against the parasitical practices of companies who* ***batten on*** *the efforts of others.* T

battle

battle it out [Vn.p] (*informal*) fight (sth) to a conclusion. **S:** armies, ships; boxers, rivals: *This weekend, eight teams* ***battle it out*** *in the sixth round of the FA Cup.* ○ (headline) *US and UK groups* ***battle it out*** *for contracts.* FT

baulk

baulk at [Vpr pass adj] ⇨ balk at.

bawl

bawl out [Vn.p pass] (*informal*) scold (sb) severely. **S:** referee, sergeant, traffic cop. **O:** player, subordinate, law-breaker: *There were people assembling to* ***bawl*** *you* ***out*** *and wave hostile banners in your face.* G ○ *Every time you give way* (ie show weakness) *I shall* ***bawl*** *you* ***out*** *in front of the company and staff.* COAA ○ *John got a* ***bawling-out*** *for dangerous driving.* □ nom form is bawling-out.

be

be about 1 [Vpr] have begun work, be busy working. **S:** workpeople, shopkeepers. **o:** one's affairs, business: *It was eight o'clock and most of the townspeople* ***were*** *already* ***about*** *their business.* ⇨ go about 4.

2 [Vp] be present here and there (and likely to endanger health, safety etc). **S:** (a lot of) 'flu; fog, smog: *'Be sure to wrap up well: there* ***is*** *a lot of 'flu* ***about****.'* ○ *'Drive home carefully: the weather report says there****'s*** *a lot of ice* ***about*** *on the roads.'* □ note the construction with *there*.

3 [Vpr] have (sth) as its subject or theme. **S:** film, play, novel. **o:** what; rivalry, loyalty: *'The Patriots'* ***is about*** *a couple of IRA bombers hiding in North London.* TES ○ *The player must know what the music he's playing* ***is about****.* BBCR

4 [Vpr] be concerned with (sth). **S:** government, management; welfare, voluntary aid. **o:** what; efficiency, improved output; concern for the poor; meeting public needs: *That in our opinion is what government should* ***be about****.* BBCR ○ *Defending hallowed differentials* (differences in pay according to skill) *is what British trade unionism often seems to* ***be*** *all* ***about****.* OBS □ *about* often preceded by *all*.

be about/around 1 [Vp, Vpr] be present in a place (though the speaker is not sure exactly where). **o:** the place, the house: *'Where's Bill?' 'Oh, he****'s*** *somewhere* ***about****.'* ○ *'I haven't seen Nick all morning.' 'I have. He****'s around*** *the house somewhere.'* □ somewhere usu present.

2 [Vp] be available, be in circulation. **S:** (consumer) article, commodity; (rare) medal, coin; picture, antique: *These sports saloons seem to be gaining in popularity. There* ***are*** *certainly plenty of them* ***about*** *on the roads.* ○ *You'll be lucky to find any of this furniture in the antique shops; there* ***isn****'t much of it* ***around****.* □ note the construction with *there*.

be above 1 be higher than or superior to (sth). **S:** performance; output, production; attendance, capacity; quality. **o:** our target, expected levels; what was forecast: *Exports of manufactured goods* ***are above*** *normal levels for this month.* ↔ be below 1.

2 [Vpr] be higher than (sb) in rank. **S:** major, sergeant. **o:** captain, corporal: *A brigadier* ***is*** *immediately* ***above*** *a colonel in rank.* ↔ be below 2.

3 [Vpr] not be open or liable to (sth). **S:** remarks, behaviour, character. **o:** ⚠ criticism, reproach, reproof, suspicion: *His handling of Government money during his term of office* ***was*** *not entirely* ***above*** *reproach.*

4 [Vpr] be too important, or morally superior, to do sth small or mean. **S:** Crown, judiciary, priest. **o:** party politics, mundane matters; taking bribes, influencing decisions: *Don't worry: Father* ***is*** *quite* ***above*** *trying to influence your choice in this matter.* ○ *Some of the staff* ***are*** *not* ***above*** *putting their hands in the cash-box.*

be above board [Vpr] be honest and open. **S:** deal, transaction: *Now we know each other's names, all* ***is*** *fair and* ***above board****.* NS

be above one/one's head [Vpr] (*informal*) be too difficult or obscure to understand. **S:** remarks, theory, lecture. **m:** miles, a long way: *The last paper he gave, on the theory of flight,* ***was*** *way* ***above my head****.*

be abreast of [Vp.pr] have up-to-date knowledge of (sth). **S:** research worker, teacher, civil servant. **o:**

trends, events, progress: *He takes several learned journals and manages to* ***be abreast of*** *developments in his field.*

be after 1 [Vpr] try to catch (sb); pursue. **S:** authorities; police, warder. **o:** prisoner, suspect, runaway: *'We're still* ***after*** *the man who broke into your shop yesterday.'* ○ *'If you trespass on my land I'll* ***be after*** *you!'* ⇨ come after 2, go after 1, keep after.

2 [Vpr] try to obtain (sb/sth); seek. **S:** employer; applicant, unemployed person; investigator. **o:** staff; post, job, vacancy; information: *Bobus had* ***been after*** *a senior legal appointment in India.* SS ○ *You may feel you are quite capable of handling the work you* ***are after***. H ○ *This was not so friendly as it sounded, and we obviously knew what they* ***were after***. SE ⇨ go after 2.

3 [Vpr] wish to steal or take away (sb/sth). **S:** rival, thief. **o:** (another's) wife, husband; job, valuables: *He's not* ***after*** *the pictures or the family silver.* OMIH

4 [Vpr] be behind (sb else); (be going to) have or enjoy sth later than (sb else). **m:** several places, some way: *'Don't let him grab your place in the queue: he's supposed to* ***be after*** *you!'* ○ *'Can I* ***be after*** *you with the paper, please?'* ↔ be before 1. ⇨ come after 1.

be against 1 [Vpr] be opposed to (sth). **m:** dead, completely. **o:** plan, scheme; alliance, merger: *'Don't expect me to approve: I've* ***been*** *dead* ***against*** *the idea from the beginning.'* ○ *Rose* ***was'nt against*** *alcohol but she* ***was against*** *pubs.* SOMP

2 [Vpr] be contrary to (sth), be in defiance of (sth). **S:** conduct, step; joining the party, signing the petition. **o:** (one's) interests, wishes, will: *Their joining the defensive pact would surely* ***be against*** *our interests.* ⇨ go against 1.

be ahead/ahead of [Vp, Vpr] have progressed beyond (sb else); have reached a stage where others cannot easily follow. **S:** artist, thinker; industry. **m:** some way, a long way. **o:** contemporary, colleague; competitor: *America* ***is*** *way* ***ahead*** *in most important aspects of space technology.* ○ *'You're* *a long way* ***ahead of*** *me there. Do you mind going back over your argument?'* = be in advance of. ↔ be behind 2. ⇨ get ahead/ahead of, keep ahead/ ahead of.

be along (to) [Vp, Vp.pr] come from one place to another, often a short distance (eg within the same building). **o:** house; office, room; meeting, reunion: *'Come along to my office when you have a free moment.' 'All right, I'll* ***be along*** *in about half an hour.'* ○ *Will he* ***be along to*** *the meeting of the housing committee this evening?* ⇨ bring along (to), come along (to).

be around 1 [Vp, Vpr] (*informal*) be active and prominent (in a particular field or profession). **S:** actor, singer; politician. **o:** (movie) business, (pop music) scene; (political) arena: *Jeffries is going to* ***be around****, at least as an active back-bench MP, for a few years yet.* ○ *Of course, he's* ***been around*** *the sports commentating scene for a good many years.*

2 [Vp] (*informal*) have acquired worldly wisdom through travel, experience, contacts etc: *I have* ***been around*** *a long time. I have known a great many interesting people.* MEF ○ *'Look, kid, I've* ***been around****. I know what happens with kids like you.'* TP □ perfect tenses only.

3 [Vp] have acquired wide experience in sexual matters: *Paul and Sarah had both had many lovers before they married. They'd certainly* ***been around*** *a bit.* □ perfect tenses only.

4 [Vp, Vpr] be present in a place. ⇨ be about/ around 1.

5 [Vp] be available, be in circulation. ⇨ be about/ around 2.

be around/round (at) [Vp, Vp.pr] come to or visit sb (at a place, generally within the same town); be with sb (at a place) having come on a visit. **o:** John's, one's grandmother's; club, pub: *'What time shall we expect you?' 'Oh, I'll* ***be around*** *by nine at the latest.'* ○ *You can't accuse him of breaking into the shop. He* ***was round at*** *my house all evening.* ⇨ bring around/round (to) 1, come around/round (to) 1.

be at 1 [Vpr] (*informal*) try to persuade (sb), in an unpleasant, nagging way. **o:** husband, wife, child. **Inf:** to change, to improve, to return: *'There you are, you see. She's* ***at*** *me again!'* ○ *Hawkins* ***was*** *still* ***at*** *her to pick up the relationship where they had left off.* NM □ inf usu present. ⇨ get at 5.

2 [Vpr] (*informal*) handle or use (sth) which is not one's property. **S:** pest, intruder, child. **o:** corn, wine, (another's) belongings: *The mice* ***are at*** *the cheese again: put it in a safer place.* ○ *Geoffrey's* ***been at*** *my shaving things again.* ⇨ get at 1.

be at attention [Vpr] (*military*) be standing in an alert position, with the feet together. **S:** soldier, airman; company, squad: *The men* ***were at attention*** *as the inspecting officer passed through the ranks.* ⇨ bring/come to attention.

be at one's/its best [Vpr] behave or perform as well as one/it is able. **S:** athlete, player; worker, teacher; machine: *He* ***is at his best*** *at the luncheon table at his London house.* NS ○ *The car* ***is*** *really* ***at its best*** *when driven hard and fast.* □ also used after *appear* etc, or after a noun: *Mary* ***felt at her best*** *when wearing her old gardening clothes.*

be at a dead end [Vpr] have reached a point where no further progress is possible. **S:** work, studies, research; inquiry, investigation: *There came a point when his research* ***was at a dead end*** *— he couldn't see how to go forward.* □ also used with *appear, seem*, or after a noun. ⇨ bring/come to a dead end.

be at an end [Vpr] have ended; have been used up or exhausted. **S:** dispute, argument; fighting, bloodshed; patience, tolerance: *Leaders hope that serious differences on the issue among their followers* ***are*** *now* ***at an end***. ○ *I must warn you that my patience* ***is*** *almost* ***at an end***. □ also used with *appear, seem.* ⇨ bring/come to an end, put an end/a stop to.

be at a halt/standstill [Vpr] (of sth moving, or in progress) have stopped. **S:** work, production; factory, yard: *Bus services in the city* ***are*** *practically* ***at a halt***. ○ *The docks have* ***been at a*** *complete* ***standstill*** *since Monday.* □ also used after *appear, seem*, or after a noun. ⇨ come/bring to a halt/standstill.

be at it [Vpr] (*informal*) behave mischievously, be a nuisance. **S:** rogue, scoundrel: *The apples keep disappearing from the trees in my garden; I suppose those children* ***are at it*** *again.*

be (hard) at it/work [Vpr] (*informal*) be very busy, be working hard. **S:** staff; team: *Rescue gangs* **were** *already* **hard at it** *when we reached the scene of the crash.* ○ *You've* **been at it** *for five hours now without a break. Surely you can take five minutes off for a cup of coffee?* ○ *'Still* **hard at work**, *Peter? Now, don't stay up too late!'* □ also used after *appear, seem.* ⇨ go to work (on).

be at large [Vpr] be free, having escaped from captivity. **S:** prisoner, criminal; lion: *Watch out: there'***s** *a tiger* **at large** *in those woods!* ○ *After last week's jail break, several men* **are** *still* **at large**. □ also used after a noun: *Prisoners still* **at large** *would be rounded up this weekend.*

be at a loose end [Vpr] have nothing to do, and have no definite plans for the future: *Christian ... has his A-levels behind him and educationally speaking,* **is at** *something of* **a loose end**. L □ also used with *appear* etc, or after a noun: *People* **at a loose end** *could come into the club and play snooker.*

be at pains to do sth [Vpr] take great care to do sth. **S:** councillor, official, inspector. **adj:** great, considerable. **Inf:** to explain, to justify, to seem fair: *The Inland Revenue* **were at** *some* **pains to point out** *how we might benefit from the revised schedule.*

be at a premium 1 [Vpr] be above the normal price. **S:** stock, share: *Shares in the telecommunications industries* **are at a premium**.

2 [Vpr] be highly valued, because of scarcity or the special needs of the time. **S:** land, building sites; skill, education: *We are moving into an era in which technology* **is at a premium**. ⇨ put at a premium, put a premium on.

be at risk [Vpr] be threatened by the possibility of failure, loss, injury, etc. **S:** worker, scientist; life, survival; experiment; industry: *People working in this industry* **are at risk** *from skin cancers.* ○ *From the moment he announced his election challenge, Joseph Yablonski realized that his personal safety* **was at risk**. ST □ also used with *appear* etc, and after a noun. = be in jeopardy.

what be at [Vpr] (*informal*) what sb is trying to do or say: *I can never understand* **what** *on earth he'***s at**. ○ *'Do you mind telling me* **what** *exactly you'***re at**?*'* □ used in direct and indirect questions. ⇨ get at 4, what be driving at.

be at grips with [Vpr] be tackling (sth); be engaged in a struggle with (sth). **o:** (**with**) problem, issue, question: *I don't think the writer* **was** *ever* **at grips with** *any serious moral issue.* ○ *At the time he* **was** *already* **at grips with** *the disease which was later to kill him.* ⇨ come/get to grips with.

be at one (with) [Vpr] have the same views or feelings (as sb). **S:** meeting, audience, follower. **m:** altogether, completely. **o:** speaker, leader: *She* **is at one with** *her husband* (or: *They* **are at one**) *in believing that this is the best course to follow.* ○ *They desire to enter, and* **be at one with**, *a vaguely conceived People, whose lives they could not even imagine.* HD □ also used with *appear* etc, and after a noun. = agree (with) 1.

be away 1 [Vp] be in a drawer etc, because one has finished using it etc. **S:** paper, book; knitting; linen, woollens: *I don't know that I can find the letters. They'***re away** *in old shoe boxes in the attic.* ⇨ put away 1.

2 [Vp] not be present; be absent: *Tommy* **is away** (ie not in school) *today.* ○ *Sarah* **is away** *in Scotland* (ie she has gone to Scotland).

be well away 1 [Vp] (*informal*) make a good start, be in advance of opponents. **S:** horse, runner; businessman: *The Queen's horse* **was well away** *at the start of the 3.15 race.* ○ *With his father's name and his mother's money, young Johnnie should* **be well away**. □ also used with *appear, seem, look*.

2 [Vp] (*informal*) enjoy oneself noisily (through having drunk too much); be drunk: *By the time we arrived at the party, Dick* **was well away**. □ also used with *appear* etc.

be back 1 [Vpr] return; have returned. **A:** soon, shortly; by lunch-time, before supper: *I'll* **be back** *in a minute with your tea.* DC ○ *He'll* **be back** *in time to put them to bed.* DC ⇨ bring back 1, come back 1, get back 1, go back 1, take back 1.

2 [Vpr] have been replaced. **S:** book, ornament, clock. **A:** where it belongs, in its rightful place, with its owner: *The grandfather clock* **was back** *in its old place.* ○ *'Make sure the dogs* **are back** *in their kennels before you go to bed.'* ⇨ get back 3, put back 1.

be before 1 [Vpr] be in front of (sb else); (be going to) have or enjoy sth earlier than (sb else). **m:** several places, some way: *'Don't push! I* **was before** *you in the queue.'* ○ *'Don't forget* **I'm before** *you with that newspaper.'* ↔ be after 4. ⇨ come before 1.

2 [Vpr] appear, be presented for a decision, the judgment of a court, etc. **S:** he etc; case; matter. **o:** court, magistrate; board, committee: *This is the third time that the accused has* **been before** *this Court.* ○ *The question* **is before** *a Select Committee of the House of Commons at this very moment.* ⇨ bring before, come before 2, go before 2, put before 2, take before.

be before sb's time [Vpr] happen or live earlier than sb was in a certain place (eg a school, university; business; club). **S:** it, that; change, event; he etc. **m:** way, long, considerably: *This used to be the master bedroom before we did the alterations upstairs. That* **was before your time**, *of course.* DC ○ *'Do you remember a French teacher with a squeaky voice? Or perhaps he* **was before your time**?*'*

be behind 1 [Vp, Vpr] be late/later than (sth); be in arrears. **S:** tenant; manufacturer, country. **m:** way, a long way, a good bit. **A:** with the rent, in repaying the loan, on delivery dates: *Everybody seems to* **be behind** *this morning.* TGLY ○ *They'***re** *often* **behind** *in making the monthly payment on the television.* ○ *By mid-January, Polanski (a film-maker)* **was** *already way* **behind** *schedule.* ST ⇨ fall behind 2, get behind 2.

2 [Vp, Vpr] be inferior (to sb/sth), be losing (to sb/sth). **S:** country, competitor. **m:** way, some way; far, well. **o:** rival, opponent: *Jones* **was behind** *on points at the end of round three.* ○ *They* **were** *well* **behind** *their nearest rivals in the development of computer technology.* ↔ be ahead/ahead of. ⇨ fall behind 1, leave behind 3.

3 [Vpr] be the explanation for (sth), be the cause of (sth). **S:** fear, greed; bid for power, clash of interests; change of policy, rise in costs: *I wonder what*

***was behind** John's sudden interest in our welfare?* ⇨ lie behind 2.

be behind bars [Vpr] be in prison. **S:** criminal, terrorist, murderer: *The last of the bank-robbers **is** now safely **behind bars**.* ⇨ put behind bars.

be behind the times [Vpr] not be modern, not be up to date (in ideas, methods etc). **S:** plan, strategy; idea, philosophy, morality. **m:** rather, somewhat; very much: *I found his thoughts on crime and punishment to **be** very much **behind the times**.* ○ *His views on marriage **are** a bit **behind the times**.* □ also used with *appear, seem.*

be below 1 [Vpr] be lower than or inferior to (sth). **S:** performance; output, production; attendance, capacity; quality. **m:** some way, a long way; well, much. **o:** normal, (former) level; expectations, what was forecast; standard: *Figures for soft drinks sales **were below** what we are used to in the summer.* ○ *Output **is** considerably **below** last year's level.* □ also used with *appear, seem.* ↔ be above 1. ⇨ fall below.

2 [Vpr] be junior to, or lower than (sb) in rank. **S:** lieutenant; corporal. **o:** captain; sergeant: *A major **is** immediately **below** a lieutenant-colonel in rank.* ○ *Jones **was below** Rogers when he joined the firm, but he was quickly promoted to a post of equal responsibility.* ↔ be above 2.

3 [Vp] (*nautical*) be below deck-level, eg in a cabin or the hold. **S:** crew, passenger; cargo: *Most of the timber **was below** in the hold, but some had to be stowed on the after-deck.* ⇨ go below (decks), ⇨ take below.

be beneath [Vpr] seem too unimportant, vulgar etc to deserve (sb's attention etc). **S:** money matters, household affairs, business dealings. **o:** ⚠ (one's) attention, notice, regard: *'Of course, the question of where the money for the next meal is coming from **is beneath** your attention!'*

be beneath contempt [Vpr] be utterly despicable. **S:** conduct, behaviour, remarks: *I've lost all respect for him: I think his criticism of the monarchy **was beneath contempt**.* ○ *To suggest that he was a petty agitator **was beneath contempt**.* UTN

be beneath one's dignity [Vpr] be sth which one feels one cannot do without some loss of dignity (usu implying that the person has a high opinion of himself). **S:** housework, manual work; (it) to help his younger brother, (it) to play party games: *A little light weeding in the garden shouldn't **be** too much **beneath your dignity**.*

be beside the point [Vpr] have nothing to do with the matter in question; be irrelevant. **S:** that, this; who it was, whoever did it. **m:** totally, completely: *Whether John or Patrick lost the tape-recorder **is beside the point**.* ○ *The judicial argument over his interpretation of the constitution **is beside the point**.* OBS □ also used with *appear, seem.*

be beside oneself (with) [Vpr] be overwhelmed (by strong feelings). **S:** widow, victim, survivor; candidate; prisoner. **m:** quite, simply. **o:** (**with**) grief, anxiety, rage, frustration: *The headmaster **was beside himself with** alarm because raindrops were falling on the school prizes.* SPL ○ *You can imagine how embarrassing it all is. **I'm** simply **beside myself**.* UTN □ also used with *appear* etc.

be between ourselves/you and me [Vpr] (of a secret) be shared by the speakers (and not with others). **S:** this, that, it; this matter: *'Now this **is** strictly **between ourselves**, but did you know that David is being promoted next month?'* ○ *Eva has invited some friends up. **Between you and me**, it's for business reasons.* RATT □ often used without a verb to introduce a confidential remark; note the extended form: between you and me and the gatepost/wall.

be beyond 1 [Vpr emph] have gone beyond a point where he/it can be saved, mended etc. **S:** patient, case; machine, meter; crew, passenger. **o:** help; remedy, cure; salvation, redemption; repair; rescue: *One wing of the car **was beyond** repair — a rear mudguard half torn off.* HD ○ *He's hopelessly addicted: surely even you can see he'**s beyond** a cure.* □ also used with *appear* etc.

2 [Vpr emph] be more than one can calculate, expect, believe, understand etc. **S:** cost, total; success, result; problem; claim, statement. **o:** reckoning, calculation; hope, (one's) expectations; understanding, comprehension; belief, credibility; him etc: *So far, twenty-eight patients have been treated, and the improvement is said to **be beyond** all expectations.* NS ○ *The intricacies of the law of libel **are beyond** my ken* (= knowledge). SD ⇨ go beyond.

be beyond a joke [Vpr] (*informal*) be too serious to joke about. **S:** behaviour, manners, dress; situation, incident: *'This **is** quite **beyond a joke**! Open the door, and let me out at once!'* ○ *Turning up at the house with that drunken pack of friends **was beyond a joke**.* ⇨ go beyond a joke.

be beyond/past caring [Vpr] have reached a point where one no longer cares (about sth). **O:** (of **caring**) whether one lives or dies, how things will turn out, what to do in another crisis: *'Don't you think we ought to find another music teacher for John?' 'Don't ask me, darling, **I'm** really **past caring**.'* ○ *When an officer **is beyond caring** for the safety of his troops, he should be removed from his command.*

be beyond endurance [Vpr] (*dated*) be more than one is prepared to bear or tolerate. **S:** behaviour, conduct; insolence, slovenliness: *Her treatment of junior staff **is beyond endurance**.* ○ *This latest outburst of his — **it's** quite **beyond endurance**.*

be down 1 [Vp] (*informal*) lack, be deficient by (some amount). **S:** stock, account. **m:** ten pounds, a thousand pairs; quite a bit: *I've checked the till and **we're** forty pounds **down**.* UTN ○ *The bar **is** ten bottles of Scotch **down**.* □ modifier usu present.

2 [Vp] have fallen, been reduced. **S:** price, cost; (level of) demand, output. **m:** some way, quite a bit: *Consumer spending **is** quite a bit **down** on last month's levels.* ↔ be up 1. ⇨ bring down 5, come down 3, go down 5.

3 [Vp] be entered or written down. **S:** name, age; opinion, view. **A:** on paper, in a notebook; in black and white: ***Is** the date of the next meeting **down** in your diary?* ○ *'Don't try to deny that you said it. Your words **are down** here in black and white.'* ⇨ get down 4, go down 9, put down 11, set down 2, take down 3.

4 [Vp] (*informal*) not be functioning. **S:** computer, printer, lines: *That's the third time the photocopier's **been down** this week. It's about time we got a new one.* = be out of action.

5 [Vp] (*sport*) be losing by (a specific amount). **S:**

visitors, touring team. **m:** two sets, one goal, 12 points: *Arsenal* ***were*** *two goals* ***down*** *at half-time.*

be down as [Vp.pr] have one's name entered or recorded as (sth), sometimes with the suggestion that the entry is false. **S:** name; he etc. **o:** Smith, Brown etc: *Her name****'s down as*** *Smythe in the telephone book, but really she's just plain Smith.* ⇨ put down as 1.

be down at heel [Vp.pr] be badly worn down; be in a generally shabby state. **S:** shoe, boot; Smith, Brown, etc: *He****'s*** *always so* ***down at heel****; is he hard up or just slovenly?* ○ *Our cases were collected by a* ***down-at-heel*** *hall porter.* □ also used with *appear* etc; adj form is down-at-heel.

be down for [Vp.pr] have one's name written down as sb interested in (a contest, outing, entry to a school etc). **S:** child, pupil, colleague; name. **o:** team; contest, outing; public school, Eton: *'****Are*** *you* ***down for*** *the school trip to Stratford-on-Avon?'* ○ *'His name's* ***been down for*** *his father's school since birth: we wanted to be absolutely sure of getting him in.* ⇨ put down for 2.

be down for a count of [Vp.pr] (*boxing*) be knocked to the floor and stay there while the referee counts (not long enough, however, to be counted out): *The challenger in the heavyweight fight* ***was down for a count of*** *six in the fifth round, got up, and walked straight into a knock-out punch.* ⇨ be out 9, count out 2.

be down (from) [Vp, Vp.pr] have left a university (esp Oxford or Cambridge): *Their son* ***is*** *just* ***down from*** *Oxford after taking a degree in chemistry.* ↔ be up 2. ⇨ come down (from), go down 8, send down 1.

be down in the dumps/mouth [Vp.pr] (*informal*) be miserable or dejected: *Bill's* ***been*** *a bit* ***down in the mouth*** *ever since they put the tax up on beer.* □ also used with *appear* etc. ⇨ get down in the dumps/mouth.

be down on 1 [Vp.pr] (*informal*) be critical of (sb); be prejudiced against (sb): *He can be a thoroughly bad writer. Some of the critics* ***are*** *terribly* ***down on*** *him.* PW □ also used with *appear, seem*; note nom form in: They have a terrible **down on** him.

2 [Vp.pr] (*informal*) criticize (sb/sth) severely, often with a threat of punishment. **S:** supervisor, manager; teacher. **o:** him etc; slip, error. **A:** at once, immediately, like a ton of bricks (= with great severity): *The examiners* ***were down on*** *his mistake in a flash.* ⇨ come down on 1.

3 [Vp.pr] (*informal*) demand money or compensation from (sb). **S:** creditor, victim (of an accident). **o:** (bankrupt) businessman, (negligent) workman: *When the news got about that the business was failing, our suppliers* ***were down on*** *us for prompt payment of bills.* ⇨ come down on 2.

be down on one's knees [Vp.pr] be very submissive or servile (to one's superiors) in the hope of gaining favours or support: *We* ***were*** *practically* ***down on our knees*** *to the management, begging them to be more flexible over holiday arrangements.* ⇨ go down on one's knees (to) 2.

be down on one's luck [Vp.pr] (*informal*) suffer a setback or misfortune: *'Well, Lumley, I'm sorry you****'re down on your luck****. I should have thought you could have got a better job than this, though.'* HD □ also used with *appear, seem* or after a noun.

be down and out [Vp] (*informal*) be destitute (without work or means and dependent on charity etc). **S:** worker, farmer; class: *After about ten years of casual work or none at all, they* ***are*** *practically* ***down and out****.* ○ *A crowd of* ***down-and-outs*** *was queuing for a meal of soup and bread.* □ also used with *appear* etc; nom form is down-and-out(s).

be down to [Vp.pr] have nothing left except (sth). **o:** our last couple of pounds, my last pair of tights: *By ten o'clock, the newsagents* ***are down to*** *the last copy of my favourite paper.*

be down with [Vp.pr] (*informal*) be ill with (sth). **o:** stomach upset, bad cold: *They****'re*** *both* ***down with*** *a nasty bout of 'flu.* ⇨ go down with.

be (all) for [Vpr] (*informal*) (strongly) favour or support (sth). **S:** minister, candidate, employer. **o:** increased pensions, reduced costs; sharing wealth, giving the young a chance: *She****'s all for*** *giving new members of the team responsibility for part of the project.* ↔ be against 1.

be for it/the high jump [Vpr] (*informal*) (be going to) be punished or reprimanded. **S:** (naughty) child; idiot, rascal: *'You'll* ***be for it*** *when your father comes home!'* ○ *'If you mess about with my typewriter again, you'll* ***be for the high jump****.'* □ often used with shall/will.

be in 1 [Vp] be fashionable. **S:** red, black; silk, leather; foreign travel: *Natural fibres* ***are in*** *at the moment; synthetics are out.* ○ *This is very much an* ***in*** *style just now.* □ note attrib use of in in last example. = be in fashion/vogue. ↔ be out 14. ⇨ bring into/come into fashion/vogue, come in 1.

2 [Vp] be gathered, be harvested. **S:** harvest, crop; grapes, potatoes: *The strawberry crop, the best they'd had for years,* ***was*** *now safely* ***in****.* ⇨ bring in 1, get in 1.

3 [Vp] be available fresh in the shops (because they are now being gathered etc). **S:** strawberries, pheasant, trout: *'Have you any peaches?' 'Sorry, I'm afraid they****'re*** *not* ***in*** *yet.'* = be in season. ↔ be out of season. ⇨ come in 2, come into season.

4 [Vpr] (*politics*) be elected; be in office. **S:** party, representative: *'Did you know our local MP* ***is in*** *again?'* ○ *The Republicans have* ***been in*** *since the hand-over of power.* ⇨ come in 4, get in/into 3, put in 7.

5 [Vp] (*cricket*) be batting. **S:** side, team; player: *The home side* ***is in*** *at the moment; but we shall be batting soon.* ↔ be out 8. ⇨ go in 4, put in 8, stay in 3.

6 [Vp] remain alight. **S:** stove, furnace: *The fire we lit last night* ***is*** *still* ***in*** *this morning.* ↔ be out 10. ⇨ keep in 2.

7 [Vp] (of the sea) have reached the highest point on the shore. **S:** the tide, water: *'Be careful about swimming when the tide****'s in****; the beach shelves quite steeply here.'* ↔ be out 16.

8 [Vp] be inside (a place). **o:** house, building; burrow, lair: *'****Is*** *John* ***in*** *?' 'No, he's out with Bill.'*

be in action [Vp] (*military*) be active, be in a position where he or it can operate. **S:** force, troops; artillery, tanks : *Our men* ***were in action*** *within an hour of arriving in the front line.* ○ *At that moment, there* ***were*** *only two guns* ***in action****.* □ also used with *appear* etc or after a noun. ↔ be out of action. ⇨ bring/come/go into action.

be in advance of [Vpr] have progressed beyond (sb else); be more highly developed than (sb else). **S:**

designer, thinker; computer, spacecraft. **m:** well, some way. **o:** contemporary, companion; ours etc: *Their space technology* **is** *well* **in advance of** *ours.* □ also used with *appear* etc, or after a noun: *Their aircraft had cooling systems well* **in advance of** *ours.* □ also used with *appear, seem* and after a noun. = be ahead/ahead of. ↔ be behind 2.

be all in [Vp] (*informal, dated*) be exhausted, be tired out: *After six weeks' training, the recruits* **were** *just about* **all in.** □ also used with *appear* etc.

be in being/existence [Vpr] exist; have started to exist. **S:** body, organization; army; industry; university: *The research unit which she had worked so hard to set up* **was** *finally* **in being.** ○ *At that time there* **was** *no procedure* **in existence** *for handling this kind of case.* □ also used after a noun: *species still* **in existence** *were....* ➪ bring/come into being/existence.

be in blossom/flower [Vpr] have blossomed, flowered. **S:** tree, shrub; rose, azalea: *On both sides of the road the cherry-trees* **were in blossom.** ○ *The crocuses* **are** *now* **in flower.** □ also used after a noun. ➪ bring/come into blossom/flower.

be in bud/leaf [Vpr] (of a bud, leaf, on a tree or bush) have appeared or shown itself. **S:** tree, shrub; branch, twig: *The roses* **are in bud** *early this year.* ○ *The plane trees lining the main street* **are** *already* **in leaf.** □ also used after a noun. ➪ come into bud/leaf.

be in employment/work/a job [Vpr] be employed, have a job: *Those who* **are in** *part-time* **employment** *should leave this part of the form blank.* ○ *The father's still* **in work**, *but the two teenage boys are finding it hard to get jobs.* □ also used after a noun: *people still* **in work....** ↔ be out of work/employment/a job.

be in fashion/vogue [Vpr] be fashionable. **S:** natural fabrics, plastic; narrow ties, miniskirt: *Styles which are now the latest thing may often have* **been in fashion** *thirty years ago.* ○ *The cult of violence in the cinema* **is** *now* **in vogue**: *let us hope it is a passing fashion.* □ also used after a noun: *styles* **in fashion** *at the time....* = be in 1. ↔ be out 14, be out of fashion. ➪ bring/come into fashion/vogue, come in 1.

be in focus 1 [Vpr] (of sth viewed through a microscope, telescope etc) be sharp and clear. **S:** microscope, specimen: *All the details of the insect's wing* **were in** *sharp* **focus.** □ also used after a noun. ↔ be out of focus 1. ➪ bring/come into focus 1.
2 be clearly visible or intelligible. **S:** question, problem, matter: *Two key aspects of the problem* **are** *now* **in** *clear* **focus**; *shall we discuss those before moving on?* □ also used after a noun. ↔ be out of focus 2. ➪ bring/come into focus 2.

be in force [Vpr] have begun to operate, and be in some way binding and enforceable. **S:** law, regulation, requirement: *A new code of practice for hoteliers* **is** *now* **in force.** ○ *There* **was** *nothing* **in force** *to stop travel-agents misleading potential bookers.* □ also used after a noun: *regulations* **in force** *forbid the use of....* ➪ bring/come/put into force.

be in hand [Vpr] have been started or undertaken. **S:** work; arrangements; checking, correction: *The editing of the manuscript* **is** *now* **in hand.** ○ *Plans* **are in hand** *to safeguard the environment against damage from heavy equipment required for the construction of pylons and oil rigs.* NS □ also used after a noun: *Plans* **in hand** *to protect the trees and shrubs include ....* ➪ have/take in hand.

be in jeopardy [Vpr] be threatened, endangered. **S:** plan, scheme; chances, prospects; trade, employment; relations: *There has been a fall in demand for their products, and thousands of jobs in the area* **are in jeopardy.** ○ *Because of infringements of the cease-fire, the peace talks* **are in** *serious* **jeopardy.** □ also used with *appear, seem.* = be at risk. ➪ put in jeopardy.

one's luck be in [Vp] (*informal*) (of sb) be fortunate, be lucky: (horoscope) ***Your luck is in*** *and you should be able to look forward to one of your smoothest weeks for some time.* WI

be in the open [Vpr] be obvious, evident; have been made public. **S:** feelings; enmity, envy; dispute, differences (between people); matter, issue: *It's far better that your disagreement should* **be in the open**; *now you both know where you stand.* ○ *The real causes of the dispute* **are** *now* **in the open.** ➪ bring/come into the open.

be in the picture [Vpr] (*informal*) have been given up-to-date information, be fully informed (about sth). **S:** staff, colleagues: *'All right, now that I'm fully* **in the picture** *what can I do to help?'* ○ *'I'm not sure that we're quite* **in the picture.** *Can you tell us exactly what was said at that meeting?'* □ also used after a noun: *people* **in the picture** *included....* ➪ put in the picture.

be in play [Vpr] be involved, be at work; have started to influence sth. **S:** force, factor, circumstance: *Important new factors, including the realignment of political forces in Central Europe, will* **be in play** *in the next round of disarmament talks.* □ also used after a noun: *The factors* **in play** *are....* ➪ bring/come into play.

be in sb's possession [Vpr] be held or possessed by sb (usu temporarily or illegally). **S:** (stolen) vehicle, firearms, drugs: *I don't know how the missing documents came to* **be in his possession** (or: *how he came to* **be in possession of** *the documents).* □ the second pattern in the example is used by the police in statements of evidence. Cf: *The accused* **was in possession of** *a quantity of cannabis resin.* □ note also use after a noun: *The cannabis* **in his possession** *was....* ➪ come into sb's possession.

be in power [Vpr] have reached or gained (political) control. **S:** party, group; clique, junta; class: *A coalition government* **was in power** *in Britain during the Second World War.* □ also used after a noun: *The party* **in power** *must not become complacent.* ➪ come/put into power.

be in progress [Vpr] be proceeding or moving forward. **S:** building, demolition; talks, discussions; sale, exchange: *Work* **was** *already* **in progress** *on a new shopping and leisure complex in the city centre.* □ also used after a noun: *Discussions now* **in progress** *are covering a wide range of issues.*

be in season [Vpr] be available fresh (in shops). **S:** oysters, (fresh) salmon; strawberries, grapes: *Don't buy imported strawberries — they're so expensive. Wait till they***'re in season** *here.* □ also used after a noun: *Fruit now* **in season....** ↔ be out of season. ➪ be in 3, come into season, come in 2.

be in service/use [Vpr] have begun to serve the public; be used. **S:** bus, lorry; railway, road; bridge, tunnel: *A new Cross-Channel link will* **be in service** *for the holiday traffic.* ○ *The footbridge over the river* **is** *no longer* **in use**. □ also used after a noun: *The two footbridges still* **in use**. . . . ↔ be out of service. ⇨ bring/come/go into service/use.

be in sight/view [Vpr] be visible; have appeared. **S:** coast; sea; train, car: *From our position on the hillside, every detail of the landscape* **was** *clearly* **in view**. ⇨ bring/come into sight/view.

be well in hand [Vpr] have been controlled. **S:** situation; crisis: *He said there was no cause for alarm: the situation* **was** *now* **well in hand**. = be under control. ↔ be out of hand. ⇨ have well in hand.

be in the wrong [Vpr] have acted wrongly; be made to feel that one has acted wrongly: *'All right, I'***m in the wrong** *— I shouldn't have lost my temper with him.'* ○ *Why* **am** *I always* **in the wrong**? *Is it something about my face that sets people against me?* □ also used after a noun: *People so clearly* **in the wrong**. . . . ⇨ put in the wrong.

be in at the finish/kill [Vp.pr] (*informal*) be present at the conclusion (usu unpleasant) of a conflict or chase. **S:** tracker, huntsman, soldier: *That's a really bloodthirsty hound you've got there; he always loves to* **be in at the kill**.

be in for 1 [Vp.pr] (*sport*) be going to compete in (sth). **S:** athlete, competitor. **o:** event, race: *I'***m in for** *the 100 metres and the high jump.* = enter for. ⇨ go in for 1, put in for 1.
2 [Vp.pr] be an applicant for (sth). **o:** job, post; vacancy: *I understand he'***s in for** *an administrative job in the Civil Service.* ⇨ put in (for).
3 [Vp.pr] (*informal*) be likely to experience (sth). **o:** fine weather, a stormy crossing; hard times, far-reaching changes: *It looked as if we might* **be in for** *a frosty spell.* TBC ○ *Anyone who thinks that Kirkaldy's a dreadful industrial town* **is in for** *a very pleasant surprise.* SC

be in charge (of) [Vpr] direct or be responsible for (some process or organization). **S:** official, businessman, academic; office, department. **o:** (**of**) business; sales, recruitment; field, area: *Jones* **was in** *complete* **charge** *while the manager was on holiday.* ○ *We are looking for an experienced person to* **be in charge of** *research and development.* □ also used with *appear* etc, and after a noun. ⇨ take charge (of).

be in control (of) [Vpr] manage or regulate the behaviour of (sb) or the movement or progress of (sth). **S:** teacher, parent; pilot, driver; scientist. **o:** oneself; child, pupil; plane, car; experiment: *How can he take control of a class when he'***s not in control of** *himself!* ○ *The police were not satisfied that he* **was in** *complete* **control of** *the car.* □ also used with *appear* etc, or after a noun. ⇨ have control of/over, take control (of).

be in on [Vp.pr] have a share in (sth); be informed of (sth). **o:** plan, scheme, venture; idea, suggestion: *Most of the staff want to* **be in on** *the new pension scheme.* ○ *The various departmental heads* **were in on** *the managing director's thinking from the start.* = participate (in). ⇨ bring/come/get/let in on.

be in on the ground floor [Vp.pr] (*informal*) have joined a business, project etc at the start. **S:** investor, shareholder; partner, associate: *You're a lucky man. The business is bound to expand and prosper, and you'***re in on the ground floor**! ⇨ come in on the ground floor, get in 3.

be in and out of [Vpr] (*informal*) be a frequent visitor to or inmate of (a place). **o:** hospital, shop: *He'***s in and out of** *jail all the time.* ○ *You're an export delivery driver. You must* **be in and out of** *every principal dock in the country.* HD ⇨ go in and out/out of.

be in accord/harmony/tune (with) [Vpr] match or agree (with sth) easily and smoothly. **S:** statement, declaration; move, action; decision. **o:** (**with**) (previous, earlier) statement etc; (others') wishes, desires: *This document* **is** *simply not* **in accord with** *our earlier agreement.* ○ *The Prime Minister's statement* **was** *not* **in harmony with** *agreed party policy.* ○ *This drawing together of the two sides* **is in tune with** *our entire policy to date.* □ also used with *appear, seem*, and after a noun. = accord with, attuned (to), fit in with.

be in collision (with) [Vpr] have struck or collided (with sth). **S:** car, lorry; train; ship: *A van* **was in collision with** *an articulated lorry* (or: *A van and a lorry* **were in collision**) *on the MI.* ⇨ come into collision (with).

be in collusion (with) [Vpr] (*legal*) have made a secret agreement (with sb), contrary to law, for some purpose: *The solicitor warned his client that he would not obtain a divorce if he was found to* **be in collusion with** *his wife* (or: *if he and his wife were found to* **be in collusion**).

be in contact (with) 1 [Vpr] touch (sth). **S:** (electrical) lead, wire. **o:** (**with**) surface, plate: *Unless both the leads* **are in contact with** *the terminals, the current will not pass through* (or: *Unless the leads and the terminals* **are in contact**, *the current* etc). □ also used after a noun.
2 [Vpr] communicate with (sb), face-to-face or by letter etc. **S:** agent, businessman. **o:** author, customer: *I* **am** *already* **in contact with** *a London agent, who is trying to secure a booking.* ○ *John and his sister* **were in** *close* **contact** *throughout the time of their parents' illness.* □ also used after a noun. = be in touch (with). ⇨ come into contact (with) 2.

be in line (with) [Vpr] follow or conform with (general views or policy within an organization). **S:** member, follower. **o:** (**with**) the majority; official doctrine: *After several shifts of position he* **is** *now* **in line with** *the rest of the party.* □ also used after a noun. ↔ be out of line . ⇨ bring/come/fall into line (with).

be in touch (with) 1 [Vpr] communicate (with sb), face-to-face, or by letter etc. **o:** (**with**) relation, friend; customer, client: *When* **were** *you and your sister last* **in touch** ? ○ **Are** *you still* **in touch with** *the people you knew at college?* ○ *I think that the next meeting of the Association should be in York. I shall* **be in touch with** *my colleagues about this.* □ also used after a noun. = be in contact (with) 2. ↔ be out of touch (with) 1. ⇨ keep/put in touch (with).
2 [Vpr] be aware of (current ideas); be sensitive to the feelings of (others). **S:** lecturer, researcher; father, teacher. **o:** (**with**) current thinking, new ideas; the latest research; one's children, pupils: *He used to attend conferences quite regularly, but he'***s** *not really* **in touch** *these days, is he?* ○ *She* **was** *always* **in touch** *with all the latest developments in her field.* □ also used after a noun: *Those*

in touch with *the latest developments say that....* ↔ be out of touch with 2.

be (well) in with [Vp.pr] (*informal*) be on familiar terms with (a particular group), and hope to benefit from the connection. **o:** crowd, set; mob, gang: *He* ***is in with*** *the bosses.* UL ○ *She****'s well in with*** *all the radio and television people, and loves to bring their names into the conversation.* □ also used with *appear, seem.* ⇨ get in with.

be inside [Vp] (*police slang*) be in prison. **S:** thief, murderer: *'****Is*** *Pearson still* ***inside****?' 'No, he was let out early.'* ↔ be out 2. ⇨ put inside.

be into [Vpr] (*informal*) have (sth) as an absorbing pastime or professional interest; be enthusiastic about (sth). **o:** karate, hang-gliding, meditation, jogging: *English artists have long* ***been into*** *Black music.* BBCTV ○ (A woman speaking of her 17-month-old son) *'He'* ***s*** *not* ***into*** *mechanical things yet but he's very musical.'* ST

be off 1 [Vp, Vpr] have fallen or been thrown from (sth). **o:** horse, pony; bicycle: *'Can he manage to stay on? No, he****'s off****!'* ⇨ come off 1.

2 [Vp, Vpr] have become detached or separated (from sth). **S:** handle, knob; hook, plug. **o:** door, wall: *'Half the buttons* ***are off*** *my shirt — can you sew them on again?'* ⇨ come off 2, take off 1.

3 [Vp] (*informal*) leave, go away, esp in a hurry: *He glanced at his watch. 'And by the way, I must* ***be off****.'* DS ○ *It's high time we* ***were off****.* ○ *Chairman Glendinning and his chief executive* ***were off*** *to advise the Australian steel city of Wollongong.* L ⇨ get off 3, set off (on) 1.

4 [Vp] be cancelled, not be going to take place. **S:** wedding, party, match: *'There is not going to be any wedding,' I told him. 'It****'s off****.'* DIL ○ *The threatened dock strike* ***is off****.* ↔ be on 1.

5 [Vp] be no longer available on the menu. **S:** meat, pudding: *'Steak pie****'s off****,' said the waitress.* ⇨ take off 9.

6 [Vp] be extinguished; be disconnected. **S:** light; central heating; water, gas, electricity (supplies): *Make sure that the lights* ***are off*** *in the children's rooms.* ○ *The gas supply will* ***be off*** *while they repair the mains.* ↔ be on 8. ⇨ go off 8, turn off 1.

7 [Vp] smell or be bad or rotten. **S:** cheese, beer, milk. **m:** a bit, slightly: *'This fish you've given me* ***is*** *slightly* ***off****.'* ⇨ go off 7.

8 [Vpr] (*informal*) lack interest in (sth), lose one's appetite for (sth). **o:** politics, golf, music, girls: *She was crazy about you then — well, now it seems, she****'s off*** *you!'* ○ *The cat****'s off*** *his food.* ⇨ go off 4, put off 5, turn off 2.

9 [Vp] (*informal*) have stopped taking or using (sth). **o:** drugs, alcohol, cigarettes: *He was an alcoholic but he****'s off*** *the booze now.*

be off one's hands [Vpr] (*informal*) have taken away from one the expense and responsibility of looking after (sb/sth). **S:** daughter, elderly relative; guest; house, car: *'I hear Mary's just got engaged. Well, that****'s*** *the last of the girls* ***off your hands****!'* ○ *We're finding it hard to get a buyer for the flat. We'll be relieved when it****'s off our hands****.* ⇨ take off sb's hands.

be off one's head etc [Vpr] (*slang*) be mad; be extremely foolish. **o:** ⚠ one's head, rocker, nut, trolley, chump: *'He must* ***be off*** *his nut to start throwing his money about like that.'* = be out of one's mind. ⇨ go off one's head etc.

be off the hook [Vpr] (*informal*) be freed from an unpleasant task, an embarrassing situation etc: *OK, Jane's agreed to do the baby-sitting instead of us, so we****'re off the hook*** *for Saturday.* ⇨ get/let off the hook.

be off the mark [Vpr] begin a sporting contest; respond to a challenge or opportunity. **S:** company, shop; manufacturer, inventor, salesman. **m:** quick; slow, late: ***Be*** *really quick* ***off the mark*** *and you'll be over the first hurdle before they realize what's happened.* ○ *The Italian landed nobility have* ***been*** *slightly late* ***off the mark*** *in realizing the potential of the stately home market* (ie opening their houses to the public). ○ *Ned* ***was off the mark*** *at once. His pottery seemed to become a vogue overnight.* CON □ also used with *appear, seem,* or after a noun.

be well etc off (for) [Vp, Vp.pr] (*informal*) be rich etc; be well etc supplied with (sth). **m:** (very, fairly) well, comfortably, badly. **o:** cash; beer, cigarettes: *My family* ***aren't well off****.* EHOW ○ *Dairy farmers will* ***be*** *particularly* ***badly off*** *because the EEC Commission proposes that they should get no price increase.* ST ○ *How* ***are*** *you* ***off for*** *money?* TC ○ *He****'s*** *pretty* ***well off for*** *food and drink.* □ also used with *appear, seem* or after a noun; adj forms: well-off, comfortably-off, badly-off.

be off (on) [Vp, Vp.pr] (*informal*) begin to speak, tiresomely and at length (about sth). **o:** favourite subject, pet theme, hobby-horse: *'Oh dear, he****'s off*** *again. Isn't there any way of stopping him?'* ○ *She****'s off on*** *her pet subject, or rather obsession — sex and violence on TV.* ⇨ set off (on) 2, start off (on) 2.

be on 1 [Vp] be going to take place. **S:** wedding; match; strike, ban: *The shut-down threatened for this weekend* ***is*** *still* ***on****, but union leaders are trying to avert a stoppage.* ↔ be off 4.

2 [Vpr] (*informal*) be paid for by (sb), be charged to (sb). **S:** drink, lunch, party. **o:** the house, the management; me: *'Now drink up and don't worry about expense: the beers* ***are on*** *me!'* ○ *When Bill got his promotion, drinks* ***were on*** *the house.*

3 [Vp, Vpr] (*racing*) be staked or bet on (sb/sth). **S:** money; his shirt; he etc. **o:** horse, dog; fighter; team: *'I want five pounds each way on "Golden Lad" in the next race.' 'Right, you****'re on****!'* ○ *My money* ***was on*** *an outsider in the last race, and I couldn't afford to lose.* ⇨ put on 8, put one's shirt on 1.

4 [Vp] (*cricket*) (have begun to) bowl. **S:** (slow, fast) bowler: *Fraser* ***was on*** *for two more overs after lunch; then he was replaced by a spin bowler.* ⇨ bring on 4, come on 9, put on 10.

5 [Vp] be on stage (in a play, opera etc). **S:** actor; Hamlet; tenor, chorus: *It's a very arduous part: he* ***is on*** *for most of the second act.* ○ *'Hurry up, Peter, you****'re on*** (ie you should be on stage)*!'* . ⇨ come on 10.

6 [Vp] be being shown or performed. **S:** film, play, ballet: *There****'s*** *a good film* ***on*** *at the Plaza this week.* ○ *'King Lear'* ***was on*** *at the Playhouse last season.* ⇨ come on 11, ⇨ put on 11.

7 [Vp] (*legal*) be being heard, considered (in court). **S:** case, lawsuit, hearing: *'Your case* ***is on*** *in Courtroom No 3, just along the corridor.'* ⇨ come on 12.

8 [Vp] be alight, be burning; be connected. **S:** light, lamp; (electric/gas) fire; central heating; electricity supply: *'The light's on in the kitchen. Please turn it off.'* ○ *'Did you know the television* **was** *still* **on** *when you came up to bed?'* ↔ be off 6. ⇨ go on 15, keep on 6, leave on 2, put on 2, turn on 1.

be on the ball [Vpr] (*informal*) be alert or wide-awake to opportunities etc. **S:** salesman, agent, negotiator: *He's not really* **on the ball** *— he lets so many chances slip by.* □ also used after a noun: *Anyone really* **on the ball** *will know that....*

be on one's feet [Vpr] have stood up; be standing. **S:** spectator; delegate, councillor; waiter, shop assistant: *As soon as the guest speaker was announced, half the audience* **was on its feet**, *clapping and cheering.* ○ *A busy waitress* **is on her feet** *for most of the day.* □ also used after a noun: *Members still* **on their feet** *were told to sit down.* ⇨ bring to his feet, come to/get on one's feet.

be on one's honour [Vpr] be trusted to do sth on pain of breaking one's oath. **S:** child, pupil. **Inf:** to behave, not to cheat: *'Now, don't forget, you're* **on your honour** *to be absolutely quiet until Miss Jones gets back.'* □ usu followed by the inf. ⇨ put on his honour.

be on ice [Vpr] (*informal*) be put aside or deferred (eg until more time or money is available to deal with it). **S:** idea, plan, project: *The plan for the new book* **is on ice** *at the moment. I've been busy with too many other things.* ⇨ put on ice.

be on the map [Vpr] (*informal*) have become well known (after being unknown, or known to very few). **S:** town, village; festival; sport: *After its well-publicized success in selling compact cars, the company* **is** *now firmly* **on the map**. ○ *Show-jumping as a spectator sport* **is** *increasingly* **on the map** *— largely because of TV coverage.* □ also used after a noun: *Resorts now firmly* **on the map** *include....* ⇨ put on the map.

not be on [Vp] (*informal*) not be possible or allowed. **S:** it, this, that: *I told the Minister that we could not make proposals within the limits of £600 million — it* **was** *simply* **not on**. MFM ○ *Any chance of a compromise* (ie with employers) **is not on**. *There is no possibility of us going back to work for ten per cent.* OBS

(the) pressure be on [Vp, Vpr] (of moral, political etc pressure) be firmly applied (to sb). **o:** government, leader; union leader, employer: *There* **is** *mounting* **pressure on** *the Government to resign.* ○ **The pressure is** *now* **on** *the union side to reach a settlement.* ⇨ put pressure on/upon.

to be on the safe side [Vpr] (*informal*) in order to be sure (of arriving in time etc); to be safe or secure (from danger): *She looked at her watch. 'We'd better be going,* **to be on the safe side**,*' she said.* QA ○ *He prefers to regard every animal as poisonous, just* **to be on the safe side**. BB □ usu an adv clause of purpose, but note: *We'd better* **be on the safe side**: *let's offer him £500.*

be on the scene [Vpr] have appeared; become involved in sth. **S:** police, ambulance; reporter, eye-witness: *The fire brigade* **were on the scene** *within minutes of being called.* ○ *Now that he***'s on the scene** *we can expect nothing but disharmony.* ⇨ come on the scene.

be on stream [Vpr] be operating actively; be producing fully. **S:** (oil)field, refinery; plant, factory; North Sea gas/oil: *When the field's fully* **on stream**, *a tanker load like this one should come ashore twice a week.* BBCTV □ also used after a noun: *Fields newly* **on stream**....

be on trial [Vpr] (*legal*) be being tried in a court of law. **S:** accused, prisoner: *'Let me remind the accused that he* **is on trial** *for his life.'* □ also used after a noun: *The people* **on trial**.... ⇨ be up 6, bring to trial.

be on about [Vp.pr] (*informal*) speak with tiresome persistence about (sb/sth). **o:** illness, money; smart friends; how clever one is: *I don't like the smart people your mother's always* **on about**. ○ *What* **is** *she* **on about**? RT ⇨ go on about, keep on (about).

be on one's guard (against) [Vpr] be wary (of sth/sb); be careful in dealing with (sth/sb). **o: (against)** infection, contagion; crook, manipulator: *'I should* **be on my guard** *if I were you. He's not the sort of man I should trust.'* ○ **Be on your guard against** *telephone salesmen with a smooth line of talk.* □ often spoken as a warning. ⇨ put on his guard (against).

be on at [Vp.pr] (*informal*) try to persuade (sb) to do sth in a persistent, nagging way. **o:** him etc; husband, girlfriend. **Inf:** to improve, to change: *My wife's forever* **on at** *me to do something about that broken fence.* ○ *I've* **been on at** *her to change her hairstyle.* □ usu followed by the inf. = be at 1. ⇨ go on at.

be well on in/into [Vp.pr] be late, be well advanced (in time). **S:** it. **o:** (**in**) the afternoon (**into**) July: *Although it* **was well on in** *the evening, we decided to try our luck at fishing again.* BM

be well (on) into [Vpr, Vp.pr] have reached a late stage in one of the later decades of one's life. **o:** fifties, sixties, seventies: *By now, he must* **be well on into** *his seventies.* □ also used with *appear, seem, look*, and after a noun: *A man* **well into** *his fifties....*

be on to 1 [Vp.pr] (*informal*) be talking to (sb) in order to inform or persuade. **o:** head office, headquarters; allies; aircraft, ships: *'I've just* **been on to** *the accounts people about your expenses, Smith; I think they'll let you have them.'* ○ *I've already* **been on to** *the spacecraft, telling it to go much slower.* TBC ⇨ get on to 1, put on to 1.
2 [Vp.pr] (*informal*) become aware of (sth/sb) and be following up that knowledge; make contact with (sb) while pursuing him. **S:** customs, tax authorities, police; reporter. **o:** dodge, fraud, little game; gang; secret hideout: *The CID* **are on to** *the men who were responsible for that break-in.* ○ *The Inland Revenue* **are on to** *him for a currency deal he thought he'd got away with some years ago.* ⇨ get on to 2, put on to 2.
3 [Vp.pr] know and be able to benefit from (sth interesting or advantageous). **o:** a certain winner (eg in a horse race); a good thing (= sth advantageous); a new investment opportunity: *He***'s on to** *a good thing, all right: a high salary, practically no income tax and a rent-free house.* ⇨ put on to 3.

be on/upon one [Vpr] have arrived (with the suggestion that the arrival may be sudden and unwelcome). **S:** dry season, winter, Christmas; election, Budget Day: *The wet season* **was on us**, *and on the Adriatic coast it became cold and damp.* MFM ○ *We'd hardly had time to get over a series of birthdays before Christmas* **was upon us**. ⇨ come on/upon one.

be out 1 [Vp] (*industry*) have stopped work, be striking. **S:** workers, clerical staff. **A:** in sympathy, in protest against dismissals: *The electricians* ***are out*** *following last night's threat to stop overtime working.* ⇨ bring out 1, come out 1, stay out 3.
2 [Vp] (*informal*) be released (from prison). **S:** prisoner, convict. **A:** of jail, on parole: *'Stevens can't have done that bank job, sergeant; he's not* ***out*** *until next week!'* ↔ be inside. ⇨ come out 2, let out/out of.
3 [Vp] (*informal*) (be sure to) be removed, thrown out (eg from a club). **S:** drunk, trouble-maker: *'Any more bad language and you****'re out*** *for good!'* ○ *I knew that if I had too much to drink and started picking fights I'd* ***be out*** . ⇨ put out 2.
4 [Vp] flower, be in bloom. **S:** rose, almond blossom, bougainvillaea: *If this fine weather keeps up, my hyacinths will* ***be out*** *in a day or two.* = be in blossom/flower. ⇨ bring out 4, come out 4.
5 [Vp] be visible (ie not covered by clouds, or made invisible against a bright sky). **S:** the sun, moon, stars: *'The sun****'s out****; now I can get on with some gardening and you can sit out in a deck chair.'* ⇨ come out 5.
6 [Vp] be on sale, be published. **S:** book, article, report: *A new magazine for the younger, smarter woman* ***is out*** *today.* ⇨ bring out 5, come out 6.
7 [Vp] be disclosed or revealed. **S:** secret, news: *The secrets they'd kept hidden from the media for so long* ***were*** *now* ***out****.* = leak out. ⇨ come out 7, get out 1, let out 2.
8 [Vp] (*cricket*) lose one's wicket. **S:** batsman, side: *Smith* ***was out*** *trying to turn a ball to leg.* ○ *The Indian touring team* ***were*** *all* ***out*** (ie they lost all their wickets) *for 260.* ↔ be in 5. ⇨ get out 3, give out 5.
9 [Vp] (*slang*) be fast asleep; be unconscious (after an exhausting day or knock-out blow). **S:** boxer, soldier, worker. **m:** right, dead. **A:** for the count, like a light: *ASTON: Sleep well? DAVIES: Yes. Dead* ***out****. Must have* ***been*** *dead* ***out****.* TC □ modifier or adjunct used, not both. ⇨ go out 3, put out 9.
10 [Vp] be no longer alight, be extinguished. **S:** fire, stove; candle, lamp, (electric) light: *The lights* ***were*** *all* ***out*** *when we got home from the theatre: Mother had gone to bed early.* ↔ be on 8. ⇨ go out 6, put out 10, turn out 1.
11 [Vp] be finished, be ended. **S:** night, week, month, winter: *There'll be some changes made in the department before the year****'s out****.* □ usu used in a dependent clause after *before*.
12 [Vp] be inaccurate, be wrong. **S:** research worker, doctor; figures, forecast. **m:** (some) way, well, not far; five minutes, several miles. **A:** by a long way, by miles; in one's calculations, when predicting recovery: *Subsequent events show how well* ***out*** *he* ***is*** *in his diagnosis.* SC ○ *His forecast of rapid growth in the public sector of industry* ***was*** *some way* ***out****.* □ when S is *worker, doctor* etc, m or A must be present; when S is *figures* etc, m or A is usu present; also used with *appear, seem.* ⇨ put out 12.
13 [Vp] (*informal*) not be possible; not be allowed. **S:** appointment, session; cheating, stealing from the poor: *'Could we meet on Monday?' 'No, that's the day the inspectors are coming.' 'Oh, well that'****s out*** *then.'* ○ *'Now we'll have a good, hard game, but any hacking or barging from behind* ***is*** *strictly* ***out****.'* = not be on.
14 [Vp] (*informal*) no longer be the fashion. **S:** baggy jeans, short hair, long skirts: *That style's* ***been out*** *for ages! You don't study fashion very closely, do you?* = be out of fashion. ↔ be in 1. ⇨ go out 7, go out of fashion.
15 [Vp] be announced, be declared. **S:** (examination) result, mark; class-list: *'The results of the Bar exams* ***are out*** *— and you're through!'* ⇨ come out 13.
16 [Vp] (of the water level at the seaside) be low, have retreated. **S:** the tide, water: *When the tide* ***is out****, you can walk across the sand to St Michael's Mount without getting your feet wet.* ↔ be in 7. ⇨ the tide go out.

be out to do sth [Vp] (*informal*) aim or propose to do sth. **S:** government, firm. **Inf:** to make changes, to improve exports, to reduce prices, to do you harm: *Like so many others involved in the case, she* ***was out to make*** *money.* T □ also used with *appear, seem* or after a noun.

be out (at) [Vp, Vp.pr] be away from home (on an outing etc). **o:** the pictures, the theatre: *'Mary****'s out*** *with her boyfriend.'* ○ *I'm sorry to have missed you. I* ***was out at*** *the pictures when you called.* ⇨ come/go/take out (for/to).

be out for [Vp.pr] (*informal*) be interested in favouring (sb) or in protecting (sb's interests etc). **S:** Government, industry; enemy, crook. **o:** better housing, good relations; oneself; one's own ends, anything he can get; your blood: *It is not money alone, but some hard thinking, which the campaign* ***is out for****.* TES ○ *He's not interested in sharing the benefits with anyone: he's just* ***out for*** *himself.* ⇨ go all out (for/to do sth).

be out from [Vp.pr] have left (a port or airfield) a stated time before; be a stated distance from (a place). **S:** ship, boat, plane. **m:** ten hours, four days; fifty miles. **o:** London, Lagos, Orly Airport: *Our aircraft* ***was*** *barely half-an-hour* ***out from*** *Newfoundland when it developed engine trouble.* ○ *We* ***were*** *a good sixty miles* ***out from*** *base.* □ also used with *appear, seem*; modifier usu present.

be out in [Vp.pr] be present in (large numbers). **S:** police, troops; supporters, teenagers. **o:** force, strength, large numbers: *Loyal party men* ***were out in*** *strength at the rally held last night.* □ also used with *appear, seem*.

be out/out of 1 [Vp, Vpr] have left (an enclosed space). **S:** owner, occupant; (caged) bird, animal; car. **o:** his etc office, house; town; cage; garage: *'I'm afraid you can't see the manager today: he's* ***out of*** *town till Monday.'* ○ *His car****'s out****, so he must have left home early.* ○ *'How long has that parrot* ***been out of*** *its cage?'* ⇨ bring out/out of, come out/out of 1, get out/out of 1, keep out/out of, take out/out of 1.
2 [Vp, Vpr] have left the place where it was fixed. **S:** nail, screw; thorn; teeth; cork, stopper. **o:** plaster, wood; flesh; gum; bottle: *'Well, the splinter****'s out of*** *your finger, so now you can run along and have some iodine put on it.'* ○ *We spent half a morning pulling carpet tacks out of the floor, so most of them should* ***be out*** *by now.* ⇨ come out/out of 2, get out/out of 2, take out/out of 2.
3 [Vp, Vpr] have disappeared, been removed (with cleaning). **S:** mark, stain; colour, dye. **o:** jacket;

carpet: *'Well, the mark***'s out***, but it certainly needed a lot of rubbing.'* ⇨ come out/out of 3.

be out of 1 [Vpr] be too far away (to hear, be seen or be reached). **o:** earshot, sight, view, range: *The French coast* **is out of** *sight from here but at Dover it's clearly in view.* ○ *The enemy positions* **were out of** *range to all but our heaviest guns.* ↔ be in sight/view, be within 1. ⇨ go out of sight/view.

2 [Vpr] (*informal*) have finished or used up one's supply of (sth). **m:** quite, right; completely. **o:** ideas, patience; spare parts, soap, petrol, tea: *'We***'re out of** *cigarettes; I'll go to the corner shop for some more.'* ⇨ run out 1, run out/out of.

be out of action [Vpr] (*military*) be no longer able to operate or function (esp because of enemy action). **S:** ship, tank; gun; radar: *'Number 2 turret* **is out of action**, *Sir.'* ○ *Thanks to accurate anti-aircraft fire, three of the raiders* **were** *already* **out of action**. ↔ be in action. ⇨ go/put out of action.

be out of the blue [Vpr] have appeared or been said suddenly or unexpectedly. **S:** arrival, appearance; statement, comment, remark; find, discovery: *His arrival was all the more pleasant for* **being** *completely* **out of the blue**. □ also used, without *be*, as an adjunct: *The coins were lost for years, then one day they turned up again, quite* **out of the blue**. ⇨ come out of the blue.

be out of breath [Vpr] find breathing difficult, eg after running, climbing etc; be breathless: *It was a steep climb to the top. We were quite* **out of breath**.

be out of character/keeping/place [Vpr] not be what one would expect of a person or occasion; be inappropriate. **S:** remark, interruption, behaviour: *His dress and manner* **were out of keeping** *with the solemnity of the occasion.* ○ *Father believed that children's conversation* **was out of place** *at the meal table.* □ also used with *appear* etc, or after a noun: *Behaviour* **out of** *keeping with the occasion ....*

be out of one's depth [Vpr] (*informal*) be in company where the discussion, knowledge etc is strange and difficult to understand: *I was drinking with a group of car enthusiasts, and for much of the time* **was** *completely* **out of my depth**. ○ *She's always* **out of her depth** *in intellectual circles.* □ also used with *appear* etc, or after a noun. ⇨ get out of one's depth.

be out of employment/work/ a job [Vpr] be unemployed, be without (work). **S:** shipyard workers, half the town. **o:** work, a job, employment: *6 677 people, most of them men,* **were** *temporarily* **out of work** *in mid-February.* SC ○ *Nor did he give any reason why he himself came to* **be out of a job**. HD □ also used after an noun: *The Department lists men* **out of work** *since June.* □ note adj form: out-of-work. ↔ be in employment/work/a job.

be out of fashion [Vpr] be no longer fashionable. **S:** flared trousers, wide lapels; scooters, rock-and-roll: *I can see I shall have to take you shopping: those boots have* **been out of fashion** *for ages.* = be out 14. ↔ be in fashion/vogue. ⇨ go out 7, go out of fashion.

be out of favour (with) [Vpr] (*formal*) have lost a privileged position (in sth or in relation to sb). **S:** minister, candidate. **o:** party; bosses, leaders: *He's in no position to help you: he's* **been out of favour** *with the authorities for some time.* □ also used with *seem* or after a noun. = fall from/out of favour (with).

be out of focus 1 [Vpr] (of sth seen through a microscope etc) not be sharp and clear. **S:** slide; specimen; microbe: *The image is blurred; the slide* **is** *a little* **out of focus**. □ also used with *appear, seem, look.* ↔ be in focus 1. ⇨ go out of focus 1.

2 [Vpr] not be clear or intelligible. **S:** question, facts: *'For me, the story* **is** *still a bit* **out of focus**. *Could you be more explicit?'* □ also used with *appear, seem, look.* ↔ be in focus 2.

be out of hand [Vpr] be uncontrolled, become uncontrollable. **S:** wages, prices; child, pupil: *The situation appears to* **be** *completely* **out of hand**. ○ *'And have you seen their children? They***'re** *quite* **out of hand**.*'* □ also used with *appear, seem, look.* ↔ be in hand. ⇨ get out of hand.

be out of line [Vpr] not behave in a normal or acceptable way; be unacceptable. **S:** he, she etc; remark, comment, criticism. **m:** well, a bit, rather, way: *I felt you* **were out of line** *in suggesting that we expected to do a lot of business with them.* ○ *I must say I thought your behaviour at the meeting* **was** *a bit* **out of line**. □ also used with *appear, seem* and after a noun: *Remarks* **out of line** *with the occasion....* = be out of order 3.

be out of one's mind [Vpr] be mad; be extremely foolish: *Some of the generals disregarded this latest order, which could only have come from a man who* **was** *already* **out of his mind**. ○ *'You must* **be out of your** *tiny* **minds** *if you think I would do anything of the sort!'* ⇨ go out of one's mind.

be out of order 1 [Vpr] not be functioning properly. **S:** system; stomach, bowels; telephone, lavatory: *There's no point in ringing the bell. There's a notice saying it***'s out of order**. ○ *The lift***'s out of order**. *Please use the stairs.*

2 [Vpr] (*legal, official*) not be allowed by a court of law as a proper statement etc; not be allowed by the rules of debate laid down for meetings. **S:** remark, comment, interruption; statement, question: *The judge ruled that the prosecution* **was out of order** *in introducing details of the accused's private life.* ○ *'You* **are out of order**,*' shouted the Chairman above the din. 'Kindly sit down.'*

3 [Vpr] not behave in a normal or acceptable way; be unacceptable. **S:** he etc; remark, behaviour: *Surely she'd think it* (**was**) *pretty* **out of order** *if I just went and banged on the door.* TWL = be out of line.

be out of play [Vpr] (*sport*) (of the ball in football etc) have crossed the line marking the edge of the playing area: *The linesman raised his flag to signal that the ball* **was out of play**. ⇨ go out of play.

be out of season [Vpr] not be available fresh (because they are not now being caught etc). **S:** salmon; grouse; peaches: *There aren't any fresh strawberries: they***'re** *just* **out of season**. ↔ be in season.

be out of service [Vpr] be no longer used; have stopped being used. **S:** bus, train. aircraft: *Most of the steam locomotives which once drew trains on this line* **are** *now* **out of service**. □ also used after a noun: *The number of buses* **out of service** *this week is unusually high.* ↔ be in service/use. ⇨ go out of service/use.

be out of stock [Vpr] not be available in a shop, warehouse etc. **S:** commodity, article, item; tool, instrument: *We regret that all the items on your list* ***are*** *at present* ***out of stock****.* □ note the pattern used in: *We* ***are*** *at present* ***out of stock of*** *all those articles.* and pattern after a noun: *The goods* ***out of stock*** *are listed below.*

be well out of it/that [Vpr] (*informal*) be lucky to avoid being involved in sth: *'So you didn't take up that job abroad after all? Well, I think we can say you****'re well out of it****.'* ○ *'Not married yet? You****'re well out of that****!'*

(be) out with it [Vp.pr] say what you want to say; say what is on your mind: *'What's the matter boy? What? Come on, now.* ***Out with it****! What's the matter — can't you tell me?'* FFE ○ *Reassured by her confusion, and really curious to know, Harold leaned back and said: 'Well,* ***out with it****.'* PW □ imperative form only.

be out of touch (with) 1 [Vpr] not/ no longer communicate regularly (with sb). **o:** (**with**) father, child; client, (former) pupil: *I'm sorry we've* ***been out of touch*** *— we must meet more regularly.* ○ *We****'re*** *completely* ***out of touch*** *with these people now.* ↔ be in touch (with) 1.

2 [Vpr] not be aware of current developments, of how others are thinking and feeling, etc. **S:** teacher, manager; father, husband. **m:** a bit, rather, somewhat. **o:** (**with**) current research, new thinking, present trends: *'That's a pretty unpleasant way to behave, isn't it?' 'Is it?' asked the old man mildly. 'I'm sorry, I****'m*** *a bit* ***out of touch****.'* HHGG □ also used with *appear* etc, or after a noun; adj form is out-of-touch. ↔ be in touch (with) 2.

be outside [Vpr] be a matter which is too difficult or unfamiliar (to understand, discuss etc). **S:** subject, topic, matter. **o:** (one's) province, competence; field, area (of interest); brief: *I can't give you a decision on anything to do with housing. That****'s*** *quite* ***outside*** *my competence.* ○ *Have a word with my colleague about that text; Old English* ***is*** *a bit* ***outside*** *my field.* ↔ be within 2. ⇨ fall outside, stand outside.

be over 1 [Vp] be ended, be finished. **S:** party, waiting, illness, winter: *That was the last window he was going to do* (ie clean) *that morning. And as it was Saturday, that meant that work* ***was over*** *for the weekend.* HD ⇨ be over and done with, get over (with).

2 [Vp] remain, be left. **S:** meat, flour; sand, bricks: *A small piece of flannel* ***was over*** *when the tailor had finished cutting out my suit.* ○ *If there****'s*** *any cement* ***over*** *when you've done, you might keep it for me.* ⇨ leave over 1.

3 [Vpr] spend a long time having or doing (sth). **A:** (too) long, a long time, ages. **o:** lunch, breakfast, coffee: *'Don't* ***be*** *long* ***over*** *breakfast; I want to get started as soon as possible.'* ○ *'How long will they* ***be over*** *their tea-break?'* ⇨ take (over).

4 [Vp] (*informal*) come, have come, to visit sb (usu by travelling some distance). **S:** friend, relative, husband: *'Will you* ***be over*** *on Saturday?' 'No, we can't manage it this weekend.'* ○ *I wasn't in Leeds last week. I* ***was over*** *with my parents in Liverpool.* ⇨ bring over, come over 1.

be all over 1 [Vpr] (*informal*) be spread or passed from one person to another (throughout a place). **S:** news, scandal, rumour, report. **o:** office, factory, camp: *'Have you heard about the inspector's report ? It****'s all over*** *the school!'*

2 [Vpr] (*informal*) greet (sb) effusively (with the suggestion that the effusiveness is rather unwelcome). **S:** dog; hostess, welcoming party: *I'd hardly set foot inside the door when that great Labrador of theirs* ***was all over*** *me.*

3 [Vpr] (*informal*) dominate (sb) completely at sport. **S:** team, players; visitors, tourists: *The visiting team* ***were all over*** *us for the first ten minutes of play.*

be all over the place [Vpr] (*informal*) be very untidy or in a disorderly state; be scattered here and there; be badly controlled. **S:** calculations, accounts; clothes, books, toys; service (at tennis), putting (at golf): *Her hair* ***was all over the place****; you would think she'd not combed it for a week.* ○ *Not a very good first over. His bowling* ***was all over the place****!* □ also used with *appear* etc.

be over and done with [Vp] (*informal*) be completely ended or forgotten, and not likely to happen again or be remembered. **S:** that, it, everything: *The bitter quarrels* ***were*** *all* ***over and done with****: nothing could mar their friendship now.* ○ *That* ***was*** *a former life,* ***over and done with****, something he had forgotten about.* HD □ also used with *appear, seem.* ⇨ be over 1, get over and done with.

be past one's/its best [Vpr] no longer be of the quality reached when fully mature or at the height of one's/its powers. **S:** actor, singer, scientist; flower, plant; fruit. **m:** way, well, a little: *Shall I cut you a few roses? They****'re past their best****, I'm afraid, but they should last a day or two.* ○ *There are many recordings of 'senior citizens' singing songs when their voices* ***are*** *well* ***past their best****.* RT ○ *He has been among the top four goalkeepers in the world . . . and, if he has any weakness at all, it is only that I think he could* ***be*** *just a little* ***past his best****.* TVT □ also used with *appear* etc, or after a noun.

be past caring [Vpr] ⇨ be beyond/past caring.

be past (one's) endurance [Vpr] ⇨ be beyond/past (one's) endurance.

be past it [Vpr] (*informal*) lack the skill or vigour (esp sexual) that one once had: *'He used to be a terrific one for the girls, but I suppose he****'s*** *a bit* ***past it*** *now, isn't he?'* □ also used with *appear* etc.

be round the corner [Vpr] have passed a difficult or dangerous point in an illness, a battle etc. **S:** patient; company, government: *What mattered was success, and to win our battles with a minimum of casualties. But we were now* ***round the corner****.* MFM ○ *He's regained consciousness, which is a good sign, but he* ***isn't round the corner*** *yet.* □ also used with *appear, seem.*

be round (at) [Vp, Vp.pr] ⇨ be around/round (at).

be through [Vp] (*informal*) reach the end of a relationship, a career etc; be finished. **S:** couple, boy and girl: *'I won't put up with any more broken promises from him: we****'re through****.'* ○ *I still think I can be Number One* (ie as a pop singer) *. . . If you don't have faith in yourself you****'re through****.* RT

be through (to) [Vp, Vp.pr] be in contact by telephone (with sb or a place). **o:** the police, fire station; New York, one's home: *After a few minutes' wait in the call-box, I* ***was through****.* ○ *'You're*

***through to** London, sir!'* ⇨ get through (to) 2, put through (to) 1.

be through (with) [Vp, Vp.pr] (*informal*) have finished talking to, dealing with etc (sb); have done (with sb). **o:** customer, client; caller, student: '*Give me another minute, will you? I'**m** not **through with** Fred yet.*' (Cf '*Fred and I **are** not **through** yet.*') ○ *I'll be here with Gabriel when they'**re through with** you.* GL ⇨ get through with 1,2.

be through with [Vp.pr] (*informal*) be tired of or dissatisfied with (sb/sth), and so determined to abandon him/it. **o:** husband, boyfriend; lies, deceit; smoking, gambling; being exploited: *'**I'm through with** hanging about all day, waiting for him to appear.'* ○ *She **was through with** trying to pretend that she loved him.*

be to the fore [Vpr] (*formal* or *jocular*) be prominent, noticeable. **S:** speaker; delegate, deputy: *If an argument develops, you can expect Stephen to **be to the fore**.* □ also used after a noun: *A scramble for seats followed, with John well **to the fore**.* ⇨ bring/come to the fore.

be under control [Vpr] be checked or mastered. **S:** fire; epidemic; riot, disturbance. **m:** well, firmly, totally: *The fire which threatened part of the business district this morning **is** now firmly **under control**.* ○ *Teachers sometimes complain that their pupils **are** not properly **under** their parents' **control**.* □ also used with *appear* etc, or after a noun. ⇨ bring/get/keep under control.

be under water [Vpr] be flooded. **S:** street, house, room. **m:** two feet, a metre: *The townspeople returned to inspect shops and houses that had **been** as much as three feet **under water**.*

be under way [Vpr] be proceeding; be developing. **S:** trial, enquiry, investigation; attack, struggle: *An internal police enquiry into the circumstances surrounding the Davis case **is** still **under way**.* G ○ *The computerization of the Inland Revenue **is** well **under way**.* IND □ also used after a noun: *The changes now **under way** in Eastern Europe make it even more desirable for Britain's role* (in the EC) *to be a whole-hearted one.*

be up 1 [Vp] have risen or increased (in price). **S:** tax, tariff; beer, petrol. **m:** ten pence, five pounds, a hundred dollars: *Cigarettes and whisky **are up** as a result of the last budget.* ○ *Share dividends **were** £86 million **up** on the year.* SC □ also used with *appear, seem*. ↔ be down 2. ⇨ go up 2, keep up 2, put up 4, send up 1.

2 [Vp] have travelled to or be in an important town (eg London); be a student (esp at Oxford or Cambridge). **S:** don, undergraduate: *'**Is** the family still **up** in Edinburgh?' 'No, they came back a couple of days ago.'* ○ *My son will **be up** at Cambridge for the next few years.* ↔ be down (from). ⇨ come up 2, go up (to).

3 [Vp] have finished or expired, have come to an end. **S:** time, leave; three weeks; term of office, period of tenure: *His time **was up**: he'd have to hand over to a younger man.* ○ *My annual leave **was up**.*

4 [Vp] remain out of bed. **A:** till all hours, all night: *She **was up** half the night with a sick child.* ○ *They **were up** until well into the small hours counting the votes.* ⇨ keep up 9, stay up 2.

5 [Vp] rise, get out of bed. **A:** late, at crack of dawn, early: *He'**s** always **up** with the lark* (ie very early). ○ *Each morning she would **be up** before dawn to sweep the hearth.* GLEG ⇨ get up 1.

6 [Vp] (*legal*) be considered (by a court). **S:** case; accused. **A:** before the court, judge; for petty larceny, on an embezzlement charge: *Two suspected terrorists **were up** on firearms charges.* □ an adjunct is usu present. = be on trial. ⇨ bring up 4, ⇨ come up 6.

7 [Vp] be about to happen, be impending. **S:** ⚠ something, what: *Something **was up** all right. The hotel bars were seething with rumours of troop movements just over the frontier.* ○ *'Have you any idea what'**s up**?'* ⇨ be up (with).

one's blood be up [Vp] (of temper) be fully aroused: *He had been slighted and ignored for so long, till now **his blood was** really **up**.* ⇨ get sb's blood up.

the game be up [Vp] (*informal*) (of a pursuit, search) be ended successfully (with the suggestion that the search has been long and the hunted person elusive). **A:** for the escaped convict, for the enemy leaders: *And now his pursuers had caught up with him; for him, at any rate, **the game was up**.* ○ *Nobody else has the financial knowledge to falsify the books. **The game's up**: you've been caught.* □ also used with *appear, seem*.

one's hand be up [Vp] be raised to attract attention etc: *'Why **is your hand up**, Jenkins? I said that nobody would be allowed to leave the room.'* ⇨ put one's hand up.

be hard up [Vp] (*informal*) be poor, be short of money. **S:** country, Exchequer; farmer: *Our nation **is** very **hard up** and we cannot afford the waste which comes from adding together the demands of three services.* MFM ○ *His father was a **hard-up** teacher.* □ also used with *appear* etc; adj form is hard-up.

the sun be up [Vp] have risen: *He's out working in the fields before **the sun's up**.* □ nom form is sun-up. ⇨ come up 13.

be up and about [Vp] (*informal*) be feeling better and able to get up. **S:** patient, invalid: *Now don't you worry about your husband, Mrs Davis. He'll **be up and about** again in a few days.*

be up against [Vp.pr] be opposed by (sth/sb), be confronted by (sth/sb). **o:** (real) problem, difficulty; (tough, formidable) opponent, competitor: *You see the kind of difficulty we **are up against**?* HOM ○ *They **were up against** a killer with the intelligence to think and plan.* TFD □ also used after *appear* etc and after a noun. ⇨ bring/come up against.

be up (as far as/to) [Vp, Vp.pr] have reached, stretched, extended (to). **S:** sea, tide; fog, gas; climber, procession. **o:** sea-wall, house; ceiling, roof; summit: *The water **was up as far as** my shoulders.* ○ *The sunflowers **are up to** the top of the kitchen window.* ⇨ bring/come up (as far as/to).

be up for [Vp.pr] be a candidate, applicant, for a post etc. **o:** re-election, admission, membership: *I believe he'**s up for** re-admission to the society at the next committee meeting.* ○ *Slutsky got caught when he **was up for** a new appointment and a member of the screening committee became suspicious of faulty statistics in his papers.* NS ⇨ come up for, put up (for) 1.

be up for auction/sale [Vp.pr] be available or offered for purchase, be on the market. **S:** house; furniture, painting, silver: *A rare collection of Chinese porcelain will* **be up for sale** *next week.* □ also used after a noun. ⇨ come/put up for auction/sale.

be up for debate/discussion [Vp.pr] be raised, be considered, during a meeting etc. **S:** subject, matter, question: *The housing policy of the council* **is up for debate** *at the next meeting.* ○ *Salaries* **are up for discussion** *at the next conference of the teacher's union.* ⇨ bring up 3, come up 5.

be up in arms [Vp.pr] (*informal*) declare opposition or disapproval; protest: *Kay* **was up in arms** *at once: her round, unmade-up face shone with high-minded intellectual disapproval.* ASA

be up in the clouds [Vp.pr] (*informal*) be out of touch with reality. **S:** thinking, ideas; all this. **m:** rather, somewhat, a bit: *Of course, he's a bit* **up in the clouds**. *All this conservatism in religion makes him think we can put the clock back* (ie go back to the past) *in everything.* ASA □ also used with *appear, seem.*

be well up in [Vp.pr] (*informal*) know a good deal (about sth), be well informed (about sth). **o:** science, languages, foreign affairs, literature: *Not very* **well up in** *the law,* **are** *you? Otherwise you'd know that it isn't possible to get divorced until you've been married three years.* TC □ also used with *appear, seem* or after a noun.

be up (to) [Vp, Vp.pr] have reached. ⇨ be up (as far as/to).

be up to 1 [Vp.pr] (*informal*) be doing, be engaged in (sth) (with the suggestion that the activity is mischievous or wrong). **o:** ⚠ mischief, something, no good; his tricks, pranks; what: *A very strange fellow your friend Libby Dobson. What's he* **been up to** *all day?* UTN ○ *I felt sure he* **was up to** *no good when I saw him hanging about the back door.* ⇨ get up to 2, put up to.

2 [Vp.pr] (*informal*) be well aware of (sb's dishonest tricks) and be capable of handling them. **S:** police, officials. **o:** ⚠ all his fiddles, dodges, tricks: *But, surely, all that's taken care of by the customs authorities and the dock police? They must* **be up to** *all the dodges.* HD

3 [Vp.pr] (*informal*) be the responsibility of (sb). **S:** (it . . .) whether we go or stay, how we manage things; (it . . .) to think about it, whether to go, how to do it: *It's* **up to** *you to find out who will lend you the money.* HD ○ *Whether you gain anything from the course* **is** *entirely* **up to** *you.* ○ *In a matter of choice, cigarettes for instance, people go to destruction their own way: that's* **up to** *them, and I'd abhor interference in free choice.* RT = rest with. ⇨ leave up to.

4 [Vp.pr] (*informal*) be deep in (sth), be overwhelmed by (sth). **o:** ⚠ here; his etc ears, eyes, neck. **A:** ⚠ in debt, in work: *He's* **up to** *his eyes in card debts.* US ○ *I* **was up to** *my ears in paperwork.* □ also used with *appear, seem.*

5 [Vp.pr] (*informal*) be of (an acceptable standard). **S:** work, performance, appearance. **o:** ⚠ standard, scratch, the mark; expectations; not much: *She had a boy who might or might not be her fiancé. He* **wasn't up to** *much, but he was her young man.* PW ○ *It's such nonsense about his household not* **being up to** *scratch.* UTN □ also used with *appear, seem*; often neg. ⇨ bring/come up to, get up to 1.

6 [Vp.pr] (*informal*) be capable of doing (sth); be equal to (sth). **m:** fully, quite; scarcely, hardly; not. **o:** task, work, responsibility; tackling the climb: *He* **was** *scarcely* **up to** *serious work, and declined rapidly in the new year.* SS ○ *None of us* **were up to** *going out in that downpour.* □ also used with *appear.* ⇨ feel up to.

be up to date/the minute [Vp.pr] be fresh or recent or modern; reflect current fashion. **S:** ideas, thought; clothes, equipment. **m:** right, bang, really: *Her clothes* **were** *bang* **up to date**. TGLY ○ *His reports from Africa* **are** *really* **up to the minute**. □ also used with *appear* etc; adj forms are up-to-date and up-to-the-minute. ⇨ bring up to date, get up to date (with).

be up (with) [Vp, Vp.pr] (*informal*) be amiss or wrong, be the matter. **S:** something, what. **o:** him etc: *I knew something* **was up** *as soon as I saw the miserable look in his eyes.* ○ *'What's* **up with** *you, now?'* ⇨ be up 7.

be all up with [Vp.pr] (*informal*) be the end of power, life, influence etc for (sb/sth). **o:** government, minister; gang; scheme, plan: *I sought a point of focus* (ie an aiming-point) *on the tiger's head, knowing now that I could not miss, and that it* **was all up with** *him.* □ also used with *appear, seem.*

be upon one [Vpr] ⇨ be on/upon one.

be with 1 [Vpr] be employed by (sb). **o:** company, corporation; ICI, Shell: *'What have you been doing since you qualified?' 'I was in insurance for a bit, but now I'm* **with** *a shipping firm.'*

2 [Vpr] (*informal*) follow or understand (sb). **S:** audience, class: *'Did you follow that bit all right?* **Are** *you still* **with** *me — or shall I go over it again?'*

3 [Vpr] support (sb). **A:** all the way, to the (bitter) end: *If you do decide to oppose him, then we're* **with** *you all the way!* = back up 2.

be within 1 [Vpr] be near enough (to be heard, seen or reached). **o:** ⚠ earshot, sight, view, range (of sth): *If we move forward we shall* **be within** *range of the enemy guns.* □ also used after a noun. ↔ be out of 1. ⇨ bring/come/get within.

2 [Vpr] be a matter which is not too difficult or unfamiliar (to understand, discuss etc). **S:** subject, topic, matter. **o:** (one's) competence, province; field, area (of interest); scope of the inquiry: *Perhaps this is something which another body should consider. It* **is** *not* **within** *the terms of reference of this committee.* □ also used after a noun. ↔ be outside. ⇨ fall within.

be within one's grasp [Vpr] (*formal*) be sth that can be achieved, controlled or understood. **S:** victory, success; difficulties; subject, problem. **m:** well, quite; comfortably: *With the junction of the allied armies, the final defeat of the enemy in North Africa* **was** *now* **within our grasp**. ○ *I'm not too worried about the maths paper: the algebra* **is** *well* **within my grasp**. □ also used with *appear, seem* or after a noun: *An achievement well* **within her grasp**.

be within one's rights (to do sth) [Vpr] have legal or moral support for sth one wishes to do. **S:** citizen, consumer, parent. **Inf:** to protest, to take the goods back, to remove one's child: *You're perfectly* **within your rights to demand** *a choice of* *schools for the child.* ○ *If you aren't satisfied with the service you're getting, you're quite* **within your rights to cancel** *the arrangement.*

bear

bear down [Vn ⇆ p pass] (*formal*) defeat, conquer (sb). **S:** forces, army. **O:** enemy, opposition: *Eventually, after much dogged fighting, our troops* **bore down** *all resistance.*

bear down on/upon [Vp.pr pass] move swiftly to attack or threaten (sb) or to control (sth). **S:** ship, tank, horse; society hostess. **o:** victim; guest; inflation, consumer spending: *The bird was* **bearing down upon** *us at a speed of twenty miles an hour.* DF ○ *Cars and buses* **bore down on** *her, but not, as far as she could see, a single taxi.* MSAL ○ *The main thrust of our policy has been to* **bear down on** *inflation and reduce it as speedily as possible.* IND

bear in mind [Vn.pr pass] remain aware or conscious of (sth). **O:** fact, truth; statement, admission; that he was not present: *He urged MPs to* **bear in mind** *the serious offences committed nowadays by young persons.* T ○ *Three factors must be* **borne in mind**. T ○ *Please* **bear in mind** *that we don't know any Mr Hawthorne.* OMIH = keep in mind.

bear on/upon [Vpr] affect or relate to (sth). **S:** action, remark, factor. **o:** matter at issue, question; what is at stake: *These were vital decisions that* **bore upon** *the happiness of everybody.* ○ *I am more concerned with how his personal experience* **bore upon** *his work and ideas than with the ideas themselves.* JUNG = have a bearing on/upon.

bear hard/severely on/upon [Vpr emph rel] (*formal*) cause hardship or suffering to (sb). **S:** shortage, rationing; unemployment, short-time working; drought, flooding. **o:** townspeople; worker; farmer: *The latest price increases* **bear** *most* **severely on** *people with fixed incomes.* ○ *It is* **upon** *the small farmer that the changes will* **bear hardest**.

bear out [Vn ⇆ p pass] support or confirm (sth/sb). **S:** evidence, facts, events; he etc. **O:** theory, supposition, hypothesis; him etc: *Indeed, the facts* **bear out** *the hypothesis.* SNP ○ *This expectation is not* **borne out**. MFF

bear a resemblance to [Vn.pr emph rel] be like, resemble (sb). **adj:** some, a good deal of; no, (not) any/much, little, small; a startling, uncanny. **o:** (one's) father, brother: *Tennessee Williams' own character* **bears no resemblance to** *the people depicted in his plays.* TO ○ *The French uniforms* **bore a** *superficial* **resemblance to** *those of Chinese regulars.* BM

bear witness to [Vn.pr emph rel] (*formal*) provide evidence of (sth). **S:** garden, house, countryside. **adj:** eloquent, mute. **o:** work, efforts, skill: *The village* **bore** *silent* **witness to** *the passage of the cyclone.* ○ *There is a hillside in Phrygia which still . . .* **bears witness to** *the time when Zeus himself came to earth.* GLEG = testify (to).

bear up [Vp] remain strong in the face of hard conditions; manage, cope. **S:** patient, soldier; plant: *The 190 men of Cottenham company appear to be* **bearing up** *well under the strain.* OBS ○ *How do they* **bear up** *against distress and shock?* AH

bear with [Vpr pass] be patient with (sb); tolerate. **o:** him etc; mood, temper: *She neither liked nor trusted Jack Corelli, but she* **bore with** *him when he came to the flat with his violent opinions and his bombastic talk.* AITC ○ *If you will all* **bear with** *me for just a few minutes, I will explain.* AITC

beat

beat about the bush [Vpr] (*informal*) go around a subject instead of coming directly to the point: *'If you've got bad news, don't* **beat about the bush**: *come straight to the point.'* ○ *'It's no use* **beating about the bush**, *Wormold, you are in trouble.'* OMIH

beat one's head against a brick wall [Vn.pr] ⇨ bang one's head against a brick wall.

beat down [Vn ⇆ p pass] make (sb) reduce the price he first asked. **O:** ⚠ owner, dealer; price, figure: *He wanted two thousand pounds for the car, but I managed to* **beat** *him* **down** *by a couple of hundred.* = knock down 3.

beat down (on) [Vp, Vp.pr rel] shine with intense heat (on sth/sb). **S:** the sun, sun's rays: *The sun* **beat down on** *our necks and backs.*

beat off [Vn ⇆ p pass] repulse (sth/sb). **S:** defender, soldier. **O:** attack; attacker, enemy: *All their attempts to break into our position were* **beaten off**. ○ *This policy is to provide a guard capable of* **beating off** *an attack, a guard that is armed, with firearms in reserve.* MFM = drive back, throw back 4.

beat out [Vn ⇆ p pass] remove (sth) by striking with a hammer etc. **S:** mechanic, panel-beater. **O:** dent, mark: *The dent on the wing of your car can be* **beaten out** *at the garage.*

beat one's/sb's brains out [Vn.p pass] (*informal*) kill oneself, or sb, by being beaten, or beating him, severely about the head (though not necessarily by knocking out the brains): *There would be nothing to stop me from plunging down the well of the staircase and* **beating my brains out** *on the stone floor at the bottom.* CON

beat out (on) [Vn ⇆ p pass adj, Vn.p.pr pass rel] produce or play (sth) by drumming. **S:** drummer, musician. **O:** tune, rhythm; message. **o:** drum; desk, table: *A small boy was* **beating out** *a tune* **on** *a tin can.* = bang out (on), hammer out (on), thump out (on).

beat to it [Vn.pr pass] (*informal*) get somewhere, reach an objective, before (sb else). **O:** opponent, rival: *They had hoped to put their model on the market within the year, but a rival company* **beat** *them* **to it**.

beat up [Vn ⇆ p pass adj] beat (sb) severely with fists, sticks etc. **S:** gang, thieves. **O:** guard, messenger, shopkeeper: *Next year another three Britons were arrested for* **beating up** *a taxi-driver.* TO ○ *The bank manager got a severe* **beating-up** *in last night's raid.* □ nom form is beating-up. = do over 2.

beaver

beaver away (at) [Vp, Vp.pr rel] work continuously and intensely (at a task). **o:** essay, thesis; accounts, records: *Charles* **beavered away** *at the Treasury addressing the economic problems that had been presented.* FAE

become

become of [Vpr] happen to, befall (sb). **S:** what, whatever. **o:** him etc; sister, wife; pet; property: *Whatever* **became of** *that house they used as a weekend cottage?* ○ *I don't know what will* *become of* her now that her husband has died. □ used only in direct or indirect questions.

bed

bed down 1 [Vp, Vn ⇆ p pass] get, put (sb), into a makeshift bed, eg of straw or sacks, and usu in temporary quarters. **S** [Vp], **O** [Vn.p]: scouts, hikers, soldiers: *We settled round the fire, making quite sure that before we **bedded down** for the night there was an ample supply of wood at hand.* BM ○ *The troops were **bedded down** in a barn.*

2 [Vn ⇆ p pass] provide with straw as bedding. **S:** groom, farmer. **O:** horse, cattle: *The horses were watered, fed, and **bedded down** with clean straw.*

bed out [Vn ⇆ p pass adj] (*horticulture*) transfer (partly-grown plants) from a greenhouse etc to beds in a garden. **S:** gardener, grower: *This is the right weather for **bedding out** your tomatoes.* ○ *'There'd better be no frost till I've got my stuff* (ie plants) ***bedded out**.'* TT

beef

beef up [Vn ⇆ p pass adj] (*informal*) make (sth) stronger; develop (sth) in size and importance. **O:** forces, defence capability; research; laboratories, clinics: *We've begun to **beef up** our naval forces.* BBCR ○ *The Defence Education Act was rushed through Congress ... to **beef up** Soviet Studies in the country's major universities.*.

beetle

beetle off [Vp] (*jocular*) hurry, scurry, away, esp to escape from trouble: *We all supposed you had **beetled off** to London as you always do when things get difficult.*

begin

begin (with) [Vpr rel, Vn.pr pass rel] (cause sth to) start or open (with a certain event). **S** [Vpr], **O** [Vn.pr]: film, play; meeting, service; meal. **o:** love scene, family reunion; speech, hymn; soup, fish: *The film **began with** a violent scene.* ○ *The chairman began his speech with a few words of welcome.* ↔ end up (with), finish off/up (with).

to begin with 1 [Vpr] at the beginning, initially: ***To begin with**, we had very little support, but later on people began to rally to us.* ○ *They had few essential supplies **to begin with**, so they had to improvise.* □ to begin with is an adv clause with no object; it may occur at the beginning or end of the sentence. = to start with 1.

2 [Vpr] in the first place, first and foremost: ***To begin with**, you must realize I have very little money.* □ to begin with is an adv clause with no object; it usu occurs at the beginning of the sentence. = to start with 2.

believe

believe in 1 [Vpr] have confidence in (sb). **o:** adviser, friend; honesty, goodness: *You can **believe in** him; he'll never let you down.* ○ *Until now, I had always **believed** firmly **in** his good intentions.* = trust in.

2 [Vpr] feel sure of the existence of (sb/sth). **o:** God; ghosts, fairies; an afterlife: *Prissie gave an excited laugh. 'Oh! One doesn't really **believe in** ghosts, does one?'* DC ○ *She was very pretty and so extraordinarily alive. She could almost make one **believe in** her world of fantasy.* DC

3 [Vpr] favour, support (an idea, a policy etc). **o:** not giving too much freedom, taxing richer people; boarding schools, penalties for motorists: *She doesn't **believe in** staying at home when her parents go to a party.* WI ○ *He also **believed in** the efficacy of corporal punishment (and the threat of it).* MRJ

believe of [Vn.pr pass rel] believe that sb is capable of a particular (kind of) action. **O:** anything malicious, nasty, underhand; it, that: *You say he's going to be a father again at forty-five? I wouldn't have **believed** it **of** him.* ○ *After all the changes of policy we've had recently I'd **believe** absolutely anything **of** that man.* □ with would; often neg.

belong

belong to 1 [Vpr emph rel] be the property of (sb); be in the control of (sb), to treat as he wishes. **o:** government; company; owner, inventor: *This land and the buildings on it **belong to** British Rail.* ○ *The world **belonged to** the young, **to** the cunning ....* MSAL

2 [Vpr] be a member of (sth); be a feature or aspect of (sth). **o:** club, society; family, tribe; youth, old age: *She **belonged to** several learned societies.* ○ *His friendship ... had the peculiar intensity which **belongs to** the almost romantic attachments of adolescence.* MLT

belt

belt out [Vn ⇆ p pass adj] (*informal*) produce (sth) with great force or vigour. **S:** singer, tenor; fire, central heating. **O:** song, aria; heat, energy: *They'll be **belting out** bits of 'Messiah'* (a musical piece for many voices) *and I should go mad.* UNXL ○ *We crouched in front of that hideous fire **belting out** unnecessary extra heat.* PPAP

bend

bend over backwards to do sth/doing sth [Vp] (*informal*) take special care to please sb, not to offend sb etc. **A:** to please the visitors, to meet their objections; trying to see their point of view: *We really **bent over backwards to meet** their conditions.* ○ *I was **bending over backwards trying** to be fair.* = fall over backwards to do sth/doing sth. ⇨ lean over backwards.

bent on [pass (Vn.pr)] having one's mind set on (sth), determined to (do sth). **o:** success, mischief; making trouble, getting on: *He declined on the grounds that he was **bent on** an early start the next day.* OBS ○ *These men are **bent on** undermining the power of union officials.* SC □ also used with *appear, seem, look*, and after a noun: *... a regime **bent on** conquest.*

benefit

benefit by/ from [Vpr pass emph rel] get some advantage from (sth). **o:** course, exchange scheme, scholarship; experience; training in London: *She **benefited** greatly **from** her time at London University.* ○ *I'm only now beginning to realize how much I **benefited from** my parents' example.* ○ *'We are trying to make sure that children who can best **benefit by** foster care, do get foster parents.'* FOX = profit from.

bitch

bitch up [Vn ⇆ p pass] (*slang*) spoil, undo (sb's good work), usu through spiteful gossip. **O:** it, the whole thing; my arrangements: *I was in a hurry to ... begin the hunt for Ned, before Robert had a chance to **bitch it up**.* CON

bite

bite back [Vn ⇆ p pass] quickly restrain oneself from saying (sth embarrassing, confidential etc). **O:** remark; oath, exclamation; admission: *John nearly launched into one of his attacks on the Church, but it struck him that Marcelle's family were Catholics and he* ***bit*** *the offending words* ***back****.*

bite sb's head off [Vn.p pass] (*informal*) show ill temper towards sb (often without good reason): *I must keep out of his way. I don't like having* ***my head bitten off*** *at the slightest provocation.* ○ *It looks like I was on the right track that night, when you* ***bit my head off*** *in the Conservative Club.* CON = snap sb's head off.

bite off more than one can chew [Vp.n] (*informal*) attempt too much, undertake more than one can manage. **S:** manager, administrator: *'You've* ***bitten off more than you can chew****,' said Bill unhelpfully, when he saw the trouble I was having with my business.*

black

black out 1 [Vp nom] suffer temporary loss of consciousness or memory (esp during flight or after a severe blow). **S:** pilot, boxer: *The pilot suffered a complete* ***blackout*** *when attempting to pull out of a steep dive.* ○ *I had a fight with the Old Man, and after it I* ***blacked out****.* LLDR

2 [Vn ⇆ p nom pass adj] make (windows, lights etc) invisible from the air at night by covering them. **S:** householder, shopkeeper. **O:** house, factory; window, car headlights: *During the war, we had to make sure windows were carefully* ***blacked out*** *at night.* ○ *Wolverhampton was the first town in Britain to impose a nightly* ***black-out****.* TBC □ nom form (usu blackout — without a hyphen) refers both to the covering which blacks out windows etc and to the appearance of blacked-out streets etc.

3 [Vn ⇆ p nom pass adj] bring (TV transmission) to a halt by strike action. **S:** technician; union. **O:** programme; speaker, performer: *Within seconds of going on the air, London Weekend Television was* ***blacked out****.* G ○ *The possibility of further screen* ***blackouts*** *by television technicians was not ruled out.* G

4 [Vn ⇆ p nom pass] not allow (news etc) to be released; suppress. **S:** government, army, news agency. **O:** news, information: *There was a complete* ***black-out*** *on information.* T ○ *Their first decision was to draw a* ***black-out*** *over today's discussions.* G □ usu nom (usu blackout — without a hyphen).

blame

blame (for) [Vn.pr pass emph rel] attach to (sb/sth) the responsibility (for sth), usu to escape blame oneself. **O:** partner, ally; staff; conditions, climate. **o:** failure, setback, disgrace; (poor) sales: *The poor health of key players can fairly be* ***blamed for*** *the disastrous opening to the season.* ○ *The Marxist analysis has nothing to do with what happened in Stalin's Russia: it's like* ***blaming*** *Jesus Christ* ***for*** *the Inquisition in Spain.* OBS ⇨ next entry

blame on [Vn.pr pass emph rel] fix or place the responsibility for (sth) on (sb/sth). **O:** disaster, setback; loss, disappearance. **o:** ally, colleague; youth, inexperience; time (of year), weather: *It's not much use* ***blaming*** *our defeat* ***on*** *the weather!* ○ *He could see nothing but impropriety and rebellion, which he* ***blamed*** *entirely* ***on*** *the Brays' influence.* GE ⇨ previous entry

blast

blast off [Vp nom] (*space technology*) (of a rocket-propelled space vehicle) be launched. **S:** spacecraft; missile, rocket: *The space shuttle will* ***blast off*** *(cf* ***Blast-off*** *for the space shuttle will be) at ten am local time.*

blaze

blaze away (at) [Vp, Vp.pr] (*informal*) fire at a rapid rate (at a target). **S:** rifleman, gunner: *The boys* ***blazed away*** *with their airguns until the tin can was full of holes.*

blend

blend in (with) [Vp, Vp.pr emph rel, Vn ⇆ p pass adj, Vn.p.pr pass emph rel] mix harmoniously (with its surroundings); not (cause sth to) clash or jar (with sth else). **S** [Vp, Vp.pr], **O** [Vn.p, Vn.p.pr]**:** building, development; design, pattern; colour. **o:** background, surroundings, setting : [Vp] 'That purple doesn't ***blend in*** *too well, does it?'* ○ [Vp.pr] The curtains ***blend in*** *perfectly* ***with*** *the carpet.* ○ [Vn.p] Various herbs are ***blended in*** *to make a good soup.* ○ [Vn.p.pr] There has been no attempt to ***blend in*** *the new office blocks* ***with*** *their Victorian surroundings.*

blink

blink (one's) tears away/back [Vn ⇆ p pass] try to control or hide one's tears by blinking: *Her voice rose higher and higher. She* ***blinked away the tears****.* THH ○ *Brigit smiled, and* ***blinked back tears****.* DC

block

block in [Vn ⇆ p pass adj] fill (sth) so that it is a solid block. **O:** outline, drawing; fireplace; window, door: *With parallel slanted strokes,* ***block in*** *the shadowy sides of the rocks on the left.* ○ *The previous owner* ***blocked in*** *most of the open fireplaces when central heating was installed.*

block off [Vn ⇆ p pass adj] separate (one place from another) by using a solid barrier etc. **O:** street, alley; pipe; trench: *Police have* ***blocked off*** *all side-streets giving access to the main procession route.* ○ *A landslide has* ***blocked off*** *traffic moving south towards the motorway.*

block out [Vn ⇆ p pass adj] (*photography* or *printing*) mask (part of a negative), when printing or enlarging, so that light does not pass through it; cover (part of a stencil etc) so that paint does not pass through it. **O:** negative; silk screen, stencil: *You can* ***block out*** *this small detail at the top of your picture.*

block up [Vn ⇆ p pass adj] fill a (pipe etc) with waste matter etc so that water cannot pass. **O:** pipe, drain; sink; lavatory: *A tree-root pierced the drain and* ***blocked*** *it* ***up****.* ○ *'Well, if the sink's* ***blocked up****, you'd better unblock it!'* = stop up 2.

blossom

blossom into [Vpr] develop or mature so as to become (sth). **o:** fine dancer, accomplished actress, sympathetic teacher: *She had* ***blossomed into*** *a charming and talented girl with a musical career.* CD

blossom out [Vp] reach a developed or mature state. **S:** girl, pupil, athlete: *I see my daughter is **blossoming out**. I see my Josephine is branching out on her own and breaking new ground.* THH

blot

blot out [Vn ⇆ p pass] make (sb/sth) invisible; dispel or blur an image in the mind. **S:** cloud, smoke; confusion. **O:** sun, stars; scene; past memories: *The summer night was **blotted out** by a driving rainstorm.* SD ○ *But his image kept **blotting out** the pages: she couldn't think of him without seeing him.* PW ○ *He could not face the possibility that Jung was still a traitor and **blotted out** the thought.* JUNG

blow

blow the cobwebs away [Vn ⇆ p pass] (*informal*) make the mind and spirits active and lively again. **S:** conversation; companionship; exercise, fresh air: *You've been cooped up in that study far too long. What you need to **blow the cobwebs away** is a couple of weeks in the open air.*

blow down [Vp, Vn ⇆ p pass] be knocked, knock (sth) to the ground. **S** [Vp], **O** [Vn.p]**:** tree; fence, gate; chimney, slate, tile. **S** [Vn.p]**:** (strong) wind, gale: *A flowering tree **blew down** and some small shrubs were flattened.* ○ *The gale raged all night and **blew down** a TV aerial from the roof.*

blow in/into [Vp emph, Vpr emph] (*informal*) arrive, come in/into (a place), esp in a lively or noisy way. **S:** politician, film-star, boss. **o:** town, New York; office: *John **blew in** to share the latest news from party headquarters.* ○ *The Adjutant General **blew into** my office.* MFM

blow off steam [Vp.n] (*informal*) release pent-up energy, tension etc (eg in drinking, dancing, argument): *Dancing started on New Year's Day. This is a traditional time to **blow off steam**.* OBS = let off steam.

blow out 1 [Vp, Vn ⇆ p pass] be extinguished with a puff of air etc; extinguish (sth) with a puff of air etc. **S** [Vp], **O** [Vn.p]**:** light; candle, lamp. **S** [Vn.p]**:** he etc; wind: *Someone opened the door and the lamp **blew out**.* ○ *'**Blow** the candles **out** before you come to bed.'* = go out 6, put out 10.

2 [Vp nom] (*oil industry*) (of petroleum vapour escaping from a well) emerge suddenly and violently at the surface. **S:** gas, vapour; well, drilling: *Gas came up the outside of the bore pipe and **blew out**, as we say in the oil industry.* ITV ○ *We have to launch a massive operation to repair the **blowout**.* ITV

blowout 1 [nom (Vp)] bursting of a tyre on a motor vehicle: *Coming over those rough mountain roads you have to be prepared for a few **blowouts**.*

2 [nom (Vp)] (*slang*) a feast, a good feed: *Even when times were bad, there was always enough money for a good **blowout** at Christmas, or whenever someone got married.*

blow one's/sb's brains out [Vn ⇆ p] kill oneself by shooting in the head: *A patient committed suicide by **blowing out his brains**.* ○ *He put his pistol to her head and **blew her brains out**.* IND

blow itself out [Vn.p] exhaust itself, dwindle to nothing. **S:** storm, wind, hurricane: *The gale had not quite **blown itself out**. Even now a hard breeze whipped at the flowers.* US

blow over [Vp] (*informal*) cease to excite feeling, no longer be thought important. **S:** scandal, controversy, trouble; business, affair: *'You've really managed to upset everyone. But I shouldn't worry: the whole thing will have **blown over** in a few days.'* ○ *The affair did not **blow over**, however, and soon the college was in ferment.* MRJ

blow to 1 [Vn.pr pass] shatter (sth) to (small pieces) by explosion. **S:** (explosive) charge; dynamite, gun-cotton. **O:** bridge, factory; dug-out, pillbox. **o:** ⚠ pieces, smithereens, atoms: *The gun emplacements were **blown to** pieces by high explosive.* = blow up 4.

2 [Vn.pr pass] kill (sb) by explosion. **S:** bomb, booby-trap. **O:** soldier, policeman. **o:** ⚠ blazes, glory, kingdom come: *We were nearly **blown to** glory by the same flying-bomb.* AH

blow up 1 [Vp] (*informal*) lose one's temper. **S:** associate, partner; wife, parent. **A:** at him; over his decision: *I **blew** right **up**, saying that I disagreed completely with the conclusion of the report.* MFM ○ *'I'm sorry I **blew up** at you this morning.'* ⇨ next entry

2 [Vn ⇆ p pass] (*informal, dated*) lose one's temper with (sb), reprimand (sb) severely. **S:** employer, parent. **O:** worker, child: *That new teacher **blew** me **up** for not saying 'Good morning' to him in the street.* ○ *I got quite a **blowing-up** for being late for practice.* □ nom form is blowing-up. ⇨ previous entry

3 [Vp] work towards a crescendo or crisis; arise. **S:** storm, gale; political storm, crisis: *It was one of those silly family rows that **blow up** over nothing and leave everyone shaking with rage.* CON

4 [Vp, Vn ⇆ p pass adj] (cause sth to) explode or smash to pieces. **S** [Vp], **O** [Vn.p]**:** bomb, mine; house, factory. **S** [Vn.p]**:** terrorist; raider, aircraft: *The bomb **blew up** with an ear-splitting crash.* ○ *Our other house was **blown up** by enemy action.* EHOW ○ *We passed the wreckage of **blown-up** bridges.*

5 [Vn.p pass adj] pump air or gas into (sth). **S:** mechanic. **O:** tyre, rubber raft, balloon: *I've got a flat tyre; I'll have to find a garage and get it mended and **blown up**.* = pump up 2. ↔ let down 3.

6 [Vn ⇆ p nom pass adj] (*photography*) make (sth) bigger; enlarge. **O:** negative, photograph, picture, snap: *'Those photographs look promising. Why not get an expert to **blow** them **up** a bit bigger?'* ○ *In this **blow-up** of the negative, you can read the date on the newspaper that Wilson's carrying.* ○ *His study walls were covered with **blown-up** pictures of sailing-ships.*

7 [Vn ⇆ p pass adj] inflate, exaggerate (sth). **S:** press, critics. **O:** reputation, achievements; story, affair: *His abilities as an actor have been greatly **blown up** by the weekend press; in fact, they are quite modest.* ○ *It didn't really happen like that: the incident's been **blown up** out of all proportion.* □ usu passive.

bluff

bluff it out [Vn.p] survive a situation (eg in which one is pretending to be sb else) by deceit: *When he was caught in the bank strong-room after hours, the cashier could tell the truth, and risk imprisonment, or try to **bluff it out**.*

bluff one's way out/out of [Vn.p, Vn.pr] escape from a difficult situation by pretence, by deceiving others. **S:** criminal, spy. **o:** tricky situation, tight corner: *She turned to the officers. 'The man is trying to* ***bluff his way out of*** *the whole thing,' she said.* PP

blurt

blurt out [Vn ⇆ p pass adj] exclaim (sth) suddenly and often nervously; reveal (sth) suddenly through nervousness. **O:** apology, confused statement; secret, confidence: *'Wonderful!' Lionel* ***blurted out****. 'It was the most wonderful experience.'* GIE ○ *In their anxiety, prisoners would often* ***blurt out*** *pieces of vital information.* □ often used after direct speech.

board

board out [Vp, Vn.p pass adj] have or give (sb) food and lodging outside one's family home; have or give (sb) food and lodging in a separate place from the school, college etc where he studies. **S** [Vp], **O** [Vn.p]**:** student, trainee, boy. **S** [Vn.p]**:** school, bursar, authorities: *The practice of* ***boarding*** *little children* ***out*** *with foster-parents was by no means unknown.* BRN ○ *Married men not living in camp receive a* ***boarding-out*** *allowance.*

board up [Vn ⇆ p pass adj] cover (sth) with boards, because a house is no longer occupied, is about to be pulled down etc. **O:** house, shop; window, door: *The windows on the ground floor have been* ***boarded up****, chiefly to stop children climbing in and making nuisances of themselves.* ○ *A dismal row of* ***boarded-up*** *shops faced the sea-front.*

boast

boast (about/of) [Vpr pass emph rel] speak in praise (of oneself, one's achievements etc). **o:** talent, (personal) quality; success, wealth; family: *He was fond of* ***boasting about*** *his war record. In fact, as far as one could gather, he had spent the war years at Clacton-on-Sea.* ○ *To little Bichet, then working in Budapest, he* ***boasted of*** *what he had done.* AF

bob

bob up [Vp emph] (*informal*) (of an elusive or irrepressible person) reappear, though often discouraged from doing so: *The Scarlet Pimpernel kept* ***bobbing up*** *in the most unlikely places.* ○ *You can't keep him down: he'll* ***bob up*** *when the police temporarily lose interest.* = pop up 1.

bog

bog down [Vp, Vn.p pass adj] (*informal*) (cause sth to) stick fast (in mud etc); (cause sb to) be heavily involved with sth. **S** [Vp], **O** [Vn.p]**:** tank, car; speaker, overworked person, ambitious youth. **S** [Vn.p]**:** driver; work, routine: *Our transport* ***bogged down*** *in the thick mud.* ○ *I hasten to reply before I get* ***bogged down*** *with other work.* ○ *I like these people here only because I'm already on my way out. If I had to stay* ***bogged down*** *here, I'd hate them.* CON

boggle

boggle (at) [Vpr pass emph rel] (*informal*) stare in amazement or perplexity at (sb/sth). **o:** face, figure; achievement; sight, spectacle: *She was fed up with men in the office* ***boggling at*** *her legs.* ○ *Science* ***boggles at*** *the problem of human nature, and tends to lose sight of the whole human being.* ESS

boil

boil down (to) [Vn ⇆ p pass, Vn.p.pr pass] (*informal*) state (sth) more briefly (as so many words etc). **O:** case, argument, proposal; article, report: *I have tried to state briefly, to* ***boil down****, the most important area of conflict.* ○ *'This report would be better if you could* ***boil*** *it* ***down to*** *about 500 words or so.'*

boil down to [Vp.pr] (may) be reduced to (sth); be essentially (sth). **S:** case, dispute, issue; advice. **o:** disagreement, misunderstanding; this, these essentials: *The good advice we gave him* ***boiled down to*** *this: that after tea he should stroll to the window.* ○ *Their disagreements over re-nationalization* ***boil down to*** *the fact that they have different views of socialism.*

boil over 1 [Vp] (of liquid in a pan) overflow the sides of the pan when the liquid reaches the boil. **S:** milk, water; saucepan; potatoes, greens: *'You'd better turn the gas down or else the vegetables will* ***boil over****.'*
2 [Vp] reach a danger or crisis point; explode. **S:** situation, quarrel. **A:** into violence, in an exchange of blows: *The Palestine Police Force was fifty per cent below strength, and this at a time when the situation was clearly about to* ***boil over****.* MFM
3 [Vp] (*informal*) be extremely angry, be furious: *John was* ***boiling over*** *and it was soon clear why; nobody had told him of our plans to move house.*

boil up [Vp] be about to happen; develop. **S:** quarrel, first-class row, crisis: *A dispute is* ***boiling up*** *over who should be exempt from payment of the tax.*

bolster

bolster up [Vn ⇆ p pass] support (sb/sth) that might otherwise collapse. **S:** government, Treasury, armed forces. **O:** ally; system, rebellion; sb's strength, self-esteem: *Our money has been used to* ***bolster up*** *unpopular regimes.* ○ *She* ***bolstered up*** *his shattered constitution so that he lived four years with her.* BLCH ○ *Micky, trying to* ***bolster up*** *his own status, assumed an assurance that he did not feel.* PE = prop up 2 .

bolt

bolt down [Vn ⇆ p pass] swallow (one's food) quickly, through hunger or greed, or because one is in a hurry. **O:** meal, snack: *You'll have violent indigestion if you* ***bolt down*** *your food like that.* ○ *The surgeon on casualty duty just has time to* ***bolt down*** *a sandwich before the first case is wheeled in.*

bomb

bomb out [Vn ⇆ p pass adj] make (sb) homeless through bombing. **S:** enemy, aircraft. **O:** family; street, neighbourhood: *Our firm was* ***bombed out*** *but we soon managed to get on our feet again.* ○ ***Bombed-out*** *families crowded into the public shelters.* □ usu passive or adj.

bombard

bombard (with) 1 [Vn.pr pass emph rel] send at (sb/sth) a heavy shower of missiles. **O:** troops; trench, fortification; prisoner; orator, actor. **o:** shell, rocket; (rotten) fruit, vegetables: *The allied positions were* ***bombarded with*** *shells of every calibre.* ○ *The crowd expressed their dissatis-*

faction with the referee's decision by **bombarding** *the pitch* **with** *beer cans.*

2 [Vn.pr pass emph rel] direct at (sth/sb) a heavy, continuous stream of (sth). **O:** office, headquarters; manager, secretary. **o:** question, inquiry, complaint: *We've been* **bombarded with** *requests for the new car all week. Unfortunately, it'll be some time before we can satisfy this level of demand.* ○ *She* **bombarded** *him* **with** *letters, first passionate, finally abusive.* BRN

bone

bone up (on) [Vp, Vp.pr pass] (*informal*) make a close study (of sth), usu for some special purpose. **o:** mathematics, French; wine and food, travel: *I must* **bone up on** *my Italian if we are going to Rome for our holiday.* □ note the adj use in: *He* (a British officer) *spent his summer holidays in Belfast. 'I used the time to get* **boned up on** *the situation before the battalion was due here,' he explained.* ST

book

book in/into [Vp, Vpr rel, Vn ⇆ p pass, Vn.pr pass rel] reserve a room, or register one's name on arrival, at (a hotel); do this on behalf of (sb). **S** [Vp, Vpr], **O** [Vn.p, Vn.pr]**:** guest, visitor. **S** [Vn.p, Vn.pr]**:** clerk, receptionist: *She* **booked into** *the lodge at the Canyon's edge; it was early evening.* SATS ○ *'Carry these cases upstairs while I* **book** *the guests* **in**.*'* ○ *Henri finally* **booked** *his friend* **into** *the Hotel Cluny.* AF

book up [Vp] reserve accommodation (on a train or aircraft, or in a hotel). **S:** traveller, holiday-maker: *If you want to go to Switzerland for your holiday this year, you ought to* **book up** *now.*

booked up [pass (Vn.p)] having no seats or rooms left, for a traveller, theatregoer etc; having no free time left, through pressure of engagements etc. **S:** hotel; steamer; theatre, stadium: *'I'm afraid we can't even offer you a seat in the balcony, sir; we're fully* **booked up**.*'* ○ *'I might go out if I had anybody to go with. Are you very* **booked up** *yourself?'* HD □ also used with *appear, seem, look,* and after a noun.

border

border on [Vpr] come close to (sth); approach. **S:** idea, suggestion; behaviour, conduct. **o:** lunacy, criminality; the fanciful, the insane: *The activities ... were at best a waste of time and money, at worst* **bordered on** *the disreputable.* TU = verge on/upon.

bore

bore to death/distraction/tears [Vn.pr pass] be utterly dreary, tedious, to (sb). **S:** story, joke; conversation, discussion; he etc. **O:** friend, audience: *I don't want to* **bore** *myself* **to death** *reminiscing about those days.* JFTR ○ *I couldn't decently leave my hosts, so I just sat there, while their television* **bored** *me* **to distraction**.

borne

borne in on/upon [pass (Vn.p.pr)] (*formal*) coming gradually to be understood by (sb). **S:** the idea of a new approach, the truth of what I had been told; it ... that he was not welcome. **A:** gradually, slowly: *The gravity of the situation was slowly* **borne in on** *him.* ○ *It had been* **borne in on** *her how little she counted for him as a human being.* PW □ also used after a noun: *It was a view* **borne in upon** *me mainly through work with children.* DL

boss

boss about/around [Vn.p pass adj] keep telling (sb) to do this or that. **S:** husband, wife; teacher: *She* **bossed** *him* **about**, *made him fetch and carry.* ○ *None of my stuffy middle-class boyfriends had ever* **bossed** *me* **around** *like that.* = order about/around, push about/around.

botch

botch up [Vn ⇆ p nom pass adj] (*informal*) spoil, mar (sth) through inattention, carelessness etc. **S:** builder, plumber; manager, executive; minister, civil servant. **O:** it, the whole thing, things; job, repairs; arrangements; discussion, treaty: *'Don't give the job to him: he'll only* **botch** *it* **up** (or: *make a* **botch-up** *of it*)*.'* ○ *The Minister said that negotiations were lengthy because he did not want a* **botched-up** *agreement.* = mess up.

bother

bother one's head about [Vn.pr] (*informal*) concern oneself in thinking about (sth). **o:** poverty, hunger; problem, issue: *Why* **bother your heads about** *what's happening on the other side of the world?* ○ *'Now, don't* **bother your** *sweet little* **head about** *that.'* ○ *This is something worth* **bothering one's head about**. □ usu forms part of a suggestion or recommendation not to be concerned.

bottle

bottle up [Vn ⇆ p pass adj] not allow (sth) to show; suppress. **O:** emotion, desire, appetite; things, it all: *It's better to express your anger now and then, rather than* **bottle** *it* **up** *and have an almighty explosion.* ○ *She shows the strain of* **bottled-up** *emotion.*

bottom

bottom out [Vp] (esp *finance*) reach its lowest level. **S:** market; trading; prices: *There were signs that the world recession would* **bottom out** *in 1981, and business confidence was already reviving.* T ○ *I think the decline in the churches has '***bottomed out***' as they say.*

bounce

bounce back [Vp] (*informal*) recover jauntily from a setback. **S:** sportsman, entertainer; economy, sterling: *He's had no end of bad luck, but he just seems to* **bounce back** *every time.* ○ *In the City share prices* **bounced back** *this morning.* BBCR

bound

bound up with [pass (Vn.p.pr)] closely connected with or related to (sth). **S:** position, life, future. **o:** his etc progress, science: *She had her own existence now, even if that existence was* **bound up with** *an unfaithful husband.* PW ○ *Their own political position is* **bound up with** *his.* SC □ also used with *appear, seem,* or after a noun.

bow

bow in/into [Vn ⇆ p pass, Vn.pr pass] welcome (a visitor etc) with low bows. **S:** porter, doorman, shopwalker. **O:** guest, client: *A crowd of flunkeys stood by the entrance waiting to* **bow** *the guests* **in**. ○ *She was* **bowed into** *a waiting taxi.*

bow out [Vp] (*informal*) give up a prominent position (eg in politics, on the stage). **S:** minister, director: *So Sir Harold* **bows out**, *at the end of a distinguished career in broadcasting.*

bow out/out of [Vn ⇆ p pass, Vn.pr pass] bow low to a visitor or customer as he leaves (a place). **S:** waiter, manager. **O:** diner, guest: *Then, collecting up our purchases, we were* **bowed out of** *the shop by the owner.* DF

bow to [Vp] accept the force of (sth). **S:** government; industry; the press. **o:** argument, pressure; demand, request: *The only way to get rid of the Algerian problem was* **bow to** *the inevitable and negotiate with the insurgents.* NS

bowl

bowl along [Vp] drive swiftly and smoothly. **S:** carriage, car: *His car* **bowled along** *at an even pace until it reached the village.*

bowl out [Vn ⇆ p pass] (*cricket*) dismiss (sb) by striking his wicket with the ball. **S:** pace-bowler; Jones etc. **O:** opening batsman, tail-ender; side: *Half the side were* **bowled out** *before lunch.*

bowl over 1 [Vn ⇆ p pass] knock (sb/sth) down and make him/it roll over or spin around. **S:** car; shot, throw. **O:** pedestrian; barrel, tin can: *He lent me his gun. I missed the first two, but then* **bowled over** *four rabbits in four shots.* RFW ○ *The Irish scrum-half was* **bowled over** *near the corner flag.* = bring down 2,3.

2 [Vn ⇆ p pass] (*informal*) overwhelm, impress (sb) deeply. **S:** beauty, charm, wit; sudden arrival, attack. **O:** admirer, audience; defender: *The chef hadn't time to prepare the kind of speciality that would be likely to* **bowl over** *the taster.* ARG ○ *You look devastating and I'm* **bowled over**. EHOW

box

box in 1 [Vn ⇆ p pass adj] prevent (sb) from going faster, manoeuvring etc, by surrounding him on three sides at the edge of a racetrack. **S:** runner; car, horse. **O:** competitor, rival: *The favourite was* **boxed in** *against the rails by three horses.*

2 [Vn ⇆ p pass adj] prevent (sb) from acting freely; constrain: **Boxed in**, *Murdoch searched for an opening.* IND ○ *The Government was effectively* **boxed-in** *to its position.* IND

box up [Vn ⇆ p pass] confine or enclose (sb) in a small space. **S:** hunter, enemy; climate, geography. **O:** prey, inhabitant: *These Islanders have been* **boxed up** *here for hundreds of years and they think they know everything.* RM □ usu passive.

branch

branch off [Vp, Vpr] turn from (one road etc) onto another usu smaller one. **S:** car, train. **o:** (main) road, line (of a railway): *'We've lost them — they must have* **branched off** *further back.'*

branch out (into) [Vp, Vp.pr] expand or develop (in a new direction). **S:** factory, enterprise; he etc. **o:** exports; banking, financial consultancy; textiles: *So far we have only been producing heavy metal parts; now we are* **branching out into** *light alloys and plastics.* ○ *I see my Josephine is* **branching out** *on her own and breaking new ground.* THH

brave

brave it out [Vn.p] confront and defy hostility, threats or suspicion. **S:** country; person: *I don't want to see him, because I know he suspects me of disloyalty. But I suppose I'll just have to* **brave it out**.

brazen

brazen it out [Vn.p] behave as if one has nothing to be ashamed of (even though one has done wrong). **S:** thief, coward, naughty child: *Everybody ignored his remark for what it was, the lowest form of wit, and contemptible into the bargain — but Miller just sat there and* **brazened it out**. TT

break

break away (from) 1 [Vp, Vp.pr rel] leave or escape (from sb/sth) suddenly. **S:** friend, acquaintance; prisoner. **o:** him etc; guard, captivity: *Suddenly John spotted his bus pulling up opposite, and* **broke away**. ○ *The prisoner* **broke away from** *his guards while being transferred to another gaol.*

2 [Vp nom, Vp.pr rel] cut one's ties or links (with sth/sb). **o:** ideas, beliefs; family, tradition; the Old Guard, the Labour Party: *He had* **broken away from** *the menial background of his parents and become a government functionary.* CD ○ *He decided to* **break away from** *the Party and seek re-election as an Independent.* ○ *A* **breakaway** *group of lorry drivers . . . is trying to organize a return to work in defiance of their union.* OBS

3 [Vp nom, Vp.pr rel] end one's political dependence (on sth), become politically separate (from sth). **S:** province, region. **o:** state, country: *One part of a federal state may attempt to* **break away** *to form an independent entity.* ○ *Several major powers have now recognized the* **break-away** *state.* □ break-away is only used attrib, as here.

break back [Vp nom] (*cricket*) (of a ball striking the pitch) change its direction sharply: *The second ball of the over* **broke back** *and took off a bail.* ○ *That delivery had a vicious* **break-back**.

break down 1 [Vn ⇆ p pass adj] knock or smash (sth) to the ground; demolish. **S:** fireman, demolition gang, police. **O:** wall, door, fence: *Firemen had to* **break down** *a wall to get to families trapped on the ground floor.* = knock down 1.

2 [Vn ⇆ p pass] overcome, conquer (sth). **S:** statesman; host, visitor; doctor; teacher. **O:** obstacle, barrier (to understanding); shyness, hostility, suspicion: *At first, there was a good deal of resistance to our pensions scheme, but by patient negotiation we* **broke** *it* **down**. ○ *The new ambassador regards as his first objective the* **breaking-down** *of suspicion and fear between the two countries.* ○ *Another woman might be able to* **break down** *their reserve and give them the sense of an unfolding love.* PW

3 [Vp] give way completely to one's feelings, lose control: *She appeared to be pretty calm, but at times she would* **break down** *and start weeping.* OBS ○ *He felt he must cut this interview short if she was not to* **break down** *in public.* RFW ⇨ break down 8.

4 [Vp nom] (*mechanical*) stop, through some mechanical or electrical failure. **S:** train, car, lorry, crane, lift: *He and Ed had gone to another race-meeting. Ed's car had* **broken down**. AITC ○ *There is a* **breakdown** *on the main through-line to Edinburgh.* ○ *A* **breakdown** *crew came to get the crane working again.* □ breakdown *crews* (*gangs, teams*) service or remove vehicles that have stopped *or* crashed.

5 [Vp nom] cease, fail; be cut; collapse. **S:** communications, contact, relations; law and order, control; resistance: *Telephone communication with all but a few outposts has* **broken down***.* ○ *A coalition of Christian Democrats and Liberals* **broke down***.* ○ *You can't imagine what it's like to feel that all your plans for the future have* **broken down***.* SPL ○ *There has been a complete* **breakdown** *of law and order.*

6 [Vp, Vn ⇆ p nom pass] (may) be analysed or presented in detail; analyse or classify (sth). **S** [Vp], **O** [Vn.p]**:** results, totals; expenditure, outlay; budget. **S** [Vn.p]**:** scientist; accountant, auditor: *Expenditure on the project* **breaks down** *as follows: wages £10m, plant £4m, raw materials £5m.* ○ *We never give a detailed sales* **breakdown** *since we don't want to give information away to our competitors.* G ○ *The results of my test can be* **broken down** (or: **break down***) under four heads.*

7 [Vn ⇆ p pass adj] (*chemistry*) change the chemical composition of (sth). **S:** body, organ, secretions. **O:** starch, fat; molecule: *The cow is an intermediary in our attempt to live off the land without having the bacteria which can* **break down** *cellulose in our stomachs.* NS

8 [Vp nom] collapse (so that the person needs rest, special treatment etc). **S:** health; sanity: *His health had been affected, and might* **break down** *altogether if the strain continued.* ○ *She suffered a total* **breakdown** *(in health).* ○ *He's heading for a nervous* **breakdown***.* □ ⇨ break down 3, where the collapse is not lengthy or serious.

break in [Vn ⇆ p pass] accustom (sb) to a new discipline, make (sb) docile; make (sth) soft and pliable. **S:** trainer, drill sergeant. **O:** horse, mount; recruit, novice; pair of boots: *New recruits are often* **broken in** *by repeated drilling on the barrack square.*

break in/into [Vp nom, Vpr pass adj] force an entry (into a place), force one's way in (to a place). **S:** burglar, intruder. **o:** shop, private house, warehouse: *Tell them that those inside need protection against desperate characters who are trying to* **break in** *from outside.* TBC ○ *There was a* **break-in** *at Smith's warehouse.* ○ *Stores were* **broken into** *and looted during the riots.*

break in (on/upon) [Vp, Vp.pr pass emph rel] interrupt (sth/sb) suddenly and disturbingly. **S:** noise, voice. **o:** thinking, meditation, conversation: *'But what's going to happen to us?' one of the miners* **broke in***.* ○ *A sudden noise from outside* **broke in upon** *his day-dream.* ○ *Their discussion was* **broken in on** *by the arrival of another medical report.* □ break in usu precedes or follows direct speech. = burst in (on/upon).

break into 1 [Vpr] suddenly change from a slower pace to (a faster one). **S:** horse, elephant, herd. **o:** a run, trot, canter, gallop: *As soon as they scented water, the whole herd* **broke into** *a gallop.* ○ *'I shall be late' — she was on the point of* **breaking into** *a run.* PW = burst into 1 .

2 [Vpr] suddenly begin (to laugh etc). **S:** audience, crowd. **o:** (loud) laughter, song, cheers; arguing: *As the President's car appeared, the waiting crowds* **broke into** *loud cheers.* ○ *His vehement discussions with his father sometimes* **broke into** *open quarrelling.* JUNG = burst into 1.

3 [Vpr] suddenly begin to produce (flowers etc). **S:** tree, shrub; hedgerow. **o:** bloom, blossom, flower; leaf: *The chestnut trees along the road were* **breaking into** *leaf.* BRH = burst into 2.

4 [Vpr pass] take time from (sth). **S:** overtime, extra duties, night-work. **o:** evenings, leisure time: *'I can't take on any extra overtime: my weekends have been* **broken into** *far too much as it is.'*

5 [Vpr pass] change (a high-value note or coin) to buy an article costing less. **S:** customer, purchaser. **o:** pound note, ten-dollar bill: *'I can't give you the forty pence I owe you without* **breaking into** *a ten-pound note, so do you mind if I pay you back tomorrow?'*

6 [Vpr pass] open and consume (sth held in reserve for emergency use). **S:** garrison, beleaguered population, expedition. **o:** (reserve stocks of) water, food, ammunition; iron-rations: *The climbers* **broke into** *their emergency supplies of food and water.*

7 [Vpr pass adj] force an entry into. ⇨ break in/into.

break off 1 [Vp, Vn ⇆ p pass adj] become separated, separate (sth), from a larger object (by breaking). **S** [Vp], **O** [Vn.p]**:** piece of brick, section of wall; mast, pole. **S** [Vn.p]**:** workman; blow; sea, high wind: *The mast had* **broken off** *at its base, and lay over the side of the boat.* ○ *He* **broke off** *a piece of chocolate and handed it to me.'*

2 [Vn ⇆ p pass adj] end (sth) abruptly; discontinue. **S:** country, firm; army; friend, fiancé. **O:** relations, association, connection; battle; negotiations, conversation, engagement (= agreement to marry): *Napier* **broke off** *the pursuit.* BM ○ *Talks with the employers were* **broken off** *an hour ago and will not be resumed today.* ○ *She* **broke off** *a previous engagement because of him.* GJ

3 [Vp] (suddenly) stop talking, interrupt one's remarks: *George rose. 'As for me,' he* **broke off** *as Christine came out of her room.* PE

4 [Vp] pause in one's work, take a break. **S:** workers, staff. **A:** for five minutes, at eleven o'clock: *Finally we would* **break off** *for coffee and to talk more informally.* CF

break out 1 [Vp] start suddenly and/or violently. **S:** fire; epidemic, disease; rioting, violence, looting; quarrel; firing: *Pandemonium* **broke out** *and there was a free-for-all fight.* DS ○ *Rationing was not introduced till some time after the* **outbreak** *of war.* ○ *The Plague* **broke out** *in London that Summer, and hundreds died.* WI □ nom form is outbreak.

2 [Vn ⇆ p pass] remove (sth), bring (sth) out, by opening a box, case etc where it is stored. **O:** stores, ammunition; food, rations: *I suppose Julian will be* **breaking out** *the champagne tonight.* ○ *Summer is just around the corner ... it's time to* **break out** *those shorts and bathing suits.* TTRIB

break out in 1 [Vp.pr] suddenly become covered in (sth). **S:** patient; face, body. **o:** spots, pimples, sores; rash: *His face had now* **broken out in** *a rash of red and purple blotches.* ⇨ break out on.

2 [Vp.pr] suddenly begin to express strong feelings. **S:** audience, listener. **o:** tears, cries, curses: *The soft music of the jazz quartet was like people who had been locked up,* **breaking out in** *tears and laughter.* THH ○ *He suddenly* **broke out in** *a rage of sobs and curses.*

break out in a cold sweat [Vp.pr] (*informal*) be suddenly overcome with fear: *He began to ima-*

gine he heard strange noises, and **broke out in a cold sweat**.

break out/out of [Vp nom, Vpr pass] free oneself (from a space), usu by forcibly removing barriers. **S:** prisoner; army; adolescent; writer, artist. **o:** cell, prison; trap, bridgehead, salient; bonds, strait-jacket: *The armies encircled at Stalingrad were not able to* **break out**. ○ *There has been a mass* **break-out** *of prisoners.* ○ *The more interesting playwrights have* **broken out of** *the strait-jackets of language.* ○ *Society was* **breaking out of** *the mould which had contained it for so long.* F

break out on [Vp.pr rel] appear suddenly upon (sth). **S:** spots; rash. **o:** face, arm: *A mass of sores had* **broken out on** *her leg.* ⇨ break out in 1.

break over 1 [Vpr] break upon, and sweep over (a floating or submerged object). **S:** sea, wave. **o:** ship, wreck; sea-wall: *Heavy seas* **broke over** *the bows as we headed in towards the shelter of the coast.* ○ *Large waves* **broke over** *him as he tried to gain a footing in the shingle.*

2 [Vpr] sweep over (sb) like waves. **S:** (waves of) cheering, applause, abuse: *He sat quietly in his place, apparently unaffected by the burst of cheering which* **broke over** *him.*

break through 1 [Vp nom, Vpr pass] make an opening in (sth) by using force. **S:** burglar, gang; army, tanks. **o:** wall, wire fence; front, defences: *Thieves* **broke through** *a wall and a steel partition to get at the safe.* ○ *There was a massive* **breakthrough** *by enemy armour on a narrow front.* = burst through.

2 [Vp, Vpr] appear from behind (sth); pierce. **S:** the sun, moon. **o:** clouds, haze, mist: *At half past eleven the sun* **broke through**, *beginning to dry at last the heavy dew on the grass.* DBM

3 [Vp nom, Vpr] be recognized, achieve prominence, by overcoming (an obstacle). **S:** actor, musician; athlete; race, ethnic group. **O:** (barrier of) hostility, ignorance, prejudice: *The talents of blacks in the United States have been short-changed* (ie not properly rewarded) *for centuries, but I've* **broken through**. *I've opened it up for blacks.* ST

4 [Vp nom] make discoveries of a new and important kind. **S:** scientist, inventor, engineer: *Chemists working on animal dye-stuffs have* **broken through** *in a number of directions.* ○ *There has been an exciting new technological* **breakthrough**. □ usu nom.

5 [Vpr pass] penetrate, overcome (sth). **S:** visitor, host. **o:** shyness, reserve, timidity; facade, front: *No matter how hard one tries to bring him out, it's almost impossible to* **break through** *his reserve.*

break up 1 [Vp] break in pieces; disintegrate. **S:** ship, aircraft: *Heavy seas . . . moved the stern section from the rocks and the remainder of the ship began to* **break up**. G

2 [Vp] crumble, disintegrate, mentally or physically. **S:** patient, old man: *I looked at his face again. If ever I saw a man on the point of* **breaking up**, *I saw one then.* CON ○ *I know what he has to endure, but there is no sign of him* **breaking up** *under the strain yet.*

3 [Vp] (of individuals in a group) go their separate ways; disperse. **S:** party, meeting, gathering, reunion. **A:** early, around eight o'clock; in disorder, in disarray: *We knew this before the party* **broke up**, *on that crucial first evening.* CON ○ *Leicester stood up, stretched himself, and ambled out. The meeting* **broke up**. TBC ⇨ next entry

4 [Vn ⇆ p pass] disperse, scatter (people), often by force. **S:** police, troops. **O:** crowd, demonstration, gathering, meeting: *The meeting was threatening to get out of hand and the police were forced to* **break** *it* **up**. ⇨ previous entry

5 [Vp] disperse (at the end of a term). **S:** school; children: *When do you* **break up** *for the Easter holidays?* SC

6 [Vp nom] come to an end, dissolve (not necessarily through outside interference). **S:** relationship, friendship; marriage: *Children should be a lifelong joy and satisfaction. But they can also be the rock on which a marriage* **breaks up**. TVT ○ *The* **break-up** *of their partnership has been expected in the City for some time.* = split up. ⇨ next entry

7 [Vn ⇆ p pass] bring (sth) to an end; destroy. **S:** rival, enemy; philanderer, adventuress. **O:** alliance, coalition; friendship: *But she* **broke up** *his home life: he had been perfectly happy until she came along.* PW ○ *Plenty of marriages have been successfully* **broken up** *that way.* AITC ⇨ previous entry

break up (into) 1 [Vn ⇆ p pass adj, Vn.p.pr pass emph rel] divide (sth) in pieces by cutting, smashing etc. **O:** beam, box; car, ship. **o:** length, firewood; piece, scrap: *The ships were* **broken up** *and sold as scrap to dealers.* ○ *The wood is* **broken up into** *short lengths.*

2 [Vn ⇆ p nom pass adj, Vn.p.pr pass emph rel] divide (sth) by analysis, administrative decision etc. **S:** scholar, scientist; grammarian; government, ministry. **O:** task, problem; word, sentence; farmland. **o:** section; syllable, phrase; plot: *Sentences can be* **broken up into** *clauses, and clauses* **into** *phrases.* ○ *And the administration is worried about the* **break-up** *of Yugoslavia.* ECON ○ *The new regime is* **breaking** *the estates* **up into** *smallholdings.*

break with [Vpr pass] end a friendship or association with (sb); cut one's links with (sth). **S:** son, elector, businessman; thinker, artist. **o:** family; party; ally; associate; tradition, the past: *Soon after this we find Fournier telling his sister that he has* **broken with** *Jeanne for ever.* AF ○ *Marx had indeed not so much* **broken with** *tradition as stood it on its head.* HA

brew

brew up [Vp nom] (*informal*) prepare a drink of tea (often in the open and by makeshift arrangements). **S:** workman, soldier: *A group of men were* **brewing up** *in a sheltered corner of the building-site.* ○ *'Eleven o'clock; time for a* **brew-up**.'

brick

brick in/up [Vn ⇆ p pass adj] block or seal (an opening) with bricks; block an opening in (sth) in this way. **S:** builder, mason. **O:** window, doorway, fireplace; house: *Now that we've changed to central heating, we've had all the fireplaces* **bricked in**. ○ *The council has* **bricked up** *several of the sturdy Victorian houses and bulldozed others.* OBS

brim

brim over [Vp] overflow. **S:** cup, jug; barrel, sack; lorry: *The boys had loaded on too much sand; the wheelbarrow was* **brimming over**. = run over 1.

brim over with [Vp.pr rel] have a great quantity of (sth). **o:** confidence; high spirits, vitality; ideas: *She was supposed to be a lady* **brimming over with** *intelligence.* AF ○ *These young designers are* **brimming over with** *bright ideas.* ○ *That last blissful summer, which* **brimmed over with** *simple pleasures.* MRJ

bring

bring about 1 [Vn ⇆ p pass] cause (sth) to happen. **S:** time, circumstances, plan. **O:** change, transformation; death, failure: *How should she present herself to him? As a lady of leisure, reading a book? Three minutes could* **bring about** *this transformation.* PW ○ *Shaftesbury was an extremely important figure in* **bringing about** *this change in attitude.* BRN ⇨ come about 1.

2 [Vn.p pass] (*nautical*) change the direction of movement of (a boat). **S:** crew, helmsman. **O:** sailing-ship; yacht, dinghy: *The helmsman* **brought** *us* **about** *and we went scudding off towards the island.* ⇨ come about 2, go about 5, put about 1.

bring a charge against [Vn.pr pass emph rel] (*legal*) formally accuse (sb) of an offence; charge. **S:** private citizen; injured party: *If you found someone loitering at the back of your house after dark, you might feel justified in* **bringing charges against** *him.* ○ *'You could* **bring a charge** *of dangerous driving* **against** *him, but you might have trouble in proving it.'*

bring along/on 1 [Vn ⇆ p pass] help or encourage (sb) to develop. **S:** tutor, coach. **O:** pupil, trainee, (young) athlete: *We're trying to* **bring along** *one or two promising young swimmers.* ○ *That boy may get an Open Scholarship if we don't ruin everything by* **bringing** *him* **on** *too quickly.* ⇨ come along/on 2, get along/on (with) 1.

2 [Vn ⇆ p pass] help (sth) to grow or flower more quickly. **S:** sun, fine weather, spell of rain. **O:** crop; vegetable, flower: *The fine spell we've been having will* **bring** *the crops* **along** *very nicely.* ⇨ come along/on 3.

bring along (to) [Vn ⇆ p pass, Vn.p.pr pass rel] lead (sb) from one place to another, often a short way (eg within the same building). **O:** brother, friend. **o:** office; house; party, meeting: *'I'm having a short staff meeting in my office at eleven. Oh, and would you* **bring** *Smith* **along**, *too?'* ○ *You can* **bring** *a friend* **along to** *the party if you like.* ⇨ be along (to), come along (to).

bring around/round (to) 1 [Vn.p pass, Vn.p.pr pass rel] lead, conduct (sb) to a place, usu within the same town etc. **O:** wife, children. **o:** our place, my house; the club: *'Do* **bring** *your wife* **around** *one evening. We're longing to meet her.'* ○ *'If you can't find room for these people you're welcome to* **bring** *them* **around** *to our place.'* ⇨ be around/round/(at), come around/round (to) 1.

2 [Vn.p pass, Vn.p.pr pass rel] persuade (sb) to share (one's view). **O:** opponent; colleague, friend. **o:** ⚠ his way of thinking, our point of view, my assessment of the situation: *At first, Dad wasn't too keen to let us have the flat for our party, but we managed to* **bring** *him* **round** *eventually.* ⇨ come around/round (to) 2.

bring away [Vp.n] return home having formed (a certain impression). **O:** (happy, pleasant) memories, (favourable, positive) impression: *We* **brought away** *rather mixed impressions of our holiday in Spain.* ⇨ come away with.

bring back 1 [Vn ⇆ p pass] cause (sth/sb) to return: *'If you borrow my electric drill don't forget to* **bring** *it* **back**.' ○ *He's gone away from home and nothing will* **bring** *him* **back** *again.* ⇨ be back 1, come back 1, get back 1, go back 1, take back 1.

2 [Vn ⇆ p pass] recall (sth) to mind, remind sb of (sth). **S:** scene, smell, conversation. **O:** memories; visit, travels; day: *The river smell* **brought back** *a night some years before.* NM ○ *How a few words can* **bring** *it all* **back**! ⇨ come back 3, take back (to).

3 [Vp.n pass] reintroduce, restore (sth). **S:** Government, the authorities, 'they'. **O:** the monarchy, one-party rule, corporal punishment: *The hardliners are very much in favour of* **bringing back** *political and economic control at the centre.* ○ *These parents believe that old-style grammar teaching should be* **brought back**. ⇨ come back 4.

bring back to health/life [Vn.p.pr pass] restore (sb) to good health; revive (sb). **S:** doctor, surgeon; devoted nursing, expert care: *And anyway he was dead. I couldn't* **bring** *him* **back to life**. DC

bring before [Vn.pr pass] present (sth) for discussion, decision or judgement. **O:** him etc; case; matter, claim. **o:** committee, board; court, magistrate: *He'll* **bring** *matters* **before** *the party meeting.* ITV ○ *'We'd better have a word together now: the proposal's being* **brought before** *the Council tomorrow morning.'* ⇨ be before 2, come before 2, go before 2, put before 2, take before.

bring down 1 [Vn ⇆ p pass] cause (sth) to fall from the sky by destroying, killing or wounding it. **S:** fighter aircraft, anti-aircraft gun; hunter. **O:** hostile aircraft, balloon; partridge, duck: *She* **brought down** *a pheasant with her first shot.* ○ *Several enemy bombers were intercepted and* **brought down**. ⇨ come down 2.

2 [Vn ⇆ p pass] cause (sth) to stop and fall over by killing or wounding it. **S:** shooting party; gamekeeper, poacher. **O:** rabbit, deer, antelope: *We managed to* **bring down** *one or two of the herd, even though they were moving fast.*

3 [Vn ⇆ p pass] (*Rugby football*) cause (sb) to fall down by tackling him; (*Association football*) cause (sb) to fall down by tackling *or* esp fouling him. **S:** defender, full-back. **O:** three-quarter, striker, winger: *The scrum-half was* **brought down** *before he had moved five yards.* ○ *Lineker was* **brought down** *by a vicious tackle just inside the penalty area.*

4 [Vp.n pass] cause the defeat or fall of (sb/sth). **S:** measure, scandal, controversy. **O:** Government, administration, tyrant: *It was mismanagement of the economy leading to large-scale unemployment that* **brought down** *the last Government.*

5 [Vn ⇆ p pass] reduce, lower (sth). **S:** government measures, increased production; wholesalers, dealers; authorities. **O:** prices, costs; deposit, premium; mileage: *Supermarket chains have* **brought down** *the cost of several basic commodities.* ○ *The approved distance between motorway stopping points is about 25 miles. The Ministry is* **bringing** *it* **down** *to 12 miles.* OBS send up 1. ⇨ be down 2, come down 3, go down 5.

6 [Vn ⇆ p pass] (*mathematics*) transfer (a figure) from one part of a calculation to another, esp in problems involving multiplication or division. **O:** next figure, next digit; eight, nine etc: *To divide 7489 by 322 you first decide how many times 322 will go into 748. Having subtracted the product of this number (2) and 322 from 748, you* **bring down** *the next figure (9) and again divide by 322.* ○ *When multiplying numbers ending in nought,* **bring** *the noughts* **down** *first.*

7 [Vn ⇆ p pass] bring (sb) to a country place from town, or to the South from the North: *'She wants a job with a pleasant family, so I've* **brought** *her* **down** *to see you.'* DC ○ *'We'd love to meet Jill, so why don't you* **bring** *her* **down** *when you next come to London?'* ↔ go up (to). ⇨ come down 5.

bring the house down [Vn.p] (*informal*) make an audience laugh, applaud etc, uproariously. **S:** joke, song; entertainer, clown: *We had a real get-together at weekends. Everybody standing up and giving a song. I used to* **bring the house down** *with this one.* TOH ○ *I remembered the joke and chucked it into the play.* **Brings the house down**, *it does.* JFTR

bring down to earth [Vn.p.pr pass] make (sb) return suddenly and perhaps painfully to reality. **A:** ⚠ with a bump, with a bang: *Losing first the job and then the house* **brought** *them* **down to earth** *with a bump.* ○ *The louder they both shouted the higher the moral plane they felt it necessary to ascend to, until only physical violence could have* **brought** *them* **down to earth**. HAA ⇨ come down to earth.

bring forth [Vp.n pass] (*formal*) cause (sth) to appear; produce, yield. **S:** committee, board; discussion, meeting. **O:** proposal, suggestion; solution, formula: *Parental neglect* **brought forth** *in Churchill an inherited tendency to depression.* BRN ○ *Our second meeting* **brought forth** *very few new ideas.* ⇨ come forth (with).

bring forward 1 [Vn ⇆ p pass] propose (sth) for discussion; raise. **S:** councillor, chairman, member. **O:** issue, question, matter; proposal, plan: *At the next Council meeting, Henderson will* **bring forward** *ambitious plans for developing the city centre.* ⇨ come forward.

2 [Vn ⇆ p pass] transfer (sth) to an earlier time or date; advance. **S:** organizer, committee. **O:** meeting, party; date, fixture: *Because of the possibility of a clash with another event, the organizers have decided to* **bring** *the barbecue* **forward** *from the 12th to the 5th June.* ○ *The meeting was* **brought forward** *by a week.* ↔ put back 3.

3 [Vn ⇆ p pass] (*accountancy*) carry or transfer (a total) from the foot of one page of a ledger to the top of the next, or from the account for one period to the account for another. **S:** accountant, auditor; bank. **O:** figure, total, amount: *A credit balance of £250 was* **brought forward** *from his September account.*

4 [Vn ⇆ p pass] (*commerce*) in business practice, record that (correspondence etc) is to be produced for sb's attention at a future date; do this at the actual date. **S:** secretary, assistant. **O:** letter, file; case: *Please* **bring** *this letter* **forward** *at the beginning of next month.* ○ *I* **brought** *this* **forward** *yesterday, and you've done nothing about it.* □ often abbreviated to B/F or b/f.

bring home (to) [Vn ⇆ p pass, Vn.p.pr pass emph rel] make (sth) clear (to sb), make (sb) realize (sth). **O:** fact, truth; realization, understanding; it . . . that the end was near. **o:** public, audience; patient, sufferer: *What he says* **brings home** *the fact that the gods of the running-track are human like to rest of us.* T ○ *These programmes do much to* **bring home to** *people the serious risks of smoking.* ○ *The . . . truth was* **brought home to** *him that he was not actually the heir to a large fortune.* HB ⇨ come/get home (to).

bring in 1 [Vn ⇆ p pass] gather (sth) in from the fields; harvest. **S:** farmer, grower. **O:** harvest, crop: *They could be sure of a few more days of fine weather in which to* **bring in** *the harvest.* ⇨ be in 2, get in 1.

2 [Vn ⇆ p pass] earn, produce, yield (sth). **S:** property, farm; investment, stock; job, profession. **O:** return; dividend, profit; wage, salary; £500 a week: *Moral indignation was as much out of place in business as the emotions were: it was all a question of what would* **bring in** *money.* PW ○ *The new Dad is busy with his touring show . . . and a vast contract that is reckoned to* **bring** *him* **in** *£3 000 a week.* H □ note Indirect Object (*him*) in the last example. ⇨ come in 6.

3 [Vn ⇆ p pass] give (sb) a part to play in some scheme. **S:** company, board; adviser, banker; doctor, consultant: *They have* **brought in** *a public relations man to advise on press coverage.* ○ *'Why* **bring** *Jones* **in**? *He'll do nothing to help, and he might mess up the whole deal.'* ⇨ come in 7.

4 [Vn ⇆ pass] introduce (sth/sb) into an argument, discussion etc. **O:** religion, politics, sex; one's wife, husband, family; the army: *It is impossible to understand the social tensions of the fourteenth century without* **bringing in** *the Church at every point.* SHOE

5 [Vn ⇆ p pass] (*police*) bring (sb) to a police station for questioning. **S:** constable, detective. **O:** wanted man, habitual offender: *'The last time we* **brought** *George* **in**, *he said he knew nothing about the car. Now we find it in his garage.'*

6 [Vn ⇆ p pass] (*Parliament*) introduce (a law). **S:** bill; measure, reform: *The Reform Bill the new government* **brought in** *was a shock to the Tories.* CD ○ *Legislation may be* **brought in** *to abolish tobacco advertising altogether.*

bring in a verdict [Vp.n pass] (*legal*) give, return, a verdict on an accused person. **S:** jury, court: *The jury* **brought in a verdict** *that Christine had died from falling off a cliff, but there was no evidence to show how she had come to fall off the cliff.* PE

bring in on [Vn.p.pr pass] give (sb) a share in or information about (sth). **S:** government; leader, manager. **O:** public; (political) party, work force. **o:** plan, scheme; discussion, negotiation; idea, proposal: *The Council greatly angered market traders by not* **bringing** *them* **in on** *the redevelopment of the city centre.* ○ *The people most likely to be affected must be* **brought in on** *our ideas from the beginning.* ⇨ be/come/get/let in on.

bring into action [Vn.pr pass] put (sth/sb) in a position where it or he can operate. **S:** (military) commander; (naval) captain; (business) manager, director. **O:** force; tank, gun; cruiser, frigate; specialist; sales force: *Because of the state of the ground, the artillery could not be* **brought into action** *at once.* ○ *These endeavours in the Roman Church have regularly* **brought into action** *priests* *who seek to integrate with the people.* HOC ⇨ be in/come into/go into action.

bring into being/existence [Vn.pr pass] cause (sth) to exist; create, establish. **S:** government, committee, board. **O:** body, organization; machinery, procedure: *The allied command had* ***brought into being*** *a whole new armoured force.* ○ *An information bureau was* ***brought into existence*** *to deal with inquiries.* = set up 2. ⇨ be in/come into being/existence.

bring into blossom/flower [Vn.pr pass] cause blossom to appear on a (bush etc); make (flowers) appear. **S:** fine spell, early Spring. **O:** bush, shrub; rose, daffodil: *The mildness of the early Spring weather will have helped to* ***bring*** *the fruit trees* ***into blossom*** *quickly.* ⇨ be in/come into blossom/flower.

bring into contact (with) [Vn.pr pass] help (one person) to meet (another). **S:** friend, colleague; work, travel; (sheer) chance. **O:** author, artist; businessman; bachelor. **o:** (**with**) publisher, dealer; customer; his future wife: *These visits* ***brought*** *me* ***into contact with*** *a large public outside the army.* MFM ○ *Alan was* ***brought into contact with*** *Jane* (or: *Alan and Jane were* ***brought into contact***) *through a shared interest in music.* ⇨ be in/come into contact (with) 2.

bring into disrepute [Vn.pr pass] give people an unfavourable impression of (sth), give (sth) a bad name or reputation. **S:** advocate, supporter; servant, agent. **O:** cause, ideology; industry, service: *The inefficiency of one individual can* ***bring*** *a whole department* ***into disrepute.*** ○ *With the advent of televising the* (House of) *Commons, people would see that the whole legislative system had been* ***brought into disrepute.*** IND ⇨ fall into disrepute.

bring into fashion/vogue [Vn.pr pass] make (sth) fashionable, make (sth) the vogue. **S:** (dress) designer, model. **O:** leather, plastic; jeans, sweaters: *People tell me I've* ***brought*** *jumpers back* ***into fashion.*** ST ⇨ be in 1, be in/come into fashion/vogue, come in 1.

bring into focus 1 [Vn.pr pass] adjust a microscope, telescope etc so that the object viewed through it is sharp and clear. **S:** scientist, technician. **O:** microscope; specimen: *To* ***bring*** *the slide* ***into*** *sharp* ***focus,*** *turn this small wheel.* ⇨ be in/come into focus 1.

2 [Vn.pr pass] make (sth) clearer and more intelligible. **S:** observer, commentator; event; treaty, truce. **O:** idea, notion; detail; the whole picture; issue, problem: *He provides the mundane detail that* ***brings*** *history* ***into*** *sharp, clear* ***focus.*** BBCR ○ *Advances in space exploration have* ***brought into focus*** *one of the most dramatic questions in human history.* TO ⇨ be in/come into focus 2.

bring into force [Vn.pr pass] make sth (which can be legally enforced) begin to operate. **S:** government, (local) council; Chamber of Commerce; Trades Union. **O:** law, bill; regulation, requirement: *If the present regulations are not effective, then new ones may have to be* ***brought into force.*** ⇨ be in/come into/put into force.

bring into line (with) [Vn.pr pass] make (sb) conform (with rules etc). **S:** leader; party. **O:** member; disciple, follower; dissident, heretic. **o:** (**with**) the rules of the club; official doctrine, the majority view; religious orthodoxy: *It will take more than promises of government posts to* ***bring*** *the rebels back* ***into line.*** ○ *It seems that nothing can* ***bring*** *him* ***into line with*** *his fellow Tories.* ⇨ be in/come into/fall into line (with).

bring into the open [Vn.pr pass] make (sth) publicly known; disclose. **S:** newspaper, reporter; meeting, speech. **O:** attitude, feeling; dispute, quarrel; matter, question: *If you hadn't allowed him to make that speech, the matter need never have been* ***brought into the open.*** ⇨ be in/come into the open.

bring into play [Vn.pr pass] make (sth) appear and have an effect. **S:** statesman, negotiator; commander; artist. **O:** force, circumstance, factor; hostility, rivalry: *Every time I try to get them to cooperate, the same jealousy and mutual suspicion are* ***brought into play.*** ⇨ be in/come into play.

bring into service/use [Vn.pr pass] introduce (sth) to serve the public; open (sth) for use. **S:** council; railway board, bus company, tunnel: *The Victoria Line was* ***brought into service,*** *as part of the Underground network, to link important parts of the city.* ○ *The canals have been* ***brought*** *back* ***into use*** *for pleasure traffic.* ⇨ be in/come into/go into service/use.

bring into sight/view [Vn.pr pass] cause (sth) to appear. **S:** movement; descent, turning. **O:** destination; coast, town: *A sudden parting of the clouds* ***brought*** *the airfield* ***into view.*** ⇨ be in/come into sight/view.

bring into the world [Vn.pr pass] cause (sb) to be born, be sb's parent(s): *'And now, Heaven forgive me, I'm* ***bringing*** *another child* ***into the world.'*** DC ○ *What a dreadful* ***world*** *to* ***bring*** *children* ***into!*** ⇨ come into the world.

bring off 1 [Vn ⇆ p pass] carry (sb) to safety, esp from a stricken ship; rescue. **S:** lifeboat, rescue launch, helicopter. **O:** crew, passengers: *The crew of the tanker were* ***brought off*** *by the Yarmouth lifeboat.* = take off 5.

2 [Vn ⇆ p pass] succeed in (sth). **S:** planner, leader, general, criminal. **O:** ⚠ it, a coup, the thing: *If we had worked more closely together, between us we could have* ***brought off*** *a real coup.* DS ○ *Now it seemed like a fine idea. He felt sure he could* ***bring*** *it* ***off.*** AITC ○ *Verdi's 'Othello' is a difficult opera to* ***bring off.*** NY = pull off 3. ⇨ come off 5.

bring on 1 [Vn ⇆ p pass] help or encourage (sb) to develop. ⇨ bring along/on 1.

2 [Vn ⇆ p pass] help (sth) to grow or flower. ⇨ bring along/on 2.

3 [Vn ⇆ p pass] cause, produce (sth); lead to. **S:** cold weather, overwork, over-eating. **O:** influenza, eye-strain; an attack of indigestion: *His heart hammered in a mad cadenza of exaltation that almost* ***brought on*** *an attack of nausea.* ARG ○ *It was pneumonia* ***brought on*** *in winter.* AH ○ *There had always been the submerged desire —* ***brought on*** *and exacerbated by administrative duties — to escape.* MRJ ⇨ come on 6.

4 [Vn ⇆ p pass] (*cricket*) ask (sb) to bowl. **S:** captain, skipper. **O:** fast bowler, spinner: *The fast bowlers were* ***brought on*** *again after the tea interval.* ⇨ be on 4, come on 9, put on 10.

bring on/upon oneself [Vn.pr] cause (difficulties) for oneself; be responsible for (the problems one faces). **O:** problems, hardships, suffering: *They* *could point out the troubles she would* **bring on herself**. GE ○ *'You needn't look to me for sympathy: you* **brought** *it all* **upon yourself**!'

bring out 1 [Vn ⇆ p pass] (*industry*) cause (sb) to strike, to withdraw labour. **S:** union official, shop-steward. **O:** workers, labour force: *He has* **brought** *the engineering apprentices* **out** *on strike*. SC ○ *It started as a strike in the foundry; then that* **brought out** *most of the assembly workers as well.* ⇨ be out 1, come out 1.

2 [Vn ⇆ p pass] help (sb) to lose shyness or reserve. **S:** husband, father, admirer. **O:** shy girl, diffident child, guest: *She's a retiring sort of girl, but he's doing his best to* **bring** *her* **out**. ○ *Not even the freedom Sydney allowed his pupil could* **bring** *him* **out** *to his father's satisfaction.* SS = draw out 1.

3 [Vn ⇆ p pass] (*dated*) introduce (a young woman) to high society, ie as a débutante. **O:** daughter, girl: *Mrs Fitzalan is* **bringing out** *her eldest daughter next season.* ○ *My mother toyed with the idea of* **bringing** *me* **out**, *but she discovered she had to be presented first before she could present me.* ST ⇨ come out 3.

4 [Vn ⇆ p pass] cause (sth) to open or flower. **S:** fine weather, sunshine. **O:** rose, tulip: *The hot weather has* **brought out** *all the blossom on the fruit trees.* ⇨ be out 4, come out 4.

5 [Vn ⇆ p pass] introduce (sth) onto the market; publish. **S:** manufacturer, makers; publisher, author. **O:** model, make; novel, biography: *Fiat are* **bringing out** *a new sporty saloon.* ○ *The book, which was an immense success, was frequently* **brought out** *in new and revised editions.* F ⇨ be out 6, come out 6.

6 [Vn ⇆ p pass adj] reveal (sth) clearly. **S:** sun, light; treatment, enlargement. **O:** detail, small mark, hidden feature: *The low sun* **brought out** *the gold of the Cotswold masonry.* ARG ○ *His photograph* **brings out** *the detail of the sculpture.* = show up 1. ⇨ come out 8.

7 [Vn ⇆ p pass] speak, utter (sth). **O:** ⚠ word, declaration, statement: *He didn't finish the sentence because if he had* **brought out** *the word it would probably have made him cry.* CON ⇨ come out 9.

8 [Vn ⇆ p pass adj] make (sth) clear or explicit; convey. **S:** teacher, lecturer; account, story. **O:** truth, sense, meaning; good points, weaknesses: *I mention this, which might seem a trivial detail . . . to* **bring out** *an important point.* CON ○ *The central theme of the poem was admirably* **brought out**.

9 [Vp.n pass] cause (some quality) to appear in sb; elicit. **S:** adversity, need, danger; her sister, his teacher. **O:** the (very) worst/best in her; (all) his cunning, his greed; the best side, the childish side (in sb): *The one person who never failed to* **bring out** *the spirit of competition in Robert was Ned Roper.* CON ○ *Flodin was the only person . . . who* **brought out** *the girlish side of Gwen's character.* GJ ○ *Disaster* **brought out** *all that was best in the family.* AITC = call forth. ⇨ come out 11.

10 [Vp.n pass] make (a flavour) more noticeable. **O:** ⚠ flavour, taste: *A pinch of salt is taken for granted in many cake recipes and is added simply to* **bring out** *the flavour of the other ingredients.* DELI

bring out in [Vn.p.pr pass] cause (sb) to be partially covered with (spots). **S:** heat, humidity; diet. **O:** skin; face, chest. **o:** ⚠ a rash; spots, pimples: *'Don't allow him to get excited: it* **brings** *him* **out in** *a nervous rash.'* ⇨ come out in.

bring out in a cold sweat [Vn.p.pr pass] (*informal*) cause (sb) to be suddenly overcome with fear: *Every time I hear the story of his execution it* **brings** *me* **out in a cold sweat**. ○ *There's one thing that* **brings** *Rigsby* **out in a cold sweat** *— and that's to be called 'unmanly'.* TVT ⇨ break out in a cold sweat.

bring out/out of [Vn ⇆ p pass, Vn.pr pass] cause (sb/sth) to leave (a place); carry from. **S:** fireman, police. **O:** owner, occupant; furniture. **o:** house, room: *He rummaged about in the attic and* **brought out** *a pile of old documents.* ○ *They gathered up the few belongings that they'd managed to* **bring out of** *the burning house.* ⇨ be out/out of 1, come out/out of 1, get out/out of 2, keep out/out of, take out/out of 1.

bring out of his shell [Vn.pr pass] (*informal*) help (sb) to overcome his shyness, or show a bolder side to his character. **O:** child; pupil: *It will take all of your patience and tact to* **bring** *John* **out of his shell**. ○ *What* **brought** *him* **out of his shell** *was an invitation to talk about his one passion — astronomy.* ⇨ come out of one's shell.

bring over [Vn ⇆ p pass] cause (sb) to come from abroad to where one now is; accompany (sb) travelling or settling overseas. **S:** immigrant, settler. **O:** wife, family: *He's been teaching in this country for a year. Next summer he hopes to* **bring** *his family* **over** *from the States.* ⇨ be over 4, come over 1.

bring over (to) [Vn ⇆ p pass, Vn.p.pr pass] cause (sb) to give his support (to sb/sth new). **O:** supporter, ally; general, scientist. **o:** us, our side; our view, our position: *'He won't support Johnson for long, you'll see, and he'll* **bring** *most of the committee* **over** *too.'* ○ *Long-standing opponents of European integration won't easily be* **brought over to** *the official party view.* = win over (to). ⇨ come over (to), go over to 1.

bring round 1 [Vn.p pass] (*nautical*) cause (a boat) to face in the opposite direction. **S:** helmsman, coxswain. **O:** vessel, boat: *They* **brought** *the ship* **round** *with a wash of water astern.* AH

2 [Vn.p pass] cause (sb) to regain consciousness. **S:** doctor, nurse, first-aider. **O:** spectator, patient: *George fainted in the heat but was soon* **brought round**. ⇨ come round 2.

bring round (to) 1 [Vn.p pass, Vn.p.pr pass rel] conduct, lead (sb) (to a place). ⇨ bring around/round (to) 1.

2 [Vn.p pass, Vn.pr pass rel] convert (sb) to one's point of view. ⇨ bring around/round (to) 2.

bring round to [Vn.p.pr pass] direct or steer (conversation) so that one's own choice of topic is discussed. **O:** conversation, discussion. **o:** one's own favourite subject; gambling, sport, cars: *I met Wells in his . . . house and* **brought** *the conversation* **round to** *Jung.* JUNG ○ *By talking about Scotland, Brown managed to* **bring** *the discussion* **round** *to salmon fishing — his favourite pastime.*

bring through [Vn.p pass, Vn.pr pass] be responsible for the survival or recovery of (sb). **S:** skilled medical care, good doctors; sound leadership. **O:** patient; firm, business; country. **o:** illness; crisis, war: *Only the daily attentions of Dr Fordyce Barker and the devoted care of Dolby* **brought**

Dickens ***through*** *the ordeal.* CD ○ *Cool heads will* ***bring*** *us* ***through*** *this crisis.* ⇨ come through.

bring to 1 [Vn.p pass] help (sb) to recover consciousness. ⇨ bring round 2.
2 [Vn.p pass] (*nautical*) make (sth) stop. **S:** captain, mate. **O:** ship, boat: *An unidentified ship was* ***brought to*** *by the firing of a warning shot across its bows.* □ usu passive. ⇨ come to 2.
3 [Vn.pr pass] make (sth) equal to (a certain sum). **S:** spending, purchase. **O:** bill, account; total. **o:** five pounds; ten dollars: *If I buy the suit, it will* ***bring*** *my bill* ***to*** *much more than I've budgeted for.* ⇨ come to 3.
4 [Vn.pr pass emph rel] approach or tackle (sth) with (a certain attitude). **S:** manager, planner; scholar, craftsman. **O:** wisdom, knowledge; fresh mind, lack of prejudice. **o:** task, work; job, post: *The designer* ***brings*** *wide experience in this medium* ***to*** *his new task.* ○ ***To*** *his new post of Foreign Secretary, he* ***brought*** *experience gained as a career diplomat.* ⇨ come to (with).

bring to sb's aid/assistance [Vn.pr pass] ask or direct (sb) to help sb in difficulties. **S:** shout, call, telephone message. **O:** (police) patrol car, breakdown van, fire brigade. **o:** (**of**) motorist, owner, occupant: *A radio appeal* ***brought*** *rescue teams hurrying* ***to the aid of*** *the flood victims.* ○ *Skilled mechanics can quickly be* ***brought to the assistance of*** *motorists.* ⇨ come to sb's aid/assistance/help.

bring to attention [Vn.pr pass] (*military*) make (soldiers etc) adopt an alert position, with the feet together. **S:** sergeant, officer. **O:** troops; platoon, company: *The sergeant* ***brought*** *the guard smartly* ***to attention*** *and saluted the inspecting officer.* ⇨ be at/come to attention.

bring to sb's attention/notice [Vn.pr pass] make sb notice, be aware of (sth). **O:** it ... that she was absent, that sth was amiss; fact, matter: *An inspector first* ***brought*** *these deficiencies* ***to the attention of*** *the management.* ○ *The majority of offences committed by police officers in this force are* ***brought to my attention*** *by other officers.* IND ⇨ come to sb's attention/notice.

bring to blows [Vn.pr pass] make (people) start fighting. **S:** disagreement, difference (of opinion); rivalry, enmity. **O:** (two) sides, parties: *The question of who should sit next to the guest of honour practically* ***brought*** *the two of them* ***to blows.*** ⇨ come to blows.

bring to the boil [Vn.pr pass] cause (sth) to reach boiling point; bring (sth) to a point of crisis. **O:** pan, kettle; vegetables, rice; situation, the whole thing: ***Bring*** *the water* ***to the boil****, put the rice in, and allow the pan to simmer until all the water has evaporated.* ○ *What really* ***brought*** *things* ***to the boil*** *was a newspaper article alleging embezzlement.* ⇨ come to the boil.

bring to a climax [Vn.pr pass] cause (sth) to reach a high level of intensity, drama etc. **S:** incident, interruption, fight. **O:** meeting, discussion, quarrel: *The meeting was* ***brought to an*** *excited* ***climax*** *by the appearance on the platform of the rebel leader.* ○ *Some brilliant writing for the brass instruments* ***brings*** *the passage* ***to a climax.*** ⇨ come to a climax.

bring to a dead end [Vn.pr pass] make the further progress of (sth) impossible. **S:** interference, opposition; stubbornness; (lack of) clues, information. **O:** inquiry; research; discussion: *The reluctance of the local people to talk had* ***brought*** *his investigation* ***to a dead end.*** ⇨ be at/come to a dead end.

bring to an end [Vn.pr pass] end (sth) (often sth unpleasant or unsatisfactory). **O:** quarrel, hostility, misunderstanding; arrangement, treaty: *Leaders were anxious to* ***bring to an end*** *the dissensions of the last few months.* T ○ *I hope we have* ***brought*** *our arguments on fundamentals* ***to an end.*** OBS ⇨ be at/come to an end, put an end/a stop to.

bring to his feet [Vn.pr pass] make (sb) stand up quickly. **S:** shock, blow; shout, cry; enthusiasm, excitement. **O:** onlooker, spectator: *It was finally a remark of Edith's that* ***brought*** *him* ***to his feet*** *in a rush of anger.* HD ○ *A jolt nearly threw me from the bed, and a second jolt* ***brought*** *me* ***to my feet.*** SD ⇨ be on/come to/get on one's feet.

bring to the fore [Vn.pr pass] make (sb) prominent, give an active part to (sb). **S:** situation; crisis, war; depression, revival. **O:** (able) leader, statesman; (dishonest) dealer, criminal: *The conditions of the post-war years* ***brought*** *many enterprising men* ***to the fore.*** ⇨ be/come to the fore.

bring to fruition [Vn.pr pass] cause (sth) to be fulfilled or realized. **S:** struggle, conflict; work, study; prayer. **O:** hope, dream; ambition; plan: *Years of patient work had at last* ***brought*** *all his plans* ***to fruition.*** ○ *The scheme was locally conceived, and* ***brought to fruition*** *with help from overseas.* ⇨ come to fruition.

bring to the ground [Vn.pr pass] make (sth) fall to the ground; cause (sth) to collapse. **S:** explosion, earth tremor; revolution, upheaval. **O:** tower, mast; regime: *The gales* ***brought*** *trees and telegraph poles* ***to the ground.*** ○ *They wanted to launch a general strike which would* ***bring*** *the State* ***to the ground.*** OBS ⇨ come to the ground.

bring to a halt/standstill [Vn.pr pass] stop the forward movement or progress of (sth). **S:** driver; operator; striker. **O:** car, lorry; machine, production-line; factory: *He* ***brought*** *the car* ***to a halt.*** HD ○ *A strike in the paint-shop* ***brought*** *production* ***to a standstill*** *this morning.* ⇨ be at/come to a halt/standstill.

bring to a head [Vn.pr pass] cause (sth) to reach a point where a decision, change etc is necessary. **S:** arrival, intervention; failure, success. **O:** matters, things, it: *The arrival of a fourth child* ***brought*** *things* ***to a head*** *. Bill would have to get a job with more money.* ○ *Matters were* ***brought to a head*** *when the boss tried to force still more work onto him. He resigned.* ⇨ come to a head.

bring to heel [Vn.pr pass] master, subdue (sb/sth). **S:** government, regime. **O:** (rebellious) subject, province: *It is no simple matter to* ***bring*** *a breakaway region of several millions* ***to heel.*** ○ *'I* ***brought*** *them* ***to heel****,' said Robert, gaily. 'I extracted some money from them, too, so drink up.'* CON = bring under control. come to heel.

bring to himself [Vn.pr pass] make (sb) aware, conscious, of what is happening. **S:** bang, explosion; light; door opening; (cold) air, water: *The mention of a name* ***brought*** *him* ***to himself****. Had he heard it before?* ⇨ come to oneself.

bring to life [Vn.pr pass] make (sth) live; give (sth) vitality. **S:** actor, story-teller. **O:** story, poem; literature, history: *She couldn't act very well, but for me she* **brought** *the whole silly play* **to life**. RATT ○ *Into the reading he* (Dickens) *threw all his genius as an actor,* **bringing to life** *the comic, oily crafty Fagin.* CD ⇨ come to life.

bring to light [Vn.pr pass] reveal (sth) which has been hidden. **S:** researcher, investigator, detective. **O:** fact, (piece of) evidence, detail: *A national newspaper claims to have* **brought to light** *some important new evidence.* ○ *Some little-known details of his early life have been* **brought to light**. ⇨ come to light.

bring to (such) a pass [Vn.pr pass] allow or cause (matters) to reach a sad or sorry state. **S:** father; manager, director; government. **O:** things, affairs, matters; us etc: *Much has been written about the errors that have* **brought** *the Chancellor* **to his** *present* **pass**. IND ○ *'And who* **brought** *us* **to such a pass**? *You did, by sheer incompetence.'* ⇨ come to a pretty pass/such a pass.

bring to prominence [Vn.pr pass] cause (sb) to be well known; make prominent. **S:** policy, view; resistance (to sth), refusal (to do sth); discovery, invention. **O:** member (of a party, of Parliament); scientist, artist: *Expressing extreme anti-European views may have* **brought** *him briefly* **to prominence**.

bring to rest [Vn.pr pass] control (sth) so that it stops, reaches a final position. **S:** driver, pilot. **O:** car, train, plane: *Wrestling desperately with the controls, the pilot finally managed to* **bring** *his aircraft* **to rest** *in a cornfield.* ⇨ come to rest.

bring to his senses [Vn.pr pass] make (sb) think and behave sensibly. **S:** experience, shock, disappointment. **O:** child, colleague, partner: *Having failed to* **bring** *Mary-Ann* **to her senses**, *he got her brothers and sisters to try.* GE ○ *Nothing but a strong letter from his bank manager will* **bring** *Fred* **to his senses**. ⇨ come to one's senses.

bring to a successful etc conclusion [Vn.pr pass] end (sth) well which is moving in a positive direction. **S:** statesman, negotiator; commander. **O:** talks, discussion; campaign: *Once a second front was opened in North-West Europe, we should be able to* **bring** *the war* **to a successful conclusion** *by the end of 1944.* MFM ⇨ come to a successful etc conclusion.

bring to trial [Vn.pr pass] (*legal*) try (sb) in a court of law. **O:** suspect, accused; case: *I sent the bomb which killed the postman. If* **brought to trial** *I should plead insanity.* ARG ○ *Before we can* **bring** *our man* **to trial**, *we must catch him in the act.* ⇨ be on trial.

bring to grips with [Vn.pr pass] make (sb) confront or tackle (sth), make him struggle with it. **S:** experience; awareness, knowledge; travel, work. **O:** statesman; scientist, scholar. **o:** (**with**) issue, problem: *Work in a developing country* **brought** *him* **to grips with** *the problems of poverty.* ⇨ come to/get to grips with.

bring together [Vn ⇆ p pass] reconcile (two parties in conflict). **O:** divorced, estranged couple; (warring, hostile) factions, parties, elements: *I'm not sure that John and Margaret can be* **brought together**. ○ *The Minister is trying to* **bring** *the two sides* **together** *to discuss a new peace formula.* ⇨ come together.

bring under [Vn.p pass] master, subdue (sb). **S:** government, police. **O:** rebel, rioter: *After an hour of unchecked street violence, the mob was* **brought under** *by squads of riot police.* = bring to heel, bring under control.

bring under control [Vn.pr pass] master, subdue (sb). **S:** fire brigade, health department; police, army. **O:** fire, epidemic; riot; crowd: *Five fire engines* **brought** *the blaze* **under control** *in just over an hour.* OBS ○ *Such bodies may sabotage the trade union movement if they are not* **brought under control**. SC = bring to heel, bring under. ⇨ be/get under control.

bring up 1 [Vn ⇆ p pass] carry, fetch (sth) to a higher level (eg from one floor to another). **O:** breakfast, lunch; mail, newspapers: *I asked Miss Matlock to* **bring** *me* **up** *a thermos of soup.* TFD ○ *The porter of our expensive block of flats ... fails to* **bring up** *our laundry.* MSAL

2 [Vn ⇆ p pass adj] raise, rear, educate (sb). **S:** parent, foster-parent, grandmother; nurse. **O:** child, family. **A:** properly, in style; single-handed, in poverty: *The nurse, suffering from conscience, adopted Prissie and* **brought** *her* **up**. DC ○ *The fact of being* **brought up** *in a shabby and dirty town was another thing that helped us to be competitive.* CON □ compound adj forms: well-brought-up, badly-brought-up; nom form: upbringing.

3 [Vn ⇆ p pass] call attention to (sth); raise. **S:** chairman, back-bencher, member of the board. **O:** question, matter, subject, proposal, point: *I* **bring** *this story* **up** *now only to compare my experience with that of some unhappy fellow on the United States Energy Commission.* NS ○ *'I think we're agreed on the main points. Does anyone want to* **bring up** *anything further?'* TBC ⇨ be up for discussion/debate, come up 5.

4 [Vn ⇆ p pass] (*legal*) make (sb) appear for trial. **S:** police, CID. **O:** habitual offender, suspected thief. **A:** before the magistrates, before the beak; on a charge of drunken driving: *They were* **brought up** *for causing a disturbance and obstructing the police.* ⇨ be up 6, come up 6.

5 [Vn ⇆ p pass] (*military*) convey or summon (sb/sth) to the front line. **S:** general; enemy; transport. **O:** armour, troops; supplies, ammunition: *We would have to blast our way on shore and get a good lodgement before the enemy could* **bring up** *sufficient reserves to turn us out.* MFM ⇨ come up 7.

6 [Vn ⇆ p pass] throw (sth) up from the stomach; vomit. **S:** child, patient. **O:** food, breakfast, everything: *'I don't seem to take my meals well,' he said. 'I* **bring up** *most of what I've taken, if you'll pardon the phrase.'* ASA ↔ keep down 7. ⇨ come up 8.

bring up the hard way [Vn.p pass] (*informal*) give (sb) a severe upbringing (ie without special help or privileges). **S:** father, family: *Father believed in* **bringing** *us* **up the hard way**. *He always said that a 'good' education would make us too soft for the harsh battles of life.* ⇨ bring up 2, come up the hard way.

bring up the rear [Vp.n pass] come last (in a procession or column). **S:** heavy transport, cavalry, car: *A short distance behind came a Peugeot, and* **the rear** *was* **brought up** *by a powerful dark-green Mercedes.* TO ○ *Ned, who had just opened the door* *to me,* ***brought up the rear*** *with a portfolio of drawings.* CON

bring up short etc [Vn.p pass] make (sb) suddenly stop talking or moving. **S:** noise, blow, interruption, sight. **A:** ! short, sharp, sharply, with a jerk: *What* ***brought*** *me* ***up short*** *and made my irritation evaporate was the sight of two bulging sacks lying at his feet.* DF ○ *We were* ***brought up short*** *by a sudden bellow from our friend.* BM

bring up to do sth [Vn ⇆ p pass] lead or persuade (sb) by deliberate training to do sth. **S:** parent, teacher, community. **O:** child, family. **Inf:** to scorn convention, to respect his parents' wishes: *He had always been* ***brought up to think*** *that his parents knew best.* ○ *They* ***brought up*** *their sons* ***to stand*** *on their own feet.*

bring up against [Vn.p.pr pass] make (sb) face or confront (sb/sth). **S:** travel, experience; marriage, courtship; work. **o:** problem, difficulty; pressure, force; opponent: *Working in a multiracial community had* ***brought*** *him* ***up against*** *the realities of intolerance.* ○ *He was soon* ***brought up against*** *her fear and mistrust of strange people.* ⇨ be/come up against.

bring up (as far as/to) [Vn.p pass, Vn.p.pr pass] lead, conduct (sb) to (a high point); cause (sth) to rise (to a certain level). **S:** road, path; bus; conditions. **O:** traveller; sea, tide. **o:** top, summit; sea-wall, houses: *Strong winds* ***brought*** *the water swirling* ***up*** *the main street.* ○ *'Did the guide* ***bring*** *you right* ***up to*** *the top?' 'No, only* ***as far as*** *that checkpoint.'* ⇨ be/come up (as far as/to).

bring up to [Vn.p.pr pass rel] help (sb) to reach (an acceptable level or standard). **S:** authorities; teacher, coach. **O:** work, performance. **o:** ⚠ standard, scratch, the mark: *His work in maths needs to be* ***brought up to*** *the standard of the others.* ○ *The committee feels that probably 80% of its inspectors do a reasonable job, and these courses help to* ***bring*** *the others* ***up to*** *scratch.* OBS ⇨ be up to 5, come up to, get up to 1, keep up to.

bring up to date [Vn.p.pr pass] revise (sth) by adding current information, figures etc; give (sb) a report with current information. **O:** pamphlet, brochure; chart, map; ideas, thinking; employer, commander: *Booklets published in the series 'Choice of Careers' are constantly* ***brought up to date****.* OBS ○ *I have only a few additional facts to add to* ***bring*** *the report* ***up to date****.* EM ○ ***Bring*** *me* ***up to date*** *quickly on the fuel crisis.* = fill in (on). ⇨ be up to date/the minute, get up to date (with).

bring within [Vn.pr pass] cause (sb) to come near enough (to be heard, seen or reached). **o:** ⚠ earshot, sight, view, range, striking distance: *Five minutes would* ***bring*** *the aircraft* ***within*** *range of our warning and interception system.* ⇨ be within 1, come within, get within.

bristle

bristle with 1 [Vpr rel] display a frightening or impressive array of (sth). **S:** army, front; task, project, scheme; book, memoir. **o:** guns, bayonets; problems, snags; impressive titles, famous names: *The first chapter, which* ***bristles with*** *names, is essentially a regimental history of the purely scientific side of the plutonium project.* NS

2 [Vpr] show, display (sth) in an extreme form. **o:** rage, anger, indignation, displeasure: *Just mention her name to him and he positively* ***bristles with*** *hostility.*

broach

broach (with) [Vn.pr pass emph rel] raise, introduce, in conversation (a matter one wishes to discuss). **O:** matter, question, issue, subject. **o:** partner, employer; wife: *I still had to* ***broach (with*** *her) the matter of her taking a job in America.* SPL ○ *I* ***broached*** *the subject* ***with*** *Elspeth one evening.* SML

brood

brood (on/over/upon) [Vpr pass emph rel] think sombrely and at length (about sth). **o:** problem, difficulty; illness, disability; failure: *She wasn't allowed to* ***brood over*** *the circumstances of the flight from Ireland.* EB ○ *The problem won't improve for being* ***brooded over****.* ○ *A nightmare scene* ***over*** *which* ***broods*** *the all-seeing, all-punishing figure of God.* BRN

browbeat

browbeat into [Vn.pr pass rel] force or bully (sb) into (doing sth). **S:** father, teacher, boss. **O:** child, pupil, staff. **o:** studying French, joining the army, accepting a new post: *Alun was the one who wanted to come and he managed to* ***browbeat*** *me* ***into*** *it.* OD ○ *I allowed myself to be* ***browbeaten into*** *subscribing £500.* = dragoon into.

browned

browned off [pass adj (Vn.p)] (*informal*) bored; annoyed. **A:** with the routine, food; with having nothing to do: *'You look* ***browned off****, Miss Traughton. Can I help?'* HAA □ also used after *appear* etc.

brush

brush aside 1 [Vn ⇆ p pass] push (sb/sth) to one side as being lighter or weaker than oneself. **S:** army, force. **O:** defences: *The enemy column* ***brushed aside*** *our defensive screen and advanced south.*

2 [Vn ⇆ p pass] treat (sth) as of little or no importance; disregard. **S:** organizer, director, manager. **O:** objections, difficulties, complaints: *We had to learn to work with others, and many of our own ideas would be* ***brushed aside*** *for the good of the whole.* MFM ○ *Gwen John* ***brushed aside*** *his objections and would not even listen to his arguments.* GJ = push aside 2. brush off 3.

brush down [Vn.p nom pass] clean (sth) with brisk strokes of a brush. **O:** oneself; jacket, coat: *Your jacket needs* ***brushing down****: it's covered with fluff.* ○ *He always looks as if he could do with a good* ***brush(-)down****.* □ the hyphen is optional in the nom form (brush down or brush-down). = dust down/off.

brush off 1 [Vn ⇆ p pass, Vn.pr pass] remove (sth) with a brush. **S:** valet, cleaner. **O:** mud, dust, fluff: *'I can't* ***brush*** *the dirt* ***off*** (or: *It won't* ***brush off****).'* ○ *'****Brush*** *the dandruff* ***off*** *your collar!'* = flick from/off.

2 [Vn.p nom pass adj] (*informal*) end a close relationship with (sb); reject, jilt; avoid meeting or forming a relationship with (sb). **S:** man, girlfriend; senior colleague, business associate. **O:** girlfriend, man; newcomer, junior: *His girlfriend has just given him the* ***brush-off****.* ○ *I've tried to* *make contact with the neighbours but they've always* **brushed** *me* **off**. □ nom form usu used in the first meaning.

3 [Vn ⇆ p pass] treat (sth) as of little or no importance; disregard. **O:** remarks, comments; objections, criticisms: *South Africa* **brushed off** *the threat of tougher economic sanctions.*

brush past [Vp, Vpr] just touch (sb) as one passes him in a confined space: *'Don't bother to move. I think I can just* **brush past**.' ○ *Something that felt like a cat* **brushed past** *him in the darkened room.*

brush up (on) [Vp.pr, Vp.n pass adj] (*informal*) revise or practise (a skill) in order to be proficient in it once again. **S:** tourist, salesman, learner-driver. **o/O:** French, Spanish; knowledge of the law, Highway Code: *To get Emily Patrick to paint you, the first thing to do is to* **brush up on** *your telephone manner.* HQ ○ *You'll have to* **brush up** *your history of art if you want a job in the museum.*

bubble

bubble over [Vp] rise to a peak, reach a climax. **S:** enthusiasm, high spirits, good humour: *Then excitement seemed to* **bubble over** *inside her. 'Life's so interesting, isn't it?' she said.* DC ⇨ next entry

bubble over with [Vp.pr rel] display a great deal of (sth). **S:** child, holiday-maker. **o:** excitement, high spirits: *With us travelled Rafael,* **bubbling over with** *enthusiasm for the whole trip.* DF ⇨ previous entry

bubble up [Vp] rise to the surface in bubbles and/or with the sound of bursting bubbles. **S:** gas, air; water, oil: *The warm gases* **bubbled up** *through the water.*

buck

buck at [Vpr pass adj] hesitate or refuse to face or accept (sth). **S:** client, customer, employee. **o:** suggestion, imposition; opportunity, challenge: *Linda accepts ... that for her wages she can't* **buck at** *being asked to perform the duties of upstairs-downstairs maid and chauffeur.* OBS = balk at, jib at.

buck up 1 [Vp, Vn.p pass] (*informal*) become, make (sb), more lively and cheerful; cheer up 1. **S** [Vp], **O** [Vn.p]**:** patient, invalid. **S** [Vn.p]**:** news; holiday, rest; meal, drink. **A:** no end, a great deal, a lot: *He'd got depressed about his work, but he* **bucked up** *at the thought that he'd soon be on holiday.* ○ *It was clear that Bennie's visit had* **bucked** *him* **up** *no end.* ILIH = cheer up 1,2.

2 [Vp] (*informal, dated*) (of people) make haste: *''Oh, do* **buck up**, *old boy, for heaven's sake! Stop loitering!'* FL ○ *'He'll have to* **buck up** *if he wants to catch that train.'* □ often imperative, or with must, have to. = hurry up.

buck one's ideas up [Vn ⇆ p pass] (*informal*) become more wideawake or alert: *If he hopes to keep his job, he'll have to* **buck his ideas up** *a bit.* □ often with have to, ought to, need to.

buckle

buckle down (to) [Vp, Vp.pr pass] begin to work seriously (at a task). **o:** ⚠ job, task, work; it: *MICK: But he won't* **buckle down to** *the job. DAVIES: He doesn't like work. MICK: Work shy.* TC ○ *They* **buckled down to** *finishing the big books and to earning as much as they could.* GE = get down to, knuckle down (to).

buckle to [Vp] make a determined effort (to tackle a problem, meet a crisis etc). **S:** family, country, partners: *Since I'm here hadn't I better* **buckle to** *and help?* GA ○ *When their father died, the children simply had to* **buckle to** *and run the farm themselves.* ○ *With Anna to lend a hand you'll be able to carry on until Laura gets here. It'll be a little adventure —* **buckling to** *and seeing it through.* TGLY

bugger

bugger about/around 1 [Vp] (*taboo*) behave in a foolish or irresponsible way: *'Now stop* **buggering about**, *Charlie. I've got work to do.'* ○ *'If you carry on* **buggering around** *with that knife, you'll do yourself an injury.*

2 [Vn.p pass] (*taboo*) treat (sb) in a foolish or casual way; behave as though one had a poor estimate of the worth etc of (sb). **S:** firm, dealer; clerk, official: *'Look, all I want is a simple answer to a simple question. Now stop* **buggering** *me* **about**!' ○ *'Don't try to be too clever with Fred. If he thinks you're* **buggering** *him* **around**, *he'll clobber you!'*

bugger off [Vp] (*taboo*) leave: *He'd* **buggered off** *before I had a chance to get a word in.* ○ *'If you're going to be rude you can* **bugger off**.' UNXL ○ *'Yah! Get away!* **Bugger off**!' PM □ often imperative. = clear off 1.

bugger up [Vn ⇆ p pass] (*taboo*) spoil, ruin (sth). **S:** workman, salesman; firm, agency. **o:** things, the whole thing, it; job, deal: *'Don't go fiddling around with that spanner — you'll* **bugger** *the whole works* **up**.' ○ *'Things can easily be* **buggered up** *by twits like you taking a hand.'* = mess up.

build

build in/into 1 [Vn ⇆ p pass adj, Vn.pr pass emph rel] make (sth) as a permanent fixture in (a house). **S:** builder, carpenter. **O:** cupboard, wardrobe, desk: *Don't bother to buy cupboards: I'm arranging to have them* **built in** *(ie* **built into** *the walls).* ○ *There was a* **built-in** *dresser in the kitchen.* □ used esp in the pass form *built in* and the adj form *built-in.*

2 [Vn ⇆ p pass adj, Vn.pr pass emph rel] make (sth) a firm and necessary part of (sth else). **S:** firm, solicitor; building-society, local authority. **O:** clause, proviso, requirement. **o:** lease, contract, agreement: *The landlord has insisted on* **building into** *our agreement a clause forbidding us to sublet.* ○ *The assembly workers will probably put in for a basic £200, with a* **built-in** *productivity arrangement.* = write in/into 2.

build into ⇨ build (up) into.

build on [Vpr pass rel] use (sth) as a foundation for further progress. **S:** team, athlete; firm, factory. **o:** achievement, success, record: *In their latest design, the company is clearly* **building on** *the success of previous years.*

build one's hopes on [Vn.pr emph rel] choose (sth/sb) as the best means of achieving an objective. **S:** country; industry, agriculture; government, party. **o:** alliance, treaty; automation, mechanization; (new) leader, policy: *City analysts are* **building their hopes** *on a revival of the Wall Street market.* ○ *It was* **on** *Mr Heseltine that this group within the Conservative Party now* **built its hopes**. OBS

build out [Vn ⇆ p pass] build (sth) as an extension to an existing structure. **O:** wing, extension; (extra) room; conservatory: *Extra classrooms were* ***built out*** *from the main block.*

build over [Vpr pass adj] cover (sth) with buildings. **o:** bomb-site, derelict land, marsh: *The woods where he used to play as a child have all gone. They're* ***built over****, of course.* ○ *This area to the left of the road is* ***built-over*** *farmland.*

build up 1 [Vp nom] accumulate, so as to form a block. **S:** traffic; queue, line: *At Easter, traffic* ***builds up*** *along the roads to the coast.* ○ *There is a serious* ***build-up*** *of cars on the M62 near Manchester.*

2 [Vn ⇆ pass adj] cover (sth) with buildings; develop. **O:** area, district, village: *The whole district is being* ***built up****; soon you won't be able to see the fields for bricks and mortar.* ○ *There is normally a speed-limit for traffic in* ***built-up*** *areas.* □ adj form built-up is usu used with area.

3 [Vn.p pass] develop the strength or physique of (sb). **S:** doctor, nurse, mother; exercise, diet: *'Must go carefully all the same. Not too much excitement. You must* ***build*** *yourself* ***up*** *for the winter.'* PW ○ *'Your brother has the nicest manners, but he needs* ***building up****; Vitamin B, I'd say.'* DC

4 [Vn.p nom pass] (*informal*) speak or write very approvingly of (sb/sth). (The praise may be exaggerated or undeserved). **S:** friend, colleague; former employer, chairman; critic. **O:** performer, actor, promising beginner; film, play: *'Don't* ***build*** *me* ***up*** *too much. I'm not that brilliant!'* ○ *He wasn't half the performer he was* ***built up*** *to be.* ○ *The film was given a terrific* ***build-up*** *in the press.*

build up (for) [Vp nom, Vp.pr] prepare (for a contest). **o:** competition, contest; match, game: *The England cricketers are now* ***building up for*** *the World Cup.* ○ *She will play at Queen's Club as part of her* ***build-up for*** *Wimbledon.* ○ *This was the perfect* ***build-up for*** *her subsequent career in television.*

build up (from) [Vn ⇆ p pass adj, Vn.p.pr pass emph rel] develop or extend (sth) gradually and steadily from a low level. **S:** leader, businessman, general, government. **O:** firm, practice; army; reputation, quality. **o:** scratch, zero, nothing: *The rebels may well be planning to* ***build up*** *this kind of army with foreign assistance.* SC ○ *We had to* ***build*** *the firm* ***up from*** *scratch after the devastation of the war.*

build (up) into [Vp, Vp.pr, Vn.pr, Vn.p.pr pass] (of parts) come together to form a whole; put (parts) together to form a whole. **S** [Vpr, Vp.pr], **O** [Vn.pr, Vn.p.pr]**:** piece, scrap; stamp, medal, book. **S** [Vn.pr, Vn.p.pr]**:** artist; collector : [Vp.pr] Eventually, these books will ***build up into*** *a fine library.* ○ [Vn.pr] The sculptor has ***built*** *these scraps of metal* ***into*** *a fine composition.*

build up (to) 1 [Vn ⇆ p nom pass adj, Vn.p.pr pass emph rel] increase, accumulate (sth). **S:** bank, City; ally, enemy. **O:** reserves, capital; force, army. **o:** level; strength: *The banks have* ***built up*** *sufficient reserves to cope with the crisis.* ○ *The army has been* ***built up to*** *its wartime strength.* ○ *A* ***build-up*** *of enemy forces has been reported.*

2 [Vp nom, Vp.pr emph rel, Vp.n pass adj, Vn.p.pr pass emph rel] develop, increase, intensify. **S** [Vp, Vp.pr], **O** [Vp.n, Vn.p.pr]**:** pressure, tension; opposition, resistance. **S** [Vp.n, Vn.p.pr]**:** overwork, stress; decision, attitude. **o:** pitch, intensity; climax : [Vp] More tightness and pressure ***build up*** *and your headache gets worse.* WI ○ [Vp] These measures will only lead to a ***build-up*** *in communal strife.* ○ [Vp.pr] Tension is ***building up to*** *a climax in this troubled city.* ○ [Vp.n] The West German Social Democrats... had ***built up*** *relations with the East German Communist Party.* IND = work up to.

bully

bully into [Vpr pass rel] make (sb) do tasks, accept sth unpleasant etc, by applying severe pressure. **O:** customer, employee, pupil. **o:** buying trashy goods, accepting low pay, playing team games: *The directors of the London Docks tried to bluster and* ***bully*** *the men* ***into*** *accepting an increase of pay.* HB

bum

bum around [Vp, Vpr] (*informal*) wander about or wait about idly. **o:** the world, the place: *She was planning to* ***bum around*** *Europe a bit before getting a regular job.* ○ *I think his idea is to* ***bum around*** *for a few years and live off his parents.*

bump

bump into 1 [Vpr pass rel] hit, strike (sb/sth) by walking, driving etc inattentively. **S:** he etc; car, bicycle. **o:** table; lamp-post, gate: *He* ***bumped into*** *one or two people on his way through, partly because of drink.* OD

2 [Vpr] (*informal*) meet (sb) by chance. (The person may be an acquaintance, or sb of whom one has heard.): *Bessie ... attended a party at the Deanery where she* ***bumped into*** *the great Master of Balliol, Benjamin Jowett.* HB = run into 4.

bump off [Vn ⇆ p pass] (*slang*) kill (sb), usu by shooting. **S:** gangster, husband, brother. **O:** crony, rival, wife: *'We'll all get* ***bumped off*** *when the balloon goes up* (ie when the war begins),*' he said.* RFW ○ *'You* ***bumped*** *the old woman* ***off****, and you're going to pay or hang!'* PE

bump up [Vn ⇆ p pass] (*informal*) increase, raise (sth). **S:** examiner, accountant; employer; shortage, scarcity, increased demand. **O:** mark, total; salary; value, shares: *Towards the close of business prices were* ***bumped up*** *by news of changes in the tax laws affecting company tax.* = put up 4.

bumped up [pass adj (Vn.p)] (*informal*) (have) risen rather quickly to a high position from humble beginnings; (be) in a job which is made to sound more important than it is (by some special title). **S:** clerk, office boy, messenger: *Mr Smythe wanted to speak to the real manager. He wasn't going to be satisfied with some* ***bumped-up*** *cashier.* ○ *'We must have struck him as rather* ***bumped up****. You know, no proper social background.'* □ used with be, appear etc.

bung

bung up [Vn ⇆ p pass adj] (*informal*) block or clog (sth). **O:** drain, pipe; nose, bowels: *'Don't throw tea leaves down the sink: you'll* ***bung*** *it* ***up****.'* ○ *'I've been* ***bunged up*** (= constipated) *since I changed my diet.'*

buoy

buoy up 1 [Vn ⇆ p pass] keep (sb) afloat. **S:** life-jacket; driftwood. **O:** swimmer, survivor (of ship-

wreck): *He seized a piece of wreckage; this would* ***buoy*** *him* ***up*** *till rescue came.*
2 [Vn ⇆ p pass] keep (sth) at a high or safe level. **S:** trading policy, improvement in the market. **O:** prices, share levels, trading figures: *These hopes have been* ***buoying up*** *share prices.* OBS
3 [Vn ⇆ p pass] keep (sb) cheerful or content. **S:** hope, thought; change of fortune: *I was* ***buoyed up*** *by thinking I might manage to get married myself.* SML

burn

burn away 1 [Vp] continue to burn. **S:** (coal-, gas-) fire: *The fire was still* ***burning away*** *cheerfully in the grate.*
2 [Vp, Vn ⇆ p pass] become, make (sth) less by burning; destroy (sth) by fire. **S** [Vp], **O** [Vn.p]**:** fuel, oil; wick, fuse; tissue, flesh: *Half the oil in the lamp had* ***burnt away***. ○ *When the pilot reached hospital, it was found that tissue had been* ***burnt away*** *from his face and hands.*
burn down [Vp, Vn ⇆ p pass adj] be destroyed, destroy (sth), to the foundations by fire. **S** [Vp], **O** [Vn.p]**:** house, factory, farmhouse. **S** [Vn.p]**:** mob, fire-raiser: *The wood-shed* ***burnt down*** *in half an hour.* ○ *Liberty ... presumes to invite the planet's poor to come and settle here* (ie in the United States)*; they came, they saw, and now they're* ***burning*** *the place* ***down***. OBS
burn for [Vpr emph rel] (*formal* or *facetious*) wish ardently that one could have. **o:** her etc; (moment of) glory, triumph: *These mercenary armies keep going because there's always some idiot* ***burning for*** *his moment of glory.*
burn off [Vn ⇆ p pass] remove, strip (sth), by burning. **O:** paint, varnish: ***Burn off*** *the old paint, fill any cracks in the woodwork, and rub down well with sandpaper.*
burn out 1 [Vp, Vn ⇆ p pass adj] (*technical*) (cause sth to) be damaged and stop working through electrical burning. **S** [Vp], **O** [Vn.p]**:** motor, coil, armature: *The high current taken by the armature when the motor is thus semi-stalled causes it to* ***burn out***. WTR ○ ***Burnt-out*** *armatures in most cases are rewound.* WTR
2 [Vp] (*space technology*) use up its fuel. **S:** rocket, missile; motor: *As the first rocket* ***burns out****, the second-stage motor ignites.*
3 [Vn ⇆ p pass adj] reduce (sth) to a shell by fire. **O:** house, factory; car, tank: ***Burned-out*** *lorries lined both sides of the road.* ○ *The factory was completely* ***burnt out***. □ usu passive or adj.
burn (itself) out [Vp, Vn.p] stop burning (because there is no more fuel). **S:** fire, flames; furnace, range: *After raging for most of the day, the fire had at last* ***burned itself out***.
burn (oneself) out [Vn.p pass] (*informal*) ruin one's health through overwork, excessive drinking etc: *His people work enormous hours for peanuts* (hardly any money) *and some have* ***burned out***. OBS ○ *The colonel had almost* ***burned himself out****, what with marching to Kandahar ... and sailing to Afridi.* SU ○ *The last time I saw him he looked completely* ***burned out***.
burn to [Vn.pr pass] reduce or spoil (sth) by burning it to (ash etc). **O:** food; meal; fuel; (wooden) furniture, fitting. **o:** ⚠ (a) cinder(s), a crisp, ash: *'Do I smell burning?' said Charmian. 'The pie and potatoes are* ***burned to*** *cinders.'* MM ○ *'You've* ***burnt*** *the bacon* ***to*** *a crisp!'*
burn to death [Vn.pr pass] kill (sb) by burning. **S:** fire, blaze. **O:** occupant; passenger: *Three people were* ***burned to death*** *in a blazing van which overturned and burst into flames late last night.* DM
burn up 1 [Vp] come to life as fuel is added. **S:** fire, stove: *He threw a log on the stove, and it* ***burned up*** *with a crackle.* = flare up 1.
2 [Vn ⇆ p pass adj] get rid of (sth) by burning; consume. **O:** rubbish; leaf, twig: *Throw the kitchen scraps in the incinerator and* ***burn them up***.
3 [Vp] catch fire and be destroyed as it enters the earth's atmosphere. **S:** meteorite; rocket: *A meteorite leaves a long, brilliant trail as it* ***burns up*** *on entering the atmosphere.*
burn with [Vpr] (*formal*) be filled with or consumed by (sth). **o:** passion, desire; ambition: *Martha was* ***burning with*** *curiosity but the solemnity of the affair checked her questions.* TP

burst

burst in/into [Vp, Vpr] enter (a place) suddenly. **S:** messenger; stranger. **o:** room, hall: *Suddenly Mr Lee* ***burst in****, in his shirtsleeves, and rushed across the living room into his bedroom.* OBS
burst in (on/upon) [Vp, Vp.pr pass] interrupt (sth) suddenly and excitedly. **o:** conversation, discussion: *A staff officer* ***burst in upon*** *their discussion with the news that the enemy was only five miles away.* ○ *'I don't see why I should be blamed,' Peter* ***burst in*** *angrily.* □ burst in usu *follows* direct speech. = break in (on/upon).
burst into 1 [Vpr] begin, suddenly and/or violently, to cry, laugh, sing etc . **S:** listener, viewer; child, old lady. **o:** tears, sobs; laughter, a guffaw, song: *Aunt Annabel, who has been nervous and jumpy lately, suddenly* ***burst into*** *tears.* DC ○ *As the comic got into his stride, the audience* ***burst into*** *hoots of laughter.* = break into 2.
2 [Vpr] begin suddenly to produce (flowers). **S:** (flowering) tree, shrub; hedgerow. **o:** bloom, blossom, flower: *The orchards seemed to have* ***burst into*** *blossom overnight.*
burst into flames [Vpr] begin, suddenly and violently, to burn. **S:** car, van; petrol tank; oil fire: *A child had knocked over an oil heater, which* ***burst*** *instantly* ***into flames***. ○ *The aircraft hit the runway, turned on its back and* ***burst into flames***.
burst into sight/view [Vpr] (of a brilliant spectacle) suddenly appear. **S:** procession, cavalcade; demonstrators, marchers: *The cavalry escort went by; then the royal coach with its outriders* ***burst into view***.
burst out 1 [Vp] declare suddenly and with feeling, exclaim (without necessarily interrupting): *'Why,' he* ***burst out****, ' don't you stop pretending you know all the answers!'*
2 [Vp] be suddenly and violently expressed. **S:** anger, frustration, resentment: *His hostility also found expression in a general aggressiveness and pugnacity which used to* ***burst out*** *with startling force.* BRN
burst out crying/laughing [Vp] suddenly begin to cry/laugh: *He looked about ready to* ***burst out crying***. TC ○ *I mentioned the incident later to a tailor friend and he* ***burst out laughing***. TO ⇨ burst into 1.

burst out/out of [Vp, Vpr emph rel] leave (a place) abruptly and/or violently, free oneself by violent efforts (from a place). **S:** crowd, mob; prisoner. **o:** gaol; cage: *The gate suddenly gave way and an angry crowd* ***burst out of*** *the yard.*

burst out of [Vpr] grow too big or fat for (sth). **S:** (growing) child, adolescent. **o:** clothes; trousers, shorts, jacket: *All the children were* ***bursting out of*** *their school uniforms and there was no money to buy new ones.*

burst through [Vp, Vpr emph rel] open (sth) and come through it with sudden violence. **S:** army; infantry, tanks; raider, bandit. **o:** front, defences; door: *Desperate efforts were made to seal off the gap* ***through*** *which the enemy divisions had* ***burst***. = break through 1.

burst upon [Vpr] occur suddenly to (sb). **S:** truth, realization; wisdom of a course of action: *The truth of what his colleagues had been saying* ***burst upon*** *him.* ○ *Those apparent discoveries which* ***burst upon*** *me with a shock of delight turned out to be ideas of which I had been told already but had not fully understood.* LIFE = dawn on/upon.

burst with [Vpr] show a great amount of (sth). **S:** child, youth; athlete. **o:** health, vitality, energy, enthusiasm, go: *Lady Emily and the Honourable Giles were* ***bursting with*** *health and good looks.* WDM

bury

bury (oneself) (away) in [Vn.pr pass, Vn.p.pr pass] move to or be situated in (a remote place). **o:** country; university, library; monastery: *What made him go and* ***bury himself in*** *the country?* ○ *We found the house at last. It was* ***buried away in*** *a remote part of the Yorkshire dales.*

bury one's face/head in [Vn.pr pass] hide one's face as a sign of grief or pain, or so that others will not see one's expression or tears. **o:** one's hands, handkerchief, the apron, bed-clothes: *Suddenly the truth struck me, and I wanted to sit down and* ***bury my face in*** *my hands.* TC ○ *Guy sat down and* ***buried his head in*** *the bed-clothes. He began to sob.* DC

bury (oneself) in [Vn.pr pass rel] become deeply involved in (sth). **o:** work; paper, book: *Right after dinner, he would go into the study and* ***bury himself in*** *his paper-work.* ○ *'Don't disturb your father: he's* ***buried in*** *''The Times'' crossword.'*

buried under [adj pred (Vn.pr)] overwhelmed by (sth). **o:** (pile, mountain of) work, marking, correcting: *'I can't get near him at the moment. He's* ***buried under*** *a pile of paperwork.'* □ used with *be, appear, seem.*

bust

bust up [Vn ⇆ p nom pass adj] (*informal*) destroy (sth). **S:** rival, competitor; philanderer. **O:** partnership; marriage: *Everything was fine between John and me until that woman stepped in and* ***bust*** *us* ***up***. ○ *Most of us could see the* ***bust-up*** *of their marriage coming.* = break up 7. ⇨ next entry

bust-up [nom (Vn.p)] (*informal*) violent quarrel: *We could hear a tremendous* ***bust-up*** *going on in the next room — china being thrown all over the place.* ⇨ previous entry

bustle

bustle about/around [Vp, Vpr] move about briskly and busily. **o:** place, house: *Debbie* ***bustled about*** *in the kitchen getting a meal together while Peter found us something to drink.*

busy

busy oneself (with) [Vn.pr emph rel] occupy oneself, be busy (with a task). **o:** preparations, housework; cooking a meal, cleaning the kitchen; car, boat; carpentry, decorating: *For some minutes he* ***busied himself with*** *his crayons.* 50MH ○ *'I brought a thermos-flask with me.' He leant over and* ***busied himself with*** *a basket.* QA

butt

butt in 1 [Vp] (*informal*) interrupt a conversation rudely: *I wish you wouldn't keep* ***butting in*** *when we are in the middle of a conversation.*
2 [Vp] (*informal*) intervene, interfere, meddle: *Of course, I don't want to* ***butt in*** *on the technical side.* RM ○ *It's better that his affairs should be handled by one man. It makes confusion if someone else* ***butts in***. PW

butter

butter up [Vn ⇆ p pass] (*informal*) praise or flatter (sb) insincerely (with the aim of obtaining favours etc). **S:** employee, junior colleague. **O:** boss, employer, professor: *'I wish he'd stop trying to* ***butter*** *me* ***up***. *I hate crawlers!'*

butter up to [Vp.pr pass] (*informal*) try to get close to (sb) by flattering him insincerely. **S:** junior, recruit. **o:** boss, foreman: *'Don't bother* ***buttering up to*** *me. Flattery never had any effect on me yet.'*

button

button up [Vn.p pass adj] (*informal*) conclude or finalize (arrangements). **S:** committee, organizer, team. **O:** it all, the whole thing, all the details: *I haven't said a word about it yet and I shan't, not till it's all* ***buttoned up***. RFW □ usu passive.

buttoned up [pass adj (Vn.p)] (*informal*) (be) secretive; (be) reserved, shy: *He hasn't said a word about our part in the plan: he's terribly* ***buttoned up***. ○ *I've always found him an awkward,* ***buttoned-up*** *sort of fellow.* □ also used with *appear, look, seem.*

buy

buy in 1 [Vp.n pass] buy a stock of (sth), often as a precaution in the event of a shortage. **O:** stock, supply; sugar, soap: *People* ***bought in*** *stocks of tinned goods in anticipation of food rationing.*
2 [Vp, Vp.n pass adj] (*finance*) purchase (stocks or shares): *BPI shareholders empowered their company to* ***buy in*** *up to 500 000 of its own shares.*

buy oneself in/into [Vn.p, Vn.pr] obtain a share in the ownership and control of (a business) by buying stock. **o:** firm, business, company: *A number of British companies are now* ***buying themselves into*** *European commerce and industry.*

buy off [Vn ⇆ p pass] (*informal*) persuade (sb), by paying him money, not to act against one's interests. **S:** intending purchaser; victim of blackmail. **O:** competitor, business rival; blackmailer: *'If you're trying to* ***buy*** *me* ***off***, *I'm afraid you've come to the wrong person.'* ○ *We can't afford to ignore his threats: I'm afraid he'll have to be* ***bought off***.

buy out 1 [Vn.p pass] (*military*) obtain the release of (sb) from the armed forces by a cash payment. **S:** soldier, sailor, airman; friend, relative. **O:** himself, themselves; son, brother: *Those who find they don't like the life can* **buy** *themselves* **out** *for $20 between their eighth and twelfth week of training.* ST

2 [Vn ⇆ p pass] pay (sb) to give up a post, or a share in a business (often to secure a controlling interest oneself). **S:** partner, shareholder, chairman: *New members can join by* **buying out** *an existing member at the current price of units.* H ○ *Balzac's associates had persuaded him to* **buy** *them* **out**, *so that he was now sole proprietor.* PTLB

buy up [Vn ⇆ p pass] buy all, or as much as possible, of (sth); obtain complete financial control over (sth). **S:** speculator, property tycoon, rival firm. **O:** land, property, office-space: *A Manchester finance house is making a bid to* **buy up** *the entire company.* ○ *All the building land for miles around has been* **bought up** *by one speculator.*

C

cake

caked in/with [pass (Vn.pr)] thickly coated with (sth), encrusted with (sth). **S:** hair, nails; clothes, shoes, boots. **o:** soap, grease, dirt, muck, soil, mud: *When he arrived home from the match, he was* **caked in** *mud from head to foot.* ○ *His ears were* **caked with** *shaving soap when he went for his interview.*

call

call (about) [Vpr] visit sb in his home, office etc (in order to discuss or investigate sth). **o:** the gas; sb's complaint, advertisement, inquiry: *'Excuse me, madam, I've been asked to* **call about** *your outstanding debt on the cooker.'*

call (at) [Vpr] ⇨ call (in) (at).

call away [Vn.p pass] summon (sb) from his place of work to attend on sb. **O:** doctor, midwife, nurse; police constable; priest. **A:** a few minutes ago; on business; to an urgent case, an accident: *'I'm afraid the doctor isn't in. He was* **called away** *a few minutes ago.'* □ very often passive, with no agent mentioned.

call back 1 [Vp] telephone (sb) again, eg having failed to contact him a first time: *'Oh, isn't Geoff in? All right, I'll* **call back** *a bit later.'* = phone back 1, ring back 1.

2 [Vn.p pass] after speaking to (sb), telephone him again, eg to give more information: *'Can I* **call** *you* **back** *in about half an hour? I'll have the answer then.'* = phone back 2, ring back 2.

call by (at) [Vp, Vpr, Vp.pr] make a stop at (a place) in the course of another, longer journey, often to collect sth/sb: *Three weeks later Uncle Leslie* **called by** *on his way to play golf.* SATS ○ *'Will you be in at five o'clock this evening? If so, I'll* **call by** *and pick up my tools, if you don't mind.'* = call (in) (at).

call down [Vn ⇆ p pass] (*military*) order (bombing) by artillery, aircraft etc onto enemy targets. **S:** (field, infantry) commander. **O:** bombardment; mortar-fire; air strike: *If the enemy advanced into the open, we would radio our field batteries and* **call down** *a pre-arranged bombardment.*

call down on sb's head [Vn.p.pr pass] (*formal* or *facetious*) summon, invoke (sth). **O:** ⚠ the wrath of god, curses, fire and brimstone, the vengeance of Heaven: *It's not much use* **calling down** *the wrath of God* **on their heads**; *something a bit more tangible is needed to make them change their minds.*

call (for) [Vpr pass rel] go to sb's house (in order to take him somewhere); go to a house, shop, cinema etc (in order to collect goods, tickets etc): *'What time shall I* **call for** *you tomorrow?'* ○ *'Has the owner* **called for** *the dog* (or: **called** *to collect the dog*) *yet?'* ○ *The goods will be* **called for** *next week.*

call for 1 [Vpr pass] summon (sb/sth), esp to perform a service. **O:** doctor; specialist; plumber, fitter; ambulance, taxi: *He carried the injured boy to a telephone kiosk where he* **called for** *an ambulance.* ○ *A more senior obstetrician was* **called for** *and he did a test.* G

2 [Vpr pass emph] demand, urge (sth). **S:** government, cabinet; committee, party; newspaper; propaganda. **O:** change, reform; spending, investment; moderation, patience: *Japan has repeatedly* **called for** *reduced US government spending to reduce its huge deficit.* ○ *The development of a national film industry has long been* **called for** *in Britain.* G □ note the alternative patterns: *Mr Marshall* **called for** *a second runway to be built* (or: **called for** *the building of a second runway*) *at Gatwick.* IND

3 [Vpr pass] require, demand, need (sth). **S:** the present conditions; the age (in which we live); his state of health; success, achievements, good luck, failure. **o:** skill, care; (careful, discreet, tactful, delicate), handling, examination; the exercise of judgement; a new approach, new thinking, immediate action; celebration, party; our gratitude, commiseration: *The identification of blood groups and the analysis of ink in forged documents can* **call for** *considerable skill.* NS ○ *Perhaps the parents felt that the intensity of the friendship between the two boys* **called for** *a separation.* MLT ○ *Something new was* **called for**, *something drastic had to be done.* G

call forward [Vn ⇆ p pass] invite or order (sb) to approach the speaker, to take some steps out of a group, row etc: *The captain of the winning team was* **called forward** *to receive the cup.*

call in 1 [Vn ⇆ p pass] summon (sb) to help in an emergency. **O:** police, army; social worker; rescue team: *Police from the specially trained armed support group were* **called in** *and they took up positions round the tower.*

2 [Vn ⇆ p pass] request or order the return of (sth), because it is now unsuitable or no longer needed. **S:** ministry, department; library, store, bank; manufacturer. **O:** all unsold tickets; (out-of-date, surplus) equipment; defective cars; empty containers. **A:** immediately, at once, without delay, urgently: *The Army is* **calling in** *all the unwanted ammunition.* ○ *How many of the models with faulty gearboxes have been* **called in**?

call (in) (at) [Vp, V.pr rel, V.p.pr rel] stop at one place on the way to another. **S:** he etc; ship, boat. **o:** café, public house; (friend's, relation's) home; the hospital, the police station; the butcher's, the chemist's; Marseilles, Karachi: *He still visited her in the evenings,* **calling in** *on the way home.*

MSAL ○ *The ship* **calls at** *several ports between Aden and London.* ○ *'***Call in** *this evening, if you can; I've something important to discuss.'* = drop in/into 1.

call in/into question [Vn.pr pass] express doubt about (sth); challenge; question. **O:** honesty, sincerity; competence, professional skill, judgement: *They do not* **call** *the defendant's integrity* **into question** *in quite the way Mr Stable did when he accused Mr Hain* (ie in court) *of trying to evade his moral responsibilities.* NS ○ *Social systems themselves are* **called in question** *and found increasingly inadequate to satisfy her heroines' needs.* JA

call off 1 [Vn ⇆ p pass] stop (sb/sth) or give the order to stop (sb/sth). **S:** officer, commander; police. **O:** pursuer; dog; chase, hunt; pursuit, attack: *As we were getting too far from our base, I decided to* **call** *my men* **off**. ○ *The pursuit was* **called off** *when it was clear that we had won the day.*

2 [Vn ⇆ p pass] order (sb) to stop searching, attacking or worrying sb. **O:** ⚠ the dogs, hounds, bloodhounds: *'Why don't you mind your own business?' he said. 'There's been no harm done, and this lady here has* **called off** *the dogs.'* TT ○ *'You can* **call** *the bloodhounds* **off**, *Inspector. I give up.'*

3 [Vn ⇆ p pass] cancel, abandon, drop (sth). **O:** the whole thing; arrangement, deal; scheme, plan, proposal; strike; journey, expedition; picnic, excursion; engagement (between a man and a woman): *Why don't we* **call off** *this competition for her love?* QA ○ *'I don't see any point in having a picnic in weather like this. Let's* **call** *it* **off**.*'*

call (on) [Vpr pass rel] visit (a place), usu for business or official reasons. **S:** salesman, traveller, our representative; (health) inspector; doctor, vicar. **o:** customers; the sick; the aged and infirm; parishioners: *Our representative will* **call on** *you in the course of the next week.* ○ *The local party makes sure that every voter in the constituency is* **called on** *at least once.*

call on/upon [Vpr pass emph rel] turn to (sth) to help one at a time of difficulty; summon. **O:** experience, knowledge; cunning, wisdom; reserves of strength: *The majority of patients . . . suffered from nervous troubles which could be treated without* **calling on** *outside help.* F ○ *She . . . would have to* **call on** *reserves of patience and cunning in which she was notably deficient.* MSAL

call on/upon to do sth 1 [Vpr pass rel] invite, request (sb) to speak etc. **S:** Chairman; Best Man. **o:** speaker, lecturer; (distinguished) guest. **Inf:** to deliver his lecture, to address us; to say a few words; to propose the health of the bride: *'I will now* **call on** *Mr White* **to propose** *a vote of thanks to the Committee.'* ○ *He was seldom* **called upon to speak** *at these gatherings.*

2 [Vpr pass rel] urge, appeal to (sb) to act in some way. **o:** organization, institution, nation; friend, relation, student, colleague. **Inf:** to help, support; protest, break away: *We* **call upon** *the masses, he writes,* **to rise** *and crush the tyrants.* RTH ○ *Violetta realizes the magnitude of the sacrifice she is* **called upon to make**. BBCR

call out 1 [Vp, Vp.n] give a greeting, make a request etc, in a loud voice: *'If you want anything from the fridge, just* **call out** *and I'll bring it.'* ○ *'A lovely evening,' the man* **called out** *to me.* ARG □ can be followed or preceded by direct speech, as in the second example.

2 [Vn ⇆ p pass] state, declare (sth) in a loud voice. **O:** (list of) names, prices, times, quantities; score, marks; results (of a competition): *'Please keep quiet while I* **call out** *the names of the successful competitors.'* ○ *When Bill's name was* **called out**, *another boy said 'Present, sir!'*

3 [Vp] (of schoolchildren) try to attract the teacher's attention; speak in a loud voice, without permission: *'How many times must I tell you not to* **call out**, *Sarah?'*

4 [Vp] try to attract the attention of (sb) by shouting. **S:** drowning man; injured child. **A:** for help; in pain: *The children were too weakened by hunger to* **call out** *for food.* ○ *She* **called out** *to people passing in the street but nobody heard her.* = cry out.

5 [Vn ⇆ p pass] summon (sb) to restore order etc. **S:** Government, Home Secretary. **O:** riot police, troops, emergency services: *A practical joker picked up the telephone and* **called out** *the fire-brigade.* ○ *Troops were* **called out** *to deal with the riot.*

6 [Vn ⇆ p pass] (*industrial relations*) order or authorize (workers) to go on strike. **S:** (Trades) Union, Executive Committee. **A:** on strike; in sympathy: *Bus-drivers may be* **called out** *on strike in support of their latest wage-claim.* = bring out 1.

call round (at) [Vp, Vp.pr] pay a visit (to a place). **o:** Kate's place, house: *'Do* **call round** *when you have the time. We're at home most evenings.'* ○ *'I'll* **call round at** *my brother's this afternoon to pick up the book.'*

called to [pass (Vn.pr)] summoned to enter a particular profession or occupation. **o:** the bar (= the profession of barrister); the ministry; task, mission: *I achieved my ambition and was* **called** *formally* **to** *the Bar in September 1953.* RFW ○ *Vocations — that is, occupations* **to** *which people feel* **called** *because of some special skill or need.* BRN

call to account [Vn.pr pass] make (sb) explain an error, loss, failure etc. **S:** manager, boss. **O:** clerk, cashier: *He may think that all this petty pilfering goes unnoticed, but one day he'll be* **called to account**. ○ *The abbot* (ie head of a monastery) *would be* **called to account**, *both for his teaching and for 'the obedience of his disciples'*. SHOE

call (sb's) attention to [Vn.pr pass emph rel] make (sb) notice (sth) in particular. **o:** shortage, abundance; fact, circumstance; failing, fault: *I write neither to defend nor condemn this sentence but simply to* **call attention to** *the Observer's method of reporting it.* OBS ○ *Finally, may I* **call your attention to** *a series of public lectures to be given in this department?* = draw (sb's) attention to.

call to mind [Vn.pr pass] recall, remember (sb/sth). **O:** him etc; the occasion; saying, promising that: *'I'm sure I've met the girl you're referring to, but I can't just* **call** *her* **to mind**.*'* ○ *'Do you know her telephone number?' 'I ought to, but I can't quite* **call** *it* **to mind**.*'* ○ *The accused said that he could not* **call to mind** *making any of the statements quoted by the police officer.*

call to order [Vn.pr pass] formally request (a meeting) to be silent so that business may begin or continue. **S:** chairman; mayor, president. **O:** meeting, assembly, gathering: *At two o'clock, the chairman* ***called*** *us* ***to order*** *and the afternoon session began.* ○ *Despite attempts to* ***call*** *them* ***to order****, the audience continued to stamp their feet.*

call up 1 [Vn ⇆ p pass] communicate with (sb/sth) by telephone. **O:** him etc; shop, restaurant, bar; airport; ticket-office: *'I tried to* ***call*** *you* ***up*** *last night, but no one answered the phone. Were you out?'* ○ *I took the phone off the hook so my folks wouldn't* ***call*** *me* ***up*** *and nag me.* AT = ring up 1.

2 [Vp.n pass] (*computing*) obtain (information) from a computer by typing commands on a keyboard, using a plastic card etc. **O:** information, data; figures; (bank) account, balance: *Jobcentre visitors can* ***call up*** *jobs page by page and get a printout of the ones they like.* ○ *You can also use your Card to* ***call up*** *the balance, print out or order a statement ...* MBNK ○ *'Patient information' can be* ***called up*** *by using the patient's name or a reference number.* WC

3 [Vn ⇆ p nom pass adj] (*military*) summon (sb) for military or national service. **S:** Government; Army. **O:** all able-bodied men, reservists, men between the ages of 18 and 25: ***Called up*** *at nineteen, Carl hated his first brief period of military conscription.* JUNG ○ *Have you received your* ***call(ing)-up*** *papers yet?* ○ *The* ***call-up*** *of medical reservists was announced on radio and television.*

4 [Vp.n pass] invite (a player) to join a team, esp for a special match, eg a cup tie or international game. **O:** striker, midfield player; bowler, batsman: *Nottingham Forest manager Brian Clough could* ***call up*** *Scottish under-21 international Terry Wilson.* ○ *Late yesterday the selectors* ***called up*** *the Worcester opener* (ie opening batsman) *Tim Curtis.* G

5 [Vn.p pass] recall (sth) to the memory. **S:** incident, smell, sound; he etc. **O:** memory, scene (from the past); past life, childhood: *The sound of seagulls* ***called up*** *happy memories of her childhood holidays.* ○ *The steps by which one* ***calls up*** *and entertains mental events now past ...* NL ⇨ bring back 2.

call upon 1 [Vpr pass rel] invite, request (sb) to speak etc. ⇨ call on/upon to do sth 1.

2 [Vpr pass rel] urge, appeal to (sb) to act in some way. ⇨ call on/upon to do sth 2.

calm

calm down 1 [Vp] become calm or quiet: *The sea* ***calmed down*** *as soon as the wind fell.*

2 [Vp, Vn ⇆ p pass] (cause sb to) become quiet, or control his temper: *'Here, Parkinson, have a cup of coffee and* ***calm down****!' 'To hell with a cup of coffee! Listen to this!'* TBC ○ *It was a real lesson in the power of a woman to* ***calm*** *a man* ***down****.* CON

camp

camp out 1 [Vp] live in a tent (usu for a holiday): *'There is no possibility of accommodating any more visitors.' 'I see,' said the young man. 'But couldn't I* ***camp out****?'* RM

2 [Vp] (*informal*) wait in a determined way, often for some time, outside a house, shop etc, in the hope of seeing sb, gaining entry etc. **S:** journalist, shopper, sightseer: *TV cameramen* ***camped out*** *all night in the gardens, competing for the best view of the President's front door.*

camp it up [Vn.p pass] (*theatre*) overact (sth) using exaggerated movements and gestures; act (sth) in an exaggeratedly effeminate way. **O:** performance, show; play; it, the whole thing: (Parliament on TV) *Mr Speaker seemed to be putting on an extra show for the occasion, as if some TV producer had told him: 'Bernie, darling,* ***camp it up*** *a bit for the cameras, will you.'* G ○ *It was a play about travelling players, so that ... the actors and actresses could have lots of verve and* ***camp it up****.* LS

cancel

cancel out [Vn ⇆ p pass adj] reduce (sth) to nothing. **S:** improvement, gain, success. **O:** failure, loss, deficit: *A large inflow of investments has* ***cancelled out*** *their indebtedness.* = wipe out 2.

cancel (each other) out [Vp, Vn.p] (of similar or identical things) make each other ineffective; reduce each other to nothing. **S:** factors, conditions, characteristics: *In the long run the two sets of factors* ***cancel out****.* ○ *'But hadn't they all been naughty, even Harold, even Irma naughty, and did not their naughtinesses* ***cancel each other out****?'* PW = balance out.

care

care about [Vpr emph rel] feel concerned about (sb/sth). **o:** outcome, result; the homeless, the less able: *Arendt constantly avoids that question and does not seem to* ***care about*** *the answer.* HA ○ *He doesn't appear to* ***care*** *very much* ***about*** *the future of the company.*

care for 1 [Vpr pass adj] do necessary things for (sb/sth); be responsible for (sb/sth). **S:** family; the State; doctor, nurse; servant. **o:** children; the sick, the elderly; house, garden: *The young brood he protected and* ***cared for*** *until they were old enough to look after themselves.* GLEG ○ *Everyone agrees that pensioners should be* ***cared for*** *by the State.* ○ *We were impressed by the well-****cared-for*** *gardens.* □ when the adj is attrib, it is always modified by an adv, as shown; note the opposite, uncared-for. = look after 1, take care (of) 1.

2 [Vpr] (*formal*) feel strongly for (sb); love. **o:** boyfriend, girlfriend; friends, family: *'If I didn't* ***care for*** *you, your new job and the move to London wouldn't matter.'* ○ *Susanna* ***cares for*** *her parents enormously, despite what she says to her friends.*

3 [Vpr] (*formal*) like to have (sth); want. **o:** cup of tea, cigarette, slice of cake: *'Would you* ***care for*** *one of my home-made mince pies?'* □ usu interrog.

not care for [Vpr] (*dated*) not think highly of (sb/sth); dislike. **o:** one's neighbours, Northerners; beer, gin; vigorous exercise: *'You* ***don't care for*** *Helena, do you?' 'You didn't seem very keen yourself, once.'* LBA ○ *Card games he did* ***not care for****, but he loved charades.* CD

carry

carry about (with one) [Vn.p, Vn.p.pr] take (sth) from place to place, take (sth) everywhere (with one). **O:** briefcase, umbrella, stick: *Why did you want to* ***carry*** *that document* ***about with you*** *all the time? You were bound to lose it sooner or later.* DC ○ *Be sure to* ***carry*** *your passport* ***about with you*** *whenever you leave the hotel.*

carry along [Vn.p pass] help (sb) to continue or complete a task, race etc; give encouragement or support to. **O:** runner, swimmer, competitor, team:

The amateur team were ***carried along*** *by the enthusiasm of their supporters and finally defeated a more highly-rated professional club.* ○ *Although he had spent years on his research, Hammond's conviction that he was on the threshold of a great discovery* ***carried*** *him* ***along****.*

carry away 1 [Vn ⇆ p pass] take, remove (sth/sb), usu by overwhelming force. **S:** river, sea; raging waters, torrent, flood, tidal wave; hurricane, whirlwind, tornado. **O:** everything in its path; structure, house, building: *Several houses were* ***carried away*** *when the swollen river suddenly changed its course.* ○ *She could see him falling into the Thames and being* ***carried away*** *by the tide.* HWKM
2 [Vn ⇆ p pass] move or fill (sb) with emotion so that he no longer has full control over his thoughts etc. **S:** speaker; occasion; feeling, sentiment: *Lionel found, during this singing, that he was completely* ***carried away*** *by the excitement of the moment.* GIE ○ *'I should have thought before I spoke. I just get* ***carried away*** *with enthusiasm.'* DC ○ *Isabel was* ***carried away*** *by the thought that almost for the first time she was having a serious conversation with her husband about books.* PW □ usu passive.

carry back (to) [Vn.p pass, Vn.p.pr pass rel] recall (sth) to mind; cause (sb) to remember (sth). **S:** incident, smell, sound, voice. **o:** childhood, early days; first encounter, last reunion: *The sound of seagulls* ***carried*** *me* ***back to*** *childhood holidays at the seaside.* = take back (to). ⇨ bring back 2, ⇨ call up 5.

carry all/everything before one [Vn.pr] advance irresistibly; sweep aside all opposition, capture all one's objectives. **S:** troops, army; team: *Thanks partly to vigorous campaigning by leading West German figures, the parties of the right* ***carried everything before them*** *in East Germany.*

carry forward [Vn ⇆ p pass] (*accountancy*) take a sum of money etc from one page or column to the next, or from one week, one year, to the next. **O:** total; (outstanding) debt; deficit, surplus: *It's no use* ***carrying*** *this debt* ***forward****; we might as well write it off.* □ often abbreviated to c/f.

carry off 1 [Vn ⇆ p pass] seize and bear (sb/sth) away, as a captive; take (sb) away as if he were a captive. **S:** enemy, gypsies, witch; bird of prey. **O:** (defenceless) women, child; small animal: *The eagle swooped and* ***carried off*** *a sleeping lizard.* ○ *At this juncture Miss Kate Martineau* ***carried*** *Marian* ***off*** *to Highbury for the weekend.* GE
2 [Vp.n pass] (*formal*) cause the death of (sb); kill. **S:** disease, epidemic; cholera, plague: *The disease* ***carried off*** *more than 7 000 people in this neighbourhood alone.* HWKM ○ *He was fatally ill with the same consumption of the lungs that had* ***carried off*** *his brother Tom.*
3 [Vp.n pass] win (sth). **S:** competitor; entry. **O:** award; trophy, cup, shield: *The Russian women gymnasts* ***carried off*** *most of the medals.*

carry it off [Vn.p] manage, handle, a difficult or embarrassing situation successfully: *If Mary's former husband had come in a little earlier, the guests would have been able to* ***carry it off*** *all right, but he had caught them off balance.* CON ○ *My remark had obviously annoyed her. I tried feebly to* ***carry it off****.* SPL

carry on 1 [Vp, Vp.n] continue (doing sth). **O:** working, writing, speaking: *'Please* ***carry on*** *as usual while I listen to the class.'* ○ *Other dogs would growl at me — but not Bruce — he just wags his lovely thick tail and* ***carries on*** *playing.* WI ○ *'Free association' ... simply allowed a patient to* ***carry on*** *talking and divulging anything and everything that came into her head.* F
2 [Vp nom] (*informal*) quarrel, argue, fuss, behave, noisily: *Old Mr Knopff was* ***carrying on*** *about his pen; he made such a fuss you'd think it was his head.* US ○ *'Did you ever hear such a* ***carry-on*** *about nothing at all?'* □ note (i) in non-standard English: carry on *something awful, something dreadful* (= in an awful or dreadful manner); (ii) the nom form carryings-on, used only in the plural: *I heard him complaining about the* ***carryings-on*** *of some town council in the paper that he was reading.* HAHA
3 [Vp, Vp.n pass] continue, maintain (sth). **S** [Vp], **O** [Vp.n]**:** life, existence; routine, pattern: *'Life on earth is not going to be impossible, but it will have to be* ***carried on*** *in far less favourable circumstances.'* TBC
4 [Vp.n pass] conduct, hold (sth). **O:** conversation, talk, discussion: *I wish you wouldn't* ***carry on*** *long conversations with your friends when I'm waiting to use the telephone!*
5 [Vp.n pass] conduct, transact, pursue (sth). **O:** business, occupation: *A great many shady businesses are* ***carried on*** *through the small-ad columns of respectable newspapers.*

carry on (with) [Vp, Vp.pr rel] (*informal*) have an extra-marital affair (with sb): *'Isn't it shocking! Everyone knows that Bill's* ***carrying on with*** *the woman next door.'* ○ *They'd been* ***carrying on*** *for years, but his wife never knew.*

carry out 1 [Vp.n pass] make (sth) a reality; implement. **O:** (one's) obligations, promises, threats; plan, agreement; instructions, specifications. **A:** faithfully; punctually; to the letter: *If this difficult phase of highways planning is to be* ***carried out*** *efficiently, the engineer has to have all the help that modern methods of survey can supply.* NS ○ *This order was not popular with the armoured units, but I was determined to see that it was* ***carried out*** *to the letter.* MFM = put into effect.
2 [Vp.n pass] perform, conduct (sth). **O:** experiment, test; research, investigation: *Before testing this method on patients, Dr Baronofsky* ***carried out*** *tests for two years on three hundred dogs.* NS ○ *The survey, which is bound to cause controversy ... was* ***carried out*** *by a team from the Bartlett School of Architecture.* OBS

carry over 1 [Vn ⇆ p pass adj] (*finance, commerce*) retain (sth) as an item to be dealt with at a later date: *'I propose that some minor matters on the agenda should be* ***carried over*** *for consideration at the next meeting.'* ○ *If you do not take your holidays at the appropriate time, you may find that you cannot* ***carry*** *them* ***over*** *to the next year.* ⇨ carry forward.
2 [Vn ⇆ p pass adj] allow or cause (sth) to survive or remain in operation at a later time. **O:** function, office; practice, ceremony: *However great the zeal of the reformers, much was* ***carried over*** *from the past.*

3 [Vn.pr pass] enable (sb) to manage or survive during (a difficult time). **S:** loan, small legacy. **o:** difficult phase, time of shortage; winter; slack trading period: *With the addition of small sums he earned as a junior assistant, the money* **carried** *him* **over** *a difficult period.* JUNG = carry through 2.

carry through 1 [Vn ⇆ p pass] pursue (sth) to a successful conclusion; complete. **O:** aim, plan, scheme, enterprise. **A:** to the (bitter) end; in the face of/in spite of every obstacle: *These aims will be* **carried through** *to the end.* MFM ○ *Scheme after scheme, absolutely foolproof, has been spoilt from the beginning by my never having enough capital to* **carry** *it* **through**. HAHA = put through 1.

2 [Vn.p pass, Vn.pr pass] help (sb) to survive (a difficult period); sustain. **S:** God, trust in God, hope (for a better life); determination, courage, grit. **o:** crisis; war: (hymn) *He* (ie God) *is willing to aid you; He will* **carry** *you* **through**. ○ *Growing confidence in the new leaders helped to* **carry** *the soldiers* **through** *an arduous campaign.* = carry over 3.

carry with one 1 [Vn.pr] obtain or keep the support of (sb); persuade (sb) to follow or agree with one. **O:** majority; committee, jury; crowd, assembled company: *Can he point to the opinion polls, ... election results, and now the local government results, as evidence that he is* **carrying** *the country* **with him**? OBS

2 [Vn.pr] be always aware or reminded of (sth); retain. **O:** memory, impression; guilt; happy recollection: *I shall always* **carry with me** *the memory of that tormented face.*

cart

cart across, along, away etc [Vn ⇆ p pass, Vn.pr pass] (*informal*) carry or take (sb/sth heavy or awkward) across etc. **O:** children, pupils; luggage, cases, boxes; papers, files: *We've got all these empties to* **cart across** *to the bottle bank.* ○ *At that stage, she was* **carting** *two young children* **about**.

carve

carve out (for oneself) [Vp.n pass, Vn.p.pr] build or create (sth) (for oneself) through strenuous efforts. **O:** ⚠ life, career, reputation; place, niche: *He'd moved up from Mexico, where he'd been out of work for quite a while. He was* **carving out** *a new life in the Californian desert.* ○ *Susie went on to* **carve out** *a reputation* **for herself** *as a serious actress.* TVT

carve up 1 [Vn ⇆ p pass] (*slang*) cut and wound (sb) seriously with a knife or razor: *We only meant to* **carve** *him* **up** *but the knife slipped.* ○ *Eddie got* **carved up** *in a street fight.*

2 [Vn ⇆ p nom pass] (*slang*) divide and share (sth), the implication usu being that those concerned are powerful and exclude weaker competitors. **O:** country, territory; estate; market; network, system: *Japanese officials plead that they do not have the power to* **carve up** *the market in this way.* ECON ○ *The busiest (air) routes are* **carved up** *by bilateral deals between the national airlines at either end.* ECON ○ *One of the consequences of World War 1 was the carve-up of Germany's African colonies.*

3 [Vn ⇆ p nom pass] (*slang*) cheat, swindle (sb) out of his share. **O:** partner, mate: *You know what they did? They* **carved** *me* **up** *.... It was all arranged, it was all worked out.* BP ○ *I didn't get a penny out of them. It was a complete bloody* **carve-up**.

cash

cash in (on) [Vp, Vp.pr pass rel] (*informal*) get the benefit of (sth); exploit. **S:** (trade) rival, competitor; colleague, associate. **o:** shortage, scarcity; boom, expansion; discovery, success: *The great problem is to prevent others* **cashing in** *before we've had time to market the product.* ○ *A few commercial enterprises have* **cashed in on** *Lawrence's reputation.* FIB ○ *If I find some woman trying to* **cash in on** *my chivalry by lashing out with her frail little fists, I lash back at her.* LBA □ note casher-in: *He's a great* **casher-in** *on people's financial difficulties: he lends money at an exorbitant rate.*

cash up [Vp] add up the cash one has taken, esp at the end of a day of trading: *A postmistress from Thilow, Cambridge, ... was shot in the head after* **cashing up** *at her post office and stores.* T

cast

cast about/round (for) [Vp, Vp.pr rel] try to find or think of (sth), usu hurriedly or in an emergency. **o:** solution, answer; expedient, device; means, method (of escape): *She* **cast about** *... in an attempt to find an image that would match her fantasy.* MSAL ○ *Macon was still at the bottle-cap factory. He'd been* **casting about for** *other occupations at the time.* AT ○ *He characteristically begins with a judgement ... and then* **casts around for** *evidence which might support it.* TSE

cast aside 1 [Vn ⇆ p pass] (*formal* or *facetious*) remove (sth). **O:** coat, gloves: *'Are those your glasses,* **cast aside** *in the heat of passion?'* TGLY = throw off 1.

2 [Vn ⇆ p pass] (*formal*) get rid of (sth/sb); abandon. **O:** cares, responsibilities; pretence, secrecy; friend, ally: *His enthusiasm waxed and waned, and in high summer he almost* **cast** *the project* **aside**. F ○ *Sainty mused much on abdications, on men who had* **cast aside** *rank and wealth.* BLCH

castaway/cast away [nom pass (Vn.p)] (sb) left, whether by accident or deliberately; (sb) washed ashore, after a wreck. **A:** on a desert island; far from civilization; somewhere in the Pacific: *Robinson Crusoe is perhaps the most famous* **castaway** *in English literature.* ○ *'If you were* **cast away** *on a desert island, would you be able to fend for yourself?'*

cast one's mind back [Vn.p] return in one's thoughts to an earlier time. **A:** a few years; to one's student days: *'***Cast** *your mind* **back** *to our first meeting with Spencer in Berlin.'*

cast down [pass adj (Vn.p)] (be) depressed, unhappy: *He was not easily* **cast down**, *but circumstances had combined to depress him.* ○ *'Oh dear.' Malcolm too seemed quite* **cast down**. OD ○ *I've never seen such a* **cast-down** (or: **downcast**) *expression!* □ used also with *appear, get, seem, look*; note alt and more usu adj form: downcast.

cast off 1 [Vp] (*nautical*) release the ropes or cables used to hold a boat or ship in position alongside a quay etc. **S:** sailor, crew; ship, boat: *The order was given to* **cast off** *and soon the ship was moving away from the quay.*

2 [Vn ⇆ p nom pass adj] remove (sth) temporarily; take (sth) off and throw it aside carelessly. **O:** clothes; jacket, shoes: *He* ***cast off*** *his clothes and dived in to the cool water of the lake.* □ nom form used to refer to clothes that are permanently discarded: *She gives her* ***cast-offs*** *to Oxfam.*

3 [Vn ⇆ p nom pass adj] abandon, reject (sb). **O:** lover, mistress; friend; employee: *Dickens could not bear to* ***cast*** *him* ***off*** *altogether after twenty years.* CD ○ *This is a tale of Christian hope brought to the* ***cast-offs*** *of the affluent society.* T ○ *He did not enjoy the role of the* ***cast-off*** *lover.*

cast off (stitches) [Vp, Vp.n pass] remove stitches from the needles, in knitting: *At last she reached the end of the sleeve, and* ***cast off*** *with a sigh of relief.* ○ *At the end of each row she* ***casts off*** *two* ***stitches.*** ↔ cast on (stitches).

cast doubt on [Vn.pr pass emph rel] (make people) question the truth or value of (sth). **S:** committee, panel; judge, inspector. **o:** findings, conclusions; claim, assertion: *The Committee also* ***cast doubt on*** *the value of her report as an independent study.* ○ *Miss Ross's experience confirms that of her young pupils* ***on*** *whose story some ... people have ventured to* ***cast doubt.*** RM

cast on (stitches) [Vp, Vp.n pass] put the first row of stitches on a knitting needle: *She had to* ***cast on*** *extra* ***stitches*** *to make the pullover wide enough.* ○ *How many* ***(stitches)*** *do you* ***cast on*** *— twenty or twenty-two?* ↔ cast off (stitches).

cast out/out of [Vn ⇆ p pass, Vn.pr pass] (*formal*) force (sb) to leave (a place); expel. **O:** animals; weaklings; misfits; criminals: *The old animals were* ***cast out*** *from the herd.* LWK ○ *Sooner or later the infant is* ***cast out of*** *the Garden of Eden* (the state in which he enjoys absolute security but has no responsibility), *and thereafter has to work his way ... to full maturity.* PS □ nom form is outcast: *The poor fellow had to live like an* ***outcast*** *when his last penny had gone.* = drive out/out of 1.

cast an eye/one's eyes over [Vn.pr] study (sth), but only superficially; examine (sth) quickly: *'Would you mind* ***casting an eye over*** *these calculations to see if you can spot any obvious mistakes?'* ○ *It isn't enough just to* ***cast your eyes over*** *that second-hand car you're thinking of buying — you should get an expert's report on it.* = pass an/one's eye over.

cast round (for) [Vp.pr rel] try to find or think of (sth), usu hurriedly or in an emergency. ⇨ cast about/round (for).

cast up (on) [Vn ⇆ p pass adj, Vn.p.pr pass emph rel] throw or deposit (sth) (in a place). **S:** sea, wave, tide. **O:** flotsam and jetsam; dead fish; body; seaweed. **o:** shore, beach; reef, rock: *The sea* ***casts up*** *the detritus of civilization on rocks and beaches all over Europe.* ○ *The shipwrecked sailors were* ***cast up on*** *the shore of a desert island.*

catch

catch at a straw [Vpr] try to grasp some slight means of rescue or escape: (proverb) *A drowning man will* ***catch at a straw.*** ○ *Close questioning had him floundering about* ***catching at straws.*** = clutch at a straw.

catch in the act [Vn.pr pass] surprise (sb) while he is committing a crime, catch red-handed: *The police* ***caught*** *the thieves* ***in the act:*** *they were just opening the factory safe.* ○ *He was* ***caught in the act*** *of breaking into a car.* □ often passive.

catch on (to) [Vp, Vp.pr] (*informal*) see the significance of (sth); understand: *'He's not very quick at* ***catching on,*** *is he?'* ○ *My young man ... didn't* ***catch on to*** *what I might have meant.* PPLA ○ *She followed the conversation rather blankly for a while, then her expression changed. She was* ***catching on.***

catch on (with) [Vp, Vp.pr emph rel] (*informal*) become popular or fashionable (with sb). **S:** (new) idea, method, suggestion, fashion. **o:** the public; young people; customers; colleagues: *The President's idea of rapid-fire legislation has not* ***caught on*** *in Congress.* SC ○ *Aerobics has* ***caught on*** *in Russia faster than yoga, dieting or vegetarianism.* LFM

catch out 1 [Vn.p pass] show that (sb) is ignorant or doing sth wrong; and, often, do this in a mean-minded way: *The little girl saw she had been* ***caught out.*** *She looked as if she were going to cry; but then her face brightened again.* PW ○ *He wouldn't know a fraud if he saw one. I know, because I've* ***caught him out.*** ASA ○ *That was one of the consolations of living alone; there was no-one to* ***catch*** *you* ***out*** *being childish.* FL

2 [Vn ⇆ p pass] (*cricket*) dismiss (a batsman) by catching the ball after he has touched it with his bat and before it touches the ground: *Three of the batsmen were* ***caught out*** *by the wicket-keeper* (= caught behind the wicket).

catch up 1 [Vn ⇆ p pass] gather (sth/sb) to oneself hastily: *The woman* ***caught up*** *her basket and ran out of the shop before anyone could stop her.* ○ *Bill* ***caught*** *the child* ***up*** *in his arms just as she was about to dash into the road.*

2 [Vn ⇆ p pass] raise and fasten (sth) hanging free or loose. **O:** hem, skirt (of a dress); hair: *Her hair was* ***caught up*** *with a long pin.*

catch up (in) [Vn ⇆ p pass, Vn.p.pr pass] trap. **O:** hair; clothing. **o:** machine, machinery; wheel, cogwheel; (overhanging) branches, undergrowth: *The poor boy had* ***caught*** *his trousers* ***up in*** *the chain of his bicycle, and this caused the accident.* ○ *She disentangled the sleeve of her jumper, which had got* ***caught up in*** *a rose bush.* = entangle in/with.

caught up in 1 [pass (Vn.p.pr)] involved in (sth) usu involuntarily and sometimes against one's will. **o:** crowd, circle, set (of people); intrigue, plotting; war, revolution; (mad) whirl, round (of activity): *For a time my father, with a young wife, was* ***caught up in*** *a circle which included many famous names.* SD ○ *In her search, she gets* ***caught up in*** *a riot and is destroyed by a machine-gun.* BRN □ also used with *seem, get, become* and after a noun: *Am I talking to an outlaw* ***caught up in*** *some feud?* ⇨ catch up (in).

2 [pass (Vn.p.pr)] lost in, completely absorbed in (sth). **o:** speculation; day-dream, reverie: *When one is adolescent, one often gets* ***caught up in*** *one's thoughts and dreams.* HAHA □ also used with *appear* etc and after a noun.

catch up (on) 1 [Vp, Vp.pr pass] (make special efforts to) do (sth) which has been left undone or neglected. **o:** reading, studies; paperwork, correspondence; sorting, tidying, cleaning; lost sleep: *The secretary had to work in the lunch hour to* ***catch up on*** *her neglected filing.* WI ○ *I must stay in*

this weekend: I've so much exam marking to **catch up on**. ○ *He . . . hardly had time to* **catch up on** *outstanding work before going into hospital.* TSE
2 [Vp, Vp.pr pass] get up-to-date with (sth); become 'au fait' with (sth). **o:** the latest news; recent developments; the latest fashions; new thinking in sth: *I wanted a full account, from start to finish . . . there was so much to* **catch up on**. CED ○ *These are clothes that you can make from fabulous American patterns — but if you don't sew you can still* **catch up on** *new fashion pointers from across the Atlantic.* WI

catch up on [Vp.pr] (*informal*) arrive and begin to change the outlook or way of life of (sb); (of sth done in the past) begin to affect (sb) now. **S:** old age; rheumatism; marriage; (misspent) youth, (dubious) past: *Marriage has* **caught up on** *her, she explained after some hesitation and a little smile that made me think I ought to sympathize.* HAHA ○ *'I think his past is beginning to* **catch up on** *him.'*

catch up (with) [Vp, Vp.pr pass rel, Vn.p pass] draw level (with sb), reach the same stage (as sb), after lagging behind. **S:** runner; cyclist, driver; car; student, worker. **o** [Vp.pr], **O** [Vn.p]**:** pack, main body (of runners); (main) party, column; rest of the class : [Vp Vp.pr] *'You go on ahead; I'll* **catch up (with** *you) later* (or: [Vn.p] I'll **catch** *you* **up** *later).'* ○ [Vp.pr] *He had to work hard to* **catch up with** *the rest* (or: [Vn.p] **catch** *them* **up**). MRJ

catch up with 1 [Vp.pr pass] (*informal*) bring (sb) to justice after pursuing him for some time. **S:** the law, the police; the Inland Revenue; Customs and Excise. **o:** crook, terrorist; tax evader; drug smuggler: *The law eventually* **caught up with** *him and he is now serving five years for conspiracy.* SC
2 clear one's arrears of (work); get up-to-date with (one's work). **o:** paperwork, marking, correspondence: *Now, at last, there was time to* **catch up with** *her correspondence.* ○ *As for vacations, for most of us it is the only time we can* **catch up with** *necessary reading and actually write something.* IND

cater

cater for [Vpr pass rel] serve (the public) by providing refreshments; aim to satisfy (particular needs). **S:** hotel, public house; club, cinema, TV. **o:** class, type (of customer); teenager, married couple; need, requirement: *The management regrets that coach-parties cannot be* **catered for**. ○ *This play centre* **caters for** *children of all ages.* ○ *What was being offered was not particularly good and . . . many needs were not being* **catered for**. OBS ⇨ next entry

cater to [Vpr pass rel] aim to satisfy (a need or demand). **o:** sb's sick mind; depraved taste, base appetite; sb's whims: *Producers of pornographic material often claim that they are* **catering to** *a psychological need.* = pander to. ⇨ previous entry

cave

cave in 1 [Vp nom] collapse. **S:** roof, mine, dug-out: *The roof of the mine* **caved in** *as a result of the explosion.* ○ *This tunnel is liable to sudden* **cave-ins**. ○ *The* **caved-in** *part of the passage was immediately beneath a row of houses.* □ the adj form is unusual in this [Vp] pattern.
2 [Vp nom] (*informal*) yield, collapse morally, under some kind of pressure. **S:** prisoner, suspect: *At the end of a month during which no bank came to his rescue Ronnie Nettlecote* **caved in** *and agreed to call in the receiver* (an official who handles the property of bankrupts). FAE ○ *We'd expected a bit of firm resistance from the employers, not a complete* **cave-in** *to the workers' demands.*

centre

centre in/on/upon [Vpr emph rel, Vn.pr pass emph rel] have (sth) as its focal point or chief concern. **S** [Vpr], **O** [Vn.pr]**:** study, research; survey; attention, interest. **o:** field, area; problem; finding a solution, ending the crisis: *For some time all my interests have* **centred in** *the people's methods of agriculture.* NDN ○ *His current work is* **centred upon** *the activity of small rodents.* ○ *Interest in linguistics among philosophers has* **centred on** *defining the limits of language.* DL ⇨ focus (on).

centre on/round [Vpr emph rel, Vn.pr pass emph rel] have or fix (sth) as its centre. **S** [Vpr], **O** [Vn.pr]**:** movement, activity; commerce, industry. **o:** (key) figure, personality; port, capital city: *The town's activities were* **centred on** *the main square.* F ○ *She became involved in the whirlpool of activity which* **centred round** *Joe.* AITC ○ *To give access to markets, the new industries had been* **centred on** *a motorway junction.* □ some purists object to the use of round with the v centre. = revolve about/around.

chain

chain up [Vn ⇆ p pass adj] restrain the movement of (sth/sb) by means of a chain, or chains. **O:** dog, hound, dangerous animal; prisoner, captive: *That dog ought to be* **chained up**; *it's dangerous.*

chalk

chalk out [Vn ⇆ p pass adj] draw the outline of (sth) in chalk. **O:** outline, plan; limit, edge; ring, square: *Goalposts were roughly* **chalked out** *on the playground wall.* ○ *To explain his design to the visitors, the architect* **chalked out** *a simple plan on the blackboard.*

chalk up 1 [Vn ⇆ p pass] (*informal*) add (sth) to the/one's record or score. **O:** victory, achievement, success, record: *In the first six months of this year the hotel-owner will have* **chalked up**, *round the world, thirteen opening ceremonies.* OBS ○ *A group of Britons have* **chalked up** *a British record by descending nearly 4 000 feet down a cave in France.* T
2 [Vn ⇆ p pass] write (sth) on a board or slate; specifically, give credit to a customer in a bar for drinks consumed: *'I see your name is* **chalked up** *on the messages board.' 'Oh, is it? Thanks very much for telling me.'* ○ *'Two double whiskies, and oh, would you* **chalk** *it* **up**, *please?'*

chance

chance on/upon [Vpr pass] meet (sb) or find (sth) by chance. **o:** old friend, acquaintance; process, method; portrait, book: *Freud* **chanced upon** *this technique when . . . one of his patients reproved him for interrupting her train of thought.* F = happen on/upon.

change

change down [Vp nom] (in driving a car) move to a lower gear: *I didn't* ***change down*** *quickly enough, and stalled the motor.* CON ○ *'That was rather an abrupt* ***change-down****. You nearly threw me through the windscreen!'* ↔ change up.

change (from) (into) [Vpr rel, Vn.pr pass rel] (of the constitution, character etc of sb/sth) alter; transform (the constitution, character etc of sb/sth). **S** [Vpr], **O** [Vn.pr]**:** pumpkin; white rabbit; patient, invalid. **S** [Vn.pr]**:** magician; drugs, alcohol; disease: *As the fairy godmother waved her wand, the mice* ***changed into*** *four splendid white horses.* ○ *Sickness had* ***changed*** *him* ***into*** *a miserable, demanding old man.* ○ *He'd suddenly* ***changed from*** *a well-behaved child* ***into*** *a loutish adolescent.* = turn into 2.

change (into) 1 [Vn.pr pass rel] break (a larger unit of money) into (smaller ones); give for the currency of one country the equivalent currency of another. **O:** pound; dollar; francs; lire. **o:** new pence; dimes, quarters; sterling; Deutschmarks: *'Could you* ***change*** *this fifty pence piece* ***into*** *five tens for me, please?'* ○ *You can* ***change*** *your sterling* ***into*** *the local currency at the airport.*

2 [Vpr rel] put on (a garment/garments) having removed another/others. **o:** (clean, fresh) clothes; (smart) suit; (casual, old) sweater: *It took him just five minutes to* ***change*** *out of one suit* ***into*** *another.* ○ *'Just a minute, I'll* ***change into*** *something smarter.'* ⇨ next entry

change (out of) [Vpr rel] remove (a garment/garments) so as to put on another/others. **o:** (old, dirty) clothes; overalls; (smart) suit: *He stamped upstairs to* ***change out of*** *his clammy trousers.* AT ○ *'Let's go for a walk.' 'All right; I'll just* ***change out of*** *these old things.'* LBA ⇨ previous entry

change over (from) (to) [Vp nom, Vp.pr emph rel] abandon (one thing) and adopt (sth new or different). **o:** (**from**) one system, diet, regime, scheme; (**to**) another, a new one: *When Britain adopted the decimal system for its money, it* ***changed over*** *relatively smoothly* (or: *the* ***change-over*** *was relatively smooth*). ○ *He used to drink tea at breakfast, but he's* ***changed over to*** *coffee.* ○ *My wife wants to* ***change over from*** *gas* ***to*** *electricity for her cooking; she says it's cleaner.* ○ *He decided against the Church, became a law student, but finally* ***changed over to*** *medicine.* SNP = go over to 2, switch over (to) 2, move over (from) (to).

change over/round 1 [Vp] (of two people) exchange places, positions or roles: *'I think I'd better drive the car into Birmingham, so if you'll stop at the next parking-place, we'll* ***change over****.'* ○ *'Perhaps you and Brown had better* ***change round****: you need more experience of office routine.'* = change places (with), swap over/round.

2 [Vp nom] (*sport*) (of opponents) change positions, change ends. **S:** players, teams, competitors, bowlers: *After a certain number of points, the players* ***changed round*** *so that neither could benefit unduly from the wind or the position of the sun.* ○ *After the* ***change-over*** *at half time, the visiting team had the benefit of the wind and scored three goals in quick succession.*

change round (from) (to) [Vp, Vp.pr] (of the direction of the wind) alter: *The wind suddenly* ***changed round from*** *westerly* ***to*** *northerly, bringing with it the threat of snow.*

change up [Vp nom] (in driving a car) move to a higher gear: *'I grind the gears whenever I* ***change up*** *from second to third. Is there something wrong with the clutch?'* ○ (a driving instructor is speaking) *'Now a nice, smooth* ***change-up*** *to third. That's fine. Now just take it quietly along this straight bit of road.'* ⇨ change down.

change places (with) [Vn.pr emph rel] (of two people or groups etc) make reciprocal changes in seats, places, positions: *'Let me* ***change places with*** *you* (or: *Let's* ***change places***) *so that you can be nearer the fire—I can see you're very cold!'* ○ *'I wouldn't* ***change places with*** *Joe for all the tea in China: working on a sewage farm must be hellish!'* = change over/round 1, swap over/round.

charge

charge (at) [Vpr pass emph rel] make a headlong attack (towards). **S:** bull, goat, horse; tank; footballer. **o:** door, barrier, fence; adversary; goalkeeper, defender: *He* ***charged at*** *me with his head down and both fists flying.*

charge (for) [Vpr pass, Vn.pr pass] ask (sth) in payment (for sth). **O:** (a heavy) price, fee; ten pounds; ten per cent commission. **o:** admission, seat; treatment, service; cleaning, repairing: *'How much do they* ***charge for*** *washing a car?'* ○ *The conductor tried to* ***charge*** *me 40p* ***for*** *a 30p journey.* □ often with an indirect object as in the second example.

charge (up) to [Vn.pr pass emph rel, Vn.p.pr pass] put (sth) on (sb's account) for later payment. **O:** goods, purchases; clothing, durables. **o:** him etc; his etc account: *'Please* ***charge*** *these goods* ***to*** *my husband's account.'* ○ *'Why were the expenses of the reception* ***charged up to*** *me?'* = debit to.

charge (with) 1 [Vn.pr pass emph rel] (*legal*) allege that (sb) is guilty (of sth). **o:** crime, misdemeanour; murder, theft, unlawful possession; being an accessory after the fact: *The police* ***charged*** *him* ***with*** *driving a car while under the influence of alcohol.* ○ *The offence* ***with*** *which she is* ***charged*** *carries a heavy penalty.* = accuse (of).

2 [Vn.pr pass emph rel] make (sth) heavy (with sth). **O:** atmosphere, air; situation; theatre. **o:** excitement, fear; tension, expectation: *His entry on stage had once again* ***charged*** *the scene* ***with*** *dramatic tension.* ○ *The atmosphere was tense and* ***charged with*** *fear.* ○ *It was a stucco wall, blank but unforgettably beautiful, empty but* ***charged with*** *all the meaning and the mystery of existence.* DOP □ usu passive.

charge with [Vn.pr pass rel] (*formal*) give or assign a duty (to sb). **o:** task, job; duty, responsibility: *A young officer was* ***charged with*** *the task of taking 200 prisoners to the rear.* □ usu passive.

chase

chase around/round (after) [Vp, Vp.pr] (*informal*) spend one's time and energy with or in pursuit of (the opposite sex). **o:** girls, women, rich widows; eligible men, good-looking drifters: *If he didn't spend so much of his time* ***chasing around after*** *girls he might have some chance of getting through his finals.* = run around.

chase up [Vn ⇆ p pass] (*informal*) make an effort to find (sth) quickly. **O:** information, latest figures, title of the book: *While Jane was setting out the* *main events of the story, Peter was* **chasing up** *details of a murder that had been committed in the village fifty years before.* = hunt up (in).

chat

chat up [Vn ⇆ p pass] (*informal*) talk to (sb) in such a way as to gain his/her confidence, esp with the aim of having a sexual relationship or of making a sale: *'Who was that girl I saw you* **chatting up** *in the bar last night?'* ○ *Please* **chat up** *your book-selling and publishing acquaintances and help sell some advertising space.* CL ○ *A young psychiatrist ... is attempting to treat his patients by* **chatting** *them* **up**, *by getting them to 'relate' to one another.* NS

chatter

chatter away [Vp] keep talking in an idle or foolish way: *I watched them* **chattering away** *as they shared a cigarette. There was nothing much on earth ... that could stop their happiness.* ARG

cheat

cheat of [Vn.pr pass emph rel] prevent (sb) from enjoying (sth). **S:** (cruel) Fate, circumstances; war, (economic) slump. **o:** achievement (of sth), success; fortune, wealth: *The cat was* **cheated of** *its prey by the warning cries of other birds.* ○ *It was the lack of a proper education,* **of** *which he had been* **cheated** *by family poverty, which he felt most keenly.*

cheat out of [Vn.pr pass rel] prevent (sb) from having (sth) by unfair or illegal means. **S:** (business) partner, associate; (dishonest) trader; relations. **o:** rights, privileges; share, portion; legacy: *The children were* **cheated out of** *their inheritance by a dishonest lawyer.* ○ *'Be careful! He'll* **cheat** *you* **out of** *your entitlement if he possibly can.'*

check

check in/into [Vp nom, Vpr rel] sign the register on arriving (at a hotel etc); report one's arrival (at an airport etc). **S:** guest, visitor: *'What time did they* **check in**?' ○ *The* **check-in** *time was fast approaching and there was no sign of him.* TVT ○ *Having got safely through the* **check-in**, *they began to feel more relaxed.* ○ *They had an accident on the road and didn't* **check into** *their hotel until after midnight.* ↔ check out/out of.

check off [Vn ⇆ p pass adj] mark (items on a list) as correct or as having been dealt with. **S:** dispatch clerk; storeman; receptionist. **O:** item, entry; spare part, tool, component; name, guest: *Please* **check off** *these parcels before they are dispatched.* = tick off 1.

check on [Vpr pass] make sure of (sth); verify. **o:** presence, absence; number, tally, score; whether/if sb is present etc: *She wanted to find out whether the children had their coats or not; she looked in the cloakroom to* **check on** *that.*

check out [Vn ⇆ p pass] make a systematic inspection of (sth); make sure that (sb) is honest, reliable etc. **O:** instruments, control systems; tyre-pressures; place; house; associate, friend: *When all the instruments had been* **checked out** *according to the established routine, the pilot signalled that he was ready for take-off.* ○ *We'd better* **check** *the whole place* **out** *in case it's been bugged.* □ note the [Vp] pattern in: *He had the address she had given him but this address did not* **check out**.

check out/out of [Vp nom, Vpr] go through the formalities, such as paying a bill, before leaving (a place). **S:** guest, visitor. **o:** hotel, self-service store, supermarket: *'Has Mr Jones left yet?' 'Yes, he* **checked out** *five minutes ago.'* ○ *We reached the* **check-out** *(counter), then discovered we hadn't got enough money for all the things we'd collected from the shelves.* ↔ check in/into.

check over [Vn ⇆ p nom pass adj] examine (sth) to find out if it is correct or working properly. **O:** bill, statement; list, page; car, engine: *The secretary always* **checked over** *the letters before putting them on the director's desk.* ○ **Check** *the manuscript* **over** *carefully before passing it to the typist.* ○ *'She* (the car)*'s missing a bit* (ie the engine's not running smoothly). *Would you just give her a* **check-over**?' BBCTV = go over 1.

check through [Vpr pass, Vn.p nom pass] ensure that the objects that are supposed to be present are in fact present; read, and look for errors in, written or printed matter: *'Please* **check through** *the laundry* (or: *give the laundry a* **check-through**) *and then put it away.'* ○ [Vn.p] 'Have you **checked** *these proofs* **through** (or: [Vpr] Have you **checked through** *these proofs*)?' ○ *'This account is full of mistakes! Wasn't it ever* **checked through**?'

check-up [nom (Vp)] medical examination (usu of sb who now feels anxious about his health): *You'd better go to the doctor for a* **check-up**; *that cough sounds serious to me.* ○ *I got a thorough medical* **check-up** *before going abroad.*

check up (on) [Vp, Vp.pr pass adj] investigate the behaviour, background etc of (sb); test the truth or soundness of (sth). **o:** him etc; story, account; movements; trustworthiness, reliability; the situation: *'You've decided not to go back to your country?' 'You've been* **checking up**?' QA ○ *An experiment was carried out to* **check up on** *the reliability of certain criteria.*

cheer

cheer on [Vn ⇆ p pass] encourage (sb) to further efforts by cheering, clapping etc. **O:** competitor; team: *The crowd* **cheered** *the runners* **on** *as they entered the last lap.*

cheer up 1 [Vp] become happier, more cheerful: *When she heard that her mother was out of danger she immediately* **cheered up**. ○ *'You must* **cheer up**, *Mrs Gaye. You'll soon be walking again.'* DC ○ (wryly humorous) *'***Cheer up**! *The worst is yet to come!'*

2 [Vn ⇆ p pass] raise the spirits of (sb); make (sb) more cheerful. **O:** patient, invalid. **A:** no end, enormously: *They sent the invalid a 'Get Well' card to* **cheer** *him* **up**. WI ○ *He longed for Fitzgerald to visit Paris and* **cheer** *him* **up**. TU ○ *I'm going to visit my father; he needs* **cheering up** (or: *to be* **cheered up**).

cheese

cheesed off [pass adj (Vn.p)] (*slang*) heartily sick or tired of sth: *'I get browned off,' he muttered. 'Voices, voices, always voices. I get* **cheesed off**.' HAHA = browned off.

chew

chew on [Vpr pass] (*informal*) consider (sth) slowly and carefully. **o:** offer, proposal, suggestion: *'I'll give you till tomorrow to* **chew on** *my offer; then you can take it or leave it.'* ⇨ next entry

chew over [Vn ⇆ p pass] (*informal*) consider (sth) slowly and carefully. **O:** offer, proposal, suggestion: *'You've had long enough to* ***chew*** *the matter* ***over****; I want my answer now.'* ⇨ previous entry

chicken

chicken out/out of [Vp, Vp.pr] (*informal*) lose one's courage (in the face of an enemy, or in a dangerous situation): *We have met men of fame and substance who freely confessed that a summons to the presence* (of a former head of the BBC) *made them quail and* ***chicken out****.* SC ○ *'You've come so far; you're not thinking of* ***chickening out of*** *the job now, are you?'*

chime

chime in (with) [Vp, Vp.pr] (*informal*) contribute (sth) to a conversation, interrupt it (with some remark): *'We* ***chimed in*** *all right, ... about the terrible injustice he was doing himself.'* OD ○ *The rest of us* ***chimed in with*** *short accounts ... of various individual ways we had developed of annoying the poor old chap.* CON

chime in with [Vp.pr] (*informal*) fit or suit (sth). **o:** mood, feelings, wishes, desires hopes, plans: *What he had said* ***chimed in*** *perfectly* ***with*** *Isabel's own immediate reaction; she exclaimed: 'Well, I am glad!'* PW

chip

chip in (with) 1 [Vp, Vp.pr] (*informal*) interrupt (a conversation); comment: *I then* ***chipped in*** *and said that in the Army whenever the Pay Code was mentioned everyone began to curse.* MFM ○ *'Who asked* you *to* ***chip in with*** *your opinion?'*

2 [Vp, Vp.pr] (*informal*) contribute (sth). **o:** loan, offer (of money): *He insisted on paying the bill; he would not dream of having them* ***chip in****.* ○ *'When Dad offered to* ***chip in with*** *$500 towards our holiday, we realized that it might just be possible to buy an old car and do a tour of Europe.'*

chivvy

chivvy along [Vn.p pass] (*dated, informal*) urge (sb), often in an irritating or officious manner, to do sth, esp work, and usu to complete it by a certain time: *The men were getting tired of being* ***chivvied along*** *by the corporal, and though they made a show of busy activity, progress in fact became slower and slower.* ⇨ jolly along.

choke

choke back [Vn ⇆ p pass] suppress or restrain (sth). **O:** tears, sobs; anger, fury: *When she saw the pitiful condition of the children, she could barely* ***choke back*** *her tears.*

choke off 1 [Vn.p pass] (*dated*) interrupt (sb) rather rudely or abruptly; reprimand (sb) severely: *Gerald felt a revulsion from the whole subject and hoped he would hear no more about it; he decided that if Vin phoned he would* ***choke*** *him* ***off****.* ASA ○ *He got a terrible* ***choking off*** *from his father for borrowing the car without permission.* = tell off (for).

2 [Vn ⇆ p pass adj] (*informal*) stop (sth) by firm, abrupt action. **O:** supply, flow; spending, expenditure; consumer credit: *The Government will almost certainly come to* ***choke off*** *consumer spending and raise interest rates.* OBS

choke the life out of [Vn.pr] kill (sb) by strangling; (*figurative*) force (sb) to stop trading or operating: *He grasped her by the throat and started to* ***choke the life out of*** *her.* ○ *The big supermarkets have practically* ***choked the life out of*** *the small grocer.*

choke up [Vn ⇆ p pass adj] fill (sth) so that nothing can pass through. **S:** mud, dirt; leaves, sticks; rubbish. **O:** drain, pipe, grid: *The drains are all* ***choked up*** *with leaves.*

chop

chop about [Vp] (*informal*) keep changing from one thing to another or from one direction to another: *'First you say you want to be a doctor; then you're going to be a teacher; then you think you'll join the Army; I wish you wouldn't* ***chop about*** *so much.'* □ the expression chop and change means much the same.

chop down [Vn ⇆ p pass adj] bring (sth) to the ground by cutting at the base. **O:** tree, bush; post, pole: *I'm going to* ***chop down*** *some of the old apple trees; they've almost stopped producing fruit.* = hack down, hew down.

chop off [Vn ⇆ p pass] remove (sth) by cutting, usu with an axe. **O:** branch, bough; leg, arm: *These branches are overhanging the road; we'd better* ***chop*** *them* ***off****.* ○ *In some countries, the hands of a thief are* ***chopped off****.* = hack off.

chop up [Vn ⇆ p pass adj] cut (sth) into small pieces, usu with a heavy knife or axe. **O:** meat, fish; fruit; mint, parsley: *This furniture is so old and useless that you might as well* ***chop*** *it* ***up*** *for firewood.* ○ *You will need a few sprigs of* ***chopped-up*** *parsley for the sauce.*

chuck

chuck away 1 [Vn ⇆ p pass] (*informal*) get rid of (sth); discard. **O:** box, carton; bottle, can; ticket, stub: *I hate to see food* ***chucked away****!* ○ *'Don't* ***chuck*** *those papers* ***away****: I haven't finished reading them yet.'* = throw away 1.

2 [Vn ⇆ p pass] (*informal*) not use (sth) properly, fail to take advantage of (sth). **O:** fortune, cash; chances, opportunities: *There were plenty of people ready to help Paul* ***chuck*** *his money* ***away****, but few to stand by him when he ended up bankrupt.* ○ *'You're young, you're attractive, you're clever, you're healthy. Don't* ***chuck*** *it all* ***away****.''* GA = throw away 2.

chuck away on [Vn.p.pr] (*informal*) waste (sth/oneself) in (foolish ventures), on (undeserving people etc). **O:** oneself, one's life: *She's a fool to* ***chuck*** *herself* ***away on*** *a smooth-talking social climber like George.* = throw away on .

chuck in 1 [Vn ⇆ p pass] (*informal*) stop doing (sth); leave, abandon. **O:** job, course (of study): *I hate this night work: I'm thinking of* ***chucking*** *it* ***in****.* = jack in, pack in 1.

2 [Vn ⇆ p pass] (*informal*) include (sth) as a free or unexpected extra feature. **O:** carpets, curtains; (cost of) cleaning, decorating, fitting (sth): *For a few pounds more, we'll* ***chuck in*** *a new set of seatcovers for the car.* ○ *A BA in Economics at 21, now front-runner* (leading striker) *for Newcastle United ... with an Under-23 cap and an MA* ***chucked in****.* OBS = throw in 1.

chuck out/out of [Vn ⇆ p pass, Vn.pr pass] (*informal*) remove (sb) forcibly, force (sb) to leave. **o:** bar, club, pub; college, university; association: *It would not be Christian charity to* ***chuck*** *you* ***out*** *now, which is what you deserve.* PPLA ○ *He's been*

chucked out of *every bar and club in town.* □ note chucker-out: *When he asked for a job at the night-club, the manager said: 'Well, you're a big strong chap, and it just happens that we need a **chucker-out**.'* HD = throw out/out of.

chuck up [Vn ⇆ p pass] (*informal*) abandon, leave (sth). **O:** one's job, post, position; everything: *John just **chucked up** his job at the factory and said he intended never to work again.* = throw up 1, give up 2, turn in 5.

chug

chug across, along, away etc [Vp, Vpr] move across etc slowly, accompanied by a deep note from the engine. **S:** (old) ship, boat; steamer, tug, tramp(-steamer): *She **chugged away** from Europe on a steamer bound for the Caribbean.* BV ○ *So we **chugged on**, through the Suez Canal, where I noticed on the left bank a train arriving at a station.* GS ○ *Connie Fox would be **chugging up** one of their driveways in his disgraceful car.* FA

chum

chum up (with) [Vp, Vp.pr] (*informal*) become friends; become the friend of (sb): *George wondered whether he would enjoy a holiday in a small fishing village; but he soon **chummed up with** the fishermen's sons* (or: *he and the fishermen's sons soon **chummed up***) *and they all had a wonderful time.* = pal up (with).

churn

churn out [Vn ⇆ p pass adj] (*informal*) produce (sth) regularly and in large quantities (usu with the implication that quality is poor). **O:** book; news, information; power; car, refrigerator, newspaper: *Some pulp writers **churn out** two or three thousand words a day.* ○ *They've got factories working round the clock, **churning out** cheap cloth for the mass market.* = pump out.

churn up [Vn ⇆ p pass adj] disturb or move (sth) violently. **O:** water, slush; mud, sand: *The ship's propellers **churned up** the water as it increased speed.* ○ *The wheels **churned up** the mud in the road as the driver tried desperately to extricate his car.* ○ *The **churned-up** mud made the country lanes impassable.*

circle

circle (round) (over) [Vp, Vpr, Vp.pr] fly (sb/sth) in circles over. **S:** plane, helicopter, glider; vulture, bird : [Vpr] *A reconnaissance plane **circled over** the enemy's position, reporting their strength and dispositions to our troops on the ground.* ○ [Vp, Vp.pr] *We knew from the number of vultures **circling round** (**over** us) that some wretched creature was nearing its end below.*

claim

claim back (from) [Vp pass, Vp.pr pass rel] ask for the return of (sth), or take (sth), to which one is or feels entitled. **O:** tax; the cost of the ticket; one's camera. **o:** the Inland Revenue; British Rail; the lost property office: *I must remember to **claim back** my expenses from the conference organizers.* ○ *Much distress was caused to the foster parents when, after six years, Susan's natural mother **claimed** her **back**.* ○ *There's quite a bit of excess tax to **claim back**.*

clam

clam up [Vp] (*informal*) become totally uncommunicative, through suspicion, fear, distrust etc. **S:** suspect, witness; patient: *When Inspector Smart began to question the arrested man's girlfriend about his whereabouts at eight o'clock the previous evening, she immediately **clammed up** and refused to say anything.* ○ *I did not dare to suggest that Paul should see a doctor — still less a psychiatrist — because from previous experience I knew that he would **clam up** for a month if I did.*

clamp

clamp down (on) [Vp nom, Vp.pr pass rel] (*informal*) use one's authority against (sb), or to suppress or prevent (sth). **S:** authorities; police, (law) court, magistrate; government; tax authorities; moral guardians (of society): *There has been much tax evasion through expense accounts, but the Government is going to **clamp down*** (or: *there's going to be a Government **clamp-down***). ○ *The police had a bit of a **clamp-down**.* ○ *This boredom could be the result of **clamping down on** creative living.* ESS

clap

clap in/into [Vn.pr pass] put (sb) swiftly in/into jail etc, often without trial. **o:** jail, prison, solitary confinement, irons: *Trouble-makers could be **clapped in** prison and kept for several months without trial.* ○ *In the old days it was commonplace for a sailor to be **clapped into** irons for some minor offence.*

clap on [Vn ⇆ p pass, Vn.pr pass] put (sth) on hastily. **O:** hat, cap; hand. **o:** head; arm; handle, knob: *He **clapped** his hat **on** and strode angrily from the room.* ○ *A detective **clapped** handcuffs **on** the man before he could escape.*

not (ever) clap eyes on [Vn.pr] (*informal*) not see (sb/sth): *'I have**n't clapped eyes on** Bill for months. What's happened to him?'* ○ *'How can I describe her? I'd **never clapped eyes on** her till five minutes ago.'* □ usu in present and past perfect tenses.

clap on/onto [Vn ⇆ p pass, Vn.pr pass] (*informal*) add (sth) to the price etc of (sth), esp in an unwelcome way. **S:** Chancellor, Treasury, County Council. **O:** tax, another five per cent, an extra ten pence; standstill order; preservation order. **o:** petrol, cigarettes; the rates; the building of any more universities; the oak tree in my garden: *We had just decided to fly to the Canary Islands for a holiday when the airlines **clapped** twenty-five per cent **on*** (or: ***onto***) *the fare.* ○ *I can't make any structural alterations to my house because it was built in the nineteenth century and a preservation order has been **clapped on** it.* = slap on/onto 2.

clapped out [pass adj (Vn.p)] (*informal*) completely worn out and apparently beyond recovery or repair. **S:** he etc; car, lorry, bus; camera, radio: *Of course, they could drag Smithers out of retirement to make the speech of welcome, but he's pretty **clapped out**, poor old boy!* ○ *A group of determined schoolchildren managed to get a **clapped-out** minibus back into working order.* □ also used with *appear* etc.

clash

clash (with) 1 [Vpr emph rel] join in combat or vigorous argument (with sb). **S:** troops, police; Prime Minister. **o:** demonstrators; Leader of the Opposition: *Backbenchers* ***clashed with*** *Government spokesmen in the debate on water privatization.*
2 [Vpr rel] not match or harmonize (with sth) because of colour, design, etc. **S/o:** colour, shade; purple, pink; blouse, skirt (because of their colour): *The red of her scarf* ***clashes with*** *the purple of her hat.* ○ *The cushion covers* ***clashed*** *violently* ***with*** *the carpet* (or: *The covers and the carpet* ***clashed*** *violently*).
3 [Vpr emph rel] occur at the same time as (sth else) thus causing inconvenience. **S:** time, hour; meeting, ceremony, party. **o:** that set aside, arranged (for sth else); his, ours, one previously arranged: *'You can't arrange a meeting for Friday: it would* ***clash with*** *my afternoon's golf!'* ○ *'Make sure his appointment doesn't* ***clash with*** *mine* (or: *our appointments don't* ***clash***).' ↔ fit in with.

class

class (with) [Vn.pr pass emph rel] put (sth/sb) in the same class or category (as sth/sb). **S:** registrar, examiner, librarian. **O:** trade, occupation; candidate, performer; document, journal. **o:** (similar) type, person: *I object to being* ***classed with*** *unskilled labourers; I'm a craftsman.* ○ *We are wrong to judge his work by the standards of people* ***with*** *whom he should never have been* ***classed*** *in the first place.*

claw

claw back 1 [Vn ⇆ p nom pass] (*finance*) recover, by taxation, government assistance paid to individuals who are not considered to need that assistance (this is done when those concerned cannot easily be identified *before* the payment is made); charge tax on excess income etc some time after it has been earned. **O:** benefit, allowance; tax: *Back in 1968 the Government increased the family allowance but it was intended that only those with lower incomes should benefit. As family allowances are paid to everyone (with children) the tax system was used to recover this increase from those paying tax at the standard rate. This '****claw-back****', as it is unattractively called, has been achieved by reducing personal allowances by £42 for each allowance received.* OBS ○ *Excess profits are periodically reviewed and '****clawed back****'. About 40 million pounds was reclaimed by the DHSS* (a government department) *when this was last reviewed.* T
2 [Vn ⇆ p nom pass] recover (a position) gradually and with great effort. **O:** ownership, control, advantage: *The Bank is engaged in the task of* ***clawing back*** *control of one of Scotland's banks from the English.*

clean

clean down [Vn ⇆ p pass adj] clean (sth) thoroughly, from top to bottom. **O:** house, place; door, wall: *We'll have to spend some time on* ***cleaning*** *the walls* ***down*** *before we start painting.*
clean out [Vn ⇆ p nom pass] clean (sth), usu by carrying or brushing dirt away. **O:** farmyard, cowshed, barn; wash-house, latrine: *The stables are in a filthy condition. When* ***were*** *they last* ***cleaned out****?* ○ *The whole place needs a good* ***clean-out*** (or: ***cleaning-out***). = do out 1.
clean out/out of [Vn.p pass, Vn.pr pass] (*informal*) take from (sb) all his money or stock. **O:** tradesman, shopkeeper. **o:** beer, spirits, tobacco; change, cash: *I haven't a penny left; buying all those books has completely* ***cleaned*** *me* ***out****.* ○ *The tobacconist was* ***cleaned out of*** *cigarettes by people who expected the price to go up.*
clean up 1 [Vp nom Vn ⇆ p nom pass] remove dirt, etc; make (a place) clean. **O:** rubbish, debris; room; work-bench, desk : [Vp] *Now that the party's over, shall we* ***clean up*** (or: *have a* ***clean-up****)?* ○ [Vn.p] *I wish you'd* ***clean up*** *your mess after you've been repairing your bicycle.* ○ [Vn.p] *I think we might give the room a bit of a* ***clean-up****.* □ one cleans up *a mess* or *a place*. ⇨ clear up 1.
2 [Vn ⇆ p nom pass] (*informal*) get rid of (sth); suppress; make (a place) free of vice etc; improve. **S:** government, city council; vice squad. **O:** corruption, vice; racket, drug traffic; town, back streets; reputation: *It's time that the police took some effective action to* ***clean up*** *this town.* ○ *There's been quite a* ***clean-up*** *around the docks: you hardly ever see a prostitute there now.* ○ *I want to see the image of our supporters* ***cleaned up*** *so we can be proud of them.* OXST
3 [Vn ⇆ p pass] (*military*) suppress an enemy, usu small groups still resisting after a major advance. **O:** nest, outpost, pocket of resistance; rearguard: *The Battle of Normandy ended on the 19th August: it was on this day that we finally* ***cleaned up*** *the remnants of the enemy trapped in the 'pocket' east of Mortain.* MFM = mop up 3.
4 [Vp, Vp.n pass] (*informal*) make money. **O:** a (small) fortune, a packet, a (cool) thousand: *Don't just stand idly by while more enterprising people* ***clean up****.* ○ *His invention was immediately successful, and in less than a year he'd* ***cleaned up*** *ten thousand pounds.* ○ *Many a fortune has been* ***cleaned up*** *by con men* (= confidence tricksters) *working on the greed and gullibility of others.*
clean (oneself) up [Vp nom Vn.p pass] (*informal*) get washed, and possibly change into cleaner clothes: *'I'm just going home to* ***clean up*** (or: *to have a* ***clean-up****). I'll meet you in an hour outside the post-office.'* ○ *'Just give me five minutes to* ***clean myself up****; I'm covered in oil.'* □ only the passive with *get* is possible: *How long will you take to get (yourselves)* ***cleaned up****?*

clear

clear away [Vp, Vn ⇆ p pass] remove (objects) in order to leave a clear space. **O:** leaves; debris; dishes, tea things: *'I'll* ***clear*** *these dishes* ***away****; then we'll be able to work at the table.'* ○ *Other people sang, and then we* ***cleared away*** *the furniture and had some dancing.* BLCH
clear (of) [Vn.pr pass emph rel] declare (sb) to be free (from sth). **O:** oneself; the accused (man); the prisoner. **o:** guilt, suspicion, responsibility, the charge: *The signalman was* ***cleared of*** *all responsibility for the collision.* ○ *The accusations you are making relate to charges* ***of*** *which my client has already been* ***cleared****.* = absolve from.
clear one's mind of [Vn.pr pass emph rel] dismiss

(sth) from one's mind. **o:** (all, any) prejudice; thought of, desire for, wish for: *The jury were told that in considering their verdict they must* **clear their minds of** *all feelings of repugnance for the behaviour of the accused during the trial.*

clear off 1 [Vp] (*informal*) run away: *When the man saw the police car, he* **cleared off** *as fast as his legs could carry him.* ○ *'You've got no right to be here.* **Clear off!***'*

2 [Vn ⇆ p pass] complete payment for (sth). **O:** debts, mortgage (on a house); remaining payments, arrears: *He had not yet* **cleared off** *the debts he had contracted at the time of his father's death.* CD = pay off 2.

clear out 1 [Vp] (*informal*) leave home; withdraw from a relationship: *'I'm fed up with you telling me what I can and can't do; I'm* **clearing out**. *Goodbye!'*

2 [Vn ⇆ p pass] remove (sth) from a place, thus leaving it clean and neat; remove sth from (a place) with this result. **O:** junk, rubbish; papers, boxes; cupboard, drawer; attic: *I went to my room to find that my mother had* **cleared out** *my toy cupboard.* AM

clear out/out of 1 [Vp, Vpr] (informal) leave quickly: *'If you've got any sense, you'll* **clear out** *before my father comes home. He'll be furious if he finds you here.'* ○ *'You'd better* **clear out of** *here before you cause any more trouble.'* HD

2 [Vn ⇆ p pass, Vn.pr pass] ⇨ clean out/out of.

clear up 1 [Vp nom, Vn ⇆ p pass] remove (rubbish etc), making things tidy or orderly. **O:** rubbish, mess; muddle: *'Aren't we going to* **clear up** (or: *have a* **clear-up**) *before we go out?'* ○ *At first she seemed to be* **clearing up** *after him* (ie removing things he had left about) *a lot.* SATS ○ *'We can't go until all the litter has been* **cleared up**.*'* □ one clears up a mess, *not* a place. ⇨ clean up 1.

2 [Vn ⇆ p pass] remove doubt about (sth); find the solution to (sth). **O:** point, matter; mystery; difficulty, misunderstanding: *So far no lunar magnetic field has been detected, but rocket experiments should be able to* **clear** *the matter* **up**. NS ○ *I decided to go and see him and get the point* **cleared up** *quickly, before trouble arose.* MFM

3 [Vp] become fine. **S:** the weather, it: *The weather was bad early on this morning but it* **cleared up** *before ten o'clock.*

clear (with) [Vn.pr pass emph rel] have (sth) inspected and approved by (sb). **O:** passport, papers, documents; goods, luggage, personal effects. **o:** authorities, police, (the) Customs, Security, Immigration: *'Have these cameras been* **cleared with** *Customs?'* ○ *You'd better get the visitors* **cleared with** *Security before you take them to the Director's office.*

climb

climb down 1 [Vp, Vpr] get down (from sth); descend: *Cats often find it easier to climb up a tree than to* **climb down**.

2 [Vp nom] admit a mistake; retract, withdraw: *Couldn't both sides of this unhappy struggle* **climb down** *a little? We will allow doctors sometimes to be wrong, if they will abdicate their omnipotent position.* NS ○ *Admit that you're wrong now and you will avoid an embarrassing* **climb-down** *later on.*

cling

cling to 1 [Vpr pass rel] keep a firm, desperate, hold on (sth); not release one's grip on (sth). **S:** shipwrecked sailor; mountaineer. **o:** raft, plank of wood; bush, projecting ledge: *Some of the survivors of the fire had climbed out of the building, and were* **clinging to** *the window ledges.*

2 [Vpr emph rel] be unwilling to abandon (sth); not relinquish. **o:** superstitious beliefs; outmoded customs; hopes, aspirations: . . . *the everyday world of ordinary common sense* **to** *which he* **clung** *obstinately.* RTH ○ *'She still* **clings to** *him in spite of all his infidelities—a sign of her own insecurity, I suppose.'*

clip

clip on/onto [Vn ⇆ p nom pass, Vn.pr pass emph rel] fasten (sth) with a clip (to sth). **O:** brooch, bangle, ear-ring; watch; microphone; paper, notice. **o:** arm, ear; lapel; board: *'Can you* **clip** *these ear-rings* **on** (or: *Do these ear-rings* **clip on**; or: *Are these ear-rings* **clip-ons**)*?'* ○ *He produced a board,* **onto** *which his secretary had* **clipped** *all the important documents.*

clock

clock in/out [Vp nom, Vn ⇆ p pass] record the time of one's arrival or departure (usu at a place of work): *Workers are expected to* **clock in** *at 8.30am.* ○ *They* **clocked** *the men* **out** *at five.* ○ *The* **clockings-in-and-out** *irritate the workforce, but they are necessary in the interests of fairness and efficiency.* ○ *'What is* **clock-in** *time* (or: **clocking-in** *time*) *at your office?'* □ clock-in and clock-out are only used attrib.

clock on/off [Vp nom, Vn ⇆ p pass] □ often used in place of. ⇨ clock in/out.

clock up (*informal*) cover (a distance); achieve or record (a figure). **O:** distance, 500 miles; figures, sales: *I* **clocked up** *over 150 thousand miles on my last car.* ○ *High street stores* **clocked up** *record sales in the week before Christmas.*

clog

clog up [Vn ⇆ p pass adj] fill (sth) in such a way as to prevent normal working. **S:** grease, dirt, oil, waste matter. **O:** works, machinery; pipes, drains, wheels; pores: *If you put too much grease into delicate machinery, it may* **clog up** *the works.* ○ *The outlet-pipe had become* **clogged up** *with kitchen waste.*

close

close about/around/round [Vpr] gradually surround (sb/sth). **S:** hunters, police; forest; darkness, fog. **o:** quarry; fugitives; explorers: *A police cordon had* **closed about** *them, making surrender inevitable.* ○ *The damp evening* **closed round** *her, numbing her responses.* MSAL

close down [Vp nom, Vn ⇆ p pass adj] (cause production or activity to) end or cease, permanently or for a time. **S** [Vp], **O** [Vn.p]**:** school; plant, factory; theatre; broadcasting. **S** [Vn.p]**:** governor; owner, management: *The factory had to* **close down** *through lack of orders.* ○ *Television* **closed down** *for the night just after eleven o'clock.* DBM ○ *We're faced with inevitable* **close-down** *because of the losses of the past three years.* ○ *A popular restaurant in the High* (Street) *was* **closed down** *for cooking its food in something described as horse oil.* SU = shut down.

close in [Vp] (of the hours of daylight as summer changes to autumn) grow shorter. **S:** the days, the evenings: ***The days** are **closing in** so that soon we shan't be able to play cricket in the evenings.* = draw in.

close in (on/upon) 1 [Vp, Vp.pr pass] move nearer to (sb), or around (sb), so as to attack or seize him. **S:** enemy; gunfire; pursuer. **o:** (defensive) position, outpost; fugitive: *The sound of mortar-fire seemed to be **closing in**.* QA ○ *Before we could establish a strong defensive position the enemy **closed in on** us.* ○ *The baying of a monster **closing in on** us in our isolation . . .* W
2 [Vp, Vp.pr pass] envelop (sb) in an unpleasant, threatening way. **S:** winter; night, darkness; jungle; city. **o:** traveller; stranger: *The night **closed in** again as the little oasis of light receded.* BM ○ *When winter **closed in on** us, with constant rain and appalling mud, I sent for a waterproof suit.* MFM

close off [Vn ⇆ p pass adj] place a barrier across (sth), thus preventing movement; stop (sth) from moving by putting up a barrier. **O:** street; approaches; trench; traffic; conversation: *Police have **closed off** all approaches to the university campus.* ○ *I would like to **close off** the dialogue by asking you one final question.* TBU = block off.

close up 1 [Vp] shut (temporarily). **S:** (a) flower; (a) petal: *These flowers **close up** at night.* □ close-up /ˈkləʊs ʌp/ is derived not from the verb close /kləʊz/ but from the adverb close /kləʊs/; thus: *Take a **close-up** (photograph) of Mary.*
2 [Vp, Vn ⇆ p pass] shut the doors etc of (a building), esp before leaving at night. **S:** trader, owner. **O:** shop, office, factory: *The Manager **closes up**; he is always the last to leave the store.* ○ *She **closes** the office **up** at five o'clock.* = shut up 1.
3 [Vp] (*military*) draw (nearer) together, usu in ranks. **S:** soldiers, troops: *The marching men had to **close up** to let the oncoming convoy go past.*

cloud

cloud over [Vp, Vn.p pass adj] (cause sth to) become covered with a thin film of moisture etc. **S** [Vp], **O** [Vn.p]**:** mirror, window; face, mind: *She opened her mouth and breathed heartily at the glass until it was **clouded over**.* SE = mist over.

one's face cloud over [Vp] lose (its) brightness; betray anxiety or worry: *When she heard the news of her friend's accident, **her face clouded over**.*

the sky cloud over [Vp] become covered with clouds: ***The sky clouded over** ominously.* PVOH ○ *Just as we were beginning to enjoy the sunshine, **the sky clouded over** and a cold wind began to blow.*

club

club together [Vp] make contributions of money so that the total sum can be used for a specific purpose. **S:** colleagues, friends, patients, neighbours, fellow-students: *All the members of the orchestra **clubbed together** to present a silver baton to their conductor on his sixtieth birthday.*

clue

clued up [pass adj (Vn.p)] (*informal*) well informed, knowledgeable (about sth): *She manages to keep **clued up** about all the new developments.* ○ *He's the most **clued-up** technician in the place.* □ also used with *appear* etc.

clump

clump across, along, away etc [Vp, Vpr] move with heavy, resounding steps across etc. **o:** kitchen floor, yard; corridor, bridge: (English country ladies) *They **clumped around** in tweeds and brogues, exercising Sealyhams* (their dogs). ○ *'I shall be in excellent comfort I do assure you,' and he turned and went **clumping down** the steps.* LA

cluster

cluster around/round [Vp, Vpr rel] surround (sb/sth) closely: *A surprising number of women, friends of hers, **clustered round** her.* MSAL ○ *We admired the roses **clustering round** the cottage door.*

clutch

clutch at a straw [Vpr] try to grasp some slight means of rescue or escape: *There was no secluded place that did not conceal some groups of broken people **clutching** at life like drowning men **at straws**.* LWK □ compare the proverb: *A drowning man will **clutch at a straw**.* = catch at a straw.

clutter

clutter up [Vn ⇆ p pass] occupy (space), giving a room, house etc an untidy appearance; (of information etc) exist plentifully but in a muddled way in (sb's mind). **S:** junk, bric-a-brac; china, silver; books; ill-digested facts. **O:** attic, study; head, mind: *Objects of every kind **cluttered up** the entrance hall, so that it was almost impossible to get in.* ○ *He said that . . . high security hospitals should not be **cluttered up** with* (medical) *cases of this sort.* OBS ○ *His head's **cluttered up** with all manner of useless information.*

coast

coast along [Vp] ride or drive without much effort; (in a car) drive without using the engine; (*figurative*) proceed in one's work, career etc, without much effort: *We **coasted along** on our bicycles with the wind behind us.* ○ *As the fuel-gauge was pointing to 'empty', he switched off the engine whenever he could and just **coasted along**.* ○ *She doesn't put in all that much effort: she's content just to **coast along**.*

cock

cock up 1 [Vn ⇆ p pass adj] raise (sth). **S:** animal; horse, dog. **O:** ears, leg: *The horse **cocked** its ears **up** several seconds before I could hear anything.* ○ *The dog **cocked** its leg **up*** (ie in order to urinate) *against the lamp-post.*
2 [Vn ⇆ p nom pass] (*informal*) spoil or ruin (sth). **S:** organizer, manager, agent. **O:** arrangements, planning; tour, holiday; ceremony: *Don't let him organize your trip; he completely **cocked up** ours* (or: *made a complete **cock-up** of ours*). ○ *Trust Smith to **cock** the whole thing **up**!* = mess up.

coil

coil around/round [Vn.pr pass emph rel] wind (sth) in a spiral around (sth). **O:** rope; wire, thread. **o:** capstan, bollard; bobbin, spool: *The wire is **coiled around** the cylinder, and then the current is turned on.* = wind around/round.

coil (itself) around/round [Vpr, Vn.pr pass emph rel] wind (itself) in a spiral around (sth). **S:** snake; rope, cable: *The constrictor **coils round** its prey and crushes the life out of it.* ○ *The rope slipped* *from my hands and* **coiled itself** (or: **got itself coiled**) **around** *the pulley.*

coil up [Vn ⇆ p pass adj] form (sth) into a coil. **O:** rope, hawser, cable: *The sailors* **coiled** *the ropes* **up** *neatly and left them on the deck.*

coil (oneself) up [Vp, Vn.p pass] form (itself) into a coil. **S:** snake, centipede: *The snake glided under a stone and* **coiled up** *there.*

colour

colour in [Vn ⇆ p pass adj] fill (sth) with colour. **O:** drawing, sketch; figure, shape: *We* **coloured in** *the elaborate ... patterns which she drew for us on our graph paper.* BRH

colour up [Vp] blush, go red in the face, as a result of shyness or feelings of guilt or embarrassment: *'You — what's your name?' called the angry headmistress. 'Me, Miss?' he said, startled, and beginning to* **colour up**. TT ○ *She* **coloured up** *at the very mention of the young man's name.*

comb

comb out [Vn ⇆ p pass] free (hair etc) of knots etc by combing; remove (knots etc) from hair, fibre etc in this way. **O:** hair; skein, hank; knot, tangle: *Josie hated having her hair* **combed out** *because her mother did it roughly, and hurt her.*

come

come aboard [Vp] board, come on board (esp a ship or plane). **S:** crew, passenger: *A relief crew* **came aboard** *at Beirut to fly the aircraft on to Singapore.* ⇨ go aboard, take aboard.

come about 1 [Vp] happen. **S:** the accident; death, defeat, disgrace, failure; success; it ... that she succeeded: *I'm not saying I'm useless, but machinery and modern techniques have* **come about** *to make me the odd man out.* ITAJ ○ *How does it* **come about** *that a person who is suffering from some profound misfortune ... nevertheless finds once more a joy in life?* CF ○ *Thus it* **came about** *that, one bright May morning, I swallowed four-tenths of a gramme of mescalin.* DOP □ often used with *how does/did it ...?*. ⇨ bring about 1.

2 [Vp] (*nautical*) change direction of movement. **S:** sailing-vessel; yacht, dinghy; motor-boat: *We* **came about** *and headed in towards the shore.* ⇨ bring about 2, go about 5, put about 1.

come across 1 [Vpr] find (sth) or meet (sb), usu by accident. **o:** (interesting) piece of information; (beautiful) wild flower; his etc name; (old) friend: *Did you* **come across** *any old photographs of the family when you were looking through the lumber-room?* ○ *I* **came across** *an old friend in Oxford Street this morning.* = run across.

2 [Vp] be communicated, understood, heard. **S:** (his) voice; message; words: *The preacher spoke with great feeling but I'm afraid his meaning did not* **come across**. ⇨ get across (to), put across 1.

come across (as) [Vp, Vp.pr] appear (to have a particular character). **o:** timid, shy; a confident man, a trustworthy woman: *She* **comes across as** *a very modest person.* ○ *How does he* **come across** *to you?* = come over (as).

come after 1 [Vpr emph rel] follow (sth) in sequence: *B* **comes after** *A; C* **comes after** *B.* ○ *Does the cheese* **come after** *the pudding in your country?* ○ **After** *the banquet* **came** *a firework display in the gardens.* ↔ come before 1. ⇨ be after 4.

2 [Vpr] (*informal*) follow in pursuit of (sb). **S:** dog; police; farmer. **o:** intruder; suspect; trespasser: *As soon as we started across the field the farmer* **came after** *us waving a big stick.* ⇨ be after 1, keep after, go after 1.

come along [Vp] arrive, present (himself etc). **S:** he etc; chance, opportunity: *He went to London whenever the chance* **came along**. ○ *Is your daughter married yet? No, she's still waiting for Mr Right to* **come along**. = turn up 5.

come along/on 1 [Vp] be quick; make an effort, try harder: **Come on** *Arthur; we can't wait all day!* ○ **Come along** *now, Nell, and leave this boy to his ... work.* GL □ usu imperative.

2 [Vp] make progress. **S:** pupil, student; work, painting. **A:** well; nicely, quickly; like a house on fire; like nobody's business: *My son has* **come along** *very well in French since that new teacher was appointed.* ○ *The horse has* **come on** *a ton* (= a great deal) *since making his debut at Wolverhampton.* DM ○ *It was as much as you could do* (= extremely difficult) *to get a word out of that girl. She has ...* **come on** *remarkably well with Miss Richards.* TT ⇨ bring along/on 1, get along/on (with)1.

3 [Vp] grow, progress, esp in the early stages. **S:** plant; flower, vegetable: *'Those seedlings are* **coming along** *well in the greenhouse; I'll plant them outside when the weather gets a little warmer.'* ○ *I forgot to put the glass back on the cold frame last night, and the frost took the tops off some tomato plants I had* **coming on**. TT ⇨ bring along/on 2.

come along (to) [Vp, Vp.pr] come from one place to another, often a short distance, eg within the same building. **o:** office; meeting, party: *Why doesn't your brother* **come along to** *the training sessions?* ○ *'We're having a few people in for drinks tomorrow. Do* **come along** *if you're free.'* ⇨ be along (to), bring along (to).

come along (with) [Vp, Vp.pr] move somewhere quickly (with sb): *'***Come along***, and please don't make a noise — you'll disturb your mother.'* DC ○ *'You'd better* **come along with** *me to the bar and have a drink. That's what you need to cheer you up.'* □ usu imperative, and used as an instruction or firm request to leave.

come apart [Vp] break. **S:** dress; table; cup, vase; car, boat: *The camera just* **came apart** *the first time I used it.* ○ *I swear I didn't drop the plate: it just* **came apart** *in my hands!* = fall apart, fall to pieces.

come apart at the seams [Vp.pr] (*informal*) collapse, disintegrate, fail. **S:** he etc; car, plane; scheme, project, idea: *He brought his Ford Escort — creaking,* **coming apart at the seams**, *but still running — into York at the conclusion of the 2 000 mile route.* G ○ *Western society is beginning to* **come apart at the seams**, *what with accelerating social and technological change.* NS

come around/round (to) 1 [Vp emph, Vp.pr] come to (a place), visit (sb), usu within the same town etc. **o:** (my) place, house: *'I'm ringing to report a burst pipe. How soon can a plumber* **come round***?'* ○ *We'd love to* **come around to** *your place tonight, but I'm afraid we're a bit tied up with work at the moment.* ⇨ be around/round (at), bring around/round (to) 1, go round (to).

2 [Vp, Vp.pr rel] agree (after disagreeing), change one's attitude (so that it matches sb else's). **o:** his etc way of thinking, point of view, assessment of the situation: *Freud had then refused to accept it (ie the idea) but after a few months' thought had* ***come round****.* F ○ *Mother* ***came around to*** *my way of thinking, thus making life a lot easier.* ○ *A few boys don't like the experiment in mathematics teaching; but some have* ***come round*** *since we started.* T ⇨ bring around/round (to) 2.

come at 1 [Vpr] attack (sb): *Two men, he has said,* ***came at*** *him from the side of the steps: one gagged him.* SCIT

2 [Vpr] reach, establish. **o:** facts; truth; causes: *The purpose of the official inquiry is to* ***come at*** *the true facts leading up to the loss of the passenger ferry.* ⇨ get at 3.

come away (from) [Vp, Vp.pr rel] part or become detached (from sth). **S:** fitting, lock, post. **o:** base, door, socket: *I pulled at the rotten wood and it* ***came away*** *in my hands.* ○ *If the chicken is properly cooked, the meat will* ***come away from*** *the bones very easily.*

come away with [Vp.pr] leave a place, the company of others etc, with (sth). **o:** feeling, impression; memories: *We* ***came away with*** *the uneasy feeling that all was not well with their marriage.* ○ *H.G. Wells went to visit Jung about this time and* ***came away with*** *very mixed impressions.* JUNG ⇨ bring away, go away 1.

come back 1 [Vp] return. **A:** soon, shortly; in a year's time: *I'm going away and I may never* ***come back****.* ○ *He told the patient that without fail he must* ***come back*** *in a year's time.* INN ↔ go away 1. ⇨ be back 1, bring back 1, get back 1, go back 1, take back 1.

2 [Vp nom] become fashionable again. **S:** fashion; style, trend: *Long skirts have been out of fashion for a long time, but they are* ***coming back*** (or: *making a* ***come-back****) this year.* ↔ go out 7.

3 [Vp] return (to the memory). **S:** it (all); former knowledge; sb's name; details: *At first I couldn't remember why everything seemed so familiar; then it all* ***came back****.* ○ *The language I used to speak at my prep school* ***came back*** *to me.* SML ⇨ bring back 2.

4 [Vp] be restored. **S:** (former) system, regime: *There are some people who would be glad to see capital punishment* ***come back*** *for certain kinds of murder.* ⇨ bring back 3.

5 [Vp nom] return successfully to prominence or fame (after a setback, retirement etc). **S:** boxer, film-star, politician: *I played the part of an artiste trying to* ***come back****.* BBCR ○ *Chris Finigan joins the few in championship boxing who've really* ***come back****.* BBCR ○ *Busby Berkeley, according to some the greatest dance director Hollywood has ever produced, retired some years ago . . . but now threatens a* ***come-back****.* TVT ○ *He has left politics for good and is about to stage a* ***comeback*** *in a field in which he became equally famous.* RT □ nom form is used with the verbs *make, stage, attempt, try.*

come-back 1 [nom (Vp)] an answer; a re-assertion of oneself: *Harold was no longer the Harold of the conference-room, dapper and self-assured. He tried to make a* ***come-back****, however.* PW

2 [nom (Vp)] means of enforcing an agreement or invoking the law; redress: *If you don't give the necessary details (date, name, address etc) when you buy the machine, you may have no* ***come-back*** *if it breaks down.*

come before 1 [Vpr] precede (sth): *A* ***comes before*** *B; B* ***comes before*** *C, and so on.* ↔ come after 1. ⇨ be before 1.

2 [Vpr] be presented for consideration, decision, judgment by (a court). **S:** he etc; case; matter, claim. **o:** court; committee, magistrate: *My claim* ***comes before*** *the court tomorrow morning.* ⇨ be before 2, bring before, go before 2, put before 2, take before.

3 [Vpr emph rel] have greater importance than (sb/sth else). **S:** (one's) country, city; interests, needs (of the community). **o:** self; all else, personal advancement: *The building of homes and schools should* ***come before*** *the building of new office blocks.* ○ ***Before*** *all else must* ***come*** *the defeat of inflation.* ⇨ put before 1.

come between [Vpr] interfere in the affairs of (sb); cause the separation or estrangement of (two people): *The two friends had never been closer; though Isabelle was with them she had never* ***come between*** *them.* AF ○ *It is often dangerous and never wise to* ***come between*** *a man and his wife.*

come between sb and sth [Vpr] prevent sb doing or enjoying sth. **o:** me etc; (**and**) my work, studies; rest, recreation: *I'm not going to let a small matter like that* ***come between me and my sleep****.* ○ *He won't let anything* ***come between him and his daily walk****.*

come by 1 [Vp] (esp of sth or sb moving towards the speaker) pass: *I moved my car out of the way so that a heavy lorry could* ***come by****.* ⇨ get by 1.

2 [Vpr] obtain (sth), usu as a result of effort. **o:** money; job; medal, coin, stamp: *Jobs are harder to* ***come by*** *now than when I left university.* ○ *It's difficult to* ***come by*** *any of their new work.* L ○ *What Jane Austen knows . . . is that, while 'domestic happiness' is an admirable ideal, it is not easy to* ***come by****.* JA ○ *I hope he* ***came by*** *all that money honestly.* □ often used in the pattern: *hard, difficult, (not) easy to* ***come by****.*

3 [Vpr] receive (sth) by accident; happen to get: *How did you* ***come by*** *that scratch on your cheek?* KLT

4 [Vp, Vpr] pay a casual visit to (a place): *She would often* ***come by*** *on her way home from work.* ○ *'Why don't you* ***come by*** *our place this evening?'* = drop by/in/in on.

come down 1 [Vp emph] collapse, drop; fall. **S:** ceiling, wall; curtain, picture; rain, sleet: *I took out just one screw and the whole thing* ***came down****.* ○ *The snow* ***came down*** *thick and fast.* ⇨ take down 2.

2 [Vp] fall to the ground (esp because of enemy fire or engine failure). **S:** (enemy) aircraft: *Two enemy intruders* ***came down*** *inside our lines.* ○ *The second engine cut out and we were forced to* ***come down*** *in the sea.* ⇨ bring down 1.

3 [Vp emph] fall, be reduced. **S:** prices, costs, expenditure: *Prices are much more likely to go up than to* ***come down****.* ↔ go up 2. ⇨ be down 2, bring down 5, go down 5.

4 [Vp] reach a decision; decide to exert one's influence. **A:** firmly, finally; after some hesitation;

against/in favour of sb or sth; on sb's side: *The Opposition has* **come down** *in support of a right to secondary* (strike) *action for workers with a 'genuine interest' in a dispute.*

5 [Vp] come to a (country) place, either from London or the North: *There's a girl* **come down** *to live here — she's married to a painter.* ASA □ in contrast, one goes up to London (as the capital), or to Scotland (if travelling north). ⇨ bring down 7, go up (to).

6 [Vp] be passed on, usu over several generations. **S:** stories, songs; myths, legends; traditions, customs. **o:** children, grandchildren; successors: *These stories* **come down** *to us from our forefathers.* ○ *The tradition has* **come down** *over several generations.* ⇨ hand down 2.

come-down [nom (Vp)] (*informal*) a loss of prestige, face, social position: *After owning her own little shop for so many years, it was quite a* **come-down** *for her to have to work for someone else.* AITC □ often modified by *rather a, a bit of a; a terrible, awful, dreadful*; note also the exclamation: *What a* **come-down**!

come down (from) [Vp, Vp.pr rel] leave (a university, esp Oxford or Cambridge): *He* **came down** *from Oxford and found lodgings in Greek Street, Soho.* TSE ○ *I have just* **come down from** *the University with a mediocre degree in History.* HD ⇨ be down (from), go down 8.

come down in the world [Vp.pr] (*informal*) suffer a change for the worse (in economic circumstances, standard of living or employment): *Poor old George has* **come down in the world** *since his business failed.* ↔ go up in the world.

come down on 1 [Vp.pr] (*informal*) criticize (sb) severely, often with a threat of punishment, for some fault; rebuke, reprimand. **o:** him etc; error, slip. **A:** like a ton of bricks (= with great severity), in a flash, instantly: *If any man was slow in obeying orders, the sergeant would* **come down on** *him like a ton of bricks.* ○ *She* **came down on** *him with the frustrated anger of a teacher whose point has not got across* (= been understood). ⇨ be down on 2.

2 [Vp.pr] (*informal*) demand money or compensation from (sb). **o:** (negligent) workman, motorists; (bankrupt) trader: *We* **came down on** *the driver of the truck for heavy damages.* ○ *Suppliers* **came down on** *him for prompt payment of their bills as soon as they heard he was in financial trouble.* ⇨ be down on 3.

come down to 1 [Vp.pr] mean, when it is stated in its simplest form. **S:** it; the accusation; his story: *So what it* **came down to**, *in the end, is that he'd got me the offer of a show from one of the better galleries.* CON ○ *It* **comes down to** *two choices: you can either stay here and obey me, or leave and never return.* TGLY = boil down to.

2 [Vp.pr] (*informal*) have one's income, self-confidence etc so reduced that one is forced to do things that would normally be beneath one. **o:** seeking my help, asking for money, begging in the streets: *I never thought she would* **come down to** *asking my advice.* ⇨ reduce to 4.

come down to earth [Vp.pr] (*informal*) return to reality. **A:** ⚠ with a bang, with a bump: *The lovers are living in a kind of dreamworld; but one day they'll* **come down to earth**. ○ cf (i) *No matter how high you jump you always* **return to earth**. DBM ○ (ii) *Never lose sight of it, or you might* **come down with a bump.** ⇨ bring down to earth.

come down with [Vp.pr] become ill with (sth); contract. **o:** measles, mumps; typhoid fever, malaria: *The Premier was* **coming down with** *a cold.* NY ○ *Chrissy and two of her children* **came down with** *typhus.* GE = go down with.

come for [Vpr] attack (sb) usu physically. **S:** ⚠ dog, bear, gorilla: *The moment I stepped inside the garden, their dog* **came for** *me.* = go for 3.

come forth (with) [Vp, Vp.pr] (*formal* or *jocular*) offer to provide (sth). **S:** thought, idea; suggestion, proposal; offer: *There was renewed hope last night that Ministry officials would* **come forth with** *a fresh offer of talks.* □ note the adj forthcoming, describing sb who provides information etc, or information etc which is being provided: *Jenny was especially* **forthcoming** *about Tom's rumoured departure.* ○ *No news of the move is* **forthcoming**. = come forward (with). ⇨ bring forth (with).

come forward [Vp] be raised for discussion, esp at a formal meeting. **S:** issue, question, matter: *The matter was deferred at last night's meeting, but will* **come forward** *at our next session.* ⇨ bring forward 1.

come forward (with) [Vp, Vp.pr] offer to provide (sth). **S:** information; idea; solution, answer; suggestion, proposal: *The true criminal has* **come forward** *and confessed.* GL ○ *The police are appealing to anyone who might have seen the raiders to* **come forward with** *descriptions.* = come forth (with).

come from 1 [Vpr emph rel] begin or originate in (a place or activity). **S:** story, account, report; money, income. **o:** journalist, diplomatic sources; commerce, industry; a family trust: *Information about twentieth century social life* **comes from** *many sources.* SHOE ○ *Much of the wealth of Priam's powerful kingdom* **came from** *trade.* GLEG = derive from 2.

2 [Vpr emph rel] be born or produced in (a place): *He* **comes from** *London.* ○ *These toys* **come from** *Hong Kong.* ○ **From** *this area* **come** *most of our best potatoes.*

come from/of 1 [Vpr] be descended from (a particular family). **o:** (good, famous, notorious) family; a long line of artists, politicians, statesmen, drunkards: *His father* **came from** *an exiled Italian family of Protestants.* MLT ○ *This chap* **came from** *a very good South African family, but he went wrong.* DS

2 [Vpr] be the result of (some action). **S:** nothing, anything; (no) good, harm; (only) good, harm; that's what. **o:** one's work, endeavours, efforts; meddling, interfering: *'I wonder if anything will* **come of** *our tea-party,' said Isabel.* PW ○ *Carry on with your present research. Nothing but good can* **come of** *it.* ○ *There was still a very strong hope, on both sides, that something would* **come of** *their attachment.* HB

come-hither [nom (Vp)] (of a girl or woman) clearly inviting a man, with a look or smile, to start a flirtation: *Sonja gave me such an obvious* **come-hither** *look that I felt myself blushing to the roots of my hair.* □ attrib use only: *a* **come-hither** *look, smile.*

come home (to) [Vp, Vp.pr rel] become gradually clear (to sb). **S:** fact, truth; message, significance; danger; it ... that he was dying. **o:** public, electorate; audience; patient, victim: *You have to look at it* (religious teaching) *carefully, ... then its meaning will **come home to** you.* CF ○ *It eventually **came home to** us that the war would be long and bloody.* ⇨ bring home (to).

come in 1 [Vp] become fashionable. **S:** long hair, whiskers; short skirts, full sleeves: *'What year did miniskirts first **come in,** in this country?'* ↔ go out 7. ⇨ be in 1, be in/bring into/come into fashion/vogue.

2 [Vp] become seasonable or available. **S:** strawberries, trout, pheasant: *'Fresh salmon doesn't **come in** before February, does it?'* ○ *'We sold the last of that wine on Saturday, and we're still waiting for fresh stocks to **come in**.'* ⇨ be in 3, be in/come into season.

3 [Vp] begin to serve the public; begin to be available or effective. **S:** car phones, cash points, student loans; the new legislation: *I bought my first car long before seat belts **came in**.* ○ *New laws banning the sale of these toys will soon **come in**.* ⇨ be in/bring into/come into/go into service/use, bring in 6.

4 [Vp] (*politics*) win an election and begin to govern. **S:** the (present) government; Labour, the Liberal Democrats, the Tories: *When the present government **came in**, the economy of the country was in a critical state.* □ note the adj incoming, as in: *the **incoming** President, administration.* ⇨ be in 4, get in/into 3, put in 7.

5 [Vp] (*sport*) finish a race in a particular position. **S:** athlete; horse, dog; yacht, car. **A:** first, second, last; where: *He led most of the way but suddenly lost his strength and **came in** last.* ○ *'Where did Peter **come in** — second or third?'* □ *first, second* etc always present.

6 [Vp] be received as income. **S:** dividend, profit; wage, salary: *He doesn't need to work: he has twenty thousand a year **coming in** from investments.* ○ *I had a tiny bit **coming in** from a few shares ... but it hardly kept us.* LBA □ note the n income (the amount that you regularly earn). ⇨ bring in 2.

7 [Vp] play one's part in some scheme. **S:** colleague, partner, member (of a team): *'Yes, I understand the scheme perfectly; but I don't see where I **come in**'.* ○ *'This is very interesting,' I said, ... but where do I **come in**?' 'You **come in**,' said Madge, 'as a scriptwriter.'* UTN □ used in a direct or indirect question after *where*, as shown. ⇨ bring in 3.

8 [Vp] (*broadcasting* or *journalism*) reach the TV studio, editor's desk etc; be received. **S:** news; details; story, report; phone call, message: *We planned to make it a reporters' and correspondents' show with much of the material **coming in** live* (ie shown on TV as it happened). SU ○ *Fresh news is just **coming in** of the severe flooding in Wales. We will give details as soon as we can.* □ note the adj incoming as in: *an **incoming** report, message, call.* ↔ go out 8.

9 [Vp] (*broadcasting*) enter a commentary, discussion etc to make one's personal contribution. **S:** reporter, commentator; member of the panel, audience: *'And now for his impressions of the first round of this championship contest, I pass you over to Jim Clark. **Come in**, Jim!'* ○ *'I should like to **come in** here, as I happen to know a good deal about how people live in these high-rise flats.'*

10 [Vp] (used in radio communication, eg between police-cars and their control points) ask sb to speak, report his position, say that he has received a message etc: *'**Come in** Victor. **Come in,** Victor. Over!'*

come in handy/useful [Vp] be found useful, especially on some future, usu unforseeable, occasion: *DAVIES: You got enough furniture here. ASTON: I picked it up. Just keeping it here for the time being. Thought it might **come in handy**.* TC ○ *'Don't throw those old jars away; they may **come in useful** one of these days.'*

come in pat [Vp] say or do sth without hesitation and just at the right moment: *'I wonder where Eileen lives?' said Mary; and her five-year-old sister **came in pat** with the answer: 'At 23 Rose Gardens.'* ○ *The press was glad to have something to print that would make a change from the international situation. Robert **came in** absolutely **pat** with his story.* CON

the tide come in [Vp] (of the sea) move higher up the beach; rise: *He could hear ... the sound of **the tide coming in** over the rocks.* FL ○ *'Don't stay on the rocks too long; **the tide is coming in** fast and you might be cut off.'* □ note the phrase: *an **incoming** (or: rising) tide.* ↔ the tide go out. ⇨ be in 7.

when one's ship comes in [Vp] when one has the money that one is constantly wishing for or dreaming about: *Perhaps, **when their ship came in,** they would be able to change some of their ugly chairs for some more beautiful ones.* PW

come in for [Vp.pr] be the object of (sth); attract. **S:** work, conduct, idea. **o:** (some, a lot of) admiration, attention; criticism, blame: *At first, his paintings **came in for** a great deal of attention from the critics.* ○ *The police ... **came in for** severe criticism from the judge.* DS

come in/into 1 [Vp emph, Vpr emph] enter (a place). **o:** house, room, hall: *Aunt Annabel **came** flying **in**, her face full of distress.* DC ○ *A patient **came into** my room and saw a tape recorder.* ESS

2 [Vp, Vpr] be relevant to (sth), play a part in (sth). **S:** money, influence, family connections; guilt, envy: *'I don't see how training costs **come in**, so please enlighten me.'* ○ *'Staff salaries over the next two years will **come into** the calculations, won't they?'* = enter into 3.

come in on [Vp.pr] have a share or part in (sth); join. **S:** public; tradesman, worker. **o:** plan, scheme, venture: *If you want to **come in on** the scheme, you'll have to decide quickly.* ⇨ be/bring/get/let in on.

come in on the ground floor [Vp.pr] (*informal*) join a venture etc at the lowest level, or at the start. **S:** partner, associate; investor, speculator: *She will have to **come in on the ground floor**. She cannot expect to be a buyer in the firm immediately.* T ○ *Those who **came in on the ground floor** have seen their capital doubled in under three years.* ⇨ be in on the ground floor, get in 3.

not have enough imagination/ intelligence/ sense to come in out of the rain [Vp.pr] (*informal*) be very foolish, or lacking in common sense or imagination: *You think he's a great scholar ...*

How could he be a great scholar? He ***hasn't enough imagination to come in out of the rain****.* ASA

come in with [Vp.pr] join (sb) in an enterprise. **o:** firm, partnership, group: *You can* ***come in with*** *us if you can put up* (= contribute) *five thousand.*

come into 1 [Vpr emph] enter (a place). ⇨ come in/into 1.

2 [Vpr] be relevant to (sth). ⇨ come in/into 2.

3 [Vpr] inherit (money). **o:** a fortune, legacy; one's share of sth: *I don't* ***come into*** *my share of the legacy until I'm twenty-one.* ○ *Whatever money he* ***came into*** *had to be applied to his debts.* CD

come into action [Vpr] (*military*) begin to act or operate. **S:** troops; guns: *There was a lull of a few seconds before the oiled machinery of pursuit* ***came into action****.* HD ↔ go out of action. ⇨ be in/bring into/go into action.

come into being/existence [Vpr] begin to exist. **S:** body, formation; industry: *Later, two more armies* ***came into being*** *— the First Canadian under Crerar and the Third American under Patton.* MFM ○ *Do you know when Parliament first* ***came into existence****?* ⇨ be in/bring into being/existence.

come into blossom/flower [Vpr] (of blossom or a bush or flowers) open, show. **S:** bush, shrub; crocus, daffodil: *The cherry trees are late* ***coming into blossom*** *this year.* ⇨ be in/bring into blossom/flower.

come into bud/leaf [Vpr] (of a bud or leaf on a tree or bush) appear, show itself. **S:** tree, shrub; branch, bough: *The rose-bushes have* ***come into bud*** *much later than usual.* ⇨ be in bud/leaf.

come into collision (with) [Vpr] collide (with sth); strike. **S:** car, lorry; ship; train: *His car* ***came into collision with*** *a bus at the crossroads.* ○ *The two vehicles* ***came into collision*** *at great speed.* ⇨ be in collision (with).

come into contact (with) 1 [Vpr] touch (sth). **S:** (electrical) lead, wire: *When this piece of metal* ***comes into contact with*** *the wires* (or: *When the metal and the wires* ***come into contact****) the circuit is complete.* ⇨ be in/bring into contact (with) 1.

2 [Vpr] meet (sb) professionally or socially. **S:** agent, official: *In her job as Public Relations Officer she* ***comes into contact with*** *all kinds of people.* ○ *We first* ***came into contact*** *in the Middle East.* ⇨ be in contact (with) 2.

come into effect [Vpr] begin to operate or take effect. **S:** regulation, provision; arrangement, schedule; timetable, programme: *The new cuts in income-tax will not* ***come into effect*** *immediately.* ○ *The revised work-schedule* ***comes into effect*** *next week.* ⇨ put into effect.

come into fashion/vogue [Vpr] become fashionable. **S:** leather, plastic; notion, ideal; theory: *Short hair and short skirts* ***came into fashion*** *at about the same time during the 1920s.* ○ *Before the new methods* (in education) ***came into vogue*** *about a decade ago, it was a simple matter to see whether a class was working or not.* ↔ go out of fashion. ⇨ be in/bring into fashion/vogue, be in 1, come in 1.

come into focus 1 [Vpr] (of sth viewed through a microscope, telescope etc) become sharp and clear. **S:** microscope; specimen; leg, head: *Draw the eyepiece towards you and the object will* ***come into*** *sharp* ***focus****.* ⇨ be in/bring into focus 1.

2 [Vpr] become clearer or more intelligible. **S:** question, problem, issue: *Now they've explained the key issues, everything* ***comes into*** *much sharper* ***focus****.* ⇨ be in/bring into focus 2.

come into force [Vpr] begin to operate, and be in some way binding or enforceable. **S:** law, regulation; requirement: *New regulations will soon* ***come into force*** *for drivers of heavy goods vehicles.* ○ *The provisions of the Act* ***came into force*** *gradually — over a period of months.* ⇨ be in/bring into/put into force.

come into one's head [Vpr] (of thoughts, words) suggest themselves, enter the conscious mind. **S:** ⚠ anything; what, whatever; the first thing: *Bruce Forsyth . . . relishes this new television series . . . 'because I can say what* ***comes into my head*** *and hope everyone's in stitches* (ie hope I make everyone laugh)*.'* RT ○ *I said whatever* ***came into my head****, in any manner that my head formed the idea and the words.* □ preceded by *say, write down* etc + *anything, what* etc.

come into line (with) [Vpr] follow the rules etc of a movement, party etc. **S:** disciple, follower, adherent. **o:** (**with**) (party, church) doctrine, the official view: *He'll never* ***come into line with*** *the majority view.* ○ *The prospect of a Cabinet post is a strong inducement for him to* ***come*** *back* ***into line****.* = conform (to/with). ⇨ be in/bring into/fall into line (with).

come into the open [Vpr] express one's thoughts or feelings openly; be expressed frankly and openly. **S:** he etc; view, attitude; feelings; hostility, greed; quarrel, controversy: *Why don't you* ***come into the open*** *and say exactly what's on your mind?* ○ *His hatred of his brother would have* ***come into the open*** *long before if he had not left home at such an early age.* TST ⇨ be in/bring into the open.

come into one's own [Vpr] show one's talents, capabilities etc, perhaps after a long period in which they are ignored or not known about: *And then, when he'd reached the point of retirement, rather like Churchill, he* ***came into his own*** *in the Second World War.* L ○ *As a picture of a great writer who was a late developer — he only* ***came into his own*** *after the age of 30 — 'My Youth in Vienna' is of considerable interest.* NS

come into play [Vpr] start to have an influence or be relevant. **S:** force(s), circumstances(s), factor(s): *All kinds of forces* ***come into play*** *when a nation's vital interests are threatened.* ○ *If we want to sell abroad, a new set of factors — different tastes, local competition and so on —* ***come into play****.* ⇨ be in/bring into play.

come into sb's possession [Vpr] (*formal*) come to be held or possessed by sb, often temporarily or illegally. **S:** money, jewels; firearms: *The police asked the arrested man how the revolver had* ***come into his possession*** (or: *how he had* ***come into possession of*** *the revolver*). □ the second pattern is used by the police in statements of evidence: *On that date the accused was said to have* ***come into possession of*** *a stolen vehicle.* ⇨ be in sb's possession.

come into power [Vpr] (*politics*) reach or gain (political) power. **S:** party; administration; clique, faction: *If a Socialist government* ***comes into power****, the law may be changed.* ⇨ be in/put into power.

come into season [Vpr] become seasonable or available (in shops). **S:** oysters, (fresh) salmon; raspberries, peaches: *Tomatoes* **come into season** *much earlier in Italy than in Northern Europe.* ⇨ be in 3, be in season, come in 2.

come into service/use [Vpr] begin to serve the public; begin to be used or available. **S:** railway, airline; ferry, bridge, road: *The new type of bus* **comes into service** *later this month.* ○ *This stretch of motorway will not* **come** *back* **into use** *until extensive tests have been carried out.* ↔ go out of service/use. ⇨ be in/bring into/go into service/use, come in 3.

come into sight/view [Vpr] appear. **S:** traveller; car, train; coast; town: *As the plane came down through the clouds, green fields and white houses* **came into sight**. ○ *The church spire* **came into view** *as we rounded the next bend.* ↔ go out of sight/view. ⇨ be in/bring into sight/view.

come into the world [Vpr] be born. **S:** infant, child: *One of the arguments in favour of birth control is that only those children* **come into the world** *who are genuinely wanted.*

come of 1 [Vpr] be descended from. ⇨ come from/of 1.

2 [Vpr] be the result of. ⇨ come from/of 2.

come of age 1 [Vpr] reach the age of legal responsibility; in Britain, reach the age of 18 — formerly 21. **S:** son, daughter, ward: *In 1848 when she* **came of age** *her father gave her an independent allowance of 300 pounds a year.* GE ○ *As soon as he* **came of age**, *Thackeray was driven down to the city to cash some of his inheritance.* TU

2 [Vpr] reach a stage where it can be taken seriously; reach maturity. **S:** government, cabinet; political party, club; organization, system: *Pollsters* (= people who measure the support given to political parties) *have* '**come of age**' *in that they are currently employed in a private capacity by both major parties.* OBS ○ *With the* (economic) *recovery came a boom that confirmed America's* **coming of age** *as an industrial and financial power.* ECON

come off 1 [Vp emph, Vpr] fall from (sth). **o:** horse, pony; bicycle: *The horse refused at the first fence, and that's when I* **came off**. ○ *I bent down to change gear, wobbled, and nearly* **came off** *the bicycle.* ↔ get on/onto. ⇨ be off 1.

2 [Vp emph, Vpr] detach itself; separate. **S:** handle, knob; paint. **o:** door; wall: *When I lifted the jug up, the handle* **came off**. ○ *The first time the baby played with the toy, a lot of the paint* **came off**. ⇨ be off 2, take off 1.

3 [Vp] be removable. **S:** handle; cover, lid; paint, varnish; glue: *'Do these knobs* **come off**?' *'No they're fixed on permanently.'* ○ *'The lid of this tin won't* **come off** *for me; can you move it?'*

4 [Vp] (*informal*) take place; occur. **S:** marriage; race, hunt; royal visit: *When does the next American shuttle launch* **come off**? ○ *'We've got a race meeting* **coming off** *next week. Will you be there?'*

5 [Vp] (*informal*) be successful; succeed. **S:** trick, scheme; effort, attempt, manoeuvre, experiment: *It was a good scheme and it nearly* **came off.** DS ○ *'You're disappointed because your match-making efforts didn't* **come off**.' DC ⇨ bring off 2.

6 [Vp] (*informal*) manage, fare (well etc). **S:** competitor, rival, opponent. **A:** well, badly; second best; how: (horoscope) *Don't argue with a superior if you can avoid it. This is a week when you are likely to* **come off** *second best.* WI ○ (cuts in school budgets) *London has* **come off** *badly. We have been cut practically every year, but never as severely as this.* T ○ *How did Mary* **come off** *in the affair?* □ *well, badly* etc always present.

7 [Vpr] finish doing (sth), no longer be involved in (sth). **S:** salesman, executive; detective. **o:** job, assignment; case: *The journalist had just* **come off** *an assignment which had taken her half-way round the world.* ○ *I want you to* **come off** *that fraud case,' said the inspector. 'I've got more urgent work for you to do.'* ⇨ take off 6.

8 [Vpr] stop taking (sth). **o:** tranquillizers; cigarettes, drugs; the (contraceptive) pill; that course of treatment: *Jenny's* **come off** *the pill: she wants to get pregnant.* ○ *Bill needs to* **come off** *the booze and cigarettes and take a bit of exercise.*

9 [Vpr] be removed from (sth) so that the overall price etc is less. **S:** fifty pence, £5; tax, surcharge, tariff. **o:** price; petrol, refrigerators; medical supplies: *I'm waiting till Budget Day to see if something will* **come off** *the price of cars.* ○ *Under the new trade agreement, the import tariff* **comes off** *certain kinds of goods.* ⇨ take off 8.

come off it [Vpr] (*informal*) do not say things which one knows can't be true; stop trying to mislead others: *'What about Squadron Leader Rusk?' 'He's a bit on the old side.' 'Oh,* **come off it**!' ST ○ *'Oh,* **come off it**,' *said Arthur, 'the chances against it were astronomical!'* HHGG □ imperative only, and used as an irritated appeal to sb not to pretend etc.

come on 1 [Vp] be quick, make an effort. ⇨ come along/on 1.

2 [Vp] make progress. ⇨ come along/on 2.

3 [Vp] grow, progress. ⇨ come along/on 3.

4 [Vp] leave a place in order to arrive at a destination later than sb else: *'You had better go to the station now; I'll* **come on** *later.'*

5 [Vp] be cheerful or strong despite hardship or stress: *The tears prophesied by Justin emerge. '***Come on**, *now, Lavinia. Bear up, dear.'* BM □ imperative only. = pull oneself together.

6 [Vp] start. **S:** fever, cold; headache, migraine; attack of hay fever: *'I think I have a touch of fever* **coming on**.' ARG □ usu continuous tenses. ⇨ bring on 3.

7 [Vp] begin to arrive. **S:** ⚠ night; winter: *We wanted to book into a hotel before night* **came on**. ○ *Winter is* **coming on**: *you can feel it in the air.* = draw on 3.

8 [Vp] begin. **S:** ⚠ (the) rain, snow, sleet: *Rain* **came on**, *as it always seemed to these evenings.* MSAL □ note: *It might* **come on** *to rain suddenly.* OI (and cf: *The rain might* **come on** *suddenly*).

9 [Vp] (*cricket*) begin to bowl. **S:** pace bowler, leg-spinner: *The spin bowlers* **came on** *and soon cut the visitors' scoring rate.* ○ *Marshall* **came on** *(to bowl) after the tea interval.* ⇨ be on 4, bring on 4, put on 10.

10 [Vp] (*theatre*) walk onto the stage, in a play, concert, opera etc; (*sport*) join a football team etc, in the course of a match. **S:** actor; player: *She had* **come on** *in that role ... and had overplayed the part.* HGW ○ *Beardsley* **came on** *as a substitute for*

Barnes ten minutes before the final whistle. ⇨ be on 5.

11 [Vp] be shown, broadcast or performed. **S:** film; programme, news; play, opera: *'The big film doesn't* ***come on*** *until three, so there's plenty of time to get to the cinema.'* ○ *There's a very good play* ***coming on*** *at The Lyric next week.* ⇨ be on 6, put on 11.

12 [Vp] (*legal*) be considered by a court. **S:** case, lawsuit; hearing, action: *They have been waiting all morning for their case to* ***come on.*** ⇨ be on 7.

13 [Vp] be lit, be switched on. **S:** light, lamp, flare: *At the touch of a button a red light* ***came on****, flickering rather.* OD ○ *You'd be waiting for the landing lights* (ie of the plane) *to* ***come on.*** STAT ⇨ be on 8, go on 15, put on 2, turn on 1.

14 [nom (Vp)] (*informal*) speak or behave in a sexually inviting way towards sb: *She had very large dark eyes. But she didn't look like a pick-up and there was no trace of* ***come-on*** *in her voice.* TLG

come on the scene [Vpr] appear and begin to take part in an activity. **S:** police, fire-brigade, ambulance; (new) child, (second) wife: *I* ***came on the scene*** *long after the treasure had been largely plundered, but I am still enchanted by the glimpses I get ... of the riches that remain.* LWK ○ *Primates* ***came on the scene*** *relatively late in the evolutionary history.* CR ⇨ be on the scene.

come on down/in/out/round/up [Vp] a more persuasive invitation than 'come in': *He gave up blocking the door. '****Come on in****,' he told Garner.* AT ○ *'****Come on up****. The front door's open.'* □ imperative only. ⇨ come in/into 1.

come on top of [Vpr] follow (sth), often as a complicating or burdensome factor. **S:** additional burden, extra expense, family illness: *This embarrassment,* ***coming on top of*** *a row with Berthe and Nicholas, was more than she could stand.* HAA

come on/upon [Vpr] meet (sb); find (sth). **o:** traveller, stranger; book; antique; coin, medal: *Round the next corner we* ***came on*** *a group of men waiting for the pub to open.* ○ *One day, being bored and poking here and there in the house, she* ***came upon*** *a fascinating jar.* GLEG = come across 1.

come on/upon one [Vpr] (of sth unwelcome) arrive and begin to affect one; afflict one. **S:** winter, chilly spell, the rains; crisis, catastrophe: *Many misfortunes* ***came upon us*** *during that harsh winter.* ⇨ be on/upon one.

come out 1 [Vp] (*industrial relations*) stop work; strike. **S:** workers; dockers, miners. **A:** on strike; in support, in sympathy: *The dockers have* ***come out*** *to a man.* CSWB = walk out. be out 1, bring out 1.

2 [Vp] be released from prison. **S:** prisoner, convict, detainee. **A:** with remission, on parole, early: *Jones got a three-year sentence, but he may* ***come out*** *early for good conduct.* ⇨ be out 2, let out/out of.

3 [Vp] (*dated*) formally enter 'high' society, ie as a debutante: *All the girls were* ***coming out*** *and talked about their own dances.* ST □ note coming-out as a modifier in: *She met her future husband at her* ***coming-out*** *ball.* ⇨ bring out 3.

4 [Vp] flower, blossom. **S:** tulip, rose; bud: *The crocuses have* ***come out*** *early this year because of the mild winter.* ⇨ be out 4, bring out 4.

5 [Vp] become visible; appear. **S:** ⚠ the sun, moon, stars: *The child loved to watch the stars* ***come out*** *at night.* ○ *During the early morning the sky was overcast, but later the sun* ***came out.*** ↔ go in 2. ⇨ be out 5.

6 [Vp] appear in the shops; be published. **S:** model, brand; book; novel, article: *We have several additions to our very successful 'Primula' range* ***coming out*** *this month.* ○ *'Have you found a title for the book?' 'No not yet.' 'When will it* ***come out****?' asked Isabel.* PW ⇨ be out 6, bring out 5.

7 [Vp] be disclosed, revealed. **S:** the (real) truth; the news, the (whole) story, all the facts: *When Puchert was killed by a bomb placed in his car in Frankfurt, the story of the Red Hand murders* ***came*** *right* ***out*** *into the open.* TO ⇨ be out 7, get out 1, let out 2.

8 [Vp] be revealed or shown up clearly. **S:** detail; spot, work; curve, moulding; letter, engraving; face, feature; subject, sitter (of a portrait painter): *The detail of the carving* ***comes out*** *very sharply in this slanting light.* ○ *Everyone* ***came out*** *well in the wedding photograph except the bride, unfortunately.* ⇨ bring out 6.

9 [Vp] be spoken. **S:** a word; a declaration, statement: *No sooner had the words* ***come out*** *than I regretted my indiscretion in speaking them.* ○ *The things she had prepared to say fled from her, and instead words* ***came out*** *which had no origin in her conscious mind.* PW ⇨ bring out 7.

10 [Vp] become clear or explicit; be revealed. **S:** truth, sense, meaning: *I think the central argument of the book* ***comes out*** *very clearly in his recent study.* ⇨ bring out 8.

11 [Vp] be shown, demonstrated; emerge. **S:** the best/worst in sb; strength, dependability, steadiness; weakness, shiftiness: *The family strain of extremism* ***came out*** *in Mrs Becher's handling of her granddaughter's love affair.* TU ⇨ bring out 9.

12 [Vp] produce a satisfactory answer. **S:** sum, calculation, problem: *'Can you help me with this sum, please? It won't* ***come out****?'* ⇨ get out 4, work out 3.

13 [Vp] be announced, be declared. **S:** (examinations) result, mark; class-list; election results: *When do the psychology results* ***come out****?* ○ *I hope my A-level marks* ***come out*** *before I go on holiday.* ⇨ be out 15.

14 [Vp] be placed (in a certain position) in an examination, test etc. **A:** top, bottom; second, fifth: *We were very disappointed when Alex* ***came out*** *bottom in French.* □ *top, bottom* etc always present.

15 [Vp] acknowledge publicly that one is homosexual: *As for declaring themselves to be gay, these people all* ***came out*** *years ago.* ○ *Sarah waited until she was over forty before* ***coming out.***

come out against [Vp.pr] show that one is opposed to (sth). **o:** proposal, suggested change; legislation, reform: *In his speech to the House, the Minister* ***came out*** *strongly* ***against*** *any change to the existing law.* = speak against.

come out at [Vp.pr] cost or be calculated at (a certain amount). **S:** total; party; excursion, move: *If you pay a pound for a hundred, they* ***come out at***

1p each. ○ *What is the cost of putting your car back on the road going to* **come out at***?* = work out at.

come out (for/to) [Vp, Vp.pr] leave home with a friend (for an excursion, etc). **o: (for)** drive, walk, picnic; (**to**) the pictures, the theatre: *Would you like to* **come out for** *a drive in the country?* ○ (old song) *'Boys and girls,* **come out to** *play, the moon is shining bright as day.'* ○ *Will you* **come out to** *dinner with me on Friday?* ⇨ be out (at), go out 2, go/take out (for/to).

come out in [Vp.pr] become (partially) covered with (sth). **S:** skin; face, chest, arms. **o:** pimples, hives, a rash, spots: *Shortly after eating the lobster I* **came out in** *spots.* ⇨ bring out in.

come out in the wash [Vp.pr] (*informal*) be put right, right itself/themselves, in the end; be made clear. **S:** it; things; everything: *The modern tendency is to avoid decisions, and to procrastinate in the hope that things will* **come out** *all right* **in the wash***.* MFM

come out in favour (of) [Vp.pr] make a decision for (sth); support. **o:** change, reform; law, Bill: *The Liberals, who held the balance of power in Parliament,* **came out in favour of** *the legislation.*

come out/out of 1 [Vp emph, Vpr] leave, emerge from (a place). **o:** house, school, cinema: *Police went into the house to try to persuade the man to* **come out***.* ○ *We were caught up in a rush of people* **coming out of** *the football ground.* ⇨ be out/out of 1, bring out/out of, get out/ out of 1, keep out/out of, take out/out of 1.
2 [Vp emph, Vpr] leave the place where it has been fixed. **S:** peg, nail, bolt. **o:** ground, wall, metal: *Jane's front tooth* **came out** *when she bit the apple.* ○ *'Can you help me to open this bottle? The cork won't* **come out***.'* ○ *The screw was rusty and wouldn't* **come out of** *the wall.* ⇨ be out/out of 2, get out/out of 2, take out/out of 2.
3 [Vp emph, Vpr] disappear (with cleaning). **S:** mark, stain, spot; colour, dye: *Do you think these ink-marks will* **come out of** *my dress if I give it a hot wash in the machine?* ○ *The colours in these materials are guaranteed not to* **come out***.* ⇨ be out/out of 3.

come out/out of badly/well [Vp, Vpr] be revealed as behaving or having behaved in a good or bad way. **S:** nobody, everyone: *In the scandal caused by the Minister's foolish behaviour, nobody* **came out well***.* ○ *In the comparisons that were made between the two women, Isabel seldom* **came out best***.* PW

come out of the blue [Vpr] (*informal*) happen, appear or be said suddenly or unexpectedly. **S:** he etc; arrival, return; comment, statement; discovery, success: *She had* **come out of the blue** *just when she was wanted but, like so many others involved in the case, she was out to make money.* T ○ *Those remarks tend to* **come** *right* **out of the blue***, and anyone not knowing him is invariably shocked.* ⇨ be out of the blue.

come out of one's shell [Vpr] overcome one's shyness; show a bolder, perhaps unexpected, side of one's character: *I think she was rather pleased with me and the way I was* **coming out of my shell***.* HAHA ○ *He* (a professional footballer) *has* **come out of his shell** *a lot this season, giving as good as he gets when the lads have a go at* (ie attack) *him.* ST ⇨ bring out of his shell.

come out on the right/wrong side [Vp.pr] (*informal*) (not) lose money. **S:** dealer, trader, salesman: *He sold his goods at very low prices but he always managed to* **come out on the right side***.*

come out on top [Vp.pr] (*informal*) win; overcome difficulties; prove oneself superior to others: *She* (a singer) *proved that she can confront an audience with totally unfamiliar material and still* **come out** *well* **on top***.* RT

come out (to) [Vp, Vp.pr] ⇨ come out (for/to).

come out with [Vp.pr] (*informal*) speak, say (sth) perhaps after some hesitation. **o:** the truth, facts; shocking, filthy language; some strange remarks, statements; the (astonishing) theory, statement that: *When Steve dropped his nonsense and* **came out with** *the truth, he was at his most engaging.* SPL ○ *Chatterway had then* **come out with** *this extraordinary story about his son taking holy orders* (entering the church). GIE

come (over) [Vpr] (*informal*) try to impress, persuade etc (sb) by assuming a false manner or behaving in an insincere or superior way. **noun complement:** it; the high and mighty, the barrack-room lawyer, the wronged wife; bully, boss: *Of course, she tries to win sympathy by* **coming** *the badly-used little woman* **over** *everybody.* ○ *Just let him try* **coming** *the big boss* **over** *me!* ○ *It gives me a pain to watch that fool* **coming** *it* **over** *people who are ten times better at the job than he is.*

come over 1 [Vp] visit sb, usu after crossing the sea or making a journey by air or land: *If you can get leave, please* **come over** *this weekend.* RFW ○ *My French pen-friend is* **coming over** *for a holiday this summer.* ⇨ be over 4, bring over.
2 [Vp] reach a country, esp England or America, as a migrant: *My ancestors* **came over** *with the Pilgrim Fathers.*
3 [Vpr] (*informal*) overtake, seize (sb); affect (sb/sth). **S:** (sudden) feeling, sense of hopelessness, futility; wave of dizziness, nausea, fear; attack of nerves; whatever?: *He would sit there, contemplating the change which had* **come over** *his life.* HWKM ○ *A little hush had* **come over** *the room; but it didn't last long.* RATT ○ *I don't know what's* **come over** *you: you used to be downright finicky* (= fussy). AT
4 [Vp] (suddenly) feel or become. **adj complement:** (all, quite, rather) tired, sick, faint, dizzy; nasty, bad-tempered; canny, crafty: *I thought of this, and thought of that, and altogether I* **came over** *quite absent-minded.* TC □ non-standard esp when *all* precedes the adj.

come over (as) [Vp, Vp.pr] appear to others (as having certain characteristics). **o:** smooth, rather bland, unsavoury; a reliable witness, a knowledgeable judge (of sth): *He usually* **comes over** *as rather indecisive.* ○ *'Is that how she* **comes over** *to you?'* = come across (as).

come over (to) [Vp, Vp.pr] change so that one is loyal (to sb else), or the ally (of sb else). **S:** country; power; agent, general, scientist. **o:** us, our side, the allies: *At a crucial point in the war, one of the enemy's most powerful allies* **came over to** *our side.* ○ *How would you like to* **come over to** *us? You could double your salary within a year.* ⇨ bring over (to), go over to 1.

come round 1 [Vp] (of a periodical event or occasion) arrive. **S:** Christmas, Easter; pay-day, my birthday; the annual Conference: *It was a relief when the Christmas holidays* ***came round*** *and he could retire to La Chapelle.* AF ○ *The Commonwealth Prime Ministers' Conference* ***comes round*** *next month.* SC

2 [Vp] regain consciousness: *On* ***coming round*** *the patient probably has a headache.* MIND ○ *'Thank goodness, dear, you're* ***coming round****. You fainted you know.'* DC = come to 1. ⇨ bring round 2.

3 [Vp] (*informal*) recover one's good humour: *He's sulking because his parents wouldn't let him see the film; but he'll soon* ***come round****.*

come round (to) 1 [Vp emph, Vp.pr] visit (sb) or come to (a place), usu within the same town etc. ⇨ come around/round (to) 1.

2 [Vp, Vp.pr rel] agree (after disagreeing), change one's attitude. ⇨ come around/round (to) 2.

come round to [Vp.pr] reach the point of (doing sth) after procrastination or unavoidable delay. **o:** inviting the neighbours to dinner; digging the garden; mending the gate: *When he finally* ***came round to*** *writing the letter, he found his feelings were easier to express than he'd expected.* = get around/round to.

come through 1 [Vp] appear on the surface; be evident. **S:** character, nature; warmth, hostility: *Jung apologized for the 'dryness' of his letter and said that there was a smile behind it even if it did not* ***come through****.* JUNG

2 [Vp, Vpr] recover from a serious illness (mental or physical); survive. **S:** patient; business, enterprise; country. **o:** illness; crisis, war: *I knew there was something that I ought to say, something that would reassure my doctor that I had* ***come through****, only I did not know what it was.* ○ *He considered himself fortunate to have* ***come through*** *two world wars unscathed.* ⇨ bring through, get through 3.

come through (on) [Vp, Vp.pr] communicate with sb (by means of sth); (of a message) arrive, be received. **S:** he etc; message, communication; news, results; order. **o:** telephone, line; screen, radio: *I was just leaving the office when Robert* ***came through on*** *the phone from London.* CON ○ *A message was* ***coming through*** *from Brazil when the signal went completely.* TBC ⇨ be through (to), get through (to) 2, put through (to) 2.

come to 1 [Vp] recover consciousness: *When he* ***came to****, he could not, for a moment, recognize his surroundings.* = come round 2.

2 [Vp] (*nautical*) stop. **S:** ship, boat: *The boat* ***came to*** *with a few feet of clear water to port.* ○ *A police patrol boat hailed to us to* ***come to****.* = heave to. ⇨ bring to 2.

3 [Vpr] be equal to or reach (a total). **S:** bill, account; shopping, purchases, goods: *The bill* ***came to*** *five pounds, fifty pence.* ○ *I didn't expect those few items to* ***come to*** *so much.* = amount to 1. ⇨ bring to 3.

4 [Vpr] reach (sth/sb), as one of a series of things or people to deal with: *I know I've got to talk about tax. I'll* ***come to*** *that in a moment.* ○ *I most definitely have not forgotten the dogs. I was* ***coming to*** *them.* GL = get to 2.

come to sb's aid/assistance/help [Vpr] give aid etc to sb. **S:** rescue team, fire brigade, police. **o:** (**of**) climber, swimmer; occupant, owner: *Firemen* ***came to the aid of*** *a man trapped on the top floor of a burning house.* ○ *The motorist was asked to give his position, so that the breakdown truck could* ***come to his assistance****.* ⇨ bring to sb's aid/assistance.

come to attention [Vpr] (*military*) adopt an alert, straight-backed posture, with the feet together. **S:** soldier; company, platoon: *'When the officer speaks to you,* ***come*** *smartly* ***to attention****, and stand still!'* ⇨ be at/bring to attention.

come to sb's attention/notice [Vpr] (*formal* or *pompous*) be noticed, remarked. **S:** it ... that he was there; fact, matter, circumstances: *It* ***came to his attention*** *that his wife was often seen in the company of another man.* ○ *It has* ***come to my notice*** *that you have not been working as well as you used to.* ⇨ bring to sb's attention/notice.

come to blows [Vpr] start fighting. **S:** (two) sides, parties, teams; rivals, opponents: *We didn't actually* ***come to blows****, but we spent the rest of the day staring out of opposite windows.* DIL ⇨ bring to blows.

come to the boil [Vpr] reach boiling-point; (*figurative*) reach crisis point. **S:** water, milk; situation, discussion: *The kettle was* ***coming to the boil****, and he made quite certain that its spout was directed out of harm's way.* TT ○ *A confrontation that had long been simmering in King's* (College) *and that now threatened to* ***come to the boil*** ... MRJ ⇨ bring to the boil.

come to a climax [Vpr] reach a high level of intensity, drama etc. **S:** noise, din; disturbance, rioting; quarrel, disagreement: *Their discussions* ***came to a*** *noisy* ***climax*** *late in the evening.* ○ *The argument* ***came to a climax*** *when she threw a plate at him.* ⇨ bring to a climax.

come to the conclusion (that) [Vpr] decide after reflection, or on the basis of evidence (that); conclude (that). **cl:** that he should retire; that it was pointless to resist; that the experiment should be repeated: *I took no further part in the war. I ...* ***came to the conclusion that*** *... the pen was mightier than the sword. I joined the staff.* MFM ○ *We have* ***come to the conclusion*** ... ***that*** *colour in dreams yields no information about the personality of the dreamer.* HAH

come to a bad etc end [Vpr] (*informal*) meet an unpleasant fate. **adj:** bad, no good; sticky (= unpleasant), nasty: *Give my regards to Carlo; tell him George* ***came to no good end****.* US ○ *I always knew that chap would* ***come to a sticky end****.* ○ *The Post Office's only contribution to the World Refugee Year* (ie a special stamp) *has* ***come to a*** *rather* ***sad end****, we are told by our stamp man.* OBS

come to a dead end [Vpr] (*informal*) reach a point beyond which no progress can be made. **S:** inquiry, investigation; survey, research; conversation: *It was puzzling; we seemed to have* ***come to a dead end****. 'Have you any idea why she did it?' 'None at all', he replied.* ⇨ be at/bring to a dead end.

come to an end [Vpr] end, finish; be exhausted. **S:** campaign, war; trouble, turmoil; patience, forbearance: *We are all relieved that the strike seems to be* ***coming to an end****.* ○ *The good relationship which existed between managers and men has* ***come to an end****.* ⇨ be at/bring to an end, put an end/a stop to.

come to one's feet [Vpr] stand up quickly. **S:** audience, crowd (at a match): *Several members of Parliament* ***came to their feet*** *at once to answer the accusation.* ○ *The audience* ***came to their feet*** *as the National Anthem was played.* ⇨ be on one's feet, bring to his feet.

come to the fore [Vpr] become prominent. **S:** member (of a group); politician, industrialist; scholar, writer: *Past memories, which are overlaid during the waking state by our sensory impressions,* ***come to the fore*** *during sleep in the form of dreams.* SNP ○ *He first* ***came to the fore*** *in a rather lean time for British politics.* ⇨ be/bring to the fore.

come to fruition [Vpr] be realized, fulfilled. **S:** hope, dream, ambition; plan, scheme: *Their hopes of a happy life together never* ***came to fruition***. WDM ○ *After years of work, he had the pleasure of seeing all his plans* ***come to fruition***. ⇨ bring to fruition.

come to grief [Vpr] be destroyed; be a failure. **S:** car, plane; scheme, plan; business; athlete, climber: *The ship* ***came to grief*** *on a hidden rock.* ○ *The patients had* ***come to grief*** *in a truck or some military vehicle.* INN

come to the ground [Vpr] fall down. **S:** pole, tent; chimney, tower: *The chimney* ***came*** *crashing* ***to the ground*** *in a cloud of dust.* □ always used with *crashing, hurtling, tumbling* etc. ⇨ bring to the ground.

come to a halt/standstill [Vpr] (of the movement or progress of sth) stop, be unable to progress further. **S:** car, convoy; production, factory: *Do not leave your seats until the aircraft has* ***come to*** *a complete* ***halt***. ○ *Production has* ***come to a standstill*** *owing to the lack of raw materials.* ⇨ be at/bring to a halt/standstill.

come to harm [Vpr] be hurt, harmed; fall under a bad influence. **adj:** (no) great, (no) real, (no) serious: *I shall really have to accompany you, if only in order to see that you* ***come to*** *no* ***harm***. US ○ *Most parents think that their children will* ***come to*** *no great* ***harm*** *if they go to a discothèque now and then.*

come to a head [Vpr] reach a critical or culminating stage. **S:** matter, argument, quarrel, crisis; (our) fears, doubts: *The matter may* ***come to a head*** *at an early meeting of the Parliamentary Labour Party.* DM ○ *This ... inspired massive enmity which festered for a couple of years or so and* ***came to a head***, *as all great issues do, in the United States Senate.* L ⇨ bring to a head.

come to heel [Vpr] obey; accept an obedient role: *He had only to speak one word and his dog would* ***come to heel*** *at once.* ○ *As I walked I threatened the universe. If it did not* ***come to heel*** *soon, my reprisals would begin and they would be terrible.* CON = fall into line (with). ⇨ bring to heel.

(if it) come to that [Vpr] (*informal*) now that I think about it ...; now that you happen to mention it ...: *He hated taking favours from her family.* ***If it came to that***, *it was her family who was to blame for the whole thing.* DC ○ *She went on to confess that she had never been to a cocktail party, and Pop said:* '***Come to that***, *neither have I!*' DBM □ used at the beginning or end of a main clause to refer back to some earlier reflection, remark by another speaker etc.

if/when it comes to the crunch/push [Vpr] (*informal*) if or when one has to make a vital decision or face a moment of crisis: *It was easy enough to visualize him blowing up the bridge* ***if it came to the push*** *and given the right company.* ILIH ○ ***When it came to the crunch***, *Britain and France went their own ways.* BBCR

come to it [Vpr] (*informal*) reach a state, usu unpleasant, as a result of a change in age, strength, ability, wealth, etc: *'Poor old Smith has had to resign from the Board because of ill-health.' 'Ah, well; I suppose we all have to* ***come to it*** *in the end.'* ○ *'So John has got to start earning his living? We all have to* ***come to it***,*' he said with a smile.*

come to life [Vpr] become lively, animated, responsive. **S:** actor, partner, speaker; show, performance; film; game: *You're very awkward with Anne and Johnny. But with Alice you really* ***come to life***. RATT ○ *Only when I have a high temperature do my mental images* ***come to*** *independent* ***life***. DOP ⇨ bring to life.

come to light [Vpr] be revealed or discovered. **S:** case, instance; fact, evidence; truth; nothing, anything; it ... that John was lying: *So far no case has* ***come to light*** *where false confessions have been produced because of the psychological effect of the instrument.* SNP ○ *Nothing has* ***come to light*** *about the death of Sally.* F ⇨ bring to light.

come to mind [Vpr] be recalled from the memory; occur to sb. **S:** event, incident; (exact, precise) impression, detail: *When she thought about Aden, all that* ***came to mind*** *were irrelevancies.* FL

(never/not) come to anything/come to nothing [Vpr] be quite unsuccessful; be a complete failure. **S:** inquiries; plan, scheme; hopes; work; agreement, deliberations, negotiations; love affair; he etc: *No one had mentioned the security inquiries, which I assumed had* ***come to nothing***. NM ○ *The two men had brave schemes for making big money quickly. They* ***never came to anything***. AITC ○ *He* ***never came to anything*** *in the end.* ⇨ next entry

(never/not) come to much [Vpr] (*informal*) (never, not) be or do anything of any importance or consequence. **S:** he etc; scheme, plan; plot, conspiracy: *As an artist, he'll* ***never come to much***: *he lacks the creative fire.* ○ *I doubt whether John's new venture will* ***come to much***; *he hasn't got enough capital to make a success of it.* ⇨ previous entry

come to oneself [Vpr] return to one's normal state; recover (full) consciousness: *I didn't realize how ill I had been, ... till I* ***came to myself*** *in that pretty, sunny sitting-room of yours.* PW ⇨ bring to himself.

come to the point [Vpr] deal directly with what is of chief importance in a discussion, speech, letter, book etc. **A:** straight, straight away; directly, immediately; after some hesitation: *The Home Secretary was both brusque and tactfully subtle at the same time. He* ***came to the point*** *straight away* (or: ***came*** *straight* ***to the point***). TBC

come to a pretty pass/such a pass [Vpr] (*informal*) reach (such) a sad or bad state. **S:** things, events, affairs; they etc: *If a man could not have a drink in his own home, things were ...* ***coming to a pretty pass***. AITC ○ *How did things* ***come to such a pass*** *that she was left entirely without money?*

□ often followed by a clause introduced by *when*. = come to something. ⇨ bring to (such) a pass.

come to sb's/the rescue [Vpr] save sb from a difficult or dangerous situation. **S:** warden, gamekeeper; fireman; bank, insurance company: *Let's not wait for somebody to* **come to our rescue** *— let's build a raft.* ○ *The International Monetary Fund* **came to the rescue** *when Britain was in financial difficulties.* SC

come to rest [Vpr] reach a final position; stop. **S:** missile; spear; ball; train, plane: *The car skidded off the road and* **came to rest** *a foot or two from somebody's front door.* ○ *Their boat floated on the tide and finally* **came to rest** *on Mount Parnassus.* GLEG ⇨ bring to rest.

come to one's senses [Vpr] behave, act, in a normal, reasonable way after having behaved unreasonably: *'Don't worry about John not wanting to work with you; he'll* **come to his senses** *before long.'* ⇨ bring to his senses.

come to something [Vpr] (*informal*) reach a sad or deplorable state. **S:** ⚠ it; (occasionally) we: *'It's* **coming to something** *when I have to ask you for a kiss,' she said. 'Are you tired?'* DBM ○ *We've* **come to something** *when car workers turn down a fourteen per cent pay increase.* □ usu in the continuous and perfect tenses; often followed by a clause beginning with *when*. = come to a pretty pass etc.

come to a successful etc conclusion [Vpr] end successfully etc. **S:** meeting, negotiations; campaign, war. **adj:** successful, peaceful, amicable, satisfactory: *Talks aimed at settling the fisheries dispute have at last* **come to a satisfactory conclusion**. ⇨ bring to a successful etc conclusion.

come to this [Vpr] reach an unsatisfactory state or ending. **S:** ⚠ it, things; he etc: *'I never thought things would* **come to this***: you asking me for advice!'* ○ *Once we dreamed of something so much greater, a paradise on earth, and it has* **come to this**. SCIT ○ *This sudden clear view of his face, coupled with his fast, wild talking, suddenly made me realize that he was half-crazed. So* **this** *was what he had* **come to**! CON

come to the same thing (as) [Vpr] equal or be equivalent to one another. **S:** it . . . if/whether you do A or B; (the two, the alternative) policies, plans, systems; answers, solutions: *Whether you drink beer or whisky, it* **comes to the same thing***; most of what you pay goes to the Government.* ○ *Helen's elaborate speeches* **came** *in the end* **to the same thing as** *Miss Small's brisk pronouncements.* AITC

when it comes to [Vpr] when one considers (sth/doing sth); in regard to (sth/doing sth). **o:** politics, sport; the French; food, wine; picking a winner, organizing a party: *She has insufficient application* **when it comes to** *such activities as reading, painting, music.* JA ○ **When it comes to** *fashion, the French mean business and their Government, unlike ours, provides hefty support.* SC

come to (with) [Vpr] approach or tackle (a task) (with sth). **S:** scholar, scientist; planner, builder. **o:** (**to**) task, problem; post, position; marriage; (**with**) an open mind, no preconceived ideas, complete lack of bias; unrealistic, romantic ideas: *His assistant* **came to** *the subject* **with** *a fresh, lively mind.* ○ *The attitude* **with** *which you* **come to** *your new job is all-important.* ⇨ bring to 4.

come to grips with [Vpr emph rel] engage in a struggle with (sth); tackle. **o:** (**with**) problem, issue, question; disease; life: *Man was really* **coming to grips with** *the question of how his newly acquired skills could help in the process of economic and social development.* T ○ *Freud's desire was to explore dreams . . . as a means of* **coming to grips with** *the unconscious mind.* F ○ *This was a problem* **with** *which he had never quite* **come to grips**. ⇨ be at/get to grips with.

come to terms with [Vpr emph rel] find a way of living with or adapting to (sth); manage, handle. **o:** life, the world; one's situation, environment; one's handicap, limitations; oneself; being isolated: *As Chris Kingsley says, 'Man will have to* **come to terms with** *his environment.'* TBC ○ *'Every great artist has* **come to terms with** *life — think of Beethoven — how tortured he was in middle-age, and how serene at the end.'* PW ○ *How, then, has it* (the white population) **come to terms with** *living in a state controlled entirely by Africans?* NS

come together [Vp] (of two parties in conflict) settle their differences; be reconciled. **S:** divorced couple; factions, sects: *I doubt if they will* **come together** *again, even for the sake of the children.* ⇨ bring together.

come under 1 [Vpr] be controlled or managed by (sth). **S:** hospital, school, college. **o:** health authority, local council; direct government control: *The Further Education Colleges used to* **come under** *local authority control.* ○ *Student scholarships don't* **come under** *this department.*

2 [Vpr] be attacked, criticized, influenced etc by sb. **S:** management, leadership; work; writing, research, sculpture. **o:** ⚠ attack, criticism, fire; pressure; influence: *If she were arrested, the organization itself would not necessarily* **come under** *attack.* HA ○ *The BBC2 programme 'Who Sank the Lusitania?'* **came under** *fire in a late night discussion chaired by Michael Dean.* L

3 [Vpr] be classified as (sth), be put in the category of (sth). **S:** item; expenditure; question, matter. **o:** heading, head; any other business: *'What heading does her trip* **come under***?' "Sales promotion"?'* ○ *'That item* **comes under** *"petty cash".'*

come up 1 [Vp] come upstairs: *'Please don't wait down there;* **come** *straight* **up**.' ⇨ go up 1.

2 [Vp] travel to town, esp London, from the country etc, or towards the north: *When you visit Britain next year, please* **come up** *to Edinburgh for a few days.* ↔ get down 2. ⇨ be up 2, go up (to).

3 [Vp] arrive to study at a university, esp Oxford or Cambridge: *He* **came up** *last year to read Modern History.* ↔ go down 8. ⇨ be up 2, go up (to).

4 [Vp] appear above the soil. **S:** bean, pea, celery: *I sowed some runner beans three weeks ago, but they haven't* **come up** *yet.*

5 [Vp] be mentioned; arise. **S:** question, problem; the issue, matter (of sth); sb's name. **A:** during the discussion, in the debate; in the course of conversation; for a decision, for review: *The issue of drug-taking is bound to* **come up** *at the next Conference.* ○ *His name* **came up** *whenever the question of emergency aid was discussed.* ⇨ be up for discussion/debate, bring up 3.

6 [Vp] (*legal*) come to be considered (by a court); appear (in court). **S:** case; the accused, offender. **A:** for review; before the court; on a fresh charge; for attempted murder: *The paper announced the cases that were to* **come up** *at the assizes the following day*. HD ⇨ be up 6 , bring up 4.

7 [Vp] (*military*) move or be carried to the front line. **S:** reserves; supplies; food, ammunition: *Roads and bridges were destroyed to prevent the enemy's reserves from* **coming up**. ○ *All our supplies have to* **come up** *by this single-line railway.* ⇨ bring up 5.

8 [Vp] (*informal*) be vomited. **S:** food; dinner: *The child doesn't seem to be able to keep anything down. Everything she eats* **comes up** *again.* ↔ keep down 7. ⇨ bring up 6.

9 [Vp] rise through water to or above the surface. **S:** diver; fish, whale: *He breathed like a diver* **coming up** *for air.* LWK ↔ go down 2.

10 [Vp] occur, arise. **S:** vacancy, opening; opportunity: *I can't offer you a job now, but I'll let you know as soon as a vacancy* **comes up**. ASA

11 [Vp] be displayed; appear. **S:** message, announcement; flight number: *I was still waiting for the Munich flight to* **come up** *on the screen.*

12 [Vp] win in a lottery, football pool etc. **S:** number, ticket, premium bond; he etc: *One of my bonds* **came up** *in the last draw: I won a £25 prize.* ○ *John's very lucky; he's always* **coming up** *on the (football) pools.*

13 [Vp] rise. **S:** the sun, the moon; the stars; the dawn: *At this time of year* **the sun comes up** *at five and goes down late in the evening.* ↔ go down 1.

come up the hard way [Vp] (*informal*) reach one's present position through hard work, without assistance or privileges etc: ***I came up the hard way***: *my father died before I was born, and I had to leave school when I was fourteen.* ⇨ bring up the hard way, bring up 2.

come up smiling [Vp] (*informal*) emerge bravely and cheerfully from an unpleasant experience, defeat etc: *He's been disappointed in love three times already, but he always* **comes up smiling**. AITC

come up against [Vp.pr] be faced with or opposed by (sth/sb). **o:** problem, question (of sth); stubbornness, will; (fierce, strong, powerful) opposition; difficulty; enemy forces: *The Hungarian government has* **come** *slap* **up against** *the problem of how to reconcile economic efficiency with the ideal of social equality.* OBS ○ *Not for the first time her will* **came up against** *her husband's.* NM ⇨ be/bring up against.

come up (as far as/to) [Vp, Vp.pr] extend all the way to (a place or point). **S:** town, houses; sea, fog; lawn, flowers: *The tide never* **comes up as far as** *the road, even though the water is only a few feet away.* ○ *The water in the swimming pool* **came up to** *my chin.* ⇨ be/bring up (as far as/to).

come up for [Vp.pr] be considered as an applicant, candidate etc, for (sth). **S:** name; member (of a board). **o:** re-election, admission: *Members of the faculty* **come up for** *election to the Board of Studies every two years.* ⇨ be up for, put up (for) 1.

come up for auction/sale [Vp.pr] become available for purchase; come on the market. **S:** house, farm; collection (of jewels, paintings): *An unusual collection of firearms dating from the 16th century* **comes up for auction** *next week.* ○ *'Is the house likely to* **come up for sale** *in the foreseeable future?'* ⇨ be/put up for auction/sale.

come up (to) [Vp, Vp.pr] extend all the way to (a place or point). ⇨ come up (as far as/to).

come up to [Vp.pr] reach an acceptable level or standard. **S:** he etc; work, performance, result. **o:** ⚠ standard, scratch, the mark; sb's expectations, hopes: *He didn't really* **come up to** *scratch in the end-of-year exam.* ○ *For one reason or another their holiday in France didn't* **come up to** *expectations.* ⇨ be up to 5, bring up to, get up to 1, keep up to.

come up with 1 [Vp.pr] draw level with (sth/sb). **o:** convoy; car, lorry; traveller, stranger: *The horseman* **came up with** *a group of people who were making the pilgrimage on foot.*

2 [Vp.pr] discover or produce (sth). **o:** suggestion, idea, information; (the right) answer; solution; (a plausible, convincing, reasonable) explanation: *Scientists will have to* **come up with** *new methods of increasing the world's food supply.* ○ *It is customary for investigations to* **come up with** *not one but a number of different factors.*.

come upon [Vpr] meet (sb); find (sth). ⇨ come on/upon.

come upon one [Vpr] (of sth unwelcome) arrive. ⇨ come on/upon one.

come with 1 [Vpr] be supplied with (sth). **S:** machine, device, appliance. **o:** fitting, attachment, push-button controls: *Made in heat-resistant glass, the jug* **comes with** *a cork mat.* ○ *The car* **comes with** *a one-year anti-rust warrantee.*

2 [Vpr] follow naturally from (sth); accompany. **S:** wisdom, insight, confidence. **o:** old age, experience, achievement: *She has to face up to the problems which* **come with** *old age.* ○ *He has the assurance which usually* **comes with** *rank and wealth.*

come within [Vpr] come near enough (to be heard, seen or reached). **o:** ⚠ earshot, sight, view, range: *At that moment a patrol* **came within** *view of our observation post.* ○ *No aircraft* **came within** *range.* ⇨ be within 1, bring within, get within.

compare

compare to [Vn.pr pass rel] say or suggest that (one person or thing) is like (another). **O:** him etc; face, nose; house, machine. **o:** monster, angel; moon, turnip; rabbit-hutch: *She was mortified when her husband* **compared** *her hairstyle* **to** *a bramble bush.* ○ *The sculpture of Rodin has sometimes been* **compared to** *that of Michelangelo.* ⇨ next entry

compare (with) [Vn.pr pass emph rel] set (one person or thing) beside (another), examine them together, so as to find similarities or differences between them. **O:** figure, rate, output; machine, device; place, climate. **o:** another, others; that of Africa: *If we* **compare** *the figures for violent crime* **with** *those for last year, we notice a marked increase.* ○ *The south of England is certainly beautiful, but it can't be* **compared with** (or: *can't* **compare with**) *the south of France for sunshine.* ○ *These losses were nothing* **compared with** *the wholesale plunder of the diamond soil outside the mines.* DS ⇨ previous entry

compensate

compensate (for) [Vpr pass emph rel, Vn.pr pass emph rel] pay (sb), offer (sb) sth, because of a loss or injuries he has suffered. **S:** employer; insurer; nothing. **O:** worker; person insured, victim. **o:** loss, injury: *Nothing will ever* **compensate** *(him)* **for** *the injuries he received in the accident.* ○ *A firm which dismisses an employee on grounds of redundancy is obliged to* **compensate** *him (***for** *loss of employment).* = recompense (for).

compensate for [Vpr pass emph rel] balance or outweigh (sth), so making it bearable, forgivable etc; redress. **S:** recent efforts, hard work; care, attentiveness. **o:** earlier neglect, idleness; deprivation, hardships: *Education ...* **compensated for** *the inferiority he felt as an unlearned farmer's boy.* 50MH ○ *My efforts were concerned with tasks which would* **compensate for** *my sins.* LIFE ○ *Those who do not particularly care for their children ... feel that by filling them with food they can somehow* **compensate for** *their lack of love.* BRN = make up for 1, recompense (for).

compete

compete against/with (for) [Vpr pass emph rel] play against (sb/sth), in the hope of winning (sth); oppose (sb/sth) in the search for (sth/sb). **S:** sportsman, athlete; business, trader: *As a young golfer he had often* **competed against** *famous players, though not often with much success.* ○ *There were many periodicals* **competing with** *each other* **for** *a rapidly expanding middle-class readership.* TU ○ *Where trees* **compete for** *space, air and light in the wild state, some are bound to fail to establish themselves.*

compete (with) [Vpr emph rel] (be able to) rival (others) successfully. **o:** trade rival; industry, store; (fellow) student, pupil: *Small suburban shops can't* **compete with** *the chain-stores in price, though they can do so in personal service.* ○ *We are satisfied that we can* **compete with** *continental firms in an enlarged market.*

complain

complain (about/of) [Vpr pass rel] speak critically (about sth/sb); express dissatisfaction (with sth). **o:** one's employer; wages, costs; poor service, dreadful food; being neglected, being woken up at night: *If old Pearson isn't* **complaining about** *one thing he's* **complaining about** *another.* ○ *The heating is so often* **complained about** *that I'm surprised it hasn't been improved.* ○ *You don't often find a woman with two children* **complaining of** *not having enough to do.*

complain of [Vpr] mention (some pain etc); give (sth) as a symptom of illness. **o:** loss of weight, of appetite; fatigue; heartburn: *There was no information ... and yet the patients* **complained of** *agonising pain.* INN ○ *Gwen John started to* **complain of** *headaches which sound very like migraines.* GJ

compliment

compliment (on) [Vn.pr pass rel] express one's admiration of (sth). **o:** hat, hair-style, new dress; success, performance; promotion, appointment: *Mrs Hunt was* **complimented on** *her choice of material for the bridesmaids' dresses.* ○ *This is an achievement* **on** *which he should be* **complimented**. ⇨ congratulate (on/upon).

comply

comply with [Vpr pass emph rel] follow or obey (sth). **o:** direction, instruction, (club) rule; request, wish, desire: *When you become a member of a club you generally agree to* **comply with** *the rules.* ○ *Certain of their conditions are not easily* **complied with**. = abide by.

compose

composed of [pass (Vn.pr)] having as members, or parts, a certain number or kind of (people, things). **S:** team, squad; family, town, city. **A:** wholly, entirely; partially: *The jury was* **composed** *entirely* **of** *men.* ○ *The village was* **composed of** *two or three groups of thatched cottages, a church, a post-office and a small general store.* □ never be comprised of; also used after a noun: *He had been brought up in a family* **composed** *entirely* **of** *females.* HB

compress

compress (into) 1 [Vn.pr pass rel] reduce (sth) to a concentrated form. **O:** wood chips, sawdust. **o:** board, sheet: *Wood cuttings and sawdust can be* **compressed into** *boards for furniture making.* **2** [Vn.pr pass rel] express (sth) concisely or briefly. **O:** story, facts. **o:** small space, a few words: *It is impossible to* **compress** *the story of the First World War* **into** *a few pages.* ○ **Compressed into** *its inexhaustibly rich few lines is a whole vision of Christianity.* MLT

compromise

compromise (with) (over) [Vpr emph rel] reach agreement (with sb) (about sth), by abandoning part of one's demands. **o:** (**with**) trades union, work force; salesman, representative; (**over**) wages, conditions; contract, conditions: *Nearly every strike is settled by employers* **compromising with** *their labour force.* ○ **Over** *fishing rights in the North Sea the trawler-men were in no mood to* **compromise**.

compute

compute at [Vn.pr pass rel] (*formal*) calculate (sth) as (a certain amount). **O:** cost, expenditure; loss. **o:** (a total of) $10 000, (a figure in excess of) $2 million: *The public were astonished when Rolls Royce* **computed** *their debts* **at** *several hundred million pounds.* = work out 2.

conceal

conceal (from) [Vn.pr pass emph rel] (*formal*) keep (sth) secret (from sb); hide (sth) (from sb). **O:** (true) facts, truth; house, building, fortifications. **o:** patient, dying man, (distraught) mother; view, road: *The doctor decided that he could not* **conceal** *the truth* **from** *the parents any longer.* ○ **From** *a person as inquisitive as Janet it's hard to* **conceal** *anything.* ○ *The house was* **concealed from** *the road by a small wood.*

concede

concede (to) [Vn.pr pass] (*formal*) acknowledge (to an opponent) that he has won. **O:** election, victory. **o:** adversary, other side, opposing party: *When three-quarters of the votes had been counted the Prime Minister* **conceded** *the election* **to** *his opponents.*

conceive

conceive of [Vpr pass] (*formal*) imagine or envisage (sth). **o:** situation, circumstances (in which); period (when); reason (why): *The modern child finds it difficult to* **conceive of** *a time when there was no radio or TV.* ○ *I can't* **conceive of** *anyone* *wanting to disturb the excellent relationship that has been built up with our allies.* □ often preceded by: *difficult, not easy, hard, (scarcely) possible, (well nigh) impossible.*

conceive of (as) [Vpr pass] consider (sth) to be (sth); reckon that (sth) is (sth). **o:** (**of**) life, childhood; work, art; (**as**) struggle, apprenticeship; intolerable burden, joyful release: *Maistre* ***conceived of*** *life* ***as*** *a savage battle at all levels.* RTH ○ *Freud had* ***conceived of*** *analysis* (ie psychoanalysis) ***as*** *an enterprise that was ... a medical enterprise.* F = regard as.

concentrate

concentrate (on/upon) [Vpr pass emph rel, Vn.pr pass emph rel] give one's full attention etc to (sth). **O:** (one's) attention, thoughts; one's mind; one's efforts, energies. **o:** the job in hand; problem, work, plans; doing a good job; book, music: *'I can't* ***concentrate on*** *what I'm doing while that noise is going on.'* ○ *The girl* ***concentrated*** *her attention* ***on*** *the swinging watch and soon fell into a trance.* ○ *If all one's efforts are* ***concentrated upon*** *reducing disharmony, there must be some improvement.* = focus (on).

concern

concern (oneself) (about/over/with) [Vn.pr pass emph rel] become occupied in an anxious way (about/over sb/sth); become interested or involved (with sb/sth) in a legitimate, straightforward, or sometimes interfering, way. **o:** loss, damage; sb's injuries; sb's movements, whereabouts: *There is no need for you to* ***concern yourself about*** *minor administrative problems.* ○ *He was much* ***concerned over*** *the plight of the refugees.* ○ *In the early days of psychoanalysis Freud* ***concerned himself with*** *three aspects of mental illness.* MP □ passive formed with *be, become, get*: *So much of Jung's later writing is* ***concerned with*** *the problems of evil.* JUNG

concerned (in) [pass (Vn.pr)] a party (to sth), having taken part (in sth). **o:** disturbance, riot; shouting, affray; demonstration: *Cecil was a successful financial administrator in India, but had been* ***concerned in*** *several dubious ventures.* SS □ also used after a noun or pronoun: *The police are anxious to interview everyone* ***concerned in*** *last night's incident.*

concur

concur (with) [Vpr emph rel] (*formal*) be of the same opinion as (sb); accept (sth). **o:** colleague, partner; opposing speaker, chairman; opinion, view; decision: *The Opposition has* ***concurred with*** *the Government in their decision to grant asylum to ten political prisoners.* ○ *My mother fully* ***concurred with*** *this judgement. The headmaster and she understood one another perfectly.* CED ○ *He* ***concurred with*** *the idea that physical ailments could be caused by sin.* F = agree (with) 1.

condemn

condemn to [Vn.pr pass emph rel] (*legal* or *figurative*) award to (sb) the punishment of (sth). **O:** prisoner, the accused (person); traitor, hostage. **o:** a month in gaol, thirty years' imprisonment; life; hard labour; death; (a lifetime of) pain, misery, loneliness: *The two were found guilty of armed robbery, and* ***condemned to*** *four years' imprisonment.* ○ *He had seen enough of Paris to fall in love with it, and now he was* ***condemned to*** *life in the provinces.* AF

condition

condition (to) [Vn.pr pass emph rel] make (a person/an animal) able to bear or endure (sth). **S:** childhood, upbringing; training. **o:** hardship, poverty; strain: *When a child has become* ***conditioned to*** *life in a city, he may feel quite out of place in any other environment.* ○ *The navy tries to* ***condition*** *its men* ***to*** *life in extreme climates.* □ often passive with *be, become, get.*

conduce

conduce to [Vpr emph rel] (*formal*) favour the development of (sth), add sth to (sth). **S:** bad management; violence, anger, ignorance. **o:** poor staff relations; racial disharmony: *Overcrowding in small houses hardly* ***conduces to*** *happy family relationships.* = contribute to 1.

conduct

conduct away (from) [Vn ⇆ p pass, Vn.p.pr pass rel] (*formal*) lead away (from a place), often with some show of force or compulsion. **S:** police, stewards, bodyguard. **O:** intruder, troublemaker, heckler. **o:** scene; meeting, platform: *The hecklers were* ***conducted away from*** *the hall at the request of the Chairman.* ○ *A steward took the man by the arm and* ***conducted*** *him firmly* ***away.***

cone

cone off [Vn ⇆ p pass] close one lane, carriageway etc of a (main) road with cone-shaped markers: *Repairs are in progress on a two-mile stretch of the M1. Police have* ***coned off*** *the fast lane.* ○ *Sections of the motorway have had to be* ***coned off.*** BBCTV

confer

confer (on/upon) [Vn.pr pass emph rel] (*formal*) give or grant (sth) officially (to sb). **O:** title, peerage, knighthood; (honorary) degree: *The title of Warden of the Cinque Ports was* ***conferred on*** *Winston Churchill.*

confer on/upon [Vn.pr pass emph rel] say or imply that (sb) possesses (some quality). **O:** fame, notoriety, respectability. **o:** hero, heroine; town, district: *The curse I carry within me is greater than any which my century has* ***conferred upon*** *me.* LTOW

confer (with) [Vpr pass emph rel] (*formal*) discuss (with sb) in order to decide a course of action; consult. **o:** solicitor; associates, board; director, manager: *For many years he had managed affairs,* ***conferring*** *almost daily* ***with*** *the Squire* (ie the landowner). GE ○ *When everyone has been* ***conferred with*** *perhaps I can give you an answer* (cf *When we have all* ***conferred****, perhaps I can give you an answer*).

confess

confess to [Vpr emph rel] acknowledge (sth). **o:** crime; stealing; killing, assaulting sb; (unreasonable) fear, dread; liking for, partiality to sth; being unable to appreciate modern art, literature etc; (a sneaking) admiration for sb; knowing nothing at all about sth: *She* ***confessed*** *readily* ***to*** *what she described as an abysmal ignorance of politics and economics.* ○ *Henderson would never have* ***con-***

fessed to *visiting strip clubs while he was in Hamburg.* = admit to.

confide

confide in [Vpr pass emph rel] tell one's secrets to (sb whom one trusts not to reveal them to sb else). **o:** sister, girlfriend, colleague: *Harold had never* ***confided*** *much* ***in*** *Isabel. He kept his business affairs from her.* PW ○ *He is not the sort of man* ***in*** *whom I would readily* ***confide****.*

confine

confine to 1 [Vn.pr pass emph rel] limit or restrict (sth) to (sth). **O:** oneself; one's attention, remarks, criticism, observations. **o:** essentials, pertinent details, the matter in hand: *I wish you would* ***confine*** *yourself* ***to*** *the matter under discussion.* ○ *The jury were instructed to* ***confine*** *their attention* ***to*** *the facts, and to ignore anything that could be described as hearsay.*

2 [Vn.pr pass emph rel] restrict (sb's movements) (to a place); keep (sb) within limits. **o:** one's room; the house; a certain area: *As a result of the accident, the child was* ***confined to*** *the house for six weeks.* ○ *As a punishment, the soldiers were* ***confined to*** *barracks for a week.* □ usu passive.

confirm

confirm in [Vn.pr pass] (*formal*) strengthen in (sb) (an opinion, habit etc). **S:** statement, revelation. **o:** suspicion, idea, belief; his tendency, habit; prejudice: *What you've told me about Bloggs* ***confirms*** *me* ***in*** *the suspicion that he's not to be trusted.*

conflict

conflict (with) [Vpr emph rel] not match (sth), be contrary (to sth). **S:** account, report, statement. **o:** evidence, facts, findings: *The policeman's story* ***conflicts with*** *that of the accused* (or: *The policeman's story and that of the accused* ***conflict***) *in several respects.* ○ *It is unfortunate for Northern Ireland that British policies, economic and financial ... so often* ***conflict with*** *her interests.* SC

conform

conform (to/with) [Vpr pass emph rel] (*formal*) be in accordance (with sth); obey, observe. **o:** specifications; rules, regulations; standards (of behaviour, manufacture etc): *Do these plans* ***conform to*** *the official specification for the building?* ○ *Mrs Jung* ***conformed to*** *all the understood conventions of the day* (as to how a woman should think, behave etc). JUNG ○ *These are very simple requirements, but they must be* ***conformed with****.* ○ *Joe's a born rebel: he just can't* ***conform*** *(****to*** *the ordinary rules of society).* = comply with.

confront

confront with [Vn.pr pass emph rel] (*formal*) bring (sb) face to face with (sth). **o:** facts; evidence, testimony: ***Confronted with*** *the evidence of half a dozen witnesses, the accused broke down and confessed.* ○ *Carl's parents constantly* ***confronted*** *him* ***with*** *the question 'What do you want to do in life?'* JUNG

confuse

confuse (with) [Vn.pr pass emph rel] be unable to distinguish (one thing) (from another). **O:** genuine, authentic (article, product). **o:** fake, imitation (product): *I always* ***confuse*** *John Waite* ***with*** *John White* (cf: *I always* ***confuse*** *the two Johns; I always* ***confuse*** *John Waite* ***and*** *John White*). ○ *This non-alcoholic cider must not be* ***confused with*** *the real stuff they drink in Somerset.* = mistake for, mix up (with) 1.

congratulate

congratulate (on/upon) [Vn.pr pass rel] give one's good wishes, express pleasure and approval, to (sb) (in connection with some event or achievement). **o:** his etc engagement, marriage; the birth of a child; being awarded first prize, coming first; her good sense, sang-froid, wise decision; promotion; appointment, nomination, election: *I am writing to* ***congratulate*** *you most sincerely* ***on*** *your recent election to the Senate.* ⇨ compliment (on).

congratulate oneself (on/upon) [Vn.pr emph rel] feel or express great satisfaction (as a result of sth one has done or that has happened): *You can* ***congratulate yourselves on*** *a very narrow escape; it's a miracle you weren't all burned alive.* ○ *The bank-robbers were just* ***congratulating themselves on*** *the success of their raid when the police burst in on them.*

conjure

conjure up 1 [Vp.n pass adj] evoke or suggest (a mental picture of sth). **O:** vision(s) of the past, of past glory, of days gone by; image, picture: *Words which when I read them* ***conjure up*** *the place and time.* ○ *He tried to imagine the night-club proprietor and could only* ***conjure up*** *a picture of a fat, oily man.* PE ○ *Hollywood's* ***conjured-up*** *visions of fabulous wealth suddenly assumed reality in Saudi Arabia.*

2 [Vp.n pass adj] cause (sth) to appear. **O:** spirits of the dead; the devil: *Witches persuaded credulous villagers that they could* ***conjure up*** *the spirits of the dead.*

conk

conk out [Vp] (*informal*) die; cease to function. **S:** he etc; car, lorry; radio, TV: *It's hard for him to get to work and he pretty nearly* ***conked out*** *in November with that pleurisy.* ○ *'As soon as that television finally* ***conks out****, I'm getting one with stereo sound.'*

connect

connect up (to) [Vn ⇆ p pass adj, Vn.p.pr pass rel] join (sth) to a main supply or system; join (one thing) (to another). **O:** telephone; wiring; electricity, gas, supply: *You won't get any current until you* ***connect up*** *the cells of the battery.* ○ *There's a phone in our new flat, but it hasn't been* ***connected up*** (***to*** the exchange) *yet.*

connect with [Vpr] arrive in time for a traveller to catch (some other convenient form of transport). **S:** bus, coach; plane: *The early bus from the village* ***connects with*** *the 8.30 train.*

connected (with) [pass (Vn.pr)] a member (of sth), having links (with sth): *'Excuse me. Are you* ***connected with*** *the visiting circus?' 'No, madam, this illuminated nose is merely to help me to see better.'* ○ *This business is in no way* ***connected with*** *the shop next door* (or: *This business and the shop next door are in no way* ***connected***). ○ *The visit of the police is not* ***connected with*** *the child's disappearance.*

connive

connive at [Vpr pass rel] give one's passive or moral support to (sth). **S:** employer; local authorities; police. **o:** deceit, fraud; pilfering; immorality: *An honest accountant will refuse to* **connive at** *a client's attempts to cheat the Income Tax authorities.* ○ *A certain amount of petty thieving is* **connived at** *by the storekeepers.*

consecrate

consecrate (to) [Vn.pr pass] (*formal*) devote (sth) to some sacred or other specified purpose. **O:** oneself, one's life; cathedral, temple: *The new church was* **consecrated** (**to** *the glory and service of God) in the presence of a large congregation.*

consent

consent (to) [Vpr pass emph rel] not oppose (sth). **o:** engagement, attachment; (his) leaving home, going abroad; proposal, scheme, plan: *The girl's parents had reluctantly* **consented to** *her marriage at the age of seventeen.* ○ *The owner wouldn't* **consent to** *our making any structural alterations to the flat.* = agree (to).

consign

consign to [Vn.pr pass emph rel] (*formal*) place or deposit (sb/sth) in (a place, esp a last resting place). **O:** coffin, body; prisoner; possessions. **o:** flames, waves; deepest dungeon; rubbish heap: *In a simple ceremony the bodies of four sailors were* **consigned to** *the deep.* ○ *He was* **consigned to** *a bleak prison in the old part of the city.*

consist

consist in [Vpr] (*formal*) be sth which is shown by (doing sth); be equivalent to (sth); mean. **S:** happiness, serenity; loyalty, service. **o:** accepting one's limitations, making do with little; putting others before self: *True patriotism* **consists in** *putting the interests of one's country above everything, including one's own life.* ○ *Education does not* **consist** *simply* **in** *learning a lot of facts.*

consist of [Vpr] comprise (sth). **S:** family, club; regiment, fleet; organism. **o:** members; tanks, ships; cells, nerves: *A sentence* **consists of** *one or more clauses and a clause* **of** *one or more phrases.* ○ *In Scotland, the jury* **consists of** *fifteen people, not twelve as in England.* = composed of.

consort

consort with [Vpr emph rel] (*formal, pejorative*) spend one's time or leisure in the company of (sb); keep company with (sb) . **o:** rogues, vagabonds, layabouts; prostitutes; professional gamblers: *He'd spent his early years* **consorting with** *petty thieves and teenage drug-pushers.* ○ *The very quality of their skin ... was different from* (ie superior to) *the human beings* **with** *whom Lionel was used to* **consorting**. GIE = associate with.

conspire

conspire (with) (against) [Vpr rel] plot or scheme (with others) (against sth/sb, or to do sth). **S:** rebels, dissidents; gang. **o:** (**against**) state, regime, established order: *A group of army officers were charged with* **conspiring against** *the newly elected government.* ○ *Bank staff are suspected of* **conspiring with** *the gang to transfer the stolen money to foreign bank accounts.*

consult

consult with 1 [Vpr] (esp *US*) seek the advice of (sb). **o:** adviser, attorney; bank; insurance company: *You'd better* **consult with** *your doctor before you take on a job in the tropics.* □ US usage; Brit speakers would normally use consult alone.

2 [Vpr] (of equal partners) hold discussions on matters of mutual interest. **o:** European Community partners; trading associates; fellow heads of state: *The Australian Attorney General is to* **consult with** *the British Government on the ending of all residual powers over the Dominion* (ie Australia) *held by Westminster.* T

contend

contend (for) [Vpr pass emph rel] (*formal*) struggle or compete with others (to win sth). **o:** prize, trophy; championship, leadership: *How many teams are* **contending for** *the Cup this year?* ○ *The boxer didn't consider such a small purse worth* **contending for**.

contend with [Vpr] handle or manage (sth/sb); bear, tolerate. **o:** much, a lot; family, in-laws; creditor, solicitor; problem, situation: *I have quite enough to* **contend with**, *without bothering myself with* your *problems.* ○ *If we've got to* **contend with** *your relatives for a week, we shall need a month's holiday afterwards.* ○ *What with one thing and another, the poor chap has too much to* **contend with**. □ usu used with *have (got) to.* = put up with.

content

content (oneself) with [Vn.pr pass emph rel] be satisfied with (sth), not want more than (sth). **o:** very little money, a sufficiency; simple fare, basic necessities; what one has: *We can't go abroad this year, so we'll have to* **content ourselves with** *a family holiday in London* (or: *we'll have to be* **contented with** *etc*).

continue

continue (with) [Vpr pass] not interrupt (sth); go on doing (sth). **o:** work, study, task; hobby, pastime: *The teacher told us to* **continue with** *our work while he was out of the classroom.* ○ *I don't propose to* **continue with** *chemistry beyond Form IV.* = go on with.

contract

contract out [Vn ⇆ p pass adj] arrange by contract for sb else to do (sth). **O:** work; catering, cleaning, repair work: *The newly privatized water authorities have* **contracted out** *maintenance of sewers to local authorities.* IND ○ *The security service on our university campus has been* **contracted out**.

contract out/out of [Vp, Vpr pass rel] withdraw (esp from a formal arrangement). **S:** country, ally; partner, associate. **o:** treaty, pact, alliance; undertaking, show, pension scheme: *I've decided that I don't want to be associated with your scheme: I'm* **contracting out**. ○ *We've had too many cases before of tenants* **contracting out of** *their obligations.*

contract (with) [Vn.pr pass emph rel] (*formal*) form or enter into (a relationship) (with sb/sth). **O:** friendship, marriage; alliance, association: *The* *heir to the throne had* **contracted** *a morganatic marriage* **with** *a commoner.* ○ *And this is the country* **with** *which they now propose to* **contract** *a trade agreement!*

contract (with) (for) [Vpr rel] make a formal agreement (with sb) (to do sth). **o:** (**with**) builder, plumber, decorator, electrician; (**for**) repairs, extension, wiring: *We* **contracted with** *a local carpenter* **for** *the woodwork* (or: *We* **contracted with** *him to do the woodwork*) *in our new boat.*

contrast

contrast (with) [Vpr emph rel, Vn.pr pass emph rel] (of one thing) be sharply different (from another); find and point out such differences. **S** [Vpr], **O** [Vn.pr]**:** appearance, outward show, manner, voice. **o:** character, record, background : [Vpr] *The wild threats* **contrast** *strongly* **with** *the mildness he always displays when brought face to face with people.* ○ [Vn.pr] *When the synthetic fabric is* **contrasted with** *the natural one, the difference is very apparent.*

contribute

contribute to/towards 1 [Vpr] give or add (sth) (to sth). **S:** presence; wisdom; ideas, suggestions; speech, remarks. **o:** success; failure; making people conscious: *The Prince's support has* **contributed** *substantially* **towards** *raising public awareness of environmental issues.* ○ *Bertrand Russell's speeches in Trafalgar Square* **contributed** *significantly* **to** *the movement against nuclear proliferation.*

2 [Vpr pass emph rel, Vn.pr pass emph rel] give (help) in support of (a cause). **O:** money, gifts, moral support. **o:** appeal, fund; resources, coffers: *A great amount of money was* **contributed to** *the Bangladesh disaster fund.* ○ *This is the kind of appeal* **to** *which most people will be glad to* **contribute** *(something).*

converge

converge on [Vpr emph rel] (all) move towards (one point) from two or more directions at once. **S:** forces; columns, patrols; assailants; shoppers. **o:** rendezvous, assembly-point, objective: *Some local insurgents* **converged on** *the house but were driven off by its inhabitants.* EB ○ *The only successful underwater launch had to be postponed last month after members of the 'Greenpeace' ecological action group* **converged on** *the testing site to protest against the missile.* G

converse

converse (with) [Vpr emph rel] (*formal*) talk (to sb). **o:** guest, visitor, stranger; class, pupils: *'If you want to* **converse with** *Japanese people, why don't you start learning Japanese?'* ○ *The tutor will be expected to* **converse with** *the students on various aspects of British life.*

convert

convert (from) (to) 1 [Vpr emph rel] change from being, doing or using sth (to sth else). **o:** (**from** and **to**) Catholicism, Judaism; solid fuel, gas; non-decimal system; Fahrenheit scale: *She* **converted from** *Christianity in order to marry a Muslim.* ○ *We're thinking of* **converting from** *solid fuel* **to** *natural gas before the cold weather sets in.* ○ *Britain* **converted to** *decimal currency on February 15th 1971.*

2 [Vn.pr pass emph rel] persuade (sb), cause (sth), to change from being, doing or using one thing (to another). **O:** wife, fiancé; house, factory; car. **o:** faith, religion; solid fuel, electricity; diesel fuel: *The preacher succeeded in* **converting** *a number of people* **to** *Unitarianism.* ○ *The transmission on his car has been* **converted from** *manual* **to** *automatic — an expensive job.* ○ *Our car has been* **converted to** *unleaded petrol.*

convert (into) [Vn.pr pass rel] change, alter (sth) (into sth else). **O:** barn, attic, bakery; pounds, dollars. **o:** house, studio, workshop; francs, lire: *They* **converted** *an old stable* **into** *a comfortable little house.* ○ *'Do you think you could* **convert** *this candlestick* **into** *an electric lamp?'* ○ *A lot of old people had difficulty in* **converting** *the old currency* **into** *the new.*

convict

convict (of) [Vn.pr pass rel] (*legal*) find or declare (sb) guilty (of sth). **o:** offence, crime; conspiracy; breaking and entering: *The woman was* **convicted of** *murdering her elderly father, despite her protests that she had ended his life out of kindness.* ○ *The offence* **of** *which he was* **convicted** *carries a stiff penalty.*

convince

convince (of) [Vn.pr pass emph rel] persuade (sb) of the truth (of sth); (in the passive) be sure (of sth). **o:** truth, validity; risk, peril; effectiveness, usefulness: *'How can I* **convince** *you (***of** *the dangers of drug-taking)?'* ○ *Nothing I could say had the slightest effect: my daughter was* **convinced of** *the young man's good intentions.* ○ **Of** *this I am* **convinced***: that Britain stands to gain by a closer association with her European neighbours.* □ passive with *appear* etc.

cook

cook up [Vn ⇆ p pass adj] (*informal*) concoct, invent (sth), often in haste. **O:** story, tale, plot; excuse, pretext: *Mr Singh earlier accused the Congress Party of* **cooking up** *a plot to create communal violence in Muslim areas of North India.* IND ○ *He arrived home at midnight with some* **cooked-up** *story of having been kept late at the office.*

cool

cool down [Vp, Vn ⇆ p pass] become or make (sb) cool or calm. **S** [Vp], **O** [Vn.p]**:** it (= the weather); passion, temper; atmosphere; situation: *'Thank heavens it's* **cooled down** *a little; I can't stand such hot weather for long.'* ○ *'Keep these men apart until they've* **cooled down** *a bit.'* ○ *'Put them in a cell for an hour or two — that'll* **cool** *them* **down***.'* = calm down 2, cool off.

cool off [Vp, Vn ⇆ p pass] become or make (sb) less warm, excited, ardent or interested: *'I've got to* **cool off***!' Mariette said, 'I'm going into the wood to* **cool off***!'* DBM ○ *After a while, these people* **cool off** *towards me and either answer in monosyllables or are plain rude.* WI ○ *The legislation provides for a* **cooling-off** *period before a strike can take place.*

coop

coop up (in) [Vn ⇆ p pass adj, Vn.p.pr pass rel] keep or confine (sb/sth) in a limited space. **o:** (this/that) place, room, house: *She would implore me to come* *outside for a 'breather' when I felt like it, and not to stay all day '**cooped up in** that furnace'*. THH ○ *I won't stay **cooped up** here for ten minutes longer even if your damned mother **is** lying in wait for me.* US ○ *She refused to spend any more of her life **cooped up** like this (**in** such a tiny house).*

co-operate

co-operate (with) [Vpr pass emph rel] work together (with sb). **o:** authorities; local council; police, security forces; staff, management: *If you will **co-operate with** us in raising funds, we will be much more successful than if we try to organize on our own.* ○ *If John can **co-operate with** me, and I **with** him* (or: *If John and I can **co-operate***), *everything should run smoothly.*

cop

cop out/out of [Vp nom, Vpr] (*informal*) withdraw (from sth) or fail to act (in sth), through timidity, cowardice etc: *I wanted him to take our complaint to the Managing Director, but he **copped out**, just as I feared he would.* ○ *Getting married in church when they've been life-long atheists is a bit of a **cop-out**, isn't it?*

cope

cope (with) [Vpr pass adj emph rel] deal effectively (with sb/sth), manage (sb/sth) adequately. **o:** crisis, situation; rush, pressure, numbers: *Our collection* (of wild animals) *had reached such proportions that it took us all our time to **cope with** it.* DF ○ *Jung hired a nurse to **cope with** the new baby and the chores.* JUNG ○ *'A few extra people for the weekend? Well, that's something that's easily **coped with**.'*

copy

copy down [Vn ⇆ p pass adj] write down sth which is spoken, or displayed on a large surface. **O:** speech, words; joke, saying; notice: *Reporters **copied down** the details in their notebooks.* ○ *'When you've **copied down** the exercise that's on the blackboard, we'll go on to the next one.'*

copy in [Vn ⇆ p pass] (*commerce*) include (sb) among those receiving a copy of a document: *Please **copy** me **in** on all the computer developments.* ○ *'Make sure that the marketing department is **copied in**.'*

copy out [Vn ⇆ p pass adj] write or type a copy of sth appearing in a book or document. **O:** chapter, paragraph; section, clause: *This passage is well worth **copying out**.* ○ *Simon is discovered **copying out** the defence plans for Paris and is arrested by the military authorities.* IND

cordon

cordon off [Vn ⇆ p pass adj] place a barrier across or round (a place) to prevent or check movement in and out. **S:** police, army, fire brigade. **O:** danger zone; street, house, beach: *The church and its precincts were already **cordoned off**, and a small crowd had gathered.* HWKM ○ *The city was devastated, fires climbing everywhere, water-mains broken, streets **cordoned off**.* BID

cork

cork up 1 [Vn ⇆ p pass] put a stopper made of cork, plastic etc in (sth) in order to keep out air. **O:** bottle; wine, beer, brew: *'It's dangerous to **cork up** these bottles while the wine is still fermenting, you know!'*

2 [Vn ⇆ p pass adj] not allow (sth) to show; suppress. **O:** feelings, (natural) emotions, (healthy) reactions; hatred, love: *It is very bad for you to **cork** your emotions **up** like that: you'd feel much better if you could 'let yourself go.'* = bottle up.

correlate

correlate (with) [Vpr emph rel, Vn.pr pass emph rel] statistically, match (sth) closely; establish such a relationship between (one thing) and (another). **S** [Vpr], **O** [Vn.pr]: results, findings; figures; linguistic ability, intelligence; size, weight. **o:** each other; (other) sets, series (of figures etc): *The results of British research into the effects of smoking **correlate with** those of scientists in other countries.* ○ *We generally find that we cannot **correlate** performance in Mathematics **with** achievement in, say, English or History* (cf: *We cannot **correlate** performance in Mathematics and English* etc). ○ *Freud attempted to **correlate** items in the dream **with** events and people in his immediate circumstances.* F

correspond

correspond to [Vpr emph rel] be equivalent to (sth); fulfil the same function as (sth). **S:** monarchy, Parliament, Foreign Office. **o:** presidency, Congress, State Department: *An infantry company **corresponds** roughly **to** a cavalry squadron.* ○ *In this engine the rotary section **corresponds to** the cylinders of a conventional model.* □ used with simple tenses only.

correspond (to/with) [Vpr emph rel] be equal or similar (to sth); match. **S:** story, report, version; figure, estimate. **o:** that given, the one made; what he had received, how I calculated it: *The witness's account **corresponded** fairly closely **to** the policeman's observations.* ○ *I'm afraid your offer doesn't **correspond with** the figure I've heard mentioned* (or: *I'm afraid your offer and the figure don't **correspond***). □ used with simple tenses only. = tally (with).

cotton

cotton on (to) [Vp, Vp.pr] (*informal*) fully understand or become fully aware of (sth). **o:** fact, danger; implication, meaning, intention; what it all means: *'Don't you understand what she's trying to do to you? Haven't you **cottoned on** yet?'* ○ *Farmers have at last **cottoned on to** the fact that they should present their animals at market in the same way a shopkeeper displays his goods at Christmas.* RT ○ *The show's writers have **cottoned on to** a basic principle of English humour.* L = catch on (to).

couch

couch (in) [Vn.pr pass emph rel] express (sth) (in particular terms). **O:** protest, application, agreement; document, letter. **o:** strong, mild terms; legal, formal language: *Another answer has been **couched** much more **in** social or political terms.* CF ○ *You'll have to **couch** your statement to the court **in** rather more diplomatic language.* □ usu passive.

cough

cough up 1 [Vn ⇆ p pass] bring (sth) from one's throat etc by coughing. **O:** blood, saliva, phlegm; particles of food: *The patient had begun to **cough up** blood.*

2 [Vp, Vp.n pass] (*informal*) pay (sth), usu reluctantly. **O:** money, cash: *She asked for a sum of money which was about the maximum that I would* ***cough up****, and then hastened to indicate a way in which I might recoup myself.* UTN ○ *'Look, you've no alternative, so* ***cough up*** *the cash and stop complaining.'* = pay up, stump up.

cough it up [Vn.p] (*informal*) say sth that is in some way difficult to reveal; confess: *'I can see that you've got something on your mind. Come on,* ***cough it up****! Stop trying to hide it!'*

count

count against [Vpr, Vn.pr pass] be considered, consider (sth), as a factor against (sb). **S** [Vpr], **O** [Vn.pr]: failing, fault; mistake, slip; background, origins: *His inability to make quick decisions* ***counted against*** *him when being considered for promotion.* ○ *The family will* ***count*** *it* ***against*** *you that you weren't at the funeral.* ○ *One careless mistake can hardly be* ***counted against*** *her.* = hold against.

count among [Vpr, Vn.pr pass] be or regard (sb) as one of (a particular group). **o:** friends, acquaintances; more valued colleagues: *Mr Heffer no longer* ***counts among*** *my friends since he refused to lend me his lawn-mower.* ○ *There was a time when we were proud to* ***count*** *Mrs Paterson* ***among*** *our supporters.* = reckon among 1.

count down [Vn ⇆ p nom pass] (esp *space technology*) count numbers in reverse order towards zero, eg in launching a rocket, detonating an explosive charge etc: *Millions of people saw Apollo 10 being* ***counted down*** *on television.* ○ *It's likely that something went wrong with Union II's* ***count-down****.* BBCTV

count for [Vpr] be of (little etc) importance. **o:** little, (not) much, nothing: *When it came to money, all his friendly promises* ***counted for*** *little: he was as mean as Scrooge.* ○ *Surely all our hard work can't* ***count for*** *nothing! We deserve* some *reward, don't we?*

count (from) (up) to [Vpr, Vp.pr] (be able to) use or say numbers as far as (a certain higher number): *Most children of five have no difficulty in learning to* ***count*** *(****from*** *one)* ***up to*** *a hundred.* ○ *Each time you feel like having a violent quarrel with somebody,* ***count (up) to*** *ten before speaking.*

count in [Vn ⇆ p pass] include (sb) as part of a group; include (sth) as part of a bill, estimate etc: *If the cost of the trip is no more than twenty pounds, you can* ***count*** *me* ***in****.* ○ *There are more than a hundred places of worship in the city, if we* ***count in*** *all the churches, mosques and synagogues.* = reckon in.

count on/upon 1 [Vpr pass emph rel] trust (sb) to help, give support etc. **o:** relative, friend; solicitor, bank manager. **A:** for assistance, for advice; to offer support, to show sympathy: *At parties Caro could* ***count on*** *her to sing gaily and play the piano.* GE ○ *This house is the only thing in my life that has stayed in the same place. It's the only thing I can* ***count on****.* EHOW ○ *You can always* ***count on*** *Bill for a pound or two when you're in difficulties.* = bank on 2, depend on/upon 1, rely on/upon.

2 [Vpr pass] make one's plans in the sure knowledge that sth will happen, or be the case. **o:** him/his being there, him/his supporting you; his help, encouragement: *You could always* ***count on*** *Fred turning up when he was least expected.* ○ *I had so* ***counted on*** *your being there ... You are just the one person I did want.* BLCH = depend on/upon 2, reckon on/upon.

count out 1 [Vn ⇆ p pass] count (things) one by one, perhaps placing them on a surface. **O:** money, change; buttons, counters: *The old lady laboriously* ***counted out*** *fifteen pence, snapped her purse shut and said 'There! Is that right?'*

2 [Vn ⇆ p pass] (*boxing*) of a referee, count up to ten over (a boxer who has been knocked down): *The poor fellow was* ***counted out*** *in the first round.*

3 [Vn ⇆ p pass] (*informal*) discount (sb) as unimportant; not include: *If the coach is not going to return before midnight, you'd better* ***count*** *me* ***out****.* ○ *He had never liked Alec as well as he did at that moment. As a rival he had* ***counted*** *Alec* ***out****.* PW

count to [Vpr] ⇨ count (from) (up) to.

count up [Vn ⇆ p pass] find the total of (several things). **O:** times, occasions; marks; coupons, stamps: *Now* ***count up*** *the points you've scored and compare them with the table. This will show you whether you are above or below average.* ○ *Try* ***counting up*** *the number of people who come into the shop each day.* = reckon up.

count (up) to [Vp.pr] ⇨ count (from) (up) to.

count upon [Vpr pass emph rel] ⇨ count on/upon 1.

counter

counter (with) [Vpr, Vn.pr pass] oppose (sth) (with sth); reply to (sth) (with sth). **O:** threat, attack, thrust; rebellion; suggestion, proposal. **o:** more powerful weapons; uppercut to the jaw, sharp jab; punitive expedition; one's own proposal, (new) idea, argument: *There was always the chance that if the enemy were too hard pressed on the ground they would* ***counter with*** *a heavy air strike.* ○ *The ginger group that had been formed by the shareholders* ***countered*** *the Board's resolution* ***with*** *one of their own.*

couple

couple on/onto [Vn ⇆ p pass, Vn.pr pass] link or attach (sth) (to sth). **O:** (railway) wagon, coach; caravan, trailer. **o:** engine; car, van: *More sleeping cars were* ***coupled on*** *at Vienna.* ○ *They covered a thousand miles with a heavy trailer* ***coupled onto*** *the back of their family saloon.* = join on/onto.

couple up [Vn ⇆ p pass] join (units) together, esp to form a railway train. **O:** wagon, coach: *When all the coaches had been* ***coupled up****, they formed a train nearly three hundred metres long.*

couple (with) [Vn.pr pass emph rel] link (sth) (to sth else) in one's words or actions. **O:** move, development; plan, proposal. **o:** demand, call, requirement; action: *The proposal, by the home affairs select committee, was* ***coupled with*** *a call to improve ethnic minority confidence in the police.* IND ○ *Public sector restraint needs to be* ***coupled with*** *measures to curb consumption and increase savings through tax incentives.* G □ usu passive. = associate with 2.

course

course through [Vpr emph rel] (*formal*) rush, run, through (sth). **S:** blood; sap; thoughts, ideas, fancies. **o:** veins, body; trunk; brain, mind: *He felt the blood* ***coursing through*** *his veins as his excitement* *grew.* ○ ***Through** his mind **coursed** all manner of confused thoughts.*

cover

cover (against) [Vn.pr pass rel] protect (oneself etc) by means of an insurance policy (against sth). **O:** oneself, life; house, property; car. **o:** accident, incapacity, illness, death; fire, storm, flood, damage, burglary; theft: *Are you **covered against** loss of earnings resulting from an accident?* ○ *Does your car insurance **cover** you **against** damage to third parties?* = insure (against).

cover in [Vn ⇆ p pass adj] place a protective covering over (sth). **O:** hall, driveway; yard, terrace: *We decided to **cover in** the passage between the main building and the annexe.* ○ *The **covered-in** area gave shelter to the cattle during the winter.*

cover in/with [Vn.pr pass rel] coat (sth) with (sth); cover (sth) with (sth); make (dirt etc) fly and fall on (sth). **o:** paint, creosote; material, protective sheeting; soot, mud, lime: *The walls had been **covered with** a dark-green paint.* ○ *The room would look much brighter if we **covered** the sofa **with** a light-coloured material.* ○ *A passing lorry ran through a puddle and **covered** us **in** mud from head to foot.*

cover oneself in/with [Vn.pr pass] achieve glory, credit, ignominy etc, by one's actions. **S:** nation; team, class; teacher, artist. **o:** ⚠ glory, credit; shame, confusion: *The regiment **covered** itself **in** glory in its first action of the campaign.* ○ *Hostile newspapers agreed that he was the only trade union leader to have **covered** himself **with** credit.* OBS

cover over/up [Vn ⇆ p pass adj] hide (sth) from view; protect (sb) with clothing etc: *'I think I'll take a look at that hole.' 'You can't. It's been **covered up**.'* DC ○ *'**Cover** the baby's feet **up**; he'll catch cold.'*

cover up (for) [Vp nom, Vp.pr pass, Vn ⇆ p pass] hide the true state of affairs (on one's own or sb else's behalf). **O:** blunder, error; inefficiency, inadequacy: [Vp] *The inefficient who successfully **cover up** are those who know how to put on a big display of efficiency when it will be noticed, and let the rest go hang.* OBS ○ *'Don't try to convince me that nothing's been happening. I suspect that it's all a big **cover-up**!'* ○ *All this assumes ... President Nixon's complicity in the original crime or in the subsequent **cover-up**.* NS ○ [Vp.pr] *If I'm late tomorrow you'll **cover up for** me, won't you?* ○ [Vn.p] *Official misdemeanours had been **covered up** because the officials concerned had connections in high places.* LFM = hush up.

cover with ⇨ cover in/with.

cover oneself with ⇨ cover oneself in/with.

cow

cow into submission [Vn.pr pass] make (sb) surrender through fear. **O:** occupied territory, conquered people: *He is not the kind of man who is likely to **be cowed into submission**.*

crack

crack down (on) [Vp nom, Vp.pr pass] (*informal*) use one's authority (against sb/sth); suppress, attack. **o:** rebels, dissidents; minority; vice, crime; prostitution, gambling: *The police are always being urged to **crack down** hard **on** the drug pushers.* ○ *Hong Kong's relations with China have grown increasingly sour in the wake of Peking's **crack-down** on the pro-democracy movement in June 1989.* IND

crack up 1 [Vp nom] (*informal*) lose one's health or mental stability: *If Angela goes on working and worrying like this, she's bound to **crack up** sooner or later.* ○ *'What's come over you? This isn't the time to **crack up**.'* YAA ○ *The **crack-up** could come quicker than you think and Joe could find himself in hospital.* = break up 2, break down 8.

2 [Vp nom] (*informal*) collapse, disintegrate. **S:** machine; organization: *Suddenly, without any warning, the plane just seemed to **crack up**.* ○ *The **crack-up** of the Rolls-Royce company surprised and shocked everyone in Britain.* = break down 4.

crack up to be [Vn.p] (*informal*) consider or estimate (sth/sb) to be (sth) (with the suggestion that the assessment is exaggerated). **O:** (new) fashion, fad, invention, pastime; town, country, area: *People will begin to wonder whether competition in the City* (ie as a major financial centre) *is all it's **cracked up to be**.* OBS ○ *She was horrified by her first bite at an apple, which her father had **cracked up to be** the finest fruit in the world.* BID □ often in the passive form after *(not) all, (not) everything.*

cram

cram into [Vn.pr pass emph rel] push or force (sth/sb) into (a space). **O:** (too much) food; (too many) people; everything, a lifetime's experience. **o:** one's mouth; bus, train; suitcase, bag; a few days: *Children often **cram** too much **into** their mouths.* ○ *It's dangerous for too many people to be **crammed into** a bus.* ○ *The lovers tried to **cram** a lifetime **into** the six months they had together.* = stuff into. ⇨ next entry

cram (with) [Vn.pr pass rel] fill (a space) overfull (with sth). **O:** drawer, room, house, desk; pocket, bag, purse; sb's head; book, encyclopedia. **o:** clothes, rubbish, furniture, letters, knick-knacks; odds and ends, scraps of paper; (useless) facts, nonsense; information, good advice: *The Victorians **crammed** their houses **with** furniture and ornaments.* ○ *Eliot's poetry is **crammed with** dreams.* TSE ○ *It's no use **cramming** your head **with** a lot of unrelated facts: what you need is a system.* ⇨ previous entry

crane

crane forward [Vp] stretch one's neck forward in order to see better. **S:** onlooker, viewer, spectator: *The audience **craned forward** as the conjuror came to the crucial part of his trick.*

crank

crank up 1 [Vp, Vn ⇆ p pass] start (an engine) by means of a starting-handle: *'The battery's flat! I'm afraid you'll have to **crank up**!'* ○ *'Once the engine has been **cranked up**, she'll probably start easily on the battery.'*

2 [Vn ⇆ p pass] start or intensify (sth) by vigorous action. **O:** board, committee; project, scheme; conflict, campaign: *If the civil war was to be **cranked up** again, anarchy might infect Europe from east to west.* HGW

crash

crash about [Vp, Vpr] move about (a place) in a clumsy, noisy manner, knocking things over etc: *'I wish you wouldn't **crash about** like that as soon as you get home from school.'*

crash about one's ears [Vpr] collapse disastrously. **S:** his etc whole world; everything that she had achieved; his dreams, ambitions: *When Bob's fiancée broke off their engagement, his whole world came* **crashing about his ears**. □ often in the form *come* crashing etc, as in the example. = fall about one's ears.

crash across, along, away etc [Vp,Vpr] move across etc, causing noise and damage: *The armoured divisions* **crashed through** *a thin defensive screen.* ○ *The maid put the tray on an unsteady table, and everything* **crashed to** *the floor.* ○ *A lorry went out of control and* **crashed into** *a shop window.*

crash down [Vp] fall noisily, heavily and often dangerously. **S:** tree, rock, house, waves: *The rocks* **crashed down** *on to the road below.* ○ *With gigantic waves* **crashing down** *upon her, the lifeboat made her way to the crippled ship.*

crash out [Vp] (*informal*) fall asleep, esp from extreme tiredness: *He wished that he was just going back to his own flat to* **crash out**. DOAP ○ *I party a little and then* **crash out** *for the remainder of the day.* IND ○ *Some people are able to* **crash out** *completely after skiing.* SKIS = flake out.

crave

crave (for) [Vpr pass emph rel] have a great desire or wish for (sth). **o:** change; (new) role, environment: *There comes a time* (ie in one's career) *when one* **craves for** *recognition.* ○ *He claimed to be a democrat, but secretly he* **craved for** *absolute authority.* AH ○ *At last she won the promotion* **for** *which she* **craved**. = long for, yearn (for).

crawl

crawl across, along, away etc [Vp emph, Vpr emph rel] move slowly across etc (esp, of humans, on hands and knees): *Somehow the wounded animal managed to* **crawl away** *from its pursuers and* **into** *a hole.* ○ *The traffic was so thick that we could only* **crawl along** *at about fifteen miles an hour.*

crawl (to) [Vpr pass] (*informal, pejorative*) act in a humble, submissive manner towards (sb) to obtain favours: *'Don't you come* **crawling** *(back)* **to** *me now that all your money's gone!'* ○ *If there's anything he loathes it's being* **crawled to** *by people impressed by his title.*

crawl with [Vpr] be full of, covered with, or 'alive' with (vermin). **o:** fleas, lice, maggots: *The children's clothes were found to be* **crawling with** *lice.* ○ *The flat was* **crawling with** *cockroaches.* □ usu continuous tenses.

cream

cream off [Vn ⇆ p pass adj] take (the best or most able) from a group of people. **S:** specialist school, good universities. **O:** the most able, outstanding candidates: *The elitist 'grandes écoles'* (university level schools in France) **cream off** *the highest fliers with selective entrance procedures.* IND ○ *With technicians* **creamed off** *from other studios, he could make cheap films so that they looked good and brought in respectable profit.* BCIN = skim off 2.

crease

crease up [Vp, Vn.p pass] (cause sb to) laugh heartily: *Whenever he appears on stage, I just* **crease up**. ○ *Debbie* (an American) *just loves these British accents on TV. It* **creases** *me* **up** *when she copies them.* GL = double up 1,2, fold up 2.

credit

credit (to) [Vn.pr pass rel] next entry

credit (with) [Vn.pr pass rel] (*finance* or *commerce*) enter in (sb's account) a sum equal to the value of (sth). **o:** the unsold goods, the damaged articles, the missing parts: *We are returning the materials covered by your invoice number 108432 as they were not according to specification. Please* **credit** *our account* **with** (or: **credit to** *our account*) *the returned goods.* ○ *We can't refund cash but we'll* **credit** *you* **with** *the value of the suit.* □ note credit *sb/sb's account.*

credit with 1 [Vn.pr pass rel] recognize that (sb) has achieved (sth) or been responsible for (sth). **o:** the introduction, improvement, achievement (of sth): *He can be* **credited with** *a long-term influence on the development of Indian publishing.* IND ○ *Archimedes is sometimes credited with inventing the lever, because of his remark that, if given a place to stand, he could move the earth.* G

2 [Vn.pr pass] believe (sb) to possess (a certain quality of mind or character). **o:** (more, so little) sense, intelligence; drive, initiative: *'What on earth did they do that for? I would have* **credited** *them* **with** *more sense!'* ○ *Why are so many of us* **credited with** *so little intelligence and self-determination?* G

creep

creep across, along, away etc [Vp emph, Vpr emph rel] move across etc gradually, steadily. **S:** ivy, honeysuckle, vine; patrol, intruder; car, train: *His particular dream was of a small country cottage, with rambler roses* **creeping along** *the fence.* ○ **Down** *the path* **crept** *a long line of ants.*

creep in/into 1 [Vp emph, Vpr emph rel] enter very quietly: *'Now,* **creep into** *the children's bedrooms and don't wake them up.'*

2 [Vp emph, Vpr emph rel] enter gradually and imperceptibly. **S:** (sour, unpleasant) tone; unpleasantness: *Once complications are allowed to* **creep in**, *the outcome is in danger.* MFM ○ *A distinct note of acrimony had* **crept into** *their conversation.*

creep over [Vpr] affect (sb) gradually. **S:** feeling, (strange) sensation; the suspicion that: *There* **crept over** *him, vaguely at first and then more strongly, the suspicion that he was being deliberately poisoned.*

creep up (on) [Vp, Vp.pr pass] approach (sb/sth) silently or unobserved: *We* **crept up** *(***on** *them) and, peering through the brambles, saw they were having a picnic.* ○ *'I dislike the feeling of being* **crept up on**. *Why don't you walk straight in and say what you have to say?'*

creep up on [Vp.pr] approach (sb) gradually and without being noticed. **S:** day of decision, time of parting, moment of truth: *One could hardly imagine the ruin that was even then* **creeping up on** *her.* 50MH ○ *Time* **creeps up on** *me ... I think, 'Oh maybe for a little while,' and next thing I know it's so late.* AT

cringe

cringe away/back (from) [Vp, Vp.pr emph rel] (of animals and human beings in a state of fear or terror) retreat (from sb/sth): *We saw the dogs* **cring-**

ing away from *a man with a whip in his hand.* ○ *If we made any overtures of friendship she would* ***cringe back****, gazing at us with wide-eyed horror, her little hands trembling with fright.* DF = draw away/back (from).

cringe (before) [Vpr emph rel] behave in a timid, cowardly or ingratiating way (to sb). **o:** father, schoolmaster, magistrate, policeman: *The sight of a big strong man* ***cringing before*** *some minor official would disgust most people.* ○ ***Before*** *such emblems of authority as a police uniform, he would invariably* ***cringe****.* = grovel (before/to).

crisp

crisp up [Vp, Vn ⇆ p pass adj] (of sth which has gone soft from a hard or crisp state) become or make crisp again; (of sth that was not previously hard, eg bacon) become or make crisp: *These cornflakes have gone soft, but they'll be all right if you* ***crisp*** *them* ***up*** *in the oven.*

crop

crop up 1 [Vp] be mentioned; arise. **S:** topic, subject, theme: *If Lucy's name* ***crops up*** *in the conversation, remember you don't know anything about her affair with John!* ○ *The pills must be good because the name was always* ***cropping up*** *in the Seattle papers.* RFW = come up 5.

2 [Vp] happen, occur, appear. **S:** opportunity, job, chance; something: *Things were always* ***cropping up*** *which forced Ned to demonstrate who was the boss.* CON ○ *Things have* ***cropped up*** *that make my position here rather difficult, for myself and others.* HD ○ *'Why don't you stay at home tomorrow? I can call you if anything* ***crops up*** *in the office.'*

cross

cross (in) [Vn.pr pass] obstruct or oppose (sb) (in sth he proposes to do). **o:** design, intention, ambition, objective: *He is a friendly enough person, so long as you don't* ***cross*** *him (****in*** *his business plans).* ○ *'What's the matter with Sally?' 'I would say she's been* ***crossed in*** *love!'*

cross off [Vn ⇆ p pass adj, Vn.pr pass] remove (sth) from a list etc by putting a line (or more rarely, a cross) through it. **O:** name; item; task, job, place. **o:** list; agenda: *I found that my name had been* ***crossed off*** *the list of players, and somebody else's substituted.* ○ *You can* ***cross*** *that job* ***off*** *— I've already fixed the lamp.* = tick off 1.

cross out [Vn ⇆ p pass adj] put a line (or more rarely, a cross) through (sth), usu because it is wrong. **O:** name, mistake, misspelt words, half the exercise: *The envelope arrived with the old address* ***crossed out****, and the new one written alongside it.* ○ *He wrote that the last three quartets were patriotic poems; then he* ***crossed out*** *the remark.* TSE ○ *The exercise was made almost illegible by many* ***crossings-out****.* □ nom form: crossing(s)-out. = score out, strike out.

cross with [Vn.pr pass rel] mix (one breed) with (another). **O:** breed, strain: *This dog looks like the result of an Alsatian being* ***crossed with*** *a spaniel.*

cross swords (with) [Vn.pr emph rel] have a dispute (with sb), enter into a verbal conflict (with sb). **o:** neighbour, colleague, (child's) teacher: *When the Prime Minister* ***crossed swords with*** *the Leader of the Opposition* (or: *When they* ***crossed swords****) across the floor of the House, the former usually got the worst of it.*

crow

crow (about) [Vpr pass emph rel] (*informal*) talk in a boastful way about (sth). **o:** achievement, success; family, business: *The buyer . . . was* ***crowing about*** *his new purchase.* SAS ○ *Nor is there any reason to* ***crow about*** *things going wrong.* FV = boast about/of.

crowd

crowd in (on/upon) [Vp, Vp.pr emph rel] push (themselves) forward into the mind (of sb); press too closely (around one). **S:** memories, thoughts, recollections; houses, traffic: *In times of stress, fantasies, dreams, symbols* ***crowded in upon*** *him.* JUNG ○ *'Where we lived before, the scenery tended to* ***crowd in on*** *us.'* T

crowd in/into [Vp emph, Vpr emph, Vn ⇆ p pass, Vn.pr emph] move in a crowd into a relatively small space. **S** [Vp Vpr], **O** [Vn.p Vn.pr]**:** spectators, audience; passengers. **o:** room, ball; carriage, compartment: [Vp] *It was as full as every other city of country people* ***crowding in*** *for high wages.* INN ○ [Vpr] *Hundreds of people* ***crowded into*** *the village hall to hear the local MP.* ○ [Vn.p] *I think we could manage to* ***crowd*** *a few more* ***in****.* ○ [Vn.pr] ***Into*** *one small van the men had* ***crowded*** *about a dozen sheep.*

crowd out/out of [Vn ⇆ p pass, Vn.pr pass] be the cause of keeping (people) out (of a place); because of one's own numbers, cause (others) to leave, or stay outside (a place). **O:** newcomers, late arrivals, would-be spectators. **o:** hall, theatre, lecture-room: *Pressure on study-space has* ***crowded out*** *new students from many university libraries* (or: *has* ***crowded*** *new students* ***out of*** *many* etc). ○ *A fairly large proportion of expectant mothers are* ***crowded out of*** *Britain's maternity hospitals.* OBS

crowd round [Vp, Vpr] form a large group (round sb). **S:** reporters, onlookers; students. **o:** celebrity; prisoner; teacher; platform, desk: *Why do people* ***crowd round****, staring blankly, whenever there's an accident?* ○ *Passers-by* ***crowded round*** *the policeman as he made his arrest.*

crumble

crumble away [Vp] fall in small pieces; disintegrate gradually. **S:** rocks, walls, cliffs; ruins; opposition: *People living in the houses on the cliff-top grow more and more worried as it* ***crumbles away*** *into the sea.* ○ *It is remarkable how completely the opposition to privatizing this industry has* ***crumbled away****.*

crumple

crumple up 1 [Vp, Vn ⇆ p pass adj] crease or break, and crush (sth); (cause sth to) lose its former recognizable shape by crushing, change of air pressure etc. **S** [Vp], **O** [Vn.p]**:** packet, tin; shell, crust; bodywork (of car): *The small car just* ***crumpled up*** *on impact with the lorry.* ○ *Eventually, I found the letter* ***crumpled up*** *into a ball in the baby's cot.*

2 [Vp] fail, collapse, give way. **S:** he etc; army, opposition, resistance: *All organized resistance* ***crumpled up*** *when the tanks went in.* ○ *One day Mr Moreton was a fine, healthy-looking man, the next* *he looked old and helpless: he had just* **crumpled up**. ○ *In the face of the numbers, audacity, and precision of the attackers, the train's security, such as it was,* **crumpled up**. T

crusade

crusade (for/against) [Vpr emph rel] take part in a vigorous campaign (in support of sth/against sth). **o:** changes (in the law, in society), reform; abolition, restoration (of sth): *In Britain, groups are constantly* **crusading for** *stricter controls on the dumping of industrial waste at sea.*

crush

crush in [Vn ⇆ p pass adj] flatten or make a dent in (sth) by pressing it very hard. **O:** door, (car) panel; chest, skull: (description of food on a supermarket shelf) ... *individual apple-pie with the crust* **crushed in**, *and a price-tag obscuring the expired date-stamp.* ST

crush in/into [Vp, Vpr, Vn ⇆ p pass, Vn.pr pass] (force people to) enter too small a space. **o:** theatre, cinema; compartment, bus : [Vp] *As soon as the train stopped, about two hundred people tried to* **crush in** (or: [Vpr] **into** *the few empty compartments*). ○ [Vn.p] *More than thirty head of cattle had been* **crushed in** (or: [Vn.pr] **into** *a lorry that was only big enough to take twenty*).

crush into [Vn.pr pass] reduce (sth) by the use of a heavy weight, or great pressure, to (sth). **o:** pieces, dust, powder; an unrecognizable shape: *The rocks were* **crushed into** *powder by a gigantic hammer.*

crush into submission [Vn.pr pass] force (sb/sth) to submit, by using superior force. **O:** subject people; opposition, hostile minority; occupied territory: *The few remaining pockets of resistance were finally* **crushed into submission**.

crush out/out of [Vn ⇆ p pass adj, Vn.pr pass] extract, remove (sth) by applying a heavy weight or great pressure. **O:** juice, moisture; spirit, life. **o:** sugar-cane, fruit, vegetable; people: *The sugar-cane is taken to the factory where the juice is* **crushed out**. ○ *When I last saw Smith he looked like a man who'd had the spirit* **crushed out of** *him.* = press out/out of.

crush to death [Vn.pr pass] kill (sb) by applying heavy weight or great pressure. **S:** rock-fall, avalanche: *There is always the danger that someone will be* **crushed to death** *whenever great crowds gather together.* □ usu passive.

crush up [Vn ⇆ p pass adj] soften (sth) or reduce it to powder by applying weight or pressure. **O:** stone, rock, rubble; chocolate, lump-sugar: (instructions in a recipe) *The root-ginger should be* **crushed up** *before it is added to the boiling jam.*

cry

cry about/over [Vpr pass] weep or lament about (sth). **o:** loss, mishap, misfortune; the unfairness of sth: *'What a noise to make. Now you've made Sarah cry too. There's nothing to* **cry about**. *We're going for a nice ride on a train.* DC ○ *I found Jenny in her room,* **crying over** *her misfortunes, both real and imagined.*

cry down [Vn ⇆ p pass] (*informal*) give little importance to (sth); belittle. **O:** attempt, initiative, move; achievement, success: *The Opposition* **cried down** *every effort of the Government to reduce inflation.* ○ *'Don't* **cry down** *the very real progress these people have made.'*

cry for [Vpr] cry or weep in an attempt to obtain (sth). **o:** food, drink; attention, a cuddle; something, nothing: *'That child is always* **crying for** *something. What does he want now?'* ○ *'Don't take any notice of Johnny; he* **cries for** *nothing* (= *he* **cries for** *no good reason*).*'*

cry for the moon [Vpr] long for the impossible: *'They're always wishing they could afford a cottage in Sardinia, or take a cruise round the world, or something equally impossible. Just* **crying for the moon**.*'*

cry off [Vp, Vpr] withdraw from some previous arrangement or agreement. **o:** attending, visiting sb, going to the cinema: *'I don't think I'll go swimming after all.' 'Oh, you're not going to* **cry off** *now are you, when I've got everyone else interested ?'* ○ *It was the only foggy night in November and Gerald was sorely tempted to* **cry off** *going to dinner but Leonie got him there somehow.* ASA □ in the [Vpr] pattern, the object is the *-ing* form of a v.

cry out [Vp] exclaim, usu involuntarily in pain or alarm: *I heard a splash, and then a man's voice,* **crying out** *for help.* GL ○ *As he drove, too fast, into the first of the bends, his passenger* **cried out** *to him to slow down.* = call out 4.

cry one's eyes/heart out [Vn.p] (*informal*) weep in misery and for a long time: *When Lucy finally came down from the bedroom she looked as if she'd been* **crying her eyes out**. ○ *The poor child* **cried her heart out** *when her father came home and told her that her dog had been run over.*

cry out for [Vp.pr rel] plainly invite (sth), be a natural subject for (sth): *Across the moors, the roads, winding, narrow, steep are perilous. If ever a stretch of country* **cried out for** *a swift, clean cut, this is it.* T ○ *His London flat near High Street, Kensington, is the sort of mess of books, records and empty wine bottles that* **cries out for** *a woman's touch.* TVT □ note alt pattern with inf: *The place* **cries out for** *redevelopment* (or: **cries out** *to be redeveloped*).

it's no use crying over spilt milk [Vpr] (*proverb*) there is no point in complaining about sth that cannot be put right or changed: *'Look! The sooner you realize that your money has gone, the better it will be for you.* **It's no use crying over spilt milk**.*'* ⇨ cry about/over.

cry oneself to sleep [Vn.pr] weep until one falls asleep: *While the parents were laughing their heads off at some nonsense on television their unhappy son lay in bed* **crying himself to sleep**.

cuddle

cuddle up (to) [Vp, Vp.pr pass] draw closer (to another person), usu for warmth or comfort. **S:** child, pet: *The twins* **cuddled up** *close together and fell asleep.* ○ *The child* **cuddled up to** *her mother.* = snuggle up (to).

cull

cull from [Vn.p pass emph rel] (*formal*) collect or gather (sth) from (a place). **O:** facts, information; examples. **o:** reports, documents: *The chairperson presented evidence* **culled from** *various official reports.*

culminate

culminate in [Vpr rel] (*formal*) reach a climax in or end in (sth). **S:** riots, disturbances; hopes, endeavours; search for; career. **o:** a lot of damage, many deaths, civil war; success, the discovery (of oil etc); his etc being promoted: *The process* ***culminates in*** *the liberation of some only at the price of the enslavement of others.* RTH ○ *The intensive search for gas and oil in the North Sea* ***culminated in*** *the discovery of several important finds.*

cure

cure (of) 1 [Vn.pr pass emph rel] restore (sb) to health (from sickness). **o:** malaria, yellow fever; stammer; shyness: *Before the discovery of antibiotics it was extremely difficult to* ***cure*** *a person* ***of*** *tuberculosis.* ○ *No sooner was I pronounced* ***cured of*** *one illness, than another, more severe, replaced it.* GL

2 [Vn.pr pass emph rel] make (sb) lose (a harmful or unpleasant habit). **o:** nail-biting, snoring: *Some people claim that they have been* ***cured of*** *smoking by hypnosis.* ○ *The black eye that Joe got last night should* ***cure him of*** *minding other people's business.*

curl

curl up 1 [Vp] from being flat or straight, turn up into a curl or sth like a curl; settle down to sleep like a dog. **S:** paper, leaves, material: *The pages of the book had* ***curled up*** *from the heat of the fire.* ○ *She could only dream of the time when she could* ***curl up*** *between clean linen sheets again.*

2 [Vp, Vn.p] (*informal*) (cause sb to) feel disgusted or nauseated: *'He's such a creep whenever the boss is around. It just makes me* ***curl up****. I tell you — it* ***curls*** *me* ***up****.'*

curry

curry favour (with) [Vn.pr] behave ingratiatingly (towards sb) for one's own advantage. **o:** superior; boss, manager; teacher: *The last Labour Government made uneasy and often desperate efforts to* ***curry favour with*** *the City and big business.* NS

curse

cursed with [pass (Vn.pr)] unfortunate in having (sth). **o:** ill luck, (every) misfortune; stammer, limp: *Mr Yates was* ***cursed with*** *a snore that shook the foundations of the house. His wife had to sleep in a separate room.* ○ *Mr Fair seems to be* ***cursed with*** *the ability to see the other person's point of view, with the result that he has no firm opinions on anything.*

curtain

curtain off [Vn ⇆ p pass adj] separate (sth) by means of a curtain. **O:** recess, cupboard; part, extension (of a room): *A corner of the room had been* ***curtained off*** *as a kind of improvised wardrobe.* ○ *He slept in a* ***curtained-off*** *alcove.* ⇨ screen off.

cut

cut across 1 [Vpr] take the short route across (sth) rather than going round it. **o:** the field(s), playing-field, meadow, ice: *Whenever the grass was dry the children would* ***cut across*** *the fields instead of keeping to the road.*

2 [Vpr] be sth that people share or agree about despite (divisions or differences). **o:** party divisions, class differences, religious affiliations: *Voting on the laws which govern Sunday trading* ***cuts across*** *political boundaries.* ○ *Feeling on the political unity of Europe* ***cuts*** *clean* ***across*** *normal party loyalties.*

3 [Vpr] be contrary to (sth); contradict. **S:** religion; doctrine, teaching. **o:** reason, common sense, scientific principles: *But the commercial interest inevitably can cut across a national one.* IND

cut at [Vpr pass] attempt to sever or open (sth), or to wound (sb), with a knife. **o:** cord, rope; covering, wrapping; face, hand: *He* ***cut*** *desperately* ***at*** *the rope in an attempt to free his foot.* ○ *One of the men* ***cut at*** *her with a razor; the blade nicked the skin.*

cut away 1 [Vn ⇆ p pass adj] remove (sth) by cutting. **O:** diseased tissue; undergrowth; dead wood, branches; torn sail, broken mast: *The surgeon* ***cut away*** *the tumour with expert skill.* ○ *You won't be able to make a good lawn here unless you* ***cut away*** *most of these overhanging branches.*

2 [Vn ⇆ p nom pass adj] remove (part of) the surface of (sth) to show the interior. **O:** engine, tail assembly: *... he made a visit to the Science Museum. There he saw a* ***cut-away*** *of a Lancaster bomber showing a section of the fuselage.* ST

cut back 1 [Vn ⇆ p pass] (*horticulture*) cut or prune (sth). **O:** tree, bush, shrub; branch: *Some gardeners believe in* ***cutting*** *rose-bushes* ***back*** *very hard indeed — almost down to the ground.*

2 [Vp, Vn ⇆ p nom pass adj] limit or reduce (sth). **O:** production, investment, expansion: *Owing to the poor state of the overseas market, the car industry has* ***cut back*** *production by fifteen per cent.* ○ *A further hefty loss would demand a* ***cut-back*** *in capital investment.* OBS

cut down 1 [Vn ⇆ p pass adj] fell (sth). **O:** tree, bush: *When I returned to my childhood home I was distressed to find that all the apple trees had been* ***cut down****.*

2 [Vn ⇆ p pass adj] (*formal*) kill (sb). **A:** in his youth, prime; in a battle: *Over the mantelpiece there was a portrait of their eldest son,* ***cut down*** *in his prime in the Second World War.*

3 [Vp, Vn ⇆ p pass] consume less of (sth); reduce. **O:** expenses; consumption, ration: *They claim that it will raise the moral tone ...* ***cut down*** *delinquency, save thousands of sinful souls from hell fire.* TO ○ *'The doctor told me to* ***cut down*** *my consumption of carbohydrates.'* ○ *'By the way, smoke if you want to — I'm trying to* ***cut down****, not with very much success as yet, I'm afraid.'* TT ⇨ cut down on.

4 [Vn ⇆ p pass adj] reduce the length of (sth). **O:** written article, report: *If you can* ***cut*** *your article* ***down*** *to about 1 000 words, we will publish it in our next issue.*

cut down on [Vp.pr] reduce one's consumption of (sth). **o:** (excessive) eating, drinking, spending, smoking: *What with increased taxation and rising prices, I'm going to have to* ***cut down on*** *quite a lot of things — clothes, records and so on.* ○ *When people* ***cut down on*** *tobacco, they often start eating too many sweets and put on weight.* ⇨ cut down 3.

cut down (to) [Vn ⇆ p pass, Vn.p.pr pass] in bargaining, persuade (sb) to reduce his price: *At first he wanted £2 000 for his car, but I succeeded in* ***cutting*** *him* ***down*** *by £300.* ○ *A tourist might* ***cut*** *a* *street trader* **down to** *$4 for a vase, little realizing that this still gave the man a hefty profit.*

cut down to size [Vn.p.pr pass] (*informal*) reduce the power or importance of (sb/sth), whether real or imagined. **O:** employee, colleague; problem; power of sth: *The college tutor . . . If he fails to be appreciative, or thinks to* **cut** *his pupil* **down to size**, *life quickly becomes hellish.* MLT ○ *In general, you tend to laugh at people above you to* **cut** *them* **down to size**, *and at those below you to express your superiority.* RT

cut for [Vpr] (in card games) lift a number of cards from the top of a pack and look at the card which is at the bottom of that 'slice' of the pack. The person who 'cuts' the card lowest (or highest) in value is entitled or obliged to do a specified thing. **o:** dealer; who makes the coffee, pays for the drinks: *As there were five of us we* **cut for** *who would not play the first rubber* (= round of games in bridge). ○ *'The drink's running out. Let's* **cut for** *who goes out to get some more.'* □ in many card games, the first step is to cut for trumps, ie select the suit which is to be trumps by following the procedure already described.

cut the ground from under sb's feet [Vn.pr pass] remove a cause of complaint, thus making it irrelevant; or, so change the circumstances that sb's action is pointless etc: *For weeks we had pressed our demands, when suddenly the Government declared such deals to be illegal, so* **cutting the ground from under our feet**. ○ *I was about to raise my offer for the farm when a neighbour* **cut the ground from under my feet** *by offering a sum that I couldn't possibly match.*

cut in 1 [Vp] (of a driver) overtake a vehicle and move sharply and dangerously in front of it: *Impatient drivers who habitually* **cut in** *are bound to cause an accident sooner or later.*

2 [Vn ⇆ p pass] (*informal*) include (sb), usu as one of a group playing a game or engaged in some money-making activity: *Next time someone drops out of the game, please* **cut** *me* **in**. ○ *The gang decided they would have to* **cut** *the Weasel* **in** *if only to keep his mouth shut about their plans.*

3 [Vp] begin to function automatically after the normal mechanism, or source of supply, has failed. **S:** generator, turbine, motor; central heating (system): *The hospital's own generators failed to* **cut in**. ↔ cut out 6.

cut in/into 1 [Vn.pr pass] divide (sth) by cutting. **o:** (a number of) pieces; halves, quarters; equal parts etc: *The destroyer hit the submarine amidships and* **cut** *it* **in** *two.* ○ **Cut** *this paper* **into** *one-inch strips, and then I'll explain how the game is played.*

2 [Vp, Vpr pass] interrupt (sb/sth). **o:** conversation, discussion: *Edith's mouth had opened to yelp out the prepared condemnation, when Robert unexpectedly* **cut in**. HD ○ *'The facts, Robert, the facts!' Ned cut in.* CON ○ *John's unwelcome voice* **cut into** *our quiet conversation.* = break in (on/upon).

cut into 1 [Vpr pass] make an incision in (sth); start to divide up, carve or slice (sth). **o:** flesh; meat; cake: *As Veronica* **cut into** *her birthday-cake, everyone cheered and clapped.* = slice into.

2 [Vpr pass] attack (sth) so as to reduce or weaken it. **o:** income, pension, legacy; reserves: *By war and legislation, the wealth of the upper classes had been effectively* **cut into**. BRN

cut off 1 [Vn ⇆ p pass, Vn.pr pass] remove (sth) by cutting. **O:** piece, section; branch, leg: *Someone* **cut off** *a succulent piece of lamb and handed it to me.* ○ *Simply to* **cut off** *their heads can only lead to a new tyranny.* RTH ○ *Her husband was* **cutting** *the crusts* **off** *a slice of toast.* OD

2 [Vn ⇆ p pass adj] make (sth) unavailable; interrupt. **O:** power; electricity, gas, water; supplies (of any commodity); sb's allowance of money, food, etc: *His parents . . . summoned him home and threatened to* **cut off** *his support.* TSE ○ *All supplies of petrol were abruptly* **cut off**. ○ *Final notice: Unless your outstanding account is paid within seven days of the date on this notice, we regret that we shall be obliged to* **cut off** *your supply of electricity.*

3 [Vp.n pass] occupy a position to prevent or block (sth). **O:** ⚠ sb's retreat; every avenue of escape, sb's escape route: *Although their retreat had been* **cut off**, *the men fought on to the bitter end.* ○ *They will* **cut off** *all our escape routes except this one— which they can't know about.*

4 [Vn ⇆ p pass] interrupt (sb) having a telephone conversation: *Just when she had reached the most interesting part of the story we were* **cut off**. ○ *'Operator! I've just been* **cut off** *while I was on the line to London. Could you reconnect me, please?'* ○ *Somebody on the switchboard must have* **cut us off** *for a minute.*

cut-off 1 [nom (Vn.p)] division, separation: *There is no hard-and-fast* **cut-off** *between semi-skilled and unskilled workers.* □ note attrib use: *The* **cut-off** *point between 'great heat' and 'excessive heat' cannot easily be defined.*

2 [nom (Vp)] exit road from a motorway: *'You've just passed an exit, but I think there's another* **cut-off** *about ten miles farther on.'*

cut off one's nose to spite one's face [Vp.n] respond to a real or assumed offence in such a way as to harm oneself only, and not the offending person or agency: *If Trades Unions refused to register under the Industrial Relations Act they were* **cutting off their noses to spite their faces**.

cut off (from) 1 [Vn.p pass adj, Vn.p.pr pass emph rel] prevent (sb) from leaving a place by surrounding it. **S:** flood, avalanche; enemy, encircling movement. **O:** town, village; forces, troops: *Although* **cut off** *by the enemy, the platoon managed to hide until nightfall and regain their own lines under cover of darkness.* ○ *Some children were* **cut off** *by the tide and had to be carried up the cliff to safety.* ○ *After the heaviest blizzard of the winter, which* **cut off** *Scotland* **from** *England . . . snowploughs and bright sunshine opened most of the border roads.* SC

2 [Vn.p pass adj, Vn.p.pr pass emph rel] prevent (sb) from having contact (with sb/sth). **O:** oneself; him etc. **o:** friends; one's family; a circle of people, a kind of life; the outside world: *If she disobeyed she had to face the prospect of being* **cut off from** *her family.* HB ○ *She's a strange person — very solitary — seems to* **cut** *herself* **off** *quite deliberately.* = shut off (from).

cut out 1 [Vn.p nom pass adj] cut from a piece of material (the shapes required for making sth). **O:** dress, skirt, jacket; back, sleeve: *Before Mary* *could **cut** her dress **out**, she had to flatten the pieces of the pattern and pin them carefully to the material.* ○ *The shoemaker carefully examines the leather before starting to **cut out** the uppers.* ○ *His bedroom floor was strewn with cardboard **cut-outs**.*

2 [Vn ⇆ p pass adj] (*informal*) defeat (sb); eliminate. **O:** his etc enemy, rival, competitor; best friend; (all) competition: *He learned to waltz in order to **cut out** her other admirers.* TU

3 [Vn ⇆ p pass adj] delete, not include (sth). **O:** word, phrase; paragraph, section; (all, any) reference to, mention of, discussion of, allusion to, description of sth: *You'd improve the article a lot by shortening the introduction and **cutting out** some of the charts and diagrams.* ○ *I think it's got the makings of a fairly good yarn, provided of course that you **cut out** this verbal tomfoolery and make it clean cut.* HD

4 [Vn ⇆ p pass adj] stop taking, eating, drinking or using (sth); stop any harmful activity or bad habit. **O:** cigarettes, tobacco, alcohol, drugs; fat, meat, sugar, carbohydrates; game, sport; watching television, going to bed late: *In a vain attempt to regain her youthful figure, she **cut out** carbohydrates completely — for about a week!* ○ *I'm afraid I shall have to **cut out** our weekly game of squash — I'm not as young as I was!* ○ (words of a man on being arrested) *'You can **cut out** the rough stuff; I'm not armed.'* T

5 [Vp] stop functioning. **S:** engine, motor: *The crash investigators established that the two port engines had **cut out** shortly after take-off.* ○ *As we were circling the field preparatory to landing, the engine **cut out**.* MFM = pack up 3.

6 [Vp nom] automatically stop providing heat, cool air etc. **S:** central heating (system); radiator, heater: *When the temperature of the room reaches 21 degrees the convector heater **cuts out**.* ○ *The central heating system is fitted with an automatic **cut-out*** (ie an electrical device which causes the boiler to ***cut out*** when a given temperature is reached). ↔ cut in 3.

cut out (the) dead wood [Vp.n pass] (*informal*) remove those parts which confuse or spoil a picture, description, test etc: *The methods used have helped enormously in making questionnaires more reliable, in **cutting out dead wood**, and generally in improving measurements along these lines.* SNP ○ *Before we can hope to make this industry more efficient and competitive, we've a tremendous amount of **dead wood** to **cut out**.*

cut it/that out [Vn.p] (*informal*) stop doing or saying sth that angers or irritates sb else: *'Can't you see that I'm trying to concentrate. Just **cut it out**, will you!'* ○ *'I'm not going to be told what I must or must not do, so you can **cut that out**!'* ○ *'You blame me for everything that goes wrong and I wish you'd **cut it out**.'*

cut out for [pass (Vn.p.pr)] (*informal*) well matched; having the right abilities or qualities for (sb/sth). **o:** each other (esp of an engaged or married couple); particular job, kind of life: *Peter and Susan seem to be **cut out for** each other.* ○ *Something reasonable always turns up once you've abandoned the idea that one particular job is the only one you're **cut out for**.* HD ○ *'I don't know that I'm **cut out for** religion, but I'd like to know a good deal more about it.* ASA □ used with *appear* etc, or after a noun: *...two people **cut out for** each other.*

cut out/out of [Vn ⇆ p nom pass adj, Vn.pr pass] remove (sth) by cutting. **O:** picture, figure, coupon, article. **o:** newspaper, magazine, book: *The children showed their teacher all the pictures of English towns that they had **cut out of** magazines.* ○ *'I'm going to **cut** this advertisement **out** and send it to Alice; she may be interested in the job.'* ○ *The table was covered with **cut-out** figures and shapes of animals, buildings and trees.*

cut through 1 [Vn.p pass, Vn.pr pass rel] open (a way) through (sth) by the removal of obstacles. **O:** one's way; a passage, route. **o:** forest, jungle, defences; ice: *Only a powerful, specially equipped ship could **cut** a way **through** such tightly-packed ice.* ○ *The Alaska Highway, which **cut** a swathe **through** solid forest, turned out to be obstructed in several places by landslides.*

2 [Vpr pass] overcome or by-pass (difficulties, esp bureaucratic ones). **o:** red tape, formalities: *Every newly-elected Town Councillor swears that he will **cut through** the red tape of the local bureaucracy, but no one ever succeeds.* ○ *If you have the patience to **cut through** all the verbiage you will find that there is much sense in the Committee's proposals.*

cut to [Vpr] (*cinema* or *TV*) change from one scene or aspect of a scene to (another): *'... so just as the escaped prisoner is about to break into the farm, we'll **cut to** the tracker-dogs following the scent.'* ○ *'While Peter and Arthur continue quarrelling, **cut to** Cynthia in close-up.'*

cut to pieces/ribbons/shreds [Vn.pr pass] defeat (sb) utterly, inflicting great losses on him; annihilate. **O:** defenders, attacking forces, armed raiders: *The heavy cavalry caught the foot soldiers out of formation, and **cut them to pieces**.* ○ *The retreat turned into a rout and our men were **cut to ribbons** by the enemy, who gave them no respite.*

cut (prices) to the bone [Vn.pr pass] (informal) reduce prices to the lowest possible level: *Competition between the supermarkets in the High Street was such that (the **prices** of) many products were **cut to the bone**, leaving practically no profit-margin.*

cut to the quick [Vn.pr pass] (*informal*) hurt the feelings of (sb) deeply: *Helen's sarcastic remarks about my efforts to help her and her family, **cut me to the quick**.* ○ *He was **cut to the quick** by such a display of callousness.*

cut up 1 [Vn ⇆ p pass adj] cut or chop (sth) into pieces. **O:** meat, vegetables, branches: *The vegetables should be **cut up** into small pieces and dropped into the boiling water.* ○ *You can **cut** this wood **up** very easily* (or: *This wood **cuts up** very easily*) *with an ordinary saw.*

2 [Vn ⇆ p pass] (*informal*) injure or hurt (sb) with cuts, bruises etc: *All the occupants of the two cars were badly **cut up** in the smash.* ○ *Those fellows weren't too gentle with him. They **cut** him **up** very badly.*

3 [pass adj (Vn.p)] (*informal*) emotionally upset: *Eve was really **cut up** at the news that Alex had been sacked.* ○ *'Sorry for the delay, Mr Weaver.' The steward looked and sounded really **cut up**.* OD ○ *There's no need to be so **cut up** about not getting* *the job: it's only a matter of time before you fall on your feet.* □ used with *appear* etc.

cut up rough [Vp] (*informal*) react violently; behave aggressively: *If Tom starts to* **cut up rough**, *for Heaven's sake don't get drawn into an argument with him.* ○ *The potential clients were lining up, tumbling over themselves, only waiting for a word from Alec. Would that word be given, if Harold started to* **cut up rough**? PW

cut no ice (with) [Vn.pr pass] (*informal*) not influence or affect (sb); carry no weight with (sb). **S:** argument, defence, submission; evidence, so-called facts: *All these statistics about increased wages* **cut no ice with** *me. What I want to know is how the government proposes to reduce unemployment.*

dab

dab off [Vn ⇆ p pass adj] absorb or remove (sth) with quick, light movements. **S:** technician; cleaner. **O:** water, excess liquid; oil, dirt, mud: *If you apply this cleaning fluid, you'll find you can simply* **dab** *the dirt* **off**. ○ *Only allow a thin film of water to settle on the plates; any excess should be* **dabbed off**. ↔ dab on/onto.

dab on/onto [Vn ⇆ p pass adj, Vn.pr pass emph rel] put on, apply (sth) lightly or gently. **S:** artist, painter; housewife, cleaner. **O:** paint, turpentine; polish, cleaning-fluid. **o:** canvas; furniture: *The painter slowly built up his landscape,* **dabbing on** *small areas of green and yellow.* ○ *The furniture cream should be* **dabbed on** *with a soft cloth.* ↔ dab off.

dabble

dabble (in) [Vpr pass emph rel] give some attention to (sth), study (sth), without becoming seriously involved. **S:** lady of leisure, gentleman of means; gentry, nobility. **o:** painting, the theatre; politics, law: *Trevor* **dabbled in** *what he called art, until he was called up, when he got into the intelligence corps.* SPL ○ *There were various pursuits* **in** *which he had* **dabbled** *from time to time — the piano was his latest.* ○ *His* **dabbling with** *socialist doctrines was not done solely to spite his father.* W

dally

dally with 1 [Vpr pass emph rel] consider or contemplate (sth) idly in the mind. **S:** manager, developer, farmer, householder. **o:** scheme, project; idea, notion: *The Department of Energy have been* **dallying with** *the notion of building a nuclear power station down here.* ○ *I brought up an idea* **with** *which he had been* **dallying** *for some time, but about which little had actually been done.* = play with 5, toy with 5.

2 [Vpr] appear to show an interest in (sb), without intending a serious relationship: *He* **dallied with** *her affections for a bit, but quickly moved on when she showed signs of wanting a more permanent relationship.* = play with 4, toy with 4, trifle with.

dam

dam up 1 [Vn ⇆ p pass adj] close (sth) by means of a dam; check, retain (waters) with a dam. **S:** government; (water, electricity) authorities; engineer. **O:** valley, gorge; river: *When a river valley is* **dammed up**, *the waters contained by the barrage rise to form an artificial lake.*

2 [Vn ⇆ p pass adj] suppress, restrain (sth). **O:** emotion, feeling; anger, resentment: **Dammed-up** *feelings will burst out at some stage in a more violent form than if they had been expressed in the first place.* = bottle up.

damp

damp down 1 [Vn ⇆ p pass adj] cause (sth) to burn more slowly, by adding ash or reducing the draught of air. **S:** stoker, caretaker. **O:** furnace, boiler, fire: *The boilers are producing too much pressure: they'll have to be* **damped down**.

2 [Vn ⇆ p pass adj] restrain, control (sth). **S:** teacher, leader. **O:** enthusiasm, high spirits, ebullience; rumour, speculation; activity, trading: *The party spirit was considerably* **damped down** *by the news that all leave had been stopped.* ○ *Now he wanted to go back, but to* **damp down** *the urge he was sent for a year to his brother's home in France.* RT ○ *New guidelines on top directors' pay have been issued by the Institute of Directors to help* **damp down** *the controversy over the recent hefty boardroom salary rises.* G

damp off [Vp] (*horticulture*) rot and die through excessive damp. **S:** seedling, cutting: *Don't give those seedlings too much water; they'll* **damp off**.

dance

dance across, along, away etc [Vp emph, Vpr emph rel] move across etc excitedly or rhythmically: *Sarah, already in her overcoat,* **danced about** *saying, 'Come on Nicky,' impatiently.* DC ○ *The bridal procession* **danced down** *the street and* **into** *the groom's garden.*

dance attendance (on) [Vn.pr emph rel] (*formal* or *facetious*) follow (sb) about attentively and/or slavishly, usu in the hope of obtaining favours. **S:** suitor; courtier, hanger-on (at court). **o:** young woman, pretty girl; prince, minister; rich relative: *Both Patrick and Alex* **danced attendance on** *her, circling each other like duellists as they vied for her attention.* PR

dangle

dangle before/in front of [Vn.pr pass emph rel] offer prospects of wealth etc to (sb) enticingly. **O:** promotion, advancement; profit, gain. **o:** employee, candidate; sb's eyes: *The days may be past when graduates had prospects of dazzling careers in industry* **dangled in front of** *them.*

dart

sb's eyes dart about/around [Vp, Vpr] sb's eyes move restlessly about (a place): **Her eyes darted** *feverishly* **about** *the room again and then settled back on the mirror.* RAEU

dart across, along, away etc [Vp emph, Vpr emph rel] move quickly, sharply, in a given direction: *Bill* **darted back** *into bed as he heard his father's footsteps on the stairs.* ○ *She opened the box and* **out darted** *a mouse.*

dart a glance/look at [Vn.pr pass emph rel] look suddenly, sharply, at (sb). **adj:** furtive, anxious, hostile. **o:** stranger, visitor; watch, clock: *She* **darted** *an interested* **glance at** *the visitor from under lowered eyelids.* ○ *I* **darted a glance at** *the* *speedometer. We were doing over eighty miles an hour.* = shoot a glance (at).

dash

dash across, along, away etc [Vp emph, Vpr emph rel] move hastily, impetuously, across etc: *Fuelled by an anguish of rage Alice* ***dashed down*** *the stairs.* GT ○ *Still the horses* ***dashed on*** *through the darkness.* GLEG ○ *Instead of time crawling, it hurries, not to say* ***dashes past*** *me.*

dash against [Vpr, Vn.pr pass] (cause sth to) crash violently against (sth). **S** [Vpr], **O** [Vn.pr]**:** boat, raft; body, skull. **S** [Vn.pr]**:** sea, wave; storm; (force of the) explosion, blast. **o:** rock, cliff; wall, pavement: *The tanker* ***dashed against*** *the reef with such a force that a great hole was opened in her side.* ○ *The force of the blast* ***dashed*** *him* ***against*** *the wall of the cave.*

dash (itself/oneself) against [Vpr, Vn.pr] throw (itself/oneself) violently against (sth). **S:** heavy sea, big wave, breaker; assault troops, wave of attackers. **o:** shore, promenade; trenches, lines: *Heavy seas* ***dashed against*** *the sea wall.* ○ *A violent rain storm broke and the rain drops* ***dashed themselves against*** *the windscreen of the car.*

dash away a tear/one's tears [Vp.n] brush tears from one's eyes with a hand or handkerchief. **S:** girl, child: *Brigit* ***dashed away her tears***. DC

dash off [Vn ⇆ p pass adj] write or draw (sth) very quickly. **S:** secretary, journalist; artist. **O:** article, letter, note; sketch, drawing: *The thing had obviously been* ***dashed off*** *but it consisted of just the right number of lines.* CON ○ *That charging of language with meaning ... is characteristic of nearly everything Lawrence wrote, even the odd* ***dashed-off*** *letter.* FIB = tear off 2.

dash one's/sb's brains out [Vn ⇆ p pass] kill (oneself/sb) by smashing the skull open. **S:** (violent) blow; bullet, stone, shell-splinter: *He fell over the cliff-edge and* ***dashed out his brains*** *on the rocks below.* ○ *One of the bodyguards* ***dashed his brains out*** *with a single blow from his club.*

dash over 1 [Vpr] throw itself violently over (sth). **S:** heavy sea, big wave. **o:** promenade, coast road, breakwater, promontory: *As the storm built up, heavy seas* ***dashed over*** *a row of cottages built near the water's edge.*

2 [Vn.pr pass] throw (sth) over (sb/sth) in a stream. **S:** car, bicycle; clumsy fellow, comedian. **O:** water, mud; paint, whitewash. **o:** suit, trousers; floor, wall: *A passing car* ***dashed*** *muddy water all* ***over*** *my clothes.* ○ *The circus clowns* ***dashed*** *buckets of whitewash* ***over*** *each other.*

date

date from/back to [Vpr emph rel, Vp.pr emph rel] have existed since (a time); originate in (a state or action). **S:** castle, church; custom, tradition; agreement, association, alliance; hostility, misunderstanding. **o:** Norman times, the Stone Age; the war, pre-war times: *The earliest municipal records* ***date back to*** *the end of the twelfth century.* SHOE ○ *Three new universities* ***date from*** *the early part of his reign.* MR ○ *The present harmony in the factory* ***dates from*** *a sensible agreement on wages and productivity.* = go back (to) 2, lead back (to).

daub

daub on/onto [Vn ⇆ p pass adj, Vn.pr pass emph rel] apply (sth) thickly and/or crudely (to sth). **S:** painter, sculptor; decorator. **O:** paint, clay, plaster. **o:** canvas, framework, wall: *The children were encouraged to* ***daub*** *the colours* ***on*** *liberally.* ○ *Modelling clay was* ***daubed*** *thickly* ***onto*** *a small metal framework and then worked into shape* (or: *A small metal framework was thickly* ***daubed with*** *clay* etc).

daub onto/over [Vn.pr pass emph rel] apply (sth) thickly (all) over a surface, staining it, or making it dirty. **S:** painter; mechanic; child. **O:** paint; oil, tar; jam, treacle. **o:** wall, woodwork; overalls; dress: *Mary had* ***daubed*** *jam and chocolate all* ***over*** *her apron* (or: *had* ***daubed*** *her apron all* ***over with*** *jam* etc). ○ *Oil and grease were* ***daubed onto*** *his shirt* (or: *His shirt was* ***daubed with*** *oil* etc).

daub with 1 [Vn.pr pass rel] ⇨ daub on/onto.

2 [Vn.pr pass rel] ⇨ daub onto/over.

dawn

dawn on/upon [Vpr] occur to (sb), become clear to (sb). **S:** sense, truth; the realization that ... ; it ... that he might be dead, it ... that she was seriously ill: *The sense of all that she had been saying suddenly* ***dawned on*** *him.* ○ *It only gradually* ***dawns on*** *the two little children that they have been left. Their grief is terrible.* BRN ○ *The truth about the human condition* ***dawns upon*** *those who have the humility to recognize their own unimportance.* RTH

deal

deal in 1 [Vn.p pass] include (sb) in a game by dealing him a hand of cards etc. **S:** banker, croupier: *Peter arrived late for our bridge party, but somebody quickly gave him a drink and then we* ***dealt*** *him* ***in***.

2 [Vpr pass rel] do business in (sth); handle;. **S:** shopkeeper; store, trading company. **o:** second-hand cars, stationery, stocks and shares: *The small post-office on the corner* ***deals in*** *a lot else besides stamps and postal orders.* ○ *Most foreign trading companies in West Africa* ***deal in*** *rubber, cocoa and vegetable oils.* = trade in 1.

deal out [Vp.n pass] administer (sth). **S:** father, boxer; magistrate. **O:** (good) hiding, thrashing; punishment, justice: *The frontier town had set up a primitive court, which* ***dealt out*** *justice of a kind.* ○ *The lighter boxer had a good deal of punishment* ***dealt out*** *to him by the end of the first round.* = mete out.

deal with 1 [Vpr rel] trade with (sb) ; talk with (sb) in order to reach a settlement etc. **o:** firm, company; supplier, wholesaler: *We've* ***dealt with*** *the same firm for years and can thoroughly recommend them to you.* ○ *They are bad people to* ***deal with****; always late on delivery dates.* ○ *'Banda in jail was a myth, but Banda out of jail is a man, and one can* ***deal with*** *a man.'* SC = do business (with).

2 [Vpr pass adj rel] handle, tackle or confront (sth), so as to settle, remedy, reform etc it. **S:** government, official; police, prison service; doctor, teacher. **o:** inquiry, complaint, grievance; crime wave, indiscipline; disease, learning problem: *Any complaints about the quality of our goods will be quickly* ***dealt with*** *by local branches.* ○ *The galloping increase of traffic in recent years must be* ***dealt with***. SC ○ *There will be mild trouble when he gets* *home, of course, but nothing he can't* ***deal with***. = reckon with 2.

3 [Vpr pass] handle or punish (some offender), with the suggestion that the reckoning will be unpleasant. **S:** father, employer, superior officer: *'I'll* ***deal with*** *you when I get home from the office!'* ○ *'I'll get Father to* ***deal with*** *him later on.'* ○ *In Cuba the police can* ***deal*** *as harshly as they like* ***with*** *émigrés from Latin America.* OMIH □ often used with *shall/will*. = reckon with 3.

4 [Vpr pass rel] have (sth) as its subject, be concerned with (sth); cover, treat. **S:** article, lecture, book. **o:** Asia, the population problem, the English Romantics, coal: *Other medieval drama included miracle plays,* ***dealing with*** *the lives of saints.* SHOE ○ *The subject isn't very well* ***dealt with*** *in his latest book.*

debar

debar (from) [Vn.pr pass emph rel] (*formal*) exclude (sb) by law or regulation from use or membership of (sth). **S:** committee, Chamber of Commerce, trades union. **O:** member, associate. **o:** voting, using club premises; membership: *New legislation may have to be introduced if clubs are to be prevented from* ***debarring*** *people* ***from*** *membership on grounds of race or colour.* ○ *'Work' as we now understand it (labour, crafts, professions and so on) was precisely what the 'well-bred woman' was* ***debarred from***. JA

debit

debit (to) [Vn.pr pass emph rel] (*finance, commerce*) subtract (sth) from the amount held in sb's account by a bank or commercial organization. **S:** bank, finance company; store. **O:** sum, amount; charge. **o:** customer; account; department: *Would you kindly explain why this large sum has been* ***debited to*** *me* (or: *why I have been* ***debited with*** *this large sum*)? ↔ credit with 1.

debit with [Vn.pr pass rel] previous entry

deceive

deceived in [pass (Vn.pr)] (*formal*) misled about the personal qualities or abilities of (sb); disappointed in. **S:** father, teacher, employer: *I've been* ***deceived in*** *Smith: he has an impressive manner, but no real staying power or brains.*

deceive into [Vn.pr pass] make (sb) believe sth which is untrue, esp for purposes of gain. **S:** enemy, rival; salesman, agent, confidence trickster. **O:** firm, purchaser, shopper. **o:** supposing, believing, thinking; buying, selling: *The Prussians* ***deceived*** *Napoleon* ***into*** *thinking they had withdrawn away from their British allies.* ○ *We were* ***deceived into*** *buying a house that was scheduled for demolition.* □ note *-ing* form of a v as object of into. = delude (into).

decide

decide against 1 [Vpr] (*legal*) deliver a verdict or judgment against (sb). **S:** judge, magistrate, jury. **o:** plaintiff, accused, defendant, Crown: *The Court* ***decided against*** *the Crown in the case of Regina v Carruthers.* = find against. ↔ decide for/in favour of.

2 [Vpr pass rel] make up one's mind not to have or do (sth). **o:** continental holiday, boarding school, efficiency campaign; having guests, sending a letter, giving a party: *We've* ***decided against*** *having a big family gathering this Christmas.* ○ *Thackeray had hoped for Fitzgerald's company, but Fitz, in a mood of depression,* ***decided against*** *the trip.* TU ↔ decide on.

decide for/in favour of [Vpr] (*legal*) deliver a verdict or judgment in favour of (sb). **S:** judge, magistrate. **o:** plaintiff, defendant: *I doubt whether any court in the country would* ***decide in his favour***. *His record must tell against him.* = find for. ↔ decide against 1.

decide on [Vpr pass rel] make up one's mind to have (sth). **o:** sports car, saloon; bungalow, flat; expansion, reduction (of activity): *Finally, she* ***decided on*** *the white and yellow striped material.* ○ *The worsening political situation ... made it impossible ... to go to Switzerland or Weimar, and Edinburgh was* ***decided on*** *instead.* SS ↔ decide against 2.

deck

deck out/up (in) [Vn.p pass, Vn.p.pr pass] put (sth) on as for a special occasion. **S:** girlfriend, young man, teenager. **O:** herself etc; child, wife. **o:** all her finery, his Sunday best, party frock: *Emily went wild when he first* ***decked*** *himself* ***out in*** *that awful uniform.* PPAP ○ *Sometimes she gets* ***decked up in*** *her black jeans and goes off to some sexy club.* FFE

deck with [Vn.pr pass rel] decorate (sth) with (sth). **S:** council, townspeople, priest, child. **O:** street, wall; house, shop; Christmas tree. **o:** flag, bunting; garland, flower; paper-chain: *The authorities gave orders to* ***deck*** *the streets* ***with*** *flags and bunting.* ○ *The table was profusely* ***decked with*** *... florists' roses.* BLCH

declare

declare war (against/on) [Vn.pr pass rel] announce officially that a state of war exists between two countries: *Britain* ***declared war on*** *Germany on 3rd September, 1939.* ○ *Hostilities were opened without* ***war*** *being* ***declared***.

dedicate

dedicate to 1 [Vn.pr pass emph rel] (*formal*) give (oneself/sth) to a purpose believed to be important. **O:** oneself; one's life, career; energies. **o:** purpose, cause; helping the needy, caring for the sick: *Members of religious communities* ***dedicate*** *their whole lives* ***to*** *God's service.* ○ *He felt that Socialism was the most important cause* ***to*** *which he could* ***dedicate*** *himself.* = devote to.

2 [Vn.pr pass emph rel] write (sb's name) at the beginning of (a work) as a mark of gratitude, admiration etc. **S:** writer, composer. **O:** novel, poems; symphony, opera. **o:** parents, wife: *Beethoven at first* ***dedicated*** *his 'Eroica' Symphony* ***to*** *Napoleon but afterwards tore out the fly-leaf in disgust.*

deduce

deduce (from) [Vn.pr pass emph rel] (*formal*) arrive at (a conclusion) by examining and weighing (evidence). **O:** knowledge, theory. **o:** facts, data; observations, measurements: *You will notice water rising in the tube; now what do you* ***deduce from*** *that?* ○ ***From*** *the presence of people of Asiatic stock in America we may possibly* ***deduce*** *that the two continents were at one time linked.*

deduct

deduct (from) [Vn.pr pass emph rel] (*formal*) take one amount, esp a compulsory levy (from a larger). **S:** employer; bursar; tax office. **O:** contribution, insurance payment, income tax. **o:** wage, salary: *The easiest way for staff to donate to the charity is to ask the Salaries Department to* ***deduct*** *a fixed amount* ***from*** *their monthly pay.* ○ *Nowadays income tax is normally* ***deducted from*** *a person's wages before he receives them.*

defect

defect (from) (to) [Vpr emph rel] transfer one's allegiance (from one country etc) (to another), esp with the knowledge and encouragement of one's intending host or employer. **S:** (intelligence) agent, (military) expert, scientist: *The year began with the bad news that two of our best agents had* ***defected to*** *the other side.* ○ *'So you are the man who is going to make Semitsa* ***defect from*** *the Moscow Academy of Sciences and come to work in the west.'* FUNB

defend

defend (against/from) [Vn.pr pass emph rel] guard, protect (sb) from attack etc. **S:** dog; fence, barbed wire; law; ombudsman, trades union, professional body. **O:** house, factory; field, emplacement; (ordinary) citizen; worker, member. **o:** thief, trespasser; attack, invasion; invasion of rights, encroachment on privacy; discrimination: *Here we are well* ***defended against*** *a surprise attack.* ○ *The association exists to* ***defend*** *the consumer* ***against*** *unscrupulous traders.*

defer

defer (to) [Vpr pass emph rel] (*formal*) out of respect, treat (sb/sth) as more important or authoritative. **S:** young man, pupil, newcomer. **o:** elder, senior; master, teacher; opinion, view: *His sister had always waited on him,* ***deferred to*** *his wishes, kept an anxious watch on his appetite.* ○ *I felt I must* ***defer to*** *my host's judgement.* ○ *Grandfather ruled his family with a rod of iron; his views were invariably* ***deferred to****.*

define

define (as) [Vn.pr pass] state the characteristics peculiar to an object, quality etc. **O:** substance, element; acid, salt; virtue, vice. **o:** lacking flavour; something which corrodes; that which corrupts: *A 'sentence' has been variously* ***defined as*** *'the expression of a complete thought', 'something beginning with a capital letter and ending with a full stop' and 'the largest unit of grammatical description'.* ○ *How can one* ***define*** *visual beauty?* ***As*** *something which arouses pleasant sensations in the viewer?*

deflect

deflect (from) [Vn.pr pass emph rel] cause (sth) to turn (from the course or direction first taken). **S:** armour-plate, steel helmet; heckler, reporter; visitor; interruption. **O:** shell, bullet; speaker, lecturer; attention. **o:** target; path, course; purpose, task; theme, topic: *Rays of light passing through water are* ***deflected from*** *their original path.* ○ *He was momentarily* ***deflected from*** *this train of thought by a knock on the door.*

degenerate

degenerate (from) (into) [Vpr rel] change in physical, intellectual or moral quality (from a higher standard) (to a low one). **S:** region, area, district; play, book; conversation, debate. **o: (into)** wilderness, slum; farce; argument, confrontation: *... a road which* ***degenerated into*** *a farm track.* GA ○ *At this stage, the debate* ***degenerated into*** *a crude slanging-match.* = deteriorate (into).

delegate

delegate (to) [Vn.pr pass emph rel] (*formal*) give (a task etc) (to a trusted subordinate). **S:** manager; commander; headmaster. **O:** duty, responsibility; task, work; organizing, planning. **o:** assistant, deputy; second-in-command: *A mark of a good leader is his readiness to* ***delegate*** *a certain amount of decision-making* ***to*** *his assistants.* ○ *The routine office work had all been* ***delegated to*** *her executive staff.*

delete

delete (from) [Vn.pr pass emph rel] (*formal*) remove (sth) (from sth). **S:** editor, censor. **O:** name; figure, amount; statement, remark; detail, reference. **o:** list, roll; report, accounts; record, transcript: *When one dictator replaces another, a fresh set of names has often to be* ***deleted from*** *the history books.* ○ *He turned to the end of the article;* ***from*** *the list of works consulted, all references to himself had been* ***deleted****.*

delight

delight in [Vpr] take (unkind) pleasure in (sth); enjoy. **S:** elder brother, bigger pupil. **o:** teasing his small sister, pulling my leg, proving us wrong: *Peter seems to* ***delight in*** *making other people suffer.* □ object of in is usu the-*ing* form of a v.

deliver

deliver oneself of [Vn.pr rel] (*formal*) state or express (sth) pompously or self-importantly. **o:** opinion, view; statement, claim, proposal: *The judge* ***delivered himself of*** *the view that young people were treated far too leniently nowadays.* ○ *A German General had* ***delivered himself of*** *an all-embracing classification about officers: the clever, the stupid, the industrious and the lazy.* MFM

deliver over/up (to) [Vn ⇆ p pass, Vn.p.pr pass rel] (*formal*) surrender (sth/sb) (to sb), usu under extreme pressure. **S:** garrison, besieged army; gaoler. **O:** castle, town; prisoner; stores: *The governor was ordered to* ***deliver over*** *the keys to the citadel.* ○ *In a painful moment he saw himself recaptured and* ***delivered up*** *again* ***to*** *his gaolers.* = hand over 1.

delude

delude (into) [Vn.pr pass emph rel] (*formal*) deliberately mislead (sb/oneself) (into thinking or believing sth). **S:** government, politician; press, radio. **O:** public; supporter, follower; oneself. **o:** belief, supposition; believing, supposing, expecting: *For years we have been* ***deluded into*** *expecting a sudden economic recovery.* ○ *They couldn't go on* ***deluding*** *themselves* ***into*** *thinking that in six months or a year their marriage would somehow improve.* = deceive into.

delve

delve into [Vpr pass emph rel] search thoroughly (in sth) for facts or knowledge. **S:** scholar, archivist. **o:** manuscript, document; past, memory: *He has been* ***delving into*** *accounts of daily life in the 16th*

Century. ○ *I had to* **delve** *pretty hard* **into** *my memory to recall where I had seen him before.*

demand

demand (of) [Vn.pr pass rel] expect (of sb) that he should give or offer (sth). **S:** work, task; office, job. **O:** sacrifice; persistence; a readiness, willingness (to do sth); that one should give up one's family life: *Have you any idea what a full-time political career will* **demand of** *you?* ○ *As director of these courses a great deal will be* **demanded of** *him.* = require (from/of).

denude

denude (of) [Vn.pr pass rel] (*formal*) remove (the covering) from (sth); strip (sth) bare of (covering). **S:** wind and rain, storm; bad husbandry. **O:** tree; hillside, countryside. **o:** leaves, branches; soil: *Intensive cultivation had* **denuded** *the hillsides* **of** *their covering of fertile soil.* ○ *Trees were* **denuded of** *their leaves.*

depart

depart from [Vpr pass adj emph rel] (*formal*) not act according to (practice); make a break from (practice). **o:** accepted practice, custom; established tradition, routine: *The chairman* **departed from** *normal procedure by allowing reporters to be present during Council business.* ○ *The rules were rigid in principle, sometimes* **departed from** *in practice.* ○ *These were hallowed traditions* **from** *which he had no intention of* **departing**. = stray from. ↔ keep to 2, stick to 2.

depend

depend on/upon 1 [Vpr pass rel] (be able to) believe that sb or sth will prove reliable. **o:** him etc; product, commodity; firm, service: *You can't* **depend on** *this bus service — it's never punctual.* ○ *He's a man who can be* **depended upon** *in a crisis.* ○ *They could* **depend on** *John to support them.* □ usu with can/could. = bank on 2, rely on/upon.

2 [Vpr pass emph rel] be sure of, confidently expect (an event). **o:** him/his turning up, him/his being on time, him/his supporting the motion; his support, co-operation, sympathy: *You can* **depend on** *his support for your Bill.* ○ *One could never* **depend on** *his arriving on time.* ○ *He'll be there when he's needed;* **on** *that you can* **depend**. □ usu with can/could. = bank on 1, reckon on/upon.

3 [Vpr emph rel] get income or material support from (sth/sb). **S:** town, port, industry; family, child; painter, writer. **o:** manufacturers, trade, coal; father, parent; steady sales, rich patron. **A:** for its existence, for his livelihood; to survive; as a source of income: *He* **depends** *for his livelihood* **upon** *a small income from investments.* ○ (someone defending his use of a car) *'I'm basically anti-social . . . and I* **depend on** *my car a lot for my freedom.'* RT ○ *To remain in existence, the theatre must continue to* **depend on** *a state subsidy.*

4 [Vpr emph rel] follow directly or logically from (sth). **S:** a great deal; whether we succeed, how we set about it. **o:** how they respond, the way it's tackled; the forces at our disposal: *A great deal will* **depend on** *the way the Government responds.* SC ○ *It all* (= the answer) **depends on** *what you mean by truth!* ○ *How successful they were would* **depend on** *the speed with which the product could be distributed to the shops.* = hang on 4, hinge on/upon, turn on 4.

depend on/upon it [Vpr] one may be sure or certain (of the fact); without any doubt: *For* **depend upon it**, *my boy, the monster won't understand a word of this new-fangled language called English.* RM ○ **Depend upon it**, *it is the intellectual element in Parliament that leavens the lump* (ie makes its debates more lively, etc). BLCH □ depend on/upon it is often followed by a main clause or a *that*-clause; imperative, as shown, or preceeded by *you may/can.*

deprive

deprive of [Vn.pr pass emph rel] stop (sb) enjoying or using (sth). **S:** gaoler, invader, tyrant; tall buildings, trees. **o:** freedom; luxuries, necessities; sunshine, heat: *The new laws threaten to* **deprive** *many people* **of** *the most elementary freedoms.* ○ *But the splendid occasion reminded him bitterly of the opportunities he had himself been* **deprived of**. CD

deputize

deputize (for) [Vpr pass emph rel] act in the place (of sb in authority) during his absence. **S:** assistant-director, sub-manager, second-in-command: *Mr Jones will be* **deputizing for** *me during my absence abroad.* ○ *I dare say Stephens can be* **deputized for** *— we seem to have managed without his guiding hand before.*

derive

derive from 1 [Vn.pr pass emph rel] (*formal*) get, obtain (sth) from (sth). **S:** patient, invalid; student, reader. **O:** relief, benefit; pleasure, instruction; income. **o:** course of treatment; studies, books; investments: *Mary has* **derived** *a good deal of benefit* **from** *her tuition.* ○ *I have* **derived** *most of my concepts* **from** *those of Freud.* ESS ○ *Lonely people listening to the wireless can* **derive** *some comfort* **from** *the fact that every wireless in the street is linking the neighbours together.* UL = draw from 2.

2 [Vpr emph rel, Vn.pr pass emph rel] (*formal*) have or take (sth) as its starting point or origin. **S** [Vpr], **O** [Vn.pr]**:** product; word, name; ceremony, ritual. **o:** mineral; (Latin, Sanskrit) root, source; ancient custom: *Margarine is* **derived from** *vegetable oils.* ○ *The word* **derives from** *a Greek noun with a quite different meaning.* ○ *The May-Day ceremonies are said to be* **derived from** *the fertility rites of the Ancient Britons.*

descend

descend on [Vpr emph rel] arrive in (a place) in an impressive way, like a monarch or conqueror. **o:** the capital; literary London: *H.G. Wells had begun his literary career and Arnold Bennett was about to* **descend on** *London.* HB ○ *Naomi Mitchison* **descended on** *London from time to time like some gypsy matriarch to visit members of her tribe.* SU

descend to [Vpr pass emph rel] allow one's behaviour to sink to (a low standard). **o:** a low level, such etc depths; vulgar abuse, gossip; cheating, fraud; personalities: *I never thought he would* **descend to** *abusing his former colleagues in public.* ○ *Who knew what depths he might* **descend to**, *given the right stimulus.* MSAL = stoop to.

describe

describe as [Vn.pr pass] say that (sb) is (sth); claim that (one) is (sth). **O:** him; oneself. **o:** clever, able;

being very tall; an expert, an authority: *You couldn't really* **describe** *her* **as** *beautiful.* ○ *Since the Commonwealth ... can hardly be* **described as** *an organization at all, there is a temptation to conclude that it does not amount to much.* SC □ often used with *can/could hardly/scarcely* + passive to make a negative or grudging judgement of sb/sth.

deserve

deserve better/well of [Vpr emph rel] (*formal*) merit good or better treatment from (sb). **o:** country, firm, employer: *He* **deserved** *rather* **better of** *his employers than to be pensioned off at a few pounds a week.* ○ *Lincoln* **deserved well of** *his country.*

despair

despair of [Vpr pass] be extremely doubtful of or sceptical about (sth). **o:** ever seeing them again, ever succeeding; success, recovery; outcome, issue: *After being cut off from the main party for two weeks they began to* **despair of** *rejoining their companions.* ○ *Don't* **despair of** *being slim again until you know what this new, reducing idea can do for you.* DM

destine

destined for [pass (Vn.pr)] (*formal*) intended by others to follow (a certain career). **S:** eldest son, brightest pupil. **o:** the church, the law, medicine, the army: *He was* **destined for** *an important career in the Church of England.* HB ○ *By family tradition he was* **destined for** *Sandhurst and a career as a regular army officer.*

detail

detail off [Vn ⇆ p pass] (usu *military*) assign, designate, appoint (sb), usu to a specific task or for a particular purpose. **S:** sergeant-major, duty NCO; manager, foreman. **O:** fatigue party, squad; ten men; team, group. **A:** as a special guard; for cookhouse duty; to design a new model: *Half-a-dozen men were* **detailed off** *for guard duty.* ○ *The best technique is to* **detail off** *known and stalwart supporters to enter into conversation with the other side before the meeting actually begins.* THH

detect

detect (in) [Vn.pr pass emph rel] find evidence of (sth) (in materials being examined, in sb's manner etc). **O:** sign, trace, mark; note, hint (of frivolity, seriousness, defiance). **o:** specimen, sample; voice, manner; suggestion: *We* **detected** *minute quantities of copper* **in** *the rock samples.* ○ *'Do I* **detect** *a certain lack of seriousness* **in** *what you're proposing?'* ○ **In** *the way they talk about the job they are doing you can* **detect** *early signs of disillusionment.*

deter

deter (from) [Vn.pr pass emph rel] (*formal*) make (sb) lose the desire (to do sth). **S:** industrial unrest, distance from markets. **O:** manufacturer, investor. **o:** moving North, investing overseas, installing new machinery: *Several factors* **deter** *new industry* **from** *coming to Cornwall.* OBS ○ *Countries have not been* **deterred from** *waging conventional wars by their opponents' possession of nuclear weapons.* □ object is the *-ing* form. = discourage (from).

deteriorate

deteriorate (into) [Vpr rel] become worse physically, morally, or intellectually. **S:** road, hotel; behaviour; discussions, argument. **o:** track, rough boarding-house; crudeness; quarrel, fight: *The debate* **deteriorated into** *a bitter quarrel between the party leaders.* = degenerate (from) (into).

detract

detract from [Vpr pass emph rel] (*formal*) lessen, diminish (sth); weaken. **S:** small size, power (of the engine), tiny cabin, awkward handling; length, difficulty, complexity. **o:** usefulness, appeal, attractiveness (to buyers); worth, value: *The underpowered engine and the bouncy suspension* **detract from** *its appeal as a general-purpose farm vehicle.* ○ *His high voice and unpleasing appearance* **detracted from** *his effectiveness as a platform speaker.* = take from 3.

develop

develop (from) (into) [Vpr rel, Vn.pr pass rel] (cause sth to) grow larger, become more powerful etc (from being small, weak etc). **S** [Vpr], **O** [Vn.pr]**:** country, city; farm, factory; school, course. **S** [Vn.pr]**:** government, regional board; owner, proprietor; director, head. **o:** (**from**) village; smallholding; family firm; obscure country. (**into**) metropolis; estate, vast complex; multi-national company; the best, most advanced of its kind: *The area to the south of the Maas has* **developed into** *Europoort, a complex of docks, refineries and warehouses.* ○ *This great industry has* **developed from** *quite modest beginnings.* ○ *The directors have plans to* **develop** *the club grounds* **into** *a stadium holding 40 000 people.*

deviate

deviate (from) [Vpr pass emph rel, Vn.pr pass emph rel] (*formal*) (cause sb to) abandon, move away (from sth). **o:** chosen course, straight path; truth; policy, course of action: *We shall not* **deviate** *by a hair's breadth* **from** *the mandate which the electorate has given us.* ○ *They could not be* **deviated from** *what they believed to be their duty.* = diverge (from).

devolve

devolve upon [Vpr emph rel] (*formal*) be passed to (sb), become the responsibility of (sb). **S:** office, job, duties, function; it ... to make sure this was done. **o:** second-in-command, Vice-Chairman, chief clerk: *When the Ambassador is on leave, his duties* **devolve upon** *the First Secretary.* ○ *It* **devolved upon** *his assistant to ensure that the guests were found hotels and entertained.*

devote

devote to [Vn.pr pass emph rel] give (oneself/sth) to (a purpose thought to be important); spend (time and effort) doing sth. **O:** oneself; energies, thoughts; a lifetime, twenty years. **o:** golf, hunting; family, children; education; improving standards, curing disease, helping the poor: *Ghandi* **devoted** *his whole life* **to** *the cause of peace.* ○ *The centre pages of this issue will be* **devoted to** *an important feature on housing.* ○ *Livestock breeders are*

***devoting** much thought and ingenuity **to** the improvement of this strain.* = dedicate to 1.

dictate

dictate to [Vpr pass] give orders to (sb). **S:** officious person, self-appointed authority. **o:** subordinate, wife, partner: *I won't have him **dictating to** me.* ○ *The shop stewards won't allow themselves to be **dictated to** by the official union leadership.*

die

die away [Vp] become fainter (or weaker) until eventually inaudible (or invisible); recede. **S:** voice; sobbing, shouting; commotion, din, tumult; anger, resentment: (stage directions) *Sound of hooves walking on hard road. They **die** rapidly **away**.* E ○ *Brigit's voice **died away** in stifled sobs.* DC ○ *The thunder and lightning **died away** in heavy rain and her mind too faded away in vague confusion.* ASA = fade away.

die back [Vp nom] (*horticulture*) (of the shoots or stems of plants) die as far as the roots, which stay alive and send out new shoots the next year: *The dahlias **died back** when we had that first cold spell.*

die down [Vp] become less intense (though without necessarily disappearing); subside. **S:** flames, fire; storm; revolution, uprising, quarrel; anger, passion, tension, excitement: *The Bill went through* (ie through Parliament)*, and the agitation **died down**.* TU ○ *Although both affairs have **died down** here, they have added to the countrywide discomfort over the ... economic situation.* OBS

die for [Vpr] (*informal*) badly need or want (sth). **o:** cigarette, pill, cup of tea; walk, bit of exercise, a sit down: *'Go and see to that coffee. I'm **dying for** a hot drink.'* TOH ○ *She was **dying for** a break, away from her family and household commitments* (cf *She was **dying** to have a break* etc). □ continuous tenses only; but note the following example where die for means 'give a great deal for': *Rugby League would **die for** the press coverage enjoyed by Union.* RW = long for.

die (from/of) [Vpr emph rel] have (sth) as the cause of death. **o:** starvation, exposure; cancer, pneumonia: *Then, when he seemed likely to **die from** sickness and grief, Athamas dreamed a dream.* GLEG ○ *One day he was attacked by a wild boar and **died of** his wounds.* GLEG

die of [Vpr] (*informal*) be in an extreme state of (sth). **o:** hunger, thirst; boredom, curiosity: *We're all **dying of** curiosity.* AITC ○ *The cleverer children had been deliberately held back from advanced work. As a result they were **dying of** boredom.*

die off [Vp] die one after the other. **S:** plant, tree; bird, animal; man, child: *A water shortage had struck the area and the wild life was **dying off** alarmingly in the intense heat.* ○ *They had to watch their young family **die off** through lack of food and proper medical attention.*

die out [Vp] become extinct; disappear, no longer be practised. **S:** family, line, species, race; custom, practice: *Only those species able to adapt to changing conditions survived. The others **died out**.* ○ *The whole ... tribe had **died out** from famine.* HHGG ○ *With the development of transport and the building of new factories many of the traditional crafts have **died out**.*

differ

differ (from) [Vpr emph rel] be different (from sth); not be of the same opinion (as sb) about sth. **S:** private industry; civilian life; university teaching. **o:** nationalized concern; service life; schoolteaching: *Russian **differs from** English in having a distinct alphabet and many inflected forms.* ○ *Patrick **differs from** his brother in many ways* (or: *They **differ (from** each other) in many ways*). ○ *The two parties **differ** very sharply **from** each other over the correct remedies to apply.*

dig

dig in [Vn ⇆ p pass adj] (*military*) position (sb/sth) below ground level by digging an emplacement or trench. **S:** commander, crew. **O:** tank, gun, mortar; troops, company: *The tanks were **dug in** so that only the gun turrets remained visible above the ground.* ○ *Our officers had **dug** their platoons **in** along the ridge.* ⇨ dig (oneself) in 1.

dig one's heels/toes in [Vn ⇆ p] (*informal*) stubbornly refuse to give way, usu on a point of principle: *I have stood a great deal from you without complaint, but after your last ridiculous and offensive letter I am going to **dig my toes in**.* US ○ *Slater* (a union leader) ***dug in his heels**. 'I don't want my union treated as a special case. All we want is justice.'* OBS = stick one's heels in.

dig (oneself) in 1 [Vp, Vn.p pass] (*military*) dig a trench for protection against enemy attack. **S:** company, platoon, troops: *As soon as they had seized the enemy position, the infantry **dug (themselves) in**.* ○ *'Get **yourselves dug in**!'* ⇨ dig in.

2 [Vn.p pass] (*informal*) establish oneself firmly in a place or job, often with the suggestion that one is determined not to move or be moved. **S:** new neighbour, employee, member of staff: *Then he manages to get **dug in**, well and truly **dug in**, in a publishing business.* PP ○ *'Do you work here or something? We all thought you would **dig yourself in** at Oxford.'* THH

dig in the ribs [Vn.pr pass] (*informal*) poke an elbow into sb's ribs to draw attention to sth: *James is awfully tiresome. Throughout the play he kept **digging** me **in the ribs** whenever anyone said anything remotely funny.* ○ *Ma **dug** him sharply **in the ribs** and started laughing like a jelly.* DBM

dig in/into 1 [Vn ⇆ p pass, Vn.pr pass] (*horticulture*) sow (sth), or mix (sth) with soil, by digging. **S:** gardener, nurseryman. **O:** vegetable, plant, tree; compost, manure. **o:** field, soil: *You'll need to **dig** those young trees **in** a bit deeper, unless you want the wind to blow them over.* ○ *Manure should be well **dug into** the soil.*

2 [Vp nom, Vpr pass] (*informal*) attack (food) hungrily. **o:** pie, cake; pile of bread and butter: *'Don't stand on ceremony — **dig in**!'* (cf *have a good **dig-in**!*). ○ *An enormous first course of turkey did not prevent them from **digging into** the Christmas pudding.* = dive in, tuck in/into 2.

dig out/out of 1 [Vn ⇆ p pass, Vn.pr pass] remove (soil etc) by digging; by doing so, form or construct (sth). **S:** navvy, miner; soldier. **O:** sand, coal; tunnel, emplacement. **o:** quarry, mine: *Ore **dug out of** these open-cast workings is loaded directly onto trucks.*

2 [Vn ⇆ p pass, Vn.pr pass] rescue (sb) by digging. **S:** rescue-party, civil defence worker, fireman. **O:**

victim, survivor, body. **o:** avalanche, fallen tunnel; wreckage, debris: *A whole family was* **dug out** *from underneath a tangle of fallen beams and masonry.* ○ *In the severe winter of 1947, farmers had to* **dig** *their livestock* **out of** *huge snowdrifts.*

3 [Vn ⇆ p pass, Vn.pr pass] catch or capture (sth) by digging. **S:** farmer, poacher, rat-catcher. **O:** rabbit, fox, rat. **o:** burrow, lair, hole: *If we can't smoke the rats out, we'll have to* **dig** *them* **out**.

4 [Vn ⇆ p pass, Vn.pr pass] obtain (sth) by diligent searching or research. **S:** student, researcher. **O:** facts, information, details, figures. **o:** library, archives: *'Where did he get hold of that information?' 'He managed to* **dig** *it* **out of** *some private library.'*

dug-out 1 [adj (Vn.p)] (*military*) shelter hollowed out of the ground, esp at the back of an open trench, and covered with material giving protection against enemy fire: *Chuikov's own command post was in a* **dug-out** *sunk into the side of the river-bed.* B ○ *While the bombardment continues, the men huddle in their* **dug-outs**. □ an adj form, but used as a noun. ⇨ dig out/out of 1.

2 [adj (Vn.p)] (boat) made by hollowing out the trunk of a tree: *In the Niger Delta,* **dug-out** *canoes* (or: **dug-outs**) *are an important means of transport: they are used for fishing, carrying goods to market, or simply ferrying people about.* □ an adj form, which may also be used as a noun. ⇨ dig out/out of 1.

3 [adj (Vn.p)] (*sport*) shelter at the side of a sports field, where trainers and substitutes sit during the game: *Peter Boyle, who came on to the pitch bearing drinks for the players after his team's first try, was waved back to the* **dug-out** *and told to stay there.* IND □ an adj form, but used as a noun.

dig up 1 [Vn ⇆ p pass adj] break and turn over (sth) by digging, often to bring under cultivation land used for other purposes, eg pasture. **O:** potato patch, field; meadow, lawn: *They were using machinery to* **dig up** *the front garden.* ○ *When food was in short supply we* **dug up** *the tennis-court in order to grow more vegetables.*

2 [Vn ⇆ p pass adj] remove (sth) from the ground by digging. **O:** plant, bulb, tree: *We must* **dig up** *those bushes; they're blocking our view of the garden.*

3 [Vn ⇆ p pass adj] reveal and remove from the ground, by digging (sth that has been deliberately hidden and/or has remained hidden for some time). **S:** dog; police; collector, explorer. **O:** bone, skeleton; firearms; coins, sculpture, pottery, human remains: *Police have* **dug up** *the body of his first wife.* ○ *A remarkable collection of terracotta heads has been* **dug up** *by archaeologists.*

4 [Vn ⇆ p pass] discover or reveal, by careful searching (sth which has remained hidden). **S:** reporter, detective. **O:** information; story; scandal: *Jeffries is said to have been living in Bristol between 1985 and 1987. See what you can* **dig up** *about those years.*

digress

digress (from) [Vpr pass emph rel] (*formal*) wander away (from a topic) when speaking or writing. **S:** speaker, lecturer, teacher. **o:** (main) theme, subject, central issue: *As boys, we had various ways of making the history master* **digress from** *the subject of the lesson.*

din

din in sb's ears [Vpr] sound, echo, in sb's ears. **S:** cry, shout; noise, tumult: *The noise of the traffic was still* **dinning in his ears** *after he had shut the doors and windows.* □ usu continuous tenses.

din in/into [Vn ⇆ p pass, Vn.pr pass emph rel] repeatedly urge (sb) to remember or be guided by (sth). **S:** teacher, parent, leader. **O:** lesson, precept, moral; need to work, necessity of honouring obligations. **o:** class, pupil, child, follower: *'Of course I remember the code numbers. I've had them* **dinned in** *enough, haven't I?'* ○ *The vital need to export more had been* **dinned into** *manufacturers by successive governments, but to little effect.* = drum in/into, hammer in/into 2.

dine

dine off/on [Vpr] (*formal*) make one's dinner of (sth); have (sth) as one's dinner. **o:** soup, melon, fish, asparagus: *He would go to the corner restaurant and* **dine off** *half a chicken and salad, washed down with white wine.*

dine out [Vp] (*formal*) dine in a restaurant, or at a friend's house: *'Don't prepare anything for me tonight, I shall be* **dining out**.*'* ⇨ eat out.

dine out on [Vp.pr] have dinner at another's expense because of one's achievements or reputation. **S:** actor, musician, novelist, painter, popular entertainer. **o:** one West End appearance, his ability to tell funny stories, the growing popularity of her work: *He would go back to town and* **dine out on** *the story of how he had freely ventured into the very heart of the industrial provinces and rubbed shoulders with the aborigines.* CON

dip

dip into 1 [Vpr pass] (*informal*) take money from (sth). **S:** government, bank, industry. **o:** gold reserves, savings, party funds, account: *The bank had to* **dip into** *its investments overseas to meet a financial crisis at home.* ○ *Mother had to* **dip into** *her holiday money to pay the milkman.*

2 [Vpr pass] (*informal*) make a brief study of (sth). **o:** author; subject; book, article: *I can't say that I know a great deal about modern painting — I've just* **dipped into** *one or two books on the subject.*

direct

direct at [Vn.pr pass emph rel] send (sth) towards sb/sth as one's target. **O:** fire, missile; criticism, abuse. **o:** target, goal; chief, director: *The violence and abuse* **directed at** *him ended only with his death in 1831.* GE = aim at 1.

direct at/to/towards [Vn.pr pass emph rel] have (sth) as the objective of one's (work etc). **O:** work, efforts, energies, resources. **o:** improvement of trade; building up one's defences, finding a new treatment: *While in office he had* **directed** *all his energies* **towards** *finding a solution to these problems.* ○ *Charcot's work ... had been* **directed at** *establishing some sort of order out of these confused ideas.* F = aim at 2.

direct to [Vn.pr pass emph rel] (*formal*) send or address (sth) to (sb), orally or in writing. **O:** remarks, comments, complaints, thanks. **o:** manager, officer, bursar: *If you have any complaints to make concerning your food or accommodation, please*

***direct** them **to** the house manager.* ○ *Inquiries about grants or scholarships should be **directed to** the College Bursar.*

direct one's/sb's attention to [Vn.pr pass emph rel] (*formal*) (cause sb to) think carefully about or look closely at (sth). **o:** problem, question, issue, matter: *The shortage has been ignored for some months, but I am glad to say that the minister is now **directing his attention to** it.* ○ *A policeman **directed our attention to** a notice which read 'No Entry'.* = call (sb's) attention to, draw (sb's) attention to.

disabuse

disabuse of [Vn.pr pass emph rel] (*formal*) free, rid (sb/oneself) of (sth). **O:** him etc; oneself; the mind. **o:** idea, notion; prejudice; opinion, attitude: *Once we can **disabuse** ourselves **of** the word, all sorts of arguments go by the board.* MFM ○ *Some followers held unacceptable political views, **of** which he sought to **disabuse** them.*

disagree

disagree (with) [Vpr emph rel] not match, not agree (with sth). **S:** statement, account, record; figure, sum. **o:** earlier, official, more reliable report, story; previous total. **A:** totally, in all respects, at all points: *I'm afraid that the total I've arrived at **disagrees with** the one on your bill.* ○ *Simon's estimate of the time it will take **disagrees with** mine* (or: *His estimate and mine **disagree***). ↔ agree (with) 2.

disagree with [Vpr rel] have a bad effect on (sb's health etc). **S:** food, meal; fish, wine; heat, humidity: *He's not feeling well: something he ate must have **disagreed with** him.* ○ *Hot climates **disagree with** her.* ↔ agree with.

disagree (with) (about/over) [Vpr emph rel] not be of the same opinion (as sb) (about sth); express such a difference of view. **S:** wife, brother; colleague, friend. **o:** (**about/over**) method, means, procedure; how to do sth, whether to take part. **A:** heartily, strongly, emphatically: *The landlord **disagreed with** his tenants* (or: *He and they **disagreed**) **over** where the new cottages should be built.* ○ *I know you **disagreed with** me yesterday **about** the terms of a settlement; can we agree today?* ↔ agree (with) 1.

disappear

disappear (from sight/view) [Vpr] no longer be visible. **S:** ship, aircraft; column, procession: *As we rounded the next bend, we found that the lorry had **disappeared** completely **from view**.* ○ *For a while Mick **disappeared from sight** — reportedly to work for his Finals.*

disapprove

disapprove (of) [Vpr pass adj emph rel] (*formal*) have or express a low opinion of (sb/sth); not think highly of (sb/sth). **S:** father; principal, headteacher; employer. **o:** (son's) friend; pastime, habit; smoking, keeping late hours; perfume, lipstick; long hair: *Tony shaved off his beard before the interview: he knew of employers who strongly **disapproved of** facial hair.* ○ *Father is unusually tolerant: there are few teenage tastes **of** which he actively **disapproves**.* ↔ approve of.

discharge

discharge (from) [Vn.pr pass emph rel] (*formal*) allow (sb) to leave (sth); make (sb) leave (sth). **S:** doctor, surgeon; army authorities, medical board; employer. **O:** patient, casualty; recruit; servant: *She was **discharged from** the intensive care unit last week and transferred to a general ward.* ○ *Rather than punish men regularly as habitual offenders, the Army may decide to **discharge** them **from** service altogether.*

discharge (from) (into) [Vn.pr pass emph rel] pass or transfer (sth) (from one place) (to another). **O:** cargo, freight; oil, coal; corn, rice; gas, electricity. **o:** (**from**) ship, hold; container, wagon; gasholder, battery; (**into**) lighter, barge; lorry; tub, bin: *Firmer action will be taken against companies **discharging** industrial waste **into** rivers.* ○ *Grain is **discharged from** giant holders **into** long lines of trucks.*

disconnect

disconnect (from) [Vn.pr pass emph rel] separate (one thing) (from another). **O:** condenser, loudspeaker; engine, coil. **o:** circuit, (source of) power; wheels, battery: *If you push down the clutch pedal, the engine is **disconnected from** the transmission.* ○ *Make sure you **disconnect** the television (**from** the mains supply) before you open up the back.* ↔ connect up (to).

discourage

discourage (from) [Vn.pr pass] try to persuade (sb) (not to do sth); make (sb) lose interest (in doing sth). **O:** motorist; climber, explorer; student, pupil. **o:** driving too fast; venturing too far; doing one's best, achieving all one might: *Try to **discourage** him **from** driving back to London tonight.* ○ *We were **discouraged from** having anything further to do with maths by his inept teaching.* □ the object is the-*ing* form of a v. = deter from.

discriminate

discriminate (against) [Vpr pass emph rel] treat (sb) differently (and usu less favourably) because of his race, religion etc. **S:** system, regime; law; police. **o:** Catholic, Jew; (coloured) immigrant, migrant worker; drug addict; woman: *There is evidence that some employers **discriminate against** women applicants.* ○ *We're not **discriminated against**, we're patronized — which is far worse.*

discriminate between [Vpr emph rel] (*formal*) because of special training, greater sensitivity etc, be able to judge which of two things is better etc. **o:** (two) performances, recordings; editions; wines; tobaccos; good and bad; ordinary and superior: *You don't need to be a professional musician to **discriminate between** two performances of the same work* (or: *to **discriminate** one performance **from** the other*). ○ ***Between** two such obviously fine instruments I find it hard to **discriminate**.*

discriminate from [Vn.pr pass emph rel] ⇨ previous entry

disembark

disembark (from) [Vpr emph rel, Vn.pr pass emph rel] go or put (sb) ashore (from a ship etc). **S** [Vpr], **O** [Vn.pr]**:** crew, passenger. **S** [Vn.pr]**:** captain, master. **o:** ship; liner, tanker: *Cars **disembarking from** the ferry jammed the approach road to the motorway.* ○ *Troops can be **disembarked from** ships* *lying off shore and carried in shore in flat-bottomed craft.*

disengage

disengage (from) [Vpr emph rel, Vn.pr pass emph rel] (*formal*) (cause sb/sth to) separate or detach (from an involvement). **S** [Vpr], **O** [Vn.pr]**:** country, political party; business, firm; army, soldier. **o:** alliance, pact; association, enterprise; struggle, battle: *De Gaulle was anxious that France should* ***disengage from*** *military dependence on the United States.* ○ *Stephen's parents tended to* ***disengage*** *him* ***from*** *any relationship that would help him to grow up.*

disentangle

disentangle (from) [Vn.pr pass emph rel] separate or free (sb/sth) (from a complicated state). **O:** truth; essential fact, central thread, main point. **o:** falsehood; garbled tale, complicated account: *Trollope discussed the difficulty that arises in novel-writing of* ***disentangling*** *men and women* ***from*** *their surroundings.* SPL ○ ***From*** *this complex pattern of events we can* ***disentangle*** *two important trends.*

dish

dish out [Vn ⇆ p pass] (*informal*) distribute (sth). **S:** storekeeper, quartermaster; employer, commander; government. **O:** tool, weapon, map, clothing; praise, commendation, thanks; medal, 'gong': *New overalls and helmets were* ***dished out*** *before the party went underground.* ○ *The boss is delighted, he's been all over the works* ***dishing out*** *bonuses and handshakes.* = give out 2.

dish it out [Vp.n] (*informal*) inflict punishment; cause pain or distress: *As Roy Jenkins suggested ... those journalists who like to* ***dish it out*** *can't take it* (ie don't like being attacked in their turn). NS ○ *I can damage people too. I can* ***dish it out*** *just like everybody else.* FFE = hand it/(the) punishment out.

dish up 1 [Vp, Vn ⇆ p pass adj] (*informal*) put (sth) onto plates. **O:** meal, supper; stew, vegetables: *I was just about ready to* ***dish up****.* TGLY ○ *Mother* ***dished*** *the food* ***up*** *straight out of the saucepan.* = serve up 1.

2 [Vn ⇆ p pass] (*informal*) offer, present (sth). **S:** newspaper, editor; producer, playwright, author. **O:** concoction, mixture; brand (of humour, entertainment): *In his latest article Smith* ***dishes up*** *a familiar mixture of reactionary opinions and thinly-disguised personal abuse.*

disinclined

disinclined (for) [pass (Vn.pr)] (*formal*) not in the mood (for sth), unwilling to undertake (sth). **o:** real effort, hard work, serious conversation: *Having just eaten a heavy meal, he felt* ***disinclined for*** *any serious work.* ○ *I had been talking all morning; I was* ***disinclined for*** *further argument* (or: ***disinclined*** *to argue any further*). □ used with *appear* etc.

dislodge

dislodge (from) [Vn.pr pass emph rel] move (sth/sb) from a place where it or he is fixed. **S:** gale, gust; attack, thrust. **O:** slate, tile; enemy. **o:** roof; position, nest: *A careless movement can* ***dislodge*** *sharp pieces of stone* ***from*** *the rock-face.* ○ *Artillery will not* ***dislodge*** *the enemy* ***from*** *his well-entrenched positions.* ○ *Emma* (ie in Jane Austen's novel of that name) *has certainly become part of our national heritage and nothing could ...* ***dislodge*** *her* ***from*** *that position.* JA

dismiss

dismiss as [Vn.pr] reject (sth) as (worthless etc). **O:** work, efforts; claim, theory. **o:** slight, puny; worthless, absurd: *The ethical standard he preached ... was* ***dismissed as*** *impractical and irrelevant.* F

dismiss (from) [Vn.pr pass emph rel] make (sb) leave his employment. **O:** official, servant. **o:** office, post; employment, service: *A maidservant ... was* ***dismissed from*** *service ... for stealing money.* F ○ *He'd had teaching jobs abroad;* ***from*** *both of them he was* ***dismissed*** *after about six months.*

dismiss from one's mind/thoughts [Vn.pr pass] not think any further about (sth). **O:** problem, difficulty; matter, question; doubt, anxiety: *'The best feeling would be if I could just* ***dismiss*** *everything else* ***from*** *my mind.'* ○ *These suspicions weren't easily* ***dismissed from*** *his thoughts. After all, Janet had been seen out with Geoff on two occasions.*

dispense

dispense with 1 [Vpr pass] (manage to) exist or function without (sth). **S:** country, industry. **o:** assistance, aid, co-operation, services: *You may dislike having to depend upon him, but it will be some time before you can* ***dispense with*** *his help altogether.* ○ *The patient's recovery has reached a point where the doctor's services can be* ***dispensed with****.* □ usu with *can/could.*

2 [Vpr pass] suspend (sth). **o:** formality, protocol, procedural rules: *I suggest we* ***dispense with*** *formality and proceed with our discussions on an informal basis.* = set aside 3.

displace

displace (from) [Vn.pr pass emph rel] move (sb/sth) (from a central or crucial position). **O:** adviser, confidant; the army, the communist party; nuclear power, fossil fuels. **o:** central role, position of dominance, unique place: *Copernicus had* ***displaced*** *the earth* ***from*** *the centre of the universe.* F

dispose

dispose of 1 [Vpr pass] settle, resolve (sth). **o:** objection, argument, criticism; difficulty, problem: *The statement does not, however,* ***dispose of*** *the doubts about the Government's earlier posture.* OBS ○ *The problem of who to select as his successor was quickly* ***disposed of****.*

2 [Vpr pass] get rid of or destroy (sb/sth). **o:** political opponent, rival contender; wife; dead body, incriminating evidence; rubbish: *He proceeded with great skill to* ***dispose of*** *the traditional anti-Catholic arguments.* SS ○ *Most of the opposition had been* ***disposed of****; only a few remained alive and out of prison.*

3 [Vpr pass] sell (sth). **o:** house, boat, land, possessions: *When the crash came, the family was forced to* ***dispose of*** *all its possessions.* ○ *The silver was* ***disposed of*** *to an antique dealer.*

4 [Vpr] have (sth) at one's disposal; possess. **S:** army, commander; industry, economy. **o:** forces, reserves; guns, men; resources: *Between them Rokossovski and Vatutin* (two Russian generals)

***disposed of** enough strength to hold off the German attack.* B ○ *The Russian artillery **disposed of** over 20 000 pieces, of which over 6 000 were 76-mm anti-tank guns.* B □ simple tenses only.

well etc disposed towards [pass (Vn.pr)] sympathetic etc towards (sth/sb); inclined to speak well etc of (sth/sb). **A:** ⚠ well, kindly, favourably; ill, unkindly, unfavourably. **o:** regime; policy, idea; change, innovation: *Students seem **well disposed towards** the idea of moving their accommodation nearer the University site.* ○ *The middle classes are **favourably disposed towards** the new military junta.* □ used with *appear* etc; an adv is present.

dispossess

dispossess (of) [Vn.pr pass emph rel] (*formal*) take away from (sb) his property etc, often in order to distribute it to others. **S:** workers' government, popular regime. **O:** landowner, industrialist, foreign investor. **o:** property; land, factory: *The upper classes may be **dispossessed of** their special powers and privileges by a slow process of evolution.*

dissociate

dissociate from [Vn.pr emph rel] (*formal*) say that (oneself/sb) opposes or is in disagreement with (sth). **O:** oneself; board, panel, committee. **o:** opinion, view; remark, statement: *Some of Stafford's sharpest critics **dissociated** themselves **from** a now divided Parliament.* SHOE ○ *The Archbishop called on other churches to **dissociate** themselves **from** the Dutch Reformed Church.* SC

dissolve

dissolve into [Vpr] gradually change or give way to (sth different). **S:** picture, image; interior scene; state; comedy. **o:** another; location sequence; tragedy, farce: *This intimate shot **dissolved into** a view of the castle steps.* ○ *Stephen lived perilously close to the border where sanity **dissolves into** insanity.* LS

dissuade

dissuade (from) [Vn.pr pass emph rel] (*formal*) persuade (sb) not to follow a course of action. **O:** child, pupil; follower, member. **o:** course, undertaking; fighting, rebelling; leaving, resigning: *Potter **dissuaded** him **from** his impulse to 'publish the truth' at once.* GE ○ *The police finally **dissuaded** the marchers **from** entering Whitehall.* ○ *John allowed himself to be **dissuaded from** taking up a post overseas.*

distinguish

distinguish between [Vpr emph rel] (be able to) tell the difference between (one thing and another). **o:** good and evil, truth and falsehood, one species and another: *He can't **distinguish between** a genuine antique and a reproduction* (or: ***distinguish** one **from** the other*). ○ *He could never **distinguish** with certainty **between** the Scandinavian colours.* OMIH □ used with *can/could.* = discriminate between.

distinguish from 1 [Vn.pr pass] ➪ previous entry **2** [Vn.pr pass emph rel] be a measure or mark of the difference between persons or things. **S:** language, higher intelligence; organizing ability, urban culture. **O:** species, mankind; race, community. **o:** non-human animals; most others, any other: *Superior intelligence and the use of language **distinguish** man **from** the other primates.* ○ *He was not easily **distinguished from** the general run of people we get here — until he began to talk.* = mark off (from).

distract

distract (from) [Vn.pr pass emph rel] draw (sb's attention etc) away (from sth). **S:** noise; explosion, report; visitor, caller; telephone, television. **O:** sb's thoughts, mind; sb's attention. **o:** work, reading; what one is saying; anxieties, fears: *His thoughts were **distracted from** this painful topic by the sudden arrival of a neighbour.* □ usu passive.

distribute

distribute (among/to) [Vn.pr pass emph rel] give (sth) among/to a number of people. **O:** leaflets, brochures; tools, weapons; food, warm clothing. **o:** crowd, audience; workers, soldiers; refugees: *Duplicated notes were **distributed to** the class at the beginning of the lecture.* ○ *Rice was **distributed among** the families thronging around the lorry.* = hand out 1.

dive

dive in [Vp] (*informal*) begin eating hungrily, attack one's food: *'Don't wait for us to join you at the table: just **dive in**.'* ○ *'Find a seat, then you can **dive in**. You want milk, don't you?'* YAA = dig in/into 2, tuck in/into 2.

dive in/into [Vp emph, Vpr emph rel] throw oneself head first into water: *'You **dive in** first and test the temperature of the water!'* ○ ***In** he **dived** and emerged spluttering half-way across the pool.* ○ *The young god, driven to the shore, escaped serious injury only by **diving into** the sea.* GLEG

dive (one's hand) into [Vpr, Vn.pr] (*informal*) thrust (one's hand) quickly into (sth). **o:** pocket, purse, handbag: *He **dived into** his jacket pocket to make sure his wallet was still there.* ○ *Someone **dived his hand into** my handbag and made off with my purse.*

diverge

diverge (from) [Vpr emph rel] (*formal*) move away (from sth), become more and more separate (from sth). **S:** path, course; views, policy; development, growth, career. **o:** that/those of one's colleagues, associates: *His thinking **diverges** increasingly **from** what is officially taught and recognized.* ○ *From that point onwards his career **diverged from** Philip's* (or: *his career and Philip's **diverged***). = deviate (from).

divert

divert (from) [Vn.pr pass emph rel] turn (sth) away from one course or purpose to another. **O:** traffic, shipping; cargo, produce; worker, scholar. **o:** route, destination; use, purpose; aim, objective: *Police have **diverted** all southbound traffic **from** the motorway for a ten-mile stretch near Nottingham.* ○ *The government were not prepared to allow these resources to be **diverted from** military use.* ○ *He could not help having his mind **diverted from** his anxieties by the rush of London life.* BLCH

divest

divest of [Vn.pr pass emph rel] (*formal*) take away from (sb/sth) (a garment etc); take away from (sb), as a mark of disgrace, (sth granted or conferred earlier). **O:** himself; scene, building; officer, public servant. **o:** mark, sign, trace; charm, mystery; honour, title: *George Orwell could never fully* **divest** *himself, as he tried to do while living amongst working-class people,* **of** *his upper-class manners and tastes.* ○ *The officers were* **divested of** *their swords and badges of rank as a visible sign that this authority had been taken from them.*

divide

divide among/between [Vn.pr pass emph rel] share (sth) among/between (people). **S:** brothers, associates, criminals. **O:** inheritance, booty, proceeds, profits. **o:** themselves; family, shareholders: *The legacy has to be* **divided between** *his two daughters.* ○ *The members of the investment club* **divide** *their profits equally* **among** *themselves.* = share out (among).

divide between [Vn.pr pass] give or allow (about the same length of time) to one thing as to another. **O:** time; day, afternoon; holiday. **o:** golf and gardening, swimming and sunbathing, reading and writing: *He usually* **divides** *his holidays* **between** *the beach and the casino.* ○ *He ...* **divided** *his time* **between** *Paris and lodgings in London.* TU ○ *His day is evenly* **divided between** *work and relaxation.*

divide from 1 [Vn.pr pass emph rel] keep (one thing) separate from (another); form a barrier between (two things). **S:** railway, the Rhine, fence, path. **O:** poorer area, Germany, his land, an airfield. **o:** fashionable district, France, my farm, surrounding ploughland: *The Red Sea* **divides** *Africa* **from** *Asia.* ○ *His study is* **divided from** *the living-room by a thin wooden partition.* = separate (off) (from).
2 [Vn.pr pass rel] make (sb/sth) separate from (sb/sth else). **S:** law, policy; resettlement, migration. **O:** mother, husband; tribe. **o:** children, wife; land: *God* **divided** *the sea* **from** *the land.* ○ *This law will* **divide** *children* **from** *their parents.*

divorce

divorce (oneself) from [Vn.pr pass emph rel] separate oneself completely from (sth/sb). **o:** ordinary life, reality; human society, companions: *The scholar ... may, in his preoccupation with intellectual matters, become equally* **divorced from** *the springs of feeling and emotion.* JUNG

do

do about [Vn.pr pass] (*informal*) act so as to overcome, solve, remove etc (sth). **O:** (not) much, a lot; enough, even less; what. **o:** it; unemployment, inflation; mess, clutter: *'I hate him going abroad all the time.' 'Well, there's not much you can* **do about** *that.'* ○ *She was never there, and in any case he would have no idea what to* **do about** *it if she had been.* HD ○ *'Well,' Charles got out at last, 'what are you going to* **do about** *it?'* HD □ the question form with *what* can be spoken as a challenging reply to an accusation: *'Is that your motorbike in our drive?' 'Yes, what are you going to* **do about** *it?'*

do (as/for) [Vpr] act in place of (sth), be a substitute for (sth). **S:** plank, stick, saucer, blanket. **o:** shelf, weapon, ashtray, tent: *'Don't throw those bricks away. They'll* **do as** *supports for my bookshelves.'* ○ *These pieces of timber will* **do** *perfectly well* **for** *the frame of the bed, but we'll need a proper spring mattress.* = serve as/for.

do away with 1 [Vp.pr pass adj] get rid of (sth); abolish. **S:** government, ministry, board. **o:** restriction, rule; institution; tax, surcharge, penalty: *The death penalty has been* **done away with** *in many European countries.* ○ *You can't* **do away with** *the House of Lords.*
2 [Vp.pr pass] kill (sb/sth); destroy (sth). **o:** oneself; cat, horse: *Hymns of the sort that made you want to* **do away with** *yourself had been sung.* TGLY ○ *The monster ... must be throttled and* **done away with**. MLT = make away with.

do well by [Vpr] (*informal*) treat (sb) kindly or generously. **S:** guardian, benefactor; employer, industry. **o:** dependant; employee: *A humane society always* **does well by** *its old people.* next entry

hard done by [pass (Vpr)] (*informal*) unfairly treated. **S:** employee, son, wife: *He claimed to be* **hard done by**. *In fact, he'd always been very generously treated by his employers.* ○ *If he's not getting more than the minimum gratuity after so many years in their service he's being* **hard done by**. previous entry

do down [Vn.p pass] (*informal*) try to make (sb/sth) appear small, mean, unimportant etc. **O:** parent, class, country: *They're all so incredibly catty and so dishonest, all trying to impress each other or* **do** *each other* **down** *the whole time.* ILIH ○ *'I hope I'm not* **doing down** *the national Exchequer,' I said anxiously.* DIL = run down 5.

do (for) ⇨ do (as/for).

do for 1 [Vpr] (*informal*) clean and keep a house tidy for (sb); keep house for (sb): *They can't afford domestic help, so they have to* **do for** *themselves.* ○ *Mrs Bloggs has* **done for** *us for over twenty years.*
2 [Vpr] (*informal*) succeed in obtaining (sth). **o:** supplies, fresh meat, water: *How will the crews* **do for** *drinking water when they're afloat in an open raft?* ○ *What shall we* **do for** *fresh fruit while the seamen's strike is on?* □ only in questions and after *what* and *how*. ⇨ do badly/well for.
3 [Vpr pass] (*informal*) act in such a way that sb is ruined, killed etc. **S:** (incompetent) doctor, surgeon; general; minister, government. **o:** patient, case; troops; industry, agriculture: *There were heavy casualties on the first day. The general nearly* **did for** *the lot of us with his plan of attack.* ○ *As soon as I feel really ill and know that I'm* **done for**, *I'll send you word, doctor.* INN ○ *The bank won't come to the rescue for ever—we'll be* **done for** *in six months.* □ usu passive; no continuous tenses.

do all right etc for oneself [Vpr] (*informal*) prosper financially, in one's career etc, esp through astuteness in business, exceptional social skills etc. **A:** ⚠ all right, (very/pretty/exceptionally) well: *I don't know what pay he gets, but if Jim wasn't* **doing pretty well for himself** *he wouldn't stay in the job for five minutes.* ○ *Born selfish, that's what he was. Dropping a pretty girl like Prissie, though from what I hear she* **did all right for herself** *last night.* DC ○ *Frank was* **doing very well for himself**. *Import-export was booming.* TO

do badly/well for [Vpr] (*informal*) have a bad/good supply of (sth); obtain a small/large number of (sth). **o:** tips, gratuities, luxuries; duty-free cigarettes, cheap drink; awards, scholarships: *We didn't* **do** *too* **badly for** *coal during the miners' strike; we'd managed to stock up.* ○ *The staff at that hotel* **did** *very* **well for** *tips and presents.* ○ *The independent schools* **do well for** *open scholarships at the older universities.* ⇨ do for 2.

never/not do enough for [Vn.pr] be unable to do as much for (sb) as one thinks that person deserves, or as one would like. **o:** one's wife, children; one's employees, colleagues: *Jim was home on leave ... Like his mother and father, he could* **not do enough for** *Virginia.* AITC

do in [Vn ⇆ p pass] (*slang*) kill (sb/oneself): *These were professional killers who '***did in***' John Regan, and they knew more about fingerprints and ballistics than I did.* CON ○ *I've thought how good it would be sometimes to* **do** *myself* **in** *and the easiest way to do it ... was to hope for a big war.* LLDR

done in/up [pass (Vn.p)] (*informal*) extremely tired, exhausted. **A:** thoroughly, completely; a bit, rather, quite, all: *'What's the matter, Simmonds? You look all* **done in***.'* ITAJ ○ *ASTON: Any time you want to get into bed, just get in. DAVIES: I think I will. I'm a bit* **done in***.* TC ○ *You look quite* **done up***, old chap; you ought to lie down before dinner.* BLCH ○ *Marian's health was far from good. She felt 'regularly* **done up***' both in body and mind.* GE □ used with *appear* etc.

do out 1 [Vn ⇆ p pass] (*informal*) make (sth) clean by scrubbing, sweeping etc. **S:** cleaner, charwoman, housewife; groom. **O:** hall, room; yard, stable: *She* **did out** *the bathroom with lots of soap and hot water.* ○ *The yard needs to be* **done out** *thoroughly* (or: *needs a thorough* **doing-out**) *with a stiff broom.* = clean out.

2 [Vn ⇆ p pass] (*informal*) make (sth) tidy or orderly by removing scrap paper, unwanted clothes etc. **S:** clerk, student, child, housewife. **O:** desk, cupboard, wardrobe, drawer: *'You must* **do out** *your desk drawer: it's full of waste paper and unanswered letters.'* ○ *It's time the children's toy cupboard was* **done out***. It looks a mess and they can never find anything they want.* = tidy out.

do out of [Vn.pr pass] (*informal*) prevent (sb) from having (sth), often by trickery or neglect. **S:** employer, landlord; colleague, rival. **o:** pension, paid holiday; grant, allowance; job, promotion: *Of course I'm furious. He just* **did** *me* **out of** *a trip to the West Indies this summer.* ○ *But I was not to be* **done out of** *the truth so easily. 'Are these illnesses curable?' I persisted.* THH

do over 1 [Vn ⇆ p pass] redecorate, refurbish (sth). **O:** house, place; bathroom, bedroom: *'Haven't you noticed how the paintwork is chipped and flaking? It really needs* **doing over** (or: *to be* **done over***).'* ○ *We'll keep this bedroom as it is and* **do** *the other one* **over***.*

2 [Vn.p pass] (*slang*) give (sb) a severe and thorough beating. **S:** gang; raider, bandit. **O:** shopkeeper, bank clerk; (innocent) bystander: *Poor old Mike, he got* **done over** *by a gang of roughs after a football match.* = beat up.

do (ample/full) justice to [Vn.pr pass emph rel] give to (sb/sth) the care, attention, fair treatment etc, that he or it deserves. **S:** report, account; observer, critic; guest, diner. **o:** achievement, character; performance; meal: *She felt that her brother's works did not* **do justice to** *the depth and courage of his humanity.* HAA ○ *The fact that we had eaten an hour earlier prevented us from* **doing full justice to** *her cooking.*

do to death [Vn.pr pass] (*formal*) kill (sb). **O:** prisoner, hostage: *The few guards soon lost their nerve and simply* **did** *their charges* **to death** *in some wood or quarry.* B ○ *It was disagreeable to be searched for weapons ... but then a young girl had just been* **done to death** *by a demonstration.* ST

do something to [Vn.pr] (*informal*) excite, stir the feelings of (sb); concern, disturb. **S:** expression, voice, figure; song, performer: (popular song) *You* **do something to** *me!* ○ *But I can hear her coughing. That little cough* **does something to** *me.* AITC

do up 1 [Vn ⇆ p pass adj] renovate, modernize (sth) by making repairs or installing modern amenities; redecorate. **S:** property developer, owner, tenant; decorator, builder. **O:** derelict cottage, old farmhouse, mews; kitchen, bathroom, front of house: *I did all this* (indicating the cottage) *for Mr Harrington. A very clever boy I was recommended to,* **did** *it* **up** *for us.* FFE ○ *We're getting a professional decorator to* **do** *the boys' bedroom* **up***.*

2 [Vn ⇆ p pass] make (sth) into a bundle or parcel. **O:** washing, books, magazines, presents, firewood: *I must* **do up** *some old clothes for the church jumble sale.* ○ *Her hair grows long and she* **does** *it* **up** *in long, complex coils.* BRN ○ *Under her arm was what looked like a framed picture* **done up** *in brown paper.* TGLY

3 [Vn ⇆ p pass] fasten (sth). **O:** zip(-fastener), shoelaces, buttons, hooks and eyes; dress, coat : *'***Do** *your flies* **up***.'* CSWB ○ *He was in his trousers and shirt,* **doing up** *his braces.* TC

4 [Vp] be fastened, may be fastened. **S:** suit, coat, dress, skirt: *The skirt* **does up** *at the back.* ○ *'How does this jacket* **do up***?'* □ usu with simple tenses.

do with [Vpr] (*informal*) need, want (sth). **o:** drink, meal, cigarette; break, holiday: *'I could* **do with** *two weeks away from the children and the washing-up.'* ○ *'You can both stop leaning against the wall: I could* **do with** *a helping hand.'* ○ *This car could* **do with** *a good polish.* □ used only with *could*.

do anything etc with [Vn.pr pass emph rel] (*informal*) (be able to) handle, control, repair etc (sb/sth). **O:** ⚠ (not) anything, not a thing, nothing. **o:** child; bicycle, car, washing-machine: *'Ask Dad to come downstairs and see if he can* **do anything with** *the television.'* ○ *'Have any of you been using my typewriter? I can't* **do a thing with** *it today.'* ○ *If you can't* **do anything with** *your hair, if it is limp, lank and lustreless, you need Estolan.* WI □ used with *can/could (not)* or *(not) be able to*.

do business (with) [Vn.pr emph rel] trade (with sb). **o:** manufacturer, supplier; store, shop: *One likes to* **do business with** *a British firm. One knows where one is.* OMIH ○ *They aren't good people to* **do business with***. They keep you waiting for your money.* = deal with 1.

what do with 1 [Vn.pr] where did you etc put, lose or hide (sth). **o:** handbag, keys, papers: *'Miss Smith,* **what** *have you* **done with** *the United Cement Holdings file?'* ○ *'***What** *did the porter* **do with** *our luggage?'* □ used with perfect tenses and simple past tense.

2 [Vn.pr pass] how shall we etc handle, treat or use (sth/sb). **o:** complaint, inquiry; delegation, visitor; prisoner, delinquent: ***What*** *on earth are we going to* ***do with*** *all these young people drifting in from the countryside?* ○ ***What*** *do the Government propose to* ***do with*** *all the surplus stores left over after the war?* ○ ***What****'s to be* ***done with*** *all this stuff in the attic?* □ usu with *will, shall, be going to* etc.

what (to) do with oneself [Vn.pr] how should one occupy one's time, give meaning to one's existence: ***What*** *do the children* ***do with themselves*** *during the holidays?'* ○ *Now that Jenny's retired, she doesn't know* ***what to do with herself***. □ what do with etc may be the Object of a larger sentence (as in the second example).

do without 1 [Vp, Vpr pass] exist, function or manage without (sth/sb). **o:** services, help; food, warmth; friends, a wife, husband: *You must buy sweets with your own pocket-money or* ***do without***. ○ *He retired into his palace and lived there alone, deciding to* ***do without*** *the company of women and not to marry.* GLEG = go without, dispense with 1.

2 [Vpr] (*informal*) not require, and resent having (sth). **o:** interference, unkind comment, criticism, innuendo; his meddling in everything: *We can certainly* ***do without*** *John poking his nose in every five minutes.* ○ *'I can* ***do without*** *that kind of advice, thank you.'* □ with *can/could* only.

dole

dole out [Vn ⇆ p pass adj] distribute, serve (sth), sometimes with the suggestion that the portions are small and grudgingly given. **O:** soup, bread; money: *Receipts from the mails go straight to the US Treasury, which then* ***doles out*** *only whatever sum is authorized by the purse-holders on Capitol Hill.* OBS ○ *She rigorously kept wine and money from him,* ***doling*** *them* ***out*** *in infinitesimal doses.* BLCH

doll

doll (oneself) up [Vn.p pass adj] (*informal*) dress smartly, as for a special occasion, sometimes with the suggestion that the dressing-up is extreme or vulgar: *She could put on her Number Ones* (= best uniform) *and* ***doll herself up*** *smartly to go home and cut a dash.* RFW ○ *She was* ***dolled up*** *without being over-dressed.* CON ○ *'P'raps you think I'm not good enough to meet your bleedin'* ***dolled-up*** *friends.'* PE

doom

doomed to [pass (Vn.pr)] bound to meet or suffer (sth). **S:** scheme, plan, enterprise. **o:** disappointment, failure, frustration: *Mary's attempts to restore the Catholic faith were ...* ***doomed to*** *failure.* SHOE ○ *This species was* ***doomed to*** *extinction* (or: ***doomed*** *to become extinct*). ○ *Every embodied spirit is* ***doomed to*** *suffering* (or: ***doomed*** *to suffer*). DOP □ used with *be, seem.*

dope

dope up (on/with) [Vn.p pass adj, Vn.p.pr pass] (*informal*) put (sb) under the influence of drugs, so that he cannot feel, think, act sensibly etc. **o:** heroin, cocaine, barbiturates, hash; medication: *They used to* ***dope up*** *the woman* ***with*** *all sorts of hormones.* BBCR ○ *I did not feel a thing because I was so* ***doped up***. RT □ used in passive with *appear* etc: *He looked* ***doped up*** *to the eyeballs.*

doss

doss down [Vp nom] (*slang*) get into a makeshift bed (eg of straw or sacking, and often on the ground); get into a rough or simple bed in a doss-house. **S:** tramp, down-and-out: *In Paris tramps would often* ***doss down*** *under the bridges or on the gratings of ventilator shafts.* ○ *She knew Harry liked to* ***doss down*** (or: *have a* ***doss-down***) *in the porch.* TFD

dot

dotted with [pass (Vn.pr)] having things scattered about it at intervals. **S:** landscape, area, meadows. **o:** trees, bushes; cottages, farms; cattle: *Clerkenwell was* ***dotted with*** *gardens and expanses of meadowland.* MLT ○ *Here was countryside* ***dotted with*** *slag heaps and scarred with railway lines.* GBART ○ *The three-mile beach is* ***dotted with*** *oil slicks.* OBS

dote

dote on/upon [Vpr pass adj emph rel] show much, or too much, affection for (sb); centre one's affections on (sb). **S:** mother, husband. **o:** children, wife: *It is not that my parents did not care for me, in fact they* ***doted on*** *me.* SU ○ *I'm afraid he* ***dotes upon*** *his wife — and she doesn't hesitate to take advantage of his affection.* ○ *Conversation centred on a much* ***doted-upon*** *first baby.*

double

double back 1 [Vp] quickly turn around and retrace one's footsteps, to elude pursuers. **S:** fox, wolf; bandit, escaped convict: *Half-way through the wood we lost the fox; it must have* ***doubled back*** *on its tracks.*

2 [Vn ⇆ p pass adj] turn (sth) back so as to form a double thickness or layer. **O:** sheet, blanket, coverlet; paper: *When making a bed you* ***double*** *the top edge of the sheet* ***back*** *over the blankets.* = fold back.

double up 1 [Vp] bend in the middle with pain etc; be convulsed (with). **S:** body; he etc. **A:** in agony, with pain, with laughter: *This made him* ***double up*** *with laughter.* BB ○ *Funny thing is that when you say it on the stage half the audience* ***double up*** *just like Fred Zombie himself.* JFTR = fold up 2.

2 [Vn.p pass] cause (sb) to bend in the middle. **S:** pain, attack, blow; comedian, joke, performance. **O:** body; audience, onlooker: *Someone struck him hard in the stomach; the pain* ***doubled*** *him* ***up***. ○ *The bystanders were* ***doubled up*** *with mirth.*

double up (with) [Vp, Vp.pr] (*informal*) form a pair (with sb) in order to share sth. **o:** colleague, fellow student; another passenger: *'We haven't any single rooms left. Do you mind* ***doubling up****?'* ○ *Jane had to* ***double up*** *with another student throughout her first year.*

doubt

doubt of [Vpr pass] (*formal*) have doubts about (sth), be pessimistic about (sth). **o:** success, outcome, result: *The enterprise had begun badly and we* ***doubted of*** *its further progress.*

dovetail

dovetail (into) [Vpr rel] fit snugly (into sth); match (sth) harmoniously . **S:** panel, cross-piece; idea, proposal. **o:** frame, upright; scheme, design: *The sides of the cigar-box* ***dovetail*** *beautifully* (***into*** *each other*). ○ *'They're interesting suggestions but* *they don't exactly* **dovetail into** *the rest of the plan, do they?'*

doze

doze off [Vp] fall into a light sleep: *After a substantial lunch, he* **dozed off** *in his armchair.* ○ *He waited, hoping desperately that he would not* **doze off**. T = drop off 2, nod off.

draft

draft in/into [Vn ⇆ p pass adj, Vn.pr pass rel] introduce (sb) into (an activity) as a support, replacement etc. **O:** fresh helpers, extra staff, additional players. **o:** team, force, side: *We played a practice match among ourselves, with local bowlers* **drafted in** *as reinforcements.* ITFL ○ *Two extra midfield players have been* **drafted into** *the England football squad.*

drag

drag down [Vn.p pass] bring (sb) to a low physical or moral level. **S:** illness; influenza, malaria; drugs, booze; drudgery, routine: *She can't stand the intense heat — it really* **drags** *her* **down**. = pull down 3.

drag in/into 1 [Vn ⇆ p pass, Vn.pr pass] (*informal*) make (sb) take part in (sth) or be the subject of (sth) against his will, or against the will of other interested persons. **O:** him etc; (his) wife, family; name. **o:** helping, working; argument, debate, discussion; controversy: *'You're free to write what you like about me. But you mustn't* **drag** *my wife's name* **in**. *Keep her out of it.'* ○ *'No, John, I won't be* **dragged into** *making polite conversation with the wives while you have one of your interminable meetings with the men.'*

2 [Vn ⇆ p pass, Vn.pr pass] (*informal*) constantly and tiresomely introduce (sth) into (a conversation etc). **O:** pet topic, favourite theory; sport, money. **o:** discussion, debate, argument: *Why must he keep* **dragging in** *references to his medals? We know he's a war hero, but must he keep reminding us?* ○ *There are some people about with only one thought in their heads: they must* **drag** *sex* **into** *every conversation.*

drag off (to) [Vn.p pass, Vn.p.pr pass] (*informal*) lead (sb) against his will (to a place). **o:** concert, film, play; meeting, service: *He will* **drag** *her* **off to** *parties, and she spends the whole evening trying to look inconspicuous in a corner.*

drag on [Vp emph] continue endlessly and tediously. **S:** quarrel, war, unhappy marriage; speech, concert: *We could take no chances; if we failed in Normandy the war might* **drag on** *for years.* MFM ○ *The partnership might have* **dragged on** *indefinitely if Peter hadn't decided on a clean break.*

drag out [Vn ⇆ p pass adj] make (sth) longer than it need be, thus causing tedium. **O:** meeting; discussion, debate; performance: *'Do you think we might end the discussion there? I see no point in* **dragging** *it* **out** *any further.'*

drag up 1 [Vn ⇆ p pass adj] (*informal*) allow (a child) to grow up without proper discipline or training. **O:** child, ward: *Their children are allowed to roam the streets and come and go as they please — they're simply being* **dragged up** *any old how.* □ usu passive.

2 [Vn ⇆ p pass] (*informal*) deliberately recall or revive (sth, usu unpleasant) from the past which is generally forgotten, and should perhaps have remained forgotten. **S:** reporter, gossip columnist. **O:** event, episode, incident: *What made you* **drag up** *that particular episode in my murky past?* ○ *Some newspapers haven't anything better to do than to* **drag up** *the past indiscretions of well-known public figures.* = rake up.

dragoon

dragoon into [Vn.p pass rel] force, bully (sb) into (doing sth). **S:** father, schoolteacher, sergeant, salesman. **o:** taking up the law, doing languages, accepting promotion, buying a second car: *He was* **dragooned into** *joining the police by his father. Left to choose for himself he would have worked in a bank.* ○ *Voices from loudspeakers* **dragoon** *housewives* **into** *buying unwanted soap powders.* □ the object is the *-ing* form of a v. = railroad into.

drain

drain away 1 [Vp, Vn ⇆ p pass] (cause sth to) flow away down a waste-pipe, or drain. **S** [Vp], **O** [Vn.p]: (dirty) water, slops, dregs: *The bath is fitted with double filters through which the waste could* **drain away**. WI

2 [Vp] decrease or disappear gradually. **S:** fear, anxiety; anger, fury; energy: *Robert yawned. His tension seemed to have* **drained away**, *leaving him, if anything, rather bored with the discussion.* CON

drain from [Vn.pr pass emph rel] gradually reduce the volume or strength of (sth) in (a place). **S:** demand, pressure; (economic) expansion, development; exertion, effort. **O:** resources, talent; strength, energy. **o:** country, area; body: *You'd be moving into a department* **from** *which the liveliest minds have been* **drained** (or: *a department which has been* **drained of** *its liveliest minds*). ○ *The very will to survive had been* **drained from** *him* (or: *He had been* **drained of** *the very will* etc).

drain of [Vn.pr pass] ⇨ previous entry.

drain off [Vn ⇆ p pass] draw (liquid) from sth until it is empty; empty (a container) of liquid. **O:** water; petrol, oil; reservoir, tank: *Fry the pork in the pan until well browned, then* **drain off** *the fat.* GC ○ *The main cylinder will have to be* **drained off** *before I can change the fittings.*

drape

drape around/over/round [Vn.pr pass emph rel] hang (a cloth etc) in folds around/over (sth). **O:** bedspread, counterpane; flag, bunting. **o:** bed, couch, table; monument: *Mary appeared at the french window, a cardigan* **draped around** *her shoulders.* COS ○ *The Union Jack was* **draped over** *the bier* (or: *The bier was* **draped with** *the Union Jack*).

drape with [Vn.pr pass rel] ⇨ previous entry

draw

draw ahead/ahead of [Vp, Vpr] move forward or in front (of sb/sth); progress beyond (sb/sth). **S:** car, bicycle, runner; competitor, trading concern. **o:** rest of the field, nearest rival: *A policeman on a motor-cycle came alongside to give us a message. Then he* **drew ahead**. ○ *We have* **drawn ahead of** *our nearest continental competitors in this field.* = get ahead/ahead of.

draw alongside [Vp, Vpr] (of sb approaching from behind) stop, or move along, at the side of (sb/sth). **S:** car, motor-cycle: *A police patrol car* **drew**

alongside *and signalled to me to stop.* = pull alongside.

draw apart (from) [Vp, Vp.pr emph rel] move away (from sb/sth); become emotionally separate (from sb). **S:** ship, vehicle; (political) group, movement; lover, friend: *A small group was seen to* ***draw apart from*** *the others and move off into the forest.* ○ *I don't share your pessimism about Peter and Hilary. Far from* ***drawing apart****, I think they're coming closer together.*

draw aside 1 [Vn ⇆ p pass] pull (sth) to one side. **O:** curtain, blanket, covering: *An inquisitive neighbour* ***drew*** *the lace curtain* ***aside*** *to see what was going on.* ○ *The sheet was* ***drawn aside*** *to reveal the patient's ribs.* = pull aside.
2 [Vn ⇆ p] take (sb) on one side to talk to him quietly or confidentially. **S:** chairman, colleague; umpire, referee: *The captain* ***drew*** *the fast bowler* ***aside*** *to warn him about throwing.* ○ *The manager* ***drew*** *me* ***aside*** *and muttered something about a proposed merger.* = take aside/to one side.

draw the line (at) [Vn.pr pass emph rel] not go beyond a certain limit in one's conduct. **o:** dishonesty, deceit; backbiting, malicious gossip; cheating one's friends, being unfaithful to one's wife: *Stephens liked to think that he was a tolerant man, but he wouldn't have that couple in his house again.* ***The line*** *had to be* ***drawn*** *somewhere* (or: ***at*** *some point*).

draw away/back (from) [Vp, Vp.pr emph rel] withdraw, move away (from sb/sth). **A:** in distaste, in horror; shyly, suspiciously: *It seemed that he* ***drew back*** *for a moment, alarmed, as if the scrappy, grubby piece of paper frightened him.* DC ○ *'Why don't you kiss me? Come.' Prissie's body stiffened. She tried to* ***draw away from*** *his embrace.* DC

drawback [nom (Vp)] disadvantage, snag, pitfall. **adj:** serious, considerable, unfortunate, irritating: *I don't see any serious* ***drawbacks*** *in the plan as you've outlined it.* ○ *Your design has two important* ***drawbacks****: the wheel-base is too narrow and too much of the car's weight is forward of the front wheels.*

draw down [Vn ⇆ p pass] lower (sth). **O:** blind, curtain; hat, veil, peak: *The batsman* ***drew*** *the peak of his cap well* ***down*** *over his eyes.* ○ *The blinds were* ***drawn down*** *to keep out the direct rays of the sun.* = pull down 1.

draw down (upon one's head) [Vp.n pass, Vn.p.pr pass] by one's conduct, attract (sb's anger etc). **S:** remark, comment; action, step. **O:** ⚠ sb's anger, fury; the wrath of God, scorn, opprobrium: *'Don't prop your feet on the Old Man's desk. You'll* ***draw down*** *the wrath of God* ***upon your head****.'*

draw from 1 [Vn.pr pass rel] ⇨ draw out/out of 4.
2 [Vn.pr pass emph rel] obtain (sth) from (sth). **O:** comfort, consolation, relief. **o:** thought, realization, knowledge: *I don't see why I should* ***draw*** *comfort* ***from*** *the fact that I'm paid in ten days' time. How do I manage for food in the meantime?* = derive from 1.

draw a conclusion (from) [Vn.pr pass emph rel] reach a decision or make a judgement (on the basis of sth); conclude. **adj:** a, the, this, what. **o:** evidence; event, circumstance: *He hasn't had a single promotion in fifteen years, and you can* ***draw*** *what* ***conclusions*** *you like* ***from*** *that.* ○ *They have a tendency to* ***draw*** *broad* ***conclusions from*** *too narrow a range of facts.* T

draw in [Vp] (of the hours of daylight as summer changes to autumn) become shorter. **S:** the days, the evenings: ***The days*** *are beginning to* ***draw in****: I shan't get so much gardening done in the evenings.* ↔ draw out 2.

draw one's horns in [Vn ⇆ p] become defensive or cautious. **S:** trader, investor; spending public, customer: *The building societies have* ***drawn in their horns*** *following the increase in the Bank Rate. You won't be able to get your mortgage now.* ○ *If Malouel was going to* ***draw in his horns*** *he would need every penny he could lay his hands on.* US

draw in/into 1 [Vp, Vpr] arrive (at a place). **S:** train; express, Pullman, Inter City. **o:** station; platform: *As I reached the ticket barrier the London train was just* ***drawing in****.* ○ *The 'Cornish Riviera'* ***drew into*** *Plymouth a few minutes ahead of schedule.* = pull in/into 1. ↔ draw out/out of 5.
2 [Vn ⇆ p pass, Vn.pr pass] cause (sb) gradually but firmly to take part in (sth). **o:** involvement; struggle, battle; debate, discussion; fighting, arguing: *Originally, the dispute was confined to the paint shop, but little by little other groups of workers were* ***drawn in****.* ○ *It is not wholly fanciful to imagine how the Queen might be* ***drawn into*** *controversy after the next election.* IND ○ *The argument* ***into*** *which he had allowed himself to be* ***drawn*** *followed the usual irritating pattern.*

draw off 1 [Vp] withdraw, retreat. **S:** enemy; troops, forces: *The enemy* ***drew off*** *as soon as we made a show of superior strength.*
2 [Vn ⇆ p pass adj] remove liquid from (sth). **S:** publican, wine-merchant; doctor, nurse. **O:** wine, beer; pint, litre; fluid, matter, blood: *The pressure inside one of the casks was building up and some liquid had to be* ***drawn off****.* ○ *Doctors were able to* ***draw off*** *the matter which had collected near the wound.*
3 [Vn ⇆ p pass adj] (*formal*) remove (sth). **O:** sock, stocking, glove (and other close fitting garments): *John* ***drew*** *his socks* ***off*** *and bathed his sore feet.* ↔ draw on 1. = pull off 1.

draw on 1 [Vn ⇆ p pass adj] put on, don (close-fitting clothes). **O:** sock, stocking, glove: *He* ***drew on*** *his gloves, picked up his umbrella and went out.* ↔ draw off 3. = pull on 2.
2 [Vn.p pass] make (sb) continue steadily forward on his course. **S:** thought, prospect; greed, curiosity, ambition: *The feeling that she was nearing her destination* ***drew*** *her* ***on****.* ○ *He was* ***drawn on*** *by the hope of making important fresh discoveries.*
3 [Vp] approach, come near; advance, move forward. **S:** night, winter: *As winter* ***drew on*** *we felt the lack of an efficient way of heating the house.* ○ *Freud's theoretical formulations were to change as the century* ***drew on****.* F = come on 7.

draw on/upon [Vpr pass emph rel] use or exploit (sth). **o:** experience, knowledge, wisdom, skill: *Your expert knowledge will be* ***drawn upon*** *increasingly as negotiations proceed.* ○ *The more good experiences a child has had, the more he has to* ***draw on*** *in times of pain and fear.* TBU ○ *It is* ***on*** *these skills that the Weizmann Institute has* ***drawn****.* NS

draw out 1 [Vn.p pass] help (sb) to feel less shy or reserved: *From his mother, Eric had learnt the* *wonderful gift of* ***drawing*** *people* ***out***. HAA ○ *He had chattered away to her in German; he had* ***drawn*** *her* ***out****, he had made her laugh.* PW ○ *She had been encouraged,* ***drawn out****, made to feel she mattered to the others.* = bring out 2.

2 [Vp] (of the hours of daylight as summer approaches) become longer. **S:** the days, the evenings: *Thank goodness the days are* ***drawing out*** *again, though. I'm so sick of the winter.* EGD ↔ draw in.

long drawn out [pass adj (Vn.p)] (be) unduly or tiresomely prolonged or protracted. **S:** fight, argument; debate, discussion: *The debate over Britain's entry to the European Exchange Rate Mechanism has been* ***long drawn out****.* ○ *There followed a* ***long-drawn-out*** *legal tussle over the compensation to be paid to the bereaved families.* □ attrib form has two hyphens.

draw out/out of 1 [Vn ⇆ p pass, Vn.pr pass emph rel] withdraw or extract (sth) (from an inner space). **O:** pistol, knife, wallet, handkerchief, pipe. **o:** holster, belt; pocket, handbag: *He opened his safe and* ***drew out*** *a petty-cash box.* ○ *He handed me a cigar* ***drawn out*** *of an ornate leather case.* = get out/out of 2, take out/out of 2.

2 [Vn ⇆ p pass, Vn.pr pass rel] remove or extract (sth) (from a place where it is fixed). **O:** cork, thorn, nail, stump (of a tooth). **o:** bottle, toe, plank, gum: *He tore his hand trying to* ***draw*** *a nail* ***out of*** *a piece of wood.* ○ *The stump was* ***drawn out*** *quite painlessly.* = pluck out/out of, pull out 1.

3 [Vn ⇆ p pass, Vn.pr pass rel] (*banking*) withdraw (money) (from sth). **O:** sum, amount, balance, savings. **o:** bank, post-office; current account: *'How much will we need to* ***draw out*** *to pay the deposit?'* = take out/out of 2. ↔ pay in/into, put in/into 2.

4 [Vn ⇆ p pass, Vn.pr pass rel] obtain or elicit (sth) slowly and with difficulty (from sb). **O:** information, story, episode; confession, admission: *The story was* ***drawn out*** *by slow degrees.* ○ *They managed to* ***draw out of*** *him* (or: ***from*** *him*) *a full account of his escape from captivity.* = get out of 2.

5 [Vp, Vpr] leave, depart (from a place). **S:** train; the 5.30, the night express. **o:** station; King's Cross, Waterloo: *The last train to Leeds was* ***drawing out*** *as I ran into the station.* = pull out/out of 1. ↔ draw in/into 1.

draw a veil over [Vn.pr pass emph rel] conceal (unpleasant etc events) when telling a story, so as not to offend or upset the hearer or reader. **S:** narrator, author; history. **o:** events, proceedings; (undignified) scene, (angry) exchange: *It would be kinder to* ***draw a veil over*** *some of Vinnie's later attempts to be stylish.* FA ○ ***Over*** *the events taking place in the bedroom the censor* ***drew a*** *discreet* ***veil***.

draw (sb's) attention to [Vn.pr pass emph rel] make sb notice, or be aware of (sb/sth). **o:** oneself; visitor, newcomer; case, situation; discrepancy, anomaly: *'You talk about this bird Reilly* ***drawing attention to*** *himself — but weren't you captain of the team?'* HD ○ *A headline on the front page* ***draws attention to*** *the fuller story inside.* CON ○ ***Mr Woodburn's attention*** *was* ***drawn to*** *this question by visiting French MPs.* SC ○ *There is another point about youth and age, ...* ***to*** *which he would* ***draw attention***. L = call (sb's) attention to.

draw to a close [Vpr] reach its end; finish. **S:** evening, weekend; holiday, visit; (period of) service, office; life: *My stay in Bafut eventually* ***drew to a close***. BB ○ *For Charles the bright sunlit days were fast* ***drawing to a close***. CD

draw to/towards [Vn.pr pass] attract (people) to (sb/sth). **S:** charm, warmth (of manner); beauty, good looks: *Many people were* ***drawn to*** *him by his lack of pretence and his fondness for plain speaking.* ○ *Those eyes of hers* ***draw*** *many poor victims* ***towards*** *their doom!* = attract (to). □ usu passive.

draw up 1 [Vp] come to a halt; stop. **S:** car, taxi, carriage: *One day we* ***drew up*** *on the quay-side at Dunkirk.* BM ○ *The dog recommenced barking ... as the car* ***drew up*** *in the yard.* UNXL = pull up 1.

2 [Vn ⇆ p pass] bring (sth) near to (sth); place (sth) close against (sth). **O:** chair, sofa, table: *Irma made her sit down in the easy chair and* ***drew up*** *the other.* PW ○ *The table was* ***drawn up*** *against the wall.* = pull up 2.

3 [Vn ⇆ p pass] place or arrange (people/things) close together in lines. **S:** officer, NCO. **O:** soldier, competitor, vehicle. **A:** in three ranks, in revue order; on the square: *10 000 men or more were* ***drawn up*** *in a hollow square and I first spoke individually to the unit commanders.* MFM ○ *The cars had to be* ***drawn up*** *close together in a dead straight line to facilitate loading.* HD □ often passive.

4 [Vn ⇆ p pass adj] prepare, draft, compose (sth). **S:** committee, board; solicitor, attorney. **O:** agreement, treaty, report, contract: *The society have* ***drawn up*** *a similar list of six conditions.* T ○ *A new arrangement was* ***drawn up***. NM ○ *He instructed a new will to be* ***drawn up***. ○ *You'll find it's a carefully* ***drawn-up*** *document.*

draw oneself up [Vn.p] straighten oneself (often in a solemn, formal or pompous way): *When I apologized for the mess in his car, he* ***drew himself up****, looked me in the face, and said: 'Sir, it's an honour.'* MFM ○ *Robert's manner changed in an instant. He* ***drew himself up*** *portentously, walked stiff-legged over to the table, and sat down.* DC

draw up sharp/sharply [Vn.p pass] make (sb) stop abruptly; cause (sb) to pause and consider or reflect. **S:** remark, comment, reflection: *A noisy interruption from the back of the hall* ***drew*** *the speaker* ***up sharp***. ○ ***Drawn up sharply*** *by the second mention of the word milord that day, Angela Snow had no time to make any sort of comment.* BFA ○ *The absence of all the familiar landmarks* ***drew*** *me* ***up sharp***.

draw oneself up (to one's full height) [Vn.p, Vn.p.pr] strike a dignified or important attitude: *The teacher had put up with quite enough indiscipline. He* ***drew himself up*** *and called for complete silence.* ○ ***Drawing herself up to her full height****, she swept from the room.*

dream

dream about/of [Vpr pass emph rel] think hopefully or longingly of (sth/doing sth). **o:** retirement, security, wealth; gaining recognition, leading a crusade, starting a family: *Wistfully (though I am forbidden to* ***dream about*** *it) I* ***dream of*** *grandchildren.* SU ○ *Her breakfasts were things to* ***dream about*** *... crisp curled bacon and fluffy scrambled eggs.* BRH

not dream of [Vpr] not, on any account, do (sth); not conceive of (doing sth). **o:** interfering, intervening; arguing, opposing; permitting: *At this age (fifteen)* ***no*** *self-respecting middle-class parent would* ***dream of*** *allowing his own children to leave school.* OBS ○ *I would****n't dream of*** *insisting on your taking a picture against your will.* MFM ○ ***No*** *man in his senses ... would ever* ***dream of*** *denying Tolstoy's intellectual powers.* RTH □ with *could/would*; the object is the *-ing* form of a v.

dream up [Vn ⇆ p pass] (*informal*) devise or create (esp sth wildly fanciful, foolish etc). **O:** scheme, project; character, plot, situation: *Everything has worked out wonderfully. This is better than anything we ever* ***dreamed up*** *in Earls Court Road.* UTN ○ *For his first play, Charles Hamblett has* ***dreamed up*** *a seedy bunch of riff-raff — drunks, lay-abouts, morons.* DM ○ *Trust you to* ***dream up*** *a script in which the hero — that's me — gets shot in the first act.*

dredge

dredge up 1 [Vn ⇆ p pass adj] raise (sth) from the bottom of the sea, or the bed of a river, by dredging. **O:** silt, sand, mud; rubbish: *The wreckage of a wooden ship was* ***dredged up*** *from the harbour bottom.*

2 [Vn ⇆ p pass adj] recall to the conscious mind some event, not necessarily unpleasant, which has been long forgotten. **O:** story, incident; moment: *What did you have to go and* ***dredge*** *his memory* ***up*** *for?* GL ○ *His grandfather was a fine raconteur,* ***dredging up*** *quite effortlessly scenes and incidents from his early life.*

dress

dress down [Vn.p pass] reprimand, admonish (sb). **S:** father, foreman, officer: *He got up and stood over him, arms akimbo like a caricaturist's washerwoman* ***dressing*** *someone* ***down****.* ASA ○ *The force of his personality was so blasting that for a moment he had me feeling that I was in for a* ***dressing-down*** *myself.* CON □ often occurs in the nom form dressing-down. = tell off (for).

dress up 1 [Vp, Vn ⇆ p pass adj] put on formal clothes, as for a party, ceremony etc; (esp of children) put on clothes normally worn by another person, or at another period: *It's not that I have anything against dinner jackets particularly, it is simply that I dislike any kind of* ***dressing up****.* NS ○ *Mary* ***dressed up*** *in Elizabethan costume for the annual Fancy-Dress Ball.*

2 [Vn ⇆ p pass adj] (try to) make (one's thoughts) seem more impressive by adding details, using special language etc. **O:** argument, statement, evidence: *It's perfectly simple and understandable. You needn't* ***dress*** *it* ***up*** *with all this nonsense.* RATT

drift

drift across, along, away etc [Vp emph, Vpr emph] move slowly or casually across etc. **S:** smoke, mist, aroma; balloon, boat; crowd, sightseers: *The smoke pall* ***drifted away*** *to reveal the blackened shell of the building.* ○ *He thought of a pleasure-garden where entertainment would vary with the weather and couples would* ***drift off*** *into the dark between a meal or a show.* OBS ○ (fig) *He was excited by novel ideas which came* ***drifting in*** *from all kinds of sources.* RTH

drift along [Vp] go through life without aim or purpose: *His upbringing seems to have left him incapable of sustained effort; he just* ***drifts along****.*

drift apart [Vp] become gradually estranged, slowly lose interest in each other. **S:** friends, husband and wife, brothers: *He and his wife have never had a serious quarrel. Through mutual indifference they've just* ***drifted apart****.* ○ *Having been close friends in the war Viola was genuinely worried to find that they had* ***drifted*** *so far* ***apart*** *that she had lost all touch with her.* RFW

drill

drill in/into [Vn ⇆ p pass adj, Vn.pr pass emph rel] teach (sth) by persistent exercise or repetition. **S:** teacher, instructor. **O:** rule, procedure; multiplication tables, irregular verbs. **o:** class, pupil: *The language patterns were thoroughly* ***drilled in****.* ○ *I simply don't believe that spoken skills can be* ***drilled into*** *learners in a language laboratory.* □ note the following pattern, where the Direct Object refers to those being taught: ... *children whom he could* ***drill*** *mercilessly* ***into*** *learning lines, movements and measures.* MLT

drink

drink down/off [Vn ⇆ p] drink (sth) until nothing remains, often at one draught. **O:** milk, medicine, beer: *I* ***drank*** *the stuff* ***off*** *in one gulp. It burned my throat.* □ suggests faster drinking than drink up, but is less likely to occur in commands.

drink in 1 [Vn ⇆ p pass] listen with eager attention to (sth). **S:** pupil, disciple, follower, party member. **O:** ⚠ his words, every word, his remarks; it all: *A packed audience* ***drank in*** *every word he uttered.* ○ *A quiet little man sat in a corner of the hall,* ***drinking*** *it all* ***in****.*

2 [Vn ⇆ p pass] absorb (sth) by eager attention. **S:** traveller, visitor. **O:** atmosphere; calm, tranquillity; beauty, picturesqueness: *They sat outside on the terrace,* ***drinking in*** *the particular quality of the light at that time of day.*

drink oneself to death [Vn.pr] kill oneself by excessive drinking: *It would be very easy, cheap and pleasant to* ***drink oneself to death*** *in Portugal.* ILIH ○ *If Finn was* ***drinking himself to death*** *somewhere, it would be my last sad act of friendship to leave him to it.* UTN

drink under the table [Vn.pr] (*informal*) drink more alcohol than (sb else) while remaining more sober than he. **O:** everyone, most people, the lot of them: *This time, if he met Tillie, she wouldn't* ***drink*** *him* ***under the table****.* PE ○ *You pride yourselves on your capacity, but he can* ***drink*** *you all* ***under the table!***

drink up [Vp, Vn ⇆ p pass] drink until nothing remains in a cup or glass, often in one draught; finish one's drink (up). **O:** milk, medicine, beer: *'I brought them to heel,' said Robert gaily, tapping his inside pocket. 'I extracted some money out of them, so* ***drink up****, lads.'* CON ○ *'****Drink*** *your juice* ***up****, Johnnie, or you won't go out and play!'* □ very often in commands. ⇨ drink down/off.

drive

what be driving at [Vpr] (*informal*) (what) is he etc trying to do or achieve; (what) is he etc trying to say or explain: *'****What*** *on earth are you* ***driving at****? Can't you come to the point?'* ○ *'You can see* ***what*** *I'm* ***driving at****, can't you? It would surely be easy* *for you to get me in on your visits to the docks.'* HD □ direct or indirect question in continuous tenses only. = what be at. ⇨ get at 4.

drive back [Vn ⇆ p pass] force (sb) to withdraw. **S:** police; troops, planes. **O:** crowd, rioters; enemy: *The attacking force was* **driven back** *to its starting point.* ○ *The police* **drove** *the spectators* **back** *behind the crash barriers.*

drive back on [Vn.p.pr pass] oblige or force (sb), as a last resort, to use sth he would prefer not to. **o:** one's own resources; subterfuge, deceit; cruder methods; local food, cheaper petrol: *I had finished all my cigarettes and couldn't find any of Robert's Gauloises lying about, so I was* **driven back on** *my pipe.* CON ○ *We couldn't go out all weekend, so were* **driven back on** *our own resources for entertainment.* □ usu passive. ⇨ fall back on.

drive a wedge between [Vn.pr pass] separate or cause disharmony between (sets of people). **S:** issue, question; movement, change (of home, of job). **o:** two wings (of a party); colleagues, partners; married couple: *Different economic priorities may* **drive a wedge between** *the various groups which make up the coalition.*

drive-in [nom (Vp)] (public facility, esp a bank, cinema, church or restaurant) into which one drives and where one is served, entertained etc, while remaining seated in one's car: *Because of their greater dependence on the motor car, Americans have a greater range of* **drive-in** *facilities than the British, though* **drive-in** *banks and fast-food restaurants are now found in Britain.* □ usu attrib, as in: **drive-in** *bank.*

drive home (to) [Vn ⇆ p pass, Vn.p.pr pass emph rel] convey (a message) forcefully and unmistakably (to sb). **O:** message, lesson, argument; importance, value (of sth); what is expected of everyone. **o:** staff, workforce; the general public: *Eloquently and intelligently though the book* **drives home** *the familiar arguments, the fact remains that they are familiar.* L ○ *There was no doubting the TUC's* (Trade Union Congress's) *determination to* **drive home to** *Jim Slater . . . what his surprise call for all-out industrial action would mean.* OBS ⇨ get home (to), go home 3.

drive in/into [Vn ⇆ p pass adj, Vn.pr pass emph rel] force (sth) to enter (sth) by striking with a hammer etc. **O:** stake, peg, nail. **o:** ground, wall, plank: *A wooden stake was* **driven** *firmly* **into** *the ground.* = hammer in/into 1, knock in/into.

drive into a corner [Vn.pr pass] (during an argument) force (sb) into a position from which it is difficult to reply effectively: *Quoting facts and figures quickly* **drove** *him* **into a corner**. ○ *When he's* **driven into a corner** *he invariably loses his temper.*

drive off 1 [Vp emph, Vn.p pass] (of a car etc) leave, go away; take (sb) away in a car: *The first of the starters in the Monte Carlo Rally were already* **driving off** *in a flurry of powdered snow.* ○ *The newly married couple were* **driven off** *in a yellow vintage Rolls Royce.* □ cf: *The married couple* **drove off**...where neither couple need be at the wheel.

2 [Vp] (*golf*) drive the ball from the tee at the start of a game or 'hole': *TV cameras were set up near the first tee, where competitors were soon to* **drive off** *in the first round of the championship.*

3 [Vn ⇆ p pass] (*military*) repel or defeat (sb). **O:** enemy; attack, assault: *Counter-attacks by mixed forces of tanks and infantry were* **driven off** *with heavy loss.* = fight off 1.

drive out/out of 1 [Vn ⇆ p pass, Vn.pr pass rel] make (sb) leave (an enclosed space) by force. **S:** government, police, soldier. **O:** alien, intruder, invader. **o:** country, position: *She needed all her courage to leave the house,* **driven out** *as she was by the even greater horror of staying in.* MSAL ○ *Russian emissaries were* **driven out of** *Afghanistan at pistol point.* TBC

2 cause (sth) to be ignored or forgotten. **S:** anxiety, preoccupation. **O:** thought, matter, question. **o:** mind, head: *The prosaic question* **drove out** *all others.* NM ○ *Any misgivings they might have felt were* **driven out** *by the sight of his cheerful face.*

drive out of his mind/wits [Vn.pr pass] make (sb) mad, drive (sb) insane; reduce (sb) to a very nervous or anxious state. **S:** noise, tension, strain, conflict: *'You're asking for a bloody good hiding, lady, just be careful. Oh! She'd* **drive** *you* **out of your mind**.*'* TOH ○ *Everyone seems completely tired out—as if he had been* **driving** *them right* **out of their wits**. HSG ○ *She was* **driven** *almost* **out of her mind** *with anxiety.*

drive round the bend/up the wall [Vn.pr pass] (*informal*) drive (sb) mad; infuriate (sb), annoy (sb) unbearably: *You two will* **drive** *me* **round the bend** *soon. I know you're going to drive me mad.* LBA ○ *I'm fed up to the back teeth with all this caper. It's* **driving** *me* **up the wall**. TT = send up the wall.

drive to despair etc [Vn.pr pass] force (sb) to the point of desperation, madness etc. **S:** state of trade, collapse of one's business; repeated disappointments, failures; (sb's) sloth, deceit, untrustworthiness. **o:** ⚠ despair, desperation, distraction, suicide, violence: *Tim's casual attitude to work had* **driven** *his serious-minded father* **to** *despair.* ○ *The merciless rioting of French schoolboys has* **driven** *saner men than Jacques* **to** *distraction.* AF ○ *Violet's childish and disgusting behaviour had* **driven** *him* **to** *violence.* EC

drive to drink [Vn.pr pass] (*informal*) make sb so desperate that he seeks forgetfulness, or relief, in drinking. **S:** failure, neglect, unkindness, insensitivity: *It is understandable that certain situations might* **drive** *anyone* **to drink**. UL

drive up the wall [Vn.pr pass] ⇨ drive round the bend/up the wall.

drone

drone on [Vp emph] speak tediously and continually. **S:** vicar, politician, tiresome acquaintance: *Is there an easy way to stop him* **droning on** *about the internal combustion engine?* ○ **On** *he* **droned** *interminably until we felt our nerves could stand no more.*

drool

drool over [Vpr pass] (*informal*) give foolish or slavish attention to (sth/sb). **S:** collector (of antiques, etc), connoisseur (of food etc); parent, proprietor. **o:** wine, food; child, new car: **Drool over** *a favourite meal, then start a cook-book of magazine and newspaper recipes.* WI ○ *He* **drools over** *his hoard of bric-a-brac like a doting parent.*

drop

drop back [Vp] be left behind; move back (deliberately). **S:** runner, member of party, car: *We found that one of the three escort trucks had* **dropped back** *in the dust with a mechanical defect.* SD ○ *The sergeant had* **dropped back** *to pick up any stragglers.*

drop behind [Vp, Vpr] be left behind (sb); (deliberately) allow others to move ahead. **S:** runner, car; country, industry. **o:** main party, rest of field; rival, competitor: *Jones had* **dropped behind** *on the back straight and Morley went on to win the race by a clear twenty metres.* ○ *John and Mary had* **dropped behind** *the others in order to be alone.* = fall behind 1.

drop by/in/in on [Vp, Vp.pr pass] (*informal*) pay a casual visit to (sb): *She should say to the parents, 'Come to tea on Friday,' rather than ask them just to* **drop in** *at any time.* WI ○ *They would just* **drop in on** *us for a chat at any odd moment.*

drop in/into 1 [Vp, Vpr] (*informal*) pay a casual visit to (a place). **o:** church, club, pub: *They hear the single melancholy church bell, and* **drop in** *and sit peacefully in some richly carved old stall.* PW ○ *In the evening we would* **drop into** *a roadside pub for a beer and sandwich.* = call (in) (at).

2 [Vn ⇆ p pass, Vn.pr pass emph rel] include (sth) casually in (one's speech or writing). **O:** a famous name, a familiar phrase. **o:** conversation, writing: *He could never resist the temptation of* **dropping in** *the names of a few fashionable acquaintances.* ○ *There was the habit, which he exhibited for the rest of his life, of* **dropping** *an occasional phrase* **into** *his letters.* F

drop off 1 [Vp] (*informal*) diminish, decrease or slacken. **S:** attendance, production, business: *Our sales of ice-cream and soft drinks start to* **drop off** *at the beginning of September.* ○ *Takings at the pier have* **dropped off** *this season.* = fall off 1.

2 [Vp] (*informal*) fall into a light sleep or doze: *I felt myself* **dropping off** *in the middle of the second act.* ○ *Just as he was* **dropping off**, *there was a loud bang from downstairs.* = doze off, nod off.

3 [Vp, Vn.p pass] (*informal*) allow to alight: *Get the driver to* **drop** *you* **off** *at the Central Station.* = set down 1.

4 [Vn ⇆ p pass] deliver (sth). **O:** parcel, letter; clothes, toys: *'I'll* **drop** *those parcels* **off** *at the post office later this morning.*

drop out/out of 1 [Vp nom, Vpr] leave school, college etc without completing the full or standard course of study. **o:** school, university; course; training: *I* **dropped out**, *right at the beginning, and said that Higher Cert. was good enough for me and they could keep Oxford and Cambridge.* CON ○ *The* **drop-out** *rate is highest in the poorest urban areas.* ○ *There is a close connection between early* **drop-out** *and delinquency.*

2 [Vp nom, Vpr] withdraw from conventional society and give up the manners, dress etc expected of its members: *'The Season of the Witch', about a girl* **drop-out** *exploring the New York drug culture, is already a period piece.* T

3 [Vp, Vpr] withdraw (from an activity, etc); leave, abandon. **S:** minister; player, competitor; runner, horse, pursuer. **o:** government; team, match; race, contest, struggle: *Peter* **dropped out** *before completing one circuit of the track.* ○ *Jack was joining our party for the theatre, but he's had to* **drop out**. ○ *He has* **dropped out of** *politics.* EHOW

the bottom drop out of the market/price [Vpr] (*informal*) (of prices) fall to a very low level: *This was Cornwall's closest brush with disaster since* **the bottom dropped out of the** *world* **price** *of tin in the nineteenth century.* OBS ○ *Are you prepared to hang on to your shares until* **the bottom drops out of the market**?

drown

drown out [Vn ⇆ p pass adj] make (sth) impossible to hear by covering it with a louder noise. **S:** (noise of) traffic, music, thunder; heckler. **O:** speaker, conversation: *I started shouting, but Mike* **drowned** *me* **out**. JFTR ○ *A gang of rowdies* **drowned out** *any speaker who tried to present a quietly reasoned case.*

drum

drum in/into [Vn.p pass, Vn.pr pass] make (sb) keep in mind or remember (sth), by frequent repetition. **S:** teacher, parent. **O:** rule, table, formula; need to be tidy, virtue of hard work. **o:** pupil, son: *Hundreds of totally unnecessary disciplines were* **drummed into** *them by their Nannies.* BRN ○ *He'd had the fear of the Lord* **drummed into** *him from an early age.* = din in/into, hammer in/into 2.

drum on [Vpr] beat against (sth) continuously. **S:** finger, foot; rain, hail. **o:** table, piano, floor; window, roof: *The rain* **drumming on** *the corrugated iron roof kept me awake last night.* = pound at/on.

drum up [Vp.n pass] obtain (sth/sb) by seeking for it/him keenly and persistently. **O:** support, backing, extra votes: *The committee has managed to* **drum up** *some support for the idea.* ○ *Did he* (a former Prime Minister who bought support by distributing titles) *find it difficult to* **drum up** *customers for his knighthoods?* BBCR

dry

dry out [Vp, Vn ⇆ p pass adj] (cause sth to) become quite free of water. **S** [Vp], **O** [Vn.p]: land, soil; corn, hay, rick; clothing. **S** [Vn.p]: sun, wind: *We waited for our wet clothes to* **dry out**. ○ *The flood-waters subsided and the hot sun* **dried out** *the wooden buildings.*

dry up 1 [Vp, Vn ⇆ p pass adj] evaporate; turn (sth) into water vapour. **S** [Vp], **O** [Vn.p]: stream, well, reservoir, pond. **S** [Vn.p]: drought, heat: *The smaller rivers and streams* **dry up** *in the summer.* ○ *I was walking over the* **dried-up** *bed of a Breckland mere recently.* G

2 [Vp, Vn ⇆ p pass adj] make (sth) dry by wiping it with a cloth. **O:** cups and saucers, tea-things: *'Help me* **dry up** *after lunch.'* □ nom form (the) drying-up commonly occurs. = wipe up 2.

3 [Vp] be exhausted, come to an end. **S:** savings, capital; wit, humour, resourcefulness: *He was very glad of Betty's allowance! This ... seemed never to* **dry up**. HD ○ *They feared a* **drying-up** *of their inventiveness.* AH □ nom form is drying up.

4 [Vp] become unable to speak (through shyness or nervousness). **S:** actor, speaker, broadcaster: *He paused, and John, knowledgeable in such things, feared that he was about to* **dry up**. ASA ○ *I babbled on about my upbringing, my schooldays and my career until I* **dried up**. SU

5 [Vp] (*informal*) stop talking, be quiet (because the speaker has said too much and further remarks will be unwelcome): *'Now I'm going to **dry up** and let someone else have his say.'* ○ *JIMMY: I will tell you the simple truth about her. She is a cow. CLIFF: You've gone too far, Jimmy. Now **dry up**!* LBA = shut up 2. □ often imperative.

duck

duck out/out of [Vp, Vpr pass] (*informal*) avoid, shirk or escape (sth). **o:** duty, obligation, responsibility, chore: *When I saw it coming I **ducked out**: I didn't want to be there when it was presented.* CON ○ *He's **ducked out of** producing the school play this year.*

dust

dust down/off [Vn ⇆ p pass] remove dust etc from (sb/sth) by brushing or flicking: *Peter was coated in cement and sand, but we picked him up and **dusted** him **down**.* ○ *Can't lose my confidence if I slip,/ I'm grateful for the pleasant trip,/ I pick myself up,/ **Dust** myself **off**,/ Start all over again.* FIELDS AND KERN = brush down.

dwell

dwell on/upon [Vpr pass adj emph rel] think, speak or write continuously or repeatedly about (sth). **o:** past glories, former achievements; failings, weaknesses, disadvantages: *He was repeating criticisms that had been made of him, **dwelling on** them, sometimes agreeing with them.* NM ○ *He had little time, and perhaps little inclination, to **dwell upon** the state of his soul.* MRJ

dwindle

dwindle (away) (to) [Vp, Vpr, Vp.pr] be gradually reduced in quantity or strength. **S:** numbers, ranks; power, reputation. **o:** a handful, a tiny fraction; nothing, zero: *She did not break completely with her though their correspondence **dwindled away**.* GE ○ *When Maggie needs her desperately she has **dwindled to** a cypher* (ie someone who is worthless). GE

E

earmark

earmark (for) [Vn.pr pass emph rel] intend (sth) to be used (for a special purpose), sometimes by using an identifying mark; intend (sb) to be given (a responsible position). **O:** supplies, stores; money, funds. **o:** customer; purpose, use: *Your article on tropical diseases has been **earmarked for** future publication.* ○ *The antique dealer's wife always **earmarked** the best pieces **for** her own collection.* ○ *Mr Parkinson had been **earmarked** by Mrs Thatcher **for** foreign secretary.* IND

earth

earth up [Vn ⇆ p pass adj] (*horticulture*) cover or partially cover (sth) with soil. **O:** roots, asparagus, celery: *The gardener conscientiously **earthed up** the young plants.* ○ *The **earthing up** should be done in the winter, to protect the asparagus from frost.*

ease

ease across, along, away etc 1 [Vp, Vpr] move across etc gently and using care: *He **eased in** behind the steering wheel.* ○ *She **eased out of** her thick jacket and hung it on the back of the chair.*

2 [Vn ⇆ p pass, Vn.pr pass] move (sth) across etc by the use of gentle pressure, careful judgement etc: *You glide down the slope before **easing** the control bar **out** prior to a stand-up landing.* CHGG ○ *My foot was rather sore, but I managed to **ease** it **into** a large slipper.* ○ *Aubrey **eased** Clara **off** his knees.* HOTC

ease back (on) 1 [Vp, Vp.pr, Vn ⇆ p pass] pull (sth) gently towards one. **o** [Vp.pr], **O** [Vn.p]: joystick, controls, throttle: (in gliding) *'We're flying too fast, so I'll **ease back (on)** the stick and gain a little height.'* ○ (in powered flight) *'You can **ease** (the throttle) **back** now that we've climbed high enough.'* □ may also be used of the throttle in cars, motor-boats etc.

2 [Vp, Vp.pr] move more slowly, or with less commitment, in dealing with (sth). **o:** scheme, project; expansion, development: *The Government appears to have **eased back** on the NHS white paper* (ie: on reform of the health service). IND

ease down [Vp] reduce speed; slow down. **S:** car; driver: *There's a narrow bridge ahead, so you'd better **ease down**.*

ease of 1 [Vn.pr pass] remove (sth) to make (sb) less sick or anxious. **o:** pain, burden; anxiety, worry, feelings of guilt: *The doctor promised that the drug would **ease** the poor man **of** his suffering.* = relieve of 1.

2 [Vn.pr pass] (*jocular*) take (sth) away from (sb) by deception. **o:** cash, savings; wallet, purse: *In London there are plenty of people ready to **ease** you **of** a few pounds, especially if they see you are foreign.* = cheat out of, relieve of 3.

ease off 1 [Vp] become less severe or intense. **S:** pressure, intensity; work, business: *The tension between the two countries has **eased off**.* ○ *He looked casually to left and right and, when the flow of traffic had **eased off**, crossed the road.* LLDR ○ *For four days and nights the curve continued to decline but on the fifth day the decline **eased off**.* TBC = slacken off.

2 [Vp] (*informal*) do sth with less severity or intensity. **S:** worker, athlete, dancer, actor: *'You're working far too hard; you'd better **ease off**.'*

ease out/out of [Vn.p pass, Vn.pr pass] (*informal*) remove (sb) from (a position) quietly and gradually, so that he is not made aware of what is happening. **o:** job, post, position; partnership, directorship; team: *After a while it became clear that the directors were **easing** him **out** to make way for a younger man.*

ease up 1 [Vp] move along, usu to make space for sb else: *'I wonder if you could **ease up** a little: there are several people without seats.'*

2 [Vp] become less pressing; be less intense about sth. **S:** work, examining, training; boss, coach: *I'm very busy just now, but when things have **eased up** a little, I'll come and see you.* ○ *Once I could be sure of … my own observations … I could **ease up**, take myself a bit less seriously.* TBU

eat

eat away (at) [Vp.pr, Vn ⇆ p pass] make (sth) grow smaller or disappear through constant pressure etc; erode. **S:** sea, river. **o** [Vp.pr], **O** [Vn.p]**:** support, base; rock, cliff: *The sea has been* **eating away at** *the coast for years, and now the houses on the cliff-top are in danger.* ○ *You can see from here how the river bank is slowly being* **eaten away**. = wear away.

eat into 1 [Vpr pass] dissolve or consume (sth). **S:** acid, caustic; rust. **o:** metal, steel; plate, pipe, superstructure: *The sulphuric acid* **eats into** *those parts of the metal that remain exposed after the wax coating has been applied.*
2 [Vpr pass] take a considerable part of (sth); consume; spend or use (sth) unwillingly. **o:** savings, reserves; nest-egg, capital: *The costs of the legal action* **ate** *deep* **into** *my savings.* ○ *These losses added to his Cambridge debt must have* **eaten into** *his inheritance quite considerably.* TU
3 [Vpr pass] damage (sb) severely in health, morale, confidence etc. **o:** him etc; body, lungs; spirit, soul: *In his late seventies, already* **eaten into** *by cancer ... he impressed his doctor by an 'enthusiastic appreciation of nature'.* F ○ *No emphasis can overstate the depth and intensity with which these experiences* **ate into** *his childish soul.* CD

eat one's head off [Vn.p] (*informal*) eat excessively: *The children came in an hour ago from their long walk, and now they're in the dining-room* **eating their heads off**.

eat out [Vp] have a meal at a restaurant etc, rather than at home: *It's a good idea to* **eat out** *once in a while: a change of scene and cooking is good for you. Not to mention the fact that somebody else has to do all the work!* ⇨ dine out.

eat one's heart out [Vn.p] grieve bitterly: *Ever since her boyfriend walked out, the poor girl has been* **eating her heart out**. *She doesn't sleep, and she's lost interest in life.*

eat out of sb's hand [Vpr] be completely docile or compliant to another person's wishes, like a wild animal that has been tamed: *Owing to the importance of Paula's position she had everyone, including the local constabulary,* **eating out of her hand**. DF □ usu in the form have (got) sb eating etc.

eat out of house and home [Vn.pr pass] (usu *jocular*) ruin (sb) by eating all his food: *'These friends of yours are* **eating** *us* **out of house and home**! *When are they going to leave?'* ○ *Whenever the children bring their friends round to play we're* **eaten out of house and home**.

eat up 1 [Vp, Vn ⇆ p pass] eat heartily; finish (the food served): *'There's plenty for everyone, so* **eat up**!*'* ○ *Many people still believe that children should be made to '***eat up***'.* BRN ○ *'You're not going out to play until you've* **eaten** *all your carrots* **up**.*'*
2 [Vn ⇆ p pass] take a large part of (sth); consume. **O:** savings, reserves; capital, trust (fund): *As for the insurance money ... a large part was* **eaten up** *by payments of compensation.* W ○ *His solicitor wanted him to get rid of his family's furniture because storage charges were* **eating up** *the trust.*
3 [Vn.p pass] bother or worry (sb); preoccupy or consume (sb). **S:** something, what; curiosity; envy, jealousy: *Curiosity was simply* **eating** *her* **up** (or: *She was simply* **eaten up** *with curiosity)—she had to know who had given me such an expensive present.* ○ *He's very embittered, and* **eaten up** *by jealousy.* □ usu passive.

eavesdrop

eavesdrop (on) [Vpr rel] listen secretly to (sb's conversation): *'How do you know that Jane's going to have a baby? You must have been* **eavesdropping on** *our conversation.'*

ebb

ebb away [Vp] weaken or fade gradually. **S:** tide, daylight; life; strength, vitality: *As daylight* **ebbed away**, *the lights of the village came on one by one.* ○ *Life, Mr Charlton felt, was* **ebbing away** *from him.* DBM ○ *Her father's feeble strength* **ebbed** *slowly* **away**. GE ○ *His party's lead* (ie in the opinion polls) *appears to be* **ebbing away**. OBS

economize

economize (on) [Vpr emph rel] reduce one's spending (on sth). **o:** housekeeping; clothes; entertainment; travel; holidays: *It was typical of Augustus to spend pounds on the meal and then try to* **economize on** *the wine.* ○ *If you have an expensive car, it's foolish to try to* **economize on** *servicing it.*

edge

edge (one's way) across, along, back etc [Vp, Vpr, Vn.p, Vn.pr] move slowly and with great care across etc: *The climber* **edged** *warily* **along** *the narrow shelf* (cf **around** *the protruding rock*), *with a fall of 2 000 feet below him.* ○ *She* **edged out of** *her seat, begging the pardon of several people.* SE

edge with [Vn.pr pass] put (sth) around the edge of (sth): *My old Grannie always used to* **edge** *her tablecloths* **with** *lace.* ○ *The plates were all* **edged with** *a rich border of gold.*

edit

edit out/out of [Vn ⇆ p pass, Vn.pr pass] remove (sth) from the text of (a book etc) while preparing it for publication. **O:** phrase, passage; offending words. **o:** text; book, play, article: *His scenes had been* **edited out** *at some late stage in the production.* FL ○ *In the 1940s and 50s, four-letter words* (ie: swear words) *were always* **edited out of** *radio scripts.*

eff

eff off [Vp] (*taboo*) leave, go away; (a euphemism for fuck off): *The leader of the gang walked up to Kevin. '***Eff off***,' he said. And Kevin* **effed off**.

egg

egg on [Vn ⇆ p pass] encourage (sb) to do sth (esp sth adventurous, foolish or criminal). **Inf:** to think for oneself, to reach a higher standard: *The two men* **egged** *each other* **on** *to perform, and criticized, or apologized for, 'dullness'.* TU ○ *He is being bullied by the other boys* **egged on** *by Harry.* BRN

eject

eject (from) 1 [Vn.pr pass] (*formal* or *jocular*) remove (sb) forcibly from (a place) because of his bad behaviour. **O:** drunk, undesirable: *Henry has been* **ejected from** *a lot of pubs in his time.* = throw out/out of.
2 [Vpr, Vn.pr pass] (*aviation*) cause (oneself) to be thrown clear of (a plane). **S** [Vpr], **O** [Vn.pr]**:** pilot,

navigator; crew: *When a pilot* **ejects from** *a fighter plane he is thrown upwards and clear of the aircraft.*

eke

eke out [Vp.n pass] make (sth inadequate) larger, more substantial, richer etc. **O:** book, article; salary, pension: *He had to* **eke out** *his tiny salary with other work.* ○ *She had arranged her six daffodils* **eked out** *in the vase with foliage.* TFD

eke out an existence/a living [Vp.n] manage to earn just enough to live on: *He lived with his parents until their death, and thereafter* **eked out a** *marginal* **living** *as a messenger.* THMAN ○ *She* **ekes out a** *bare* **existence** *by taking in student lodgers.*

elbow

elbow one's way across, along, back etc [Vn.p, Vn.pr] move across etc using one's elbows to move people aside: *Bill* **elbowed his way to** *the front of the room.* ○ *The ambulance-men had to* **elbow their way through** *the huge crowd standing round the crashed cars.*

elect

elect (to) [Vn.pr pass emph rel] give enough votes to (sb) to give him a place (in sth). **o:** Council, Parliament, Senate; Presidency: *Ronald Reagan was* **elected to** *the Presidency for a second term of office.*

elevate

elevate to [Vn.pr pass] (*formal*) increase the status of (sb) by promoting him to (sth). **o:** the peerage, House of Lords, position of President of the company: *When a politician becomes an embarrassment to his party in the Commons, he may be 'kicked upstairs', ie* **elevated to** *the peerage.*

eliminate

eliminate (from) [Vn.pr pass] extract or remove (sth) from (sth). **O:** waste matter; poison; lead; possibility of suicide; candidate; competitor. **o:** body; liquid; paint; our considerations; election; race: *Once you have* **eliminated** *the obvious causes of death* **from** *your list you must, I am afraid, consider the possibility of foul play.* ○ *In the first round of the FA Cup most of the amateur teams were* **eliminated** *(***from** *the competition).*

elope

elope (with) [Vp rel] leave home (with sb) in order to marry him/her: *Dorelia had* **eloped with** *Leonard to a secret address in Bruges.* GJ = run away (with).

emanate

emanate from [Vpr emph rel] (*formal*) come from (sb/a place). **S:** light; smell; influence, power. **o:** a hidden source; a vase of gardenias; a group of high ranking officers: *There was very loud music* **emanating from** *the house.* OSOF ○ *The strength of the European Community* **emanates from** *the prosperous economies of relatively few member states.*

emancipate

emancipate (from) [Vn.pr pass emph rel] make (sb) free (from sth). **O:** women; working class, minority groups, black people. **o:** drudgery, tyranny of the home, child-rearing; slavery, inferior status, inequality, exploitation, ignorance, prejudice: *The Women's Liberation Movement struggles to* **emancipate** *women* **from** *the injustices of a world run by and for men.* ○ *The aim of Black Power is to* **emancipate** *(***from** *an inferior status) those whose skin is not white.* = release (from) 2.

embark

embark on/upon [Vpr pass rel] make a start on (sth); begin. **o:** project, scheme, campaign; journey, voyage: *Whatever made John* **embark on** *such a hair-brained scheme? He'll be ruined!* ○ *In Vienna Freud* **embarked upon** *his education.* F

embed

embed (itself) in [Vn.pr pass rel] stick or secure (itself) in (sth). **S:** arrow, bullet, splinter. **o:** tree; leg, finger: *A shell splinter* **embedded itself in** *the wall above his head.* ○ *The sword was so deeply* **embedded in** *the rock that no one could move it.*

embedded in [pass (Vn.pr)] (be) firmly fixed in (sth); (be) rooted in (sth). **S:** principle, rule, notion. **o:** charter, constitution; law, act: *The principle ... is* **embedded in** *the foundations of this chapter.* CF ○ *The more solidly* **embedded** *a fact is* **in** *the actual world ... the less we can imagine how things might have turned out if something different had happened.* RTH □ used with *appear* etc.

embody

embodied in [pass (Vn.pr)] (be) made a part or feature of (sth); (be) contained in (sth). **S:** rights, law, principles. **o:** constitution, charter, treaty: *The rights and obligations of all the member countries of the European Community are* **embodied in** *the Treaty of Rome* (or: *The Treaty of Rome* **embodies** *the rights and obligations ...*).

embroil

embroiled in [pass (Vn.pr)] (*formal*) (be) engaged or involved in (sth), possibly unwillingly or through lack of foresight etc. **o:** argument, row; futile discussion, somebody else's fight: *Members became* **embroiled in** *a heated debate over the issue of political union within the European Community.* □ used with *appear* etc.

emerge

emerge (from) 1 [Vpr emph rel] (*formal*) come out of (a place); leave. **o:** house, room; meeting, session: *She would* **emerge from** *her room only at dinner and retire as soon as the meal ended.* 50MH
2 [Vpr emph rel] (*formal*) be the result (of sth); become apparent (from sth). **o:** discussion, correspondence; negotiations, exchanges: *It was clear that no agreement was likely to* **emerge** *before the weekend* **from** *talks between the foreign ministers.* ○ *It* **emerged from** *John's letter to his wife that he had already made up his mind to leave her for good.*

emigrate

emigrate (from) (to) [Vpr emph rel] go away permanently (from one country) (to another): *The tendency for young people to* **emigrate from** *Ireland* **to** *England shows no sign of being reversed.* ○ *The family decided to uproot themselves en bloc and* **emigrate to** *Australia.*

empty

empty (itself) into [Vpr rel, Vn.pr rel] (of the contents of one river etc) pour into (another body of water). **S:** river, stream; Indus. **o:** sea, ocean, lake: *The river Ganges* **empties (itself) into** *the Bay of Bengal.*

empty out [Vn ⇆ p pass] remove all the contents of (sth). **O:** room, attic, barn; bag, pockets: *The bookcase will have to be* **emptied out** *before we can carry it upstairs.* ○ *The boys suspected of stealing were made to* **empty out** *their pockets in the headmaster's study.*

enamour

enamoured of [pass (Vn.pr)] (*formal* or *jocular*) greatly attracted by (sth/sb); in love with (sb): *I must confess that I am not greatly* **enamoured of** *life in the tropics: the heat is too great for my northern blood!* □ used with *become, appear, seem.*

encase

encase in [Vn.pr pass rel] cover completely with (sth); enclose in. **O:** coffin; baked chicken; packet. **o:** sarcophagus; clay; waterproof covering: *The chest was richly* **encased in** *leather, protected at the corners with ornamental metalwork.* ○ *Medieval knights,* **encased in** *armour from head to foot, had to be lowered into their saddles on ropes.* □ often passive.

encroach

encroach on/upon [Vpr pass] (*formal*) take or consume part of (sth). **S:** sea; visitors; neighbours; legislation. **o:** land, coast; his time; civil rights: *If the sea* **encroaches** *any further* **on** *the cliff, the houses at the top will be in great danger.* ○ *I apologize for* **encroaching upon** *your valuable time, but I should appreciate your advice in an important matter.*

encumber

encumber (with) [Vn.pr pass rel] (*formal*) place on (oneself/sb/sth) the burden or liability of (sth). **O:** oneself; troops; room. **o:** responsibilities, obligations; family; debts, large mortgage; excessive baggage, useless equipment; old-fashioned furniture: *One should not* **encumber** *oneself* **with** *large interest repayments at the beginning of a marriage.* ○ *The army was* **encumbered with** *tanks that could move at only half the speed of the enemy's.* ○ *The estate was so* **encumbered with** *debts that it was not worth inheriting.* □ often passive. = load down (with).

end

end in 1 [Vpr] have as its extremity, tip or termination. **S:** cylinder, thermometer; path, road. **o:** bulb; field, farmyard: *The tube* **ended in** *a large bulb, where the gas condensed into a colourless liquid.* ○ *The track became less and less distinct,* **ending** *finally* **in** *an impassable marsh.* ○ *The scorpion's tail* **ended in** *a menacing point, and the child sensibly decided to leave it alone!* ○ *Not all English words which* **end in** *-ly are adverbs.*
2 [Vpr] have (sth) as its result or culmination. **S:** long struggle; battle; trial, jury's deliberations; argument, discussion, debate; marriage. **o:** failure, success; victory, defeat, chaos, the capture of a thousand prisoners, the route of the enemy; a verdict of guilty/not guilty; uproar, confusion, pandemonium; divorce-court: *The Liberals Democrats' attempts to improve their position in Parliament* **ended in** *a gain of only two seats.* ○ *The argument between the two drunks* **ended in** *a free-for-all in which about twenty people became involved.* ○ *It was obvious to everyone that the marriage would sooner or later* **end in** *separation if not divorce.*

end up [Vp] finally be or do (sth); finish (as sth). **A:** Prime Minister; dead, bankrupt, in jail; like everyone else, the same as his father; paying the bill: *The nuts are pressed for their vegetable oil, which* **ends up** *as margarine.* NS ○ *If we take her too seriously, we'll all* **end up** *in a mental home.* YAA ○ *'Carry that box of explosives carefully or we'll* **end up** *dead ourselves!'* ○ *JIMMY: That's how you'll* **end up**, *my boy — black-hearted, evil-minded and vicious.* LBA ○ *He reckons this catastrophe will* **end up** *making a mint* (a lot of money) *for him, one way or the other.* NATC = finish up, wind up 7.

end up (with) [Vp, Vp.pr, Vn ⇆ p, Vn.p.pr] finish by doing or having (sth). **S** [Vp], **O** [Vn.p]**:** concert, meal, party: *The party* **ended up with** *the singing of Auld Lang Syne.* ○ *'I don't know what he* **ended up** *his speech* **with** *— a funny story I expect.'* = finish off/up (with). ↔ begin (with).

endear

endear to [Vn.pr] inspire liking or affection in (sb). **S:** habit, practice; character, temper. **O:** him, himself; child, guest, lodger: *My father played the host, with the grave courtesy which later* **endeared** *him* **to** *many children.* BRH ○ *It was Thérèse's simplicity of heart which* **endeared** *itself* **to** *Elodie.* HB

endow

endowed with [pass (Vn.pr)] (be) the possessor of (sth), (be) fortunate enough to have (sth). **o:** second sight, a sixth sense; the gift of beauty, eloquence: *Florence . . . seems to have been* **endowed with** *gumption as well as inventiveness and charm.* EB

enfold

enfold in one's arms [Vn.pr pass] hold (sb) close and protectively. **O:** baby, child, woman: *When she found the abandoned child on her doorstep, she lifted it up and* **enfolded** *it* **in her arms**.

engage

engage in [Vpr] be a participant in (sth); be a party to (sth). **o:** hostilities, warfare; politics; backbiting: *If you* **engage in** *politics, you cannot expect to have much time for your family.* ○ *I've no time to* **engage in** *gossip, so please don't come to me with your rumours and complaints.*

engaged in [pass (Vn.pr)] busy doing (sth), occupied with (sth). **o:** petty theft; preparing for the party, building a garage: *John and his brother are* **engaged in** *some plan for acquiring land and starting in business as market gardeners.* ○ *'Those men are behaving very suspiciously. They're* **engaged in** *some fishy business, I reckon.'*

engage with 1 [Vpr] make effective contact with (sth) : *If the big cogwheel does not* **engage with** *the small one, the clock stops.*
2 [Vpr] begin fighting (sb): *The plan was to* **engage with** *the enemy at dawn, thus achieving surprise.* = join battle (with).

engrave

engrave on 1 [Vn.pr pass emph rel] cut (a mark/marks) on (sth). **O:** name, date. **o:** presentation cup, plate: ***On*** *one side of the cup were* ***engraved*** *the names of all the teams who had won the championship.*
2 [Vn.pr pass emph rel establish (sth) firmly on or in (sth). **O:** incident, place. **o:** memory, mind: *The old man's words were* ***engraved on*** *my memory: I could never forget them.*

engross

engrossed (in) [pass (Vn.pr)] (*formal*) completely occupied (with sth). **o:** work, problem; book, story; one's thoughts: *He appeared totally* ***engrossed in*** *the problem.* ○ *That a man should become so* ***engrossed in*** *a pursuit that he risks his life on a mountain ... needs explanation.* CR □ used with *appear* etc.

engulf

engulfed in [pass (Vn.pr)] so covered in (sth) as to be obliterated by it; overwhelmed by (sth). **S:** town, city, village; coast; fields, crops. **o:** lava, water, mud: *The countryside was* ***engulfed in*** *a sea of mud left by the receding flood-water.* ○ *The country was* ***engulfed in*** *an economic crisis of the utmost severity.* □ used with *appear* etc.

enlarge

enlarge on/upon [Vpr pass emph rel] (*formal*) add details to (sth). **o:** statement, original version; theory, proposal: *I should be grateful if you could* ***enlarge*** *a little* ***on*** *your suggestions for improving the club's premises.* ○ *It would be in everybody's interests if the unfortunate incident in which two members came to blows was not* ***enlarged upon****.*

enlighten

enlighten (about/on) [Vn.pr pass] (*formal*) give (sb) the important facts (about sth/sb). **o:** what happened; the events of the past week; their private relations: *Nobody seemed anxious to* ***enlighten*** *me* ***about*** *the events leading up to the dispute.* ○ *It was obvious that Helen had been* ***enlightening*** *my wife* ***about*** *why I was so often 'delayed at the office'.*

enlist

enlist in [Vpr rel, Vn.pr pass rel] (*military*) (cause sb to) join (the armed forces). **o:** army, navy, air force; his father's regiment: *The three brothers* ***enlisted in*** *the navy at the outbreak of war.* ○ *A boy can't be* ***enlisted in*** *the Army without his parents' consent.*

enmesh

enmeshed in [pass (Vn.pr)] (*formal*) inextricably caught or trapped in (sth). **S:** youths; debaters; litigants. **o:** crime; argument; the toils of the law: *Switzerland became* ***enmeshed in*** *the French Revolution and Napoleonic Wars.* JUNG ○ *Let's not get too* ***enmeshed in*** *legal niceties: we need a quick decision in the interests of the children.*

enquire

enquire ⇨ inquire.

enrol

enrol in [Vpr rel, Vn.pr pass rel] enter (one's/sb's name) in (sth). **o:** evening class, Mr Jones's Art class: *Have you* ***enrolled in*** *the car maintenance class this year?* ○ *Mrs Jones has* ***enrolled*** *her daughter* ***in*** *the Elementary Ballet class.*

ensconce

ensconce (oneself) in [Vn.pr pass rel] (*formal* or *jocular*) settle or install oneself well and comfortably in (sth): *Father had* ***ensconced himself in*** *his favourite corner of the bar, with a pint of bitter on the table in front of him.* ○ *I at once spotted him* ***ensconced in*** *a deep armchair.* CED

enshrine

enshrined in [pass (Vn.pr)] (*formal*) (be) stated or described formally and solemnly in (sth). **o:** law, statute; account, record: *The rights of the ordinary individual were acquired over centuries and are* ***enshrined in*** *law and privilege.* MIND ○ *The history of the regiment is* ***enshrined in*** *the official records.*

ensnare

ensnare (in) [Vn.pr pass rel] (*formal*) catch (sth/sb) (in sth), generally through deception, trickery etc. **O:** bird, rabbit; the gullible, the unwary. **o:** net, trap; her toils; wild scheme: *A whole flock of Icelandic geese was attracted by the decoys and* ***ensnared in*** *the cleverly contrived tunnel of nets.* ○ *Confidence tricksters have little difficulty in* ***ensnaring*** *the greedy* ***in*** *their schemes.*

entangle

entangle in/with [Vn.pr pass rel] (cause oneself/itself/sth to) become intertwined in such a way that separation is difficult or impossible. **O:** itself, oneself; clothes, hair. **o:** bushes, branches: *'How did Alice manage to* ***entangle*** *her hair so badly* ***in*** *the brambles?' 'She was playing hide-and-seek with her brother.'* = catch up (in). ⇨ next entry

entangled (with) 1 [pass (Vn.pr)] be intertwined or connected (with sth) so that the two cannot easily be separated: *The weeds were so* ***entangled with*** *the plants* (or: *The weeds and the plants were so* ***entangled***) *that it was impossible to remove them without damaging the flowers.* ⇨ previous entry
2 [pass (Vn.pr)] involved (with sb) in such a way that one cannot easily free oneself. **S:** legitimate business; husband, secretary. **o:** criminal operations; woman next door, boss: *It was at Clarence Terrace that Rosamund Lehmann met Cecil Day Lewis,* ***with*** *whom she was* ***entangled*** *throughout the forties.* □ also used with *become, get, appear, seem.* = caught up in 1.

enter

enter for [Vp, Vn.pr pass rel] officially present (oneself/sb) as a competitor in (sth). **o:** race, contest, competition: *Not as many students* ***entered for*** *the exam as had been hoped.* G ○ *I'd like to know what joker* ***entered*** *me* ***for*** *the cake-making competition!* = put in for 1.

enter in/into [Vn.pr pass] write (sth) in (sth) as a record. **O:** note, transaction, name. **o:** diary, ledger, register: *Before she went to sleep, Mary* ***entered*** *the events of the day* ***in*** (or: ***into***) *her diary.* ○ *When the last item had been duly* ***entered in*** *the ledger, the clerk closed it and put it in its usual place before locking up and going home.*

enter into 1 [Vpr pass] (*formal*) begin or undertake (sth). **o:** conversation, discussions, negotiations; relationship, commitment: *Everyone who comes to believe in the Christ is obliged to* ***enter into*** *the deepest and fullest relationship with him.* CF ○ *The* *two governments* ***entered into*** *preliminary talks in the hope of reaching complete agreement at a full conference.* ○ *Wrong commitments are* ***entered into****; being decent doesn't save you from disaster.* EB

2 [Vpr] (*formal*) give, provide or mention (sth). **o:** details, particulars; a long account: *'There's no need to* ***enter into*** *a lot of detail: just tell the court the main facts of the case.'*

3 [Vpr] form a (necessary or vital) part of (sth). **o:** calculations, considerations; plan, scheme; it: *The possibility of an air-attack from the west did not* ***enter into*** *the calculations of the General Staff. So they were entirely unprepared when the apparently impossible actually happened.* ○ *'If you had any charity at all, you'd forgive him for what he did.' 'Charity doesn't* ***enter into*** *it. It's a matter of sticking to one's principles.'* = come in/into 2.

enter into the spirit (of) [Vpr] behave with a spirit or attitude which suits the occasion: *Some local authorities remain reluctant to* ***enter into the spirit of*** *... public participation in planning.* SC ○ *When George arrived home and found a party in progress, he soon* ***entered into the spirit of*** *it.*

enter on/upon [Vpr pass rel] begin, commence (sth). **o:** route; course of study; career, duties, term of office; period of peace, prosperity: *The train* ***entered on*** *a straight stretch of track between Headcorn and Staplehurst.* CD ○ *The President* ***entered upon*** *his second term of office, with many hoping that he would show more wisdom in it than in his first.*

enter up [Vn ⇆ p pass] record (sth) in a book etc provided for the purpose. **S:** nurse; warden; chemist. **O:** temperature, blood pressure, pulse rate; names of visitors; drugs, poisons sold: *It is very important that every sale of a dangerous poison should be* ***entered up*** *at the time of sale.*

entice

entice away [Vn ⇆ p pass] cause (sb) to leave another person (or his home or employment) by means of promises, often unfulfilled. **O:** girlfriend, boyfriend; employee: *Fred is so obsessed by money that he'd be* ***enticed away*** *by the first man who offered him a couple of hundred above his present salary.* ○ *Mrs Brown is not speaking to Mrs Green any more. She reckons it was Mrs Green who* ***enticed*** *her gardener* ***away****.*

entitle

entitle to [Vn.pr pass emph rel] give (sb) the right to enjoy (sth). **S:** rank, position. **o:** privileges; a fair hearing: *His position as a friend of the family doesn't* ***entitle*** *him automatically* ***to*** *a share of the inheritance.* ○ *He was different and better, he told himself; more, he was therefore* ***entitled to*** *special treatment.* 50MH

entrap

entrap into [Vn.pr pass rel] (*formal*) make (sb) do or say sth by a trick. **S:** interrogator, police. **O:** suspect, thief, prisoner. **o:** giving himself away, confessing to the crime: *Experienced guerrilla fighters are not easily* ***entrapped into*** *revealing their positions.* = trap into.

entrust

entrust to [Vn.pr pass rel] give (sth/sb) to (sb) for safe keeping. **O:** money, documents; children. **o:** (the care of) a solicitor; friend: *I wouldn't advise you to* ***entrust*** *anything of value* ***to*** *Kingsley-Smith.* ⇨ next entry.

entrust with [Vn.pr pass rel] make (sb) responsible for the safety, custody etc, of (sth/sb). **O:** messenger; pilot; inexperienced maid. **o:** delivering money; one's life; children: *Kingsley-Smith is not the kind of man who can be* ***entrusted with*** *money or secret information.* ○ *My father* ***entrusted*** *me* ***with*** *a letter to give to her.* GL ○ *He had become a sort of sub-editor,* ***entrusted with*** *hiring other members of staff.* CD ⇨ previous entry.

envelop

enveloped in [pass (Vn.pr)] surrounded by (sth). **S:** countryside, lake; house; affair, subject. **o:** mist, fog; flames, smoke; mystery, obscurity, confusion: *In a second, poor Semele withered as though* ***enveloped in*** *flames.* GLEG ○ *The whole business of the Director General's appointment has been* ***enveloped in*** *mystery from start to finish.* □ used with *become, appear, seem.* = wrapped in.

equate

equate (to/with) [Vpr rel, Vn.pr pass rel] (of one thing) correspond to or be equivalent (to another); claim that (one thing) corresponds to or is equivalent (to another): *Cleanliness does not* ***equate with*** *godliness.* ○ *It is no longer possible to* ***equate*** *death* ***with*** *the lack of a heart beat.* MIND ○ *We cannot simply* ***equate*** *religion* ***with*** *immaturity and science* ***with*** *maturity as Freud wished to do.* PS

equip

equip (for) [Vn.pr pass rel] give (to sb) the necessary equipment for (sth). **o:** task, work; climb; campaign, attack: *Can the Council really claim that they* ***equipped*** *their road-workers adequately* ***for*** *such conditions* (or: *to face such conditions*)? ○ *I shall have to remind her myself, and I don't honestly feel* ***equipped for*** *the task any more.* GL

equip (with) [Vn.pr pass rel] provide (sb/sth) with (sth). **O:** expedition; hospital; school; every normal child. **o:** many tons of supplies; latest apparatus, devices, kidney machine; every luxury, splendid laboratories, bright classrooms; what is necessary for his survival: *Nature had* ***equipped*** *the boy* ***with*** *two hands, but not, apparently,* ***with*** *the brains to use them properly.* ○ *Deep-sea trawlers are now* ***equipped with*** *electronic devices.* = fit up (with).

escape

escape (from) [Vpr emph rel] break free (from sb/sth); be released involuntarily (from sth). **S:** prisoner; lion, pet hamster; cry of pain. **o:** captors, jail, captivity; cage; lips: *Within a period of three weeks, five prisoners succeeded in* ***escaping from*** *the 'top security' prison.* ○ *Jane never* ***escaped from*** *her mother's arbitrary and capricious rule.* TU ○ *An involuntary exclamation of joy* ***escaped from*** *her lips.*

escort

escort (from) [Vn.pr pass rel] accompany or lead (sb) away (from a place). **S:** police; guard. **O:** arrested man; distinguished visitor. **o:** magistrates' court; platform: *Several policeman had to* ***escort*** *the referee* ***from*** *the field to protect him from angry spectators.* ○ *The young woman was* ***escorted from*** *the court by her solicitor.* ⇨ next entry

escort (to) [Vn.pr pass rel] accompany (sb) as a partner, guard or protector (to a place). **O:** prisoner; young lady; ambassador. **o:** cells; car; airport: *At the eleventh hour a suitable partner was found to* ***escort*** *Laetitia* ***to*** *the ball.* ○ *The ambassador was* ***escorted to*** *the plane by the Foreign Secretary.* ⇨ previous entry

estimate

estimate at [Vn.pr pass rel] roughly guess, assess or calculate (sth) to be (sth). **O:** attendance, crowd; profit; size, capacity. **o:** 10 000; £2 million; number 14, ten gallons: *The police put the number of demonstrators at about 2 000 though the organizers* ***estimated*** *it* ***at*** *5 000.* ○ *The tax inspectors* ***estimated*** *Sir Joseph's income* ***at*** *£250 000 for the year just ending.* = put at.

estrange

estranged (from) [pass (Vn.pr)] (*formal*) no longer on close and affectionate terms (with sb). **o:** wife, husband; children: *I didn't realize that Arthur was* ***estranged from*** *his wife* (or: *that Arthur and his wife were* ***estranged***). *They seemed a perfect match. What went wrong?* ○ *A young friend phoned to tell me about the wonderful summer holiday he had just had with his father. They had for many years been* ***estranged from*** *each other.* ISOH □ used with *become, appear, seem, feel.*

etch

etch in [Vn ⇆ p pass adj] draw (sth) in, with a pen, pencil etc. **O:** background, details, horizon, trees: *'Your drawing would look better,' he said, 'if you were to* ***etch*** *something* ***in*** *over on the left, to give the composition more balance.'*

evacuate

evacuate (from) (to) [Vn.pr pass rel] remove (sb) (from a dangerous building, or area) (to a safer one). **O:** troops, women and children, non-combatants, inhabitants: *During the war hundreds of thousands of children were* ***evacuated from*** *industrial* ***to*** *rural areas.*

even

even out [Vn ⇆ p pass] spread (sth) evenly over a period or among people. **O:** payments; load, work; responsibility: *Not everyone likes to pay large sums for electricity or gas. It is much better if payments can be* ***evened out*** *on a monthly or weekly basis.*

even up [Vn ⇆ p pass] obtain or restore a balance between (things or people); make equal. **O:** things, matters; sides, teams: *We gave the Smiths a bottle of gin last Christmas, so this year they gave us a bottle of Scotch to* ***even*** *things* ***up*** *a bit.* ○ *When the German relay team dropped their baton, we managed to* ***even*** *the score* ***up****. Then everything depended on the result of the marathon.*

evict

evict (from) [Vn.pr pass rel] compel, force (sb) to leave (a place). **O:** farmer; tenant, occupier; squatter. **o:** farm; house, flat; office block, building: *All the tenants on the estate marched in protest when the Council* ***evicted*** *an old man (****from*** *his home) because he had neglected the garden.*

evolve

evolve (from/out of) [Vpr rel] grow or develop slowly (from sth). **S:** life-form; mammal, primate; machine, process. **o:** more primitive form; crude prototype: *This industrialized method of manufacture* ***evolved*** *by trial and error* ***from*** *a simple process carried on in the home.* ○ *The present highly complex forms of life* ***evolved from*** *minute unicellular creatures.*

exact

exact (from) [Vn.pr pass] (*formal*) require or force (sb) to give (sth). **O:** money, taxes; an apology; homage, obedience: *If the government goes on* ***exacting*** *so much* ***from*** *the taxpayer, it will not last long.* ○ *The customer* ***exacted*** *an apology* ***from*** *the store for questioning her honesty.*

examine

examine (in) [Vn.pr pass rel] test the knowledge of (sb) (about a given subject). **o:** physics, chemistry; business management, accountancy: *My son was* ***examined in*** *First Aid last week. He's got about six Scout badges now.*

examine on [Vn.pr pass] test sb's knowledge of (a specific point). **o:** detail, point, aspect: *Each student was* ***examined on*** *a different aspect of the nervous system.*

excel

excel (at) [Vpr emph rel] perform outstandingly well (in some activity). **o:** games; cricket, archery, gymnastics; throwing the javelin: *John did not make much of a mark at school in his studies, but he* ***excelled at*** *playing the fool!* ○ *Gloves were the sort of thing* ***at*** *which the English* ***excelled****.* GIE

excel in [Vpr emph rel] reach a high standard, in an academic subject etc. **o:** French, Latin; music, painting: *Churchill, who had such a distinguished career as a statesman and writer,* ***excelled in*** *nothing at all at school.*

exchange

exchange (with/for) [Vn.pr] give (sth) (to sb) in return (for sth similar). **O:** badges, souvenirs; shirt, jacket: *His first thought after appointment had been to* ***exchange*** *his living* (ie the church where he served) ***for*** *one more convenient to London.* SS ○ *After the final whistle blew, the England captain* ***exchanged*** *shirts* ***with*** *his opposite number* (cf *the two captains* ***exchanged*** *shirts*).

exchange ideas etc (with) [Vn.pr rel] have some form of communication (with sb). **O:** ⚠ ideas, thoughts, views; (a few) words: *I usually* ***exchange*** *a few* ***words*** *of greeting* ***with*** *my neighbour after breakfast.* ○ *'I found it very refreshing to* ***exchange ideas with*** *your father.'* ⇨ next entry

(not) exchange more than a few/half a dozen words (with) [Vn.pr] (not) have much communication (with sb); (not) really become acquainted (with sb): *A lot of people in England don't know their neighbours. I'm ashamed to say that I have****n't exchanged more than half a dozen words with*** *the chap who lives next door since last Christmas!* □ usu used in the perfect tenses. ⇨ previous entry

excuse

excuse (for) [Vn.pr pass emph rel] forgive (sb) (for sth/doing sth). **o:** his offensive remarks, her bad behaviour; failing to recognize sb, arriving late: *Please* **excuse** *me* **for** *not writing earlier to thank you for your kind invitation.* ○ *Nothing could* **excuse** *him* **for** *bursting in on the meeting like that.* = pardon (for).

excuse (from) [Vn.pr pass emph rel] allow (sb) not to fulfil some duty or obligation: *As you were kept working so late today, you will be* **excused from** *attending the early meeting tomorrow morning.* ○ *I'd like to be* **excused from** *any further participation in this scheme: it takes up too much of my time.*

exempt

exempt (from) [Vn.pr pass emph rel] officially or legally, free (sb) from the obligation or duty to do sth. **o:** military service; preliminary examinations; any further jury service: *Bill was* **exempted from** *National Service because he was in a 'reserved occupation'.* □ also be exempt from: *Nobody should* **be exempt from** *doing some of the unpleasant jobs around the camp.*

exercise

exercise in [Vn.pr pass rel] give (sb) practice in (sth/doing sth). **O:** horse; team; students. **o:** jumping over ditches; new tactics; giving ready responses to questions: *The recruits are* **exercised** *every day* **in** *the art of self-defence.*

exercise over [Vn.pr pass rel] use (sth) in dealing with (sb). **O:** influence, authority, power: *People with strong personalities should be careful how they* **exercise** *their influence* **over** *less assertive people.* ○ *The problem … is directly connected with the 'power'* **exercised** *by some men* **over** *others.* RTH

exile

exile (from) (to) [Vn.pr pass rel] send (sb) away (from one place) (to another) as a punishment or precaution. **o:** (**from**) Court, his native land; (**to**) the country, France: *Many political rebels of the time ended their days* **exiled from** *their native regions.*

exonerate

exonerate (from) [Vn.pr pass emph rel] (*formal*) pronounce (sb) free from or not guilty of (sth). **o:** (all) blame, responsibility; charge: *After a lengthy inquiry, the management was* **exonerated from** *any responsibility for the fire that destroyed the factory.*

expand

expand into [Vpr, Vn.pr pass] (cause sth to) become larger. **S** [Vpr], **O** [Vn.pr]**:** short story; small town. **o:** full-length novel; large industrial centre: *The BBC has decided to* **expand** *its programme on the political changes in Eastern Europe* **into** *a full-scale studio discussion.* ○ *This once small family business has* **expanded into** *a public company employing many thousands.*

expatiate

expatiate upon [Vpr emph rel] (*formal* or *jocular*) talk at length and with (sometimes boring) authority or enthusiasm about (sth). **o:** the delights of the English countryside; the virtue of moderation in all things; his latest discovery: *'There goes James again! What is he* **expatiating upon** *this time?' 'How the Romans made glass, I believe. I haven't been listening really!'* = hold forth.

expect

expect (of) [Vn.pr pass] hope that sb will do sth or behave in a certain way. **O:** too much, a great deal; great things: *Bill's parents* **expected** *too much* **of** *him, with the inevitable result that they were disappointed, and he left home at the earliest opportunity.* ○ *Religious commitment was* **expected of** *the children and encouraged in every way.* MRJ = ask (of).

expel

expel (from) [Vn.pr pass emph rel] force (sb) to leave (a place). **O:** air; enemy; boy, girl; member. **o:** tube; occupied territory; school; club: *In such a small house it is important to have some method of* **expelling** *cooking smells* **from** *the kitchen.* ○ *Two forwards were* **expelled from** *the club following violent play during a home match.*

expend

expend energy etc (on) [Vn.pr pass emph rel] (*formal*) use or consume (energy etc) in order to achieve (sth). **O:** ⚠ energy, effort, time. **o:** task, work; building, reorganizing: *It isn't worth* **expending** *too much* **effort on** *redecorating the house if you're going to move out in a year's time.* ○ *He is a travesty of a father whose minimal* **energy** *is* **expended in** *speaking out against marriage.* JA

experiment

experiment on/upon [Vpr pass rel] test the effectiveness of techniques, drugs etc, on (sb/sth). **o:** criminals, human beings, guinea-pigs: *Animal rights campaigners are opposed to research which involves* **experimenting on** *live animals.* ○ *My wife* **experiments on** *me before she serves a new dish to our guests. She calls it 'trying it out on the dog'!*

experiment with [Vpr pass] adopt or use (sth) to test its effectiveness or discover its effects. **o:** fresh methods, new forms of government, traffic control, drugs: *The children were warned not to* **experiment with** *dangerous drugs.* ○ *East European countries find themselves in the novel position of being able to* **experiment with** *various electoral systems.*

explain

explain away [Vn ⇆ p pass] give a satisfactory reason for (sth); remove objections to (sth) by means of a convincing argument. **O:** behaviour, slip of the tongue, attitude; difficulty, apparent inconsistencies: *There are always those who are anxious to* **explain away** *the divine nature of the Church.* CF ○ *He had* **explained away** *his mother's habit of lying in bed as sheer idleness.* JUNG

explain (to) [Vn.pr pass emph rel] make (sth) clear (to sb); tell (sb) the facts about (sth). **O:** the workings; plan, situation; meaning: *'Would you be kind enough to* **explain** *the meaning of this expression* **to** *me?'* ○ *The teacher* **explained** *the basic principles of nuclear fission (***to** *the class), but only a few seemed to understand.* □ not: * **explain** *me the meaning of this expression.*

explode

explode with [Vpr] exclaim loudly as a result of (sth). **o:** anger, fury, rage; frustration: *When I* *arrived home at midnight I found my father purple in the face and about to* ***explode with*** *rage at his guests' failure to leave at a reasonable hour.*

export

export (from) (to) [Vn.pr pass emph rel] send (sth) (from one country) (to another). **O:** foodstuffs, raw materials; cars, trucks; luxury items; culture: *Japan* ***exports*** *large quantities of electrical equipment* ***to*** *countries all round the world.* ○ *Timber* ***exported from*** *Scandinavia may end up as building material or wood-pulp.* ↔ import (from) (into).

expose

expose to [Vn.pr pass emph rel] put (sb) in a vulnerable position with regard to (sth). **O:** child; population; country; colleagues, oneself. **o:** danger, corruption, vice; the cold of winter; disease, starvation; invasion; accusation, charge: *In 1971 the people of East Bengal (now Bangladesh) were* ***exposed to*** *every kind of danger — flood, famine, disease and war.* ○ *No one so startlingly blond . . . should* ***expose*** *himself* ***to*** *sunburn.* AT

expunge

expunge (from) [Vn.pr pass rel] (*formal*) remove (sth) (from a record) and thus treat it as never having been stated or recorded. **O:** name, words; conviction. **o:** record(s), minutes: *He has willingly* ***expunged*** *all revolutionary sentiments* ***from*** *his poems.* ○ *Time had* ***expunged from*** *his memory all recollections of these terrible events.* = delete (from).

extort

extort from [Vn.pr pass emph rel] (*formal*) obtain (sth) from (sb) by means of threats or violence. **O:** money; confession, admission of guilt: *The gang specializes in* ***extorting*** *money* ***from*** *men in important positions, by threatening to reveal activities which they prefer to keep secret.* ○ *The Court . . .* ***extorted*** *large sums of money* ***from*** *reluctant landowners.* SHOE

extract

extract (from) [Vn.pr pass emph rel] obtain (sth) (from sth) by means of a mechanical or chemical process. **O:** oil; dyes; juice; essence. **o:** earth; coal; orange; flowers: *It is one thing to locate oil, but quite another to* ***extract*** *it (****from*** *the earth) and transport it to the centres of industry.*

extract from [Vn.pr pass emph rel] obtain (sth) from (sb) by any means ranging from gentle persuasion to physical violence . **O:** money; information, confession; present; promise: *The union* ***extracted*** *that concession* ***from*** *a reluctant government after a 12-day strike.* ○ *When he has* ***extracted*** *everything he can* ***from*** *a new acquaintance, he drops him like a hot brick.*

extricate

extricate (from) [Vn.pr pass emph rel] (*formal* or *jocular*) free or remove (sb/sth) (from sth). **O:** himself; friend, colleague; lorry; lump of meat. **o:** difficulties; an embarrassing situation, this predicament; mud, quagmire; child's throat: *Mr Mason discovered he had no money in his pocket to pay for lunch. He was wondering how to* ***extricate*** *himself* ***from*** *this difficulty when he saw an old friend sitting at another table. 'Saved!' he exclaimed to himself.*

exult

exult at [Vpr rel] (*formal*) feel overjoyed or triumphant because of (sth). **o:** the prospect of winning a fortune, the thought of completing the task; one's new-found freedom: *Most people would* ***exult at*** *the overthrow of the ruling junta.*

exult in [Vpr pass rel] (*formal*) take pride in (sth); derive pleasure from (sth). **o:** the defeat, humiliation, of his enemy; one's own strength, one's ability to overcome difficulties: *Mr Smith* ***exulted in*** *his release from a lifetime of office drudgery.* ⇨ next entry

exult over [Vpr pass rel] (*formal*) meanly enjoy the sight or thought of (sth). **o:** his disgrace, downfall, misfortune, defeat; defeated enemy, team, champion: *I left the scene quickly, not wishing to witness the crowd* ***exulting over*** *the capture and lynching of the unfortunate bandits.* ⇨ previous entry

F

face

face away from [Vp.pr emph rel] (turn, so as to) look or point in the opposite direction from (sth/sb). **S:** listener, spectator; building. **o:** platform, speaker; street, traffic: *The estate is so designed that the front of each house* ***faces away from*** *busy roads.*

face down [Vn ⇆ p pass] (esp *US*) make (sb) yield by confronting him confidently and boldly: *Like most women, she would not have had the experience of* ***facing down*** *an enemy.* MAA

face up to [Vp.pr pass adj] accept (sth) honestly and courageously. **S:** parent, teacher; government, local council. **o:** responsibility, burden, task; prospect, possibility (of loss, failure): *He had to* ***face up to*** *the depressing possibility of the monster's death.* RM ○ *There's no running away from the facts; they just have to be* ***faced up to***. ○ *He won't* ***face up***, *can't* ***face up***, ***to*** *them being gone.* BONE

fade

fade away [Vp] gradually become less visible, less audible or weaker. **S:** shape, vision; music, cheering; strength, vitality; inventiveness, inspiration: *I just saw him down the end of the passage. I screamed and he sort of* ***faded away.*** DC ○ *The clip-clop of the horse's hooves* ***faded away*** *into the distance.* ○ (saying) *Old soldiers never die, they only* ***fade away***. = die away.

fade in [Vn ⇆ p pass adj] gradually make (sth/sb) visible or audible, esp on radio, TV etc. **O:** voice, music; sound effects; scene, shot; announcer: *At this point you* ***fade in*** *the background music and street noises.* ⇨ next entry

fade out [Vp nom, Vn ⇆ p pass adj] gradually (cause sth/sb to) become invisible or inaudible, esp on radio, TV etc. **S** [Vp], **O** [Vn.p]**:** voice, music, sound effects; image, picture; speaker, performer. **S** [Vn.p]**:** broadcasting company, studio; producer: *When you turn on a transistorized radio the sound comes on immediately; when you turn off, it* ***fades out*** *gradually.* ○ *I hope that during his television appearance, there will be no* ***fade-outs*** *or black-*

outs! ○ ***Fade out*** *the storm effect here, and turn up the music.* ⇨ previous entry

fade up [Vn ⇆ p pass] gradually make (sth/sb) louder, esp in a radio or TV studio. **S:** technician, sound effects man. **O:** music, voice; announcer: *As the signature tune was faded out, the voices of a group talking around a table were* ***faded up****.*

fag

fag out [Vn.p pass adj] (*informal*) make (sb) very tired; exhaust. **S:** exercise; game, race; entertaining, being sociable: *Standing on your feet all day really* ***fags*** *you* ***out****.* ○ *After ten minutes of his conversation I feel quite* ***fagged out****.* ○ *She wanted me to have a bath every night, and that caused a bit of trouble because I was too ...* ***fagged out*** *even to change my clothes.* LLDR □ usu passive or adj. = tire out.

fall

fall about one's ears [Vpr] collapse utterly. **S:** his (whole) world; their achievements: *Soon the secure, enclosed life he had built up for himself would* ***fall about his ears****.* = crash about one's ears.

fall about (laughing/with laughter) [Vp, Vp.pr] (*informal*) laugh uproariously, uncontrollably. **S:** audience; listener, viewer: *People* ***fell about*** *when he told them he was doing 'O' Level woodwork and music.* BBCR ○ *The audience* ***fell about laughing*** *but no laughter came from me. I was in love with her.* BID

fall apart [Vp] disintegrate. **S:** car, house; alliance, coalition; defence, case; marriage, partnership: *The school oboe was unused, so I tried that for a term or two; but ... it* ***fell apart*** *in my hands.* SU ○ *Ann did what she could to keep the marriage from* ***falling apart****. If she and Robert broke up, she decided, it wouldn't be her fault.* = come apart, fall to pieces.

fall away [Vp] crumble, collapse. **S:** structure, defence; basis (of a case); grounds (for an appeal); hostility: *Any personal opposition gradually* ***fell away*** *as people got to know him.* ○ *At night, after two or three glasses of wine, she would feel her defences* ***fall away****.* MSAL

fall away (to) 1 [Vp, Vp.pr rel] slope steeply (towards sth). **S:** field, meadow; garden, orchard. **o:** river, road: *Beyond the garden, an area of woodland* ***fell*** *sharply* ***away to*** *the river bank.*
2 [Vp, Vp.pr] sink, drop (to a lower level). **S:** demand, supply; production, output. **o:** level; zero, nothing: *Output from the power stations* ***fell away*** *steeply as restrictions on the supply of coal took effect.* ○ *As demand for funds slackened off, the rate* ***fell away to*** *the clearing banks' basic level of 3.38 per cent.* T

fall back [Vp] withdraw; retreat. **S:** crowd, spectators; troops; army, division: *They had* ***fallen back*** *to let her through.* TFD ○ *The Russians were finding an offensive war of movement very different from the fluid fighting of 1941 and 1942, when they had been* ***falling back*** *towards their dumps and railheads.* B = pull back 2.

fall back on [Vp.pr rel] approach or consult (sb) for support or comfort in difficult times; use (sth) as a last resort if other things fail. **o:** mother, family; religion; pension, savings; simpler plan, more straightforward approach, threat of dismissal: *He grasps at things greedily, like a child, just because he hasn't any inner certainty to* ***fall back on****.* PW ○ *He could always* ***fall back on*** *his wife's money.* JUNG ○ *And if the scheme didn't work there was always the Home Secretary's plan to* ***fall back on****.* TBC □ fall back on often occurs as an inf immediately following a n; less often as a main (finite) v. ⇨ drive back on.

fall behind 1 [Vp, Vpr] move back behind (others); be overtaken by (others). **S:** runner, horse; company, industry. **m:** a long way, very far. **o:** rest of the field; competitor, rival: *His black three-legged dog ...* ***fell*** *so far* ***behind*** *that it was only a black dot on the plain.* GJ ○ *We have already* ***fallen behind*** *our competitors in the production of advanced computer hardware.* = drop behind, get behind 1. ↔ get ahead/ahead of. ⇨ be behind 2.
2 [Vp] fail to pay, complete or deliver (sth) for some time. **A:** with payments, instalments; in repaying a debt; on deliveries: *Teenagers were more likely to* ***fall behind*** *with the rent.* H ○ *He'd stopped deliveries, because I* ***fell behind*** *with the bill.* CON = get behind 2. ⇨ be behind 1.

fall below [Vpr emph rel] drop lower than (a permitted or desired level etc). **S:** oil, water; wage, earnings; intake, recruitment; production, demand. **o:** point, level; figure, percentage; standard: *Engineering workers in the state sector are determined that their earnings will not* ***fall below*** *the average for the whole industry.* ○ *Output for the current year will* ***fall below*** *that for last year.* ↔ rise above 1. ⇨ be below 1.

fall between two stools [Vpr] fail to be either of two satisfactory alternatives. **S:** policy, scheme, plan; show, performance; speech, statement: *The display* ***falls between the two stools*** *of an historical exhibition and a survey of the visual arts of the period — it is not wholly satisfactory as either.* T ○ *The British Government look like* ***falling between two stools*** (in Northern Ireland). *Their security measures are not ruthless enough to be effective, though they alienate the minority.* SC

fall by the wayside [Vpr] (*euphemism*) fail to make progress in life; slip into dishonest ways: *In Mr Robert Hollis's play 'June Fall' on BBC television, the discards are the people who* ***fall by the wayside*** *and stop developing, the world's rejected guests.* T ○ *'It's a funny thing, but even the best of us can* ***fall by the wayside*** *and yours truly* (= the speaker) *is no exception.'* OBS

fall down 1 [Vp emph] fall to the ground; collapse. **S:** building, tent, scaffolding; old man, cripple: *Bits of the steel scaffolding* ***fell down*** *and narrowly missed a couple of bystanders.* ○ *His grandmother* ***fell down*** *in the street and broke her leg.*
2 [Vp] be shown to be false or inadequate; collapse. **S:** argument, case; policy, approach: *The Council's answer to the population expansion was to build high blocks of flats, but that's where the plan* ***fell down*** *— nobody wanted to live in them.* ○ *'I'd rather be happy than right any day.' 'And are you?' 'No. That's where it all* ***falls down****, of course.'* HHGG = fall to the ground.

fall down on it/the job [Vp.pr] (*informal*) fail to make a success of sth, not be able to handle it. **S:** employee, workman, contractor: *I don't want Jeremy to be Prime Minister or anything of that sort. He'd only* ***fall down on it****.* PW ○ *Don't put him* *in charge of planning: he's sure to* **fall down on the job**.

fall for (in a big way) [Vpr rel] (*informal*) be (strongly) attracted to (sb); come to admire (sb) (wholeheartedly): *A man who's on the way up is continually raising the standard of the women he can* **fall for**. CON ○ *About this time I* **fell for** *Keats —* **fell for** *him as you do for the first poet who really means something to you.* ○ *I* **fell for** *Irma* **in a big way**, *Harold.* PW = fall in love (with).

fall for (hook, line and sinker) [Vpr rel] (*informal*) allow oneself to be persuaded by (sth). **o:** line of talk, argument; propaganda; trick: *The garage said the car had been driven carefully by one previous owner, and of course I* **fell for** *it* **hook, line and sinker**. ○ *Had we been listening to gullible Westerners* **falling for** *the same tricks Stalin was pulling in the Thirties?* L ○ *If you* **fall for** *that, you'll* **fall for** *anything!*

fall from grace [Vpr] lose one's position as a trusted favourite of those in power. **S:** minister, adviser, courtier, favourite: *Thomas More* **fell from grace** *because of his opposition to the royal divorce.* = lapse from grace.

fall from power [Vpr] lose a position of power; relinquish office. **S:** Government, party: *This administration* **fell from power** *over its handling of the economic crisis.*

fall from/out of favour (with) [Vpr] (*formal*) lose a favoured or privileged position. **S:** minister, courtier: *I had* **fallen from favour** *and would be lucky to pass out of the College at all.* MFM ○ *Jones has* **fallen out of favour with** *the party leadership.* = fall from grace. ⇨ be out of favour (with).

fall in 1 [Vp] collapse, give way. **S:** roof, ceiling, wall; sides of a trench: *The roof of the new tunnel hasn't been properly supported: it shows signs of* **falling in**.

2 [Vp, Vn ⇆ p pass] (*military*) (cause people to) form into ranks, as when on parade. **S** [Vp], **O** [Vn.p]**:** soldier, troops; platoon, battalion. **S** [Vn.p]**:** sergeant-major, officer: *The company* **fell in** *and stood at ease.* ○ *Platoon sergeants* **fell** *their men* **in** *on the barrack square.* ↔ fall out 2.

3 [Vp] (*legal*) expire. **S:** lease, leasehold: *As the leases of these old properties* **fall in**, *they are being pulled down to make way for office blocks.*

fall in alongside/beside [Vp.pr] join a person or group that is already walking or marching along: *I* **fell in beside** *him and the three of us, with the kid sitting aloft, walked over the line.* CON ○ *Onlookers left the pavement and* **fell in alongside** *the marching demonstrators.*

fall in/into [Vp emph, Vpr emph rel] drop accidentally into (sth), eg by tripping over an obstacle. **A:** head over heels, head first, headlong. **o:** river, swimming-pool: *He thrust the hands forward, tore at the water and* **fell** *flat* **in** *the pool.* PM ○ *This reminded me of a rather fat boy who had once* **fallen** *head foremost* **into** *a muddy puddle.* SNP

fall in with 1 [Vp.pr rel] encounter, meet (sb); join or rejoin (sb) after an absence: *We* **fell in with** *a party of nomads encamped by a water-hole.* ○ *I crossed into Assam and* **fell in with** *our forces in Imphal.* ARG

2 [Vp.pr pass rel] show support for (sth). **o:** scheme, arrangement; proposal, suggestion: *He believed he had been looking forward to* **falling in with** *Alec's request.* PW ○ *For if Isobel had fallen in love with Alec, would she have* **fallen in with** *his scheme for getting hold of Irma?* PW

fall in love (with) [Vpr] feel a sudden, strong sexual attraction (for sb). **A:** madly, deeply, head over heels. **o:** (one's) pupil, neighbour, secretary: *But if Guy were* **falling in love with** *her, was she genuinely returning Guy's affection?* DC ○ *You're still crazy about Fergus. What are you going to do if he* **falls in love with** *another woman?* DC ↔ fall out of love (with).

fall into 1 [Vpr emph rel] (may) be divided into (parts); have a certain number of (components). **S:** lecture, article, subject. **o:** three sections, two parts, four main sections: *The present talk* **falls into** *three parts.* ○ *His works this century* **fall** *conveniently* **into** *three specific categories.* F

2 [Vpr emph rel] suddenly enter (a specific state). **o:** ⚠ a deep sleep; a trance; a coma: *The patient was given an injection and afterwards* **fell into** *a deep sleep.* ○ *When she* **fell into** *a trance, she was wholly possessed by the god.* GLEG = pass into 3. ⇨ go into 4.

3 [Vpr] acquire or develop (sth). **o:** ⚠ (bad, undesirable) habits, ways; the habit of doing sth: *It was to be expected that a young man with easy-going parents and considerable private means should keep bad company and* **fall into** *undesirable habits.* ○ *Paul had* **fallen into** *the habit of calling at his brother's flat on Thursday evenings.* = get into 7.

4 [Vpr emph rel] drop accidentally into sth. ⇨ fall in/into.

fall into decay [Vpr] become rotten or decayed, physically or morally. **S:** house, boat, factory, installation; monarchy, parliament, university: *During the long period of the Depression, the sheds and warehouses were allowed to* **fall into decay**. ○ *The laws and institutions of the republic had long* **fallen into decay**.

fall into a decline [Vpr rel] sink to a low level. **S:** country, economy; morals, arts: *Intense competition from overseas has caused much of our manufacturing industry to* **fall into a decline**. ○ *Without government help, these local theatres will not recover from the serious* **decline into** *which they have* **fallen**.

fall into a (deep) depression [Vpr rel] become dispirited or morally depressed: *After the loss of her second child, she* **fell into a depression** *from which it was difficult to rouse her.*

fall into disfavour [Vpr] ⇨ fall from/out of favour (with).

fall into disgrace [Vpr] reach a state where one is no longer respected or well regarded. **S:** minister, official; schoolboy: *A little indiscreet gossip isn't enough to make you* **fall into disgrace** *with all your friends.* ○ *After a well-publicized scandal, the minister* **fell into disgrace** *and was forced to resign.*

fall into disrepair [Vpr] through neglect, reach a state where repairs are needed. **S:** building; church, palace; machinery, mechanism: *The stonework of the tower was crumbling, and the great clock had* **fallen into disrepair**.

fall into disrepute [Vpr] lose one's good name or reputation. **S:** press, television; police, civil service: *The company has* **fallen into disrepute** *in* *recent years.* ○ *An examination system which cannot provide an objective measurement of aptitude must* **fall into disrepute**. ⇨ bring into disrepute.

fall into disuse [Vpr] reach the state of no longer being used. **S:** expression, phrase; practice, custom; ceremony: *Words which* **fall into disuse** *may sometimes be revived with a new meaning.*

fall into place [Vpr] (begin to) form an orderly, intelligible pattern. **S:** (scraps of) evidence, (parts of) the story, (pieces of) the puzzle: *'Of course, now that you tell me about the man's relationship with his wife, the whole picture* **falls into place**. *It explains, for instance, why he was always desperately short of money.'*

fall into sb's/the right etc hands [Vpr emph rel] be seized by sb; pass into sb's possession, care etc. **S:** document, map; evidence; refugee, escapee. **adj:** (the) right, wrong; enemy, foreign; friendly, allied: *Old Mother Curry's always there to help. It's a good thing you've* **fallen into the right hands**. HAA ○ *It is important that these letters should not* **fall into** *the wrong hands.*

fall into conversation (with) [Vpr] begin, esp on first meeting, to talk to (sb). **o:** (**with**) one's neighbour, fellow guest, visitor: *Next day at breakfast they presented Miss Evans, who* **fell into** *earnest* **conversation with** *him.* GE

fall into line (with) [Vpr] start to accept or follow (the views of others). **A:** tamely, abjectly; reluctantly. **o:** (**with**) the others, the majority; public opinion, the general view; what others think: *When the Chairman proposed a tightening-up of credit facilities, most of the Board* **fell into line**. ○ *After a period in the political wilderness, he has* **fallen** *back* **into line with** *the rest of the party.* = fall into step (with). ⇨ be in/bring into/come into line (with).

fall into step (with) [Vpr] begin to walk in step with sb; start to accept or follow (the views etc of others). **o:** (**with**) companion; marchers, procession; committee, political masters: *Charles followed him into the street, and* **fell into step** *as they trudged along.* HD ○ *Mr Powell ... gave the impression that he is just waiting for the day when England will* **fall into step with** *him.* OBS = fall into line (with).

fall off 1 [Vp] become smaller or fewer; lessen, decrease. **S:** orders, exports, takings, income: *Attendances at afternoon lectures have* **fallen off** *this term.* ○ *For the first and only time the circulation ... began to* **fall off**. CD ○ *Brian Phillips at Pan* (a paperback publisher) *notes a distinct* **falling-off** *in the south and especially in the south east.* BOOK □ nom form is falling-off. = drop off 1.

2 [Vp] get worse; deteriorate. **S:** standard, quality; service, catering: *The cooking* **fell off** *remarkably; I remember I several times had to go out to a restaurant to quell my hunger.* CON ○ *Our customers complain of a distinct* **falling-off** *in quality.* □ nom form is falling-off.

fall on [Vpr rel] take place on (a certain date); occur on. **S:** Easter, New Year's Day, Bank Holiday; his birthday, their anniversary. **o:** Monday, weekday: *His birthday* **falls on** *a Sunday this year.* ○ *What day does Christmas* **fall on**?

fall on deaf ears [Vpr] not be heard or noted, because others do not wish to listen. **S:** cry, shout (for help); appeal, plea; request, application: *His suggestion for a three-Power world-wide Western directorate* **fell on deaf ears**. SC ○ *Claims for a twenty per cent salary increase are likely to* **fall on deaf ears**.

fall on one's feet [Vpr] (*informal*) make a quick recovery after difficult times, often through good luck: *'He came back from the war penniless and landed a good job right away.' 'Yes, he has the knack of* **falling on his feet**, *hasn't he?'* ○ *'You got extra* (food etc, as a prisoner) *because you looked so clean and Nordic. Oh yes, you always* **fell on your feet**.*'* RATT = land on one's feet.

fall flat on one's face 1 [Vpr] (*informal*) fall to the ground suddenly and in an undignified way: *With a mighty heave, he succeeded in lifting both feet from the ground, and promptly* **fell flat on his face**. DF ○ *He had not gone many steps before he stumbled on the uneven ground and* **fell flat on his face**. BM

2 [Vpr] (*informal*) suffer an undignified setback or defeat (esp after attempting sth which is beyond one's powers). **S:** (young, inexperienced) politician, negotiator, salesman: *Don't imagine that you can get the better of him in argument. More experienced debaters than you have* **fallen flat on their faces** *before now.* ○ *If he tries to tackle that kind of market before he's made a thorough study, he'll* **fall flat on his face**.

fall on good/stony ground [Vpr] (of ideas etc) be well (or badly) received, so that they flourish and spread (or wither and die). **S:** teaching, preaching; ideas, philosophy: *Some seeds ...* **fell upon stony places**, *where they had not much earth ... But others* **fell into good ground**, *and brought forth fruit ....* BIBLE (MATT 13:3) ○ *He introduced me also to modern literature. ... This was an overwhelming experience because ... the seed* **fell on good ground**. *The books we loved grew and sprouted in the mind.* ST

fall on/to one's knees [Vpr] kneel down (to beg for favours or mercy). **S:** slave, suppliant, subject: *The prisoners* **fell on their knees** *to beg for clemency.*

fall on/upon 1 [Vpr] attack (sb) fiercely; seize (sth) greedily. **S:** soldier; bandit, thief; hungry child. **o:** convoy, column; booty, plunder; food: *Perseus was enraged. He* **fell on** *Dionysus with his sword, and the two fought together.* GLEG ○ *The 2nd Cavalry roamed the marshy length of the river Teberev,* **falling upon** *isolated units of German infantry.* B

2 [Vpr emph rel] be borne by or incurred by (sb). **S:** expense, cost; blame, burden, work; attack, fighting: *When anything goes wrong, the blame usually* **falls on** *his younger brother.* ○ *The full cost of the wedding* **fell on** *me.* ○ *It was* **on** *this part of the front that the main weight of the attack* **fell**.

3 [Vpr rel] (*formal*) (of sb) catch sight of (sb/sth). **S:** ⚠ his etc eye, gaze: *His eye* **fell on** *the letters he had not yet thought of opening.* BLCH ○ *His gaze* **fell upon** *a small party of men moving up the hillside.* ○ *His eyes* **fell on** *the looking-glass.* EHOW

fall on/upon sb's ears [Vpr emph] (*formal*) be heard, become audible. **S:** sound, noise; cry, shriek: *As we entered the temple, a curious chanting* **fell upon our ears**. ○ **Upon their ears fell** *a low, humming sound.*

fall on/upon evil days/hard times [Vpr] (*formal*) suffer hardship, misfortune. **S:** country; industry, farming; class, family: *West Point* (the US military academy) *has* ***fallen on hard times***. NS ○ *It was a nobleman's house, though* ***fallen upon evil days***. WDM

it fall on/upon sb to do sth [Vpr] (*formal*) be or become one's responsibility to do sth: ***It fell upon me to open*** *the exhibition in the mayor's absence* (or: *The responsibility for opening etc* ***fell upon me***). ⇨ fall on/upon 2.

fall out 1 [Vpr] (*formal*) happen, occur. **S:** ⚠ things, events; everything. **A:** thus, in this way; as arranged, as we had anticipated: *I was pleased with the way things had* ***fallen out***. UTN ○ *Everything* ***fell out*** *as we had planned.* □ an adv phrase or clause is usu present. ⇨ it fall out that.

2 [Vp, Vn ⇆ p pass] (*military*) (cause sb to) go off parade; dismiss. **S** [Vp], **O** [Vn.p]**:** soldier, platoon. **S** [Vn.p]**:** sergeant, officer: *At the end of the drill parade, the battalion* ***fell out***. ○ *The troops had been* ***fallen out*** *by the roadside.* ↔ fall in 2.

fall-out [nom (Vp)] radioactive dust, resulting from a nuclear explosion: *The claim made for the shelters is that they will protect people from radioactive* ***fall-out***. OBS ○ *'Dirty' bombs produce a higher level of* ***fall-out*** *than 'clean' ones.*

it fall out that [Vp] (*formal*) it happen that: *Thus* ***it fell out****, to Muriel's delight,* ***that*** *she was able to cross to Little Todday without arousing any possible suspicion.* RM ○ *How did* ***it fall out that*** *the two men arrived to address the same meeting at the same time?* = come about 1. ⇨ fall out 1.

fall out/out of [Vp, Vpr] fall from an enclosed space at a high level to a lower level. **S:** bird; baby, spectator. **o:** nest; cot, window: *'I'm so glad you didn't hurt yourself when you* ***fell out of*** *bed, Mrs Baye.'* DC ○ *'Hold on to the side of the boat. You'll* ***fall out****!'*

fall out (with) [Vp, Vp.pr rel] (*informal*) get on bad terms (with): *Mr J. L., a good-looking young man aged thirty -six, began to* ***fall out with*** *his wife.* BRN ○ *He has a knack of* ***falling out with*** *everyone.* PP ○ *'Did you and mother* ***fall out****?'* R

fall out of favour (with) [Vpr] ⇨ fall from/out of favour (with).

fall out of love (with) [Vpr] no longer be strongly attracted to (sb), convinced by (sb) etc. **o:** wife, witness; politician, party: *Sarah's not particularly fickle. She's just of an age when girls* ***fall*** *in and* ***out of love*** *all the time.* ○ *How would the leader's own morale stand up if there are to be repeated demonstrations that the voters are* ***falling out of love with*** *him?* OBS ↔ fall in love (with).

fall outside [Vpr] not be sth which one can handle, understand etc. **S:** matter, question; finance, housing. **o:** (one's) province, competence; field, area (of interest): *The improvement of school buildings and facilities* ***falls outside*** *the scope of the present inquiry.* = stand outside. ↔ fall within. ⇨ be outside.

fall over 1 [Vp] fall forward and to the ground, usu after slipping or tripping. **S:** old lady, small boy, footballer: *Johnny slipped on a banana skin and* ***fell over***. ○ *Mrs Jenkins missed her footing and* ***fell over***.

2 [Vp] (of a stationary object) fall from an upright to a horizontal position. **S:** vase, lamp-standard; monument: *A suit of armour* ***fell over*** *with a loud crash.*

fall over backwards to do sth/doing sth [Vp] (*informal*) take special care, go to great pains, esp to please sb. **A:** to appease, to placate others; to meet objections; trying to be fair: *But I think everybody* ***falls over backwards to be*** *fair to female doctors.* DIL ○ *They* ***fall over backwards to lay on*** *gracious service on a few favoured express trains.* T = bend over backwards to do sth/doing sth. ⇨ lean over backwards.

fall over oneself to do sth [Vpr] (*informal*) strive anxiously or eagerly, esp to achieve or obtain sth. **S:** host, salesman, employer. **Inf:** to buy, to win, to acquire; to retain, to protect: *The oil firms were* ***falling over themselves to obtain*** *concessions from the Government.* ○ *These people are* ***falling over themselves to keep*** *the British space effort confined to small satellites.* NS

fall overboard [Vp] (*nautical*) fall from the deck of a ship etc into the water: *The spaces between the rails on the promenade deck are so wide that it would be easy for a child to slip through and* ***fall overboard***. = go overboard.

fall through [Vp] fail, miscarry. **S:** scheme, plan, project; marriage, merger: *The scheme* ***fell through*** *because of some big business deal Ned had to stay and attend to.* CON ○ *We're not going to Spain after all — the whole thing's* ***fallen through***.

fall to 1 [Vp] (*dated*) begin (to eat, fight, work). **S:** guest, diner; contestants, team. **A:** with gusto, with enthusiasm: *A meal had been prepared. I* ***fell to*** *with ravenous appetite.* DOP = set to 1 .

2 [Vpr] (*dated*) start, begin. **o:** asking, thinking, considering, quarrelling: *I* ***fell to*** *brooding.* PP ○ *And she* ***fell to*** *wondering again who her enemy might be.* MM □ the object is the -ing form of a v.

fall to the ground [Vpr] collapse, crumble, for want of proof or evidence. **S:** theory; argument, case, contention: *This hypothesis* ***falls to the ground*** *because intelligence correlates only to a slight extent with 'good taste'.* SNP □ simple tenses only. = fall down 2.

fall to one's knees [Vpr] ⇨ fall on/to one's knees.

fall to sb/sb's lot [Vpr emph rel] (*formal*) become the concern or responsibility of (sb). **S:** task, work; arranging, organizing; to arrange, to organize; to design, to devise: *The work of investigation and social criticism* ***falls to the novelist***. NOED ○ *Other practical matters* ***fell to the lot of Alan****, who tackled them well and efficiently.* EB □ when the Subject is an inf, *it* is placed before fall to sb/sb's lot and the inf after it: *It* ***fell to my lot*** *to form an administration.* EM ○ *Anthony Trollope was doing his turn of duty, and it* ***fell to him****, a mere junior, to show the visiting royalty around.* TRO

fall to pieces [Vpr] be broken or shattered utterly. **S:** jug, cup; car, van; defence, argument, case: *No wonder the car's* ***falling to pieces***. *Have you seen how he drives it?* ○ *He was the coward whose cloak of broadminded, humane conduct had* ***fallen to pieces*** *in one moment.* HAA = fall apart.

fall (a) victim to [Vn.pr emph rel] be harmed or destroyed by (sth), either physically or in one's career, a relationship etc. **o:** attack, assault; wild animal; malaria, cancer; malice, intrigue: *A surviving brother of his* ***fell victim to*** *an unfriendly buffalo in Africa.* L ○ *The second son, a scientist uninvolved in any political action, . . .* ***fell a victim to*** *Stalin's vengeance.* ST ○ *Avoid the emotion, the* *sham rhetoric,* **to** *which politicians … have also* ***fallen victim.*** L

fall under [Vpr] be classified as (sth); be placed within the category of (sth). **S:** matter, question; item. **o:** heading, head; (the heading of) petty cash, foreign trade: *Does the entertainment of visitors* ***fall under*** *the heading of miscellaneous expenditure?* ○ *'No, we're not discussing the Christmas appeal just yet. That* ***falls under*** *"any other business".'* = come under 3.

fall under sb's/the spell [Vpr rel] be charmed, captivated, by (sb). **S:** follower; pupil, patient: *The newly-selected candidate addressed the women's branch, and the entire audience* ***fell under his spell.*** ○ *His fellow-townsmen* ***fell under the*** *same* ***spell****, but finally it was broken and he had to carry out his great plans in actual fact.* SNP

fall upon 1 [Vpr] attack (sb) fiercely. ⇨ fall on/upon 1.
2 [Vpr emph rel] be borne by (sb). ⇨ fall on/upon 2.
3 [Vpr rel] catch sight of (sb/sth). ⇨ fall on/upon 3.

fall upon sb's ears [Vpr emph] ⇨ fall on/upon sb's ears.

fall upon evil days/hard times [Vpr] ⇨ fall on/upon evil days/hard times.

it fall upon sb to do sth [Vpr] ⇨ it fall on/upon sb to do sth.

fall within [Vpr] be sth which one is able to discuss or handle. **S:** question, matter. **o:** (one's) competence, province; field, area (of interest): *The allocation of funds for research projects does not* ***fall within*** *the competence of this committee.* ↔ fall outside. ⇨ be within 2.

fan

fan out [Vp] move away from each other, while advancing. **S:** troops, search party, hunters: *The Army was* ***fanning out*** *north of Naples.* SD ○ *Police with tracker dogs were* ***fanning out*** *over the moor.* = spread out 3.

fancy

fancy oneself as [Vpr] (*informal*) consider that one is well suited to a certain role, or that one does a particular job well, even though one may have little aptitude, training etc. **o:** lover, father; actor, painter; driver, handyman: *He was a clerk at the works.* ***Fancied himself as*** *a writer.* RATT ○ *If you* ***fancy yourself as*** *a nurse then go down to Aldgate, we've got a first-aid post there.* CSWB ○ *He thought she rather* ***fancied herself as*** *a Hero's Widow.* BRH

farm

farm out [Vn ⇆ p pass] give (sb/sth) to others to be responsible for or to manage. **S:** mother; firm. **O:** child; work, responsibilities: *You are* ***farming*** *your baby* ***out*** *on that unspeakable woman.* AITC ○ *Fostering. This is the* ***farming out*** *of little babies, more or less from birth, for almost any length of time.* BRN ○ *The work of producing the many electrical components has been* ***farmed out*** *to small manufacturers.*

fasten

fasten on/upon [Vpr pass emph rel] choose (sth/sb) in a keen, alert way for special comment, criticism or attention. **o:** idea, suggestion, proposal; weakness; girl, student: *A more serious problem was* ***fastened upon*** *by the treasurer. 'Have you considered the likelihood of rising interest rates?' he asked.* ○ *Some wealthy, fair-haired girl would* ***fasten on*** *him and marry him before he knew what he was doing.* INN = seize on/upon.

father

father on/upon [Vn.pr pass emph rel] claim that (sb) is the father, author or originator of (sb/sth). **O:** child, offspring; manuscript, book; device, gadget: *'Don't look at me: I had nothing to do with the idea. Try* ***fathering*** *it* ***on*** *someone else.'*

fathom

fathom out [Vn ⇆ p pass] (try to) discover, or devise, an explanation for (sth). **O:** it, things; why he had done it, where they had gone: *I could have sworn I left my keys on the desk. I can't* ***fathom out*** *where they've got to.* ○ *Don't tell me the answer; let me try to* ***fathom*** *it* ***out*** *for myself.*

fatten

fatten on/upon [Vpr emph rel] grow fat, rich etc at the expense of (sb else). **S:** idler, parasite, sponger. **o:** efforts, toil, sweat (of others, of the poor): *It is a distortion to represent the owners of industry in western countries as a small and indolent class* ***fattening on*** *the labours of others.*

fatten up [Vn ⇆ p pass adj] give (sb/an animal) plenty to eat, causing him/it to gain weight. **O:** underweight child; livestock: *I'm trying to* ***fatten*** *him* ***up*** *as fast as I can.* BFA ○ *The pigs are being* ***fattened up*** *for market.*

fawn

fawn (on) [Vpr pass] attempt to win the favour of (sb) by servile behaviour. **o:** employer, teacher; the rich, the powerful: *He* ***fawns on*** *anyone in an influential position.* ○ *Don't try to win his support in that way — he hates to be* ***fawned on****.*

fear

fear for [Vpr] feel anxious about the health etc of sb, or the future development of events. **o:** sb's health, life, survival; the future, the development (of sth): *The miners' families* ***fear for*** *the lives of the men trapped underground.* ○ *'Don't attempt to climb on that very difficult rock-face. I should* ***fear for*** *your safety.'* ○ *He is downcast, and* ***fears for*** *his job as a concert hall director.* LFM

feature

feature in [Vpr emph rel, Vn.pr pass emph rel] (cause sb to) play a part in (sth). **S** [Vpr], **O** [Vn.pr]**:** actress; dancer, pianist. **o:** play, film; series; article, journal: *Fred Astaire and Ginger Rogers* ***featured in*** *three movie musicals before 'Top Hat' secured their reputation as an international starring team.* ○ *He was* ***featured in*** *one of the Sunday colour supplements happily engraving glass.* SU

feed

feed back (into/to) 1 [Vn ⇆ p nom pass, Vn.p.pr pass] (*radio, electronics*) return part of the output of a circuit as an input to the preceding stage of that circuit. **O:** signal, oscillation; information. **o:** stage; circuit; appliance, device: *Part of the output of an amplifier can be* ***fed back*** *to get rid of sound distortion* (cf *Amplifier* ***feedback*** *can get rid of sound distortion*). □ usu nom or passive as here.
2 [Vp nom, Vp.pr] (of a hearer's unconscious gestures or expressions, or conscious comments) indicate to a speaker, teacher etc how well he is being received, so enabling him to adapt to his audience; (of ideas etc) return in an altered or extended form to their point of origin, so making

possible still more progress. **S:** response, reaction; experience, knowledge; ideas, techniques. **o:** research, industry: *The teachers complain that nothing is* **feeding back to** *them from the classroom* (cf *that there is no* **feedback** *from the classroom*). ○ *A lot of ideas are* **feeding back** *from the applied sciences (such as agriculture or metallurgy)* **into** *the pure sciences (such as botany or chemistry)* (cf *There is a lot of* **feedback** *from the applied to the pure sciences).* □ usu nom.

feed in/into [Vn ⇆ p pass, Vn.pr pass emph rel] introduce or deliver (sth) into (a machine, process etc). **O:** cloth, tubing, wire; bullets; components; information. **o:** sewing machine, cutter; machine gun; workshop; computer: *It's simple. You* **feed in** *the information and out comes the answer.* HWKM ○ *Materials are* **fed into** *the processor from a revolving drum.*

feed off [Vpr pass rel] use (sth) as a source or supplier of food, materials, energy etc. **S:** outpost, station, factory, machine; newspaper, radio station; author, teacher. **o:** base, depot; power-station, generator; news agency; idea, thought: *When fresh food and water are not available, the camel can* **feed off** *its hump.* ○ *The central services of the BBC to some extent* **feed off** *the regional stations.* ⇨ feed on.

feed on [Vpr emph rel, Vn.pr pass emph rel] (cause sb to) have as (food etc). **S** [Vpr], **O** [Vn.pr]**:** cattle, chickens; dog, goldfish; child; public, electorate; student. **S** [Vn.pr]**:** farmer; owner; parent; dictator, propaganda machine; teacher. **o:** cake, corn; scraps; milk, meat; lies, pap; information: *'Of course the children look undernourished. Their mothers can't afford to* **feed** *them* **on** *meat and fish every day!'* ○ *I'm not surprised that his classes never express an original thought when the stuff they're* **fed on** *is second and even third hand.* ⇨ feed off 1.

feed up [Vn.p pass] bring (sb) to his proper weight by giving him nourishing food. **O:** patient, convalescent; orphan, refugee: *'I think he looks half-starved. Wants* **feeding up**. *I'll find him a good fat kipper.'* DBM

fed up (with) [pass adj (Vn.p)] (*informal*) depressed or irritated (by sth/sb); having had enough (of sth/sb). **o:** manner, attitude; climate, place, job; wife, husband. **A:** thoroughly, utterly; to the back teeth: *They were getting a bit* **fed up with** *her by that time, so they wrote her rather a sharp letter.* RFW ○ *I'm* **fed up with** *being wholesome. I long to be seductive and tempting.* RATT ○ *The public is* **fed up** *to the back teeth* **with** *the dispute.* BBCR □ used with appear etc. = tire of.

feel

feel for 1 [Vpr rel] search for (sth) with the hands. **o:** light-switch, door-knob; wallet, purse; wall, door: *Prissie's fingers pressed the catch of the locket and from habit* **felt for** *the folded paper within.* DC ○ *In the gathering darkness he had to* **feel for** *the kerb with his walking-stick.*

2 [Vpr] feel sympathy for (sb); sympathize with. **o:** unhappy, distressed (person); the bereaved, the homeless; orphan, refugee: *It's easy enough to* **feel for** *people in need; it's harder to bring yourself to do something practical about it.*

feel in one's bones (that) [Vn.pr emph] (*informal*) sense or suspect instinctively or intuitively (that sth is the case). **O:** it; that he is untrustworthy, that something was amiss, that trouble was afoot: *I* **felt in in my bones that** *Archer didn't do him justice and I wanted to make sure.* HAA ○ *I knew that something of the sort would happen. I* **felt** *it* **in my bones.**

feel like [Vpr] feel in the mood for (sth); fancy. **o:** party, night out, drive in the country; walking, drinking, dancing: *He didn't* **feel like** *anything to eat.* TO ○ *Those who* **felt like** *hearing the story again came over and added themselves to the audience.* HD

feel on top of the world [Vpr] (*informal*) feel very light-hearted, in good spirits: *'You look depressed, Peter.' 'I'm not depressed. I'm* **feeling on top of the world**.*' 'Are you? You don't sound at all convincing.'* ○ *'He's got every reason to* **feel on top of the world** *— a beautiful wife, talented children, no financial worries.' 'It all sounds marvellous. Where's the catch?'*

feel out of it/things [Vpr] (*informal*) feel that one is not fully sharing in an experience, either because of shyness, or because one is unused to the company, conversation etc: *Not that she* **felt out of it**; *her nature was a silent one and she could sit quietly while people talked without* **feeling out of things** *herself or making other people feel embarrassed.* WDM

feel out of place [Vpr] not feel at home, comfortable, at one's ease etc, because the place, or one's companions, are foreign, of a different social background etc: *Many of us would* **feel out of place** *in a duke's drawing room or a bishop's palace.* ○ *I want to work here, where I know what people are like. Not in another country, where I would* **feel out of place**. AITC

feel up to [Vp.pr] (*informal*) feel able to (do sth), feel capable of (undertaking sth). **o:** much; sustained effort, long journey; meeting, working; it: *I don't know whether George* **feels up to** *opening presents.* EGD ○ *When I suggested that I should walk part of the way, he said: 'Of course, if you* **feel up to** *it.'* NM ⇨ be up to 6.

fence

fence in 1 [Vn ⇆ p pass adj] enclose (a space, or animals) with a fence. **O:** garden, orchard; field, meadow; stock, cattle: *Thousands of acres of open prairie were* **fenced in** *to prevent cattle grazing freely.* ○ *It was some two acres in extent, neatly* **fenced in** *with tall palms.* DF ⇨ hedge in 1.

2 [Vn ⇆ p pass adj] restrict the freedom of (sb). **S:** regulation; rule; manners, customs; requirement, duty: *He felt* **fenced in** *by domesticity, by his nine-to-five daily routine, by the social demands of suburban living.* ○ *'Don't* **fence** *me* **in**, *Mary, don't make me feel trapped.'* = hedge in 2, hem in.

fence off (from) [Vn ⇆ p pass adj, Vn.p.pr pass rel] separate (one area) (from another) by means of a fence. **O:** playground, flower-garden; private land; rubbish tip: *The children can't play in the front garden until its been* **fenced off from** *the main road.* ⇨ rail off (from), wall off (from).

fend

fend for oneself [Vpr] keep house, feed oneself etc, without outside help: *The old couple have no one to do the washing and heavy cleaning: they have* *to **fend for themselves**.* ○ *The rations issued to the patrols would last for two days; after that they would **fend for themselves**.*

fend off 1 [Vn ⇆ p pass adj] turn (sth) aside to protect oneself; deflect. **O:** blow, thrust; rapier, dagger: *D'Artagnan neatly **fended off** a thrust at his chest.* = ward off 1.

2 [Vn ⇆ p pass adj] prevent (sth) from affecting or hurting one. **O:** question, challenge; jibe, attack, criticism: *Instead of bothering to **fend off** the sneer, I just said simply, 'Yes'*. CON = ward off 2.

ferret

ferret out [Vn ⇆ p pass] find, discover (sth) by searching carefully. **O:** letter, document; reference, detail; information, fact: *He **ferreted out** my address from somewhere, and wrote to ask how I was doing.* CON ○ *They have overlooked another aspect, one that's more difficult to **ferret out**.* HD

festoon

festoon with [Vn.pr pass rel] decorate (sth) with chains of flowers etc, which hang in loops. **O:** street, house; wall, door; curtain; book. **o:** flowers, leaves; ivy; paper-chains, ribbons; squiggles, notes: *The children had **festooned** the Christmas tree **with** tinsel and fairy lights.* ○ *The margins of his notebook were **festooned with** doodles.*

fetch

fetch up [Vp] (*informal*) eventually arrive (in a place): *We all **fetched up** simultaneously at the same spot.* SPL ○ *She left him a little time before she **fetched up** in Forfar and came to you.* RFW = land up.

fight

fight back 1 [Vp nom] respond vigorously to an attack made on oneself; retaliate: *'His attack on our work came as a great shock, but we have every intention of **fighting back** through the media.'* ○ *'We are meeting this afternoon to organize our **fight-back**.'*

2 [Vp.n pass] try hard not to let (a feeling) overwhelm one. **O:** tears; emotion; panic, nerves: *As the train began to draw out, she **fought back** the impulse to jump aboard.* ○ *The children **fought back** their tears.*

fight (one's way) back (to) [Vp, Vp.pr emph rel, Vn.p, Vn.p.pr emph rel] return, by struggling hard (to a position held previously). **S:** country, firm; politician; patient. **o:** position, place; the top; perfect health: [Vp] *Still he **fought back**, and there were even moments when he felt, fleetingly, the old symptoms of vitality and spiritual health.* HD ○ [Vn.p.pr] *After several reverses, they **fought their way back to** their old seats on the Board.*

fight down [Vn ⇆ p pass] control (strong feelings); suppress; hold in check. **O:** anger, rage, disappointment, revulsion: *He told me what the trouble was. He **fought** it **down** and as the minutes passed I thought he was going to win out.* TBC

fight off 1 [Vn ⇆ p pass adj] force (sb/sth) to withdraw; repel, defeat. **O:** attack, assault; tank, aircraft; insect, pest: *All the infantry attacks were **fought off** with heavy loss.* = drive off 3.

2 [Vn ⇆ p pass] prevent (sb/sth) from approaching one or gaining control. **O:** girlfriend, boyfriend; salesman; cold, bug: *He's been **fighting** Monica **off** for months but no doubt she'll catch him in the end.* ○ *'Everyone's been going down with this virus, but I think I've **fought** it **off**.'*

fight it out [Vn.p] (*informal*) fight until a conclusion is reached. **S:** troops, armies; lawyers, accountants: *Mixed groups of tanks and infantry **fought it out** with the enemy in sub-zero temperatures.* ○ *Don't interfere in a matrimonial squabble — let husband and wife **fight it out** between themselves.*

figure

figure in [Vpr emph rel] have a role in (sth); feature in. **o:** play, novel; account, report; list, programme; talks, negotiations: *Many characters in Balzac's 'Human Comedy' **figure in** more than one novel or story.* ○ ***In** the negotiations leading to Britain's accession to the European Community Mr Heath **figured** prominently.*

figure out 1 [Vn ⇆ p pass] calculate, reckon (sth). **S:** accountant, bursar, treasurer. **O:** pay, allowance; cost, expense; that it will cost £300, how much to spend: *We'd already **figured out** that the trip would cost £2 000.* ○ *The cost of the operation will need to be **figured out** very precisely.* = work out 2.

2 [Vn ⇆ p pass] find the answer to (sth); solve. **O:** problem, riddle, code; what to do, how to react: *We can't **figure out** why he's been behaving so oddly.* = puzzle out, work out 3.

file

file across, along, away etc [Vp emph, Vpr emph rel] go across etc in a single line: *The men **filed across** a narrow footbridge.* ○ *The staff **filed into** the canteen for their mid-morning break.*

file away [Vn ⇆ p pass] put (sth) away in an office file. **S:** secretary, clerk. **O:** letter, circular; report, record: *'Just **file** this correspondence **away** under 'Forecasts of Sales', will you please?'* ○ *Heaven knows what the Ministry does with our production figures. **Files** them **away** somewhere, I suppose.*

fill

fill in 1 [Vn ⇆ p pass] enter (sth) in writing. **O:** particulars, details; name, occupation: *There were many details to be **filled in** and a detailed plan to be drawn up.* MFM ○ ***Fill in** your address at the bottom of the application form.* = write in/into 1. ⇨ fill in/out/up.

2 [Vn ⇆ p pass adj] make (a hole etc) level with the surrounding surface by filling it. **O:** hole, trench, fireplace: *If we **fill in** that old fireplace, we'll have a wall free for bookshelves.* ○ *The ruts must be **filled in** so that traffic can pass.*

fill in time [Vp.n] spend the interval between two stages in one's career in a temporary job: *Girls who are not so much in demand often **fill in time** working in department stores and coffee bars.* H ○ *Tim is just doing odd jobs — **filling in time** before he starts at university.*

fill in (for) [Vp, Vp.pr] do the work of (sb) on a given occasion, eg because that person is ill or absent: *'Betty's off sick; we'd better find someone to **fill in**.'* ○ *'Would you **fill in for** me at this week's research meeting?'* = stand in (for) 1.

fill in (on) [Vn ⇆ p pass, Vn.p.pr pass] (*informal*) give (sb) up-to-date information (about sth). **o:** latest exploit, recent move, future plan, actual situation: *She always **fills** us **in on** what her programme is.* TGLY ○ *As we drove off, I was **filled in on** the latest developments at the London office.* = bring up to date.

fill in/out/up [Vn ⇆ p pass adj] complete (a form) in writing by supplying the information required. **O:** form, application, tax-return: *What's a doctor for? Not to sit all day* ***filling out*** *forms for the National Health.* AITC ○ *We asked Mr Charlton if he had yet* ***filled up*** *the forms.* BFA ○ *'I'm afraid your application for benefit is incorrectly* ***filled in****.'* ⇨ fill in 1.

fill out 1 [Vp] gain in weight; grow rounder or fatter. **S:** he etc; face, cheeks: *He's* ***filled out*** *a lot with all the good food and regular exercise he's been having.*

2 [Vn ⇆ p pass] make (sth) fuller, more substantial, by adding material. **O:** story, account; treatment. **A:** a bit, a little, a lot: *The manuscript might be usable, the editor wrote, if the author could* ***fill*** *it* ***out*** *a little.* ARG ○ *As a series of episodes, I find this book entertaining; it would be much more successful if the story-line were* ***filled out*** *a bit.*

fill up 1 [Vp, Vn ⇆ p pass] (cause sth to) become completely full. **S** [Vp], **O** [Vn.p]**:** gutter, channel; reservoir; stadium, theatre: *Following the recent heavy rains, the storage tanks are* ***filling up*** *again.* ○ *All parts of the theatre were quickly* ***filling up****.* ○ *'I've* ***filled up*** *all the buckets I can lay my hands on.'* ○ *'Please* ***fill up*** *(the hall) from the front — the speaker's voice won't carry to the back.'*

2 [Vn ⇆ p nom pass] make (sth) completely full, esp with drink or fuel. **O:** glass, jug; (petrol-)tank, radiator: (request to a barman to refill glasses) *'****Fill*** *'em* ***up*** *again!'* ○ (request to a garage attendant to fill one's tank) *'****Fill*** *her* ***up*** *with unleaded, please!'* ○ *'Let's stop at the next garage for a* ***fill-up****.'* ○ *'Here's a glass that needs* ***filling up*** (or: *needs* ***a fill-up***).'

find

find against [Vpr] (*legal*) find (sb) guilty in a court of law. **S:** court; magistrate, jury. **o:** plaintiff, defendant: *We* ***find against*** *the defendant and order him to pay costs in the sum of £1000.* = decide against 1. ⇨ next entry

find for [Vpr] (*legal*) reach a verdict in favour of (sb). **S:** court, jury. **o:** plaintiff, defendant: *When the case went to Appeal, the judges* ***found for*** *the defendant.* = decide for/in favour of. ⇨ previous entry

(not) find it in oneself/one's heart to do sth [Vn.pr] be unable, through kindheartedness or delicacy of feeling, to do sth. **Inf:** to criticize, to blame, to punish, to kill: *I cannot* ***find it in myself to condemn*** *a mother who steals food for a hungry child.* ○ *He nearly* ***found it in his heart to apologize.*** OMIH

find out 1 [Vp, Vp.n pass] learn (sth) by study, calculation, or inquiry. **O:** answer, cost, size; when we leave, whether to go; that the disease is curable, that resistance is futile: *I know nothing about this job, but* ***finding out*** *will be enjoyable.* ○ *When you can't account for money, do you feel a need to* ***find out*** *what you have done with it?* WI ○ *It was* ***found out*** *that many evacuees progressed faster at school than children who had not left the home environment.*

2 [Vp, Vp.n] discover a mistake, a loss, sb's dishonesty etc. **O:** where the money went, what has been happening, how the loss occurred: *You'd better send on another fifty pounds to stop their* ***finding out****.* DC ○ *One day someone will start asking questions and* ***find out*** *precisely why we've been losing so much money.*

3 [Vn.p pass] discover that sb has been misbehaving, acting dishonestly etc: *He can't go on making false tax returns. The tax inspector is bound to* ***find*** *him* ***out*** *sooner or later.* ○ *'You won't get away with this. You'll be* ***found out****!'*

find an answer/a solution (to) [Vn.pr pass emph rel] be able to solve (sth). **S:** science, technology; religion, philosophy; government, industry. **o:** question; riddle, puzzle; dilemma, quandary: ***A solution*** *has not yet been* ***found to*** *the fundamental problems of industrial relations.* SC ○ *These are questions* ***to*** *which we shall not* ***find*** *easy* ***answers****.*

find favour with [Vn.pr emph rel] (*formal*) appear favourable to (sb) and so be well received by him. **S:** petitioner, suitor; scheme, project; proposal, idea. **o:** king, court; committee, board; public, electorate: *The king's new mistress did not* ***find favour with*** *the court.* ○ *This was obviously a reasonable suggestion; it didn't however,* ***find favour with*** *the men.* ARG

finish

finish off 1 [Vn ⇆ p pass] bring (sth) to a conclusion; end. **O:** conflict, battle; discussion, dispute: *I finally said we must* ***finish off*** *the war in Italy quickly.* MFM

2 [Vn ⇆ p pass] destroy, kill (sb/sth). **O:** victim, prey, prisoner: *This last unhappy warrior had been* ***finished off*** *by a cut on the head.* SD ○ *That last climb nearly* ***finished*** *me* ***off****.*

finish off/up [Vn ⇆ p pass] eat or drink every bit or drop of (sth): *Smith came round for a chat and* ***finished off*** *the remains of my whisky.* ○ *'Do* ***finish up*** *the fruit salad — it'll only go to waste if you don't.'* = polish off 1. ↔ begin (with).

finish off/up (with) [Vp, Vp.pr emph rel] end, conclude, a festive occasion, performance etc (by having or doing sth). **o:** cigar, brandy, port; loyal toast, rousing speech, Auld Lang Syne: *The Male Voice Choir* ***finished off with*** *a rousing chorus* (or: ***finished off*** *by singing* etc). ○ *We had Madeira and nuts to* ***finish up with****.* = end up (with).

finish up [Vp] eventually become or do (sth); end (as sth). **o:** exhausted, dead; broke, penniless; a pauper; in prison; like his father; digging ditches: *'Be careful how you carry that tray — you could* ***finish up*** *spilling the lot!'* = end up, wind up 7.

finish with 1 [Vpr] end a relationship or connection with (sb/sth). **o:** girlfriend, husband; firm, business; academic life: *'I've* ***finished with*** *our greengrocer for good: half the potatoes he sold me yesterday were rotten right through.'* ○ *Helen's* ***finished with*** *schoolteaching — she's looking for a nice, well-paid job in industry.*

2 [Vpr] finish using, consulting etc (sth); have no further need of (sb). **o:** newspaper, book: *'Have you* ***finished with*** *our lawn-mower yet? We shall be needing it this week-end.'* ○ *Scobie stood up. 'May I go, Sir, if these gentlemen have* ***finished with*** *me?'* HOM □ usu with perfect tenses.

3 [Vpr] finish chastising or punishing (sb): *'Before I've* ***finished with*** *you, you'll regret the day you were born!'* ○ *'No, he can't go. I haven't* ***finished with*** *him yet!'* □ usu with perfect tenses.

fire

fire ahead/away [Vp] (*informal*) start questioning: *'I want to ask you something.' 'Ask on', Pop said. '**Fire away**.'* BFA □ usu imperative.

fire off [Vn ⇆ p pass] use up (sth), esp by shooting; expend. **O:** ammunition; magazine, belt (of cartridges); bullets, rockets; questions, curses: *With this machine gun you could never **fire off** more than two magazines without a break. The barrel would get too hot, and you'd need to change it or allow it to cool down.* ○ *'Now then, ladies and gentlemen, if you've **fired off** all your questions I think we might let the speaker have a rest.'*

firm

firm up [Vn ⇆ p pass adj] put (sth) in a fixed and settled form. **O:** deal, arrangement, agreement: *'We've agreed on the essentials. We can **firm** the deal **up** by letter in a few days.'*

fish

fish for [Vpr pass adj] (*informal*) try to obtain (sth) by hints etc. **o:** compliments, applause; story, information: *Don't be taken in by his charm: he's **fishing for** an invitation to the big party.* ○ *She was a vain but constantly sought after young woman: the **fished-for** compliments were never slow in coming.* = angle for.

fish out/out of [Vn ⇆ p pass, Vn.pr pass] (*informal*) take out, raise (sth/sb) (from a place). **O:** coin, handkerchief; tin can, dead body. **o:** pocket, drawer; river, canal: (stage direction) *Mrs Bryant leaves washing up to **fish out** some curtains.* R ○ *Several derelict cars are **fished out of** the canal every month.*

fit

fit in/into 1 [Vn ⇆ p pass, Vn.pr pass amph rel] find space or room for (sth) in (a place). **O:** table, bed; case, box. **o:** room, office; boot (of a car), chest, trunk: *'I don't see how we can **fit in** any more chairs.'* ○ *'Try to **fit** the stereo **into** the space beside the bookcase.'*

2 [Vn ⇆ p pass, Vn.pr emph rel] find a time for (sb) in (a programme). **O:** patient, customer. **o:** programme, list (of appointments), schedule: *'Sorry, I can't **fit in** any more callers this morning.'* ○ *Mrs Smith will have to be **fitted in** next week.* ○ ***Into** that one hour on Monday I shall have to **fit** about five appointments.*

3 [Vp, Vpr rel] live in harmony (in a particular group) because one's background, interests etc are similar to those of the other members. **S:** newcomer, immigrant. **o:** group, class; project, programme: *How would they **fit in**, in this new land?* WI ○ *She's **fitted into** our new set-up very well.*

fit in with [Vp.pr] match, suit (sth). **S:** statement, claim; behaviour; arrangement, plan. **o:** facts, record; sb's appearance, the declared aim; yours: *The answer disappoints you or doesn't appear to **fit in with** your temperament.* WI ○ *At least my ideas work. Because they **fit in with** the way life's lived.* TGLY ○ *Our holiday must be timed to **fit in with** yours.* ↔ clash (with) 3.

fit out [Vn ⇆ p pass adj] supply to (sb/sth) new equipment, stores, or clothes. **O:** ship, garrison; house; children, recruit: *The 'Discoverer' is being **fitted out** for a new expedition to the Arctic.* ○ *I went to a large clothes shop where they could **fit** you **out** for anything.* DIL □ an outfit is a suit of clothes etc with which one has been fitted out. = kit out (with).

fit up 1 [Vn ⇆ p pass] install, mount (sth). **O:** lamp, wash-basin, desk: *There's room at the end of the garage to **fit up** a work-bench.* ○ *The most up-to-date appliances have been **fitted up** in the new flats* (cf *The new flats have been **fitted up with** the appliances*). ⇨ fit up (with).

2 [Vn ⇆ p nom pass] (*informal*) by providing false evidence etc, make (sb) seem guilty of a crime: *'I was nowhere near the West End that night, and they know it. I've been **fitted up**.'* = frame up, stitch up 2.

fit up (with) [Vn ⇆ p pass, Vn.pr pass rel] give (sth) as equipment to (sb/sth). **O:** patient, handicapped person; house, workshop. **o:** artificial limb, hearing aid; appliance, gadget: *If you speak to your oculist he'll see that you're **fitted up with** new spectacles.* ○ *He's had the new place **fitted up with** every labour-saving device.* = equip (with). ⇨ fit up 1 .

fix

fix on/onto [Vn ⇆ p pass adj, Vn.pr pass emph rel] attach, fasten (sth) (to sth). **O:** button, clip; switch, dial. **o:** jacket, dress; radio, motor: *' **Fix** me **on** a new zip — the old one's broken.'* ○ *I want the garage to **fix** a rev-counter **onto** the dashboard — a sports car should look sporty.* □ note the Indirect Object (*me*) in the first example.

fix on/upon [Vn.pr pass emph rel] (*formal*) look intently at (sb/sth). **O:** ⚠ one's gaze; one's eyes, attention. **o:** her face; the scene, spectacle: *Throughout the display his gaze was **fixed on** the horsemen in the foreground.* ○ ***On** this golden prospect all his attention was now **fixed**.* = gaze at.

fix up 1 [Vn ⇆ p pass] make (sth) quickly from any materials that are available. **O:** workroom, darkroom, playroom; bench, desk, shelter: *She's **fixed up** a temporary desk for herself from packing cases and an old plank.* ○ *The boys have **fixed up** a den among the trees at the bottom of the garden.* = rig up.

2 [Vn ⇆ p pass] (*informal*) arrange for (sth) to take place; organize. **O:** meeting, talks; lunch; trip, tour: *'I haven't done anything about my trip to Madrid yet.' 'Why not get a travel agent to **fix** it **up** for you?'* ○ *'Try to **fix** me **up** an appointment for eleven tomorrow morning.'* □ note the Indirect Object (*me*) in the second example.

fix up (with) [Vn ⇆ p pass, V n.p.pr pass] (*informal*) arrange for (sb) to have (sth/sb). **O:** friend, relative; oneself. **o:** room, job, meal; girlfriend: *He's **fixed** himself **up with** a very smart flat on the seafront.* ○ *Charlie had **fixed** him **up with** one of his former girlfriends.* ○ *'You can sleep here if you like ... Till you ... get yourself **fixed up**.* TC

fix it/things up (with) [Vn.p pass, Vn.p.pr pass] (*informal*) arrange for sth (not) to take place, by using persuasion, influence etc: *'You won't go to gaol. I've **fixed it up**.'* AITC ○ *The whole team can leave school early today. John's **fixed things up with** the Headmaster.*

fix with [Vn.pr] (*formal*) look intently at (sb), esp in an unfriendly or hostile way. **o:** ⚠ a (cold, fishy) stare, an (intent, angry) look; a (terrifying) glare: *She **fixed** him **with** a fierce, censorious eye. 'Out of the question,' she said again.* BMTD

fizzle

fizzle out [Vp] (*informal*) end in a feeble and unsatisfactory way. **S:** scheme, attack, argument, enthusiasm: *His protest* ***fizzled out****.* NM ○ *The first and only attempt to tax the British gambler* ***fizzled out****.* SC

flag

flag down [Vn ⇆ p pass adj] stop (sth/sb) by waving with a flag or, more usually, the hand. **S:** traffic police, hitchhiker. **O:** passing car, taxi: *A student hitchhiking to London* ***flagged*** *me* ***down*** *on the A1.* = wave down.

flake

flake away/off [Vp] separate, detach itself, in flakes. **S:** paint, stucco, pebbledash, rust: *We scraped at the woodwork, and the paint just* ***flaked away****.*

flake out [Vp] (*informal*) fall asleep from exhaustion; faint: *After the guests had gone and the dishes were cleared away, we simply* ***flaked out*** *in a couple of armchairs.* ○ *Some poor old dear had* ***flaked out*** *in the waiting room.*

flare

flare up 1 [Vp] suddenly begin to burn more brightly or fiercely. **S:** fire, candle, lamp: *We blew hard with the bellows until the charcoal* ***flared up****.* ○ *The flames* ***flared up*** *briefly, then finally died away.* = burn up 1.

2 [Vp nom] suddenly enter an angry or violent state. **S:** boss, husband; fighting, battle: *Robert looked as if he were about to* ***flare up*** *and tell me to mind my own business.* CON ○ *The war will all* ***flare up*** *again and everyone says it will be much worse than before.* RFW ○ *The Southern Area commander reported a sudden* ***flare-up*** *of fighting on his front.*

flash

flash across [Vp, Vpr emph] cross (a surface etc) like a sudden, bright light. **S:** lightning, meteor; jet, rocket; expression, smile. **o:** sky, horizon; face: *A flight of aircraft* ***flashed*** *low* ***across*** *the field.* ○ *A sudden smile of recognition* ***flashed across*** *his face.*

flash (at) [Vn.pr emph rel] send a sudden bright look etc (at sb). **O:** ⚠ a look, glance; a smile: *Mother* ***flashed*** *a reassuring smile* ***at*** *the child.* ○ *She* ***flashed*** *a discreet glance* ***at*** *the young man seated in the corner of the compartment* (or: *She* ***flashed*** *the young man a discreet glance*).

flash back (to) [Vp, Vp.pr rel] return quickly in one's thoughts (to some earlier event). **S:** ⚠ mind, thoughts. **o:** event, episode, incident; meeting, reunion; remark, comment; what Peter had said: *Her mind* ***flashed back to*** *something that had taken place only the week before.* ○ *My thoughts* ***flashed back to*** *the meeting in his New York office.*

flashback [nom (Vp)] (*cinema*) a return during a film either to events that have already been shown, or to events that occurred before the main action of the film began: *The main action of the film portrayed the hero's adult life; scenes from his boyhood were shown in* ***flashback****.*

flash into [Vpr emph] enter (a place) like a sudden bright light. **S:** aeroplane, train; thought, idea; recollection. **o:** ⚠ sight, view; sb's mind: *A small, brilliantly coloured bird* ***flashed into*** *view.*

flash on [Vp] be lit with sudden brightness. **S:** light, illuminations: *Someone pressed a switch and all the lights on the Christmas tree* ***flashed on*** *together.*

flash out 1 [Vp] appear like a sudden bright light. **S:** brilliance, radiance; anger, temper: *The humour and high spirits* ***flash out*** *whenever you speak to him.*

2 [Vp] say (sth) suddenly and with feeling: *She* ***flashed out*** *at Martin: 'Do you really believe that no one has any idea what's in the wind?'* NM = burst out 1.

fleck

flecked with [pass (Vn.pr)] marked with small patches of (sth). **S:** sky; ground. **o:** small clouds; flowers, leaves: *The grass underneath the trees was* ***flecked with*** *patches of sunlight.*

flesh

flesh out [Vn ⇆ p pass adj] make (sth) fuller and more solid by providing specific details. **O:** account, story; analysis, report: *'The report's fine, but it needs* ***fleshing out*** *a bit. How about some more tables?'* ○ *In a learner's dictionary, grammatical patterns should be* ***fleshed out*** *with plenty of examples.*

flick

flick from/off [Vn.pr pass] remove (sth) with a sharp tap or brushing movement of the finger(s). **O:** dust, fluff; fly, wasp; ash. **o:** sleeve; cheek; cigar: *The waitress* ***flicked*** *the breadcrumbs* ***from*** *the table cloth and brought plates and glasses.* = brush off 1.

flick out [Vp, Vn ⇆ p pass] (cause sth to) come out and forward in a sudden, sharp, light movement. **S** [Vp], **O** [Vn.p]: tongue, tail, paw: *The lizard's tongue* ***flicked out*** *and trapped an insect.* ○ *The cat* ***flicked out*** *a paw and drew the ball of wool towards it.*

flick through [Vpr nom pass] scan (a book etc), turning the pages with a quick movement of the thumb. **o:** magazine, review; (pile of) photographs, exam scripts: *Patients in the waiting room idly* ***flicked through*** *magazines as they waited for their names to be called.* ○ *'Have you read the report yet?' 'I've hardly had time to do more than* ***flick through*** *it* (or: *give it a* ***flick(-)through***)*.'* = leaf through, thumb through.

flicker

flicker out 1 [Vp] (of a naked light) gradually go out with small spurts of flame. **S:** flame; match; candle, lamp: *The candles* ***flickered out*** *one by one and the room was plunged in darkness.*

2 [Vp] be extinguished little by little. **S:** fighting; opposition, resistance: *The flame of resistance never entirely* ***flickered out*** *in occupied Europe.*

flinch

flinch from [Vpr pass emph rel] try to avoid (sth) through fear, moral cowardice etc. **o:** truth; the facts, reality; an unpleasant task, responsibility: *'Don't* ***flinch from*** *the facts!'* ○ *It's not an easy decision to take, but it shouldn't be* ***flinched from****.* □ usu neg.

fling

fling (at) [Vn.pr pass emph rel] express (sth) (to sb) in a sudden, violent way. **O:** accusation, charge; taunt, jibe; insult, curse. **o:** prisoner, accused; servant, menial: *Perhaps he should check his facts* *before **flinging** charges of corruption **at** half the Board of Directors.* ○ *'You'd think that all the criticism that has been **flung at** him might have dented his self-esteem — but nothing of the kind!'*

fling one's head back [Vn ⇆ p pass] stand generally erect, with the head pressed back, usu from feelings of pride, arrogance etc: *'That story you told about your royal blood isn't true, is it?' Prissie **flung back her head** and seemed momentarily to gain height.* DC

fling down a challenge [Vp.n pass] challenge sb dramatically. **S:** politician; boxer, promoter; newspaper: *The party has **flung down a challenge** to its political rivals to debate the issue on television.*

fling out/out of [Vp, Vpr] (*dated*) leave in an angry and dramatic manner. **o:** room, meeting: *Following an angry exchange with the Chairman, Jones gathered up his papers and **flung out of** the room.* = sweep out/out of 2 .

fling one's arms up in horror [Vn.p.pr] express surprise and shock on hearing news: *Peter **flung his arms up*** (or: ***flung up his arms***) ***in horror** at the news that developers had been given planning permission to build in the fields opposite.*

flip

flip over [Vp, Vn ⇆ p pass] (cause sth to) turn over with a sharp, sudden movement. **S** [Vp], **O** [Vn.p]**:** plane, glider; screen; card. **S** [Vn.p]**:** (gust of) wind, breeze; player: *The plane stalled, **flipped over** onto its back and crashed near the perimeter fence.* ○ *He **flipped over** the thin piece of pasteboard and read the address scribbled on the back.*

flip through [Vpr nom pass] ⇨ flick through.

flirt

flirt with 1 [Vpr pass rel] (usu of a woman) talk or behave in an attractive, enticing way, without intending a serious involvement. **o:** sb else's boyfriend, older men: *Don't take her too seriously, she's only **flirting with** you.* ○ *Deal gently with the poor boy — he's not used to being **flirted with**.*

2 [Vpr pass rel] consider (an idea), but not very seriously. **o:** idea, notion; scheme, proposal: *He **flirted** for a time **with** the idea of setting up in the antique business.* = dally with 1, play with 5, toy with 3.

flock

flock in/into [Vp emph, Vpr emph rel] enter (a place) in large numbers. **S:** audience, spectators; fans; students. **o:** theatre, cinema; stadium, ground; lecture-hall: *Hotels were unable to cope with the huge numbers **flocking in** for the Olympic Games.* ○ *Thousands of Scots **flocked into** Barcelona for the European Cup tie.*

flock together [Vp] (esp of people with common interests or loyalties) gather, come together, in a crowd. **S:** scientists, teachers; trade unionists, (political) party members: *Brighton was full of Conservative Party stalwarts, **flocking together** for their annual conference.* ○ (proverb) *Birds of a feather **flock together**.*

flog

flog to death [Vn.pr pass] (*informal*) try to persuade sb of the worth or desirability of (sth) so persistently that he loses interest in it. **S:** advertiser, salesman; politician; inventor. **O:** product; scheme; idea: *The need to 'export or perish' has been dinned into manufacturers so fervently that this worthy cause may have been **flogged to death**.*

flood

flood in/into [Vp, Vpr emph rel] arrive in great quantities (at a place). **S:** letters, entries, applications, offers of help. **o:** office, bank, college: *Donations have been **flooding in** since our last appeal for help over the radio* (or: *We have been **flooded with** donations* etc). ○ *If oil pollution does eat into that £50 million **flooding into** Cornwall each year, everyone in the county will feel it in his pocket.* OBS

flood out [Vn ⇆ p pass adj] (of flood waters) force (sb) to leave his home. **O:** villager, farmer: *Hundreds were **flooded out** when the sea-wall collapsed.* □ usu passive.

flood with [Vn.pr pass emph rel] ⇨ flood in/into.

flop

flop about/around [Vp] make a dull, flapping sound as one moves about, usu because one is wearing loose shoes: *Grandmother **flopped around** comfortably in a pair of old carpet slippers.*

flop down [Vp emph] fall heavily or clumsily, eg through tiredness: *At the end of a working day all he feels like doing is **flopping down** in an armchair to watch television.*

flounder

flounder about/around [Vp, Vpr] move about clumsily, and often helplessly, as when walking in mud. **S:** walrus, seal: *A heavy lorry was **floundering around** in thick mud at the entrance to the building site.*

flow

flow across, along, away etc [Vp emph, Vpr emph rel] move across etc in a steady stream. **S:** water, oil, lava; pedestrians, traffic; reinforcements, supplies: *Requests for blankets, tents and medical supplies are **flowing into** the offices of the relief organizations.* ○ *Fresh material and drafts of infantry continued to **flow up** to the front.* B

flow from [Vpr emph rel] follow logically from (sth). **S:** improvement, benefit; wealth, prosperity; conclusion, result. **o:** change, decision; development, expansion; argument: *This is an important technical innovation **from** which will **flow** many benefits to industry.* ○ ***From** the court's decision these consequences must surely **flow**.*

flow over [Vpr] (of noisy or disturbing events) take place all around (sb) without greatly affecting him. **S:** noise, hubbub, din; tensions, jealousies; rebukes, reprimands: *He doesn't allow himself to be excited by the children's squabbles. The bickering and fisticuffs simply **flow over** him.* = wash over.

fluff

fluff out/up [Vn ⇆ p pass adj] shake (sth) into a soft mass like fluff. **S:** bird, animal; maid. **O:** feather, fur; pillow, cushion: *Birds **fluff out** their feathers as a protection against the cold.* ○ *A nurse smoothed out the sheets and **fluffed up** the pillows.*

flutter

flutter about/around [Vp, Vpr] move here and there in a nervous, restless way: *Our hostess **fluttered about**, taking quick nervous puffs at her cigarette.* ○ *'Stop **fluttering about** the place. Sit down, and I'll buy you a drink.'*

flutter down [Vp emph] come down, descend, with sharp irregular flapping movements. **S:** bird, leaf, petal; letter, paper: *Tons of ticker-tape* ***fluttered down*** *into Fifth Avenue from office windows.*

fly

fly in the face of [Vpr] oppose sth which is well-established, customary, reasonable etc. **S:** he etc; action, step; decision. **o:** (**of**) tradition, custom; reason, logic; fact, evidence; unity, comradeship: *Revolutionization of long distance road haulage would* ***fly in the face of*** *all common sense.* SC ○ *Being more hard-headed than Dr Heck, they will avoid attempting to* ***fly in the face of*** *international unity.* TES

fly in/into 1 [Vn ⇆ p pass, Vn.pr pass] cause (an aircraft) to land (at an airfield). **S:** pilot, co-pilot. **O:** aircraft, plane, jet; passenger, cargo. **o:** Gatwick, Orly; Madrid, Kano: *The pilot* ***flew*** *the badly crippled bomber* ***in*** *on one engine.* ○ *Tons of freight are* ***flown into*** *this airport every day.* ⇨ next entry
2 [Vp, Vpr] (of a pilot) cause an aircraft to land (at a place); (of a passenger) arrive aboard an aircraft; (of an aircraft) come in to land. **S:** pilot; tourist, visitor; jet, cargo-plane. **o:** Rome: *My partner has just* ***flown in*** *from London; we can begin discussions at once.* ○ *Aircraft arriving later today will have to* ***fly into*** *Gatwick through heavy fog.* ⇨ previous entry

fly into [Vpr] begin to show, display (strong feeling). **o:** ⚠ a (fit of) temper, rage, passion; an angry fit: *The child* ***flew into*** *a rage and began scattering its toys about.* ○ *He'll* ***fly into*** *a temper and tell me the contract for the murals is off.* CON

fly off the handle [Vpr] (*informal*) lose one's temper. **S:** wife, husband, school-teacher: *She's always* ***flying off the handle*** *at the children.* ○ *Don't* ***fly off the handle*** *every time you run up against a small problem.*

flyover [nom (Vp)] bridge carrying one (main) road over another at an important junction: ***Flyovers*** *or underpasses will be built wherever the motorway cuts across existing trunk-roads.*

fly past [Vp nom] fly in formation as part of a ceremonial parade, often over the route of the parade on the ground. **S:** fighter, bomber: *The crowd looked up as a squadron of jet-fighters* ***flew past.*** ○ *The ceremony ended with a* ***flypast*** *of new aircraft.* □ usu nom.

foam

foam at the mouth 1 [Vpr] send out foam from the mouth, as during an epileptic fit. **S:** epileptic, rabid dog: *A symptom of rabies is* ***foaming at the mouth.***
2 [Vpr] (*informal*) show extreme anger — though without literally foaming at the mouth: *When Smith was told that children had been trampling on his prize vegetables, he practically* ***foamed at the mouth.***

fob

fob off onto [Vn.p.pr pass] trick or deceive (sb) into buying or accepting (sth). **S:** dishonest trader, door-to-door salesman, confidence trickster. **O:** inferior goods, shoddy article. **o:** gullible customer, innocent shopper: *Unscrupulous firms are* ***fobbing*** *these goods* ***off onto*** *the unsuspecting customer.* ○ *Last year's model was* ***fobbed off onto*** *us instead of the one we ordered.* = foist (off) on, palm off (on). ⇨ next entry

fob off (with) [Vn.p pass, Vn.p.pr emph rel] trick or deceive (sb) into buying or accepting (sth); stop sb achieving his aim or purpose by trickery or delaying tactics. **S:** dishonest trader, confidence trickster. **O:** gullible customer. **o:** inferior goods; half-truth, yarn, tale; (empty) promises: *Let me make my point, and I am not to be* ***fobbed off*** *this time.* TBC ○ *We were entitled to be treated as equals and we would not be* ***fobbed off with*** *Skybolt* (a military rocket). T ○ *He might* ***fob*** *Madame La Botte* ***off with*** *50 francs, if he happened to be in the mood.* US = palm off (with). ⇨ previous entry

focus

focus (on) [Vpr emph rel, Vn.pr pass emph rel] think of (one thing) to the exclusion of others. **O:** (one's) attention, thoughts; one's mind; one's efforts, energies. **o:** problem; question, matter; speaker, lecturer; process: *He finds it hard to* ***focus*** *his thoughts* ***on*** *one thing for longer than five minutes.* ○ *Public attention at the moment is* ***focused on*** *the problems of a declining economy.* = concentrate (on/upon).

foist

foist (off) on [Vn.pr pass emph rel, Vn.p.pr pass emph rel] trick or deceive (sb) into buying, accepting or shouldering (sth). **S:** dishonest trader etc; superior. **O:** inferior goods etc; problems, difficulties. **o:** gullible customer etc; subordinate: *He* ***foisted off*** *a few cases of inferior scotch* ***on*** *a too eager customer.* ○ *I'm sorry all this has been* ***foisted on*** *you.* EHOW = fob off onto, palm off (on).

fold

fold back [Vn ⇆ p pass adj] turn one (part of a) thing back over itself. **O:** page, sheet (of paper); canopy, hood (of a vehicle); cover, sheet (on a bed): *They drove in bright sunshine, with the hood of the car* ***folded back.*** = double back 2.

fold in/into [Vn ⇆ p pass, Vn.pr pass emph rel] (in cooking) mix (sth) with (existing ingredients). **S:** chef, cook. **O:** eggs, sugar. **o:** flour, mixture: (recipe) *Then* ***fold in*** *the rest of the sugar and flavouring.*

fold up 1 [Vn ⇆ p pass adj] make a neat, and perhaps portable, package etc of (sth) by turning parts of it back upon themselves. **O:** newspaper; sheet, tablecloth; deck-chair, camp bed, tent: *The table linen was neatly* ***folded up*** *and put away.* ○ *'Would you* ***fold up*** *the garden chairs and put them in the conservatory?'*
2 [Vp] (*informal*) collapse with mirth or pain. **S:** audience, spectator; boxer, patient: *From the moment he appeared on stage, the audience* ***folded up*** *in their seats.* ○ *He jabbed me just once, in the solar plexus, and I* ***folded up.*** = double up 1.
3 [Vp] (*informal*) collapse morally or economically. **S:** country, enemy, industry: *They felt that if she didn't* ***fold up*** *when her boy died, she wouldn't* ***fold up*** *when the balloon went up* (= when war began). RFW ○ *Several national newspapers have* ***folded up*** *in the past ten years.*

follow

follow in sb's footsteps [Vpr] continue a tradition or process established by a predecessor; adopt the same trade or profession as one's father etc: *We shall not recount the many experiments carried out by Rhine and by others who have* **followed in his footsteps** *over the years.* SNP ○ *One of my passes was in Maths, so my old lady decided that I should* **follow in** *my poor* **father's footsteps**. JFTR

follow on [Vp nom] (*cricket*) (of the second side to bat in a match) bat again, having failed in the first innings to come close enough to one's opponent's score: *Australia were all out for 120 in their first innings and had to* **follow on**. ○ *He defended his decision not to enforce the* **follow-on** *against India at Edgebaston.* G

follow through 1 [Vn.p pass] continue doing (sth) until a conclusion is reached. **S:** thinker, scientist; designer, builder. **O:** argument, experiment; project, development: *'Don't keep breaking off. I'd like to hear you* **follow** *the argument* **through** *to a conclusion.'* ○ *He takes several schemes in hand, but lacks the persistence to* **follow** *them* **through**.
2 [Vp nom] (*sport*) continue a stroke to the full extent of one's arm after hitting the ball. **S:** batsman, tennis player, golfer: *To hit the ball clean and hard you must develop a smooth* **follow-through**.

follow up 1 [Vn ⇆ p nom pass adj] continue, develop (sth) by doing sth better or more ambitious; extend, exploit. **O:** process, series; campaign; achievement, success, victory: *This production team have had one successful television series; how will they* **follow** *it* **up** (or: *what will they do for a* **follow-up**)? ○ *Don't rest on your laurels:* **follow up** *your success and start looking for new markets now.*
2 [Vn ⇆ p pass] investigate (sth) closely; follow where sth leads. **O:** story, rumour; lead, clue: *I decide to* **follow up** *one or two hints that had been dropped at her cocktail party.* ○ *The night editor decides which of the stories that are phoned in should be* **followed up**.

fool

fool about/around (with) [Vp, Vp.pr] behave in a casual or irresponsible way (with sth/sb). **A:** with a revolver, in a sports car, on a golf course: *He should know that you don't* **fool around** *on a rifle range.* ○ *'What the blazes are you* **fooling about** *at, Joe?'* CON ○ *Everyone knows he's been* **fooling around** *with Bill's wife.* = play about/around (with).

forbear

forbear (from) [Vpr emph rel] (*formal*) not begin to do, or stop doing, sth, esp sth which offends or irritates others. **o:** interference (in sth), over-attention (to sth), indulgence (in sth); comment, criticism; being drawn in, giving an opinion: *This was a warning to* **forbear from** *being too deeply involved in the company's affairs.* = refrain from.

force

force down sb's throat [Vn.pr pass] (*informal*) compel an unwilling listener etc to accept (sth). **S:** regime, (political) party; radio, TV; advertiser, public relations man. **O:** dogma, doctrine; slogan, catchphrase; product, merchandise: *We would have to walk delicately and not* **force** *our ways* **down the throats of** *all and sundry.* MFM ○ *You're not obliged to sit in front of a television set and have that rubbish* **forced down your throat**. = ram/stuff down sb's throat.

force on/upon [Vn.pr pass] compel (sb) to accept (sth). **S:** shopkeeper, salesman; victorious power, strong neighbour. **O:** goods; terms, conditions; war. **o:** customer, public; small country: *Madge had* **forced** *a crisis* **on** *me.* UTN ○ *This country didn't want the war. It was* **forced upon** *us by powers that needed our coal and iron.*

force up [Vn ⇆ p pass adj] cause (sth) to rise, by applying strong pressure. **S:** shortage; bad harvest; strike; wage increase. **O:** price, cost: *Increasing the wages of the bus crews will* **force up** *fares.* ○ *The gloomiest forecast was that the oil crisis would* **force** *the cost of living* **up** *very considerably.*

forge

forge ahead [Vp] go forward, progress, in a impressive way. **S:** country; company, industry; department; troops: *Japan continues to* **forge ahead** *in the manufacture of new electronic equipment.* ○ *We've* **forged ahead** *since that much-needed management shake-up.*

forget

forget about [Vpr] no longer remember (sth); not think any further about (sth). **o:** the past; experience, event; visit, arrangement, appointment; (unpleasant) experience, (nasty) shock: *Helping his son with his physics homework reminded him of things he'd long* **forgotten about**. ○ *'Thanks for reminding me—you know, I'd* **forgotten** *all* **about** *him coming this afternoon.'* ○ *'Don't worry,' she said soothingly, 'just go away and* **forget about** *all this.'* DC = dismiss (from one's mind/thoughts).

fork

fork out [Vp, Vp.n pass] (*informal*) pay (sth), usu unwillingly. **S:** public, tax-payer. **O:** cash, money: *'That will be another half-crown.' Brownsworth* **forked out**. RM ○ *It would be laughable if we weren't always having to* **fork out** *money for the police which ought to be spent on roads.* RM = shell out.

form

form from [Vn.pr pass emph rel] make (a whole) from (parts). **O:** grouping, consortium, conglomerate, association. **o:** (smaller) units, elements; companies, firms: *There is talk of* **forming** *a new radical party* **from** *those breaking away from the Conservatives.* ⇨ form into.

formed from [pass (Vn.pr)] composed of (certain elements). **S:** rock, stone; cloud; lake, sea. **o:** liquid; drop, particle; pool: *These substances are* **formed from** *a mixture of liquids solidifying under great pressure.*

form into [Vpr rel, Vn.pr pass rel] (cause people to) come together in (a group). **S** [Vpr], **O** [Vn.pr]**:** followers, young people. **o:** committee, club, brotherhood; company, brigade: *On the word of command, the company* **formed** *smartly* **into** *three ranks.* ○ *The children were* **formed into** *small groups, which went from door to door collecting money and old clothes.* ⇨ form from.

form (a) part of [Vn.pr emph rel] be part of (sth), be an element in (sth). **S:** episode, incident; chapter, section; limb, organ; company. regiment. **o:** story, film; book, article; trunk, abdomen; army: *There is discussion over whether the new Department should* **form part of** *the Faculty of Arts.* ○ *There is a* complex rehousing plan ***of*** *which this development* ***forms*** *only* ***a*** *small* ***part***.

form up [Vp, Vn ⇆ p pass] (cause people to) get into parade order or a formation. **S** [Vp], **O** [Vn.p]: troops, company, battalion; demonstrators, protesters. **S** [Vn.p]: officer, sergeant; steward: *The procession* ***formed up*** *near Hyde Park Corner.* ○ *The battalion was* ***formed up*** *on the barrack square.*

fortify

fortify (against) [Vn.pr pass emph rel] make (sth/sb) stronger, more able to resist (sth). **O:** town, position, emplacement; oneself. **o:** attack, invasion; cold, flu: *The forward positions were strongly* ***fortified against*** *artillery bombardment.* ○ *There were more difficult times ahead,* ***against*** *which his upbringing and training would do little to* ***fortify*** *him.*

foul

foul up [Vn ⇆ p nom pass adj] (*informal*) spoil, mar (sth). **O:** things; arrangements, organization; relationship, marriage: *When everything is running smoothly, why must he step in and* ***foul*** *things* ***up****?* ○ *His easy-going ways with other women have* ***fouled up*** *a good working partnership.* ○ *We'll finish the building on time provided there are no* ***foul-ups*** *or hang-ups.* = mess up.

frame

frame up [Vn ⇆ p nom pass adj] (*informal*) arrange, by falsifying evidence, corrupting witnesses etc, to make an innocent person appear guilty. **S:** enemy, rival; policeman, official: *It's hard to* ***frame*** *you* ***up****.* BBCTV ○ *In most cases in which a person is* ***framed up*** *by the police, the victim is too surprised, or ignorant, to help himself.* BBCTV ○ *We have been expecting a* ***frame-up*** *for a long time. But this time we have got witnesses.* G □ the verb alone is commonly used in this sense: *She was sure that she was being* ***framed****.* = fit up 2, stitch up 2.

freak

freak out [Vp nom] (*slang*) move into a heightened or depressed state of mind (esp after taking drugs); behave in a lively, fanciful or abandoned way, eg during a party or celebration: *He took a lot of acid* (LSD) *and really* ***freaked out****.* ○ *John's party last weekend was wild — a real* ***freak-out****.*

free

free from [Vn.pr pass emph rel] make (sb/sth) free, independent, of (sth). **O:** oneself; country, people; client; patient. **o:** slavery, dependence; obligation, undertaking; anxiety: *A local authority grant* ***freed*** *John* ***from*** *financial dependence on his parents.* ○ *They were* ***freed from*** *some of their anxieties about the future by taking out another insurance policy.*

freeze

freeze off [Vn ⇆ p nom pass] (*informal, dated*) keep (sb) at a distance by being too unfriendly or remote; drive away. **O:** suitor, visitor, customer: *If this were all, outsiders could hardly succeed with working-class people; they would be likely to impress them but also to* ***freeze*** *them* ***off****.* UL ○ *Before he had got half-way through his sentence she was giving him the Siberian* ***freeze-off****, a routine she must have known all about.* CON

freeze out [Vn ⇆ p pass] (*informal*) prevent (sb) from doing business by making his goods too expensive etc; exclude (sb) from society by unfriendly behaviour. **S:** rival, competitor; neighbour, club member: *Many of the smaller traders are being* ***frozen out*** *by the big supermarket chains.*

freeze over [Vp] become covered with ice. **S:** lake, river, sea: *During the severe winter of 1947 even the sea* ***froze over****.* = ice over. ⇨ next entry

frozen over [pass adj (Vn.p)] covered with ice. **S:** pond, lake, river: *The drinking troughs were* ***frozen over****. Farmers had to break the ice to water their cattle.* ○ *Even heavy lorries could cross the* ***frozen-over*** *rivers.* ⇨ previous entry

freeze to death [Vpr] die through exposure to extreme cold. **S:** men, livestock: *Flocks and herds were cut off by deep snowdrifts and* ***froze to death*** *in the open.* □ the passive of a [Vn.pr] pattern is also used: *Our men just stand about miserably burning the precious petrol to keep warm. Several times we found the sentries had fallen asleep . . . literally* ***frozen to death****.* B

freeze up [Vp nom, Vn ⇆ p pass] become hard and blocked with ice; cover or block (sth) with ice and make it unworkable. **S:** pipe, tank; road, river: *In the winter of 1947, everything* ***froze up****, even the sea.* ○ *I must do something about protecting the water-pipes in case we have another bad* ***freeze-up****.* = ice up.

freshen

freshen up [Vp nom] wash, shave etc, so as to feel fresh after a journey etc: *I'll put on a clean shirt and* ***freshen up****.* ○ *I shall have time for a quick* ***freshen-up*** *at the hotel before the meeting begins.*

frighten

frighten away/off [Vn ⇆ p pass] frighten (sb) thus making him stay away or go away. **S:** dog, guard; loud noise. **O:** intruder, thief; stranger: *Of course the job won't* ***frighten*** *her* ***away****. She likes babies, otherwise she wouldn't be here.* DC ○ *The sound of us moving about upstairs must have* ***frightened*** *the burglar* ***off****.*

frighten into [Vn.pr pass] force (sb) into (doing sth) by means of threats, terrorization etc. **O:** population; child; victim. **o:** submission, obedience; stealing; handing over the money: *The older boys* ***frightened*** *the younger ones* ***into*** *stealing money from their parents.* ○ *The villagers were* ***frightened into*** *surrendering their grain by the drunken troops.*

frighten to death [Vn.pr pass] frighten (sb) very severely. **S:** crowd, traffic; air travel; animal, bird: *The baby monkeys would get stricken with all sorts of complaints and* ***frighten*** *us* ***to death****.* BB ○ *His wife is* ***frightened to death*** *on the rare occasions when she has to travel by air.*

fritter

fritter away [Vn ⇆ p pass] (*informal*) waste (money etc) by spending it in a number of separate and unrewarding ways. **O:** money, time, energies: *I didn't want us to* ***fritter*** *it* (the money) ***away*** *on things we don't really need.* AITC ○ *I do hope that all you've got to give the world won't be* ***frittered away*** *in side-tracks and bypaths.* HAA

frost

frost over [Vp] become covered with frost. **S:** window(-pane), gate, pavement: *The windows had **frosted over** in the night; Mary breathed on them and scraped at the crystals with her finger nails.* ⇨ next entry

frosted over [pass adj (Vn.p)] covered with frost. **S:** window, glass: *After the severe cold of last night, all the windows are **frosted over**.* ⇨ previous entry

fuck

fuck about/around 1 [Vp] (*taboo*) behave in a foolish or irresponsible way: *'When's he going to stop **fucking about** and do an honest day's work?'* ○ *'Is it you that's been **fucking around** with my camera?'* = mess about/around.

2 [Vn.p pass] (*taboo*) treat (sb) in a foolish or thoughtless way; behave as though one has a poor estimate of sb's worth etc. **S:** boss, sergeant, teacher: *'Now don't **fuck** me **about**! I came here looking for proper service, not to be palmed off with dud equipment.'* ○ *'Don't **fuck** me **around**, Harry. Give me the money and we'll leave you in peace.'* = mess about/around (with) 2.

fuck off [Vp] (*taboo*) leave, go away: *'If he comes here bothering you again, tell him to **fuck off**.'* ○ *'We wanted to have a word with Geoff, but he'd **fucked off** home.'*

fuck up [Vn ⇆ p nom pass] (*taboo*) mismanage, spoil, ruin (sth). **O:** things, the whole works; engine, suspension; scheme, project: *He said he didn't want his motor **fucked up** by some kid with oil on his hands.* ○ *'The meeting was a complete **fuck-up** from start to finish.'* = mess up.

fume

fume (at) [Vpr rel] show irritation, without fully expressing it, in response (to sth). **S:** motorist; shopper, consumer. **o:** delay, hold-up; incompetence, rudeness: *We **fumed at** the casualness of waitresses who could keep us waiting for half an hour and then serve up half-cold soup.*

fur

fur up [Vp] become coated with a white crust, the result of being used to boil water which contains lime. **S:** kettle, saucepan: *In areas where the water is 'hard' pots and kettles quickly **fur up**.*

furnish

furnish (to) [Vn.pr emph rel] (*formal*) give, hand (sth) (to sb) for his use or exploitation. **O:** supplies, stocks; equipment; excuse, pretext, justification. **o:** customer; store, factory; rival, opponent: *The firm won a contract for **furnishing** boots **to** the army* (or: ***furnishing** the army **with** boots*). ○ *Don't go out of your way to **furnish** opportunities **to** your rivals* (or: ***furnish** them **with** opportunities*). = supply (to).

furnish with [Vn.pr pass emph rel] ⇨ previous entry.

fuss

fuss about [Vp] move about or behave in a nervous, excited way: *'Stop **fussing about**: the taxi will arrive on time, and we shan't miss the train.'*

fuss over [Vpr pass] unsettle, irritate (sb) by giving him too much attention. **S:** wife, mother; teacher: *She does **fuss over** the children so — making sure they're well wrapped up, and worrying about their minor illnesses.*

G

gabble

gabble away/on (about) [Vp, Vp.pr] (*informal*) talk rapidly and possibly indistinctly (about sth): *The two women **gabbled away** twenty to the dozen, oblivious to what was happening around them.* ○ *I couldn't hear what the operator at her end* (of the telephone line) *was **gabbling on about**.* GL

gad

gad about [Vp nom] (*informal*) go from place to place, usu for pleasure: *The way Tom **gads about**, I can't see how he will ever pass his finals.* ○ *It's only too easy to become a **gadabout** — going from one party to another, from one friend's house to another, and never doing anything useful.* = gallivant about.

gain

gain in 1 [Vpr] become heavier, taller etc. **S:** child; company, firm; army. **o:** weight, size, girth; height; strength, power: *You seem to have **gained** a lot **in** weight since I last saw you.* ○ *The army has **gained** greatly **in** striking power with the acquisition of five hundred of the latest tanks.*

2 [Vpr] acquire more of (a moral or intellectual quality). **S:** parent; manager; politician. **o:** experience; knowledge, wisdom, understanding; cunning, astuteness; (moral) stature, authority: *By the time he left London he had **gained** enormously **in** poise and confidence.* SS ○ *The Leader of the Opposition **gained** greatly **in** stature as a result of his handling of the so-called Hard Left.* = grow in.

gain on 1 [Vpr] draw closer to (sth or sb one is pursuing). **S:** our car, ship; runner; Labour; police. **o:** the car in front, the ship ahead; the leaders in the race; the Conservatives; thieves: *The police-launch was clearly **gaining on** the boat when the shots were fired from it.* ○ *I gradually began to **gain on** him — maybe he was nursing* (trying to conserve) *his fuel or something.* SATS

2 [Vpr] move further ahead of (sb/sth). **S:** car, ship; runner; Labour. **o:** others; the enemy; the rest of the field; the Conservatives: *The leading group of three continued to **gain on** the rest of the runners and were soon half a mile clear of them.*

gain on/upon [Vpr] (*formal*) consume part of (sth); erode. **S:** sea, river, floods. **o:** land, cliffs, bank: *Year by year the North Sea **gains upon** this part of the Suffolk coast.*

gain access to [Vn.pr rel] (*formal*) reach (sth), sometimes by overcoming difficulties. **o:** safe, filing cabinet; computer records; roof, bedroom: *A burglar had **gained access** to personal details kept in a secret file.* ○ *It was an unlocked office, to which anyone could **gain access**.* = get access to. ⇨ have access to.

gallivant

gallivant about [Vp] (*informal*) go from place to place, usu for pleasure: *If she spent more time* *looking after her family and less time* **gallivanting about**, *everyone would be a lot happier.* = gad about.

galvanize

galvanize into action/activity [Vn.pr pass] cause (sb) to act instantly: *A shot rang out and* **galvanized** *the patrol* **into action**. *They rushed for cover and began to move in the direction from which the firing had come.*

gamble

gamble away [Vn ⇆ p pass] lose (sth) by gambling. **O:** fortune, inheritance; his week's wages: *Having* **gambled away** *half his salary at cards, Bottomley had to borrow from his friends to buy food and pay the rent.* ○ *Many a family fortune has been* **gambled away** *on the Stock Exchange.*

gamble on 1 [Vpr, Vn.pr pass] bet (money) on (a horse etc) in the hope that it will win. **O:** money; one's savings, a fortune. **o:** horses, dogs; the outcome: *He* **gambled on** *the horses when he was a bit younger.* ○ *Only a fool would* **gamble** *his life's savings* **on** *a single shake of the dice.* = put on 8, stake on, wager on 1.

2 [Vpr] take a risk, hoping that sth will happen. **o:** it, that; that happening; his paying; the result: *'We must allow plenty of time to get to the airport—we can't* **gamble on** *the road being clear.'* ○ *Both* (parties in the dispute) *are* **gambling on** *winning the support of the travelling public for their rival peace efforts.*G = wager on 2.

gang

gang up against/on [Vp.pr pass] (*informal*) form a group or alliance against (sb/sth): *Henri ... felt betrayed: as if his best friend and his old confidante had* **ganged up against** *him.* AF ○ *She had favourites; and I was one of them. That was partly the cause of the one time that I was* **ganged up on** *by my own kind.* BRH

gape

gape (at) [Vpr pass rel] look open-mouthed (at sb/sth): *'Don't just stand there* **gaping at** *the poor man, help him to his feet!'* ○ *The frontier guards were so astonished at the appearance of a Rolls Royce that they could only* **gape at** *it.* = stare (at).

garnish

garnish with [Vn.pr pass] add (sth) as a trimming to (food); decorate with. **O:** dish; roast chicken, lamb, sole meunière: *The salmon was brought to the table whole,* **garnished with** *parsley and slices of tomato and cucumber.*

gasp

gasp (at) [Vpr pass rel] show great surprise, horror etc, by a sudden involuntary release of one's breath. **o:** news; his nerve; risk; the intensity of the bombing, the physical state of the children: *When theatre audiences first saw the play they* **gasped at** *the audacity of some of the scenes.* ○ *CLIVE: Let us not* **gasp** *too excitedly* **at** *the loftiness of Mother's family tree. ... it has, you see, feet of clay.* FFE

gasp for breath [Vpr] have great difficulty in breathing; be very surprised by sb's remarks, behaviour etc: *The low punch made him* **gasp for breath**. ○ *The sheer intensity of his performance leaves one* **gasping for breath**.

gasp out [Vp.n pass] say (sth) while struggling for breath. **O:** message, warning, last request: *The messenger had enough breath left to* **gasp out** *his warning.* ○ *'You'll never make it in time,' he* **gasped out**. □ may follow direct speech, as shown.

gather

gather (from) [Vn.pr pass emph rel] learn, understand (from sth said or written). **O:** nothing, very little; how much, what; that he means to attend. **o:** remark, statement, report: *'Did you* **gather from** *what she said that they intend to make a bid for the house?'* ○ **From** *what John said I* **gather** *he'll be giving up his job in the summer.*

gather in [Vn ⇆ p pass] harvest, collect (a crop). **O:** crop; oats, barley: *There was a week of rain which ruined the wheat crop before it could be safely* **gathered in**.

gather round 1 [Vp, Vpr rel, Vn.p pass, Vn.pr pass rel] (cause people to) assemble around (sb/sth). **S** [Vp, Vpr], **O** [Vn.p, Vn.pr]**:** crowd, group, spectators. **o:** accident; entrance to the theatre, newly-arrived ship: [Vp] *The cast had* **gathered round** *to hear the director's opening remarks.* ○ [Vn.pr] *The street trader had managed to* **gather** *a small group of passers-by* **round** *his stall.*

2 [Vp] come to sb's side and give moral, physical or material support. **S:** the family; friends, comrades, companions; Masons, Rotarians: *'A man ought to be given a chance to be born at home, and he certainly ought to have a chance to die there. The family* **gathers round**, *you know, and it's only right he should feel the event is something of an occasion.'* DIL

gather together collect, assemble (things). **O:** tools, books, toys; thoughts, ideas, impressions: *At the end of the school day the children are taught to* **gather** *all their things* **together** *and put them tidily away.* ○ *Melanie Klein ... has* **gathered together** *her ideas on the subject* (ie in a book). ESS

gawk, gawp

gawk/gawp (at) [Vpr pass rel] (*informal*) look open-mouthed (at sb/sth): *'Don't just* **gawp at** *the child, pick him up!'* = stare (at).

gaze

gaze around/round [Vp, Vpr] look round in surprise, amazement etc: *Unable to believe his good fortune, he* **gazed round** *at the gifts that his friends had showered upon him.*

gaze at [Vpr pass rel] look at (sb/sth) in a steady, concentrated way: *When we found Joe, he was sitting on a rock,* **gazing at** *the sea.* ○ *She dropped the sheet of paper as if she had been stung. She* **gazed at** *it in complete horror, as if it were some horrible insect.* DC = fix on/upon.

gaze on/upon [Vpr pass rel] (*formal*) look continuously and with wonder at (sb/sth). **o:** survivor, victim; beauty, perfection; sight, view, prospect: *He was being* **gazed upon** *as a spectacle: the man who had defied the divine order and been stricken blind.* MLT

gaze round [Vp, Vpr] ⇨ gaze around/round.

gear

gear to [Vn.pr pass emph rel] organize (sth) in such a way that some purpose, or the needs of some group, are served. **O:** life, work; daily routine, study programme. **o:** the needs of management, the export programme; patients, older students: *The work at Temple Grove* (a preparatory school) *was* **geared to** *the requirements of the public* *schools.* MRJ ○ *Life in the city was* ***geared to*** *the student.* GJ □ often passive.

gear up [Vp, Vn ⇆ p pass] (cause sth to) increase in operating efficiency. **S** [Vp], **O** [Vn.p]**:** industry; economy; administration; army: *The Department is* ***gearing up*** *for an increased intake of students.* ○ *The party organization is ready to be* ***geared up*** *for the General Election, whenever that takes place.*

gen

gen up (about/on) [Vp, Vp.pr, Vn ⇆ p pass, Vn.p.pr pass] (*informal*) (cause sb to) obtain or learn the essential facts (about sb/sth): [Vp.pr] *The visitors had* ***genned up on*** *the project very thoroughly and there was little that I could tell them that they didn't already know.* ○ [Vn.p.pr] *I went in to see MacGilvery, and he was all* ***genned up about*** *my genius and how Braithwaite was going to turn my book into a best-seller.* JFTR

get

get about/around [Vp] move from place to place, often with the implication of overcoming difficulty to do so: *Considering his age, my father still manages to* ***get about*** *a great deal.* ○ *Now that traffic has been restricted in the centre of the city, it's easier to* ***get about***. ○ *A car seemed a good idea for* ***getting around***. GL

get about/around/round [Vp] circulate, spread. **S:** news, rumour, story; it; word: *It* ***got about*** *that the British Centre was recruiting more teachers.* ○ *I don't know how that rumour* ***got around***. *There's absolutely no truth in it.* ○ *Word* ***got around*** *that she was thinking of retiring early.* ⇨ go about 2, put about 2.

get above oneself [Vpr] have too high an opinion of oneself: *That young man is* ***getting above himself***. *He's only been in the firm two weeks and already he's telling everyone how to do their work.*

get across 1 [Vp, Vn.p pass, Vn.pr pass] (cause or help sb to) cross (an obstacle). **o:** bridge, river, street; border, frontier: [Vp] *The frontier is so well guarded that no one can* ***get across***. ○ [Vpr] *Only half the company* ***got across*** *the bridge before it was blown up.* ○ [Vn.pr] *A young officer succeeded in* ***getting*** *all the men* ***across*** *the river.* ⇨ go/send/take across (to).

2 [Vpr] (*informal*) annoy, offend, irritate (sb): *Those two men are so different in temperament that they were bound to* ***get across*** *each other.* ○ *Be careful how you talk to Mr Swann. He's an unpleasant man to* ***get across***. = get on the wrong side of.

get across (to) [Vp, Vp.pr, Vn.p pass, Vn.p.pr pass] (cause sth to) be understood (by sb); communicate, transmit. **S** [Vp, Vp.pr], **O** [Vn.p, Vn.p.pr]**:** message, joke, information: [Vn.p] *So if this Cloud contains separate individuals, the individuals must be able to communicate on a vastly more detailed scale than we can. What we can* ***get across*** *in an hour of talk they might* ***get across*** *in a hundredth of a second.* TBC ○ [Vn.p.pr] *The comedian didn't seem to be able to* ***get*** *his jokes* ***across to*** *his audience — they all fell flat!* = get over (to). ⇨ come across 2, put across 1.

get ahead/ahead of [Vp, Vpr] advance, progress (beyond sb else): *As soon as he settled down to the routine of his new job, Alex* ***got ahead*** *splendidly.* ○ *By doing just a little extra homework each day, Jane* ***got*** *well* ***ahead of*** *the rest in maths.* = draw ahead/ahead of, pull ahead/ahead of 2. ↔ get behind 1, fall behind 1. ⇨ be ahead/ahead of, keep ahead/ahead of, stay ahead/ahead of.

get along [Vp] succeed in doing sth; manage: *'How are you managing to do your work without an assistant?' 'Oh I* ***get along*** *somehow.'* ○ *John's* ***getting along*** *pretty well, considering he could hardly speak a word of French when he arrived.* = get by 3.

get along/away with you! [Vp.pr] (*informal*) an exclamation of mild rebuke or disbelief: *'Henry's paying for the wine.'* ***'Get along with you!*** *Henry never bought anyone a drink in his life.'* = go along with you!. ⇨ get on! 5, go on! 14.

get along/on (with) 1 [Vp, Vp.pr] make progress (with a task). **o:** work, studies; German; new novel, painting: *'How is Tim* ***getting along with*** *the car? Has he got it into working order yet?* ○ *I'm not* ***getting on*** *very fast* ***with*** *this pile of marking.* ⇨ bring along/on 1, come along/on 2.

2 [Vp, Vp.pr emph rel] have a harmonious relationship (with sb), live or work well etc (with sb). **S:** child, schoolboy, employee. **o:** parents, classmates, colleagues. **A:** (not) very well; splendidly, badly; like a house on fire; like nobody's business, like one o'clock: *She did not* ***get along with*** *Vivienne, whom Eliot whisked away to the country whenever he could.* TSE ○ *My mother and I don't always* ***get on*** *very well, but I believe in the saying, 'Home is where the heart is.'* H ○ *If only 'them' and 'us' had the same ideas we'd* ***get on*** *like a house on fire, but they don't see eye to eye with us and we don't see eye to eye with them, so that's how it stands and how it will always stand.* LLDR ○ (reading from a letter) *'We're* ***getting on*** *like a house on fire.' How peculiar, she thought, similes are: why should* ***getting on*** *like a house on fire mean that everything was going well? And again, 'The children are* ***getting on*** *like one o'clock, especially Janice.'* PW ○ *She* ***got on*** *well* ***with*** *Aunt Ellen* (or: *She and Aunt Ellen* ***got on*** *well*)*, but she found her rather a sick woman with mysterious internal pains.* RFW

get along without [Vp.pr] succeed reasonably well, manage to live or work, without (sth/sb). **o:** (any) help, assistance; equipment, spare parts; electricity, (regular) water supply; friends, other people: *I don't know how Mrs Briggs* ***gets along without*** *domestic help in that large house.* ○ *I have to* ***get along without*** *even proper equipment and work in a damned shack like this.* HD

get around [Vp] travel to many places, eg in connection with one's work: *She was in Milan last week and she's off to Oslo today. She certainly* ***gets around***.

get around/round 1 [Vpr pass] (*informal*) gain the confidence, trust or favour of (sb), usu for a special purpose: *Sarah told her boyfriend that she would try and* ***get round*** *her father to lend them the car for the day.* ○ *'You seem to have* ***got round*** *Mrs Williams all right. Tea in bed every morning! It's unheard-of.'*

2 [Vpr] tackle (sth) successfully; overcome. **o:** problem, obstacle, difficulty: *They haven't yet* ***got around*** *the costly inconvenience of running two* *homes — one in Leeds and one in London.* ○ *There seems to be no way of* **getting round** *the difficulty of keeping prices down while the cost of imports goes on rising.*

get around/round to [Vp.pr pass] find the necessary time, usu after some delay, for (doing sth). **o:** thinking about our holidays; taking out an insurance policy; digging the garden over; writing to my parents: *It was a pity, really, that Sheila had never* **got around to** *telling him about the baby.* FL ○ *I did plenty of designs he hasn't* **got around to** *using yet.* CON ○ *It was a week ... before Charles* **got round to** *looking for a job.* 50MH ○ *When I finally* **got round to** *buying the Christmas cards it was too late. The shops were all sold out.* □ the object is usu the *-ing* form of a v; usu neg, as in the first two examples, or used with *eventually, finally, at last* etc, as in the second two.

get at 1 [Vpr pass] reach (sth), possibly to steal, eat etc, it. **S:** curious eyes; thieving hands; children; mice. **o:** private papers, books; jewellery, deeds of the house, family silver, housekeeping money; jam, honey; dangerous medicines; flour, cheese: *All those streets, and no country to be* **got at** *save by car on special occasions.* BRH ○ *A sensible man keeps his savings in the bank — not in the house where some thief can* **get at** *them.* ○ *I'm afraid that rabbits have been* **getting at** *your chrysanthemums again.* □ note the unusual adj forms get'atable and unget'atable (= that can/cannot be got at). ⇨ be at 2.

2 [Vpr] start work on (sth); tackle. **o:** job; roof, garden, hedge: *I wish the snow would thaw so that I could* **get at** *the garden.*

3 [Vpr pass] discover or identify (sth). **o:** truth, facts; real wishes, intentions; the root of the trouble; the cause of the disturbances: *The official board of inquiry had the greatest difficulty in* **getting at** *the truth of the matter: there seemed to be a conspiracy of silence.* ○ *The only reason I relate these tiresome adventures is to* **get at** *the effect they had on us.* SU ⇨ come at 2.

4 [Vpr] suggest (sth) in an indirect way: *'I don't know what you're* **getting at** *exactly, but if you're suggesting that my brother is involved in this, you'd better think again.'* ○ *'Don't you see what I'm* **getting at**? *If we shared a flat we could both live much more cheaply.'* □ nearly always used in a direct or indirect question introduced by *what.* = what be driving at. ⇨ what be at.

5 [Vpr pass] (*informal*) criticize (sb) persistently; nag: *Olive is always* **getting at** *her husband because he doesn't keep the garden tidy.* ○ *Salvatore felt, in the course of this conversation, that he was being* **got at**. INN ⇨ be at 1.

6 [Vpr pass] (*informal*) (try to) influence (sb), esp by improper means. **o:** witness, jury: *'You didn't use to be so anti-religious. Who's been* **getting at** *you?'* ○ *The judge said it was obvious from the man's behaviour in the witness-box that he had been* **got at**.

getaway [nom (Vp)] escape (by criminals) from the scene of a crime: *Their* **getaway** *was obviously very well planned.* ○ *The* **getaway** *car was found abandoned not far from the scene of the robbery.* ○ *They made their* **getaway** *in a fast car under cover of darkness.* ⇨ get away with 1.

get away (from) 1 [Vp nom, Vp.pr rel] manage to leave (a place). **o:** house, office; his family, her husband; work, routine: *He was the big trout that always* **got away** *the moment you thought you had him hooked.* FL ○ *There's so much still to be done before we go on holiday that I can't see us* **getting away** *on time.* ○ *He needed ... an excuse to* **get away from** *London,* **from** *his office,* **from** *the insistent telephone.* TFD = escape (from).

2 [Vn.p pass, Vn.p.pr pass] help (sb) to leave (a place), esp for his own good. **O:** patient, invalid; parent. **o:** the fighting, the danger; relatives, children: *'Can't you* **get** *him* **away** *for a bit. He needs a complete rest.'* ○ *The poor woman must be* **got away from** *her children for a while. They're a dreadful strain.*

get away (from) [Vn.p.pr pass] win, secure (sth) in a struggle (from sth/sb). **O:** bone, stick; rifle, sword. **o:** dog, retriever; opponent, attacker: *'***Get** *the ball* **away** *from the dog!'* ○ *'The first thing was to try to* **get** *the gun* **away from** *the intruder.* ⇨ take away (from) 2.

get away from it all [Vp.pr] (*informal*) go away in order to gain relief from one's worries, responsibilities, excessive work etc: *He just couldn't wait for the day when he would pack his bags and* **get away from it all**. *The rat race had finally got him down.* ○ *It's no use* **getting away from it all** *if the cause of your troubles lies within yourself.*

get away with 1 [Vp.pr] steal and escape with (sth). **S:** thieves, burglars, bandits, confidence tricksters, con-man, (armed) gang, smash-and-grab raiders. **o:** property; jewellery, antiques, pictures, gold to the value of £10 000; the contents of the safe; £2 000 in notes and money-orders; one of the biggest hauls this year: *Bandits wearing stocking-masks raided the Midland Bank in Beckenham this morning and* **got away with** *over £100 000.* ⇨ getaway.

2 [Vp.pr] (*informal*) go unpunished for (sth), even if caught. **o:** anything, it; a piece of cheek; swearing at the referee: *What was amusing him was the thought that he, forty years old and weighing twelve stone, had punched a fourteen-stone international footballer of twenty-eight in the mouth and* **got away with** *it.* PE ○ *'If he can* **get away with** *defying the director's authority, he can* **get away with** *anything.'* ○ *Other men knocked off early and* **got away with** *it. Joe was always the one who got pulled up.* AITC ⇨ next entry

3 [Vp.pr] receive the relatively light or negligible punishment of (sth). **o:** a reprimand; seven days in gaol; suspension for a month: *'As it's a first offence,' the solicitor said, 'I think she'll* **get away with** *a fine. It'll be a heavy one, though; the magistrate'll aim at frightening her.'* ASA = get off 6. ⇨ previous entry

get away with murder [Vp.pr] (*informal*) do anything, however outrageous, and not be punished for it, or be thought any less of because of it: *With that innocent, smiling face of his, he could* **get away with murder**. ○ *'You have no real sense of justice, James. People you don't happen to like never get a bloody chance, and the others can* **get away with murder**.*'* ILIH □ usu with *can/could.*

get away with you! [Vp.pr] ⇨ get along/away with you!

get back 1 [Vp] return to one's starting point: *'When Tom* **gets back**, *please tell him that Jill phoned.'* ○ *'Good heavens! It's nearly midnight! I must be* **getting back**. *My wife will be wondering what's happened to me!'* ○ *Johnny's mother told him that he was to* **get back** *home before dark.* ○ *There was a letter of dismissal ... waiting when she* **got back** *to the room.* GJ ⇨ be back 1, bring back 1, come back 1, go back 1, take back 1.
2 [Vp] move back to a reasonable, sensible distance: *The police had some difficulty in making the crowd* **get back** *and let the ambulance through.* ○ *'***Get back**! *There's a bomb in the building!'* □ usu in direct or indirect commands.
3 [Vn.p pass] return (sth/sb) to its/his place: *'You took the spring out of the clock; now you must* **get** *it* **back**.*'* ○ *'If you take Mary out you must promise to* **get** *her* **back** *in time for her music lesson.'* ○ *'I'm afraid we can't* **get** *your TV* **back** *to you for this evening; but we can lend you one.'* ⇨ be back 2, put back 1.
4 [Vn ⇆ p] recover sth which belongs to one: *Don't lend Bill your umbrella! If you do, you'll never* **get** *it* **back**.*'* ⇨ give back (to) 1, have back 1.

get one's breath back [Vn ⇆ p] after a period of physical exertion, be able to breath normally again: *'Give me a couple of minutes to* **get my breath back**!*'* ○ *Dickens was so prostrated that he could not* **get back his breath** *for some time.* CD

get one's own back [Vn.p] (*informal*) get one's revenge; retaliate: *Margaret had a habit of snubbing her lover in public; perhaps it was her way of* **getting her own back** *for the way he completely dominated her in private.* ⇨ next entry

get back at [Vp.pr pass] (*informal*) get one's revenge on (sb); retaliate against. **o:** her critics, boss; shopkeeper, supplier; bully, know-all: *Joe* **got back at** *his more adventurous and successful colleagues by sniping at them in committee meetings.* ○ *Civil servants have no way of* **getting back at** *individuals who criticize them, so they sometimes take it out on the public in general.*

get back into circulation [Vp.pr] (*informal*) return to normal life, mix once more with one's friends and colleagues: *You could have a few things done to your face by a surgeon and* **get back into circulation** *again, but even false passports have to be renewed from time to time, and the whole business is pretty tricky.* DS ○ *It's about time you* **got back into circulation**, *isn't it? After all, you can't spend your whole life here sitting against that wall, ...*THH

get back to 1 [Vp.pr] return to (an activity); resume. **o:** work, one's studies; the job in hand; the main point in the argument; what you were saying: *The students were glad to* **get back to** *their books after a vacation that had seemed too long.* ○ *'But to* **get back to** *the question of your immediate plans ... What are you doing next week?'* ○ *He woke up at half past three and couldn't* **get back to** *sleep.*
2 [Vp.pr] (*informal*) call (sb) again after the telephone conversation one has been having with him is interrupted: *'Bill, I'll* **get back to** *you just as soon as these visitors have left.'* ○ *He caught sight of Macon. 'Macon!' he said. 'Stefanie, I'll* **get back to** *you.' He hung up.* AT □ often used, with *will/'ll*, to make a promise to resume the conversation.

get back to the grindstone [Vp.pr] return to one's job, with the implication that the job is uninteresting, difficult or tiring: *To think that in three days' time our holiday will be over and we'll have to* **get back to the grindstone** □ sometimes simply 'Back to the grindstone!' ⇨ keep one's nose to the grindstone.

get behind 1 [Vp, Vp.pr] move back behind (others); be overtaken by (others). **m:** badly; a long way, very far: *Owing to his illness, Peter* **got** *badly* **behind** *in English and maths.* = fall behind 1. ↔ get ahead/ahead of. ⇨ be behind 2.
2 [Vp, Vpr] fail to pay, complete or deliver (sth) for some time. **S:** customer; supplier; borrower. **A:** with one's payments; on deliveries; in repaying a loan: *If you* **get behind** *with your repayments on the machine, the dealer will repossess it.* ○ *The company undertook to deliver a thousand components a month but* **got** *badly* **behind** *on deliveries.* = fall behind 2. ⇨ be behind 1.

get by 1 [Vp] pass an obstacle: *There was such a crowd outside the shop window that the young woman with the pram couldn't* **get by**. ○ *Traffic had come to a complete halt. A lorry had broken down and nothing could* **get by**. ⇨ come by 1.
2 [Vp] be considered acceptable: *Ramsbottom didn't possess a dinner-jacket, but he was told that he would* **get by** *in a dark suit.* ○ *Liz thought that she could* **get by** *with the minimum of work. Her tutor quickly disabused her!*
3 [Vp] (*informal*) manage to survive, though only narrowly: *'Don't worry, Johnnie,' she said, 'I'm not prophesying ruin. You'll* **get by** *— indeed, you'll probably drift from strength to strength.'* ASA ○ *My parents never seemed to have much money, but somehow they managed to* **get by**. = get along. ⇨ next entry

get by on/upon [Vp.pr emph rel] (*informal*) manage to survive by means of or with the help of (sth). **o:** small income, pension; allowance, grant; a handful of rice; native intelligence, wit: *Without the breakdown she would have* **got by upon** *her native wit, and with her competence she would have made her way in peace time.* RFW ○ *'You've got a job, haven't you, on that fancy magazine? We can* **get by on** *that for a start.'* AITC ⇨ previous entry

get down 1 [Vp emph, Vpr] descend: *'Who said you could climb up there? Now,* **down** *you* **get** *at once.'* ○ *Several people escaped from the burning building by* **getting down** *a ladder.* = climb down 1. ↔ get up 3,4.
2 [Vp] visit a place in the country from the capital, or one in the South from the North: *It's not often that we* **get down** *to see my son in London.* ○ *'It'd be nice if you could manage to* **get down** *there ... I know she'd like to see more of you.'* FL = come down 5. ↔ come up 2.
3 [Vp emph] adopt a stooping or kneeling position. **A:** on all fours; on one's knees: *I thought I heard a mouse under the bed, and* **got down** *on all fours to have a look.* ○ *'You should* **get down** *on your knees and pray that we've enough money left to see us through.'* ⇨ go down on one's knees (to) 1.
4 [Vn ⇆ p pass] record (sth) on paper, esp quickly or with difficulty. **O:** everything, the main points, the gist of what he said; lecture; message, confession; the number of the car, her address: *'***Get** *this* **down** *in your notebooks!'* ○ *I didn't* **get down**

every word, but I certainly **got** *a lot of the conversation* **down**. = write down. ⇨ be down 3, go down 9, put down 11, set down 2, take down 3.

5 [Vn ⇆ p pass] swallow (sth), usu with difficulty. **O:** medicine, pill; wine, whisky; meat, rice: *Fred* **got** *his medicine* **down** *with the help of a spoonful of jam.* ○ *I could hardly* **get** *the last of the couscous* **down** *It was delicious, but I had taken too much.* ⇨ go down 4.

6 [Vn.p] (*informal*) depress, demoralize (sb). **S:** weather; things in general, life, work; sb's attitude, behaviour; disease, drink: *Going straight* (ie being honest) *was* **getting** *Vin* **down** *a little.* ASA ○ *Don't let your work* **get** *you* **down**. *You must try to forget about it when you leave the office.* ○ *It's a terrible state of affairs when you let drink* **get** *you* **down** *like that.* DBM

get down in the dumps/mouth [Vp.pr] (*informal*) become depressed, miserable: *He's one of those people who can't stand his own company. As soon as he finds himself alone he* **gets down in the dumps**. ⇨ be down in the dumps/mouth.

get down to [Vp.pr pass] (*informal*) take steps to manage or settle (sth); tackle. **o:** work, job, task; his writing; things, it; thinking about the future: *From the day our schooldays began, we were taught, implicitly, that every other boy was a potential rival and that we must all* **get down to** *the sacred task of outdoing one another.* CON ○ *'Look! You'll never finish that job unless you drop everything else and really* **get down to** *it.'*

get down to brass tacks [Vp.pr] (*informal*) discuss, talk about (sth) in practical, businesslike terms: *'It's time George stopped all this theorizing and* **got down to brass tacks**. *What we want to know is how much the job will cost, not how scientific the method is going to be.'*

get down to business [Vp.pr] start serious discussion about sth, perhaps after some time has been spent on irrelevant or social talk: *The two men had a couple of drinks together, talked about their families and their holidays for a while, and finally* **got down to business**. ○ *'I hope you don't mind if we* **get down to business** *straightaway, as I've got to catch the four o'clock train.'*

get down to a fine art [Vn.p.pr pass] learn to do (sth) with perfection. **O:** carving the joint; catching rats; getting money out of his father; making beer: *Becky always manages to have something urgent to do — homework, music practice, feeding her pets — when it's time to wash the dishes. She's* **got** *it* **down to a fine art**. □ usu in the perfect tense, as in the example.

get home 1 [Vp, Vn.p pass] return to one's house; help (sb) return to his house: *'What time did you* **get home** *last night?'* ○ *'If you'll come round for coffee, I'll promise to* **get** *you* **home** *before ten o'clock.'*

2 [Vp] (*racing, athletics*) reach the winning-post, target, etc, first. **S:** favourite, champion, record-holder: *My horse* **got home** *by a nose!* ○ *The hundred metres champion managed to* **get home** *by a tenth of a second.*

get home (to) [Vp, Vp.pr, Vn.p pass, Vn.p.pr pass] (cause sth to) be understood; (cause sth to) hit its target. **S** [Vp, Vp.pr], **O** [Vn.p, Vn.p.pr]**:** point; criticism, barb, satire: [Vp] *The TV enquiry* **got home** *all right. The next morning, the papers were full of it.* ○ [Vn.p] *Politicians are adept as* **getting** *their point* **home**, *even in the face of constant interruptions from their opponents.* ○ [Vn.p.pr] *We left the meeting confident that we had at last* **got** *the essential part of our proposal* **home to** *the more conservative members of the Council.* = drive home (to). ⇨ bring/come home (to).

get in 1 [Vn ⇆ p pass] gather, harvest (a crop). **O:** crops, fruit; tomatoes, potatoes; hay, wheat: *The growers have to employ casual labour to help* **get in** *the strawberries.* ○ *The farmers were delighted to* **get** *the hay* **in** *so early in the year.* ⇨ be in 2, bring in 1.

2 [Vn ⇆ p pass] obtain the services or advice of (sb). **O:** specialist, another doctor; plumber, electrician; management consultants: *When he saw how ill his mother was he told the doctor he would like to* **get** *a specialist* **in**. ○ *'There's a leak somewhere under the kitchen sink. We'd better* **get in** *a plumber to fix it.'* ⇨ have in.

3 [Vp] (*informal*) gain an advantage by being the first, or one of the first, to do sth. **A:** ⚠ first; early; on the ground floor; at the start: *A Manchester charter firm* **got in** *first, offering a £250 return fare to the Caribbean.* ○ *Reg had* **got in** *on the ground floor, and as the firm had progressed, so had he.* ⇨ be/come in on the ground floor.

4 [Vn ⇆ p pass] (*boxing*) succeed in landing (a blow) on one's opponent. **O:** blow, punch; jab, right hook: *The challenger was so outclassed that he couldn't* **get** *a single blow* **in**. ○ *The champ* **got in** *one or two sharp jabs with his left.*

get a blow in [Vn ⇆ p pass] make a verbal attack on sb; strike a blow (for): *We tackled the Minister on the issue of river pollution during his recent visit, and* **got a blow in** *for our anti-pollution policy.*

get one's eye in [Vn.p] (*sport*) reach the point in a ball-game where one can judge distances, the speed of the ball etc, well enough to play easily and successfully: *Once Gooch* **gets his eye in**, *he'll score a century or more off this bowling.* ○ *The sunlight out on court is very strong — she'll take a while to* **get her eye in**. □ in games such as cricket and tennis, one normally needs to get one's eye in every time one plays. ⇨ keep one's hand/eye in. ⇨ next entry

get one's hand in [Vn.p] develop skill with one's hands: *Once the girl* **gets her hand in** *she'll be getting through as much work as the more experienced machinists.* ⇨ previous entry

get a word in (edgeways) [Vn.p] (*informal*) succeed in saying something when many people are talking, or when another person will not stop talking: *The scorn, ridicule, slander and threats poured over him in a remorseless stream that flowed so steadily he had no chance to* **get a word in**. DF ○ *The three of them had so much to talk about that I couldn't* **get a word in edgeways**. □ usu neg.

get in/into 1 [Vp emph Vpr] enter (a place): *The thieves* **got in** *by tunnelling under the floor.* ○ *They* **got into** *the strongroom by tunnelling under the floor.* ○ *'Don't stand there dithering!* **Get in**! *The water's not all that cold.'* ○ *I believe in* **getting into** *the water as quickly as possible.* ↔ get out/out of 1. ⇨ come in/into 1, let in/into.

2 [Vp, Vpr, Vn.p pass, Vn.pr pass] (cause sth to) arrive (at a place). **S** [Vp, Vpr], **O** [Vn.p, Vn.pr]**:** train;

ferry; bus. **o:** station; Dublin; town. **A:** on time; late, early, punctually: [Vp] *'What time does the 2.05 from Euston* **get in**, *please?'* ○ [Vpr] *The coach* **gets into** *Carlisle at about 6.15.* ○ [Vn.pr] *In spite of heavy seas the Captain* **got** *the ferry* **into** *Liverpool on time.*
3 [Vp, Vpr, Vn.p pass, Vn.pr pass] (*politics*) (cause sb to) be elected (to office). **S** [Vp, Vpr], **O** [Vn.p, Vn.pr]**:** the present Government; the Tories, Labour, the Liberal Democrats. **S** [Vn.p, Vn.pr]**:** the floating vote; the employment issue, the Government's handling of the economy: [Vp] *The Conservatives* **got in** *with a small majority.* ○ [Vpr] *The independent candidate* **got into** *Parliament with a thumping majority.* ○ [Vn.p] *The Prime Minister's support* **got** *the official party man* **in**. ⇨ be in 4, come in 4, put in 7.

get in on [Vp.pr, Vn.p.pr pass] (*informal*) become involved in an activity, with the implication that joining is desirable but possibly difficult. **o:** debate, discussion; new organization; grants for restoring old property; the play; the trip to Italy: *It's important that you should* **get in on** *the discussion about the future development of the department.* ○ *Don't let Matthew know we are thinking of forming a new society. He would* **get** *his wife* **in on** *it and they would end up running it.* ⇨ be/bring/come/let in on.

get in with [Vp.pr] (*informal*) (try to) form a relationship with (sb), perhaps with an ulterior motive for doing so: *'Everyone likes a drink. You come over to the Golf Club with me, you'll soon find that out. I'll make you a member. You'll* **get in with** *them in a jiffy if you'll only try.'* FFE ○ *He managed to* **get** *well* **in with** *local business leaders by joining the golf club.* □ note also (*US informal*): get in bad with: *The new man was unfortunate enough to* **get in bad with** *the boss on the first day.* ⇨ be (well) in with.

get in contact/touch (with) [Vpr, Vn.pr pass] (help sb to) meet or contact (sb): *I've been meaning to* **get in contact** (**with** *you) about some changes I'd like to make to the first-year course.* ○ *Bill and Sally miss each other badly. Somebody ought to* **get** *them* **in touch with** *each other again.* ↔ lose contact/touch (with). ⇨ be in/bring into/come into contact (with), be/put in touch (with).

get into 1 [Vp] enter (a place). ⇨ get in/into 1.
2 [Vpr, Vn.pr pass] (cause to) arrive at (a place). ⇨ get in/into 2.
3 [Vpr, Vn.pr pass] (*politics*) (cause sb to) be elected to (office). ⇨ get in/into 3.
4 [Vpr, Vn.pr pass] (help sb to) get dressed in (sth). **O:** himself, feet; baby; actor. **o:** suit, shoes; clothes; mask: *I* **got into** *my shirt and shorts and wandered out into the hotel garden.* ○ *At the end of the six-hour flight, my feet had swollen so much that I couldn't* **get** *them back* **into** *my shoes.* ○ *'Have you got this dress in a size 14? I don't think I'll get into a size 12.'* = put on 1.
5 [Vpr] enter, penetrate (sth). **S:** sand, dust; flies, wasps; smell, gas, fumes. **o:** hair, eyes, nose, mouth, ears; everything; jam, honey; room, hall; every corner of the house: *The molten lava* **got into** *every nook and cranny on its downward path.* ○ *Spiders seem to* **get into** *every corner of the woodwork. They're everywhere.*
6 [Vpr, Vn.pr pass] (cause sb to) become involved in (sth). **o:** trouble, quarrel, fight; hopeless mess, tangle; debt: *He was a little too fond of drink and would occasionally* **get into** *fights.* TFD ○ *It's easier to* **get into** *debt than to get out of it again!* ○ *Oswald was no sooner out of one pickle than he had* **got** *himself* **into** *another.* GL ○ *'Please don't make so much noise. You'll* **get** *me* **into** *trouble.'* ↔ keep out of.
7 [Vpr, Vn.pr pass] (cause sb to) acquire, learn (sth). **o:** (the way, hang, of) it; the habit (of doing sth): *The children* **got into** *the dreadful habit of switching on the television as soon as they came in from school.* ○ *They too were on their own, and we* **got into** *the way of going on our daily walks together.* BRH ○ *Painting is a fascinating hobby once you* **get into** *it.* = fall into 3. ↔ get out of the habit/way of doing sth.
8 [Vpr, Vn.pr pass] (cause sb to) enter (a certain emotional state). **o:** rage, fury, temper; tizzy, stew, paddy: *Nick had* **got into** *a blind fury and started smashing the furniture up.* ○ *'Try not to* **get** *your father* **into** *a temper tonight. I want a bit of peace and quiet.'* ○ *'You shouldn't* **get into** *a stew about nothing. It's bad for your blood pressure!'*
9 [Vpr] seize, possess (sb's emotions or thoughts). **S:** ⚠ something, the Devil; I don't know what: *We could not understand why the child was being so uncooperative. Something must have* **got into** *her.* ○ *'What's* **got into** *him?' he asked. 'He never used to do this.'* AT

get into the act [Vpr] (*informal*) involve oneself, often in an unwelcome way, in an activity started by sb else: *'The trouble with Stephen is that whenever someone has a new idea, like a training programme for overseas staff, he wants to* **get into the act**. *Then he ends up running it.'* ⇨ get in on.

get into deep water [Vpr] become involved in matters that are too difficult or complicated to handle: *'We'd better not talk about starting up a new company before the first one is operating smoothly, or we'll be* **getting into deep water**.

get into one's head [Vn.pr] (*informal*) come to believe, understand fully (that sth is the case). **O:** these facts; it ... that I'm not God; it ... what this meant: *'I wish you would* **get** *it* **into your head,** *once and for all, that I'm not made of money.'* ○ *How did Tom* **get** *it* **into his head** *that medicine was an easy profession?* ○ *It was years before I really* **got** *it* **into my head** *what this second kind of attention really was like.* LIFE

get one's hooks into [Vn.pr] (*informal*) succeed in dominating or controlling (sb), esp sexually. **o:** man; boss, tutor: *Once Barbara's* **got her hooks into** *him he'll have a devil of a job getting free.*

get into hot water [Vpr, Vn.pr pass] (*informal*) (cause sb/oneself to) be in serious trouble: *The receptionist* **got into hot water** *for handing over the documents without insisting on a receipt.* ○ *'You'll be* **getting** *yourself and me* **into hot water** *if you take the car out again. The insurance doesn't cover a second driver.'*

get into a rut [Vpr] (*informal*) be trapped in one's routine, in a set pattern of life, at home or at work: *By the time Harold was forty, he realized that he had* **got into a rut** *and that there was very little he could do about it.*

get into one's stride [Vpr] reach the stage, when speaking, playing, working etc, when one is performing at one's best: *Once the preacher* **got into his stride** *it became obvious that we were in for a very long sermon.* ○ *CLIVE: Let us therefore not gasp too excitedly at the loftiness of Mother's family tree. . . . it has, as you see, roots of clay (Clive pours himself some coffee, Walter stares at him in silence, as he* **gets into his stride***).* FFE

get one's teeth into 1 [Vn.pr] grip (sth) firmly with the teeth; attack (food) hungrily. **S:** dog; hungry boys. **o:** leg; dinner: *The postman is terrified of that great mastiff* **getting its teeth into** *his ankle.* ○ *When I left them the children were* **getting their teeth** *into a roast chicken.* ○ *'Here,* **get your teeth into** *that; it should keep you going till the morning.'*

2 [Vn.pr] (*informal*) approach (sth) with determination; work with concentration on (sth). **S:** secretary, manager; researcher; detective. **o:** task, job; problem; investigation, case: *Being put in complete charge of the office obviously gave her something to* **get her teeth into**. ○ *These are the sorts of situation that one likes to* **get one's teeth into**. L □ often preceded by *give sb/have/there be anything/nothing/something to . . . .*

get the better of 1 [Vn.p pass(o)] defeat (sb) in a quarrel, a struggle for power etc. **o:** boss, colleague, rival: *It was natural for Tom not to let pass an opportunity for* **getting the better of** *me.* SPL ○ *Don't always try and* **get the better of** *her over every stupid incident.* H ○ *He was* **got the better of** *by a more experienced dealer.*

2 [Vn.pr] overcome, defeat (sb). **S:** curiosity, fear, anxiety, exhaustion: *Soon, tiredness* **got the better of** *me and I fell into a deep sleep.* ○ *At times her jealousy would* **get the better of** *her.* GJ

get the better/best of [Vn.pr rel] be the winner in (a contest). **o:** it, things; argument, quarrel, fight: *When Alex and Robert argue, Alex always manages to* **get the better of** *it.* ○ *Bill and Jane fought again, and you know who always* **gets the best of** *their fights!* ↔ get the worst of. ⇨ have the best/worst of.

get the hang of [Vn.pr] (*informal*) understand or appreciate (sb/sth); grasp how to do (sth). **o:** him, what he said; this type of art, architecture; driving this car, riding a horse: *'I can't exactly make him out. Just can't* **get the hang of** *him, that's all.'* TC ○ *That lecture was beyond me. I just couldn't* **get the hang of** *what he was saying at all.* ○ *I shall probably quite enjoy driving the car once I* **get the hang of** *the automatic gearbox.*

get hold of [Vn.pr pass(o)] (*informal*) obtain (sth); reach or contact (sb). **o:** name, telephone number; duplicate, copy; waiter, policeman: *He'd have no problem* **getting hold of** *a key.* TFD ○ *At that time travel permits were not easily* **got hold of**. ○ *If it's very urgent, I may be able to* **get hold of** *the doctor for you during the lunch-hour.*

get hold of the wrong end of the stick [Vn.pr] (*informal*) completely misunderstand a situation or something said: *'If you owe John fifty pounds, why don't you stop arguing and just pay him?' 'Me pay him! You've* **got hold of the wrong end of the stick**! *It's John who owes* me *fifty pounds!'* ○ *He has an exasperating habit of* **getting hold of the wrong end of the stick**!

get rid of [Vn.pr pass (o)] free a place or oneself of (sb/sth). **o:** hanger-on, sponger; parasite, vermin; smell; headache, cold: *His letters home refer to the difficulty of* **getting rid of** *unwelcome callers.* TU ○ *He tore round the garden . . . shouting in his desperate need to* **get rid of** *surplus energy.* BRH ○ *'I wish those press photographs could be* **got rid of**!*'* = rid of.

get wind of [Vn.pr pass(o)] hear news of (sth), usu in an indirect or roundabout way. **o:** changes, developments; his involvement, intentions; them/their being with me: *Whenever we* **got wind of** *a fat parcel of diamonds on its way out of Africa towards Monsieur Diamant or his friends, we tipped off London.* DS ○ *Georgina had* **got wind of** *a plan among the villagers to meet Dickens at Higham Station.* CD ○ *It was amazing that preparations for the landing were not* **got wind of** *by the enemy.*

get the worst of [Vn.pr] be defeated, be overcome, in (a contest); suffer the most as a result of (events). **o:** it, things; argument, fight: *Joe had been adopting a non-belligerent attitude, and* **getting the worst of** *things. The women were taking unfair advantage of him.* ○ *When two armies come to blows, it is usually the ordinary civilians who* **get the worst of** *it.* ↔ get the better/best of. ⇨ have the best/worst of.

get off 1 [Vp emph, Vpr] dismount, alight (from sth). **o:** horse, bicycle; train, bus: *They were* **getting off** *at the new stop near the Luxembourg Gardens.* AF ○ *'***Off** *you* **get** *and let me have a ride!'* ○ *A policeman told me to* **get off** *my motorbike.* ↔ get on/onto. ⇨ let off 1, put off 6.

2 [Vpr] move from (a place). **o:** father's chair; your behind; ladder, wall, roof; grass, flowerbeds, tennis-courts: *'We'd better* **get off** *the lake before the storm breaks, or we'll get soaked.'* ○ *The children were told to* **get off** *the scaffolding round the building.* ⇨ keep off 2.

3 [Vp, Vn.p pass] (cause sb to) leave or start a journey: *'What time are you leaving tomorrow?' 'We hope to* **get off** *before seven o'clock.'* ○ *The children had to* **get** *themselves* **off** *to school as both their parents went out to work at eight o'clock.* ○ *'***Get** *yourself* **off** *to bed now, there's my good Gabriel.'* GL ⇨ be off 3, set off (on) 1.

4 [Vn ⇆ p pass, Vn.pr pass] (manage to) remove (sth) (from sth). **O:** feet; clothes; paint; hands; boots. **o:** the mantelpiece; the floor; the door; my property; feet: *Her finger had swollen so much that she couldn't* **get** *her ring* **off**. ○ *'***Get** *that stinking animal* **off** *the table and back into its cage.'* ↔ get on 1. ⇨ take off 2.

5 [Vp, Vn ⇆ p pass] (cause sth to) go by post, radio etc; supervise the sending of (sth) by post etc. **S** [Vp], **O** [Vn.p]**:** message, cable, wire, letter: *'Please make sure these letters* **get off** *by the five o'clock post.'* ○ *Our man in Sydney is the obvious person to make the contacts in Papua-New Guinea. Let's* **get** *a fax* **off** *to him immediately.* ⇨ send off 1.

6 [Vp, Vn.p pass] escape or nearly escape punishment; save (sb) from punishment. **A:** lightly; with a suspended sentence, with a warning, with a caution, with a fine; scot-free: *Considering his record, he was lucky to* **get off** *with a six-month sentence.* ○ *It was her youth that* **got** *her* **off***, not her innocence.* = get away with 3. ⇨ let off 2, let off with.

7 [Vp] escape or nearly escape injury in an accident. **A:** lightly, unscathed; with only a few scratches and bruises, with a broken rib or two, with minor injuries: *Fortunately the two cars did not crash head on, so Bill* **got off** *with nothing worse than a bad fright.* ○ *The patrol was ambushed but* **got off** *fairly lightly. One man was killed and four wounded.*

tell sb where he gets off/where to get off [Vp] (*informal*) reproach, reprove, admonish (sb): *Joe's been throwing his weight around for far too long. It's high time somebody* **told him where he got off**. ○ *The old lady* **told the policeman where he got off** *in no uncertain terms.*

get off sb's back Vpr (*informal*) stop harassing or or bothering (sb): *The cricketers are telling the politicians 'Get off our backs!'* ↔ get on sb's back.

get off one's chest [Vn.pr pass] (*informal*) say (sth) which one has long wanted to say and thus relieve one's feelings; not suppress. **O:** ⚠ it, everything, the whole thing: *'Don't just sit there brooding! If you've got something you want to tell me, now's your chance to* **get** *it* **off your chest**.' ○ *These are desperately hurt people ... Part of my effectiveness is that they can* **get** *everything* **off their chest**. ST

get off the ground [Vpr, Vn.pr pass] (*informal*) (cause sth to) begin to succeed clearly and noticeably. **S** [Vpr], **O** [Vn.pr]**:** show, performance; discussion, debate; plan, scheme. **S** [Vn.pr]**:** producer; chairman; organizer: *A discussion of jokes failed to* **get off the ground**. ST ○ *This hardly seemed the best way to* **get** *the international festival* **off the ground**. BBCR = take off 13.

get off the hook [Vpr, Vn.pr pass] (*informal*) (allow sb to) escape, get free, from an unpleasant task, a firm commitment etc: *Parliamentary action was required* (to change the power of local councils). *Some councils struggled and wriggled to* **get off the** *administrative* **hook**. NS ○ *'She'll have to stay in charge of the project till next year, unless somebody comes back from the States early and* **gets** *her* **off the hook**. ⇨ let off the hook.

get the weight off one's feet/legs [Vn.pr] (*informal*) sit or lie down; often said to a pregnant woman, or anyone who has some weakness or who has been standing for a long time: *'Come on, sit down, Kathy.* **Get that weight off your legs**.' LLDR ○ *'You're looking a bit tired. Why don't you* **get the weight off your feet**?' ⇨ take the weight off one's feet.

get off on the right/wrong foot [Vp.pr, Vn.p.pr pass] (cause sb/sth to) begin sth, esp a relationship, in the right/wrong way: *The professor seems to have a gift for* **getting off on the wrong foot** *with a new colleague.* ○ *Stalin was deliberate in making the best of his disadvantages and often he liked to* **get** *his interlocutor* **off on the wrong foot**. OBS ○ *The marketing director took pains to* **get** *the campaign* **off on the right foot**. = start off on the right etc.

get off to a good etc start [Vp.pr, Vn.p.pr pass] (cause sb/sth to) begin well etc. **S** [Vp.pr], **O** [Vn.p.pr]**:** runner, horse; enterprise, campaign, scheme, project. **S** [Vn.p.pr]**:** steward, official; manage, organizer. **adj:** good, bad, poor, slow, splendid, flying: *The whole evening had* **got off to a bad start** *when Mousie had arrived half an hour too early.* MSAL ○ *Milton's marriage, very evidently,* **got off to a poor start**. MLT ○ *The widespread publicity failed to* **get** *the fund* **off to a good start**.

get off (to sleep) [Vp, Vp.pr, Vn.p pass, Vn.p.pr pass] fall asleep; send (sb) to sleep : [Vp.pr] I was absolutely exhausted from the long journey, but I simply couldn't **get off to sleep**. *That's what happens to me when I'm overtired.* ○ [Vn.p.pr] It took the nurse half an hour to **get** *the baby* **off to sleep**.

get off with [Vp.pr, Vn.p.pr pass] (*informal*) succeed in attracting (sb) sexually; arrange such a relationship for (sb): *He* **got off with** *my secretary, a thing he no doubt imagined I was secretly burning to do myself.* ○ *'It's time Sam had a girlfriend. Can't you* **get** *him* **off with** *that nice girl you keep talking about?'* ○ *Eddie has to* **get off with** *people because he can't get on with them.* EB □ the last example plays on the contrast between the meanings of get off with and get on with (have a harmonious relationship with).

get on 1 [Vn ⇆ p pass] get dressed in (sth); put (sth) into position. **O:** things (ie hat and coat); something warm, bathing costume, swim-suit; lid, cover: *'I'll just* **get** *my things* **on** *and we'll go for a short walk.'* ○ *He got the top off the jar but couldn't* **get** *it* **on** *again.* ↔ get off 4. ⇨ have on 1, put on 1.

2 [Vp, Vn.p] make progress physically, socially, professionally etc; advance. **A:** nicely; at work, in business; in life, in the world: *She is* **getting on** *so well; a few weeks more of good air and rest will do everything for her.* BLCH ○ *They say he is making money and will* **get on**. BLCH ○ *To become an instituteur* (primary schoolteacher) *was the established way for a bright child of poor parents to* **get on** *in the world.* AF

3 [Vp] manage, perform, in a particular situation: *'How did you* **get on** *in your oral examination?' 'Not too badly. I don't think I failed, anyway!'* ○ *I didn't* **get on** *too well in France. My school French was quite useless; nobody could understand a word I said.* = make out 6.

4 [Vp] (of time) become late; (of people) advance in age, grow old. **S:** it, time; father: *'Time's* **getting on**, *so will you all start getting ready, please? The bus will be here in twenty minutes.'* ○ *It was* **getting on** *towards midnight when Bill called round.* ○ *'The director's* **getting on** *a bit, isn't she? Must be close to retirement.'* ○ *When a woman's* **getting on** *in years, and not very well, it's a great comfort to have a girl about the place who's sensible and responsible.* RFW □ usu in continuous tenses. ⇨ get on for, go on (for).

5 [Vp] (*informal*) (used as an exclamation of disbelief, surprise etc): *'Guess how far I walked yesterday?' 'Ten miles?' 'No, thirty-two!'* '**Get on!**'. = go on! 14. ⇨ get along/away with you!, go along with you!.

get on sb's back [Vpr] (*informal*) harass or bother (sb): *'You were a bit late arriving at work today, Nick.' 'Oh, Lord, are you going to* **get on my back**, *too? I had two hours of complaints from my wife last night, and a load of bills by this morning's post!'* ○ *FLINT: Look, George — nobody else has seen these reports, especially Grace, thank God. Far as I'm concerned they were never written, but man, what's happened to you? DIXON: Don't* **get on my back**, *Sarge* (= Sergeant) — *I've had enough.* BBCTV ↔ get off sb's back.

get on one's feet [Vpr] stand up for a special purpose, eg to speak in a debate: *When the member for Sefton* **gets on his feet** *in the Commons, there's no knowing when he will sit down again.* ⇨ be on/come to one's feet, bring to his feet.

get on one's/his feet [Vpr, Vn.pr pass] (cause or help sth/sb to) recover. **S** [Vpr], **O** [Vn.pr]**:** firm, company; the wounded, injured; patient: *After the recent recession the car industry will need time to* **get on its feet** *again.* ○ *Exercise and a sensible diet will help* **get** *Phil* **on his feet** *again.*

get a grip on [Vn.pr] gain or regain full control of (oneself/sb/sth). **o:** oneself; things, affairs, events: *'I could see years ago that you hadn't* **got a grip on** *things. But I didn't think you would have come down to this.'* HD ○ *'Look here, Bill! You really must* **get a grip on** *yourself. You can't let your wife see you in this state.'*

get one's hands on 1 [Vn.pr rel] obtain (sth), often as a fulfilment of one's desires or as an essential part of a long-cherished plan. **o:** money; a first edition, her private diary; a nice plot of land, a cottage in the country: *He's a second-hand dealer. It doesn't matter what it is: anything he can* **get his hands on**, *he sells.* ○ *If only I could* **get my hands on** *a couple of thousand pounds, I'd be able to get married.* = lay one's hands on 1.

2 [Vn.pr] (*informal*) get near enough to (sb/sth) to seize or hit him/it: *'That woman's got a nerve. Just let me* **get my hands on** *her!'* ○ *'Those damned cats kept me awake again all last night. If I could* **get my hands on** *them, I'd throttle them.'* = lay one's hands on 3.

get one's hooks on [Vn.pr] ⇨ get one's hooks into/on.

get a move on [Vn.p] (*informal*) take urgent steps to do sth; be quick: *'If you don't* **get a move on**, *you'll miss the last bus.'* ○ *Martin is going to have to* **get a move on** *if he wants to pass his finals.*

get on the move [Vpr, Vn.pr pass] (cause sb/sth to) start moving. **S** [Vpr], **O** [Vn.pr]**:** army; family; holiday-makers; animals; swallows; traffic: *After that terrible pile-up in the fog, it was several hours before the traffic could* **get on the move** *again.* ○ *It was dawn before the men could be* **got on the move** *over the difficult, unfamiliar terrain.*

get on sb's nerves [Vpr] annoy or irritate (sb): *She* **gets on your nerves**, *doesn't she, the way she never stops talking about her brilliant son?* ○ *The constant noise of aircraft flying overhead* **gets on everyone's nerves**. ○ *The letter* **got on my nerves**. *It was far from stupid and therefore dangerously persuasive.* JUNG

get on the right side of [Vpr] make oneself popular with (sb), avoid offending him, often in the hope of getting favourable treatment etc. **o:** boss, captain; cook, matron: *He* **got on the right side of** *the camp guards early on, so he was never short of food.* ○ *If you want to stay up late to see the Bond film on TV, you'd better* **get on the right side of** *your father.* ↔ get on the wrong side of. ⇨ keep on the right side of.

get one's skates on [Vn.p] (*informal*) be quick; make haste: *If you're going to meet your friends at the station, you'll have to* **get your skates on**, *because the train is due in five minutes!*

get on sb's wick [Vpr] (*slang*) annoy or irritate (sb): *'The boss* **gets on my wick** *with his everlasting complaints about timekeeping. He thinks nothing of rolling up at the office at ten o'clock himself.'* = get on sb's nerves.

get on the wrong side of [Vpr] form a poor relationship with (sb): *Poor Jane* **got on the wrong side of** *her mother-in-law from the start by ignoring her advice about a suitable flat.* ○ *I'd advise you not to* **get on the wrong side of** *Smith. He can be very awkward and is capable of making life very uncomfortable for you.* = get across 2. ↔ get on the right side of.

get on for [Vp.pr] draw near to, approach (a stated time or age). **S:** it (of time); old : *'What time is it?' 'I don't know exactly, but it must be* **getting on for** *midnight.'* ○ *'I've got to go. It's* **getting on for** *five and I promised to meet my wife at the bowling-club.'* ○ *Jessie continued to look after herself in her own home although she was* **getting on for** *a hundred.* ⇨ get on 4, go on (for).

get on/onto [Vp, Vpr, Vn.p pass, Vn.pr pass] (cause or help sb to) mount or board (sth). **o:** horse, bicycle; bus, tram, train; boat, ship, hovercraft, hydrofoil; plane: [Vp] *The bus was full when it stopped at the school gates, so the children couldn't* **get on**. ○ [Vpr] *Before you can learn to ride a horse you have to be able to* **get on** (or: **onto**) *it.* ○ [Vn.pr] *The plane wasn't large enough to take 50, so the travel agent couldn't* **get** *us all* **on** *the same flight.* ↔ get off 1.

get on to 1 [Vp.pr pass] make contact with (sb/sth), esp by telephone but also by letter etc. **o:** electricians, suppliers; emergency service, police, fire-station; HQ, our man in Bristol: *The garage didn't carry the necessary spare parts, but they promised to* **get on to** *the makers and order them straight away.* ○ *If the fire-station had been* **got on to** *at once, the hotel might have been saved.* = get in contact/touch (with). ⇨ be on to 1, put on to 1.

2 [Vp.pr] trace, find or detect (sth/sb); become aware of the presence or activity of (sth/sb). **o:** the scent, trail; his movements, whereabouts; spy, smuggler: *The murder squad followed up every bit of information and eventually* **got on to** *the man's trail in a remote area of Scotland.* ○ *The secret service* **got on to** *the agent shortly after he arrived in this country and watched his every move.* ⇨ be on to 2, put on to 2.

3 [Vp.pr] move from one activity, or stage, to (another). **o:** more important matters, something more interesting; the next item on the agenda; cleaning out the cellar: *'Now that we've cleared up those routine matters we can* **get on to** *what we've all been looking forward to: Mr Cowley's report on his visit to Thailand.'* ○ *'I hate all this theory. When do you think we're going to* **get on to** *something useful?'* ○ *We don't* **get on to** *anatomy until next year.* = pass on (to) 5.

get on (with) 1 [Vp, Vp.pr] make progress (with a task etc). ⇨ get along/on (with) 1.

2 [Vp, Vp.pr rel] have a harmonious relationship (with sb). ⇨ get along/on (with) 2.

get on with [Vp.pr] continue to make, pursue, perform etc (sth), often after an interruption. **o:** work, job; life; homework, the gardening, housework: *She insisted that he remained in Paris, and* **got on with** *his book.* HB ○ *The majority of men had come back from the war to finish their degrees in a hurry and* **get on with** *their lives.* SU ○ *'Excuse me if I* **get**

***on with** this letter, but the post goes in twenty minutes. Then we'll have a cup of tea and a chat.'* ⇨ go on 5, go on with.

let sb get on with it [Vp.pr] (*informal*) (an expression used forcefully and rather disapprovingly to imply that if sb is intent on doing sth he should be allowed to do it, regardless of the consequences): *'If Sarah and Jenny think they can run the shop without any help, well, all I can say is, **let them get on with it**.'* □ often used at the end of a sentence after *if sb thinks/imagines/supposes ... well/then*.

get on without [Vp.pr] manage, survive or keep going without (sb/sth): *How will Mr Andrews **get on without** a housekeeper? He's never had to look after himself before.*

get out 1 [Vp] become known despite efforts to keep it secret. **S:** news, secret, information; it ... that you were abroad; word ... about Mary being here: *Somehow the news **got out** that the Prince was in the hotel, and a crowd gathered outside in the hope of seeing him.* ○ *'If it ever **gets out** that you were behind the raid on Barclay's Bank, you'll be in real trouble, because one of the clerks got shot.'* = leak out. ⇨ be out 7, come out 7, let out 2.

2 [Vn ⇆ p] speak, utter (sth). **O:** ⚠ a word, the words; the message; it; anything, nothing: *Martha was in such a state of shock after the accident that she couldn't **get** a word **out**.* ○ *When John finally plucked up enough courage to ask for an increase in salary, he had quite a job **getting** the words **out**.* ⇨ get out of 2.

3 [Vp, Vn.p pass] (*cricket*) (cause a batsman to) lose his wicket; be dismissed, dismiss (sb): *'How did Gooch **get out**?' 'He was caught behind the wicket.'* ○ *When England **got** Richardson **out**, there was a faint chance they would win the match.* ⇨ be out 8, give out 5.

4 [Vn.p pass] find the correct answer to (sth); succeed in solving (sth). **O:** calculation, sum; puzzle, problem: *Not a single child in the class could **get** the problem **out**.* ○ *'You have a go: I can't **get** this thing **out**.'* = work out 3. ⇨ come out 12.

get out/out of 1 [Vp emph, Vpr, Vn.p pass, Vn.pr pass] (help sb to) leave, esp a building, room etc; (help sb to) escape from danger. **S** [Vp, Vpr], **O** [Vn.p, Vn.pr]**:** passenger, inmate; hostage, prisoner. **o:** burning aircraft; captivity, gaol: [Vp] *'**Get out**,' spluttered Creon, '**get out**, you insolent fool.'* GLEG ○ [Vp] *'I advise you to **get out** while the getting is good* (= while it is still possible to do so).*'* AITC ○ [Vpr] *'Anyone with poor nerves should not stay in the motor manufacturing business. He should **get** the hell **out of** it!'* ○ [Vn.p] *'Don't wait for the troops to arrive. **Get** your family **out** now.'* ○ [Vn.pr] *'**Get** Belinda the hell **out of** here!'* BBCR ↔ get in/into 1. ⇨ be out/out of 1, bring out/out of, come out/out of 1, take out/out of 1.

2 [Vn.p pass, Vn.pr pass] withdraw or extract (sth) (from an enclosed space). **O:** rabbit; screw; splinter. **o:** burrow; wood; finger: *A couple of the screws were pretty rusty. I didn't manage to **get** those **out**.* ○ *Our car couldn't be **got out** (**of** the garage) because there were several other cars parked in front.* ⇨ be out/out of 2, come out/out of 2, take out/out of 2.

3 [Vn ⇆ p pass, Vn.pr pass] clean or remove (sth) (from sth). **O:** stain, spot, mark; grease, oil. **o:** carpet, curtain; fabric, cloth: *We used a special cleaning fluid to **get** all the stains **out**.* ⇨ be out/out of 3, come out/out of 3.

4 [Vn.p pass, Vn.pr pass] obtain or gain (sth) (from sth/sb). **O:** much, a lot; something, anything; (next to) nothing, very little; ten per cent; a nice profit. **o:** experience, life; trip, expedition; deal, transaction: *In most jobs you only **get out** as much as you put in.* ○ *He **got** little **out of** his conversations with Eckermann, who was in the last few months of his life, his mind failing fast.* GE ↔ put in/into 2.

get out of 1 [Vpr pass] succeed in not doing (what one ought to do); manage to avoid (sth). **o:** unpleasant chores, all the dirty work; night duty, military service; going to school, helping with the washing-up: *Her sons were experts at **getting out of** hard work.* ○ *I wish I could **get out of** going to the party this evening; I don't feel like standing around making polite conversation for three hours.* ○ *Going to the dentist is something which can't be **got out of**.* = wriggle out of.

2 [Vn.pr pass] make (sb) reveal (sth), sometimes by dubious means. **O:** truth; admission, confession; the whole story: *She bombarded the doctor with questions ... and almost **got out of** him the straight answer she craved.* GL ○ *Nothing further could be **got out of** the Secretary of State. All he would say was that talks with his Russian opposite number would continue in the morning.* ○ *I held my breath. I had to step carefully now if I was to **get out of** him the full confession for which I thirsted.* UTN = draw out/out of 4. ⇨ get out 2.

get out of bed (on) the wrong side [Vpr] (*informal*) be in a bad mood or temper from the moment one gets up: *'What's the matter with Mick? He's cursing at everyone.' 'I don't know. He must have **got out of bed on the wrong side** this morning.'* □ an alt construction is get out of the wrong side of the bed.

get the best/most/utmost out of [Vn.pr pass] use (sb/sth) to the best advantage; employ (sb/sth) most effectively. **o:** him, employee; car, horse; computer; life, holiday: *You don't **get the best out of** trainees by treating them like a bunch of idiots.* ○ *To **get the best out of** your Kenwood mixer, follow the directions carefully.* ○ *The doctors have told him that he has only six months to live, so he's trying to **get the most out of** the time he's got left.*

get blood out of a stone [Vn.pr pass] (*informal*) obtain (money etc) from sb who does not have it or is unwilling to hand it over: *Persuading John to part with his annual subscription to the Labour Party is like **getting blood out of a stone**.* ○ *It's no use asking your father for a contribution. You can't **get blood out of a stone*** (or: ***Blood** can't be **got out of a stone***).

get out of one's depth [Vpr] (of a non-swimmer) be in water in which one cannot stand or walk, and thus be in danger of drowning; be in a situation which one cannot manage or which one cannot understand: *Peter managed quite well in chemistry at school, but when he went to university he soon **got out of his depth**.* ⇨ be out of one's depth.

get out of the groove/rut [Vpr] (*informal*) abandon a boring, repetitive type of life: *'I don't suppose I'll like America, but it's time I **got out of the***

***groove** here.'* RFW ○ *'Why don't you do something to **get out of the rut** if you're so dissatisfied with your job?'* ↔ get into a rut.

get out of the habit/way (of doing sth) [Vpr, Vn.pr pass] (make sb) lose or abandon the habit (of doing sth): *'If only you could **get out of the habit of smoking during meals**, you'd enjoy your food more.'* ○ *'Can't you **get** this child **out of the habit of repeating** everything I say?'* ○ *After two years of living in hotels I had **got out of the way of doing** things for myself.*

get out of hand [Vpr] become uncontrollable, unmanageable. **S:** children, horse; business, organization: *The children quickly **get out of hand** when there isn't an adult around.* ○ *Lady Naylor ... intervenes in the tiresome business between a moneyless suitor and her niece Lois before it **gets out of hand**.* EB ⇨ be out of hand.

get out of one's head/mind [Vn.pr] stop thinking about (sb/sth), forget him/it if only for a short time. **O:** him etc; it, idea ... that she was involved; picture; fear, prospect, thought (of losing sb): *I wish I could **get** the picture of that awful accident **out of my head**.* ○ *You must try to **get** work completely **out of your mind**. You ought to take up a sport!* ○ *Try as he might, he could not **get** the idea **out of his head** that there was a conspiracy to cheat him of his rightful share of the money.* ○ *'If you think I'm going to pay all your debts, you can **get** the idea **out of your head** now, because I'm not.'*

get out of it! [Vpr] (*slang*) do not exaggerate, do not say things that nobody can believe: *'I'm going to give Harry a piece of my mind next time I see him.' '**Get out of it!** You couldn't give a sick mouse a piece of your mind!'* □ imperative only. = get along/away with you!.

get a kick out of [Vn.pr pass] (*informal*) find great etc pleasure in (sth/sb); greatly etc enjoy (sth/sb). **adj:** no, not much of a; a big, terrific, tremendous. **o:** jazz, swing; 1940s movies; watching you dance, going to parties: (popular song) *'I get no kick from champagne, Mere alcohol doesn't thrill me at all, So tell me why should it be true, That I **get a kick out of** you.'* COLE PORTER ○ *'I'm no good,' said Bill, 'no good at all and, as you well know, I don't even **get a kick out of** admitting it any more.'* HAA

get no change out of [Vn.pr pass] (*informal*) be unsuccessful in one's attempts to persuade, manipulate, seduce or exploit (sb). **adj:** no, not any/much, (very, precious) little: *'He was a critic who tried to take liberties with all the lady novelists ... You'll remember him, I daresay.' 'Vaguely,' said Lettie. 'He **never got much change out of** me.'* MM ○ *'I suppose several people have been inquiring about him since he died?' 'A lot from the newspapers did, but they **got no change out of** me. I keep meself to meself.'* PP ○ *'I can see there's **not much change** to be **got out of** him!'*

get out of sb's sight [Vpr, Vn.pr pass] remove (oneself/sb) from another person's presence: *I'm going to **get out of your sight** as soon as I can get a bit of money in my pocket.* TOH ○ *'I wish you would **get** these quarrelling kids **out of my sight** for an hour or two.'* □ often imperative.

get out of one's system [Vn.pr pass] (*informal*) try to banish the strong feelings one has for (sth/sb); succeed in overcoming the attraction one feels towards (sth/sb): *'Do you think you'll want to go back and live in England?' he asked. 'I don't think so,' I said. 'I think I've **got** that much **out of my system**.'* RFW ○ *'You look so miserable! I suppose it's that man again. Why don't you try and **get** him **out of your system**?'* ○ *A religious upbringing — now that's something that can't easily be **got out of one's system**.* RFW

get out of sb's/the way [Vpr, Vn.pr pass] remove (oneself/sb/sth) from the path of (sb/sth); complete (a job, task etc): *'If you don't **get out of the way**, you're liable to be knocked down by a bicycle or something.'* ○ *'I wish you'd **get** your boxes **out of the way**. I trip over them every time I go into the hall.'* ○ *'Once I've **got** this pile of marking **out of the way**, I'll come for a walk with you.'* ⇨ keep out of sb's/the way.

get over 1 [Vp emph, Vpr pass, Vn.p pass, Vn.pr pass] (cause sth/sb to) climb or cross (sth). **S** [Vp, Vpr], **O** [Vn.p, Vn.pr]**:** sheep, horse; children, troops. **o:** wall, fence; stream, bridge: *How did the cattle manage to **get over** the bridge?* ○ *We **got** the children safely **over** the fence and back towards the security of the house.*

2 [Vpr pass] surmount, overcome (sth). **o:** obstacle, difficulty, problem: *Three scientists at Stanford University think they can **get over** the barrier by exploiting the properties of macrophages.* NS ○ *There were a number of linguistic problems to be **got over** in preparing the text of the treaty.*

3 [Vpr pass] become calm, healthy etc, again. **A:** soon, quickly; not quite, not entirely; never. **o:** shock, disappointment, surprise; handicap, illness; effort; it; being made redundant, being disinherited; him doing this to us: *I can't **get over** a thing like that happening to him.* QA ○ *His mother was quite distraught with grief and kept on sobbing, 'We'll never **get over** it, we'll never **get over** it.'* CF ○ *Monsieur Rue ... gets mad at this sometimes, but he soon **gets over** it.* PPLA □ often neg. = recover (from) 1.

4 [Vpr] (not) fully believe, appreciate or understand (sth). **o:** sb's impudence, madness, bad behaviour; the fact that ...; his being there all along: *'I can't **get over** that woman's cheek. Coming in here and complaining about a dress she bought six months ago!'* ○ *We couldn't **get over** the fact that nothing had been taken from the car — despite the driver's window being left open.* □ usu neg with *can/could*.

5 [Vpr pass] overcome, master or govern (sth). **o:** one's embarrassment, confusion; shyness, inhibitions; stutter; disinclination to work: *When I last saw Marie she had almost completely **got over** her nervousness in the presence of strangers.*

6 [Vpr] travel over (ground); cover. **o:** a lot of ground, the distance; mileage, acreage: *These new tractors **get over** twice the acreage that the old ones used to cover.* ○ *The athlete failed to **get over** the distance in the minimum time to qualify for the final.*

get over (to) [Vn.p pass, Vn.p.pr pass] make (sth) clear or intelligible (to sb); make (sth) felt (by sb). **O:** oneself; one's personality, sincerity; anger, distress: *Dressed in deepest black, possessing more personal force than anyone else in court, and more ability to **get** it **over**, she made a great im-*

pression. PW ○ *Though he knows his subject inside out, James seems quite incapable of* ***getting*** *anything useful* ***over to*** *his students.* = get across (to). ⇨ put over (to).

get over (with) [Vn.p pass, Vn.p.pr pass] (*informal*) complete sth necessary but possibly unpleasant. **O:** it; work; formalities; ordeal, operation, trial: *'We'd better* ***get*** *lunch* ***over****,' said Rose.* SE ○ *'If we must visit your parents today let's go early and* ***get*** *it* ***over with****.'* ○ *He looked upon the marriage ceremony as a mere formality — something to be* ***got over with*** *as quickly as possible.* ○ *'Let's* ***get*** *the goodbyes* ***over with*** *and go!'* □ in get over with, with has no object of its own. ⇨ next entry.

get over and done with [Vn.p pass] (*informal*) do (a necessary but unpleasant task) finally, once and for all. **O:** work, chores; formalities, the serious business: *Let's* ***get*** *all this form-filling* ***over and done with****, then we can go off somewhere and have a drink.* ○ *If your tooth is aching you should go to the dentist, and soon! You might as well* ***get*** *it* ***over and done with****.* □ note that with has no object of its own. ⇨ be over 1, be over and done with. ⇨ previous entry

get round 1 [Vp, Vpr pass] (*sport*) succeed in completing (a course, test etc) for a stated score or in a given time. **o:** course, track, circuit; dartboard: *Nick Faldo* ***got round*** *the course in 67 — five under par.* ○ *The runners* ***got round*** *the first lap in just under sixty-one seconds.* ○ *The champion* ***got round*** *the board with 25 throws.*

2 [Vpr pass] avoid (sth), legally if not honourably; circumvent. **o:** law, regulations, rules: *The lawyer was well known for his skill at* ***getting round*** *the law, usually on technical points.* ○ *He believed that there were very few tax-laws that couldn't be* ***got round****, one way or another.* = scrub round.

3 [Vpr pass] gain the confidence of (sb). ⇨ get around/round 1.

4 [Vpr] tackle (sth) successfully. ⇨ get around/round 2.

get round the table [Vpr, Vn.pr pass] (persuade two or more groups in a dispute to) sit down together in order to discuss a problem and find a solution to it. **S** [Vpr], **O** [Vn.pr]**:** workers and employers; the management and the unions; the warring factions: *What the strike committee are demanding is for the dismissed men to be reinstated. Until they are, they've no intention of* ***getting round the table*** *with anybody.* ○ *'Surely what we all want is to* ***get*** *the two sides* ***round the table*** *and talking?'*

get one's tongue round [Vn.pr pass] (esp *jocular*) pronounce, articulate (sth). **o:** word, name, title: *Chinese students of English have great difficulty in* ***getting their tongues round*** *some English words — especially those containing r and l. 'Rival librarians' is for them an almost unpronounceable phrase.* ○ *English* ***tongues*** *simply can't be* ***got round*** *the sounds of some African languages.*

get round to [Vp.pr pass] ⇨ get around/round to.

get through 1 [Vp, Vpr] manage to pass through (sth). **o:** hole, aperture; gap, opening, crack; eye of a needle: *We wondered how such a large animal could* ***get through*** *such a small hole.* ⇨ go through 1.

2 [Vp, Vpr, Vn.p pass, Vn.pr pass] (help sb to) be successful in (sth); (help sb to) pass (sth). **o:** the first round; the entrance exam; one's driving-test: [Vpr] I ***got through*** *the written papers but failed the oral examination.* ○ [Vn.p, Vn.pr] I wouldn't expect that instructor to ***get*** *anyone* ***through*** *(the driving-test).*

3 [Vpr] manage to live through (a difficult period); survive. **o:** war, siege; famine; epidemic: *He* ***got through*** *four years of war without suffering so much as a scratch.* ○ *They* ***got through*** *the earthquake unscathed but lost everything except the clothes they stood up in.*

4 [Vp, Vpr, Vn.p pass, Vn.pr pass] (cause a bill to) be approved by Parliament and so become an Act of Parliament; pass (sth) into law. **S** [Vp, Vpr], **O** [Vn.p, Vn.pr]**:** a bill to privatize water; new laws on child abuse; the reform of the law on divorce: [Vp] *People began to doubt that the bill would ever* ***get through****.* ○ [Vn.pr] *The Government rarely has any difficulty in* ***getting*** *its annual Finance Bill* ***through*** *Parliament.* ⇨ go through 6, put through 2.

5 [Vpr pass] consume, drink, eat, spend etc (sth). **o:** ten aspirins a day; a bottle of gin a week; enough for two people; a fortune, a lot of money: *Charles* ***got through*** *a fortune when he was young, and lived in poverty for the rest of his life.* ○ *I marvelled that so much food could be* ***got through*** *by such a small child.* ⇨ go through 2.

6 [Vpr pass] manage to do, read, write etc (sth); complete. **o:** homework; all these files; fifty letters a day; a lot of reading: *My new secretary is very quick; she* ***gets through*** *a stack of mail in a morning.* ○ *'I've brought you a very interesting book on the Sudan.' 'Thanks, but I haven't* ***got through*** *the one you brought yesterday yet!'* ○ *When I've* ***got through*** *the 'get through' entries I'll get on with the 'get to' ones!*

get through (to) 1 [Vp, Vp.pr pass, Vn.p pass, Vn.p.pr pass] (cause sth/sb to) reach its/his destination, after overcoming difficulties. **S** [Vp, Vp.pr], **O** [Vn.p, Vn.pr]**:** message; survivor; supplies, reinforcements : [Vp] Things were not easy ... It seemed unlikely that Quinn's money would ***get through****.* GJ ○ [Vn.p.pr] Ammunition couldn't be ***got through to*** *the garrison, and they were forced to surrender.*

2 [Vp, Vp.pr, Vn.p, Vn.p.pr] (help sb to) make contact, by telephone, radio etc (with sb/sth). **o:** hospital, police, London: [Vp] A messenger arrived from the radio station to say that the American had ***got through*** *to inform them that there was a lull in the fighting.* DF ○ [Vp, Vp.pr] 'International Enquiries told me all the lines were engaged. That's why I couldn't ***get through to*** *you.)'* ○ [Vn.p, Vn.p.pr] At the fifth attempt the operator ***got*** *me* ***through*** *(****to*** *New York).* ⇨ be through (to), put through (to) 1.

get through to 1 [Vp.pr, Vn.pr pass] (*sport*) (help sb to) reach or get as far as (a certain stage). **o:** the final (round), the semi-final(s): *Colchester were lucky to* ***get through to*** *the fifth round of the Cup.* ○ *How many times has Lendl* ***got through to*** *the final of the men's singles at Wimbledon?* ○ *The new manager* ***got*** *the team* ***through to*** *Wembley in his first season.*

2 [Vp.pr] make (sb) understand the meaning of what one is saying; communicate effectively with (sb): *The boy's an idiot: I can't* ***get through to*** *him at all, even when I explain things in words of one syllable.* ○ *The police were told that the injured* *man was in a critical state and that no one had been able to* **get through to** *him.* ⇨ get through (to) 2.

get through with 1 [Vp.pr pass] finish, complete (a task). **o:** job, assignment; shopping, housework; painting the windows, selling the house: *By the time we had* **got through with** *the formalities, all we wanted to do was go to the hotel and rest.* ○ *No sooner had the tedious job of decorating the house been* **got through with** *than a pipe burst in the attic and ruined everything.* ⇨ be through (with).
2 [Vp.pr pass] (*informal*) finish dealing with (sb) (implying physical attack or verbal correction): *'When I've* **got through with** *that bastard even his own mother won't recognize him.'* ⇨ be through (with).

get to 1 [Vpr] reach (a place or stage). **o:** village, hotel, destination; coffee; the most interesting part: *We didn't* **get to** *the hotel until midnight.* ○ *She has no right to be late ... Where on earth could she have* **got to** *?* GL □ note the idiom: *Cut the cackle and* **get to** *the horses* (or: *'osses),* often reduced simply to: *Cut the cackle,* meaning 'cut out the unnecessary preliminaries, and tell us the important news or facts'. = arrive (at).
2 [Vpr] reach the point of (doing sth). **o:** wondering, asking herself; the point where ..., the stage of thinking ...: *In his disturbed state, he* **got to** *screaming obscenities at anyone who entered the room.* ○ *Only yesterday I* **got to** *thinking how nice it would be to get everyone together for a celebration.*

get access to [Vn.pr pass rel] (*formal*) reach (sth), sometimes by overcoming some obstacle. **o:** attic, roof, secret room; the White House; classified information, state secrets; rival's plans: *The men need to* **get access to** *the roof to fit the new television aerial.* ○ *We realized too late that* **access** *could easily be* **got to** *our stronghold by means of a long-forgotten tunnel.* = gain access to. ⇨ have access to.

get to the bottom of [Vpr pass(o)] find the cause of (sth); solve, fathom. **o:** mystery, affair; it, this: *'I'm determined to* **get to the bottom of** *this outrageous rumour.'* ○ *Sherlock Holmes had a reputation for* **getting to the bottom of** *any crime, however baffling it might seem to others.* ○ *'I shan't be satisfied till this whole business is* **got to the bottom of***!'*

get to the top (of the ladder/tree) [Vpr] reach the highest position in one's chosen career: *'My ambitions are the same as they were in football — to* **get to the top** *and stay at the top as long as possible.'* G ○ *From the earliest age, you could see that he would* **get to the top of the tree** *— no matter what profession he chose.*

get to work (on) [Vpr] start working, operating, studying etc (sth); begin work (on sth): *The men piled out of the coach, rushed into the restaurant and immediately* **got to work on** *the meal that was laid out for them.* ○ (book review) *I wish that she would chuck her tape-recorder off Brighton pier and* **get to work on** *a real book again.* OBS

get to first base with [Vpr] (esp *US informal*) begin to make progress towards achieving an objective (used esp of a man making amorous advances to a woman): *Sam was crazy about Helen, but he never even* **got to first base with** *her.* ○ *The discussions* (of a possible takeover of a car plant) *will not* **get to first base** *if the Rover car is a fundamental part of the deal.* DT □ from the game of baseball; usu neg or with neg implications.

get to grips with [Vpr pass(o)] tackle (sth/sb) in earnest. **o:** problem, work; opponent, enemy: *It's time you stopped tinkering about with those trifling repairs on your car, and* **got to grips with** *the basic trouble by decarbonizing the engine.* ○ *When Nikki* **gets to grips with** *a problem, she doesn't leave it alone until she's found a solution.* ○ *The question of where our energy is coming from in the next decade needs to be* **got to grips with** *in a serious way.* ⇨ be at/come to grips with.

get together 1 [Vp nom] meet socially, for a discussion etc: *'Hello, Bill! Haven't seen you for ages!' 'That's a fact. Look! Let's* **get together** *later and have a drink and a chat.'* ○ *The younger members of staff decided to* **get together** *over the question of weekend duty. They didn't see why the older teachers shouldn't do their fair share.* ○ *The firm had its annual* **get-together** *at the Anchor Inn. A good time was had by all.*
2 [Vn ⇆ p pass] assemble, collect (sb/sth). **O:** body, party, group, army of men; papers, documents; impressive amount of information: *'I want you to* **get** *your things* **together***, so that we can leave at a moment's notice.'* ○ *Enough volunteers were* **got together** *to keep the beaches clean all through the summer.*
3 [Vn.p] (*informal*) (be able to) manage or organize (sth) satisfactorily. **O:** things, it; career, game: (a model girl in an interview) *'I didn't seem to get on at all well during my session with Cecil Beaton* (the photographer)*. Perhaps I was too young to see what he wanted. I couldn't* **get** *it* **together***.'* BBCTV ○ *Virginia Wade assesses how she was able to* **get** *her game* **together** *and win the Wimbledon crown* (ie the Women's Tennis Championship). OBS

get under [Vpr, Vn.pr pass] (cause sb/sth to) pass beneath (sth); (help sb to) shelter or hide under (sth). **o:** barbed wire, rope, hedge; tree, tarpaulin, stairs: *The rabbits couldn't* **get under** *the wire netting, so for once we were able to grow a few vegetables.* ○ *The dog had the sense to* **get under** *some old boxes to shelter from the storm.* ○ *The children had to be* **got under** *the stairs whenever there was an air-raid.* ↔ get over 1.

get under control [Vn.pr pass] subdue, master (sth/sb). **O:** fire, floods; people, children; mob, crowd; riot, uprising, rebellion, mutiny, revolt: *The fire-brigade arrived within minutes of the alarm and quickly* **got** *the blaze* **under control***.* ○ *The government hasn't enough troops to* **get** *the rebellious province* **under control***.* ○ *The mob was* **got under control** *and several of the ring-leaders were arrested.* ⇨ be/bring/keep under control.

get under sb's feet [Vpr] (*informal*) annoy or inconvenience sb by one's presence: *'Damn that cat! It will keep* **getting under my feet***.'* ○ *'***Don't get under Dad's feet** *while he's trying to fix the sink.'*

get under sb's skin [Vpr] be a constant source of irritation to sb: *I don't know what it is about that fellow Fotheringay, but he always manages to* **get under my skin***.* □ note that the words *I've got you under my skin,* the title of a song, mean 'I can't stop thinking about you'.

get under way 1 [Vpr, Vn.pr pass] (*nautical*) (cause a boat to) start moving through the water; gather speed. **S** [Vpr], **O** [Vn.pr]**:** dinghy, cruiser; steamer, destroyer: *At Calais the ferry was late* ***getting under way****, so we missed our connecting train at Dover.*
2 [Vpr, Vn.pr pass] (cause sth to) begin. **S** [Vpr], **O** [Vn.pr]**:** campaign, war; investigation, experiment; manufacture, distribution. **S** [Vn.pr]**:** commander, general; scientist, laboratory; plant, industry: *The post-war rise in prices* ***got under way*** *in the mid-1950s.* T ○ *A radical experiment in public transport has just* ***got under way*** *in the north of England.* OBS ○ *But before production could really be* ***got under way****, the war intervened.* L ⇨ be under way.

get up 1 [Vp emph, Vn.p pass] rise from one's bed; call or awaken (sb), and possibly lift him out of bed. **S** [Vp], **O** [Vn.p]**:** baby; father; boys. **A:** early, late; at the crack of dawn, in time for: *What to do? His first answer was sleep: quite simply to* ***get up*** *as late as possible in the morning.* AF ○ *'Isn't it time you* ***got*** *the baby* ***up*** *for its bottle* (= for its milk)*?'* ○ *'If I'd been* ***got up*** *earlier I wouldn't have missed my train.' 'It's high time you were able to* ***get*** *yourself* ***up****, Steve!'* ↔ go to bed, lie down. ⇨ be up 5.
2 [Vp emph] rise to one's feet from a chair or the ground: *When the Chairman asked if there were any questions, about four people* ***got up*** *at once.* ○ *Would a man dare to* ***get up*** *in public and claim to have raised the dead if he had not?* GIE ○ *I* ***got up*** *from the table and left the room as quickly as possible.* = stand up 1. ↔ sit down 1.
3 [Vp, Vpr, Vn.p pass, Vn.pr pass] (help sb/sth to) climb (sth). **S** [Vp, Vpr], **O** [Vn.p, Vn.pr]**:** old man; car, lorry; load, furniture. **o:** hill, mountain, incline, cliff; stairs, steps, ladder : [Vpr] Your car will never ***get up*** *that hill* .... ○ [Vp] ... but mine will ***get up*** *in second gear!* ○ [Vn.pr] 'How do you expect to ***get*** *this filing-cabinet* ***up*** *all those stairs?'* ○ [Vn.p] 'I don't know. All I know is that it has got to be ***got up****! And it's your job to* ***get*** *it* ***up****!'* ↔ get down 1. ⇨ go up 1.
4 [Vp, Vn.p pass] (cause or help sb to) mount a horse, bicycle etc: *'Can you* ***get up*** *by yourself, or shall I help you?' 'Thanks, I think I can manage to* ***get up*** *by myself.'* ○ *'Quick!* ***Get*** *the girl* ***up*** *behind me and let's start before her father arrives!'* ↔ get down 1.
5 [Vp] rise, increase in force; become violent. **S:** ⚠ the wind, storm, sea: *Although the wind was obviously* ***getting up****, and with it the sea, the foolish couple left harbour in their flimsy catamaran.* □ get the wind up has an entirely different meaning.
6 [Vn ⇆ p pass] organize, arrange (sth). **O:** party, concert; show, exhibition; appeal, petition (against/on behalf of/for): *The prisoners-of-war kept their spirits up by* ***getting up*** *bingo sessions, art classes and sing-songs.* ○ *He* ***got up*** *a day of foot races and rustic sports each Christmas season.* CD ○ *The students* ***got up*** *a country-wide campaign on behalf of the famine victims.*
7 [Vn.p nom pass adj] dress (oneself/sb) in a special way; make (oneself/sb) beautiful or attractive. **O:** daughter, child; oneself; book, present, room. **A:** in one's Sunday best; in evening-dress; to kill: *She saw people* ***got up*** *in national dress in the Dublin streets.* EB ○ *'Do you like my* ***get-up****? 'It's lovely. The colour suits you perfectly.'* ○ *Arthur was* ***got up*** *to kill* (ie in a rather exaggerated way, designed to impress others)*, with a vast expanse of shirt-front illuminated by a single jewel.* BLCH ○ *'I envy you the village,' Gerald said; 'it's charming.' 'Is it?' Dollie asked. 'It always seems to be a bit* ***got-up*** *for tourists.'* ASA = dress up 1.
8 [Vn ⇆ p pass] prepare or study (sth); memorize. **O:** German, chemistry; part, role: *When we went to see John he was busy* ***getting*** *the Law of Torts* ***up*** *for his exam.* ○ *She would* ***get up*** *a new role in a matter of days. She had an almost photographic memory.*

get up a(n)/one's appetite/thirst [Vn ⇆ p pass] develop an appetite or thirst, do sth which produces an appetite: *Mariette has gone for a ride now to* ***get her appetite up****.* DBM = work up 3.

get one's/sb's back up [Vn.p] (*informal*) get oneself into a difficult or antagonistic mood; annoy or antagonize (sb): *If your mother* ***gets her back up****, as she inevitably will, you'll have the devil of a time with it.* BLCH ○ *No, Borstal* (a kind of prison for young offenders) *didn't* ***get my back up****, because it's always been up, right from when I was born.* LLDR ○ *'Why should a simple request* ***get your back up****? I only asked if you would like to wash the dishes.'* ⇨ put sb's back up.

get sb's blood up [Vn.p pass] make sb feel aggressive; enrage, anger: *His insolent manner really* ***got my blood up****. For two pins I would have punched him on the nose.* ⇨ one's blood be up.

get up sb's nose [Vpr] (*informal*) annoy, irritate (sb). **S:** manager, supervisor; routine, working methods; it ... that he never consults anyone: *I very much wanted to go home ... I had had enough of hospital routine; it was* ***getting up my nose****.* L ○ *DREW: They will never tell us these things* (ie how to plan a murder)*. STONE: I know, it* ***gets up anyone's nose****.* BBCTV = get on sb's wick.

get up steam [Vp.n] develop enough pressure of steam to drive sth; (*informal*) (of persons) prepare oneself to make an effort. **S:** ship; ferry, tug; he etc: *We saw the ferry in the harbour* ***getting up steam*** *for the daily crossing to the island.* ○ *'Do you think you could* ***get up*** *enough* ***steam*** *to take these letters along to the post-office for me?'*

get the wind up [Vn.p] (*informal*) become frightened, alarmed: *The Minister of Defence* ***got the wind up*** *and asked the Chiefs of Staff ... to reduce the period of active National Service.* MFM ○ *With the approach of the General Election, the Government* ***got the wind up*** *and cut taxes by a further one per cent.* ⇨ have/put the wind up.

get up against 1 [Vp.pr, Vn.p.pr pass] stand, sit or huddle very close to (sth); place (sth) very near to (sth). **O:** piano, sacks, ladder. **o:** wall, partition: *The child* ***got up against*** *the radiator in her efforts to keep warm.* ○ *'Help me* ***get*** *this ladder* ***up against*** *the wall, will you?'*
2 [Vp.pr] form a bad relationship with (sb); annoy, offend. **S:** new shop-steward; French assistant; students. **o:** manager, management; headteacher, head of the French department; authorities, Vice-Chancellor: *I'd only been working in the hotel for a week when I* ***got up against*** *the head waiter, and he began to make life unbearable.* ○ *She's hope-*

lessly headstrong; she always **gets up against** *people in authority.* = get across 2.

get up on one's hind legs [Vp.pr] (*informal*) rise to one's feet in order to speak to a group of people: *You'd know what work meant if you'd been in industry, where what you do affects thousands of people, instead of* **getting up on your hind legs** *in the House of Commons, where you can say what you like because it affects nobody.* ASA = get on one's feet. ⇨ get up 2.

get up to 1 [Vp.pr, Vn.p.pr pass] (cause sb to) reach (a certain level). **o:** (degree, diploma) standard; (university) level: *Emma despaired of ever* **getting up to** *the high standard required for entry to university.* ○ *Don't pay too much attention to job advertisements that promise to* **get** *you* **up to** *management status in a couple of years.* ⇨ be up to 5, bring up to, come up to, keep up to.

2 [Vp.pr] be occupied in or busy with (sth) (usu with the implication that the activity is undesirable, foolish or surprising). **o:** what; mischief; his old tricks: *Dad doesn't deserve to be made a fool of ... Heaven knows what sort of nonsense he'll* **get up to** *if he has much more of this* (adverse) *publicity.* ASA ○ *Jim would jump out of his hiding place ... and frighten the life out of them and* **get up to** *his dirty tricks.* LLDR ⇨ be up to 1, put up to.

get up to date (with) [Vp.pr, Vn.p.pr pass] do (sth) which is due or overdue; inform (oneself) about (sth). **o:** the latest developments, news; prices, trends, fashions: [Vn.p.pr] *Teachers spent five hours on Sunday* **getting** *their marking* **up to date** (or: [Vp.pr] **getting up to date with** *their marking).* ○ *'What's been going on in the world while I've been ill? I really must* **get** *myself* **up to date**!' ⇨ be up to date/the minute, bring up to date.

get with child [Vn.pr pass] (*formal* or *jocular*) make (sb) pregnant. **O:** girl; fiancée, wife, mistress: *'Sin' is* **getting** *a girl* **with child** *before marriage and then not marrying her.* UL ○ *She couldn't name the father; all she knew was that she'd been* **got with child** *during an all-night party.*

get within [Vpr] reach a position where one can hit or be hit, see or be seen etc. **o:** ⚠ striking distance, earshot, range, sight: *It was obvious that they would never* **get within** *striking distance of the guest of honour, so they just sat on the stairs and enjoyed the free drinks.* ○ *We were now* **getting within** *range of the enemy batteries* (ie we could hit or, more likely, be hit by, them). ⇨ be within 1, bring within, come within.

gibe

gibe (at) [Vpr pass rel] mock, scorn (sb). **o:** sb's modest attempts, efforts; misfortunes, poverty; mistakes: *Children can be very cruel; they often* **gibe at** *the feeble efforts of their younger brothers and sisters.* = jeer (at).

ginger

ginger up [Vn ⇆ p pass adj] (*informal*) put more life, energy, enthusiasm, into (sb/sth). **O:** him, the Party; fund-raising campaign, movement for equal pay for women: *'It's obvious that the Liberal Democrats need* **gingering up**; *they're dying on their feet.'* ○ *He asked me to '***ginger up***' the evacuation of the* (Nile) *Delta cities.* MFM

gird

gird on [Vp.n pass] (*dated* or *formal*) fix or fasten (sth) on. **O:** sword, armour, suit of mail: *The Minstrel Boy to the war is gone, In the ranks of death you'll find him; His father's sword he has* **girded on**, *And his wild harp slung behind him.* TMB

gird up one's loins [Vp.n pass] (*dated* or *figurative*) prepare for a battle or serious conflict: *He* **girded up his loins** *and ran before Ahab.* BIBLE (1 KINGS 18: 46) ○ *With* **your loins girded**, *your shoes on your feet, and your staff in your hand.* BIBLE (EXODUS 12:11) ○ *It was becoming clear that the Government was* **girding up its loins** *for another confrontation with the EC Commissioners.*

girdle

girdle about/around [Vn.p pass] (*formal*) surround (sth) as if with a belt. **O:** island, lake, castle: *A thick forest* **girdled** *the castle* **about**. ○ *The loch was pleasantly* **girdled about** *with beech, fir and aspen.* ○ *The tiny tropical island was* **girdled round** *with a coral reef.* □ usu passive.

give

give away 1 [Vn ⇆ p nom pass adj] give (sth) free of charge; sell (sth) at a very low price. **O:** money, possessions, old clothes; everything; samples, free packets: (letter) *Why do politicians, and newspapers, give the impression that a Chancellor has money to* **give away**? T ○ *'Twenty pounds for that book! It isn't exactly* **given away**, *is it?'* ○ *'Please don't bring any more of those plastic* **give-away** *tulips into the house.'* ○ *'Have you seen the latest* **give-away**? *A packet of bird-seed with every jar of coffee. Grow your own hemp, I suppose!'*

2 [Vn ⇆ p pass] distribute or present (sth). **O:** prizes, medals, diplomas, certificates: *'Do you really think it necessary to drag the Mayor in, just to* **give away** *a few certificates to kids who've passed their first swimming test?'*

3 [Vn ⇆ p nom pass adj] betray or reveal (sth), voluntarily or involuntarily. **O:** secret; someone, something, nothing; oneself, itself: *He had invented secrets, he hadn't* **given** *them* **away**. OMIH ○ *I have slipped in the word 'science',* **giving away** *my own view that Freud really did start up a new science.* ESS ○ *She was aware as she spoke that the tremble in her voice was the* **give-away** *that the police had been waiting for.*

4 [Vn ⇆ p pass] fail to take or use (sth), through foolishness or neglect. **O:** opportunity, the chance of a lifetime; game, match: *Whether from laziness or ineptitude Sam* **gave away** *his last opportunity to become a serious actor.* ○ *If you* **give** *chances* **away** *like that, how can you expect to win the game?* = throw away 2.

5 [Vn ⇆ p pass] in a marriage ceremony, lead the bride to the groom's side and 'give' her to him. **S:** Mr Jones; the bride's father, brother, uncle, guardian. **O:** bride; daughter, sister, niece, ward: *She was* **given away** *by her father, who signed the register as witness.* GE

6 [Vp] yield or collapse; give way. **S:** wall, floor, roof; ground, river bank: *The floor of the wardrobe was rotten and had* **given away** *with Nurse Ellen's heavy body.* DC □ the form give way is more usual than give away in this meaning.

give the game/the show away [Vn.p pass] (*informal*) betray a plan or sb's intentions, voluntarily or involuntarily: *Hour after hour we lay in silence, waiting for some movement from the enemy. If only they would open fire and* ***give the show away****.* SD ○ *It was a secret document that* ***gave the game away****: a document that was never meant to be there at all.* IRANCN. ⇨ give away 3.

give back (to) 1 [Vn ⇆ p pass, Vn.p.pr pass emph rel] return (sth) to its owner. **O:** confiscated goods; tennis ball; pen, book, suitcase: *'Isn't it time you* ***gave*** *Mary her ear-rings* ***back****? She may want to wear them herself!'* ○ *The equipment was* ***given back to*** *the tourist once he had proved that it belonged to him.* □ the second example has an Indirect Object (Mary) and a Direct Object (ear-rings); cf: *'Isn't it time you* ***gave*** *her ear-rings* ***back to*** *Mary?'* = hand back (to). ↔ take away (from) 2. ⇨ get back 4, have back 1.

2 [Vn ⇆ p pass, Vn.p.pr pass emph rel] allow (sb) to have (sth) again; restore. **O:** sight; freedom, liberty; dead son: *There was nothing the doctors could do to* ***give*** *me* ***back*** *the use of my legs. The paralysis was complete and irreversible.* ○ *The popular cry was '****Give*** *us* ***back*** *the vote!'* □ the second example has an Indirect Object (us) and a Direct Object (the vote); cf: *'****Give*** *the vote* ***back to*** *us!'*

give back (to) with interest [Vn ⇆ p pass, Vn.p.pr pass] reply to (an insult, offence etc) but with greater force or effectiveness: *I've only got to finish this novel and I'll be famous; then I'll* ***give*** *her it all* ***back with interest****.* HD □ note the Indirect Object (her) and the Direct Object (it all), and cf: *I'll* ***give*** *it all* ***back to*** *her* ***with interest****.* = pay back (for).

give cause for [Vn.pr pass] be the reason for (sth); arouse. **o:** alarm, anger, concern: *The state of the Defence Services of Britain* ***gave cause for*** *'grave concern' and unless steps were taken to put the matter right we could look forward only to great disasters if we became involved in war.* MFM ○ *During the night Mother took a turn for the worse and today her condition* ***gives*** *us* ***cause for*** *some anxiety.* □ the second example has an Indirect Object (us) and a Direct Object (cause); note the passive transform: *We were* ***given cause for*** *some anxiety.*

give credit for [Vn.pr pass emph rel] believe that (sb) possesses (sth). **o:** intelligence, common sense, ability, determination, initiative, performance: *I wouldn't have* ***given*** *him* ***credit for*** *such fine feelings. I always thought he was rather insensitive. But I was wrong.* □ the example has an Indirect Object (him) and a Direct Object (credit) followed by the prep phrase with for; often used in an active or passive pattern with than: *The customers are better informed than they are* ***given credit for****.* G ○ *Eisenhower was a much more able president than he is* ***given credit for*** .G = credit with 2. ⇨ give credit (to) (for), take credit for.

give grounds for [Vn.pr pass emph rel] (*legal* or *formal*) provide (sb with) evidence that can be used in court for (obtaining a divorce etc); give (sb) a reason or pretext for (believing sth etc). **o:** divorce; hostile action; mistrusting him, acting in a warlike manner: *She wanted a divorce, but would he* ***give*** *her* ***grounds for*** *one?* ○ *She has been careful to* ***give*** *the rulers ... no* ***grounds for*** *the accusation that she is trying to destroy their country.* L □ the first example has an Indirect Object (her) and a Direct Object (grounds); note the passive transform: *Would she be* ***given grounds for*** *one?*

give scope for [Vn.pr pass emph rel] allow or encourage the use of (sth). **o:** imagination, invention; expansion, development; his talents: *The search for a neat code of rules of civilized behaviour, though it would* ***give scope for*** *ingenuity, would be largely a waste of time.* SC ○ *We've* ***given*** *our young men no* ***scope for*** *the spirit of adventure.* □ the second example has an Indirect Object (young men) and a Direct Object (scope) followed by the prep phrase with for; note the passive transform: *Our young men have been* ***given*** *no* ***scope for*** *the spirit of adventure.*

give for/to do sth [Vn.pr emph rel] sacrifice or exchange (sth) for (sth)/to do sth. **O:** ⚠ one's eyes, eye-teeth, back teeth, right arm; one's life, one's all, a great deal: *Sarah would have* ***given*** *her eyes* ***for*** *a ballet dress.* DC ○ *There is a golf club (to which half the community would* ***give*** *their eye-teeth* ***to belong****) ....* OBS ○ *She missed the company of children so much that she would have* ***given*** *her right arm* ***for*** *the slightest sound from the tiniest throat.* HSG ○ *'What a very romantic story! And now of course he would* ***give*** *his life* ***for*** *you.'* OMIH □ usu used with *would (have)*; when the Object is one's life or one's all, the expression usu indicates the literal sacrifice of one's life: *He would* ***give*** *his life* ***for*** *his country.*

give forth [Vp.n pass] (*formal* or *jocular*) utter (sth); emit, produce (sth). **O:** cry, yell; smell, stench: *The animal did not run away, but stood its ground* ***giving forth*** *a mooing sound.* ○ *On summer evenings the flowers* ***gave forth*** *an almost intoxicating scent.* ○ *The engine* ***gave forth*** *a horrible grinding noise, and stopped.* = give off.

give in [Vn ⇆ p pass] give (sth) to a person who is authorized to receive it. **O:** script, exercise; kit: *All papers must be* ***given in*** *before 12.30 p.m. Candidates failing to observe this rule may be disqualified.* ○ *'Who* ***gave*** *my name* ***in*** *for the cross-country run on Saturday?* I *certainly didn't!'* = hand in.

give in (to) [Vp, Vp.pr pass] allow oneself to be overcome (by sth). **o:** pressure, force; persuasion, argument; self-pity: *All sorts of other things I've had — tempers, scenes, reconciliations,* ***giving in*** *sometimes, sometimes holding out, ...* PW ○ *It would have been easy to* ***give in to*** *sentimental melancholy.* ILIH ○ *Blackmail is something that should never be* ***given in to****; but that is easier said than done.* = give way (to), yield to 1.

give of one's best/utmost [Vpr] work or perform as well as one possibly can: *If a man is not properly nourished, you can hardly expect him to* ***give of his best*** *at work or play.* ○ *The general* ***gave of his best*** *in order that the army should be well prepared for all eventualities.* MFM ○ *There is a large number of women who would* ***give of their utmost*** *in another job providing it could be done during school hours.* TVT

give evidence of [Vn.pr pass emph rel] produce witnesses or other proof in support of (sth). **o:** court, magistrate; **(of)** identification, negligence: *The prosecution* ***gave*** *the court* ***evidence of*** *identification before proceeding with the case against the accused.* □ the example has an Indirect Object (the court) and a Direct Object (evidence) followed by the prep phrase with of; note the passive transform: *The court was* **given evidence of** *identification.*

give off [Vp.n pass] emit, release, produce (sth). **O:** smoke, vapour; fumes, odour, scent, aroma; radiation, gamma rays: *The Daimler* (a car) *stood patiently in the sun outside, its leather* **giving off** *a hot smell.* H ○ *The acid* **gives off** *a characteristically pungent odour.* ○ *Pavements dried,* **giving off** *a smell of concentrated damp.* MSAL = give forth.

give on to [Vp.pr] allow sb to reach or see (sth) easily; give access to; overlook. **S:** entrance, door; window, french window. **o:** garden, street, stream, park, courtyard: *The front of the house* **gave on to** *the street, and the back* **on to** *a long, narrow garden, with a gate opening on a rough sandy path.* CON ○ *The windows* **gave on to** *a small square courtyard.* AF ⇨ look onto/out on.

give out 1 [Vp] be ended, broken or exhausted. **S:** road, track; engine, machine; body; supply, stock; energy, strength; patience, memory, ingenuity: *His liver was not too good but it could have stood a few more years' abuse before it actually* **gave out** *on him.* TFD ○ *The engine spluttered ominously. We exchanged anxious glances. The petrol was* **giving out**. ○ *Conversation came to a halt as reminiscence and invention both* **gave out**. *An embarrassed silence fell on the company.* = run out 1.

2 [Vn ⇆ p pass] distribute or circulate (sth). **O:** pencils, examination papers, books; leaflets, handbills, brochures; free cigars: *When the papers had been* **given out** *the supervisor rang a bell and the examination began.* ○ *Several demonstrators have been arrested for* **giving out** *leaflets.* = hand out 1.

3 [Vn ⇆ p pass] make (sth) known; announce. **O:** news, figures; it . . . that the Minister had resigned: *He* **gave out** *that he would come to my headquarters and investigate the matter with my staff.* MFM ○ *I have been informed by two totally reliable sources that this story was* **given out** *by Downing Street.* IND

4 [Vp.n pass] radiate, release or emit (sth). **O:** heat, glow; scent, aroma; radiation: *The log fire* **gave out** *a warm glow.* ○ *The stew* **gave out** *a delicious odour of garlic.* ○ *She was so intensely occupied . . . that she rarely noticed the signals she* **gave out** (the information about herself she unconsciously conveyed). MSAL = give off.

5 [Vn.p pass] (of an umpire) say that a batsman (*cricket*) or striker (*baseball*) is dismissed, and that his innings (*cricket*) or inning (*baseball*) has ended: *The umpire raised his hand without hesitation. The last hope of the England side had been* **given out**. ⇨ be out 8, get out 3.

give over [Vp, Vpr] (*non-standard*) stop (doing sth); be quiet. **o:** shouting, playing about, fiddling with the engine: *'We want boiled eggs, too!' the twins said, as in one voice. 'Can we have boiled eggs?'* '**Give over**. *Can't you see I'm cutting the pineapple?' Ma said.* DBM ○ '**Give over** *shoving! You'll have me off this chair in a minute.'*

give over to [Vn.p.pr pass] devote or abandon (oneself/sth) fully to (sth). **O:** oneself; life, existence. **o:** work, pleasure; domestic concerns; fasting, prayer: *He had* **given** *himself* **over** *entirely* **to** *work. The needs of his family had been pushed to the back of his mind.* ○ *Jane led a rather circumscribed life,* **given over** *almost completely* **to** *the house and children.* □ often passive. = give up to.

given over to [pass (Vn.p.pr)] reserved especially for (sth); having (sth) as its particular activity or purpose. **S:** building, plant, theatre; day, weekend; season, term: *A large part of our productive capacity is being* **given over to** *the new model because of its enormous popularity.* ○ *The evenings were* **given over to** *card- and paper-games, always an enthusiasm of Elizabeth's.* EB ○ *We have to make a translation of the electrical activity in our brains. To do this, quite a bit of the brain is* **given over to** *the control of the lip muscles and of the vocal chords.* TBC □ also used with *appear, seem.* = given up to.

given to [pass (Vn.pr)] in the habit of (doing sth), having a tendency to (do sth); liable to (sth). **o:** making bets, smoking cigars; black moods, bouts of melancholy: *'I'm not* **given to** *making predictions, so don't ask me what's going to happen in the next general election.'* ○ *She was a clever woman and a scholar, but* **given to** *furious outbursts of rage.* BRN □ also used with *appear, seem* or after a noun: *A type of emotional gangster,* **given to** *hijackings and other acts of terrorism.* MSAL

give birth (to) [Vn.pr] be delivered (of young); produce. **S:** woman, wife; ewe, cow, mare. **O:** baby, twins; lamb, calf, foal: *In the third year of their marriage his wife had* **given birth to** *twin boys.* ○ (song) *'The South Lands* **gave birth to** *the blues.'*

give credence to [Vn.pr pass emph rel] (*formal*) believe or support (sth), perhaps in spite of certain factors that may make this difficult. **S:** he, etc; evidence, corroboration. **adj:** no; some, little. **o:** tale, story; account, claims: *The corroboration of four out of five of the witnesses* **gave** *some* **credence to** *the man's alibi.* ○ *Little* **credence** *should be* **given to** *such wild rumours.* □ should not be used instead of believe in informal contexts.

give currency to [Vn.pr pass emph rel] be responsible for circulating (sth). **o:** rumour, story; accusations; ideas, theories, proposals: *Any newspaper that* **gives currency to** *such inflammatory reports should be brought before the Press Council.*

give the lie to [Vn.pr pass emph rel] (*formal*) show (sth) to be untrue. **o:** rumour, story, statement: *There were discussions of how to counteract this rumour and* **give the lie to** *it.* HAA ○ *Such loyalty, he argued,* **gave the lie to** *his critics.* F ○ *The Government's efforts to reduce unemployment have* **given the lie to** *Opposition charges of callous indifference.*

give place/way to [Vn.pr rel] be replaced or succeeded by (sth). **S:** town; sunshine; laughter; sorrow; joy. **o:** countryside; rain; tears; happiness; sadness: *Flat-fronted terraced houses reached by steep flights of steps* **gave place to** *semi-detached brick villas.* OD ○ *Everywhere small family businesses are* **giving way to** *larger and more impersonal supermarkets.*

give rise to [Vn.pr rel] be the cause of (sth). **S:** travel, education; inflation; greed; floods. **o:** inventiveness, enlightenment; alarm, panic; crime, corruption; disease, cholera; starvation, homelessness: *Under the new secular government, the exchange* *of ideas from Europe* **gave rise to** *an unprecedented richness of expression in literature.* RT ○ *Japan and Germany are still fighting inflation,* **giving rise to** *differences in interest-rate policies.* ECON

give teeth (to) [Vn.pr pass] (*informal*) make (sth) truly effective or enforceable. **o:** rules, regulations, law, emergency measures: *The Press Council, as a self-regulatory body, would be more useful if it had more power. Some new measures are needed to* **give teeth to** *it* (or: **give** *it* **teeth**).

give thought (to) [Vn.pr pass emph rel] think (about sth); consider. **adj:** some, any, much; careful, serious. **o:** one's future career; Christmas, Tom's birthday-present; getting ready for one's guests; where one will spend the holidays: *Have you* **given** *any* **thought to** *which university you'd like to attend when you leave school?* ○ *I was just* **giving thought to** *the problem of next term's timetable when my brother arrived.* ○ *I haven't* **given** *much* **thought to** *the problem* (cf *I haven't* **given** *the problem much* **thought**).

give tongue to [Vn.pr] (*formal*) say (sth) aloud. **o:** one's suspicions, reservations, fears; words that were better left unsaid: *'Soho' they tell us, was once a hunting call. I felt like* **giving tongue to** *it.* CON ○ *If I had* **given tongue to** *my doubts about the plan, a great deal of money might have been saved.*

give voice to [Vn.pr pass emph rel] (*formal*) utter or express (sth), not necessarily aloud. **o:** feeling, annoyance, anger, anguish; objection, suspicion, doubts: (a musician) *He wanted to* **give voice to** *spontaneous ... experience, yet also to serve radical causes.* IND ○ *If the Professor had objections to some 'new-fangled' scheme he could always be relied upon to* **give voice to** *them.*

give way (to) [Vn.pr pass emph rel] allow oneself to be overcome (by sb/sth). **o:** parent, colleague; emotion; anger, fear, hysterics; pressure, argument, persuasion: *He was to become firm in the determination that not he but they must always* **give way**. CD ○ *Even if they occasionally seemed to* **give way to** *the mother, they always preserved the substance of power.* BRN ○ *It was no use. She didn't shout, but she* **gave way to** *a low controlled anger.* DC = give in (to), yield to 1.

give weight to [Vn.pr pass emph rel] provide strong(er) evidence for (sth); strengthen. **adj:** more, some; added, further, extra. **o:** theory, statement, movement, warning, probability: *The facts that he had not been seen in his usual haunts and had answered the phone at ten o'clock* **gave weight to** *his claim that he had not been out on the evening in question.* ○ *Added* **weight** *was* **given** *last year* **to** *the possibility that there is vegetation on Mars by the American astronaut, William Sinton.* TO ○ **To** *this speculation recent discoveries* **give** *further* **weight**.

give credit (to) (for) [Vn.pr pass emph rel] ensure that sb's effort is properly recognized. **adj:** all (of) the, some (of the); (not) enough, insufficient: *'Will you be famous?' 'I doubt it. Unlike most writers I shall* **give** *all the* **credit to** *my ghosts.' 'Ghosts?' 'That's what they call those who do the real work while the author takes the pay.'* OMIH ○ **Credit for** *the success of the concert should be* **given to** *the teacher who organized it.* ○ *They haven't* **given** *the police sufficient* **credit for** *keeping essential services running.* □ the last example has an Indirect Object (the police) and a Direct Object (sufficient credit); note the passive transform: *The police haven't been* **given** *sufficient* **credit for** *keeping ....* ⇨ give credit for, take credit for.

give up 1 [Vn ⇆ p pass] allow (sth) to be taken; surrender. **O:** disputed territory, island; advanced positions: *The general was content to* **give up** *a few miles of desert and retreat to a stronger, fortified line.*

2 [Vn ⇆ p pass] leave, abandon (sth). **O:** job, appointment, career: *Laura* **gave up** *a promising career in the City and emigrated to Canada.* ○ *Jacques was forced to* **give up** *his teaching job ... because he could not keep order in the class.* AF = resign (from).

3 [Vn ⇆ p pass] sacrifice (sth), esp by selling it. **O:** car, boat; house, home: *'I'm afraid that business is so bad that we'll have to* **give** *something* **up**. *We'd better sell the horses.'* ○ *Nothing could persuade her to* **give up** *her home: it was much too big, but it was where the family had always lived.*

4 [Vn ⇆ p] reveal, disclose (sth). **O:** information, jealously guarded secret, treasure: *It was not until the twentieth century that Tutankhamun's tomb* **gave** *its secrets* **up** *to the world.* ○ *'Harold,' commanded Isabel, 'I insist on knowing the exact sum.' 'One thousand three hundred and forty-nine pounds six shillings, if you want to know,' said Harold, with the air of a stone* **giving up** *its blood* (a reference to the expression **get blood out of a stone**). PW = yield up 2.

5 [Vn ⇆ p pass] hand over custody of (sb); abandon one's claim to (sb). **O:** child(ren), ward, foster-child(ren): *When she realized that she would have to* **give up** *her children, she dropped all idea of getting a divorce.* ○ *If the natural mother of a child claims custody, it is often very painful for the foster-parent to* **give** *the child* **up**.

6 [Vn ⇆ p pass] no longer seek to avoid capture, or protect (sb) from capture. **O:** oneself; escaped prisoner; spy, agent: *The desperate man forced his hostages to drive on through the night. He was afraid, hungry and thirsty, but he had no intention of* **giving** *himself* **up**. ○ *A neighbour had concealed the man in the attic of her home and vowed never to* **give** *him* **up** *to the police.*

7 [Vn.p pass] no longer expect, or hope for, the arrival of (sb): *It was a sound she had been waiting for all the morning ...; yet it took her by surprise for she had almost* **given** *him* **up**. PW

8 [Vn.p pass] lose hope that a person will recover: *Everyone — the doctors, the nurses, his own family — had* **given** *him* **up**, *but he surprised them all by suddenly taking a turn for the better.*

9 [Vp, Vp.n pass] stop eating, drinking, using or indulging in (sth); abandon. **O:** starchy foods, meat, alcohol; wine, beer; smoking, cigarettes; trips to London, one's daily swim; gambling, cards, roulette: *I'm still smoking twenty a day. All my attempts to* **give up** *have failed.* ○ *'You'd better* **give up** *wearing your new suit to work or it'll soon look as shabby as all your other clothes.'* ○ *It's easy to say that dairy products are bad for the heart, but the eating habits of a lifetime are not so easily* **given up**.

10 [Vn ⇆ p pass] no longer hold (sth); renounce. **O:** religion; belief(s), convictions, principles: *Just because the man she's going to marry is an atheist, there's no need for Elizabeth to* **give up** *her own beliefs.*

11 [Vp.n pass] no longer pursue (one's efforts etc); abandon, renounce. **O:** all thought of sth, all attempt to do sth, any pretence of doing sth; the search for sb; trying to please sb, trying to understand what he was talking about; it: *I decided to* **give up** *all attempt to behave responsibly, keep my attention fixed on what went on, or think and talk coherently.* CON ○ *She had* **given up** *her social life because Uncle Saunders, with his growing miserliness, had said it cost too much.* DC ○ *Mr Charlton, soporific as well as fearful, made no hint of a move and Ma* **gave** *it all* **up**, *at last, in disgust (it* = her attempt at match-making between Mr Charlton and her daughter). DBM

12 [Vp] admit defeat or one's inability to do sth (eg in a guessing game, or in an attempt to convince sb of something): *'Look! I've mentioned every possible kind of seat I can think of. I* **give up**. *What's the answer?' 'A chaise-longue.'* ○ *'I've explained the situation to John a hundred times if I've explained it once. He does not or will not understand. I* **give up**!*'* ○ *If any of these things were true Guy would not have* **given up** *so easily. In the past he had had more tenacity than that.* DC
⇨ give up on.

give up (all) hope [Vp.n pass] abandon hope, lose hope: *Even though the hostages had been missing for three years, their families refused to* **give up hope** *that one day they would return safely.* ○ *After three days of continuous flights over the Atlantic,* **all hope** *of finding the missing aircraft was* **given up** *and the search abandoned.*

give up the fight/the (unequal) struggle [Vp.n] abandon the fight etc; be defeated: *I tried a variety of materials as leads, and the one that took him* (= a captured animal) *longest to get through was a thong of rawhide, but even this* **gave up the unequal struggle** (ie was eaten through) *eventually.* DF ○ *After years of trying to make a living from a small farm, Timothy finally* **gave up the fight** *and turned to catering for tourists.*

give up for dead/lost [Vn.p.pr pass] assume that sb is dead or has been lost; consider sb to be 'past redemption', ineducable, past help etc: *When the climbers were three days overdue at the rendezvous, they were* **given up for lost** (or: **dead**). ○ *When Sue's father — a pillar of the Church — heard that she had been living with an avowed atheist, he* **gave her up for lost**. ⇨ give up 7.

give up on [Vp.pr pass] (*informal*) admit defeat in one's efforts to affect, harm, change, improve etc (sb/sth). **o:** one's children, pupils; house, farm: *She wondered why mosquitoes didn't* **give up on** *victims who had reached a certain age.* SATS ○ *It was as if the forces of evolution had* **given up on** *them ..., and turned aside in disgust and written them off as an ugly and unfortunate mistake.* HHGG
⇨ give up 12.

give up to [Vn.p.pr] devote or abandon (oneself/sth) fully to (sth). **O:** oneself; life, career. **o:** spell, magic; research, writing, composition: *Swayed by the faintly hypnotic melody, the crowd* **gave** *themselves* **up to** *its power.* GIE = give over to.

given up to [pass (Vn.p.pr)] (be) reserved or set aside for (a purpose). **S:** house, church, factory; season, weekend, evening. **o:** activity, celebration; leisure pursuits: *Every house with as much as one small bedroom ... was* **given up to** *this seasonal occupation* (ie accommodating visitors). SE ○ *The week was entirely* **given up to** *lectures and practical demonstrations.* = given over to.

glance

glance at [Vpr pass adj rel] look quickly at (sth/sb). **o:** book, article; clock: *I* **glanced at** *my watch and was surprised to see it was nearly midnight.*

glance off [Vp, Vpr] change course after striking (a sloping surface); be deflected from (sth). **S:** arrow, bullet, shell, stone; her barbed remarks. **o:** armour, wall, tank; head; his thick skin: *The bullet* **glanced off** *the soldier's helmet and buried itself in a nearby tree.* ○ *It was impossible to insult Roger. Every remark, however barbed, just seemed to* **glance off** *his incredibly tough hide.*

glance over/through [Vpr nom pass adj rel] scan (sth) quickly or casually. **o:** book, article, newspaper, report, letter; poem, short story, script: *'Do you think you could* **glance over** *the minutes that I've drafted of our last meeting, before I have them typed out?'* ○ *As a conscientious parent, she always* **glanced through** *her daughter's homework and signed it.* ○ *'You might just give the article a quick* **glance-through**.*'*

glance round [Vp, Vpr] look quickly round (a place etc). **o:** room, hall, theatre; assembly, gathering: *She walked into the room,* **glanced round**, *saw nobody that she knew, and left again at once.* ○ *The actor* **glanced round** *the audience and spotted his wife in the third row.*

glare

glare (at) [Vpr pass] look, with an intense expression of enmity or hostility (at sb). **S:** teacher; sergeant-major; husband; thief. **o:** child; the offending soldier; his wife; the policeman: *The two men stood* **glaring** *drunkenly* **at** *each other, while the crowd looked on with amusement.*

glare contempt/defiance/hate (at) [Vn.pr] look with an intense expression of contempt etc (at sb). **o:** rival, enemy: *The three accused* **glared defiance at** *the court as the judge handed down sentences of up to twenty years.*

glare down [Vp] pour light and heat down. **S:** ⚠ sun; spot-lights, arc-lights: *The sun* **glared down** *with merciless intensity on the six men adrift in the lifeboat.*

glass

glass in [Vn ⇆ p pass adj] enclose (sth) with glass. **O:** verandah, porch, entrance, patio: *If we were to* **glass in** *the back entrance, the kitchen would not be so cold.* ○ *Although they lived in the north of Scotland, they could sit in their* **glassed-in** *verandah even in the middle of winter.*

glaze

glaze in [Vn ⇆ p pass adj] ⇨ glass in.

glaze over [Vp] (*formal*) assume a fixed, trance-like, sightless appearance, perhaps because of boredom or indifference. **S:** ⚠ one's eyes, expression: *The dying man's eyes* **glazed over** *as he sank deeper into unconsciousness.* ○ *She observed her guests' expressions* **glazing over** *with boredom* *as her husband embarked on yet another anecdote.*

glean

glean (from) [Vn.pr pass emph rel] obtain (sth) (from sth/sb), usu with difficulty and in small amounts at a time. **O:** information, knowledge; details, facts. **o:** old books, newspapers; overheard conversation, passing remarks; questioning the staff: *Reporters managed to* ***glean*** *a few details* ***from*** *interviewing the butler.* ○ *The emotions Freud felt when gazing at the pictures may be* ***gleaned from*** *... the reactions of a friend.* F

glide

glide across, along, away etc [Vp, Vpr, Vn.p, Vn.pr] move very smoothly across etc: [Vp, Vn.p] The pilot managed to ***glide*** *(the plane)* ***down*** *to a safe landing.* ○ [Vpr] The ghostly apparition ***glided out of*** *the library,* ***down*** *the passage,* ***up*** *the stairs and* ***through*** *the wall at the top.*

glisten

glisten in/on [Vpr emph rel] ⇨ next entry

glisten with [Vpr] be covered, filled or specked with (drops or particles reflecting light). **S:** eyes; grass; trees. **o:** tears; dew, raindrops; frost: *The branches* ***glistened with*** *newly-fallen snow* (or: *Newly-fallen snow* ***glistened on*** *the branches*). □ note the figurative use, as in: *George's eyes* ***glistened with*** *amusement as he heard the tale of our accident with the dinghy.*

glitter

glitter in/on [Vpr emph rel] ⇨ next entry

glitter with [Vpr] give out or reflect (light); shine with. **S:** sky; Christmas tree; tiara, diadem, crown; dress; neck: *The sky* ***glittered with*** *a myriad stars* (or: *A myriad stars* ***glittered in*** *the sky*). ○ *The filmstar's neck* ***glittered with*** *a million pounds' worth of diamonds* (or: *A million pounds' worth of diamonds* ***glittered on*** *her neck*).

gloat

gloat over 1 [Vpr pass rel] look at (one's possessions) with greedy, miserly delight. **o:** hoard, haul; treasure; collection: *The gang* ***gloated over*** *their haul from the jeweller's, little realizing that the diamonds were mainly worthless paste.* ○ *She had a natural and greedy pleasure in words,* ***gloating over*** *their sounds and shapes.* BRN

2 [Vpr pass rel] derive a sadistic pleasure from (sth). **o:** her rival's downfall, the ruin of his neighbour; the Prime Minister's embarrassment, James's misfortunes: *'I can't understand why you should* ***gloat over*** *John losing his job. You could be next on the list of "redundant workers".'*

glory

glory in 1 [Vpr] draw great pleasure from (sth/doing sth); be proud of (sth). **o:** her ability to speak five languages; his attractiveness to women; devoting his life to others: *St Francis of Assisi* ***gloried in*** *his love for all God's creatures.* ○ *For a few brief years, Stephen* ***gloried in*** *his success with London theatre audiences. Then, suddenly, he faded from the limelight.*

2 [Vpr] (*jocular*) possess, by accident, some 'glorious' or amusing attribute (esp one's name): *Sarah Smith went to Spain and fell in love with a young man who* ***gloried in*** *the name of Juan Luis Velázquez de Albornoz y Madariaga.* ○ *One of the characters in The Mikado* ***glories in*** *the title of Lord High Executioner.* = rejoice in 2.

gloss

gloss over [Vpr pass adj] try to conceal or lessen (sth); ignore. **o:** faults, mistakes, errors, inconsistencies; humble origins, murky past; unsuitability for the job: *I deplore the modern tendency to* ***gloss over*** *the low standards in some of our schools.* ○ *He tended to remind people of things they'd prefer to* ***gloss over***. FL ○ *Weaknesses ... should be thoroughly probed, and not* ***glossed over*** *in public.* T = varnish over 2.

glow

glow with [Vpr] show, throw out, reflect or be filled with (sth). **S:** face, whole body, eyes; forest, trees. **o:** health, pride, joy, pleasure, enthusiasm; colour: *The children ran into the house from the beach, their faces* ***glowing with*** *health and vigour.* ○ *The whole countryside* ***glowed with*** *the russet tints of autumn.*

glower

glower (at) [Vpr pass] stare in a threatening or defiant way (at sb): *The child would not go, but stood by the door* ***glowering at*** *his father.*

glue

glue down [Vn ⇆ p pass adj] fasten (the cover etc of sth) with glue. **O:** edge, flap, cover; envelope: *One of the photographs has come unstuck: you'll have to* ***glue*** *it* ***down***. ○ ***Glue down*** *the corner of the carpet.* = stick down 1.

glue in/into [Vn ⇆ p pass adj, Vn.pr pass emph rel] fix or fasten (sth) into an enclosed space with glue. **O:** fitting, part; piece, fragment. **o:** assembly, frame; side, back: *A small piece of wood has come out of the base of the clock. I'll try to* ***glue*** *it back* ***in***. ○ *These small cannon have to be* ***glued into*** *the hull of the model.* = stick in.

glue on/onto [Vn ⇆ p pass adj, Vn.pr pass emph rel] fasten (sth) onto a surface with glue. **O:** photograph, map; fitting, catch. **o:** board, wall; door, bag: *If the veneer peels away from the surface of the wood, you have to* ***glue*** *it* ***on*** *with a special adhesive.* ○ *A plastic strip was* ***glued onto*** *his office door bearing his name and title.* = stick on.

glue to [Vn.pr pass] join (sth) to (sth) with glue. **O:** poster, stamp, photograph; (table) leg; false beard. **o:** wall, envelope, passport; table; chin: *When you've* ***glued*** *the spindles* ***to*** *the chair, put a couple of screws in to hold them on firmly.*

glued to [pass (Vn.pr)] (appear to be) attached to sth as though with glue. **S:** maid, child, young man. **o:** keyhole, television: *Half the nation was* ***glued to*** *the television, watching the World Cup.* ○ (advertisement for a TV rental service) *You'll be* ***glued to*** *our sets — not stuck with them* (ie not forced to keep them). ITV □ also used with *appear, seem, become*; note the expressions *with/have one's eyes* glued to *sth* and *sit* glued to *one's seat.*

gnaw

gnaw away [Vn ⇆ p pass] (of certain animals) destroy (sth) with the teeth. **S:** rat, beaver. **O:** wood(work); floorboards: *Parts of the wooden support of the house had been dangerously* ***gnawed away***. *Immediate repair was essential.* □ often passive.

gnaw (away) at 1 [Vpr pass, Vp.pr pass] bite at (sth) continuously, as a rodent does. **S:** rat, mouse; rabbit; lion. **o:** wood; bone: *The bark had been* ***gnawed at*** *by young squirrels.* ○ *A tiger in the corner of the cage* ***gnawed*** *listlessly* ***at*** *an old bone.*
2 [Vpr, Vp.pr] hurt or trouble (sb) without rest or relief; consume. **S:** a sense of guilt, remorse, injustice; hatred, sorrow, despair. **o:** him etc; conscience, heart, mind: *The sense that he had been punished for another man's crime* ***gnawed at*** *him until he became obsessed with thoughts of revenge.*

go

go aboard [Vp, Vpr] get on (a ship etc); board. **o:** ship, plane; (esp *US*) train, bus: *'The ship's leaving in half an hour, so we'd better* ***go aboard*** *and find our cabin.'* ○ (In US, call to passengers to board a train) *'All aboard that's* ***going aboard****!'* ⇨ come/take aboard.

go about 1 [Vp] go, walk, travel from place to place; move in society, among friends etc. **A:** in shabby clothes, in jeans and tee-shirt; in an old van, on a bicycle; claiming to have royal blood: *Is it dangerous to* ***go about*** *bareheaded in the tropics?* ○ *He was very good at drawing and painting, and used to* ***go about*** *saying he was going to be an artist.* CON □ cf the second example with go about *doing sth* as in go about 3. = go around/round 1.
2 [Vp] circulate or be current. **S:** ⚠ story, rumour, lie: *The rumour is* ***going about*** *that John and Mary are getting divorced.* ○ *Stories were* ***going about*** *concerning his involvement in a currency racket.* = go around/round 2. ⇨ get about/around/round, put about 2.
3 [Vpr] approach, tackle or make a start at (sth). **o:** problem, job, matter; it; solving the problem, repairing the car: *I've got a big brown mole on my cheek. It's not very flattering and I want to get rid of it. How should I* ***go about*** *it?* H ○ *Peter hasn't the faintest idea how to* ***go about*** *finding a better job.* □ cf the second example with go about *doing sth* in go about 1; often used with *(in) the right/wrong way* : *He was* ***going*** *the right way* ***about*** *it* (or: *He was* ***going about*** *it (in) the right way*). = set about 1.
4 [Vpr] be or keep busy with (a task) normally. **o:** affairs, business; work, chores, everyday job: *Those who* ***went about*** *their ordinary business without feeling heroic emotions ... were the most useful to their country.* RTH ○ *While the bombs were exploding in Belfast, housewives* ***went about*** *the everyday job of keeping their homes going.* ⇨ be about 1.
5 [Vp] (*nautical*) change direction; move onto a fresh tack. **S:** ship; captain, helmsman: *When the boat is turned from one tack to another the operation is termed '****going about****' and it invariably involves bringing the bow of the boat over the wind.* SAIL ⇨ bring about 2, come about 2, put about 1.

go about (together/with) [Vp, Vp.pr] court (sb) with a view to marriage; have a regular sexual or romantic relationship (with): *I'm afraid your daughter is* ***going about with*** *a man old enough to be her father.* ○ *How long have Eric and Hilda been* ***going about (together/with*** *each other)?* = go around/round (together/with).

go above sb's head 1 [Vpr] (*informal*) be too difficult or obscure for sb to understand. **S:** lecture, book; theory, ideas. **m:** way, miles; totally: *These points ...* ***go*** *completely* ***above the heads of*** *Labour supporters or indeed* ***of*** *voters generally.* NS ⇨ be above one/one's head.
2 [Vpr] ask for advice or support from sb higher in rank than one's immediate senior: *If I don't get a satisfactory answer from the departmental manager I shan't hesitate to* ***go above her head****.*

go abroad [Vp] leave one's own country to visit or live in another: *Emma felt that she needed to get away for a while, so she decided to* ***go abroad*** *for a holiday.* ⇨ take abroad (with).

go across (to) [Vp emph, Vpr, Vp.pr] pass from one side (of sth) (to the other). **o:** (**across**) road, bridge; river; Channel; (**to**) shop; other bank; France: [Vpr] Planks were laid so that the villagers could *go across the marshy area.* ○ [Vp.pr] 'I'm just ***going across to*** *the pub for half an hour.'* = go over (to). ⇨ get across 1, send across (to), take across (to).

go after 1 [Vpr] try to catch (sb); pursue. **o:** suspect, runaway, wanted man: *The police warned the public not to* ***go after*** *the escaped prisoner, as he was armed and dangerous.* ⇨ be after 1, come after 2, keep after.
2 [Vpr] try to get (sth); pursue. **o:** job, position; championship; girl. **A:** with a will, with determination; as though her life depended on it: *Once Sam decided what he wanted, he* ***went after*** *it with a single-mindedness that reminded me of his father.* ⇨ be after 2.

go against 1 [Vpr] be contrary to (sth); be out of harmony with (sth). **S:** scheme, plan, idea; way of life. **o:** my principles, beliefs; philosophy, religion: *The idea of trying to cheat the income tax authorities* ***went against*** *her principles — she had a strong sense of civic responsibility.* ○ *That one could be protected from disease by the injection of a serum seemed to* ***go against*** *all logic.* ⇨ be against 2.
2 [Vpr] be lost by (sb); be unfavourable to (sb). **S:** war; fight; election; (legal) case, action: *The notion that the battle could* ***go against*** *them never for a moment entered into the generals' calculations.*
3 [Vpr] disregard or oppose (sb/sth). **o:** ruler; authority; order, decree: *My power is secure ... No man in the city dare* ***go against*** *my orders or my wishes.* GLEG

go against the grain [Vpr] be contrary to sb's wishes or natural inclinations. **S:** it ... to give money to the council; giving money away, paying high prices, doing as one is told: *The children finally went and changed their wet clothes, though it obviously* ***went against the grain****.* ○ *Staying in bed may* ***go against the grain*** *but that's what you must do if you want to get better.* □ sometimes found in the form go against sb's grain as in: *It* ***went against my grain*** *to spend thirty pounds on a meal.*

go aground (on) [Vp, Vp.pr emph rel] (*nautical*) become stuck on mud, sand or rocks. **S:** ship, boat; tanker, liner, dinghy, launch: *The coaster, on its first trip up the estuary, missed the narrow channel and* ***went aground on*** *a mud-bank.* ⇨ run aground.

go ahead 1 [Vp nom] proceed (to do what one wants to do). **A:** with one's plans; without further delay: *He told me to* **go ahead** *and design a small mass-production car.* ST ○ *The government has decided to* **go ahead** *with its plans to develop manufacturing in the North-East.* ○ *We can't do anything about your proposal until we get the* **go-ahead** *from the local Council.* □ go-ahead often used with *give sb/get/have*.

2 [Vp nom] make progress; proceed. **S:** he etc; company, firm; scheme, building; work. **A:** like a house on fire, (very) fast; at a good speed, vigorously: *Once our policy is formulated we intend to* **go ahead** *full steam* (or: **go** *full steam* **ahead**). TBC ○ *With the strike settled, work on the new bridge* **went ahead** *like wildfire.* ○ *The best way to get ahead yourself is to join a really* **go-ahead** *company* (or: *a company that's really* **go-ahead**). □ nom form usu used as an adj, as in the last example. = go forward (with).

go ahead/ahead of [Vp, Vpr emph] continue a journey in advance (of others). **o:** main party, the others, the rest: *A few carefully chosen men* **went ahead** *while the main body remained concealed in the valley.* ○ *Scouts* **went ahead of** *the main force and reported back the strength of the enemy.* ○ **Ahead of** *the main group* **went** *an advance party to test the new route to the South Col.* = go on 3. ⇨ send ahead/ahead of.

go along [Vp] move forward, proceed, on a journey, in one's work etc: *As they* **went along**, *they kept up their spirits by singing and telling jokes.* ○ *You'll get more skilful at this job as you* **go along**.

go along (with) [Vp, Vp.pr] accompany (sb) to a certain place: *As everyone else was going to the pub, I decided to* **go along** *too.* ○ *'I have to go to the dentist this morning.' 'Would you like me to* **go along with** *you?'*

go along with 1 [Vp.pr] (*informal*) be provided together with (sth); accompany. **S:** furniture, carpets; a free supply of detergents. **o:** flat, house; the washing-machine: *A splendid bookcase* **goes along with** *the complete Encyclopedia — if you pay cash.*

2 [Vp.pr pass emph rel] have the same opinion as (sb); act in agreement with (sb). **o:** him etc; policy, scheme, proposal; view, opinion: *I don't necessarily* **go along with** *all you say about politics.* TBC ○ *That is an argument* **with** *which Sir Geoffrey Howe might* **go along**. OBS ○ *If we* **go along with** *your party on the improvement of street-lighting, we shall expect you to* **go along with** *us in providing more funds for libraries.* = agree with 1.

go along with you! [Vp.pr] (a mild rebuke or expression of disbelief): *'Thirty thousand pounds a year?* **Go along with you!** *The job isn't worth fifteen thousand!'* = get along/away with you! ⇨ get on! 5, go on! 14.

go around/round 1 [Vp] go from place to place; move in society, among friends etc. **A:** doing, saying, that kind of thing; pretending that sex doesn't exist; with one's head in the clouds, with a face like thunder: *You can't* **go around** *making up things about being assaulted by people who don't exist.* DC ○ *I would hate to* **go round** *saying I was a chicken magnate* (ie claiming to make a fortune from chickens). AT = go about 1.

2 [Vp, Vpr] pass from person to person (in a place); circulate. **S:** news, word; story, rumour: *Word* **went round** *that something important was in the offing, so the meeting was well attended.* TCB ○ *She had no idea what ugly stories were* **going round** *town about her.* GE = go about 2.

go around/round (together/with) [Vp, Vp.pr emph rel] keep company (with sb); have a regular sexual or romantic relationship (with sb). **o:** him/her; girl, fellow; the wrong sort of people: *Alex has been* **going around with** *the same group of friends since he started at the High School.* ○ *They've been* **going around** *for two years now, but they still haven't decided whether to marry or not.* = go about (together/with). ⇨ take around/round (with).

go astray 1 [Vp] get lost; be mislaid: *A good sheep-dog never lets any sheep* **go astray** *from the flock.* ○ *I'm sorry that I haven't answered your letter. Unfortunately, it has* **gone astray** *and I don't remember exactly what you said in it.*

2 [Vp] get into undesirable company, have trouble with the police etc: *It's only too easy for young people to* **go astray** *if they arrive in London with no friends and nowhere to live.* ⇨ lead astray.

go at 1 [Vpr] attack (sb) physically; argue about or discuss (sth) heatedly. **o:** her/him; each other; it. **A:** hammer and tongs, hell for leather, tooth and nail: *The two drivers lost their tempers and really* **went at** *each other.* ○ *'We had two teams from rival estate agents down here the other week. They really* **went at** *each other hammer and tongs.'* NS

2 [Vpr] make great efforts to do (sth); tackle (sth) vigorously. **o:** job, work, task; it. **A:** with a will, with determination, with renewed vigour; for all he was worth, as though her life depended on it: *The villagers* **went at** *the building of the dam with a will, once they had realized that the rising waters could be stemmed.* ○ *'I know you're keen to help, but there's no need to* **go at** *it like a madman!'*

go away 1 [Vp emph] leave a place or sb's presence; depart: *'Oh,* **go away** *and leave me in peace!'* ○ *Only by speaking to them like 'an angel' could Gwen get them to* **go away**. GJ = go off 1. ⇨ send away.

2 [Vp] (specifically, of a bride with her bridegroom) leave the wedding-guests and go on one's honeymoon: *Mary bought a very smart outfit to* **go away** *in.* ○ *This is the most beautiful blue, it's* **going-away** *blue.* DPM □ going-away used attrib with *dress, hat, shoes* etc.

go back 1 [Vp emph] return. **S:** children; books; one, you. **A:** to school; to the library; to one's childhood home; to the scene of the accident: *'This machine is* **going back** *to the shop where I bought it. It's no good!'* ○ *You should never* **go back**, *they say, to the scene of a past romance.* ○ *He sometimes* **went back** *to the hospital to check that everything had been done according to instructions.* INN ⇨ be back 1, bring back 1, come back 1, get back 1, take back 1.

2 [Vp] (of clocks and watches) be set to an earlier time in order to allow for changing hours of daylight (eg in Britain at the end of British Summer Time): *'Oh dear, the clocks* **go back** *tonight. Awful, isn't it?'* EGD ○ *'I'm looking forward to the clocks* **going back** *next Sunday: it means an extra hour in bed!'* ↔ go forward. ⇨ put back 2.

go back on [Vp.pr pass] fail to keep or fulfil (a promise); retract. **o:** one's word, promise; solemn undertaking, solemn pledge; one's previous choice: *'He'd promised her a free rein; he couldn't* **go back on** *his word.* EC ○ *If you witness a drunkard signing the pledge* (ie that he will stop drinking), *you feel personally responsible when he* **goes back on** *it.* CON ○ *I promised you, didn't I? I'm not* **going back on** *that.* AITC

go back (to) 1 [Vp, Vp.pr emph rel] return to an earlier point in space, time, a discussion etc. **o:** the start; first principles, basics; carpentry; teaching chemistry: *'Now that you've done a year in Medicine, you can't very well* **go back** *and start an Arts course.* ○ *'But to* **go back to** *what I was saying about life in the country ....'* ○ *He had simply* **gone back to** *restoring old harpsichords, which were his true passion.* MSAL

2 [Vp, Vp.pr] extend back (over a certain period) or (to a certain date). **S:** our family; the company; custom, belief, practice; devotion, attachment to sth; taste, liking for sth; hatred of sth. **A:** several centuries, decades; a long way. **o:** 1965; an earlier time: *'The fifteenth century! Good Lord, I didn't realize that his title* **went back** *that far.'* ○ *The Pipe Rolls* (annual records of the king's revenue and expenses) **go back to** *1129-30 and as a complete series to 1154.* SHOE ○ *Ann's love of horses* **goes back** *as far as she can remember.* H = date from/back to, lead back(to).

go before 1 [Vp, Vpr] (*rhetorical*) live (and die) before one's own time. **S:** those who have ...; many; our ancestors: *We have endeavoured to live up to the high standards of those who have* **gone before** (or: **gone before** *us).* MFM □ usu perfect tenses.

2 [Vpr] appear before (sb) in order to explain one's actions or to receive punishment; be presented for discussion, approval etc. **S:** thief, miscreant; plan, draft; application, request. **o:** court, magistrate; council, senate: *In my day, a boy who was caught smoking in school* **went before** *the headmaster and was probably beaten.* ○ *My application to build an extension to my house* **goes before** *the planning committee next week.* ⇨ be before 2, bring before, come before 2, put before 2, take before.

go behind sb's back [Vpr] act unfairly, unethically or deceitfully: *'I know that you and I don't agree about everything, but I thought I could trust you to discuss our problems frankly, and not to* **go behind my back** *complaining to the manager.'*

go below (decks) [Vp, Vpr] (*nautical*) on a ship, leave the deck and go down to the living quarters etc: *A seaman* **went below** *to fetch the mate a cup of cocoa.* ⇨ be below 3, take below.

go between [Vpr] fit well into a position between (A and B): *This picture* **goes** *nicely* **between** *the portraits of your father and mother.*

go-between [nom (Vpr)] an intermediary or messenger, esp between lovers: *The child was quite unaware that she was being used as a* **go-between** *by her elder sister and the married man next door.*

go beyond [Vpr] exceed, surpass (sth). **o:** one's brief, instructions; the scope of (sth), the bounds of (sth); expectations, intentions; all reason; anything I could have imagined: *We expected Mr Graham to be displeased with our decision, but his anger* **went beyond** *all reason.* ○ *A prize of £1 000 would have been marvellous, but the announcement that I had won £10 000* **went beyond** *my wildest dreams.* □ a soldier is often 'decorated' for actions that go beyond the call of duty. ⇨ be beyond 2.

go beyond a joke [Vpr] become a serious matter; be no longer funny: *This teasing of Sarah has* **gone beyond a joke**. *I wish he'd stop it!* ⇨ be beyond a joke.

go by 1 [Vp, Vpr] pass before, in front of, near to (sb). **S:** procession, cavalcade, parade; band; car, train: *As each contingent* **went by**, *there was a burst of applause from the watching crowd.* ○ *In the playing field* (at school) *I was always caught watching trains* **go by**. SU

2 [Vp] pass, elapse. **S:** time; days, weeks, months; seconds, minutes; an age, an eternity: *Scarcely a month* **goes by** *without a fisherman being drowned.* T ○ *They used to be pirates in days* **gone by** (or: *In* **bygone** *days), but what I say is they've never stopped being pirates.* RM ○ *We used to eat solidly, making up for the lean week* **gone by**, *and the lean week stretching ahead.* BRH □ note the form bygones in: *Let* **bygones** *be* **bygones** (ie Let us forget past quarrels or disagreements and make a fresh start). = go on 7.

3 [Vp] pass without being used or grasped. **S:** opportunity, chance, opening: *Mr Simpson hesitated just a little too long over accepting a partnership in the firm; when he finally made up his mind, the opportunity had* **gone by**.

4 [Vpr] be guided by (sth); take one's course or direction from (sth). **o:** star; map, compass: *We had no compass, and only the distant gunfire to* **go by** (ie to judge our position). BM

5 [Vpr] form an opinion according to (sth). **o:** advice, recommendation; past experience; appearances; what John says: *If the FAO experts' report is anything to* **go by**, *there's going to be another terrible famine in Ethiopia.* ○ *'Please don't* **go by** *what I say! My taste in films is not very reliable.'* ○ *It's often a mistake to* **go by** *appearances: that poor-looking individual is anything but poor.* = judge by/from 1.

go-by [nom (Vp)] the act of ignoring, disregarding, not selecting sb (eg for promotion): *Gilbert's accepted me in his rather pompous way, even when my own family have given me the* **go-by**. ASA □ only in the phrase *give sb the* go-by.

go by the board [Vpr] be abandoned or sacrificed. **S:** rule, principle; ceremony, tradition; luxury: *Normally I love a glass of sherry ... when my husband comes home before dinner. That will* **go by the board** *now!* RT ○ *Apart from one hotel and five blocks of luxury flats, the whole front has been devoted to offices. And so, at a stroke, the Borough's excellent proposals* **go by the board**. OBS

go by the book [Vpr] act in a rigid, strictly correct, or bureaucratic manner: *'If you* **go by the book** *you shouldn't have any trouble with the authorities.'*

go by the name of [Vpr] be known as (sth); be called: *This wild flower* **goes by the name of** *Old Man's Beard.*

go down 1 [Vp] disappear below the horizon; set. **S:** the sun, moon, stars: *As the sun* **went down** *the whole sky became suffused with a red glow.* ↔ come up 13.

2 [Vp emph] (*nautical*) disappear below the surface of the sea; sink; (of men) drown. **S:** ship, boat, vessel; captain, crew, yachtsman, fisherman: *The* *ship struck a hidden reef and* **went down** *with all hands.* ○ *In the tradition of the sea, the captain stayed on board until all the passengers and crew had left; but he himself* **went down** *with his ship.* ↔ come up 9.

3 [Vp emph] fall, collapse; be defeated: *Tyson hit the challenger once with a right hook, and he* **went down** *like a felled ox.* ○ *This was the batsmen's first taste of body-line bowling* (hostile bowling meant to intimidate) *and they* **went down** *like ninepins.* SC ○ *The home team* **went down** *2-0* (or: *went down by 2 goals to nil*). ↔ get up 2. ⇨ bring down 3.

4 [Vp] be swallowed; be consumed. **S:** soup, fish, dinner; wine, cocktail, drink; pill, medicine. **A:** very well, famously; badly; the wrong way: *John was delighted that his wife's cooking should* **go down** *so well. The main guest was his boss!* ○ *Either from the sherry* **going down** *the wrong way or from pure rage, Tom's face turned purple.* SPL ○ *It was Portuguese champagne and* **went down** *like mother's milk.* ILIH ⇨ get down 5, go down (with).

5 [Vp] be reduced in amount; fall. **S:** prices, charges; fees, subscriptions; taxes, rates: *It's a strange thing, but prices always seem to be going up. They never* **go down**! ↔ go up 2. ⇨ be down 2, bring down 5, come down 3.

6 [Vp] be lowered (in level). **S:** wine, whisky; sugar, flour; reserves, trading balance: *Now and then Pop decided that the punch was* **going down** *rather too fast and added another harmless dash of rum, a little Kirsch, or a glass of brandy.* BFA ○ *If our stocks of food* **go down** *much further, we shall have a hard winter.*

7 [Vp] be reduced in force or degree; fall. **S:** temperature; the glass (= barometer), the mercury: *The glass is* **going down**, *so we must expect a change in the weather.* ↔ go up 3.

8 [Vp] leave university at the end of a term or finally: *He was trying to remember, first, who this was, and secondly, whether he was one of the present generation of undergraduates or had* **gone down**. HD ○ *'We were living together all through my third year.' 'I suppose that helps to account for your* **going down** *without taking a degree?'* HD □ used esp of Oxford or Cambridge students. ↔ come up 3. ⇨ be/come down (from), send down 1.

9 [Vp] be written down, recorded. **S:** statement, speech; evidence, complaint: *Every word uttered in court* **went down** *for future reference.* ○ *Nothing of this must* **go down** *on paper.* ⇨ be down 3, get down 4, put down 11, set down 2, take down 3.

10 [Vp] become less swollen or inflated. **S:** finger, wrist, knee; tyre, ball: *I've bandaged his wrist up but it'll be a while before the swelling* **goes down**. ○ *My back tyre keeps* **going down**. *There must be a puncture somewhere.* ↔ swell up 1, pump up 2. ⇨ let down 3.

go down on one's knees (to) 1 [Vp.pr] adopt a kneeling position (in front of sb): *'Come here darling. Bring Sarah.' As Nicky came dragging the unwilling Sarah, Prissie* **went down on her knees** *to them.* DC ⇨ get down 3.

2 [Vp.pr] (*informal*) behave in a submissive way (towards sb), esp to beg for favours or support: *You had to* **go down on your knees** *for a ham sandwich, and for a hot meal you had practically to sign an undertaking that the landlord could be ... your sole legatee.* CON ⇨ be down on one's knees.

go down to 1 [Vp.pr] be defeated by (sb/sth). **S:** champion, record-holder, challenger; batsman. **o:** newcomer, younger man; faster ball: *The reigning champion* **went down to** *a hammer-blow in the twelfth round.* ○ *The Roman Empire finally* **went down to** *the barbarians.*

2 [Vp.pr] approach, esp a river or the sea: (children's rhyme) *Adam and Eve and Pinch-me-tight* **went down to** *the river to bathe. Adam and Eve were drowned. Who do you think was saved?* ○ *They that* **go down to** *the sea in ships: and occupy their business in great waters* (= earn their living as sailors and fishermen). PRAYER BOOK

3 [Vp.pr] get as far as (a certain date or stage); reach. **S:** book, volume, article. **o:** the sixteenth century; 1945: *This book is no use to me; it only* **goes down to** *the General Election of 1951.* ○ *The membership list was useless: it only* **went down to** *letter G.*

go down to posterity [Vp.pr] be remembered for many years to come: *She would* **go down to posterity** *as the only party leader to win three consecutive elections.*

go down (with) [Vp, Vp.pr emph rel] (*informal*) be accepted or welcomed (by sb). **S:** he etc; suggestion, proposal; scheme, plan; offer; explanation, story, account; my divorce, their decision to emigrate. **A:** (none too) well; a treat; all right; (very) big. **o:** mother, my family; the public: *They don't recognize a Mexican divorce in New York, and a Reno divorce doesn't* **go down** *all that well in the Motherland* (ie in Britain). TGLY ○ *These toys are a big hit in the United States. 'They could* **go down** *even bigger than skateboards,' says the firm importing them.* YP ○ *I gave my name as Jessie Proctor. It* **went down** *all right, and it matches the initials on my case.* RFW

go down with [Vp.pr] become ill with (sth). **o:** measles, mumps; a severe chill, flu; cholera, malaria, typhoid: *Beckwith* **went down with** *a bad case of malaria.* JUNG ○ *'For God's sake, don't you* **go down with** *the flu too.'* PPLA □ usu restricted to illnesses that strike quickly. ⇨ be down with, come down with.

go for 1 [Vpr] leave one's home or place of work to take (exercise etc). **o:** walk, stroll, run; drive in the country; a sail: *He* **went for** *picnics and days out in the car.* BRH ○ *'My husband's just* **gone for** *a walk, but he'll be back in half an hour.'*

2 [Vpr] go somewhere to obtain or fetch (sb/sth). **o:** newspaper; drink; help, assistance: *Tom stayed with the injured climber while Jane* **went for** *help.* ○ *After lunch, Bill* **went for** *a quick one* (drink) *to the local pub.* HAA ⇨ send for 1.

3 [Vpr pass] attack (sb), physically or verbally. **S:** dog, youth; journalist; wife. **o:** intruder, old man; Prime Minister; husband. **A:** with a razor, a two-handed sword; with venom: *'What do you want me to do? Throw the furniture about, or* **go for** *you with a kitchen knife?'* AITC ○ *When Robert* **went for** *him bald-headed, ... his attacks were attended by a certain risk.* CON ○ *I didn't mean to kill Micky; he* **went for** *me with a razor.* PE ○ *She had already been twice* **gone for** *by Mrs Thompson for trying to make herself useful.* TGLY

4 [Vpr] be true for (sb); include. **S:** ⚠ this, that; what I say: *'Tell the men that they can knock off for an hour.' 'Does that* **go for** *me, too?'* ○ *'Your sister is a thoroughly selfish girl — and that* **goes for** *you, too.'*

5 [Vpr] be attracted by (sb/sth); have a taste for (sb/sth). **o:** him etc; pop music, modern art; every new gadget: *I don't* **go for** *horror films, and I can't understand why anyone else does.* ○ *'There's a terrific girl sitting by herself over there. Why not offer to buy her a drink?' 'Thanks, but I don't* **go for** *blondes.'* ○ *He* **goes for** *its full, delicious flavour. I* **go for** *its economy.* WI □ often neg.

6 [Vpr] be sold for (a certain sum). **S:** house, land; second-hand car, antique. **o:** far more/less than we expected, a mere twenty pounds, a price I couldn't possibly afford: *The old cottage, dilapidated as it was,* **went for** *over £50 000.* ○ *'How much do you think these Chinese vases will* **go for***?'* □ note esp go for a song meaning go for very little money, be sold very cheaply.

go for a Burton [Vpr] (*slang*) be killed; be damaged or destroyed. **S:** airmen, crew; aircraft; radio, car: *A very great friend of mine was with that squadron ... Thoroughly decent chap ...* **Went for a Burton** *over the Ruhr* (ie during a bombing raid over Germany). RATT ○ *Down the corridor came this blast of music ... and suddenly the music stopped as though something* (ie the record-player) *had* **gone for a burton**. TT □ alt spelling: go for a burton; originally an RAF expression meaning that a companion had not returned from a mission; favoured by officers rather than NCOs.

go for nothing/very little [Vpr] have no/little importance. **S:** (all one's) work, effort, endeavour, sacrifice, devotion; influence, position, money: *When the company was taken over by Giant Containers Ltd, a lot of people lost their jobs. Their loyalty and hard work* **went for nothing**. ○ *The niceties of business ethics* **go for very little** *in the world of large-scale property development.* = count for.

go for a song [Vpr] ⇨ go for 6.

go forth [Vp] (*dated* or *rhetorical*) be issued, be created, emerge. **S:** order, command, edict; an army, a fleet: *We must call the whole people to our help, as partners in the battle; only from an inspired Nation can* **go forth** *... an inspired Army.* MFM

go forward [Vp] (of clocks and watches) be set to a later time to allow for changing hours of daylight (eg in Britain at the beginning of British Summer Time): *All clocks and watches should* **go forward** *one hour tonight.* ↔ go back 2.

go forward (with) [Vp, Vp.pr] make progress (with sth); progress. **S** [Vp], **o** [Vp.pr]**:** work, plans; reorganization of a plant, rationalization of production methods: *Work on the new hospital is* **going forward** *at a satisfactory pace.* ○ *The Committee decided to* **go forward with** *its plans for the compulsory purchase of land, so that the road could be widened.* = go ahead 1,2.

go from bad to worse [Vpr] continue to deteriorate. **S:** matters, things, situation; behaviour; the condition of the homeless: *What does all this tell us about West Ham* (football club)*? That they are* **going from bad to worse**. IND ○ *With inflation and already high interest rates, the situation is* **going from bad to worse** *for millions of people.*

go from strength to strength [Vpr] go from an already strong position to an even stronger one. **S:** army, team, society; writer, composer; player: *Sherlock Holmes* **went from strength to strength** *in the years before the First War.* RT ○ *Watching him* (a golfer) **going from strength to strength** *in the final it was impossible not to think back to ... when he trailed from the field plunged in despair.* SC

go home 1 [Vp] go to the place where one lives; return to one's country: *'It's terribly late! I must* **go home***! My father gets furious if I'm out after midnight.'* □ used in taunts addressed at particular groups of unwelcome foreigners: *For the first three years they said to me 'Scotchman* **go home**.' ST

2 [Vp] (*euphemism*) die; go to heaven: *'Poor old Joe's* **going home** *at last. It's a pity he couldn't have lived to be a hundred.'* ○ *I'm afraid those old rose bushes are* **going home**; *but they've been marvellous for the last twenty years.*

3 [Vp] hit the target aimed at; have the intended effect. **S:** barb, taunt, jibe; reply: *Rufford was a skilful debater, and his calculated sarcasm* **went home**. *His opponent flushed under the attack.* ⇨ drive home (to).

go in 1 [Vp emph] enter a house, school, shed etc: *'We can't discuss your problems standing here in the rain. Let's* **go in** *and make ourselves comfortable.'* ○ *I* **went in** *by the back door and found myself in the kitchen.* ↔ come out/out of 1. ⇨ get in/into 1, go into 1.

2 [Vp emph] disappear behind a cloud. **S:** ⚠ the sun, moon, stars: *Just as we were about to be photographed, and all saying 'cheese' to produce those fake smiles, the sun* **went in**! ↔ come out 5.

3 [Vp emph, Vpr] fit; enter. **S:** cork; key; foot; plug; suit. **o:** bottle; lock; shoe; socket; bag: *'The piano's too big; it won't* **go in** *(this room).'* ↔ come out/out of 2. ⇨ put in 4.

4 [Vp emph] (*cricket*) take one's turn to bat etc. **S:** batsman; side; team: *My uncle used to* **go in** *number four for Beckenham* (ie he was the fourth batsman). ○ *Then* **in went** *the skipper at six wickets down to try and prevent a total collapse.* ↔ get out 3. ⇨ be in 5, put in 8, stay in 3.

5 [Vp] be understood or assimilated. **S:** facts, information, news: *'It's no use. I've read and reread the chapter on the life-cycle of the river fluke, but it won't* **go in**!' ⇨ take in 7.

go in sb's favour [Vp] (*legal*) be decided in sb's favour. **S:** case, action, suit: *After many anxious days when things looked very black, the case finally* **went in my friend's favour**.

go in fear of one's life [Vpr] be afraid that one may be killed, esp by assassination or murder: *As her husband became more and more violent every time he had too much to drink, the poor woman* **went in fear of her life**.

go in (at) one ear and out (at/of) the other [Vpr, Vp.pr] (of sth said to an inattentive, uninterested or unintelligent person) be unheeded or unlearnt: *It's no use asking Tim to deliver any messages. Everything you say* **goes in at one ear and out at the other**.

go in for 1 [Vp.pr] enter (sth) as a candidate or competitor. **o:** examination, competition; tournament, event; the 5 000 metres: *He **went in for** too many events, and so won none.* ⇨ be in for 1, put in for 1.
2 [Vp.pr] (*informal*) have (sth) as one's chosen career. **o:** teaching, medicine, architecture, politics, the law: *My son is **going in for** catering, and part of his course takes him to France.*
3 [Vp.pr] have (sth) as a sport; play; have (sth) as a hobby, pastime etc. **o:** cricket, golf, tennis, swimming; keeping rabbits, breeding dogs, collecting stamps; bird-watching: *'Why don't you **go in for** collecting antiques or something? You need something to take your mind off your work.'*
4 [Vp.pr] regularly practise (sth). **o:** smoking; exercise; that sort of thing; scandal-mongering, gossip; flag-waving, name-dropping: *I'm not one of those people who **go in for** dieting — I'm much too fond of eating!* ○ *'You smoke too much.' ... 'Yes,' she said. 'I've never **gone in for** doing things by halves* (ie in moderation).*'* FL

go in and out [Vp] shine intermittently. **S:** light, lamp, sign: *The neon lights **went in and out**, one moment turning the square into day and the next plunging it back into darkness.*

go in and out/out of [Vp, Vpr] move about from one place to another, usu entering and leaving premises, or cover of some kind: *I wish that child would keep still for a while, and stop **going in and out** like a dog at a fair.* ○ *The visitors **went in and out of** the various pavilions so fast that they could not have appreciated everything they saw at the Exhibition.* ⇨ be in and out of.

go into 1 [Vpr] insert a part of oneself (esp one's hand) into (sth); enter. **o:** room, corner, den; drawer, desk, cupboard: *The owner **went into** a room at the back of the shop and returned with a beautiful Meissen figure which she placed carefully on the counter.* ○ *Somebody keeps **going into** my desk and pinching my pencils.* ⇨ go in 1.
2 [Vpr] make (violent) contact with (sth); enter. **o:** wall, tree, barrier; crowd, oncoming traffic: *The car must have **gone into** the side of the house at tremendous speed. The car was unrecognizable and the wall reduced to rubble.*
3 [Vpr] be admitted to (a place), usu temporarily; go to live in (a place). **o:** hospital; a mental home, a convalescent home; college; lodgings, digs: *I hear that old Mrs Smith has had to **go into** hospital again; evidently she wasn't completely cured last time.* ○ *Most University students have to **go into** digs for at least one or two years.* ↔ come out/out of 1.
4 [Vpr] enter (a mental or physical state); begin (a pattern of behaviour), usu involuntarily. **o:** a trance, a coma; hysterics, a fit, convulsions; a decline; peals, shrieks, fits of laughter: *A hypnotist will remind us that, if he can be induced to stare intently at a shiny object, a patient may **go into** a trance.* HAH ○ *She **went into** a decline of spirits from which she did not recover.* 50MH ⇨ fall into 2, go off into.
5 [Vpr] adopt (sth) as a career; join; start, organize. **o:** the Army, Navy, Air Force, Merchant Navy; the Church; politics, the family business; business (for oneself): *Nothing would induce me to **go into** the family business!* ○ *... on the other hand, I would not be opposed to **going into** business on my own account.*
6 [Vpr] adopt a different kind of dress. **o:** mourning; long trousers; lighter clothes: *People don't **go into** mourning these days. It's all part of our wanting to forget about death.* ○ *In those days boys didn't **go into** long trousers until the age of twelve or thirteen.*
7 [Vpr pass adj] examine, consider or discuss (sth). **o:** details, particulars; the why and the wherefore of sth; question, problem, evidence; accusations, allegations; the cost, usefulness of a scheme; it: *Jones does not **go into** the incident in any kind of detail.* F ○ *'I know you want to tell me about your father's illness; but please don't let's **go into** it now.'* ○ *The Chancellor said that these proposals would have to be **gone into** very carefully.*
8 [Vpr emph] be capable of dividing (another, given figure) so that the result is greater than one: *Six **goes into** twelve, twice. But thirteen **into** twelve doesn't **go*** (or: *won't **go***).
9 [Vpr] appear in, be published in (a new edition etc). **S:** book; dictionary, novel; collection. **o:** second edition; third impression: *'Great Expectations' **went into** a fourth edition within a few weeks of its appearance in book form.* CD

go into abeyance [Vpr] be suspended, shelved or postponed indefinitely. **S:** laws, draft legislation; the citizen's right to a quick trial, the government's plans to expand the economy: *I'm afraid that our new pension scheme will have to **go into abeyance** until the present depression is over.* ○ *'No imprisonment without trial' is a principle that **goes into abeyance** when the nation's security is in danger from terrorists.*

go into action [Vpr] begin an attack; start a planned operation: *The commandos **went into action** at night with their faces blackened for better concealment.* ○ *The proposal is very attractive, but before we can **go into action** we shall need to secure the agreement of all our overseas partners.* ⇨ be in/bring into/come into action.

go into a (flat) spin [Vpr] (of an aircraft) get out of control by spinning; (of a person) lose one's usual self-control or balanced way of life: *The first time Jane flew solo she **went into a spin** and only just succeeded in getting the aircraft under control 500 feet above the ground.* ○ *When Mary broke off the relationship, John seemed to **go into a flat spin**. He would hardly speak to anyone for three months.*

go into a huddle [Vpr] (*informal*) consider what action to take; confer: *The professors **went into a huddle** and decided that a breach of the exam regulations could not be overlooked.*

go into service/use [Vpr] begin to be used. **S:** new model; vehicle, gun, machine: *The Boeing 747s could not **go into service** before the crews agreed on a new salary structure.* ⇨ be in/bring into/come into service/use.

go near 1 [Vp, Vpr] approach (sb/sth). **o:** the edge of the cliff; dog, bull; nettles: *'Don't **go** too **near** that dog; it's very fierce.'* ○ *'I told you not to **go near** your father's study while he's working.'* □ usu neg; often preceded by *too, very*.
2 [Vpr] offer a good chance of (helping etc); come close to. **o:** solving the problem, meeting sb's

wishes, fulfilling the conditions: *Her idea doesn't* **go** *anywhere* **near** *solving the problem.*

go off 1 [Vp emph] leave (a place). **A:** to look for his friends; to Japan; for a short holiday; in a foul temper: *They sold up their house and* **went off** *to live in Canada.* ○ (stage directions) *John* **goes off** *L.* (= left) *as a face appears at the window C.* (= centre). ○ *'This* (discussion) *is unbearably scientific,' said Ann Halsey. 'I'm* **going off** *to make tea.'* TBC = go away 1. ⇨ take off (to).

2 [Vp] take place; proceed. **S:** match; conference, meeting, visit; interview. **A:** well, as expected, without a hitch: *'How did the meeting* **go off**? *Did Bill lose his temper as usual?'* ○ *Harold was relieved . . . that the visit had* **gone off** *so well.* PW ○ *Aunt Ellen had the operation this morning and it all* **went off** *quite well.* RFW □ adv or prep phrase is always present. = pass off 2.

3 [Vp] fall asleep: *He didn't seem to be able to* **go off**, *so he went down to the kitchen and made himself a cup of tea.* ○ *'As soon as the baby's* **gone off** *we'll be able to relax and watch television.'* = drop off 2. ⇨ put off 8.

4 [Vpr] lose one's appetite for (sth) or one's interest in (sth/sb). **o:** coffee, beer, cheese; the cinema, pop music; Fred: *The children seem to have* **gone off** *cornflakes for breakfast.* ○ *We've* **gone off** *Spain — the beaches are so terribly overcrowded.* ○ *She* **went off** *driving altogether after her accident.* ⇨ be off 8, turn off 2.

5 [Vp] explode. **S:** bomb, grenade; (explosive) charge: *The mine could* **go off** *just because of vibration caused by a train at the village station.* ARG ○ *The tins of food had been booby-trapped and would* **go off** *the moment you tried to open them.* = blow up 4. ⇨ let off 4, set off 1.

6 [Vp] make a sudden ringing noise. **S:** burglar alarm, fire alarm; alarm-clock: *If anyone tries to break into the boot of the car, the alarm will* **go off**. ○ *We awoke the next morning before the alarm* **went off**. SML

7 [Vp] turn sour; go bad. **S:** milk, beer; meat, fish: *'That fish we bought yesterday — it's* **gone off**.' ⇨ be off 7.

8 [Vp] become disconnected. **S:** water, gas, electricity, power: *The water will* **go off** *for a couple of hours this morning. The men are repairing a broken pipe.* ⇨ be off 6, cut off 2, turn off 1.

go off the boil 1 [Vpr] stop boiling. **S:** vegetables; potatoes, sprouts; pudding: *'Don't let the potatoes* **go off the boil**, *will you?'*

2 [Vpr] (*informal*) no longer be interested, enthusiastic, sexually excited etc; lose momentum. **S:** colleague, lover; investor, backer; scheme, project: *If you don't get on with your book now, the publishers could very easily* **go off the boil**. ○ (a woman is expecting a child but, after feeling the first pangs of childbirth, has stopped experiencing them) *'She's just* **gone off the boil**, *as they say in the midwifery trade.'* DIL

go off one's head etc [Vpr] (*slang*) go mad. **o:** ⚠ head, nut, rocker, chump, trolley: *'When I told him someone had nicked* (stolen) *his new car, he practically* **went off his nut**.' ○ *'If anyone as much as speaks to his wife, he* **goes off his trolley**.' ⇨ be off one's head etc.

go off the deep end [Vpr] (*informal*) show extreme anger; rant and rave: *PETER: You should have heard her the other night. You know what happened ? Her wandering boy returned. He hadn't been home for two weeks. And she* **went off the deep end**. TOH

go off the rails [Vpr] (*informal*) (begin to) behave in an antisocial, immoral or dishonest way: *It was odd how Harold, who had never since his marriage . . .* **gone off the rails** *in any way or wished to, proved himself a past-master of intrigue.* PW ○ *'As for leaving him, that's a lot of bilge* (nonsense) *. . . Suppose* you *had* **gone off the rails** *— do you suppose it would have made any difference to me?'* AITC = run off the rails. ↔ keep on the rails.

go off at half-cock [Vp.pr] (*informal*) (of a process) begin before preparations for it are complete, thus resulting in failure, danger to others etc. **S:** display, show; parade, festival; play, show: *If we don't get the preparations finished tonight, the meeting could* **go off at half-cock** *tomorrow.* ⇨ go off 2.

go off at a tangent [Vp.pr] abruptly change the subject under discussion; take up a minor point, losing track of the main argument: *We were talking about the cost of tomatoes when Laura* **went off at a tangent** *and started talking about the revival of wine-making in England.*

go off into [Vp.pr] (*informal*) suddenly begin to behave in a certain way. **o:** hysterics; fits of laughter; a dead faint: *Cissy* **went off into** *peals of laughter in which Sainty could not help joining.* BLCH ⇨ go into 4.

go off with 1 [Vp.pr] leave with the sexual partner of sb else. **o:** Jane, John; one's best friend's wife: *'If somebody tried to* **go off with** *you, I'd black his eye.'* = run away (with).

2 [Vp.pr] steal (sth) and carry it away. **o:** sb's bike, car; radio, stereo: *'Someone's broken into the flat and* **gone off with** *my video recorder.'* ○ *'Lock your bike: somebody might* **go off with** *it.'* = run away with 1.

go on 1 [Vpr] depart for a certain purpose. **o:** holiday, vacation, safari; trip, excursion; course: *Laura Graham's father* **goes on** *a trip to Rome.* BRN ○ *It's time I* **went on** *a refresher course — I'm getting out of touch with modern techniques.* ⇨ send on 1.

2 [Vp] continue a journey, career etc; progress: *We all agreed to* **go on**, *despite the signs of a thunderstorm on the horizon.* ○ *He had occupied the Presidential chair from which men had* **gone on** *to hold the highest office in the land.* HB

3 [Vp] continue a journey ahead of others: *'I've got a meeting at eleven, so I'll have to* **go on**. *We can meet up later in the restaurant.'* = go ahead/ ahead of. ⇨ send on 2.

4 [Vpr] mount and travel on (sth), esp as a treat. **o:** donkey, horse, elephant, camel; speed-boat, yacht; roundabout, slide; the Big Dipper, the Ghost Train: *The children* **went on** *all the rides at the fair, and then found they hadn't enough money to get the bus home.*

5 [Vp] continue (an activity or relationship). **A:** walking, working, talking; as before, like that; as though you weren't here: *I want to* **go on** *being a teenager, because I am enjoying every minute of it.* H ○ *Like some infernal monster, still venomous in death, a war can* **go on** *killing people for a long time after it's all over.* RFW ○ *'We can't* **go on** *as* *though nothing has happened. It has happened. You've broken your promise.'* = carry on 1. ⇨ get on with, go on with.

6 [Vp] continue without change or relief. **S:** noise, interruptions; affair; rivalry, jealousy; war, hostilities: *The chatter **went on** for several minutes.* DC ○ *She felt that she could not keep up the pretence much longer. How long, she wondered, could it **go on**?* ○ *The hostility and suspicion seemed to **go on** and **on**.*

7 [Vp] pass (by). **S:** time; days, weeks, months, years: *As time **went on**, the more athletically inclined began to train.* CON ○ *As the years **go on** we grow sadder, and perhaps wiser.* = go by 2.

8 [Vp] continue speaking, esp after a short pause: *'Of course I had to be decently educated,' Prissie **went on**, speaking half to herself.* DC ○ *She was angry with herself for her voice being a little stiff. Yet she couldn't help **going on**, 'My husband says Nicky must get over these things.'* DC □ follows direct speech (and its own subject), or precedes direct speech, as shown.

9 [Vp] continue by adding some new point to what has already been said or written. **Inf:** to say, to remark; to explain, to observe: *He **goes on** to say that political historians who write in this way explain nothing.* RTH ○ *In a letter …, Fournier **went on** to describe an incident with a certain Josepha.* AF □ inf always present.

10 [Vp] take place; occur, happen. **S:** something very strange, fishy, interesting, important; what, not much, nothing: *'There's something very odd **going on** between those two.'* ○ *Something wasn't right there, and she wanted to know what was **going on**.* WI ○ *'Where are you? What's **going on** and is there any way of stopping it?'* HHGG ○ *'If you never read the newspapers, you'll never know what's **going on** in the world.'* □ usu continuous tenses, but note the following use of the simple present tense: *'I can't fathom what **goes on** in that skull of yours, I really can't.'* GL ⇨ goings-on.

11 [Vpr] be helped or guided by (sth). **o:** hearsay, rumour, gossip; what you read in the papers: *The spitting image of my mother, dad had said, and I believed him but only had her photograph to **go on**.* PPLA ○ *Police admitted that after questioning the staff of the hotel they still had no real evidence to **go on**.* ○ *What I suddenly saw then was … that the belief I had been **going on** all my life … had no foundation.* KLT □ often in the pattern *no* + n/*hardly anything*/*nothing*/*very little* etc to go on.

12 [Vpr] be spent on (sth). **S:** money, income; half of what she earns; pension; legacy. **o:** the car, the house; food, heating, clothes; luxuries, (non-) essentials: *A lot of my grant **goes on** books; but I think it's money well spent.'* ○ *In the winter a lot of their pension has to **go on** just keeping warm.*

13 [Vpr] begin to receive (money) esp from an official source. **o:** unemployment benefit, the dole; famine relief: *Thousands of skilled workers, who never expected to be unemployed, have had to **go on** the dole.*

14 [Vp] (*informal*) I don't believe you!; Don't exaggerate; I dare you to do it; Please do it!; Stop hesitating! Do it!: *'Not garden party weather.' '**Go on**,' said Phyllis. 'Lovely day.'* SE ○ *'How old are you?' 'I'm forty.' '**Go on**! You don't look a day over thirty!'* ○ *'**Go on**! Have a brandy snap* (a sort of biscuit). *Be a devil!'* HWKM □ used as an exclamation in various meanings, depending on context; there is a mid to low falling tone on go on in the first two examples and a fall-rise tone on on in the third. = get on! 5. ⇨ get along/away with you!, go along with you!.

15 [Vp] be lit. **S:** light, lamp: *A light **went on**. Nurse Ellen, blinking and full of alarm, rushed to the bedside.* DC ○ *We'd been sitting for a couple of hours in candlelight when to our relief the lights **went on** again.* ↔ go out 6. ⇨ be on 8, keep on 6, leave on 2, put on 2, turn on 1, stay on 2.

goings-on [nom (Vp)] behaviour, usu of an extraordinary or unpleasant kind. **adj:** (such) odd, frightful, peculiar, disgusting, strange, queer, inexplicable: *Accounts of strange **goings-on** at church services had begun to circulate.* ○ *There have been some peculiar **goings-on** in the village recently, I can tell you!* ⇨ go on 10.

gone on [pass (V.pr] (*informal*) captivated by (sb), emotionally and/or sexually: *'He's completely **gone on** her, of course. Won't talk about anyone or anything else.'* □ also used after *appear, seem.*

go on record as [Vpr] let it be known publically that one is saying sth. **o:** stating, declaring, advocating: *I would like to **go on record as** saying that I have worked in good faith on these operas.* L ○ *The South African Economics Minister … **went on record as** declaring he had no objections.* NS □ go on record also followed by *with*: *Aristotle … **went on record with** the statement that men have more teeth than women.* L

go on tour [Vpr] travel from place to place to entertain or do business. **S:** the Royal Ballet, the circus; play; pop group; director, publicity manager: *The Royal Shakespeare Company **goes on tour** for several weeks every year.* ○ *'I'm afraid you can't see the Manager until next week; he's **gone on tour**.'*

go on about [Vp.pr] talk endlessly about (sth/sb), usu in a tiresome or complaining way: *'All right, you two, I'll help, only don't **go on about** it, please.'* EGD ○ *'I come from a planet called Earth, you know.' 'I know,' said Marvin, 'you keep **going on about** it. It sounds awful.'* HHGG ⇨ be on about, keep on (about).

go on at [Vp.pr] (*informal*) worry, pester or harass (sb) continuously with complaints, suggestions, requests etc: *Lyn's **going on at** me to fix the garden gate.* ○ *'Why do I have to **go on at** you? Because you're foolish, that's why.'* OD ⇨ be/keep on at.

go on (for) [Vp, Vpr] be approaching (a certain age): *'I'm sixteen, **going on** seventeen.'* ○ *'You wouldn't think it to look at him, but David's **going on for** seventy.'* □ usu in the continuous tenses as in the examples. ⇨ get on 4, get on for.

go on for [Vp.pr] (of time) get near, approach: *'Good Lord! It's **going on for** one o'clock and I promised to see George at half past twelve!'* □ usu in the continuous tenses as in the example. = get on for.

go on (to) 1 [Vp, Vp.pr] pass from one subject or item (to the next), on an agenda etc: *'If nobody has any objection, we'll **go on**.'* ○ *The Chairman said that as time was short, we should **go on to** the next item.* ○ *'I don't want any pudding, thank you. I'd like to **go** straight **on to** the coffee.'*

2 [Vpr, Vp.pr] adopt (sth) as a new or temporary practice. **o:** a fat-free diet; solids, liquids; the pill (ie contraceptive pill): *The doctor warned me I'd have to* **go on** *a strict diet.* ○ *The baby will be* **going on to** *solids* (ie solid foods) *shortly.* ○ *Many women* **go** *back* **on** *the pill after they've had a couple of children.*

go on to [Vp.pr] change working arrangements to (another system). **S:** industry, factory; half the employees. **o:** overtime, short time, full production: *If cheap imports of coal continue to build up, more mines will* **go on to** *short time working or stop production altogether.*

go on with [Vp.pr] continue doing (sth). **o:** the cooking; your book; what you were doing: *Sure enough Prissie came back and* **went on with** *her letter.* DC ○ *I hope you'll find time while you're in America to* **go on with** *your writing.* = continue (with). ⇨ get on with, go on 5.

enough/something to go on with [Vp.pr] sth that is sufficient for the present, with the suggestion that more is to follow: *'I can't let you have the whole amount now, but I can give you* **something to be going on with**. *Will ten pounds do?'* ○ *'Have you got plenty to read?' '***Enough to go on with**, *thanks.'* ○ *'Here's a cup of tea* **to be going on with**. *I'll give you something to eat shortly.'*

go out 1 [Vp] leave a place: *'They were still playing in the garden at half past three. I know because I had to* **go out** *and tell them to make less noise.'* DC ↔ come in/into 1.

2 [Vp] leave one's home etc, for recreation, to visit friends etc: *'What a pity you didn't come half an hour ago. Mary's* **gone out** *riding and won't be back until six.'* ○ *'You are a fine pair!' Prissie exclaimed. 'We're only* **going out** *for some fresh air.'* DC □ often followed by the -ing form of a v. ↔ stay in/indoors. ⇨ go out (for/to).

3 [Vp] become unconscious. **A:** like a light; within a minute: *No sooner had I tucked Sam up in bed than he* **went out** *like a light.* ○ *They gave me this injection and before I could count to five I* **went out** *cold.* ↔ come to 1. ⇨ be out 9, put out 9.

4 [Vp] (*euphemism*) die: *'It's the one thing that will make me* **go out** *with an easy mind, Sarah, the knowledge that you and Terry and Pauline will not suffer financially.'* WI ○ *'I wish I'd been less of a workaholic. As it is, I shall* **go out** *thinking of all the fun I've missed.'*

5 [Vp] end, close. **S:** the year, the month; 1990: *The year* **went out** *with the news of catastrophic flooding in Bangladesh.* ○ (*proverb*) *When March comes in like a lamb, it* **goes out** *like a lion.* □ the following example (where went out means 'left') contains a humorous variant of the proverb: *GEOFF: Has anybody ever tried? JO: What? GEOFF: Taking you in hand. JO: Yes. GEOFF: What happened to him? JO: He came in with Christmas and* **went out** *with the New Year.* TOH

6 [Vp] stop burning or shining; be extinguished. **S:** candle, lamp; light, sun: *Then the last flame of the fire* **went out** *and the shadows leaped on them.* DC ○ *I was just about to go upstairs when all the lights* **went out**. ○ *The sun* **went out**. FL ↔ go on 15. ⇨ be out 10, put out 10, turn out 1.

7 [Vp] cease to be fashionable. **S:** miniskirts, woollen underwear; that theory; wearing black, dressing up in suits: *The idea that women can't do the same work as men* **went out** *with the dodo.* ○ *Great train robberies were thought to have* **gone out** *with the silent films.* OBS ↔ come in 1. ⇨ be out 14, be/go out of fashion.

8 [Vp] (*broadcasting, journalism*) be broadcast; be printed and distributed. **S:** news, details; edition, story: *This programme is* **going out** *live.* ○ *There are news bulletins* **going out** *twenty-four hours a day.* ○ *Our next edition* **goes out** *at four o'clock.* ↔ come in 8.

9 [Vp] be stated or sent. **S:** message, announcement; order: *Orders have* **gone out** *to all unit commanders.* ○ *The call would* **go out** *to her once more and she would be invited to give her opinion.* MSAL

the tide go out [Vp] (of the sea) move lower down the beach; ebb: ***The tide****, at certain parts of the coast,* **goes out** *several miles.* ↔ the tide come in. ⇨ be out 16.

go out and about [Vp] leave one's house, visit friends, go shopping etc (usu after a period of confinement): *I'm glad to hear that your mother can* **go out and about** *once more. She's made a wonderful recovery from her illness.*

go out (for/to) [Vp, Vp.pr rel] leave a building, go into the open (for a purpose/to a place). **o:** (**for**) ride, trip, run; (**to**) beach, park; pictures: *'We're only* **going out** *for some fresh air.'* DC ○ *'I'm just* **going out to** *the post. If anyone calls, ask them to wait.'* ⇨ be out (at), come/take out (for/to), go out 2.

go all out (for/to do sth) [Vp, Vp.pr] (*informal*) make a strong, determined effort (to achieve sth). **o:** results, a win, success; what he can get. **Inf:** to finish the job, to win the order: *'***Go all out** *in the sprints and see if you can bring back at least one medal.'* ○ *They didn't ask whether such and such a job would suit the boy. They just* **went all out for** *one that wouldn't get snatched away every time trade slumped.* CON ○ *She'll* **go all out to prove** *her approach is the only one possible.*

go out of [Vpr] no longer be present in (sth). **S:** the sting; venom, fury; heat, passion, tension; the (sour, harsh) note, tone. **o:** correspondence, remarks; argument, debate, discussion: *The venom has* **gone out of** *the debate.* ○ *As time went by and the old man became mellow, the fury* **went out of** *his parliamentary speeches.* ○ *The moment it became clear that nobody had anything to lose from the changes, the heat* **went out of** *the discussion.*

go out of action [Vpr] cease to operate or function. **S:** submarine, ship; gun; fighter; pump: *Two machine-guns have* **gone out of action***: they tend to overheat when fired continuously.* ⇨ be/put out of action.

go out of business [Vpr] fail in business; stop trading or operating. **S:** store, company, factory; trader, supplier: *Many small grocers have* **gone out of business** *since the advent of the supermarkets.* ○ *If there is another crisis in world stockmarkets, a lot more small- to medium-size City firms will* **go out of business**. ⇨ put out of business.

go out of fashion [Vpr] cease to be fashionable. **S:** leather, miniskirts; theory, notion, belief: *Morality has* **gone out of fashion**. *Permissiveness is all.* ↔ come into fashion/vogue. ⇨ be out of fashion, be out 14, go out 7.

go out of focus 1 [Vpr] cease to be sharply focused: *Just as we were about to take a photograph of the diseased cell, the microscope* **went out of focus**. ↔ come into focus 1. ⇨ be out of focus 1.

2 [Vpr] no longer be clearly perceived or understood. **S:** idea, problem, issue: *I had the problem all sorted out in my mind, then Matthew came in, and everything* **went out of focus**. ↔ come into focus 2. ⇨ be out of focus 2.

go out of one's mind [Vpr] become mad; become enthusiastic about sb/sth: *When Jennifer heard the dreadful news the poor girl* **went** *clean* **out of her mind**. ○ *It appears Conrad has even been translated into Japanese, and the Hawaiians* **go out of their minds** *when they read him.* RT ⇨ be out of one's mind.

go out of sb's mind [Vpr] be forgotten. **S:** appointment, meeting; promise to do sth; message: *I'm so sorry I forgot to come to the meeting. I fully intended to, but it* **went** *right* **out of my mind**. ○ *Harold. She had forgotten him. He had* **gone** *clean* **out of** *her mind.* PW

go out of play [Vpr] (of the ball in football, tennis etc) go over the lines marking the pitch or court: *Lineker took a quick shot at goal but the ball* **went** *harmlessly* **out of play**. ⇨ be out of play.

go out of service/use [Vpr] cease to be used. **S:** old models, obsolete equipment; tram, steam locomotive: *The 'slow' jets of the 1960s* **went out of service** *to be replaced by more modern machines.* ↔ come into service/use. ⇨ be out of service.

go out of sight/view [Vpr] disappear from sight; pass from view. **S:** ship, plane; bus; house, shop; coastline: *For a few seconds the aircraft had* **gone out of sight** *behind a cloud.* ↔ come into sight/view. ⇨ be out of 1.

go out of one's way to do sth [Vpr] take particular trouble to do sth. **Inf:** to be helpful; to be as pleasant, unpleasant, as possible; to look one's best; to make a success of sth: *Most specimens are fairly straightforward and are not much trouble once they are used to the routine, but occasionally we would get a creature which appeared to* **go out of its way to cause** *extra work.* DF ○ *He had* **gone out of his way to irritate** *the dons* (college tutors) *and then been astonished that they did not elect him to a Fellowship* (a teaching post in college). HB

go out (to) 1 [Vp, Vp.pr] leave a building, go into the open air. ⇨ go out (for/to).

2 [Vp, Vp.pr] go overseas (esp to some distant place): *My son* **went out to** *Australia ten years ago.* ○ *'Are you* **going out** *by plane or by ship?'* ○ *Jenny has decided to* **go out to** *South America as an English teacher.*

go out to [Vp.pr] be extended to (sb), be offered to (sb). **S:** ⚠ one's sympathy, heart(s): *Our hearts* **go out to** *all the victims of the earthquake in California.*

go out (together/with) [Vp, Vp.pr emph rel] keep company (with sb); have a regular sexual or romantic relationship (with sb). **o:** one's cousin, an older man, a Dutch girl: *He was* **going out with** *a girl he wasn't in love with but whom he liked.* AF = go about (together/with), go around/round (together/with).

go over 1 [Vpr pass] check, examine or inspect (sth). **o:** accounts, inventory; contents of a house; claim, appeal: *I've* **gone over** *the statement, and it seems to be in order.* ○ *You'll have to* **go over** *the figures again; they don't balance.* = look over 2.

2 [Vpr] survey or inspect (sth) with a view to renting or buying it. **o:** house, flat, castle; boat: *The prospective buyers* **went over** *the property pretty thoroughly but made no comment except to thank the agent for her trouble.* ○ *The surveyor gave the house a thorough* **going-over** *and advised us not to buy.* = look over 1.

3 [Vpr pass] clean (sth). **o:** room, kitchen; car, boat: *'The girl has only* **gone over** *the room with a duster. No attempt to wash down the paintwork or anything like that.'* ○ *'Would you mind giving my study a quick* **going-over**? *I'm expecting a visitor in half an hour.'*

4 [Vpr pass] ponder or consider (sth); examine or re-examine (sth). **o:** the facts; the same ground; his story, account, allegation: *We* **went over** *every detail of his story in an effort to discover whether it was true or not.* ○ *'Please don't mention Aubrey to me. I'm not* **going over** *all that again. I'm finished with him; do you understand?'* ○ *His 'Times' letter is a good one,* **going** *once again* **over** *old ground.* SS

5 [Vpr pass] search (sb/sth). **S:** police, detective; custom's officer. **o:** suspect, prisoner; baggage: *A woman police-officer* **went over** *the girl from head to toe, but wouldn't say what she was looking for.*

6 [Vpr pass] test one's/sb's knowledge of sth learned or studied; rehearse. **o:** lines, part; scene two; French homework: *The boys' mother used to* **go over** *their sums with them every evening.* ○ *I can't come out this evening. I'm in the college play and I must* **go over** *my lines again.* = go through 5.

7 [Vp] be received. **S:** (maiden) speech; performance; proposal, plan. **A:** (extremely) well; rather badly; big: *How did Susan's talk at the British Council* **go over**? ○ *Your idea of a sponsored walk to raise funds* **went over** *big! Everyone was in favour.* = go down (with). ⇨ get over (to), put over (to).

going-over [nom (Vpr)] questioning; physical attack: *The police gave the suspect a long* **going-over**, *but didn't get the expected confession.* ○ *It was obvious that Joe had been given a savage* **going-over** *by several people.* □ usu in the patterns give sb/get a going-over.

go over one's head [Vpr] be too difficult or technical for one to understand. **S:** lecture, book; theory, subject. **m:** way, miles, a long way; completely: *The last lecture* **went** *completely* **over my head**. = be above one/one's head.

go over the top [Vpr] (*informal*) act or behave in an exaggerated manner. **S:** actor, performer; writer: *The production had three players who are more than capable of* **going over the top** *when in front of the cameras.* NS ○ *Some critics feel he overwrites, and even that he had* **gone** *slightly* **over the top** *in both the words and the pictures he painted of wartime evacuation.* RT

go over (to) [Vp, Vp.pr] cross a road, a river, the sea etc (so as to reach the other side). **o:** the other side; the mainland, the island: *He felt hungry and, seeing a fig tree, he* **went over to** *it to pick some figs.* CF ○ *A boat* **goes over to** *the island once a week with mail and provisions.* = go across (to). ⇨ take over (to).

go over to 1 [Vp.pr] transfer one's loyalties to (sth). **S:** rebel MP, Communist; spy, agent; brigade, regiment, army; priest, bishop. **o:** other side, the Labour Party; enemy, allies; Rome (= Roman Catholicism), Methodism: *Peter had appalled me* *by quitting as a reporter and* **going over to** *the editorial side.* SU ○ *Italy* **went over to** *the Allies in 1944.* ○ *'It's the first time I've ever joined a couple in Holy Matrimony according to the rites of the Anglican Church,' the Canon persisted, 'and heard the bridegroom say, barely an hour later, that he's thinking of* **going over to** *Rome.'* CON ⇨ bring/come over (to).

2 [Vp.pr] abandon one thing or practice and adopt another. **o:** violin; pop art; vegetarian diet; bicycle: *Sarah's given up the piano and* **gone over to** *the flute.* ○ *I'm afraid you'll have to* **go over to** *a vegetarian diet if the price of meat goes on rising!*

3 [Vp.pr] (*broadcasting*) transfer to (another speaker or station). **o:** our reporter on the spot, news desk; New York, Tokyo; Westminster, Wembley: *'We're interrupting the programme to* **go over to** *our news desk for an important announcement.'* ○ *'Let's* **go over to** *Lords to hear the latest on the Test Match from Brian Johnston.'*

go overboard [Vp] (*nautical*) fall or be thrown from a ship: *During the storm a lot of the deck cargo* **went overboard**. ○ *'Why has the ship stopped?' 'I think somebody must have* **gone overboard**.*'* = fall overboard.

go overboard about/for [Vp.pr] be enthusiastic about (sth/sb), commit oneself totally to (sth/sb). **o:** the new play; Australia; modern architecture: *It would be very foolish of the Government to* **go overboard about** *nuclear energy to the extent of running down the coal industry altogether.* ○ *Jane has* **gone overboard for** *some new Japanese restaurant.*

go round 1 [Vp, Vpr] walk, drive etc, along the outside edge of (sth); make a detour round (sth). **o:** centre of the city; park, prison; island; military installations: *The front gate was shut, so we had to* **go round**.

2 [Vp, Vpr] walk inside a building etc in order to inspect it or its contents. **o:** museum, castle; Westminster Abbey, Hyde Park; Flower Show, exhibition; school, hospital, prison: *'While you're here, would you like to* **go round**?*'* ○ *So many distinguished visitors* **go round** *the school, that the children hardly look up from their work when a stranger is brought into the classroom.* = look around/round 2. ⇨ take round.

3 [Vp] spin, or seem to spin; be dizzy or confused. **S:** the world; the room, everything; my head: *It's love that makes the world* **go round**. ○ *After a couple of glasses of whisky, the bar began to* **go round**. *He had forgotten that he was drinking on an empty stomach.* ○ *His head seemed to* **go round**, *and he clutched at the nearest passer-by.*

4 [Vp, Vpr] be sufficient (for a number of people). **o:** the guests; starving children; all these people: *'Don't worry! There's enough coffee to* **go round**.*'* ○ *There are 90 councillors, with precious few posts of real responsibility to* **go round**. OBS ○ *How can India possibly find enough rice to* **go round** *these millions of refugees?* □ often in the pattern *(not) enough/sufficient to* go round.

5 [Vp] go from place to place or person to person. ⇨ go around/round 1.

6 [Vp] circulate. ⇨ go around/round 2.

go round the bend/twist [Vpr] (*informal*) become mad; be annoyed unbearably: *There is always the situation where one can lose control,* **go round the twist** *if you like.* RT = go up the wall. ⇨ drive round the bend/up the wall.

go round (to) [Vp, Vp.pr] visit (sb/sth): *'Let's* **go round** *and see Mary. She's always ready for a chat.'* ○ *Afterwards they all* **went round to** *1 Pembroke Gardens to tell William and Alice the good news.* GJ ⇨ be around/round (at), bring around/round (to) 1, come around/round (to) 1.

go round (with) [Vp, Vp.pr] ⇨ go around/round (together/with).

go through 1 [Vp, Vpr] pass from one side of an object to the other, sometimes forcefully. **S:** thread; piano; lorry; ship; motor-cyclist. **o:** needle; door; gate; canal; shop-window: *This rope is too thick to* **go through** *the hole.* ○ *The piano* **went through** *the door easily, but the sideboard wouldn't* **go through** *at all.* ⇨ get through 1.

2 [Vpr pass] use, consume (sth). **o:** stock, store; food, beer; fortune: *'Do you mean to say that we've* **gone through** *all those envelopes I bought last week?'* ○ *It didn't take James very long to* **go through** *his inheritance.* ⇨ get through 5.

3 [Vpr pass] examine, explore or search (sth). **o:** every room; all my pockets; his papers: *The woman* **went through** *every drawer and cupboard in the house, but she could not find the missing silver.* ○ *The police* **went through** *the building with a fine tooth-comb, but they found no evidence that would help them build up a case.* ○ *It was obvious that the room had been* **gone through** *by a professional thief.*

4 [Vpr pass] perform, enact (sth). **o:** marriage, initiation, matriculation, degree (ceremony): *Tom and Sarah had been living together for years, but finally* **went through** *the marriage ceremony for the sake of their children.* ○ *I hate the idea of attending the funeral but I suppose it'll have to be* **gone through**. ⇨ go through with.

5 [Vpr pass] review or rehearse (sth). **o:** facts, arguments, pros and cons; scene, text: *They* **went through** *the details of the plan over and over again to make sure that there was no possibility of failure.* ○ *'Let's* **go through** *the last scene in Act Two again. We haven't got it right yet.'* = go over 6. ⇨ take through.

6 [Vp] be completed, concluded (usu successfully). **S:** appointment, application; Bill (the form of legislation before it becomes an Act of Parliament); scheme, deal, agreement; divorce: *As soon as Joe's divorce has* **gone through**, *he's going to marry Alice.* ○ *You'd better see that Luke's scheme* **goes through**. NM ○ *Surely my application for a visa has* **gone through** *by now? I can't understand the delay.* ⇨ get through 4, put through 2.

7 [Vpr] be published in (a certain number of editions etc). **S:** book, title; article. **o:** three printings; ten editions: *The book* **went through** *twelve editions and was translated into seven languages.* F ⇨ go into 9.

8 [Vpr pass] experience, endure or suffer (sth). **o:** operation; years of pain; ordeal; fire; boring performance: *Lower interest rates would bring fast relief to the consumer industries, which have been* **going through** *a bad period recently.* ○ *'Well, I'm glad we don't have to* **go through** *that again for another year! Speech Days bore me to death.'* ○ *'After what he* **went through** *with his first wife,* *you'd think he would have steered clear of marriage for the rest of his life.'*

go through sb's hands [Vpr] be handled by (sb) in the course of his duties. **S:** thousands of pounds; jewellery, diamonds; (secret, confidential) papers, documents; patients, cases: *More than a million pounds' worth of diamonds* **went through his hands**, *and around forty thousand of them stuck to his fingers.* DS ○ *'I should check on the new man before letting these documents* **go through his hands**.*'*

go through the mill [Vpr] (*informal*) do a succession of lower-level jobs before reaching senior status: *The best people at running an industry are those who have had to* **go through the mill** *themselves.* ⇨ put through the mill.

go through the motions [Vpr] do sth without interest or serious commitment: *Her husband* **went through the motions** *of welcoming the guests, but left the room at the earliest opportunity.*

go through (the) proper channels [Vpr] (*formal*) follow the correct, prescribed procedures. **S:** document, letter; application, complaint: *'It's no good applying to me for leave. You'll have to* **go through the proper channels**.*'* ○ *Applications for leave must* **go through proper channels**.

go through with [Vp.pr pass] take (sth) through to its conclusion. **o:** deal, arrangement; wedding, party; aim, intention: *I did tell Norman he didn't have to* **go through with** *it if he didn't want to.* AT ○ *If Mrs Thatcher ...* **goes through with** *her intended aim of fighting on in a second ballot, it would cause a bloody party battle.* OBS ⇨ go through 4.

go to 1 [Vpr] visit, attend (a place). **o:** school, university; market: *The children are too young to* **go to** *school yet.* ○ *Does your son* **go to** *university?* ⇨ send to.

2 [Vpr pass] take trouble, put oneself to inconvenience, when doing sth. **o:** (a lot of, no end of, endless, infinite) trouble; great pains to do sth; ridiculous lengths: *The British Council* **goes to** *no end of trouble to arrange suitable programmes for academic visitors.* ○ *Why* **go to** *all that trouble, Jean thought, as she got out of the car.* SATS ○ *She* **went to** *absurd lengths to please her new boss; but he sacked her within a month.* ⇨ put to 4.

3 [Vpr] be given or awarded to (sb). **S:** special prize, gold medal; honour, privilege: *Book Trust is also organizing a Booker Prize display competition ... with a prize of £500* **going to** *the winner.* BOOK ○ *The distinction of being the first to split the atom* **went to** *Rutherford.*

go to bed [Vpr] retire to bed for a rest or sleep, or because one is ill: *'I don't feel well; I'm* **going to bed**.*'* ↔ get up 1. ⇨ send to bed.

go to bits [Vpr] ⇨ go to pieces.

go to the country [Vpr] (*politics*) call a general election: *The government knew that if they were defeated on this crucial issue they would be forced to* **go to the country**.

go to the dogs [Vpr] (*informal*) decline in power, influence, efficiency etc. **S:** the country, the school, family life: *From the way some people talk, you'd think that the country had been* **going to the dogs** *for the last fifty years.* ○ *I had to resign my membership because the club was* **going to the dogs**. □ associated with rather pompous, old-fashioned, middle-class speakers.

go to earth/ground [Vpr] (of animals) take refuge underground, in a burrow, lair etc; (of people) hide away. **S:** fox, quarry, hunted animal; escaped criminal, wanted man, refugee: *When the master of hounds realized that the quarry had* **gone to earth** *and the dogs had lost the scent, he called off the hunt.* ○ *The police believe that the terrorists have* **gone to ground** *somewhere in North London.* ⇨ run to earth/ground.

go to the expense (of) [Vpr] spend (a good deal of) money; incur expense. **adj:** much, great; a great deal of, a lot of: *We* **went to** *a lot of* **expense** *having the roof retiled.* ○ *'Why don't you hire a caravan for a couple of weeks instead of* **going to the expense of** *buying one?'* ○ *'Don't* **go to** *too much* **expense** *on our account.'*

go to extremes [Vpr] be immoderate in one's actions: *He is the kind of man who cannot do anything in moderation. If he drinks, he drinks too much; if he drives a car, he drives too fast; if he goes out for a meal, he goes to the most expensive hotel. He always* **goes to extremes**. ⇨ next entry

go to the other extreme/go from one extreme to another/the other [Vpr] pass from one exaggerated view or position to its opposite: *Before we* **go to the other extreme** *of assuming that Mr Khruschev's power was absolute, there is one important difference to remember between him and Stalin.* BM ○ *'Last week you wanted to marry him as soon as you could; now you wouldn't marry him if he was the last man on earth. You do* **go from one extreme to the other**, *don't you?'* ⇨ previous entry

go to sb's head [Vpr] affect a person's balance or judgement. **S:** strong drink, beer, champagne; success, praise, money; sudden fame, notoriety: *The wine* **went to Susan's head**. *What with that and the heat, she simply passed out at the table.* ○ *Don't let the manager's congratulations* **go to your head**. *Next week he's just as likely to bite your head off.*

go to the heart of [Vpr] reach the central point of (an issue). **o:** ⚠ the matter, question, problem: *'You're getting married?' 'Yes.' 'To whom?' asked Donna Rachele, who liked to* **go to the heart of** *a question.* ARG ○ *His recent series of articles* **goes to the heart of** *the problem of urban homelessness.*

go to hell etc [Vpr] (*informal*) an offensive expression dismissing or rejecting a person or his ideas, wishes etc. **o:** ⚠ hell, blazes, the devil: *'As far as I am concerned, if you aren't willing to work for a living, you can* **go to hell**!*'* ○ *'I'm sick to death of this place. I'm going out!' 'But what shall I tell Mr James if he wants to see you?' 'Tell him to* **go to hell**!*'*

go to it [Vpr] give energy and time to doing sth (eg taking part in a sporting event or completing a piece of work): *After dinner we* **went to it** *again, carting paints and easels about.* CON ○ *They* **went to it** (ie love-making) *with such a vengeance, that it was almost Biblical, the way they multiplied.* GL □ seldom now used to urge sb on to a special effort.

go to pieces [Vpr] lose one's self-control, health, sense of purpose in life etc: *When he lost his wife, James* **went** *completely* **to pieces**. ○ *Following* *their defeat in the election the Party seemed to* **go to pieces** *for a time.* □ also, occasionally, go to bits.

go to the police [Vpr] inform the police: *The blackmailer warned his victim that if he* **went to the police** *he would regret it.*

go to the polls [Vpr] (*politics*) cast one's vote at an election: *The number of people who actually* **go to the polls** *seems to depend on the weather. That, in a democracy, is surely absurd!* ○ *The country was in no mood to* **go to the polls** *for a second time in less than six months.*

go to pot [Vpr] (*informal*) be spoilt, ruined: *MYRA: It would take you six months to study for that examination. TONY: A year, after my brain's* **gone to pot** *in the army.* EHOW

go to press [Vpr] (*publishing*) (be sent to) be printed. **S:** paper, book, article; last edition; the Times: *It's too late to include the announcement in tomorrow's paper. It's* **gone to press**.

go to rack and ruin [Vpr] reach a state of disrepair, decay or disorganization through neglect. **S:** house, store; company, firm: *Now the house was* **going to rack and ruin**. *Aunt Annabel patiently inquired how it could be expected to do anything else, with only a cook-housekeeper, one maid, and a daily.* DC ○ *Our fine organization is* **going to rack and ruin** *and all my son Max wants to do is go yachting.* NS

go to sea [Vpr] earn one's living on a ship: *'You can't plan anything because you never know just when you will be putting out to sea again.'* ○ *He says he wouldn't want either of his sons to* **go to sea**. RT

go to seed 1 [Vpr] go beyond the edible stage and produce seeds. **S:** cabbage, parsley, lettuce: *'What a pity you let all those cabbages* **go to seed**. *Nobody can eat them now.'*

2 [Vpr] fall below a previous high standard, through neglect; deteriorate. **S:** actor, lover; figure, looks; business, estate: *She was recognizable, he saw thankfully, not* **gone to seed**. MSAL ○ *The place had* **gone** *completely* **to seed**, *with lawns uncut and gates hanging off their hinges.* □ often used as an adj after *be, appear, seem, look.* = run to seed.

go to town [Vpr] (*informal*) do sth with enthusiasm, vigour, thoroughness and relish: *She's really* **going to town** *over Alan's room. First of all she said it needed new curtains.* RFW

go to trial [Vpr] (*legal*) be tried in a court of law; stand trial: *'If I'm caught, I have my own plan. You can be sure that I shall never* **go to trial**.*'*

go to the wall [Vpr] be crushed or destroyed through weakness, inefficiency, inability to adapt etc. **S:** institution; company, firm; weaker states: *Our universities are realising that unless they justify their activities to the general public they are going to* **go to the wall**. EFLG ○ (Conservative Party election broadcast) *If prices and incomes were uncontrolled, it would be the old-age pensioners, the lowly paid, the people without powerful trade unions — it is these people who would* **go to the wall**. BBCTV ○ *War was very much in the air ... it was felt that the appeasers* (those not prepared to resist Hitler) *would ultimately* **go to the wall**. EB

go to war [Vpr] start or engage in a war. **S:** country, nation; people; statesmen: *No modern army has* **gone to war** *so inadequately equipped and so poorly trained and led.* □ used of groups rather than individuals.

go to waste [Vpr] be wasted, unused. **S:** food aid; work, effort; energy resources; man, woman: *'How can you let this food* **go to waste** *when there are so many people starving in the world?'* ○ *I didn't like to see a performer with her talent* **going to waste** *in a provincial theatre company.*

go to work (on) [Vpr] begin to tackle (a job): *Intelligence* (ie secret service) *agents* **went to work** *and traced the leak of information back to headquarters.* ○ *Nick, a young architect,* **went to work** *with a will* **on** *his first commission.* □ a famous advertisement, 'Go to work on *an egg*', had three meanings: (a) go to work riding on an egg; (b) have an egg (for breakfast) before you leave for the office, factory etc; (c) tackle, ie eat, an egg. = set to 1.

go together 1 [Vp] be good, right, pleasing etc when worn, eaten etc, at the same time; match. **S:** red and green; oysters and champagne; coffee and liqueur: *'Do you think this hat and coat* **go** *well* **together**? *Or do they clash?'* ○ *Potatoes and rice don't* **go together**. *They make a stodgy meal.* ⇨ go with 5.

2 [Vp] accompany each other in one person, place, environment etc. **S:** poverty and disease; sunshine and health; wealth and selfishness: *Bullying and cowardice often* **go together**. ○ *Speed and efficiency do not always* **go together**. ⇨ go with 4.

3 [Vp] spend time in each other's company, often with a view to a permanent relationship. **S:** Paul and Pamela; those two: *While he had been away on this last trip to America, she had had a chance to take stock of herself, and it had come as a shock when she realized they had been* **'going together'** *for over a year.* WI ⇨ go with 2.

go towards [Vpr] be a contribution to (sth). **S:** salary, pay; cash; donation: *'This week's pocket money will have to* **go towards** *the cost of repairing your bicycle.'* ○ *'The ten pounds that's left over can* **go towards** *your holiday clothes.'*

go under 1 [Vp] sink below the surface of the sea, river etc. **S:** helpless child; boat: *Two of the men hanging on to the lifeboat* **went under** *and were never seen again.*

2 [Vp] lose consciousness: *It seems as if you're just about to* **go under**, *to fall asleep, and then for some reason you pull yourself back.* 50MH ○ *His voice saying quietly, 'Breathe deeply, Deeply.' ... is a better way of* **going under** *than a jab in the arm* (ie 'gas' is a better anaesthetic than an injection). BRH = go out 3.

3 [Vp] become bankrupt; fail. **S:** he etc; company, business, firm, organization, aircraft industry: *Poor Donaldson had no head for business, and it wasn't long before he* **went under**. ○ *The Grand Hotel had struggled ... but had finally* **gone under** *and was now merely a collection of holiday flatlets.* SE

4 [Vpr] be known by (a certain name); hide one's identity behind (sth). **S:** flower, criminal, writer. **o:** name, title; sobriquet, nom de plume, guise: *Willow-herb also* **goes under** *the name of old man's beard.* ○ *One of the robbers* **went under** *the guise of a respectable dealer in antiques.* = pass by/under the name of.

go under the hammer [Vpr] be sold at auction. **S:** sb's home; pictures, silver, collection of antiques; all sb's worldly possessions: *Every stick that Joss possessed* **went under the hammer** *to pay his debts.* ○ *We must do everything we can to prevent the farm* **going under the hammer**.

go up 1 [Vp emph, Vpr emph] climb upwards, on or through (sth). **o:** stairs, ladder; hill, cliff; wall; tree; side of a ship, rigging; chimney: *Freud ... had gone up the 6 000 foot Raxalp* (mountain) *three times in some weeks.* F ○ *The squirrel* **went up** *the tree like greased lightning.* ○ *The brush was too big to* **go up** *the tube.* ⇨ get up 3.

2 [Vp emph] rise, increase. **S:** prices, expenses; production, demand; sales, exports; the cost of living: *Though some towns — and exports — seem to have declined, home demand* **went up**. SHOE ○ *We'd only just got over the last increase when* **up went** *the price again!* ⇨ be up 1, keep up 2, put up 4, send up 1.

3 [Vp] reach a higher level; rise. **S:** pressure, barometer, glass; temperature, mercury: *I see the mercury is* **going up**. *Perhaps we're going to get a spell of good weather at last.*

4 [Vp] be constructed. **S:** buildings, skyscrapers; new schools, hospitals: *Everywhere you looked, you could see glass and concrete monstrosities* **going up**. ○ *New universities* **went up** *at a fantastic rate two decades ago.* ⇨ put up 3.

5 [Vp] be destroyed, be blown up. **S:** building, bridge, ship, ammunition dump. **A:** in flames, in smoke; with a bang, with a roar: *The gelignite store received a direct hit and* **went up** *in a spectacular explosion.* ○ *Many houses of the Anglo-Irish* **went up** *in flames as a destructive urge took hold of the Republican movement.* EB □ this literal meaning and the figurative go up in flames/smoke may be linked: *James O'Hare, a Roman Catholic, owned a greengrocer's shop in a Protestant area. It was burnt down. Mr O'Hare said: 'Six years' hard work* **gone up** *in smoke.* OBS ⇨ blow up 4, send up 2.

6 [Vp emph] (*theatre*) be raised; be lit. **S:** ⚠ the curtain, the lights: (stage directions) *The curtain* **goes up** *on the sitting-room of a small English semi-detached house.* ○ *The stage is set; regal chairs await the entry of the two actors; the curtain has* **gone up**. ECON

7 [Vp] be uttered, be heard. **S:** cry, shout, roar: *As the two teams ran out out onto the field, a great roar* **went up**. ○ *When the strikers saw them coming* (ie those who wished to work), *the cry of 'Scabs!'* **went up**. 50MH

the balloon go up [Vp] (of a war, a major offensive) begin: *I shamelessly snatched an extra twenty-four hours from my office on Sunday in order that I might see Bill before 'Overlord'* (= the invasion of Europe), *before* **the balloon went up**. RFW ○ *All the officers instinctively parked their cars facing back home, ready for a quick getaway should* **the balloon go up**. IND

go up in flames/smoke [Vp.pr] be utterly defeated or destroyed. **S:** hopes, dreams; plans; agreement, treaty; marriage: *With the outbreak of renewed hostilities on the border all our hopes for peace have* **gone up in flames**. ○ *I could see the commission for the murals* **going up in smoke**. CON ⇨ go up 5.

go up the wall [Vpr] (*informal*) go nearly mad from frustration, overwork, annoyance etc: *When I arrived home, I found Jane* **going up the wall**. *The baby was crying, Johnny had just cut his knee and our visitors were due to arrive at any moment.* ⇨ send up the wall.

go up in the world [Vp.pr] reach a higher position in society, in one's profession etc: *Arnold's* **gone up in the world**. *It's quite something to start as an apprentice and end up as the head of an industry with 50 000 employees.* ○ *Three women in my life, but the one I want doesn't want me. Who cares? That's the way it goes. I'm* **going up in the world** *before the world goes up before me.* DBM □ in the second example there is play on two meanings of go up: rise (in society) and blow up.

go up (to) [Vp, Vpr rel] go to a university, or to London ('town') from the provinces, or towards the north: *At New College, Gaitskill (who* **went up** *a year earlier) became passionately interested in politics, ballroom dancing and social life.* OBS ○ *'I'm* **going up to** *town for a few days. Is there anything I can do for you while I'm there?'* ○ *My parents have* **gone up to** *Scotland for a short holiday.* ↔ go down 8. ⇨ be up 2, come up 2, 3.

go with 1 [Vpr] accompany (sb) on an outing, journey etc: *The younger children stayed with their uncle while the older ones* **went with** *their parents to Spain.* ○ *Spencer often had tickets for Covent Garden and sometimes asked her to* **go with** *him.* GE

2 [Vpr] (*dated*) spend time in sb's company, perhaps with a view to a more permanent relationship: *'How long has Alice been* **going with** *Steven? I thought her boyfriend was Adam.'* ⇨ go together 3.

3 [Vpr] be a fixed part or accompaniment of (sth). **S:** fields, paddock, two acres; belt; company car. **o:** house; dress; job: *We were delighted to find that a large rock garden* **went with** *the house.* ○ *The sixteen illustrations were to* **go with** *the two volumes.* CD

4 [Vpr] be normally associated with (sth); attend. **S:** disease, crime, influence. **o:** poor hygiene, poverty, money: *This phase* (of the illness) *will be very painful for the patient, ... and a risk of suicide* **goes with** *it.* MP ○ *I had my reputation to think of, and the status in society that* **went with** *it.* GL ⇨ go together 2.

5 [Vpr] combine well with (sth); match, suit. **S:** hat; lipstick, powder; his voice. **o:** dress; shoes; complexion; his distinguished appearance: *The tie* **goes** *well* **with** *the green shirt.* ○ *She had put on a pair of new shoes which did not* **go** *very well* **with** *her coat.* INN ⇨ go together 1.

6 [Vpr] (*informal*) have the same opinion as (sb); accept (sth). **o:** you, your party; that idea, your views: *If you mean sex and violence on the screen means sex and violence on the streets, I don't* **go with** *that.* BBCTV = agree (with) 1.

go with a bang/swing [Vpr] (*informal*) be very successful and enjoyable. **S:** party, concert, pop festival: *The pop festival on the Isle of Wight* **went with a bang**. ○ *When we arrived at 9 o'clock the party was well under way and* **going with a swing**.

go with the tide [Vpr] follow the lead taken by others; not adopt an independent course: *Max has* *no ideas of his own on any matter of importance; he just* ***goes with the tide****.*

go without [Vp, Vpr] suffer the lack of (sth). **o:** food; shoes, clothes; shelter: *Thousands of refugees were given food, but many hundreds had to* ***go without****. ○ Police on the murder enquiry team* ***went without*** *sleep answering the calls that came in from the public.* = do without 1.

it/that goes without saying [Vpr] it is so obvious that it is not, or it is hardly, necessary to say it: ***It goes without saying*** *that the period from 1885 to 1900 is of crucial significance.* F ○ *When you visit England you will stay with us —* ***that goes without saying****.*

goad

goad into [Vn.pr pass rel] provoke (sb) to do sth or into a certain state. **S:** jeers, mockery, complaining tone; hunger, need, despair. **o:** losing my temper, retaliating, striking out; stealing food, breaking into a shop; a fury, passionate anger: *The riot police were well trained and refused to be* ***goaded into*** *attacking the demonstrators. ○ His mean-spirited attacks on our work finally* ***goaded*** *us* ***into*** *an angry response.*

goad on [Vn ⇆ p pass] challenge or provoke (sb) to do sth foolish, antisocial, illegal etc. **O:** mob; demonstrators; prisoners, rebels. **Inf:** smash windows, turn over barriers, burn buildings: *Sergeants along the assault course were* ***goading*** *the men* ***on*** *to climb a lot faster and run a lot harder. ○ Quite young children were being* ***goaded on*** *to break into shops and private houses.*

gobble

gobble up [Vn ⇆ p pass] consume, devour (sth). **S:** geese, dogs; children; large countries; companies; computer. **O:** grain, meat; dinner; small neighbours; family businesses; facts: *Imperial powers throughout history have always tended to* ***gobble up*** *their weaker neighbours. ○ The newest computers can* ***gobble up*** *work at a quite fantastic rate.*

goggle

goggle (at) [Vpr pass] (*informal*) stare wide-eyed (at sb/sth): *The boys sat on the hotel terrace,* ***goggling at*** *the girls as they went down to the beach.* = gape (at).

gorge

gorge (oneself) on [Vpr, Vn.pr] eat (sth) until one is full. **S:** vultures; rats; children. **o:** rotting carcasses; grain; ice-cream and chocolate: *We came across a crocodile scarcely able to move after* ***gorging on*** *some dead animal. ○ The boys* ***gorged themselves on*** *the cakes, and left the bread and butter uneaten.*

gorged with [pass (Vn.pr)] having eaten (sth) to excess; sated with: *The guards were* ***gorged with*** *rich food and were easily overcome.* □ also used after *appear, seem*, or after a noun.

gouge

gouge out [Vn ⇆ p pass] force (sth) out, with one's fingers or a sharp instrument. **O:** eyes; channel, groove: *Some vandal had* ***gouged*** *his initials* ***out*** *on the newly finished altar. ○ The monster machine* ***gouged out*** *a deep trench across the field, revealing a rich layer of coal.*

grab

grab at [Vpr pass] attempt to seize (sth). **o:** falling child; branch of a tree; chance, opportunity: *A passer-by* ***grabbed at*** *the child, and was just quick enough to pull him out of the path of a lorry. ○ He recognized the offer of a job in Professor Norman's department as a chance to be* ***grabbed at*** *straight away.* = grasp at.

graduate

graduate (in) (from) [Vpr rel] complete a degree course (in a subject) (at a university etc): *He* ***graduated in*** *metallurgy* ***from*** *Birmingham in 1973.*

graduate from [Vpr] (*jocular*) move from (one stage in one's career) to a higher one: *Joe* ***graduated*** *into the drugs racket* ***from*** *the back streets of Glasgow. ○ This is Nurse Barker, into whose position Simpson* ***graduates from*** *nursery maid.* BRN

graft

graft in/on (to) [Vn ⇆ p pass, Vn.p.pr pass] attach living tissue taken from one part of the body (to another); attach part of one plant (to another plant). **O:** skin, piece of bone; cutting: *The tendon had been so skilfully* ***grafted in*** *that she was able to flex her finger quite normally after four weeks. ○ The gardener could* ***graft*** *as many as twenty cuttings an hour* ***on to*** *briar stems.*

graph

graph out [Vn ⇆ p pass] plot or display (sth) in the form of a graph. **O:** figures, statistics; forecast: *When the results of the previous six months' trading had been* ***graphed out****, it was clear that the firm was heading rapidly for bankruptcy.*

grapple

grapple with 1 [Vpr] try to control or overpower (sb). **o:** thief, intruder; invaders, enemy: *The public were warned not to* ***grapple with*** *the fugitive, as he was armed and dangerous.*

2 [Vpr pass rel] struggle to solve (sth); tackle. **o:** problem, difficulty; issue, question; implication: *It is high time that the government* ***grappled with*** *the ever-growing problem of unemployment in Scotland.* = come to grips with.

grasp

grasp at [Vpr pass] try to seize (sth). **o:** opportunity, chance, offer: *When my daughter was offered a trip to Hong Kong by her employers, she* ***grasped at*** *it with both hands.* = grab at.

grass

grass on [Vpr pass] (*informal*) give information to the police about a companion's crimes, plans etc: *He would certainly* ***grass on*** *his mates if he thought he was going to get more lenient treatment from the police.*

grate

grate on [Vpr pass] be hard to bear; irritate. **S:** his voice, manners, behaviour. **o:** my nerves; everybody present, his wife: *Everything about him* **grated on** *her now.* FL

gravitate

gravitate to/towards [Vpr rel] move towards (sth/sb) as though drawn by some natural force. **o:** house, room; bar, saloon; her, their mother: *You could be sure that if Norman and his pals were in the hotel, they would have* **gravitated** *quite rapidly* **to** *the bar.* ○ *London was swarming with refugees ... many of whom* **gravitated towards** *this centre of enlightenment.* GE

greet

greet with [Vn.pr pass rel] offer (sb) (sth) in the form of a 'welcome'. **o:** a smile, a warm welcome; jeers and catcalls, enthusiasm; a burst of applause; a barrage of stones: *When the visiting speaker entered the hall he was* **greeted with** *ironic cheers by the students.* □ usually passive.

grieve

grieve for/over [Vpr pass] feel sorrow on recalling (sb/sth). **o:** dead friend; the passing of one's youth: *'It's no use* **grieving over** *"the good old days", you know. They've gone for ever, and anyway were they really so good?'*

grin

grin all over one's face [Vpr] (*informal*) smile broadly, showing great pleasure or amusement: *'Yes, I'm angry, damned angry,' she stamped her foot, 'and what are you* **grinning all over your face** *for, I'd like to know.'* ○ *Cosmo, the oldest ..., was* **grinning all over his face** *as he trotted to keep pace.* US

grind

grind away (at) [Vp, Vp.pr] work with intense determination (at sth). **o:** translation, essay; French, Russian; revision: *'James has a biology exam on Friday, and he's* **grinding away** *to make up for lost time.'* ○ *He continued to* **grind away** *without ceasing* **at** *his shorthand.* CD

grind down [Vn ⇆ p pass] make life miserable for (sb); oppress. **S:** tyranny, government; military forces; poverty, taxation: *In the sixteenth century the European invaders ruthlessly* **ground down** *and exploited the Indians of South America.* ○ *The peasants were* **ground down** *by oppressive landlords.*

grind into [Vn.pr pass] press (sth) with great force into (sth). **O:** cigarette; fist; heel. **o:** saucer, ashtray; sb's face: *He dropped the photograph and* **ground** *his foot* **into** *it.*

grind into/to [Vn.pr pass] reduce (sth) to (smaller pieces), by grinding. **O:** corn; stone. **o:** flour; powder, pieces: *When the stone had been* **ground to** *a fine powder it was used as the base for cosmetics.*

grind on [Vp] move slowly and tediously forwards. **S:** machine, juggernaut; bureaucratic procedures; process of law: *The war machine* **ground** *slowly* **on** *towards disaster.* ○ *The trial* **ground on** *endlessly.*

grind out 1 [Vn ⇆ p pass] play (sth) heavily or drearily. **S:** band; gramophone, jukebox. **O:** tune, song, number, the latest hit: *The hurdy-gurdy men used to come and* **grind out** *their melancholy tunes.* AF

2 [Vn ⇆ p pass adj] extinguish (sth) by pressing down hard on it. **O:** cigarette, cigar; burning twig: *Charles* **ground out** *his cigarette before answering.* 50MH ○ *The floor was littered with* **ground-out** *cigarettes.* = stub out.

grind to [Vn.pr pass] ⇨ grind into/to.

grind to a halt 1 [Vpr] come slowly, inevitably and perhaps noisily to a stop. **S:** car, lorry, machine; motorized forces; invasion, army: *As supplies of petrol gave out, the retreating columns* **ground to a halt**. ○ *After the first 400 yards of brisk running he was still with me ... I was about to call it a day and surrender when he* **ground to a halt**. NS

2 [Vpr] stop working efficiently. **S:** dock, mine, shipyard; parish, school: *Heathrow Airport* **grinds** *slowly* **to a halt**. *How serious is overmanning in British industry?* BBCR ○ *Although revered greatly as a person, his leadership had* **ground to a halt**. CF

gripe

gripe (at) [Vpr pass] (*informal*) complain about (sth), usu unreasonably. **o:** treatment, proposal; the way the matter is being handled: *'No matter how generous the financial terms are, you'll always find somebody ready to* **gripe at** *them.'* ○ *'What's old Bloggins* **griping at** *now? Last week it was women being taken on as mechanics.'*

groan

groan in/with [Vpr] produce a long, low sound from the throat, deliberately or involuntarily, expressing pain or unhappiness. **S:** injured man; audience. **o:** dismay, misery, pain; mock dismay: *Wounded men* **groaned in** *agony as the stretcher-bearers tried to move them.* ○ *The audience* **groaned with** *mock pain at the comedian's ancient jokes.*

groan with [Vpr] be heavily laden with (sth). **o:** food and drink; good things; jelly and trifle: *The children could hardly believe their good fortune when they saw the tables* **groaning with** *cakes and jellies.*

grope

grope for [Vpr] try to find (sth) in a blind, fumbling way. **o:** switch; right word, expression; formula, name; the truth: *I slipped into the darkened room and* **groped for** *the light switch.* ○ *The lecturer paused,* **groping for** *the precise word to express her meaning.*

ground

well etc grounded in [pass (Vn.pr)] having a deep knowledge of (sth). **A:** well, solidly, thoroughly. **o:** logic, the law, politics, comparative religion: *Every educated man of the nineteenth century was* **well grounded in** *Latin and Greek.* □ also used after *appear, seem* and after a noun: *a woman* **solidly grounded in** *company law.*

ground on [Vn.pr pass emph rel] use (sth) as a basis or foundation for (sth). **O:** theory, belief, policy; appeal, argument. **o:** observation; facts, evidence; prejudice, hearsay: *The government claimed that its policies were* **grounded on** *the realities of the situation and not on wishful thinking.* ○ *They* **grounded** *their religion* **on** *Nature.* = base on/upon.

group

group around/round [Vpr, Vn.pr pass rel] (cause sb/sth to) surround (sth) in a group. **S** [Vpr], **O** [Vn.pr]: class, men; tanks, divisions. **S** [Vn.pr]: teacher; commander. **o:** blackboard, desk; village, forest: *The class was* **grouped around** *the front bench, watching the teacher demonstrate a chemical reaction.* ○ *Before setting out, we* **grouped** *ourselves* **round** *the guide to hear his final instructions.*

group together [Vn ⇆ p pass] place (people/things) in the same category, or in one place. **O:** infections, illnesses; fish, insects; books, articles: *It is absurd to* **group** *all murderers* **together**, *as though they were all equally wicked or antisocial.* ○ *It would be better if the books were* **grouped together** *under 'author' rather than 'subject'.*

grouse

grouse (about) [Vpr pass] complain about (sth/sb), usu with little justification. **o:** food, conditions, lodgings, beds; weather; the BBC; the hotel staff: *He's the kind of chap who will always find something to* **grouse about**, *no matter how perfect the arrangements are.*

grovel

grovel (before/to) [Vpr] behave (towards sb) with a show of humility or shame. **o:** manager, boss: *'Why should I have to* **grovel to** *him to get an extra week's holiday when I'm entitled to it anyway?'*

grow

grow apart (from) [Vp, Vp.pr] come gradually to have a less intimate or close relationship (with sb): *It became clear to her how much they had* **grown apart** *in the time he was away.* ⇨ next entry

grow away from [Vp.pr] come gradually to have a less intimate or close relationship with (sb). **o:** parents, former friends, the gang: *It often happens that a girl who in her early teens has been very close to her mother suddenly* **grows away from** *her as she makes new friends and her horizons widen.* ○ *After only one term at university, David was conscious that he had* **grown away from** *his old school friends and that things would never be the same again.* ⇨ previous entry

grow from 1 [Vpr, Vn.pr pass] (cause sth to) germinate and reach fruition. **S** [Vpr], **O** [Vn.pr]: flowers, fruit, vegetables, plants. **o:** seed; a cutting: (proverb) *Great oaks* **from** *little acorns* **grow**. ○ *'How do you like my tomatoes? I* **grew** *them* **from** *seed.'* ○ *Were these roses* **grown from** *seed or from cuttings?* ↔ grow into 1.

2 [Vpr emph rel] have (sth) as its origin. **S:** interest; fear; admiration; desire. **o:** reading sth, meeting sb; an unpleasant experience as a child; what he had heard about her; ambition to succeed: *His interest in ships* **grew from** *talking to his father, who had always longed to go to sea, and from reading the innumerable books about them that he found on his father's shelves.* = arise from, grow out of 3.

grow in [Vpr] acquire more of (a moral or intellectual quality). **o:** wisdom, stature, importance, authority: *John has* **grown in** *strength, but not, unfortunately,* **in** *wisdom. He's as foolish as ever with his money.* ○ *The Prime Minister was not an impressive figure when he took office, but he has* **grown** *greatly* **in** *stature over the past three years.* = gain in 2.

grow into 1 [Vpr] become (sth), with the passing of time. **S:** she, he; actor; politician; corner shop; sapling. **o:** strapping girl, handsome young man; polished performer; clever statesman; flourishing business; sturdy tree: *We did not meet again for ten years. By then, the rather puny boy had* **grown into** *a six-footer weighing 220 pounds.* ○ *That small family business has* **grown into** *a company of international repute.* ↔ grow from 1.

2 [Vpr] become large enough to fit (sth). **o:** jacket, suit, shoes: *The coat's a bit large now, but Alex will soon* **grow into** *it.* ↔ grow out of 1.

3 [Vpr] come gradually to fit a role etc that is now beyond one. **o:** role, part; job: *She didn't perform badly on the opening night, but she needs time to* **grow** *more fully* **into** *the part.*

grow on [Vpr] become gradually more attractive, interesting, likeable to (sb). **S:** John, Liverpool; style of painting, writing, speaking, acting; country life: *When I first went to live in Glasgow I found it rather a dreary place, but after a while it began to* **grow on** *me.* ○ *The Portuguese 'fados' sound strange at first, but they quickly* **grow on** *you.*

money doesn't grow on trees [Vpr] (*saying*) it is not easy to obtain money, it has to be worked for: *'I can't give you twenty pounds for a trip to London, Jill.* **Money doesn't grow on trees**, *you know!'* ○ (a mother, exasperated at her sons' excessive consumption of expensive apples) *'Apples* **don't grow on trees**, *you know!'*

grow out of 1 [Vpr] become too big for (sth). **o:** clothes, suit, dress, shoes: *'It's terrible the way Sheila's* **growing out of** *her shoes; she needs a bigger size every three months!'* □ outgrow is used in the same meaning: *She's* **outgrown** *all her clothes.* But note: *She's* **outgrown** *all her friends* can mean 'She's grown taller than all her friends' or 'She's become more mature than them' (and consequently does not associate with them). ↔ grow into 2. ⇨ next entry

2 [Vpr pass] lose (sth) with the passage of time or with maturity; abandon. **o:** bad habits; asthma; dependence on his mother; the need for excitement: *Her sister in Oxford had suffered from migraines as a child but had* **grown out of** *them.* MSAL □ outgrow is used in the same meaning: *He's* **outgrown** *his habit of wetting the bed.* ⇨ previous entry

3 [Vpr emph rel] have (sth) as its origin or cause. **S:** war between A and B; financial troubles; love affair. **o:** an unresolved border dispute, the persecution of minorities; rash investments; daily contact: *The plot to kill the President* **grew out of** *the inordinate ambition of a few colonels.* ○ *We began with an informal link with a single French school, and* **out of** *this* **grew** *a complex scheme for exchanging pupils and teachers.* = arise from, grow from 2.

grow over [Vpr pass, Vn.pr pass] (cause a plant etc to) cover (sth). **S** [Vpr], **O** [Vn.pr]: ivy, wisteria; climbing plants; hair. **o:** tree, wall, side of the house; scar : [Vpr] *Bracken, brambles, ivy and a variety of clinging plants had* **grown** *all* **over** *the garden and given it the appearance of an impenetrable jungle* (or: *The garden had become* **overgrown/grown over** *with bracken* etc, *giving it the appearance* etc). ○ [Vn.pr] *To avoid recognition he had* **grown** *his hair* **over** *the scar on his forehead.* □ note the passive transform grown over and the alt form overgrown, both with *be/become*; the latter is more usual in horticultural contexts.

grow up 1 [Vp] become adult; go through one's formative years: *'What are you going to be when* *you **grow up**, Anne?' 'I'm going to be a nurse.'* ○ *'How is it that you are so fond of South America?' 'I **grew up** there.'* ○ *Sarah is only fifteen, but her opinions and reactions are surprisingly **grown-up**.* ○ *The children can stay up late and watch the Bond movie with the **grown-ups**.* □ grown-up can be used as an adj; there is also a noun grown-up(s).

2 [Vp] behave or think as an adult ought to, face the realities of life as they are: *'It's no good, George. There's only one thing you can do about it, and that's **grow up**. Stop being the kind of person that people play practical jokes on.'* HD

3 [Vp], **S:** empire; market; sect, movement: *These were small sects that **grew up** and flourished in the last century.* ○ *A dealing market **grew up** in these products of instant consumption.* NTG

grow up into [Vp.pr] become (sth), when one is an adult. **o:** thief, crook, scrounger: *'What sort of person is he going to **grow up into** if I don't try to control him now?'* ○ *'I think you were rather unkind,' said Isabel. 'No! I can't let her **grow up into** a liar, can I?'* PW

grow upon [Vpr] become stronger, more firmly fixed, in (sb's mind). **S:** conviction, belief; suspicion; realization: *The conviction **grew upon** him that if he had known the work would be so different from his expectations he would never have embarked upon it.* DL

grub

grub about [Vp] busy oneself in some obscure way, perhaps in search of sth or to organize things, and getting dirty in the process. **A:** under the bushes; among old books; in the cellar: *'I don't know where your mother is. Probably **grubbing about** in the vegetable garden or somewhere.'* ○ *A fat sow was **grubbing about** near the gate and refused to move out of our way.*

grub up [Vn ⇆ p pass] pull (sth) out of the ground, and get dirty in doing so. **O:** weeds; turnips, potatoes; tree stump: *The last time the old man was seen alive he was **grubbing up** some roots of heather on the mountainside.*

grumble

grumble (at) (about) [Vpr pass rel] complain (to sb), usu in a surly, ill-tempered way (about sth). **o:** (**about/over**) food, lodging; treatment, low pay; weather: *Old Scrooge was for ever **grumbling at** Bob Cratchit **about** his work.* ○ *'It's no good **grumbling at** me **about** your treatment in hospital. Write to the hospital management.'*

guard

guard against [Vpr pass rel] be careful to avoid (sth); take precautions against (sth). **o:** illness; colds, infection; scandal, suspicion; developing bad habits; the invasion of one's privacy, prying eyes: *A doctor must always **guard against** passing on disease to his family.* ○ *Her mother was always telling her to **guard against** over-excitement.* SATS ○ *Hasty reactions to provocation should be **guarded against**.*

guess

guess at [Vpr pass rel] try to imagine (sth); estimate. **o:** her age; likely effects of sth; his probable reaction; the cause of the explosion: *If you want me to **guess at** John's reaction to your suggestion, I think he would probably welcome it.* ○ *Two leaves have been cut from the Diary, so we can only **guess at** how he soothed her ruffled feelings.* GE ○ *His origins can only be **guessed at**. French, perhaps?*

guide

guide across, along, away etc [Vn ⇆ p pass, Vn.pr pass] (of a person with knowledge and experience) lead (sb) across etc. **O:** search-party, police, climbers: *The police-dog **guided** its handler **to** the hidden drugs.* ○ *'Give me your hand and I'll **guide** you **through** the tunnel.'*

gull

gull into [Vn.pr pass] (*formal*) deceive (sb) into (doing sth). **O:** shopper, housewife, pensioner. **o:** parting with money, signing away their inheritance: *People were **gulled into** investing their savings in worthless pension schemes.* = trick into. ⇨ next entry

gull out of [Vn.pr pass] (*formal*) make (sb) give up (sth) by trickery. **O:** drunken man, young boy, innocent peasant. **o:** money, horse; everything he had: *Street traders **gull** the unsuspecting tourists **out of** every penny they have.* = cheat out of. ⇨ previous entry

gulp

gulp down [Vn ⇆ p pass] swallow (sth) quickly. **O:** dinner, food; tea, medicine: *The firemen paused for a couple of minutes, **gulped down** a cup of hot soup and returned to the job of fighting the fire.*

gum

gum down [Vn ⇆ p pass adj] secure (sth) with gum. **S:** envelope; stamp, label: *The stamp had not been properly **gummed down** and had come off the parcel, so we had to pay the postage again.* = stick down 1.

gum up the works [Vp.n pass] (*slang*) make progress impossible; spoil everything: *Just when some stability seemed to have been reintroduced into industry, the Civil Service **gummed up the works** by going on strike for more pay.*

gun

gun down [Vn ⇆ p pass] (*informal*) shoot (sb) ruthlessly (the implication often being that the victims are defenceless). **o:** women and children, villagers; prisoners, suspects; rival (gangster, politician); presidential candidate: *As the Colonel emerged from the meeting, the guerrillas, concealed behind the grill of an air-shaft, **gunned** him **down**.*

gun for [Vpr pass] (*informal*) seek an opportunity to attack or criticize (sb): *'Old Sanders is **gunning for** you, so don't give him an easy excuse to report you to the boss.'* ○ *Poor Harry! He had no idea he was being **gunned for** until the blow fell!* □ continuous tenses only.

gush

gush from/out/out of [Vp emph, Vpr empr rel] pour suddenly and with some force from (sth). **S:** blood; water; oil; curses, abuse. **o:** severed vein, wound; broken pipe; newly-drilled well; mouth: *There was a shout from the men on the rig and the next thing we knew was that water was **gushing from** the well to a height of fifty feet.* ○ *An artery was severed and the blood **gushed out**.* ○ *She had to* *stick her fingers in her ears to muffle the stream of obscenities that came* ***gushing out of*** *him.* FL

gush (over) [Vpr pass] (*pejorative*) talk with excessive enthusiasm (about sb/sth). **o:** new baby; son's fiancée; visiting celebrity; achievement: *'I wish Mummy wouldn't* ***gush over*** *Peter's little successes at school: it makes him feel such a fool in front of his friends.'* ○ *Being* ***gushed over*** *like that was a new experience for him.*

gutter

gutter out [Vp] (of a naked light) gradually go out with small spurts of flame. **S:** flame; match, candle, lamp: *He sat and watched his candle dwindle to its base and then* ***gutter out*** *completely.* MOB = flicker out.

H

habituate

habituate to [Vn.pr pass emph rel] (*formal*) make (sb) learn to accept or expect (sth). **S:** he etc; experience, event; war, famine, drought; achievement, success. **O:** oneself; population, citizens. **o:** hardship, deprivation, shortage; flattery, applause: *He had* ***habituated*** *himself* (cf *He was* ***habituated***) ***to*** *the solitary life.* ○ *The responsibility of command had* ***habituated*** *him* ***to*** *making quick decisions.* = accustom to, used to.

hack

hack down [Vn ⇆ p pass adj] cut (sth) to the ground with rough blows. **O:** tree, branch: *Men were* ***hacking down*** *an old privet hedge to make way for an ugly modern fence.* = chop down, hew down.

hack off [Vn ⇆ p pass adj] remove (sth) with rough chopping blows. **O:** branch; limb; length, section (of rope, piping): *The cook* ***hacked off*** *a piece of the roasted carcass and handed it to me in his fingers.* = chop off.

haggle

haggle (over) [Vpr pass rel] attempt, by making proposals and counter-proposals, to settle the price of goods, the terms of an agreement etc, in one's favour. **S:** traders, merchants; negotiators. **o:** price; wage, conditions: *Let's not* ***haggle over*** *the odd few pounds in the price. Shall we settle at a round figure of £500?* ○ *The trade union side did not consider it a waste of time to* ***haggle over*** *the finer points of the package deal.*

hail

hail from [Vpr rel] (usu *jocular*) have (sth) as a place of origin. **S:** visitor, tourist; ship. **o:** abroad, the North; foreign port: *Judging from his speech, I should say he* ***hails from*** *North of the Border* (= Scotland).

ham

ham up [Vn ⇆ p pass adj] (*informal*) act (sth) on the stage in a crude or exaggerated way (either through inexperience or for deliberate effect). **S:** actor, performer. **O:** it, the (whole) thing; part, passage: *We sat through a dreadful TV comedy show containing a* ***hammed-up*** *extract from grand opera.* ○ *'Don't on any account* ***ham*** *this scene* ***up****. If anything, underplay it — play it down.'*

hammer

hammer down [Vn ⇆ p pass] secure or fasten (sth) by striking it or driving in nails. **O:** lid, top, cover: *The cover, which had already been roughly fitted into position, was now* ***hammered down****.*

hammer in/into 1 [Vn ⇆ p pass, Vn.pr pass] force, drive (sth) in by striking it. **O:** post, stake; nail, rivet: *First the pegs were* ***hammered into*** *the ground in a large circle, then the tent was raised and the ropes fastened.* = drive in/into.

2 [Vn ⇆ p pass, Vn.pr pass] force (sb) to learn (sth) by tiresome repetition. **S:** teacher, preacher, pedant. **O:** lesson; moral, point; French, grammar. **o:** class, flock; head: *'Don't you start on me Martin! My parents have been hammering the point in long enough already.'* ○ *We had French* ***hammered into*** *our heads for five years. How much of it do we still remember?* = din in/into, drum in/into.

hammer on/onto [Vn ⇆ p pass, Vn.pr pass] fasten (sth) in position by beating or striking it. **S:** blacksmith, carpenter. **O:** lid, top, metal cap: *When you've packed the box,* ***hammer*** *the lid* ***on****.* ○ *A protective copper strip was* ***hammered onto*** *the end of the post.*

hammer out 1 [Vn ⇆ p pass] make (sth) flat or smooth by beating it; remove (an irregularity) by beating. **S:** panel-beater, coach-builder. **O:** metal sheet, panel, wing; bump, dent: *The gold leaf has to be* ***hammered out*** *to the thinness of a sheet of paper.* ○ *That dent is not big enough to be worth* ***hammering out****; we can fill it in.*

2 [Vn ⇆ p pass] evolve or agree (sth) through hard discussion or negotiation. **S:** conference, negotiators. **O:** new proposals, compromise solution, final draft: *After prolonged discussion, the delegates* ***hammered out*** *a form of words that was acceptable to everyone.*

hammer out (on) [Vn ⇆ p pass, Vn.p.pr pass emph rel] produce (sound etc) by striking on (a surface etc). **O:** tune, chorus, rhythm. **o:** piano, drum: *I took hours* ***hammering out*** *the opening bars of a piano concerto.* SU = bang out (on), beat out (on), thump out (on).

hand

hand back (to) [Vn ⇆ p pass, Vn.p.pr pass] return (sth) (to its owner). **S:** official, policeman; teacher. **O:** passport, driving licence; exercise-book, examination script: *Please remember to* ***hand back*** *your room key before leaving the hotel.* ○ *'I haven't managed to mark your essays yet. I'll* ***hand*** *you them* ***back*** *(or: I'll* ***hand*** *them* ***back to*** *you) on Thursday.'* □ the second example shows the Indirect Object construction. = give back (to) 1.

hand down 1 [Vn ⇆ p pass adj] pass (sth) on to a child below one in age or size. **O:** clothes, shoes; book, toy: *In poor families, clothes may be*

***handed down** from one child to the next.* ○ *Peter was dressed in a pair of his brother's* **hand-me-downs** (**handed-down** *trousers* etc). ○ *The kids had to wear* **hand-me-down** *jackets.* □ nom form is hand-me-down(s).
2 [Vn ⇆ p pass adj] transmit (sth), usu over several generations. **O:** custom, tradition; enmity, prejudice: *These ceremonies have been* **handed down** *through the centuries, and remain practically unchanged.* □ usu passive. = pass down 1.
3 [Vn ⇆ p pass] (*legal*) pass sentence on sb convicted of a crime. **S:** court; judge, magistrate. **O:** judgment; sentence (of thirty years): *After the jury had returned its verdict the judge* **handed down** *sentences ranging from fifteen to twenty-five years.*

hand in [Vn ⇆ p pass adj] submit (sth); tender (sth); surrender (sth) because it is worn out or no longer required. **O:** exam script, form; resignation, protest; uniform, equipment: *The Minister* **handed in** *his resignation in protest against the Cabinet's European policy.* ○ *Hitherto such* (temporary) *passports have been issued only for the duration of a trip abroad and must be* **handed in** *immediately upon return.* IND = give in.

hand off [Vn ⇆ p nom pass] (*rugby football*) push away (a would-be tackler) with straightened forearm and spread fingers: *Smith* **handed off** *the full-back and raced for the corner-flag.* ○ *Jones was penalized for a too vigorously administered* **hand-off**.

hand on (to) 1 [Vn ⇆ p pass adj, Vn.p.pr pass emph rel] give (sth) to the next person, or another person; get rid of (sth) by handing it to another person. **O:** note, file; task, job: *'Perhaps I'd better leave a note. . . . I hardly feel you could be trusted to* **hand** *a message* **on**.*'* HD = pass on (to) 1.
2 [Vn ⇆ p pass adj, Vn.p.pr pass emph rel] give (sth) to the generation following one's own. **O:** burden, trust, responsibility; knowledge, skill: *The parent indeed* **hands** *something* **on** *to the child: haemophilia, syphilis, hay fever.* SATS ○ *Each new generation coming into the Sixth will have this body of experience* **handed on**, *and they'll be able to make their own contribution.* CON = pass on (to) 2.

hand out 1 [Vn ⇆ p nom pass] distribute, circulate (sth). **S:** lecturer, salesman. **O:** duplicated sheet, summary, sales brochure: *Duplicated material illustrating the lecture was* **handed out** *to the students* (cf *Illustrative* **hand-outs** *were given to the students*). ○ **Hand-outs** *were pushed through our letter-boxes as the first stage in this new trade war.* □ the hand-out is the written or printed material itself. = give out 2.
2 [Vn ⇆ p nom pass] offer (sth) as charity (to famine victims etc). **O:** soup, bread; clothing, blankets; gift parcels: *Relief workers* **handed out** *gifts of food and clothing to the survivors of the flooding.* ○ *During the thirties, many thousands of workers survived on* **hand-outs**. □ the hand-out is the food, clothing etc itself.

hand it/(the) punishment out [Vn ⇆ p pass] (*informal*) give a severe beating to sb; thrash sb soundly: *Smith was really going for his opponent,* **handing it out** *with both fists.* ○ *This new class of ship is built to* **hand out (the) punishment**. = dish it out.

hand over 1 [Vn ⇆ p pass] surrender (sth/sb). **S:** breadwinner; captor, enemy; intruder, assailant. **O:** money, pay-packet; prisoner, hostage; gun, knife: *This was the day of the week that Uncle Saunders was expected to* **hand over** *the housekeeping money.* CON ○ *Having expelled the student, the authorities almost literally* **handed** *him* **over** *to the secular arm.* OBS
2 [Vp nom, Vn ⇆ p nom pass] transfer (authority or power); make or complete (checks on cash etc) as part of this transfer. **S:** government, administration; governor, minister; storekeeper. **O:** territory, colony; office, post; stores, plant: *The time had now come for* **handing over** *power* (or: *a* **hand-over** *of power*) *to a local, elected government.* ○ *I shall be glad to* **hand** *this job* **over**. ○ *The stores were properly* **handed over** *to the new man—even the nuts and bolts were checked.*

hand it to [Vn.pr] (*informal*) (one must) give credit or praise to (sb): *'They're a clever lot, you've got to* **hand it to** *them.'* ILIH ○ *'She's been wonderfully cheerful, and interested in everything — you've really got to* **hand it to** *her.'* ILIH □ always used with with *must* or *have (got) to*.

hang

hang about/around [Vp, Vpr] (*informal*) wait idly (eg for sth to happen). **S:** (would-be) customer, spectator. **o:** door, entrance; gym, stadium: *Cai* (an animal) *only saw that I had put something in her cage which was alive, and she was not going to* **hang about** *and see what it was.* DF ○ *Desmond had spent several weeks* **hanging around** *the garage making friends with the rest of the ring* (ie gang of diamond smugglers). DS = stick about/around, wait about/around.

hang back (from) [Vp, Vp.pr emph rel] hesitate through timidity or fear (to do sth). **o:** people; fight; discussion; involvement: *She no longer* **hung back from** *people, she was open and friendly.* TP ○ *He's a solitary child — always* **hangs back from** *any group activities.* = hold back 2.

hang behind [Vp] linger in a place after others have left. **S:** spectator, student: *One or two of the audience* **hung behind** *after the lecture to have a word with the speaker.* = remain behind, stop behind.

hang in the balance [Vpr] (of events) have reached a critical point, where the result may go either way. **S:** future; result, outcome, issue; life, career: *If your heart begins to fail when the issue* **hangs in the balance**, *your opponent will probably win.* MFM

hang on 1 [Vp] (*informal*) wait, pause. **A:** a second, a sec, a bit: *Mrs Roth said she'd* **hang on** *a bit.* TT ○ *'Got a match, Bob?' he asked.* '**Hang on**,' *Bob replied.* BM □ often imperative. = hold on 1.
2 [Vp] (*informal*) grip sth firmly, hold tight; survive a crisis, hold fast: *'***Hang on** *with your knees. Don't let go.* **Hang on** *tight. Like grim death.'* DBM ○ *The most we can hope for is that by staying put, by digging our caves, we shall be able to* **hang on**. TBC = hold on 2.
3 [Vp] remain in a place when it is no longer sensible or safe to do so: *She* **hung on** *year after year in a small furnished room, hoping for fame.* GJ
4 [Vpr emph rel] require that some condition should first be met. **S:** future; career; result, out-

come. **o:** vote, election; decision, resolution; support, backing; whether one is supported, what happens later: *The survival of the government* **hangs on** *tonight's crucial vote.* ○ **On** *our ability to compete in difficult markets* **hangs** *our future as a trading nation.* = hinge on/upon.

hang on to [Vp.pr pass] (*informal*) not give or sell (sth) to sb else; keep, retain. **o:** (one's) lead, advantage; shares, profits; what one has: *Was Wouvermans keeping his word to* **hang on to** *the picture?* US ○ *I'm* **hanging on to** *those shares—I think they'll show a sizeable gain after the Budget.* = hold on to 2.

hang out 1 [Vn ⇆ p pass] spread (damp washing) on a clothes line, so that it can dry. **O:** washing, clothes: *'I've just got one or two shirts to* **hang out** *—then we can go shopping.'*

2 [Vp nom] (*informal*) live, reside in a place, usu temporarily; visit a place frequently: *'What did you say you were doing? And where are you* **hanging out***?'* THH ○ *'If I were you I'd look for him in the union bar. It's a favourite* **hang-out** *for students.'*

hang over 1 [Vpr emph rel] envelop (sth); possess (sb). **S:** (cloud, atmosphere, spirit, of) gloom, depression; elation, jubilation. **o:** proceedings; gathering, meeting; company: *Robert tried with a few good-humoured remarks to break through the cloud of gloom* **hanging over** *his colleagues, but his words struck no response from them.* ○ **Over** *everything* **hung** *the haunting magic of those final summer nights.* MRJ

2 [Vpr emph] seem likely to occur soon; be imminent. **S:** (prospect, possibility, of) ruin, disaster, failure; (threat of) dismissal, expulsion; examination, interview. **o:** army, industry; employee, member; student: *The threat of bankruptcy was* **hanging over** *Major Carmichael-Smyth.* TU ○ *Now that my Bar exams are* **hanging over** *me I don't want to take on any new outside commitments.*

3 [Vn.pr pass emph rel] suspend (things) from a surface so that they cover it. **O:** carpet, tapestry; picture, drawing, poster; medal, cross. **o:** wall, ceiling; chest; uniform: **Over** *one wall of the study he had* **hung** *a set of framed prints.* ○ *Trophies were* **hung** *all* **over** *the walls* (or: *The walls were* **hung with** *trophies*). RATT

hangover/hung over [nom pass (Vn.p)] (suffer) the consequences of drinking heavily the evening before: *I woke up with a dreadful* **hangover** *this morning.* ○ *This gifted 27-year-old guessed that the frontier guards would be too* **hung over** *to prevent him crossing.* ST

hang together 1 [Vp] co-operate, support one another: *It was better to* **hang together** *than separately* (ie *than be* **hanged** *separately*). DS ○ *We can come through any crisis if we* **hang together***.* = stand together, stick together.

2 [Vp] form an intelligible whole or coherent pattern. **S:** evidence, clues; story, picture; everything, it all: *'The two parts of his statement don't quite* **hang together***, do they?' said the inspector. 'We'll have to question him again.'*

hang-up/hung up [nom pass (Vn.p)] (*informal*) (feel or suffer from) confusion, bewilderment : *Another* **hang-up** *students complain of is too little personal contact with the teaching staff.* ○ *She's strangely* **hung up** (or: *has a strange* **hang-up***) about meeting new people.*

hang up [Vp] end a telephone conversation with sb by replacing the receiver: *'See you tomorrow,' she said. She* **hung up***.* AT

hang up (on) [Vp, Vp.pr pass] put down the telephone receiver abruptly, and possibly rudely, so ending a conversation (with sb): *She's incorrigible on the telephone. You literally have to* **hang up** *in her ear.* DC

hang upon [Vpr pass] listen with devoted attention to (sth said). **S:** audience; follower, supporter; admirer, lover. **o:** ⚠ (sb's) every word, words, reply; sb's lips: *They* **hung upon** *their leader's words.* EM ○ *Certainly he knew how to captivate Irma: she seemed to* **hang upon** *his lips.* PW

hanker

hanker after/for [Vpr pass emph rel] have a strong desire for (sth). **o:** steak, chicken; fame, wealth: *She got rid of nearly all the raw fish without* **hankering** *much* **after** *a gravy dinner and cider.* TGLY ○ *They* **hankered for** *the excitement of criminal investigations.* TFD

happen

happen along [Vp] (*informal*) appear by chance; happen to arrive: *He was obviously annoyed that the child had* **happened along***.* CON ○ *He had to* **happen along** *and ruin things just as we were about to settle the quarrel amicably!*

happen on/upon [Vpr] (*dated*) meet (sb), discover (sth), by chance. **o:** old friend, acquaintance; rare commodity, congenial job; answer, solution: *I* **happened on** *some uncut emeralds in a small jeweller's in Zanzibar.'* ○ *I* **happened** *one day* **upon** *another approach to this same fundamental question.* LIFE = chance on/upon, come on/upon.

happen to [Vpr] take place and affect (sb/sth). **S:** something dreadful, nothing of significance; what?. **o:** brother, colleague; department, firm: *Gwen John claimed in a letter to Rodin that nothing of importance* **happened to** *her before she was twenty-seven.* GJ ○ *'What's been* **happening to** *the place? I can hardly recognize it.'*

harden

harden off [Vp, Vn ⇆ p pass] (*horticulture*) (make a plant) become strong enough to be planted out of doors. **S** [Vp], **O** [Vn.p]**:** plant, bush; rose: *Now that these plants have* **hardened off** *we can plant them out in the garden.*

harden (oneself) to [Vn.pr pass emph rel] make (oneself) tough or resilient, physically or morally, so that one can face (sth). **o:** harsh conditions; extremes of climate; hardship, privation, solitude: *The miners had to* **harden themselves to** *the harsh winters of Alaska.* ○ *Lytton must by now have been* **hardened to** *Thackeray's attacks.* TU

hark

hark at [Vpr] (*informal*) just you listen to X! (implying that what X says is untrue, conceited, or otherwise not worth listening to): *'Just* **hark at** *him — anyone would think he owned the place!'* □ imperative only.

hark back (to) [Vp, Vp.pr pass emph rel] mention (sth) again; recall. **o:** past event, earlier tradition, former achievement: *To understand this entails* **harking back to** *a revelation I made earlier on.* SPL

○ *But the tradition is not entirely dead. It is* **harked back to**, *leaned upon as a fixed and still largely trustworthy field of reference.* UL

harmonize

harmonize (with) [Vpr emph rel, Vn.pr pass emph rel] (make sth) blend or fit in pleasingly (with sth else). **S** [Vpr], **O** [Vn.pr]: colour, shade, tone; note; mood, feelings; behaviour. **o:** one another; the other; background, surroundings: *These notes don't* **harmonize** *(***with** *each other).* ○ *His temperament does not* **harmonize with** *a slow, even pace of life.* ○ *Modern architects often make little attempt to* **harmonize** *the old* **with** *the new.*

harness

harness (to) [Vn.pr pass emph rel] connect a source of energy (to sth) so that the latter is driven. **O:** horse, ox; energy, power. **o:** cart, wagon; economy, industry: *The farmer* **harnessed** *a pair of oxen* **to** *the heavy wagon.* ○ *The productive energies of a whole people were* **harnessed to** *the war effort.*

harp

harp on [Vpr pass adj] talk persistently and tiresomely of (sth). **o:** an old string, the same string; grievance, suffering; one's lack of money: *She's always* **harping on** *the family's neglect of her. In fact everyone goes to visit her once a week.* ○ *His friends, perhaps, wearied of his* **harping on** *the same string.* HB

hatch

hatch out [Vp, Vn ⇆ p pass] (cause or help a shell to) break open; (cause or help a young bird to) break through the egg shell. **S** [Vp], **O** [Vn.p]: egg; batch; chick, grub, caterpillar: *The eggs* **hatch out** *in the warm mud of the river-bank.* ○ *The mother hen* **hatches out** *her young by covering the eggs with her warm feathers.* ○ *Several batches a day can be* **hatched out** *with the new incubator.*

haul

haul over the coals [Vn.pr pass] (*informal*) reproach or reprimand (sb) severely. **S:** father, employer; chief, boss: *He* (the Minister) *said it was a new experience to be* **hauled over the coals** *in the Cabinet room.* MFM ○ *'What was all the fuss about?' 'Oh, just Dad* **hauling** *me* **over the coals** *for borrowing his car again.'*

haul up (before) [Vn ⇆ p pass, Vn.p.pr pass] (*informal*) bring (sb) for trial in a court of law. **O:** thief, bigamist; defaulter; truant. **o:** judge, magistrate; commanding officer; headteacher: *This is the second time that Matthew has been* **hauled up** *on a dangerous driving charge.* ○ *The most that can happen is that you'll be* **hauled up before** *an officer and given a severe reprimand.* = bring up 4.

have

have doubts about [Vn.pr emph rel] be uncertain or unsure about (sth/sb). **adj:** some, no, one's; grave, serious. **o:** integrity, truthfulness, reliability; (sb's) work, research; your successor; how things will develop, whether to continue: *We may* **have** *serious* **doubts about** *the quality of working-class life today.* UL ○ *They had always* **had** *their* **doubts about** *George; others refused to believe in his guilt.* PE □ note the pattern with with: *She was a woman* **with** *no serious* **doubts about** *her role in the enterprise.*

have misgivings etc about [Vn.pr emph rel] be checked or restrained by moral uncertainty or principles from (doing sth). **O:** ⚠ (some, serious, certain) misgivings, reservations, qualms, scruples. **o:** interfering, intruding; accepting, receiving; advising, proposing: *I wouldn't* **have** *any* **qualms about** *taking his money.* DC ○ *We* **had** *no serious* **misgivings about** *recommending him for promotion.* □ note the pattern with with: *There were others* **with** *serious* **misgivings about** *what we were undertaking.*

have a/this thing about 1 [Vn.pr] (*informal*) feel esp attracted to, fond of or interested in (sb/sth). **o:** dark girls, tall men; wine, rich food; sea, desert; astronomy, antiques: *Of course he* **has a thing about** *her. He always* **has a thing about** *petite brunettes who need looking after.* ○ *David's always* **had this** *terrific* **thing about** *the army — ever since his grandfather gave him his first set of model soldiers.*

2 [Vn.pr] (*informal*) feel a particular and often irrational fear or dislike of (sb/sth). **o:** strangers, foreigners; snakes, spiders; travelling, being left alone: *'She* **has this** *silly* **thing about** *men with beards. Won't let one anywhere near her.'* ○ *It's the particular one* (ie girl) *he doesn't like at the time that he calls Clementine. It's just* **a thing** *he* **has about** *that name.* DC

have one's wits about one [Vn.pr] be alert and shrewd; be sharp-witted. **S:** salesman, dealer; sailor, airman: *You need to* **have your wits about you** *in the market. The last time I bought from a market trader I was given rotten fruit from the back of the pile.* ○ *'He's an awful fellow, Alec is, a real smart-alec, when he* **has his wits about him**.*'* PW □ note the pattern with with: *She's a girl* **with her wits about her**.

have feelings about/on [Vn.pr emph rel] feel a certain way about (sth); adopt a particular attitude about (sth). **adj:** (any, no) decided, particular, strong. **o:** divorce, abortion; capital punishment; disarmament; drugs, drink, smoking: *I* **have** *no* **feelings** *one way or the other* **about** *what you are suggesting.* ○ *It* (the aristocracy) *was not a matter* **on** *which he* **had** *any strong* **feelings**. US □ note the pattern with with: *They were people* **with** *no strong* **feelings on** *the matter.*

have anything etc against [Vn.pr rel] consider (sth) as a reason for mistrusting or disliking (sb). **O:** ⚠ anything, something, nothing; what?: *'I've* **nothing against** *him as an individual; I just don't happen to think he's suitable for the job.'* ○ *'***What have** *you* **got against** *her?' 'Nothing especially.'*

have a grudge against [Vn.pr emph rel] feel ill-will towards (sb), for no good reason, or because of sth he has done. **S:** teacher, prefect; police, magistrate, traffic warden; boss, foreman. **o:** pupil, class; motorist; student, hippy; workman: *Mark's been put into detention so many times that he's beginning to feel his form teacher must* **have a grudge against** *him.* ○ *Mary never forgot that she* **had a grudge against** *Africans in general, and she used to pick on any strange ones that came to camp.* BB

□ note the pattern with with: *He's a man* **with a grudge against** *authority.*

have around/over/round [Vn.p] entertain (sb) at one's house, usu for a short time, eg for a meal or drinks: *'I'll be* **having** *a few people* **round** *for a beer one of these evenings,' said the man.* HD

have a bash etc at [Vn.pr] (*informal*) try to achieve or do sth different and challenging. **O:** ⚠ a bash, crack, go, shot, stab, try. **o:** title, championship; trophy, cup; exam; persuading, convincing, converting, sb: *At the next meeting, he's going to* **have a stab at** *the 5 000 metres record.* ○ *As things stand, I don't mind* **having a go at** *doing up the place.* TC

have it away/off (with) [Vn.p, Vn.p.pr] (*slang*) make love to (sb), the suggestion being that the love-making is illicit, or at least furtive: *While Smith was in the North on business, Jones was* **having it away with** *his wife.* ○ *There was a spate of detail about how and where she'd* **had it off with** *her long string of lovers.*

have back 1 [Vn ⇆ p] have (sth) returned which has been borrowed. **O:** book, paper; car, lawnmower: *You can make use of my typewriter, but I must* **have** *it* **back** *by the weekend.* ○ *When can you let me* **have back** *the money that I lent you?* □ often used with *let*; not in continuous tenses. ⇨ get back 4, ⇨ give back (to) 1.
2 [Vn.p] allow a spouse or lover from whom one is separated to return. **O:** wife, husband; boyfriend; fiancée: *She wouldn't* **have** *him* **back** *if he was the last man on earth.* ⇨ take back 2.

have by [Vn.pr emph rel] have a child by X (ie X is the father of the child): *She* **had** *a daughter* **by** *her first husband and two sons* **by** *her second.* ○ *Bess* **had** *a boy* **by** *the fellow who's walking around the Court today.* WI

have down [Vn.p] have (sb) to stay at one's house as a guest, either from London or the north. **A:** for a few days, at Christmas: *They're planning to* **have** *their grandchildren* **down** *for the weekend.* ⇨ come down 5.

have their tails down/up [Vn.p] (*informal*) be dispirited, depressed; be confident, elated: *The troops* **had their tails down** *and there was no confidence in the higher command.* MFM ○ *Having won the President's Cup, the team* **had their tails up** *for the final of the league championship.* □ note the pattern with with: *They were a team* **with their tails up**.

have an appeal etc for [Vn.pr emph rel] be interesting or attractive to (sb). **S:** book, music, play; writer, composer; woman; face, figure. **O:** ⚠ (certain, great, tremendous) appeal, attraction, fascination, interest: *The topic seemed to* **have a fascination for** *her.* TST ○ **For** *me, the poetry of Keats has always* **had** *an enormous* **appeal**.

have an ear/an eye/a nose for [Vn.pr emph rel] be able to detect or appreciate (sth) because one's senses are alert or well trained. **adj:** no; good, sensitive; discerning, sharp. **o:** music, opera; colour, design; scandal, gossip: *He* **has no ear for** *music.* ○ *I've not* **got** *much of* **an eye for** *dresses.* OI ○ *The writer* **had a** *keen* **eye for** *evidences of superstition.* NDN ○ *A good reporter* **has a nose for** *news.* □ note the pattern with with: ... *children* **with an ear for** *music.*

have a flair/gift for [Vn.pr emph rel] be naturally gifted in some respect. **adj:** no, (not) any; special, remarkable. **o:** languages, mimicry; making things, handling machinery; foolery, saying the wrong thing: *'Did you have any difficulty in learning to shoot?' 'No, sir.' She* **had a flair for** *it.* RFW ○ *He* **had no gift for** *making polite conversation at parties.* □ note the pattern with with: ... *an actor* **with no gift for** *mimicry.*

have no terrors for [Vn.pr emph rel] not alarm or frighten (sb). **S:** mathematics, science; flying, motoring; tests, exams; speaking in public, meeting new people. **adj:** no, (not) any, few: *Unknown hazards must* **have no terrors for** *us.* MFM ⇨ have a dread etc of.

have no time/use for [Vn.pr emph rel] think very little etc of (sb); have a poor etc opinion of (sb). **adj:** some, a lot of; (not) much, little. **o:** shirker, coward; bigot, show-off; (upper, lower) class; boss, trade unionist; democracy, the monarchy: *The colonel never* **had any time for** *officers who had risen from the ranks.* ○ *He* **had no use for** *girls who did not know their way around.* AITC

have a soft/weak spot for [Vn.pr emph rel] (*informal*) feel a special fondness for (sb). **o:** (one's) youngest child, baby, orphan; vagrant, down-and-out: *Valerie sends her regards. She has always* **had a weak spot for** *you.* US ○ *People* **have a soft spot** *in their hearts* **for** *alcoholics.* OMIH □ note the pattern with with: *She was a woman* **with a soft spot for** *younger men.*

have in [Vn.p] have (sb) working in one's house. **O:** decorator, builder, plumber, carpenter: *I'm afraid we can't have you to stay after all: we'***ve got** *the decorators* **in** *all this week.* ⇨ get in 2.

have confidence in [Vn.pr emph rel] be sure in one's mind that sb is capable, or that things will turn out well. **adj:** a lot of; (not) any/much; considerable. **o:** manager, officer; parent, teacher; sb's ability, capabilities; future: *His personal authority would need to be great enough for the public to* **have confidence in** *him.* SC ○ *He* **has** *very little* **confidence in** *himself.* ○ *The vote indicates that the House* **has** *no* **confidence in** *the Government.* □ note the pattern with with: ... *a people* **with** *no* **confidence in** *its rulers.*

have faith (in) [Vn.pr emph rel] believe in the power, effectiveness etc, of (sb/sth). **adj:** no, little; (not) any/much; absolute, minimal. **o:** God; leader; promise, word: *Such men must* **have faith in** *God and they must think rightly on the moral issues involved.* MFM ○ *After so many disappointments, he finds it hard to* **have faith in** *doctors.* □ note the pattern with with: **With faith in** *God, we shall eventually triumph.*

have in hand [Vn.pr] have started or undertaken (sth); have (sth) in progress. **S:** contractor; agent, organizer; editor, examiner. **O:** work; alterations; arrangements; checking: *There's no need to worry about the electrical fittings. We'll* **have** *the work* **in hand** *by the end of July.* □ note the pattern with with: **With** *another scheme now* **in hand**, *he's clearly very busy.* ⇨ be/take in hand.

have a hand/part in [Vn.pr emph rel] be partly responsible for (sth); be involved in. **adj:** no, (not) any. **o:** decision; move, step; development, enterprise; forming opinion, changing conditions: *Sir Roy says that his government* **had no hand in** *the decision.* OBS ○ *The man* **had a hand in** *shaping my* *ideas.* ITAJ ○ *The rehousing programme was something* ***in*** *which he was proud to have* ***had a part****.*

have it in one (to do sth) [Vn.pr] be capable (of doing sth), have the ability (to do sth). **Inf:** to succeed, to go far; to hold sb's attention for long: *You'll find you can make good if you* ***have it in you****.* HD ○ *She never had the certainty that she* ***had it in her to*** *draw the love she coveted.* MM

have it in mind to do sth [Vn.pr] ⇨ next entry

have in mind [Vn.pr] be considering or contemplating (sth); propose, intend. **O:** idea, proposal; remedy, answer; it ... to warn sb, to increase spending: *Don't give your confidence to others regarding a plan you* ***have in mind****.* WI ○ *It was this weapon that the Minister of Defence* ***had in mind****.* NS ○ *He* ***had*** *it* ***in mind*** *to initiate staff talks with the Americans.* MFM

have a place in [Vn.pr emph rel] appear as an important etc feature of (sth). **S:** parent, child; upbringing, schooling; accident, disaster. **adj:** some, no, little; important, significant, special, minor. **o:** affections; biography, novel; report, record: *The working-class mother* ***has an*** *honoured* ***place in*** *most accounts of working-class childhoods.* UL ○ ***In*** *the Report now published, training provision for language teachers* ***has a*** *prominent* ***place****.* □ note the pattern with with: ... *a leader* ***with a place in*** *everyone's affections.*

have a say/voice in [Vn.pr emph rel] be involved in deciding future events. **S:** general public, ordinary person; consumer, user (of public services). **adj:** some, little; (not) any/much; considerable. **o:** (future) developments; what should happen, how things should develop; deciding, shaping, controlling, planning (sth): *They will* ***have a*** *determining* ***say in*** *their own future.* SC ○ *The ordinary MP may feel he* ***has no*** *effective* ***voice in*** *determining policy.* □ note the pattern with with: ... *ordinary people,* ***with no say in*** *shaping the future of their country.*

have in one's spell [Vn.pr] exert a magic power or control over (sb). **S:** girl; actor, orator; sportsman. **O:** lover; audience, onlookers; opponent: *Well, well, Bessie girl, Solly'****s got*** *you* ***in his spell****.* HSG ○ *For twenty minutes of the first half, the Brazilian forwards* ***had*** *a packed stadium* ***in their spell****.*

have a stake in [Vn.pr emph rel] have invested money, effort etc in (sth) and therefore stand to lose or gain. **S:** businessman, industrialist; inventor, designer, craftsman; investor; public, taxpayer. **adj:** some; no, not much of a; considerable, sizeable. **o:** region; economy; industry, business; venture, enterprise: *He'd invested in local property. Unlike other European traders, he* ***had a*** *genuine* ***stake in*** *the country.* DS ○ *Involving workers in management decisions may help them feel they* ***have a*** *bigger* ***stake in*** *the success of the company.* □ note the pattern with with: ... *workers* ***with a*** *real* ***stake in*** *the future of the business.*

have well in hand [Vn.pr] be easily able to control (sth). **O:** situation; crisis; game, contest: *Hopalong was trying to give the impression that he* ***had*** *the situation* ***well in hand*** *really and was just about to do what his friends had merely saved him the trouble of doing.* TT □ note the pattern with with: ... ***with*** *everything* ***well in hand****.* ⇨ be well in hand.

have it in for [Vn.p.pr] (*informal*) intend to make trouble for (sb), often through sheer ill-will: *They (the police)* ***have got it in for*** *your blue-eyed Larrie.* ASA ○ *The teachers* ***have it in for*** *this class. They must have taken a dislike to us on sight.*

have the best/worst of [Vn.pr emph rel] profit or benefit most from (sth); suffer most from (sth). **S:** country; army; industry, business; contestant. **o:** it, things; struggle, conflict, argument; deal, arrangement: *You can depend on it that when we come to divide the spoils Philip will* ***have the best of*** *the share-out.* ○ *Most of these forces had serious problems on their hands, but of those plagued by difficulties, Sierra Leone* ***had*** *easily* ***the worst of*** *it.* DS ⇨ get the better/best of, get the worst of.

have the courage of one's convictions etc [Vn.pr] be courageous enough to act according to (one's feelings etc). **o:** ⚠ one's convictions, desires, feelings, instincts, inclinations: *He was a sensualist who never* ***had the courage of his desires****.* ASA ○ *I should have* ***had the courage of my instincts****, cancelled the old plan, and started again from scratch.* LWK □ note the pattern with with: *This was a woman* ***with the courage of her convictions****.*

have control of/over [Vn.pr emph rel] direct, control or command (sb/sth). **S:** civil power, army, church, ordinary people. **adj:** some; no, (not) any/much; absolute, total. **o:** city, district, area; (people's) lives, movements: *The Constitution must give citizens confidence that they will* ***have control of*** *their own destinies.* ○ *She* ***has*** *very little* ***control over*** *the children; they seem to decide how they will behave.* □ note the pattern with with: *Soldiers were in charge,* ***with control over*** *the lives of ordinary people.* ⇨ be in/take control (of).

have a dread etc of [Vn.pr emph rel] be frightened of (sth/sb); fear. **O:** ⚠ a dread, fear, horror, terror. **o:** isolation, the dark, open spaces; snakes, spiders: *I might sleep and wake again before the night really started. I* ***had a horror of*** *this.* UTN ○ *She* ***has this*** *inexplicable* ***fear of*** *the empty house next door.* □ note the pattern with with: ... *a child* ***with a*** *healthy* ***fear of*** *snakes.* ⇨ have no fears/terrors for.

have off (by heart) [Vn.p, Vn.p.pr] learn (sth) (word for word). **O:** poem, speech; role, part: *She had read the essay to him a thousand times, so often that she almost* ***had*** *it* ***off by heart****.* GL

have it off (with) [Vn.pr, Vn.p.pr] ⇨ have it away/off (with).

have on 1 [Vn ⇆ p] be wearing (sth). **O:** clean shirt, bow tie; nothing: *She may* ***have on*** *a fur coat.* AITC ○ (*figurative*) *Fergus* ***had*** *his light-hearted face* ***on*** *again.* DC ○ *'You shouldn't feel hot. You'****ve*** *nothing* ***on****.'* RATT □ note the pattern with with: *Speak to the woman* ***with*** *the red jacket* ***on****.* ⇨ get on 1, put on 1.

2 [Vn.p] have (sth) arranged; have (sth) on one's programme or as a commitment. **O:** meeting, appointment, engagement; anything, nothing: *'****Have*** *you* ***(got)*** *anything* ***on*** *this evening?' 'Yes, one or two short meetings.'*

3 [Vn.p pass] (*informal*) tease, play tricks on (sb): *He was doing what he'd been paid for, but half the time I reckoned that he was* ***having*** *me* ***on****.* JFTR ○ *'I've just heard they're moving your whole department to Manchester.' 'Get away — you're* ***having me on****!'* □ normally used in continuous tenses.

4 [Vn.pr] (*informal*) have (no) reason or evidence to suggest that sb is responsible, etc. **S:** police; rival organization, firm. **O:** ⚠ (not) anything, nothing, something; what, how much: *'Belfounder **hasn't** anything **on** us legally; and if he starts making complaints I can make plenty of counter-complaints about the way I was treated.'* UTN ○ *Joe couldn't be sure how much the police **had on** him, but the suspicion that they might have something was enough to make him leave town.*

have on the brain [Vn.pr] (*informal*) be greatly preoccupied, or obsessed, with (sth/sb). **O:** power, money, sex; blondes, men: *'Some boy?' Terence echoed scornfully. 'You've **got** sex **on the brain**.'* HAA □ note the pattern with with: *He's a guy **with** sex **on the brain**.*

have pity on [Vn.pr emph rel] have kind and tender feelings for (sb in distress). **adj:** no, (not) any/much; little, great. **o:** the poor, the homeless; hungry people: *MYRA* (breaking down and crying): *Tony, **have pity on** me sometimes.* EHOW

have a crush on [Vn.pr rel] (*informal*) love (sb) in a passionate but immature way. **S:** schoolgirl, girl student, young parishioner. **adj:** big, serious, terrific, tremendous. **o:** teacher, lecturer, vicar: *It was the story of a schoolgirl who'd **had a crush on** an old man.* PP □ note the pattern with with: ... *a boy **with a crush on** an older woman.* = infatuated (with).

have designs on [Vn.pr rel] (*informal*) plan or propose to win control of (sb/sth). **adj:** no, (not) any; serious. **o:** girl, woman; man; top position, controlling interest: *I can assure you that I **have** no **designs on** Peter's job.* ○ *Darling, I want to go unattached. Maybe the devil'**s got designs on** me.* DPM □ note the pattern with with: *He's a young driver **with designs on** the World Championship.*

have one's eye on [Vn.pr rel] (*informal*) have chosen (sb/sth) as a desirable conquest, acquisition etc. **o:** girl, man; house, business; job, vacancy: *I looked around, wondering which young starlet the Baron **had his eye on**.* PP ○ *There was this nice little corner shop he'd **had his eye on** for some time.* □ note the pattern with with: ... *a woman **with an eye on** a job in marketing.*

have one eye on [Vn.pr] give part of one's attention to (sth/sb), while the rest is engaged somewhere else. **o:** clock, time; saucepan, kettle; baby, toddler: *It was a tricky experiment — he had to **have one eye on** the thermometer all the time.* ○ *He had a double motive, he **had one eye on** his own future.* NM □ note the pattern with with: *He always works **with one eye on the** clock!* ⇨ keep one eye on.

have feelings on [Vn.pr emph rel] ⇨ have feelings about/on.

have on the go [Vn.pr] (*informal*) have (sth) on which one is working; have (sth) in progress. **O:** picture, film; novel, article; embroidery, knitting: *He always **has** a book **on the go** and now he's joined by his second wife, Sheila, who is also writing a book.* TVT □ note the pattern with with: *He's doing well — **with** one film behind him and another **on the go**.*

have on hand (to do sth) [Vn.pr] have (sb) available that one can call on (to do sth). **Inf:** to help, to support one, to back one up: *I was glad to **have** an experienced teacher **on hand to deal with** the rowdier children.* □ note the pattern with with: ***With** someone **on hand to deal with** the rowdier children ....*

have on one's hands [Vn.pr] have goods that one does not need and would like to sell; (*figurative*) have a responsibility that one finds irksome. **O:** (spare, surplus) stores, supplies; elderly relative, maiden aunt, (sb else's) children: *'I've an extra gas cooker **on my hands**. Do you want to take it off me?'* ○ *I now **have** a ghost **on my hands** — another father would have the decency to die and stay dead.* HSG □ note the pattern with with: ***With** three children **on her hands**, she could do with a holiday.*

have on one's mind [Vn.pr] be thinking about, and worried or concerned by, (a problem). **O:** something, nothing; a lot, a great deal; arrangements, organization; party, wedding: *'You've **got** something **on your mind**. You aren't still worrying, are you?'* OMIH ○ *'Don't bother your father now — he **has** too much **on his mind**.'* □ note the pattern with with: *I left the finance committee meeting **with** a lot **on my mind**.*

have on one/one's person [Vn.pr] be carrying (sth), esp in a pocket or handbag. **O:** money, change; passport, ticket; comb, nail-file: *'I suppose you wouldn't **have** the price of a drink **on you**?'* ○ *'**Have** you **got** the key of the sideboard **on you**?'* MM □ note the pattern with with: ***With** only a pound **on me**, I couldn't afford a meal.* ⇨ have about one.

have time on one's hands [Vn.pr] (*informal*) have little (work) to do; not be under pressure of work: *'Still here then, I see,' he said conversationally. 'You must **have** plenty of **time on your hands**.'* TGLY ○ *'Now that Father's retired he'll **have** more **time on his hands**.' 'That's what worries me. He'll feel miserable with so little to do.'* □ note the pattern with with: *He's retired, **with** a lot of **time on his hands**.*

have a bearing on/upon [Vn.pr emph rel] be related to (sth); affect or influence (sth). **S:** (sb's) presence, participation, involvement; belief, feeling. **adj:** (not) any/much, little; direct, important. **o:** outcome, result; case, affair, issue: *The points you are raising **have some bearing on** the case now being tried.* ○ *Whether you love him **has no bearing on** whether he's good or bad.* AITC □ note the pattern with with: *The evidence was presented, most of it **with little bearing on** my investigation.* = bear on/upon.

have an effect/impact (on/upon) [Vn.pr emph rel] affect or influence (sth) in some way. **adj:** some; (not) any/much, little; slight, marginal; strong, favourable; adverse, contrary. **o:** production, demand, sales; (foreign) relations, policy; strategy, planning: *The measures which the Chancellor has taken should **have a** favourable **impact upon** the balance of payments.* SC ○ *These provisions have **had no** marked **effect on** the unemployment figures.* ○ *We can see **the effect** the difficulties of his early life **had on** him.* BRN □ note the pattern with with: *Exports were down, **with a** serious **impact on** our overall trading balance.*

have out [Vn.p] get (sth) removed by a surgeon or dentist. **O:** tooth, appendix: *He was **having** his tonsils **out**, which is a severe operation for an ageing man.* HD

have out (with) [Vn.p, Vn.p.pr] (*informal*) discuss (a matter) frankly and often angrily (with sb) until an understanding is reached. **O:** it; the thing, the question, the whole issue: *'I'm going round to Ned's. We've got to* **have** *this thing* **out**.' CON ○ *Their determination to* **have** *the apartheid issue* **out** *has not been changed in any degree.* SC ○ *'I* **had** *it* **out with** *her about the pilchard tins,' said Frank petulantly.* ASA

have over/round [Vn.p] ⇨ have around/over/round.

have control over [Vn.pr emph rel] ⇨ have control of/over.

have an/the edge over [Vn.pr emph rel] be in a position of advantage compared with (sb else). **adj:** (a) distinct, noticeable, considerable. **o:** neighbour, rival, competitor: *As far as having influence among those top half-dozen men, Sir Harold Johnson* **had the edge over** *Annette's father.* SML ○ (with reference to the US investment drive abroad) *Germany* **has a** *comfortable* **edge over** *France.* SC □ note the pattern with with: *Germany is a country* **with a** *comfortable* **edge over** *its industrial competitors.*

have a hold over [Vn.pr emph rel] be able to restrict sb's freedom, decide how he will act etc, because of some special advantage one has (eg information which could be used to damage him). **adj:** no, (not) any, (not) much of a; slight, considerable. **o:** enemy, rival, competitor: *'He* **has a hold over** *you, you realize that?' 'I don't see how.' 'His family own the land adjoining yours, and in time you will need that land to expand your workshops.'*

have access to [Vn.pr emph rel] be able to reach or use (sth). **adj:** some; no, not any/much; free, open, direct, restricted. **o:** garden, garage; shop, bank; paper, document, book; evidence, facts: *The café was a large room opening out on to the street, and the public* **had access to** *it.* T ○ *Thanks to the owner of a private library, I now* **have access to** *personal correspondence from that period.* ○ *From the flat, we* **have** *easy* **access to** *shops and schools.* □ note the pattern with with: *He lives in the country,* **with** *limited* **access to** *cinemas and theatres.* ⇨ get access to.

have recourse to [Vn.pr emph rel] (*formal*) use or adopt some means, usu unpleasant, to achieve one's ends. **o:** device, ruse, trick; argument, excuse, pretext; lawyer, solicitor, agent; the law: *He held the attention of the company round the bar without* **having recourse to** *any tricks to make guests listen.* RM ○ *He hoped the affair could be settled without either of them* **having recourse to** *legal proceedings.* = resort to.

have a right to sth/to do sth [Vn.pr rel] be entitled to possess or enjoy (sth). **adj:** some; no, (not) any; a perfect, an undeniable. **o:** share, part (of property); money; assistance, help: *'You had so many beautiful things, and Clementine . . .'* **'Had a right to** *some,' said Fergus softly.* DC ○ *France* **has** *as* **much right to** (or: **to have**) *nuclear weapons as Britain.* SC □ note the pattern with with: *And there was France,* **with the** *same* **right to** *the weapons as us.*

have their tails up [Vn.p] ⇨ have their tails down/up.

have the wind up [Vn.p] (*informal*) be frightened: *I don't mind actual flying, but every time the plane takes off or lands I* **have the wind up**. ⇨ get/put the wind up.

have up (for) [Vn.p pass, Vn.p.pr pass rel] (*informal*) cause (sb) to appear in court charged with an offence. **o:** armed robbery, petty larceny: *'If I see you hanging about these shops again, I'll* **have** *you* **up for** *loitering with intent.'* ○ *That's the second time he's been* **had up for** *dangerous driving.*

have a bearing upon [Vn.pr emph rel] ⇨ have a bearing on/upon.

have an effect/impact upon [Vn.pr emph rel] ⇨ have an effect/impact on/upon.

have an affair (with) [Vn.pr rel] have a sexual relationship with sb to whom one is not married (the implication is that the couple are emotionally involved, but that the relationship is impermanent: at least one of the partners may already be married). **S:** (married) man, woman; boss. **o:** friend's wife, husband; assistant: *'I'm glad you are being married. In Havana I thought you were just* **having an affair**.' OMIH ○ *Paul's first reaction to the discovery that his wife was* **having an affair with** *an old family friend was one of bewilderment rather than shock.* ⇨ live together/with.

have no truck with [Vn.pr rel] (*informal*) not (be prepared to) deal with, recognize, or accept (sb/sth). **adj:** no, (not) any, little. **o:** vagrant, slacker; brutality, insensitivity, thoughtlessness, bad manners: *The lighthouse men* **had no truck with** *the islanders and in no sense 'belonged'.* SD ○ *He'll* **have no truck with** *art or religion; for him everything that cannot be weighed or measured is suspect.* □ adj sometimes omitted, as in: *Protestant, professional Dublin . . . refused to* **have truck with** *swank or fuss.* EB

have a way with one [Vn.pr] (*informal*) be able, through charm or force of personality, to lead or captivate others: *Even as a small boy he* **had a way with him** *— he charmed every elderly lady in sight.* ○ *She was the sort of woman who* **had a way with her** *— which meant that she usually got what she wanted.* LLDR

have a word with [Vn.pr rel] speak to (sb), esp to make inquiries, seek advice, or reprimand. **adj:** quick, quiet, private. **o:** bank manager, house agent, solicitor; child, pupil: *'I wonder whether I could* **have a word** *or two* **with** *you, sir.'* EM ○ *'John's left his room in a mess again. You promised to* **have a word with** *him about it, darling.'*

have words (with) [Vn.pr emph rel] (*informal*) talk angrily (with sb), esp to reproach or reprimand. **o:** child, pupil; employee, subordinate: *'If you fiddle with my camera again you and I are going to* **have words**, *young man* (cf *I am going to* **have words with** *you*)!'

head

head for/towards [Vpr] be on a course that leads to (sth); move towards. **o:** London, Spain; trouble, disaster; show-down, clash: *We* **headed for** *Turkey.* BM ○ *'If you go on with him, Jinny, you're* **heading for** *disaster.'* AITC ○ *You're* **heading for** *serious trouble.* TGLY □ in US English: *We were* **headed for** *Turkey/You're* **headed for** *trouble etc.*

head off 1 [Vn ⇆ p pass] (*informal*) reach an important place before sb else, thus giving him important news, preventing him from escaping etc. **O:** enemy, thieves, bandits; stampeding herd, runaway car: *The first thing to be done was to **head off** the enemy from the tender spots and vital places.* MFM ○ *'If you take the next turning to the right, you'll be able to **head** them **off** at the big crossroads.'*

2 [Vn ⇆ p pass] (*informal*) prevent (sb) from moving to a topic that is boring, or embarrassing, by getting him to think about sth else: *This grandfather was slightly easier to deal with, because it was sometimes possible to **head** him **off**; he did have one other topic that interested him — the career of Stanley Matthews.* CON

head up [Vp.n pass] (*informal*) be in charge of (an enterprise); head, direct. **O:** organization, industry, business; government: *Inevitably if you **head up** a business like this you become personally identified with it.* BBCTV ○ (Israeli politics) *Mrs Meir should **head up** a new cabinet with Mr Dayan in some post.* BBCR □ avoided by some speakers (who prefer to use head alone).

heal

heal over [Vp, Vn ⇆ p pass] (cause sth to) close or be sealed, ie with the growth of scar tissue; (cause a quarrel etc to) end or be mended. **S** [Vp], **O** [Vn.p]: cut, wound; rift, breach: *The deep gash in his arm would take weeks to **heal over**.* ○ *With the passage of time the divisions between the two countries have **healed over**.*

heal up [Vp, Vn ⇆ p pass adj] (help sth) become completely better. **S** [Vp], **O** [Vn.p]: wound, sore, cut; leg, arm: *Within a few weeks their feet had **healed up** nicely, and we had no recurrence of the trouble.* DF ○ *I had no more bother with the rash. The swims in salt water must have **healed** it **up**.*

heap

heap on/upon 1 [Vn.pr pass emph rel] place (sth) in heaps on (sth). **O:** food; rice, meat; earth, sand, rock. **o:** tray, plate; bank, slag-tip: *They **heaped** more food **on** my plate* (or: ***heaped** my plate **with** more food) than I could eat.* = pile on/onto 1.

2 [Vn.pr pass emph rel] (*formal*) award or address (sth) to (sb) in abundance. **O:** honours, praise; curses, opprobrium. **o:** guest, explorer; disgraced leader: *He had a deep-rooted dissatisfaction with the world that **heaped** rewards **upon** him.* CD

heap up [Vn ⇆ p pass adj] form (sth) into a heap. **O:** money, coins; clothes, blankets: *Hermes **heaped up** in the stable what meat was left.* GLEG ○ *She wore a huge hat **heaped up** with white roses.* AH = bank up/.

heap with [Vn.pr pass rel] ⇨ heap on/upon 1.

hear

hear about [Vpr emph rel, Vn.pr pass emph rel] receive news or information about (sb/sth). **O:** a lot, a good deal; much, little; nothing, anything: *So this is the pianist we've **heard** so much **about**.* ○ *'Yes, I've **heard about** the restaurant. How good is it?'* = hear of 1.

hear from [Vpr pass rel] receive news, esp a letter, from (sb): *Mother hasn't **heard from** you for quite some time. She's beginning to think you must be ill.* ○ *Until we **hear from** head office we can't give you your permit.* ○ *When the telephone rang, she was quite surprised; she had not expected to **hear from** anyone.* MSAL

hear of 1 [Vpr] receive news or information about (sth). **o:** product, commodity; disappearance, death; : *He was saddened to **hear of** the death of his old friend Chauncy Townshend.* CD = hear about.

2 [Vpr pass] have news of (sb); have reports of the (continuing) existence of (sb): *He disappeared from Europe about a year ago, but the police have been **hearing of** him in South America.* ○ *They started out to cross the Sahara in a saloon car, and have not been **heard of** since.*

3 [Vpr] know of the existence of (sb/sth). **o:** the painter Tissot; a composer called Stanford: *My host asked me if I had **heard of** a painter called John.* GJ ○ *'Do you know Jim Patterson?' 'No, I've never **heard of** him.'*

not hear of [Vpr] refuse to consider or allow (sth). **o:** any such thing, such a thing; his paying, your resigning: *'Smith leave our service after all these years? I wo**n't hear of** such a thing!'* ○ *She would**n't hear of** his sharing in the expenses.* □ neg, with *will/would/could.*

hear out [Vn.p pass] listen to (sb) until he has finished his remarks. **A:** attentively, silently: *The rest of the company **heard** the Astronomer Royal **out** with interest.* TBC ○ *Their chief **heard** them **out**, scowling impressively.* DF

heat

heat up 1 [Vp, Vn ⇆ p pass adj] (cause sth to) become hot, or hotter. **S** [Vp], **O** [Vn.p]: stew, beans; coffee, milk: *'I'll **heat up** some coffee,' said Angela, rising with energetic grace.* SE = warm up 1.

2 [Vp] (*informal*) become more exciting or lively; become excited or intense. **S:** game, match; campaign, struggle; he etc: *With only two weeks to go to polling day, the electoral battle is now really **heating up**.* ○ *He seemed to calm down as quickly as he had **heated up**.* SATS = hot up.

het

het up [pass (Vn.p)] (*informal*) irritated, excited; bothered, annoyed. **A:** all, quite, so, very: *Father seemed terribly **het up** over something last Saturday. What was bothering him?* ○ *We needn't have got so **het up** about it! He **did** say he would like to come and stay with us again.* PW □ used with be, seem, look, sound, get.

heave

heave to [Vp] (*nautical*) come to a standstill, without anchoring or mooring. **S:** skipper, master; (sailing-)ship, clipper, barque: *The frigate fired a warning shot across the privateer's bows to make her **heave to**.* ○ *He **hove to** in the lee of a palm tree.* FL

heave up [Vp, Vn.p] (*informal*) be violently sick; vomit: *John must have been mixing his drinks. I found him **heaving up** in the kitchen.* ○ *Some politicians make you want to **heave up**.* = throw up 2.

hedge

hedge about/around/round [Vn.p pass] restrict or limit (sb), preventing him from acting freely. **S:** control, restriction; problem, difficulty: *Their life was **hedged around** with petty restrictions.* ○ *Starting a small business is **hedged about** with financial and staffing problems.* = hem about/around/round.

hedge in 1 [Vn ⇆ p pass adj] put a hedge around (sth). **O:** garden, field, plot: *These fields were* ***hedged in*** *during my grandfather's time.* ○ *She began to climb the hill to Tilecotes, between the* ***hedged-in*** *gardens.* WI ⇨ fence in 1, wall in 1.
2 [Vn ⇆ p pass adj] restrict the freedom of action of (sb). **S:** regulation, protocol; fear, inhibition: *Custom* ***hedged*** *her* ***in*** *and made her helpless.* WI ○ *He felt* ***hedged in*** *on financial matters.* SC ○ *We were being increasingly* ***hedged in*** *by government controls and restrictions.* = fence in 2, hem in.

heel

heel over [Vp] (esp *nautical*) lean over to one side. **S:** ship, vessel; steamer, ferry; lorry, van: *The boat* ***heeled over*** *in a strong wind blowing up the channel.*

help

help along [Vn.p pass] assist the progress of (sth/sb). **O:** process, development, reaction; things, matters: *The experiment was not* ***helped along*** *by Smith opening a door at the crucial moment.* ○ *Then, to* ***help*** *matters* ***along****, his wife's father offered to pay the deposit on a new house for them.*
help off with [Vn.p.pr pass] help (sb) to remove (a garment). **S:** doorman, valet, flunkey. **O:** guest, visitor. **o:** overcoat, jacket: *'Let me* ***help*** *you* ***off with*** *your coat.'* ↔ help on with.
help on with [Vn.p.pr pass] help (sb) to put on (a garment). **S:** footman, valet. **O:** guest, visitor. **o:** coat, cloak: *He quickly selected the least tatty-looking raincoat, which was Ned's, and began to* ***help*** *me* ***on with*** *it.* CON ○ *The ladies were* ***helped on with*** *their coats and wraps.* ↔ help off with.
help out [Vp, Vn ⇆ p pass] help (sb) to face and overcome a difficulty. **O:** friend, wife, ally. **A:** with the harvest; during the vacation, over Christmas: *The dentist's wife* ***helped out*** *with great pride when the receptionist took her holiday.* MSAL ○ *Janet finished her work and crossed to* ***help*** *May* ***out*** *with hers.* RFW
help to [Vn.pr pass] serve (sb) with (sth). **O:** guest, diner; oneself. **o:** fish, meat, pudding: *The fair-haired sergeant* ***helped*** *himself* ***to*** *one of his own cigarettes.* RFW ○ *'The children should only be* ***helped to*** *pudding when they've eaten all their vegetables.'*

hem

hem about/around/round [Vn.p pass] surround (sb), thus limiting his freedom of movement. **S:** obstacle, problem, difficulty: *His position was precisely the same as it had been before his attempt to face the problems that* ***hemmed*** *him* ***around****.* HD ○ *He felt* ***hemmed about*** *by forces that he was powerless to overcome.* = hedge about/around/round.
hem in [Vn ⇆ p pass adj] restrict the freedom of action of (sb). **S:** enemy; fire, forest, snowdrifts; financial commitments, unhappy relationship: *The man looked round him with the desperate, hunted eyes of an animal* ***hemmed in*** *by a ring of fire.* PW ○ *His marriage had* ***hemmed*** *him* ***in****.* NM = fence in 2, hedge in 2.

herd

herd together [Vp, Vn ⇆ p pass] gather together as, or like, a herd of animals. **S** [Vp], **O** [Vn.p]**:** cattle; prisoners, refugees; guests: *Try to stop the men* ***herding together*** *around the bar.* ○ *The school party was* ***herded together*** *and shepherded on board the ship.*

hew

hew down [Vn ⇆ p pass adj] cut (sth) down with rough chopping blows. **O:** tree, branch: *A line of poplars was* ***hewn down*** *to make way for an ugly parade of shops.* = chop down, hack down.
hew out [Vn ⇆ p pass] form (sth) by cutting with rough chopping blows. **O:** path, entrance; step, ledge: *The climbers used their axes to* ***hew out*** *steps in the ice.*

hide

hide away (in) [Vp nom, Vp.pr emph rel] take cover or shelter (in a place); conceal (oneself) (in a place). **S:** guerrilla, partisan, bandit; escaped convict; deposed ruler. **o:** the mountains, the jungle: *Rather than be taken into captivity, the bulk of the army* ***hid away in*** *the mountains and forests.* ○ *The gang returned to their secret* ***hideaway in*** *the shanty town.*
hide behind [Vn.pr pass] use (sth) as a mask or cover for (embarrassment etc). **O:** nervousness, timidity, embarrassment. **o:** (serious, stern) expression, (awkward, nervous) smile, grin: *She* ***hid*** *her shame* ***behind*** *a nervous smile.*

hinge

hinge on/upon [Vpr emph rel] require that some condition should first be met. **S:** result, success, outcome; everything. **o:** co-operation, response, reaction: *The success of the conference* ***hinges upon*** *a Cabinet decision which is expected at any moment.* ○ *Everything* ***hinged on*** *the speed with which the tanks could complete their flanking movement.* = depend on/upon 4, hang on 4, turn on 4.

hint

hint at [Vpr pass rel] indicate or mention (sth) in a slight or indirect way. **S:** minister, manager, headmaster. **o:** tax reduction, wage standstill, further expansion, far-reaching changes: *In his annual address to the employers' federation, the Minister* ***hinted at*** *an increase in the capital grants for new factories.* ○ *The possibility of an early election was inadvertently* ***hinted at****.*

hire

hire out [Vn ⇆ p pass adj] allow the temporary use of (sth) in return for payment. **S:** sailors; council, parks department. **O:** rowing-boats, canoes; deck chairs, umbrellas: *Punts are usually* ***hired out*** *by the hour.* ○ *Hotel owners* ***hire out*** *changing-cabins and beach umbrellas by the season.* = let out 5.

hiss

hiss off (the stage) [Vn ⇆ p pass, Vn.pr pass] force (sb) to leave the stage by hissing in disapproval. **S:** audience, claque. **O:** actor, singer, dancer: *When he first appeared in a starring role he was* ***hissed off*** *by an unsympathetic audience.* ○ *Several of the French plays he saw were* ***hissed off the stage****.* TU

hit

hit back (at) [Vp, Vp.pr] (*informal*) counter-attack (sth/sb) vigorously; reply with vigour to verbal attacks (eg in the press or on TV). **S:** bomber; tank, gun; government; trades unionist. **o:** airfield; emplacement; critic, opposition; employer: *As soon as an enemy battery opens fire fighter-*

bombers can be ordered into the air to ***hit back****.* ○ *In a speech to party loyalists the Prime Minister* ***hit back at*** *those who 'sought to undermine the Government's fight against inflation'.* = strike back (at).

hit off [Vn.p pass] (*informal*) imitate (sb) successfully: *'You're a natural mimic, my love. You've a gift for* ***hitting*** *people* ***off****.'* GL = take off 15.

hit it off (with) [Vn.p, Vn.p.pr emph rel] (*informal*) enjoy good relations (with sb): *How well do he and his boss* ***hit it off*** (or: *does he* ***hit it off with*** *his boss)?* ○ *I did not know she was suffering like this when we were working together, though I realized we did not quite* ***hit it off****.* SU = get along/on (with) 2.

hit the nail on the head [Vn.pr pass] (*informal*) make a point or interpret a remark precisely. **A:** ⚠ right, squarely: *The report spoke of a period of unfulfilled promise. That* ***hit the nail*** *squarely* ***on the head****.* T ○ *'Not that Ibsen doesn't* ***hit the*** *moral* ***nail on the head****, every time.'* HAA

hit on/upon [Vpr pass] suddenly devise or discover (sth). **o:** scheme, idea, solution: *The committee eventually* ***hit upon*** *a formula that was acceptable to everyone.* ○ *Then an idea was* ***hit upon*** *that seemed the answer to all our problems.*

hit out (at) 1 [Vp, Vp.pr] (*cricket*) attack (the bowling) vigorously. **o:** pace bowling, spin attack: *The opening batsmen seemed reluctant to* ***hit out at*** *the seam bowlers.*

2 [Vp, Vp.pr] (*informal*) make a vigorous attack in the press, on TV etc (against sb or sth). **S:** minister, church leader, trade unionist. **o:** restrictive practices, industrial sabotage; moral laxity; government policy: *He* ***hit out*** *to right and left, assailing the vulgarity of commercial imperialism.* HB ○ (pay rises for Britain's top executives) *The Prime Minister* ***hit out at*** *spectacular increases emerging in the country's boardrooms.*

hitch

hitch up [Vn ⇆ p pass adj] pull up (trousers) at the knees before sitting so as to preserve the crease; pull up (sleeves) to free the hands, etc. **O:** trousers, slacks, pants; shirt-sleeves: *He sat down on a kitchen chair,* ***hitching up*** *his trousers, carefully, as if afraid of destroying a knife-edged crease.* CON ○ *He* ***hitched up*** *his sleeves with a pair of elasticated steel bands.* SATS

hive

hive off [Vp, Vn ⇆ p pass adj] (cause sth to) detach itself and form a separate body. **S** [Vp], **O** [Vn.p]: swarm, colony; department, branch, section. **S** [Vn.p]: beekeeper, farmer; management, planners: *Next year, the biochemistry section will* ***hive off*** *to form an independent department.* ○ *National Power is the larger of the two companies to be* ***hived off*** *from the Central Electricity Generating Board.*

hold

hold against [Vn.pr pass] allow (sth) to affect one's judgement of (sb). **O:** past failings, criminal record; it ... that he's taught abroad; the fact that he's worked for a rival firm: *She* ***held*** *it* ***against*** *me that I took her son away.* AT ○ *The fact that he's let you down once before shouldn't be* ***held against*** *him.* = count against.

hold back 1 [Vn ⇆ p pass] prevent (sth/sb) from advancing; check, restrain. **S:** dam; barrier, fence; police, troops. **O:** river, flood-waters; crowd, mob: *Millions of tons of water are* ***held back*** *by a complex system of dykes.* ○ *The thin cordon of police could do nothing to* ***hold back*** *the crowd; they flooded on to the pitch.* = keep back (from).

2 [Vp] hesitate to act through caution or fear: *Because of the uncertain state of the market, buyers are* ***holding back****.* ○ *She* ***held back****, not knowing what to do or say.* = hang back (from).

3 [Vn ⇆ p pass] prevent (sb) from making progress. **S:** poor education, unpleasant manner, unsuitable background. **O:** candidate, ambitious youth: *John felt that he was* ***held back*** *from further promotion because of his working-class background.* ○ *Now that the end's in sight, nothing can* ***hold*** *him* ***back****.* = keep back 1.

4 [Vn ⇆ p pass] withhold or delay the release or payment of (sth). **S:** government, ministry; state corporation, employer. **O:** information, report; result; increase (in salary), wage award: *The laboratory has been advised to* ***hold back*** *any announcement of its findings.* ○ *There will be sharp resentment if they have their salaries* ***held back*** *for too long.* BBCTV

hold down 1 [Vn ⇆ p pass] keep (sth) at a low level; restrain. **S:** firm, department, school. **O:** wages; costs, prices; numbers; pressure: *More salaries have been* ***held down****.* BBCTV ○ *They were blamed for their failure to* ***hold down*** *expenditure.* SC ○ *Last year we had to* ***hold down*** *student intake because of the cuts in the grants.* OBS = keep down 3.

2 [Vn ⇆ p pass] hold (sth/sb) in submission; repress. **S:** tyrant, dictator; police, army. **O:** country, district; people: *How long can a small force of mercenaries* ***hold down*** *an entire people?* = keep down 4.

hold a/the job down [Vn ⇆ p] (*informal*) (manage to) remain in one job for some length of time. **S:** ex-convict, vagrant: *Many Borstal boys have been unable to* ***hold down a job****.* T ○ *For two whole years, he* ***held down the job*** *of literary columnist* (ie in a newspaper). AF □ often neg; with can/could.

hold (good/true) (for) [Vpr] apply (in the case of sb/sth), be valid (for sth/sb). **S:** remark, statement; promise, guarantee, undertaking; warning: *This is a reproach which* ***holds good*** *to this day.* JUNG ○ *The same requirement* ***holds good for*** *any applicant wishing to study natural sciences.* ○ *'What I have said* ***holds*** *as much* ***for*** *houses to rent as* ***for*** *houses to buy.'*

hold no brief for [Vn.pr emph rel] (*formal*) not support (sth/sb); feel no sympathy for (sb). **adj:** no, (not) any, little. **o:** system, government; violence, disruption; anarchist, pacifist: *'You do****n't hold any brief for*** *him?' 'I don't know. Maybe he was sincere.'* PP ○ *'Don't look surprised. You know I* ***hold no brief for*** *people with extreme views.'*

hold no fears/terrors for [Vn.pr emph rel] ⇨ have no fears/terrors for.

hold forth [Vp] speak pompously, as if one's hearers were an audience, and at some length. **S:** commentator, pundit, critic, teacher. **A:** at (great, considerable, some) length: *Newby was* ***holding forth*** *to a small knot of admirers.* BLCH ○ *Paula introduced the carpenter, and* ***held forth*** *at great length on his prowess, personality, and intelligence.* DF

hold in [Vn ⇆ p pass adj] restrain or check (sth). **O:** emotions; resentment, frustration: *Eventually these feelings could be* ***held in*** *no longer; there were outbreaks of violence everywhere.* = keep in 4.

hold in high/low esteem/regard [Vn.pr pass emph rel] (*formal*) feel considerable/little respect for (sb/sth). **O:** president, official; office, post; degree, diploma; skill, craftsmanship: *Not that the Land Dayaks resent European authority. They* ***hold*** *it* ***in*** *the* ***highest regard****.* NDN ○ ***In*** *such* ***high esteem*** *is the university* ***held*** *that the number of applicants greatly exceeds the available places.* □ the combination low regard is unusual.

hold off 1 [Vp] be delayed, not occur; delay, restrain oneself. **S:** rain, storm, winter; enemy: *The monsoon* ***held off*** *for a month; then the rain fell in torrents.* ○ *The Nationalists had* ***held off*** *while their troops rested and reinforcements arrived.*
2 [Vn ⇆ p pass] prevent (sb) from defeating oneself. **S:** beleaguered garrison; goalkeeper; celebrity, hero; government. **O:** attackers; forwards; press, fans; inflation, unemployment: *For several days a small force* ***held off*** *the attacks of a numerically superior enemy.* ○ *He's been* ***holding*** *her* ***off*** *for years, but sooner or later he'll have to give in.* = keep at bay.

hold on 1 [Vp] (*informal*) wait, pause. **A:** a second, a minute: *'Just* ***hold on*** *a second while I get my breath back.'* ○ *'Tell him to* ***hold on*** *a minute: I haven't written down a single word he's said.'* □ often imperative. = hang on 1.
2 [Vp] stay in an exposed or dangerous position; stand firm in the face of danger. **S:** surrounded troops, shipwrecked sailors; government: *The party cut off by the tide were told to* ***hold on****; help would soon reach them.* ○ *At the height of the financial crisis, all they could do was* ***hold on*** *and hope that conditions would improve.* = hang on 2.
3 [Vn ⇆ p pass] fasten (sth); keep (sth) in position. **S:** glue; pin, bar; clasp, buckle. **O:** knob; medal, brooch; strap: *The soles of his shoes were just* ***held on*** *by a few stitches.* ○ *Use special adhesive for this job: ordinary glue won't* ***hold*** *the handle* ***on****.*

hold on to 1 [Vp.pr pass] keep grasping (sth), not let it go. **o:** rope; branch, root: *'Don't panic; just* ***hold on to*** *that rock and I'll come and fetch you down.'* ○ *He was* ***holding on to*** *a window-ledge for dear life when the fireman got to him.*
2 [Vp.pr pass] (*informal*) not give or sell (sth) to sb else; keep, retain. **o:** advantage, lead; property, shares: *It's not enough to take over the lead; we must* ***hold on to*** *it!* ○ *She had a few shares in Babcock and Wilcox Boilermakers, which she* ***held on to*** *for forty years.* SU = hang on to.

hold out 1 [Vp] resist in the face of physical force or moral pressure; hold firm, stand fast. **S:** force, defence: *From a purely military point of view, the* ***holding out*** *in North Africa once the Mareth Line had been broken through could never be justified.* MFM ○ *Jane is quietly but resolutely* ***holding out*** *against Mrs Elton's planning for her employment.* JA
2 [Vp] last, remain. **S:** stocks, supplies, rations: *We can stay here for as long as our supplies of food and water* ***hold out****.* = last out 1.
3 [Vp.n pass] offer (sth). **O:** ⚠ (the) hope, prospect, possibility: *Radio astronomy investigations seem to* ***hold out*** *the best hopes of obtaining such proof.* NS ○ *The prospect of a further reduction in interest rates was* ***held out*** *by the Chancellor speaking in the City yesterday.*

hold out for [Vp.pr rel] deliberately delay reaching an agreement in the hope that one can get more. **S:** politician, trades union leader, negotiating team. **o:** greater concessions, the full amount; granting of one's demands: *Mr Smith rejected one splendid deal and is now* ***holding out for*** *the lot.* G ○ *Magazine pay was mostly low, and Thackeray was not at first in a position to* ***hold out for*** *good terms.* TU = stand out for, stick out for. ⇨ hold out 1.

hold out (on) [Vp, Vp.pr pass] (*informal*) refuse to yield or surrender (to sb). **S:** dealer, seller, owner. **o:** customer, buyer: *'He's an obstinate old fool; he insisted in* ***holding out****, partly from sentiment, and partly from conceit. So we've busted him.'* ASA ○ *'The little minx, she's been* ***holding out on*** *me. She with her delusions of grandeur.'* DC ⇨ hold out 1.

hold over [Vn.p pass adj] defer or postpone (sth). **S:** committee, council. **O:** question, matter; decision, vote: *The final item on the agenda will be* ***held over*** *until our next meeting.* ⇨ stand over 2.

hold to 1 [Vpr pass adj rel] not abandon or change (sth). **o:** choice, decision; course of action; principles, beliefs: *We shall* ***hold*** *firmly* ***to*** *what has already been agreed.* ○ *One obstacle to a settlement is the strongly* ***held-to*** *conviction that the employers have already decided to close the factory.* = adhere to 2, keep to 2, stick to 2.
2 [Vn.pr pass rel] make (sb) keep or be faithful to (sth). **o:** promise, guarantee, assurance; offer, proposal: *'You can have the car when I go abroad.' 'I'll* ***hold*** *you* ***to*** *that.'* ○ *One promise* ***to*** *which they must be* ***held*** *is that there will be no more staff redundancies.*

not hold a candle to [Vn.pr] (*informal*) not (be able to) match or emulate (sb/ sb's achievements). **S:** industry, transport; organization, set-up; method, process. **o:** rival, competitor: *In speed and efficiency of delivery we ca****n't hold a candle to*** *our European competitors.* ○ *'What about Arsenal's chances for the Cup?' 'They ca****n't hold a candle to*** *Liverpool.'* □ with can/could.

hold together [Vp, Vn ⇆ p pass] remain united; unite (sth/sb). **S** [Vp], **O** [Vn.p]**:** country, political party; membership, followers: *The Party has* ***held together*** *wonderfully during the current crisis.* ○ *What has* ***held*** *the Christian Democrats* ***together****?* SC = stick together.

hold under [Vn.p pass] hold (sb) in submission; suppress. **S:** regime, dictatorship; police, troops. **O:** (subject, colonial) people, race: *The country is* ***held under*** *by appeals to patriotism, some economic inducement, and, where necessary, force.* = keep under 3.

hold up 1 [Vn ⇆ p nom pass adj] delay or halt (sth). **S:** strike, working to rule; flooding, landslide; narrow road, pressure of traffic. **O:** production, delivery; traffic, travellers: (headline) *Rugby League: Cup Final* ***held up*** *by crowd trouble.* IND ○ (headline) *Industry hit by docks* ***holdup****.* G ○ *'What's the* ***hold-up****? We're usually on our way by now.'* BBCTV ○ *The worst road* ***hold-ups*** *were on the A74 Glasgow to Carlisle road.* SC □ in current usage nom form is usu hold-up — with a hyphen.

2 [Vn ⇆ p nom pass] force (sb) by the threat of violence to hand over money or valuables. **S:** gang, bandit. **O:** bank, post-office; coach, train: *Masked men* **held up** *a wages van in South London.* ○ *After the* **holdup**, *the gang got away in a fast car.* □ in current usage nom is holdup — without a hyphen. = stick up 2.

hold up as an example [Vn.p.pr pass] offer (sb) as a model (of conduct, success etc) to be imitated: *I wish they'd stop* **holding up** *the older boy* **as an example** *to emulate: it's bad for the younger one's confidence.*

hold up to ridicule/scorn [Vn.pr pass] mock or scorn (sb/sth) and try to make others do the same. **O:** colleague, associate; values, standards; work, achievement: *It's common to hear socialism* **held up to ridicule**. *The fall of communism in Europe has led to a disenchantment with all parties of the left.*

(not) hold with [Vpr] (*informal*) (not) support or favour (sth). **o:** plan, scheme, idea; blood sports; socialism; religion: *I do***n't hold with** *laxatives. Never have.* OD ○ *'Why did you enter* (for the contest) *if you do***n't hold with** *it?'* CON □ hardly ever positive except when used in questions. = approve (of).

hold one's own (with) [Vn.pr emph rel] be able to compete successfully or on equal terms (with sb). **S:** industry, factory; worker, designer; athlete, footballer; soldier. **o:** anyone, everybody; opposition, competition: *Scottish teams cannot* **hold their own with** *the best in Europe.* SC ○ *Those who liked champagne were able to* **hold their own with** *those who preferred whisky.* RM

hole

hole out [Vp] (*golf*) sink the ball in the hole: *A young man sees no reason why he should not* **hole out** *and, in his ignorance, he does so more often than most. If he retains his faith in his ability to* **hole out** *then he remains a good putter.* OBS

hole up [Vp, pass (Vn.p)] (informal) go into hiding, esp from the police. **S:** terrorists, gangsters: *He'd* **holed up** *at a local motel.* BBCTV ○ *They now believe the gang is* **holed up** *somewhere in Melbourne, but so far have few clues to work on.* G ○ *'The Patriots'* (a play) *is about a couple of IRA bombers* **holed up** *in North London, the terror and destruction they cause.* TES □ holed up may be used after a noun (third example).

home

home in (on) 1 [Vp, Vp.pr rel] locate (a signal) and be directed by it to a destination. **S:** aircraft, spacecraft. **o:** (radar) beam; signal, impulse: *In fog, or at night, an approaching aircraft will* **home in on** *a radar beam and be guided to its destination.* □ also home onto.

2 [Vp, Vp.pr rel] think of or deal with one thing in particular. **S:** speaker; debate, discussion. **o:** issue, problem; housing, hospital provision, education: *What we need to do is* **home in on** *the problems of our larger cities.* BBCR = concentrate (on/upon), focus (on).

hook

hook up [Vn ⇆ p pass] fasten (a garment) by means of 'hooks and eyes'. **O:** dress; girl: *Her evening dress had to be* **hooked up** *at the back — a much slower process than zipping it up.* ○ *'Do you mind* **hooking** *me* **up**?' *she said.* ⇨ zip up.

hook-up/hooked up [nom pass (Vn.p)] linking of/linked by radio or TV stations to transmit the same programme: *There was a nation-wide* **hook-up** *to carry the President's state of the Union message.* ○ *I* (a BBC radio presenter) *will be in Brussels for an important Council meeting, and Brian will be in London,* **hooked up** *to the rest of the world.* BBCR

hoot

hoot off [Vn.p pass, Vn.pr pass] force (sb), with hoots of disapproval, to leave or stop speaking. **S:** audience, public. **O:** actor, speaker. **o:** the stage, the platform: *Whenever the Minister tries to explain his policies in public he's* **hooted off** *the platform.* ⇨ hiss off.

hop

hop off [Vp] (*informal*) leave, go away: *'***Hop off** *before you get a thick ear.'* ○ *'If you see anyone hanging around here tell them to* **hop off**.' □ usu imperative. = clear off.

hope

hope (for) [Vpr pass adj rel] hope that sth will take place, be granted etc. **o:** change, improvements; success, victory; reduction, easing (of tension, strife): *The suitable marriage her family was* **hoping for** *soon took place.* TU ○ *The best one could* **hope for** *was to attract no attention either way.* SU ○ *Where is the* **hoped-for** *takeover by a moderate administration?* G

hope for the best [Vpr] hope that all will end well: *I don't know how the negotiations will go. All we can do is sit back and* **hope for the best**. ○ *Virginia knew that Ella came to see Joe; but there was nothing she could do about it, except* **hope for the best**. AITC

horn

horn in (on) [Vp, Vp.pr pass] (*informal*) by cunning or force get oneself into a situation which seems profitable. **S:** trader, publisher, writer. **o:** deal, racket, market: *They had come up for the day with no other motive than to* **horn in on** *Myra's second wedding* (ie attend the party uninvited). CON ○ *Mike started planning my campaign like a Desert General who hasn't yet* **horned in on** *the memoir racket* (ie made money from writing his war memoirs). JFTR = muscle in (on).

horse

horse about/around [Vp] (*informal*) play about in a noisy, clumsy way; engage in horseplay: *There was a certain amount of* **horsing about** *in the dressing-room after the game was over.* = lark about/around.

hose

hose down [Vn ⇆ p nom pass] wash (sth) from top to bottom with water from a hose. **O:** car, shop-front, window: *The Indian woman was* **hosing down** *a glowing threadbare carpet that she'd spread across the sidewalk.* AT ○ *I give the car a good* **hose down** *every Sunday morning.* □ no hyphen in nom form.

hot

hot up [Vp] (*informal*) intensify, increase. **S:** struggle, contest; trade, business: *Competition in the*

British sea cruise market is ***hotting up*** *visibly after the successful launching of the Travel Savings Association.* T = heat up 2.

hound

hound out/out of [Vn.p pass, Vn.pr pass] (*informal*) force (sb) to leave (sth), often by means of a conspiracy to damage his good name etc. **S:** envious colleague, political rival. **o:** job, Cabinet post, office: *Do you want to get me* ***hounded out of*** *the Civil Service altogether?* SML ○ *By digging up a few unsavoury details about his private life they managed to have him* ***hounded out****.*

howl

howl down [Vn.p pass] prevent (sb) from being heard by shouting scornfully. **S:** crowd, audience. **O:** speaker: *The guest speaker was* ***howled down****, and it was some time before the chairman could restore order.* = shout down.

huddle

huddle together [Vp, pass (Vn.p)] move or press close together for warmth or protection; pressed close together. **S:** sheep, cattle; children, refugees: *The children* ***huddled together*** *on a pile of old sacks.*

hum

hum with [Vpr] be in a state of intense activity. **S:** factory, classroom, kitchen. **o:** life, activity: *The mill is very streamlined, scientific, and it fairly* ***hums with*** *wheels.* WI

hunger

hunger for [Vpr emph rel] desire to have (sth) strongly. **o:** news, information; (new) experience, change; excitement, sensation: *He* ***hungered for*** *experience outside his narrow, circumscribed world.* ○ *She behaved as if to expect or* ***hunger for*** *anything else were quite simply beneath her dignity.* MSAL = long for.

hunt

hunt down [Vn ⇆ p pass] pursue and find (sb). **S:** police, guard, tracker dog. **O:** escaped prisoner, criminal: *Whitehall felt it necessary to* ***hunt down*** *and jail one of its employees for disclosing that the missiles were arriving.* G

hunt out [Vn ⇆ p pass] search for and find sth that was previously used and has been put away. **O:** documents, clothes, family photographs: *I've packed my suitcase, but I've still got to* ***hunt out*** *my passport'.* ○ *I've got the application form for you somewhere, but it'll need a bit of* ***hunting out****.*

hunt up (in) [Vn ⇆ p pass, Vn.p.pr pass rel] search for (sth/sb) (in a place). **S:** scholar, research worker; visitor. **O:** reference, quotation, detail; friend, contact. **o:** library, archives; dictionary, atlas; town: *He had little inclination to* ***hunt up*** *his friends.* TU ○ *He's* ***hunting up*** *details of Elizabethan household expenditure* ***in*** *a document of the time.*

hurl

hurl (at) 1 [Vn.pr pass emph rel] throw (sth) violently (at sb). **O:** spear, stone; oneself. **o:** troops, police: *The streets were littered with stones and bottles* ***hurled at*** *the soldiers.* ○ *The full-back* ***hurled*** *himself full length* ***at*** *the man's legs.*

2 [Vn.pr pass emph rel] direct (sth) (at sb) in a sudden, violent way. **O:** taunt. jibe; insult, curse. **o:** prisoner, captive; servant, pupil: *In a sudden fit of rage he began* ***hurling*** *insults and accusations* ***at*** *his partners.* = fling (at).

hurry

hurry up [Vp, Vn.p pass] (cause sb/sth to) move or act more quickly: *'I wish the bus would* ***hurry up*** *and come; I've been waiting here for hours.'* ○ *'****Hurry*** *those children* ***up****!'* ○ *The estate agent seems helpful enough, but he needs* ***hurrying up****.*

hush

hush up [Vn ⇆ p nom pass] prevent (a crime, error, etc) from becoming known. **O:** official blunder, criminal behaviour; matter, thing; it (all); loss, theft: *You can't* ***hush*** *a thing like this* ***up****.* EM ○ *It'd all be* ***hushed up****.* NM ○ *Much of the credit goes to Geoffrey Howe's refusal to connive in a bureaucratic* ***hush-up****.* OBS = cover up (for).

I

ice

ice over [Vp] become covered with ice. **S:** lake, pond, pool, river; road: *When a road* ***ices over*** *it can be extremely dangerous, because drivers may mistake the coating of ice for dampness.* ○ *The children were delighted to find that the pond had* ***iced over*** *during the night; perhaps, after all, they would be able to try out their new skates.* = freeze over.

ice up [Vp, Vn ⇆ p pass] be covered with ice and be unworkable or unusable because of it; cover (sth) with ice and make it unworkable etc. **S** [Vp], **O** [Vn.p]**:** wings, machinery, rigging; fridge, lock: *The superstructure of the boat had* ***iced up*** *during the night, putting it in danger of capsizing.* ○ *The flying spray had* ***iced up*** *every inch of the deck and bridge.* = freeze up.

identify

identify with 1 [Vpr emph rel] find one's own feelings reflected in or in some way represented by (sb); take (sb) as a model. **o:** character (in a play); father, teacher: *One of the dominant themes in his psychology was his willingness to* ***identify with*** *heroes.* F ○ *I found the play totally unsatisfactory: there wasn't a single character* ***with*** *whom I could* ***identify****.*

2 [Vn.pr pass emph rel] accept (sb/sth) as representing one's ideas, intentions etc. **O:** army, military commander; central government, party, movement, revolution; oneself. **o:** progress, the forces of reaction: *The Governor refused to* ***identify*** *himself* ***with*** *the policies of the Central Government.* ○ *The university authorities are* ***identified*** *in the students' minds* ***with*** *the government's cost-cutting programme.* □ often passive.

idle

idle about/around [Vp, Vpr] spend one's time idly; not do anything energetic. **S:** young man, lazy fellow, unoccupied soldiers: *John's the energetic sort who can't bear to see others* ***idling about*** *when he's working.* ○ *Fred was just* ***idling around*** *the place for most of the weekend. I'm sure it* *makes his father furious.* = laze about/around, loiter about/around.

idle one's/the time away [Vn ⇆ p] pass the time in an idle or wasteful way, whether voluntarily or not. **S:** soldier, student: *The troops had nothing to do but* ***idle the time away*** *while waiting for ships to come and take them off the beaches.* ○ *In Paris he* ***idled away his time*** *with expatriate friends and relatives.* TU

imbue

imbued with [pass (Vn.pr)] (*formal*) having a good deal of (sth), filled with (sth). **o:** a desire to do good; a driving ambition; patriotism; hatred of ignorance and superstition: *The true scientist is* ***imbued with*** *the desire to discover something new about man and his environment.* □ also used after *appear*, etc and after a noun: *What the generals are looking for are men* ***imbued with*** *the fighting spirit.* □ active occasionally used.

immerse

immerse (oneself) in [Vn.pr pass emph rel] involve (oneself) so fully in (sth) that one is hardly aware of anything else. **o:** work, sport; book, newspaper: *For six months, he* ***immersed himself in*** *detailed planning.* ○ *In the study, I found Mr Johnson fully* ***immersed in*** *his writing, as usual.*

immersed in [pass (Vn.pr)] placed below the surface of (sth), usu for a long time. **S:** one's head; clothes. **o:** liquid, water: (Archimedes' Principle) *When a body is* ***immersed in*** *a fluid it apparently loses weight.* ○ *To prepare for his attempt to reach the North Pole, Sir Ranulph Fiennes* ***immersed*** *himself for long periods* ***in*** *an ice cold bath.* T □ active occasionally used, as shown.

immure

immure in [Vn.pr pass emph rel] (*formal* or *jocular*) shut (oneself/sb) away in (part of) a building. **O:** himself; his daughter. **o:** attic, study; convent: *Old Silas had* ***immured*** *himself* ***in*** *the attic, never going out from one year's end to the next.* ○ *He would probably have been* ***immured in*** *some convent of holy monks.* BLCH

impale

impale on [Vn.pr pass emph rel] stick (sb/sth) on the end of (sth). **O:** victim; tyrant; child. **o:** pole, spear, spiked shaft: *In 'Lord of the Flies', the children* ***impaled*** *a pig's head* ***on*** *a spear.* ○ *After the Restoration of the monarchy, it is said that Cromwell's head was* ***impaled on*** *a pole and displayed to the public.*

impart

impart to 1 [Vn.pr pass emph rel] (*formal*) pass (sth) on to (sb). **O:** information, news; secret, confidence; fervour, zeal: *He was not willing to divulge information* ***imparted to*** *him in confidence by colleagues.* ○ *Among Mr Jones's ardent disciples was Maria Lewis, whose enthusiasm was* ***imparted to*** *her young pupil Mary Anne Evans.* GE **2** [Vn.pr pass emph rel] (*formal*) give (sth) to (sth). **O:** movement, spin; a semblance of order, an aura of authenticity: *The batsman completely failed to realize that strong leg-spin had been* ***imparted to*** *the ball.* ○ *The presence of leading Conservatives* ***imparted*** *an air of drama* ***to*** *what was otherwise a routine local meeting.*

impel

impel to [Vn.pr pass emph rel] (*formal*) drive (sb) to (do sth), sometimes against his wishes or inclinations. **o:** firm measures, drastic steps, greater efforts: *The feeling that the moment was ripe for action* ***impelled*** *the Party* ***to*** *still greater efforts.* ○ *The extreme measures* ***to*** *which the Cabinet was* ***impelled*** *by rapidly rising inflation made the government extremely unpopular.* □ the verb can also be followed by an inf with the same meaning as the prep phrase: *The Cabinet was* ***impelled to*** *extreme measures* (or: ***impelled to take*** *extreme measures*).

impinge

impinge on/upon [Vpr emph rel] (*formal*) affect (sb/sth) in some way; strike, touch. **o:** group, class; life, routine; consciousness, awareness: *She described historical events as they* ***impinged on*** *a particular group in Ireland — the gentry of north-east County Cork.* EB ○ *In his sleepy state, the noise of a car driving up to the door hardly* ***impinged upon*** *his consciousness.*

implant

implant (in) [Vn.pr pass emph rel] put (an idea or feeling) (in sb), in such a way that it is not easily removed. **O:** idea, notion; desire, terror, fear. **o:** mind; them: *Milton* ***implanted in*** *his daughters a great fear of, if not respect for, their father.* ○ *The revolutionary leaders* ***implanted in*** *the peasants the determination to take and own the land on which they worked.* = inculcate (in), instil (in,into).

implicate

implicate (in) [Vn.pr pass emph rel] (*formal*) cause (sb) to be involved (in an illegal or immoral activity). **O:** others; colleague, workmate. **o:** crime; murder, fraud; plot, scandal: *'His own part in the affair is bad enough, but his attempts to* ***implicate*** *his partners* ***in*** *it is beneath contempt.'* ○ *He was deeply* ***implicated in*** *the affair of the missing diamonds* (ie He shared the responsibility for their disappearance). □ also used after *appear*, etc or after a noun.

import

import (from) (into) [Vn.pr pass emph rel] bring (sth) (from one country, culture, language etc) (to another). **O:** transistors, cotton goods, cars; drugs, cannabis; cholera; fashions: *Excise officers have detained a young couple suspected of trying to* ***import*** *heroin* ***from*** *the Far East.* ○ *In many countries there are people who would like to prevent foreign words being* ***imported into*** *their language.* ↔ export (from) (to).

impose

impose (on) [Vn.pr pass emph rel] (*formal*) place (sth) (on sth/sb). **O:** tax, levy, duty; purchase tax, value added tax (VAT); task, burden, obligation: *The government would not dare to* ***impose*** *taxes* ***on*** *such necessities as bread or milk.* ○ *I am sorry to* ***impose*** *a new burden* ***on*** *you so soon after your illness, but there is no one else capable of doing the work.* ○ *He spoke of the handicaps* ***imposed on*** *Jesuit missions in China and India.* CF = put on 6.

impose on/upon [Vpr pass] (*formal*) obtain a favour from (sb), esp by using undue pressure. **o:** a generous, kind person; his generosity, kindness, good nature: *'You shouldn't be so generous towards people who come asking you for money. You're allowing yourself to be* **imposed on***!'* ○ *'Could I possibly* **impose upon** *you for a little help with this letter? I don't quite know how to phrase it without causing offence.'*

impose oneself/one's company on/upon [Vn.pr rel] (*formal*) inconvenience or annoy (sb) by one's presence: *As there was no train until the late evening he had to* **impose himself on** *his hosts for longer than he had intended.* ○ *The outing was ruined by a drunken tourist who* **imposed his company on** *us.*

impress

impress on/upon [Vn.pr pass emph rel] in saying or writing sth to sb, try to stress or fix (some aspect) in (his mind). **O:** the importance of sth, the need to do sth, the desirability of doing sth; his parting words: *They* **impressed on** *their children the importance of getting good marks in English and maths.* ○ **On** *all the witnesses the judge* **impressed** *the necessity of saying everything they knew about the movements of the accused.* ⇨ impress with.

impress (itself) on/upon [Vn.pr pass emph rel] become firmly set or fixed in (sb's mind). **S:** fact, circumstance; remark, utterance; figure, statistic. **o:** mind, consciousness; audience, gathering: *It was extraordinary how many details simultaneously* **impressed themselves on** *Dalgliesh's mind.* TFD

impress (with) [Vn.pr pass] make (sb) feel positively or favourably (because of some quality one has). **o:** her strong character; beauty, intelligence, learning, gaiety, ingenuity, resilience: *The girl* **impressed** *her boyfriend's family* **with** *her liveliness and sense of humour.* ○ *The spectators were greatly* **impressed with** (or: **by**) *the jockey's skill in controlling a difficult mount.*

impress with [Vn.pr pass] fix in (sb's mind) (a particular need etc). **o:** the need for secrecy; the urgency, importance (of the task): *The project manager* **impressed** *the research team* **with** *the importance* (or: **impressed upon** *the research team the importance*) *of keeping accurate records.* ○ *I want to* **impress** *this fellow* **with** *the fact that I am not acting alone in this matter.* RM ⇨ impress on/upon.

improve

improve on [Vpr pass] produce sth of a better standard or quality than (sth else); do better than (sth). **S:** athlete; candidate; artist; hairdresser. **o:** previous best time, performance; earlier attempt; early work; nature: *All the women swimmers have* **improved on** *their previous best performances.* ○ *'We've done very well this year, but I'm sure the sales figures can be* **improved on** *still further.'*

impute

impute to [Vn.pr pass emph rel] (*formal*) consider or claim that (sth) is the fault of (sth/sb). **O:** failure, accident, debacle. **o:** inattentiveness, idleness, incompetence: *Never one to see his own weaknesses, he had no hesitation in* **imputing** *the failure of his marriage* **to** *his wife's shortcomings.* ○ *No insincerity can be* **imputed to** *him for a seemingly casual response to their call.* ss = ascribe to, attribute to 1.

incarcerate

incarcerate (in) [Vn.pr pass emph rel] (*formal* or *jocular*) imprison (sb) (in a place). **o:** dungeon, cell; convent, house in the country: *Allied prisoners with a record of escape attempts were* **incarcerated in** *Colditz castle, a bleak German fortress from which escape seemed impossible.*

inch

inch (one's way) across, along, back, etc [Vp, Vpr emph rel, Vn.p, Vn.pr emph rel] move carefully across etc inch by inch: *We* **inched our way across** *a fallen tree spanning the stream.* ○ *Jeff* **inched his way along** *the window-ledge.* ⇨ edge (one's way) across etc.

incite

incite to [Vn.pr pass] encourage or urge (sb) to participate in (sth). **o:** crime; murder, mutiny, rebellion: **Inciting** *others* **to** *violence is a serious criminal offence.* ○ *Their punishment was all the more severe because they had* **incited** *other normally well-behaved inmates* **to** *defiance of the prison authorities.*

incline

incline forward [Vp] lean towards sth or sb: *As the old lady's voice grew weaker, her solicitor* **inclined forward** *in an attempt to catch her last words.*

incline to [Vpr, Vn.pr pass] (*formal*) tend to support or accept (sth); tend to develop. **S** [Vpr], **O** [Vn.pr]: court, jury; assessor, examiner. **S** [Vn.pr]: evidence, observation. **o:** view, opinion: *'I've listened to all your arguments in favour of releasing the prisoner, but I'm afraid that I still* **incline to** (or: *am* **inclined to**) *the opposite view. He will go to prison for three months.'* ○ *The screen idol of the 1930s* **inclined to** *plumpness in his later years.*

incline towards 1 [Vpr emph rel] bend or lean in the direction of (sth/sb). **o:** speaker, chairman; platform: *As the noise outside the hall increased we all* **inclined towards** *the speaker, straining to catch every word.*

2 [Vpr emph rel, Vn.pr pass emph rel] (cause sb to) support or favour (an action, cause etc). **o:** radical solutions; an immediate response; communism, liberal democracy: *There are clear signs that the party is* **inclining towards** *more liberal policies.*

include

include among [Vn.pr pass emph rel] name or specify (sb/sth) as one of (a category). **O:** friend, uncle; film-star, pop-singer; Greek; playing the tuba. **o:** the missing; guests, acquaintances; his talents: *Two of my closest friends were* **included among** *those reported missing after the raid.* ○ **Among** *John's talents was* **included** *the ability to tell you the name of any footballer playing in the First Division.*

include (in) [Vn.pr pass emph rel] treat or consider (sth/sb) as part (of sth). **O:** tools, supply of spare parts; latest composition; difficult questions; me. **o:** purchase price; concert; examination; list of contributors: *Are the books* **included in** *the sale of the bookcase, or are they a separate lot?* ○ *Harrington* **included** *the gentry* **in** *his 'nobility', but historians of the 1940s and 1950s often dis-*

tinguished between the two. SHOE □ Sam Goldwyn, a Hollywood film magnate, when invited to take part in something of which he did not approve, exclaimed 'Include me out!'.

incorporate

incorporate (in/into) [Vn.pr pass emph rel] make (sth) a part or feature (of sth). **O:** new ideas, theories, proposals; methods, processes; subsidiary companies. **o:** article, book, plan, thesis; scheme, project; main organization: *The Government has* ***incorporated in*** *the Bill many of the suggestions put forward by the Opposition* (cf *The Bill* ***incorporates*** *many of the suggestions* etc). ○ *Much of Freud's work ... had become* ***incorporated into*** *the accepted order of things even before his death.* F

inculcate

inculcate (in) [Vn.pr pass emph rel] (*formal*) establish or fix (sth) (in sb) by example, precept and repetition. **O:** principles; duty, respect, obedience; understanding. **o:** disciple, follower, pupil: *He undoubtedly* ***inculcated*** *a thorough knowledge of Scripture* ***in*** *his youngest son.* MRJ = implant (in), instil (in/into).

indoctrinate

indoctrinate (with) [Vn.pr pass emph rel] (*formal*) deliberately teach (sb) to hold certain views, attitudes etc, possibly using methods that leave the person unable to resist, or to maintain opposite ideas. **o:** Catholicism; Communism, Socialism: *It was clear that our guests had been* ***indoctrinated with*** *some strange notion that the end of the world would come in the year 2000.* ○ *It is against the Geneva Convention for prisoners to be* ***indoctrinated with*** *ideas alien to their culture and cherished beliefs.*

induce

induce (in) [Vn.pr pass emph rel] (*physics, formal*) cause (sth) to enter (sth). **O:** current, magnetism; certain attitudes. **o:** wire, filings; the mind: *it is a simple matter to* ***induce*** *magnetism* ***in*** *an iron bar, given the necessary equipment.* ○ *Perhaps a new morality can be* ***induced in*** *those* (people) *... one that puts care for their fellow men and women above political expediency.* IND

indulge

indulge in [Vpr pass rel] allow oneself to have or enjoy (sth). **o:** an occasional glass of wine, a Mediterranean cruise, the luxury of a sauna bath; criticism of others: *One thing was to go to a certain bank ... where four times the official rate in Turkish currency was to be had for the asking. ... Why should Syrian bankers, most worldly of men,* ***indulge in*** *such philanthropy?* BM ○ *On Sunday afternoons, Joe would* ***indulge in*** *a short sleep in his armchair.*

infatuated

infatuated (with) [pass (Vn.pr)] strongly attracted (to sb); foolishly affected (by sth). **o:** younger woman, older man; self-esteem: *He was profoundly and physically* ***infatuated with*** *her.* MLT ○ *When a man becomes passionately* ***infatuated with*** *a commonplace girl, his friends may say to each other, 'What can he see in her?'* JUNG □ used after *appear* etc, or after a noun: *It is impossible to reason with a man so* ***infatuated with*** *his own importance as your brother.*

infect

infect (with) [Vn.pr pass rel] give or pass (a disease) (to sb); cause (sb) to behave or feel in a similar way (to oneself). **O:** water; air; him, others. **o:** disease, cholera; germs; good humour, enthusiasm; need, desire: *Some of the refugees were suffering from cholera and it was not long before they had* ***infected*** *the drinking-supply* ***with*** *the bacteria.* ○ *During an epidemic of influenza the air in trains and buses quickly becomes* ***infected with*** *germs.* ○ *The whole class was* ***infected with*** *the teacher's enthusiasm for the subject.* □ often passive.

infer

infer from [Vn.pr pass emph rel] (*formal*) draw (a conclusion) from (sth). **O:** pattern, picture; that something had happened. **o:** his behaviour; your comments; the reports I have heard: *It would be wrong to* ***infer from*** *this that she had no interest in, or awareness of, the larger society.* JA ○ *Reconstructions of significant events in his life ... were* ***inferred from*** *his actions.* 50MH = deduce (from).

infiltrate

infiltrate into [Vpr emph rel, Vn.pr pass emph rel] (cause sb/sth to) enter (sth) in a furtive, secretive way; (cause sb to) pass into (sth) in small numbers or quantities. **S** [Vpr], **O** [Vn.pr]**:** troops, spies, agents; ideas: *A company might* ***infiltrate*** *two or three men* ***into*** *a rival's Research and Development unit, and so be kept informed of everything that went on.* ○ *If only a handful of commandos could* ***infiltrate into*** (or: *be* ***infiltrated into***) *the enemy's defences, the attack might have a good chance of success.*

inflict

inflict on/upon [Vn.pr pass emph rel] cause (sb) to suffer or undergo (sth). **O:** wound; irreparable damage; defeat; a long recital. **o:** him etc; country, city; enemy; drug smuggler; captive audience: *In the four days of carnage that followed ... millions of rupees worth of damage was* ***inflicted on*** *Sikh businesses and homes.* IND ○ *Most of us are wounded and indeed defeated by the wounds* ***inflicted upon*** *us.* CF

inform

inform against/on [Vpr pass] betray (sb) to his enemies, the police etc. **o:** one's friends, comrades, fellow-conspirators: *The IRA* (Irish Republican Army) *deals ruthlessly with anyone who* ***informs on*** *one of its members.*

infringe

infringe on/upon [Vpr pass emph rel] affect (sb) in such a way that his freedom is restricted. **o:** rights, privileges; freedom; domain, area of responsibility: *There was concern that our right to join a trade union was being* ***infringed upon***.

infuse

infuse into [Vn.pr pass emph rel] give (a feeling or outlook) to (sb) by means of inspiring words etc. **O:** renewed interest, curiosity; enthusiasm, spirit. **o:** men, followers, army, class: *The leader had the gift of being able to* ***infuse*** *enthusiasm* ***into*** *the most sceptical member of the group* (or: *being able to* ***infuse*** *the most sceptical member of the* *group* **with** *enthusiasm).* ○ *Even our highest aspirations are* **infused with** *the baser, more fundamental instincts.* F = inspire (in).

infuse with [Vn.pr pass emph rel] ⇨ previous entry

ingratiate

ingratiate oneself (with) [Vn.pr emph rel] (*formal*) seek to obtain the support (of sb), even at the cost of one's dignity, principles etc: *It was sickening to watch Stevenson trying to* **ingratiate himself with** *the senior members of the department.* ○ *Eddie duly arrives and* **ingratiates himself with** *everyone, and especially* **with** *Daphne.* EB

inhibit

inhibit (from) [Vn.pr pass] make (sb) hesitate or be reluctant (to do sth). **S:** upbringing; (previous) failures, rebuffs. **o:** talking to women; expressing his opinion, saying what he feels, fulfilling his desires; evil impulses: *His strict upbringing* **inhibited** *him* **from** *asking questions, with the result that he tended to get left out of any serious discussion.*

initiate

initiate (into) [Vn.pr pass emph rel] make (sb) familiar (with sth), make sb a member (of sth), esp in a ceremonial way. **o:** the mysteries of antique-collecting; the art of fencing; the family circle; club, society, masonic order: *The poet Laurie Lee was* **initiated into** *the mystery of love by a young girl called Rosie.* ○ *A future American Ambassador* **initiated** *the Prince of Wales* **into** *the mysteries of the black bottom* (a dance), *with suggestions and corrections by the Maestro* (Fred Astaire). BBCR

inject

inject into 1 [Vn.pr pass emph rel] make (sth) enter (the body), by means of a hypodermic needle etc. **O:** drug, serum, solution. **o:** arm, finger; vein, bloodstream; child: *A nurse has to take care not to* **inject** *air* **into** *the patient's bloodstream.* ○ *Be careful not to* **inject** *too strong a solution* **into** *a young child* (or: *not to* **inject** *a young child* **with** *too strong a solution*).

2 [Vn.pr pass emph rel] (*formal*) change the tone of (sth) by adding a positive, brighter element. **O:** some life; a little gaiety, enthusiasm. **o:** proceedings, performance, meeting: *The meeting was incredibly dull until old Mrs Appleby started to* **inject** *a little life* **into** *the discussion.*

inject with [Vn.pr pass rel] ⇨ inject into 1.

ink

ink in [Vn.p pass adj] use ink to write words on a map, fill an empty space in a drawing etc; go over with ink anything already drawn or written in pencil. **O:** place-names, background: *'Your drawing would look better if you were to* **ink in** *the area to the left of the mill, perhaps with some bushes or distant mountains.'* ⇨ pencil in.

inlay

inlay with [Vn.pr pass rel] set (sth) in the surface of (sth). **O:** tray, table, cigarette-box. **o:** gold, silver; ivory, bone: *The tomb of Jehangir Khan was* **inlaid with** *semi-precious stones.* □ usu passive; also used after a noun: *Chiniot, in the Punjab, is famous for its trays* **inlaid with** *metal.*

inoculate

inoculate (against) [Vn.pr pass rel] (*medicine*) protect (sb) (against a disease) by means of an injection. **O:** population, refugees, inhabitants. **o:** smallpox, cholera, yellow fever: *The Red Cross nurses worked throughout the day,* **inoculating** *tens of thousands of people* **against** *cholera.* ○ *'Have you been* **inoculated against** *typhoid fever?'*

inquire

inquire (about) [Vpr rel] seek information (about sth). **o:** times of trains, package holidays to Greece; the possibility of getting a job: *'There was a lady in here a few minutes ago* **inquiring about** *domestic help. I told her that we weren't an employment agency.'* ○ *'Where should I go to* **inquire about** *London bus-tours?'*

inquire after [Vpr pass rel] ask about the welfare or state of health of (sb): *I met your old friend Joshua the other day. He was* **inquiring after** *you, and sent his kind regards.* ○ *It's reassuring to have friends* **inquiring after** *you when you're ill. It shows that they haven't stopped being concerned about you.* = ask after.

inquire into [Vpr pass rel] investigate (sth). **S:** police; headteacher; assistant manager. **o:** attack on a girl, robbery; the leak of the examination questions; complaint; the matter: *I told the police that I was worried by the noises from the empty house next door, and they said they would* **inquire into** *it.* = look into 2.

inquire (of) [Vpr, Vn.pr] (*formal*) put questions (to sb) in connection with a certain matter. **O:** why the train is late, whether he will attend; whether to go or not, how to resolve the dispute: *He had been encouraged to* **inquire** *freely* **of** *his parents on religious matters.* MRJ ○ *You should* **inquire of** *the hotel staff whether arrangements have been made to forward your luggage.* □ note that the Object in the [Vn.pr] pattern follows the prep phrase.

inscribe

inscribe in/on [Vn.pr pass emph rel] make letters, marks etc in/on (sth). **O:** name, year; record; tribute. **o:** tomb, stone, tablet, wall; silver cup, plate, cigarette-box, watch: *When Mr Fotheringay retired he was presented with a gold watch* **in** *which his name and the dates of his service (1924-1974) were* **inscribed**. ○ *The story of Adam and Eve was* **inscribed on** *the door of the Cathedral* (or: *The door was* **inscribed with** *the story* etc).

inscribe with [Vn.pr pass rel] ⇨ previous entry

insert

insert (between) [Vn.pr pass emph rel] push or place (sth) (between one thing and another). **O:** comma; wad of cotton, paper, cloth; piece of rubber. **o:** two words; teeth; wires: *These plugs would be safer if you could* **insert** *some kind of insulating material* **between** *the wires.*

insert in/into [Vn.pr pass emph rel] push or place (sth) in/into (sth). **O:** plug; key; hand; advertisement; extra paragraph; coin. **o:** socket; lock; bag; magazine; article; slot: (instructions on a vending machine) ***Insert*** *a 20p piece* **into** *the slot and pull* *the drawer out.* ○ *Chapman got Hukson to promise that he would* ***insert*** *Marian's article ...* ***in*** *the July number* (of the magazine). GE

insinuate

insinuate oneself into [Vn.pr emph rel] gradually enter (sth) by stealth or deceit. **o:** organization, meeting; sb's favour, confidence: *She resented the way in which he seemed to be taking over,* ***insinuating himself into*** *the family.* TFD

insist

insist on/upon [Vpr pass emph rel] do, require or maintain (sth), in spite of objections from others. **o:** going for a walk, helping me with my work; a replacement for the broken part; an answer; his innocence; absolute secrecy: *'If you* ***insist on*** *doing things like that,' she said, 'I'd be glad if you did them when I wasn't around.'* DF ○ *She didn't really want tea, but Nurse Ellen* ***insisted on*** *making it.* DC ○ *During the build-up to the invasion, total secrecy was* ***insisted upon****.*

inspire

inspire (in) [Vn.pr pass emph rel] produce (some feeling) (in sb), as a result of one's behaviour, example etc. **S:** he etc; example; courage, spirit; authority, assured manner. **O:** confidence, enthusiasm, hope; the desire to emulate him: *It was my father's courage and devotion that* ***inspired in*** *his men the determination* (or: ***inspired*** *his men* ***with*** *the determination) to hold out against what seemed like overwhelming odds.* ○ *The doctor's clumsy handling of the syringe did not* ***inspire*** *confidence* ***in*** *his nervous patient* (or: *did not* ***inspire*** *his nervous patient* ***with*** *confidence*). = infuse into.

inspire (with) [Vn.pr pass emph rel] ⇨ previous entry

install

install (in) [Vn.pr pass emph rel] place or settle (sb/sth) (in a place). **O:** oneself; visitor, newcomer; new bookcase; television. **o:** the easy chair; back room, new home; library, lounge; a corner of the room: *The mistress of the house reluctantly* ***installed*** *the two refugees* ***in*** *a spare room.* ○ *'Don't forget that the men are coming to* ***install*** *the refrigerator (****in*** *the kitchen) this morning.'* □ *visitor, newcomer,* etc can function as the Subject when the Object is a reflexive pronoun: *The newcomer* ***installed*** *himself* ***in*** *the large leather chair.*

instil

instil (in/into) [Vn.pr pass emph rel] establish or fix (sth) firmly (in sb's mind) by teaching and repetition. **O:** the fear of God, a healthy respect for the law, obedience. **o:** him, his mind: *My parents were very puritanical and* ***instilled in*** *me the value of a God-fearing, self-denying sort of existence.* ○ *The old feeling of fear* ***instilled*** *itself* (or: *was* ***instilled***) ***into*** *her mind again.* MSAL = implant (in), inculcate (in).

instruct

instruct in [Vn.pr pass emph rel] give (sb) lessons in (sth). **O:** children; soldiers; students. **o:** hygiene; the use of weapons; computer technology: *Fournier had just one pupil, a certain Dubois whom he* ***instructed in*** *philosophy.* AF ○ *When the visitor entered, a group of handicapped patients were being* ***instructed in*** *weaving.*

insulate

insulate (from) (with) [Vn.pr pass emph rel] keep (one thing) separate (from another); protect (one thing) (from another). **O:** (power) drill, radio; experimental laboratory, space vehicle. **o: (from)** the main current; the surroundings; (**with**) fuse, pvc (polyvinyl chloride); heat shield: *It is important to* ***insulate*** *the furnace* ***from*** *any neighbouring woodwork* ***with*** *brick and asbestos.* ○ *The recording studio should be well* ***insulated from*** *any source of noise.* ○ *If the wires are not well* ***insulated with*** *pvc or some other non-conductor, there will be a risk of fire.*

insure

insure (against) [Vpr pass emph rel, Vn.pr pass emph rel] protect (sb/sth) (against sth) by means of an insurance policy (a contract which guarantees the payment of money in certain circumstances). **O:** oneself; possessions; car, house, yacht. **o:** death, loss of a limb; theft, fire, total loss, damage (by flood or storm): *Make sure you have arranged...* (insurance) *cover and, if possible,* ***insure*** *yourself* ***against*** *sickness, redundancy or accident.* MBNK = cover (against).

insure (oneself) against [Vpr pass, Vn.pr] take measures so that one is protected from (sth). **o:** all possibilities, eventualities; failure, defeat: *Take care that all eventualities are* ***insured against****.* ○ *We tried to* ***insure ourselves against*** *surprise attack by posting additional sentries.*

integrate

integrate (with) [Vn.pr pass emph rel] (*formal*) make (sth) an essential part (of sth); cause (sth) to form a whole (with sth). **O:** building; river; college. **o:** setting; canal system; university: *The new residential blocks were skilfully* ***integrated with*** *the rest of the College to form a pleasing, self-contained whole.* ○ *An attractive feature of the course was the way the practical work had been* ***integrated with*** *the theoretical aspects* (or: *the way the practical work and the theoretical aspects had been* ***integrated***).

intend

intend for [Vn.pr pass emph rel] wish (sb) to have or receive (sth); propose that (sb) should enter or join (sth): *'I* ***intended*** *these flowers* ***for*** *your mother* (or: ***intended*** *your mother to have them), but as she is away I'd be glad if you would accept them.'* ○ *The letter bomb did not reach the man* ***for*** *whom it was* ***intended****.* ○ *In the nineteenth century, younger sons were often* ***intended for*** *the Church, the Army or the colonies.*

inter

inter (in) [Vn.pr pass emph rel] (*formal*) bury (sb/sth) (in sth). **O:** body, mortal remains, ashes; victims of the air disaster: *His son's body was brought home to be* ***interred in*** *the family grave.*

intercede

intercede (with) [Vpr emph rel] (*formal*) approach (sb in authority) on behalf of sb else. **o:** Home Secretary; girl's father; men's leader; Governor: *A group of MPs promised to* ***intercede with*** *the*

Home Office on behalf of several prisoners who were said to be mentally ill. ○ *We approached a friend, hoping that he would* ***intercede (with*** *the headmaster) to prevent John's expulsion, but he refused to help.*

interest

interest in [Vn.pr rel] help or lead (sb) to study (sth) with interest. **O:** oneself; one's pupils; customer; visitor; the public. **o:** local history; new car; buildings; environment: *Mr James was a gifted teacher of economics, who managed to* ***interest*** *his students* ***in*** *every aspect of the subject.* ○ *Astronomy was one of the subjects* ***in*** *which he had* ***interested*** *himself while in the Sixth Form.*

interfere

interfere in [Vpr rel] show an undue interest in sth which is not one's concern. **o:** his affairs; things that don't concern you; their marriage: *I'd be glad if you didn't* ***interfere in*** *matters that don't concern you.* ○ *There are certain aspects of nature* ***in*** *which it is, to say the least, unwise for men to* ***interfere****.* = meddle in.

interfere with 1 [Vpr pass] disturb or mishandle (sth) without sb's permission. **o:** my bicycle; these papers; the manager's private correspondence: *She was always telling Jack to ... stop* ***interfering with*** *the balance of nature.* SE ○ *'Please tell Mary not to touch the papers on my desk. Once they've been* ***interfered with****, I can never find anything I want.'* = meddle with.

2 [Vpr pass] (*euphemistic*) molest or assault (sb), usu sexually; sexually abuse. **o:** girl, woman; boy, child: *The man admitted taking the child away from her home but denied* ***interfering with*** *her.*

3 [Vpr] be an obstacle to (sth); get in the way of (sth); hinder. **o:** business, duty; important matters, progress; his research: *He was completely exhausted by work ... which he felt might* ***interfere with*** *his contribution to the congress.* JUNG ○ *'Nothing must be allowed to* ***interfere with*** *our search for the truth!'*

interlard

interlard with [Vn.pr pass rel] (*formal* or *jocular*) make (sth) part of a text, with the aim, or effect, of impressing, shocking, etc. **O:** book, poem, speech, writings. **o:** purple passages, biblical allusions, foreign phrases, slang expressions: *The Chairman* ***interlarded*** *his speech* ***with*** *patently insincere compliments to all and sundry.* ○ *The talk was a substitute for the social life withheld from them — chatter and gossip* ***interlarded with*** *sex.* 50MH

interleave

interleave with [Vn.pr pass rel] place or fasten between (the leaves of a book) (sheets of another colour etc). **O:** book, volume; pages. **o:** tissue paper, tracing paper; colour plates: *Meg enjoyed my gift: a little drawing book* ***interleaved with*** *transparent paper for tracing.*

intermarry

intermarry (with) [Vpr rel] make or allow marriages (with members of another group): *Many a tribe or ruling house has survived by* ***intermarrying with*** *its rivals, rather than waging war on them.* ○ *The priestly caste does not normally* ***intermarry with*** *the warrior caste* (or: *The priestly and the warrior castes do not normally* ***intermarry***).

intermingle

intermingle (with) [Vpr emph rel, Vn.pr pass emph rel] mix (with others) in such a way that one is not easily identified; (cause ideas to) mix freely and fully (with others). **S:** detectives, agents; ideas, policies, beliefs. **o:** crowd, audience; football supporters, holiday-makers; other philosophies: *Several glamorously dressed policewomen* ***intermingled with*** *the gamblers, looking out for the drug-pushers who were known to operate in the club.* ○ *People from over a hundred countries* ***intermingle (with*** *each other) at the Olympic Games.* ○ *We can leave them* (ideas from other religions) *undisturbed until they are* ***intermingled with*** *the new presuppositions of the Christian truth.* D

intern

intern (in) [Vn.pr pass emph rel] shut (sb) up (in a prison etc), often as a preventive measure and without trial. **O:** aliens, suspected terrorists, anarchists. **o:** camp, prison: *In World War II, many people of German or Austrian background were* ***interned in*** *special camps in Britain.*

intersperse

intersperse among/between [Vn.pr pass emph rel] ⇨ next entry

intersperse with [Vn.pr pass emph rel] (*formal*) place (one thing) here and there in the midst or course of (another). **O:** trees; speech; report; book. **o:** bushes, shrubs; jokes, amusing comments; biographical notes and references: *The trees were* ***interspersed with*** *evergreen shrubs* (or: *Evergreen shrubs were* ***interspersed among*** *the trees*). ○ *I could never have completed the work if it had not been* ***interspersed with*** *regular visits to the pub for a chat with friends.* □ often passive; also used after a noun: *Nick told us how he'd fallen into the river — an account liberally* ***interspersed with*** *fits of sneezing.*

intervene

intervene (between) [Vpr] place oneself (between two or more people) to settle a dispute etc. **S:** policeman, bystander; boy; referee. **o:** two drunken men; mother and father; contestants: *Margaret tried to* ***intervene*** *(****between*** *her husband and son), but she was roughly pushed aside.* ○ *'I'd advise you not to* ***intervene between*** *those two drunks. You might get hurt.'*

intervene (in) [Vpr emph rel] enter (sth), to try to influence or settle it. **o:** debate, discussion; the affairs of another country; quarrel, dispute: *The Prime Minister decided that it was unnecessary for him to* ***intervene*** *personally* ***in*** *the debate.* ○ *Gwen also sent in paintings but they were not hung* (in the exhibition). *Her brother was indignant and for once* ***intervened in*** *art politics.* GJ

intimidate

intimidate (into) [Vn.pr pass emph rel] make (sb) act in a particular way, through fear or by means of threats. **O:** small boy; employee; witness. **o:** giving away his sweets; acting as an accomplice; keeping quiet: *'My Lord, it is obvious that the witness is being* ***intimidated into*** *remaining silent. I would request that he be given police protection.'* ○ *The children cannot be blamed for performing illegal acts* ***into*** *which they were* ***intimidated*** *by their father.* □ often passive. = frighten into.

intoxicate

intoxicated by/with [pass (Vn.pr)] very excited by (sth); carried away with. **o:** success, good news, freedom, joy; fresh air, the Christmas spirit: *The crowd were* **intoxicated by** *the news of the victory and filled the streets of the capital in celebration.* ○ *He was* **intoxicated with** *the completeness and perfection of his portrait.* BRN □ also used as an adj after *appear* etc, and after a noun: *This was a man* **intoxicated by** *success.* ⇨ carry away 2 .

intrigue

intrigue against [Vpr pass rel] (*formal*) plan secretly to remove etc (sb): *A small group of dissatisfied officers were* **intriguing against** *the government. On the appointed day they arrested the President and seized power.* ○ *The Director was aware that he was being* **intrigued against**, *but he had no means of finding out how and by whom.* = conspire (with) (against).

introduce

introduce (into) [Vn.pr pass rel] make (sth) available (in a place), perhaps for the first time. **O:** potatoes, tobacco; disease; cannabis. **o:** Britain; school; the community: *It is not known precisely how the disease was* **introduced into** *Britain.* ○ *The police have a good idea how most of the cannabis that is* **introduced into** *the country gets past customs.*

introduce into 1 [Vn.pr pass] push (sth thin or fine) into (sth/sb). **O:** tube, catheter; key, wire. **o:** wound, artery; lock, hole: *A thin, hollow needle was carefully* **introduced into** *the patient's abdomen, and some fluid was drawn off.*

2 [Vn.pr pass emph rel] make (sth) a part of or an element in (sth). **O:** topic, subject; a new factor, fresh ideas; his name.. **o:** the conversation, argument: *You had no right to* **introduce** *my name* **into** *the discussion. You know very well that I want to be kept out of your family quarrels.* ○ **Into** *the curriculum for the sixth form a number of new, non-examinable subjects were* **introduced**.

introduce (to) [Vn.pr pass rel] make (sb) known by name (to sb else). **O:** girlfriend; new officer; teacher; lecturer. **o:** parents; the mess; class; audience: *'Well, John,' said Mary, who had been listening to the conversation for a minute or more, 'aren't you going to* **introduce** *me* **to** *your friend?'* ○ *The chairman* **introduced** *the speaker* **to** *the audience in a few, well-chosen words.* ○ *'I don't think we've been* **introduced** *(***to** *each other),' said my neighbour at dinner. 'My name's Stephen Black.'*

introduce to [Vn.pr pass] make (sb) aware of (sth) for the first time. **O:** students; children; listeners. **o:** the latest theories on the origin of the universe; the mysteries of the laser-beam; the intricacies of international trade; the song-birds of the region: *When I visited Japan I was quickly* **introduced to** *the etiquette of the tea-ceremony.* ○ *Who* **introduced** *you* **to** *the differences between Lancashire and Yorkshire accents?*

intrude

intrude into [Vpr emph rel] (*formal*) enter (sth) uninvited, often in a rude manner. **o:** meeting, king's presence, confidential discussion: *He* **intruded into** *the conversation without a word of apology.*

intrude on/upon [Vpr pass emph rel] (*formal*) enter (sth) in an unwelcome way. **o:** his privacy, time; a private celebration: *One of the dreadful facts about murder is that the police are obliged to* **intrude on** *grief.* TFD ○ *He never tried to* **intrude on** *their thoughts and feelings.* TU = obtrude (upon).

inundate

inundate (with) [Vn.pr pass rel] (*formal*) cover (sth) as if with a flood of water; overwhelm. **O:** staff; Post Office; BBC; Leader of the Party. **o:** work; Christmas mail; complaints; telegrams of congratulation: *When Charlie won £50 000 on the pools, he was* **inundated with** *begging-letters.* ○ *The public* **inundated** *the Foreign Office* **with** *requests for news of relatives who had been unable to leave the area before the fighting began.* ○ *'Have you had many replies to your advertisement?' 'I've been* **inundated (with** *them)!'* □ usu passive. = flood with.

inure

inure to [Vn.pr pass emph rel] (*formal*) make (sb/oneself) hard and resilient, so that he can withstand (sth). **o:** living on a pittance; the cold climate; the hardships that go with old age: *She had been brought up untidily,* **inured to** *disorder.* SE ○ *So much early death . . . not only* **inured** *parents* **to** *it but led them to feel less about their children in the first place.* BRN □ also pass after *appear* etc; also used after a noun: *Freud,* **inured to** *attack, smiled and turned away.* F = harden (oneself) to.

invalid

invalid out/out of [Vn.p pass, Vn.pr pass] remove (sb) from a job etc because of illness. **O:** soldier, airman; civil servant: *'Did Brown resign from the British Council?' 'No; he was* **invalided out**.*'* ○ *George had been* **invalided out of** *the band of the Grenadier Guards.* SU □ usu passive.

inveigh

inveigh against [Vpr pass emph rel] (*formal*) attack (sth/sb) violently, in speech or writing. **o:** corruption; the permissive society; the ruling class; the police: *The first speaker was an Italian, . . . who* **inveighed against** *both men, their books, their work — and even their income!* JUNG

inveigle

inveigle into [Vn.pr pass] (*formal*) persuade or trick (sb) by flattery or deception into (doing sth). **O:** his inexperienced partner; my younger brother; the old lady. **o:** raising an unnecessarily large loan; stealing sweets; parting with her life's savings: *A couple of bank employees were* **inveigled into** *handing over the combinations of the two safes.* □ the object is the *-ing* form of a v.

invest

invest in 1 [Vpr emph rel, Vn.pr pass emph rel] put (money) in (sth) with the aim of earning interest or increasing one's capital; use (time or energy) in (some activity) in the hope of profiting in some way. **O:** savings, weekly sum, inheritance; time, energy. **o:** stocks, shares, property, small shop; studying for a degree, learning Spanish, building an extension to his house: *What you* **invest in** *depends entirely on your needs — basically, whether you want to increase your income or your capital.* ○ *He* **invested** *every spare minute* **in** *trying to improve his knowledge of Russian.*

2 [Vpr] buy, acquire (sth). **o:** new clothes; stereo system; sports-car: *We've decided to* ***invest*** *our winnings* ***in*** *a dishwasher. It'll give us a chance to watch television after supper.*

invest with 1 [Vn.pr pass rel] (*formal*) formally declare that (sb) possesses (sth); give (sth) to (sb) as an award. **O:** governor, viceroy; consul-general, ambassador. **o:** (full) powers (to do sth); authority; an order (of chivalry): *When the officer commanding was wounded, his second-in-command was automatically* ***invested with*** *his authority.* ○ *The Queen* ***invested*** *the Prime Minister* ***with*** *the Order of Merit.*

2 [Vn.pr pass rel] (*formal*) give to (sth/sb) (a certain quality). **O:** history; partnership, alliance; participant, player. **o:** romance; an air of permanence, an aura of respectability; dignity: *The presence of the Vice-Chancellor* ***invested*** *the proceedings* ***with*** *an importance they might otherwise have lacked.* ○ *He looks so distinguished that one* ***invests*** *him* ***with*** *more wisdom than he could possibly possess.* MSAL

invite

invite in/over/round [Vn.p pass] ask (sb) to come into a house, study, office etc: *'Don't stand talking at the gate, Mary!* ***Invite*** *your friend* ***in****!'* ○ *Don't* ***invite*** *him* ***over*** *when nobody's home.* H ○ *Our parents have* ***invited*** *us* ***round*** *for a meal on Sunday.*

involve

involve in [Vn.pr pass rel] get (sb/sth) into a difficult situation or condition. **O:** himself; his parents; them. **o:** trouble, robbery, conspiracy; other people's affairs; expense; debt: *Somehow he managed to* ***involve*** *several of his friends* ***in*** *his matrimonial troubles.* ○ *Eustace Folville ... had been* ***involved in*** *crimes that included robbery, kidnapping, rape and murder.* SHOE ○ *An accident* ***in*** *which more than fifty vehicles were* ***involved*** *caused the death of six people on the M1 last night.* ○ *The accountant's errors* ***involved*** *everyone* ***in*** *a great deal of extra work.* = mixed up in.

iron

iron out 1 [Vn ⇆ p pass] remove or smooth (sth) with a hot iron. **O:** crease, wrinkle; garment, shirt: *'I should be ready in a minute. Just got a few creases to* ***iron out****.'*

2 [Vn ⇆ p pass] settle (sth) by means of discussion, compromise etc. **O:** issue, matter, problem; differences, misunderstandings: *'What about the other mess?' 'Well, there's nothing much else really,' he said, 'nothing we can't* ***iron out*** *at the Staff meeting.'* TT ○ *Problems in working life will be* ***ironed out****.* TO ○ *Subtleties* (ie in an argument) *can be ignored and inconsistencies* ***ironed out****.* CF

isolate

isolate (from) [Vn.pr pass rel] make (sb/sth) separate (from others/another thing); prevent (sb/sth) from coming into contact with (others/another thing). **O:** patient; case of typhoid; dangerous criminals; significant facts. **o:** others; the rest of the hospital; harmless petty thieves; the mass of data: *Convicted terrorists will be* ***isolated from*** *other members of the prison population.* ○ *It is wrong to try to* ***isolate*** *drug-taking* ***from*** *the general condition of society; cure the ills of society and you cure drug-taking.*

issue

issue from 1 [Vpr emph rel] come from (sth) in a stream. **S:** smoke; blood; stream of pure water. **o:** chimney, every window in the building; his wounds; the side of the mountain, rock: ***From*** *the upstairs windows* ***issued*** *a dense cloud of black smoke.*

2 [Vpr emph rel] come from (sb/sth) without a pause. **S:** orders, complaints; advice, abuse. **o:** director, husband; head office: *As John put on his coat and got ready for work, the usual barrage of complaints and instructions* ***issued from*** *the bathroom.*

itch

itch for [Vpr] (*informal*) wait impatiently for (sth). **S:** children; staff; young couple. **o:** Christmas Day; five o'clock; a house of their own: *Milly had been* ***itching for*** *a chance to get Pat to herself, so that she could tell her exactly what she thought of her.* ○ *He stood by the window,* ***itching for*** *the arrival of the postman and, he hoped, a reply to his proposal of marriage.* = long for.

J

jab

jab at [Vpr pass, Vn.pr pass] thrust sth sharp towards (sb/sth), often repeatedly. **O:** fist, elbow; umbrella. **o:** opponent; face, stomach, solar plexus, ribs: (boxing instructor) *'Keep* ***jabbing at*** *him with your left. You're bound to get under his guard.'* ○ *'Don't* ***jab*** *your finger* ***at*** *me: I'm not on trial and you're not the prosecutor!'*

jack

jack in [Vn ⇆ p pass] (*slang*) abandon (sth) finally. **O:** job; business; course (of study): *I can't take any more of this night-work. I'll have to* ***jack*** *the job* ***in****.* ○ *He often felt he was approaching the point of* ***jacking*** *it all* ***in*** *completely.* OD = pack in 1.

jack up 1 [Vn ⇆ p pass adj] lift one side of (sth) using a (screw-)jack. **S:** mechanic, driver. **O:** car, lorry: *'****Jack*** *her* ***up*** *a bit more. The wheels are still touching the ground.'* ○ *A* ***jacked-up*** *car stood at the kerb-side; the driver was changing a wheel.*

2 [Vn ⇆ p pass adj] (*informal*) raise, increase (sth). **O:** salary, wage; allowance; payment: *'We know you're not happy about the money you're getting. We think it could be* ***jacked up*** *a bit.'* ○ *Her son's an old skinflint. Always waiting to* ***jack up*** *the price.* AT = put up 4.

jam

jam in/into [Vn ⇆ p pass, Vn.p pass] press (sb/sth) tightly into a small space. **O:** audience; passengers; belongings, clothes. **o:** hall; car, bus, (railway) compartment; box, case: *'Don't* ***jam in*** *too much clothing; you won't be able to close the lid.'* ○ *'Give the papers to me; I can* ***jam*** *a few more* ***into*** *my briefcase.'*

jam on/onto [Vn ⇆ p pass, Vn.pr pass] press (sth) firmly or tightly onto sth. **O:** lid, cover; hat, cap. **o:** jar, tin; head: *'I can't get the lid off: you've* ***jammed*** *it* ***on*** *too tightly.'* ○ *He looked down at his cap, and after a moment he* ***jammed*** *it abruptly* ***on*** *his head.* AT

jam the brakes on [Vn ⇆ p pass] (*informal*) apply the brakes of a vehicle suddenly and forcefully: *I had to* ***jam on the brakes*** *sharply to avoid hitting two schoolchildren.* = slam the brakes on.

jar

jar on/upon [Vpr] be discordant or unpleasant to (sb). **S:** sound, music; voice, accent. **o:** him etc; sb's ears, nerves: *I had to turn the radio off. The music* ***jarred on*** *my nerves.*

jar (with) [Vpr emph rel] not be in harmony (with sth); not match. **S:** colour, pattern; arrangement; view, opinion: *The stripes on his tie* ***jarred with*** *the checks on his jacket* (or: *The stripes and checks* ***jarred***).

jazz

jazz up [Vn ⇆ p pass adj] (*informal*) make (sth) more lively or colourful; brighten. **O:** music, tune; party, celebration; room, decorations: *'Go out and get some more to drink: this party needs* ***jazzing up*** *a bit.'* ○ *The room decorations had been* ***jazzed up****. The overall effect was loud and restless.* = liven up.

jeer

jeer (at) [Vpr pass rel] mock, taunt (sb). **S:** spectators, audience. **o:** prisoner, victim; speaker, performer: *The man was* ***jeered (at)*** *by the crowd as the police bundled him into a car.* = gibe (at).

jerk

jerk out [Vp, Vn ⇆ p pass] (make words) come out in short, sharp bursts. **S** [Vp], **O** [Vn.p]: a reply; a few words: *'She's gone — left?'* ***jerked out*** *Hugh, visibly shocked.*

jib

jib at [Vpr pass] hesitate or refuse to face or accept (sth). **S:** horse, mount; car, tank; employee. **o:** fence, obstacle; extra work, wage freeze; working overtime, losing wages: *The banks* ***jibbed at*** *providing more than £2 million to support our expansion plans.* = balk at, buck at.

jibe

jibe with [Vpr] (esp *US*) be in agreement with (sth); match. **S:** account, story; behaviour, manners; appearance; position, status. **o:** record, transcript; pretensions, claims (for oneself); merits, deserts: *'His account of what happens* ***jibes*** *pretty closely* ***with*** *what I've got written down here.'* ○ *The optimistic picture painted by the chairman doesn't* ***jibe with*** *forecasts by the economic experts.* = accord with, correspond (to/with).

jockey

jockey for [Vpr pass rel] move about, manoeuvre, pushing others aside in order to improve (one's position). **S:** rider, runner; politician, courtier. **o:** position, place; power, privilege, advantage: *The cease-fire agreement hasn't meant much because the two sides are jumbled up and they've gone on* ***jockeying for*** *position and shooting.* L ○ *The break between the two of them was . . . unedifying with both of them* ***jockeying*** *and manoeuvring* ***for*** *power.* F

jog

jog along/on [Vp] (*informal*) make steady but unexciting progress in business, a relationship etc. **S:** factory, business; worker, employee; couple: *The industry is happy to* ***jog along*** *in its old way.* ○ *'Eleanor and I* ***jog along*** *pretty comfortably in spite of our differences.'* GOV

join

join in [Vp, Vpr emph rel] add oneself, or give one's support, to (sth taking place). **S:** audience, crowd. **o:** race, entertainment; applause, conversation: *We had a street carnival . . . and everyone* ***joined in****.* SE ○ *A group of tourists was invited to* ***join in*** *the dance.* ○ *This is an exciting game* ***in*** *which the whole family can* ***join****.*

join on/onto [Vp, Vpr, Vn ⇆ p pass, Vn.pr pass emph rel] (of a smaller thing) be fixed or attached to (a larger); fix or attach (a smaller thing) to (a larger). **S** [Vp, Vpr], **O** [Vn.p, Vn.pr]**:** part, component; wagon, carriage; caravan, trailer. **o:** body; train; lorry: [Vp] *'Where does this bit of the model* ***join on****? Is it part of the chassis or part of the engine?'* ○ [Vpr, Vn.pr] *The dress pattern doesn't really explain how the cuff* ***joins onto*** (or: *is* ***joined onto***) *the sleeve.* ○ [Vn.p, Vn.pr] *Two extra carriages were* ***joined on*** (ie ***onto*** the train) *at Doncaster.*

join together/to [Vn ⇆ p pass, Vn.pr pass emph rel] bring (two things) together; attach one thing to another (so as to form a continuous whole). **O/o:** rail, rod, pipe, wire: *The welding is so smooth that you can hardly see where the sections of pipe are* ***joined together*** (or: *where one section of pipe is* ***joined to*** *another*). ○ *One rail is* ***joined to*** *the next by means of a metal plate; space is left between them to allow for expansion.*

join up [Vp] (*military*) join the armed forces; enlist: *He* ***joined up*** *as a private in a county regiment.* DS ○ *Why should I hope for a big war so that I could* ***join up*** *and get killed?* LLDR

join up (with) [Vp, Vp.pr emph rel] meet and unite (with sb/sth), esp for a common purpose. **S:** force, body (of men); company, firm; road, branch line. **o:** army; neighbour, competitor; motorway, main line: *The commando force* ***joined up with*** *the airborne troops near the captured bridges.* ○ *'Grants' the boiler makers* ***joined up with*** *a small transport firm in order to save on delivery costs.* ○ *The M62* ***joins up with*** *the M1* (or: *The M62 and the M1* ***join up***) *a few miles south of Leeds.* = link up (with).

join battle (with) 1 [Vn.pr pass rel] begin fighting (sb). **o:** enemy; infantry, armour: ***Battle*** *was* ***joined****, shortly after ten o'clock,* ***with*** *advance elements of two enemy divisions.* = engage with 2.
2 [Vn.pr pass rel] begin a serious struggle or argument (with sb). **o:** neighbours, in-laws; employer, trades union: *As for my instinct in* ***joining battle with*** *Sammy and Sadie, it has been a sound enough instinct.* UTN ○ *The letter from Mr A. D. Walker contains more naiveté and bad logic . . . Perhaps, therefore, I may* ***join battle with*** *him.* SC

join forces (with) [Vn.p emph rel] meet sb and unite one's followers and resources with his; come together (with sb) in a common enterprise. **S:** army; division, regiment; manufacturer, tradesman. **o:** garrison, defenders; neighbour, competitor: *A force sent round on a flanking march* ***joined forces with*** *the main body two days later.* ○ *I never thought seriously about* ***joining forces with*** *Wales — I've been boss of my own works too long to relish being a co-director.* RATT = join up (with).

join hands (with) [Vn.pr rel] be united (with sb), esp in friendship. **S:** nation, people; army, force. **o:** neighbour, (old) enemy: *The leading troops of the English Army* ***joined hands with*** *the right flank of the Fifth U.S. Army.* MFM

joke

joke about [Vpr pass] talk about or treat (sth) in a light-hearted way, perhaps when seriousness is called for. **o:** matter, things; loss, misfortune, hardship, infirmity: *'John's lost his job, but it's nothing to* ***joke about****. Show a little sympathy instead.'* ○ *'Look, he's made a mistake. There's no need to* ***joke about*** *it.'*

jolly

jolly along [Vn.p pass] (*informal*) keep (sb) in a good humour so that he will continue to collaborate, agree to work etc. **O:** parent; wife; employee: *The job won't be finished on time unless you* ***jolly*** *the staff* ***along*** *with an occasional bonus.*

jot

jot down [Vn ⇆ p pass adj] make a quick written note of (sth). **S:** policeman, reporter. **O:** address, particulars, details: *A milkman had several times seen a dark-green Mercedes. ... He had* ***jotted down*** *the licence number: FAX 160.* TO ○ *'I'll just* ***jot*** *that time* ***down*** *before I forget it.'*

judge

judge by/from 1 [Vpr] take (sth) as evidence, base one's opinion on (sth). **o:** testimony, press report; what has come down to us, what has emerged: ***Judging by*** *the look on his face, he doesn't think much of our local wine.* ○ *'Thirty years ago,' he said. 'That's a lot of years* ***judged by*** *anybody's standards.'* PP ○ ***To judge from*** *the evidence of the experts, the deceased was still alive at three o'clock.* □ judge is in a non-finite form (*-ing* form, pp or *to*-inf).

2 [Vn.pr pass emph rel] form one's estimate or view of (sb/sth) according to (evidence). **O:** age, quality, freshness; truth, reliability; that he is telling the truth; whether he can be trusted. **o:** appearance, smell, taste; statement, testimony: *People still* ***judge*** *a man* ***by*** *the company he keeps.* FFE ○ *'I* ***judge*** *trees* ***by*** *their fruit,' Louie said.* HAA ○ ***From*** *the finger marks high on the cupboard we can* ***judge*** *that he was a tall man.*

juggle

juggle with 1 [Vpr] in a music-hall or circus act, pass (objects) skilfully from one hand to the other so that at least one is in the air at any time. **o:** hoop, ball, club china; plate, cup: *The older brother rode round the stage on a bicycle while the younger one sat on his shoulders* ***juggling with*** *four silver hoops.*

2 [Vpr pass] handle or manage (several things) at the same time, with difficulty. **O:** china; plate, cup; jobs, tasks: *'Help Mum carry the things into the dining-room. She's in the kitchen* ***juggling with*** *a pile of hot dishes.'* ○ *It is still mothers who have to* ***juggle with*** *difficult family budgets, buy the family food, children's shoes and clothing.* IND

3 [Vpr pass] (*informal*) move (things) around skilfully, for pleasure or in order to deceive sb etc. **S:** (public) speaker, writer; (dishonest) accountant, salesman. **o:** words; figures, accounts; facts: *Peter loves* ***juggling with*** *words, so much so that you often lose the thread of his story.* ○ *Anyone running an eye down these columns could see that the cash entries have been* ***juggled with****.*

jumble

jumble up (with) [Vn ⇆ p pass adj, Vn.p.pr pass rel] throw (things) together in confusion. **O:** papers, documents; clothes; ideas: *'Don't* ***jumble up*** *your ties and socks now that I've sorted them out!'* ○ *Recent events were* ***jumbled up*** *in her mind* ***with*** *scenes recalled from early childhood.* = muddle up (with), mix up (with) 2.

jump

jump at [Vpr pass adj] (*informal*) seize (sth) eagerly. **o:** ⚠ the opportunity, the chance, the offer: *If he offered me a job sweeping out the theatre I'd* ***jump at*** *the chance.* ○ *This looks like a genuine offer of international inspection. Russia should* ***jump at*** *it.* SC = leap at.

jump down sb's throat [Vpr] (*informal*) address or answer (sb) sharply and aggressively: *'Stop pitying yourself.' 'Don't* ***jump down my throat****.'* TOH ○ *'Guy—now don't* ***jump down my throat****—you're not in debt, are you?'* DC

jump off [Vp nom] (*show-jumping*) compete in an additional round of jumping when two or more horses have tied in the first round. **S:** horse; rider: *Four competitors had a clear first round and will be* ***jumping off*** *later this evening.* ○ *In the* ***jump-off*** *the winner had a lead of two seconds over his nearest rival.*

jump on [Vpr pass] (*informal*) turn one's attention sharply to (sb) so as to challenge or reprove him. **S:** teacher, drill-sergeant, coach. **o:** inattentive pupil, recruit: *The teacher,* ***jumping on*** *individuals at random, would set them impossible problems.* ○ *His wife* ***jumped on*** *him if he seemed to be taking Virginia's side.* AITC

jump to conclusions/the conclusion [Vpr pass] be over-hasty in judging a person or event: *'I know I was standing near the till when you came back into the shop, but don't* ***jump to conclusions****.'* ○ *You seem to have* ***jumped to the conclusion*** *that because of what happened to this young man there must have been foul play.* EM = rush to conclusions.

jump to it [Vpr] (*informal*, esp *military*) move quickly; look sharp: *'I want you in three ranks by that wall. Come on—****jump to it****!'* ○ *'Shun, stand at ease!' The thought of her* ***jumping to it*** *gave him a delicious thrill.* PW □ usu imperative. = get a move on.

jump up [Vp emph] spring to one's feet, stand up suddenly: *Then suddenly Fergus* ***jumped up****. 'I have the answer!'* DC ○ ***Up jumped*** *Peter with an angry look on his face.*

justify

justify (to) [Vn.pr pass emph rel] (*formal*) explain one's actions etc (to sb) so that they seem reasonable. **O:** oneself; (one's) behaviour, conduct. **o:** colleague; audience; critic: *'I don't have to* ***justify*** *my actions* ***to*** *you!'* ○ *We'll have to* ***justify*** *the additional expenditure* ***to*** *the Board.*

jut

jut out [Vp] project, protrude. **S:** balcony, roof; rifle, cannon; chin: *The stern of the ship* ***juts out*** *over the water.* ○ *He was sitting very nearly in the aisle, with his knees* ***jutting out*** *to the side.* AT = stick out 1.

K

keel

keel over 1 [Vp] overturn completely or partially; capsize. **S:** boat, ship, lifeboat: *The old Queen Elizabeth liner burnt out and* **keeled over** *while anchored off Hong Kong in January 1972.*
2 [Vp] (*informal*) lose one's balance and fall: *John walked into the room unsteadily, fixed me with a glazed stare, and* **keeled over** *at my feet.*

keep

keep one's head above water [Vn.pr] remain solvent; just manage to cope with one's duties etc: *High interest charges made expansion difficult, but we* **kept our heads above water** *thanks to a reviving export market.* ○ *Mr Chester has taken on a great deal of extra work recently, but he's just about managing to* **keep his head above water**. ○ *Virginia's life was a whirlpool which centred round Joe, but she struggled to* **keep her head above water**, *and to appear as if she had nothing on her mind.* AITC

keep abreast of 1 [Vp.pr, Vn.p.pr pass] (cause sb to) stay level with (sb/sth). **o:** boat, car; rival, competitor: *In the stiff breeze the catamaran skimmed over the water,* **keeping abreast of** *the motor-launch.* ⇨ be/get/stay abreast of 1.
2 [Vp.pr, Vn.p.pr pass] inform (oneself/sb) about (sth). **o:** events; the news, the times; fashion: *He continued to* **keep abreast of** *modern technology.* ○ *Is the opera company's first duty to make available the acknowledged operatic masterpieces or should it concentrate on* **keeping** *the public* **abreast of** *current developments?* T = keep up with 2.

keep after [Vpr pass] continue resolutely to pursue (sb); chivvy. **o:** escaping prisoner; pupils, servants: *The police* **kept after** *the terrorists until they at last trapped them in a North London flat.* ○ *'If you want to get any essays out of that crowd of layabouts, they'll have to be* **kept after**.*'* ○ *'Please don't* **keep after** *me so. I'm telling you everything I know.'* 50MH ⇨ be after 1, come after 2, go after 1.

keep ahead/ahead of [Vp, Vpr] not lose one's position in front (of others). **S:** favourite; newspaper; designer; bank robbers. **o:** other horses; rivals, competitors; pursuers: *Barrier Reef led the field from the start and* **kept ahead** *right to the winning-post.* ○ *If you want to* **keep ahead of** *your rivals, you'll have to work a good bit harder.* ○ *Don't try to* **keep ahead** *in the rat race — it isn't worth it!* ⇨ be/get/stay ahead/ahead of.

keep one jump/step ahead/ahead of [Vp, Vpr, Vn.p pass, Vn.p.pr pass] (cause sb to) retain his position in front (of others) by a small margin. **o:** opponents, competitors, pursuers: [Vp, Vp.pr] *Not knowing much Italian, it was all I could do to* **keep one step ahead** (**of** *the class*). ○ [Vp.pr] *Gibbs* **kept one step ahead of** *the police for years, but they finally tracked him down in Australia.* ○ [Vn.p.pr] *Up to now, Johns's studied air of neutrality has* **kept** *him* **two jumps ahead of** *all likely criticism.* L
□ one jump and one step show the extent to which sb keeps ahead.

keep at 1 [Vpr, Vn.pr pass] (make sb) work persistently at (a task); (make sb) continue persistently in his efforts. **S** [Vpr], **O** [Vn.pr]**:** students, workers, troops. **o:** the job, the task; your studies; it: *The only way to get a dictionary written is to* **keep at** *it, day after day.* ○ *Our professor was a martinet. He* **kept** *his students* **at** *their studies when they would rather have gone out to the pub.* = stick at.
2 [Vpr] worry, pester or harrass (sb). ⇨ keep on at.

keep at arm's length/a distance [Vn.pr pass] not allow (sb/sth) to come near to one or influence one. **O:** neighbour; danger, disease; temptation: *She called Fergus by his name while she* **kept** *Brigit* **at arm's length**. DC ○ *I had none of the frustration that Luke felt and perhaps Martin also, because they were being* **kept at arm's length** *from a piece of scientific truth.* NM

keep at bay [Vn.pr pass] cause (sb/sth) to remain some distance away. **O:** attackers; rats, mosquitoes; hunger, poverty; inflation, unemployment: *When fiddling about with lens and exposure meters I found it essential to have someone stand over me with a hat, to* **keep** *at least some of the insects* **at bay**, *otherwise it was impossible to concentrate and my temper frayed rapidly.* DF ○ *Industry as a whole is trying to* **keep** *rising costs* **at bay**. = hold off 2.

keep away (from) [Vp, Vp.pr, Vn.p pass, Vn.p.pr] not go near, touch, use etc (sth/sb); prevent (sb) from going near, touching, using etc (sth/sb). **S** [Vp, Vp.pr], **O** [Vn.p, Vn.p.pr]**:** children; crowd; insects; cats. **o:** fire; baby; distinguished visitor; flowers; food: ○ [Vp, Vp.pr] *The spectators have to* **keep away** (**from** *the players*). ○ [Vn.p] *'What's been* **keeping** *you* **away**? *You haven't been round to see us for ages.'* ○ [Vn.p.pr] *You know you can't expect to* **keep** *Arthur* **away from** *women.* BLCH ⇨ stay away (from) 1,2.

keep back 1 [Vn.p pass] prevent (sb) from making the progress expected of him. **S:** poor education, inadequate coaching, unsympathetic treatment. **O:** pupil, athlete, patient: *Poor teaching at the secondary level* **keeps** *many bright pupils* **back**. = hold back 3.
2 [Vn ⇆ p pass] control, restrain (feelings). **O:** ⚠ feelings, emotions; tears: *So Antigone was taken ... to her living death – and those who saw her could not* **keep back** *their tears.* GLEG = keep down 5.

keep back (from) 1 [Vp, Vp.pr, Vn ⇆ p pass, Vn.p.pr pass] stay at a distance (from sb/sth); prevent (sb/sth) from getting too close (to sb/sth). **S** [Vp, Vp.pr], **O** [Vn.p, Vn.p.pr]**:** crowd; enemy; small craft. **o:** the Prime Minister; our positions, the river; the round-the-world yacht: [Vp] *'***Keep back***!' the doctor ordered, as the onlookers crowded round. 'Give the man some air!'* ○ [Vp.pr] *The conjuror liked to* **keep** *well* **back from** *the front of the stage so that the audience could not follow all his movements.* ○ [Vn.p] *There were so many demonstrators that the stewards could not* **keep** *them all* **back** *as they pressed forwards towards the barriers.* ○ [Vn.p.pr, Vp.pr] *The President's security men did their best to* **keep** *the crowds* **back from** *him, but they despaired when he refused to* **keep back from** *the crowds.* = hold back 1.

2 [Vn ⇆ p pass, Vn.p.pr pass emph rel] not tell (sth) (to sb), not let (sb) know about (sth). **S:** husband; doctor; witness. **O:** the news; information, vital details; the truth. **o:** wife; patient; police, court: *The President decided not to* **keep back** *the facts concerning the secret negotiations any longer, and announced them on January 25th.* ○ *The news of the army's defeat was* **kept back from** *the people for several days.* ↔ let out 2. ⇨ keep from 1.

3 [Vn ⇆ p pass, Vn.p.pr pass emph rel] not pay (to sb); retain (from sth). **O:** a certain percentage; 50p a week. **o:** contractor, employee; wage packet, salary: *It is quite normal to* **keep back** *ten per cent of the cost of a building for a period of six months after completion, in case faults are found in it.* ○ *We agreed to let our employer* **keep back** *fifty pence a week* **from** *our wages to go into a special welfare fund.*

keep down 1 [Vp] not reveal one's position; lie low; not raise oneself: *'There's somebody coming!* **Keep down** *and don't make a sound!'* ○ *'When we reach the footbridge over the canal,* **keep down** *or you'll bang your head on it!'* (ie 'we' are on a boat).

2 [Vn.p pass] not raise (sth). **O:** one's head; voice; arms: *My father's parting words as I left to join my regiment were '***Keep** *your head* **down** *and your eyeballs moving!'* ○ *'I wish you two would* **keep** *your voices* **down**. *I can hardly hear myself think!'*

3 [Vn ⇆ p pass] prevent (sth) from increasing. **O:** prices, taxes, rates, the cost of living; one's weight: *The government seems to be making little effort to* **keep** *the cost of living* **down**. *Prices have gone up by fifteen per cent in the last year.* ○ *The doctor ... played a good deal of golf as a pretence of getting exercise and* **keeping** *his weight* **down**. DBM = hold down 1. ↔ keep up 2.

4 [Vn.p pass] repress (sb/sth). **O:** population; conquered country, occupied territory: *The peasants were* **kept down** *ruthlessly by the occupying power, which found allies among the landowning class.* = hold down 2.

5 [Vn ⇆ p pass] control, restrain (feelings). **O:** anger, fury: *It was all I could do to* **keep** *my anger* **down** *when I heard how the visitors had been treated in my absence.* = keep back 2.

6 [Vn.p pass] remove or kill (sth); not allow (sth) to multiply or grow. **O:** flies, mosquitoes; rabbits, foxes; weeds: *There is no absolutely foolproof way of* **keeping** *the flies* **down** *during the summer.* ○ *'If you want good crops of vegetables you must* **keep** *the weeds* **down**.*'*

7 [Vn.p pass] retain (sth) in the stomach. **S:** baby, invalid, dying man. **O:** milk, food, solids; (not) anything; medicine: *Unless we can find some way of getting the baby to* **keep** *her food* **down**, *she's simply going to starve to death.* ○ *'Can you prescribe something else for me, doctor? I can't* **keep** *this medicine* **down** *at all.'* ↔ bring up 6. ⇨ stay down 2.

keep from 1 [Vn.pr pass] not let (sb) know (sth); not tell (sth) to (sb). **O:** it; the news, the truth: *This is terrible in childhood: ... the feeling that something is being* **kept from** *you because it is too bad to be told.* EB ○ *Harold never confided much in Isabel. He* **kept** *his business affairs* **from** *her.* PW = keep back (from) 2.

2 [Vpr, Vn.pr pass] avoid (doing sth); stop or prevent (sb/sth) (from doing sth). **O:** partner, husband; children; thoughts; ambition, greed. **o:** overworking, taking on too much responsibility; quarrelling; distracting one; dominating, controlling one's life: *He should* **keep from** *interfering in matters that don't concern him.* ○ *He seemed to have forgotten who it was whose name he wanted to know, and also how to* **keep** *his head* **from** *nodding.* CON □ the object is the *-ing* form of a v.

keep the wolf from the door [Vn.pr pass] be enough to feed oneself and one's family; earn or obtain enough to feed oneself etc. **S:** wages, food; worker, housewife: *George didn't care for the job he was offered but at least it would* **keep the wolf from the door** *until he found something more to his liking.* ○ *During the Depression of the 1920s and 1930s many families found it almost impossible to* **keep the wolf from the door**.

keep in 1 [Vp, Vpr] remain inside (a place); not emerge (from a place). **S:** children, old people; rabbit, mouse: *You'd be wise to* **keep in** *while the temperature is so far below freezing point.* ○ *The rabbits* **kept in** *their burrows most of the day, and only came out to eat as darkness fell.* ↔ keep out/out of, let out/out of. ⇨ keep indoors, stay in/indoors.

2 [Vp, Vn.p pass] stay alight, continue to burn; keep (sth) alight, not allow it to be extinguished. **S** [Vp], **O** [Vn.p]**:** lamp, fire; furnace. **S** [Vn.p]**:** maid, servant; stoker, caretaker: *The stove will* **keep in** *all night if you put enough anthracite on in the evening.* ○ *'Whose job is it to* **keep** *the fires* **in**?*'*

3 [Vn ⇆ p pass] detain (sb) after normal school hours, as a punishment. **O:** pupils, class, culprits: *'Our teacher was in a terrible temper today. She* **kept** *us all* **in** *for half an hour.'* ⇨ stay in 1.

4 [Vn ⇆ p pass] not allow (sth) to express itself; restrain. **O:** anger, annoyance, feelings of indignation: *The policeman was sorely provoked by the crowd but he managed to* **keep** *his anger* **in**, *and dealt with the situation coolly and competently.* = hold in.

5 [Vn.pr pass] (*informal*) give or allow (sb) a regular supply of (sth). **o:** cigarettes, beer, chocolates: *Such jobs as he had from time to time barely* **kept** *him* **in** *drink and cigarettes.* AITC ○ *He won first prize in a lottery—enough to* **keep** *him* **in** *beer for a year.*

keep in check 1 [Vn.pr pass] avoid an excess of (sth); control. **O:** expenditure, inflation; strikes, wage demands; consumption of carbohydrates; drinking: *Unless imports are* **kept in check** *we are in danger of losing our favourable balance of trade.* ○ *If I hadn't* **kept** *myself* **in check**, *I might have said something I would have regretted later.*

2 [Vn.pr pass] prevent any further advance by (sb/sth). **O:** enemy; wastage, erosion; cholera, Aids: *By prompt action the Indian authorities managed to* **keep** *the threatened epidemic* **in check**. ○ *The enemy was* **kept in check** *by the floodwaters, which made the terrain impossible for armoured vehicles.*

keep in the dark [Vn.pr pass] (*informal*) deliberately not inform (sb): *'Let me tell you that I don't like being* **kept in the dark** *about matters that affect my daughter's future.'* ○ *He must* **keep** *Bunder absolutely and permanently* **in the dark** *about Dog-*

son and his mission to reveal the secrets of the drug traffic. HD

keep one's eye/hand in [Vn.p] retain one's skill by exercising it from time to time, though not as frequently as before: *I don't find much time to play squash these days, but I do try to* **keep my hand in** *at the weekends.* ○ *Peter* **keeps his eye in** *by joining in the occasional game of darts at the pub.* ⇨ get one's eye in, get one's hand in.

keep in ignorance [Vn.pr pass] withhold information or education from (sb). **O:** population; child, husband: *In medieval times it was the policy of the Church to* **keep** *the people* **in ignorance**. *Education represented the greatest danger to their entrenched position.* ○ *You can't* **keep** *children* **in ignorance** *of the facts of life indefinitely.*

keep in line [Vpr, Vn.pr pass] (cause sb to) stay in his allotted position; (cause sb to) observe the rules or conventions of a group: *If everyone* **keeps in line**, *we'll get through the Customs more quickly!* ○ *The girls are the firmest of friends, and woe betide any of the men in the cast who doesn't* **keep in line**. RT ○ *The Chief Whip can be depended on to* **keep** *recalcitrant members of the Labour Party* **in line**.

keep in luxury/style [Vn.pr pass] enable (sb) to live in considerable ease or luxury: *The pop-singer took pride in the fact that he* **kept** *his mother and sister* **in luxury**. ○ *If Charlotte marries Fred, she certainly won't be* **kept in the style** *to which she is accustomed.*

keep in mind [Vn.pr pass] not forget (sb/sth); constantly remember (sb/sth). **O:** me; dangers, possibilities, difficulties; what you told me about, why you're here: *'We've got to* **keep in mind** *how very small a disturbance — small from the astronomical point of view — could still wipe us out of existence.'* TBC ○ *'You'll* **keep** *my son* **in mind**, *won't you — just in case a vacancy should occur in your firm?'* = bear in mind.

keep in order [Vn.pr pass] not allow (sb) to behave in an uncontrolled way; discipline. **O:** class, group, crowd; troops, children: *The headmaster was astounded to see how well this notoriously difficult class was being* **kept in order** *by the new teacher — inexperienced though she was.* ⇨ put in order.

keep in his place [Vn.pr pass] not allow (sb) to forget his lower professional or social status: *Mrs Curry would have enjoyed discomfiting* (= embarrassing) *Hubert with Ron's presence, but she conceded the priority to* **keeping** *Ron* **in his place**. *'I shan't want the car until five, Ron,' she said; 'you'd better go to the cinema.'* HAA ⇨ put in his place.

keep in sight 1 [Vn.pr pass] not allow (sth/sb) to remain unobserved or to disappear from view. **o:** land, ship; enemy: *He wasn't a good navigator, so he* **kept** *the coastline well* **in sight** *as he moved from one harbour to the next.*

2 [Vn.pr pass] not forget about (sth). **o:** goal, objective, purpose: *You have to* **keep** *your main goal* **in sight** *and not allow yourself to be distracted.*

keep in sight of [Vpr] remain where one can see (sth/sb), or be seen by (sb). **o:** the coast, the lifeguards: *The children had been warned to* **keep in sight of** *the land in case they were caught in a storm.*

keep in suspense [Vn.pr pass] cause (sb) to be in a continual state of fear, worry, expectation etc: *'Don't* **keep** *me* **in suspense**, *please! If you know my exam results, tell me!'* ○ *We were all* **kept in suspense** *as Fred wrestled with the string around his birthday parcel.*

keep in training [Vpr, Vn.pr pass] maintain (oneself/others) in a state of fitness for competitive sports etc: *The girls* **keep in training** *all the year round in the hope of being picked for the national athletics squad in the summer.* ○ *'What's the best way of* **keeping** *a team of footballers* **in training**?' ○ *'I just can't remember at the moment ...' 'You should* **keep** *your memory* **in training**,' *she said.*

keep in with [Vp.pr pass] (*informal*) remain on good terms with (sb), either to gain some advantage or to avoid being victimized. **S:** pupil; customer; actress; lodger. **o:** teacher; grocer; theatrical agent; landlady: *We'll have to* **keep in with** *her in case we can't ever pay the rent.* AITC ○ *If you're hoping to get an exit visa, you'd better* **keep in with** *the authorities.* ⇨ keep on the right side of.

keep in step (with) [Vpr] move forward (with sth/sb), like soldiers on the march. **S:** pay, wages, salary; flow of raw materials; supply of experts; country. **o:** cost of living, other forms of income; rate of production, expanding industry; needs of society; allies, rivals, competitors: *There have been a number of movements in the constable's pay which have* **kept** *broadly* **in step with** *average industrial earnings.* DM ○ *The political consensus ... was that state incomes should* **keep in step with** *rising living standards.* IND

keep in touch (with) [Vpr emph rel, Vn.pr pass emph rel] (help sb to) remain aware or informed (about sth/sb) through visits, meetings, correspondence etc: *He* **kept in** *constant* **touch with** *... developments through letters to his mother.* TU ○ *If Anna and Sadie were friends, then to consort with Sadie was one way of* **keeping in touch with** *Anna.* UTN ○ *This was the prosperous Fluss family,* **with** *whom Freud had* **kept in touch** *since leaving Moravia.* F ○ *Documentary and current affairs programmes* **keep** *me* **in touch with** *more serious subjects.* L

keep indoors [Vp, Vn.p pass] not (allow sb to) leave the house: *On a day like this, with the rain pouring down, it's best to* **keep indoors**. ○ *We always* **keep** *the children* **indoors** *after dark. You never know who's hanging about in the streets.* ⇨ keep in 1, stay in/indoors .

keep track of [Vn.pr pass (o)] follow closely the progress or whereabouts of (sb/sth). **o:** vehicle, ship, satellite; sb's whereabouts, movements; one's friends: *'Don't Special Branch* (a police department) *make it their business to* **keep track of** *all these people?'* TFD ○ *There are so many pieces of hardware circling the earth that only a computer could possibly* **keep track of** *them all.* ○ *He's working on so many projects that it's a wonder they're all* **kept track of**.

keep off 1 [Vp] not begin. **S:** ⚠ the rain, snow; storm: *Thick clouds passed overhead, but fortunately the rain* **kept off** *the whole day.* ○ *The thunderstorm which had been brewing all evening* **kept off** *until we were indoors.* = hold off 1.

2 [Vp, Vpr] stay at a distance from (sth); not trespass on: *Two large* **KEEP OFF** *signs had been at-*

tached to the sides of the boat. □ public notice: ***Keep off** the grass.* ⇨ get off 2.

3 [Vn ⇆ p pass, Vn.pr pass] cause (sb) to stay at a distance. **O:** wild animals; squatters, intruders; pests, vermin. **o:** farm; territory, property; food: *'**Keep** those blasted squatters **off** my land!'* ○ *'How can I **keep** the flies **off** the jam?'* ○ *Her letters to Thackeray are those of a tease, alternately **keeping** him **off** and drawing him on.* TU

4 [Vpr, Vn.pr pass] refrain from eating, drinking, smoking etc; persuade (sb) not to do these things. **o:** fats, stodgy foods; whisky, cigarettes; narcotics: *The only way to get your weight down is to **keep off** fattening foods, and cut out alcohol altogether.* ○ *The patient was to be **kept off** all solid food for at least twenty-four hours.* ⇨ stay off.

5 [Vpr, Vn.pr pass] (ensure that sb does) not mention (sth); avoid. **o:** topic, issue, question; tricky subject, embarrassing matter; the question of who pays: *The negotiators **kept off** the religious issue, and concentrated instead on economic and political matters.* ○ *The conversation had to be **kept off** the subject of Mr Smith's bankruptcy. It was a source of embarrassment to the whole family.*

keep one's eyes off [Vn.pr] refrain from looking at (sb/sth) with interest or longing. **o:** girl, man; dancer, acrobat; newcomer: *'**Keep your eyes off** Carmen. She's somebody else's girl.'* ○ *'He was a stunning dancer. I couldn't **keep my eyes off** him.'* □ usu neg and with *can/could*. = take one's eyes off.

keep one's hands off [Vn.pr] (*informal*) not touch (sb); not take or use (sth). **o:** him etc; money, food; car: *'And George, **keep your hands off** Dora. Her boyfriend has a nasty temper.'* ○ *'I wish she'd **keep her hands off** my clothes. I can never find anything to wear for the weekend.'*

keep on 1 [Vp] continue one's journey: *Some of the climbers favoured returning to base-camp; others were for **keeping on** in the hope of reaching the top before nightfall.* ○ *'Is this the way to Willersey?' 'Yes. Just **keep on** till you reach Broadway; then you'll see the sign to Willersey.'*

2 [Vn.p pass] continue to wear (sth). **O:** best clothes; wet swim-suit; hat, boots; dark glasses: *In a church men take their hats off; in a synagogue, they **keep** them **on**.* ○ *I've told you before not to **keep** your socks **on** if they get wet.'* ○ *'Do you think I should change my dress for dinner?' 'No. **Keep** that one **on**. You look fine in it.'*

3 [Vn ⇆ p pass] continue to employ (sb). **O:** servants, employees; old retainer, farm-hand: *When Lord Lamont gave up his country seat he **kept on** only two of his servants.* ○ *They're **keeping** Paul **on** for a bit, taking him back to America.* MSAL ○ *Some of the older men are **kept on** to do simple maintenance jobs around the plant.*

4 [Vn.p pass] not remove (from a place). **o:** school, university, college: *There's no point **keeping** you **on** at that expensive school if you're not prepared to work for your exams.* ⇨ stay on (at).

5 [Vp] persist in the face of difficulties. **A:** through thick and thin; in the face of great odds; despite all setbacks: *Helen Keller was born with the most appalling physical handicaps, but **kept on** in spite of every difficulty until she became a well-educated, useful member of society.*

6 [Vn ⇆ p] leave (a light etc) burning. **O:** light, lamp; electric fire, television: *Every street has its corner-shop ... if the light is **kept on** at nights the children make it a meeting place.* UL ⇨ be on 8, go on 15, put on 2, turn on 1.

keep on doing sth [Vp] do sth repeatedly or continually: *'Religion is poppycock, Harvey, as I **keep on insisting**.* GL ○ (one child is talking to another) *'I've told you over and over again, and I **keep on telling** you, they wouldn't want to marry you, you aren't old enough to marry, is she Mummy?'* PW ○ *I **keep on forgetting** to post my wife's letters!* ○ *'Do be quiet, Sally, and don't **keep on asking** such silly questions.'*

keep an/one's eye on [Vn.pr pass] observe (sb/sth) and if necessary take appropriate action. **adj:** ⚠ (a) careful, professional, sharp, watchful. **o:** old people; children; house; things; what others are doing: *I asked him why he didn't come back home; at least he had friends there who could **keep an eye** on him.* CON ○ *I don't know what would happen if we weren't here to **keep an eye** on you.* US ○ *An agent provocateur, or police spy, might join an extremist party in order to **keep an eye on** it: you could not expect him to share its views and attitudes.* SNP ○ ***A** careful **eye** will have to be **kept on** the younger brother — he's the dangerous one.*

keep one eye on [Vn.pr pass] give part of one's attention to (sth/sb). **o:** the time, the clock; the kettle; the baby: *I was finishing my cornflakes while **keeping one eye on** the garden gate — my taxi was expected at any moment.* ⇨ have one eye on.

keep on its feet [Vn.pr pass] (*informal*) prevent (sth) from collapsing financially. **O:** firm, school, country; project: *An Australian financier bought the newspaper and promised to **keep** it **on its feet** for at least two years.* ○ *The Scots fought a long battle to **keep** shipbuilding **on its feet**.*

keep on one's feet [Vpr] (*boxing*) not be knocked out; not collapse: *The young challenger was not in the same class as the champion, and the wonder was that he managed to **keep on his feet** for three rounds.*

keep one's finger on the pulse of [Vn.pr pass] be fully aware of (sth), have an up-to-date knowledge of (sth). **o:** the country's mood; public opinion; the Stock Market: *A commander must always **keep his finger on the** spiritual **pulse of** his armies.* MFM ○ *A successful politician is one who **keeps his finger on the pulse of** the electorate.*

keep a firm/tight grip/hold on [Vn.pr pass pass(o)] exercise close, careful, strong control over (sth/sb). **o:** the purse-strings, household expenditure; the youngsters: *Unless a **tight hold** is **kept on** the purse-strings, the committee will soon find that its expenditure exceeds its income.* ○ *Those boys are pretty wild - they need a **firm grip keeping on** them* (or: ***a firm grip** needs to be **kept on** them*).

keep one's hair/shirt on [Vn ⇆ p] (*informal*) not lose one's temper or composure; keep calm: *'**Keep your hair on**! I'll move my car when I'm ready, not before.'* ○ *'If that's the way you treat my radio, I won't ever lend it to you again.' '**Keep your shirt on**! I'll get it fixed for you.'* □ usu imperative.

keep one's mind on [Vn.pr pass] not let one's attention wander from (sth). **o:** business, work; the matter in hand; what one is doing: *I found it hard to **keep my mind on** what the colonel was saying.*

QA ○ ***Your mind*** *should be* ***kept*** *firmly on the matter in hand.*

keep on the rails [Vpr, Vn.pr pass] (*informal*) (cause sb to) observe the laws and conventions of society: *We have all* ***kept on the rails****. There have been no scandals in the family; ... none of us have been in the divorce courts.* MFM ○ *By taking a constant interest in his son's progress, he helped to* ***keep*** *him* ***on the rails*** *when so many of his friends were in trouble with their teachers.* ↔ go off the rails.

keep on the right side of [Vpr] (*informal*) avoid offending (sb), often in the hope of being rewarded or favoured by him: *We must* ***keep on the right side*** *of the chairman. He could make things very uncomfortable for us if we were to annoy him in any way.* ○ *He believed in* ***keeping on the right side of*** *his wealthier relations!* = keep in with. ⇨ get on the right side of.

keep on the right side of the law [Vpr] not break the law, act legally: *'Look! I don't mind how you get this information, so long as you* ***keep on the right side of the law****.'*

keep a tab/tabs/a tag on [Vn.pr] (*informal*) follow closely the movements, activity, development of (sb/sth). **o:** criminals, suspects; associates, companions; movements: *'Alec seems to be* ***keeping tabs on*** *his wife these days. Does he think she's got a lover?'* ○ *I've* ***kept a*** *pretty close* ***tab on*** *most of what he's said these last twenty years.* PP

keep on one's toes/his toes [Vpr, Vn.pr pass] (make sb) continue to be alert, observant, ready for action etc. **S** [Vpr], **O** [Vn.pr]**:** students, pupils; trainees, recruits; department: *'The Chairman's visiting the warehouse today, so* ***keep on your toes*** *and be ready to answer any questions.'* ○ *What the children need is plenty of variety to* ***keep them on their toes****.* ○ *The sergeant-major* ***kept*** *the cadets constantly* ***on their toes****. They never knew what was coming next.*

keep on (about) [Vp, Vp.pr] (*informal*) talk endlessly (about sb/sth) in an irritating way: *'Bill's a nice enough chap, but oh dear, he does* ***keep on****, doesn't he?'* ○ *'I wish you wouldn't* ***keep on about*** *that computer you want me to buy. You know very well that we can't afford it.'* ⇨ be/go on about.

keep on at [Vp.pr pass] (*informal*) worry, pester or harass (sb) continuously with suggestions, requests, complaints etc. **o:** their father, older brother; friend, teacher. **Inf:** to mend the lock, to find a replacement, to talk to the head: *'Jane's been* ***keeping on at*** *me all week to mend the cupboard doors in the kitchen.'* ○ *'Don't* ***keep on at*** *me about Simon getting a bike for his birthday. He's not getting one, and that's final.'* ⇨ be/go on at.

keep on top (of) [Vp, Vpr] continue to manage or control (sb/sth) comfortably. **o:** opponent, opposition; job, events, developments: *The Prime Minister* ***keeps on top of*** *the Opposition more through their ineptitude than his own superior debating skills.* ○ *'Charlie's looking a bit worn out, isn't he? How much longer do you think he'll be able to* ***keep on top of*** *his job?'* = stay on top (of).

keep out/out of [Vp, Vpr, Vn ⇆ p pass, Vn.pr pass] (make sb/sth) remain outside (a place); exclude. **S** [Vp, Vpr], **O** [Vn.p, Vn.pr]**:** the public; crowds; undesirables; rabbits; gas, liquid: [Vp] *There was a notice on the railings round the power-station bearing the words '****Keep out****! 20 000 volts'.* ○ [Vn.p] *The pub landlord said he had no intention of* ***keeping*** *football supporters* ***out*** *so long as they behaved themselves.* ○ [Vn.p] *The rain darkened the room and* ***kept out*** *the air.* HOM ○ [Vn.pr] *We've tried everything to* ***keep*** *the moles* ***out of*** *the garden, but without much success.* ↔ keep in 1. ⇨ be out/out of 1, bring out/out of, come out/out of 1, take out/out of 1.

keep out of [Vpr, Vn.pr pass] (help sb to) avoid (sth harmful). **S** [Vpr], **O** [Vn.pr]**:** children; staff; troops. **o:** the sun, the cold; mischief, trouble; danger; other people's quarrels; debt: *I didn't come to Spain in August to* ***keep out of*** *the sun. Quite the contrary, in fact.* ○ *Half of all morality is negative and consists in* ***keeping out of*** *mischief.* DOP ○ *He begged Ida to marry him secretly and* ***keep*** *him* ***out of*** *trouble.* GJ ↔ get into 6. ⇨ stay out of.

keep out of harm's way [Vpr, Vn.pr pass] (cause sb to) stay in a safe place, engaged in some harmless activity etc: *I don't much like the children watching comedy videos all weekend, but I suppose it* ***keeps*** *them* ***out of harm's way****.*

keep one's nose out of [Vn.pr] (*informal*) not take an unwelcome part in (sth). **o:** her business; other people's affairs; matters that don't concern one: *'It happens to be nothing to do with Ed, but you* ***keep your nose out of*** *it, anyway.'* AITC ○ *She could never learn to* ***keep her nose out of*** *her son's private life, though she was always made unhappy by what she discovered.*

keep out of sb's/the way [Vpr, Vn.pr pass] avoid obstructing or being a nuisance to sb; ensure that sb avoids obstructing etc sb: *On the wedding morning will you please ensure that the children* ***keep*** *well* ***out of my way****?* ○ ***Keep*** *the cat* ***out of the way*** *when we bring the china downstairs.* ⇨ get out of sb's/the way.

keep to 1 [Vpr pass] not leave or wander from (sth). **o:** the main road, route; the point, the facts; familiar ground: *We did our best to* ***keep to*** *the recommended route but we strayed off it from time to time.* ○ *George* ***kept to*** *the shadows on the far side of the street.* FL ○ *I have always tried to* ***keep to*** *the facts as I know them.* LIFE ○ *The author gives a lively airing to one or two of the bees in his bonnet but on the whole his Olympic Diary* ***keeps to*** *the point with admirable discipline.* T = stick to 1. ↔ wander from/off.

2 [Vpr pass] follow or observe (sth). **A:** firmly, closely, resolutely. **o:** prearranged plan, agreed schedule; timetable, deadlines; strict regime, diet: *The success of our enterprise depends on everyone* ***keeping*** *faithfully* ***to*** *the plan.* ○ *Try to ensure that this timetable is strictly* ***kept to*** *by the whole party.* = adhere to 2, stick to 2. ↔ depart from.

3 [Vpr] remain in (a place); not leave. **o:** ⚠ one's bed; one's bedroom; the house: *Next day, when they told her she must* ***keep to*** *her bed she protested louder.* MM ○ *During the winter a lot of old people are forced to* ***keep to*** *the house, the weather being so cold and treacherous.*

4 [Vpr, Vn.pr pass] limit (sth) to a (certain amount). **O:** numbers, admission; price, dividend; costs, expenses. **o:** the agreed quota; a low figure; a minimum: *In admitting undergraduates, we have to* ***keep to*** *the figures laid down by the University.* ○

We must **keep** *costs* **to** *the absolute minimum.* ○ *There has to be some verbal guidance to the action, but descriptive comment is* **kept to** *a minimum.* UL

keep an ear/one's ear(s) (close) to the ground [Vn.pr] (*informal*) notice signs of coming events or tendencies (as an American Indian used to detect the approach of others by placing an ear against the ground): *When we want to know what the students are thinking about the authorities, we only have to consult Fraser, who always* **keeps an ear close to the ground**. ○ *'What's the gossip of the market, Tom? You fellows certainly do* **keep your ears to the ground**.*'* QA

keep one's/sb's nose to the grindstone [Vn.pr pass] (cause sb to) work persistently and hard, with the implication that the work is difficult, monotonous, or disliked: *Only by* **keeping one's nose to the grindstone** *can one hope to improve one's standard of living.* ○ *Miss Pennington was one of those teachers who enjoyed seeing that the children's* **noses** *were* **kept** *firmly* **to the grindstone**. ⇨ get back to the grindstone.

keep to oneself [Vn.pr pass] not tell others about (sth); not let others know of (sth). **O:** information, news; intentions, plans: *Later in the day, he thought of introducing a few private harmless jokes of his own. What these were he was* **keeping to himself**. DBM ○ *One's sins and consequent feelings of guilt are often best* **kept to oneself**. ○ *London suffered much less than a number of other European cities, and I will* **keep** *my bomb stories* **to myself**, *except to say that I made the acquaintance of more than one 'near miss'.* AH

keep (oneself) to oneself [Vpr, Vn.pr] not concern oneself with other people's business; not meet or join other people socially; maintain a veil of secrecy around oneself: *'I suppose several people have been enquiring about him since he died?' 'A lot from the newspapers did, but they got no change out of me. I* **keep meself to meself** (non-standard = myself)*.'* PP ○ *Nobody knows much about old Smout. He* **keeps to himself** *most of the time.*

keep to the straight and narrow (path) [Vpr, Vn.pr pass] (cause sb to) live a blameless though perhaps unexciting life: *I was surprised to hear that Peter had been having an affair. I thought he always* **kept to the straight and narrow**. ○ *The chaplain tried hard, but unsuccessfully, to* **keep** *the boys* **to the straight and narrow path**. □ also, occasionally, keep in the straight and narrow path: *Australian wool producers ... got such an economic fright as would* **keep** *them* **in the straight and narrow path** *for the rest of their lives.* RFW

keep together 1 [Vp, Vn.p pass] not (allow things to) become dispersed or scattered. **O:** stamp collection; books, papers, files; toys: *'Children, do try to* **keep together** *when we leave the train.'* ○ *'John, I do wish you'd learn to* **keep** *your things* **together** *and not scatter them all over the house.'* ○ *It is incredible how these old records have been* **kept together** *through the centuries.*

2 [Vp, Vn.p pass] (cause people to) work or behave in harmony or unison. **S** [Vp], **O** [Vn.p]: oarsmen, orchestra, choir: *The Oxford crew* **kept together** *immaculately throughout the boat race.* ○ *The conductor found it more and more difficult to* **keep** *the players* **together**.

keep body and soul together [Vn.p pass] (*informal*) stay alive, but with some difficulty; scrape a living: *Somehow the millions of unemployed of the 1930s managed to* **keep body and soul together**, *though on the meanest possible diet.* ○ *'So you got that contract for the million-pound office block? Well that should help you to* **keep body and soul together** *for a while!'*

keep under 1 [Vp, Vpr, Vn.p pass, Vn.pr pass] remain or hold (sb/sth) below the surface : [Vp] *The escaping prisoners, swimming across the river, managed to* **keep under** *as the searchlight raked the surface.* ○ [Vn.pr] *The crocodile killed its prey by* **keeping** *it* **under** *the water and drowning it.*

2 [Vn.p pass] maintain (sth) in a state of unconsciousness or strong sedation: *The patient's injuries were so severe that she was* **kept under** *by regular pain-killing injections.*

3 [Vn.p pass] maintain control over (sb/sth); suppress. **S:** regime, dictatorship; tyrant; outbreak of fire. **O:** people, population; his children: *The population were* **kept under** *by the invaders for a few months, and then armed resistance began to spring up.* ○ *Local volunteers managed to* **keep** *the outbreak* **under** *and prevent it reaching a nearby petrol-station.* = hold under, keep under control.

4 [Vn.pr pass rel] maintain (a constant watch etc) over (sb/sth); keep observing (sb/sth). **O:** suspect; patient; premises. **o:** ⚠ observation, surveillance, scrutiny: *Plain-clothes officers* **kept** *the suspects* **under** *constant observation.* ○ *Bookshops displaying pornographic material were* **kept under** *police surveillance for two weeks.*

keep under control [Vn.pr pass] not allow (sth) to spread. **O:** fire, epidemic, outbreak; locusts: *The threatened epidemic was* **kept under control** *by the authorities' vigorous action.* = keep under 3. ⇨ be/bring/get under control.

keep under one's hat [Vn.pr pass] (*informal*) remain secret about (sth), not tell anyone about (sth). **O:** it; the terms of the agreement; the news, plan; our intentions: *'Mary and I are getting married; but please* **keep** *it* **under your hat** *until we've told her parents.'* ○ *'It's almost certain that you will get the manager's job when he leaves: but* **keep** *it* **under your hat** — *I'm not supposed to tell you!'* □ often imperative.

keep up 1 [Vp, Vn ⇆ p pass] not fall or sink; prevent (sth) from falling or sinking. **S** [Vp], **O** [Vn.p]: swimmer; construction, house: *The survivors managed to* **keep up** *by clinging to pieces of wreckage.* ○ *The children use floats to* **keep** *themselves* **up** *in the water whilst they're learning to swim.* ○ *Those houses are so badly built that one wonders how they* **keep up** *in a strong wind.* ○ *You can* **keep** *your trousers* **up** *with a belt or braces.* ⇨ stay up 1.

2 [Vp, Vn ⇆ p pass] (cause sth to) remain at a high level. **S** [Vp], **O** [Vn.p]: costs, wages, prices; production: *So long as the cost of raw materials* **keeps up**, *prices of consumer goods will* **keep up**, *too.* ○ *Despite inflation, we have managed to* **keep** *output* **up**, *even raising it a little above last year's level.* ↔ keep down 3. ⇨ be up 1, go up 2, put up 4, send up 1.

3 [Vn ⇆ p pass] not allow (sth) to weaken or decline; maintain. **O** [Vn.p]**:** spirits, courage, morale, determination, strength: *Women patients in hospitals are encouraged to use make-up to* **keep up** *their morale.* ○ *'Do drink this soup I've made, dear. You must* **keep** *your strength* **up**, *you know!'* ○ *That I* **kept** *my spirits* **up** *at all was largely due to three of the younger masters.* SU ○ *I tried to* **keep** *my courage* **up** *by telling myself that the war would be over within a few weeks.*

4 [Vn ⇆ p pass] maintain (sth) in a proper state by spending money on repairs, decoration etc. **O:** two establishments; a large estate, a town house; extensive gardens: *He found a companion ... in Sir George Bluff-Gore, who owned a large red-brick Georgian mansion that was too expensive to* **keep up**. DBM ○ *He can't afford to* **keep up** *a house in the country* (or: *afford the* **upkeep** *of a house in the country*). □ used esp of large establishments; nom form is upkeep (sing only).

5 [Vp] continue unchanged, unabated. **S:** storm, hurricane; fine weather; sunshine, rain: *If this rain* **keeps up**, *all the crops will be ruined.* ○ *The hurricane* **kept up** *for several days, leaving a swathe of destruction across the country.*

6 [Vp.n pass] cause (sth) to continue at a high level of intensity. **O:** attack, onslaught, bombardment; propaganda; interruptions, heckling, catcalls, insults; constant flow of information, criticism, questions: *There wasn't much traffic, and they crowded the narrow streets, calling across to one another,* **keeping up** *an endless flow of sharp little fragments of repartee.* CON ○ *All the time he was doing this, he'd* **keep up** *a long, snarling monologue, usually about Baxter.* CON ○ *The world, the flesh and the Devil* **kept up** *their traditional assaults upon the spirit.* GIE

7 [Vp.n pass] continue to pay (sth) regularly. **O:** instalments, monthly payments; rent: *'If we don't* **keep up** *the payments on the car, the Finance Company will repossess it.'* ○ *I regret that I can no longer* **keep up** *my annual subscription to the golf-club, so I am tendering my resignation.*

8 [Vp.n pass] continue to practise or observe (sth); not allow (sth) to lapse or be neglected. **O:** the old customs, traditions; correspondence; friendship, acquaintance; my French: *Although the children knew all about the myth of Father Christmas, they still liked to* **keep up** *the old seasonal customs.* ○ *While the younger John Milton was still at Christ's College* (Cambridge), *the older* **kept up** *his Oxfordshire contacts.* MLT ○ *You have a tradition to maintain. You have standards to* **keep up**. GL ○ *If only I'd* **kept up** *my German, I might have got that job in Berlin.*

9 [Vn.p pass] prevent (sb) from going to bed at the usual time. **S:** (sick) child; noise, celebrations. **O:** parents; guests, visitors. **A:** till the early morning, into the small hours, half the night: *'Good heavens! It's nearly half past midnight. I must go and I do hope I haven't* **kept** *you* **up**!' ○ *The friend always visited Freud on his annual trips to Vienna,* **keeping** *him* **up** *until three in the morning.* F ○ *... she knew about having to be gay and lively for him and always ready to listen when he wanted to talk, and being sometimes* **kept up** *half the night if he felt like a party.* AITC ⇨ be up 4, stay up 2.

keep up appearances [Vp.n pass] continue to observe the conventions; present an unchanged front or appearance in public, esp after some loss of status, prestige or fortune: *She would rather go hungry and* **keep up appearances** *than eat properly and wear last year's fashions.* ○ *When I was a girl everyone was pure, today virgins are as rare as unicorns — still, I'll give white clothes* (as a wedding present) *to* **keep up appearances**. DPM

keep one's chin/pecker up [Vn.p] (*informal*) not lose one's courage, hope, determination, optimism: *'I don't think I'll ever be able to pass my exams.' 'You've got nothing to worry about. You've done all the work you were asked to do. So* **keep your pecker up**. *It'll be all right.'* ○ *'Bill's just been sacked; what are we going to do?' 'Something will turn up. Just* **keep your chin up** *— for the sake of the children, at least.'* □ usu imperative.

keep one's end up [Vn ⇆ p] (*informal*) perform well, appear cheerful (esp in a difficult situation); defend oneself against attack, implied criticism, or rivalry: *He* **kept his end up** *as host, even when Goodrich was retailing the diverting and fantastic adventures which had made him miss his train.* PW ○ *Charles* **kept his end up** *fairly well. The invaluable 'News of the World' provided them with topics.* HD ○ *He laughed ... whenever Alec's name was mentioned, and sometimes in Alec's face, and called him 'poor old Alec', just to* **keep up his end** *with him, and drown his sense of inferiority — which was strengthened by the benefits Alec had conferred on him.* PW

keep up the good work/keep it up [Vp.n, Vn.p] maintain a high level of effort and achievement: *'I see your sales figures are well up on the last quarter. Splendid!* **Keep up the good work**!' ○ *Robert's father studied the report and looked up. 'This is excellent, Bob. I hope you'll* **keep it up**.' □ usu imperative.

keep up to [Vn.p.pr pass] ensure that (sb) works or behaves as well as he is able to. **S:** coach; general; director; headteacher. **O:** team; officers; actors; staff and pupils. **o:** ⚠ standard, scratch; the mark; expectations: *You can trust Stephen to* **keep** *his sales force* **up to** *scratch.* ○ *Once the research team are appointed, it'll be your job to ensure they're* **kept up to** *the mark.* ⇨ be up to 5, bring up to, come up to, get up to 1.

keep up (with) 1 [Vp, Vp.pr] work, play, walk, dance etc with the same vigour, speed, skill etc as (sb else). **o:** the youngsters; the experts; my cousin: *Margaret began to have to take running steps to* **keep up**. GOV ○ *Even when Josh was in his sixties he took part in swimming competitions, and a lot of younger people couldn't* **keep up with** *him.* ○ *Johnny finds it difficult to* **keep up with** *the rest of the class in mathematics.*

2 [Vp, Vp.pr] progress or rise at the same rate as (sth else). **S:** wages; exports; supply. **o:** prices; imports; demand: *The main cause of industrial unrest is that workers' incomes are not* **keeping up** *(***with** *rising prices).* ○ *The government said they would try to ensure that old age pensions* **kept up with** *the ever-increasing cost of living.*

keep up with 1 [Vp.pr] maintain the same social and material standards as (sb else). **o:** one's neighbours, friends: *Most people, in this competitive so-*

ciety, think they must **keep up with** *the people next door.* ○ *'It's no use expecting me to buy a new car just because the neighbours have got one. My salary's only about half Bill's, and we just can't* **keep up with** *them, that's all.'* ⇨ keep up with the Joneses.

2 [Vp.pr] inform oneself about (sth); learn about (sth); be 'au fait' with (sth). **o:** the news; latest developments; public opinion: *She's read all sorts of books on the subject. She sort of* **keeps up with** *it.* OD ○ *There is so much going on in the London theatrical world that I just can't find time to* **keep up with** *it.* = keep abreast of 2. ⇨ keep up with the times.

3 [Vp.pr] maintain contact with (sb), through visits, correspondence etc. **o:** their friends in Venezuela, one's schoolfriends; old acquaintances, former colleagues: *Between whiles — for Alec was writing hard — she visited her old friends. She had scarcely* **kept up with** *them at all, so alien had been the mere thought of them to the life she led at Marshport.* PW ○ *For some years after retirement he* **kept up with** *a number of his old workmates, but as time went by he dropped them one by one.*

keep up with the Joneses [Vp.pr] (*informal*) try to maintain the same material and social standards as one's (richer) neighbours: *It is hard these days* **keeping up with the Joneses**. *Even Conrad N. himself, head of the dynasty, must find it a strain; in the first six months of this year he will have performed round the world 13 ... opening ceremonies* (ie opened 13 new plants or stores) OBS □ the following gives a fresh twist to the expression by providing a contrasting phrase: *Certainly working-class people have a strong sense of being members of a group. The group does not like to be shocked or attacked from within. There may be little of the competitive urge to* **keep up with the Joneses** *but just as powerful can be the pressure to* **keep down with the Atkinses**. UL □ it is now common for Joneses to be replaced by the name of any other group who are in the public eye on account of their luxurious mode of living etc. = keep up with 1.

keep up with the times [Vp.pr] adapt oneself in order not to become out of date or old-fashioned: *It's no use hoping that you can go on without changing your business methods. If you don't* **keep up with the times**, *you'll get left behind.* ○ *'I see you've introduced self-service in your restaurant.' 'Yes; you've got to* **keep up with the times**.*'*

keep faith with [Vn.pr] not break one's promises to (sb). **S:** government; company. **o:** the electorate; workers: *We* **kept faith with** *our allies by going to their help when they were invaded.* ○ *By withholding the promised bonus, management has failed to* **keep faith with** *the employees.*

keep pace with [Vn.pr pass(o) emph rel] progress at the same rate as (sth/sb else). **S:** sales; supply; building. **o:** production; demand; requirements: *Design must* **keep pace with** *technological innovation; it should neither lag behind it nor try to anticipate it.* ○ *The provision of student accommodation has simply not* **kept pace with** *the demand for places at universities and polytechnics.* ○ *The tremendous demand for the new model just couldn't be* **kept pace with**.

keep within bounds [Vn.pr pass] not allow (sth) to become excessive or unreasonable. **O:** claims; enthusiasm, excitement; celebrations; consumption of alcohol, tobacco; expenditure: *The government claims to be doing its best to* **keep** *price increases* **within bounds**. ○ *If your claims for expenses are* **kept within** *reasonable* **bounds**, *the Insurance Company will probably meet them in full.*

key

key in [Vp, Vn ⇆ p pass] enter (words etc) in a computer by typing them on a keyboard. **O:** information, data; word, letter, figure: *You* **keyed in** *your social security number.* SATS ○ *She spent the day* **keying in** *entries for a new edition of the dictionary.*

keyed up [pass adj (Vn.p)] extremely tense because sth important or dangerous is about to happen: *The troops were* **keyed up** *by the announcement that they were leaving camp the next day.* ○ *Suddenly Mike pops his head round the door. He was looking all* **keyed up** *and I knew it wasn't excitement over my pink body either.* JFTR □ also used with *appear* etc. ⇨ tense up.

kick

kick about/around [Vp, Vpr] (*informal*) be present (in a place); be alive; be in existence. **S:** books, clothing; Joe, old Jolyon; idea: *'Alex, is that your dirty washing* **kicking about** *on the stairs?'* ○ *'You don't mean to say that old Thompson is still* **kicking around**! *He must be a hundred if he's a day.'* ○ *The idea of flight had been* **kicking around** *for centuries before man actually achieved it.* □ in continuous tenses only. = knock about 1.

kick against [Vpr pass] protest strongly about (sth) to show one's dislike of it. **o:** authority, the law, the rules; fate, nature: *It's no use trying to* **kick against** *the rules; you'll be the sufferer in the end.* ○ *'Don't* **kick against** *fate. What will be, will be.'*

kick around/round [Vn.p pass] (informal) discuss (sth) in a tentative, informal way. **O:** idea, notion, suggestion: *After the clinical examination, the consultant invited his students to put forward any suggestions they had about the nature of the disease, so that they could* **kick** *them* **around** *for a while.*

kick back 1 [Vn.p] kick (sb) in retaliation: *'David says it isn't true. And he keeps kicking me!' 'Tell him it is and* **kick** *him* **back**!*'* ILIH

2 [Vp.n nom] (*informal*) illegally give back part of the cost of sth to the purchaser as an inducement to buy: *You have to* **kick back** *about ten per cent of the price to secure an undertaking to do business.* ○ *'Most of the ministries they sell to expect the promise of a substantial* **kick-back** *before they will agree to place an order.*

kick downstairs [Vn.p pass] give (sb) a job at a lower level; demote: *Poor old Richard was* **kicked downstairs** *to a job in Accounts.* ↔ kick upstairs.

kick in [Vn ⇆ p pass] break (sth) open with a kick; dislodge (sth) with a kick. **O:** door; face, teeth: *As the door was locked, and I could hear someone screaming for help, I* **kicked** *it* **in** *and rushed into the house.* ○ *Some of these thugs are quite capable of* **kicking** *your teeth* **in** *if you try to resist.*

kick in the teeth [Vn.pr pass] (*informal*) treat (sb) with a brutal lack of respect or gratitude: *'I pay these people good money, and what happens? They* ***kick*** *me* ***in the teeth****!'* ○ *Anyone hoping for promotion on merit in this place is likely to get* ***kicked in the teeth****.* ⇨ previous entry

kick off 1 [Vn ⇆ p pass] remove (sth) with a kick. **O:** shoes, slippers: *The woman threw her coat on a chair,* ***kicked off*** *her shoes, lit a cigarette.* 50MH
2 [Vp nom] (*sport*) start a game of football or rugby by kicking the ball from the centre of the field; (of a game) be started in this way. **S:** the captain, the Mayor; game, match: *A television personality was invited to* ***kick off*** *in the final.* ○ *We were delayed by the traffic and missed the* ***kick-off****.* ○ *The game is due to* ***kick off*** *at 2.15.*
3 [Vp, Vn ⇆ p nom pass] (*informal*) (cause sth to) start or open. **S** [Vp], **O** [Vn.p]**:** party, celebration; show; display, exhibition: *The show* ***kicked off*** *with an outstanding musical act.* ○ *Fashion designer Karl Lagerfeld* ***kicked off*** *the Paris week in high spirits with a superbly sophisticated collection.* OBS □ compare for a kick-off = 'for a start', 'as the first point or argument of many': *'Why don't you believe what Tom says?' 'Well, I know he wasn't anywhere near the place,* ***for a kick-off****. And besides, everyone knows he's a liar!'*

kick out/out of [Vn ⇆ p pass, Vn.pr pass] (*informal*) drive (sb) out forcibly (from a place); expel. **O:** employee; interloper, intruder, unwanted guest: *'You're only allowed one mistake in this firm. If you slip up a second time they* ***kick*** *you* ***out*** *without any hesitation.'* ○ *'And supposing I did go to prison. You know the Templars. I'd be* ***kicked out****, just as mother was. I'd be disinherited.'* DC ○ *His father* (a god)*, in a rage,* ***kicked*** *him* ***out of*** *heaven, and he became lame and crippled.* GLEG = throw out/out of.

kick over the traces [Vpr] disobey, or rebel against, people in authority, esp one's parents: *I couldn't see eye to eye with the old man* (= my father)*. I* ***kicked over the traces****, and I've lived my life in the entertainment business.* HD ○ *Maybe I was too confident, and showed it. But I had received many rebuffs and there is no doubt they were good for me; they kept me from* ***kicking over the traces*** *too often and saved me from becoming too overbearing.* MFM

kick round [Vn.p pass] ⇨ kick around/round.

kick up 1 [Vn ⇆ p pass] make (sth) uneven; disturb. **O:** carpet; cloud of dust, sand, gravel: *I was forever straightening the fringes of the carpet, but five minutes later the children had inevitably* ***kicked*** *it* ***up*** *again.* ○ *A man sat at a table in a corner of the saloon idly* ***kicking up*** *the sawdust at his feet.*
2 [Vp.n] create, produce (sth). **O:** ⚠ a row, fuss, stink, shindy: *She* (a baby) ***kicked up*** *a terrible fuss, which was all it was, because as soon as I went into her room she stopped, and started giving me flirtatious smiles, so it couldn't have been wind or anything.* WI ○ *These Portuguese are pretty efficient at police work, so people don't get a chance to do much damage or* ***kick up*** *a row.* ILIH

kick up its heels [Vp.n] (of a horse) kick into the air with its heels and run about, enjoying its freedom; (of a person) break away from the routine of work, family life etc and enjoy oneself: *As soon as Ned was released into the field he* ***kicked up his heels*** *and ran off to join the other horses near the stream.* ○ *Everyone needs to* ***kick up his heels*** *once in a while, just get away, have some fun and forget everything.* 50MH

kick upstairs [Vn.p pass] (*informal*) promote (sb) to a position which carries greater prestige or financial reward, but which carries less power (esp from the House of Commons to the House of Lords). **O:** manager, former Minister of Defence: *The only way for us to get rid of old Smith is to* ***kick*** *him* ***upstairs****; then we'll be able to appoint Brown, and put some life back into the business.* ↔ kick downstairs.

kid

kid (on/up) [Vn.p] (*informal*) tell (sb) sth in jest but with a serious expression on one's face. **O:** me; the poor child; his brother's friends: *'If he tells you that you've won first prize, don't believe him. He's probably* ***kidding*** *you* ***on****.'* ○ *BOY: And you really will marry me? JO: I said so, didn't I? You shouldn't have asked me if you were only* ***kidding*** *me* ***up****.* TOH □ kid up is regional (north of England).

kill

kill off [Vn ⇆ p pass] destroy all, or nearly all, of (a number of things or people). **O:** insects, pests, mosquitoes, locusts; buds, early shoots; inhabitants, prisoners: *A late frost* ***killed off*** *nearly all the apple-blossom, with the result that we had a very poor crop this year.* ○ *Since the mosquitoes were* ***killed off****, the island has become a far pleasanter place to live in.*

kill with kindness [Vn.pr pass] be so indulgent towards (sb) that one causes him great harm: *Her idea of being a good wife and mother was to heap the table with food. But as it was mostly starch and fat she was literally* ***killing*** *her family* ***with kindness****.*

kill two birds with one stone [Vn.pr] do two things, achieve two objectives, by means of a single action: *'Why don't you come and discuss your idea when you're next in Edinburgh?' 'Well, I have to see my solicitor there next week, so perhaps I could drop in and have a chat with you as well.' 'That's right.* ***Kill two birds with one stone****.'*

kip

kip down [Vp nom] (*informal*) lie down and go to sleep, esp in a makeshift bed. **S:** tramp, hippy; student; team: *We were given straw-filled mattresses and* ***kipped down*** *for a couple of hours* (or: *had a* ***kip-down*** *for a couple of hours*) *in a corner of the barn.* ○ *The hippies were tough. They could* ***kip down*** *anywhere — on grass or on concrete.*

kip out [Vp] (*slang*) sleep in the open air: *Every night during the summer thousands of young people* ***'kip out'*** *on the beaches. It costs nothing and it makes them feel adventurous.* ○ *DAVIES Yes, well, you'd be well out of the draught there. ... You'd be well out of it. It's different when you're* ***kipping out****.* TC

kiss

kiss away [Vn ⇆ p pass] remove (a painful feeling etc) by kissing. **O:** tears, frown; jealousy, anger: *John walked into the house with a thousand worries written across his face. His wife helped him off with his coat and tried to* ***kiss*** *the anxiety* ***away****.*

kit

kit out (with) [Vn ⇆ p pass, Vn.p.pr pass rel] provide (sb/sth) with special clothing and equipment ('kit'); equip. **O:** oneself; expedition, troops: *Aquascutum, the 140-year-old tailoring business,* ***kitted out*** *officers* ***with*** *showerproof wool coats in the Crimean war.* T ○ *The men were* ***kitted out with*** *the latest gear for high-altitude climbing.* = fit out.

kit up (in) [Vn.p pass adj, Vn.p.pr pass rel] (*informal*) dress (oneself/sb) in expensive, conspicuous clothes etc. **O:** oneself; child: *'Look at that trendy couple —* ***kitted up in*** *all the latest sportswear!'* ○ *Some of these would-be skiers had* ***kitted*** *themselves* ***up*** *absurdly* ***in*** *the most expensive equipment you can imagine.*

kneel

kneel down [Vp] get on to one's knees; (continuous tenses) be or remain on one's knees. **S:** child; congregation, worshippers; cleaner: *Mary* ***knelt down*** *at the side of the bath and supported the baby's head in one hand as she gently washed it with the other.* ○ *When the young man entered the church he saw that the congregation were already* ***kneeling down*** *in prayer.*

knit

knit together [Vp, Vn ⇆ p pass] (cause sth to) join or unite. **S** [Vp], **O** [Vn.p]: brows; bones; thread, strand (of a story); elements in society: *The surgeon said that it would be six months before the two parts of the broken femur* ***knitted together*** *firmly.* ○ *War, more than anything else, seems to* ***knit*** *the various strata of society* ***together****. When peace returns, the old divisions return with it.*

knit up [Vn.p pass] make (sth) by knitting; use (sth) completely by knitting. **O:** a pair of socks; wool; a few odd ounces (of wool, nylon etc): *Susan was amazingly quick with her needles. She could* ***knit up*** *a baby's jacket in an afternoon.* ○ *Martha spent several hours a day* ***knitting up*** *odd scraps of wool into little squares, which she would later join together to make a blanket for her grandchild.*

knock

knock about 1 [Vp, Vpr] (*informal*) wait idly in (a place); move or travel about (an area) in a casual way: *There are always a few old men* ***knocking about*** *the Grassmarket in Edinburgh; it's a sort of open-air club for tramps and down-and-outs.* ○ *'Our elder son has been* ***knocking about*** *the Continent for several months. We don't know exactly where he is or what he's doing.'* = hang about/around, kick about/around.

2 [Vn.p nom pass] (*informal*) beat (sb) in a severe, brutal way: *I was called to attend to a woman whose husband had* ***knocked*** *her* ***about****, and had to stitch up a scalp wound.* TBU

knockabout [nom (Vn.p)] broadly humorous film or play involving chases, comic fights etc; slapstick: *This kind of rip-roaring* ***knockabout*** *is beloved of local audiences.* IND ○ *Charlie Chaplin appeared in several* ***knockabout*** *comedies, in which he was pursued by irate shopkeepers, head-waiters and policemen.* □ often used attrib, as in: ***knockabout*** *humour, farce, comedy, comedian.* next entry

knock about/around together/with [Vp, Vp.pr rel] (*informal*) (of two or more people) be often in each other's company. **o:** the same old crowd, bunch; his old cronies; some undesirable characters; that girl: *ASTON: Some of these men, from the cafe, we used to* ***knock about together*** *sometimes. I used to tag along* (accompany them) *on some of their evenings.* TC ○ *'It's amazing! Julie is still* ***knocking about with*** *that good-for-nothing Dave* (cf: *She and Dave are still* ***knocking about together***). *What on earth does she see in him?'* ○ *'Sarah's* ***knocking around with*** *some pretty unsavoury characters in London.'* = go about (together/with).

knock one's head against a brick wall [Vn.pr] ⇨ bang one's head etc.

knock against/on [Vpr, Vn.pr] (cause sth to) hit or strike (sth), often causing damage or pain. **S** [Vpr], **O** [Vn.pr]: head, shin; jug, bucket: *A branch was* ***knocking against*** *the garage door in the strong wind.* ○ *Tom* ***knocked*** *his head* ***on*** *a protruding iron bar and had to have six stitches.*

knock at/on [Vpr] strike at/on (sth), esp to gain entry to a room or house. **o:** door, window, entrance: *He would come bounding up the stairs,* ***knock at*** *our door and spend at least one evening ... with us.* AP7 ○ *He was strongly tempted to go and* ***knock on*** *the door of Michael's office.* TB ○ (children's rhyme) *One, two, buckle my shoe; Three, four,* ***knock at*** *the door; Five, six, pick up sticks ....*

knock back 1 [Vn ⇆ p pass] (informal) swallow (liquid, esp alcohol) quickly; swig. **O:** whisky, beer; pint: *There was nothing for Charlie to do but chat to the customers and* ***knock back*** *the Scotch.* OD ○ *He mixed two Ma Chéries, double strength, adding an extra dash of brandy to hold the feeble things together. 'There you are.* ***Knock*** *that* ***back****!'* DBM = throw back 3, toss off 1.

2 [Vn.p pass] (*informal*) cost (sb) a certain amount. **S:** new car; court case; daughter's wedding; dress, suit. **A:** 50 dollars; a good bit, a good few quid; how much?: *'I like your new stereo equipment. It must have* ***knocked*** *you* ***back*** *a couple of hundred pounds.' 'No, it didn't. I put it together myself.'* ○ *'If we take them out to the theatre and a meal, how much will that* ***knock*** *us* ***back****?'* = set back 2.

knock down 1 [Vn ⇆ p pass] cause (sb/sth) to fall to the ground; demolish. **O:** opponent, challenger, champion; building; fence, obstacle: *Jeffries was* ***knocked down*** *by a much stronger opponent in the first round of the contest.* ○ *He was elected to Lambeth Council ... with the ambition of* ***knocking down*** *the house in Brixton where he and his parents had lived in penury.* OBS = pull down 2.

2 [Vn ⇆ p pass] hit (sb) with a vehicle and cause him to fall, often inflicting injuries or causing death: *I think she must have been hurrying over to Harrods* (a store in London) *and been* ***knocked down*** *by a car. Probably she's still unconscious.* DC ○ *Your brother is the hit-and-run driver who* ***knocked down*** *a man and killed him outside Dorking.* DC

3 [Vn ⇆ p nom pass] persuade (sb) to reduce the price of sth; cause (a price) to be reduced by persuasion. **O:** dealer, stallholder; price, figure; vase, picture: *'Don't be too quick to agree a figure. You should be able to* ***knock*** *him* ***down*** *a few pounds on his asking price.'* ○ *It can be worthwhile to* ***knock down*** *the price of your current home if you're travelling abroad.* OXTM ○ *In the depression of the* *thirties, when everyone was going broke and all the properties were coming under the hammer at a* **knockdown** (cf ***knocked-down***) *price* (ie at a low price), *the McConchies were prudently buying land.* RFW □ knockdown used attrib, as in: ***knockdown*** *price, figure, sum.* = beat down.

4 [Vn ⇆ p pass adj] sell (sth) to sb by auction. **O:** lot number thirty-four; table, antique mirror, picture; farm, homestead: *'There is no way an auctioneer is going to* ***knock down*** *something to you without you knowing.'* OXTM ○ *The violin was* ***knocked down*** *to a Bond Street firm of dealers.* PTLB

5 [Vn ⇆ p nom pass adj] dismantle (sth) for ease of transport. **O:** machine, car, apparatus: *In many Asian countries there are assembly plants for the construction of cars which are imported in* ***knocked-down*** (*cf* ***knockdown***) *form from Europe, America and Japan.* ○ ***Knock-down*** *furniture from Sweden has become very popular in recent years.* □ nom form is used attrib, as in these examples.

knock for six 1 [Vn.pr pass] (*cricket*) (of a batsman) score six runs from a single ball bowled: *He attempted to* ***knock*** *the next ball* ***for six****, missed, and was clean bowled.* ○ *One spin bowler was* ***knocked for six*** *off three successive balls.*

2 [Vn.pr pass] (*informal*) deal a severe blow to (sb/sth); affect (sb/sth) deeply or devastatingly. **O:** enemy, competitor, rival; hopes, plans; scheme, project: *'Didn't you get to know of the Hampden Cross housing estate? The Council are putting one up all the way round here. It will* ***knock*** *the value of the property* ***for six****, of course.'* DIL ○ *Stock markets round the world were* ***knocked for six*** *by the news of the bank's collapse. .*

knock them in the aisles [Vn.pr] (*theatre*) score a great success with 'them' (ie the audience, the public), usu by a humorous performance, play etc: *When the mass did the right thing, they were the 'public'; when they did not react satisfactorily they were simply 'them' ('just can't get them moving tonight', 'if this doesn't* ***knock them in the aisles****, well, blast 'em').* HD

knock in/into [Vn ⇆ p pass, Vn.pr pass] drive (sth) into (sth) with a hammer etc. **O:** nail; joint; bung. **o:** wood; socket; hole: *I tried hard enough, but I couldn't* ***knock*** *the nail* ***in*** *straight.* ○ *The plugs had been accurately made and it was easy to* ***knock*** *them* ***into*** *their sockets.* = drive in/into.

knock sense into [Vn.pr pass] (*informal*) force (sb) to behave in a sensible way. **adj:** some, any, a little, a bit of: *I've been trying for years to* ***knock*** *some* ***sense into*** *my youngest daughter, but she insists on going her own way.*

knock off 1 [Vn ⇆ p pass, Vn.pr pass] remove (sth) with a blow (from sth). **O:** cup; man; insect. **o:** table; horse, deck; wall, coat: (traditional song) *'Every time that I go out,/ The monkey's on the table./ Get a stick and* ***knock*** *it* ***off****./ Pop goes the weasel!'* ○ *The cat's* ***knocked*** *the jug* ***off*** *the table.*

2 [Vp] (*informal*) stop work. **S:** workers, staff; pupils: *'We always* ***knock off*** *early on Christmas Eve. Nobody's in the mood to do any work, and we usually have a drink and a bit of an office party before we go home.'* ○ *The whistle went, the machines stopped and the men* ***knocked off*** *for lunch.*

3 [Vn ⇆ p pass, Vn.pr pass] reduce (a price) by (a stated amount). **O:** ten per cent, a few pence, a pound or two. **o:** the price, estimate, bill: *The greengrocer always* ***knocks*** *a bit* ***off*** *the price of his fruit for the pensioners.* ○ *'Did you pay the full price for the book?' 'No. The girl* ***knocked off*** *a pound because it was shop-soiled.'* ○ *'You overcharged me 70p last week.' 'Oh did I? Sorry. I'll* ***knock*** *it* ***off*** *your next bill.'*

4 [Vn ⇆ p pass] (*informal*) write or compose (sth) rapidly or easily. **O:** song, couple of verses; short story, article: *'Wait a minute while I* ***knock off*** *a letter to the bank.'* ○ *The script shows every sign of being* ***knocked off*** *in great haste. It is very badly written.* = throw off 4, toss off 2.

5 [Vn ⇆ p pass] (*slang*) kill (sb). **O:** policeman, guard, watchman: *The thieves broke into the back of the building and* ***knocked off*** *the night watchman, who must have surprised them.*

6 [Vn ⇆ p pass] (*slang*) steal (sth); steal from (a place). **O:** load of bullion; video, television; bank, security van: *He'd* ***knocked off*** *a couple of computers and was caught trying to sell them locally.* ○ *'They're a tough mob: they* ***knocked off*** *a bullion van last month.'*

knock sb's block/head off [Vn.p] (*slang*) (threaten to) strike sb, usu in punishment or retaliation: *'If I see that kid hanging round my car again, I'll* ***knock his block off****.'* □ usu with *shall/will.*

knock it off [Vn.p] (*slang*) stop doing sth irritating or unpleasant: *'Do me a favour! You've been whistling that tune all morning.* ***Knock it off****, will you?'* □ usu imperative. = pack it in, pack it up, turn it in.

knock spots off [Vn.pr] (*informal*) be far better than (sb/sth); surpass. **o:** all of you, the opposition, the competition; the local beer, home cooking: *This restaurant is impressive, but any little French café would* ***knock spots off*** *it.* ○ *When it comes to foreign languages, the girls can usually* ***knock spots off*** *the boys.*

knock on 1 [Vpr] strike at/on (sth). ⇨ knock at/on.

2 [Vn.pr] (cause sth to) hit or strike (sth). ⇨ knock against/on.

3 [Vp nom] (*rugby football*) knock the ball forwards with the hands — play not permitted by the rules of the game: *Jerry thought he'd scored a try, but the referee had blown his whistle for a* ***knock-on*** *some seconds earlier.*

knock-on effect [nom (Vp)] a consequence which has followed step by step from some original action; domino effect: *The increase in interest rates is bound to have a* ***knock-on effect*** *throughout manufacturing industry.* ○ *The* ***knock-on effect*** *of the delays is leaving many planes stranded.* BBCR

knock on the head [Vn.pr pass] (*informal*) destroy, demolish (sth). **O:** idea, scheme, plan; superstition, belief: *The increase in car prices has* ***knocked*** *our hopes for a new one right* ***on the head****.* ○ *'It's high time this myth about eighteenth-century design was* ***knocked on the head****.'* HAA

knock out 1 [Vn ⇆ p nom pass] make (sb) unconscious by means of a blow, very strong drink etc. **S:** boxer; challenger; punch; drug, pill; bug, virus; drink: *The fight ended with the challenger* ***knocking out*** *the champ* (cf *ended in a* ***knock-out*** *victory over the champ*). ○ *The driver was* ***knocked out*** *at the moment of impact, and could remember* *nothing of how the accident happened.* ○ *He was equally concerned about Gwen John's health . . . agreeing that there was nothing like a cough to* **knock** *you* **out**. GJ ○ *I've got Aunt Ellen's* **knock-out** *drugs, a whole bottle of them.* RFW □ knock-out can modify a noun, as shown. .

2 [Vn ⇆ p nom pass] stop (sb) as if with a blow; overwhelm (sb) with shock or admiration. **S:** news, dismissal; car, bike; house; painting, film: *I was completely* **knocked out** *by the news of Peter's death.* ○ *John's new flat* **knocked** *me* **out**. *I'd never seen anything so luxurious in my life.* ○ *She's beautiful, anyway, but in that dress she's a* **knock-out**. ○ *'The new musical at the Drury Lane Theatre is a* **knock-out**. *You must see it.'*

3 [Vn ⇆ p pass adj] seriously damage or destroy (sth). **O:** radio installation, missile launching site; tank, armoured vehicle: *The first rocket* **knocked out** *an armoured car.* ○ *The battlefield was littered with* **knocked-out** *tanks.*

knock out/out of 1 [Vn ⇆ p pass, Vn.pr pass] remove (sth) from (sth) by means of a blow or repeated blows. **O:** contents, ashes; tooth: *Several of Bill's teeth were* **knocked out** *in the accident.* ○ *'***Knock** *the powder* **out of** *the tin gently. We don't want it all over the room.'* ○ *Sam* **knocked** *the ashes* **out of** *his pipe* (cf *Sam* **knocked** *his pipe* **out**).

2 [Vn ⇆ p nom pass, Vn.pr pass] remove (sb/sth) at some stage in a contest; eliminate: *He would consider standing in a second round if the Prime Minister is* **knocked out** *in the first.* OBS ○ *Ipswich* **knocked** *Chelsea* **out of** *the competition in the third round, and were* **knocked out** *themselves in the fourth.*

knock the bottom out of [Vn.pr pass] (*informal*) suddenly remove the basis of (sth); weaken, undermine. **o:** case, argument; one's confidence; her world; the market: *The evidence of a passer-by* **knocked the bottom out of** *the boy's claim that he was nowhere near the place at the time.* ○ *'You always think that you're immune, and that things like this only happen to other people. Then, when they happen to you, it* **knocks the bottom out of** *your confidence.* AITC ○ *When John's wife left him,* **the bottom** *seemed to have been* **knocked out of** *his world.*

knock hell/the living daylights out of [Vn.pr pass] (*slang*) give (sb) a severe, brutal thrashing; drum heavily on (sth): *I'll kill her. I'll* **knock the living daylights out of** *her.'* TOH ○ *My dad . . . would be on the stage* **knocking hell out of** *the old joanna* (piano). PPLA

knock the spirit/the stuffing out of [Vn.pr pass] (*informal*) demoralize (sb) by physical attack or psychological shock: *Four days of continuous bombardment had* **knocked the stuffing out of** *the defenders, who surrendered without even a show of resistance.* ○ *I released his shoulder, letting my hand fall helplessly to my side as if his words had* **knocked** *all* **the spirit out of me**. CON

knock over [Vn ⇆ p pass adj] make (sb/sth) fall over by accidentally striking him or it. **O:** child; pot, vase, lamp: *Ermyn got up very quickly,* **knocking over** *her chair.* SE ○ *It was too dangerous to rely on oil lamps — we were drinking a lot of the time and tended to* **knock** *them* **over**.

knock through [Vp, Vn.p pass] remove a wall, partition etc, of (a room) in order to enlarge its area, or in order to make a new door, serving-hatch etc: *The apartment was occupied by a designer, who had* **knocked through** *between the two small bedrooms, and ripped out the simple plumbing, installing in its place an elegant decor of white tiles and chromium.* OBS ○ *The only major disagreement we had was what to do when we* **knocked** *the room* **through**. ST ○ *The middle interior wall has gone, and one can see through into the back garden with its breakfast patio. The* **knockers through** *are here.* L

knock together [Vn ⇆ p pass] prepare or construct (sth) rapidly and roughly. **O:** meal, snack; some kind of shelter; a sledge for the children; a few bookshelves; a rough bed: *I don't claim to be much of a handyman, but I reckon I could* **knock** *a rough table* **together**. ○ *The hut looked as if it had been* **knocked together** *in a great hurry.* = knock up 3.

knock their heads together [Vn.p pass] (*informal*) force two quarrelling people to behave sensibly by this or some similar violent action: *You could sense the women were longing to grab the children by the hair and* **knock their heads together**. ○ *Sometimes one feels that the leaders of the political parties should have* **their heads knocked together**.

knock up 1 [Vn ⇆ p pass] drive or hit (sth) upwards with a blow. **O:** fist, arm, weapon; latch, bar: *As the intruder rushed at me with a knife, I* **knocked** *his arm* **up**, *and hit him in the stomach with the poker.*

2 [Vn ⇆ p pass] awaken (sb) by knocking on a door or window. **O:** us; mill-workers; travellers; visitor: *'Would you mind* **knocking** *me* **up** *at about 7 o'clock tomorrow? I've got to catch an early train to London.'* ○ *In some Lancashire towns the mill-owners employed their own* **knockers-up** *who went round banging on the windows of the workers every morning to wake them up.*

3 [Vn ⇆ p pass] prepare or construct (sth) quickly and without much planning. **O:** snack, meal, dinner; shelter, hen-house, kennel, rabbit-hutch: *My mother was a marvel at* **knocking up** *a meal for the unexpected guest.* ○ *'Have you see the garage that George has built? It looks more like a shack* **knocked up** *out of driftwood.'* = knock together.

4 [Vp.n pass] (*cricket*) make, score (runs). **O:** a good score; twenty runs, a century (= a hundred runs): *At last the Sussex captain found his form and* **knocked up** *his best score of the season — a faultless 70.*

5 [Vn.p pass] make (sb) tired, exhausted or ill. **S:** climb, swim; experience, shock; overwork: *'Don't try to dig up the whole garden in one day: you'll* **knock** *yourself* **up**.' ○ *At half past ten that night Dickens arrived at his hotel in Albany 'pretty well* **knocked up**'. CD

6 [Vn.p pass] (esp *US, slang*) make (a woman) pregnant: *'His sister was going to drama school in six months — that's if she didn't get* **knocked up** *first.* = bang up.

knock-up [nom (Vp)] (*tennis*) a short period of practice before starting to play a game: *While the players were having a* **knock-up**, *the crowd were settling down in expectation of a first-class match.*

knot

knot together [Vn ⇆ p pass] join (two or more things) by means of a knot. **O:** two pieces of rope, string; laces: *People escaped from the burning hotel by* **knotting** *sheets* **together** *and using them as a rope.*

know

know about [Vpr pass, Vn.pr pass emph rel] have knowledge of, be aware of. **O:** anything, nothing; a lot, a good deal: *'Did you* **know about** *your son's behaviour at the club last night?' 'Yes, thank you. I* **know** *all* **about** *it.'* ○ *'Two weeks ago Britain* **knew** *nothing* **about** *John Major; now the whole world* **knows** *nothing* **about** *John Major.'* OBS ○ *Not much is* **known about** *the mountainous region to the north.*

not know about [Vpr] not recognize or accept the truth or sense of (sth). **o:** that; (any words used by a previous speaker): *'Joan's a pretty girl, isn't she?' 'I do***n't know about** *pretty. She's certainly got plenty of money.'* ○ *'Steve should make a good Chairman.' 'I do***n't know about** *that. He's not particularly decisive.'* □ usu first person, neg, simple present tense; used to express doubt about a claim sb has made.

know by sight [Vn.pr pass] know (sb) without being an acquaintance. **O:** her; film-star; your friend; the Vice-Chancellor: *'Have you ever met Professor James?' 'No, but I* **know** *him well enough* **by sight**.*'*

not know from [Vn.pr] not know (sb) because one has never seen him before. **O:** one brother, twin; goldfinch. **o:** another; yellowhammer: *'That nurse's head is always in the clouds. She never seems to* **know** *one patient* **from** *another.'* ○ *'He's hopeless at jobs around the house. Doesn't* **know** *a plane* **from** *a chisel.'* ⇨ next entry

not know from Adam [Vn.pr] not be at all familiar with sb's character, habits etc: *He sent me some business without* **knowing** *me* **from Adam***; I might have been a complete crook for all he knew.* PW ○ *'What do you want to go trusting me for? Hardly* **know** *me* **from Adam**.*'* HD ⇨ previous entry

know of [Vpr] be familiar with (sth); have heard about (sb) without having met him. **o:** a nice, quiet spot for a holiday; a good way to make money; an interesting restaurant: *'There is only one way that I* **know of** *to get out of this building and that's to keep turning right.'* ○ *'Excuse me. Do you by any chance* **know of** *a short cut to the post office?'* ○ *'Do you know Sir Ralph Thomas?' 'No; I* **know of** *him, but I've never met him.'* □ where know of is contrasted with know, as in the last example, the word of is pronounced /ov/.

not that I know of [Vpr] not as far as I am aware: *'She's been married happily now for four years — or at least* **not** *unhappy* **that I know of**.*'* RATT ○ *'Do twins run in your family, Charley?'* **'Not that I know of**,*' Charley said.* DBM □ used at the end of a sentence or as a separate reply.

know through and through [Vn.p] know and understand (sb) perfectly. **O:** him etc; her husband, the boss, men: *She had only been with him once, for a weekend — but her thoughts had been so constantly with him ... that she felt she* **knew** *him* **through and through** PW ○ *Mary* **knew** *children* **through and through** *After all, she'd brought up six of her own.*

known to [pass (Vn.pr)] on the records of (sb). **S:** tramp, suspect; applicant. **o:** the police, authorities; the Home Office: *We are anxious to interview in connection with this incident two men who are already* **known to** *the police.* □ cf the more straightforward passive of know: *Mr Jones has been* **known to** *me for several years, and I can write with confidence about his suitability for the vacancy in your office.*

knuckle

knuckle down (to) [Vp, Vp.pr pass] begin to work seriously (at a task). **o:** work, study; task; it; getting the job done: *I shall just have to* **knuckle down** *and get the marking done over the weekend.* ○ *He could not* **knuckle down to** *mastering the Law of Tort.* HB = buckle down (to), get down to.

knuckle under (to) [Vp, Vp.pr pass] (*informal*) yield in the face of pressure (from sth/sb). **o:** menaces, threats; pressure, authority; the bosses: *He's a very stubborn character, not the kind to* **knuckle under** *easily.* ○ *The British Government had* **knuckled under to** *threats of violence, which had created insurmountable obstacles to progress.* SC

kowtow

kowtow (to) [Vpr pass] behave in servile way (towards sb). **o:** the gentry, the clergy; people in authority, the bosses: *He ...would not wish to* **kowtow to** *the customers, though some of his fellows do that.* UL ○ *He may have made a lot of money but that doesn't mean he has to be* **kowtowed to** *all the time.*

L

labour

labour over [Vpr pass rel] work hard and continuously at (some difficult task). **o:** paper, document; draft, communiqué; marking, corrections: *The editor* **laboured over** *the manuscript till early morning.* ○ *Some kinds of writing are all the better for being* **laboured over**. = toil over.

labour under 1 [Vpr emph rel] (*formal*) have (sth) as a disadvantage or handicap. **o:** disability, infirmity: *The new regime removed many of the injustices* **under** *which the population had* **laboured**.

2 [Vpr emph rel] (*formal*) be misled or blinded by (sth). **o:** (mistaken, false) idea, supposition; misapprehension: *Our political opponents* **labour under** *the delusion that support for our policies is dwindling.*

lace

lace up [Vn ⇆ p nom pass] close up or fasten (sth) with laces. **O:** shoe, jacket: *His swimming-trunks are* **laced up** (or: **lace up**) *at the side.* ○ *Her new boots can be* **laced up** (or: *are* **lace-ups**). □ the form lace-up(s) refers to footwear only.

lace with 1 [Vn.pr pass] add (spirits) to (a hot beverage). **O:** tea, coffee. **o:** rum, whisky, brandy, vodka: *Someone had* **laced** *my drink* **with** *a stiff tot of brandy.* ○ *On night watch, the sailors drank hot tea* **laced with** *rum.* □ esp passive.

2 [Vn.pr pass] fill (one's talk) with (slang, oaths etc). **O:** speech, talk; conversation. **o:** oaths, curses; slang; jokes, humour: *The whole conversation was* ***laced with*** *quips and jokes.* JUNG □ esp passive.

laden

laden with [pass adj (Vn.pr)] (*formal*) bearing heavy loads or burdens; loaded with, burdened with. **S:** table, tree; businessman, official. **o:** food, fruit; care, responsibility: *The traditional picture of an English Christmas includes a table* ***laden with*** *food and drink.* ○ *One doesn't normally think of Stephen as a man* ***laden with*** *anxieties.* □ used with *appear* etc or after a noun. ⇨ load down (with).

ladle

ladle out [Vn ⇆ p pass adj] serve (sth) with a ladle or serving spoon. **O:** soup, beans, rice: *Martha stood at the head of the table,* ***ladling out*** *soup.*

lag

lag behind 1 [Vp, Vpr] fail to keep level (with sb), stay to the rear (of sb). **S:** runner, car. **m:** way, some way, far. **o:** leader, pack: *I was* ***lagging*** *some way* ***behind*** *as we entered the last lap.*

2 [Vp, Vpr] be inferior (to sb/sth), be losing (to sb/sth). **S:** plant, factory; industry; figure; production. **o:** rival, competitor; trading partner: *In steel production, we* ***lag behind*** *the rest of Europe.* ○ *Our figure* ***lags behind*** *the national average.* SC

lam

lam into [Vpr pass] (*informal*) attack (sb) violently, with the fists or verbally. **S:** boxer; listener, critic: *In the last round, Smith really* ***lammed into*** *his opponent.* ○ *'What did the poor fellow say that made you* ***lam into*** *him like that?'* = lay into.

land

land in [Vn.pr pass rel] (*informal*) make things end unhappily, badly etc for (sb). **S:** firm; colleague, friend; oneself. **o:** mess, muddle; court, prison; (*taboo*) the shit: *'Just look at the mess you've* ***landed*** *us* ***in****!'* ○ *'You know where he'll* ***land*** *himself next time?* ***In*** *jail.'*

land on one's feet [Vpr] (*informal*) make a quick recovery after difficult times or after being put in a difficult or challenging position: *She arrived here with just a few hundred pounds and is now running a thriving business. But then, she always did* ***land on her feet****.* = fall on one's feet.

land onto [Vn.pr pass] ⇨ land with.

land up [Vp] (*informal*) reach (a final point) after a journey, career etc. **S:** (lost) parcel, letter; crook, petty thief; wanderer, vagabond. **A:** in France; in prison; working on the land: *His hat blew off in a strong wind and* ***landed up*** *on top of a lorry.* ○ *After knocking about the world for a few years Michael* ***landed up*** *teaching in his home town.* ○ *The probation officer had a warning for Bill. 'One more appearance in court and you could* ***land up*** *in prison.'* = end up, fetch up.

land with [Vn.pr pass] (*informal*) oblige (sb) to accept (a burden). **S:** boss, colleague. **o:** task; arrangement, organization; child, invalid: *I've been* ***landed with*** *two extra sets of papers to mark.* ○ *Someone has* ***landed*** *me* ***with*** *the job of finding hotel rooms for the visitors* (or: ***landed onto*** *me the job of finding hotel rooms* etc) . ○ *The family were* ***landed with*** *mother-in-law* (or: *Mother-in-law was* ***landed onto*** *the family) for the entire weekend.* = saddle with.

lap

lap up 1 [Vn ⇆ p pass adj] drink (sth) by taking liquid on the tongue. **S:** cat, dog. **O:** milk, water: *The milk you put out in the saucer was quickly* ***lapped up****.*

2 [Vn ⇆ p pass adj] (*informal*) absorb or learn (sth) greedily or eagerly. **S:** spoilt child, favourite; student. **O:** flattery, praise; compliments; facts, knowledge: *Irma could call him the silliest things — 'treasure', 'little sparrow' — and he would* ***lap*** *them* ***up****.* PW ○ *He'll take all the instruction you can give him — he just* ***laps*** *it* ***up****.*

lapse

lapse into [Vpr emph rel] fall to a lower level of (feeling, seriousness, proficiency etc). **o:** a tearful state, tearfulness; crudeness, insensitivity: *The children were portrayed with a tenderness that never* ***lapsed into*** *sentimentality.* GJ ○ (She remembers) ***lapsing into*** *a state from which others have to rescue her.* MSAL

lapse from grace [Vpr] fall from a position in which one is highly thought of, favoured etc. **S:** adviser, associate, favourite: *Gunning spoiled his chances for promotion by writing articles highly critical of the party leadership. Then having* ***lapsed from grace*** *he found it hard to climb back up again.* = fall from grace.

lard

lard with [Vn.pr pass emph rel] (*formal*) add sth pompous, flowery etc to (one's words). **O:** speech, address. **o:** compliment, praise; anecdote, quotation: *The chairman* ***larded*** *his opening remarks* ***with*** *references to the visitor's qualities and achievements.* ○ *The sailors' language was richly* ***larded with*** *oaths.*

lark

lark about/around [Vp] (*informal*) play in a lively, carefree manner. **S:** children, students: *We were roach fishing,* ***larking about*** *perhaps more than anything else, and could catch nothing.* EDTH ○ *'Remember, no* ***larking about*** *at school today!'* ⇨ horse about/around.

lash

lash down 1 [Vn ⇆ p pass adj] tie (sth) firmly in position with ropes etc. **O:** sail, canvas; tarpaulin, awning; hatch; load; box, bale: *A tarpaulin was spread over the hay-rick and* ***lashed down*** *to prevent it blowing off in a high wind.* ○ *The crew* ***lashed down*** *the cargo of timber stowed on the foredeck.*

2 [Vp] be blown by wind so that it falls with some force. **S:** rain, sleet, hail: *The hail* ***lashed down****, drumming fiercely on the garage roof.*

lash out (at) [Vp, Vp.pr emph rel] make a sudden and violent attack, physical or verbal (upon sb). **S:** horse, mule; speaker, politician; husband, teacher. **o:** rider, stranger; tax-evader, slacker, child: *He had* ***lashed out*** *and severely mauled* (= hurt) *his publisher for daring to disobey.* CD ○ *It seemed that he was going to* ***lash out at*** *her, but he controlled himself.* DC ⇨ hit out (at) 2.

lash out (on) [Vp, Vp.pr] (*informal*) spend freely or lavishly (on sth); pay a lot, and more than one is willing to pay (for sth). **o:** food, wine; perfume, cigars, luxuries, fripperies: *When David goes on one of his European trips he* **lashes out on** *presents for the whole family.* ○ *Many parents resent having to* **lash out on** *expensive items of school uniform which their children will in any case grow out of in a year.* = splash out (on).

last

last out 1 [Vp] not be consumed or used up. **S:** supply, store; money; food, water, fuel: *We can hold this position for as long as the ammunition* **lasts out**. ○ *The petrol should just about* **last out** *till we get to the next village.* = hold out 2.

2 [Vp] (be able to) complete some difficult task without collapsing etc; remain alive, survive. **S:** climber, explorer; sick, elderly, person: *'We shall have to call a halt soon. Some of the youngsters haven't enough breath in them to* **last out** *till the end of the climb.'* ○ *The group at the bedside could see that Paul's condition was deteriorating: he'd probably not* **last out** *the afternoon.*

latch

latch on (to) [Vp, Vp.pr pass] (*informal*) perceive, understand, or feel sympathy for (sb/sth). **o:** talk, remarks; humour, wit; mood; ideas, philosophy: *As the mists cleared from my brain, I* **latched on to** *their conversation.* CON ○ *Elizabeth Bowen, after her 1920s frivolity and smartness, quickly* **latched on to** *the troubling ... spirit of the next decade.* EB

laugh

laugh (at) 1 [Vpr pass emph rel] show amusement (at sb/sth) by laughing. **o:** comedian; joke, story: *They were engaged in animated conversation, the old lady* **laughing at** *what the girl was telling her.* AF

2 [Vpr pass emph rel] mock, ridicule (sb/sth). **o:** him etc; misfortune, impediment; speech, dress: *They all* **laughed at** *Christopher Columbus/ When he said the world was round./ They all* **laughed** *when Edison recorded sound.* G GERSHWIN, I GERSHWIN ○ *People ridiculed his manners and* **laughed at** *his provincial accent.* = make fun of.

laugh away [Vn ⇆ p pass] drive away, by laughing, some unpleasant feeling or sensation in oneself or others. **O:** anxiety, fear, misgivings; depression, tears: *'I know you're very brave but you can't just* **laugh** *a toothache* **away** *— you'll have to see a dentist.'* ○ *Jane had this tremendous fear of the dark, and her husband would try to* **laugh** *it* **away**, *saying it was just her overdeveloped imagination.*

laugh in sb's face [Vpr] (*informal*) reject (sb) with cruel mockery. **S:** captor; boss; (cruel) lover: *'Just try asking them for a bit longer to pay back the loan. They'll just* **laugh** *in your* **face**.*'*

laugh off [Vn ⇆ p pass adj] (*informal*) try, by laughing, to pretend that sth for which one is responsible has not happened or is not important. **O:** blunder, faux pas; neglect, responsibility: *That's a mistake that can't easily be* **laughed off**. ○ *'Don't worry,' he said, trying to* **laugh off** *his resentment at the intrusion.* AITC ○ *'Well, I've something to tell you. Your incompetence has set the project back a month. Now try* **laughing** *that* **off**!*'*

laugh one's head off [Vn.p] (*informal*) laugh noisily and cheerfully, often at sb else's expense. **S:** onlooker, listener: *As he picked himself up from the floor, he saw a couple of boys* **laughing their heads off**.

laugh on the other side of one's face [Vpr] (*informal*) be made to appear ridiculous because one's supposed reason for being pleased with oneself etc is shown to have no real basis: *'Laugh as much as you like, I've got some news here that will make you* **laugh on the other side of your face**!*'* ○ *If Robert thinks he has outwitted his teacher, he is due for a surprise. Mr Prescott will make him* **laugh on the other side of his face**. □ often with *will/would* (*make*), as in the examples; note the plural: *'This'll make them* **laugh on the other side of their faces**.*'*

laugh out of [Vn.pr pass] make (sb) forget his unhappiness etc by laughing at it. **o:** mood, state; depression, misery; embarrassment: *He could tell she was in a depressed state and did his best to* **laugh** *her* **out of** *it.* ○ *She tried to* **laugh** *him* **out of** *this infantile episode.* FL

laugh out of court [Vn.pr pass] (*informal*) dismiss (sth) scornfully as false, ridiculous etc. **O:** charge, accusation; claim, statement: *The story was untrue — the villagers had* **laughed** *it* **out of court**. HAA ○ *Any attempt to charge us with some legal offence would be* **laughed out of court**. TBC

launch

launch (out) into [Vpr pass, Vp.pr pass] begin (a long and involved speech etc), often in a vigorous or violent way. **S:** orator, critic. **o:** tale, account; rigmarole; (verbal) tirade, onslaught: *Mr Blearney* **launched into** *another of his stories.* HD ○ *Before she could speak he had* **launched into** *a long and circumstantial narrative.* HD ○ *He* **launched out into** *a tirade ... on the barbarism of the English upper classes.* BLCH

launch out (into) [Vp, Vp.pr pass rel] (*informal*) change to sth involving challenge and risk. **S:** firm, businessman; producer, writer. **o:** manufacture, politics; journalism: *Why must a dancer* **launch out** *as choreographer as well?* OBS ○ *You'll want to* **launch out into** *something with a proper salary.* THH

lavish

lavish on/upon [Vn.pr pass emph rel] give, devote (sth) in abundance to (sb/sth). **O:** sympathy, kindness; care, attention. **o:** child, ward, pupil; car, house: *Rodin had furnished the garden with a care he never* **lavished on** *the house.* GJ ○ *The kindnesses which his father has* **lavished upon** *him are numberless.* MLT

lay

lay about [Vp, Vpr] (*informal*) fight or struggle with (sb), physically or verbally. **o:** one (= oneself); opponent, assailant: *Aren't you* **laying about** *for your discharge from hospital?* THH □ also lay about oneself meaning 'fight people around one': *With his free arm he proceeded to* **lay about** *him.* SD

layabout [nom (Vp)] (*informal*) person who habitually avoids work, and who may be a petty criminal: *He's a wretched, idle* **layabout** *— never done a day's work in his life.* ○ *'Get on your feet, you crowd of* **layabouts**!*'*

lay aside 1 [Vn ⇆ p pass] place (sth) to one side. **O:** reading, needlework: *She* **laid aside** *her knitting for a moment to rest her eyes.* ○ *After he* **laid** *his papers* **aside**, *she would read aloud to him.* GE = put aside 1, set aside 1.

2 [Vn ⇆ p pass] relinquish, abandon (sth). **O:** burden, responsibility, cares of office: *Now that he's nearing retirement, some of his responsibilities can be* ***laid aside****.*

lay aside/by [Vn ⇆ p pass] save (sth) for future needs. **S:** parent, young couple. **O:** money, cash: *We must* ***lay*** *something* ***aside*** *for the boy's education.* ○ *They've a little money* ***laid by*** *for emergencies.* = put by.

lay at sb's door [Vn.pr pass emph rel] say that sb is responsible for (sth). **O:** the blame, the responsibility, the guilt: *The blame for these accidents should be* ***laid at the door of*** *careless drivers.* ○ *With so many misleading reports circulating, it is hard to say* ***at whose door*** *the responsibility should be* ***laid****.* = attach to 3 . ⇨ lie at sb's door.

laid back [adj (Vn.p)] relaxed, easy-going: *I am living by the ocean in Southern California. People tell me I speak like the natives. They say I look '****laid back****'.* LC ○ *Max Wall, exuding* ***laid-back*** *magic, runs off with* (ie dominates) *the last 15 minutes of the play.* OBS □ laid-back used before a noun; laid back used after *appear* etc.

lay before [Vn.pr pass] present (sth) to an official body for discussion, passing into law etc. **O:** plan, proposal; bill. **o:** committee, council; Parliament, the House: *His proposals were* ***laid before*** *a select committee of members.* ○ *Here is a draft of the legislation he intends to* ***lay before*** *Parliament.*

lay by [Vn ⇆ p pass] ⇨ lay aside/by.

layby [nom (Vp)] recess at the side of main road where vehicles may be parked: *We parked the car in a* ***layby*** *and had a picnic lunch.*

lay down 1 [Vn ⇆ p pass] place (sb/sth) on a flat surface, eg a table; set down (sth) which may be a danger or nuisance: *Knowing that there was no bringing the boy back to life, Apollo sorrowfully* ***laid*** *him* ***down****.* GLEG ○ *Most of the men had already* ***laid down*** *their weapons.* = put down 1. ⇨ lay down one's arms.

2 [Vn ⇆ p pass adj] prescribe, indicate (sth). **O:** rule, principle; what action to follow, how to proceed: *We had to* ***lay down*** *the general direction in which the answer lay.* MFM ○ *Follow the procedure* ***laid down*** *in our booklet.* ○ *You don't have to think about what to do, or when or why. It is* ***laid down****.* BRN

3 [Vn ⇆ p pass] store (sth) in a cellar to mature. **O:** claret, burgundy, port: *Father had managed to* ***lay down*** *a few good bottles of claret before the war.* = put down 6.

4 [Vn ⇆ p pass] construct, build (sth). **O:** ship, vessel; railway: *Several of the giant tankers are being* ***laid down*** *in Korean yards.*

lay down one's arms [Vp.n] (*military*) surrender. **S:** army, regiment; troops: *The majority of their soldiers simply* ***laid down their arms*** B ⇨ lay down 1.

lay down the law [Vn ⇆ p] say, with real or assumed authority, what should be done. **S:** (so-called) expert, specialist; critic, rebel. **A:** on pollution, on law and order: *It is not right for the soldier to* ***lay down the law*** *in political matters.* MFM ○ *Churchill tended to talk as if Great Britain and France could still* ***lay down the law*** *in Europe.* EH = hold forth.

lay down one's life (for) [Vp.n, Vn.p.pr emph rel] (*formal*) sacrifice one's life (on behalf of sth/sb). **S:** patriot, fanatic. **o:** country, king; cause, convictions: *Young men flocked to the recruiting offices, ready to fight and, if need be, to* ***lay down their lives****.* ○ *It was a cause* ***for*** *which he was prepared to* ***lay down his life****.*

lay down to [Vn.p.pr pass] convert (land) into (pasture), ie for cattle or sheep. **O:** field, big acreage. **o:** grass, clover: *The farmers decided to* ***lay*** *a big acreage* ***down to*** *grass.*

lay the blame (for) (on) [Vn.pr pass emph rel] regard (sb) as the one responsible (for an error, evil etc). **o:** (**for**) loss, setback; mistake, blunder; decision, plan, policy; (**on**) one's wife, partner; government: *There was no one person* ***on*** *whom* ***the blame*** *could be* ***laid****; responsibility for the failure was evenly shared.* ○ *The churches are united and vocal in ...* ***laying the blame for*** *the recent tragic events where it belongs.* SC = put the blame on.

lay in [Vn ⇆ p pass adj] provide oneself with a stock of (sth). **O:** winter fuel, food supplies, provisions; drink, cigarettes: *We* ***laid in*** *a good supply of table wine just before the Budget increases took effect.*

lay into [Vpr pass] (*informal*) attack (sb) violently, with one's fists or verbally: *I saw Jones* ***laying into*** *a man twice his size.*

lay hold of 1 [Vn.pr pass(o)] seize, grasp (sth). **S:** porter, gaoler. **o:** bundle, case; prisoner, victim: *We* ***laid hold of*** *the rope and pulled lustily.* BB ○ *As he left the building he was* ***laid hold of*** *and hurriedly bundled into a van.*

2 [Vn.pr pass (o)] obtain, acquire (sth). **S:** speculator, developer. **o:** property, land: *He was lucky to* ***lay hold of*** *a block of shares before the price went up.*

lay off 1 [Vp, Vpr] (*informal*) stop doing (sth harmful, unpleasant, irritating etc). **o:** it; drink, cigarettes, drugs; all-night parties; bullying, shouting: *A teacher came in. 'There's far too much noise here', he said. '****Lay off****, or I'll put the lot of you in detention.'* ○ *She was always telling Jack to* ***lay off*** *the insecticide and stop interfering with the balance of nature.* SE ○ *So long as I can make good my threat they'll* ***lay off*** *the use of force.* TBC

2 [Vpr] (*informal*) stop troubling, molesting (sb/sth); leave (sb/sth) alone. **o:** family, girlfriend; chickens, sheep: *'Take it easy, then he'll soon* ***lay off*** *you.'* AITC ○ *'****Lay off*** *my tie and give me a kiss.'* SC

3 [Vn ⇆ p nom pass adj] dismiss (sb) from work, usu temporarily, while trading conditions are bad. **S:** firm, management. **O:** workers, staff: *The factory was* ***laying*** *people* ***off****.* AITC ○ *He is a skilled worker* ***laid off*** *from his job in a Belfast shipyard.* T ○ *Rolls-Royce says the* ***lay-offs*** *will start from 22 December, the day its factories close for Christmas.* IND

4 [Vp nom] aim to one side of a target to allow for wind or movement of the target. **S:** gunner, hunter: *I bowled over four rabbits by* ***laying off*** *enough ahead of them.* RFW ○ *It came straight at us. One couldn't miss: no* ***lay-off*** *at all sideways.* RFW □ the lay-off is the amount one has to aim to one side.

lay on 1 [Vn ⇆ p pass] supply, provide, furnish (sth). **S:** landlord, council; firm, host. **O:** water, electricity, gas; car, transport; driver, escort: *We had electricity* ***laid on****.* H ○ *'I'll* ***lay on*** *a car tomorrow and have you run down to London.'* DIL

2 [Vn ⇆ p pass adj] make arrangements for (sth); organize. **O:** concert, display, exhibition, outing, party: *They decided to get married and we* **laid on** *an old-fashioned family wedding.* SU ○ *It's his birthday. That's why I* **laid on** *a party.* QA

3 [Vn ⇆ p pass adj] (*informal*) make (sth) seem bigger, worse etc, than it really is; exaggerate. **O:** it; pathos, sorrow, regret; pleasure, gratitude. **A:** (rather, a bit) thick, with a trowel: *The only sin he ever had to confess was the sin of Pride: and he* **laid** *it* **on** *thick.* US ○ *That's how we like our humour —* **laid on** *with a trowel.* OBS ○ *He's* **laying** *it* **on** *a bit, with all this talk of wanting to help the underprivileged.*

lay the blame (on) [Vn.pr pass emph rel] ⇨ lay the blame (for) (on).

lay one's cards on the table [Vn.pr pass] (*informal*) declare openly one's assets, intentions etc: *How did Alec know that Harold wouldn't take advantage of these confidences? How foolish to* **lay** *all* **his cards on the table**! PW ○ *The negotiators felt they had nothing to lose by* **laying** *some of* **their cards on the table** *at the beginning of the talks.* = put one's cards on the table.

lay emphasis/stress on [Vn.pr pass emph rel] treat (sth) as specially important; give special attention to (sth); emphasize, stress. **S:** government, council; planner, developer; report, survey. **adj:** much, little; great, special, particular. **o:** wishes, consent (of the governed); cost, profit; lack, absence (of amenities); achieving results, making a profit: *She and Dr Gager* **lay** *great* **emphasis on** *developing confidence and mathematical skill.* G ○ *Too little* **stress** *has been* **laid on** *preserving an existing sense of community in the planning of new estates.*

lay eyes on [Vn.pr emph rel] perceive, see (sb). **A:** never; first, next. **o:** his etc wife, brother; prisoner, accused man: *'Do you deny having spoken to the witness on the day in question?' 'Yes, sir, I do. In fact I've never* **laid eyes on** *him before.'* ○ *'He's a hooligan. When I first* **laid eyes on** *him, I thought he's certainly not the type for my Cairy. Too damn rough.'* YAA = set eyes on.

lay (one's) hands on 1 [Vn.pr rel] take or obtain (sth) for one's use. **o:** extra capital, spare cash; office space, building land: *It was a purely mercenary desire to* **lay hands on** *valuable manuscripts.* ○ *The mob pelted police with poles and anything they could* **lay their hands on**. G ○ *Wimbledon* (ie those in charge of the tennis championships) *should allocate him official tickets. He can* **lay his hands on** *400 unofficially for the men's finals.* G □ often used with *can/could, be able to.* = get one's hands on 1.

2 [Vn.pr rel] find (sth) one is looking for. **o:** book, paper, reference; money: *'I don't carry a fortune around. You've got everything I could* **lay hands on** *this morning.'* CTD ○ *I arranged these shelves, and I could* **lay my hands on** *anything.* EM ○ *I was never able to* **lay my hands** *quickly and accurately* **on** *quotations.* SML □ often used with *can/could, be able to.*

3 [Vn.pr] (*informal*) seize or arrest (sb) in order to punish or hurt him. **o:** criminal, mischief-maker: *All she wanted to do was* **lay hands on** *Victoria and shake her into recognition of what she had done.* TP ○ *The place is swarming with policemen just waiting to* **lay their hands on** *some of us.* CSWB ○ *Heaven help that boy if ever I* **lay my hands on** *him!* = get one's hands on 2.

never/not lay a finger/hand on [Vn.pr] (*informal*) not harm or molest (sb) at all: *We have firm discipline, but the staff* **never lay a finger on** *the boys.* ○ *He* **never laid a finger on** *her but would like us to think he did.* OD ○ *'Nobody has* **laid a hand on** *me. Yet.'* TOH

lay out 1 [Vn ⇆ p nom pass adj] arrange (parts) in relation to each other and to the whole in a convenient and pleasing manner. **S:** editor, printer; architect, landscape-gardener, planner; shopkeeper, window-dresser. **O:** front page, contents; suburb, street, park; wares, stock, goods: *The empty ashtrays were* **laid out** *neatly on the little tables.* CON ○ *Oswald took an unskilled job doing photo* **lay-out** *work.* OBS ○ *... the leafy and historic park of Sceaux,* **laid out** *to the south of Paris by Le Nôtre.* AF = set out 2.

2 [Vp.n pass adj] present (sth) in words; declare, state. **S:** speaker, lecturer; delegate; article. **O:** ideas, thoughts; wishes, requirements; criticisms: *They support more dialogue with the West on disarmament and* **lay out** *a vision of a world free of nuclear and chemical warfare.* G ○ *Let's be sure that we've got a good basic design, that we did* **lay out** *our requirements properly.* CHAL = set out 3.

3 [Vp.n pass adj] spread out (clothes) ready for the wearer to put on. **S:** valet, chambermaid. **O:** clean underclothes; evening dress, dinner jacket: *The drill is to* **lay out** *the clothes that he'll be wearing in the evening.* RFW ○ *'Why don't you have a shower and I'll* **lay out** *that nice new uniform for you?'* CH

4 [Vn ⇆ p pass] spend (sth); invest (sth). **O:** cash, a lot (of money); capital, resources: *He had to* **lay out** *all he had on the airline tickets.* ILIH ○ *Last year there was a considerable* **outlay** (= expenditure) *on school uniforms.* ○ *It's not likely that many countries would* **lay out** *the funds for a structure of that size.* □ nom form is outlay.

5 [Vn ⇆ p pass adj] prepare (a dead person) for burial. **S:** undertaker, family. **O:** ⚠ the deceased; corpse, body: *Word had to be sent to Woods to come and* **lay out** *the body.* AW ○ *She can set a limb and deliver a child, ... and* **lay out** *a corpse and resuscitate the drowned.* POS

6 [Vn ⇆ p pass] (*informal*) make (sb) unconscious by striking him: *I* **laid** *one of them* **out** *and I had another one round the throat.* TC ○ *If you slap my face — by God, I'll* **lay** *you* **out**! LBA = knock out 1.

lay claim to 1 [Vn.pr pass(o) emph rel] (*legal*) maintain that in law one is entitled to (sth). **S:** relative, associate; government. **o:** estate, fortune; title (of nobility); territory: *There was little doubt that Gray's will would be contested: his former wife would surely* **lay claim to** *the large sum he had left to his housekeeper.* ○ *'If the property was ever* **laid claim to** *by a surviving relative you might have difficulty proving your title to it.'* ○ *Britain and Argentina* **lay claim to** *the same area.* G

2 [Vn.pr emph rel] maintain, assert, that one knows, understands etc, (sth). **o:** knowledge, understanding, expertise; familiarity (with); being a connoisseur, having some competence: *'I* **lay** *no* **claim to** *expert knowledge of the stock market, but it strikes me that these companies have an excellent record of growth.'* ○ *The Oxford Archaeological Unit say* *that Abingdon can* ***lay claim to*** *being the the oldest town in Britain.* OXTM

lay to rest 1 [Vn.pr pass] (*formal*) bury (sb). **O:** body, remains: *The victims of the disaster were* ***laid to rest*** *in the village churchyard.*

2 [Vn.pr pass] finally show (sth) to be false, unjustified etc; finally settle or resolve (sth). **S:** explanation; statement, communiqué. **O:** story, tale; rumour, scandal; doubt, uncertainty: *An official statement* ***laid to rest*** *the remaining fears about possible redundancies in the industry.* ○ *Sweden will today attempt to* ***lay to rest*** *the messy affair of the Olof Palme murder* (ie the murder of its Prime Minister). G

lay up 1 [Vp.n pass adj] accumulate (supplies etc), eg for an emergency. **O:** foodstuffs, fodder; provisions, fuel; store, supply: *We'll need to* ***lay up*** *a good supply of feed if this winter's going to be like the last.* ○ *He began to* ***lay up*** *... a quite extraordinary store of miscellaneous antiquarian knowledge.* MRJ = store up 1.

2 [Vn ⇆ p pass adj] take (a vehicle) off the road; put (sth) out of commission. **O:** motor vehicle, ship: *He's had to* ***lay*** *his* ***car up****: he can't afford the insurance premiums.* ○ *For thirteen years the flying boat has been* ***laid up*** *on the Isle of Wight.* BBCTV

3 [Vn.p pass adj] make (sb) inactive; make (sb) keep to his bed. **S:** flu, a severe cold; a broken leg, a stiff neck: *George was* ***laid up*** *with a sore throat.* GE ○ *A bout of malaria had* ***laid*** *me* ***up*** *for a few weeks.* ○ *He was* ***laid up*** *with a bad knee.* MFM □ often in the passive form followed by *with* + the name of the illness or injury.

lay up for oneself [Vn.p.pr] (*formal*) ensure by one's present conduct, or neglect, that trouble will follow. **O:** trouble, difficulty, problems, bother: *You are* ***laying up for yourselves*** *the most appalling economic problems.* BBCTV ○ *He's* ***laid up*** *no end of trouble* ***for himself****.*

laze

laze about/around [Vp, Vpr] spend one's time idly; not do anything energetic. **o:** the place, the house; town: *For most of the holiday he watched videos or just* ***lazed about*** *in his room.* = idle about/around, loiter about/around.

lead

lead astray [Vn.p pass] tempt (sb) to do wrong. **S:** criminal, con man; charmer. **O:** young people, innocent girls: *He's* ***led*** *many girls* ***astray*** *with his easy, superficial charm.* ⇨ go astray.

lead back (to) [Vp, Vp.pr] have its origin (in some earlier stage or time). **S:** practice, custom, belief; affection, hostility. **o:** Saxon times, the Norman Conquest; early childhood: *We find a long line of evolving creatures whose ancestry* ***leads back to*** *the simplest living organisms.* F = date from/back to, go back (to) 2.

lead in (with) [Vp nom, Vp.pr emph rel] introduce or open one's remarks, a performance etc. **o:** a few words of welcome; a reference to the guest's achievements; a few notes on the flute: *The chairman* ***led in with*** *some flattering references to the visiting speaker's record in the industry.* ○ *There was a long* ***lead-in*** *on the piano; then the strings and woodwind came in together.*

lead off [Vp nom] begin, start: *Ned, the General Editor,* ***led off*** *with a general survey of the objectives to be aimed at.* CON ○ *The town band* ***led off*** *by playing the National Anthem.*

lead on [Vn.p pass] (*informal*) (try to) persuade (sb) to do, believe etc, sth by making false promises. **S:** advertiser, salesman; poster, brochure; playboy: *Travel brochures do* ***lead*** *you* ***on*** *with their promises of five-star treatment in luxury hotels.* ○ *'Haven't you noticed the predatory gleam in his eye? He's probably* ***leading*** *you* ***on****.'*

lead up the garden path [Vn.pr pass] (*informal*) mislead, deceive (sb). **S:** rogue, imposter; politician, expert. **O:** police; electorate; consumer: *We have been* ***led up the garden path*** *before with such promises* (ie of magnificent cricket). SC ○ *Someone posing as a television reporter has been* ***leading*** *us* ***up the garden path****.*

lead up to 1 [Vp.pr] guide or direct a conversation so that one can introduce (sth). **o:** matter, issue, question; subject, topic: *We could tell that he was* ***leading up to*** *to a favourite theme: his opposition to European unity.* = bring round to.

2 [Vp.pr pass] occur, one after the other, before (sth); have (sth) as a consequence; prepare. **S:** incidents, events; discussion, argument. **o:** conflict, war; agreement: *The report describes the negotiations which* ***led up to*** *the settlement.* ○ *Every event in Oswald's life* ***led up to*** *that moment.* OBS

leaf

leaf through [Vpr nom pass] read (sth) in a brief, inattentive way, turning the pages quickly. **o:** book, magazine: *Mary* ***leafed*** *idly* ***through*** *some old magazines as she waited for her taxi to arrive.* ○ *I can't claim that I've read the article at all carefully: just given it a quick* ***leaf-through****.* □ compare: *a quick* '***leaf-through***/ *a quick* ***leaf*** '***through***. = flick through, thumb through.

leak

leak out [Vp] (*informal*) become known despite efforts to keep it secret. **S:** news, information; secret: *The news* ***leaked out****.* WDM ○ *Stringent precautions were taken to prevent the details of the meeting* ***leaking out****.* = get out 1.

lean

lean on [Vpr pass] (*informal*) make (sb) act as one wishes by the threat or use of force, by blackmail etc. **S:** gangster, racketeer; politician, minister. **o:** bookmaker, small-time crook; colleague, ally: *'Joe's soft. He'll co-operate. He just needs* ***leaning on*** *a little.'* ○ *There is a deliberate strategy of offering the least possible public offence to these people while* ***leaning on*** *them hard in private.* G

lean on/upon [Vpr pass emph rel] choose (sb reliable) for moral support. **o:** colleague, parent, teacher: *In a crisis, the headmaster tends to* ***lean*** *rather too much* ***on*** *senior members of staff.* ○ *It was reassuring to have someone* ***upon*** *whom he could* ***lean*** *for a while.*

lean out/out of [Vp, Vpr] thrust the head and shoulders out (of sth); have the head and shoulders projecting (from sth). **o:** window, porthole: (safety of doors on railway coaches) *Passengers have to pull down a window,* ***lean out*** *and turn a handle, and the door opens outwards.* OBS ○ *If we* ***leant*** *a long way* ***out of*** *our hotel window we could just glimpse a small triangle of blue sea.*

lean over [Vp, Vpr] slant, incline, one's head and shoulders (so that one can more easily hear sb, see what he is doing etc): *Peter* ***leant*** *(or:* ***leaned)*** ***over*** *and whispered something in Felicity's ear.* ○ *I do so hate people* ***leaning over*** *me when I am trying to read the paper.*

lean over backwards [Vp] (*informal*) try one's hardest (to help, understand, co-operate etc). **S:** assessor, examiner; court, jury. **A:** to be fair, to see his side of the question; trying to help her: *The examiners* ***leant over backwards*** *to find some saving merit in the candidate's literature paper.* ○ *People were* ***leaning over backwards*** *trying to be pleasant to this odious little man.* □ usu followed by *to*-infin or *-ing* form. ⇨ bend over backwards to do sth/doing sth, fall over backwards to do sth/doing sth.

lean towards [Vpr rel] tend to support (a cause); favour. **o:** the Left, the Right; communism, federalism, liberalism: *In his student days he* ***leaned towards*** *socialism; but with the passing of time he became increasingly conservative.* = incline towards.

leap

leap at [Vpr pass adj] accept or seize (sth) eagerly. **o:** ⚠ the opportunity, the chance, the offer: *If he offered me a small part in his new production, I'd* ***leap at*** *the chance.* ○ *The opportunity was laid before him and eagerly* ***leapt at***. = jump at.

learn

learn from [Vpr] by studying (one's mistakes etc), and those of others, ensure that they are not repeated. **o:** experience(s); mistake, blunder: *'At my age,' Milly said, 'one has to* ***learn from*** *other people's experiences.'* OMIH ○ (Helen has just learnt that her teenage daughter is pregnant) *'Oh, Jo, you're only a kid. Why don't you* ***learn from*** *my mistakes?'* TOH = profit by.

learn off (by heart/rote) [Vn ⇆ p pass, Vn.p.pr pass] memorize (sth) perfectly. **O:** part, lines (in a play); formula, theorem: *'****Learn*** *these words* ***off by heart****.'* BFA ○ *'Can you* ***learn off*** *the part by the end of the week?'*

lease

lease back [Vn ⇆ p nom pass] (*commerce*) sell the freehold, or sometimes the long lease, of a property in order to free the capital tied up in it, and obtain in return the temporary use of the property on a lease. **O:** property, office block: *The Managing Director suggested to the Board that the best way of obtaining capital for the expansion programme would be to sell the company's headquarters to a finance house and then* ***lease*** *them* ***back***. ○ *In recent years there has been a spate of* ***leaseback*** *deals as more and more firms cash in on the value of the properties they own.*

leave

leave about/around [Vn.p pass, Vn.pr pass] fail to put (sth) away carefully and tidily. **O:** clothes; book, paper. **o:** place; room, house: *'Don't* ***leave*** *your toy soldiers* ***around*** *the house: I walk on them all the time.'* ○ *The nurse took pride in her work: she wouldn't have* ***left*** *things* ***about***. DC

leave aside [Vn ⇆ p pass] not consider or calculate (sth). **O:** matter, question; cost, inconvenience: ***Leaving*** *the matter of cost* ***aside***, *we still have to find time off from other work.* ○ *I don't see how you can* ***leave aside*** *his neglect of his family.*

leave it at that [Vn.pr pass] (*informal*) say or do nothing further; let matters rest there: *The insurers weren't prepared to compensate him for loss of earnings, so he had to* ***leave it at that***. ○ *'It isn't like that,' I said wearily. 'I did love you, but I can't now. Let's* ***leave it at that****.'* RATT

leave behind 1 [Vn ⇆ p pass] fail or forget to bring or take (sth); abandon (sth), eg in a retreat. **O:** raincoat, umbrella; wallet, key; wounded, dying: *'It's a fine day: you can* ***leave*** *your mac* ***behind****!'* ○ *In their withdrawal, much of the heavy equipment had to be* ***left behind***.
2 [Vp.n pass, Vn.pr pass emph] (*formal*) leave (sth) as a sign or record that sb has acted or sth has occurred. **S:** government, regime; invader; typhoon, storm. **O:** record, legacy; devastation, damage: *Some rulers have* ***left behind*** *no lasting memorial.* ○ *The cyclone* ***left behind*** *it a trail of destruction.*
3 [Vn ⇆ p pass] leave (sb) in an inferior position financially etc. **A:** far, well; way, a long way; miles. **O:** contemporaries, schoolfellows; rivals, competitors: *Those on fixed incomes, including old age pensioners, are being* ***left*** *well* ***behind***. SC ⇨ be behind 2, fall behind 1.

leave down [Vn.p pass] allow (sth) to remain in a lowered position. **O:** handle, lever, switch: *All switches should be* ***left down*** *during the experiment.* ↔ leave up. ⇨ stay down 1.

leave (for) 1 [Vpr, Vn.pr] depart (to travel to another place). **O:** home; London. **o:** office, work; New York: *We* ***leave for*** *Madrid by the next plane.* ○ *He* ***left*** *home* ***for*** *the station a few minutes ago.*
2 [Vn.pr pass rel] abandon (sth/sb) in order to follow sth or sb new. **O:** army, law; wife, family. **o:** Church, politics; another woman: *He* ***left*** *business* ***for*** *a new career as a social worker.* ○ *My husband* ***left*** *me* ***for*** *a young woman with a degree in computer sciences.* MSAL

leave for dead [Vn.pr pass] abandon (sb) in the belief that he is dead: *He'd been* ***left for dead*** *near the enemy lines but had later turned up at a military hospital.* ○ (*figurative*) *Christie was fastest off the blocks,* ***leaving*** *the rest* ***for dead***. □ usu passive.

leave in [Vn ⇆ p pass] allow (sth) to remain where it is. **O:** application, proposal, bid; passage, reference: *I shouldn't* ***leave in*** *that reference to your employer: I should take it out.* ⇨ stay in 2.

leave in the lurch [Vn.pr pass] abandon, desert (sb) at a time of difficulty. **O:** family; mistress, partner; company, department: *'You're just as callous as the rest of them: you're just going to walk out on a poor old man and* ***leave*** *him* ***in the lurch****.'* TST ○ *She'd just gone away, and that was that. She hadn't* ***left me in the lurch*** *with a mountain of debts or any such thing.* LLDR

leave in peace [Vn.pr pass] allow (sb) to remain undisturbed. **S:** child, pupil, student. **O:** parent, teacher, tutor: *'If only I could trust Janice to* ***leave*** *you* ***in peace****,' Isabel began, and at that moment there was a scampering of feet.* PW ○ *'No, I don't want a nice warm drink. I just want to be* ***left in peace****, if that's not too much to ask.'*

leave off 1 [Vn ⇆ p pass] no longer wear or put on (a garment). **O:** jumper, winter woollens, overcoat: *Cardigans and sweaters can be* ***left off*** *when* *the warmer weather comes.* ↔ keep on 2. ⇨ get off 4, take off 2.

2 [Vp, Vp.n] (*informal*) stop, cease (sth). **O:** work; arguing, interrupting; being a nuisance: *The rain hadn't* **left off** (or: *It hadn't* **left off** *raining*). PW ○ *'I've told you before about interfering in my affairs. Now,* **leave off**!' ○ *Ned* **left off** *talking about the firm.* CON □ object is usu the *-ing* form of a verb. ↔ keep on doing sth.

3 [Vp, Vp.n] stop, be interrupted; stop, interrupt (sth). **S** [Vp], **O** [Vp.n]**:** relationship, friendship; discussion, narrative: *My part of the story of our escape begins where John's* **leaves off**. ○ *The two girls picked up their friendship where they'd* **left** *it* **off**. EB □ often used in the construction: *start/continue/resume ... where something* **leaves off**.

leave on 1 [Vn ⇆ p pass, Vn.pr pass emph rel] allow (sth) to stay in position. **O:** lid, cover; kettle, pot; cloth; coat, gloves. **o:** saucepan; gas-cooker; table: *'Where did you* **leave** *the keys?'* **'On** *the desk.'* ○ **'Leave** *the cloth* **on**. *I want to lay the table for supper.'* ○ *When they entered the new house they* **left** *their coats* **on** *because the heating system had not been installed.* ↔ leave off 1, take off 2. ⇨ stay on 1.

2 [Vn ⇆ p pass adj] allow (sth) to stay alight or keep burning. **O:** light, lamp; gas fire; television: *The electric fire had been* **left on** *overnight.* ○ *'You can* **leave** *the hall-light* **on**.' ↔ turn off 1. ⇨ be on 8, go on 15, stay on 2, turn on 1.

leave out [Vn.p pass] leave (sth) in the open, eg through forgetfulness. **O:** toy, pram; washing: *If you* **leave** *your car* **out** *in all weathers, you'll soon have trouble with rust.* ↔ put away 1. ⇨ stay out 2.

leave out in the cold [Vn.p.pr pass] exclude (sb) from a group or activity; ignore. **O:** ally, supporter; partner, colleague: *The government has discriminated in favour of its own supporters. That* **leaves** *the two-thirds of the electorate who did not vote for it* **out in the cold.** OBS ○ *There we were, knowing that we were being talked about—sensing as fully as we could the feeling of being* **left out in the cold**. L

leave out/out of [Vn ⇆ p pass adj, Vn.pr pass] not include or mention (sb/sth) (in sth). **o:** guest-list; party, group; arrangements; story: *'When you wrote the invitations, did you* **leave** *anyone* **out**?' ○ *He would hate it if he were* **left out** (ie **left out of** *the party*) *and simply heard about the evening from Barbara.* MSAL ○ *'You realize you forgot to invite her? She must be feeling terribly* **left out**.' □ note pred use of adj in last example. = miss out/out of, omit (from). ↔ put in 2.

leave out of account/consideration/the reckoning [Vn.pr pass] not consider (sth). **O:** (possible) reaction, response; the fact that ... ; what sb will do: *He had* **left out of consideration** *the likely hostility of his former colleagues.* ○ *'And don't* **leave out of account** *the fact that he'd probably like a job in the South.'* ↔ take account of.

leave over 1 [Vn ⇆ p pass adj] leave (sth) as a remainder, the best part having been consumed. **O:** oddment, scrap; bone, crumb: *The force must have all it needed. Other armies would do their best with what was* **left over**. MFM ○ *The older children had the lion's share; the small ones had to make do with* **left-overs**. □ usu passive; left-overs (always pl) is the adj form used as a noun. ⇨ be over 2.

2 [Vn.p pass adj] reserve (sth) for attention at a later date. **S:** council, committee. **O:** business; item, question: *I regret that these matters will have to be* **left over** *until our next meeting.* ⇨ lie over.

leave to [Vn.pr pass emph rel] give the responsibility for doing (sth) to (sb). **O:** arrangements, organization, staffing; everything, things, it (all): *'You* **leave** *it* **to** *me; I'll see what can be done.'* BLCH ○ *The catering can safely be* **left to** *Mother.* ○ *It is* **left to** *the new Parliament to make a European electoral law.* OBS □ note construction with it in the last example.

leave to chance [Vn.pr pass] allow (sth) to happen by chance by not taking too much care over details. **O:** issue, outcome, result; something, (not) anything: *Nelson prepared against every contingency, but recognized that something must be* **left to chance**. MFM ○ *In the experiment, we* **leave** *nothing* **to chance**: *weights are checked twice over.*

leave to it [Vn.pr pass] (*informal*) let (sb) proceed with a task, without help or interference: *He gave the new crew their instructions and then went off,* **leaving** *them* **to it**. ○ *I suppose we could have gone out and* **left** *her* **to it**, *but neither Jimmy nor I would have enjoyed the party if we had.* WI

leave to his own devices [Vn.pr pass] allow (sb) to solve a difficult problem unaided; leave (sb) alone to do as he wishes. **O:** staff; assistant, trainee; pupil, guest: *He* **left** *us* **to our own devices**; *he didn't mind how the work was done as long as it was finished when we'd promised.* RATT ○ *Unmarried officers posted to the War Office were* **left to their own devices** *to find accommodation.* MFM ○ *Altogether I was not in the most jovial of moods, and Jacquie had long since* **left** *me* **to my own devices**. DF

leave up [Vn.p pass] allow (sth) to stay in a raised position. **O:** picture, notice; flag, curtain; switch, lever: *The decorations can be* **left up** *for another day.* ↔ leave down. ⇨ put up 1, stay up 3.

leave up to [Vn.p.pr pass] let important decisions etc about (sth) be made by (sb). **O:** organization, distribution; it ... how to divide the money, it ... whether to go or stay: *'How shall I raise the money?' 'I don't know. I'll* **leave** *that entirely* **up to** *you.'* ⇨ be up to 3.

leave word (with) [Vn.pr pass emph rel] leave a message (with sb): *John had* **left word** *of his departure* **with** *the departmental secretary.* ○ **Word** *was* **left with** *a neighbour that we would be back soon.*

left to oneself [pass (Vn.pr)] if allowed or obliged to do a difficult task unaided; if allowed to be alone: **Left to myself**, *I couldn't even get access to the docks when the ships were being unloaded.* HD ○ **Left to himself**, *he could have driven through the dry belt* (ie near the Equator) *in a week.* ARG ○ *He works in ... the vast Airways building on the Great West Road at Brentford, but* **left to himself** *he sails strange boats at Portofino.* OBS □ equivalent to the conditional clause if left to oneself, and followed by a finite clause. ⇨ leave to his own devices.

lecture

lecture at [Vpr pass adj] (*informal*) address (sb) in a formal, pompous manner, esp to scold or reproach. **o:** wife, child; employee: *'He doesn't talk to me, he **lectures at** me!'* ○ *'I don't mind having things explained to me when I make mistakes, but I don't like being **lectured at**.'*

lecture (to) [Vpr pass emph rel] give a formal talk (to a group): *He **lectures to** undergraduates on the Elizabethan theatre.*

leech

leech onto [Vpr pass] attach oneself firmly and persistently — like a leech — to (sb). **S:** child, pupil; neurotic. **o:** teacher; doctor: *The girl's really **leeched onto** Philip. He can't shake her off. I suppose it goes to show you can take too close an interest in problem children.*

leer

leer (at) [Vpr pass rel] look (at sb) in a crude, unpleasant way suggesting desire or ill-will. **o:** pretty woman; victim: *She was tired of feeling **leered at** all the time.* ○ *A face **leered at** him through a grating in the door.*

lend

lend (to) 1 [Vn.pr pass emph rel] let (sb) have the temporary use of (sth); let (sb) borrow (money) at interest. **S:** friend, neighbour; bank, building society. **O:** lawn-mower, bicycle; money: *I don't mind **lending** these papers **to** you* (or: ***lending** you these papers*)*, but do be sure to return them.* ○ *Building societies attract deposits at one rate of interest and **lend** the funds thus accumulated **to** house buyers at a higher rate of interest.*

2 [Vn.pr pass emph rel] give (support etc) to (sth). **S:** government; industry; scholar, scientist. **O:** his etc backing, support; authority, name; prestige; oneself. **o:** venture, scheme, project; speculation, swindle; theory: *There are proposals to develop new industries away from the existing major centres. **To** these kinds of development, the government will **lend** its full support.* ○ *He refused to **lend** himself or his organization **to** such blatant profiteering.*

3 [Vn.pr pass emph rel] (*formal*) make (sth) more significant, believable etc. **S:** event, development. **O:** meaning, significance; credibility, genuineness. **o:** view, interpretation, analysis: *It is these considerations that **lend** particular significance **to** the annual congress opening in Perth today.* SC ○ *What **lends** some plausibility **to** this historian's view of events* (or: ***lends** his view some plausibility*) *is that trade links with Britain were well developed at this time.*

lend itself to 1 [Vn.pr emph rel] (*formal*) be suitable for (sth), be well suited to (sth). **S:** park, garden; room, attic; subject, theme, topic. **o:** solitary walks; conversion, extension; extensive treatment: *The cellars **lend themselves to** conversion into a workroom and store.* ○ *The play **lent itself** admirably **to** presentation on an open stage.*

2 [Vn.pr emph rel] (*formal*) because of inherent weaknesses etc, be liable or subject to (ill use). **S:** democracy, free enterprise, universal education. **o:** abuse, misuse: *Any system of taxation **lends itself to** manipulation by clever or unscrupulous individuals.* ○ *The various malpractices **to** which the election arrangements could **lend themselves** were pointed out by neutral observers.*

let

let down 1 [Vn ⇆ p pass adj] let (sth) fall; lower, drop. **O:** bucket; rope, ladder; dress; hair; standard: *The hem of your dress needs to be **let down** an inch.* ○ *Her parents had maintained their standards of value. She had **let** hers **down**.* PW ↔ put up 1.

2 [Vn ⇆ p nom pass adj] fail (sb who believes that one is reliable). **O:** friend, husband, wife; audience, readers: *'You won't go to gaol. I fixed it up. I didn't **let** you **down**.'* AITC ○ *The hostages had felt **let down** by the Government's lack of effort to free them.* OBS ○ *He's been **let down** so much* (or: *had so many **let-downs***) *in the past that he trusts no one.*

3 [Vn ⇆ p pass adj] release the air from (sth); deflate. **O:** tyre, balloon: *'Some joker has **let down** the back tyres of my car!'* ↔ blow up 5. ⇨ let out/out of.

4 [Vn ⇆ p nom pass adj] (*informal*) make sb's spirits sink; depress: *He felt at once relieved and **let down**.* PW ○ *A feeling of **let-down** had followed years of boisterous vigour.* OBS ○ *It was a tremendous **let-down** to be told we had failed.* □ usu passive or nom.

5 [Vp] lose height, so as to land. **S:** aircraft; pilot: *Eleven hours out of Paris, the Air France plane **let down** into Rio de Janeiro.* T

let one's hair down [Vn.p] (*informal*) relax and enjoy oneself, eg at a party: *There will be a celebratory dinner at the Campana Restaurant for everyone involved to really **let their hair down**.* CLSH ○ *This is the night that the Cricket Club really **lets its hair down**.*

let the side down [Vn.p] (*informal*) disappoint or fail one's friends, colleagues etc; behave in a way regarded as unacceptable by one's family, social class etc: *He will always do his part — he never **let the side down**.* MFM ○ *If you* (a graduate) *take a job as a window-cleaner, you're just **letting the side down**.* HD

let in [Vn ⇆ p pass] allow (sth) to enter or penetrate. **S:** window; roof, wall; leather, shoe. **O:** light; cold, rain; water: *My kitchen wall **lets in** the damp.* ○ *Air is **let in** through vents at the side of the car.*

let the clutch in [Vn ⇆ p pass] (*motoring*) release the clutch pedal of a motor vehicle, so connecting the engine and transmission: *Pop **let in the clutch** and began to steer a course of slow elegance.* DBM

let in for [Vn.p.pr pass] (*informal*) make (sb) assume responsibility for (sth). **O:** firm, colleague; oneself. **o:** (extra) work, expense, trouble: *'I hope you realize what you're **letting** yourself **in for**!'* ○ *'While you've been abroad, I've been **let in for** a lot of extra duty.'*

let in/into [Vn ⇆ p pass, Vn.pr pass rel] allow (sb) to enter (a place); admit. **O:** guest, spectator; oneself. **o:** club, theatre; house: *If they try to buy tickets don't **let** them **in**.* ○ *He **let** himself **into** the study with a spare key.* ⇨ come in/into 1, get in/into 1.

let in on [Vn.p.pr pass] (*informal*) allow (sb) to know about or take part in (sth that was previously hidden from him). **O:** stranger, new partner. **o:** scheme, plans; the act: *That would have involved*

***letting** a third person **in on** the act: my mother.* CON ○ *We both know there's a trick involved; **let** me **in on** the secret.* SATS ○ *He was **let in on** the arrangements without our knowledge.* ⇨ be/bring/come/ get in on.

let into [Vn.pr pass emph rel] set (sth) in a hollowed-out place in (sth). **O:** cupboard, lighting; tube, pipe. **o:** wall, ceiling; body (of patient): *The figure stood on a shelf **let into** the study wall.* ○ *A tube is **let into** his leg to carry off fluid.* □ usu passive.

let into a/the secret [Vn.pr pass] share with (sb) one's secret: *Don't **let** Peter **into the secret**: it won't remain a secret for long.* ○ *I'll **let** you **into a secret**: I'm being sent abroad.*

let off 1 [Vn ⇆ p pass, Vn.pr pass] allow (sb) to disembark or alight (from sth). **S:** skipper, crew; conductor. **O:** passenger. **o:** boat, plane; bus: *I asked the captain to **let** me **off** at the next port of call.* ○ *The guard won't **let** anyone **off** the train between stations.* ⇨ get off 1, put off 6.

2 [Vn ⇆ p pass] (*informal*) release (sb) without punishing him. **S:** court, judge. **O:** prisoner, accused: *He was charged with dangerous driving, but the court **let** him **off**.* ○ *'I'll be lenient this time, but you won't be **let off** again.'* ⇨ get off 6, let off with.

3 [Vn ⇆ p pass, Vn.pr pass] (*informal*) allow (sb) not to do (an unpleasant task). **O:** prisoner, defaulter. **o:** chore, fatigue; peeling potatoes: *'Is he on guard duty tonight?' 'No, he's been **let off**.'* ○ *'What's he been **let off** doing this time?'*

4 [Vn ⇆ p pass] fire (sth); explode (sth). **S:** soldier; engineer. **O:** rifle, gun; charge, explosives: *A brass cannon was **let off** dangerously with real gunpowder.* SD ○ *Some small boys **let** a few fireworks **off**.* ⇨ go off 5, set off 1.

5 [Vp, Vn ⇆ p pass] (*informal*) break wind; fart. **O:** a fart; one: *If I **let off** in the parlour she'd have me shipped off to the hospital to be disembowelled.* JFTR

6 [Vn ⇆ p pass] allow others to rent a building in portions. **O:** flat; room, office: *The three floors of this large Victorian house were **let off** as separate flats.* ○ *The agent isn't keen to **let** the offices **off** one by one; he wants to find one tenant for the whole building.*

let off the hook [Vn.pr pass] (*informal*) free sb from an unpleasant task, an embarrassing situation etc: *I thought I'd have to talk to old Mrs Jenks all evening, until Penny came along and **let** me **off the hook**.* ○ *'Don't think, just because you've been **let off the hook** once, that you can always slide out of the dirty jobs!'*

let off steam [Vp.n] (*informal*) release tension, feelings that have been restrained etc: *Still fuming with frustration, I sat down and applied for the vacancy, rather as a means of **letting off steam**.* SD ○ *I **let off steam** by mimicking and muttering silently.* OBS = blow off steam.

let off with [Vn.p.pr pass] give (sb) a lighter sentence than the law allows. **S:** court, judge. **O:** offender, prisoner. **o:** a caution, a fine; six months (in prison): *My pal Mike got **let off with** probation because it was his first offence.* LLDR ⇨ get off 6, let off 2.

let on (about) [Vp, Vp.pr pass, Vp.n] (*informal*) reveal, disclose (sth). **O:** that he knew, that we are friends; how you were going to manage. **o:** plan, scheme; how we did it : [Vp] *I've been dating this guy: Claude McEven. Only I didn't **let on** to Ma.* AT ○ [Vpr] *We didn't **let on about** how rich we were.* LLDR ○ [Vp.n] *Do not **let on** that I have given away his secret ingredient.* ARG = give away 3.

let sb get on with it [Vp.pr] ⇨ get on with.

let out 1 [Vp.n] utter (sth); emit. **O:** cry, yell, scream: *He **let out** a spontaneous cry.* NM ○ *She **let out** a yelp of pain.*

2 [Vn ⇆ p pass] allow sb to know (sth); reveal, disclose. **O:** news, information; secret; (it . . .) that John was leaving: *Who **let out** the details of the reshuffle in the department? It was confidential news.* ○ *Keep this to yourselves — don't **let** it **out** to the press.* □ note outlet, a means of expressing sth: *He was allowed no **outlet** for his emotions.* ↔ keep back (from) 2. ⇨ be out 7, come out 7, get out 1.

3 [Vn ⇆ p nom pass] (*informal*) release (sb) from an unpleasant obligation: *He appeared just in time to propose the vote of thanks, which **let** me **out** nicely* (cf *gave me a welcome **let-out***).

4 [Vn ⇆ p pass adj] make (sth) wider or looser. **S:** tailor. **O:** dress, trousers: *I've got so fat that I'll have to **let** the waistband **out** several inches.* ↔ take in 3.

5 [Vn ⇆ p pass] make (sth) available for hire. **O:** horse, donkey; boat: *Farm machinery is **let out** by the week.* = hire out.

let out/out of [Vn ⇆ p pass, Vn.pr pass] allow (sth/ sb) to leave (a place); release (from). **O:** gas, water; animal, prisoner. **o:** tyre, tank; cage, gaol: *'Who **let** the air **out of** my tyres?'* ○ *'**Let** me **out of** here! **Let** me **out**!'* □ note outlet, a pipe through which liquid or gas can escape. ↔ keep in 1. ⇨ be out 2, come out 2.

let the cat out of the bag [Vn.pr pass] (*informal*) reveal a secret, let it be known, through carelessness: *'I wanted Mother's present to be a surprise; now you've gone and **let the cat out of the bag**!'*

let through [Vn ⇆ p pass, Vn.pr pass] allow (sb/sth) to pass. **O:** visitor; car; goods; defective items. **o:** immigration; customs; control-point; quality control: *A number of mistakes in the proofs were **let through**.* ○ *Most of their party were **let through** customs without an examination.*

let up [Vp nom] (*informal*) relax one's alertness or efforts; ease, slacken. **S:** worker, team; (bad) weather, storm; pressure, volume (of work): *Petrie's mind never **let up** for an instant.* SD ○ *We will never stop, or **let up*** (cf *there will be no **let-up***), *till Tunis has been captured.* MFM

level

level an accusation/a charge/a criticism against/at [Vn.pr pass rel] accuse (sb) of an offence or a failing: *She did not admit **the charge** of disloyalty when it was **levelled against** the Irish.* EB ○ *He was bothered by **the accusations** which were to be **levelled at** him by the ignorant or the prejudiced.* SS □ usu passive.

level down [Vp, Vn ⇆ p pass adj] lower, reduce, (the high standards of a few) to the level of the many, esp to achieve equality. **S:** government, firm, school. **O:** wage, benefit; mark, standard: *Does the country as a whole benefit from **levelling down** the rewards and privileges of the rich?* ○ *Some believe* *that the extension of higher education has* ***levelled down*** *university standards.* ↔ level up.

level off [Vn ⇆ p pass adj] make level sth which is uneven, rough etc. **O:** board; surface, top: *Rub with sandpaper to get a smooth,* ***levelled-off*** *surface.*

level off/out [Vp] move horizontally after climbing; remain steady after a rise. **S:** aircraft; price, wage: *We climbed steeply after take-off, and* ***levelled out*** *at 25 000 feet.* ○ *It looks as though the unemployment figures are at last beginning to* ***level out.*** BBCR

level up [Vp, Vn ⇆ p pass adj] raise (the standards of the poorest, least able etc) to the level of the few, esp to promote equality. **O:** standard, mark; salary, benefit: *To achieve excellence with equality, we need to* ***level up*** *the state schools—not level down the independent schools.* ↔ level down.

level with [Vpr] (*informal*) be honest with (sb), tell (sb) the truth: *'If you won't* ***level with*** *me we're not going to get anywhere.'* ○ *'She wasn't* ***levelling with*** *us—anyone could see that.'*

lick

lick into shape [Vn.pr pass] (*informal*) raise (sb/sth) to the right standard of discipline, efficiency, organization etc. **S:** instructor; coach; sergeant; organizer. **O:** trainee; runner, footballer; recruit; project, scheme. **A:** quickly, soon; in a few weeks: *They're not a very promising bunch but we'll soon* ***lick*** *them* ***into shape.*** ○ *If Ann and Yvette will make another brew of coffee, perhaps we can do something towards* ***licking*** *this business* ***into shape.*** TBC

lick off [Vn ⇆ p pass adj, Vn.pr pass] remove (sth) by licking. **O:** glue, gum; jam, sugar: *I can't use this stamp: the gum has all been* ***licked off.*** ○ *Someone's* ***licked*** *the chocolate* ***off*** *the cream buns!*

lick up [Vn ⇆ p pass] take (sth) up into the mouth by licking. **S:** cat, dog. **O:** milk, water: *'Don't mop up the spilt milk; the cat will* ***lick*** *it* ***up.'***

lie

lie about/around/round 1 [Vp, Vpr] lie or sit in a casual lazy manner (in a place). **o:** the place; house, bar: *Students were* ***lying about*** *on the lawns behind the lecture theatre.* = loll about/around, lounge about/ around.

2 [Vp, Vpr] be left here and there in an untidy way. **S:** books, papers; rubbish, dirty shirts: *'I suppose you know your dirty clothes are* ***lying about*** *all over the bedroom floor?'* ○ *'Don't leave any money* ***lying around*** *for Jim to pick up!'* □ often used in the construction *leave sth* lying around.

lie ahead/ahead of/before [Vp emph, Vpr emph rel] (*formal*) be going to confront or happen to (sb) in the future. **S:** difficulty; hazard, danger; death: *She saw his astonishment at the enormity of the complications that* ***lay ahead*** TFD ○ *He thought of the disease that might* ***lie ahead of*** *him.* NM ○ ***Before*** *him* ***lay*** *the prospect of continuing hardship.*

lie at anchor/its moorings [Vpr emph] (*nautical*) be anchored or moored, usu off shore. **S:** ship, boat: *The fleet* ***lay at anchor*** *half a mile off the headland.*

lie at death's door [Vpr] be at the point of death, be close to dying: *For weeks her father* ***lay at death's door.***

lie at sb's door [Vpr emph rel] (*formal*) be borne by (sb). **S:** the blame, the responsibility, the guilt: *The responsibility for the present crisis* ***lies*** *squarely* ***at the door of*** *the government.* ○ ***At whose door*** *does the blame* ***lie?*** ⇨ lay at sb's door.

lie back [Vp] move back so that one is supported on a bed, or by the back of a chair: *Alone, Blanche* ***lay back*** *gratefully, but again sleep did not come.* MSAL ○ *She was so weak and exhausted she had to* ***lie back.*** DC

lie before [Vp emph, Vpr emph rel] ⇨ lie ahead/ ahead of/before.

lie behind 1 [Vp emph, Vpr emph] (*formal*) have happened to (sb), be in the past. **S:** achievement, exploit; hardship, suffering: *And* ***behind*** *them* ***lay*** *bitter memories of what midwinter was like.* B ○ ***Behind lay*** *nothing but defeat; ahead lay the certainty of victory.*

2 [Vpr] be the explanation for (sth), be the cause of (sth). **S:** ambition, desire for power; necessity, expediency; incompetence, mismanagement. **o:** move, event; retreat; failure, price-rise: *I'm not sure what* ***lay behind*** *his remarks, but it certainly wasn't good will.* ○ *Repressed sexual feelings or experiences* ***lie behind*** *much mental disease.* F ⇨ be behind 3.

lie down [Vp nom] be or move into a horizontal position on a bed, to rest or sleep: *'You're going to* ***lie down*** *for a bit.'* PE ○ *He was* ***lying down*** *on the sofa when we came in.* ○ *She likes to have a* ***lie-down*** *after lunch.* ↔ get up 1.

lie down on the job [Vp.pr] (*informal*) neglect to do a job properly, not put all one's effort into a job: *These men are hardly* ***lying down on the job*** *— they're working all hours to finish it.*

lie down (under) [Vp, Vp.pr] accept (sth) without protest or resistance. **o:** tyranny, oppression; abuse, insult: *We have no intention of* ***lying down under*** *these accusations* (cf *We have no intention of taking these accusations* ***lying down***). □ note the equivalent patterns: lie down under sth = take sth lying down.

lie in 1 [Vp nom] stay in bed after the normal time for getting up: *They let us* ***lie in,*** *but I got up for breakfast.* RFW ○ *Sally will be bound to sleep late and give us a nice Sunday* ***lie-in.*** WI

2 [Vpr emph rel] have its source or origin in (sth). **S:** problem, difficulty, trouble. **o:** design, planning; poor maintenance; convincing one's employer, finding a backer: *Our destiny* ***lies in*** *original sin—in the fact that we are human—finite, fallible, vicious, vain.* RTH ○ *The trouble is often found to* ***lie in*** *the problem of the patient's attitude to psycho-analysis.* DL

3 [Vpr emph rel] have (sth) as its future direction. **S:** future course, further development (of one's work). **o:** research, exploration: *Her duty* ***lay,*** *not* ***in*** *helping with household work, but* ***in*** *earning more money through writing.* GE

lie in ruins [Vpr] be completely destroyed or ruined. **S:** city; factory, house; policy, programme: *In Tibet ... the authorities could not avoid acknowledging the hundreds of monasteries that* ***lay in ruins.*** IND ○ *By this time, the Government's policy for the statutory control of incomes* ***lay in*** *complete* ***ruins.***

lie in store (for) [Vpr] be going to happen (to sb): *No one knew what* ***lay in store for*** *us round the next bend in the river.*

lie in wait (for) [Vpr] wait (as if) in a concealed place (for sb), so as to obtain sth from him, or force one's attentions on him. **o:** visitor, tourist; customer: *She* **lay in wait for** *unsuspecting travellers and lectured them.* SE ○ *'I'm sorry we're* **lying in wait for** *you like this, but we did want to get hold of you rather urgently.'* TGLY

lie over [Vp] await attention at a later date. **S:** business, matter, item: *There are several important matters* **lying over** *from last week.* ⇨ leave over 2.

lie to [Vp] (*nautical*) have halted, be anchored; halt, anchor. **S:** ship; cruiser, launch, dinghy: *The yacht was* **lying to** *in about six fathoms.* ○ *They reached the other side at about midnight and* **lay to** *about four miles off shore.* RFW

lie up 1 [Vp] go into hiding, eg to escape pursuers or to attack enemies. **S:** bandit; soldier, guerrilla: *Nobody saw him all through the war. I think he* **lay up** *in the mountains.* RM ○ *The partisans* **lay up** *by day, and by night ventured out to attack convoys.*
2 [Vp] stay in bed to rest during an illness. **S:** patient, sick child: *John must* **lie up** *for a few weeks until his leg mends.*

lie with [Vpr emph rel] be carried or held by (sb); be located in (sth). **S:** fault, blame; power, responsibility; decision; difficulty, problem. **o:** the President; committee, board; system, structure, arrangement: *Overwhelming power* **lies with** *Mr Gorbachev and his allies.* IND ○ *The problem* **lies with** *our present system of academic examinations.* IND

lift

lift down (from) [Vn ⇆ p pass, Vn.p.pr pass emph rel] move (sth), usu with the hands, from a higher to a lower level. **O:** crate, box, drum, bale. **o:** shelf, lorry: *'That looks a heavy case: let me* **lift** *it* **down** *for you.'* ↔ lift up 1.

lift off [Vp nom] (*space technology*) rise vertically from the launching-pad. **S:** rocket, missile: *Twenty minutes to go before the rocket* **lifts off**. ○ *The space vehicle made a perfect* **lift-off**. = blast off.

lift up 1 [Vn ⇆ p nom pass] raise (sth) physically. **O:** child; arm, leg; box: *'If you* **lift** *me* **up** *(or: give me a* **lift-up***) I can just get a leg over the wall.'* ○ *'***Lift** *your foot* **up***: you're standing on the hem of my dress.'* ↔ lift down (from).
2 [Vn ⇆ p pass adj] stimulate or inspire (sb) spiritually. **S:** preacher, statesman; sermon, address; presence. **O:** congregation, audience: *His very presence* **lifted** *us all* **up** (cf *We all found his very presence* **uplifting**). ○ *Talking to her gave me a tremendous* **uplift**. □ nom form is uplift.

light

light on/upon [Vpr pass emph rel] discover (sth) by chance. **o:** treasure, manuscript; (secret) passage, tunnel: *Her rinsed blue eyes had only to* **light on** *something costly, ugly and tasteless and she must have it.* EC ○ *He had* **lighted** (or: **lit**) **upon** *a new method of refining the metal.* = happen on/upon.

light out/out of [Vp, Vpr] (*esp US, informal*) leave (a place), esp hurriedly, and to escape from sb. **S:** bandit, raider; police, cavalry: *The gang didn't waste any time over farewells. Just packed their bags and* **lit out of** *town.*

light up 1 [Vp, Vp.n pass adj] apply a flame to tobacco in order to smoke. **O:** cigar, pipe: *He settled comfortably in an armchair and* **lit up**. ○ *Pop had* **lit up** *one of his best Havanas.* BFA
2 [Vn ⇆ p pass adj] make (sth) brighter with lights; illuminate. **S:** council; trader. **O:** building; shop: *Public buildings were* **lit up** *for the Victory celebrations.* ○ *Not many shop windows were* **lit up** *last Christmas because of the Government restrictions on the use of electricity.*
3 [Vp] switch on the head- (or side-) lights of a motor-vehicle at dusk; switch on the street lighting. **S:** motorist, lorry-driver: *It's seven o'clock, and still one or two cars haven't* **lit up**. ○ *At this time of the year, official* **lighting-up** *time is six-thirty.*
4 [Vp,Vn ⇆ p pass adj] (cause sth to) become bright or flushed with emotion. **S** [Vp], **O** [Vn.p]: face, eyes. **S** [Vn.p]: anger, passion: *His eyes were still able to* **light up** *under the influence of curiosity or greed.* RM ○ *His face was* **lit up** *with sudden excitement.*

light upon [Vpr pass emph rel] ⇨ light on/upon.

liken

liken to [Vn.pr pass emph rel] (*formal*) say that (one thing) is like (another): *Someone* **likened** *his voice* **to** *the croaking of a bull-frog.* ○ *The nervous system can be* **likened to** *a telephone exchange.*

limber

limber up [Vp nom] (*sport*) make one's muscles loose through exercise, eg before a race. **S:** athlete, footballer: *He always* **limbered up** (or: *had a* **limber-up**) *before his afternoon match.* = loosen up 1.

limit

limit (to) [Vn.pr pass emph rel] keep (sth) at a low level. **O:** number, entry; participants, competitors; applications. **o:** a few; 100, a dozen: *The number of visitors given passes has had to be* **limited to** *ten for security reasons.* = restrict (to) 1.

line

line-out [nom (Vp)] (*Rugby football*) parallel lines of forwards formed at right angles to the touch line, to receive a ball which has just gone out of play: *The hooker throws the ball in at* **line-outs**. ○ *There was a* **line-out** *just inside the Welsh half.*

line up 1 [Vp, Vn ⇆ p pass adj] (cause people/things to) form into lines or ranks. **S** [Vp], **O** [Vn.p]: soldiers; visitors; vehicles. **S** [Vn.p]: officer; attendant; policemen: *The sergeant* **lined** *his platoon* **up** *on the parade-square.* ○ *The lorries were* **lined up**, *ready to move off.*
2 [Vp] form a queue to get transport, buy food etc. **S:** passenger, shopper, spectator: *Fans began* **lining up** *early in the morning to buy their cup-tie tickets.* = queue (up) (for).
3 [Vn ⇆ p pass adj] move (part of sth) so that it is in line with another part; move (sth) so that it points directly towards sb/sth; get (sb/sth) in view by pointing sth towards him/it. **O:** sights (on a gun); gun, camera; target, subject, scene: *He pressed the rifle butt into his cheek and* **lined up** *the sights on the distant target.* ○ *You just* **line up** *the group in your viewfinder and press this button.* ⇨ line up in one's sights.
4 [Vn ⇆ p nom pass] (*informal*) bring together, assemble (people/things) for a special event; organize, arrange (sth). **S:** impresario, producer. **O:** performer, artist; item, turn; scheme, project:

They've **lined up** *some excellent entertainers for our show.* ○ *There was a good* **line-up** *of musical and comedy acts on television tonight.* ○ *Mum tells me you've got some scheme* **lined up** *for visiting places of scenic and historical interest.* OD
5 [Vp nom] (*sport*) be arranged or positioned within a team. **S:** players; team; Germany, Arsenal: *This is how the England team will* **line up** *for tonight's crucial game.* ○ *The French have an impressive* **line-up** *of young players.*

line up (against) [Vn ⇆ p pass, Vn.p.pr pass] place (people) in line (against sth) for execution by a firing-squad. **S:** invader, soldier. **O:** hostage, prisoner. **o:** wall, barn: *They pulled out the first five civilians,* **lined** *them* **up** *on the lawn, and shot them.* SD ○ *Old men and women were* **lined up against** *a wall and shot.*

line up alongside/with [Vp.pr] (*informal*) be the ally or associate of (sb). **S:** deputy, delegate, member. **o:** majority, minority; extremist, moderate: *He's* **lined up with** *some of the most reactionary people in the party.* ○ *They're not the sort of folk I'd expect a confessed liberal to* **line up with**.

line up behind [Vp.pr rel, Vn.p.pr pass rel] (cause sb to) follow or support (sb). **S** [Vp.pr], **O** [Vn.p.pr]**:** group, party; conference, meeting; rebel, dissident. **S** [Vn.p.pr]**:** leader, chairman: *The majority of rank-and-file members are happy to* **line up behind** *the new leadership.* ○ *Have you noticed the kind of support he has got* **lined up behind** *him?*

line up in one's sights [Vn.p.pr pass] point a rifle etc directly at (a target). **S:** marksman, hunter. **O:** target, prey: *For a moment, he had the deer* **lined up in his sights** *— then it vanished.* ○ (*figurative*) *Once Freda's got you* **lined up in her sights** *there is nothing I can do to save you!* ⇨ line up 3.

line up with [Vp.pr] ⇨ line up alongside/with.

linger on 1 [Vp] continue to live, though physically weak or seriously ill. **A:** (for) a few days longer, into the summer: *He* **lingered on** *five months longer, with Mary Ann watching over him constantly.* GE
2 [Vp] stay, remain, after others have gone; stick, persist, in the mind etc. **S:** guest, visitor; smell, scent; tradition: *Harold* **lingered on and on***, and even treated himself to a third half-pint* (ie of beer). PW ○ *Today these practices are no more, but their memory* **lingers on**.

linger

linger over [Vpr pass emph rel] take more time than is normal or desirable (over sth), esp when completing a task or describing events. **o:** meal; ceremony, speech; (gory, unsavoury) details, facts: *'You've* **lingered** *long enough* **over** *breakfast. Eat up. We're leaving in five minutes.'* ○ *'Don't you feel that newspaper accounts of these disasters tend to* **linger** *rather nastily* **over** *the details?'*

link

link together/with [Vn ⇆ p pass, Vn.pr pass rel] say or suggest that different persons or events are connected. **S:** newspaper; report, rumour. **O:** name, celebrity, public figure. **o:** girl, pop star; creation, institution (of sth): *There is nothing to suggest that her death was* **linked with** *the outbreak of smallpox* (cf *that the two events were* **linked together**). ○ *More than anything, Aneurin Bevan is* **linked** *in the public mind* **with** *the setting-up of the National Health Service* (cf *the name and the event are* **linked together** *in the public mind*). □ often passive.

link up (with) [Vp nom, Vp.pr emph rel, Vn ⇆ p nom pass adj, Vn.p.pr pass emph rel] (cause sth to) form one whole (with sth else). **S** [Vp, Vp.pr], **O** [Vn.p, Vn.p.pr]**:** town, village; force, army; business, firm. **o:** another, a neighbour; allied troops; (chief) competitor : [Vp.pr] *12 Army Group would* **link up with** *the Dragoon force* (cf [Vp] *The two units would* **link up**; or: *do a* **link-up**). MFM ○ [Vn.p] **Link up** *the islands as far as possible.* SC ○ [Vp, Vn.p] *This American leader announces a first major* **link-up** *of supermarkets in this country.* T ○ [Vn.p.pr] *Arrangements were well advanced for* **linking up** *this newly opened length* (of motorway) **with** *the Lancaster by-pass.* T = join up (with).

listen

listen in (to) [Vp nom, Vp.pr pass rel] listen on the telephone to (sth private); listen to sth on the radio which one is forbidden to hear. **o:** other people's conversations; foreign radio stations; the BBC: *'I wish you'd stop* **listening in** *to my private conversations.'* ○ *'Half a sec, I think Fred's* **listening in** *on the other phone.'* ○ *Despite the government ban, people continued to* **listen in to** *the World Service.*

listen out for [Vp.pr] pay attention so that one be will be ready to hear sb/sth that one is expecting. **o:** doorbell, knock; footsteps; car, taxi: *'***Listen out for** *the phone: John should be ringing any moment now.'* ○ *She would lie awake,* **listening out for** *the sound of his footsteps on the landing.* ⇨ look out (for), watch out (for).

listen to [Vpr pass] pay careful attention to (sb/sth). **o:** father, adviser; advice, counsel: *'He never* **listens to** *anyone. How can you expect him to improve?'* ○ *Whenever we went back to the bank for additional funding, we were always* **listened to** *sympathetically.*

listen to reason [Vpr] be prepared to hear and be guided by reasonable arguments: *'I'm glad to say the headmaster has* **listened to reason** *over the reorganization. He asked me to take over both jobs.'* SPL ○ *'Sonia, now you've got rid of your son maybe you'll* **listen to reason***. Marry me.'* 'DPM

litter

litter about/around [Vn ⇆ p pass, Vn.pr pass] scatter (things) here and there untidily. **O:** books, papers, clothes: *He just* **litters** *his stuff* **around** *— no wonder he can never find anything!* ○ *Papers were* **littered about** *the study in the utmost confusion.*

live

live above/beyond one's income/means [Vpr] spend more than one can afford: *Although he had received a final salary increase in 1820 to £350 a year, he was again* **living beyond his means**. CD

live apart (from) [Vp, Vp.pr] (of a married couple) live in separate houses, though without obtaining a divorce: *After leading a cat and dog existence for about five years Philip and Mary decided it might be better if they* **lived apart**. ○ *Jane's only been* **living apart from** *her husband* (cf *they've only been* **living apart**) *for a while, but already she finds she can manage pretty well on her own.*

live down [Vn ⇆ p] behave so well that one's earlier failings etc are forgotten. **O:** one's past; shame, disgrace; a lot, too much: *We can never hope to* ***live down*** *these shortcomings.* FFE ○ *'You can't walk out on the committee after all you've promised to do for them. You'd never* ***live it down****!'* □ usu with *can, could, will,* or *would* + *never*.

live for [Vpr] have (sth) as one's main reason for living. **o:** work, sport; one's family: *He* ***lives for*** *the day when he can retire and grow roses.* ○ *If you took away his job, you'd leave him with nothing to* ***live for****.*

live (in) [Vpr emph rel] have (sth) as one's home or dwelling. **o:** flat, digs; caravan, tent; area, district: *He* ***lives*** *over there,* ***in*** *the most expensive part of town.* ○ *The houses* ***in*** *which they are forced to* ***live*** *are rat-infested.*

live in [Vp nom] reside in the building etc where one works or studies. **S:** cook, housemaid, chauffeur; student, tutor: *They've had a nurse* ***living in*** *for the last six months.* ○ *'What's against us having a servant to* ***live in****? There's room for one.'* PW ○ *They do have a housekeeper: they need to have a* ***live-in*** *one.* G □ live-in used only as an attrib adj. ↔ live out.

lived in [pass adj (Vpr)] having the comfortable, settled look of a home: *Their place really looks* ***lived in*** *— nothing expensive or fashionable just to impress people.* ○ *It takes time for a house to acquire that* ***lived-in*** *appearance.*

live in hope(s) (of) [Vpr] look optimistically (for an improvement). **o:** (**of**) early election; radical change, some reform; fresh trial: *The prisoner* ***lives in hope of*** *an early release.* ○ *The exam results haven't come through yet, but I* ***live in hopes****.*

live in the past [Vpr] behave as though conditions, values etc have not changed from what they were earlier. **S:** (retired) politician, army officer, official; philosopher, theorist, artist: *'Time passes. You are* ***living in the past****, Taylor.'* MM ○ *How could I* ***live in the past*** *when you and Bernie are so good to me?* HAA ⇨ next entry.

live in the present [Vpr] accept conditions as they are now and arrange one's life accordingly: *He seems incapable of* ***living in the present****: always hankering after a glorious past which in fact existed only for a privileged few.* ○ *He's a robust, down-to-earth fellow,* ***living*** *very much* ***in the present****.* ⇨ previous entry.

live in sin [Vpr] (usu *jocular*) live together without being married: *These days the Government are making it so much cheaper for people to* ***live in sin****.* DIL ○ *Do I detect a growing, satanic glint in her eyes? Do you think it's* ***living in sin*** *with me that does it?* LBA

live off the country [Vpr] support oneself by obtaining food from the country one is staying in or passing through. **S:** traveller, explorer; soldier, partisan: *Why take so much tinned food with you to France? Buy local fruit and vegetables —* ***live off the country****.*

live off/on [Vpr rel] have (sth) as one's diet; survive by eating (sth). **o:** raw fish, root vegetables: *Do these people* ***live off*** *human flesh?* LWK ○ *Apart from stolen fruit they* ***lived*** *chiefly* ***on*** *bread.* GJ ○ *'I can't* ***live on*** *air!'*

live off/on the fat of the land [Vpr] (*informal*) enjoy the best food, drink, lodging, entertainment etc: *The poor people starved, while a few* ***lived off the fat of the land****.* ○ *He could get out of London,* ***living on the fat of the land*** *in George's house.* PE

live on 1 [Vp] survive, endure. **S:** family; work, reputation, name: *She had survived . . . the Bolshevik Revolution, and now in 1937* ***lived on*** *in Tiflis.* BRN ○ *He* ***lives on*** *in the affectionate and grateful memory of many.* MRJ

2 [Vpr emph rel] feed and support oneself on a stated amount, or from a certain source. **o:** income, salary; profit, rent; charity, hand-outs: *'I can't* ***live on*** *a hundred pounds a week!'* ○ *'Do you know how little they manage to* ***live on****?'*

live on one's nerves [Vpr] live in a constant state of anxiety, because of threats to one's safety etc: *As time went on and we received so many more threatening phone calls, we* ***lived*** *so much* ***on our nerves*** *that we accepted police protection.* L

live out [Vp] reside away from the place where one works or studies, though it might be possible to live there. **S:** servant, student, soldier: *All married students are allowed to* ***live out*** *after the first two terms in College.* BM ○ *Workers who don't use company accommodation are given a* ***living-out*** *allowance.* ↔ live in. □ nom form, living-out, usu used to modify a noun.

live out one's days/life [Vp.n] spend one's whole life or the rest of one's life. **A:** in one's native town, as an ordinary worker, in humble circumstances: *These two old men had* ***lived out their lives*** *as industrial labourers.* CON ○ *No doubt he would* ***live out his days*** *in the same Welsh valley.* □ an Adjunct of place is usu present.

live out of a suitcase etc [Vpr] not have a settled life, or fixed address, so that one's belongings are kept in suitcases. **o:** ⚠ suitcase, trunk, box: *That's all we do,* ***live out of*** *a travelling-bag.* TOH

live out of cans/tins [Vpr] (*informal*) exist on tinned foods — which are easily prepared — usu because other foods are hard to buy or cook. **S:** camper, explorer; (front-line) soldier; homeless person; vagrant: *Their home was a shack on a piece of waste land, and they* ***lived out of tins****.* ○ *I shall be glad when we get a proper cooker and can stop* ***living out of tins****.*

live over again [Vn.p pass] experience (sth) again in the imagination; relive. **O:** life, career; experience; it all: *If I had to* ***live*** *my life* ***over again*** *I wouldn't choose to spend it in a cold climate.* ○ *Hearing these old soldiers talk, Father was* ***living over again*** *his experiences as a young recruit.*

live through [Vpr pass] experience and survive (difficult times); endure. **o:** famine, war, revolution: *He had* ***lived through*** *the worst years of the depression.* ○ *He was* ***living through*** *a period of mental and physical bewilderment.* GJ

live to a/the ripe old age (of) [Vpr] live to be very old: *I can't see him* ***living to a ripe old age****: he smokes too much.* ○ *Grandfather* ***lived to the ripe old age of*** *ninety.*

live together/with [Vp, Vpr emph rel] live in the same house, as husband and wife, but without being married; cohabit: *This isn't the provinces, you know. I'm* ***living with*** *Celia, as you can see* (or: *We are* ***living together*** etc) CON ○ *My father wasn't really getting married. What he was going to do was just* ***live with*** *a woman who kept a pub.* PPLA

live under [Vpr] experience the rule of (sth/sb). **S:** citizen, subject. **o:** system, regime, government;

king, emperor, dictator: *The country is now* **living under** *a military dictatorship.* ○ *He's* **lived under** *three monarchs, and survived them all.*

live under the same roof (as) [Vpr] reside in the same house (as sb): *We had* **lived** *on terms of close friendship* **under the same roof**. *It was not an easy parting.* AH

live it up [Vn.p] (*informal*) lead an easy, pleasure-filled life: *He was in London,* **living it up** *on his winnings from the football pools.* ○ *The advertisements invite one to* **live it up** *in the rich playgrounds of Jamaica.*

live up to [Vp.pr pass adj] reach a standard that one has set, or that is expected of one. **S:** he etc; machine, device. **o:** standard, claim (made for sth), expectations, position (in life): *We cannot* **live up to** *our moral pretensions.* NM ○ *The beast had* **lived up to** *his reputation for stupidity.* DF ○ *If you have a complaint to make . . . about a product which fails to* **live up to** *its maker's claims, write to this address.* L

live with 1 [Vpr rel] accept the limitations or opportunities of (sth). **o:** fact, situation; disability, disease; shortcomings, failings; technology, automation: *You've lost all your money; now you must learn to* **live with** *the situation.* ○ *You must* **live with** *the fact that you're no longer as active as you were.* ○ *The railways must learn to* **live with** *the motorist and lorry-owner, and offer him advantages which will induce him to foresake his car.* NS □ usu after have to, must (learn to).

2 [Vpr emph rel] live in the same house as husband and wife. ⇨ live together/with.

liven

liven up [Vp, Vn ⇆ p pass adj] (*informal*) (make sth/sb) become more cheerful or lively. **S** [Vp], **O** [Vn.p]**:** things; proceedings, party, evening; guest; audience, class: *How he likes to* **liven** *things* **up**! DC ○ *Another drive and the evening would have* **livened up** *no end.* ILIH = perk up.

load

load down (with) [Vn ⇆ p pass adj, Vn.p.pr pass rel] place many heavy burdens on (sb/sth); overburden (sb), making him strained, depressed etc. **O:** lorry, cart; staff, colleague; person. **o:** parcel, box; care, worry, responsibility: *The van moved off,* **loaded down** *to the springs* **with** *every stick of furniture they possessed.* ○ *He was* **loaded down with** *administrative jobs.* □ esp passive. = weighdown 1,2.

load up (with) [Vp, Vp.pr rel, Vn ⇆ p pass adj, Vn.p.pr pass rel] fill (sth) to the top; place a full load upon (sth). **S:** warehouseman, driver, (freight) handler; removal man, packer. **O:** lorry, truck, goods van, hold (of an aircraft); oneself. **o:** cargo, merchandise; cloth, whisky, butter : [Vp] *'Lower the tail-board and start* **loading up**'. ○ [Vp.pr, Vn.p.pr] *The Nepalese porters* **loaded** *(themselves)* **up with** *food, medical supplies and oxygen equipment.* ○ [Vn.p] *The van seems fully* **loaded up**.

load with [Vn.pr pass rel] give (sth) to (sb) in abundance, either as a reward or as a burden. **S:** government; college; country. **O:** general; student; public servant. **o:** medal; prize; responsibility, problem: *She'd been a lonely child . . . her mother used to* **load** *her* **with** *toys.* EC ○ *Deaths in the family* **loaded** *him* **with** *more griefs and responsibilities.* CD

loaf

loaf about/around [Vp, Vpr] (*informal*) spend one's time idly. **S:** crowd, gang; teenager; vagrant; petty criminal. **o:** the place; town, the streets: *Parents seem to get particularly irritated when their teenage sons* **loaf around** *with their hands in their pockets.* ○ *As there wasn't anything to do in the place but work, they were uncomfortably conspicuous* **loafing about** *the streets.* CON = idle about/around, loiter about/around.

lock

lock away/up (in) 1 [Vn ⇆ p pass, Vn.p.pr pass emph rel] put (sth) for safe keeping in a drawer etc, which is then locked. **O:** jewels, silver. **o:** bank; safe, vault, strong-room: *Take good care to* **lock away** *your jewellery before going away on holiday.* ○ *'You're old enough to take a drink if you want one. I don't keep it* **locked up**.' FFE

2 [Vn ⇆ p pass, Vn.p.pr pass emph rel] imprison (sb); keep (sb) in a mental institution. **O:** felon, criminal. **o:** gaol, prison; cell, dungeon; institution: *By 1950 the* (US communist) *party was in a state of disintegration and many of its leaders had been* **locked away**. 50S ○ *'Where is he now,* **locked up**?' *'No he's dead.'* TOH ○ *'She isn't mad is she, Aunt Kathleen?' 'She's never been* **locked up** *if that's what you're asking.'* ⇨ lock-up 1.

lock in 1 [Vn.p pass, Vn.pr pass emph rel] deliberately put (sb) in a room etc, and then lock the door from the outside. **O:** prisoner, escapee; wayward child. **o:** cell, guardroom; bedroom: *Prisoners were* **locked in** *their huts at night to discourage further attempts at escape.* ↔ lock out/out of 1.

2 [Vn.p pass, Vn.pr pass] prevent (sb) from leaving a room etc, by accidentally locking the door, losing the key etc. **O:** him etc; oneself. **o:** flat; cellar, lavatory: *'Open the door, you idiot! You've* **locked** *me* **in**.' ○ *The cashier spent an uncomfortable night* **locked in** *the basement. The porter had turned the key in the door.* ↔ lock out/out of 2.

lock out [Vn ⇆ p nom pass adj] (*industrial relations*) prevent (workers) from entering (their workplace) eg in response to a threat of strike action. **S:** owner, employer. **O:** workforce, worker: *Workmen have been* **locked out** *until they agree to the employers' terms.* ○ *There has been a* **lock-out** *at the Liverpool firm of Smith and Weston.* G

lock out/out of 1 [Vn.p pass adj, Vn.pr pass] deliberately prevent (sb) from entering (a place) by locking the door etc on the inside. **S:** parent, warden (of a hostel etc), porter. **O:** child, student. **o:** house, college, hall of residence: *Father threatened to* **lock** *us* **out** *if we didn't get back from the party before midnight.* ○ *In some university towns, landladies are requested to* **lock** *students* **out** *if they do not return to their lodgings by a certain time.* ↔ lock in 1.

2 [Vn.p pass, Vn.pr pass] accidentally or mistakenly prevent (sb/oneself) from entering (a place), eg by losing the key. **O:** him etc; oneself. **o:** flat, office, bedroom: *He'd* **locked** *himself* **out of** *the house and had to get in by breaking a window.* ↔ lock in 2.

lock up [Vp, Vn ⇆ p pass adj] make (a house etc) secure by locking doors and windows. **O:** house, garage; shop, store; car: *He always **locks up** last thing at night.* ○ ***Lock** everything **up** securely before going away on holiday.*

lock-up 1 [nom (Vn.p)] place where prisoners may be kept temporarily; prison: *The suspects were kept in the station **lock-up** overnight.* ⇨ lock up (in) 2.

2 [nom (Vn.p)] shop or garage, usu at some distance from the house of the tradesman or owner: *Her father has a small **lock-up** tobacconist's in the old part of town.* ○ *I pay ten pounds a week for the rent of a **lock-up** garage.* □ a lock-up (no second noun) is a lock-up *shop*.

lock up (in) 1 [Vn ⇆ p pass, Vn.p.pr pass emph rel] put (sth) in a drawer etc. ⇨ lock away/up (in) 1.

2 [Vn ⇆ p pass, Vn.p.pr pass emph rel] imprison (sb); keep (sb) in a mental institution. ⇨ lock away/up (in) 2.

3 [Vn ⇆ p pass, Vn.p.pr pass emph rel] enclose or trap (sth) (in sth). **S:** mechanism; process. **O:** power, energy: *Our new process **locks up** pounds of energy **in** every grain of the breakfast food.* ○ *Many ignore the beauty **locked up in** every minute speck of material around us.* HAH □ usu pass.

4 [Vn ⇆ p pass adj, Vn.p.pr pass rel] invest (money) in such a way that it cannot easily be changed into cash. **S:** firm, company; investor. **O:** capital; estate, fortune; savings. **o:** business; plant, machinery; shares: *He had most of the money from the profitable years **locked up in** the building and expansion programme. For working capital he had to borrow from the bank.*

lodge

lodge (against) (with) [Vn.pr pass emph rel] (*formal*) present a statement, usu of protest or complaint, to (sb) so that he can take action. **S:** committee, action group; citizen, consumer. **O:** complaint, protest; petition. **o:** (**against**) intimidation, brutality; plan; (proposed) extension, development; (**with**) local council; police; solicitor: *Police action in controlling the crowd was unnecessarily severe. A formal complaint is being **lodged with** the Chief Constable.* ○ *Following the recent explosion, statements have been **lodged against** the Gas Board accusing them of negligence.*

lodge (in) [Vpr emph rel] enter and become stuck fast (in sth). **S:** bullet, shell fragment. **o:** skull, bone; foot, chest: *A piece of shrapnel had **lodged in** the brain, causing damage to the centres controlling movement.*

log

log off [Vp] (*computing*) leave a computer system, usu by keying a special word or sequence of words: *Before **logging off** for the day, remember to copy your completed file to the backup disk.* ↔ log on.

log on [Vp] (*computing*) enter a computer system, usu by keying a special word or sequence of words: ***Log on** by typing your user name and password.* ↔ log off.

log up [Vp.n pass] travel for (a specified time or distance); have (times and distances travelled) recorded, ie in a log-book. **S:** pilot, driver. **O:** flight, run, journey; hours, miles: *The pilot of the crashed aircraft had **logged up** several hundred hours' flying time on jets.* ○ *'I see you've **logged up** a thousand miles on this truck since the last service. You'd better bring it into the garage straight away.'*

loiter

loiter about/around [Vp, Vpr] spend one's time idly, perhaps with the aim of causing mischief. **o:** the place; door, entrance-way: *Small boys would **loiter about** in the entrances of smart hotels, hoping to pick up a few tips.* ○ *'Who's that shifty-looking character **loitering around** outside?'* = idle about/around, loaf about/around.

loll

loll about/around [Vp, Vpr] sit, lie or lean on sth lazily. **o:** the place; room, bar: *There are too many of these people **lolling about** the place with nothing to do but plan trouble.* ○ *He **lolls around** in an armchair; she does the washing-up.* = lie about/around/round 1, lounge about/around, sprawl about/around.

long

long for [Vpr pass adj emph rel] desire to have (sth/sb) strongly. **o:** success, money, fame; horse, car; husband, wife, family: *One **longs for** the South of France.* NM ○ *Even such high praise and recognition was not enough for Freud, who **longed for** public recognition for his hard-won ideas.* F ○ *This **longed-for** change was slow in coming.* = die for.

look

look about/around/round [Vp nom, Vpr] examine (things) or search for (sth/sb), while standing still or moving around. **o:** office, study; town, castle; store, department; : *You **looked round** you as you stood waiting for the bus to take you to school* (cf *You had a **look round** as you stood* etc). TC ○ *'Fergus, what are you doing with that torch?' 'Just having a **look around**.'* DC ○ *He spent the first few days **looking round** the sights* (of the city). F □ nom forms look around, look round, not usu hyphenated.

look after 1 [Vpr pass adj] be responsible for (sb). **S:** nurse, doctor, mother. **o:** patient, old person, sick child: *I thought the nurse was **looking after** you.* DC ○ *He seemed well **looked after**.* ○ *He knows how to **look after** himself* (= protect himself, his interests). □ adj always modified by *well, carefully, badly* etc: *a well-**looked-after** garden.* = attend to 1, care for 1, take care (of) 1.

2 [Vpr pass] take responsibility for doing (sth). **S:** trustee, agent. **o:** affairs, finances; shop, business; campaign: *'I'll **look after** the bill.'* ○ *Gould was asked to **look after** the publicity for Labour's last election campaign.* . = attend to 2, take care (of) 2.

look ahead [Vp] think about events that will take place in the future, and perhaps plan for them. **A:** ten years; several decades: *You can expect to find a multi-storey building on this site. Of course, I'm **looking ahead** five years when I tell you this.* ○ *Their love of short-term solutions is based on a genuine inability to **look ahead**.* MSAL

look at 1 [Vpr pass] examine (sth) closely to confirm its genuineness or value. **S:** valuer, expert. **o:** porcelain, silver, painting; collection: *I can't tell you what it's worth, you must get an expert to **look at** it.* ○ *Ask a museum to **look at** your coins.*

2 [Vpr pass] examine (sth) closely for possible disease, damage or faults etc, or in the hope of finding a solution. **S:** doctor, dentist; plumber, mechanic; committee, problem. **o:** shoulder, tooth; tap, engine; question, problem: *You must get that tooth* **looked at** *at once.* ○ *Get a carpenter to* **look at** *those floorboards.* ○ *The more I look at the problem, the more I feel that we'll never find a solution.* **3** [Vpr] (*informal*) consider, think of (sth). **o:** trouble, difficulty; fuss, bother; mess, chaos: *'Fancy Philip bringing all that wine back from France.' 'Yes, and* **look at** *the trouble we had getting it through customs!'* ○ *'I'll ask Mary to book you a flight.' 'Not Mary!* **Look at** *the mess she made of it last time.'* □ always imperative; an indignant appeal to sb to consider a blunder etc.

not look at [Vpr] not consider or entertain (sth). **o:** proposal, suggestion, offer: *They would***n't** *even* **look at** *our bid.* ○ *I will* **not look at** *any price under £5000.* □ usu after will/would.

to look at [Vpr] (*informal*) superficially, on the surface: ***To look at*** *him, you wouldn't think he'd just suffered a major setback.* ○ *He's not much* **to look at**, *I have to admit.* □ inf only.

not look at twice/not look twice at [Vpr emph rel] (*informal*) show very little interest in (sth/sb); not pay serious attention to (sth/sb). **o:** house, furniture; book, poetry; girlfriend, companion: *These old bitches would as soon go without their clothes as without their make-up, and* **no one** *in their senses would* **look at** *them* **twice** *whichever they did.* HAA ○ *It was a pile of old furniture that hundreds of people, happy with their 'contemporary'* (ie modern furniture) *would* **not look twice at**. RT □ used with *would*.

look away [Vp] turn one's eyes away; avert one's gaze: *The sunlight on the water was so dazzling that one had to* **look away**. ○ *Bill belched again. Laura* **looked away** *in embarrassment.*

never/not look back [Vp] (*informal*) move forward steadily in one's profession etc; progress continuously. **S:** actor, writer; businessman: *He's the youngest comedian ever to have his own television series . . . He's* **never looked back**, *scooping up audiences, awards and money wherever he goes.* RT ○ *The public realized that a new star had arrived, and since then Ann has***n't looked back**. H ○ *From now onwards there was* **no looking back**. SD

look back (on/upon) [Vp, Vp.pr pass emph rel] return (to an earlier time) in one's thoughts, cast one's mind back (to such a time). **o:** event; time, period; one's childhood, early days: ***Looking back***, *it is a privilege to have lived such a life.* SU ○ *The people would soon begin to* **look back** *with longing* **on** *the old regime.* MFM

look beyond [Vpr pass rel] place oneself imaginatively in the future. **o:** the present, the here and now; actual circumstances; where we are now: *Try to* **look beyond** *present hardships to future happiness.* = see beyond.

look down [Vp] lower one's eyes, one's gaze. **S:** child, girl. **A:** shyly, modestly; with a blush: *Sarah* **looked down** *in embarrassment. When would this terribly intense young man stop talking to her?* ○ *John* **looked down** *to hide his confusion. He hadn't realized the door led to the ladies' changing-room.*

look down one's nose (at) [Vpr] (*informal*) regard (sb/sth) in a superior, condescending way. **o:** (**at**) poorer people, the 'lower orders'; speech, remarks, habits (of others): *The English neighbours would say 'Mrs Middleton's quite mad', and* **look down their noses**. ASA ○ *'Don't* **look down your nose at** *a fat woman, Flo.'* RM

look down on/upon 1 [Vp.pr] from a higher level, observe or dominate (sb/sth) at a lower level. **o:** landscape; town; streets: *Zeus, the father of the gods,* **looking down upon** *the world, fell in love with the Princess Semele.* ○ *Paternoster Row, at the top of Ludgate Hill,* **looks down upon** *Fleet Street.* HB
2 [Vp.pr pass] consider (sb) as inferior; despise. **o:** one's father; working people; the poor, the illiterate: *Parents scrape and save and sacrifice themselves, and then their children* **look down on** *them.* PW ○ *The really unskilled people in the industry are* **looked down on** *by just about everyone.*

look for [Vpr pass adj emph rel] try to find (sth); seek. **o:** new job, house by the sea, business; lost cat, handkerchief: *'What are you* **looking for**?' *'A little sympathy.'* ○ *They* **looked for** *a harmonious society, but everywhere found war and disorder.* RTH ○ *Traditional Japan needs* **looking for**. BBCTV

look for trouble [Vpr] (*informal*) behave in a way which suggests that one seeks unpleasantness, a violent response etc: *You could see from his face that he was* **looking for trouble**. ○ *There's no sense coming into a new place just* **looking for trouble**.

look forward to 1 [Vp.pr pass adj rel] anticipate (sth) with pleasure. **o:** holiday, meeting, evening out; going abroad, returning home. **A:** eagerly; with pleasure, with keen anticipation: *She had been* **looking forward to** *leaving the hospital wards for a holiday in the Orkneys.* WI ○ *The third baby, Brigit had almost* **looked forward to** *with a timorous pleasure.* DC ○ *Retirement was eagerly* **looked forward to**, *especially after the mounting pressures of recent years.*
2 [Vp.pr] (be able to) expect (sth) confidently. **o:** regular leave, decent conditions, good pay: *Once in the trade an apprentice could* **look forward to** *becoming a journeyman.* SHOE ○ *Instead of the shore leave which crews of mixed cargo ships can* **look forward to**, *all that the tanker men can expect is an unbroken voyage.* OBS □ used with *be able to*, *can/could*.

look-in [nom (Vp)] (*informal*) a chance to take part or be involved. **Verb:** get, have; give sb: *I wanted to talk to her but with all those guys around I didn't get a* **look-in**. ○ *John would like a match with one of the teams but the club won't give him a* **look-in**. □ used in the sing only.

(not) look in the eye/face [Vn.pr] (*informal*) (not) look at (sb) or contemplate (sth) fearlessly and without shame. **O:** boss, father; questioner, challenger; facts, truth: *'The sure sign of a liar — you can***'t look** *me* **in the eye**, *can you?'* E ○ *When I had signed the contract, I felt I could hardly* **look** *Hugo* **in the face** *any more.* UTN ○ *This truth has been disguised . . . by Liberal unwillingness to* **look** *a fact* **in the face**. L □ often with (not) be able to/dare to.

(not) look a gift-horse in the mouth [Vn.pr] (*saying*) (not) look too critically at sth offered to one as a free gift: *It was one of mother's maxims* **never** *to* **look a gift-horse in the mouth**. HAHA ○ *'Why did you let Nora stay on after I'd gone?' 'Why* **look a gift-horse in the mouth**?' AITC

look in (at/on) [Vp, Vp.pr pass] (*informal*) pay a short visit (to a place); visit (sb) briefly. **o:** (**at**)

Mother's; headquarters, the factory; (**on**) Mother, Bill; my boss: *I suppose the doctor will* **look in** *when he gets a chance?* HOM ○ *We* **looked in at** *Burlington House.* AH ○ *I ought to visit the Mediterranean countries where British troops were stationed, and also* **look in on** *Jordan.* MFM ⇨ next entry

look into 1 [Vpr] (*informal*) make a brief call or visit to (a place). **o:** office, surgery; mother's (house); club: *I must* **look into** *the garage on the way home to book a service for the car.* ⇨ previous entry

2 [Vpr pass] investigate (sth). **o:** case, matter, question: *Police are* **looking into** *the disappearance of a quantity of uncut gems.* ○ *Perhaps you wouldn't mind* **looking into** *it for me?* TT ○ *All these complaints will have to be* **looked into**. = inquire into.

look on [Vp] be a spectator: *Most people aren't good enough to play in first-class matches; they have to be content to* **look on** (or: *to be* **lookers-on**, *to be* **onlookers**). ○ *I was merely* **looking on**. AH □ onlookers is the more common nom form.

look on/upon (as) [Vpr pass] regard, consider (sb/sth) (to be sth). **o:** (**on/upon**) his rival, their brother; this country (as) an enemy of the state, a popular hero; a safe refuge, an island of democracy: *People* **look upon** *him almost* **as** *a traitor to the cause.* ○ *He is* **looked upon as** *something of an authority on rare books.* ○ *The other servants* **look on** *the nursery* **as** *a separate and almost alien world.* BRN ⇨ next entry

look on/upon (with) [Vpr pass] regard, consider (sth/sb) (in a positive or negative way). **o:** (**on/upon**) scheme, plan; idea, thought; colleague; (**with**) favour, approval; disfavour, mistrust, suspicion: *Though I knew such an idea was* **looked upon with** *suspicion I felt it was a possibility not to be ignored.* LIFE ○ *The God Apollo* **looked with** *favour* **on** *his work and blessed it.* GLEG ○ *'Tell me, how do people* **look upon** *him in general?'* ⇨ previous entry

look onto/out on [Vpr, Vp.pr] give a view of (sth); overlook. **S:** bedroom, dining-room. **o:** alley, wall, garden: *Her attic bedroom* **looks onto** *rows of chimney pots.* ○ *The long low windows* **looked out on** *a driveway at the side of the house.* OBS ⇨ back on to, give on to.

look out 1 [Vp] take care, beware: *'***Look out***, Peter, that step's not safe!'* ○ *'Tell them to* **look out***, the ceiling's threatening to fall in.'* □ usu in imperative sentences. = mind out, watch out.

2 [Vp.n pass] (*dated*) search for and produce (sth/sb). **O:** old clothes, books, photographs, stamps; friend: *I must* **look out** *some bits and pieces for the church jumble sale.* ○ *Perhaps he'll* **look out** *one of his old girl friends.* LBA

look-out 1 [nom (Vp)] one who keeps watch, sentry; place from which a watch is kept. **Verb:** post, relieve: **Look-outs** *were posted at night in our forward positions.* ○ *They were manning a* **look-out** (or: *a* **look-out** *post*) *in the front line.*

2 [nom (Vp)] (*informal*) prospect, outlook. **adj:** poor, grim; bright: *It's a bleak* **look-out** *for anyone hoping for quick profits.* ○ *It's not a very bright* **look-out** *if you're thinking of a career in the coal industry.*

it/that be sb's look-out [nom (Vp)] (*informal*) that is sb's (own) concern and responsibility (often with the implication that the person involved does not deserve to succeed etc): *The salesman's incentive is to get any business, not any good business: if the customer doesn't keep up the payments,* **that is** *the company***'s look-out** *and loss.* OBS ○ *If he can't be bothered to write, and misses his chances,* **that's his look-out**. □ when the idiom begins with *that*, it is used in a main clause after *if* + negative, as shown; when it begins with *it*, it is used in a main clause before *if* + negative: **It's his look-out** *if he can't be bothered to turn up on time!*

look out (for) [Vp.pr pass] watch or search carefully (for sth/sb). **o:** new car, second-hand radio; talent, capable player; criminal, fugitive: *The policemen are* **looking out for** *burglars.* CON ○ *Jeremy will soon be old enough to go to boarding school. We must be* **looking out for** *one.* PW ○ *Keep a sharp* **look-out for** *Peter.* ○ *Mother is always on the* **look-out for** *bargains.* □ nom form look-out comes from a [Vp] pattern. = watch out (for).

look out/out of [Vp, Vpr] direct one's gaze through (sth). **o:** window, door, porthole: *He got up, went to the cavern's entrance and* **looked out**. GLEG ○ *He drew back the curtains and* **looked out of** *the window.*

look out on [Vpr, Vp.pr] ⇨ look onto/out on.

look over 1 [Vpr nom pass] make a tour of inspection of (a place); survey, inspect. **o:** house, garden; estate, farm; factory: *We were allowed to* **look over** *their new plant near Coventry.* ○ *The surveyor will come back later to do a full inspection. He just had time to give the place a quick* **look-over** *before lunch.* = go over 2.

2 [Vn ⇆ p pass] examine (sth/sb) closely; scrutinize. **O:** document, letter; claim, appeal; arm, heart; visitor, newcomer: *A sheet of photocopies was given to her, and Hawksmoor* **looked over** *each one rapidly.* HWKM ○ *Her green eyes* **looked** *them* **over** *indifferently from under her dusty lashes.* ARG = go over 1.

look over one's shoulder [Vpr] look back when running a race to see if one is being overtaken by a competitor; (*figurative*) be unduly concerned about possible threats and dangers: *'Don't* **look over your shoulder***: you could be giving vital seconds to the opposition.'* ○ (*figurative*) *British exports are not large enough to allow us to enjoy our boom without this constant* **looking over our shoulder**.

look round 1 [Vp nom, Vpr] examine what is round one. ⇨ look about/around/round.

2 [Vp nom, Vpr] inspect or survey (sth). ⇨ look about/around/round.

3 [Vpr rel] observe cautiously around (an obstacle). **o:** screen, door, pillar; newspaper, fan: *The door was half open and I* **looked** *carefully* **round** *it.* ○ *With a periscope you can* **look round** *corners without being seen.*

4 [Vp] turn to look at sth/sb behind one: *I made a rustling sound and the lady in front* **looked round** *angrily.* ○ *'Don't* **look round** *now but there's a police car following us.'*

look through 1 [Vp, Vpr pass emph rel] turn one's gaze through (sth). **o:** window; telescope, field glasses: *He* **looked through** *the living-room window at a rain-soaked garden.* ○ *The skylight*

through *which he was now* ***looking*** *was directly above the staircase.*

2 [Vpr nom pass] survey or scan (sth), often briefly. **o:** book, paper; stamp-collection, notes: *He gave his notes a quick* ***look-through*** *before giving his lecture.* ○ *He* ***looks through*** *several newspapers before breakfast* (or: *He gives them a* ***look-through***).

3 [Vn ⇆ p pass] inspect (sth) carefully, part by part; scrutinize. **o:** application, proposal, recommendation; document, letter: *'Have you read the man's references?' 'I haven't finished* ***looking through*** *them yet.'* = go over 1, look over 2.

4 [Vpr] not see sb/sth that is clearly visible; deliberately ignore (sb) whom one can plainly see. **o:** friend, acquaintance: *'You must be as blind as a bat. I was standing ten yards away, and you* ***looked*** *straight* ***through*** *me.'* ○ *'In that icily superior way of his, he* ***looked*** *right* ***through*** *us.'*

look to for sth/to do sth [Vpr pass rel] choose (sb/sth) to give one (support etc). **o:** (**to**) government, private industry; personal enterprise, individual courage; (**for**) assistance, guidance; success, survival. **Inf:** to explain the regulations, to guide us: *Musicians, writers and painters* ***looked for*** *patronage* ***to*** *courtiers and gentlemen.* SHOE ○ *Let this be a warning against* ***looking to*** *personal diplomacy* ***to settle*** *issues.* SC ○ *It was* ***to*** *Freud that many members of the family* ***looked****, not only* ***for*** *cash but* ***for*** *advice.* F = turn to 1.

look to one's laurels [Vpr] beware of losing one's reputation. **S:** athlete, sportsman; industrialist, inventor: *One or two younger scientists are challenging him in this field, so he must* ***look to his laurels****.* ⇨ rest on one's laurels.

look towards 1 [Vpr] have its front towards (sth); face. **S:** house, entrance. **o:** river, golf course, open country: *The front of the house* ***looks towards*** *the open sea.*

2 [Vpr] focus one's attention on (some future event). **o:** introduction, arrival; change, move: *Many teachers ... are now* ***looking towards*** *the implementation and implications of the National Curriculum as a more urgent priority.* G

look up 1 [Vp] raise one's eyes: *He didn't* ***look up*** *from his newspaper when I entered the room.* ○ *I* ***looked up*** *from my desk and found myself gazing at grey roofs and chimneys.* LIFE

2 [Vp] (*informal*) get better; improve. **S:** trade, business; turnover, figures; things: *Prospects for the small builder are* ***looking up****.* ○ *It's a completely new beginning and perhaps things will soon begin to* ***look up*** *for them.* F

3 [Vn ⇆ p pass] try to find (sth), usu in a work of reference; seek information about (sth). **O:** detail, account; quotation, expression; train, bus, plane; him etc: *He comes back with an enormous dictionary, sits down and* ***looks up*** *the word.* KLT ○ *All I can do is* ***look up*** *the figures and find that we were the richest country in the world.* CON ○ *I* ***looked*** *him* ***up*** *in 'Who's Who'.* ○ *Evidently he'd* ***looked up*** *the train; it wasn't all a matter of wild impulse.* CON

4 [Vn ⇆ p pass] (*informal*) search for sb's house so as to visit (him). **O:** old friend, acquaintance: *I've promised that the next time I go to London I'll* ***look*** *him* ***up****.* ○ *Mine was not the kind of life where you 'ran into old friends', or were* ***'looked up'*** *by them.* THH

look up and down [Vn.p pass] examine (sb) in an admiring, sexually calculating, or contemptuous way: *Standing with her hands on her hips, she* ***looked*** *George* ***up and down*** *in mock admiration.* PE ○ *I was staring out of the driver's seat, taking in every word she said. She* ***looked*** *me* ***up and down****.* THH

look up to [Vp.pr pass adj] regard (sb) with respect; admire. **o:** leader, teacher, father: *He was still a leading member of the local organization, much* ***looked up to*** *for his maritime war experience.* RFW ○ *People you can* ***look up to****, with no frills, no snob-stuff, are pretty rare.* PW

look upon [Vpr pass] ⇨ look on/upon (as), look on/upon (with).

loom

loom ahead [Vp emph] (*formal*) await one as a danger or challenge in the future. **S:** adult responsibilities; matrimony, military service: *I had just attained the glory of the sixth form at school, with scholarships* ***looming ahead****.* SD ○ *The Second Front in Europe, the invasion across the Channel, was* ***looming ahead****.* MFM

loom up [Vp] appear suddenly and threateningly. **S:** ship; rock, iceberg: *Another rock* ***loomed up*** *and they only missed it by a fraction.* PW

loose

loose off [Vp, Vn ⇆ p pass adj] fire (sth); explode (sth). **O:** shell, round (of ammunition); rocket, grenade: *Trigger-happy resistance fighters were* ***loosing off*** *bullets all over the place.*

loosen up 1 [Vp, Vn ⇆ p pass] make (oneself/sb) more physically relaxed or supple: *He* ***loosened up*** *with a few exercises before the big match.* ○ *I got to* ***loosen*** *myself* ***up****, you see what I mean? I could have got done in* (= killed) *down there.* TC = limber up.

2 [Vp, Vn ⇆ p pass] (help sb to) become less stiff, formal or solemn; (help sb to) relax: *When I told her that I was his brother from Australia she* ***loosened up*** *and invited me into the parlour.* RFW ○ *'Perhaps I'm beginning to* ***loosen up****,' Pyle said. 'Your influence. I guess you're good for me, Thomas.'* QA ○ *'A few drinks will* ***loosen*** *them* ***up****.'*

lop

lop off [Vn ⇆ p pass adj] cut (sth) off cleanly with a bill-hook or sword. **O:** branch; arm: *The ground was littered with* ***lopped-off*** *branches.* ○ *His arm was* ***lopped off*** *at the elbow.* = chop off.

lord

lord it over [Vn.pr] (*jocular*) behave in a superior way towards (sb). **S:** butler; matron; prefect. **o:** lesser servant; nurse; junior boy: *She'd be Queen and* ***lord it over*** *all the other servants, and live in luxury.* RFW ○ *Pendennis, home from school after his father's death, was* ***lording it over*** *the household as the young squire.* TU ⇨ queen it over.

lose

(not) lose any sleep about/over [Vn.pr emph rel] (*informal*) (not) be greatly worried or concerned about (sth). **o:** news, announcement; proposal, suggestion; change, move; him/his being appointed: *There's* ***no*** *need to* ***lose any sleep over*** *the aircraft. I think it was probably trying to land.*

RFW ○ *'I should have thought you might wish it hadn't happened?' 'Oh, I have**n't lost any sleep about** it.* NM □ usu negative.

lose by [Vpr, Vn.p pass] suffer financially or personally through (some action). **O:** nothing, not anything; not much, not a lot. **o:** the change, the move; joining us, leaving your present job: *Why not join us? I promise you that you won't **lose by** it* (ie it will be to your advantage). ○ *How much do they stand to **lose by** this merger?* ○ *I suppose there's nothing to be **lost by** sending a small patrol to the other side of the island.* □ usu in neg/interr sentences.

lose confidence etc in [Vn.pr pass emph rel] no longer have confidence, faith etc in (sb/sth). **O:** ⚠ confidence, faith, interest, trust. **o:** leader, management; course, programme; enterprise, project: *Customers are **losing confidence in** our ability to meet delivery dates.* ○ *Now that she'd got him involved it seemed she'd **lost interest in** the problem itself.* AT

lose (oneself) in [Vn.pr pass emph rel] become fully absorbed in (sth). **o:** game, sport; story, book: *I soon **lost myself in** the rediscovered pleasures of the game.* ○ *Mick was **lost in** the intricacies of a new electric motor.*

lost in [pass (Vn.pr)] filled with (sth), overwhelmed with (sth). **o:** ⚠ thought; admiration, wonder: *We were **lost in** admiration for his achievements.* □ also used after *appear* etc, or after a noun: *. . . people **lost in** wonder at his exploits.*

lose all trace of [Vn.pr pass emph rel] have no clues as to the whereabouts of (sb/sth). **S:** family; police; search-party; secretary. **o:** (missing) child; escapee, suspect; climber, explorer; record-card, letter: ***All trace** has been **lost of** the climbing party missing since last weekend.*

lose count (of) [Vn.pr emph rel] be unable to remember how many things or people there are because there are so many of them. **o:** (number of) times, occasions (sth has happened); (his) cars, yachts; wives, husbands: *'I've **lost count of** the times he's bored us with that particular story.'* ○ *'How many holiday homes did you say they had? I've **lost count** of them.'*

lose sight of 1 [Vn.pr pass(o) emph rel] no longer be able to see (sth). **o:** land, ship, quarry: *We **lost sight of** the enemy in some thick scrub about half a mile to our front.* ○ *The fugitive was **lost sight of** in the crowd.*

2 [Vn.pr pass(o) emph rel] not keep (sth) fresh or uppermost in one's mind. **o:** objective, aim, goal; advantage, merit: *My mind could take such decisions without **losing sight of** the main question.* QA ○ *The end-product — doing as many good things for as many patients as possible — can be **lost sight of**.* OBS = forget about.

lose track of [Vn.pr pass(o) rel] no longer be able to trace or follow (sb/sth whose progress one is interested in). **o:** him etc; movements, progress; aircraft, ship: *I can follow his career up to 1958, then quite abruptly I **lose track of** him.* ○ *His plane was **lost track of** about two hours out from Kennedy Airport.*

lose the use of [Vn.pr] be unable, through illness or injury, to use (a limb). **o:** hand, arm, leg: *The doctors did what they could, but he **lost the use of** both legs.*

lose on [Vpr emph rel, Vn.pr pass emph rel] lose (money) as a result of (some activity). **O:** a fortune, a packet, one's shirt; investments, savings. **o:** gamble, venture; deal, transaction: *He **lost** heavily **on** the deal.* ○ *It's a project **on** which we stand to **lose** a large sum of money.* ○ *You can **lose** a packet **on** racing whether you study the horses or not.*

lost on [pass (Vn.pr)] wasted on (sb), unnoticed by (sb). **S:** remark, comment, observation; charm, attentiveness; finesse, subtlety (of manner): *'It's like having a television set you never look at.' The illustration was **lost on** Sir George, who had no television set.* DBM ○ *This impressive display of western air power was not **lost on** the Russians.* MFM □ used as adj after *appear, seem*: *The comment seemed totally **lost on** Frank.*

lose one's hold on/over [Vn.pr] no longer control (sb); not master or dominate (sth) any longer. **S:** teacher, leader; scholar, craftsman. **o:** class, (political) party; subject-matter, material: *Some parents hate to relinquish control: the more they **lose their hold on** their children, the more they seek to retain it by unfair means.*

lose out (to) [Vp, Vp.pr emph rel] (*informal*) be overcome and replaced (by sth). **S:** live theatre, music hall; tradition, family; small trade, private initiative. **o:** television; the new morality; big combines: *Faced with competition from the supermarkets the small neighbourhood shop is bound to **lose out**.* ○ *The hard way, the grind, the moral lesson, duty, all were **losing out to** the easy way, money, charm, a well-known name.* ASA

lose one's hold over [Vn.pr] ⇨ lose one's hold on/over.

(not) lose any sleep over [Vn.pr emph rel] ⇨ (not) lose any sleep about/over.

lose ground (to) [Vn.pr pass emph rel] retreat, give way, because of pressure (from sth/sb). **S:** trade, industry; product, commodity; army. **o:** (overseas) pressure, competition; invader: *We have been **losing ground** fast **to** foreign producers and we must do something to stop the rot.* T ○ *We've already **lost** a lot of **ground to** cheap imports from the Far East.*

lose contact/touch (with) [Vn.pr pass emph rel] no longer be closely connected (with sth); no longer be talking or writing to (sb). **S:** ship, aircraft; actor, writer; politician; teacher, parent. **o:** shore, base; audience, public; the masses, his origins; class, child: *Radio **contact with** the lightship has been **lost** but will soon be restored.* ○ *Her letters betray a desperate desire not to **lose touch with** her beloved.* HB ○ *No one whom Dave has taught seems ever to **lose touch with** him.* UTN

lose patience with [Vn.pr emph rel] no longer be able to deal patiently with (sb/sth). **o:** parent, child; boss, employee; machine, car, radio: *Prissie had **lost patience with** the boy, and had told him to stop in the nursery and mind Sarah.* DC ○ *It is easy to **lose patience with** Jung, as I have myself at times.* JUNG

lost without [pass (Vn.pr)] unable to live happily, work efficiently etc, without (sth). **o:** daily paper, sporting news, television; tobacco, whisky; conversation, companionship: *Anna's life worked to schedule; like a nun, she would have been **lost without** her watch.* UTN ○ *Oh, don't try and take his* *suffering away from him — he'd be* ***lost without*** *it.* LBA □ also used after *appear*, etc.

lounge

lounge about/around [Vp, Vpr] (*informal*) lie, sit or lean on sth lazily. **o:** the place; sitting-room, bar: *'Do you think that instead of* ***lounging about*** *you could give a hand with the dishes?'* ○ *If my son wants to* ***lounge around*** *at home, he doesn't have to monopolize my favourite armchair.* = lie about/around/round 1, loll about/around, sprawl about.

louse

louse up [Vn ⇆ p pass] (*slang*) spoil, ruin (sth). **S:** (clumsy, inconsiderate) fool, idiot. **O:** chance, prospects (of success); party, celebration; things, the whole thing: *We'd just got Monica settled with a few comforting words when Dan had to* ***louse*** *everything* ***up*** *by opening his big mouth!* = mess up.

lull

lull to sleep [Vn.pr pass] send (sb) to sleep by rocking. **S:** (movement of) train, aircraft; mother. **O:** passenger; infant: *The swaying motion of the train must have* ***lulled*** *me* ***to sleep****. The next thing I knew was waking up with a jerk at King's Cross.*

lumber

lumber (with) [Vn.pr pass] (*informal*) pass to (sb else) an awkward or inconvenient person, object or task. **o:** relative, pet animal; ugly furniture, unusable china; organizing, arrangements: *'Why* ***lumber*** *me* ***with*** *all this paperwork?'* ○ *Every summer we get* ***lumbered with*** *Aunt Mabel for a fortnight.* = saddle with.

lump

lump together [Vn ⇆ p pass] (*informal*) treat (separate things) as one. **O:** items, belongings; towns, states; accounts, bills: *Their incomes are* ***lumped together*** *for tax purposes.* ○ *They've* ***lumped*** *the two districts* ***together*** *under one administrator.*

lunge

lunge at [Vpr rel] throw oneself forward at (a target), as when thrusting with a sword. **S:** adversary, assailant: *The intruder* ***lunged at*** *Stevens with a knife; Stevens snatched up a briefcase to ward off the blow.*

lure

lure away (from) [Vn ⇆ p pass, Vn.p.pr pass emph rel] persuade (sb) to leave (a place etc) by making false or genuine promises. **S:** manufacturer, publisher, director of research. **O:** executive, author, scientist: *I've heard many stories of bright young research workers being* ***lured away*** *only to find their position change for the worse.* ○ *You'll need to be very seductive or very devious to* ***lure*** *her* ***away from*** *Peter. She's crazy about him.*

lust

lust after [Vpr pass] strongly desire (sb/sth); covet. **o:** woman; money; fame, glory: *He* ***lusted after*** *those things which people born to money took for granted and didn't greatly desire.*

M

make

make no bones about [Vn.pr] act or speak about sth frankly and vigorously. **o:** blaming sb, accusing sb, coming to sb's defence: *Mr Justice Danckwerts* ***made no bones about*** *stigmatizing its use as dishonest trading.* T ○ *He* ***made no bones about*** *describing her in 'The Times' as an incomparable singer.* T □ object is usu the *-ing* form of a verb.

make a fuss (about/over) [Vn.pr pass emph rel] become very excited or worried (about sth), for no good reason. **adj:** much, a deal of, a lot of, no end of (a): *Jean Pierre was* ***making a fuss about*** *one of the translations.* UTN ○ *The unexpected rise in British factory investment,* ***about*** *which so* ***much fuss*** *has been* ***made****, should be greatly welcomed.* OBS ○ *They are* ***making a lot of fuss over*** *nothing!*

make a song and dance (about/over) [Vn.pr pass] (*informal*) become unreasonably and absurdly excited or worried (about sth): *Kay's parents* ***made a*** *dreadful* ***song and dance about*** *her being out after midnight.* ○ ***A*** *tremendous* ***song and dance*** *was being* ***made over*** *the change in the licensing laws.*

make one's way across, along, back etc [Vn.p, Vn.pr emph rel] move across, along, back etc. **o:** road; river, sea; room, corridor: *It was an hour and a half or so later that the company* ***made its way back*** *to the transmitting station.* TBC ○ *Armed with lengths of string and fish-hooks, we would* ***make our way down*** *to the river-bank in the morning.* DF ○ *The session is finishing and the swimmers* ***make their way to*** *the changing rooms.* RT

make after [Vpr] chase, pursue (sth/sb). **o:** quarry, prey, thief: *A rabbit shot from the burrow and the two dogs* ***made after*** *it at top speed.*

make at [Vpr] move towards (sb) as if to attack him: *He* ***made at*** *the man with a heavy ruler snatched from the table.* ○ *The dog* ***made at*** *the postman with his teeth bared.*

make eyes at [Vn.pr] (*informal*) look at (sb) flirtatiously or coquettishly. **o:** good-looking man, beautiful woman: *'Stop* ***making eyes at*** *the waiter, Mary. We shan't get our meal any quicker!'* ○ *There's nothing for the French boys to do but* ***make eyes at*** *Mariette.* BFA ○ *Claude had no right to come* ***making eyes at*** *this fair young creature.* BLCH

make a grab at [Vn.pr rel] (*informal*) suddenly stretch out a hand and try to grasp (sth/sb). **adj:** quick, sharp, sudden. **o:** rope, handle; hand, sleeve: *I could do nothing more than* ***make a*** *wild* ***grab at*** *him with my arms.* BB

make a pass (at) [Vn.pr] (*informal*) suggest by word or gesture that one wants to have a sexual relationship (with sb): *'If he ever* ***makes a pass at*** *you I'll wring his neck.'* AITC ○ *'I was quite shameless, wasn't I? The owner's wife* ***making a*** *big* ***pass at*** *one of the salesmen.'* PE □ pass may be pl, as in: *Men don't* ***make passes at*** *girls in glasses.*

make away/off (with) [Vp, Vp.pr pass] steal (sth) and hurry away with it. **o:** cash, valuables, luggage: *They snatched the cashbox and* ***made off*** *in a white van.* ○ *While we were having coffee two small boys* ***made off with*** *our suitcases.*

make away with [Vp.pr] kill (oneself): *'You don't think she had any motive for* **making away with** *herself, Mother?'* RFW = do away with 2.

make for 1 [Vpr pass] move towards (sth), eg to escape. **S:** audience, crowd; vehicle; ship. **o:** exit, gate; sea: *'I can't listen to any more of this rubbish!' he said, and* **made for** *the door.* EM ○ *He* **made for** *the Western Highway by a short cut through suburban roads I did not know.* RFW ○ *The bar was instantly* **made for** *by the thirsty audience.*
2 [Vpr pass] rush towards (sth/sb) so as to attack it/him. **S:** aircraft, tank; elephant, bull: *Two sentries* **made** *straight* **for** *him with drawn revolvers.*
3 [Vpr pass] help to make (sth) possible; ensure. **S:** good management; improved motorways; enlightened teaching. **o:** better labour relations; safer driving; sound education: *The Government's refusal to consider major changes in the Bill and the uncompromising opposition of the TUC have . . .* **made for** *bitterness.* SC ○ *A big family's a wonderful interest. It* **makes for** *the stability of marriage.* QA

make allowances (for) [Vn.pr pass emph rel] consider (a factor) when measuring, assessing or judging (sth/sb). **adj:** some, no, (not) any, few; certain, due. **o:** growth, shrinkage; wind, tide; age, inexperience: *Now that I had seen this attitude abroad, I was even less ready to* **make allowances for** *it.* AH ○ *The financing of road improvements is just as much of a burden to one place as another when* **allowances** *are* **made for** *size and revenue.* SC □ allowances occasionally sing, as in: *When every* **allowance** *has been* **made for** *his inexperience . . . .* = allow for, take into account/consideration, take account of.

make amends (for) [Vn.pr pass emph rel] ⇨ make amends (to) (for).

make a bee-line for [Vn.pr pass emph rel] (*informal*) hurry directly towards (sth/sb). **o:** door, exit; bar; best-looking girl: *Most of the children, being normal, healthy little hooligans,* **made a bee-line for** *all the percussion instruments.* TVT ○ *It was the time when the younger sons of noble but impoverished French families were* **making a bee-line** *for the arriving American heiresses.* L ○ ***A bee-line*** *was* **made for** *the best seats.*

make a bolt/dash for [Vn.pr] (*informal*) hurry to reach, arrive at (a place) or to escape from (a place). **o:** bus, train; freedom, open door; it: *I became oblivious of the passage of time and had to* **make a bolt for** *it to get the bus.* WDM ○ *The moment the guard's back was turned, Steve* **made a dash for** *the open window.*

make a break for it [Vn.pr] escape from captivity while one's captors' attention is elsewhere: *He was looking at her frequently, perhaps to make sure of catching her eye if she decided to* **make a break for it.** TGLY ○ *I am not so daft as to* **make a break for it** *on my long-distance running.* LLDR

make a name for oneself [Vn.pr] earn oneself a reputation in a particular field. **A:** on the stock exchange, in the theatre, as an after-dinner speaker: *The Prime Minister favoured Gott, who had* **made a** *great* **name for himself** *in the desert.* MFM ○ *Lanny Watkins has quickly* **made a name for himself** *in the professional game* (ie golf). OBS

make a/one's play for [Vn.pr] (*informal*) try by some special action to secure or capture (sth), or win the interest (of sb). **o:** job, vacancy; sb's attention; pretty girl: *'Stephens has been with the company for about a year now. How long will it be before he* **makes a play for** *the top job?'* ○ *'Did you see how Bill's eye lighted on the girl in the yellow dress? He'll be* **making his play for** *her in just a minute.'*

make room (for) [Vn.pr pass pass(o) emph rel] make space or time (into which sb/sth can be fitted). **o:** passenger, visitor, speaker; furniture, junk; activities: *The car was sold to* **make room** *in the garage* **for** *rabbits.* SU ○ *More* **room** *needs to be* **made** *in the TV schedules* **for** *serious drama.* ○ *Somehow the extra children will have to be* **made room for***—perhaps on the sitting-room floor.*

make tracks (for home) [Vn.pr] (*informal*) leave sb's company or house (to return home): *'It's time we were* **making tracks for home.** *Thank you for a delightful evening.'* ○ *'Come on,' said Finn, 'let you and I be* **making tracks**.' *We had been there nearly three-quarters of an hour.* UTN

make way for 1 [Vn.pr pass] create space for (sth). **o:** new roads, housing, an industrial estate: *Farmers had ripped out hedges and woods to* **make way for** *arable crops.* ○ *The trees were felled to* **make way for** *a road improvement scheme.*
2 [Vn.pr pass] move aside (eg by resigning) so that sb else can take one's place. **o:** a younger colleague, one's partner: *He decided that his role in life would be to die young and* **make way for** *the younger brother.* BLCH

make capital from/of/out of [Vn.pr pass rel] use (sth) to one's own advantage; exploit. **S:** press, critic, opponent. **adj:** much, a lot of, no end of. **o:** slip, blunder; confession, remark; resignation, move: *The newspapers have* **made** *much* **capital from** *a few indiscreet remarks.* ○ *A lot of* **capital** *will be* **made of** *their unwillingness to testify before the Committee.*

make a dent in 1 [Vn.pr pass rel] (*informal*) make (sth) less; reduce. **o:** savings, bank balance: *'All these bills for repairs to the house have* **made a** *big* **dent** *in our holiday money.'*
2 [Vn.pr pass rel] make (sth) weaker; damage. **o:** reputation, credibility, authority: *Stories of official corruption have* **made a** *serious* **dent in** *the government's high-minded campaign against lawlessness.*

make one's way in the world [Vn.pr] progress in one's career, make a success of one's working life: *He hasn't the determination to* **make his way in the world**. ○ *If he hasn't* **made his way in the world** *by now, he never will.* MM

make into [Vn.pr pass rel] cause (sb/sth) to become (sb/sth else). **O:** boy, trainee, recruit; mild person; loft, barn. **o:** man, manager, leader; tiger, bully; flat, studio: *He wasn't always a bully. You* **made** *him* **into** *one.* FFE ○ *Many of the cinemas have been* **made into** *bowling alleys and bingo halls.* = transform (into), turn into 2.

make inroads (into) [Vn.pr pass emph rel] absorb or consume a large part (of sth). **adj:** serious, extensive. **o:** savings, reserves, capital: *Our recent economic difficulties have caused serious* **inroads** *to be* **made into** *our gold and currency reserves.*

make of [Vn.pr pass emph rel] understand (sth) to a stated extent; form an impression of (sb). **O:** nothing; very little, hardly anything; something. **o:** behaviour, character; work, art; writing, sound: *He tired very quickly ... of the popular records and could* **make** *nothing* **of** *the others.* TST ○ *Nothing much could be* **made of** *the scribble in his notebooks.* ○ *'What did you* **make of** *the old lady?'* PP ⇨ make sense of.

make the best of [Vn.pr] do one's best in difficult conditions, or with limited means. **o:** situation; confinement, isolation; resources, gifts: *He was sorry his talents were not greater, but he was ready to* **make the best of** *them.* ○ *We must* **make the best** *we can* **of** *the few natural resources we have.* ↔ make the worst of.

make the best of a bad job [Vn.pr] (*informal*) do the best one can in unfavourable circumstances: *Aubrey Clover, resigned to* **making the best of a bad job**, *said, 'We'll have to rehearse on the day itself.'* WDM ○ *They were not well suited to each other, but both had determined to* **make the best of a bad job**.

make the best of both worlds [Vn.pr] combine the best aspects of different ways of life, philosophies etc: *Some have tried to* **make the best of both worlds** *— the best of Indianism, the best of Christianity.* DOP ○ *This device is really an invitation to* **make the best of both worlds**, *the telescopic and the microscopic, at a single glance.* HAH

make capital of [Vn.pr pass rel] ⇨ make capital from/of/out of.

make a clean breast of it/the whole thing [Vn.pr] confess (sth) in full: *'If you don't* **make a clean breast of it** *to the police I shall have to give them the information.'* EM

make a clean sweep (of) [Vn.pr pass pass(o) emph rel] remove (sth) entirely by vigorous action. **o:** rubbish, rubble, waste; rules, controls, restrictions: *His desk was quite bare. 'You've* **made a clean sweep**,*' I said.* QA □ sometimes sweep is pl, as in: *Government grants will hasten the disappearance of old buildings. Local authorities ... are apt to* **make clean sweeps of** *these ruins.* OBS = sweep away 2.

make effective etc use of [Vn.pr pass pass(o) emph rel)] use (sth) effectively etc. **adj:** ⚠ effective, good, proper. **o:** superior strength, reserve troops; spare capital, new machines: *The composer* **makes effective use** *of the augmented brass section.* ○ *How can an underdeveloped country* **make the best use of** *science?* NS ○ **Proper use** *is not being* **made of** *development aid from overseas.* = put to effective etc use.

make an evening etc of it [Vn.pr] (*informal*) devote a whole evening etc to a party, celebration, outing etc. **O:** ⚠ an evening, a night, a weekend: *Tharkles, released from supervision by Edith's absence, had suggested that they should* **make a weekend of it** *(ie spend the weekend together).* HD ○ *'Say you'll be back by one — unless you decide to* **make a night of it**.*'* OMIH

make an example of [Vn.pr pass pass(o) emph rel] punish (sb) severely for an offence in order to deter others. **S:** magistrate, court; headteacher. **o:** offender, culprit: *'Wasn't it high time,' said one letter, 'for* **an example** *to be* **made of** *these juvenile thugs?'* ○ *Those responsible for the disturbance in the main prison block were* **made an example of** *(or:* **made examples of***) by the governor.*

make an exhibition of oneself [Vn.pr] draw attention to oneself through loud, vulgar behaviour. **adj:** disgusting, dreadful, fearful: *'Did you have to* **make** *such* **a** *disgusting* **exhibition of yourself** *at the party? Why must you always be the centre of attention?'* ○ *'Do try to stop the children* **making exhibitions** (or: **an exhibition**) **of** *themselves in front of their grandparents!'*

make a fool of [Vn.pr pass(o)] make (sb) appear foolish by making him expect sth which does not come: *I wanted to laugh now: what* **fools** *we had both* **made of** *each other!* QA ○ *His friends were always ready to believe the best of him, but they were* **made fools of**. OBS

make a fool of oneself [Vn.pr] make oneself appear ridiculous through clumsy or thoughtless behaviour: *Aisgill had a watchful coldness about him which almost frightened me; he looked utterly incapable of* **making a fool of himself**. RATT ○ *There was a sort of tug-of-war between rival organizations. The result was that we both* **made fools of ourselves**. DS

make a friend of [Vn.pr] put oneself on close and friendly terms with sb one already knows (eg a pupil): *He never bothered to* **make a friend of** *his son.* ○ *A probation officer best succeeds if he tries to* **make friends of** *the young people in his care.*

make fun of [Vn.pr pass(o)] mock, ridicule (sb). **o:** sister, husband; speech, gestures; ambition, aspiration: *We all* **make fun of** *him, behind his back, of course.* OBS ○ *'You're* **making fun of** *me,' she said in a low voice. 'I'm quite serious.'* RATT ○ *His efforts to improve himself are constantly* **made fun of**. = laugh (at) 2.

make a fuss of [Vn.pr pass pass(o)] give much, perhaps too much, attention, hospitality etc to (sb). **adj:** much, a lot of; (not) any. **o:** guest, visitor; son: *We* **made** *such* **a fuss of** *them. Gave them cigarettes and mugs of tea.* CSWB ○ *Too* **much fuss** *can be* **made of** *very young children.* ○ *We were* **made** *a big* **fuss of** *by my husband's family.*

make a go of [Vn.pr pass(o)] (*informal*) make (sth) succeed. **o:** it; marriage, partnership, life together; business, venture: *Valerie will give me her support. She has been meeting a number of people in the business, and ... feels I could* **make a go of** *it.* TVT ○ *I think Helena and Tony will* **make a go of** *it* (ie their relationship). NM

make a good etc job of [Vn.pr pass rel] (*informal*) perform (a task) well, badly etc. **adj:** good, excellent, satisfactory; poor, dreadful. **o:** car, cooker; bathroom, kitchen; report, revision: *Many machines wash, rinse, spin-dry — but the new Acme Twin Speed Combination* **makes a better job of** *all three.* DM ○ *You can hand over to her any rewriting that needs to be done, knowing that a* **first-class job** *will be* **made of** *it.*

make a habit/practice of [Vn.pr pass pass(o) emph rel] do (sth) regularly, as a habit. **o:** it, this; turning up on time, greeting one's colleagues: *Use my telephone by all means, but don't* **make a habit of** *it.* ○ *He* **made a practice of** *doing his exercises in front of an open window.* ○ *He* **made a habit of** *taking a nap after lunch (cf He* **made** *it* **his habit** *to take a nap etc).*

make a hash/mess of [Vn.pr pass pass(o) rel] (*informal*) mismanage, mishandle (sth). **adj:** dreadful, complete, absolute. **o:** arrangements;

finances, accounts; booking, reservation: *Considering* ***the mess*** *he has* ***made of*** *explaining his vital programme, how strange he should be chairman of the group.* NS ○ *The travel agents have* ***made a*** *complete* ***hash of*** *our bookings.* ○ ***An*** *absolute* ***mess*** *was* ***made of*** *the seating plan.* = mess up.

make head or tail of [Vn.pr pass(o)] (*informal*) (not) understand (sth) at all. **o:** report, lecture; note, letter: *He was for some time completely unable to* ***make head or tail of*** *the blotted scrawl.* EM ○ *She'd taken some notes, which she subsequently could not* ***make head or tail of.*** WDM □ with *can/could* and *not/hardly*.

make heavy weather of [Vn.pr pass] (*informal*) make (a task) seem more difficult than it really is. **o:** problem, sum; packing, removals; painting, repairs: *He picked up the briefcase and began to* ***make heavy weather of*** *the straps to have something to do.* TT ○ *You're* ***making*** *terribly* ***heavy weather of*** *a perfectly simple calculation.*

make an honest woman of [Vn.pr pass] (*dated* or *jocular*) marry a woman with whom one has been having an affair: *Come on down to the church and I'll* ***make an honest woman of*** *you.* TOH ○ *Even the silliest little shopgirl has the sense to try and get* ***an honest woman made of*** *herself.* ASA

make light of [Vn.pr pass(o)] treat (sth) as slight or unimportant. **o:** discomfort, pain, inconvenience: *This he put forward as a youthful folly. In fact, he* ***made light of*** *the whole episode.* ASA ○ *These terrible injuries were* ***made light of*** *in his talks with reporters.*

make a meal of it [Vn.pr] (*informal*) do sth to excess; overdo: *'Listen Phil, all I wanted was a short report — let's not* ***make a meal of it****!'* ○ *He wasn't content with saying a few words in reply. He had to* ***make a meal of it****!*

make a mental note of [Vn.pr pass pass(o) rel] record (sth) carefully in one's mind. **o:** remark, saying; number, time: *I* ***made a mental note of*** *the phrase.* RATT ○ *Here's something else that ought to be* ***made a mental note of.*** ⇨ make a note of.

make mention of [Vn.pr pass emph rel] (*formal*) speak of (sb/sth); mention. **adj:** some; no, (not) any: *I was sitting on one of the walls of the partially excavated bath-building* ***of*** *which I have* ***made mention.*** SD ○ ***Mention*** *was* ***made*** *earlier* ***of*** *the other surviving members of the family.* = refer to 1.

make mincemeat of 1 [Vn.pr pass pass(o)] (*informal*) destroy (sb/sth) utterly. **o:** infantry; attack: *The assault troops were* ***made mincemeat of*** *by accurate machine-gun fire.* ○ *Yorkshire* ***made mincemeat of*** *the Surrey attack in piling up a score of 434 for 4 declared.* DM

2 [Vn.pr pass pass(o)] defeat (sb/sth) by argument, by producing evidence etc. **o:** prosecutor, defence counsel; argument, case; essay, report: *Mahler . . . has* ***made mincemeat of*** *most of the prosecution witnesses.* ST ○ *A good lawyer would* ***make mincemeat of*** *your case.*

make a mockery of [Vn.pr pass pass(o) emph rel] treat (sth) with no seriousness or respect; flout, mock. **S:** behaviour; treatment, handling; trial. **adj:** complete, total. **o:** democracy, justice, free speech: *The conduct of the elections* ***made an*** *absolute* ***mockery of*** *democratic procedures.* ○ *The law was being* ***made an*** *open* ***mockery of*** . BBCR

make the most of [Vn.pr pass pass(o) rel] get as much from (an experience) as one can. **o:** opportunity, chance; freedom, youth; being here, having them to stay: ***Make the most of*** *your life — because life is a holiday from the dark.* HSG ○ *'I never met a girl like you, so I might as well* ***make the most of*** *having you here.'* AITC

make much of [Vn.pr pass pass(o) emph rel] stress, emphasize (sth). **o:** idea, notion; factor, element; one's expertise; one's family background: *Whatever their economic or political motives, the Romans* ***made much of*** *their mission to 'civilize'.* SHOE ○ *Too* ***much*** *has been* ***made of*** *the notion that the English novel is obsessed with class.* JA ○ *Running has always been* ***made much of*** *in our family, especially running away from the police.* LLDR

make nonsense of [Vn.pr pass pass(o)] render (sth) worthless. **S:** facts, evidence; police, investigator. **adj:** complete, absolute. **o:** pretensions; story, account, version: *His extravagant style of life* ***makes nonsense of*** *his claim to be a simple man of the people.* ○ *The official report was* ***made nonsense of*** *by investigative journalists.*

make a note of [Vn.pr pass pass(o) emph rel] record (sth) in one's mind or on paper; note. **o:** size, shape, position (of a place); time, destination (of a train etc): *Still Charles hung back,* ***making a note of*** *the obviously complex traditions of the place.* HD ○ ***A*** *careful* ***note*** *was* ***made of*** *the exact dimensions of the emplacement.* ⇨ make a mental note of.

make nothing of [Vn.pr pass(o)] overcome with ease some apparently difficult obstacle; make (sth) seem unimportant. **S:** athlete; boxer; student, scientist, inventor. **o:** obstacle, jump; opposition; problem, difficulty: (commentary on a horse and rider jumping obstacles) *'She comes round again to take that fence and of course* ***makes nothing of*** *it.'* BBCTV ○ *No, better to limit the danger, control his anger,* ***make nothing of it****, pretend he didn't mind.* NW ⇨ make of.

make a nuisance of oneself [Vn.pr] disturb others by making a noise, interrupting, criticizing authority etc: *The children are* ***making*** *confounded* ***nuisances of themselves.*** ○ *If the Council goes ahead with its plans to demolish the hall, there are plenty of people who are prepared to* ***make a nuisance of themselves.***

make a point of [Vn.pr pass] take particular care to (do sth). **o:** being punctual, greeting people by name; it, this: *Do you* ***make a point of*** *being on time for work and social appointments?* WI ○ *She* ***makes a point of*** *having someone around to sort things out for her.* EHOW

make a secret of [Vn.pr pass emph rel] try to hide (sth). **adj:** no, (not) any, little. **o:** plans, intentions, designs; wishes, feelings: *Uncle Saunders had* ***made no secret of*** *his disapproval and disappointment.* DC ○ *You knew I was doing that at the club. I never* ***made a secret of*** *it.* AITC

make sense of [Vn.pr pass pass(o) emph rel] understand, interpret (sth) to a stated extent. **adj:** some, no, (not) any, little; perfect. **o:** conversation, message, language: *I can never* ***make sense of*** *a word he says.* ○ *The code couldn't be* ***made sense of*** *by our experts.* ⇨ make of.

make a success of [Vn.pr pass pass(o) emph rel] be successful in (sth/doing sth). **adj:** considerable, remarkable, outstanding. **o:** job, task, project: *He* *was given the job last year and has since* **made a** *great* **success of** *it.* ○ **The** *tremendous* **success** *she's* **made of** *the project has delighted her backers.* ○ *I rather doubt if such an ambitious scheme could be* **made a success of**.

make use of 1 [Vn.pr pass pass(o) emph rel] employ and benefit from (sth/sb). **adj:** some; wide, extensive; frequent, occasional. **o:** techniques, processes; foreign labour, teenage workers: *The chapels had ministers who were not Oxford-trained, and* **made** *wide* **use of** *lay preachers.* UL ○ *Very few operators* **make use of** *all the facilities the machine offers.*

2 [Vn.pr pass(o)] exploit a weaker or less experienced person. **S:** boss, director; husband, lover: *A trusting and innocent girl is being manipulated by a more sophisticated and unscrupulous one. Becky* **makes use of** *Amelia.* TU ○ *Anyone can see you're just being* **made use of** *by these people.*

make a virtue of necessity [Vn.pr] pretend or believe that sth which one is obliged to do or accept is good for one's character, moral development etc: *The Churches enjoined fasting partly to allow the faithful to* **make a virtue of necessity** *and partly, too, so that the wealthy might have a taste of what their poorer brothers and sisters had to put up with.* OBS

make the worst of [Vn.pr] fail or refuse to make any effort when faced with difficulties. **o:** situation, crisis, setback: *Some element in her character forced her to* **make the worst of** *a bad day.* AITC ○ *Dave was now changing over from* **making the worst of** *the affair to making the best of it.* UTN ↔ make the best of.

make demands (of/on) [Vn.pr pass emph rel] ask for help, so placing a burden (on sb/sth). **adj:** excessive, heavy, repeated. **o:** staff, helpers, supporters; resources, funds: *Dave is an old friend but he has no money. I felt perhaps I oughtn't to* **make demands on** *Dave.* UTN ○ *Isabelle seemed to have been able to cope with life as long as too many* **demands** *were not* **made on** *her.* TU

make off [Vp] leave in a hurry, esp to escape from other people: *Suddenly Myrtle slid down from the gate and quietly* **made off** *beside the hedgerow.* SPL ○ *The priest struggled up the cliff alone and* **made off**. RFW

make off (with) [Vp, Vp.pr pass] ⇨ make away/off (with).

make (on) [Vn.pr pass emph rel] make (a profit) (from a transaction). **O:** nothing; profit, return; pile, packet (of money). **o:** deal, transaction; investment, sale: *John was willing to sell me the car for what he'd paid for it: he wouldn't* **make** *a penny* **on** *the deal.* ○ *There wasn't very much money to be* **made on** *property transactions in London immediately after the war; redevelopment was strictly controlled till 1954.*

make an attempt on [Vn.pr pass] try to break or exceed (a record). **o:** record; time, speed, distance (set up by sb): **A** *fresh* **attempt** *is being* **made on** *the land speed record later this year.* ○ *The Kenyan runner* **made** *two further* **attempts on** *the world record that summer.*

make an attempt on sb's life [Vn.pr pass] try to assassinate a prominent person: *Last night* **a** *fresh* **attempt** *was* **made on the life of** *the Crown Prince.* ○ *That was the palace where the President had never slept since* **the** *last* **attempt** *was* **made on his life**. OMIH □ often passive, as shown; attempt also pl: *Further* **attempts** *have since been* **made on his life**.

make demands (on) [Vn.pr pass emph rel] ⇨ make demands (of/on).

make an impression (on) 1 [Vn.pr pass emph rel] affect (sb) in a particular way by one's appearance or behaviour. **adj:** favourable, good; deep, lasting; bad, unfortunate. **o:** jury, selection board, prospective buyer: *The Russians were clearly anxious to* **make a** *good* **impression** (ie **on** the British). MFM ○ *It's important that* **the** *right kind of* **impression** *should be* **made on** *the French.*

2 [Vn.pr emph rel] get people to notice one; impress. **o:** newcomer, visitor: *'He does like to* **make an impression** *(***on** *people), doesn't he? Notice the way he enters a room.'* ○ *Tom's stock method of* **making an impression on** *anyone was to indicate that he understood them perfectly.* SPL

make a start (on) [Vn.pr pass emph rel] begin (to do sth); start. **adj:** no, (not) any; fresh, new; early, belated. **o:** task, job; notes, corrections; writing a report, repairing a machine: *There was work to do, awaiting him in his room. He had better* **make a start on** *it now.* EM ○ **A start** *has yet to be* **made on** *building a much-needed relief road to the south of the city.*

make out 1 [Vn ⇆ p pass adj] write (sth) in full; complete. **O:** cheque, receipt; application, claim: *He won't know I've gone except when he comes to* **make out** *the pay cheques.* TC ○ *Applications have to be* **made out** *in triplicate.* ○ *He picked up a laundry list* **made out** *on the back of an envelope.* = write out.

2 [Vp.n pass] claim, assert, maintain (sth). **O:** that one is overworked, that one can cure all ills; themselves to be badly treated, him to be cleverer than he is: *I'd just tell them to* **make out** *that they were taking the risk themselves.* CON ○ *It was not the cure everyone* **made** *it* **out** *to be.* TGLY ○ *They* **make** *themselves* **out** *to be poorer than they really are.*

3 [Vn ⇆ p pass] manage to see or read (sth). **O:** figure, face, building. **A:** just, barely, scarcely; in the mist, half-light, gloom: *I could* **make out** *the expression on his face.* NM ○ *The outline of the house could just be* **made out**. □ usu with can/could.

4 [Vn.p] understand the nature or character of (sb): *'I really can't* **make** *him* **out**. *Why does he offend the very people who try to help him?'* □ usu with can/could not. = work out 4.

5 [Vp.n] understand (sth). **O:** it; what he was after; how she came to be there, why we always disagreed: *I could never* **make out** *if they needed money or not.* ○ *'Where's the sense in that?' 'None, that I've been able to* **make out**.*'* HHGG □ usu with can/could not.

6 [Vp] (*informal*) progress, prosper. **S:** business, firm; family, son; things: *I wonder how Paula is* **making out** *in her new practice?* ○ *How are you* **making out** *with Kate?* (ie How is your love-affair progressing?). □ usu in direct and indirect questions after *how*. = get on 3.

make out a case [Vp.n pass] argue or plead (for or against sb/sth). **adj:** strong, good, excellent: *I can't agree with them, but I grant you they've* **made out** *a very good* **case**. ○ **A case** *could be* **made out** *that* *it's more humane to kill off these wild animals.* TES ○ *He has* **made out a** *strong* **case** *for the repeal of the law.* □ case may be followed by a *that*-clause, *in favour of, for* or *against*.

how make that out [Vn.p] how (does/did one) arrive at a certain conclusion or statement: *'You say that we shall be making a loss for the next three years. Well,* **how** *do you* **make that out**?' ○ *'He thinks we'll make a profit. Well, I want to know* **how** *he* **makes that out**.' □ direct or indirect question.

make capital out of [Vn.pr pass rel] ⇨ make capital from/of/out of.

make a mountain out of a molehill [Vn.pr pass] make a small difficulty, problem etc seem much more serious than it is: *He said the Government were frightened of nothing. The real trouble was we were* **making a mountain out of a molehill**. MFM □ note pl: *'Don't* **make mountains out of molehills**.'

make over [Vp.n pass adj] change, transform (sth). **O:** house, room, garden; face, manner, appearance: *They were the new energetic middle class who were* **making over** *the industrial city for their own ends.* SCIT ○ *Though you say you've* **made over** *your outside in a week, no one can do that with the inside* (ie the personality). PTTP

make a fuss (over) [Vn.pr pass emph rel] ⇨ make a fuss (about/over).

make a song and dance (over) [Vn.pr pass] ⇨ make a song and dance (about/over).

make over (to) [Vn ⇆ p pass adj, Vn.p.pr pass emph rel] transfer the ownership of sth (to sb). **O:** income, property, business, house: *To avoid death duty, grandfather* **made over** *the bulk of his property as soon as he retired.* ○ *The best farming land was* **made over to** *the eldest son.* ○ **To** *which of the partners is he* **making over** *the residue of his estate?*

make advances (to) [Vn.pr pass emph rel] approach (sb) in the hope of seducing, taking control etc. **adj:** cautious, timid, bold. **o:** girl, woman; smaller firm, shareholders (of a business one wishes to control): *'When he* **made advances to** *me, I turned my back on him and his set,' Catherine said roundly.* PATM ○ *Tentative* **advances** *have already been* **made to** *our shareholders by a multinational company.*

make application (to) [Vn.pr pass emph rel] (*formal, official*) write (to sb) asking for information, a form, an allowance etc. **o:** office, department; Registrar, Town Clerk: *To obtain a new birth certificate for your son,* **make application to** *the Adopted Children's Register.* TO ○ **Application** *should be* **made** *in the first instance* **to** *the local office of the Department.* = apply (to) (for).

make a difference (to) 1 [Vn.pr pass] affect or alter (sth). **adj:** no, (not) any, (not) much; considerable, significant. **o:** relationship, friendship; prospects, future: *My secret activity had* **made no difference** *at all* **to** *my friendship with Hugo.* UTN ○ *The move could* **make** *quite* **a difference to** *our income.*

2 [Vn.pr] be of importance (to sb), matter (to sb). **adj:** no, (not) any; big, considerable: *He was brought up in a fashionable district. That didn't* **make any difference to** *me.* CON ○ *It* **makes a difference to** *voters whether they elect Progressives or Socialists.* SC

make love (to) [Vn.pr pass(o) rel] have sexual intercourse (with sb). **adj:** ardent, passionate: *What did come naturally, too naturally, was his urge to* **make love to** *her.* LM

make amends (to) (for) [Vn.pr pass emph rel] (*formal*) repay or compensate (sb) (for sth one has failed to do in the past). **adj:** generous, handsome. **o:** (**to**) him etc; (**for**) failure, neglect: *There was the College putting forth all its beauty as if to* **make amends to** *him* **for** *all it had denied.* HD ○ *Whatever disappointment he had been in life, he was certainly beginning to* **make** *some* **amends** *(***for** *it) in death.* PP = atone for, make up for 2.

make up 1 [Vn ⇆ p pass adj] provide (a road) with a hard surface of bitumen etc to make it suitable for motor traffic. **O:** road, street; drive, carriageway: *Half the roads in the estate are still waiting to be* **made up**. ○ *There's a good* **made-up** *road from the capital to the main port.* □ usu passive or adj.

2 [Vn ⇆ p pass adj] compose or invent (sth), possibly to deceive others. **O:** words, tune, story; the whole thing, things, it: *These entertainers* **make** *their stories* **up** *as they go along.* ○ *You can't go around* **making up** *things about being assaulted by people who don't exist.* DC ○ *There isn't any little girl called Clementine. He's just* **made** *her* **up**. DC

3 [Vn ⇆ p nom pass adj] arrange type, illustrations etc to form pages for printing. **O:** page, column: *The way the front page is* **made up** *may need to be altered several times* (or: *The* **make-up** *of the front page may need* etc).

4 [Vp.n nom pass] form, compose (sth larger). **S:** cell, tissue, sinew; man, individual; island, atoll. **O:** body; tribe, nation; chain, archipelago: *'The American family is* **made up** *of hopelessly lonesome people,' he says.* T ○ *There are plans to change the* **make-up** (= composition) *of the Board.* ○ *There is something in his* **make-up** (= nature, character) *that repels people.* □ in the passive, often followed by *of*.

5 [Vn ⇆ p pass adj] add more fuel to (a fire etc). **O:** fire, stove, boiler: *The fire needs* **making up**. ○ *If the stove isn't* **made up**, *it'll go out.*

6 [Vp nom, Vn ⇆ p nom pass adj] prepare (one's face etc) for a performance in the theatre, or on film or television; apply cosmetics to (one's face) to make it more attractive. **S:** actor, cast; woman. **O:** himself; face, nose, eyes: *It takes the actor more than an hour to* **make up** (or: *do his* **make-up**) *for the part of 'Othello'.* ○ *The actor applies several kinds of* **make-up** *to his face* (eg cream, greasepaint, powder). ○ *I* **make up** *to the nines* (ie heavily), *put on false eyelashes, have my hair done, wear really glamorous clothes — everything.* TVT ○ *Just give me two seconds to* **make** *my face* **up**.

7 [Vn ⇆ p pass] prepare (sth) by mixing together various ingredients. **S:** chemist, druggist (US). **O:** medicine; prescription: *The doctor writes out a prescription and you get it* **made up** *at the chemist's.*

8 [Vn ⇆ p pass] prepare a bed which is not now in use, eg for a patient; prepare a makeshift bed, eg for an unexpected guest. **O:** bed, cot, campbed: *Sister sat down on the wireworks of the bed. I had*

not had time to **make** *it* **up** *yet.* DC ○ *I had a bed* **made up** *for me on the sofa.*
9 [Vp.n pass] prepare (a light meal), esp for a journey or outing. **O:** (picnic-)basket, hamper; a packed lunch; some sandwiches: *We've got a dozen picnic lunches to* **make up**. ○ *The hotel will* **make** *you* **up** *a packet of sandwiches for the journey.* □ note the Indirect Object (*you*) in the second example.
10 [Vn ⇆ p pass] make (sth) complete. **O:** (full) strength, numbers, complement; (required, total) sum, amount: *The 7th Armoured Brigade, supported by a US Marine Brigade,* **makes up** *the division strength.* OBS ○ *Local recruits* **made up** *our full complement of labourers.* ⇨ make up to 1.
11 [Vn ⇆ p pass] replace or make good (sth lost). **O:** loss, deficiency, wastage; leeway: *Our losses will have to be* **made up** *with fresh drafts* (ie of troops). ○ *There's a tremendous amount of leeway to* **make up** *if he's to have a chance of winning.*

make up a four (at bridge) [Vp.n] (*cards*) make a game of bridge possible by offering or agreeing to be the fourth player: *Ask Geoffrey if he'd mind* **making up a four**.

make one's/sb's mind up [Vn ⇆ p pass] (cause sb to) reach a decision: *'Look, I've* **made up my mind**. *I want to have the party here.'* TOH ○ *He had been pondering the great decision. Now* **his mind** *was* **made up**. TO ○ *He wants somebody to* **make up his mind** *for him.* □ make one's mind up may be followed by clauses introduced by that, what, whether, how etc: *At just what age people* **make up their minds** *that they have finally said goodbye to youth varies according to temperament.* OBS

make up for 1 [Vp.pr pass] help to balance (a disadvantage). **S:** strong personality; hard work; inventiveness. **o:** unattractive appearance; lack of intelligence; shortage of natural resources: *My face is a bit thinner, but the rest of me is rapidly* **making up for** *that.* AITC ○ *Pay increases will not always* **make up for** *poor working conditions.* NS = compensate (for).
2 [Vp.pr pass adj emph rel] repay (sb) for one's past failures etc. **S:** he etc; kindness, considerate treatment. **o:** neglect, rudeness; what she has suffered: *In the BBC, I found myself working for Gerard once again and I hoped I* **made up for** *letting him down.* SU ○ *This display of bad manners was hardly* **made up for** *by his subsequent behaviour.* = atone for, make amends (to) (for).

make up for lost time [Vp.pr] make a special effort to do sth after starting late: *Now that we're practically neighbours, we must* **make up for lost time**. *Do look us up!* ○ *We came into this field late, so we must work hard to* **make up for lost time**.

make up (from) 1 [Vn ⇆ p pass, Vn.p.pr pass emph rel] assemble, put together (a finished article) (from raw material). **O:** screen, gate; bracelet, locket. **o:** fragments, scraps; coin, chain: *Their wrought-iron gate was* **made up** *by a blacksmith.* ○ *She wore a necklace* **made up from** *silver coins.* ⇨ make up (into) 1.
2 [Vn ⇆ p pass, Vn.p.pr pass emph rel] assemble, fashion (a garment) (from cloth). **O:** suit, trousers, skirt. **o:** material, stuff; piece, length: *The suit will take about a week to* **make up**. ○ *Two full-length dresses can be* **made up from** *this piece.* ⇨ make up (into) 2.

make up (into) 1 [Vn ⇆ p pass adj, Vn.p.pr pass] assemble, put together (raw material) (into a finished article). **O:** dough; scraps, pieces. **o:** cake, pudding; sculpture; jewellery: *'There's no cement left over; it's all been* **made up**.' ○ *You could get these pieces of old gold* **made up into** *a bracelet.* ⇨ make up (from) 1.
2 [Vn ⇆ p pass adj, Vn.p.pr pass] fashion (cloth) (into a garment). **O:** cloth; worsted; piece, length. **o:** coat, jacket, dress: *A friend is* **making up** *the dress-length Jane bought on holiday.* ○ (notice outside tailor's shop) *Customers' own materials* **made up**. ⇨ make up (from) 2.

make up to 1 [Vn.p.pr pass] raise, increase (sth) to (a particular level). **O:** mixture, liquid; sum, amount. **o:** consistency, concentration; figure, level: *You can* **make** *the lemonade* **up to** *full strength if you add more juice.* ○ *If you contribute a few pounds, I'll* **make** *the collection* **up to** *the total required.* ⇨ make up 10.
2 [Vp.pr pass] (*informal*) make oneself pleasant to (sb) in order to win favours. **o:** pretty girl; employer, officer, prefect: *On his first day in the department he started* **making up to** *the secretaries.* ○ *He's not the sort of man who responds well to being* **made up to**.

make it/this up to [Vn.p.pr pass] (*informal*) give sth to (sb) to compensate for sth he has missed or suffered: *When I get you home safely in the country I'll* **make** *all* **this up to you**. DC ○ *I am sorry you missed the outing.* **It** *will be* **made up to** *you at Christmas.*

make (it) up (with) [Vp, Vp.pr, Vn.p, Vn.p.pr] settle a quarrel (with sb): [Vp.pr] *She never overcame her dislike for Joseph Kennedy, though she was eventually to kiss and* **make up with** *his sons.* L ○ [Vn.p Vn.p.pr] *I don't know if Philip and Rosemary have* **made it up** *or not* (cf *I don't know if Philip has* **made it up with** *Rosemary or not*). EHOW = make one's peace (with).

make with [Vpr] (esp *US informal*) deliver or produce (sth). **o:** money; food; music, jokes: *'We need some slogans for the promotion of the new shampoo, so start* **making with** *the ideas.'* ○ *'Listen,' said Dusty, 'this bloke was at College with Goldilocks.* **Make with** *the dirt* (the scandal about her).' TT

make a deal (with) [Vn.pr pass emph rel] agree terms for doing business (with sb). **o:** client, trading partner; competitor, enemy: *'I'll* **make a deal with** *you. You can have the plans if you split the profit with us.'* DM ○ *United Copper* **made a deal with** *a European consortium* (cf *United Copper and a consortium* **made a deal**) *to share the mineral rights.*

make friends (with) [Vn.pr rel] get on pleasant, intimate terms (with sb): *'You'll find us all wanting to* **make friends with** *you. Do you like the idea?'* PW ○ *John* **made friends with** *Bill* (or: *John and Bill* **made friends**). ○ *The letter was probably from one of the patients* **with** *whom she had* **made friends** *in the hospital.* DC

make great etc play with 1 [Vn.pr pass pass(o) emph rel] stress (sth) in a dramatic way, and esp in an argument or debate. **adj:** great, much, a good deal of. **o:** one's achievements, privations, sufferings; figures, estimates: *She* **made great play with** *the years of work she had given to Mrs Portway.*

ASA ○ *The Prime Minister* **made a good deal of play with** *the contrast between the backward-looking Opposition and the new thinking amongst Conservatives.* OBS

2 [Vn.pr pass emph rel] handle (sth) for dramatic effect. **adj:** much, a great deal of. **o:** gold watch and chain, eye-glass, document: *She took off and put on her spectacles a hundred times a day,* **making as much play with** *them as a barrister in court.* AITC

make a hit (with) [Vn.pr emph rel] (*informal*) impress (sb) favourably. **S:** speaker, actor, politician. **o:** audience, public: *My daughter Janice asks me to send you her love—you* **made a** *big* **hit with** *her.* = make an impression (on) 1.

make (a) peace (with) [Vn.pr pass emph rel] end hostilities (with another state etc). **o:** neighbour; aggressor; employee: *The new government was prepared to* **make peace with** *the invaders at almost any price.* ○ **A** *more lasting* **peace** *could be* **made with** *the unions if the restrictions on wage settlements were lifted.*

make one's peace with [Vn.pr emph rel] settle a quarrel with (sb) by apologizing, agreeing to co-operate etc. **o:** church, political party; leader, father, wife: *He had no intention of* **making his peace with** *the director simply to give an impression of harmony within the department.* ○ *'Have you* **made your peace with** *your wife yet?' 'I've tried, but she refuses to talk to me.'* = make (it) up (with).

make shift (with) [Vn.pr pass(o) rel] use (one thing) for lack of sth better; make do (with). **o:** synthetic materials, plastic components: *We can't get the proper ingredients so we'll have to* **make shift with** *local substitutes.* ○ *He can't afford copper, but aluminium will do as a* **makeshift** (= substitute) . □ nom form is makeshift(s).

map

map out [Vn ⇆ p pass adj] arrange, organize (sth) in one's mind or on paper. **O:** journey, route; programme, plan (of events): *We must get the whole expedition clearly* **mapped out** *on paper before we start to order equipment.* ○ *It was a well* **mapped-out** *itinerary, taking in all the places of interest in the area.*

march

march on [Vpr] move on foot towards (a place), esp to attack or seize it. **S:** troops, rebels, revolutionaries: *The rebels* **marched on** *London and the revolt reached its climax in three stormy days.* SHOE

march past [Vp nom, Vpr] (*military*) move ceremonially past a senior officer, who 'takes the salute'. **S:** troops, column, contingent, parade. **o:** sovereign, inspecting officer; saluting base: *The battalion* **marched past** *their commanding officer.* ○ *After the inspection, there is a* **march-past** *of all troops on parade.* ⇨ fly past.

mark

mark down 1 [Vn ⇆ p pass] choose (sb) in a deliberate way, especially as someone to punish, exploit etc: *He was certain the man had* **marked** *him* **down**, *was out to wring his neck.* LLDR ○ *Having* **marked down** *Blanche as inadequate to her purposes, Sally had to make use of her.* MSAL ⇨ mark out (for).

2 [Vn ⇆ p pass] choose (sth) as suitable for a particular purpose. **O:** place, hall, square: *I drove on to the Aosta Palace, which I had* **marked down** *for my brigade headquarters.* SD

3 [Vn ⇆ p nom pass adj] indicate that the price of (an article) has been reduced. **O:** dress, suit; linen, china: *Many household articles are* **marked down** *during summer sales at the big London stores.* ○ *There's a* **mark-down** *of 15% on kitchen furniture.* ↔ mark up 2.

4 [Vn.p pass] reduce the marks awarded to (sb) in a test etc. **O:** pupil, form: *The children at the top of the form were* **marked down**, *as the gap between them and the rest did not reflect their true merits.* ↔ mark up 3.

mark in [Vn ⇆ p pass adj] add (small details) to a map, picture etc. **O:** road, track, conventional sign; leaf, twig: *The district boundaries are* **marked in** *with a fine mapping pen.*

mark off 1 [Vn ⇆ p pass adj] separate (one thing) from another with a line or boundary. **O:** place, space; enclosure, car-park; period, stage: *They'd* **marked off** *an area at the end of the site as a future playground.* ○ *This phase in his life was* **marked off** *by the death of his father.*

2 [Vn ⇆ p pass adj] place a tick or cross against (an item) to remind oneself of it or to show it has been dealt with. **O:** article, item; entry; task, job: *'All right, that job's been* **marked off**. *What's next?'* = cross off, tick off 1.

mark off (from) show (sb/sth) to be different (from sb/sth else). **S:** intelligence, business acumen, organizing ability. **O:** mankind, community, group. **o:** animals, any other, most others: *She was* **marked off** *by a fiery temper and a strain of intolerance.* ○ *There were other qualities too which* **marked** *him* **off from** *his brothers.* = distinguish from 2, mark out (from).

mark out [Vn ⇆ p pass adj] draw the internal dividing lines within (a space), eg the places where windows are to go on a drawing of a wall. **O:** tennis-court, football pitch, gymnasium floor; elevation, plan: *The sports field is being* **marked out** *for an athletics meeting by the ground staff.*

mark out (for) [Vn.p pass, Vn.p.pr pass] identify (sb) as likely to succeed (in sth). **S:** firm, employer. **O:** trainee, recruit, entrant. **o:** early promotion, special treatment, management training: *They had a spiky and memorable argument which* **marked** *Major* **out** *as someone Mrs Thatcher could do business with.* OBS ○ *He's the bosses' blue-eyed boy: you can tell he's been* **marked out for** *quick promotion.* □ usu passive. ⇨ mark down 1 .

mark out (from) [Vn.p pass, Vn.p.pr pass] show (sb/sth) to be special or different (from sb/sth else). **S:** temperament, intelligence, wit; persistence, courage. **O:** brother, colleague, partner. **o:** the others, the rest: (The play) *was directed with the lucidity and intensity which has* **marked** *Warner* **out** *and catapulted her from the fringe to the major theatre companies.* IND ○ *The irrational side of his nature ...* **marked** *Carl Jung* **out from** *most of his conforming colleagues.* JUNG = distinguish from 2, mark off (from).

mark up 1 [Vn ⇆ p nom pass adj] (in retail trading) decide the selling price of sth after taking all costs into account; (in overseas trade) decide the selling price in relation to the cost of importing. **O:** price, figure: *The* **mark-up** *price of British books abroad has been fluctuating considerably in recent months as the value of the pound strengthens or weakens.*

2 [Vp.n nom pass adj] increase the existing price of (sth), in order to absorb higher costs, earn more profit etc. **O:** food, clothes, soft furnishings: *Spirits have been* **marked up** *following tax increases announced in the Budget.* ○ *The City, which* **marked** *the shares* **up** *a modest 38p to 400p, is wise to see a bid (of say 500p) is still at least 12 months away.* IND ↔ mark down 3.

3 [Vn ⇆ p pass] increase the marks awarded to (a student etc). **O:** pupil, form; script, paper: *If we* **mark up** *Jones on this paper he will just scrape a pass.* ↔ mark down 4.

4 [Vn ⇆ p pass adj] (*publishing*) prepare (a manuscript) for the printer by making corrections, inserting new material etc. **O:** manuscript (ms); book, article: *When a manuscript has been accepted for publication, it is passed to an editor for detailed scrutiny. The editor's subsequent* **marking up** *of the manuscript consists of deletions or additions to the author's text, together with instructions to the printer on the typefaces to be used.*

5 [Vn ⇆ p pass adj] make items on (a list) prominent by using coloured marks etc. **O:** list, programme; item; name, team: *He used to* **mark up** *the wireless programmes in different-coloured pencils.* OD

marry

marry above [Vpr] marry sb in a higher social class than (one's own). **o:** him, her; themselves; one's (own) class: *People who* **marry above** *themselves socially have similar kinds of problems to those who marry outside their religion or ethnic group.*

marry beneath [Vpr] marry sb in a lower social class than (one's own). **o:** him, her; themselves; one's (own) class: *John's father threatened to disinherit him if he* **married beneath** *himself.*

marry in/into [Vp, Vpr rel] become a member of (a particular group) through marriage. **o:** aristocracy, landed gentry; Sikh community, Catholic faith: *She wasn't born into the nobility, she* **married in**. ○ *He* **married into** *a rich farming family.*

marry off [Vn ⇆ p pass] find husband(s) for one's daughter(s): *She had been* **married off** *at an early age to a man she heartily detested.*

marry out/out of [Vp, Vpr] leave (one's own religious community) by marrying a member of another faith etc. **o:** faith, church: *Strictly speaking, a Catholic is only* **marrying out** *if his partner is a non-Catholic* and *refuses to be married according to the rites of the Catholic Church.*

marry up [Vp nom, Vn ⇆ p nom pass adj] (cause things to) combine; unite. **S** [Vp], **O** [Vn.p]: components, parts; halves of the train; forces. **S** [Vn.p]: fitter, assembly worker; railwayman; military commander: *The regular troops* **married up** *with partisans pressing down from the hills.* ○ *The two parts of the project are not well* **married up**. ○ *We've achieved the first* **marry-up** *of our separate television networks.* = join up (with), link up (with).

marvel

marvel (at) [Vpr pass emph rel] find (sth) wonderful or impressive. **S:** spectator, layman. **o:** speed, efficiency, ingenuity, fluency: *Ninety-eight per cent will* **marvel at** *the accuracy with which we have been able to diagnose their handwriting.* SNP ○ *We* **marvel at** *man's ingenuity in putting complex pieces of machinery into space.*

mash

mash up [Vn ⇆ p pass adj] crush (food) to make it soft and smooth. **O:** potatoes, turnips, parsnips: *Add milk and butter to the potatoes and* **mash** *them* **up** *with a fork.*

mask

mask out [Vn ⇆ p pass adj] (*photography*) when printing or enlarging, cover (part of the negative), so that light does not pass through it. **O:** portion, part (of a negative, photograph): *We can get rid of the unwanted detail in the foreground by* **masking out** *the bottom of the negative during processing.*

match

match against [Vn.pr pass emph rel] set (sb/sth) to compete against (sb/sth). **O:** boxer, wrestler; fighting cock; strength, wits, brains, cunning: *He's prepared to* **match** *his skill and strength* **against** *all comers.* ○ *You've been* **matched against** *one of the best amateur fighters in the tournament.* = pit against.

match up [Vp, Vn ⇆ p pass adj] (cause things to) fit together to form a pleasing ensemble, or a complete and intelligible whole. **S** [Vp], **O** [Vn.p]: garments, furnishings, curtains; gems, ornaments; parts, aspects (of a story, of the evidence): *'Have you noticed how well the blouse goes with her long skirt? The whole outfit* **matches up** *beautifully.'* ○ *'I can't* **match up** *the two halves of the photograph. A bit is missing from the middle.'* ○ *The police had some difficulty in* **matching up** *the statements taken from the two witnesses.*

match up (to) [Vp, Vp.pr pass rel] be of the right size, standard, quality etc (when compared with sth). **S:** work, performance; output; personality, appearance. **o:** expectations, requirements; our standards; what is required: *She was keen enough, but she simply didn't* **match up to** *the demands of the job.* ○ *He wanted to study law, but his A-levels didn't* **match up to** *the course requirements.* = measure up (to).

measure

measure against [Vn.pr pass emph rel] compare (sth) with (a certain standard). **O:** work, performance; production, output. **o:** efforts; yield; level: *For much of the 1970s and early 1980s profitability was poor... when* **measured against** *the earnings of companies overseas.* IND □ often passive.

measure off [Vn ⇆ p pass adj] measure (a certain distance) along a length of cloth etc and cut at that point. **O:** half, three-quarters; 2 feet, six and a half metres; piece, length (of cloth, wallpaper etc): *The assistant* **measured off** *two metres from the roll.* ○ *He had a 4-foot length* **measured off** *from an oak plank.* ○ *'How much shall I* **measure** *you* **off**?' □ note the Indirect Object (*you*) in the last example.

measure out [Vn ⇆ p pass adj] take (a specific quantity) of sth. **O:** ten grams, a litre; a glass, a tot: *The assistant* **measured out** *50 millilitres of the liquid.* ○ *I* **measured out** *a little more of the black powder.*

measure up [Vp, Vn ⇆ p pass] measure the dimensions of (a place), so that one can fit carpets, hang wallpaper etc, in it. **S:** floor, window, wall; room: *'We'll have to get someone in to* ***measure up*** *for new curtains.'* ○ *'We'll* ***measure up*** *the bathroom next and fit vinyl tiles.'*

measure up (to) [Vp, Vp.pr emph rel] be of the right size, standard, quality etc (when compared with sth/sb). **S:** place; food, service; appearance, character. **o:** reports, expectations, hopes; him etc: *Visually the fellow* ***measured up****: he was tall, slightly stooping.* ILIH ○ *Differentiate between the genuine private detectives and others who do not* ***measure up to*** *our standards.* T = match up (to).

meddle

meddle in [Vpr pass rel] show undue interest in (sth which is not one's concern). **o:** (sb else's) business, affairs, concerns: *I'm furious with her for* ***meddling in*** *a purely private dispute.* ○ *'That's just like him, isn't it? Always* ***meddling in*** *other people's affairs.'* = interfere in.

meddle with [Vpr pass rel] handle sth which does not concern one, and which one may know very little about. **o:** papers, documents, collection; fitting, circuit, machine: *Somebody's been* ***meddling with*** *the photographs I laid out so carefully.* ○ *The filing system I took so much trouble over has been* ***meddled with*** *by some incompetent busybody.* = interfere with 1.

mediate

mediate (between) [Vpr] (*formal*) try to help two parties holding conflicting views to reach a settlement. **o:** husband and wife, employer and trades unionist; rival firms, hostile powers: *If the two sides reach deadlock this weekend, the Secretary of State will attempt to* ***mediate between*** *them.* ○ *It would take someone with the wisdom of Solomon to* ***mediate between*** *these two: both are so utterly convinced they're in the right.*

meet

meet up (with) [Vp, Vp.pr pass] make contact (with sb), esp by chance; encounter: *By 1954, when we* ***met up with*** *him, he had six German clerks working for him.* DS ○ *Macon was worried they'd* ***meet up with*** *Rose, but she was nowhere to be seen.* AT □ cf: *John* ***met up with*** *Mary/John and Mary* ***met up****.*

meet with 1 [Vpr pass] experience or be received with (sth). **o:** kindness, generosity; a good reception; hostility, resistance; approval: *They* ***met with*** *stubborn resistance.* BM ○ *These techniques* ***met with*** *little success, although in theory they were sound.* NS ○ *Here are some happy suggestions for snacks, sandwiches or main dishes, sure to* ***meet with*** *all the family's approval.* TO
2 [Vpr pass] be overcome by (sth); suffer. **o:** accident, misfortune, disaster: *'Mrs Portway is very ill,' she said. 'She* ***met with*** *an accident.'* ASA ○ *Every attempt to rescue the climbing party* ***met with*** *further misfortune.*

melt

melt away [Vp] disappear, vanish. **S:** crowd, throng; fog, mist; fear, anxiety: *Mrs Dixon gave me a whisky, ... and then deferentially* ***melted away****.* BRN ○ *As the sun rose the early mist* ***melted away****.* ○ *Her suspicion* ***melted away*** *as he began to talk.*

melt down [Vn ⇆ p pass adj] melt (gold or silver articles) to use the metal as raw material; melt (stolen bullion etc) so that it is no longer recognizable to the owners. **O:** jewellery, ring, old gold; gold bar, plate: *The bars are stamped with distinguishing marks and will have to be* ***melted down*** *before the thieves can hope to dispose of them.* T

meltdown [nom (Vp)] (*technology*) melting of, and damage to, the overheated core of a nuclear reactor: *One incident, in the reactor at Greifswald, nearly caused a* ***meltdown*** *in 1976.* DTW

melt in sb's/the mouth [Vpr] (*informal*) be so light or soft that it dissolves readily in the mouth; be delicious. **S:** cake, pastry; fudge, caramel: *This birthday cake simply* ***melts in the mouth****.*

mess

mess about/around [Vp] (*informal*) behave in a foolish, boisterous or idle way: *'Tell the boys to stop* ***messing about*** *upstairs: I'm trying to work.'* ○ *The rest of the party thought it would be amusing to* ***mess about*** *on the river.* TFD

mess about/around (with) 1 [Vp, Vp.pr pass] work in a pleasant, casual, disorganized way (with sth): *He spends most weekends* ***messing about with*** *his car.* ○ *SARAH: He didn't half upset them: they wouldn't let him* ***mess around with*** *the radio so he ... threw their books on the floor.* CSWB
2 [Vp.pr pass rel, Vn.p pass] (*informal*) treat (sb/sth) clumsily, irresponsibly etc. **o** [Vp.pr]**:** girl; engine, car; tooth, leg. **O** [Vn.p]**:** wife, girlfriend; patient: *'If he was your lover why couldn't you have been kinder to him? You can't* ***mess about with*** *people like Guy.'* DC ○ *The house was a modest brick building ... with a few unobtrusive innovations in the cause of comfort, ... but no* ***messing about with*** *the outside.* HD ○ *'Stop* ***messing*** *my daughter* ***about****.'*

mess up [Vn ⇆ p nom pass adj] spoil, ruin (sth). **O:** bookings, travel arrangements, flight schedules, seating plan: *'I've sorted the list out; now don't* ***mess*** *it* ***up*** *again!'* ○ *Don't ask them to organize your itinerary: they made a complete* ***mess-up*** *of ours.*

mete

mete out [Vp.n pass] (*formal*) administer (sth). **O:** punishment, hard blows, harsh treatment; justice; rewards: *The king and his court moved about the country,* ***meting out*** *justice at the assizes.* ○ *The punishment was duly* ***meted out****.* = deal out.

militate

militate against [Vpr] (*formal*) make (sth) less likely to take place or develop. **O:** growth, progress; understanding, harmony; our being involved: *There were fashions in infant feeding and pot training which* ***militated against*** *the freedom this programme suggests.* BRN

mill

mill about/around [Vp] move about in a disorderly or confused way. **S:** children, crowd, spectators; thoughts, ideas, impressions: *The first of the girls were* ***milling about*** *in the corridor.* TT ○ *Conflicting fancies* ***milled around*** *in his mind.*

mind

mind out [Vp] (*informal*) take care to avoid danger etc: *'****Mind out****, the dish is hot!'* ○ *'You'll trip over* *the cat if you don't* **mind out**!' □ usu imperative. = look out 1, watch out.

miss

miss out/out of [Vn ⇆ p pass adj, Vn.pr pass] not include or mention (sth/sb) in (sth). **S:** printer, compositor; host; singer. **O:** comma, word; name, title; verse, line. **o:** sentence, text; introduction; song: *The more I read scientific books on psychology the more I felt that the essential facts of experience were being* **missed out**. LIFE ○ *No one is to be neglected or made to feel* **missed out**. ○ *Through an oversight his name was* **missed out of** *the guest list*. = leave out/out of, omit (from).

miss out (on) [Vp, Vp.pr pass rel] not be present at or notice (sth), and thus fail to enjoy or profit from it. **S:** visitor; businessman; editor. **o:** celebration, reception, welcome; bonanza, oil-strike; scoop, story: *Only a distinguished visitor can hope for such a reception and even he may* **miss out** *if the people find him too grand*. NDN ○ *If he finds that his own paper has* **missed out on** *some important fact, his day is soured to begin with*. L

mist

mist over 1 [Vp] become covered with mist, tears, or a thin film of water. **S:** landscape, view; eyes; spectacles, looking-glass, windscreen: *His glasses kept* **misting over** *in the steam from the boiler*. ○ *His eyes were already* **misting over** *at the awful prospect*. GL □ also used in the passive of a [Vn.p] pattern: *His glasses were all* **misted over**.

2 [Vp] become darkened or obscured. **S:** mind, brain: *His brain* **misted over** *for a moment, then cleared suddenly*. HD

mist up [Vp] become completely obscured by a film of water, usu resulting from condensation. **S:** windscreen, window; goggles, spectacles: *A fan directs a stream of warm air over the car's windscreen to prevent it from* **misting up**. ○ *'I'm as blind as a bat: my glasses have* **misted up**!' □ also used in the passive of a [Vn.p] pattern: *My goggles were completely* **misted up**. = steam up.

mistake

mistake for [Vn.pr pass emph rel] wrongly suppose that (sth/sb) is (sth/sb else): *People are always* **mistaking** *him* **for** *his twin brother*. ○ *He was* **mistaken for** *an enemy scout and shot at by our sentries*. = confuse (with), mix up (with) 1.

mix

mix in 1 [Vn ⇆ p pass adj] add (one substance) to another, stirring as one does so. **O:** seasoning, herbs; cream: *Now* **mix in** *the nuts and the dried fruit*. ⇨ mix with 1.

2 [Vpr rel] be seen regularly in the company of (rich or influential people). **o:** artistic circles, the right company, the world of fashion: *He* **mixed in** *the glittering world ended by the crash of 1929*. IND ○ *No wonder the record companies are so keen to* **mix in** *the right company*. IND ⇨ mix with 2.

mixed up [adj pred (Vn.p)] (*informal*) muddled, confused, in one's thoughts or feelings: *I think that she's been very* **mixed up** *and she feels as if she's had to fight the whole world*. DC ○ *He discussed personal problems with a group of very* **mixed-up** *teenagers*. □ also used with *appear*, etc.

mixed up in [pass adj pred (Vn.p.pr)] involved in sth secret or illegal. **o:** robbery, conspiracy, plot, intrigue; organization, spy ring: *What a business to get (yourself)* **mixed up in**! ○ *He was* **mixed up in** *that horse-doping case*. □ adj also used with *appear, seem*, or after a noun: ... *people* **mixed up in** *drug smuggling*. = involve in.

mix up (with) 1 [Vn ⇆ p pass adj, Vn.p.pr pass rel] be unable to distinguish (sb/sth) (from sb/sth else). **O:** colour, twin, name: *He's always* **mixing** *me* **up with** *my brother*. ○ *One fault with his reading is that he still* **mixes up** *'b' and 'd'* (or **mixes up** *'b'* **with** *'d'*). = confuse (with), mistake for.

2 [Vn ⇆ p nom pass adj, Vn.p.pr pass rel] mix (two or more things) together so that one does not know which is which. **S:** organizer, agency, official. **O:** ticket, luggage, children, papers: *The office* **mixed up** *our flight documents* (or: *There was a* **mix-up with** ... *in the office*)*: John got mine and I got his*. ○ *The porter got our bags* **mixed up***: I nearly walked off with someone else's*. = jumble up (with), muddle up (with).

mixed up with [pass adj pred (Vn.p.pr)] involved with (sb), esp for an immoral or illegal purpose. **o:** man, (sb else's) wife; gang, crowd: *The Colonel got worried about that woman Hector was getting* **mixed up with** *in Tallulagahabad*. RM ○ *I've no reason to believe that the set she's* **mixed up with** *go in for razor slashing*. TFD □ adj also used after *appear to be, seem to be*.

mix with 1 [Vn.pr pass emph rel] put (one substance) with (another) and shake or stir them so that they blend. **O:** flour, wine, coffee. **o:** butter, water, milk: *You* **mix** *a measure of gin* **with** *two measures of vermouth*. ○ *The animals had to be fed on milk* **mixed with** *calcium and codliver oil, and this was no easy task*. BB ⇨ mix in 1.

2 [Vpr], **o:** everyone; all social classes, people from every background: *He* **mixes** *easily* **with** *all kinds of people*. ○ *In her job you have to be able to* **mix with** *everyone — from cleaners to managing directors*. ⇨ mix in 2.

mock

mock-up [nom (Vn.p)] full-size model of an aircraft etc, made of wood and cardboard — or other materials that are ready to hand: *The* **mock-up** *is particularly useful in the development of the flight compartment*. INTERNATIONAL JOURNAL OF AVIATION ○ *I want to propose a vote of thanks to Sergeant Wilson for an excellent* **mock-up** *of a boat*. BBCR

model

model on/upon [Vn.pr pass emph rel] use (sth) as a pattern or basis for (sth). **O:** aircraft; course of study; TV series. **o:** successful RAF fighter; an existing MA; an Australian soap opera: *He would have deplored any attempt to* **model** *girls' schools* **on** *the great public schools*. TU ○ *They discredit historical theories* **modelled upon** *the natural sciences*. RTH = base on/upon.

monkey

monkey about/around [Vp] (*informal*) play mischievously: *'Stop* **monkeying about** *with those matches!'* ○ *It's dangerous to* **monkey around** *in a workshop*.

moon

moon about/around/round [Vp, Vpr] (*informal*) wander about (a place) unhappily and aimlessly.

o: house, place: *Pull your socks up ... and stop* ***mooning about****.* GL ○ *He's no longer* ***mooning round*** *at Kenspeckle, thank goodness.* RM

mop

mop up 1 [Vp, Vn ⇆ p pass adj] absorb (liquid) using a sponge, mop, or rag. **O:** (spilt) coffee, milk, orange juice: *She* ***mopped up*** *the pools that had formed under the leak in the ceiling.*

2 [Vp.n pass adj] absorb (excess money) in an economy, by additional taxation etc: *This may* ***mop up*** *some of the money that's about.* BBCR ○ *The savings scheme will* ***mop up*** *some of the surplus cash that's washing about in the economy.*

3 [Vn ⇆ p nom pass adj] (*military*) clear small enemy groups left behind in a general advance. **O:** isolated pockets of resistance: *There are still some enemy remaining and they are being* ***mopped up****.* MFM ○ *There were still some* ***mopping up*** *operations to be undertaken.* MFM □ mop-up usu attrib, as in: *a* ***mop-up*** *operation.* = clean up 3.

mope

mope about/around/round [Vp, Vpr] wander here and there in a dispirited, aimless way. **o:** house, place: *'Can't you get Jenny's mind off Alex? She's been* ***moping about*** *the place all weekend.'*

motion

motion aside/away [Vn ⇆ p pass] direct (sb) to move away or to one side, with a gesture. **S:** steward, flunkey, doorkeeper, attendant: *A steward* ***motioned*** *us* ***aside*** *and ushered in the guests.* ○ *The photographers were* ***motioned away*** *by the policeman on duty.*

mount

mount up [Vp] form a bigger and bigger amount; accumulate. **S:** expenses, costs; savings, pounds: *The small loss of weight from her day's production wouldn't be noticed, but the stolen carats* (ie diamonds) *would* ***mount up*** *fast.* DS ○ *Put aside a few pounds a week and you'll be surprised to find how quickly your savings* ***mount up****.*

move

move about/around/round [Vp, Vn.p pass] (cause sb to) move from one place or task to another, esp in connection with work: *Salesmen are constantly* ***moving around*** *from one town to another.* ○ *The families of servicemen are* ***moved about*** *a good deal.* ○ *As a bright young recruit, she was* ***moved around*** *from one department to another to gain experience.*

move along 1 [Vp, Vn ⇆ p pass] (cause sb to) go away; disperse: *'Now,* ***move along*** *there, please,' said the policeman.* ○ *A screen of police kept would-be spectators* ***moving along****.* □ said to, or about, onlookers who have gathered near the scene of an accident etc. ⇨ move on.

2 [Vp] progress satisfactorily. **S:** work, project; business; painting; things. **A:** well, smoothly, nicely: *I'd got the office organized and things were beginning to* ***move along*** *very nicely.*

move along/up [Vp] go along from where one is sitting on a bench etc, so that another person can sit down: *'Why don't you* ***move along*** *a bit, so that this lady can sit down?'* ○ (to someone sitting on the back seat of a car) *'****Move up****, Alex, so that the other boys can get in.'*

move away (from) [Vp.pr pass emph rel] stop following or favouring (sth); abandon. **S:** planner, scientist; teacher; management; committee. **o:** interest (in sth), concern (with sth); written exams; old methods, present system: *At postgraduate level we're now* ***moving away from*** *the old pattern of three taught courses spread over two terms.* ○ *We need to* ***move away from*** *formal dance exercises towards freer types of movement.* ↔ move towards.

move down 1 [Vp, Vpr, Vn.p pass, Vn.pr pass] (cause sb to move) to a lower professional and/or social level. **o:** the employment ladder, the social scale: [Vpr] *She wants a job here with us, and she's prepared to* ***move down*** *the salary scale a bit to get it.* ○ [Vn.p] *'Moving Jane up will mean* ***moving*** *Bill* ***down****. I hope you realize that.'* ↔ move up 1.

2 [Vp, Vpr] (*finance*) decrease in value or strength; fall. **S:** price, rate; share; copper, silver: *Industrial shares* ***moved down*** *on news of depressed trading in New York.* ○ *House prices are stationary or actually* ***moving down****.* ↔ move up 2.

move in (on) 1 [Vp, Vp.pr] move closer (to sb/sth) so as to handle, tackle or treat him/it. **S:** demolition team, bulldozer; riot squad, police; (film, television) camera. **o:** building, rubble; demonstrators; actors: *Tanks* ***moved in*** *to flush the snipers from their nests.* ○ *The camera* ***moved in on*** *the sofa for a close-up sequence.*

2 [Vp, Vp.pr] (*informal*) begin to be interested in (sth) and to take control of it. **S:** multinational company; property syndicate; racketeers, organized crime. **o:** national industry; electronics; City, West End; arms dealing, drugs trade: *Major Japanese companies have already* ***moved in on*** *the British car and truck business.* ○ *Important changes are* ***moving in on*** *the industry* (ie are about to affect it). OBS

move in (with) [Vp, Vp.pr, Vn.p pass, Vn.p.pr pass] (cause sb to) occupy a house etc (with others). **S** [Vp, Vpr], **O** [Vn.p, Vn.p.pr]**:** family, couple. **S** [Vn.p, Vn.p.pr]**:** council, church: [Vp] *The new lodger is* ***moving in*** *on the first of the month.* ○ [Vp.pr] *She had to suffer the humiliation of* ***moving in with*** *the parents of the man who had jilted her.* GJ ○ [Vn.p] *'Won't the agricultural people have something to say if they're shot out* (= made to leave) *and we're* ***moved in****?'* TBC ↔ move out/out of 1. ⇨ move into 1.

move into 1 [Vpr rel, Vn.pr pass emph rel] (cause sb to) enter (a place) and find a home there. **S** [Vpr], **O** [Vn.pr]**:** family, retired couple, homeless couple. **o:** another part of town, a smaller house, a flat: *We're thinking of* ***moving into*** *a quieter district.* ○ *Father's been* ***moved into*** *a retirement home.* ↔ move out/out of 1. ⇨ move in (with).

2 [Vpr] enter (a specialist area) and become active there. **o:** specialist field, area; market, business; electronics, robotics: *John's* ***moved into*** *an entirely new area of research.* ○ *Some years ago the United States* ***moved into*** *the field of interplanetary exploration.* ↔ move out/out of 2.

move on [Vn.p pass] tell (sb) to move from where he is causing an obstruction, unlawfully parked etc. **S:** police, traffic warden. **O:** motorist, onlooker, loiterer: *We tried to park in front of the* bank, but a traffic warden **moved** *us* **on**. ○ *Before the crowd could get big enough to pose a threat to law and order, the police* **moved** *everyone* **on**. ⇨ move along 1.

move on (to) [Vp, Vp.pr] move, progress (to another job, experience, style of life etc). **o:** another job, field; a different challenge; a new environment: *I've been in this job for five years now; it's time I was* **moving on**. ○ *We were leaving one world and* **moving on to** *another.* BRH ○ *Her main concern was to* **move on** *smoothly* **to** *happier times.* MSAL

move out/out of 1 [Vp, Vpr, Vn ⇆ p pass, Vn.pr pass] (cause sb to) leave (a house etc). **S** [Vp, Vpr], **O** [Vn.p, Vn.pr]**:** tenant, occupant, owner; family, couple. **o:** district, area; house, flat: [Vpr] *'I think it's time we* **moved out of** *the area and found a bigger house.'* ○ [Vn.p] *The tenants of the condemned houses are being* **moved out**. ↔ move into 1.

2 [Vp, Vpr] leave (a specialist field) in which one has been active. **o:** field, area; dentistry, teaching; optics, electronics: *'This is a pretty stagnant field of research: you'd do well to* **move out** *while you can.'* ○ *She wants to* **move out of** *schoolteaching and into textbook publishing.* ↔ move into 2.

move over [Vp] move away so as to leave more room for another occupant of a bed, bench etc: *'***Move over***: you're taking up more than half the bed!'*

move over (from) (to) [Vp, Vp.pr rel] abandon (one thing) and adopt (sth new and different). **o: (from)** one system, pattern; regime; (**to**) another; an entirely different one: *We are now* **moving over to** *a new examination system.* ○ *The school has recently* **moved over from** *oil* **to** *gas-fired central heating.* = change over (from) (to).

move round [Vp, Vn.p, Vpr, Vn.pr] ⇨ move about/around/round.

move towards [Vpr rel] move nearer to (sth); approach. **S:** powers, parties; negotiators. **o:** settlement, agreement, compromise: *After days of discussion, I sense we're* **moving towards** *a formula acceptable to both sides.* ○ *We are* **moving towards** *a better understanding of the issues.* ↔ move away (from).

move up 1 [Vp, Vpr rel] progress professionally and/or socially. **o:** the social scale, pyramid, ladder, hierarchy: *He'll* **move up** *a rung or two when his qualifications are confirmed.* ○ *She's* **moved** *very rapidly* **up** *the promotion ladder.* ○ *They've* **moved up** *in the world.* ↔ move down 1.

2 [Vp] (*finance*) improve its position; rise. **S:** price, rate, cost; share, stock, copper, rubber: *The exchange rate of the pound* **moved up** *sharply to well over 2.91 dollars.* SC ○ *Mining shares* **moved up** *to a new level after brisk trading.* ↔ move down 2.

3 [Vp, Vn ⇆ p pass] (*military*) (cause troops to) move into the battle area. **S** [Vp], **O** [Vn.p]**:** division, battalion; armour, guns. **A:** into the (front) line, to the front: *Two companies were* **moved up** *under cover of darkness to reinforce the front line troops.* ○ *As they* **moved up**, *they tangled with troops coming out of the line.* RFW

4 [Vp] ⇨ move along/up.

mow

mow down [Vn.p pass] (*military*) cut (people) down as if with a scythe. **S:** machine-gunners; rifle fire. **O:** assault troops, attackers: *The first wave of infantry was* **mown down** *before it had passed through its own wire.*

muck

muck about/around [Vp] (*informal*) occupy oneself in a sloppy, idle or foolish way: *A lot of accidents are caused by children* **mucking about** *on railway lines.* ○ *It is becoming increasingly difficult in the modern classroom to distinguish precisely when purposeful activity shades into '***mucking about***.'* SC = mess about/around.

muck about/around (with) [Vp.pr pass, Vn.p pass] (*informal*) handle (sb/sth) roughly, clumsily, incompetently etc.[Vp.pr], **o:** girl; car, motor, radio; wound [Vn.p], **O:** girl; patient; customer: *'Stop* **mucking about with** *that stereo: I've just paid £40 to get it fixed.'* ○ *'That dealer has been* **mucking** *me* **about** *for days: I despair of getting a satisfactory answer out of him.'* = mess about/around (with) 2.

muck in (with) [Vp, Vp.pr] (*informal*) put oneself on close, friendly terms with workmates etc, sharing their work and pleasures: *On better-tempered ships he used to* **muck in with** *the men and play cards in their mess.* G ○ *'He's a bit of a loner: never* **mucks in with** *the others.'*

muck out [Vp, Vn ⇆ p pass] clean dung from (stables etc). **O:** cowshed, pigsty, farmyard; pig, cow: *He has to* **muck out** *the horses* (ie the stables) *every morning at six.* ○ *'Give the yard a thorough* **mucking-out***.'* = clean out.

muck up [Vn ⇆ p nom pass adj] (*informal*) spoil, ruin (sth) . **O:** garden, study; layout, arrangement; holiday, outing, weekend: *While I considered that the allies could win the war by the end of 1944, I was fairly certain we would* **muck** *it* **up**, *and would not do so.* MFM ○ *The weather really* **mucked up** (or: *made a real* **muck-up**) *of our weekend.* = mess up.

muddle

muddle through [Vp] reach one's goal despite inefficiency, the lack of a plan etc: *The Labour Party had a theory fifty years ago, but it's no use for them now. They're just hoping to* **muddle through** *without it.* SPL

muddle up (with) [Vn ⇆ p pass adj, Vn.p.pr pass emph rel] (*informal*) mix (one thing) (with another) so that one does not know which is which. **S:** official, porter, agency. **O:** tickets, reservations: *The stamps were found* **muddled up** *in a drawer.* ○ *My personal letters got* **muddled up with** *a batch of circulars.* = jumble up (with), mix up (with) 2.

muffle

muffle (oneself) up [Vn.p pass] wrap a thick scarf etc about one's neck and face: *Veronica had* **muffled herself up** *in a thick scarf.* ○ *His face was* **muffled up** *against the extreme cold.*

mug

mug up [Vn ⇆ p pass adj] (*informal*) learn (sth) by intensive study, esp before an exam. **O:** chemistry, law; formulae, figures: *I'm* **mugging up** *my medicine, too.* DIL ○ *All the candidate could offer were a few facts hastily* **mugged up** *before the examination.* = swot up.

mull

mull over [Vn ⇆ p pass] consider (sth) slowly and carefully. **O:** remark, statement, proposal: *A group of us **mulled** the thing **over**.* MEF ○ *He wanted the chance of **mulling over** his conclusions about the old boy.* ILIH ○ *Many Inter-City trains have full air-conditioning with adjustable seats so that you can sit back and **mull over** a business idea.* ST = ponder on/over.

muscle

muscle in (on) [Vp, Vp.pr pass] (*informal*) use force or cunning to get a share of, or participate in, sth important or profitable. **S:** gang, hoodlum; rival, colleague. **o:** market, racket, money; project, scheme: *I see red when I think anyone is trying to **muscle in on** my property.* AITC ○ *The Association has been trying to **muscle in** for years now, but we have always rejected their applications to be affiliated.* RM

muse

muse on/over [Vpr pass adj rel] (esp *jocular*) think about (sth) in an absorbed, dreamy way. **o:** past adventures, pleasant events: *The prospect of a week in their seaside cottage was pleasant to **muse on**.* ○ *We **mused on** the hospitality awaiting us at the end of the day's drive.* = ponder on/over.

muss

muss up [Vn ⇆ p pass] (esp *US, informal*) make (sth) untidy; disarrange. **O:** hair, clothes: *'I'm not crawling about in that dusty attic and **mussing up** my new dress.'* ○ *'Keep your hands to yourself. You're **mussing** my hair **up**!'*

muster

muster up 1 [Vn ⇆ p pass] gather (people) together for a particular purpose. **O:** members, supporters; students: *At times we couldn't **muster up** the required six members for a quorum.* POL
2 [Vn ⇆ p pass] collect or call up (some quality) in a determined way. **O:** energy, strength; willpower: ***Mustering up** her last reserves of strength, she pushed the massive door shut and slid both bolts.*

N

nag

nag (at) [Vpr pass adj] criticize (sb) continuously and irritatingly. **S:** wife, girlfriend, children: *She never stops **nagging** (**at** her husband and children)!* ○ *He feels constantly **nagged at** by his staff.* □ often, though not always, used of the behaviour of women.

nag at [Vpr pass], **S:** worry; thought; suspicion, doubt: *Worry about Steve's health **nagged at** her, making her lose sleep and miss appointments.*

nag at to do sth [Vpr pass] press (sb) irritatingly to do sth. **S:** wife, girlfriend, children: *The children have been **nagging at** me **to give up** smoking.* ○ *She's been **nagging at** him for days **to mow** the lawn.* □ often, though not always, used of the behaviour of women.

nail

nail back [Vn ⇆ p pass adj] fasten (sth) back with nails. **O:** door, shutter, flap: *The shutter kept banging to and fro in the wind, so we **nailed** it **back** against the wall.* ○ ***Nail** the edges **back** at right angles to the cover.*

nail down 1 [Vn ⇆ p pass adj] fasten (sth) flat onto another surface with nails. **O:** carpet; lid, cover: *If the corner of the carpet curls up, **nail** it **down**.*
2 [Vn.p pass] get (sb) to say precisely what he believes or intends to do: *John's very difficult to **nail down**: you can never get him to speak his mind on anything.* ○ *Try to **nail** him **down** on the subject of religious education. You won't find it easy.* = pin down 3.
3 [Vn.p pass] define the character of (sb/sth) precisely. **O:** him etc; character; problem, subject: *Harold had **nailed** him **down**, robbed him of his mystery. His secret was out.* PW ○ *Can we **nail** it* (the concept) ***down** a little more precisely?* SNP = pin down 2.

nail on/onto [Vn ⇆ p pass adj, Vn.pr pass] fasten (sth) to (sth else) with nails. **O:** shelf, cupboard, box. **o:** wall, door: *Don't **nail** the uprights **onto** the wall; screw them on.*

nail one's colours to the mast [Vn.pr pass] make one's views known on a subject, and abide firmly by them: *The Home Secretary **nailed his colours** firmly **to the mast** on the question of arming the police.* □ the idiom may be playfully varied, eg: *They have all **nailed their colours to a mast** erected in honour of the philosophy that money stinks.* SC

nail up 1 [Vn ⇆ p pass adj] secure (sth) with nails so that it cannot easily be opened. **O:** door, window, shutter; box, trunk: *Doors of derelict houses may be boarded and **nailed up** to prevent children getting in.* ○ *Mr Fiske sat down on a **nailed-up** crate and beat his hands gently upon his knees.* AITC
2 [Vn ⇆ p pass adj] fasten (sth) to a surface so that it hangs from that surface. **O:** painting, tapestry, awning: *He **nailed up** a sign over the door which read: 'No Admission'.*

name

name (after) [Vn.pr pass] give (sb) the same first name as (sb else); give (sth) the same name as (sb/sth). **S:** child, daughter; town, square. **o:** father, grandmother; a French statesman, a British general: *They **named** the girl Mary — **after** her mother.* ○ *French departments are often **named after** the rivers that run through them.* AF

narrow

narrow down (to) [Vn ⇆ p pass, Vn.pr pass] reduce the number of people being questioned or options being considered etc (to a few). **S:** police; detectives; rescue party; scientists, engineers. **O:** investigation, inquiries; search. **o:** small number of suspects; one area; possible solutions; options; very few: *Police have **narrowed** the search for the missing boy **down to** a few streets near the school.* ○ *The consultants ... looked at a number of options for new or improved roads and **narrowed** them **down to** two or three in each area.* IND

negotiate

negotiate (with) (for) [Vn.pr pass emph rel] (*formal*) conclude or arrange (sth) by formal discussion (with sb). **O:** contract, deal; treaty, settlement; release, transfer. **o:** (**with**) firm, labour force; (foreign) power, government: *It was* *announced that Tyneside shipyards had* **nego-tiated** *deals worth $30m* **with** *a major oil company.* ○ *The British have* **negotiated** *satisfactory terms* **with** *the French* (or: *The British and the French have* **negotiated** *satisfactory terms)* **for** *the man's release.* ○ *We are* **negotiating** *Paul's transfer* **with** *an Italian club.*

nestle

nestle down [Vp] settle oneself comfortably under bedclothes, a rug etc: *Robin had* **nestled down** *in his father's sleeping-bag on the floor of the dinghy.* = snuggle down.

nestle up (against/to) [Vp, Vp.pr pass] press close (to another person) for warmth or comfort. **o:** husband, lover; mother: *The children* **nestled up** *close together and fell fast asleep.* ○ *Liza* **nestled up against** *her mother and dozed fitfully.* = cuddle up (to), snuggle up (to).

nibble

nibble (at) [Vpr pass] take small bites (from sth); eat sparingly and without appetite. **o:** biscuit, sausage; bait: *Dad never had much for breakfast. He would drink a cup of black coffee and* **nibble at** *a piece of dry toast.* ○ *The cheese left out on the kitchen table had been* **nibbled at**. *Mice again.*

niggle

niggle (over) [Vpr pass] (*informal*) be fussy, behave in a petty way (about sth). **o:** terms, conditions; price: *'I don't see why they should* **niggle over** *paying a few pounds into the fund. They're rich enough, Heaven knows.'* ○ *'We had tremendous difficulty getting the agreement signed. Every little clause was* **niggled over**.*'*

nip

nip across, along, away etc [Vp, Vpr] (*informal*) move sharply, hurry, across etc: *'I must just* **nip out** *to the shops before the children come home from school.'* ○ *Finding himself without money, Belloc* **nipped off** *to the provinces to give some lectures.* HB

nip in the bud [Vn.pr pass] stop (sth) from going any further, because the action, development etc may become harmful, inconvenient etc. **S:** authority; parent, teacher. **O:** revolt, escapade, adventure; scheme, development: *He sat down with the air of having* **nipped** *some possibly dangerous nonsense* **in the bud**. ASA ○ *His new-found intimacy with his son had been* **nipped in the bud**. ASA

nip off [Vn ⇆ p pass adj] (*horticulture*) remove (sth) with a sharp cutting or pinching action. **S:** gardener. **O:** shoots, growth: *He* **nipped off** *the side shoots from the geraniums.*

nod

nod off [Vp] (*informal*) fall asleep, esp in one's chair, letting one's head fall forward at the same time: *I must have* **nodded off**, *I sometimes do, on a Sunday, over my paper.* HD ○ *I managed to make my mind a blank, even* **nodding off** *for a moment at one point.* CON = doze off, drop off 2.

noise

noise abroad [Vn ⇆ p pass] (*formal* or *jocular*) make (sth) known; announce. **O:** reputation, fame; result, outcome; announcement; it ... that he was retiring: *Rumours of his dismissal had been* **noised abroad** *in the department.* ○ *It was* **noised abroad** *that he was taking up a new post.*

nose

nose about/around/round [Vp nom] (*informal*) go about searching or prying, often into matters which are not one's concern: *I wish I could stop him* **nosing about** *— he's not wanted here.* ○ *The children had a good* **nose-around** *(or:* **nose around**) *in the attic.* = poke about/around.

nose out 1 [Vn ⇆ p pass adj] discover (sth) by smell. **O:** rat, ferret, rabbit: *The dog* **nosed** *a rat* **out** *from behind a pile of old newspapers.*

2 [Vn ⇆ p pass] (*informal*) discover (sb/sth) by persistent searching. **O:** information, evidence; story; scandal, sensation: *He's* **nosed out** *a choice piece of scandal!* ○ *The change was well under way, and Sydney was quick to* **nose it out**. SS

notch

notch up [Vp.n pass adj] (*informal*) record (a score), formerly by cutting notches in a stick; achieve, attain. **S:** hunter, marksman; player, team. **O:** bull's eye, hit; pheasant, grouse; big score, several wins: *We* **notched up** *one or two rabbits in a day's shooting.* ○ *Our teams have* **notched up** *a number of wins in matches against visiting sides.*

note

note down [Vn ⇆ p pass adj] record (sth) in writing. **O:** detail, particulars; recipe, formula: *He* **noted down** *every word I said.* ○ *The date of the meeting was carefully* **noted down**. = put down 11, write down.

noted for [pass (Vn.pr)] well known for (sth); famous for. **S:** area, locality; soil; people, family. **o:** fruit, wine; fertility; generosity, musical talent: *The region is* **noted for** *its cattle.* ○ *Frank was* **noted for** *his interest in the opposite sex.* SU □ also used with *become*, or after a noun.

nurse

nurse through [Vn.p pass, Vn.pr pass] help (sb) to recover from (an illness) by caring for him. **o:** sickness, fever; malaria, hepatitis: *She was always having to* **nurse** *him* **through** *illnesses and once her devotion saved his life.* BRN

object

object (to) [Vpr pass adj emph rel] express one's dislike (of sb/sth); oppose. **o:** newcomer, neighbour; noise, disturbance; being interrupted, having to stay on at school: *No one could* **object to** *him; but no one had any particular reason for liking him.* SATS ○ *His father reputedly* **objected to** *a legal career and urged Sydney to go into the church.* SS ○ *The new transport plan is* **objected to** *by nearly all the interested parties.* = raise an objection (to).

oblige

oblige (by) [Vn.pr] (*formal*) it would be less of a nuisance or irritation (if you did sth); you will please (do sth). **o:** asking your children to make less noise, parking your car elsewhere, not smoking in the building: *You'd* **oblige** *me* **by** *keeping your thoughts on the subject to yourself.* ○ *You would* **oblige** *me* **by** *giving more time to your work* (or: ***oblige*** *me if you gave more time to your work*). □ used with *you* + *would;* an apparently polite request which is in fact threatening or sarcastic.

oblige (with) [Vn.pr] (*dated*) (would you) please lend or give (sth) to (sb). **o:** match, light; lift in one's car: *'Could you* ***oblige*** *me* ***with*** *20p for the coffee machine?'* ○ *I asked him if he could* ***oblige*** *us* ***with*** *a lift to* (or: ***oblige*** *us by taking us to*) *the nearest garage.* □ direct or indirect question with *can/could*; a polite request for help.

obtrude

obtrude (upon) [Vpr emph rel, Vn.pr emph rel] (*formal*) force or push (itself etc) forward, esp in an unwelcome way. **S** [Vpr], **O** [Vn.pr]**:** ideas, thoughts, opinions; presence, personality: *Painful memories* ***obtruded upon*** *his attempts to reflect calmly.* ○ *His vulgar presence* ***obtruded*** *(itself)* ***upon*** *us at the worst possible moment.* = intrude on/upon.

occupy

occupy (oneself) with [Vn.pr pass emph rel] spend time and effort on (sth). **o:** task; business, shop; controlling, administering: *COLONEL: A sweet-stall. It does seem an extraordinary thing for an educated young man to be* ***occupying*** *himself* ***with***. LBA ○ *The magistrates were much* ***occupied with*** *the administration of road tax.* SS □ passive also with *appear, become, seem.* = busy oneself (with).

occur

occur to [Vpr emph rel] come into one's mind, enter one's head. **S:** thought, idea, plan; (it ...) that he should know; (it ...) to ask why: *It had never* ***occurred to*** *her to ask herself why she was so unpopular.* ○ *That he should have some deep personal objection had never* ***occurred to*** *me.*

offend

offend against [Vpr pass emph rel] behave in a way that is contrary to (sth); flout. **o:** code (of behaviour); conventions, manners, proprieties: *He seems to take pleasure in* ***offending against*** *the conventions of middle-class life.*

offer

offer up [Vn ⇆ p pass adj] (*religious worship*) present (a prayer etc) to God. **O:** prayer; sacrifice: *A priest* ***offered up*** *a slaughtered chicken.* ○ *Short but fervent prayers were* ***offered up***. GIE

officiate

officiate (at) [Vpr emph rel] (*formal*) conduct a ceremony (esp a religious one). **S:** priest, minister, rabbi. **o:** wedding, funeral; dedication, unveiling: *The bride's father, the Reverend Peter Masters,* ***officiated*** *yesterday* ***at*** *the wedding of Miss Cynthia Masters to Mr Stephen Drew.*

omit

omit (from) [Vn.pr pass emph rel] (*formal*) not mention or state in (sth). **S:** author, speaker. **O:** reference, mention; statement, claim; charge, accusation. **o:** book, report, speech: *The finance minister was careful to* ***omit from*** *his speech any reference to the immense trading deficit.* ○ ***From*** *the most recent edition of Maitland's book the chapter dealing with his arrest and imprisonment has had to be* ***omitted***. = leave out/out of, miss out/out of.

ooze

ooze out/out of [Vp, Vpr] (of a heavy gas or thick fluid) come out (of sth) slowly. **S:** gas, smoke; blood; oil. **o:** window; wound, cut; flaw: *Black oil was* ***oozing out of*** *a crack in the engine casing.* □ also ooze from: *Blood* ***oozed from*** *a cut on his finger.*

open

open off [Vp, Vpr] (of a space) lead directly from (a path etc). **S:** room, dining area; garden, square. **o:** corridor, passage; pathway, street: *Bedrooms* ***opened off*** *to left and right along the corridor.* ○ *Here a small square* ***opens off*** *the paved street.*

open fire (on) [Vn.pr pass pass(o) rel] (*military*) begin firing (at sth/sb). **S:** enemy; infantry, sniper; gun; ship. **o:** position; trench, strong point: *It would not have surprised me if someone had* ***opened fire on*** *us from an upstairs window.* UTN ○ *A searchlight picked her* (the ship) *up, and* ***fire*** *was* ***opened on*** *her from the shore.* RFW = open up 10.

open on to [Vp.pr] allow one to reach (a place). **S:** door, french-window, gate. **o:** backyard, garden; stream, street: *The back gate* ***opens on to*** *a private road.* ○ *The cottage door* ***opens on to*** *an uninterrupted stretch of countryside.* □ also open onto. = give on to.

open out 1 [Vp] become wider; broaden. **S:** river, valley: *The river* ***opens out*** *suddenly into a broad estuary.* ○ *At that point, the road* ***opens out*** *and becomes a dual carriageway.*

2 [Vn ⇆ p pass adj] unfold (sth). **O:** map, blueprint, chart: *He* ***opened*** *the road-map* ***out***, *and laid it on his knee.*

3 [Vp, Vn ⇆ p pass adj] (cause sth to) spread or separate. **S** [Vp], **O** [Vn.p]**:** flower, bloom; petals; fan: *In the warmth of the room, the roses* ***opened out*** *in a few hours.* ○ *You* ***open*** *the fan* ***out*** *with a quick flick of the wrist.*

4 [Vp] show more of one's feelings, character etc to people. **S:** character, personality: *She* ***opened out*** *a good deal while she was with us.* PW

open up 1 [Vp] open the door of a building to admit sb: *Mother!* ***Open up****! Let me in, I'm home.* DPM ○ *'****Open up*** *or we'll break the door down!'* □ direct or indirect command only.

2 [Vn ⇆ p pass adj] unwrap, unfasten or unlock (sth) so that one can see what is inside. **O:** packet, package; suitcase, trunk; wing, room: *'****Open up*** *the boot of the car, and let me look inside.'* ○ *Some of the smaller state rooms in the palace have not been* ***opened up*** *for years.*

3 [Vp, Vn ⇆ p pass] (cause a business to) start trading. **S:** business; shop, supermarket; café, restaurant; factory, plant: *New service areas are* ***opening up*** *on this motorway.* ○ *She's thinking of* ***opening up*** *a boutique catering specifically for teenagers.*

4 [Vp.n pass adj] make (a gap) appear in sth by cutting etc. **O:** gap, breach, passageway: *The infantry* ***opened up*** *a corridor across the minefield for the armour to pass through.* ○ (*figurative*) *They* ***open up*** *a chink in the defensive armour of the Exchequer.* SC

5 [Vn ⇆ p pass] (*informal*) cut open (a body) in order to repair or take out part of it. **O:** patient; body; abdomen; heart, stomach, bladder: *The surgeon had to* ***open up*** *the windpipe to clear a blockage.*

6 [Vn ⇆ p pass adj] make (a new area) known to people, so that they can explore, settle or develop it. **O:** territory, land; the West (US); coalfields, oilfields: *The government is* **opening up** *a whole new region for settlement by peasant farmers.* ○ *There was the new middle-class tourist, for whom the Continent was* **opened up** *by . . . the increasing ease and speed of travel.* TU ○ *His stories* **open up** *new worlds of the imagination.* AH

7 [Vp.n pass] create (opportunities etc) for people to progress in their work etc. **O:** possibilities, opportunities; path, avenue: *The Conservative Party . . . was more inclined to* **open up** *opportunities to enable you to move* (ie progress in life). OBS ○ *Freud's work . . . was* **opening up** *an avenue for him to advance himself — as an academic.* F

8 [Vp, Vn ⇆ p pass adj] (*sport*) (make play) become more lively and mobile. **S** [Vp], **O** [Vn.p]: play, game, match: *In the second half the game* **opened up** *and several attacking moves developed.*

9 [Vp] talk more freely and openly: *She hoped that he would* **open up** *at once about his visit, but he didn't.* PW ○ *It was only after he'd had a few drinks that he could* **open up**.

10 [Vp] (*military*) begin to fire. **S:** gun, battery, artillery: *His battery of rockets* **opened up** *over their heads.* BM ○ *A machine gun* **opened up** *from a concealed position.* = open fire (on).

11 [Vp, Vn.p] (*informal*) (cause a vehicle to) go faster; accelerate: *As soon as the boat had cleared the harbour entrance, I* **opened up**. ○ *'When you get onto the motorway, you can* **open** *her* **up** *a bit.'*

open oneself up to [Vn.p.pr] make oneself vulnerable with regard to (sth). **o:** accusation, charge; criticism: *In offering an interpretation . . . he would inevitably* **open himself up to** *the charge of being an evil man.* F ○ *If you do it that way, you* **open yourself up to** *the complaint that you're putting your own family first.* = expose to.

operate

operate (on) [Vpr pass rel] (*medicine*) perform surgery (upon sb). **S:** surgeon; heart specialist, obstetrician. **o:** patient: *'Has Mr Cutler* **operated** *yet?' 'Yes, but only* **on** *one patient.'* ○ *Mr Smith was* **operated on** *for a constriction of the intestine.*

oppose

opposed to [pass (Vn.pr)] disapproving of (sth), not favouring (sth). **o:** change; plan, scheme; treaty, agreement; his going, my being there: *He is totally* **opposed to** *any change in the existing law.* ○ *The Church of England is on record as being* **opposed to** *apartheid.* SC □ also used with *appear, become, remain, seem*, and after a noun: *. . . a man resolutely* **opposed to** *the regime.*

opt

opt in favour of/for [Vpr pass] choose, select (sth) from a number of alternatives. **o:** fuller participation, better schools, the alternative plan: *He* **opted for** *the artillery and he joined the 10th Battery of the 8th Regiment.* HB

opt out/out of 1 [Vp, Vpr pass adj] refuse to be involved or concerned, to take responsibility etc. **o:** commitment, responsibility; struggle, fight: *To* **opt out** *at this critical moment would be quite indefensible.* ASA ○ *She was protecting herself and her feelings by* **opting out of** *the situation.* GOV

2 [Vp, Vpr] choose not to be under the control of some official body (esp, in the UK, an elected council or a local health authority). **S:** schools, hospitals; employees; ambulance service. **o:** local government control; the existing pension scheme: *We guarantee the right of hospitals to* **opt out of** *district control.* OBS ○ *Labour is promising to repossess more than 50 hospitals that the Government will . . . allow to* **opt out of** *local health authority control.* OBS

order

order about/around [Vn.p pass adj, Vn.pr pass] keep telling (sb) to do this and that in a bossy way. **o:** ⚠ the house, the place: *A military mood came over him and he longed to* **order** *her* **about**: *'Shun! Stand at ease!'* PW ○ *'I mean, he's got no right to* **order** *me* **about** *the place.'* TC = boss about/around, push about/around.

order off (the field) [Vn ⇆ p pass, Vn.pr pass] (*sport*) order (sb) to leave the field of play. **S:** referee. **O:** player: *Jones was* **ordered off** *in the second half after repeated fouls on the opposing winger.* = send off (the field).

order out [Vn ⇆ p pass adj] order (police etc) to assemble, usu to control a demonstration, civil disturbance etc. **S:** government, military governor. **O:** riot police, soldiers: *A dangerous situation was developing in the city and security forces were* **ordered out** *to control it.*

order out/out of [Vn.p pass, Vn.pr pass] tell (sb) to leave (a place). **o:** hall, room; presence: *He entered his parents' bedroom from curiosity, after which he was* **ordered out** *by an irate father.* F ○ *While cooking was in progress, the children were* **ordered out of** *the kitchen.*

order up [Vn ⇆ p pass] (*military*) order (troops) to move from a position in the rear to the front line. **S:** general, commander. **O:** division, brigade; tanks, infantry: *Two battalions were* **ordered up** *to strengthen a weak point in the line.*

oust

oust (from) [Vn.pr pass] remove (sb/sth) abruptly (from a position). **O:** intruder, newcomer; ruler, minister; subject, course (of study). **o:** seat, place; position, office, power; programme, syllabus: *Smith was* **ousted from** *his post as a result of manoeuverings by departmental rivals.* ○ *Copernicus* **ousted** *the earth* **from** *the centre of the universe.* F = drive out/out of 1.

owe

owe to [Vn.pr pass emph rel] have (sb/sth) to thank for (an achievement). **O:** success, pre-eminence; discovery, invention. **o:** colleague, friend; hard work, ingenuity: *We* **owe** *the increase in exports* **to** *the energy of our sales force.* ○ *What do we* **owe** *this sudden upsurge of interest* **to**?

owe it to sb to do sth [Vn.pr] feel obliged or bound to do sth for (sb/oneself). **o:** one's family, children; pupils, employer; oneself. **Inf:** to set an example, to work harder; to buy insurance, to get a house; to buy a product: *I* **owed it to** *my parents* **to come** *home, for they were getting tired and old.* RFW ○ *I felt I* **owed it to** *my family* **to get** *a bigger house.* ○ *You're lucky to be fair — you* **owe it to** *yourself* **to use** *'Stablond' shampoo always.* H

own

own up (to) [Vp, Vp.pr pass] admit or confess that one is to blame (for sth). **o:** one's envy, treachery; being mistaken, having lied: *Sometimes the mistakes are much more important than that. What is important is that we* **own up**, *and say we are sorry.* TT ○ *Greed, ... the thing we are all frightened to* **own up to**. ESS ○ *He was faced with one incriminating detail after another — but none of it was* **owned up to**, *or even reacted to.*

P

pace

pace off [Vp.n pass] measure in paces (part of a total distance or length). **O:** part, section; twenty feet, fifty metres: *'**Pace off** about four feet along the side of the marquee and knock in a peg. Then* **pace** *the same distance* **off** *again, and so on all the way round.'*

pace out [Vp.n pass] measure (the full extent of sth) in paces or steps. **O:** room, field; distance, dimensions: *He* **paced out** *the length and width of the room, and decided it was just large enough.*

pace up and down [Vp emph, Vpr emph] walk backwards and forwards, esp out of impatience, restlessness etc. **S:** prisoner; exam candidate, interviewee. **o:** cell; waiting-room, corridor: *'Stop* **pacing up and down** *like a caged tiger, David. The train will be here in a minute.'*

pack

pack away [Vn ⇆ p pass] put (sth) in a box, cupboard etc, because it is no longer needed, for safe keeping etc. **O:** toy, book; shirt, dress; machine, rifle: *'**Pack away** your books, children. It's time for break.'* ○ *All the glass and china was carefully* **packed away** *in cases and stored in the attic.* = put away 1.

pack down [Vp] (*rugby football*) (of opposing packs of forwards) form a set scrum: (match commentary) *'The referee's bringing the forwards back five yards, and they're* **packing down** *just inside the England half.'*

pack in 1 [Vn ⇆ p pass] (*informal*) abandon, renounce (sth). **O:** job, work; smoking, gambling; racing, football: *The grandfather used to work at the cattle market and bring home sweetbreads, a great source of protein. When he* **packed** *the job* **in**, *the cheap protein ran out.* IND ○ (a fruit farm manager's crop) *'Last year was a complete washout. Had to* **pack** *it all* **in** *and send everyone home.'* G = jack in.

2 [Vn.p] (*informal*) draw (people) in large numbers to a theatre, stadium etc. **S:** comedian, singer; club. **O:** the crowds; them: (one performer to another) *'Do you remember the way we used to* **pack** *them* **in** *at the old Alhambra?'* ○ *Leeds United will be* **packing** *the crowds* **in** *this Saturday at Elland Road.* = pull in 2.

pack it in [Vn.p] (*informal*) stop doing or saying sth noisy, destructive etc: *'You're giving me a headache with your caterwauling; why don't you* **pack it in**?' ○ **Pack it in** *old son, Mister what's-his-name'll be here soon to have a look at this chair of his.* ITAJ = knock it off, pack it up, turn it in.

pack off to [Vn ⇆ p pass, Vn.p.pr pass rel] (*informal*) send (sb) away briskly or urgently to (a place). **O:** refugee, patient; children, husband. **o:** quiet spot, safe retreat; the seaside, the mountains: *He* **packed off** *his wife with Mrs Paine and left a few days later.* OBS ○ *I* **packed** *them* **off** *with notes* **to** *the appropriate hospitals.* DIL ○ *When I was five, I was* **packed off to** *school to learn to read, write and tell my tables.* SU

pack out [Vn ⇆ p pass adj] fill (sth) to capacity. **O:** concert hall, theatre, stadium: *A throng of first-years* **packed out** *the lecture theatre and overflowed into the corridors.* ○ *The Albert Hall was* **packed out** *for the first concert of the season.* ○ *The company played to* **packed-out** *houses for more than a year.* □ esp passive or adj.

pack up 1 [Vp, Vn ⇆ p pass] put (belongings) into cases etc, before leaving home etc. **O:** books, goods; stall; home: *Several dealers found the business left over inadequate to pay their overheads, and they* **packed up** *and left.* DS ○ *He* **packed up** *the few possessions he had and moved out.*

2 [Vp] (*informal*) abandon everything one is doing and not try to start again: *I shall tell him straight out that if he doesn't take this on, he may as well* **pack up**. ASA ○ *'You just didn't try, did you? It makes me sick, I can tell you. We might as well* **pack up**.' OBS □ usu with may/might (just) as well. = give up 12.

3 [Vp] (*informal*) stop, fail. **S:** motor, engine; central heating: *Fifty miles out from land our port engine* **packed up** *on us.* = cut out 5.

pack it up [Vn.p] (*informal*) stop an activity, esp one causing an unpleasant noise or disturbance: *The children were making a dreadful din and I told them to* **pack it up**. = knock it off, pack it in, turn it in.

pad

pad out 1 [Vn ⇆ p pass adj] pack material into (part of a garment etc). **O:** shoulder, sleeve: *The shoulders of his jacket were* **padded out** *to make them look square.* ○ *The bedhead was covered with silky fabric and the surface then* **padded out** *with wadding.* = pack out.

2 [Vn ⇆ p pass adj] make (sth) larger by adding material that is trivial, irrelevant etc. **S:** novelist, journalist. **O:** book, paper; report, account: *The chapter is irritatingly* **padded out** *with references to her smart friends.*

paint

paint in [Vn ⇆ p pass adj] add or insert (sth) in paint. **O:** detail, figure: *The standing figure to the right was* **painted in** *some years after the picture was completed.* ○ *They give a form to the world,* **painting** *it* **in** *excitingly and often amusingly.* NDN

paint on/onto [Vn ⇆ p pass adj, Vn.pr pass rel] apply (sth) with paint to (a surface). **O:** title, name; moustache, eyebrow; stripe, square: *Groucho Marx's moustache was* **painted on**. ○ *Windows and doors had been* **painted onto** *an end wall of the house.*

paint out [Vn ⇆ p pass adj] cover or hide (sth) with paint. **O:** name, figure, detail: *Parts of old paintings which appear unpleasing to later artists are sometimes* ***painted out****.*

pair

pair off (with) [Vp, Vp.pr rel, Vn ⇆ p pass adj, Vn.p.pr pass rel] (get people to) form pairs. [Vp] : *The sentries* ***paired off*** *and began to patrol the area.* ○ [Vp.pr] *Angela* ***paired off with*** *Douglas and Jane* ***with*** *Stephen.* ○ [Vn.p.pr] *Each girl in the party was* ***paired off with*** *a boy.* = partner off (with).

pal

pal up (with) [Vp, Vp.pr] (*informal*) become friends; become the friend of (sb): *Two or three of us who'd* ***palled up*** *went off at the weekends to the sea.* ○ *In his first week in school he* ***palled up with*** *a boy from the same street.* = chum up (with).

pale

pale at [Vpr emph rel] become pale or white at (sth); show signs of fear at (sth). **o:** the (very) thought (of), the mention (of), the sight (of): *She was no coward, but she* ***paled at*** *the mention of an injection.* ○ *Meeting his mother-in-law for the first time was a prospect* ***at*** *which he* ***paled****.* □ usu simple tenses.

pale beside [Vpr rel] seem slight or insignificant when compared with (sth). **S:** achievement, record; work; poetry, painting. **o:** his brother's, yours; that of the last century: *All his prose would* ***pale beside*** *the serious verse he wrote in this decade.* HB □ simple tenses only.

pall

pall (on) [Vpr emph rel] (*formal*) become dreary or uninteresting (to sb) because it is used, spoken etc, too long. **S:** voice, manner; conversation, music: *His funny stories begin to* ***pall*** *(****on*** *his listeners) after the second time of telling.* ○ *The lush harmonies* ***pall on*** *you after a bit. You begin to long for something simple and austere.*

palm

palm off (on) [Vn ⇆ p pass adj, Vn.p.pr pass emph rel] (*informal*) persuade (sb) to accept (sth/sb) by deceit, misrepresentation etc. **O:** shoddy goods, surplus stock; unwelcome guest. **o:** unsuspecting public, gullible customer; friend: *Export rejects may be* ***palmed off*** *in the street markets.* ○ *We* ***palmed off*** *the unimportant Carter* ***on*** *somebody else.* OMIH = fob off onto. ⇨ next entry

palm off (with) [Vn ⇆ p pass, Vn.p.pr pass emph rel] (*informal*) persuade (sb) to accept (sth/sb) by deceit, misrepresentation etc; quieten or pacify (sb) with (sth). **O:** consumer, customer; voter. **o:** inferior stuff, trash; half-truth, excuse: *The salesman tried to* ***palm*** *us* ***off with*** *some shop-soiled sheets.* ○ *We couldn't have our Superstore just yet and we were* ***palmed off with*** *promises.* DPM = fob off (with). ⇨ previous entry

pan

pan out [Vp] (*informal*) develop. **S:** events, the future; it, things. **A:** well, badly; how: *Nobody knows how the economy will* ***pan out*** *over the next few years.* ○ *Don't spend too much time worrying how things are going to* ***pan out****.* = work out 5.

pander

pander to [Vpr pass adj emph rel] aim to satisfy (sth). **S:** newspapers, television, pulp literature. **o:** taste for violence, interest in crime, fondness for scandal; whim, caprice: *The tabloid press* ***panders to*** *popular interest in the seamy and sensational.* ○ *There wasn't a whim of hers he didn't* ***pander to****.* GL ○ *This is exactly the kind of low taste* ***to*** *which television so often* ***panders****.* = cater to.

pant

pant for [Vpr] show by one's rapid breathing that one needs to drink (sth). **o:** drink, glass of water: *'If you'd spent the day working in the open you'd be* ***panting for*** *a drink, too!'*

pant out [Vp.n pass] deliver (sth) in short, quick breaths. **S:** messenger, scout. **O:** story, message: *Steve was almost breathless after the climb: it was as much as he could do to* ***pant out*** *a few words.*

paper

paper over 1 [Vpr pass adj] cover (sth) over with (wall)paper. **O:** door, ceiling; crack, opening: *The cracks aren't very deep; we can* ***paper over*** *them.* ○ *The stains on the wall had been* ***papered over****.*
2 [Vpr pass adj] cover or hide (sth) thinly and imperfectly. **S:** statement, agreement. **O:** crisis; split; divisions, differences; cracks: *Some vague formula may be found to* ***paper over*** *the disagreements.* SC ○ *The split had only been* ***papered over*** *by declarations that could hardly be reconciled.* OBS ○ *The* ***papered-over*** *cracks in front-bench unity were by this stage beginning to show through.*

parcel

parcel out [Vn ⇆ p pass adj] divide (sth) into small plots. **O:** estate, land: *Some landowners voluntarily* ***parcelled*** *their land* ***out*** *among the local peasants.* ○ *An extensive tract of land was* ***parcelled out*** *into small holdings.*

parcel up [Vn ⇆ p pass adj] make a parcel of (sth). **O:** old clothes, rags, toys: *We* ***parcelled up*** *some games and toys to take to the Children's Home at Christmas.* ○ *She wore so many bulky sweaters and scarves that she always presented a* ***parcelled-up*** *appearance.*

pardon

pardon (for) [Vn.pr pass emph rel] (*formal*) forgive (sb) (for sth/doing sth). **o:** mistake; forgetfulness, laziness; being late: *'Please* ***pardon*** *me* ***for*** *not arriving sooner. I got held up in the traffic.'* ○ *We could be* ***pardoned for*** *thinking that no one in the shop is interested in serving us.*

pare

pare down 1 [Vn ⇆ p pass adj] make (sth) smaller by removing thin strips. **O:** stick, panel, (carved) figure: *A lean-looking man at the next table was* ***paring*** *his chop right* ***down*** *.* ○ *The neck of the figure was* ***pared*** *right* ***down*** *with chisel and mallet to make it appear lean and withered.*
2 [Vn ⇆ p pass adj] reduce (sth) considerably. **O:** budget, allowance, finances, investment: *The committee have* ***pared*** *our travelling allowances* ***down*** *to the bare minimum.* ○ *Expenditure on new building is being* ***pared*** *right* ***down*** *to the bone.* ○

Even with a **pared-down** *budget, we shall have trouble making ends meet this year.*

pare off [Vn ⇆ p pass adj, Vn.pr pass] remove (sth) in thin strips, usu with a knife. **O:** skin, peel; bark: *First,* **pare off** *the peel with a sharp knife.* ○ *Plastic surgeons have perfected the technique of* **paring** *strips of skin* **off** *one part of the body and grafting them on elsewhere.*

parley

parley (with) [Vpr pass emph rel] (*military*) discuss the possibility of a truce, an exchange of prisoners etc (with sb). **o:** enemy, opposing forces: *An officer came forward with a white flag to* **parley** *(***with** *our general).* ○ *The encircled forces were in no mood to* **parley** *or be* **parleyed with**.

part

part from [Vn.pr pass emph rel] make (sb) leave or abandon (sb) or give away (sth). **o:** child, wife; money, cash: *'You must kill me too. I love her, and I cannot be* **parted from** *her.'* GLEG ○ *He's not easily* **parted from** *his money.* ○ *... my books,* **from** *which I could not bear to be* **parted**, *even for a few days.* GL □ usu passive. ⇨ next entry

part with [Vpr pass rel] spend (sth); relinquish. **o:** money, cash; pet; furniture, ornament: *She made them listen and even on occasion* **part with** *money for her objects of charity.* ASA ○ *He's not the sort who's happy to* **part with** *hard-earned cash.* ○ *To raise money, Aunt Martha had to* **part with** *some of her most treasured possessions.* = give away 1. ↔ hold on to 2. ⇨ previous entry

part company (with) 1 [Vn.pr emph rel] separate oneself (from sb); leave. **o:** expedition, convoy; employer, firm: *I* **parted company with** *the other climbers* (or: *We* **parted company**) *after completing the first stage of the ascent.*

2 [Vn.pr emph rel] take a different view, hold different opinions (from sb) (about sth): *She* **parts company with** *her colleagues over the need for additional investment.* ○ *We agree about most things, but we* **part company** *on the issue of full European unity.* = differ (from).

partake

partake of 1 [Vpr pass emph rel] (*formal*) share (sth). **o:** meal, feast; success, triumph, joy: *They invited us to* **partake of** *their simple fare.* ○ *The world is so marvellous, I want to grasp it, to* **partake of** *it, to embrace it.* LIFE

2 [Vpr] (*formal*) be partly like (sth); suggest. **S:** conduct, behaviour, action; appearance, manner. **o:** arrogance, presumption, conceit: *I can't help thinking that his generosity* **partakes** *somewhat* **of** *patronage.* = smack of.

participate

participate (in) [Vpr emph rel] (*formal*) be involved (in sth). **o:** activity; demonstration, match; show, display; enterprise, undertaking, venture: *The Council decided not to* **participate in** *the building of a new pool, but to leave this entirely to private initiative.* ○ *Despite their financial and other problems, Henri and Jeanne were still able to* **participate in** *the social life of Paris.* AF = take part (in).

partition

partition off [Vn ⇆ p pass adj] divide (sth) by means of a partition or partitions; separate (one area) from another in this way. **O:** room; office, kitchen; corner, bay: *Down one side, the restaurant has been* **partitioned off** *into small booths.* ○ *Emma had* **partitioned off** *one corner of her room to form a washing and cooking area.*

partner

partner off (with) [Vp, Vp.pr rel, Vn ⇆ p pass adj, Vn.p.pr pass rel] make a pair, a couple; form (people) into couples. **S:** organizer, host: [Vp.pr] *Most of the guests had* **partnered off with** *somebody before the weekend was over.* ○ [Vn.p] *The organizers* **partnered** *everyone* **off** *for the afternoon excursion.* = pair off (with).

pass

pass along/down [Vp] (instruction from bus conductor to passengers) move to the far end of the bus, and don't block the entrance: *'Now,* **pass** *right* **along** *inside, please.'*

pass around/round [Vn ⇆ p pass, Vn.pr pass] hand (sth) from person to person in a group. **O:** drinks; sandwiches, cake; document, photograph. **o:** room, table: *Coffee and sandwiches were* **passed around** *and we began to discuss the programme for the next day.* ○ *The letter was* **passed round** *the table in silence.*

pass as/for [Vpr] appear to be (sth), be regarded as (sth), even though one, or it, may be quite different in fact. **o:** scholar, gentleman, native-speaker; gold, silver: *They are ignorant of half the things that* **pass as** *common knowledge.* SC ○ *She* **passes for** *normal ... but she knows I know she's loony* (= mad). GL ○ *He looked at the collection of odds and ends that* **passed for** *china.* TT

pass away [Vn ⇆ p pass] spend or occupy (time), esp in a pleasant, easy way. **S:** he etc; cards, conversation. **O:** the time; the evening, the night; a few days: *He* **passed** *the evening* **away** *looking through his collection of stamps.* ○ *A game of cards can* **pass away** *the time pleasantly enough.*

pass away/on/over [Vp] (*euphemism*) die: *As soon as the old Queen* **passed on**, *poor old lady, there seemed an almost audible sigh of relief all round.* GOV ○ *'You'll be sorry to hear that Mr Barker's* **passed over**,*' she said.* ASA

pass between [Vpr] be exchanged by (writers or speakers). **S:** letters; angry words; secret, confidence: *No more letters have* **passed between** *us.* ○ *They'll never speak to each other again after what's* **passed between** *them.* ○ *'Remember! No one must ever know what has* **passed between** *us.'*

pass by 1 [Vp, Vpr] go past (sth/sb). **S:** pedestrian, vehicle. **o:** door, house: *The procession* **passed** *right* **by** *my door.* ○ *Somebody* **passing by** (= *A* **passer-by**) *asked me the way to the Town Hall.* □ nom form is passer-by, pl passers-by.

2 [Vn.p pass] not touch or affect (sb); leave alone. **S:** great event; excitement, commotion, disturbance: *She feared commitment, and hoped that the great challenges of life would* **pass** *her* **by** (or: **bypass** *her*). ○ *Life's colourful pageant would best oblige him by continuing to* **pass** *him* **by**. ILIH □ alt v form is bypass.

3 [Vn.p pass adj] avoid approaching or tackling (sth) because it is too complicated, painful etc. **O:** area, field; passage, episode; problem, difficulty: *We cannot neglect whole areas of aesthetic appreciation, but we must* **pass** *them* **by** *in our attempt to isolate one aspect of aesthetics.* SNP ○ *If you try to*

***pass** these problems **by** (or: **bypass** them), you'll only have to sort them out later, at greater cost to the company.* □ alt v form is bypass.

4 [Vn.p] avoid or shun (sb). **S:** friend, colleague; girl: *John neglects his friends but he gets terribly upset when others **pass** him **by**.* ○ *'Don't **pass** me **by**, don't make me cry, don't leave me blue, 'Cause darling, I love only you!'* LENNON AND McCARTNEY

life pass by [Vn.p] (*informal*) (of the various opportunities and pleasures of life) go by without one having gained from them, or enjoyed them: *You seem to be afraid that **life** might **pass** you **by** without giving you time to enjoy it to the full.* WI ○ *I used to remind him of the good luck he'd had, but he was unimpressed: he was convinced that **life** had **passed** him **by**.*

pass by on the other side [Vp.pr] fail or refuse to go to the aid of people in need: *And by chance there came down a certain priest that way; and when he saw him, he **passed by on the other side**.* BIBLE (LK X 31) ○ *People in the famine areas will die if we in the richer countries **pass by on the other side**.*

pass by/under the name of [Vpr] (esp *jocular*) be known by a particular name, though it is not, in fact, one's own: *At that stage in his criminal career, he **passed by** the **name** of Bloggs.* ○ *What **name** is he **passing under** at the moment?* = go by the name of, go under 4.

pass down 1 [Vn ⇆ p pass] transmit (sth) from generation to generation. **O:** standards (of service, of scholarship); craft; myth, tale, saga; jewellery, silver. **A:** from father to son; by oral tradition, by word of mouth: *There was also the rigid conscience which a long line of … ancestors had **passed down** to her.* BLCH ○ *These high standards of craftsmanship have been **passed down** over four generations.* ○ *Nothing is as tenacious … as knowledge **passed down** by word of mouth.* BRN = hand down 2, pass on (to) 1.

2 [Vp] move to the far end of the bus. ⇨ pass along/down.

pass for [Vpr] ⇨ pass as/for.

pass (the ball) forward [Vp, Vn.p pass] (*rugby football*) when throwing the ball to another member of one's team, make it move forward (rather than back, as the rules require). **S:** scrum half, three-quarter: *If **the ball** is **passed forward** (or: If there is a **forward pass**) the referee orders a set scrum.*

pass in review [Vn.pr pass] consider (things) one by one; review, survey. **O:** events, developments; successes, achievements; setbacks: *Let me, as briefly as I can, **pass** these new developments **in review**.* ○ *In his address to the Board, the Chairman **passed in review** the principal events of the trading year.* = pass over 5, run through 3.

pass into 1 [Vpr] be admitted to (an institution) by passing an examination. **o:** college, school; military academy: *He **passed into** Sandhurst by the narrowest possible margin.* ↔ pass out 2.

2 [Vpr] become a part of (sth) because of its importance, notoriety, etc. **o:** ⚠ history, legend, folklore: *William Howard Russell's words 'the thin red streak', used of the 93rd Regiment at Balaklava, have **passed into** history as 'the thin red line'.*

3 [Vpr] move from a conscious state into an unconscious one. **S:** patient; injured, wounded man. **o:** ⚠ a deep sleep; a coma; a trance: *Patients under hypnosis **pass into** a trance-like state.* = fall into 2.

pass off 1 [Vp] not be felt any longer; disappear. **S:** pain, irritation; anger, depression: *This bout **passes off**.* NM ○ *Mescalin is completely innocuous, and its effects will **pass off** after eight or ten hours.* DOP = wear off 2.

2 [Vp] take place; proceed. **S:** meeting, discussion, debate; party, celebration. **A:** peacefully, well; in an orderly manner, without fuss: *By the grace of God, the rally **passed off** quietly.* T ○ *The Soviet leaders are clearly very anxious that the year should **pass off** smoothly.* OBS □ adv or prep phrase usu present.

3 [Vn ⇆ p pass] turn sb's attention away from (sth), by suggesting it is not very important. **O:** incident, moment; comment, remark. **A:** with a shrug, with a jest; lightly: *Even if someone else raised the subject of the lecture, he would **pass** it **off** as easily as he could.* ASA ○ *He had jokingly asked her … when the novel was coming out. Marian tried to **pass** it **off** with a jest.* GE

pass off (as) [Vn.p pass, Vn.p.pr pass] speak or act as if one/sb has a different job, status, income etc from the true one. **O:** oneself; wife, friend. **o:** tourist, millionaire, VIP; blind, penniless: *He has been **passing** himself **off as** a deaf mute.* T ○ *He **passed** his wife **off as** an official member of the party.*

pass on [Vp] ⇨ pass away/on/over.

pass an opinion (on) [Vn.pr pass emph rel] state one's views (on a subject). **S:** expert, specialist; auctioneer, valuer. **o:** subject, matter; purchase, requisition: *A research student will ask his supervisor to **pass an opinion on** material collected during fieldwork.* ○ *There are few matters **on** which our friend will not **pass an** unsolicited **opinion**.*

pass sentence (on) [Vn.pr pass emph rel] (*legal*) say what the punishment of (a convicted person) is to be. **S:** court; judge, magistrate. **o:** accused, defendant: *'Have you anything further to say before I **pass sentence on** you?'*

pass on (to) 1 [Vn ⇆ p pass adj, Vn.p.pr pass] give (sth) to the next person, or another person; get rid of (sth) by giving it to another person. **O:** note, memorandum, file; message, advice, news; job, task: ***Pass** the letter **on to** whoever's next on the distribution card.* ○ *In his usual way he **passed on** some gratuitous advice **to** Bichet.* AF ○ *If you can't do the job yourself, **pass** it **on to** someone who can.*

2 [Vn ⇆ p pass adj, Vn.p.pr pass rel] transmit (sth) from one generation (to another). **O:** company, firm; skill, craft; (personal) qualities, characteristics; genes: *Fathers are taking the time and trouble to **pass on** these skills.* ○ *Grandfather's money was **passed on to** the two surviving daughters.* = hand down 2, pass down 1.

3 [Vn ⇆ p pass adj, Vn.p.pr pass] enable (sb) to benefit from a decrease in costs etc; oblige (sb) to pay, or share, an increase in costs etc. **O:** saving, economy; increase (in price, cost); tax. **o:** general public; consumer; taxpayer: *There would be a saving to the airlines of about £70 million a year, some of which could be **passed on to** the public in lower fares.* OBS ○ *The retailer can absorb some of* *the increase in costs, but he is bound to* ***pass on*** *a percentage* **to** *the customer.*

4 [Vn.p pass, Vn.p.pr pass rel] tell (sb) to consult another person or body for help or a decision. **o:** (another) department; lost property, environmental health; doctor, dentist: *'I can't help you, but I'll* ***pass*** *you* ***on to*** *someone who can.'* ○ *She spent the whole day in the hospital being* ***passed on*** *from one specialist* **to** *another.* = refer to 4.

5 [Vp, Vp.pr pass] move from one activity or stage (to another). **o:** (another) point, matter; post, stage (in one's career); object of interest: *'If nobody has anything further to add, perhaps we can* ***pass on****.'* ○ *He had found time to* ***pass on to*** *her later.* TGLY ○ *Logically the next step was for her to* ***pass on*** *from the theatre* **to** *television.* = get on to 3.

pass out 1 [Vp.n pass] give (things) freely. **O:** drinks, cigarettes; tickets (for a show, or a football match); samples (of merchandise): *He's a generous spender: when he wins money at the races, he starts* ***passing out*** *the beer and cigarettes.* ○ *The exhibitors at the trade fair* ***pass out*** *free samples to stimulate interest.* = give out 2, hand out 1.

2 [Vp, Vn.p pass] (*military*) successfully complete a course of training at a military academy etc; appear in the parade which marks the completion of the course; post (sb) to a unit after completion. **S** [Vp], **O** [Vn.p]**:** cadet, recruit, trainee: *At the end of the course he* ***passed out*** *top in Navigation.* FL ○ *I decided to get back to England in time to take the* ***Passing Out*** *Parade myself, so that I could fasten the Belt of Honour on my son.* MFM ○ *A number of selected cadets of my batch were to be* ***passed out*** *in December, 1907.* MFM □ nom form, used attrib with *parade, ceremony*, is passing(-)out. ↔ pass into 1.

3 [Vp] (*informal*) lose consciousness; faint: *'My, fancy that being a real burglar last night. I'd have* ***passed out*** *if I'd known.'* DC ○ *'I'd only have to point a gun at him and say bang, bang, and the little twerp would* ***pass out*** *cold from fright.'* AITC ⇨ be out 9.

pass over 1 [Vn ⇆ p pass adj] fail to include or notice (sth); disregard. **O:** fact, detail, particular: *If there's something here I must see, then rest assured I shan't* ***pass*** *it* ***over****.* ○ *I would ask every person who came along to tell me where Chesterfield Mews was. I wouldn't* ***pass over*** *anyone.* CON

2 [Vp.n pass] not face or deal with (sth) because it is too painful or embarrassing; avoid. **O:** feeling; disturbance, conflict; subject, topic. **A:** without comment, in silence, too quickly: *You can't* ***pass over*** *the underlying causes of conflict, and hope they'll just vanish.* ○ *Emotion was something to be covered up, or* ***passed over*** *with a few short words.* PW ○ *The mother's death was* ***passed over*** *almost without comment.* BRN = skirt around/round.

3 [Vn.p pass adj] not consider (sb) for promotion who is, or might think himself to be, qualified for it; reject: *When the senior appointments were made, I was* ***passed over*** *in favour of a younger person.* ○ *Bill is going around with that gloomy look of the* ***passed-over*** *executive.* □ usu pass or adj.

4 [Vn.p pass adj] fail to grasp (sth), let (sth) slip by. **O:** chance, opportunity, opening: *The halt gave an opportunity for further speech which Patrick, being Patrick, felt he could not afford to* ***pass over****.* TGLY = pass up 2.

5 [Vpr pass adj] review, survey (sth). **o:** paragraph, section, sentence; (sequence of) events, happenings: *I must* ***pass*** *quickly* ***over*** *the next few years of my military life.* MFM ○ *The Chairman* ***passed*** *quickly* ***over*** *the first few items to leave more time for the main business of the meeting.* = pass in review, run through 3.

6 [Vp] (*euphemism*) die. ⇨ pass away/on/over.

pass an/one's eye over [Vn.pr rel] scan, survey (sth) briefly. **o:** letter, form; essay, exercise: *I can't say I've examined the document at all closely; I just had time to* ***pass my eye over*** *it.* = cast an eye/one's eyes over, run an/one's eye over.

pass the hat round [Vn ⇆ p pass] (*informal*) collect money, usu for a fellow employee who is sick, retiring etc: *When George died, they* ***passed the hat round*** *to buy a wreath.* = take the hat round.

pass through 1 [Vp, Vpr pass] go through (a town etc), perhaps making a brief halt, but not staying: *'Why don't you stay the night?' 'No, thank you: we're just* ***passing through****.'* ○ *He had always been a lodger and had picked up the lodger's habit of* ***passing through*** *without leaving tracks.* FL

2 [Vpr] take and complete a course of training at (an institution). **o:** officer cadet school, staff college; medical school; university: *His brother had* ***passed through*** *police college to qualify for promotion to Inspector.*

3 [Vpr pass rel] experience or suffer (sth). **o:** a (difficult, testing) period, time, phase: *Mike* ***passed through*** *a difficult period shortly after his marriage broke down, but after a year or so his health and spirits picked up.* ○ *The astronauts* ***passed through*** *an anxious hour when the onboard computer started to malfunction.* = go through 8.

pass under the name of [Vpr] ⇨ pass by/under the name of.

pass up 1 [Vn ⇆ p pass] hand (sth) to sb positioned above oneself. **O:** hammer, nails, ladder, bucket: *'****Pass up*** *the paint pot and brush, and I'll put another coat on the ceiling.'* ○ *The top section of the derrick had to be* ***passed up****, piece by piece.*

2 [Vn ⇆ p pass adj] (*informal*) fail to grasp (sth), let (sth) slip by. **O:** chance, opportunity, occasion; deal, contract, sale: *It doesn't do to be too modest. You can* ***pass*** *a lot of business* ***up*** *that way.* ASA ○ *You can't afford to* ***pass up*** *too many openings like that.* ○ *If all his* ***passed-up*** *chances were placed end to end they'd stretch to the moon.* = pass over 4.

paste

paste up 1 [Vn ⇆ p pass] attach (sth) to a surface, usu at or above eye-level, with paste. **O:** poster, notice; wallpaper: *There were posters advertising the bullfight* ***pasted up*** *all over town.*

2 [Vn ⇆ p nom pass] (*publishing*) arrange (printed matter etc) by pasting it onto pages for photographing and printing, eg by offset, or as a rough guide for the printer to arrange the pages himself; paste (printed pages) onto larger sheets to enable an author or editor to insert corrections etc, eg for a new edition. **O:** typeset matter, illustrations, headings: *'Has the Art Department* ***pasted up*** *the captions to the illustrations yet? I want them to go to the printer tomorrow.'* ○ *The underground press* *produces its magazines by the cheapest method possible—typing the text on ordinary typewriters, using photographs from many printed sources and* **pasting** *the lot* **up** *together to make camera-ready copy for cheap offset litho printing.* ○ *The publishers agreed to provide the author with a* **paste-up** *of the pages that he wanted to make corrections to.*

pat

pat down [Vn ⇆ p pass] flatten, settle or replace (sth) with a pat. **O:** hair; turf, wicket: *She* **patted down** *one or two unruly wisps of hair.* ○ *The batsman walked out to* **pat down** *some bumps in the pitch.*

pat on the back [Vn.pr pass] express one's approval or appreciation of (sb), often, though not necessarily, by tapping him on the back. **O:** child, pupil, colleague; oneself: *When you least expect it, he'll give you a word of encouragement and* **pat** *you* **on the back**. □ pat in this idiom is often used as a noun: *'Yes, praise! It would hurt you, any of you? There isn't enough generosity to spare a little* **pat on the back***?'* ITAJ

patch

patch together [Vn ⇆ p pass adj] put (sth) together roughly or hurriedly. **O:** components, elements; alliance, government, organization: *The book consisted of material from other articles,* **patched together** *and polished up.* ○ *The Prime Minister is trying to* **patch together** *another coalition with the smaller religious parties.*

patch up 1 [Vn ⇆ p pass adj] repair (sth) roughly or temporarily. **O:** wall, floor; car, plane; wound, injury: *He was little use at emergency* **patching up** *of electrical equipment.* HD ○ *A few squares of glass had been* **patched up** *with treacle-brown paper.* BFA

2 [Vn ⇆ p pass adj] treat (sb/an injury) temporarily, eg after an accident. **O:** patient; injury, wound, cut: *I do not want to be saved, but the damned doctors might* **patch** *me* (ie my body) **up**. ARG

3 [Vn ⇆ p pass adj] settle, resolve (a dispute). **O:** quarrel, argument, difference; matter, things: *The matter was* **patched up** *without resort to the police.* ARG ○ *They* **patched** *things* **up** *pretty quickly.* EB

patter

patter about/around/round [Vp, Vpr] move about etc with quick, light, tapping footsteps. **S:** mouse, rat, kitten; child: *We could hear mice* **pattering about** *in the attic above our heads.* ○ *'Sarah, is that you* **pattering around** *downstairs?'*

paw

paw about/around [Vn.p pass] (*informal*) handle (sth/sb) in a clumsy, insensitive way. **O:** fruit, produce; girl: *'I don't want tomatoes that have already been* **pawed around** *by other customers!'* ○ *A firm kiss was one thing, thought Helen, irresolute* **pawing about** *was quite another.*

pay

pay back (for) [Vn ⇆ p pass, Vn.p.pr pass] punish (sb) in return for some injury one has suffered. **o:** neglect, humiliation, slight: *You may think you can get away with neglecting your responsibilities, but events will* **pay** *you* **back**. HD ○ *'I shouldn't try anything on with him, if I were you. He would* **pay** *you* **back** *with interest.'* = pay out (for).

pay back (to) [Vn ⇆ p pass adj, Vn.p.pr pass] repay, return (money) (to sb). **O:** loan; the amount outstanding; what is owing. **o:** relative, partner; bank, building society: *'I'll have some luck and* **pay** *you* **back**,*' he promised.* DC ○ *'It's high time he* **paid** *me* **back** *the £1000 he owes me.'* ○ *The amount was* **paid back to** *the bank by the date agreed.* □ note the position of the Indirect Object in the first two examples.

pay for 1 [Vpr pass adj rel, Vn.pr pass rel] give (money) in exchange for (sth). **O:** £100; a good deal; hard-earned cash; a fortune, the earth: *'No friends of mine could possibly* **pay for** *me to go into a private ward* (ie in a hospital)*.'* HD ○ *'Have those articles been* **paid for**, *Sir?'* ○ *'How much did you* **pay** *him* **for** *the watch?'*

2 [Vpr] suffer for (sth), be punished for (sth). **A:** dearly, heavily. **o:** blunder, omission, failure, neglect: *Sometimes you have to* **pay** *dearly* **for** *mistakes.* WI ○ *If we do nothing now, we shall find ourselves* **paying for** *our inaction later on.*

pay for itself [Vpr] cover the money paid for it, by enabling one to save on other costs, over a period of time. **S:** new technology; retooling; computer. **A:** in time, eventually; over five years: *Computerization of the routine operations of the bank will quickly* **pay for itself** *through savings in staff costs.*

pay in/into [Vn ⇆ p pass, Vn.pr pass emph rel] give (money) to a bank, to be kept in an account; deposit. **O:** cash, banknote, cheque. **o:** current account, savings account; bank, Giro, building society: *I'll* **pay** *the cheque* **in** *as soon as the bank opens.* ○ *Her monthly salary is* **paid into** *her account by her employers.* = put in/into 2. ↔ draw out/out of 3.

pay off 1 [Vn ⇆ p pass adj] pay (sb) in full and discharge him from service. **O:** worker; gang, (ship's) crew: *The crew were* **paid off** *at the end of the trip and a fresh one engaged.* ○ *It's all most regrettable but it looks as though I'm compelled to* **pay** *you* **off** *for your caretaking work.* TC

2 [Vn ⇆ p pass adj] clear, settle (a debt) in full. **O:** debt, overdraft (at a bank), loan: *You'll have to* **pay off** *your old loan before being allowed a new one.* ○ *All our outstanding debts have been* **paid off**.

3 [Vn ⇆ p nom pass] (*informal*) give money to (sb) to prevent him from carrying out a threat. **O:** protection gang, blackmailer: *Publicans are know to have* **paid off** *one gang of terrorists to stop their pubs being blown up by another.* ○ *A girl was sent out to collect the* **pay-off** *— a parcel of notes thrown onto the pavement from a passing car.*

4 [Vp nom] (*informal*) succeed, work. **S:** preparation, effort, planning; scheme, idea, gamble: *Occasionally the checking* **pays off** *and there is the excitement of a chase or an arrest.* T ○ *The good early upbringing, abundant in care and attention, was* **paying off**. EB ○ *This is the* **payoff** *for all our work* (on breeding peregrine falcons). BBCTV

pay out 1 [Vp.n pass adj] pass or release (sth) through the hands. **O:** rope, cord, cable: *He placed the gelignite carefully on the seat and* **paid out** *the wire.* TO ○ *Knotting the rope round a projecting stone cornice, he* **paid** *it* **out** *into the darkness.* ARG

2 [Vp, Vn ⇆ p pass adj] give (accumulated payments) to a member of a savings club etc. **S:** club, association; treasurer: *You can save up for toys by paying into a Christmas club over the year; the club* ***pays out*** *in December.* ○ *We can't* ***pay out*** *more than we take in.*

3 [Vp, Vp.n pass adj] (*informal*) spend (money) on sth; give (money) to sb; the suggestion is that one has to pay too much or too often. **O:** thousands of pounds; a fortune; most of one's income. **A:** for uniforms; on school fees; to charities: *I'm tired of* ***paying out*** *for new trainers every month.* ○ *Mr Charlton had already* ***paid out*** *millions to this swindle in weekly contributions.* DBM ○ *An awful lot of money gets* ***paid out*** *to these people.* DBM

pay out (for) [Vn ⇆ p pass, Vn.p.pr pass] (*informal*) punish (sb) in return for some injury one has suffered. **o:** thoughtlessness, unkindness: *They'll* ***pay*** *you* ***out*** *if you try to take advantage of their generosity.* ○ *Joe felt that he had been more than* ***paid out for*** *a few thoughtless remarks.* = pay back (for).

pay attention (to) [Vn.pr pass emph rel] look (at sb/sth); listen (to sb/sth); consider. **S:** host; audience; fashion model, actress; manager, student. **adj:** some, no; little, scant; close, careful. **o:** stranger, guest; remark, speech; appearance, dress; event, development: *'Please* ***pay*** *no* ***attention to*** *her, my lady,' Briggs interrupted, obviously distressed.* EM ○ *A creative moment had arrived and he* ***paid*** *no* ***attention to*** *the world beyond it.* OMIH ○ *Close* ***attention*** *is being* ***paid to*** *fluctuations in the exchange rate.* = attend (to).

pay court to 1 [Vn.pr pass(o) emph rel] (*formal*) treat (sb) with the respect, admiration etc, usu shown to a prince. **o:** minister, tycoon; actor, artist: *He represented the power of money as Jack did: he was another king. As I watched them all* ***paying court to*** *him, I wondered how on earth he came to marry Alice.* RATT

2 [Vn.pr pass(o) emph rel] (*formal*) try to get (a woman) interested in oneself by being attentive towards her, offering her gifts etc; woo, court: *The handsome young farmer ...* ***pays court to*** *a spinster ten years his senior.* TRO ○ *Augustus proceeded to* ***pay court to*** *two members of the group in quick succession.* GJ

pay heed (to) [Vn.pr pass emph rel] attend to sth which it is important not to ignore; heed. **adj:** no; little, small; careful, greater. **o:** warning; portent, sign; safety, well-being: *It is all to the good that the Conservative Party is to* ***pay*** *greater* ***heed to*** *the voice of youth.* SC ○ *When his sister* ***paid*** *no* ***heed to*** *him, Apollo became both jealous and angry.* GLEG ○ *These are the 'submerged'* (ie subconscious) *portions of themselves* ***to*** *which professional historians have ...* ***paid*** *so little* ***heed***. RTH

pay lip service to [Vn.pr pass emph rel] declare that one regards (sth) as important while not treating it as important in fact. **o:** need (for change); desirability, usefulness (of the measure); idea, notion (of freedom); expansion, development; friendship, brotherhood: *Trades unionists* ***pay*** *only* ***lip service to*** *the need for research.* SC ○ *The authorities must cease to* ***pay lip service to*** *Allied co-operation and must instead embark on a policy of unselfish solidarity.* MFM ○ *Most people, while they* ***pay*** *it* ***lip service*** (or: ***pay lip service to*** *it*), *are reluctant to face up to the importance of infant and child upbringing in character formation.* BRN □ note the Indirect Object construction in the last example.

pay one's respects (to) [Vn.pr pass emph rel] greet (sb) in a polite and formal way: *'Is your mother at home? I just called in to* ***pay my respects****.'* ○ *'Do I intrude? Don't mind me Jo-Jo. I just came down to* ***pay my respects to*** *the bride.'* AITC

pay tribute to [Vn.pr pass pass(o) emph rel] express one's admiration for (sb), one's recognition of (sb's qualities etc). **S:** employer, commander; successor, opponent. **adj:** his etc, this; generous, handsome, warm. **o:** staff; ally, partner; wisdom, vision: *I want to take this opportunity to* ***pay*** *a public* ***tribute to*** *him.* MFM ○ *His personality and achievements are* ***paid tribute to***. BBCR

pay up [Vp] hand money to sb; usu one is under some obligation or pressure to pay: *I must* ***pay up****, and without argument or comment.* UTN ○ *My goods have vanished and the insurance company will have to* ***pay up***. DC ○ *Though her contribution was frequently several terms in arrears, she generally* ***paid up*** *in the end.* BLCH

peal

peal out [Vp] (of bells) resound one after the other; have the resonant sound of bells. **S:** bells; voice, laughter: *The church bells* ***pealed out*** *to mark the end of the war.* ○ *Miss Maxwell's voice* ***pealed out*** *over the cocktail party chatter.*

peck

peck at [Vpr pass adj] take small mouthfuls of (sth); eat only part of (sth) from lack of appetite. **o:** food; breakfast, dinner: *She* ***pecked*** *daintily* ***at*** *a salad.* ○ *He* ***pecked*** *listlessly* ***at*** *his breakfast of egg and bacon.* = pick at 1.

peel

peel off 1 [Vp, Vpr, Vn ⇆ p pass adj, Vn.pr pass] (make the outer covering of sth) separate (from the surface). **S** [Vp Vpr], **O** [Vn.p Vn.pr]**:** covering, skin; peel, husk; bark: [Vp Vpr] *The paint is beginning to* ***peel off*** *(the legs of the chairs).* ○ [Vn.p] *'I don't need a knife, I can* ***peel*** *the skin* ***off*** *with my fingers.'*

2 [Vn ⇆ p pass] (*informal*) remove all or part of (one's clothing). **O:** glove, wet suit, jacket, pullover, sock: *She came further into the room and* ***peeled off*** *her remaining glove.* NW ○ (cricket) *Benjamin bowled three satisfactory overs and had barely* ***peeled off*** *his sweater before Andy Lloyd brought on Reeve in his place.* IND = strip off 1.

3 [Vp nom] leave a formation by curving away to the side. **S:** fighter, interceptor (aircraft); cavalry escort; motorcyclist: *As soon as an enemy bomber formation was sighted, the squadron leader gave the order to* ***peel off***.

peep

peep (at) 1 [Vpr pass adj rel] look quickly (at sth/sb): *She* ***peeped*** *quickly* ***at*** *the sleeping child.*

2 [Vpr pass adj] look slyly and inquisitively (at sb). **o:** neighbour, lover: *Newcomers to the area sensed that they were being* ***peeped at*** *from behind lace curtains.*

peep out [Vp] come partly and suddenly into view. **S:** ⚠ the stars, moon, sun: *The sun* ***peeped out*** *through a gap in the clouds.*

peer

peer (at) [Vpr pass adj] look closely (at sb/sth), as if unable to see well or recognize him/it, or out of curiosity: *She* **peered at** *him closely, as if not believing he could really be Fletcher.* ○ *They were used to being* **peered at** *on arriving in a strange town.*

peg

peg away (at) [Vp, Vp.pr pass] (*informal*) work or struggle persistently (at sth). **o:** writing, research; training, exercise: *'You're bound to find the answer in the end: just keep* **pegging away**.*'* ○ *Between fights the boxers* **pegged away at** *roadwork and exercises in the gym.* = plug away (at).

peg down [Vn ⇆ p pass adj] fasten (sth) in position on the ground with pegs. **O:** flap, fly-sheet; tent: *In the rain and wind it was hard to* **peg down** *the walls of the tent.* ○ *A plastic sheet was* **pegged down** *over the compost heap to hasten decomposition.*

peg (down) (at) [Vn ⇆ p pass, Vn.pr pass, Vn.p.pr pass] hold or fix (prices etc) at a relatively low level. **S:** government; dealer, supplier; industry. **O:** price, cost; wage, salary. **o:** level; percentage: *The Government agreed to* **peg down** *the retail price of certain basic foodstuffs.* ○ *As an anti-inflationary measure, prices of basic commodities would be* **pegged at** *their present level.*

peg out [Vp] (*informal*) faint or collapse from exhaustion; die: *At this height, a climber can* **peg out** *from lack of oxygen.* ○ *His family would be glad if he would just* **peg out** *quietly and let them get on with spending his money.* RT

pelt

pelt down [Vp] fall very heavily. **S:** ⚠ rain; it: *The rain was* **pelting down** *all morning* (or: *it was* **pelting** *with rain all morning.*).

pelt (with) [Vn.pr pass rel] throw (objects) at (sb) in a continuous shower. **o:** bricks, stones, mud; eggs, tomatoes: *The crowd lost patience with the speaker and started to* **pelt** *him* **with** *rotten eggs.* ○ *The prisoner in the stocks was* **pelted with** *anything the crowd could lay their hands on.* = bombard (with) 1.

pen

pen in 1 [Vn ⇆ p pass adj] confine, enclose (sth/sb) in a pen. **O:** sheep, goats, cattle: *The flocks were* **penned in** *for the night as a protection against marauding wolves.*

2 [Vn ⇆ p pass adj] restrict the movements or freedom of (sb). **O:** wife, child; employee: *She feels* **penned in** *by domesticity, permanently tied to the cooker and washing machine.* ○ *The sense of being* **penned in** *. . . was universal.* IND □ esp passive and adj.

pencil

pencil in [Vn ⇆ p pass adj] write (sth) in a diary etc in pencil, eg because the arrangements noted down have still to be confirmed. **O:** time, date; arrangement, rendezvous: *'Tuesday at ten seems fine. I'll* **pencil** *it* **in** *and confirm tomorrow.'* ○ *There was a* **pencilled-in** *note to one side that I could barely decipher.* ⇨ ink in.

pension

pension off 1 [Vn ⇆ p pass adj] discharge (sb) from service, esp at the end of a career and with a pension. **S:** government; company; army. **O:** civil servant; employee; officer: *'Pollard is past his best, and he'll certainly never be promoted, but it's a bit too soon to* **pension** *him* **off**.*'* ○ *A number of* **pensioned-off** *teachers were brought back into the schools to fill the places of younger men called up for military service.*

2 [Vn ⇆ p pass adj] (*informal*) stop using (sth) because it is old and worn. **O:** machine, weapon, car: *Half the machinery in the works is ready to be* **pensioned off**, *but for the moment we can't afford to invest in anything new.*

pent

pent up [pass adj (Vn.p)] restrained, repressed. **S:** emotion; resentment, frustration; energy: *All this anger that's* **pent up** *inside him has to break out from time to time.* ○ *'Were you blazing with* **pent-up** *desire like people in books?'* RATT

people

people with [Vn.pr pass emph rel] (*formal*) fill (sth) with people etc. **S:** migration; author; travel, time. **O:** area, region; tale, narrative; mind, imagination. **o:** fisherman, trader; character; fancies: *The westward expansion of the nineteenth century* **peopled** *the Mid-West* **with** *farming communities.* ○ *The waterlogged streets were* **peopled with** *dozens of small children. . . chasing each other through the water.* PTN ○ *His dreams were* **peopled with** *strange, terrifying fantasies.*

pep

pep up [Vn ⇆ p pass adj] (*informal*) make (sb/sth) more interesting, lively or powerful. **O:** him etc; food, drink; conversation, entertainment; proceedings: **Pep up** *jaded palates with this exotic salad.* GF ○ *'You're the sort of chap they ought to have. New blood to* **pep** *them* **up**.*'* DBM ○ *I would consider drastically curtailing the number of* (radio) *series and taking steps to* **pep up** *those that were left.* L

pepper

pepper with 1 [Vn.pr pass rel] strike (sb/sth) with a stinging shower of (sth). **o:** shot, stones: *The dog went off to fetch in the dead rabbit. It was* **peppered with** *shot all down one side.*

2 [Vn.pr pass rel] mark (sth) in several places, as if with grains of pepper. **O:** book, story, account, narrative. **o:** anecdotes, reminiscences, jokes: *His letters to Martha in this period are* **peppered with** *references to his hopes.* F □ esp passive.

perk

perk up [Vp, Vn ⇆ p pass adj] (*informal*) (cause sb/sth to) become more lively and cheerful; enliven. **S** [Vp], **O** [Vn.p]**:** guest, class; things; party, evening. **S** [Vn.p]**:** speaker; news; music, drink: *She was very huffy, so I suggested she could use some of the money. She* **perked up** *at that.* JFTR ○ *I felt liberated. And so life had* **perked up** *again.* SML ○ *'I need a stiff drink to* **perk** *me* **up**!*'* = liven up.

permit

permit of [Vpr] (*formal*) leave room for (sth). **S:** situation, circumstances; moment, time. **o:** delay, hesitation; compromise, makeshift: *The present crisis does not* **permit of** *weakness or indecision.* □ usu neg. = allow of.

persist

persist in [Vpr pass adj] (*formal*) continue stubbornly to do sth, or to follow a course of action. **o:** interrupting, behaving unpleasantly; habit, conduct, line of action: *'If you* **persist in** *heckling every time that someone tries to speak, I shall have you removed.'* ○ *Bakunin* **persisted in** *trying to stir up rebellion.* RTH ○ *This line of action, if* **persisted in**, *could lead to disaster.*

persuade

persuade (of) [Vn.pr pass] make (sb) accept or believe in (sth). **o:** sincerity, truth; practicality, futility: *He'd managed to* **persuade** us **of** *the practicality of the scheme; now* we *had to* **persuade** *the boss.* ○ *You don't have to* **persuade** *me* **of** *the likelihood of an outbreak* (or: *that an outbreak is likely*). = convince (of).

pertain

pertain to 1 [Vpr] (*formal*) be connected with (sth). **S:** document, paper; evidence; discussion, meeting. **o:** enquiry, case; investigation, research; event, proposal: *Documents* **pertaining to** *that enquiry were never produced in court.* ○ *Our findings do not* **pertain** *directly* **to** *her line of research.* = relate to.

2 [Vpr] (*formal* or *jocular*) be associated with (sth); be appropriate to (sth). **S:** wildness, enthusiasm, freedom. **o:** age, time, season: *The fire and dash* **pertaining to** *youth are not very much in evidence in this team.*

pester

pester the life out of [Vn.pr pass] (*informal*) bother or trouble (sb) unbearably, esp to obtain some gift or service from him. **S:** child, pupil; salesman, newspaperman: *Players leaving the stadium had* **the life pestered out of** *them by small boys looking for autographs.* ○ *Never again would a journalist* **pester the life out of** *the mother of a week-dead son.* PP □ note the passive with have.

peter

peter out [Vp] dwindle to nothing; gradually lose its force or momentum. **S:** stream, path; talk, chat, story; attack, offensive: *The boom of the 1920s* **petered out** *at about the same time.* OBS ○ *My search for Janet Prentice seemed to have* **petered out**. RFW ○ *The Victorian age seemed to be* **petering out** *at about the end of 1918.* AH

petition

petition (for) [Vpr pass emph rel, Vn.pr pass emph rel] appeal (for sth) by submitting a written document signed by many people. **O:** MP, Parliament. **o:** release of detainees, change in the law, pensions for the disabled: *Many organizations are* **petitioning for** *the case to be reopened.* ○ *The families have* **petitioned** *the Government* **for** *the early release of the detainees.*

phase

phase down [Vn ⇆ p pass adj] gradually reduce (sth). **O:** production, output; payment, support: *We must* **phase down** *the subsidies* (ie to the nationalized industries), *which encourage inefficiency and cost dear in taxes and inflation.* DT

phase in [Vn ⇆ p pass adj] gradually introduce (sth). **O:** charge, tax; increase; model, pattern, process; organization, set-up: *The main* (increases) *... are caused by the phasing in of major re-equipment programmes.* BDD ○ *It is thought that the rise will be* **phased in** *over the next two years.* BBCR

phase out [Vn ⇆ p pass adj] gradually stop making or supplying (sth). **O:** manufacture, provision (of sth); (model of a) car, aircraft; organization, set-up: *The anti-tank company was armed mainly with the 75mm, although production of this gun was being* **phased out** *in 1942.* B ○ *There are plans to* **phase out** *the now separate Department of Economic Geography.* ○ *There must be a* **phasing out** *of export subsidies.* IND

phone

phone around/round [Vp, Vpr] telephone one address after another, esp to find which of a number of suppliers offers the best service, cheapest goods etc. **S:** shopkeeper, storekeeper, buyer. **o:** supplier, dealer, wholesaler: *There are lots of bargains on offer at the moment, so before you buy your stereo* **phone around** *to see what prices are being asked.* = ring around/round.

phone back 1 [Vp] telephone (sb) again, having failed to contact him the first time: *'Deborah isn't at home at the moment. Could you* **phone back** *this evening?'* = call back 1, ring back 1.

2 [Vp, Vn.p pass] after speaking to sb on the telephone, call him again later, eg to give him more information etc: *'I'm teaching at the moment — I'll* **phone back** *later.'* ○ *'Could you* **phone back** *when you've put all the figures together?'* = call back 2. = ring back 2.

phone (for) summon (sb) by telephoning him. **o:** doctor, ambulance; the police, fire brigade: *I've already* **phoned for** *the doctor. He should be here any minute.*

phone in [Vn ⇆ p nom pass adj] send (sth) by telephone, esp to a radio or TV programme. **O:** question, inquiry, problem; news item, story, report: *Listeners are invited to* **phone in** *their questions to the Shadow Foreign Secretary from six o'clock this evening.* ○ *This new* **phone-in** (or: **phone-in** *programme*) *is designed to elicit listeners' views on the important issues of the day.*

phone up [Vp, Vn ⇆ p pass] call (sb) on the telephone: *Alison just* **phoned up** *to say they're coming this weekend.* ○ *I'll* **phone** *you* **up** *if there's anything new to report.* = call up 1, ring up 1.

pick

pick at 1 [Vpr pass adj] take small, or a few, mouthfuls of (sth) either from fastidiousness or lack of appetite. **o:** lunch, supper; meat, pudding: *'Did she finish her rice pudding?' 'No, she just* **picked at** *it.'* ○ *My friend* **picks** *sourly* **at** *her cocktail.* SCIT = peck at.

2 [Vpr pass adj] find fault with (sb); criticize. **o:** wife, child, employee: *'Leave the child alone: you're always* **picking at** *her!'* ○ *She's been* **picked at** *so often by parents and teachers that her confidence is destroyed.* = nag (at).

pick holes in [Vn.pr pass] (*informal*) comment adversely on (sth); criticize. **o:** scheme, plan; speech, report; book, film: *It's easy for an outsider to* **pick holes in** *our programme. What you don't under-*

stand is the technical difficulties we have to face. ○ ***Holes** can be **picked in** any scales of pay.* TES

pick off [Vn ⇆ p pass adj] shoot (persons/animals) one by one with deliberate aim. **S:** sniper, marksman. **O:** officer, specialist: *They had probably been **picked off** by American snipers at the head of our advance.* SD ○ *They **pick off** the officers first, so as to throw the attack into confusion.*

pick on [Vpr pass adj] (*informal*) choose (sb) repeatedly for criticism, blame, punishment, or an unpleasant task. **A:** always, forever. **o:** smaller brother, weaker person: *He ignored his wife's plea to stop **picking on** his daughter and lifted his hand to settle her with a blow.* LLDR ○ *'What's she **picking on** him for? ... Why doesn't she let him alone?'* 50MH ○ *He's constantly being **picked on** to do the dirty jobs.*

pick out 1 [Vn ⇆ p pass] choose (sth) from a number of similar objects; select. **O:** (largest, least expensive) fruit, vegetables; dress, suit: *Cyril had a lot of azaleas in pots. I **picked out** a big red one just coming into bloom.* RFW

2 [Vn ⇆ p pass] separate, distinguish (sb/sth) from surrounding persons or objects: *We **pick** someone **out** from the crowd because they possess one significant ... quality.* SCIT ○ *His house was easily **picked out** from the others: it had a large blue door.*

3 [Vn ⇆ p pass] (of a person who plays an instrument by ear) find the notes of a tune by trial and error. **A:** on the piano, on the guitar: *He was trying to **pick out** a tune he had heard on the radio.*

4 [Vp.n pass] make (sth) prominent; highlight. **O:** detail; feature, shape; brickwork, moulding, tracery: *The sun **picked out** the skin around her eyes.* FL ○ *The colour scheme was brown, with the mouldings **picked out** in orange.*

pick over [Vn ⇆ p pass adj] lift and turn over (things) so as to examine and make a choice from them. **O:** fruit, vegetables; clothing: *The women **pick** the fruit **over** carefully before making their minds up which to buy.* ○ *... the shame of beggary, the humiliation of **picking over** the contents of waste cans and garbage dumps.* 50MH

pick up 1 [Vn ⇆ p pass] take hold of and raise (sth): *She **picked up** the half-finished letter and put it on the mantelpiece.* DC ○ *'You dropped the plate on the floor; now you can **pick** it **up**.'* ↔ put down 1.

2 [Vp.n nom pass adj] collect (sth). **S:** delivery van, lorry. **O:** groceries, newspaper; load, cargo: *After leaving the church Dalgliesh went briefly back to the Yard to **pick up** his files.* TFD ○ *We **picked up** a consignment of cigarettes at the warehouse.* □ nom form used attrib, as in: *a **pick-up** truck, service, point.*

3 [Vp.n pass] (*informal*) collect (sth) as wages; earn: *There are men in that factory **picking up** three hundred pounds a week.* ○ *'He earns good money, he does. He **picks up** a packet.'* PW

4 [Vn ⇆ p pass] take (sb) on board; stop to give a lift to (sb). **O:** passenger, crew member; hitchhiker: *The giant tankers have to start slowing down some 15 miles before they reach a rendezvous point to **pick up** a pilot.* OBS ○ *You can walk or ride the mile or two to the crossroads where the school bus will **pick** you **up**.* WI ○ *He **picked up** two students outside Doncaster and dropped them off in Central London.*

5 [Vn ⇆ p pass adj] rescue (sb) from the sea. **S:** lifeboat, helicopter. **O:** shipwrecked sailor, aircrew; survivor: *A naval helicopter **picked up** the downed airman after receiving his SOS message.* ○ *Survivors of the disaster were **picked up** by small boats.*

6 [Vn ⇆ p nom pass] (*informal*) make sb's acquaintance, usu with a view to having sexual relations: *The story opens with Grace being **picked up** by a good-looking Frenchman.* BRN ○ *'I'd be grateful if you'd keep your street **pick-ups*** (ie the women you ***pick up*** on the street) *out of my wife's house,' he said in a whisper of rage.* ASA

7 [Vn ⇆ p nom pass] find (sb) and arrest him or return him to custody. **S:** police, prison authorities. **O:** suspect, escaped prisoner: *He was implicated in a murder, and sooner or later they would **pick** him **up**.* HD ○ *The prisoners missing from the working party were **picked up** within forty-eight hours.* ○ *They complain that the **pick-up** operation netted only small fry* (= caught only rank-and-file terrorists). BBCTV

8 [Vn ⇆ p pass] receive or intercept (sth). **S:** radar, radio receiver. **O:** signal, message; plane, ship: *'Point all our aerials upwards. Then we'll **pick up** reflections of our own transmissions.'* TBC ○ *It should have been possible to **pick up** signals telling us more about the moon itself.* NS

9 [Vn ⇆ p pass] hear or gather (sth). **O:** story, rumour; (scrap of) information: *He's always on the prowl, **picking up** scraps of gossip.* ○ *'I hear their house is to be turned into a museum.' 'Where did you **pick** that **up**?'*

10 [Vn ⇆ p pass] acquire a knowledge of or skill in (sth), usu casually and without special study. **O:** some knowledge of politics, the law; painting, carpentry; (a smattering of) a language; philosophy, religion: *I **picked up** scraps of knowledge from a variety of sources.* SD ○ *Branson seems to have **picked up** his philosophy of food during his career with the Indian Civil Service.* OBS ○ *She isn't very quick at **picking up** the language.* PW

11 [Vp.n pass] buy or acquire (sth), usu as a bargain. **O:** bargain, snip; antique, objet d'art, furniture: *There are still some charming things to be **picked up** in Bruges itself, for a mere song* (ie for very little money). US ○ *Bric-a-brac **picked up** on his many journeys abroad filled the room.*

12 [Vp.n pass] acquire (sth) as one grows and develops; be infected by (sth). **O:** habit; accent, whine; allergy; virus: *He realized that he'd **picked up** the local accent; that was when he stopped noticing it in other people.* AF ○ *As she grew up she **picked up** the anxiety that young parents lavish on their firstborn.* SU

13 [Vp.n pass] win, secure (sth) in a contest. **O:** ⚠ support; votes: *Heseltine's campaign managers say they are **picking up** support from loyal Thatcherites.* OBS ○ *I think the Liberal Democrats will **pick up** a lot of votes, though perhaps not so many as in the by-election.* BBCR

14 [Vp.n] pay for meals, drinks, hospitality in hotels etc; be responsible for paying the large-scale debts of a business or country. **O:** ⚠ bill, check, (*US*) tab: *It's not strictly true that I have to **pick up** the checks. Quite often I get a free lunch and there's nothing to pay at the cocktail parties.* ST ○ *Small islands dependent on one crop can fall* *into serious difficulties of foreign exchange, and whoever* **picks up** *the bill can pick up political influence with it.* NS

15 [Vp, Vn ⇆ p pass] continue telling (a story etc) after an interruption (eg at the end of one episode in a series); manage to continue following (a story) etc after an interruption. **O:** story, tale; conversation; (thread of the) argument: *Terry expects us to* **pick up** *where we left off.* RT ○ *We* **pick up** *the story again at the point where John has lost his job at the newspaper office.* ○ *Because of the clatter outside I lost the thread of the discussion and had difficulty* **picking** *it* **up** *again.* = take up 8.

16 [Vp nom] get better; become more lively. **S:** child; health, condition: *'You'll soon* **pick up** *after a day or two in bed.'* ○ *Her health and spirits* **picked up** *after a week at the seaside.* ○ *Another draught of alcohol injected fire into his body. 'My God, this is a perfect* **pick-me-up**,*'* Pop said (ie a perfect way to make him ***pick up***). BFA □ note unusual nom form. = perk up.

17 [Vp nom] improve or recover. **S:** sales, exports; the market; sterling: *The shares* **picked up** *after an early spate of panic selling.* ○ *Consumption of wines and spirits* **picked up** *again before the New Year.* ○ *We're still waiting for the promised* **pick-up** *in trade.*

18 [Vp] start to function again. **S:** motor, engine: *The port engine spluttered and seemed about to cut out; then it* **picked up** *again.*

pick-me-up [nom (Vp)] ⇨ pick up 16.

pick oneself up [Vn.p] get to one's feet after a fall: */Can't lose my confidence if I slip, /I'm grateful for the pleasant trip,/ I* **pick myself up**, */Dust myself off,/ Start all over again.* D FIELDS, J KERN

pick up the pieces [Vp.n] (*informal*) repair a relationship, organization etc that has been badly damaged: *There is just one man bold enough to try to* **pick up the pieces** *and launch the left wing on a new departure: François Mitterand.* L

pick up speed [Vp.n] move more quickly; accelerate. **S:** train, ship: *The train* **picked up speed** *as it reached open country.* ○ *The car wallowed through the slush ... then out on the main road, it* **picked up speed**. AT

pick up the threads [Vp.n] readjust to a job, a way of life or a relationship after a period of absence or separation: *'You must realize that I've been away from the job for five years. It'll take me a little time to* **pick up the threads** *again.'* ○ *With some lingering mistrust on both sides Bill and Jane set about* **picking up the threads** *of their marriage.*

pick-up (truck) [nom (Vn.p)] small commercial vehicle with, at the back, an open top and low sides and tail-board: *Plumbers, electricians and jobbing builders often use* **pick-up trucks** *to transport their tools and materials.* ○ *A young man in a top hat plays jazz on a piano wedged into the back of a parked* **pick-up truck**. OBS ⇨ pick up 2.

pick up on 1 [Vp.pr] return to (an issue) for special comment or discussion. **o:** point, issue, matter, question, topic: (TV discussion following the Budget speech to Parliament) *'Shall we* **pick up on** *some of the main points the Chancellor has made already?'* BBCTV

2 [Vn.p.pr pass] (*informal*) comment critically on (sth) said by (sb). **O:** him etc; speaker, chairman. **o:** an earlier, remark; something he said a moment ago: *'I'd like to* **pick** *you* **up on** *something you said about immigration.'* ○ *'She went on to speak about funding for the Health Service, and of course she was* **picked up on** *that.'*

pick up with [Vp.pr pass] (*informal*) make the acquaintance of (sb); meet. **o:** curious fellow, odd creature, shady character: *He's liable to bring home any odd character that he* **picks up with** *in a pub.*

pick an argument/a quarrel/a fight (with) [Vn.pr pass] look for a reason or excuse for quarrelling or fighting (with sb): *'We've got our chance at last. Why do you have to spoil it by* **picking quarrels with** *me about nothing?'* AITC ○ *'Peter's going through a tiresome stage. Always* **picking fights with** *his brother for no reason at all.'*

picture

picture to oneself [Vn.pr] summon a picture of (sth) into one's mind; imagine. **O:** effect, result; scene; devastation, congestion: *Readers can* **picture to themselves** *the utter confusion that would result if the procession were routed through these narrow streets.*

piece

piece out [Vp.n pass adj] complete (sth) by adding pieces or parts. **O:** story, account; picture, design: *You must* **piece out** *the full story from your own imaginations.*

piece together 1 [Vn ⇆ p pass adj] assemble, fit together (parts); form (a whole) by fitting parts together. **O:** patches, scraps (of material); rug, blankets: *Bits of wood and metal were* **pieced together** *to form a roof.* ○ *She* **pieced together** *a blanket from knitted woollen squares.*

2 [Vn ⇆ p pass adj] join together (parts of a story etc); compose a (story etc) by joining parts together. **O:** clues, shreds of evidence; episodes, events; case; story, account: *I gradually* **pieced together** *the hints and clues which led to my final conclusions.* LIFE ○ *It was only much later that we were able to* **piece together** *the full story.*

pile

pile in/into [Vp, Vpr, Vn ⇆ p pass, Vn.pr pass] (get a group etc to) press into a space too small to take the group in comfort. **o:** car, boat, flat : [Vp] *'**Pile in**! There's room for a few more on the floor.'* ○ [Vpr] All five of us ***piled into*** *Peter's car and headed back to the flat.* ○ [Vn.p] We ***piled*** *all the luggage* ***in*** *and drove off.* = crowd in/into.

pile on the agony [Vp.n] (*informal*) make the description of an event more painful than it need be: *She* will ***pile on the agony*** *when she describes her visits to the dentist: she makes a filling sound like a major operation.* ⇨ next entry

pile it on [Vn.p] (*informal*) make sth seem more important or dramatic than it is; exaggerate: *John* does ***pile it on***: *anyone would think he's the only one with domestic problems.* ○ *'Stop* **piling it on**: *it's not half as bad as you make out.'* ⇨ previous entry

pile the pressure on [Vn ⇆ p pass] make sb work or struggle harder by giving him more tasks etc to do. **S:** employer, teacher; opposing team: *The tutors* **piled on the pressure** *from the very beginning of the course.* ○ *The French forwards really* **piled the pressure on** *in the second half of the Scotland match.*

pile on runs [Vp.n pass] (*cricket*) add quickly to one's total of runs. **S:** batsman, (batting) side: *There was no fall in the scoring rate when the new ball was taken: the West Indies continued to* ***pile on runs***.

pile on/onto 1 [Vn ⇆ p pass, Vn.pr pass] place (sth) in heaps upon (sb/sth). **O:** coal, wood; luggage. **o:** fire, stove; bed: *Wood was* ***piled on*** *the bonfire* (cf *The bonfire was* ***piled with*** *wood*) *till the flames roared.* ○ *The verandah outside my bedroom was* ***piled*** *high* ***with*** *a strange variety of cages* (or: *A strange variety of cages were* ***piled*** *high* ***on*** *the verandah*). BB = heap on/upon 1.

2 [Vn ⇆ p pass, Vn.pr pass] (*informal*) place an undue amount of (sth) on (sb). **O:** work; responsibility. **o:** staff; colleague: *Why is it that all the extra work gets* ***piled onto*** *me at Christmas time?*

pile out/out of [Vp, Vpr] (*informal*) emerge in a mass or crowd, usu from a confined space. **o:** room, car, aeroplane: *We* ***piled out of*** *the back of the car and stretched our cramped limbs.*

pile up 1 [Vp nom] collect in one place because work has stopped or large quantities of goods etc are arriving. **S:** goods, exports; mail. **A:** at the docks, in warehouses: *Perishable goods are* ***piling up*** *at the docks because of the seamen's strike.* ○ *Posting at peak times often leads to a* ***pile-up*** *of mail at the Post Office.*

2 [Vp] grow in size or number; accumulate. **S:** fears, anxieties; tensions; responsibilities: *I began to doubt my ability to contain the curiosity that had been* ***piling up*** *within me.* 50MH ○ *Domestic troubles* ***piled up*** *on her.* EB

pile-up [nom (Vp)] crash involving several vehicles (often because they have been travelling too close to each other): *There was a* ***pile-up*** *on the M25 involving a van and four cars.*

pile with [Vn.pr pass] ⇨ pile on/onto 1.

pilot

pilot through [Vn.p pass, Vn.pr pass] pass (sth) through various legislative etc stages. **S:** minister, back-bencher; councillor. **O:** Bill, measure; scheme, project. **o:** second reading, committee stage: *Mr Ashley successfully* ***piloted*** *his Private Member's Bill* ***through*** *its various stages.* = put through 2.

pin

pin against [Vn.pr pass rel] press (sth/sb) firmly to (sth), so that he/it cannot move away. **o:** tree, wall, door: *She remembered the pitiless wind* ***pinning*** *her dress* ***against*** *her body.* FL ○ *He was* ***pinned against*** *the fence by a boy twice his size; he could hardly breathe.*

pin down 1 [Vn ⇆ p pass] prevent (sb) from moving from cover or showing himself; trap. **S:** beam, tree, girder; rubble, masonry; machine-gun fire, shelling: *They seemed to have* ***pinned*** *his legs* ***down*** *under a heavy weight.* HD ○ *Our troops were* ***pinned down*** *in their trenches by accurate mortar fire.*

2 [Vn ⇆ p pass adj] define the nature of (sth/sb) exactly; specify. **O:** essence, character, tone; him etc: *And — this is the part I can't* ***pin down*** *in words — he had conveyed, to the right onlooker, that he knew what he was doing.* CON ○ *He remains a difficult person to* ***pin down****, largely because of the contradictory opinions held by those who knew him.* EB □ often neg, or preceded by *hard, difficult, impossible,* as in the second example. = nail down 3.

3 [Vn.p pass] get (sb) to say exactly what he believes or intends to do. **O:** official, politician; expert, pundit: *He's not the easiest man to* ***pin down*** *politically; he changes his views all the time.* ○ *Have you tried* ***pinning*** *him* ***down*** *on the question of local taxation?* = nail down 2.

pin one's faith in/on/to [Vn.pr pass emph rel] trust or depend on (sb/sth) to help one. **o:** a new messiah; religion, socialism; a political movement: *Charles* ***pinned his faith in*** *the Advertiser* (a newspaper) *to tell him what happened.* HD ○ *'But we objectors over here in this corner are* ***pinning our faith to*** *Yvette's question. It seems to me a very good one.'* TBC ○ *The fundamental point remained unchanged; it was* ***to*** *that that I* ***pinned my hopes***. MFM

pin on/upon [Vn.pr] say that (sb) is responsible for (sth). **O:** blame, responsibility; crime, robbery, break-in; it: *'How like you to* ***pin*** *the blame* ***on*** *me!'* ○ *He was harmless enough. The police have no call to be* ***pinning*** *it* ***on*** *Harry.* TFD = blame on.

pin up 1 [Vn ⇆ p pass adj] keep (sth) at a higher level with pins. **O:** skirt, hem, flap: *In the afternoon the ladies walked, ...* ***pinning up*** *Gwen John's skirts so that she could keep up.* GJ

2 [Vn ⇆ p nom pass adj] attach (sth) to a surface with pins. **O:** drawing, photograph, map; hanging, curtain: *The photograph of Therese Martin was* ***pinned up*** *on one wall.* HB

pin-up [nom (Vn.p)] photograph of an attractive young man or woman, or of a film or pop star, attached to a wall; person represented in the photograph: ***Pin-ups*** *used to be, and still are, standard decoration for servicemen's billets and the cabs of lorries* UL

pine

pine away [Vp] grow pale and thin through sorrow: *'She would just have* ***pined away*** *in that desert without the sparkle of London life.'* GOV

pine for [Vpr pass adj emph rel] desire to have (sth) strongly. **o:** attention, companionship; peace, seclusion; former times, the good old days: *I knew you'd be* ***pining for*** *my company, so I've come early.* GL ○ *Working-class people do not much* ***pine for*** *their lost freedom; they never regarded it as more than temporary.* UL = long for.

pip

pipped at/on the post [pass (Vn.pr)] narrowly beaten in a contest: *Most people feel that their worth is not always being appreciated and that they have sometimes been* ***pipped at the post*** *by people less able than they.* SNP ○ *Her pale green eyes were as baleful as the eyes of a cat* ***pipped on the post*** *by a record-breaking mouse.* PP □ there is a humorous reference in the second example to the origin of the idiom in racing; at racecourses, a post marks the finish of the race, where a horse can be narrowly beaten, or pipped, by another.

pipe

pipe down [Vp] (*informal*) make less noise or be quiet: *Ashore, '****Pipe down****' means silence. Afloat it means several things: men working aloft to return on deck, washed clothes or hammocks to be removed, or simply 'hands turn in'.* RFW ○ *'Have* *you come to see Mariette?' 'No, **pipe down**, you loony. Nobody knows anything about that.'* DBM □ usu imperative.

pipe up [Vp] begin to speak, usu in a thin, high voice: *The still small voice **piped up**.* PP ○ *Suddenly Irma **piped up** and said: 'Please, what is a harpy?'* PW □ may follow or precede direct speech: *'What are you doing about us?' she **piped up**.*

piss

piss about/around [Vp] (*taboo*) behave in a foolish, boisterous way: *'Look, just stop **pissing about**, will you? I've got work to do.'* = mess about/around.

piss about/ around (with) [Vp.pr pass, Vn.p pass] handle or treat (sb/sth) clumsily, incompetently etc. **o** [Vp.pr]: bloke, fellow, girl; delivery, order; staff. **O** [Vn.p]: people, guys: *'Smith and Murray have been **pissing around** with that order since January. Tell them, if they don't bloody well get a move on we'll take our business somewhere else.'* ○ *'Stop **pissing** me **about**, Charlie, I'm not in the mood for it today.'* = mess about/around (with) 2.

piss off 1 [Vp] (*taboo*) go away: *He told me to **piss off**, or he'd clobber me.* ○ *'I've had about as much of you as I can stand. Now, **piss off**!'* □ usu imperative. = clear off 1.

2 [Vn.p pass adj] (*taboo*) bore or irritate (sb). **S:** work, routine; voice, music: *'It really **pisses** you **off**, doesn't it, the way he thinks we've got to jump like trained monkeys every time he snaps his fingers!'* ○ *By this time Bill was really **pissed off** with the job and was looking for a way out — any way out.*

pit

pit against [Vn.pr pass emph rel] (*formal*) set (sb/sth) in competition against (sb/sth). **O:** strength; wits, intelligence; will, courage; oneself: *He was an adventurer **pitting** his brains **against** authority.* ARG ○ *The human intellect was but a feeble instrument when **pitted against** the power of natural forces.* RTH ○ *In the shed is a new electronic brain, **against** which Harry is eager to **pit** his wits.* TVT = match against.

pitch

pitch in/into 1 [Vp, Vpr pass] (*informal*) attack (sb) physically or with insults etc. **o:** opponent; leader, organizer: *Then Bill **pitched in**, waving his arms about.* ○ *By this stage, she was so furious with the delays that she was ready to **pitch into** the chairman of the travel company himself.* = lam into, lay into.

2 [Vp, Vpr] start to eat (food) greedily, with appetite. **o:** meal, spread; stew, rice: *'Dinner's on the table. **Pitch in**!'* ○ *After a day out in the fields, they **pitched into** the food with a rare appetite.* = dig in/into 2, tuck in/into 2.

3 [Vp] (*informal*) begin working (on sth) energetically. **O:** job, task: *He'd never need telling: he'd just take his coat off and **pitch in**.* ○ *They grabbed spades and **pitched into** the digging.*

pitch in (with) [Vp, Vp.pr] give help or support (in a particular form). **S:** friend, neighbour, ally. **o:** story, report; figures, statistics; donation, subscription: *They asked people to help ... build a barricade and there was lots of collaboration. Even little boys **pitched in**.* IND ○ *Local businessmen **pitched in with** an offer of £1000 to cover advertising costs.*

place

place above □ in this and all of the following place entries, the grammatical patterns, definitions, collocates etc, are the same as for the corresponding put entries (to which cross-reference is made). ⇨ put above.

place at a premium ⇨ put at a premium.

place before ⇨ put before 2.

place sb in an awkward etc position ⇨ put in an awkward etc position.

place in inverted commas ⇨ put in inverted commas.

place in jeopardy ⇨ put in jeopardy.

place one's trust in ⇨ put one's trust in.

place one's cards on the table ⇨ put one's cards on the table.

place a construction on ⇨ put a construction on.

place a premium on ⇨ put a premium on.

place on one side ⇨ put on one side 1.

place pressure on/upon ⇨ put pressure on/upon.

place a strain on/upon ⇨ put a strain on/upon.

place a/one's finger to one's lips ⇨ put a/one's finger to one's lips.

place a match to ⇨ put a match to.

plague

plague with [Vn.pr pass emph rel] address (so many questions etc) to sb that they burden and irritate him. **O:** office, department; employer, teacher. **o:** questions, inquiries; suggestions; fears, doubts: *At this time of year university admissions offices are **plagued with** inquiries from anxious applicants.* ○ *The manufacturers are **plagued with** supply problems: they can't get hold of enough electrical components of the right quality.* □ usu passive.

plan

plan ahead [Vp] arrange things in advance: *A general may have to **plan** months **ahead**, a platoon officer only a few hours.* ○ *You should **plan ahead** for really good cold-meat-and-salad eating.* TO

plan for [Vpr pass] consider (sth), take (sth) into account, when arranging things. **o:** expansion, contraction; increased demand; falling numbers: *They're **planning for** a three-fold increase in student numbers.* ○ *I'll be honest: ... my baby was not exactly **planned for**.* AT

plan on [Vpr pass] intend to (do sth). **o:** meeting him, eating here, staying overnight: *'I hadn't exactly **planned on** spending the weekend in Leeds.'* ○ *'Do you **plan on** staying with Muriel forever?'* AT □ object is the *-ing* form of a v.

plan out [Vn ⇆ p pass adj] organize (sth) in detail or in stages. **O:** dinner, party; course of lectures, programme of work; weekend, evening: *He took care to **plan out** his teaching for the following week.* ○ *They sat down at the kitchen table to **plan out** the meal.* = plot out.

plane

plane away/off [Vn ⇆ p pass adj] remove (sth) with a woodworker's plane. **S:** carpenter, cabinet-maker. **O:** irregularity, rough patch: *The cuts and scratches that the packers made on the desk can be **planed away**.*

plane down [Vn ⇆ p pass adj] make (sth) thinner, reduce it, with a woodworker's plane. **O:** surface, edge; board, beam: *You need to* **plane down** *the edges until all the roughness disappears.* ○ ***Plane*** *one side of the panel* **down** *until it fits snugly into place.*

plant

plant out [Vn ⇆ p pass adj] (*horticulture*) take (a young plant) from a pot or seed tray (in a greenhouse or glass frame) and plant it in open ground. **O:** seedling, young plant; patch, flower-bed: *Sow sweetcorn in pots from now until May, for* ***planting out*** *in early June.* GF ○ *Container-grown roses can be* ***planted out*** *at any time.* BEST

plaster

plaster one's hair down [Vn ⇆ p pass adj] (*informal*) make one's hair lie flat by coating it with hair gel etc: *The gang wore leather jackets and had long* ***hair plastered down*** *over their ears.*

plaster over/up [Vn ⇆ p pass adj] cover or seal (sth) with plaster. **O:** crack, blemish, hole: *The cracks in the ceiling have to be* ***plastered up*** *before you can start painting.*

play

play about/around (with) [Vp, Vp.pr pass] handle, treat (sb/sth) in a casual and irresponsible way. **o:** young girl, sb else's wife; other people's money, property; dangerous drugs, explosives: *It's time he stopped* ***playing around*** *and began to take life seriously.* ○ *He's* ***playing around with*** *a girl young enough to be his daughter.* ○ *This is not a substance that should be* ***played about with***. = fool about/around (with).

play along (with) [Vp, Vp.pr pass] (*informal*) agree with (sb), or accept (sth), and act accordingly. **o:** leader, majority; scheme, system, arrangement: *But he did have the sense to* ***play along with*** *the school system to the extent of going into the Sixth.* CON ○ *Your grandmother prefers to believe her son wasn't a murderer. She may even persuade the police to* ***play along with*** *her fantasies.* TFD = go along with 2.

play at 1 [Vpr] pretend for fun to be (sb) or do (sth). **o:** mothers and fathers, cops and robbers, pirates, cowboys; keeping a shop, camping out: *At this age, children enjoy* ***playing at*** *pirates or cowboys.* **2** [Vpr pass] do, perform (sth) casually or half-heartedly. **o:** marriage, business; being a father, being a businessman: *Business is just something he* ***plays at****; the one thing that really interests him is golf.* ○ *This is a job that needs to be tackled whole-heartedly—not* ***played at*** *in an amateurish way.*

what be playing at [Vpr] (*informal*) expression of anger at sb who is behaving foolishly and/or dangerously: (mother finds small boy playing with matches) *'And* ***what*** *do you think* ***you're playing at****?'* ○ *'There's a lot of banging and crashing coming from Fred's room. Do you mind asking him* ***what*** *on earth* ***he's playing at****?'* □ used in direct or indirect questions.

play back 1 [Vn ⇆ p nom pass adj] run (sth) forward through a recorder again, so that the material recorded on it can be heard or seen. **O:** tape, recording; film, video; conversation, discussion: *I'm going to* ***play back*** *to you part of the statement you made to the inspector.* ○ *Let's have a* ***play-back*** *of the first half of Act One.* □ the nom form play-back refers to the action of playing sth back; note attrib use in: *The engineer put our edited cassette into the* ***play-back*** *machine and ran through it.* OBS = run back. **2** [Vn ⇆ p pass adj] (*sport*) return (the ball) with a kick or stroke. **O:** ball, shot; volley, lob: *He* ***played*** *a good-length ball* ***back*** *to the bowler.* ○ *There is always the danger of being caught by the bowler from a* ***played-back*** *ball.*

play down [Vp.n pass adj] make (sth) appear less important than it is. **O:** one's part, contribution; danger, crisis, defeat: *Major* ***plays down*** *the significance of the event.* OBS ○ *The letters to his mother deliberately* ***play down*** *his feelings for both.* TU ↔ play up 3.

play for laughs [Vpr] act, perform, in a way that is intended to make people laugh. **S:** actor; comedy team; show: ***Playing for laughs*** *on Monday is Benny Hill, whose shows are always worth a second look.* TVT ○ *By low-brow comedy I mean down-to-earth films that* ***play for laughs****. No messages, no nonsense.* RT

play for safety [Vpr] behave in such a way that one is secure, free from harm: *They continue to be married and buried in church and chapel, to have children baptized there. ... Are they simply ...* ***playing for safety****?* UL

play for time [Vpr] try to delay defeat, an embarrassing admission etc, by keeping one's opponent or questioner at a distance. **S:** boxer, cricketer; commander, army; politician, government: *'I can't hear a word,' said Madge. This was untrue. She was* ***playing for time****.* UTN ○ *I* ***played for time*** *a bit more, but finally he got me to admit that I could come, and that I didn't have to return till the next day.* CON

play the New Year in [Vn ⇆ p pass] play to celebrate and announce the start of a New Year. **S:** band, orchestra, Scots piper: *Veteran of* ***playing in the New Year****, Jimmy Shand, along with his band, will be playing for dancers at Perth.* RT ○ *They* ***played*** *the Old Year out with Auld Lang Syne and* ***the New Year in*** *with Roll Out the Barrel.*

play a part (in) [Vn.pr pass emph rel] be an important factor or element in (sth). **S:** idea, feeling; belief, faith; her involvement, commitment. **adj:** some, any; a large, considerable; little, no. **o:** book, play; thought, philosophy; changing attitudes, reforming the system: *Investment considerations* ***played*** *no* ***part in*** *the acquisition of works of art* (by banks). NTG ○ ***The part played*** *by religion* (ie ***in*** the opening up of Africa) *was very great.* BN = figure in.

play a part/role (in) [Vn.pr pass emph rel] be prominent and active (in sth). **S:** colleague, partner. **adj:** leading, prominent, important, significant; slight, negligible. **o:** success, recovery; making this possible: ***The*** *active* ***part*** *which the Trades Unions have* ***played*** *has certainly served to make Scotland's economic needs much better understood.* SC ○ ***In*** *bringing about such a change the Churches* ***have a*** *very important* ***role*** *to* ***play****.* SC

play into sb's hands [Vpr] act to sb's advantage, usu by doing sth which that person has planned or hoped for. **o:** (**of**) rival, enemy; authorities: *She deliberately got transferred to the same airline as me, and I* ***played into her hands*** *right away by falling for her hints about wanting a quiet home and children.* DC ○ *A vast armaments programme* *should not be allowed to undermine economic development. This would be to* **play** *right* **into the hands of** *the Chinese.* T

play off [Vp nom] (of teams or competitors that have obtained the same number of points or won the same number of matches in a championship) play the deciding match: *Uruguay and Brazil came out on top and had to* **play off** *for the Championship.* BBCTV ○ *There will be a* **play-off** *between Smith and Peters next week.*

play off against [Vn.p.pr pass] make (sb) argue with or fight against (sb else) for one's own advantage. **O:** competitor, rival; firm, country: *Freud* **played** *the two* **off against** *each other.* F ○ *One way of securing the market was to* **play** *our rivals* **off against** *each other.*

play on [Vp] (*sport*) continue to play; resume play: *A linesman signalled 'off-side', but the referee overruled him and ordered '***play on***'.*

play on/upon 1 [Vpr pass] explore for humorous or poetic effect the various meanings of particular words or phrases. **o:** meanings; ambiguity, contrast: *The poem* **plays on** *the various possible meanings of the verbs 'bend', 'break' and 'mend'.* ○ *The writer* **plays upon** *the contrasts between the ordinary meanings of words and their technical senses.*

2 [Vpr pass] exploit or develop (sth), usu to harm sb. **o:** fear, suspicion; credulity, superstition: *The Empire* **played upon** *its neighbours' fears of military expansion to obtain trade concessions from them.* ○ *Their memories of past injustices were cleverly* **played upon***.*

play out 1 [Vp.n pass] perform (sth) over which one has little control; enact. **O:** episode, interlude, scene, drama: *He was conducted past the dingy form rooms where the pitiful farce of his childhood had been* **played out***, act after endless act.* HD ○ *It is clear that a vast human tragedy is being* **played out** *in the north of the country.* BBCR □ usu passive.

2 [Vp.n pass] express in action (an inner vision). **O:** role, part; fantasy: *Fräulein Preiswerk* **played out** *in various trance-like states a number of roles.* JUNG

played out [pass adj (Vn.p)] having lost one's talent, vitality etc. **S:** footballer, athlete; businessman; painter: *He's not the writer he was. People are beginning to say he's* **played out***.* ○ *She drifted from one affair to another, finally setting up house with a* **played-out** *opera singer.* □ used with *appear*, etc. = clapped out.

play the Old Year out [Vn ⇆ p pass] play to celebrate the end of an Old Year. ↔ play the New Year in.

play up 1 [Vp, Vn.p] (*informal*) cause discomfort or pain. **S:** back, leg; rheumatism, arthritis: *My shoulder's* **playing up** *horribly.* ○ *His old war wounds have been* **playing** *him* **up** *again.*

2 [Vp, Vn.p] (*informal*) try to anger or annoy (sb). **S:** son, sister; pupil: *Since he resented his mother trying to bully him into obedience, he* **played up***.* BRN ○ *Don't you see how unhappy he must be with this woman? That's why he had this breakdown—because she* **played** *him* **up***.* PW

3 [Vp.n pass adj] make (sth) appear more important than it is; exaggerate. **O:** contribution, role, part; incident, success; loss, defeat: *How like George to* **play up** *the importance of his contribution!* ↔ play down.

play up to [Vp.pr pass] flatter or encourage (sb) so as to to win an advantage for oneself. **o:** employer, boss; pretty woman: *'***Play up to** *her, won't you? Be the husband who's taking a holiday—playing while the cat's away.'* PW ○ *He's the sort of man who hates being* **played up to***. He prefers a more straightforward approach.*

play upon 1 [Vpr pass] ⇨ play on/upon 1.

2 [Vpr pass] ⇨ play on/upon 2.

play with 1 [Vpr pass rel] amuse oneself through games, make-believe etc (with sb). **o:** son, daughter; neighbour's child: *In Hyde Park there were children they could* **play with***.* BRN ○ *Riding absorbed him completely, and he found no time to* **play with** *Mary Ann.* GE

2 [Vpr pass rel] amuse oneself by handling or using (sth). **o:** (toy) soldier, doll; computer: *'Where's Stephen?' 'Up in the attic* **playing with** *his toy railway, I expect.'*

3 [Vpr rel] handle (sth) in a casual, absent-minded way. **o:** necklace, ring; food: *While we spoke, the manager* **played with** *a carved paper-knife.* = toy with 1.

4 [Vpr pass] treat (sb/sth) lightly or insincerely. **o:** him etc; feelings, affections: *You can* **play with** *a woman's affections once too often.* = dally with 2, toy with 2, trifle with.

5 [Vpr rel] consider (sth) but not very seriously. **o:** notion, idea, scheme: *She's often* **played with** *the idea of emigrating to Canada, but that's as far as it's gone.* = dally with 1, flirt with 2, toy with 3.

play the devil/hell with [Vn.pr] (*informal*) reproach, reprimand (sb) very severely. **S:** parent, boss. **o:** child, employee: *'Dad'll* **play** *merry* **hell with** *you when he finds out you've broken his favourite record.'* ○ *Alice would accept these things* (ie self-pity and class-consciousness)*, though she'd* **play the devil with** *me for my stupidity.* RATT □ *merry* only used before hell.

play hell with [Vn.pr] (*informal*) seriously disturb or upset (sth/sb). **S:** climate; altitude, pressure; food, water. **o:** experiment, test; digestion: *The salt water has* **played hell with** *my books and papers.* ○ *I've had enough dope* (= drugs) *to* **play hell with** *my nervous system.* TST

play with fire [Vpr] do things that might lead to trouble: *She gave him what was intended as an affectionate kiss, but ... it turned into a soft deep gently pushing one. ... Oh, they were* **playing with fire** *all right.* TGLY

plead

plead (with) (for) [Vpr pass emph rel] beg (sb) to grant some special favour. **o:** (**with**) guard, captor; (**for**) one's life; mercy, forgiveness; release, freedom. **Inf:** to spare her life, to forgive you, to let you go: *With that kind of man you will* **plead** *in vain.* ○ *'You can try* **pleading with** *the landlord* **for** *more time to pay, but I doubt whether he'll listen.'* □ *to forgive you* etc can be used instead of *for forgiveness* etc. = appeal (to) (for).

plod

plod away (at) [Vp, Vp.pr pass] (*informal*) work in a slow, dull, laborious way (at sth). **o:** studies; French, maths; job; banking: *He's not the kind to make sharp leaps forward. Just keeps* **plodding**

away. ○ *Mike's not content to* ***plod away at*** *a desk job for ever*.

plod on [Vp emph] continue to walk, work etc at a steady slow pace: *There Péguy eventually spent the night before* ***plodding on*** *to Chartres*. AF

plonk

plonk down [Vn ⇆ p pass] (*informal*) place (sth) roughly or heavily on a surface. **O:** dish, bag, box; money: *The postman was able to compel any citizen to assist him to carry the mail bags just for one mile. After that the citizen could* ***plonk*** *them* ***down*** *on the road*. WI ○ *'Come on the trip if you like, but you'll have to share in the expenses. So* ***plonk down*** *your money!'* = plump down.

plonk (oneself) down [Vp, Vn.p] sit down heavily: *She* ***plonked down*** *on a convenient sofa*. ○ *'I just feel like* ***plonking myself down*** *in a pub and having a beer.'* = plump (oneself) down.

plot

plot out [Vn ⇆ p pass] plan (sth) in advance, in one's mind or on paper. **O:** plan, programme; arrangements; evening; celebration: *We had already* ***plotted out*** *the weekend programme*. ○ *She mischievously invented a game called Bad Parties, which involved* ***plotting out*** *frightful combinations of guests*. EB = map out, plan out.

plough

plough back (into) [Vn ⇆ p pass adj, Vn.p.pr pass] spend (profits etc) on developing (sth). **O:** takings, earnings, profits. **o:** business; development, research; retooling (the plant): *We must increase the rate of* ***ploughing back*** *new money* ***into*** *re-equipment and expansion*. OBS ○ *My father had been* ***ploughing back*** *much of the profits* ***into*** *the land and saving the rest for death duties*. RFW

plough in/into [Vn ⇆ p pass adj, Vn.pr pass] cover or bury (sth) with earth from a plough. **O:** crop; stubble, manure. **o:** soil, land: *That year the farmers couldn't get the right price for their cabbages and had to* ***plough*** *them* ***in***. ○ *The* ***ploughing-in*** *of a quick growing crop as green manure… is sometimes used to increase fertility*. COS

plough into [Vpr pass] drive violently into (sth). **S:** car, lorry; train; tank: *A delivery van* ***ploughed into*** *the back of the car*. ○ *Coaches hurtled off the track and* ***ploughed into*** *the embankment*.

plough through [Vpr pass] (*informal*) read, study (sth) laboriously. **o:** book, essay, thesis; legislation: *We* ***ploughed through*** *every document that could possibly have a bearing on the case*. = wade through 2.

plough up 1 [Vn ⇆ p pass adj] open up (the ground) for planting with a plough. **O:** ground; field: *The ground beneath the trees had been* ***ploughed up*** *for potatoes*. INN

2 [Vn ⇆ p pass adj] uncover (sth) with a plough. **O:** potato, turnip; metal objects: *In parts of Northern France, farmers still* ***plough up*** *shell fragments, bullets and grenades*.

pluck

pluck out/out of [Vn ⇆ p pass adj, Vn.pr pass] withdraw (sth) sharply or quickly. **O:** nail, thorn, needle. **o:** flesh, limb: *He bent over and* ***plucked*** *the thorn* ***out*** *with his teeth*. ○ *He* ***plucked*** *the box* ***out of*** *the fire seconds before the flames caught it*. = draw out/out of 2.

pluck up courage [Vp.n] overcome one's fears sufficiently to say or do sth. **Inf:** to speak to her, to protest, to intervene: *At last Gerald* ***plucked up courage*** *to say, 'Well, for me, Miss Dollie hasn't changed at all, Mrs Salad.'* ASA ○ *STANLEY: You told him you thought the furniture we make was shoddy and vulgar? CLIVE: (****plucking up*** *a little* ***courage****) Well, those terrible oak cupboards*. FFE ⇨ summon up.

plug

plug away (at) [Vp, Vp.pr pass] (*informal*) work persistently (at sth). **o:** homework, housework, accounts; German, physics: *'How is the French coming on?' 'Oh, I keep* ***plugging away****.'* ○ *'Don't you want to be read?' Mrs Jones demanded. 'Can't think why you* ***plug away at*** *your book if you don't.'* US = peg away (at).

plug in/into [Vn ⇆ p pass adj, Vn.pr pass] connect (sth) to the power supply by means of a plug. **O:** (electric) cooker, kettle; radio, TV; earphones. **o:** mains, socket; portable radio: *She* ***plugged in*** *the radio and switched on, and there was the familiar hum*. TT

plug up [Vn ⇆ p pass adj] fill (sth) with a plug of wood, plaster, etc. **O:** hole, gap, crack: ***Plug up*** *any cracks in the panel with plastic wood*.

plumb

plumb in/into [Vp.n pass adj, Vn.pr pass] connect (an appliance) to the water and drainage systems of a house. **O:** washing machine, dish-washer, shower: *Most washing machines … are better permanently* ***plumbed in***. STDIY ○ *Overflows from baths and cisterns can now be* ***plumbed*** *back* ***into*** *their own waste pipes, thus avoiding soaking brickwork*. SWIA

plump

plump down [Vn ⇆ p pass] (*informal*) place (sb/sth) down quickly and decisively. **O:** baby; shopping bag; (playing-)card, entrance fee, membership card: *The child was* ***plumped down*** *on the counter while Jane rummaged in her bag*. ○ *He* ***plumped*** *his money* ***down*** *to secure one of the few remaining tickets*. = plonk down.

plump (oneself) down [Vp, Vn.p] (*informal*) sink quickly and heavily. **A:** into an armchair; onto the floor: *She glanced quickly around the room and* ***plumped down*** *on the only available chair*. = plonk (oneself) down.

plump for [Vpr pass adj] (*informal*) choose (sth) with decision and confidence. **o:** a week in the country, a trip to Paris; a new dish-washer: *I wanted the red car, but Mary* ***plumped for*** *the blue one with grey seats*. ○ *He offered André Gide English lessons for five francs an hour, but Gide* ***plumped for*** *the Berlitz School instead*. AF

plump up [Vn ⇆ p pass adj] pat (sth) with the hands to make it round and fat. **O:** cushion, pillow: *She smoothed out the sheets and* ***plumped up*** *the pillows*.

plunge

plunge in/into [Vp emph, Vpr emph rel] throw oneself head first in (to water). **o:** water; sea, river: *Robin dashed from the cabin, clambered onto the handrail, and* ***plunged in***. ○ *The van broke through the parapet and* ***plunged into*** *twenty feet of water*.

plunge into 1 [Vn.pr pass rel] make (sth) suddenly go dark. **O:** room, hall; house. **o:** ⚠ (total) dark-

ness, blackness; gloom: *A power failure* ***plunged*** *the whole house* ***into*** *sudden darkness.*
2 [Vpr rel, Vn.pr pass rel] (make sb) suddenly become unhappy, depressed etc. **S:** news; development, crisis; death, tragedy. **o:** (the depths of) despair, (deep) gloom, depression: *His death* ***plunged*** *Freud* ***into*** *a period of depression and intense introspection.* F ○ *I thought this kind of happiness must be unstable — just as suddenly as it had come it would collapse and* ***plunge*** *her* ***into*** *deeper despair.* SPL
3 [Vpr rel, Vn.pr pass rel] (make sb) suddenly begin to fight. **S** [Vpr], **O** [Vn.pr]**:** continent, country, people. **o:** ⚠ war, conflict, strife: *The country had* ***plunged*** *swiftly* ***into*** *open conflict with its neighbours.* ○ *We were* ***plunged into*** *civil war by the attempted break-away of the eastern provinces.*
4 [Vpr rel] begin (an activity) suddenly and energetically. **o:** activity; discussion, study; speculation, gambling: *No sooner had they returned ... than Dickens* ***plunged into*** *games.* CD ○ *He* ***plunged into*** *every debate organized by the society.* JUNG
5 [Vpr rel, Vn.pr pass rel] (cause sb to) be suddenly overwhelmed by (poverty). **S** [Vpr], **O** [Vn.pr]**:** country, firm. **o:** debt, (financial) crisis: *The Government can surely not let things go on as they are, with the balance sheet* ***plunging*** *deeper and deeper* ***into*** *the red* (ie debt). NS ○ *... the poverty* ***into*** *which his wife and family were* ***plunged*** *by Maginn's irresponsibility.* TU

ply

ply between [Vpr] (*nautical*) travel regularly, provide a regular service, between (one place and another). **S:** steamer, ferry. **o:** the island and the mainland; Dover and Calais: *Ferries carrying passengers and commercial lorries* ***ply*** *daily* ***between*** *Hull and Rotterdam.*

ply with 1 [Vn.pr pass rel] give (sb) a steady supply of (sth). **o:** food, drink; cigarettes: *The visitors were sat down in armchairs and* ***plied with*** *food and drink.*
2 [Vn.pr pass rel] direct (sth) at (sb) in a steady stream. **o:** questions, queries, enquiries: *Relatives besieged the shipping offices and* ***plied*** *the staff* ***with*** *anxious inquiries.*

point

point the finger at [Vn.pr] accuse a particular individual or group of being responsible for a crime etc. **o:** leader, boss; organization, mob: *He said it was not his intention to* ***point the finger*** *at any individual for the deaths of the three miners.* G ○ *Mr Whitelaw could and did* ***point the*** *accusing* ***finger at*** *the Provisionals* (ie the Provisional IRA, in Northern Ireland), *and wondered aloud what kind of men they were.* L

point out 1 [Vn ⇆ p pass] show, indicate (sth/sb). **O:** beauty spot, place of interest; (principal) sights, attractions; boss, teacher: *The guide* ***pointed out*** *the best known paintings in the gallery.* ○ *'If you wait here, I'll* ***point*** *him* ***out*** *to you.'*
2 [Vn ⇆ p pass] make (sth) clear (to sb); explain. **O:** fact, truth; aspect, side (of a question); that the figures were wrong; how best to tackle the problem: *Not that he wasn't quick to see his own advantage, when it was* ***pointed out*** *to him.* PW ○ *The Mortonstowe transmitters were capable of handling an enormous quantity of information, as Kingsley was not slow to* ***point out***. TBC ○ *He rightly* ***pointed out*** *that the club would never have any difficulty selling the shares should it wish to.* H

point to 1 [Vpr pass] indicate (sth) when making a case or defending one's position etc. **o:** growth, increase; figure, amount: *In defence of her policy, the Minister* ***pointed to*** *the sharp decrease in road deaths.*
2 [Vpr] suggest, indicate (sth). **S:** (various) signs; evidence; statement, report. **o:** guilt, involvement; quick election, early withdrawal: *All the signs at the moment* ***point to*** *an early resumption of the fighting.*

point up [Vp.n pass] show (sth) more sharply; emphasize, underline. **O:** contrast, difference, change: *The recent wage increases* ***point up*** *still further the difference between past and present economic policies.* ○ *This admission only serves to* ***point up*** *an aspect of police work that the public fails to understand.* L

poke

poke about/around [Vp nom] (*informal*) search inquisitively; pry. **A:** among papers, possessions; in one's study, spare room: *'What are you doing* ***poking about*** *among my private papers?'* ○ *I only left them alone for a couple of minutes and when I came back they were having a* ***poke around*** *in my writing-desk.* = nose about/around/round.

poke fun at [Vn.pr pass(o) emph rel] ridicule, mock (sth). **o:** appearance, manner, speech; traditions: *Loyalty, patriotism, the old school tie — these were all things which we loved in our superior way to* ***poke fun at***. ○ *He was often* ***poked fun at*** *at school because of his shabby clothes.*

poke one's nose in/into [Vn.p, Vn.pr] (*informal*) take an unwelcome interest in (the concerns of others). **o:** ⚠ (sb else's) affairs, business, concerns: *'If you'd stop* ***poking your nose in*** *where it's not wanted, we might get some work done.'* ○ *JO: I don't want her* ***poking her nose into*** *my affairs.* TOH = pry (into).

poke up 1 [Vp, Vn ⇆ p pass] (make sth) appear out of or above the level of (sth). **S** [Vp], **O** [Vn.p]**:** head, hand; spear, gun; brush, rod: *Suddenly a head* ***poked up*** *out of the grass ahead of us.* ○ *Jim* ***poked*** *a long brush* ***up*** *through the pipe.*
2 [Vn ⇆ p pass] jab at (a fire) with a poker so that it burns more brightly: *He* ***poked*** *the fire* ***up*** *into a blaze.*

polish

polish off 1 [Vn ⇆ p pass adj] (*informal*) finish eating, writing etc (sth) quickly. **O:** dish, course; scrap, left-overs; work: *I can* ***polish off*** *the rest of the typing in no time.* ○ *The rest of the Christmas pudding was* ***polished off*** *by the children.* = finish off/up.
2 [Vn ⇆ p pass adj] (*informal*) defeat (sb) convincingly. **O:** opposition, contender: *Having got rid of the main opposition, he could* ***polish*** *the others* ***off*** *at his leisure.* ○ *In his first fight, he* ***polished off*** *a much more experienced boxer.* = finish off 2.

polish up 1 [Vp, Vn ⇆ p pass adj] become clean and bright with polishing; rub (sth) with polish until it becomes clean and bright. **S** [Vp], **O** [Vn.p]**:** (metal) ornament; weapon, armour; (varnished) table, chair: *These old pieces of brass have* **polished up** *beautifully.* ○ *The silver will need to be* **polished up** *for the dinner party.* ○ *The furniture could do with a good* **polishing-up**.

2 [Vp.n pass adj] (*informal*) work at (sth) to improve its quality or effectiveness. **O:** French, German; essay, report; (knowledge of) administration, business methods: *I'll have to* **polish up** *my Italian: it's getting a bit rusty.* ○ *Had he only* **polished up** *his verse, . . . he might have achieved great things.* HB ○ *Our sales techniques need* **polishing up**.

ponce

ponce about/around [Vp] (*taboo*) behave in a sloppy, idle or foolish way: *If Julian would just stop* **poncing about**, *we might get some work done.* = mess about/around.

ponder

ponder on/over [Vpr pass adj emph rel] consider (sth/sb) slowly and thoughtfully. **o:** past error, event; (future) outcome, result: *Brigit did not* **ponder on** *these things too long. The morning was too lovely for problems or gloom.* DC ○ *I* **pondered on** *William, stranded perhaps in Mesopotamian wastes, a lonely speck in that desert.* BM = muse on/over.

pop

pop across, along, away etc 1 [Vp emph, Vpr emph] (*informal*) move across etc quickly: *'I'll just* **pop across** *to get an evening paper.'* ○ *'Would you* **pop round** *to the baker's and pick up the cake?'* = nip across etc.

2 [Vn ⇆ p pass, Vn.pr pass] (*informal*) bring or take (sth) across etc quickly. **O:** book, parcel, letter: *'I'll just* **pop** *this letter* **into** *the post.'* ○ *John* **popped** *his head* **round** *the door.* ○ *'I'll* **pop** *the results* **over** *when I get a minute.'*

pop along, around, down, in, over, round [Vp] (*informal*) make a brief, casual visit to sb or a place: *'There's a meeting tonight, and I was thinking of* **popping along** *for half an hour or so.'* ○ *'I just* **popped in** *to say hullo.'* EHOW ○ *'They'll* **pop over** *in person if they don't get an answer.'* AT □ pop in this sense combines esp with the particles shown. ⇨ come along (to), come around/round (to) 1.

pop off 1 [Vp] (*informal*) die: *'Now you can all stop fighting over my money: I've no intention of* **popping off** *yet.'*

2 [Vp, Vn ⇆ p pass] (*informal*) (cause sth to) explode with a sharp sound. **S** [Vp], **O** [Vn.p]**:** firework; rifle, gun; (champagne) bottle, cork: *A brilliant flare* **popped off** *right over our heads.* ○ *There were children running all over the place,* **popping off** *toy guns.* ⇨ go off 5, let off 4, set off 1.

pop out/out of [Vp emph, Vpr] come out (of sth) with a sharp, explosive sound. **S:** cork, stopper. **o:** bottle, tube: *The cork* **popped out** *and the champagne gushed from the bottle.*

pop up 1 [Vp emph] (*informal*) appear, esp in unlikely places, when one is unexpected etc; surface: *Rogers disappeared for a whole year, then* **popped up** *in Bolivia, of all places.* ○ *'Then, when finally we've given him up for lost,* **up** *he* **pops**!' = bob up.

2 [Vp nom] (esp of illustrated pages in a book) rise into three-dimensional form as the book is opened: *'There you are, you see. You just press the pages flat and all the animals* **pop up**.' □ nom form is used attrib, as in: *a* **pop-up** *book, picture.*

pore

pore over [Vpr pass adj] study (sth) with close attention. **o:** book, document; figure, table; painting, sketch: *He* **pored over** *drawings.* BB ○ *We* **pored over** *the sketches for a long time.* BB

portion

portion out (among) [Vn ⇆ p pass adj, Vn.p.pr pass emph rel] divide (sth) in portions (among people). **O:** food, rations; land; work. **A:** evenly, fairly, justly: *The standard ration pack had to be* **portioned out among** *fourteen recruits.* ○ **Portioning** *land* **out** *equally* **among** *one's children leads to a proliferation of small, uneconomic holdings.* = share out (among).

possess

possessed of [pass (Vn.pr)] (*formal* or *jocular*) having some quality of body, mind or character; gifted with. **o:** great talent, miraculous powers, superhuman patience: *He was a large Buddha-like figure* **possessed of** *both learning and an irrepressible sense of life's absurdities.* SU ○ *Mrs Hatchett was* **possessed of** *impressive vocal chords.* DC □ also used with *seem, become* or after a noun.

post

post up [Vn ⇆ p pass adj] attach (sth) to a wall or board so that it is easily seen. **O:** notice, announcement; names; results: *They haven't* **posted up** *the results yet.* ○ *A number of students clustered around a notice* **posted up** *outside the chairman's office.* = put up 2.

potter

potter about/around [Vp nom, Vpr] (*informal*) move in a leisurely, unorganized way from one little job to another. **A:** in the garden, in one's study: *I imagine that he enjoys life.* **Pottering about** *and buying his drawings.* ASA ○ *I'll take it easy today; perhaps have a* **potter-about** *in the garden.*

pounce

pounce (on/upon) [Vpr pass emph rel] make a sudden attack on (sth/sb), often from above. **S:** eagle, hawk; tiger; aircraft; raider, bandit: *The big cats wait for the right moment, then* **pounce** *swiftly (***on** *their prey).* ○ *Guerrillas* **pounced on** *the convoy from both sides of a narrow ravine.*

pounce on/upon [Vpr pass emph rel] choose (sth) in a keen, alert way for criticism etc. **o:** (every) error, slip, mistake: *The class teacher would* **pounce on** *every slip the child made, however slight.* ○ *This is the kind of careless mistake* **on** *which examiners love to* **pounce**. = fasten on/upon, seize on/upon.

pound

pound at/on [Vpr pass] strike heavily and repeatedly (at sth). **o:** door, table; drum, piano: *Must he always* **pound on** *the table to make his point?* ○ *'My ears have been* **pounded at** *for the past hour; when is he going to switch off that damned drill?'* = drum on.

pound (away) (at) [Vp, Vpr pass, Vp.pr pass] (*military*) bombard (sth) heavily and continuously. **S:**

artillery; bomber. **o:** line, position; fortification: *Heavy artillery* ***pounded away*** *in the distance.* ○ *Waves of rocket-firing aircraft* ***pounded at*** *the enemy columns.*

pour

pour across, along, away etc 1 [Vp, Vpr emph rel] move in a continuous stream across etc. **S:** crowd, refugees, city workers; ants, termites: *For countless Czechs who* ***poured into*** *Wenceslas Square yesterday . . . the first visit by a US President was a moving occasion.* OBS ○ *The fans* ***poured out of*** *the stadium.*

2 [Vn ⇆ p pass, Vn.pr pass emph rel] cause (sth) to move across etc in a stream. **O:** water, oil; grain, sand: *Molten metal is* ***poured into*** *moulds.* ○ *Any unused sugar can be* ***poured back*** *into the tin.*

pour down [Vp] fall in a continuous stream, in torrents. **S:** ⚠ the rain; it: *The rain* ***poured down*** *steadily* (or: *There was a steady* ***downpour***) *all afternoon* (cf *It* ***poured with*** *rain all afternoon*). ○ *It was* ***pouring down*** *non-stop* (cf *It was* ***pouring with*** *rain non-stop*). □ nom form is downpour. = sheet down, teem down.

pour forth/out [Vp, Vp.n pass] (cause sth to) emerge in a stream. **S** [Vp], **O** [Vp.n]**:** music; propaganda, lies; hatred, mistrust. **S** [Vp.n]**:** choir; radio-station, loud-speaker; orator: *A continuous programme of martial music* ***poured forth*** *from the loudspeakers.* ○ *If they* ***poured out*** *their private life to one of the circle, they could be sure that their secret was safe.* H ○ *Strong feelings were* ***poured out*** (or: *There was an* ***outpouring*** *of strong feelings*).

pour in/into [Vp, Vpr emph rel] arrive in a stream (at a place). **S:** application, inquiry; donation, gift: *The switchboards were jammed as angry protests* ***poured in*** *from all over the country.* ○ *Thousands of pounds* ***poured into*** *our London office in response to the broadcast appeal.*

pour off 1 [Vpr] flow freely from (the pores of the skin). **S:** ⚠ (the) sweat, perspiration: *After a few laps of the running-track, the sweat was* ***pouring off*** *us.*

2 [Vp.n pass] separate (one liquid) from another by tilting the container; remove (liquid) in this way from a solid substance etc. **O:** fat, oil, cream: ***Pour off*** *the cream from the milk.* ○ *Dry-fry or boil mince and* ***pour off*** *resulting fat.* BEST

pour on [Vn.pr pass emph rel] speak of (sth/sb) scornfully; ridicule, scorn. **S:** commentator, critic; expert. **O:** ⚠ contempt, ridicule, scorn. **o:** effort, attempt; achievement; rulers, management: *The republican Belloc* ***poured*** *scorn* ***on*** *the titles of the English aristocracy.* HB ○ *Despite the ridicule often* ***poured on*** *the leaders of the feminist movement, it has a serious case which deserves serious attention.*

pour out 1 [Vp, Vn ⇆ p pass adj] serve (a beverage) from a pot, bottle etc. **S:** hostess, waitress. **O:** (cup of) tea, coffee: *'Shall I* ***pour out*** (ie Shall I serve the tea)*?'* ○ *'Let me* ***pour out*** *the tea at least.'* TGLY ○ *'Tea? Do sit down and I'll* ***pour*** *you some* ***out****.'* □ note the position of the Indirect Object in the third example.

2 [Vp, Vn ⇆ p pass] (cause sth to) emerge in a stream. ⇨ pour forth/out.

pour with [Vpr] ⇨ pour down.

prance

prance about/around [Vp, Vpr] (*informal*) dance about in a light-hearted or foolish way: *'Tell those children to stop* ***prancing around*** *upstairs and get into bed.'* ○ *There was a certain amount of* ***prancing about*** *in the corridors when the exam results were announced.*

pray

pray (for) [Vpr pass emph rel] make a request to God (for sth or on behalf of sb). **o:** food, water; help, forgiveness; the sick, the refugees: *The farmers are* ***praying for*** *rain.* ○ *To this temple came long-robed Greeks to worship and* ***pray for*** *protection.* GLEG ○ *She's past* ***praying for*** (ie can no longer be helped).

preach

preach (at) [Vpr pass] give moral advice (to sb) in an aloof, superior way: *'Please don't* ***preach at*** *me,' Virginia said. 'I came home to get some help.'* AITC ○ *We were tired of being* ***preached at*** *by sanctimonious ushers* (ie teachers) *with no knowledge of life outside the school gates.* CON

preclude

preclude from [Vn.pr pass] (*formal*) prevent (sb) from (doing sth); make it impossible for (sb) (to do sth). **o:** participation, attendance; having a share, standing for office: *Something in her temperament* ***precluded*** *her* ***from*** *taking a socialist view.* EB ○ *Retiring members of the Board were* ***precluded from*** *seeking re-election for three years.*

predispose

predispose to/towards [Vn.pr pass] (*formal*) (of an earlier event) make (sb) likely or inclined to do or accept (sth) at a later time. **S:** upbringing, training, indoctrination. **o:** acceptance, refusal; scholarship, music, the law, medicine: *His father's harsh treatment of him* ***predisposed*** *him* ***to*** *a rejection of authority in later life.* ○ *She was* ***predisposed towards*** *literary studies by the bookish environment of her early years.*

preface

preface with [Vn.pr pass emph rel] (*formal*) place (sth) before the main body of a speech, text etc. **S:** speaker; chairman; editor. **O:** address, speech; chapter. **o:** (short) reference (to sth), (brief) mention (of sb): *'If I may, I should like to* ***preface*** *my remarks* ***with*** *a short tribute to my predecessor in the chair.'*

prepare

prepare (for) [Vpr pass adj emph rel, Vn.pr pass emph rel] (cause sb to) get ready (for sth). **O:** oneself; pupil, class; follower, subject; article, book; room. **o:** exam; ordeal, hardship; the press; guest: *'****Prepare for*** *a shock!'* ○ *He's* ***preparing*** *a paper* ***for*** *the next meeting of the Association.* ○ *The children will have to be carefully* ***prepared for*** *the new type of assessment.* ○ *These long-****prepared-for*** *discussions open in Brussels on Monday.*

present

present to [Vn.pr pass emph rel] ⇨ next entry

present with [Vn.pr pass rel] give or offer (sth) to (sb) as a present or reward. **o:** medal, scroll (of honour), sum of money: *He was* ***presented with*** *the keys of the city* (or: *He had the keys of the city* ***presented to*** *him*). ○ *The company* ***presented*** *him*

***with** a gold watch* (or: ***presented** a gold watch **to** him*) *on the day he retired.*

preside

preside over 1 [Vpr pass emph rel] be the chairman (at a formal meeting); sit at the head of the table (at a formal meal). **o:** meeting, session; dinner, banquet: *He was a brilliant industrial diplomat, who **presided over** banquets and regally entertained foreign potentates.* OBS

2 [Vpr pass] be the head of (sth); govern. **o:** organization, group of companies; clan, family: *Franz Joseph, the last of the Habsburgs, had **presided over** this Empire for twelve years.* F ○ *The Raeburns were a large and artistic family **presided over** by Walter, the Labour lawyer.* SU

3 [Vpr] witness, from an important position, events over which one has little control. **S:** government, administration; minister, director. **o:** decline, collapse, break-up; shambles: *Successive post-war governments **presided over** the gradual dissolution of the British Empire.*

press

press across, along, away etc 1 [Vp, Vpr] move with a steady pressure across etc. **S:** spectator, demonstrator; crowd, mob: *The advance guard **pressed forward** to maintain contact with the enemy.* ○ *The fans **pressed through** the tunnels and **onto** the terraces of the stadium.* ○ *A mass of new sights and sounds **pressed in** upon them.*

2 [Vn ⇆ p pass, Vn.pr pass] using firm pressure, make (sb/sth) move across etc steadily. **O:** crowd; demonstrators, troops; assault: *The police **pressed** the students **back** behind the barriers.* ○ *The movement of wheeled vehicles was impossible. The attack, however, had to be **pressed forward** under all circumstances.* B

press ahead/forward/on (with) [Vp, Vp.pr] continue steadily and with determination (to carry sth out). **o:** proposals, plans; efforts, endeavours: *They appear determined to **press ahead with** plans to increase the standard rate of income tax.* OBS ○ *He had time enough ... to **press on with** his researches.* MRJ = push ahead/forward/on (with).

press (for) [Vpr pass emph rel, Vn.pr pass emph rel] make repeated and urgent requests (for sth). **O:** ministers, Government. **o:** debate, discussion, inquiry: *We are **pressing** (the Government) hard **for** a renewal of talks.* ○ *Reporters **pressed** him **for** an explanation* (or: ***pressed** him to give an explanation*). ○ *The engineers' representatives have won all the concessions **for** which they were **pressing**.* = push (for).

press home [Vp.n pass] launch or express (sth) forcefully. **O:** attack, assault; accusation, charge: *This particular charge was **pressed home**.* LWK ○ *The attacks were **pressed home** in the face of determined resistance.* = push home.

press home an/one's advantage [Vp.n pass] use well or exploit an opportunity or advantage: *She was rather more concerned with her appearance than with the strong-room key, so he **pressed home his advantage** and took the key.* TO ○ *The employers were prepared to discuss wages with the staff, and they **pressed home the advantage** this gave them by raising the question of productivity.*

press on (with) [Vp, Vp.pr] continue steadily and with determination to do sth. **o:** work, task, project; fight, struggle: *But if the Government refused to come to the negotiating table it should be under 'no illusions about our determination to **press on**'.* IND ○ *It* (The Japanese Government) *urged the US to **press on with** efforts to reduce its budget deficit.* IND

press on regardless [Vp] (*informal*) continue in a determined and stubborn way despite risk or the advice of others: *He was blessed and cursed with the politician's talent of **pressing on regardless**.* NS

press on/upon 1 [Vn.pr pass] offer (sth) insistently to (sb), out of gratitude, or in the hope of gaining sth. **O:** attentions, favours; money, gifts: *The crowds **pressed** food and wine **on** the liberating troops.*

2 [Vn.pr pass] oblige or force (sb) to accept (sth) against his will. **O:** opinions, beliefs: *He* (a clergyman) ***pressed** his reforms **on** the parish with more zeal than wisdom.* GE = thrust upon.

press out/out of [Vn ⇆ p pass adj, Vn.pr pass] force (sth) to leave (sth else) by applying pressure. **O:** part, component; oil, juice. **o:** (sheet of) metal, card; seed, fruit: *The parts of the model have been printed on cardboard; all you have to do is **press** them **out** and assemble them.* ○ *This machine **presses** the oil **out of** palm kernels.*

presume

presume on/upon [Vpr pass] (*formal*) test or strain too much (the goodwill etc) of sb. **o:** patience, indulgence; kindness, good nature; hospitality: *I don't think we should **presume** overmuch **on** the good nature of these people.* ○ *I think we have already **presumed** too much **on** your generosity.*

pretend

pretend to [Vpr pass emph rel] (*formal*) claim to have (sth). **o:** wit, understanding, knowledge; talent, gift: *He couldn't **pretend to** a detailed knowledge of the road system.* ○ *There was Mark Pattison, the old Rector of Lincoln, who **pretended to** no Christian faith whatever.* GIE

pretty

pretty up [Vn ⇆ p pass adj] (*informal*) make (sth) pretty or charming, esp in a pretentious way. **O:** child; street, house; story: *Here was a row of simple cottages, **prettied up** for sale to commuting stockbrokers.* ○ *The script will have to be **prettied up** to give it box-office appeal.*

prevail

prevail on/upon [Vpr pass emph rel] (*formal*) persuade (sb) to do sth. **Inf:** to join in, to contribute; to retire, to withdraw: *At dinner he **prevailed on** her to take some wine. It wasn't easy.* PW ○ *Severus, his constitution much undermined, ... was **prevailed upon** to undergo a cure.* GIE ○ *He allowed himself to be **prevailed upon**.* □ the object is usu followed by an inf.

prey

prey on/upon 1 [Vpr pass adj] pursue and attack (sb/sth) regularly. **S:** hawk, eagle; tiger, lion;

pirate, bandit. **o:** small bird; antelope; merchant shipping: *Owls* **prey on** *small rodents, especially mice.* ○ *Helicopters* **preyed upon** *the columns of refugees.* ○ *Bullion ships plying out of the Caribbean were* **preyed upon** *by pirates.*

2 [Vpr pass] deeply trouble (sb); agitate, beset. **S:** doubt, fear, anxiety. **o:** ⚠ him etc; sb's mind, thoughts: *Was it the accident with the car and the blackmailing letters that were* **preying on** *his mind?* DC ○ *It would appear that his impending trial* **preyed on** *his mind* (or: **on** *him*). T

price

price out of the market [Vn.pr pass] set one's prices so high that no one buys one's goods. **O:** oneself; product, goods: *Higher labour costs will* **price** *us clean* **out of** *the market.* ○ *If you don't accept a lower profit, you'll* **price** *yourself right* **out of the market**.

prick

prick out [Vn ⇆ p pass] (*horticulture*) plant (sth) in the earth, in holes made with a pointed stick. **O:** seedling, young plant: *'I'm just going to* **prick out** *some cabbage plants.'*

prick one's ears up [Vn ⇆ p pass] (of a dog, horse) raise the ears — a sign that it is listening attentively; (of a person) pay careful attention: *The horse seemed so interested in what was going on that after being led away some paces she turned,* **pricked up her ears**, *and looked around.* DBM ○ *'I've been thinking about Myrtle for some time, Joe.' 'Oh?' I* **pricked up my ears**. SPL

pride

pride oneself on/upon [Vn.pr emph rel] regard (sth) as a special reason for pride or satisfaction. **o:** skill, craft; sensitivity, finesse; being tactful, knowing the best places to eat: *I* **pride myself on** *being very English and even try to speak some French with an English accent.* PPLA ○ *He* **prided himself** *justly* **on** *his skill at negotiation.* □ the idiom is sometimes used with that: *He* **prided himself that** *his voice sounded quite ordinary.* PE

print

print off 1 [Vn ⇆ p nom pass adj] (*photography*) make (prints etc) on sensitive paper from a negative film. **O:** print, enlargement; copy: *How many copies of the wedding group do you want* **printed off**? ○ *I want to do a* **print-off** *from that negative* (or: **print off** *photographs from that negative*).

2 [Vn ⇆ p nom pass adj] (*printing*) print copies of a book etc — with the suggestion that another printing is to be made from the same plates: *We* **printed off** *10 000 copies* (cf *did a* **print-off** *of 10 000) from the existing plates.* □ note the special nom form offprint meaning an extra printing of (usu) a single article from a journal, in a small number of copies for the author's own use.

print out [Vp.n nom pass adj] (*computing*) produce a printed version of a document etc stored in a computer. **O:** document, data; letter, bill, circular; analysis: **Printing out** *quite complex documents under Locoscript should always be a simple matter.* AUG ○ *The computer is programmed to* **print out** *an analysis of the orders received and invoiced and the resulting stock levels.* ○ *The texts were fed into the computer and several* **printouts** *were obtained, showing, among other things, word-frequency distribution and sentence lengths.*

prise

prise off [Vn ⇆ p pass adj, Vn.pr pass] remove or raise (sth), usu by applying force to a lever. **O:** lid, cover, top. **o:** tin, box, cask: **Prise off** *the cover with your thumbs.* ○ *Scratches on the neck … could have been made by the victim trying to* **prise off** *the attacker's hands.* HWKM □ alt spelling prize: *We* **prized** *the lids* **off** *the packing cases with a tyre lever.*

prise out/out of 1 [Vn ⇆ p pass adj, Vn.pr pass] extract (sth) (from a place), usu by applying force to a lever. **O:** stone, nail. **o:** (animal's) hoof, tyre: *Sharp pieces of grit should be* **prised out of** *the tyre treads.* □ alt spelling: prize.

2 [Vn ⇆ p pass, Vn.pr pass] obtain (sth) with difficulty from (sb), by applying moral pressure etc. **O:** secret, confession suspect, prisoner: *Foreign espionage would do its utmost to* **prise out** *these secrets.* TBC ○ *She* **prised** *the story* **out of** *him by threatening to inform his employers.* □ alt spelling: prize.

probe

probe into [Vpr pass] investigate or explore (sth). **o:** complaint, problem; disappearance; robbery, break-in; health, condition; state of mind: *It is helpful in* **probing into** *the problem to make a statement about* (the patient's) *mental health and ill health.* ESS ○ *She had known from the start how to disturb him, how to* **probe into** *delicate areas.* EC = inquire into, look into 2.

proceed

proceed against [Vpr] (*legal*) take steps to bring (sb) to trial; prosecute. **S:** police; (solicitor's) client, plaintiff. **o:** suspect, prisoner: *'Before we go to the trouble and expense of* **proceeding against** *this man I must be satisfied that your charges are well founded.'*

proceed from [Vpr emph rel] (*formal*) have (sth) as a cause or starting-point. **S:** event; agreement, treaty. **o:** decision, plan; meeting, discussion: **From** *one small error many unfortunate misunderstandings have* **proceeded**. ○ *These were the plans* **from** *which the momentous events of 1944 were to* **proceed**.

proceed to 1 [Vpr] (*formal*) take the next item etc in succession. **o:** next item (on the agenda); vote, election: *'May we* **proceed**, *then,* **to** *the election of a committee?'* ○ *'Let us* **proceed to** *nominations for President.'*

2 [Vpr] (*formal*) go forward from a lower university degree to a higher one. **o:** the (degree of) MA, PhD: *Graduates wishing to* **proceed to** *the MA may do so on payment of the necessary fees and dues.*

profit

profit by [Vpr] by studying one's mistakes etc, ensure they are not repeated. **o:** one's mistakes, experience; sb's advice, counsel: *We ought to* **profit by** *our mistakes.* ○ *He's been married twice, but he doesn't seem to have* **profited** *much* **by** *the experience.* = learn from. ⇨ next entry

profit by/from [Vpr pass emph rel] get some benefit from (sth). **o:** course, training, instruction; trip, stay: *When people could* **profit by** *doing so, they accepted the benefits of government.* LPOL ○

*Volunteer teachers can **profit** personally as well as professionally **from** their year overseas.* = benefit by/from. ⇨ previous entry

prohibit

prohibit from [Vn.pr pass] (*formal*) forbid (sb) to do (sth). **o:** smoking, walking on the grass, using public transport: *The court issued a writ **prohibiting** the press **from** publishing extracts from the book.* ○ *Seven days before the election newspapers were **prohibited** by law **from** printing further opinion poll results.* G □ object is the -ing form of a verb.

pronounce

pronounce on/upon [Vpr pass emph rel] (*formal*) give a considered opinion or verdict on (sth). **S:** expert, adviser, consultant. **o:** health, safety; efficiency, viability: *The air is heavy with the voices of experts, **pronouncing on** everything from the effect of fluoride on drinking water to the future of motor traffic in cities.*

prop

prop up 1 [Vn ⇆ p pass adj] raise (sb/sth) and keep him/it in a raised position by means of supports. **S:** nurse, mother; farmer, building. **O:** patient, child; fence, outhouse: *Nurse Ellen had tucked her up and left her to sleep, but she **propped** herself **up*** (on the pillows). DC ○ *The gardener **propped up** the apple tree with a stout plank.*

2 [Vn ⇆ p pass] support (sth/sb) which would otherwise collapse or fail. **O:** (failing) company, business; uneconomic enterprise; badly-run organization; inefficient colleague. **A:** with public money, with government support: *The Minister said that it was not the job of the Government to **prop up** failing companies.* ○ *'I can't afford to **prop** him **up** with extra cash. He'll just have to manage on his own.'* = bolster up.

prospect

prospect for [Vpr] (*mining*) search for (minerals). **o:** diamonds, gold; copper, bauxite; oil: *Where in the nineteenth century amateur fortune hunters **prospected for** gold, today professional geologists **prospect for** oil, uranium and industrial metals.*

protect

protect (against/from) [Vn.pr pass emph rel] act as a shield or defence for (sb) (against sth). **S:** armour plate, barricade; law, regulation; police. **O:** passenger, crew; customer, retailer; citizen. **o:** shellfire, explosion; unfair trading; violence: *An armoured shield will **protect** the driver **against** all but a direct hit.* ○ *Is the tenant adequately **protected from** exploitation?* ○ *Pensions tied to the cost-of-living index can **protect** retired people **from** the effects of inflation.*

protest

protest against [Vpr pass emph rel] express opposition (to sth), eg by means of an organized demonstration. **o:** intrusion, rudeness; rent increase, armed intervention, sexual harassment, racial discrimination: *Crowds of young demonstrators **protested against** the increase in students' fees.* ○ *Thousands took to the streets, . . . **protesting against** the UN Security Council Resolution.* OBS □ cf US usage: *Demonstrators **protested** the increase in fees.*

provide

provide for 1 [Vpr pass adj emph rel] take care, by earning enough and by spending carefully, that one's family etc has enough to live on now, and/or if one is separated from them or dies. **A:** well, generously, adequately. **o:** wife, children, parent; widow: *He had **provided for** her, after his own fashion, handsomely.* GIE ○ *The children are **provided for**.* OMIH ○ *He's always **provided** well **for** his family* (cf *He's always been a good **provider***).

2 [Vpr pass] make such efficient arrangements that all possible difficulties can be overcome. **o:** every eventuality, all contingencies; increase, shortfall: *Every possible failure of the electrical system has been **provided for**, generally by duplicating the circuits.*

3 [Vpr pass] (*legal*) establish the legal basis or authority for the later actions or conduct of Government or individuals. **S:** Act (of Parliament), Bill. **o:** the hand-over of power, confiscation of property; easier divorce, wider parental choice of schools: *The Bill **provides for** the eventual self-government of the territory.* ○ *A clause in the agreement **provides for** the arbitration of all disputes by an independent body* (or: ***provides** that all disputes shall be arbitrated* etc). ○ *Equal job opportunities for women are **provided for** in the party manifesto.*

provide with [Vn.pr pass rel] give (sth) to (sb) for his use; ensure that (sb) has (sth). **O:** staff, colleagues; children, animals. **o:** adequate facilities, comfortable quarters; food and shelter, recreation: *Augustus had **provided** them only **with** a small amount of money and some cakes.* GJ ○ *I could not **provide** the Pouched Rats **with** a stream so they used the next best thing, which was their waterpot.* BB = furnish with, supply (to).

provoke

provoke into [Vn.pr pass rel] irritate, annoy (sb) so much that he reacts angrily, behaves violently etc. **o:** temper, rage, outburst; slapping, beating: *Jibes about his scruffy appearance always **provoked** him **into** violent displays of temper.* ○ *The continual noise in the classroom **provoked** him **into** slapping one or two hands* (or: ***provoked** him to slap* etc).

prowl

prowl about/around [Vp] go about carefully looking for food or an opportunity to steal. **S:** lion, tiger; thief, mugger: *The big cats **prowl about** in the savannah grass, looking for an incautious prey.* ○ *'What's going on down there? Who's **prowling about** downstairs?'* DC

pry

pry (into) [Vpr pass emph rel] show too much interest (in other people's affairs). **o:** others' affairs, matters that don't concern one: *She **pries** too closely **into** the private life of her friends.* ○ *'This is something you weren't supposed to **pry into**.'* = poke one's nose in/into.

psych

psych out/out of [Vn ⇆ p pass, Vn.pr pass] (*informal*) make (sb) lose interest or confidence so that he abandons (sth). **o:** a relationship, marriage; competing (with sb), taking part (in sth): *You may opt out of sexuality because you wish to,... or are sick, but it's a pity to be* ***psyched out of*** *something you value by anxiety and wrong information.* ST

psych (oneself) up [Vn.p pass adj] (*informal*) get ready for a task by putting oneself in a confident, aggressive mood. **S:** team, crew; singer, dancer: *Like their Cambridge counterparts, they* (the Oxford rowing crew) *have been in London... getting* ***psyched up*** *for tomorrow's race.* THES

pucker

pucker up [Vp, Vn ⇆ p pass adj] (make one eyes etc) come together into small folds or wrinkles. **S** [Vp], **O** [Vn.p]**:** eyes, lips; brow; skin: *His eyes were* ***puckered up*** *against the strong sunlight.* ○ *She had the little* ***puckered-up*** *face of a seal, very worried-looking.* CON

puff

puff across, along, away etc 1 [Vp, Vpr] go across etc, sending out smoke etc and/or panting noisily. **S:** engine, train; runner, messenger: *Our train* ***puffed into*** *the station ten minutes late.* ○ *Steam* ***puffed up*** *from a crack in the metal.* ○ *A few weekend athletes* ***puffed along****, unhappy at the unaccustomed exercise.*

2 [Vn ⇆ p pass, Vn.pr pass] send (sth) across etc, in short, sudden gusts. **S:** pipe, tube, chimney; smoker. **O:** smoke, fumes, smog, gas: *The factory chimneys* ***puff*** *dense smoke* ***into*** *the air.* ○ *'Don't* ***puff*** *your tobacco smoke* ***into*** *my eyes.'* ○ *Air is* ***puffed up*** *through the liquid.*

puff (at/on) [Vpr] draw smoke (from a pipe etc), usu in short gusts. **o:** pipe, cigar, cigarette: *He was* ***puffing*** *nervously* ***at*** *a cigarette.* ○ *'Stop* ***puffing*** *(****on*** *that pipe) for a moment, and listen to me.'*

puff out 1 [Vn ⇆ p pass adj] (*informal*) make (sb) short of breath. **S:** exercise, exertion; race, climb: *Climbing up the long staircase to his office quite* ***puffed*** *me* ***out****.* ○ *We were completely* ***puffed out****: we had to sit down for a few minutes to get our breath back.* □ usu passive or adj.

2 [Vn ⇆ p pass] make sth go out with a sharp gust of air; extinguish. **O:** light, flame; lamp, candle: *A sudden gust of wind from the open window* ***puffed*** *the candle* ***out****.*

puff one's chest out [Vn ⇆ p pass adj] make one's chest expand with air, from pride, or in order to appear smart on parade: ***His chest*** *was* ***puffed out*** *with pride on the day they gave him his medal.* ○ *Little boys marched up and down with* ***puffed-out chests****.*

puff up 1 [Vn ⇆ p pass adj] make (sth) larger and rounder by patting, heating etc. **O:** pillow, cushion; pastry case: *She tidied and dusted,* ***puffed up*** *the cushions and straightened the furniture.* ○ *Bake for 12-15 minutes until the cheese filling is* ***puffed up*** *and the pastry golden.* GF

2 [Vn ⇆ p pass adj] fill (sb) with conceit, with too great a sense of his importance. **S:** money, success, status: *Uncle Saunders is only a noisy pompous ass,* ***puffed up*** *by too much money.* DC ○ *They're a couple of* ***puffed-up*** *idiots — very much in need of deflating.* □ usu passive or adj.

pull

pull about/around [Vn.p pass adj] handle (sb) roughly; mistreat. **O:** wife, child; furniture: *'If you don't stop* ***pulling*** *me* ***about****, I'll scream the place down.'* ○ *'I wish the dogs would leave the cushions alone: they're looking terribly* ***pulled-about****.'*

pull ahead/ahead of 1 [Vp, Vpr] move in front (of sb/sth that is also moving). **S:** car; runner. **o:** opposition, rival; the field: *'That driver's trying to overtake. Slow down a bit and let him* ***pull ahead****.'*

2 [Vp, Vpr] make more progress (than a competitor). **S:** business, company; economy. **o:** rival, competitor: (headline) *Heseltine* ***pulls ahead*** *with backing of Tory big guns.* OBS ○ *Arsenal has* ***pulled*** *well* ***ahead of*** *Liverpool in the race for the League championship.* = get ahead/ahead of.

pull alongside [Vp, Vpr] stop, or move along, at the side of (sb/sth). **S:** car; tug, launch. **o:** lorry; steamer: *A motor-cyclist* ***pulled alongside*** *and signalled that my off-side door wasn't properly shut.* ○ *'We'll* ***pull alongside*** *her and put a salvage crew aboard.'* = draw alongside.

pull apart 1 [Vn.p pass] use force to separate the parts of (sth). **O:** box, cupboard; garment; flower: *The table is made so that you can easily* ***pull*** *it* ***apart*** (or: *that it easily* ***pulls apart****).* = pull to pieces 1.

2 [Vn.p pass] criticize (sth) severely. **S:** tutor, supervisor. **O:** idea; plan, scheme; work, achievement: *There's nothing more demoralizing than having your essays* ***pulled apart*** *in front of other students.* = pull to pieces 2, take apart 2.

pull around [Vn.p pass adj] ⇨ pull about/around.

pull aside [Vn ⇆ p pass] move (sth) to one side, esp to reveal what is behind it. **O:** curtain, hanging; mask, veil (of secrecy, deceit): *We* ***pulled aside*** *a dingy curtain to reveal a flight of steps running downwards.* ○ *The cloak of secrecy was* ***pulled aside*** *by a news photographer who spotted a prototype of the car while working in Austria.* = draw aside 1.

pull at/on [Vpr] draw smoke steadily from (a pipe etc). **o:** pipe, cigar: *The old man* ***pulled*** *thoughtfully* ***at*** *his pipe before replying.*

pull away (from) 1 [Vn.p pass, Vn.p.pr pass] use force to move (sth/sb) away, esp from danger. **O:** bomb; pilot, passenger. **o:** house; wreckage, ruins; fire: *With great presence of mind a fireman* ***pulled*** *the driver* ***away from*** *his burning cab.*

2 [Vp, Vp.pr rel] move away (from a place where one is parked) into the stream of traffic; move forward (from a stationary position). **S:** car, lorry, bus; driver. **o:** kerb, side of the road: *The police car* ***pulled away*** *and disappeared round the next bend.* ○ *We settled the children on the back seat and* ***pulled away from*** *the kerb.* ↔ pull in/into 2.

pull back 1 [Vn ⇆ p pass adj] take hold of (sb/sth) and draw him/it backwards. **O:** child, spectator; curtains, bedclothes; hair: *Her hair was* ***pulled back*** *from her skull in plaits.* FL

2 [Vp, Vn ⇆ p pass] (*military*) (cause sb to) retreat; withdraw. **S** [Vp], **O** [Vn.p]**:** tanks, infantry. **S** [Vn.p]**:** commander, general: *The battalion* ***pulled back*** *two miles during the night and took up prepared positions.* ○ *The bad condition of the roads made relief impossible without* ***pulling*** *the division* ***back*** *to Orel, so the 4th Panzer had struggled on.* B

pull back (from) [Vp, Vp.pr emph rel] decide not to continue (with sth), out of caution or fear. **o:** the edge, the brink; an agreement, a deal; commitment, marriage: *'I think he'll leave, but he might* *just decide to* **pull back** *at the last minute.'* ○ *Would he* **pull back from** *marrying? He had once before.*

pull down 1 [Vn ⇆ p pass adj] lower (sth). **O:** blind, shade; hat: *Passengers have to* **pull down** *a window, lean out and turn a handle, and the door opens outwards.* OBS ○ *Comfortably hatted, with the peak* **pulled down** *low over his eyes, George began to unpack.* FL = draw down.

2 [Vn ⇆ p pass adj] demolish, destroy (sth). **O:** theatre, monument, house: *A row of back-to-back houses is being* **pulled down** *to make way for new flats.* ○ *Many people are opposed to the* **pulling-down** *of buildings of historical interest.* = knock down 1, tear down. ↔ put up 1.

3 [Vn.p pass adj] (*informal*) leave (sb) in a poor physical or moral state; weaken. **S:** malaria, influenza; poor diet, feeding: *'Bit thinner, aren't you? You look a bit* **pulled down**, *you know.'* PW ○ *That long spell in hospital* **pulled** *him* **down** *a lot.* = drag down.

4 [Vn.p pass] (*informal*) cause (sb) to fall to a lower position, eg in a class. **S:** mark, score; written test, oral: *He seemed all set to win a gold medal, but his performance in the third round* **pulled** *him* **down**. ○ *It was the written paper that* **pulled** *me* **down**. ↔ pull up 4.

pull in 1 [Vn ⇆ p] (*informal*) earn (sth) from one's job. **O:** a good wage; twenty thousand a year: *He's* **pulling in** *a regular salary.* NM ○ *'They're* **pulling in** *a lot of overtime* (money paid for working extra hours) *on that job.'*

2 [Vn ⇆ p pass] (*informal*) attract, draw (sb) to a place of entertainment, an opportunity to make money etc. **O:** crowd, audience; investor, saver; investment: *'We used to* **pull in** *a good Saturday crowd at the Palace Theatre.'* ○ *They need to have a high rate of interest in order to* **pull in** *money from investors.* BBCTV

3 [Vn ⇆ p pass] (*informal*) fetch (sb) to a police station for questioning. **O:** suspect, habitual offender: *'The two lads we found inside the warehouse have been* **pulled in** *for questioning.'* ○ *'Come on,* **pull** *him* **in**, *let's have a word with him.'*

pull in/into 1 [Vp, Vpr] arrive (at a place); enter. **S:** train; express, monorail. **o:** station, terminus: *As we* **pulled in**, *an hour late, our connection to Rome was pulling out.* ○ *Our train* **pulled into** *Paddington dead on time.* = draw in/into 1. ↔ pull out/out of 1.

2 [Vp nom, Vpr] move closer to (the side of the road etc). **S:** boat; car, lorry; skipper, driver. **o:** shore, quay; kerb, lorry-park: *The steamer* **pulled in** *towards the quay-side.* ○ *'***Pull into** *the side of the road and I'll drive for a bit.'* □ a café where you pull in for refreshments is a pull-in. ↔ pull away (from) 2. ⇨ pull up 1.

pull off 1 [Vn ⇆ p pass adj, Vn.pr pass] remove (sth) with some force. **O:** shoe, jumper; leaf, bud: *'Here, help me* **pull** *these boots* **off**.' ○ *'See if you can* **pull** *the cloth* **off** *the table without disturbing these glasses.'* ↔ pull on 2.

2 [Vp, Vpr] drive, be driven, a short distance from (a road). **S:** driver; car lorry. **o:** road, motorway: *'Why don't we* **pull off** *just here and have our picnic?'* ○ *I was in danger of falling asleep at the wheel, so I* **pulled off** *the road and had a nap.*

3 [Vn ⇆ p pass] (*informal*) achieve what one sets out to do. **O:** it; coup, deal, speculation; scoop; murder: *Every time he* **pulled off** *a big deal it made a paragraph in the 'Sentry'.* CON ○ *'We did it, we've* **pulled** *it* **off**, *we've won.'* BBCTV = succeed (in).

pull on 1 [Vpr] draw smoke steadily from (a pipe etc). ⇨ pull at/on.

2 [Vn ⇆ p pass] put on (clothing). **O:** boot, sock, shirt: *He* **pulled** *a sweater* **on** *over his woollen shirt.* = draw on 1. ↔ pull off 1.

pull out 1 [Vn ⇆ p pass] extract (sth). **S:** dentist; carpenter. **O:** tooth; nail, tack: *I was afraid he was going to* **pull out** *one of those big back teeth.* = draw out/out of 2.

2 [Vn ⇆ p nom pass] remove, detach (sth). **O:** supplement, (comic-, magazine-)section: *The map is at the back of the book, and may be* **pulled out** (or: **pulls out**) *for easy reference.* ○ *In this special* **pull-out** *section* (or: *section you can* **pull out**) *we publish a complete episode.* OBS □ nom form usu attrib, as shown.

pull out all the stops [Vp.n] (*informal*) use all one's power, resources etc, to achieve an objective: *An army spokesman said: 'Whether it's a last desperate effort or not we cannot be sure. But they are certainly* **pulling out all the stops**.' ST ○ *Helen, desperately afraid that Archie would leave her,* **pulled out all the stops** *to keep her hold over him.*

pull one's finger out [Vn.p] (*informal*) stop behaving in a lazy, inefficient way. **S:** firm; manager, accountant, storekeeper: *'He's got till the end of the month to get his research project written up and typed, so he'd better* **pull his finger out**.' ○ *So come on, shoe companies,* **pull your finger out**. RUN

pull out/out of 1 [Vp, Vpr] depart from (a place); leave. **S:** train; bus, coach. **o:** station: *Then the train* **pulled out**. TC ○ *The three-thirty was* **pulling out of** *platform five as I ran into the station.* = draw out/out of 5. ↔ pull in/into 1.

2 [Vp, Vpr] move out (of a line of traffic) in order to overtake the vehicle in front or enter a faster traffic lane. **S:** driver, motorist; car, lorry: *The car in front* **pulled out** *to overtake just as I was about to overtake it.* ○ *Don't* **pull out of** *a line of stationary vehicles unless the road behind you is clear.*

3 [Vp, Vpr pass] (*informal*) force oneself to overcome (low spirits etc). **o:** illness; mood, depression: *He's been dogged by a sense of failure; now he's working strenuously to* **pull out**. ○ *'But he'll* **pull out of** *it. He has these spells, you know. He's never been strong.'* AITC

4 [Vp nom, Vpr pass, Vn ⇆ p nom pass adj, Vn.pr pass] (cause sb to) withdraw (from a place). **S** [Vp Vpr], **O** [Vn.p Vn.pr]**:** troops, force; trade mission; diplomatic representative. **o:** colony, base, occupied territory : [Vp] I had lain in the grass and impotently watched the enemy *pulling out below me.* SD ○ [Vp] If he agrees, Britain will be failing to make the clean **pull-out** (or: *to* **pull out** *cleanly*) *which is essential to the Government's strategy.* OBS ○ [Vn.p] The 'withdrawal' now talked about in Britain is the far more radical step of **pulling out** *British troops.* ST = withdraw (from) 1.

pull over [Vp, Vn.p pass] move towards the roadside, either to stop or to allow other vehicles to overtake. **S** [Vp], **O** [Vn.p]**:** car, lorry. **S** [Vp Vn.p]**:** driver, motorist: *I shouted to the driver of the tractor to* **pull over** *and let me through.* ○ *The traffic* *police asked if we would mind* ***pulling*** *the car* ***over*** *to the side of the road.*

pull the wool over sb's eyes [Vn.pr pass] (*informal*) conceal one's true actions or intentions from sb by a display of virtue. **o:** (**of**) employer, teacher, wife, husband: *'I'm afraid you can't* ***pull the wool over the eyes of*** *the Tax Inspectors. They have ways of finding out.'* ○ *'She's had* ***the wool pulled over her eyes*** *for years. You don't imagine he always travels to London on business, do you?'*

pull round 1 [Vn.p pass] force (sb/sth) to face another way, esp in the opposite direction. **O:** nose, tail (of an aircraft); bow, stern (of a boat): *A tug* ***pulled*** *the bow of the ship* ***round***. ○ *A hand descended on his shoulder, and he was* ***pulled round*** *to face a pair of glaring eyes.*

2 [Vp] (*informal*) regain consciousness: *'How long will she take to* ***pull round*** *after her operation?'* ○ (of a person injured in an accident) *'Loosen his clothes and give him a little brandy: that'll soon help him to* ***pull round***.*'* = come round 2. ⇨ bring round 2.

pull through [Vp, Vpr pass, Vn.p pass, Vn.pr pass] (help sb to) recover (from a serious illness); (help sb to) survive (a crisis). **S** [Vp, Vpr], **O** [Vn.p, Vn.pr]: patient; country, firm. **o:** sickness; tough time, emergency, crisis : [Vp] The patient has an excellent chance of ***pulling through***. ○ [Vn.p] Only a powerful will to live could ***pull*** *her* ***through***, *and she had no desire to live.* GJ = come through 2, bring through.

pull to [Vn.p pass] close or nearly close (sth). **O:** door, window; curtains, blinds: *'****Pull*** *the door* ***to*** *and come and sit down.'* ○ *The curtains were* ***pulled to***.

pull to pieces 1 [Vn.pr pass] separate the parts of (sth) by force. **O:** model, construction; garment, cloth; prey: *The rags are washed and* ***pulled to pieces*** *by machine.* ○ *A tiger can* ***pull*** *a roebuck* ***to pieces*** *in a matter of minutes.* = pull apart 1.

2 [Vn.pr pass] criticize (sb/sth) severely, find serious faults in (sb/sth). **O:** persons; theory, argument, case; evidence: *The new theory was* ***pulled to pieces*** *by many of the world's leading astronomers.* ○ *The poor woman was* ***pulled to pieces*** *by all her neighbours. Her hair-style, clothes, make-up, accent, political opinions — nothing escaped criticism.* = pull apart 2.

pull together 1 [Vpr] act as one person; combine the efforts of several people: *If we all* ***pull together***, *we should be able to get the country out of the mess it's in.* ○ *The old habit of looking well after the wage earners* (ie in working-class families) *is still alive; so is the stress on the need for all to* ***pull together***. UL

2 [Vn ⇆ p pass] restore the morale or unity of (an organisation). **O:** assembly, party, regiment, (industrial) company, country: *There is the NATO alliance, which will soon disintegrate unless we do something to* ***pull*** *it* ***together***. MFM ○ *It was he more than anybody who* ***pulled*** *the Party* ***together*** *after our big electoral defeat.*

3 [Vn ⇆ p pass] combine or assemble (things) so as to form a whole; form (a whole) by combining things. **O:** themes, topics; material, data; case, story: *'Try to* ***pull*** *the various points* ***together*** *into one argument.'* ○ *The police haven't yet managed to* ***pull together*** *all the eye-witness reports.*

pull oneself together [Vn.p] (*informal*) take firm control of one's feelings and impulses and begin to behave sensibly: *She had her ups and downs, but she had always managed to* ***pull herself together*** *and have a good time.* H ○ *'Come on,' she repeated sharply. 'You've got to* ***pull yourself together*** *for a minute. You can't catch a train as you are now.'* PE

pull under [Vn.p pass] drag (sb) below the surface of a river or the sea. **S:** ⚠ the current, undertow: *The currents were deceptively strong at this point, and nobody would swim for fear of being* ***pulled under***.

pull up 1 [Vp nom, Vn ⇆ p pass] (make sth) stop, halt. **S** [Vp], **O** [Vn.p]: car, lorry. **S** [Vp Vn.p]: driver, motorist: *More slowly than usual he drove towards his office. At last he* ***pulled up***. PW ○ *She* ***pulled*** *her car* ***up*** *within a few yards of the wreckage.* ○ *His pursuer* ***pulled up*** *short to greet us with an affable little bow.* BM = draw up 1. ⇨ pull in/into 2.

2 [Vn ⇆ p pass] move (a seat) nearer to sb/sth. **O:** ⚠ chair, armchair, stool: *'****Pull*** *a chair* ***up*** *to the table.'* = draw up 2.

3 [Vn.p pass] (stop sb in order to) check or reprimand him: *ALISON: I'm sorry. I'll go now. (She starts to move upstage. But his voice* ***pulls*** *her* ***up****).* ○ *JIMMY: You never even sent any flowers to the funeral.* LBA ○ *Even his wife had to* ***pull*** *him* ***up*** *over his wrong-headed notions this afternoon.* RM

4 [Vp, Vn.p pass] (help sb) improve a position in a race, contest etc. **S** [Vp], **O** [Vn.p]: pupil, competitor. **S** [Vn.p]: marks, points; performance, effort: *He* ***pulled up*** *to within a few yards of the leaders.* ○ *Her mark in the geography paper* ***pulled*** *her* ***up*** *several places.*

pull one's socks up [Vn ⇆ p] (*informal*) deal with difficulties by becoming more serious, business-like etc: *PENNY: Please Peter, pull yourself together. PETER: Leave me alone. ALEX:* ***Pull up your socks***, *son.* DPM ○ *We had no money in the bank, there were instalments on the car and there were the kids. So we decided to* ***pull up our socks***. ST □ socks occasionally modified: *The country collectively needs to* ***pull up its*** *industrial* ***socks***. BBCR

pull oneself up by one's own bootlaces/bootstraps [Vn.p] (*informal*) try to improve one's position by one's own unaided efforts: *Sandwell has to . . .* ***pull itself up*** *out of 100 years of industrial pollution* ***by its own bootstraps***. ST ○ *Unable to borrow capital to repair and modernize its plant, the company was forced to* ***pull itself up by its own bootlaces***.

pump

pump in/into 1 [Vn ⇆ p pass adj, Vn.pr pass emph rel] cause (sth) to flow in(to sth) by using a pump. **O:** gas, air; oil, water. **o:** tank, reservoir: *Too much oil had been* ***pumped in***, *and it overflowed everywhere.* ○ *Millions of gallons of liquid oxygen were* ***pumped into*** *the fuel tanks.*

2 [Vn ⇆ p pass, Vn.pr pass] (*informal*) cause (sb) to learn or acquire (sth) by force or persuasion. **O:** facts, information. **o:** head, brain: *Keep* ***pumping*** *the propaganda* ***in***: *it's really all they understand.* ○ *It's a hard job,* ***pumping*** *facts and figures* ***into*** *unwilling pupils.*

3 [Vn ⇆ p pass, Vn.pr pass] put (money) in (sth), with the aim of providing support, earning interest etc; inject. **O:** money, capital. **o:** industry, company: *The economy is booming and foreign companies are confidently* ***pumping in*** *capital.* ○ *There may be strong social reasons why the Government should* ***pump*** *money* ***into*** *industries which, economically, are no longer viable.*

pump out [Vn ⇆ p pass] (*informal*) produce (things) regularly and in large amounts. **O:** goods, cheap toys; news, pop music; books, stories; words: *He's got a factory* ***pumping out*** *plastic toys for export.* ○ *There are half a dozen private radio stations* ***pumping out*** *music round the clock.* = churn out.

pump out/out of [Vn ⇆ p pass adj, Vn.pr pass] cause (sth) to flow out (of sth) by using a pump. **O:** gas, air; oil, water. **o:** balloon; tank, sump, hold: *They pursued two ideas: the first was to* ***pump*** *the oil* ***out****; the second was to refloat the ship.* OBS ○ *The petrol is* ***pumped out of*** *the spare tank and into the main tank.*

pump out of [Vn.pr pass] (*informal*) cause (sb) to reveal (sth) by applying pressure. **O:** information, story: *We* ***pumped*** *the full story* ***out of*** *him little by little.*

pump up 1 [Vn ⇆ p pass adj] cause (sth) to rise by using a pump. **O:** (crude) oil, water: *The oil is* ***pumped up*** *from deep underground reservoirs.*

2 [Vn ⇆ p pass adj] fill (sth) with air etc, using a pump; inflate. **O:** tyre, balloon, (air-)mattress: ***Pump*** *the tyres* ***up*** *hard before going out on the road.* ○ *The* ***pumped-up*** *balloons began to burst as the heat increased.* = blow up 5.

punch

punch down/in [Vn ⇆ p pass adj] drive (sth) below the surface of a plank etc, using a tool called a 'punch'. **O:** nail, tack: *You should* ***punch down*** *any old nails or screws before attempting to lay a carpet.* ○ ***Punch in*** *the nails and then fill the holes with putty.*

punch out/out of [Vn ⇆ p pass adj, Vn.pr pass] cut (sth) from wood, metal etc, using a sharp tool called a 'punch'. **O:** disc, strip; coin, button: *The machine* ***punches out*** *hundreds of coins in an hour.* ○ *The figures are* ***punched out of*** *a continuous strip of cardboard.* = stamp out/out of.

punch up 1 [Vn ⇆ p pass] make a machine register (an amount) by striking a key or button sharply. **O:** £2.25, ten dollars fifty; bill: *She* ***punched up*** *the cost of our groceries on the cash register.*

2 [Vp nom, Vn ⇆ p] (*informal*) have a fist fight, exchange punches (with sb): *If there is any* ***punching up*** *between the two (sides), it's going to be here.* BBCTV ○ *He hires himself out to* ***punch up*** *people.* BBCR ○ *He was involved in a* ***punch-up*** *after an all-night party.* □ usu nom.

purge

purge (of) [Vn.pr pass] (*formal*) free or cleanse (sb) from (sth). **o:** guilt, shame, sin: *She felt* ***purged of*** *all feelings of guilt.* ○ *He looked for the finishing of the Reformation in England, the* ***purging of*** *the last odours of popery* (ie Catholicism). MLT

push

push about/around [Vn.p pass] (*informal*) order (sb) to do this and that in a bullying tone: *'I wish he'd stop* ***pushing*** *us* ***about*** *as though we were kids.'* ○ *'He established himself as ... a bully, a swaggering tough whom no one could* ***push around****.'* 50MH ○ *'I won't be* ***pushed around*** *by him any longer!'* = boss about/around, order about/around.

push ahead/forward/on [Vp] advance in a steady, determined way. **S:** team, expedition, army: *I was asked to* ***push on*** *and help the Fifth Army.* MFM ○ *We* ***pushed on*** *and now there was no doubt about the right direction: we came in sight of the walls of Peking.* BM = press ahead/forward/on.

push ahead/forward/on (with) [Vp, Vp.pr pass] continue in a determined way (to carry sth out). **o:** proposals, plans, scheme: *Now that particular problem is solved, there is nothing to stop us* ***pushing ahead****.* ○ *We are* ***pushing forward with*** *our plan to complete an inner ring road.* ○ *Redevelopment must be* ***pushed on with*** *as fast as money permits.*

push along [Vp] (*informal*) (of a guest) leave one's host: *'I'm afraid I really ought to be* ***pushing along*** *now.'* ○ *'It's time I was* ***pushing along****.'* □ used as shown in the examples as a polite though informal way of taking leave; also, even more informally, push off 2.

push around [Vn.p pass] ⇨ push about/around.

push aside 1 [Vn.p pass] push (sb) firmly, or roughly, out of one's way. **S:** steward, guard. **O:** spectator, bystander: *Young men* ***pushed*** *the older people* ***aside*** *in the scramble for food.* ○ *The order came to clear the hall. People standing in the aisles were roughly* ***pushed aside****.*

2 [Vn ⇆ p pass] treat (sth) as if it is of little or no importance; disregard. **O:** idea, suggestion; principle, consideration: *Moral considerations get* ***pushed aside*** *in the scramble for new arms contracts.* = brush aside 2.

push back 1 [Vn ⇆ p pass] move (sb) back under firm pressure; make (sb) retreat. **S:** police; army. **O:** crowd; enemy: *Police* ***pushed*** *the demonstrators* ***back*** *behind the crush barriers.* ○ *The invaders were* ***pushed back*** *beyond their own frontiers.*

2 [Vn ⇆ p pass adj] move (sth) back that has slipped forward out of its usual place. **O:** glasses, hair, hat: (radio review of a play)*'And then, the little habit he had of* ***pushing*** *his spectacles* ***back*** *on his nose.'* BBCR ○ *She kept* ***pushing back*** *wisps of hair that fell over her eyes.*

push by/past [Vp, Vpr] move past (sb), pressing against him, or pushing him to one side: *A large woman* ***pushed by*** *on her way to the bar.* ○ *A waiter* ***pushed by*** *me, almost knocking the glass from my hand.* ○ *A number of latecomers* ***pushed past*** *us to reach their seats* (ie at the cinema).

push (for) [Vpr pass, Vn.pr pass] make repeated and urgent requests (for sth). **O:** chairman; creditor. **o:** debate, adjournment; payment: *The teachers' union is* ***pushing*** *hard* ***for*** *new talks* (or: ***pushing*** *hard to get new talks).* ○ *Don't* ***push*** *him too hard* ***for*** *a settlement.* = press (for).

push forward 1 [Vp] advance in a steady way. ⇨ push ahead/forward/on.

2 [Vn ⇆ p pass] make (sb/sth) be noticed by others, so as to gain approval, help, business etc. **O:** oneself; child, relative; claim, case; product, goods: *He's never been one to* ***push*** *himself* ***forward****.* ○ *She's* ***pushing forward*** *a claim for extra compensation.*

push forward (with) [Vp, Vpr pass] ⇨ push ahead/forward/on (with).

push home [Vn ⇆ p pass] make (an attack etc) forcefully. **O:** attack; charge, accusation: *Resistance had been obstinate and the attack was* ***pushed home*** *with every sort of savagery.* SD ○ *He had now found the weakness in his adversary's case, and* ***pushed home*** *his points with vigour.* = press home.

push in [Vp] force oneself into a line, group or activity where one is not wanted: *'Don't let anyone* ***push in*** *or we'll never get to the head of the queue!'* ○ *'If there's a fund-raising event, he* ***pushes in*** *and tries to run everything.'*

push into [Vn.pr pass] persuade (sb) forcibly to do sth. **o:** a response; reacting, speaking, writing: *She... lay awake wondering to what extent she had let events* ***push*** *her* ***into*** *resuming her affair with Wickham.* CTD ○ *Baldwin himself was* ***pushed into*** *action by Dawson, editor of The Times.* EH

push off 1 [Vp, Vn ⇆ p nom pass] move (sth) out into the stream by pushing against the bank with a pole or oar. **S** [Vp Vn.p]**:** boatman, sailor. **O:** punt, dinghy: *'****Push off*** *as soon as you're ready!'* ○ *Bill* ***pushed*** *us* ***off*** (or: *gave us a* ***push-off****) and we went skimming away from the bank.* = shove off 1.
2 [Vp] (*informal*) leave, go away: *'Why don't you* ***push off****! You're not wanted here.'* ○ *'Well, I'll* ***push off****,' the girl said. 'See you later, Charlie.'* DBM ○ *He comes into town, looks up a few friends, and then* ***pushes off*** *again.* = shove off (which is even more informal), push along.

push on [Vp] ⇨ push ahead/forward/on.

push on (with) [Vp, Vp.pr pass] ⇨ push ahead/forward/on (with).

push the boat out [Vn.p] celebrate regardless of the expense: *'Bill and Jane are giving another party this weekend.' 'They're* ***pushing the boat out*** *a bit lately aren't they?'*

push over [Vn ⇆ p pass] make (sb/sth) overturn or fall to the ground by pushing him or it. **O:** him etc; vase, ornament; bucket, jug: *They* ***pushed over*** *one or two tables in the scramble.* ○ *I was nearly* ***pushed over*** *by a crowd of boys surging through the school gates.*

pushover [nom (Vn.p)] (*informal*) an easy triumph or victory (for sb): *Saturday's match should be a* ***pushover*** *for Leeds: they're playing a fourth division team.* ○ *'What do you mean, you couldn't persuade Joe? He should have been a* ***pushover****!'*

push past [Vp, Vpr] ⇨ push by/past.

push through 1 [Vp, Vpr] go though (an obstacle) by pushing firmly. **o:** long grass, hedge; gap, opening: *There was a gap in the wooden fence and one of the dogs managed to* ***push through****.* ○ *As Emlyn* ***pushed through*** *the hedge two crows rose and flapped slowly away.* SE
2 [Vn ⇆ p pass, Vn.pr pass] get (an official body) to accept (sth) or make it law, by applying pressure. **O:** measure, reform; Bill. **o:** Parliament, committee: *We're trying to* ***push*** *the legislation* ***through*** *before the Christmas recess.* ○ *Some serving generals demand ... hefty commissions for* ***pushing through*** *government contracts.* OBS ○ *You can't* ***push*** *proposals on this sort of scale* ***through*** *the Finance Committee.*

push to [Vn.p pass] close or nearly close (sth) by pushing on it. **O:** door, gate: *'Please* ***push*** *the door* ***to*** *behind you.'*

push up [Vn ⇆ p pass] increase (sth) at a steady rate. **O:** temperature, pressure; price, wage: *Demand for monastic land ... certainly* ***pushed up*** *land prices and rents.* SHOE ○ *The usual drinking parties at New Year will* ***push*** *the road death figures* ***up****.* BBCTV

put

put about 1 [Vp, Vn ⇆ p pass] (*nautical*) (cause a boat to) change direction. **S** [Vp], **O** [Vn.p]**:** boat, ship: *The ship* ***put about*** *to avoid icebergs reported in the area.* ⇨ bring about 2, come about 2, go about 5.
2 [Vn ⇆ p pass] pass (sth) from one person to another; circulate. **O:** tale, rumour; it ... that she was resigning, it ... that wages were going up: *Somebody* ***put*** *the story* ***about*** *that the Department was being closed down.* ○ *It was* ***put about*** *that he was seeing too much of another woman.* ⇨ get about/around/round, go about 2.

put above [Vn.p pass emph rel] regard or treat (sth) as more important than (sth else). **O:** (national) survival, recovery; honour, integrity. **o:** all else; safety, self-interest: *The investigations showed that few men were prepared to* ***put*** *the integrity of the Administration* ***above*** *its survival.* ○ ***Above*** *such considerations of cost we should* ***put*** *the safety of the men who have to work in the plant.* = put before 1.

put across 1 [Vn.p pass] communicate (sth) effectively to others. **O:** ideas, thoughts; material; subject: *He may be a good researcher, but he's very poor at* ***putting*** *the stuff* ***across*** *to a class.* = put over (to). ⇨ come across 2, get across (to).
2 [Vn.p pass] persuade (others) to like or accept (sth/oneself). **O:** scheme, plan; oneself: *Sarah's the one who's most likely to* ***put*** *the scheme* ***across*** *to the Board.* ○ *He finds it hard to* ***put*** *himself* ***across*** *at interviews.*
3 [Vn.pr pass] (*informal*) trick (sb) into accepting or believing (sth). **O:** ⚠ it; this, one; anything, something. **o:** teacher, employer, judge: *'You'd better not try to* ***put*** *anything* ***across*** *him!'* ○ *He* ***put*** *one* ***across*** *the police once, but they're not likely to be caught a second time.* = put over (on).

put the cat among the pigeons [Vn.pr pass] (*informal*) produce a strong reaction in people, esp of shock, dismay or anger: *'By jove, if the monster started rutting next October that would* ***put the cat among the pigeons****, what?'* RM

put aside 1 [Vn ⇆ p pass] place (sth) to one side; abandon. **O:** book, knitting; study, subject: *She* ***put*** *her needlework* ***aside****, and we had a talk.* ○ *He* ***put aside*** *his textbooks when he left school and never reopened them.* = lay aside 1, set aside 1.
2 [Vn ⇆ p pass] save (sth) for spending or use later. **O:** money, cash; food: *I've a nice little sum of money* ***put aside*** *for a rainy day.* ○ *The rest of the soup can be* ***put aside*** *for tomorrow's lunch.* = put on one side 1, set aside 4.
3 [Vn ⇆ p pass] save, reserve (an article) for a customer who cannot pay for it now. **O:** stereo, fridge, washing-machine: *'If you can pay me a small deposit, I'll* ***put*** *the camera* ***aside*** *for you.'* = put on one side 2.

4 [Vn ⇆ p pass] stop regarding (sth) as important; disregard. **O:** grievance, difference; bitterness, hatred: *At times like this, we have to* **put aside** *party political differences.* ○ **Put aside** *all that has happened and try to start again.* = put on one side 3, set aside 3.

put at [Vn.pr pass] calculate or estimate (sth) to be a certain size, weight etc. **O:** fifty, 12 by 10 metres, thirty feet, ten gallons: *'What would you* **put** *the outer radius* **at**?' TBC ○ *I'd* **put** *the weight* **at** *about fourteen pounds.* = estimate at.

put at his ease [Vn.pr pass] make (sb) feel free from anxiety or embarrassment. **S:** ruler, commander, manager; distinguished guest. **O:** subordinate, member of staff; hosts, audience: *Being well aware that those on the civil side were apprehensive of what I might do, I took great trouble to* **put** *them* **at their ease**. MFM ○ *They were seated in armchairs, offered cigarettes, and generally* **put at their ease**.

put at a premium [Vn.pr pass] make (sth) especially important, set a special value upon (sth). **S:** situation, circumstances; crisis, emergency. **O:** skill, intelligence; cunning, deception: *Our dependence on overseas trade* **puts** *drive and resourcefulness in the export industries* **at a premium**. ○ *In these communities loyalty to the family is* **put at a premium**. = put a premium on. ⇨ be at a premium 2.

put away 1 [Vn ⇆ p pass] put (sth) in a box, drawer etc, because one has finished using it, or to make a room tidy etc. **O:** paper, book; doll, toy: *The kitchen table was littered with dishes and no one had* **put** *the cream* **away**. AT ○ *The other day I found an old doll. I had to* **put** *it* **away** *again because he wouldn't touch it.* DC ↔ leave out. ⇨ be away 1.

2 [Vn ⇆ p pass] save (sth). **O:** a good amount, a tidy sum, a fortune: *She's got a couple of thousand* **put away** *in the building society.* ○ *I'll have to* **put** *something* **away** *for my retirement.* = put by.

3 [Vn ⇆ p pass] (*informal*) shut (sb) up, esp in a mental home or prison. **O:** mental patient, psychotic, criminal: *It was like those nightmares in which the dreamer sees himself* **put away** *for lunacy.* HD ○ *People who were disrespectful of the power of money were mad or bad . . . and deserved to be* **put away** . SE □ esp passive.

4 [Vn ⇆ p pass] (*informal*) consume large quantities of food and drink. **o:** stacks of food; pints of beer: *I don't know how he manages to* **put** *it all* **away**. ○ *He* **put away** *half a dozen cakes while my back was turned.* = tuck away 1.

5 [Vn ⇆ p pass] (*informal*) kill (sth/sb), because of old age, sickness or injury; destroy. **S:** vet, doctor, soldier. **O:** dog, cat; wounded man: *The dog Billy was dying, and in September he had to be* **put away**. RFW ○ *We knew of a couple of men being* **put away** *because they were too badly wounded to survive.* = put down 10.

put back 1 [Vn ⇆ p pass] replace or return (sth). **O:** book, record: *'Kindly* **put** *the book* **back** *in its proper place.'* ○ *I recaptured the animal and* **put** *him* **back** *in the tin without much opposition.* DF ⇨ be back 2, get back 3.

2 [Vn ⇆ p pass] move the hands of a clock back to conform with the end of official Summer Time, or to give the correct time. **O:** clock, watch: *The clocks should have been* **put back** *one hour last night.* ○ *'Your watch is fast; you need to* **put** *it* **back** *ten minutes.'* ↔ put forward 3. ⇨ go back 2.

3 [Vn ⇆ p pass] move (an event) to a later time or date; defer. **O:** party, wedding; programme, exercise; date, time: *The invasion was* **put back** *twenty-four hours while the chiefs waited for better weather reports.* ○ *The date had been* **put back** *from March to April.* NM ↔ bring forward 2.

4 [Vn ⇆ p pass] hamper the progress of (sth) or reverse it by some amount. **O:** programme; production, output. **A:** six months, a whole year: *Drought has* **put** *our agricultural programme* **back** *to where we started from.* ○ *The seamen's strike has* **put** *our deliveries* **back** *at least a month.* = set back 1.

put the clock back [Vn ⇆ p pass] return to the practices, values etc of an earlier period: *All this* Anglo-Catholicism (a form of Christianity which revived certain medieval features of Christian worship) *makes him think we can* **put the clock back**, *but there's a tough core of common sense there, all the same.* ASA ○ *The 'Mirror' says nobody can* **put back the clock** *and get rid of decimal currency.* BBCR ⇨ put back 2.

put before 1 [Vn.pr pass emph] treat or regard (sth) as more important than (sth else). **O:** country, national interest; economic revival, military strength. **o:** self; all else, all other aims: *Our determination is to* **put** *the development of the European Community* **before** *all other considerations.* ○ **Before** *everything else we must* **put** *the reconstruction of our damaged cities.* = put above. ⇨ come before 3.

2 [Vn.pr pass emph] present (sth) for sb to consider. **O:** plan, proposal, scheme. **o:** committee, board: *The hungry public gobbled avidly whatever he* **put before** *them.* GE ○ *A whole set of new demands were* **put before** *the management.* ⇨ be before 2, bring before, come before 2, go before 2, take before.

put the cart before the horse [Vn.pr pass] (*informal*) reverse the proper order of events, cause and effect etc: *To speak of one language for the world as leading to one purpose is to* **put the cart before the horse**. SC ○ *Emotion comes first, the physiological concomitants come second. James and Lange maintain that this is* **putting the cart before the horse**. SNP

put one foot before/in front of the other [Vn.pr] (*informal*) (not) be able to walk properly. **S:** elderly person, invalid: *She was hardly able to* **put one foot before the other** *because of the tightness of the skirt above the ankles.* AH ○ *He'd had so much to drink that he couldn't* **put one foot in front of the other**. □ with *can/could not, hardly, scarcely.*

put behind bars [Vn.pr pass] (*informal*) put (sb) in jail; imprison. **S:** authorities; magistrate, court. **O:** bank-robber, gunman: *We shall all sleep more soundly in our beds when this lunatic has been* **put behind bars**. ⇨ be behind bars.

put behind one [Vn.pr pass] not allow sth that has upset or concerned one in the past to affect one in the present. **O:** (past) disappointments, failures; disagreements, differences; suspicion, hatred: *'His 'O' level results were disappointing, but of course he's* **put** *all that* **behind him** *now.'* ○ *The hour of crisis is past. The ship of state is back on* *an even keel, and we must* **put behind us** *the fear of capsizing.* NS

put by [Vn ⇆ p pass] save (sth). **O:** a few pounds, a couple of thousand; a small nest egg: *'It's all right, love. I've got a bit of money* **put by**.' TOH ○ *Have a bit* **put by** *for a rainy day.* = lay aside/by, put away 2.

put down 1 [Vn ⇆ p pass] place (sth) on a table, shelf etc: *She had* **put** *the sewing needle* **down** *on the chair by the window.* DC ○ *I* **put down** *the phone and made a note of the caller's name.* ↔ pick up 1.
2 [Vn ⇆ p pass] set down (sth) which is a danger or nuisance to oneself or others. **O:** gun, knife: *'***Put down** *that knife before you hurt somebody!'*
3 [Vp, Vn.p] (cause sth to) return to land; land. **S** [Vp], **O** [Vn.p]: plane, helicopter: *The helicopter hovered over us looking for a place to* **put down**. ○ *He* **put** *the glider* **down** *in a corn-field.* ↔ take off 12. ⇨ let down 5.
4 [Vn ⇆ p nom pass] allow (sb) to alight. **S:** driver, pilot; bus. **O:** passenger, crew: *The bus stopped at the crossroads to* **put down** *one or two passengers.* □ nom used attrib as in: *a* **put-down** *point.* = set down 1. ↔ pick up 4.
5 [Vn ⇆ p pass] pay part of the cost of sth — the remainder being paid in regular amounts later on. **O:** a deposit; 20% of the total price; £50: *You can* **put down** *the money you get for your old camera as a deposit.* ○ *We had to* **put** *a couple of hundred* **down** *to get the keys of the flat.*
6 [Vn ⇆ p pass] place (wine) in a cellar to mature. **O:** wine, port, brandy: *When you see what they're charging for French wines, I'm glad I* **put down** *a couple of cases of claret last year.*
7 [Vn ⇆ p pass] force (sb) to remain silent or inactive; force (sth) to stop; suppress. **O:** opponent, critic, rebel; uprising, rebellion: *They also employed small family groups as retainers... to run estates, bear arms,* **put down** *any resistance....* RI ○ *The demonstration was* **put down** *by armed riot police.*
8 [Vp.n pass] get rid of (sth); suppress, abolish. **O:** organized crime, vice; gambling, prostitution: *They introduced measures aimed at* **putting down**, *or at least restricting, organized gambling.*
9 [Vn.p nom pass] (*informal*) (try to) make (sb) feel foolish or inadequate; humiliate. **O:** husband, daughter, girl-friend: *She's the kind of girl who* **puts** *you* **down** *when friends are there. You feel a fool.* LENNON AND MCCARTNEY ○ *'Mind your own business,' Savundra shouted, adding his favourite* **put-down**: *'Don't get in the ring with heavy-weights* (ie don't try to compete with stronger or cleverer people).' OBS
10 [Vn ⇆ p pass] kill (sth) because it is old, sick or injured; destroy; kill (sth) because it is a nuisance or danger; exterminate. **O:** cat, dog; pest, vermin: *We tried* **putting down** *mice and other small vermin with poison.* ○ *They have become pests and have to be* **put down**. OBS = put away 5.
11 [Vn ⇆ p pass] record (sth) in writing. **O:** name, address; thought, impression: *When the lists were first drawn up, you* **put** *your name* **down** *mechanically.* CON ○ *One feels almost ashamed of* **putting** *it* (this view) **down** *in black and white again.* SNP ○ **Put down** *the date in your diary so that you don't forget it.* = note down, write down. ⇨ be down 3, get down 4, go down 9, set down 2, take down 3.
12 [Vp.n pass] (*Parliament*) include (sth) in the agenda for a meeting so that it can be debated and voted on; table. **O:** motion, resolution: *Some MPs are in favour of* **putting down** *a resolution which would come before the Parliamentary Labour Party.* OBS ○ *The Conservatives may* **put down** *a censure motion on the Government's handling of the Torrey Canyon affair.* OBS

put one's foot down 1 [Vn.p] (*informal*) press down the accelerator, causing the vehicle to travel faster: *Don't think, when you reach the motorway, that you can just* **put your foot down** *and relax.* ○ *She* **put her foot** *right* **down** *on the accelerator and felt the car surge forward.*
2 [Vn.p] (*informal*) act firmly to oppose some course of action: *Isobel was longing to be called up for service. But here her father unexpectedly* **put his foot down** (and forbade her to join up). PW ○ *'Robin doesn't seem to see that there has to be some hierarchy in the place!' 'Then you must* **put your foot down**, *darling.'* ASA

put down roots [Vp.n] adopt a settled way of life, eg by buying a house or starting a family: *Once I took a wife I should have to* **put down roots** *and settle for a definite way of life.* CON

put down as 1 [Vn.p.pr pass] write (sb/sth) in a record or on a form, often with a view to misleading or deceiving sb else. **O:** private spending, holiday trip; oneself; girlfriend. **o:** business expenses, necessary journey; self-employed; wife: *When travelling abroad, Smith often* **puts down** *entertainment costs* **as** *business expenses.* ○ *He* **put** *himself* **down** *on the Income Tax form* **as** *'unemployed'.* ○ *His secretary was* **put down** *in the hotel register* **as** *Mrs Jones.* ⇨ be down as.
2 [Vn.p.pr pass] consider (sb) to be (sth). **o:** sales representative, retired officer: *Noticing his military bearing, I* **put** *him* **down as** *a retired major.* ○ *He was* **put down as** *an ordinary waiter and passed almost unnoticed among the others.*

put down for 1 [Vn.p.pr pass] record that (sb) is willing to contribute (sth) to charity, buy (sth) at a sale etc. **o:** a dozen raffle tickets; fifty pounds; two suits: *'How many tickets shall I* **put** *you* **down for**?' *'Half a dozen.'* ○ *You can* **put** *me* **down for** *fifty Preference Shares.*
2 [Vn.p.pr pass] enter (sb's name) on a list as sb interested in (studying at a school, going on an outing etc). **O:** son, daughter; name. **o:** Westminster, St. Paul's; trip to Edinburgh: *He changed his mind ... and* **put** *no fewer than three of us* **down for** *Charterhouse.* SU ○ *Children need to be* **put down for** *some schools almost as soon as they are born.* ⇨ be down for.

put down to 1 [Vn.p.pr pass] enter (an amount) in (a particular account). **o:** expenses, petty cash: *You can* **put** *the lunch* **down to** *my account.* ○ *Expenditure on Christmas decorations was* **put down to** *petty cash.*
2 [Vn.p.pr pass] regard (sth) as being due to (sth). **O:** outburst, scene; behaviour, conduct; epidemic, famine; poor health. **o:** temper, ignorance, poor breeding; inadequate precautions, civil war; living in the tropics: *I did notice that you were depressed, but I* **put** *it* **down to** *drink.* ASA ○ *I know he'd got a bit pompous, but I* **put** *that* **down to** *Marie Hélène* (his wife). ASA ○ *My dad had pains in his stomach*

. . . *which he* **put down to** *eating too many ripe bananas.* PPLA

put forth [Vp.n pass] (*formal*) produce (sth); display. **O:** shoot, bud, (young) leaf: *In the Spring, the hedgerows* **put forth** *new buds.* ○ *The day was superb, and here was the College* **putting forth** *all its beauty.* HD = put out 3.

put forward 1 [Vn ⇆ p pass] propose, suggest (sth) for discussion; advance. **O:** argument, theory; proposal, suggestion; plan, scheme; answer, solution: *I will not* **put forward** *any solutions; if we have these problems we must live with them.* ESS ○ *It's an explanation that's often* **put forward** *by Geoff: he's convinced that economics is at the bottom of everything.* = put up 7.

2 [Vn ⇆ p pass] recommend or propose (sb); nominate. **O:** oneself; colleague, employee. **A:** as a candidate; for promotion; for an award, honour, title: *They're* **putting forward** *three names for the Shelley Prize.* ○ *He was* **put forward** *as the man most likely to win the ear of the conference.*

3 [Vn.p pass] move the hands of a clock forward, to correct the time shown by it, or by one hour at the beginning of British Summer Time etc. **O:** clock, watch: *Summer Time begins tomorrow, so* **put** *your clocks* **forward** *one hour tonight.* ○ *'***Put** *your watch* **forward***: you're five minutes slow.'* ↔ put back 2.

put one's best foot forward [Vn.p] make haste, hurry: *If you want to get home by nightfall, you'll have to* **put your best foot forward***.* ○ *The work force* **put its best foot forward** *to meet the promised delivery date.*

put in 1 [Vp] say (sth) as a contribution to a discussion etc, usu by interrupting another speaker; interpose, interject: *'It's the firm's time,' Baxter insisted. 'He's carrying out an experiment,' I* **put in***.* CON ○ *'He said you'd have to sign the Official Secrets Act,'* **put in** *Derek.* SATS □ usu follows direct speech, as shown.

2 [Vn ⇆ p pass, Vn.pr pass] include (sth) in (a story etc). **O:** comma, full stop; detail, episode; that he offered to help. **o:** paragraph; account, story, article: **Put in** *the proper punctuation marks.* ○ *'Don't forget to* **put in** *the bit about Jim falling into the river!'* ○ *'And you can* **put in** *that I was prepared to be helpful!'* ↔ leave out/out of.

3 [Vn ⇆ p pass] devote, spend (a period of time). **O:** two weeks, some time, an hour a day: *Harold consciously tried to* **put in** *a quarter of an hour each day improving his putting* (ie at golf). PW ○ **Put in** *a few hours of careful weeding and he'll be pleased!* WI ○ **Put in** *some time asking yourself why.* EHOW □ often followed by the -ing form of a verb.

4 [Vn ⇆ p pass] fit, install (sth). **O:** cork, plug; central heating, new plumbing: *'***Put** *the cork back* **in** *the bottle.'* ○ *We're* **putting in** *a completely new system of wiring and switches.* ○ *We've pulled the old pipes out and* **put** *copper ones* **in***.* ↔ take out/out of 2. ⇨ go in 3.

5 [Vn.pr pass] cause (sb) to enter (an institution). **o:** boarding school; old people's home, nursing home; jail: *Joe had always had learning difficulties, so we thought of* **putting** *him* **in** *a special school.* ○ *If the authorities think you're a troublemaker, you might get* **put in** *jail.*

6 [Vn ⇆ p pass] give duties to (sb), usu in a building, office block etc. **O:** guard, night-watchman: *They've* **put in** *a caretaker to keep an eye on people coming in and out of the building.* ○ *A security man was* **put in** *to check on doors and windows.*

7 [Vn ⇆ p pass] (*politics*) elect (sb) to office. **O:** Labour, the Conservatives: *The Conservatives were* **put in** *with a reduced majority at the last General Election.* ⇨ be in 4, come in 4, get in/into 3.

8 [Vn ⇆ p pass] (*cricket*) ask the opposing team to bat at the start of a match; tell a member of one's own side to bat. **S:** captain, skipper. **O:** side, team; (fast-scoring) batsman: *The home side* **put** *the visitors* **in** *to bat on a fast wicket, and had half of them out before tea.* ⇨ be in 5, go in 4, stay in 3.

put (all) one's eggs in one basket [Vn.pr pass] (*informal*) give all one's attention to a single aim (eg loving one person only); risk all that one has in a single venture (eg by using all one's troops in one attack): *I'm* **putting all my eggs in one basket***,/ I'm betting everything I've got on you./ I'm giving all my love to one baby,/ Heaven help me if my baby don't come through.* IRVING BERLIN ○ *Office development in the City — now that's* **one basket** *you shouldn't* **put all your eggs in***.* ○ *Leeds has never suffered very deeply from the recession;* **its eggs** *have been* **put in** *too* **many baskets***.* □ note the pl forms: *several, too many* baskets, suggesting the spreading of interests or money.

put in an/one's appearance [Vp.n] appear, often briefly, at a party, ceremony etc because one feels obliged to do so, and not for pleasure or out of genuine interest. **S:** VIP, minister, director: *Jeremy* **put in a** *brief* **appearance** *towards the end of our party, and was then swept off to a more important one.* ○ *'Wait five minutes — just to show you've* **put in an appearance** *— and then go for a drink.'* ○ *He waited for the right moment to* **put in his appearance** *— just as supper was about to be served.*

put in an awkward etc position [Vn.pr pass rel] make things appear awkward etc for (sb). **adj:** awkward, difficult, embarrassing, impossible: *The support given to the rebels by outside forces* **puts** *the government* **in an impossible position***.* ○ *We are* **put in an intolerable position** *by her refusal to co-operate.* ○ *Is that all you can say, 'I'm sorry'? Such* **an awkward position** *I* **put** *you* **in***, don't I?* FFE

put one's foot in it [Vn.pr] (*informal*) say sth embarrassing or hurtful, out of thoughtlessness or insensitivity, thus making oneself appear foolish: *I just said what came into my head, and there I go,* **putting my foot in it** *as usual.* AITC ○ *There is a dazzling reward for allowing your best friend to make advances to your young woman in your presence — that of seeing him* **put his foot in it***.* SPL

put a (good) word in [Vn ⇆ p pass] (*informal*) speak or testify on behalf of (sb). **A:** for me, on my behalf, in his defence, in support of Linda: *'Here, Lumley,' he called, as the policeman marched him away, 'you* **put in a word** *for me, will you?'* HD ○ *The head teacher was always prepared to* **put a good word in** *for her former pupils.*

put in inverted commas [Vn.pr pass] place (a word or phrase) between quotation marks to indicate that one is specially conscious of it, eg because it is foreign or a slang term; in speech, pronounce (a word etc) with special intonation, for the same reasons as above: *Until borrowed words are fully assimilated into the language they are often* **put in inverted commas**. ○ *He was so ashamed and suspicious of the word 'love' that he had to* **put** *it* **in inverted commas**. PW

put in jeopardy [Vn.pr pass] threaten, menace, endanger (sth). **O:** campaign, project; trade, communications; security, vital interests. **adj:** grave, serious: *The hold-up in the supply of fuel* **puts** *our whole advance* **in jeopardy**. ○ *The chances of an important representative match at Twickenham are* **put in jeopardy** *by the weather*. T ⇨ be in jeopardy.

put in mind of [Vn.pr pass] suggest to (sb) a similarity to (sth). **S:** conversation, lecture; appearance, posture, movements. **o:** something I'd heard before in London; a bear, an eagle, a crab: *Sudden ... immersion in country air and country silence* **puts** *me* **in mind of** *an observation by Norman Douglas*. AH ○ *She made love strenuously; I was* **put in mind of** *a hard set of mixed tennis*. RATT = remind of.

put in a nutshell [Vn.pr pass] state (sth) in a few words, express (sth) succinctly. **O:** ⚠ it, the whole thing; the matter, problem, question: *Alexis* **puts** *it* **in a nutshell**: *losing power is the most dreadful prospect that a politician can think of*. TBC ○ *The whole position was* **put in a nutshell** *by none other than Daniel Defoe*. SNP

put in order [Vn.pr pass] arrange (things) tidily, according to a pattern. **O:** papers, books; study, office; affairs, business: *His study is a chaos: his housekeeper has long since given up trying to* **put** *his papers* **in order**. ○ *Delegates retorted that the union should first* **put** *its own affairs* **in order**.

put one's (own) house in order [Vn.pr pass] organize one's (own) affairs efficiently. **S:** government; management, administration; military command: (headline) *Daimler-Benz to* **put its house in order**: *the German carmaker is to start using international standards for its accounts*. IND ○ *There is a feeling that the press... has decided it is in its interests to* **put its own house in order**. G

put in the picture [Vn.pr pass] (*informal*) give (sb) up-to-date information about sth. **O:** staff, colleagues; one's family: *The battle plan was kept secret until the last moment; then the men were* **put in the picture**. ○ *You've got to* **put** *me* **in the picture**. *What's this business with your Philip?* EHOW ⇨ be in the picture.

put in his place [Vn.pr pass] by exerting one's authority, remind (sb) that he is in a subordinate position, without power: *The Italian nobility had been* **put in their place**, *and no longer held important public office*. INN ○ *His manner indicated that the subject was closed, and I'd been* **put in my place**. RATT □ note pl form: *We were* **put** *firmly* **in our places**. ⇨ keep in his place.

put oneself in sb's place/shoes [Vn.pr] try, by an effort of sympathy, to share the feelings of another person: *Try to* **put yourself in his shoes**. *Would you have behaved any differently in the circumstances?* ○ *Remembering our own bereavements and humiliations, we can condole with others, we can* **put ourselves in their places**. DOP

put in the shade [Vn.pr pass] by one's/its own success, importance etc, make (the achievements of others) seem small. **S:** he etc; performance, interpretation. **O:** achievement, effort: *You can do a big dash* (= sprint) *later that* **puts** *everybody else's hurry* **in the shade**. LLDR ○ *The first part of the programme was* **put in the shade** *by the appearance of the star attraction*.

put a sock in it [Vn.pr] (*informal*) stop speaking or making a noise; be quiet: *George Formby* (a comic actor) ... *dreams a sequence in which he flies over Berlin ... lands at a Nuremburg rally and challenges the Führer himself, 'You, Adolf,* **put a sock in it**!' BCIN □ usu direct or indirect command.

put a spoke in sb's wheel [Vn.pr pass] (*informal*) stop or hinder sb's activities, which may be unpleasant or dishonest: *'No, you can't get out of it as easily as all that, Miss Richards — it's about time that someone* **put a spoke in your** *little* **wheel**.' TT ○ *She did not spare him, and if he lost his flicker of self-assurance, she welcomed it. She had* **put a spoke in that wheel**, *anyway*. PW

put that in one's pipe and smoke it [Vn.pr] (*informal*) tell sb in a determined, stubborn way that one is not going to change and that people must accept that fact: *I'm not going to become a Catholic so they can* **put that in their pipe and smoke it**. HAA ○ *We weren't going to shift our ground one bit, and he could* **put that in his pipe and smoke it**. □ usu in imperative form, or with can/could. □ Note pl form: *'You can* put that in your pipes and smoke it' and compare the first example.

put one's trust in [Vn.pr emph rel] treat (sb/sth) as reliable or dependable; trust. **adj:** one's; no, (not) any/much, (not) a lot of. **o:** God, Church; friend, ally; sb's story, account: *They did not* **put their trust in** *the information they received from the well-tried and veteran staff of the Eighth Army*. MFM ○ *He was still* **putting his trust in** *material efficiency, in 'getting on'*. CON ○ *There was no one around* **in** *whom he felt he could* **put** *very much* **trust**.

put in the wrong [Vn.pr pass] make it seem, perhaps unjustly, that (sb else) is to blame for sth; act wrongly, thus losing any moral advantage for (oneself). **O:** colleague, wife; oneself: *He's always trying to* **put** *me* **in the wrong**; *that way, he hopes to spoil my relationship with my students*. ○ *If I hadn't* **put** *myself* **in the wrong** *by doing that, I might have taken a high moral line about the typescript*. UTN ⇨ be in the wrong.

put in (for) [Vp, Vp.pr pass, Vn ⇆ p pass, Vn.p.pr pass] make (an application etc) (for sth). **O:** application, claim, request, demand. **o:** job, promotion; leave; expenses : [Vp.pr] *I'd like to* **put in for** *a posting up north or somewhere, but they'd never let me go*. RFW ○ [Vp, Vn.p] *He's due for some leave and is thinking of* **putting in** *(an application)*. ○ [Vn.p.pr] *A claim has been* **put in for** *a wage increase*. ⇨ be in for 2.

put in for 1 [Vn.p.pr pass] (*sport*) enter sb's name as a competitor in (an event). **S:** coach, club. **O:** athlete; runner. **o:** event, race; long jump, 3 000 metres: *We're thinking of* **putting** *Peter* **in for** *the 100 metres and the discus*. = enter for. ⇨ be in for 1, go in for 1.

2 [Vn.p.pr pass] recommend (sb) for (a post etc) as a suitable and deserving person. **S:** superior officer, employer. **o:** award, decoration; post, job, transfer: *His commanding officer is* **putting** *him* **in for** *the Victoria Cross.* ○ *He's being* **put in for** *a job on the administrative side.*

put in touch (with) [Vn.pr pass] help (sb) to meet (sb else): *I got put on to the idea of Alcoholics Anonymous. They* **put** *me* **in touch with** *a marvellous woman.* ASA ○ *He* **put** *Father* **in touch with** *another collector* (or: **put** *Father and another collector* **in touch**). ○ *They were* **put in touch** *by a church organization.* = bring into contact (with), put on to 1. ⇨ be in touch (with).

put one foot in front of the other [Vn.pr] ⇨ put one foot before/in front of the other.

put in/into 1 [Vn ⇆ p pass, Vn.pr pass] place (sth) in (an enclosed space). **O:** hand, fingers; fruit, vegetables; components. **o:** pocket, glove; bag, box; container: *'That's the nest, but don't* **put** *your hand* **in** *unless you want to get bitten.'* ○ *In those days eggs were* **put into** *paper bags not* **into** *plastic boxes.* PPLA ↔ take out/out of 2.

2 [Vn ⇆ p pass, Vn.pr pass] give (money) to a bank, to be kept in an account; deposit. **O:** cash, cheque; savings, earnings. **o:** current account, savings account; building society: *I'll* **put** *these two cheques* **in** *and draw out a bit of cash.* ○ *We try to* **put** *money regularly* **in/into** *a savings account for the children.* = pay in/into. ↔ draw out/out of 3.

3 [Vn ⇆ p pass, Vn.pr pass] invest (money) in (sth). **O:** money; millions (of pounds); people's savings. **o:** industry, commercial development; property, shipping: *If you're prepared to invest in the water privatisation, I might* **put in** *a few pounds of my own.* ○ *Investment is drying up: nobody is* **putting** *anything* **into** *industry.*

4 [Vp, Vpr] (*nautical*) call, dock (at a port). **S:** ship, boat. **o:** harbour, port. **A:** at a port, at Singapore; for a refit, for supplies: *We'll* **put in** *at the next port for refuelling.* ○ *Their ships* **put into** *Lagos, Dakar and Bom Porto.* FL ○ *The 'Norfolk Yeoman'* **put into** *Newlyn yesterday with a catch of gleaming fresh mackerel.* OBS

5 [Vn ⇆ p pass, Vn.pr pass] devote (effort) to (doing sth). **O:** effort, work, thought. **o:** arranging, finishing, organizing, planning: *August is a month ... to relax in the garden and reap the rewards of all the hard work you* **put in** *earlier in the season.* GW ○ *A lot of careful planning was* **put into** *making the day a success.*

put the fear of death/God in/into/up [Vn.pr pass] (*informal*) thoroughly frighten sb; force sb to give way or to obey through the strength of one's authority. **S:** explosion, accident; boss, schoolteacher, sergeant-major: *'The question is,' said Rose, 'who's the fellow that's trying to* **put the fear of God in** *us?'* MM ○ *The drill sergeant begins by* **putting the fear of death into** *every new recruit.* ○ *He'd had* **the fear of God put up** *him by a domineering mother. It seemed a natural transition to marry a shrewish wife.*

put inside [Vn.p pass] (*police slang*) put (sb) in prison. **O:** criminal; burglar, shoplifter: *One of your scientists has been giving us away. They're going to* **put** *him* **inside** *soon.* NM ○ *He's been* **put inside** *for breaking and entering.* ⇨ be inside.

put into effect [Vn.pr pass] make (sth) really happen; implement. **S:** administrator, engineer. **O:** plan, programme; phase, stage (of an operation): *'It's a first-rate scheme, and he's just the man to* **put** *it* **into effect**.' ○ *Your proposal looks good on paper, but I'm not yet convinced it can be* **put into effect**. = carry out 1, put into practice. ⇨ come into effect.

put into force [Vn.pr pass] introduce (sth) with the backing of the law. **O:** law, regulation; speed limit: *There is pressure on the Government to* **put** *new safety measures* **into force**. ○ *A new upper limit on price increases has been* **put into force**. ⇨ be in/bring into/come into force.

put heart into [Vn.pr] make (sb) more cheerful and optimistic, esp in difficult times; encourage. **adj:** fresh, new. **o:** team, crew; troops; survivors; supporters: *His arrival* **puts heart into** *his subordinates.* RTH ○ (a shipwrecked sailor is speaking) *Then I heard my own name on the radio programme ... That* **put** *fresh* **heart into** *me. I determined that the sea should not have me.* SC

put one's heart and soul into [Vn.pr pass emph rel] undertake (a task) with total dedication. **o:** profession, business; building a home, bringing up a family: *If each one of us* **puts his** *whole* **heart and soul into** *this next contest, then nothing can stop us.* MFM ○ **Into** *the work of rebuilding their cities the peoples of war-ravaged Europe* **put their heart and soul**.

put the idea/thought into sb's head [Vn.pr pass] make sb think or believe (sth): *'She says I've fallen in love with Alec? What could have* **put that idea into her head**?' PW ○ *It was a question about the cost of houses in York that first* **put into my head the thought** *that he was applying for another job.*

put ideas into sb's head [Vn.pr pass] (*informal*) persuade sb to think that he is specially important, that sth pleasant is going to happen to him, that he is in danger etc. **adj:** (such) absurd, odd, strange: *Now don't go* **putting ideas into people's heads**: *nobody's going to pay us any extra money.* ○ *I hope this fellow doesn't go* **putting ideas into the heads of** *these islanders that the monster is going to pay them a visit.* RM

put into power [Vn.pr pass] give political control to (sb), esp through an election. **S:** voter, votes. **O:** party, administration: *An electoral landslide* **put** *the Labour Party* **into power** *in 1945.* ○ *Before de Gaulle was* **put into power** *in 1958, France was often governed by unstable coalitions.* ⇨ be in/come into power.

put into practice [Vn.pr pass] make (sth) actually happen; implement. **o:** idea, concept; theory; plan, design: *Unlike most philosophers, Jung was also a man who* **put** *his theories* **into practice**. JUNG ○ *He had an opportunity of* **putting into practice** *some of his ideas on prison reform.* SS = carry out 1, put into effect.

put into words [Vn.pr pass] express (sth) in words. **O:** emotion; fear, love, hatred, anxiety; thought, idea: *He could not now* **put into words** *his intense fear of the witch doll in the cupboard.* DC ○ *Though they could not have* **put** *it* **into words**, *their objection to him was that he did not wear uniform.* HD

put words into sb's mouth [Vn.pr pass] suggest that sb has said or implied sth when in fact he has not: *'I'll understand if you haven't a place for me,' she said. 'Who said I hadn't? Don't* **put words into my mouth**, *Virginia.'* AITC ○ *'Now you're* **putting**

***words into my mouth**. When did I say anything about moving?'* □ note pl form of mouth: *'Don't go **putting words into people's mouths**!'*

put off 1 [Vn ⇆ p pass adj] postpone or delay (sth). **O:** decision; party, appointment; making a move, tidying the study: *He **put off** for as long as he could the pain of admitting to himself his father was wrong.* INN ○ *I've been **putting** it **off** and not thinking about it, hoping that something would turn up.* RFW ○ *The question was to be **put off** and decided later.* NS
2 [Vn.p pass] discourage or prevent (sb) from talking to one, making contact, collecting a debt, discussing an important matter etc. **O:** wife, boyfriend; landlord, tradesman; visitor. **A:** with a promise, an excuse; by pretending to be ill, busy: *Maybe he had **put** her **off** too often when she had wanted to talk.* TO ○ *They went out eight or ten times and then she started **putting** him **off**, just a little: he was getting possessive.* H ○ *The store won't be **put off** with promises any longer; they want their money.*
3 [Vn.p pass] displease or repel (sb). **S:** appearance, language; manners, bad breath: *He could be a good salesman, but his manner **puts** customers **off**.* ○ *Many people are **put off** by his surly behaviour* (or: *find his surly behaviour **off-putting***). ○ *Harold realized to his surprise that instead of being **put off** by Irma's lack of English he rather enjoyed teaching her.* PW □ note unusual adj form off-putting.
4 [Vn.p pass] distract (sb) from doing sth; disturb (sb) while doing sth. **S:** noise, interruption; heat; insects: *She was trying to write, but the continuous noise outside her window **put** her **off**.* ○ *His opponent's delaying tactics are designed to annoy him and **put** him **off**.*
5 [Vn.pr pass] cause (sb) to lose an interest in (sth), or appetite for (sth). **S:** experience, incident; teacher, instructor. **o:** food, drink; French, maths; driving, smoking: *My drill sergeant **put** me **off** the army for good.* ○ *She was **put off** learning languages by incompetent teaching.* ⇨ be off 8, go off 4, turn off 2.
6 [Vn ⇆ p pass, Vn.pr pass] allow or cause (sb) to alight or disembark (from sth). **S:** captain, pilot. **O:** passenger, stowaway. **o:** bus, boat, aircraft: *I asked the taxi driver to **put** me **off** in the town centre.* ○ *The stowaways were **put off** the ship at the next port of call.* ○ *If he makes trouble he'll be **put off** the plane.* ⇨ get off 1, let off 1.
7 [Vp.n] (*formal*) remove or abandon (sth). **O:** uniform, regalia; care, worry, responsibility: *The war was over but Harold was still in khaki; he never looked so nearly a gentleman again when he **put** it **off**.* PW ○ *He had **put off** all personal cares.* RFW = lay aside 2.
8 [Vn.p pass] send (sb) to sleep; anaesthetize. **S:** hot drink; injection, pill; exhaustion: *'What about a nice cup of tea to **put** you **off** to sleep again?'* DC ○ *A whiff of gas'll soon **put** you **off**.* ⇨ go off 3.
9 [Vn ⇆ p pass] extinguish (sth); disconnect (sth). **O:** light; television: *Don't forget to **put off** the heating before you come to bed.* = switch off 1, turn off 1. ↔ put on 2.

put off the scent/track/trail [Vn.pr pass] prevent sb from following a fugitive etc by giving false clues. **O:** policeman, detective: *Nothing would **put** Mr Blearney **off the scent**.* HD ○ *We managed to **put** our pursuers **off the track** by walking our horses up river for a few hundred yards.*

put off his stride/stroke [Vn.pr pass] disturb the rhythm or steady progress of sb's work; spoil sb's composure. **S:** noise, disturbance, interruption: *These telephone calls **put** him completely **off his stroke** and ruined a morning's work.* ○ *She coloured faintly, and seemed **put off her stride**.* US ⇨ put off 4.

put on 1 [Vn ⇆ p pass] get dressed in (sth); don. **O:** coat, hat; suit, trousers: ***Put on** some clothes.* EHOW ○ *I don't know what dress to **put on**.* ↔ take off 2. ⇨ get on 1, have on 1.
2 [Vn ⇆ p pass] connect or light (an electric or gas appliance). **O:** light, lamp; (electric/gas) fire, radiator: *'Half a tick and I'll **put on** the light.'* PW ○ *I'll **put** the light **on**.* TOH = switch on. ↔ put off 9, turn off 1. ⇨ be on 8, go on 15, keep on 6, turn on 1.
3 [Vn ⇆ p pass] grow heavier or fatter by (some amount); gain. **O:** (a lot of) weight; ten pounds, two kilos; two inches (round the waist): *In the month she had been with them she hadn't **put on** any weight.* DC ○ *How much (weight) did you **put on** over Christmas?* ↔ take off 7.
4 [Vn ⇆ p pass] (*cricket*) add (runs) to the score for an innings. **O:** fifty, one hundred (runs): *The tail-end batsmen **put on** 48 between them.* ○ *Ninety was **put on** for the first wicket.*
5 [Vn ⇆ p pass, Vn.pr pass] add (some amount) to the price or cost of (sth). **S:** Government, company; budget, legislation. **O:** several pounds, two pence in the pound, ten per cent. **o:** price, total, bill; cost of living: *Their latest measures will **put** several pounds **on** the weekly food bill.* ○ *The bill came to ten pounds but the waiter **put on** a bit extra.* ○ *This'll **put** a couple of per cent **on** the cost of living.* ↔ take off 8.
6 [Vn ⇆ p pass, Vn.pr pass] place (a tax) on (sth); impose. **O:** tax, duty, levy. **o:** wine, tobacco, betting: *What'll they be **putting** a tax **on** next?* ○ *The Government has decided not to **put on** a local income tax.* ↔ take off 8.
7 [Vn ⇆ p pass, Vn.pr pass] add (sth) to existing services. **O:** extra train, holiday flight, ten coaches. **o:** line, route, run: *Southern Region are **putting on** ten extra trains to cope with the holiday traffic.* ↔ take off 4.
8 [Vn ⇆ p pass, Vn.pr pass] (*racing*) place (money) with a bookmaker, as a wager on (sth). **O:** money, a fortune; £1000. **o:** horse, dog: *I've **put** a couple of pounds **on** Mountain King in the three-thirty.* ○ ***Put** a fiver to win **on** Running Wild.* ○ *'Are you a betting man?' 'Oh, I **put** a few pounds **on** in the course of a year.'* = stake on, wager on 1. ⇨ be on 3.
9 [Vn ⇆ p pass, Vn.pr pass] (*informal*) apply physical or moral pressure to (sb), in order to be unpleasant, extract money or favours etc. **O:** ⚠ the screw(s), the squeeze, the heat, the arm: *'I take it you have your fighting boots on this morning? Has the Old Man been **putting** the screw **on**?'* TT ○ *He could live off the fat of the land in George's house, and see just exactly what George was worth, and **put** the screws **on** him good and proper.* PE ○ *I'm not doing this because Meyer has **put** the arm **on***

me because of our family relationship. He can't. OBS
10 [Vn ⇆ p pass] (*cricket*) give a spell of bowling to (sb), bring (a bowler) into action. **O:** pace bowler, spinner: *He* **put** *Marshall* **on** *to bowl from the Kirkstall Lane end.* ○ *Gooch took the new ball after tea, and* **put** *the fast bowlers back* **on**. ⇨ be on 4, ⇨ bring on 4, come on 9.
11 [Vn ⇆ p pass] present (a spectacle); stage, mount. **O:** show, display; play, pantomime; exhibition: *He was generous with advice and assistance in* **putting on** *'The Master of Ravenwood', a dramatization of a Scott novel.* CD ○ *It was all agreed that this gallery was to* **put on** *a one-man show* (an exhibition of paintings). CON ↔ take off 11. ⇨ be on 6, come on 11.
12 [Vp.n pass adj] (*informal*) assume (a manner of behaving) in order to impress or deceive sb. **O:** it; act, facade; airs; voice, accent; anger, annoyance: *She was obviously very good for Bill. He didn't have to* **put on** *an act for her.* RFW ○ *She* **put on** *rather a good act of taking me for a door-to-door brush salesman.* FL ○ *'He does* **put** *it* **on**, *doesn't he?'* ○ *There was something seriously wrong with her . . . she was not just* **putting on** *the symptoms.* F ○ *Zhdanov enthuses his listeners with a* **put-on** *heartiness.* IND

put on the back burner [Vn.pr pass] (*informal*) keep (sth) to be discussed and resolved at a later stage; defer. **O:** issue, question; peace initiative, defence debate: *The Government does not share the view that it* (Northern Ireland) *should be* **put on the back burner**. BBCR ○ *'She doesn't know what to* **put on the back burner** *and what on the front.'* OBS

put the blame on [Vn.pr pass emph rel] treat (sb) as responsible (for sth). **o:** leader, government; poor communications, bad weather: *Calamity after calamity descended upon the village, and the highly superstitious people* **put** *all* **the blame on** *Anak Agung Nura.* TO ○ *Some of* **the blame** *must be* **put on** *the manager for not anticipating the shortage.* = lay the blame (for) (on).

put a bold/brave/good face on [Vn.pr pass] appear brave and cheerful on the surface, even though one is unhappy, disappointed etc. **o:** ⚠ it, things; events, proceedings: *He wouldn't have been pleased, of course, but he would have shrugged his shoulders and for Isobel's sake* **put a good face on** *it.* PW ○ *There is not much optimism in the air, but at least both sides are* **putting a brave face on** *proceedings.* DT

put a/the brake on [Vn.p pass, Vn.pr pass] (*informal*) reduce the speed or activity of (sth). **S:** government; employee; general. **o:** development; investment; advance: *He asserted that scaling down nuclear power would* **put a brake on** *economic development in third world countries.* IND ○ *Because the Government cannot restrain the City . . . they have to* **put the brake on** *the economy as a whole.* SC

put one's cards on the table [Vn.pr pass] (*informal*) declare openly one's assets, intentions, proposals etc: *'I think I ought to* **put** *all* **my cards on the table**. *I'm not rich. But when my father dies I'll have about fifty thousand dollars.'* QA ○ *She didn't seem excited, but this was a business deal, and he couldn't expect her to* **put** *all* **her cards** *down* **on the table**. PW = lay one's cards on the table.

put a construction on [Vn.pr pass emph rel] interpret (sth) in one's own individual way. **adj:** one's own, this, what; certain, particular; special, different. **o:** event, occurrence; crisis, drama: *The same drama may be played out before two spectators each of whom will* **put his own construction on** *it.* MFF ○ **On** *the same body of evidence each of the witnesses* **put a** *quite different* **construction**. ○ *'You say that you borrowed the car, believing it to belong to a friend. Now* **what construction** *am I to* **put on** *that?'*

put on a diet [Vn.pr pass] advise (sb) to take food of a particular kind, to improve or safeguard his health. **adj:** new, experimental; fat-free, meatless: *Mr Bury forbade him to climb the stairs and* **put** *him* **on a** *new* **diet** *without meat or wine.* GE ○ *Dr Ambrosic* **put** *him* **on a** *strange* **diet** *consisting entirely of grapes.* BRN

put (back) on his/its feet [Vn.pr pass, Vn.p.pr pass] restore (sb/sth) to health or prosperity. **S:** treatment, rest; loan, capital. **O:** patient; country, economy: *Special measures were introduced to help* **put** *the banking sector* **back on its feet**. ○ *The factory was* **put back on its feet** *through the joint efforts of management and workforce.* = set on his/its feet.

put one's finger on [Vn.pr rel] (*informal*) indicate (sth) precisely, specify (sth) exactly. **o:** trouble, source of danger; anomaly, fallacy: *I thought there was a contradiction somewhere, as there was in most of Tom's counsels, but I could not* **put my finger on** *it.* SPL ○ *'Then what is the trouble?' 'Nothing explicit that I can* **put my finger on**.*'* TBC □ often neg, or in the pattern: . . . *nothing that one can/could* **put one's finger on**.

put the finger on [Vn.pr pass] (*slang*) point an accusing finger at (sb); name. **o:** accomplice, associate: *Questioned by the special investigators, Ulrich* **put the finger on** *the Attorney-General.* TO ○ *I became distinctly uneasy, sensing that* **the finger** *would next be* **put on** *me.*

put on his guard (against) [Vn.pr pass] warn (sb) of a danger: *His words* **put** *me* **on my guard against** *speaking too freely over the telephone.* ○ *He was* **put on his guard** *by reports of missing drugs that had been appearing in the paper.* ⇨ be on one's guard (against).

put on his honour [Vn.pr pass] trust (sb) to do sth, or not to do it, on pain of breaking an oath. **O:** pupil; employee; prisoner. **Inf:** not to talk, to go to bed by eight; to record all periods of absence, not to speak to other candidates: *'Your teacher is not feeling very well, and so I am going to* **put** *you* **on your honour** *to go on with your work.'* TT ○ *A prisoner on parole is* **put on his honour** *to return to custody by a certain date.* □ often followed, as here, by an inf. ⇨ be on one's honour.

put on ice [Vn.pr pass] (*informal*) suspend, shelve (sth), possibly with the intention of reviving it later. **O:** proposal, scheme, plan: *The Prime Minister is speaking in a way that suggests* **putting** *the famous Peace Treaty* **on ice**. OBS ○ *The plans will be* **put on ice** *until money is available to implement them.* ⇨ be on ice.

put on the map [Vn.pr pass] (*informal*) bring (sth/sb) to the notice of the public; make prominent. **O:** resort, festival, fair; sport, pastime: *Barbara Goalen* **put** (fashion) *modelling* **on the map**. H ○ *'This* *will hit the world's press. You've* **put** *General Thé* ***on the map*** *all right, Pyle.'* QA ⇨ be on the map.

put one's money on [Vn.pr] (*informal*) confidently expect (sb/sth) to succeed. **adj:** one's; any, (not) much. **o:** him etc; candidate; plan, idea: *I suppose he could end up as chairman, but I'm not* ***putting any money on*** *it.* ○ *I'm* ***putting my money on*** *the Tories to win the next by-election.* ⇨ put on 8.

not to put too fine a point on it [Vn.pr] (*informal*) to speak bluntly, to speak the plain truth: ***Not to put too fine a point on it****, we're finished, all washed-up — it's the end of the road.* ○ ***Not to put too fine a point on it****, Querini lives by a now diminishing talent (he is nearly fifty-two) and by his wits.* US □ idiom is a subordinate (adv) clause.

put on one side 1 [Vn.pr pass] save (sth) for use or spending later. **O:** product, part, component; money, cash: *The outside skin, or husk, George said, is* ***put on one side*** *to make bran.* WI ○ *He tries to* **put** *a few pounds* **on one side** *for his old age.* = put aside 2.

2 [Vn.pr pass] reserve (an article) for a customer who cannot pay for it now. **O:** stereo, TV, dishwasher: *'Would you like me to* **put** *the camera* ***on one side*** *for you?'* = put aside 3.

3 [Vn.pr pass] forget or ignore (sth). **O:** jealousy, suspicion, strife, dissension: *The detailed arguments which have been tearing the party in two could be* ***put on one side****.* T ○ *Let us* ***put on one side*** *the suspicions which have divided us in the past.* = put aside 4.

put a premium on [Vn.pr pass] make (sth) seem more important or worthwhile. **o:** careful husbandry, skill; courage, endurance: *The immediate and present nature of working-class life* ***puts a premium on*** *the taking of pleasures now, discourages planning for the future.* UL ○ *The sort of weather we have been having alters the character of rugby,* ***putting a premium on*** *forwards, with backs at a disadvantage.* T = put at a premium. ⇨ be at a premium 2.

put one's shirt on 1 [Vn.pr] (*informal*) gamble all the money one has on (a particular horse etc): *I was* ***putting my shirt on*** *a well-fancied Irish horse running at Doncaster.* = put on 8. ⇨ be on 3.

2 [Vn.pr] (*informal*) be thoroughly convinced that (sth/sb) will succeed. **o:** scheme, project; idea; him getting the contract, the plan being accepted: *You may not think the product will sell, but I'd* ***put my shirt on*** *it.* ○ *The scheme must have some merits: the committee are* ***putting their shirts on*** *it.*

put the (tin) lid on it/things [Vn.pr] (*informal*) be the final event in a series of mishaps, disasters etc; be the last straw: *'After the distance I've covered today all I want is to go to bed.' That* ***put the lid on it****: he was in a bad temper.* ARG ○ *On the way back, I had a flat tyre. And I found the spare was flat, too. That pretty well* ***put the tin lid on things****.* TGLY

put years on [Vn.pr pass] make (sb) feel or appear older; say sth which makes (sb) appear older than he is or would like to feel. **adj:** several; ten, twenty: *The terrible events of the last few months have* ***put years on*** *him.* ○ *GEOFF: It's your grandchild. HELEN: Oh, shut up, you* ***put years on*** *me.* TOH ↔ take years off.

put pressure on/upon [Vn.pr pass emph rel] persuade by constant argument, by the threat of force etc (to do sth). **adj:** a lot of, some; no, (not) any/much. **o:** employer; leader, governing body; neighbour, children: *Parents are* ***putting pressure on*** *the council to create more places in nursery schools.* ○ *Does any government care about the protests of nice-minded humanitarians? They care about having* ***pressure put on*** *them.* EHOW

put one's stamp on [Vn.pr pass emph rel] work, perform in such a way that people are constantly reminded later of one's achievement. **o:** sports commentating, middle-distance running; television documentaries, radio drama: *John Reith* ***put his stamp upon*** *a kind of broadcasting ... whose value is recognized not only in Britain but in many other parts of the world.* L

put a strain on/upon [Vn.pr pass emph rel] place (sb/sth) under force or pressure so that he or it is tested and stretched. **adj:** a lot of, some; no, (not) any/much. **o:** resources, capacity; industry, agriculture; forces, nerves: *The opening of the Channel Tunnel would* ***put an*** *intolerable* ***strain on*** *the existing rail network.* ○ ***A*** *sudden and severe* ***strain*** *was* ***put on*** *us by the cutting off of these supplies.*

put on to 1 [Vn.p.pr pass] help (one person) to meet or speak to (another). **S:** receptionist, inquiry desk, telephone operator. **O:** caller, visitor. **o:** manager, secretary: *All I had to do was ring him up and he would* ***put me on to*** *his private secretary and she would read out a specially prepared 'release'.* CON ○ *He always insisted on being* ***put on to*** *the person in charge.* = put in touch (with). ⇨ be on to 1, get on to 1.

2 [Vn.p.pr pass] inform (one person) of the whereabouts or activities of (another) so that he can be caught. **S:** enemy, police informer. **O:** police, law. **o:** escapee, fugitive; sb's track, trail: *Sooner or later she will be spotted in the street, and the police will be* ***put on to*** *her.* ○ *He can't go on defrauding the Inland Revenue for ever: somebody some day will* ***put*** *the tax man* ***on to*** *him.* ⇨ be on to 2, get on to 2.

3 [Vn.p.pr pass] inform (sb) of the existence of sth interesting or advantageous. **S:** agent, broker; friend, colleague. **o:** a good thing; bargain, snip; opening in industry, vacant post; club, holiday resort: *It was Randall who had* ***put*** *Stocker* ***on to*** *this afternoon drinking club.* CON ○ *I was* ***put on to*** *this cheap line in printed cotton by a friend in the trade.* ⇨ be on to 3.

4 [Vn.p.pr] arrange for (sb/sth) to be employed in (a certain way). **O:** staff, crew; resources; extra transport, shipping. **o:** task, project; relief operation, rescue work; carrying war supplies: *We had to* ***put*** *a few more cars* ***on to*** *ferrying elderly voters to the polling stations.* ○ *We agreed to cancel all plans for airborne drops ... and* ***put*** *all available aircraft* ***on to*** *transport work.* MFM ↔ take off 6.

put out 1 [Vp] (*nautical*) move towards the open sea. **S:** captain, crew; boat, ship. **A:** to sea; from harbour, from the shore: *We* ***put out*** *from Plymouth on the early morning tide.* ○ *'You can't plan anything because you never know when you will be* ***putting out*** *to sea again.'* RT ↔ put in/into 4.

2 [Vn.p pass] remove (sb) by force; eject. **S:** doorman, bouncer. **O:** troublemaker, gatecrasher, drunk: *The next time he brings his unpleasant friends to the club we'll have them* ***put out****.* ⇨ be out 3.

3 [Vp.n] sprout (sth); display. **S:** tree, shrub. **O:** leaf, bud, shoot: *The plants* **put out** *early shoots.* AH ○ *Without her help the barley could not ripen, ... nor the trees* **put out** *new leaf in springtime.* GLEG

4 [Vn ⇆ p pass] issue or publish (sth), usu for a special purpose, eg to explain one's policy, apologize for delays etc. **S:** government department, official news agency, public relations firm. **O:** pamphlet, document; report, statement: *The Department of Health and Social Security have* **put out** *a pamphlet explaining the new rates of pension for retired people.* ○ *Head Office has* **put out** *an official statement denying press reports of a possible take-over.*

5 [Vn ⇆ p pass] issue, circulate (sth). **S:** police, army. **O:** general call, SOS; description: *A description of the wanted man has been* **put out** *to all mobile patrols.*

6 [Vn ⇆ p pass] transmit (sth) by radio or television; broadcast. **S:** BBC, Yorkshire Television; studio, station. **O:** news bulletin, sports report, talk; play, concert: *They clustered around the radio, listening to the news of the invasion* **put out** *by the BBC.* RFW

7 [Vp.n pass] produce, generate (sth). **S:** power station, generator; motor, engine; battery. **O:** 100 kilowatts, 15 horsepower: *The engine of a wartime fighter aircraft* **put out** *more than one thousand horsepower* (or: *had an* **output** *of more than one thousand* etc). □ nom form is output.

8 [Vn ⇆ p pass] remove (sth) from inside a house and leave it outside for exercise, collection etc. **O:** cat; rubbish, old newspapers: *It's Alex's job to* **put** *the cat* **out** *last thing at night.* ○ *'Don't forget to* **put out** *the empty milk bottles.'*

9 [Vn ⇆ p pass] make (sb) unconscious, by striking with the fists, giving an anaesthetic etc. **S:** boxer, assailant; doctor, anaesthetist. **O:** opponent; patient: *A whiff of ether will* **put** *you* **out** *in a few seconds.* ○ *The champion* **put** *the guy* **out** *in the fifth round — and he stayed out.* ⇨ be out 9, go out 3.

10 [Vn ⇆ p pass] extinguish (sth). **O:** light, lamp; (gas, electric) fire; flame, candle; cigarette, cigar: *Nurse Ellen, in Brigit's room, drew the curtains and* **put out** *the lights.* DC ○ *The fire brigade were still* **putting out** *small fires started by the plane crash.* = blow out 1, stub out, switch off 1. ↔ turn on 1. ⇨ be out 10, go out 6, turn out 1.

11 [Vn.p pass adj] dislocate (sth). **S:** accident, fall, blow. **O:** shoulder, knee, ankle: *He* **put** *his back* **out** *badly, falling down the stairs like that.*

12 [Vn ⇆ p pass] cause an inaccuracy in (sth). **S:** movement, shock; temperature, pressure. **O:** instrument, dial; figure, calculation, reading. **A:** (by) a long way, (by) ten seconds: *Any inaccuracy in the measuring vessels would be bound to* **put** *his results* **out**. ○ *The final totals can have been* **put out** *by as much as five per cent.* = throw out 6. ⇨ be out 12.

13 [Vn.p pass adj] spoil or complicate sb's arrangements; inconvenience. **S:** his sudden arrival; extra guests; a change in the programme: *'I hope it hasn't* **put** *your housekeeper* **out**, *Mr Alexander, having three extra suddenly thrust upon her.'* WI ○ *The hotel was seriously* **put out** *by a sudden cancellation of holiday bookings.* ⇨ put oneself out.

14 [Vn.p pass adj] upset, dismay or worry (sb). **S:** rudeness, insensitivity, tactlessness: *'Come and lunch with me,' she said. He pleaded an urgent engagement. She looked so* **put out** *that he felt he had been rude.* ASA ○ *She muttered all the way upstairs, ... and I could see she was most* **put out**. GOV □ often passive or adj after *appear* etc.

put out feelers [Vn ⇆ p pass] (*informal*) take exploratory steps to see if conditions are right for trade, a peace settlement etc: *Their government is* **putting out feelers** *through a neutral delegation; they are clearly anxious to renew negotiations.*

put one's hand out [Vn ⇆ p] extend one's hand on first being introduced, to congratulate sb etc: *He poked his head forward ...* **put out his hand** *and said, 'Good afternoon.'* PP

put oneself out [Vn.p] inconvenience oneself (in order to achieve sth, to help others etc). **Inf:** to be of service, make us welcome: *Jung had a gift for communicating with people in many walks of life when he* **put** *himself* **out** *to do so.* JUNG ⇨ put out 13.

put out of action [Vn.pr pass] (*military*) cause (sth) to stop working, firing etc. **S:** (enemy) fire, bombardment; artillery, aircraft. **O:** installation, emplacement; gun; radio: *Accurate gunnery had already* **put** *three of the leading tanks* **out of action**. ⇨ be/go out of action.

put out of business [Vn.pr pass] (*commerce*) force (sb) to stop trading. **S:** economic slump, decline in efficiency, labour troubles, rising prices. **O:** company, firm; store, shop; artisan: *If a major manufacturer is in serious difficulties, the suppliers and contractors dependent on him may be* **put out of business**. ⇨ go out of business.

put sb's nose out of joint [Vn.pr pass] (*informal*) ruffle or upset an interfering or unduly sensitive person: *The next time he comes around cadging, I'll remind him of all the money he owes us already: that'll* **put his nose out of joint**. ○ *It was one of the most popular plays with amateurs ... It was because all the parts were of equal length, so* **nobody's nose** *was* **put out of joint**! RT □ note pl form: *She would turn up in her new car, more expensive than anything they could aspire to. That would* **put their noses out of joint**.*'*

put out (to) 1 [Vn ⇆ p pass, Vn.p.pr pass emph rel] pass all or part of a job to a manufacturer or worker who is not one's employee, and who will not do the work on one's premises. **S:** (large) manufacturer, factory. **O:** work, job; fitting, finishing; (making of a) part, fitting, component. **o:** subcontractor, small business: *The expansion of the market led not to the concentration of production in factories, but to work being '***put out**.*'* SHOE ○ *Already contractors are queuing outside Crook's door and about fifty per cent of the work will be* **put out**. ST □ often passive.

2 [Vn ⇆ p pass, Vn.p.pr pass emph rel] lend (money) at interest (to sb). **S:** government, bank, insurance company. **o:** public; borrower: *The building societies attract deposits from investors and then* **put out** *this money, at a higher rate of interest,* **to** *people wishing to buy houses.*

put over (on) [Vn ⇆ p pass, Vn.p.pr pass] (*informal*) get (sb) to accept a story, statement, claim etc that is untrue or worthless. **S:** con man, (dishonest) sales representative. **O:** ⚠ one, something. **o:**

uncritical public, gullible customer: *They have the air of people determined to make the best of what they could get and not have anything* **put over on** *them.* SE = put across 3.

put over (to) [Vn ⇆ p pass adj, Vn.p.pr pass] convey, communicate (sth) effectively (to sb). **S:** speaker, critic, narrator. **O:** point, case, argument; story, tale; sincerity, conviction. **o:** listener, viewer: *John was waving across the room and smiling with all the charm he already* **put over** *at twelve years old.* ASA ○ *This evening he was not* **putting over** *a story* **to** *an untried audience.* ASA = put across 1. ⇨ get over (to).

not put it past [Vn.pr] (*informal*) consider (sb) quite capable of doing sth malicious, illegal etc. **O:** it . . . to cause trouble, it . . . to upset people's feelings: *I would***n't put it past** *him to steal money from his own grandmother.* ○ *'She thinks you may be the culprit.' 'I doubt it,' he said. 'Well,' she said, 'I would***n't** *have* **put it past** *you.'* MM □ used with would.

put through 1 [Vn ⇆ p pass] conclude, complete (sth). **S:** department, firm. **O:** programme, plan; change, reorganization: *At the moment we are trying to* **put through** *a mass literacy programme.* ○ *The harbour redevelopment was* **put through** *in record time.* = carry through 1. ⇨ go through 6.

2 [Vn ⇆ p pass, Vn.pr pass] cause (sth) to pass through various legislative or administrative stages. **O:** Bill, Act, measure; scheme, idea. **o:** stage, phase, process: *These proposals have to be* **put through** *several committees before they become part of the constitution.* ○ *John'll* **put** *your scheme* **through** *the Faculty Board, if anybody will.* ⇨ get through 4, go through 6.

3 [Vn.pr pass] provide for (sb) so that he can complete his schooling etc. **o:** school, college, university: *He managed to* **put** *all four of his children* **through** *boarding school.* ○ *She was* **put through** *university with money left by her grandfather.*

put through the mill [Vn.pr pass] (*informal*) give to (sb) the severe training of practical experience. **O:** child, trainee; aspirant to leadership: *Most of his present officers were* **put through the mill**; *he considers battle experience more valuable than college training.* ○ *I'd been through a Remand Home* (institution for young offenders) *before; and Mike was* **put through the** *same* **mill**, *because all the local cops knew he was my best pal.* LLDR ⇨ be/go through the mill.

put through his paces [Vn.pr pass] make (sb) display all his skills or expert knowledge. **O:** class, crew, squad; musician, dancer; athlete: *A dance instructor was called in to* **put them through their paces**. RT ○ *Aged between 12 and 18, the entrants have been* **put through their paces** *. . . and judged by a jury of celebrated musicians.* RT

put through (to) 1 [Vn.p pass, Vn.p.pr pass] connect (an outside caller) (with sb on an internal extension). **S:** operator; switchboard. **O:** caller; call: *'An outside call, Mr Murdoch.' 'Oh,* **put** *him* **through**.*'* BBCTV ○ *'When Mr Parkinson comes on the line, you will* **put** *the call* **through to** *me.'* TBC = switch through (to). ⇨ be through (to), get through (to) 2.

2 [Vn ⇆ p pass, Vn.pr pass] convey (a message) (to sb), esp by telephone. **O:** call, message; enquiry, request; requisition, order. **o:** London, Paris; office, shop: *'Shan't keep you waiting long: there are one or two orders I've got to* **put through**.*'* ○ *Marlowe next* **put through** *a call* **to** *Bill Barnett of Caltech.* TBC

put to 1 [Vn.pr pass rel] convey, express, communicate (sth) to (sb). **O:** point, suggestion, proposal; situation; it . . . that there are better times coming, it . . . that inflation will fall. **o:** meeting, audience; board, committee: *Let me* **put** *the situation* **to** *you as I saw it in January and February. In February I planned to take over control.* TBC ○ *The committee's proposals were* **put to** *us briefly and forcefully.* ○ *The Prime Minister can* **put** *it* **to** *his supporters that there will almost certainly be a considerable swing back to the Government.* OBS

2 [Vn.pr pass emph rel] ask (sth) of (sb); submit. **O:** question, query, inquiry. **o:** panel, chairman; tribunal, board of inquiry: *The audience was now invited to* **put** *its questions* **to** *the visiting speaker.* ○ *'***To** *which of our experts do you wish to* **put** *that question?'*

3 [Vn.pr pass] ask (a meeting etc) to vote on (a particular proposal). **O:** matter, question; proposal, resolution. **o:** the vote; the assembly, meeting: *'I propose that the matter be* **put to** *the vote, Mr Chairman.'* ○ *The secretary rose to* **put** *the motion* **to** *the assembly for its approval.*

4 [Vn.pr pass rel] make (sb) suffer or undergo (sth). **o:** extra expense; unnecessary bother, some inconvenience, endless trouble: *She is ready to oblige anyone provided this doesn't* **put** *her* **to** *any trouble.* UTN ○ *You can't imagine the trouble I've been* **put to** *by the Council.* ○ *He's been* **put to** *no end of expense by subsidence under the front of his new house.* ⇨ go to 2.

5 [Vn.pr] (*legal*) suggest (sth) to (a witness etc). **O:** it . . . that you were in Brighton on that date; it . . . that the door was in fact open. **o:** you; the witness, the accused: *The counsel for the defence harries her: 'I* **put** *it* **to** *you that you acted out of spite?'* PW ○ *'I* **put** *it* **to** *the witness, My Lord, that he was nowhere near York at the time.'*

put to bed [Vn.pr pass] (*informal*) send a newspaper in its final edited form to be printed. **O:** paper, late (extra) edition; 'Guardian', 'Mirror': *'I suppose you've been* **putting** *the ''Independent Socialist''* **to bed**,*' said Dave.* UTN

put to death [Vn.pr pass] execute (sb) by order of the civil or military authorities. **O:** prisoner, hostage; rebel, critic: *They* **put to death** *anyone appearing in the streets after curfew.* ○ *On a scaffold in Tyburn the first English monks were* **put to death** *by order of the King.* WI

put to effective etc use [Vn.pr pass] use (sth) well or profitably. **O:** time, interval, break; forces, labour; money, savings. **adj:** ⚠ effective, good, better, excellent: *The 3rd Division certainly* **put** *that first winter* **to good use** *and trained hard.* MFM ○ *His medical talents were* **put to good** *general* **use** *in 1816.* SS = make effective etc use of.

put an end/a stop to [Vn.pr pass pass(o)] end, stop (sth). **o:** episode, saga; quarrel, unpleasantness; war, riot, disturbance: *This appeared to* **put an end to** *one of the most disturbing intervals in recent British politics.* OBS ○ *Is there any hope of* **putting a stop to** *this mad triple arms race?* OBS ○ *It's high time this leaking of information was* **put a stop to**. ⇨ be at/bring to/come to an end.

put the final/finishing touches to [Vn.pr pass emph rel] complete the final details of (sth). **o:** arrangements; meal, food; cake; account, story: *Heinz Wolf was **putting the finishing touches to** his report.* TO ○ *While **the finishing touches** are **put to** the dinner, we'll stroll round the garden.* CON ○ *The centre piece was to be a massive cake, **to** which the caterers were now **putting the final touches**.*

put a/one's finger to one's lips [Vn.pr pass] signal to sb to be quiet by raising a finger to one's lips: *Hugo followed, making a noise like a bear. I turned back and **put my finger to my lips**.* UTN

put to flight/rout [Vn.pr pass] cause (sb) to flee in disorder. **O:** enemy, invader: *In a sharp counter-attack our men had **put** the enemy **to flight**.* ○ *The twentieth century, vulgar, discordant and disquieting, had invaded the stronghold of the eighteenth and **put** it **to rout**.* EM ○ *All their fears were **put to flight** by the news that help was on the way.*

put a match to [Vn.pr pass] light (sth) with a match. **o:** fire; wood, coal; paper, document, record: *I've laid the fire in the hearth; all you have to do is **put a match to** it.* ○ *The gas popped loudly as he **put a match to** it.* FL = set fire/light to.

put one's mind to [Vn.pr pass] give one's full attention to (sth). **o:** task, job; studies, revision: *I'm sure we can get it all sorted out if we **put our minds to** it.* ILIH ○ *They were confident that, once **his mind** was **put to** it, the work would be finished in a few days.* = set one's mind to.

put a name to [Vn.pr rel] identify (sth/sb) by name. **adj:** definite, exact, precise. **o:** noise, smell; foodstuff, liquid: *The silence became full of sound: noises you couldn't **put a name to** — a crack, a creak, a rustle.* QA ○ *He was somebody you read of every other day in the newspaper, yet we couldn't **put a name to** him.* □ usu with can/could not.

put paid to [Vn.pr pass(o) emph rel] finish or destroy (sth). **o:** hope, plan, prospect; holiday, excursion: *One blow and you'd be dead, which would **put paid to** any thoughts of Australia.* LLDR ○ *Our tour was finally **put paid to** by a series of arguments with theatre managers.*

put pen to paper [Vn.pr] begin to write sth: *His Newark pupils just wouldn't **put pen to paper**.* OBS ○ *Poor Lewes fell ill and was forbidden to **put pen to paper** for a month.* GE

put to rights [Vn.pr pass] settle, resolve or arrange (sth) properly. **O:** matter, question; grievance, wrong, injustice; the world: *They would often sit chattering over a beer, **putting** the world **to rights**.* ○ *A family-run business which faced bankruptcy in 1985, had been **put to rights** by the application of sound Thatcherite principles.* IND

put to shame [Vn.pr pass] make (sb/sth) seem slight or insignificant by comparison. **O:** him etc; efforts, achievement; resistance, resilience: *This little man with his variety of games and complex music **puts** many other so-called 'superior' cultures **to shame**.* LWK ○ *'How smart,' said Angela acidly. 'You **put** us all **to shame**.'* SE ○ *The face was dominated by a pair of tremendous eyes that would have **put** any self-respecting owl **to shame**.* BB

put to sleep [Vn.pr pass] (*euphemism*) destroy an animal, generally a household pet, painlessly. **O:** dog, cat: *The head-waiter poisoned his own dog. That's not the way to **put** a dog **to sleep**.* OMIH ○ *Their cat was growing old and blind, and would have to be **put to sleep**.* = put away 5, put down 10.

put to the test [Vn.pr pass] try the strength of (sth/sb); test. **O:** readiness, preparedness; theory, idea; defence, army. **adj:** final, ultimate, supreme: *She is also, as she shows when **put to the test**, extremely brave.* BRN ○ *Soon it is likely that all suppositions about extra-terrestrial life will be **put to the test**.* TO

put to use [Vn.pr pass] employ, use (sth). **O:** talents, skills; lessons, findings; experience: *It was a suffocating society, where there was no opportunity of **putting to use** one's natural gifts.* RTH = make use of 1.

put together 1 [Vn ⇆ p pass] fit (pieces) together to make a whole; assemble. **O:** part, component, piece; model, bookcase, vase: (nursery rhyme) *All the King's horses and all the King's men/Couldn't **put** Humpty **together** again.* ○ *He collected . . . old broken-down clocks and watches in the hope of one day **putting** them **together** again.* BRH ↔ take apart 1.

2 [Vn ⇆ p pass] combine (pieces of evidence etc) to make a coherent whole; make (a whole) by combining pieces. **O:** scraps, pieces (of evidence); events, incidents; case, argument; story, narrative: *We managed to **put together** a convincing case from the accounts of eye-witnesses.* ○ *I now want to **put together** the material I have collected in the form of case material.* ESS

3 [Vn ⇆ pass] organize (people) so that form a group; assemble. **O:** group, team, outfit, unit: *Essex have **put together** a terrific team this season.* ○ *The right blend of talents was quickly **put together**.*

put our etc heads together [Vn.p] (*informal*) combine our etc thinking so as to solve a problem more quickly; think together: *We shall have to sit down sometime and **put our heads together** and think about ways and means.* THH ○ *If only our leaders would **put their heads together** we might find a way out of our difficulties.*

put two and two together [Vn.p] (*informal*) make the simple connection between related facts and draw the obvious conclusion: *'The police can **put two and two together**, you know; they'll be on his track in no time.'* ○ *There was a theft from the safe just before he went on an expensive holiday: it's only a matter of time before somebody **puts two and two together**.*

put towards [Vn.pr pass] give (money) as a contribution to (a particular fund). **O:** fifty pounds; (part, a fraction of) one's income. **o:** cost, expense; holiday, education (of one's children); trousseau, dowry: *'You'd think he could have **put** something **towards** the outing, wouldn't you?'* ○ *'You take care of the household expenses and I'll **put** half my salary **towards** the cost of the holiday.'*

put up 1 [Vn ⇆ p pass] hang, fasten (sth) at a high level. **O:** flag, banner; curtain: *'It's time we **put up** the Christmas decorations in the living-room.'* ○ *On the other wall was a blanket, **put up** to hide a hole in the plaster.* ↔ take down 1.

2 [Vn ⇆ p pass] fasten (sth) in a place where it will be seen; display. **O:** notice, announcement; banns; result; poster, picture; team, name (of winner etc): *The supermarket chain will be relabelling new* *packs and* **putting up** *shelf warning stickers.* OBS ○ *The names of the successful candidates will be* **put up** *on the College notice board.* = post up . ⇨ stay up 3.

3 [Vn ⇆ p pass] build (sth); erect. **O:** house, factory; tent, marquee; statue, column: *A hundred years ago, people* **put up** *... brownstone houses along wide wooded avenues.* SCIT ○ *These were buildings* **put up** *in Czarist days.* AH ○ *They're having a memorial to him* **put up** *by public subscription.* ↔ take down 2. ⇨ go up 4, set up 1.

4 [Vn ⇆ p pass] raise, increase (sth). **O:** cost, price, rent, tax, premium: *Every time a new tenant moves into the flat, the landlord* **puts up** *the rent a bit more* (or: *he* **ups** *the rent* etc). ○ *The rate of interest was* **put up** *in the last Budget.* □ up (as a v) is sometimes used, informally, for put up in this sense. ⇨ be up 1, go up 2, keep up 2, send up 1.

5 [Vp.n pass] pretend to be, feel, or have done (sth) in order to hide one's true origins, activities etc. **O:** ⚠ a front, façade, show, smoke-screen: *Royal blood, indeed! Her grandfather had more likely been a poverty-stricken actor. But one had to admire the girl for the façade she* **puts up**. DC ○ *The fundamental secret of covering up inefficiency is the art of* **putting up** *a front.* OBS ○ *Tom gave loud commands, and Steve* **put up** *a token show of obedience.* SPL

6 [Vp.n pass] offer (sth). **O:** (stout) resistance, (good) fight, struggle: *The smuggler* **put up** *a fight but was finally overcome and carried off to jail.* DS ○ *Sir Paul* **put up** *a desperate struggle for life.* TFD

7 [Vp.n pass] state, advance, advocate (sth). **O:** case, argument, proposal: *He supported the case which scientists were* **putting up** *in Washington.* NM ○ *I'll see that your idea is* **put up** *at the next meeting of the Board.* = put forward 1.

8 [Vp.n pass] advance, lend (money). **O:** capital, funds, cash, money: *When we'd spent this huge sum, they* **put up** *another half-million.* DS ○ *The directors refused to* **put up** *any more money to save the club.* TU ○ *How much can you* **put up**? UTN

9 [Vp, Vn ⇆ p nom pass] take food and lodging; provide (sb) with food and lodging. **S** [Vp], **O** [Vn.p]**:** visitor, traveller; friend, relative. **A:** at a guest house, hotel; with relatives; for the night, a weekend: *They had* **put up** *at a hotel in Fermoy.* EB ○ *Mother will* **put** *you* **up** *for the night.* SML □ note nom form put-up, used attrib: *We always gave the father a* **put-up** *bed, in the single room, with his wife.* BBCR

put sb's back up [Vn.p] (*informal*) make (sb) angry, usu by clumsy or insensitive conduct. **S:** rudeness, thoughtlessness, insensitivity: *If you had pressed him for a reply, you would have* **put his back up**. PW ⇨ get sb's back up.

put the fear of death/God up [Vn.pr pass] ⇨ put the fear of death/God in/into/up.

put one's feet up [Vn.p] (*informal*) rest, relax, on a bed or in a chair, though not necessarily with one's feet supported: *'**Put your feet up** for five minutes: you've earned a rest.'* ○ *'I should advise you to* **put your feet up** *and sleep it off.'* ASA

put one's hand up [Vn ⇆ p pass] raise one's hand in order to attract attention, or to indicate one can answer a question etc. **S:** pupil, student; member of the audience: *'**Put up your hand** if you think you know the answer.'* ○ *Someone at the back tried to catch the chairman's eye by* **putting his hand up**. ○ *The French teacher asked if there was any support for another trip to Paris, and several* **hands** *were* **put up**. □ note imperative form in: *'**Hands up** if you think you know the answer!'* ⇨ (one's) hand be up.

put one's hands up [Vn ⇆ p] raise one's hands above one's head as a sign of surrender. **S:** soldier, criminal, fugitive: *'Drop your weapons and* **put your hands up**.*'*

put the wind up [Vn.pr pass] (*informal*) scare, frighten (sb). **S:** illness, relapse, accident; disturbance, demonstration: *'Mrs Batey, I wish you'd stop trying to* **put the wind up** *Virginia.' 'That child is ill, young man,' replied Mrs Batey.* AITC ○ *The news from New York of falling share prices* **put the wind up** *everybody.* ⇨ get/have the wind up.

put up (for) 1 [Vn.p pass, Vn.p.pr pass] propose, nominate (sb) (for a position). **O:** present holder, 'sitting member'. **o:** (re-)election; secretary, chairman; membership; club, society: *We'd like to* **put** *him* **up**, *but he won't accept nomination.* ○ *He* **put** *Wills* **up for** *membership of the Garrick Club in the autumn of 1864.* CD ⇨ be/come up for, next entry

2 [Vp, Vp.pr, Vn.p, Vn.p.pr] offer oneself as a candidate (for election). **S:** (all patterns): (party) member, officer. **O:** oneself. **o:** (re-)election; membership: [Vp.pr] *She isn't* **putting up for** *re-election to the Council this year.* ○ [Vp.pr, Vn.p.pr] *John is* **putting** *(himself)* **up for** *election to the Academic Committee.* ⇨ previous entry

put up for auction/sale [Vn.p.pr pass] offer (sth) for sale (by auction); sell. **O:** house, flat; site, plot; furniture, jewellery: *They're* **putting** *the family silver* **up for auction**. ○ *They can't possibly afford to keep the thing, but he won't hear of* **putting** *her* **up for sale** . FL ⇨ be/come up for auction/sale.

put up to [Vn.p.pr pass] encourage (sb) to behave mischievously or unlawfully. **o:** it; prank, escapade; trouble-making, skullduggery: *He wants to get off income-tax. Somebody* **put him up to** *it.* PW ○ *He's not been out of trouble all term, and he's been* **put up to** *it by some of the older boys.* ⇨ be up to 1, get up to 2.

put up with [Vp.pr pass adj] (*informal*) bear, tolerate (sth/sb). **o:** noise, disturbance; bad manners, inconsiderate behaviour: *He just wasn't going to* **put up with** *all the caterwauling.* TC ○ *There are some things that are not easily* **put up with** *— and his damned impertinence is one.* □ often neg, with will/would. = stand for 3.

put upon [adj pred (Vn.pr)] (*informal*) feeling resentful or aggrieved, because one is being expected to do more for sb than one had originally been led to expect: *This always happened when he felt miserable or* **put upon**, *and he had never been able to explain it to himself.* HHGG ○ *Like most people who feel themselves* **put upon** *or harbour a grievance against life, Anthony Trollope was ... excessively touchy.* TRO □ note the use of put-upon before a noun: *He was wearing his most* **put-upon** *expression.* ⇨ impose on/upon.

put pressure upon [Vn.pr pass emph rel] ⇨ put pressure on/upon.

put a strain upon [Vn.pr pass emph rel] ⇨ put a strain on/upon.

puzzle

puzzle out [Vn ⇆ p pass] solve (a problem) or obtain (an answer) by careful reasoning or experiment. **O:** answer, result, solution; how it works, why he did it, where the trouble started: *He spent the afternoon trying to* ***puzzle out*** *what had gone wrong with his car.* ○ *She found everything interesting, though she was quite without curiosity and never tried to* ***puzzle*** *things* ***out***. HD ○ *Follow that line of inquiry and I think you should be able to* ***puzzle out*** *an answer*. = figure out 2, work out 3.

puzzle over [Vpr pass adj] think carefully about (a problem) in an attempt to solve or understand it. **o:** matter, difficulty; document, plan, diagram: *He'd* ***puzzled over*** *the figures for hours without being able to make head or tail of them.* ○ *I* ***puzzled over*** *that bit of the letter for quite a while. As usual, John's handwriting was proving hard to decipher.*

Q

quail

quail (at) [Vpr rel] become fearful or feel dismay (because of sth unpleasant which seems likely to happen). **o:** ⚠ the prospect, possibility; the thought: *The tunnel on the left might lead deeper into the side of the mountain rather than back towards our starting point. We* ***quailed at*** *the thought.* ○ *There was a possibility that Jenkins might fill the vacancy left by Harrison's retirement — a prospect* ***at*** *which we all* ***quailed***.

qualify

qualify (as) [Vpr] pass examinations and take the title enabling one to practise (a calling or profession). **o:** accountant, dentist, teacher: *He had* ***qualified as*** *a barrister, but had been unable to practice his profession because of ill health.* HB ○ *She* ***qualified*** *in London* ***as*** *a teacher of English overseas* (cf *She* ***qualified*** *in London to teach English overseas*).

qualify (for) 1 [Vpr emph rel] reach, or be of, the standard required for (a post, reward etc) by passing a test, reaching a particular age etc. **o:** post, career; membership, associateship; vote; pension, grant: *You* ***qualify for*** *the vote, but John won't* ***qualify*** *till he's eighteen.* ○ *When the Second World War broke out, we did not* ***qualify for*** *a petrol ration and the car was sold.* SU ⇨ next entry
2 [Vn.pr pass emph rel] enable (sb) to undertake or obtain (sth). **S:** exam, test; diploma, degree; age, experience. **o:** job, post; reward, pension: *'I'm afraid this certificate doesn't* ***qualify*** *you* ***for*** *admission.'* ○ ***For*** *that kind of course his ordinary degree does not* ***qualify*** *him.* ⇨ previous entry
3 [Vpr] (*informal*) deserve (sth) by one's actions. **o:** stiff reprimand; punch on the jaw, black eye: *'Another crack like that and you'll* ***qualify for*** *a punch on the nose.'*

quarrel

quarrel with [Vpr emph rel] question or challenge (sth). **o:** statement, account, version (of what happened); estimate, figure: *They would not have found much to* ***quarrel with*** *in Emerson's rather crude diagnosis.* JA ○ *'I won't* ***quarrel with*** *your estimate of costs: it seems reasonable enough.'* □ usu with *will/would + not*.

quarrel (with) (about/over) [Vpr emph rel] disagree strongly (with sb) and argue angrily with him (about sth). **o: (with)** friend, colleague, workmate, wife, husband: *George is always* ***quarrelling with*** *his wife.* (This does not imply necessarily that she quarrels with him; cf *George and his wife are always* ***quarrelling***). ○ *There are very few people* ***with*** *whom he hasn't* ***quarrelled*** *at some time or other.* ○ *'That's just like Frank and Jane, isn't it? Always* ***quarrelling over*** *trifles.'*

queen

queen it over [Vn.pr] (*informal*) (of a woman) behave in a superior way towards (sb). **S:** housekeeper, cook; matron. **o:** (lesser, other, junior) servants, staff: *'She's not the kind of girl to let promotion go to her head. Not the sort to* ***queen it over*** *the ordinary nurses.'* ○ *Nan still* ***queened it over*** *the rest of the staff.* BRN ⇨ lord it over.

query

query (with) [Vn.pr pass emph rel] ask (sb) questions about (sth) with the aim of getting a clear answer, an authoritative decision etc. **O:** order, instruction; invoice, bill. **o:** superior; manager, accountant: *'I'm not sure I can issue the replacements on this authority. I shall have to* ***query*** *it* ***with*** *head office.'*

quest

quest for [Vpr rel] (*formal*) look about to find (sth) in a determined way. **S:** explorer, hunter, collector. **o:** gold, precious stones; ruins, remains: *The travellers pushed inland,* ***questing for*** *signs of human settlement.* = search (for).

queue

queue (up) (for) [Vp, Vpr pass rel, Vp.pr pass rel] form a line to get transport, buy food etc. **o:** bus, taxi; cinema, theatre; bread, fruit: [Vp] *Over seven hundred animals quietly* ***queued up*** *to drink.* NS ○ [Vpr] *She* ***queued*** *to get in the shop, and then had to* ***queue*** *again* ***for*** *fruit.* = line up 2.

quibble

quibble (about/over) [Vpr pass] ask trifling questions, raise petty doubts (about sth). **o:** unimportant details; small sums of money, a matter of a few pounds; who should be given precedence: *'I'm not questioning your claim for travel expenses. It's such a small amount that it's not worth* ***quibbling about***.*'* ○ *When we got down to discussing the details of the agreement we found that we were* ***quibbling over*** *the precise meaning of quite minor clauses.*

quicken

quicken up [Vp, Vn ⇆ p pass adj] (cause sth to) become much faster. **S** [Vp], **O** [Vn.p]**:** pace, rate; trade, commerce; activity, movement. **S** [Vn.p]**:** leader, officer, director: *The order came back to* ***quicken up*** *the pace of our advance.* ○ *We've noticed a distinct* ***quickening-up*** *in the turn-round of shipping.* ○ *The whole process needs to be* ***quickened up***. □ nom form is quickening-up. = speed up.

quieten

quieten down [Vp, Vn.p pass] (cause sth/sb to) become more quiet and calm. **S** [Vp], **O** [Vn.p]: meeting, assembly, crowd; class, child. **S** [Vn.p]: chairman, steward; teacher, parent: *The meeting* ***quietened down*** *after repeated warnings that the hall would be cleared.* ○ *'****Quieten*** *those children* ***down****: I can't hear myself think.*

quiver

quiver (with) [Vpr] shake or tremble, esp with strong emotion. **o:** rage, fury, indignation: *Peter* ***quivered with*** *scarcely concealed rage. What right had they to question his methods or results?* ○ *I had one letter . . . which* ***quivered with*** *the pain of still torn feelings.* BRN

quote

quote (from) [Vpr pass adj emph rel, Vn.pr pass emph rel] repeat aloud or write down words used by another person, esp an author. **O:** extract; page, verse. **o:** play, poem; speech: *He wished to* ***quote from*** *the seventeenth century version of the Tractatus.* GE ○ *I shall* ***quote*** *a short extract* ***from*** *the address you gave at Brighton on Friday.* ○ ***From*** *'Hamlet' he* ***quoted*** *the best-known soliloquies.*

R

rabbit

rabbit on (about) [Vp, Vp.pr] (*informal*) talk continuously and boringly (about sth/sb). **o:** garden, pets, record collection; family, children: *'Could you try to stop her* ***rabbiting on about*** *her children?'* ○ *He had* ***rabbited on and on about*** *going boating.* FL

race

race about/around/round [Vp] go quickly from place to place, usu on some urgent task such as warning people of danger: *As soon as the alarm went, the crew* ***raced around*** *shutting the watertight doors.* ○ *The children have been* ***racing round*** *all day, collecting signatures for the petition.*

race up (into/to) [Vp, Vp.pr] rise rapidly (to a particular level). **S:** temperature, pressure; consumption, inflation. **o:** (**into**) the sixties, eighties; (**to**) a new level, an all-time high: *The temperature of the outer parts of the atmosphere'll go* ***racing up to*** *hundreds of thousands of degrees.* TBC ○ *Expenditure* ***raced up and up to*** *an unprecedented level.* = shoot up 2.

radiate

radiate from 1 [Vpr emph rel] spread outwards (from sth), have (sth) as its source. **S:** heat, light; authority; charm, friendliness. **o:** sun, radioactive material, fire; face, eyes; personality, character: *Dangerous emissions* ***radiate from*** *plutonium* (or: *Plutonium* ***radiates*** *dangerous emissions*), *necessitating the use of protective clothing.* ○ *I was greatly impressed by the way he* ***radiated*** *confidence and kindness* (or: *by the way confidence and kindness* ***radiated from*** *him*). MFM
2 [Vpr emph rel] point outwards at various angles from (a centre). **S:** spoke; road, railway; cable, wire. **o:** hub; capital, terminus; communications centre, switchboard: *Most of Britain's motorways* ***radiate from*** *London.* ○ ***From*** *this headquarters* ***radiated*** *the communications system which kept airfields informed of the movements of enemy aircraft.*

rage

rage against/at [Vpr emph rel] (*formal*) express violent anger about (sth). **o:** illness, disability; confinement, restriction; inefficiency: *He* ***raged*** *helplessly* ***against*** *the disability which kept him confined to a wheelchair.* ○ *This was the kind of bureaucratic pettiness* ***at*** *which she had always* ***raged***. = rave against/at.

rage through [Vpr emph rel] pass or sweep violently through (a place). **S:** storm, hurricane; fire; plague, pestilence. **o:** street, town, country: *A cyclone* ***raged through*** *the Mid West, destroying houses, uprooting trees and flattening crops.*

rail

rail against/at [Vpr emph rel] (*formal*) protest or complain bitterly (about sb/sth). **o:** leader, colleague; condition; restriction, control; tax, charge: *I caught myself* ***railing against*** *others as if I were being compelled by them to do this thing that I hated.* LIFE ○ *Many family doctors* ***rail*** *vehemently* ***at*** *the amount of paperwork connected with running a surgery.* ○ *He now sat like a prisoner in his own house . . .* ***railed at*** *by his daughters, defied by his wife.* GIE

rail in [Vn ⇆ p pass adj] enclose (sth) with railings or a fence. **O:** field, garden; herd, flock: *They* ***railed in*** *part of the pasture to prevent the cattle from wandering.* ○ *Behind the house was a small* ***railed-in*** *garden.* ⇨ fence in 1.

rail off (from) [Vn ⇆ p pass adj, Vn.p.pr pass emph rel] separate (one place) (from another) by means of rails or a fence. **O:** garden, orchard, field. **o:** path, road: *The bottom of the garden was* ***railed off*** *to stop the children straying into the road.* ○ *They had* ***railed*** *the meadows* ***off from*** *the motorway.* ⇨ fence off (from).

railroad

railroad into [Vn.pr pass] (*informal*) persuade (sb), esp by applying strong or improper pressure, to do (sth). **S:** commercial interests, pressure group; (impatient, ambitious) colleague, associate. **O:** government, council; company, firm. **o:** (hasty, precipitate) action, decision; buying, selling: *The Council was* ***railroaded into*** *a decision that it was later to regret.* ○ *In the course of the evening he was* ***railroaded into*** *throwing down spiced-beef hot dogs, cream cakes and sparkling wine.* ILIH

railroad through [Vn.p pass, Vn.pr pass] (*informal*) enact (legislation) by applying improper pressure. **S:** government; clique, junta. **O:** Bill, Act; scheme. **o:** legislature, chamber: *The Bill giving emergency powers to the military government was* ***railroaded through*** *with little respect for parliamentary niceties.*

rain

rain down (on/upon) [Vp, Vpr, Vn ⇆ p pass, Vn.p.pr pass] (cause sth to) fall in great quantities (on sb/sth). **S** [Vp, Vp.pr], **O** [Vn.p, Vn.p.pr]: stones, masonry; arrows, spears, shells; blows, curses; demands, appeals: [Vp] *He would hammer a nail* *into the wood with a series of blows that continued to* ***rain down*** *long after the head was flush with the boards.* DF ○ [Vp.pr] *Bits of plaster* ***rained down on*** *our heads from the ceiling, filling our hair and eyes.* ○ [Vp.pr] *Government handouts and diplomatic communiqués ...* ***rained down upon*** *our desks.* SU ○ [Vn.p.pr] *Accurate mortar fire was* ***rained down upon*** *reinforcements moving up through the valley.* □ [Vn.p.pr] pattern usu passive.

rained off [pass adj (Vn.p)] cancelled or abandoned because of rain. **S:** match, game; race; picnic: *Looks as if that trip is going to be* ***rained off***. FL ○ *Yesterday's* ***rained-off*** *match has been rescheduled for Friday.* ⇨ snowed off.

rain upon [Vpr emph rel, Vn.pr pass emph rel] be sent or offered in great quantities to (sb); send or offer (sth) in great quantities to (sb). **S** [Vpr], **O** [Vn.pr]**:** hospitality; food, drink; compliment; request, letter. **S** [Vn.pr]**:** host; visitor: *We couldn't complain of the hospitality; food and drink* ***rained upon*** *us from the moment we entered the house.* ○ *She began early in the May term to* ***rain*** *letters* ***upon*** *her son.* BLCH = shower on/upon.

raise

raise one's voice against [Vn.pr pass emph rel] speak firmly, boldly, in opposition to (sth). **o:** sale of arms, traffic in drugs; neglect of the old; capital punishment: *Not* ***many voices*** *were* ***raised against*** *that decision.* SC ○ *This was an undoubted social evil* ***against*** *which* ***many voices*** *were* ***raised***. □ voices (pl) may be modified by *many, several, few, no*.

raise a/one's glass to [Vn.pr] drink a toast to sb, thus indicating one's approval or admiration. **o:** friend, benefactor, host: *'Mr Charlton, I think we should* ***raise a glass*** (or: ***our glasses***) ***to*** *our hostess.'* DBM ○ *We* ***raised our glasses to*** *the memory of a great man.*

raise one's hat to [Vn.pr] show one's approval of or admiration for (sb), though without literally removing one's hat: *If you're prepared to work in that place for so little money, I* ***raise my hat to*** *you.* ○ *It was a fine gesture: something worth* ***raising one's hat to***. □ take one's hat off to is more commonly used. = take one's hat off to.

raise an objection (to) [Vn.pr pass emph rel] express one's disapproval (of sth). **adj:** no, (not) any; serious. **o:** statement; draft, wording; proposal, scheme: *'If you won't* ***raise any objections***, *I'm going to buy the champagne. OK?'* SML ○ *I tried to* ***raise objections to*** *the situation, but it was no good.* ASA ○ *There was nothing in the first draft* ***to*** *which one could* ***raise any objection***. = object (to).

raise to the peerage [Vn.pr pass] give to (sb) the rank and title of peer. **O:** commoner, knight: *Sir Peter Stainer was* ***raised to the peerage*** *in the Birthday Honours List* (a list of honours made public on the Queen's official birthday).

raise to the surface [Vn.pr pass] bring (sth) up from the bottom to the surface of the sea, river etc. **O:** wreck; sunken ship, submarine: *Divers place an inflatable jacket around the wreck as it lies on the seabed. Then by filling the jacket with air we can* ***raise*** *the wreck* ***to the surface***. ⇨ rise to the surface 1.

raise (with) [Vn.pr pass emph rel] introduce (a subject) in a discussion (with sb). **O:** ⚠ the issue, matter, point, question, subject: *'I took the liberty, sir, of* ***raising*** *the subject* ***with*** *his lordship just now when I brought him his tea.'* EM ○ *These matters have been* ***raised***, *notably* ***with*** *the Canadians, before.* OBS = bring up 3.

rake

rake about/around/round (for) [Vp nom, Vp.pr rel] search carefully here and there (for sth). **o:** trace, sign, evidence: *He spent the afternoon* ***raking around*** *in the attic* ***for*** *some old family photographs.* ○ *The police had a good* ***rake-round*** *in the cellar, but they didn't turn anything up.*

rake in [Vp.n pass] (*informal*) take (sth) as the proceeds of one's business. **O:** a few pounds, a lot of money, a good percentage: *How much do you expect to* ***rake in*** *over the weekend?* ○ *The dealers can* ***rake in*** *another ten or fifteen per cent on the takings.* TT

rake-off [nom (Vn.p)] (*informal*) share of profit, fee, commission, esp in an illegal deal: *The paintings could be disposed of through a crooked art dealer in London, but he would expect a fat* ***rake-off*** *for his trouble.* ○ *'You could try selling your car through Jeff, but his usual* ***rake-off*** *is about ten per cent.'*

rake over old/the ashes [Vp.n pass] revive unpleasant or painful memories of the past: *'I don't want to* ***rake over old ashes***, *Norah, but whilst we are discussing personal matters, have you heard from Jim at all lately?'* TT ○ *We stood by in silent embarrassment as* ***old ashes*** *were* ***raked over***.

rake round (for) [Vp nom, Vp.pr rel] ⇨ rake about/around/round (for).

rake through [Vpr nom pass] examine (documents etc) carefully in search of evidence etc. **o:** book, paper; report, transcript; clothing, possessions: *The police* ***raked through*** *the company files looking for evidence of a massive transfer of funds.* ○ *We'll give the place another* ***rake-through*** *before we give up the search.*

rake up [Vn ⇆ p pass adj] (*informal*) revive sth which is now forgotten, and which is best left forgotten. **O:** one's past, unpleasant memories; old grievances, past enmities: *Old scores were* ***raked up***. *Before I knew where I was, I had a fight on my hands.* DIL ○ *'Why did you have to* ***rake up*** *all this stuff about his divorce?'* = drag up 2.

rally

rally round [Vp, Vpr] come together, unite, in order to support or defend (sb/sth). **S:** colleagues, friends, family: *When their mother fell ill, the children* ***rallied round*** *and helped with household chores and expenses.* ○ *The Visual Aids Group had* ***rallied round*** *and made no end of slides and a film-strip.* TT ○ *He had expected them to* ***rally round*** *and sympathize with him.* FL

rally to [Vpr] increase one's efforts to support a cause, to defeat an enemy etc. **S:** followers, supporters, members; backers, investors. **o:** ⚠ the support/defence of sb/sth; the attack; the task: *Even when the party's election prospects were threatened the rebels couldn't be depended on to* ***rally to*** *the support of the leader.* ○ *I was really concerned for him and I* ***rallied to*** *the attack.* CON ○

I said . . . the bad days were over; we must all **rally to** *the task and finish off the war.* MFM

ram

ram down [Vn ⇆ p pass adj] strike (sth) firmly so that its parts pack tightly together, usu by applying force at the end of a rod. **O:** (explosive) charge; stones, pebbles, ballast: *In muzzle-loading firearms, ball and powder were placed in the barrel and* **rammed down** *with a steel ramrod.* ○ *Broken bricks were* **rammed down** *in the trench to make a base for the concrete.*

ram down sb's throat [Vn.pr pass] (*informal*) repeat (sth) often in the hope of impressing it upon the hearer. **O:** view, opinion; history, science; moral, truth: *He's* **rammed** *his opinions* **down my throat** *so many times that I could repeat them in my sleep.* ○ *There's no point in trying to* **ram** *abstract information* **down the throats of** *young children.* = force/stuff down sb's throat.

ram home [Vn ⇆ p pass] (*informal*) make (a point) absolutely clear by example or illustration. **S:** accident; fall, (car-)crash; loss, bankruptcy. **O:** lesson, moral; urgency, necessity (of sth): *The loss of all his belongings* **rammed home** *the need to insure against fire and theft.* ○ *The instructor's point about sound navigation was* **rammed home** *by the disappearance of an aircraft over the sea.*

ram into [Vpr pass rel, Vn.pr pass rel] drive (one's vehicle) with great force into (sth). **S** [Vpr], **O** [Vn.pr]**:** car, van, lorry: *Her car was* **rammed into** *from behind by a lorry with faulty brakes.* ○ *He turned too sharply and* **rammed** *the car* **into** *a gatepost.*

ramble

ramble on [Vp] continue to speak or write in a wandering, incoherent way: *'We thought of asking Peter to make the speech of welcome, but he does* **ramble on**, *doesn't he?'* ○ *Mark's tutor had difficulty in reducing his draft chapter to coherent shape. The original had* **rambled on** *for fifteen pages.*

range

range against [Vn.pr pass emph rel] assemble (people/things) in opposition to (sb). **O:** (strong) forces, army; tanks, artillery; strength, resources: *We had* **ranged against** *us elements from several enemy divisions.* ○ **Against** *us were* **ranged** *the resources of two major banks.*

range from to [Vpr] cover the range from (one stated limit) to (another). **S:** price, cost; demand, yield; mood, reaction. **o:** (**from**) ten pounds; 20 000 tons; elation, optimism; (**to**) fifty pounds; 1 m tons; gloom, pessimism: *Increases in compulsory contributions* **range from** *thirty pence* **to** *one pound.* ○ *Reactions to the news that a new oil terminal is to be built* **range from** *outright hostility* **to** *cautious optimism.* = vary from to.

range in (on) [Vp, Vp.pr pass, Vn.p pass] (*military*) establish the exact range between one's guns and an enemy position. **S:** artillery, rocket batteries. **o** [Vp.pr], **O** [Vn.p]**:** target, position; emplacement, fortification: [Vp.pr] *'We still hadn't been* **ranged in on** *from the ground. It was a very peaceful atmosphere, really pastoral.'* ST ○ [Vn.p] *'They had both shores* **ranged in**. *The moment a barge set out from one shore there'd be a terrific barrage on it.'* ST = zero in (on) 1.

range over [Vpr rel] move about among (various things); cover, include. **S:** talk, discussion; book, article; interest, experience. **o:** (several) fields, topics, areas: *The four essays* **range over** *a wide variety of topics.* F ○ *It would be difficult to list all the fields* **over** *which his scholarly interests* **range**.

rank

rank among/with [Vpr, Vn.pr pass] (consider sth/sb to) be in the same class or category as (sth/sb): *He* **ranks among** *the best tactical commanders of the last war.* ○ *I wouldn't* **rank** *it* **with** *the very finest white wines from Burgundy.* ○ *She can be* **ranked among** *the best students of her year.* = rate among/with.

rank as [Vpr, Vn.pr pass] (consider sb/sth to) have the qualities or standing of (sth). **o:** (great) statesman; painter, novelist; masterpiece: *He* **ranks as** *one of the most remarkable Presidents of our time.* ○ *It's an exceptionally fine novel, but it can't be* **ranked as** *a work of genius.* = rate as.

rap

rap at/on [Vpr] make a sudden, sharp, blow upon (sth). **o:** door, window, table: *Then Mrs Thurgood would* **rap on** *the window and nod and beckon.* BRH ○ *He* **rapped** *sharply* **on** *the table and the room fell silent.*

rap on/over the knuckles [Vn.pr pass] (*informal*) reprimand, reprove (sb) (for sth): *My report fell short in some parts of its record and he very properly* **rapped** *me* **over the knuckles** *for it.* SD ○ *Some final-year students were* **rapped on the knuckles** *for not submitting their long essays on time.*

rap out 1 [Vn ⇆ p pass adj] signal (a message) by means of a number of sharp taps, eg on a Morse key. **O:** message; sentence, (a few) words: *The prisoners communicated with each other by messages* **rapped out** *on the heating pipes.* ○ *It is claimed that at seances spirits send the messages* **rapped out** *on the table.*

2 [Vn ⇆ p pass] utter (sth) suddenly and sharply. **O:** order, command; oath, curse: *'Stand still!' he* **rapped out**, *in a voice that froze the troops on parade.* ○ *He always* **raps** *his instructions* **out**, *as though he was still in the army.*

rat

rat on 1 [Vpr pass] (*informal*) betray (sb) to people in authority. **o:** friend, mate: *Nobody likes being* **ratted on**, *and he's done it more than once.* = inform against/on.

2 [Vpr pass] (*informal*) fail to honour (an agreement). **o:** promise, deal, agreement: *We thought we could count on Bridger, but he* **ratted on** *the deal at the last minute.*

rate

rate among/with [Vpr, Vn.pr pass] (consider sb/sth to) be in the same class or category as (sb/sth): *He* **rates among** *the best heavyweight boxers of the past fifty years.* ○ *'Would you* **rate** *him* **with** *the best of our MA students?'* = rank among/with.

rate as [Vpr, Vn.pr pass] (consider sb/sth to) have the qualities or standing of (sb/sth). **o:** (good) scholar, sportsman, pilot, sailor; (very) able, competent: *He* **rates as** *one of the best runners over the distance.* ○ *He is* **rated as** *outstanding by the best judges.* = rank as.

rate at [Vn.pr pass rel] reckon (sth) to be at (a particular level of power, capacity etc). **O:** motor, engine; output, capacity, horsepower; income, fortune. **o:** (so many) kilowatts; tons, cubic feet; pounds, dollars: *'What would you* **rate** *the engine* **at**?' *'About twenty horsepower.'* ○ *Output was* **rated at** *about 5 000 bales per working day.*

rate with [Vpr, Vn.pr pass] ⇨ rate among/with.

ration

ration out [Vn ⇆ p pass adj] distribute (sth) as rations, or fixed allowances, in a time of shortage. **O:** food, water; cigarettes: *The remaining stores of tinned milk were carefully* **rationed out** *among the children.* ○ *They had to* **ration** *the petrol* **out**: *twenty litres to each motorist while stocks lasted.*

rattle

rattle away (at/on) [Vp, Vp.pr rel] operate (sth) energetically and with a sharp, rhythmical noise. **o:** typewriter, teleprinter, computer; loom: *Jane was* **rattling away at** *a battered typewriter.*

rattle off [Vn ⇆ p pass] say or repeat (sth) in a fast, rhythmical, sometimes careless, way. **O:** report, story; poem; list: *I got potential criminal Lamb on to the subject of agents, and he* **rattled off** *a few names for me.* JFTR ○ *'Now read the poem again, and this time don't* **rattle** *it* **off** *like a machine-gun.'* ○ *Lady Eccleston* **rattled off** *a list that seemed to contain everyone of any celebrity.* BLCH

rattle on 1 [Vpr emph rel] strike sharply upon (sth), one after the other. **S:** rain, hail; stone, pebble; finger. **o:** roof, window; key: *A shower of rocks and stones* **rattled on** *the roof of the dug-out.* ○ *Her fingers* **rattled on** *the keys of the piano.*

2 [Vp] talk continuously and fast, and usu thoughtlessly: *I found his company unbearable. He could* **rattle on** *for hours about absolutely nothing at all.*

rave

rave about/over [Vpr pass emph rel] (*informal*) talk with foolish enthusiasm about (sth/sb). **o:** holiday, trip; art, architecture; food, wine: *She* **raved about** *her little dressmaker, who could copy a Paris model for next to nothing.* ○ *I might make an injudicious remark or start* **raving** *on* **about** *Henry James.* MSAL ○ *Their house in the country is nothing to* **rave over**.

rave against/at [Vpr emph rel] oppose (sb/sth) violently and possibly incoherently. **o:** young people, (supposed) criminals, imaginary enemies; loose morals, lax standards: *The aging tyrant* **raved against** *his closest associates, accusing them of unimaginable crimes.* = rage against/at.

rave-up [nom (Vp)] (*slang*) wild party, outing etc, esp for young people, and often with pop music: (caption to a picture) *It's a great day for a* **rave-up** *—Julie takes in the scene with other pop fans at a show at Chelmsford, Essex.* EXP ○ *George claims he can 'still shake a leg with all the youngsters at the discos. I enjoy a bit of a* **rave-up**.' TVT

raze

raze to the ground [Vn.pr pass] reduce (sth) to ruins, esp by fire or explosives. **S:** fire; shell, bomb. **O:** city; house, factory: *Memories of the war of 1870 were still vivid at Meudon, where the famous Chateau had been* **razed to the ground**. GJ ○ *Fires swept through the outskirts, where the houses, being mostly of wood, were* **razed to the ground**.

reach

reach down [Vn ⇆ p pass] fetch (sth) from a higher point by stretching one's hand. **O:** book, magazine; cigarette, match: *'Would you mind* **reaching down** *my knitting from the top shelf?'* ○ *The remaining files had to be* **reached down** *from the top of a cupboard.*

reach for [Vpr] stretch out one's hand to grasp (sth). **o:** gun, knife; bottle, glass; cigarettes, pills: *One or two false alarms had the men* **reaching for** *their guns.* ○ *She* **reached for** *Craig's hand.* CH ○ *Hortense* **reached for** *a cigarette and smiled up at Genevieve coldly.* CH

reach for the moon [Vpr] try to reach a goal which is remote and possibly unattainable: *Record-breaking too was becoming old-fashioned: men were now* **reaching for the moon**. OBS ○ *Our modern technological age has expanded human possibility and now '***reaching for the moon***' is a practicality.* SC □ in the second example the literal meaning of the idiom is humorously recalled.

reach out (for) 1 [Vp, Vp.pr rel, Vn ⇆ p pass, Vn.p.pr pass rel] extend a hand etc (to take sth). **O:** ⚠ a hand, an arm. **o:** glass, knife: [Vp] *David* **reached out** *and took down a small leather-bound book.* ○ [Vn.p.pr] *'Would you mind* **reaching** *an arm* **out for** *my tobacco pouch?'* = stretch out 1.

2 [Vp, Vp.pr rel] be ambitious to obtain (sth) or be (sth): [Vp] *The moment has come for* **reaching out**, *even for the moon.* ESS ○ [Vp.pr] *The farm means ease and security and wealth. I think that's what I've been* **reaching out for**, *really.* RFW

reach out (to) [Vp,Vp.pr emph rel] try to give help or comfort (to sb). **S:** regime, (political) party; church. **o:** masses, rank and file; poor, underprivileged: *A party which doesn't* **reach out** *and take account of grass-roots feeling is like a head without a body.* ○ *The worker-priest movement was a largely unofficial attempt from within the Catholic Church to* **reach out to** *the urban working class.*

reach to [Vpr rel] stretch as far as (a certain point). **S:** voice, music; wire; carpet, curtain; dress, coat. **m:** all the way, halfway; nearly, almost. **o:** the back of the hall; wall; floor; below the knee: *'Your voice won't* **reach to** *the back of the auditorium; we'll have to use an amplifier.'* ○ *Boxed into a corner with plywood* **reaching** *three-quarters of the way* **to** *the ceiling, there was . . . an office.* AITC

react

react against [Vpr pass emph rel] respond to (a system or a set of influences) by acting in a contrary or hostile way. **o:** regime, government; parents, upbringing: *People* **reacted against** *wartime austerity by spending freely on clothes and holidays abroad.* ○ *The Courts were both* **reacting**, *and* **reacting** *violently,* **against** *liberal optimism.* RTH

react on/upon 1 [Vpr pass emph rel] produce a chemical change in (sth). **S:** acid; heat, light. **o:** metal, wood: *Heat* **reacts upon** *certain substances to change their chemical composition.* ○ *The acid quickly* **reacts on** *the thin layer of copper and dissolves it.*

2 [Vpr pass rel] act in response to (sb/sth that has acted on one/it). **S:** speaker, actor. **o:** audience, crowd: *Good actors and sympathetic audiences* ***react upon*** *each other.*

react (to) [Vpr pass emph rel] act in response (to sth/sb) by behaving differently, eg in a kinder or more lively fashion. **S:** organism, plant; listener, viewer; patient. **o:** light, heat; display, drama; treatment: *Observe carefully how the bacteria* ***react to*** *this stimulus.* ○ *Children* ***react*** *well* ***to*** *a lively teacher.* ○ *'How is your patient* ***reacting to*** *the course of treatment?'* = respond (to).

read

read about [Vpr pass rel, Vn.pr pass rel] read (sth) on the subject of (sth). **O:** something, a little; article, letter: *I know it's true, because I* ***read about*** *it in the official report.* ○ *Heart transplants have now been* ***read about*** *and discussed throughout the world.* ○ (newspaper-seller's cry) *'****Read all about*** *it!'*

read back [Vn ⇆ p pass] read aloud (a message that has just been received) so that the sender can check its accuracy. **O:** telegram; paragraph, section: *When you send a telegram by phone, the operator will normally* ***read*** *it* ***back*** *to you.* ○ *Do you mind* ***reading*** *the message* ***back****?*

read between the lines [Vpr, Vn.pr] gather meanings from a text that are not actually stated but implied: *I* ***read between the lines*** *of her letter that she had driven him out, and I rejoiced.* ASA ○ ***Reading between the lines****, it was obvious the poor chap was desperately anxious about the future.* ASA

read for [Vpr] study in order to obtain a university degree. **o:** a degree, a diploma; the bar: *She spent three years* ***reading for*** *a degree in history.* ○ *He* ***read for*** *the Bar in his spare time.*

read from [Vpr rel, Vn.pr pass emph rel] read, usu aloud, (an extract) of (a book etc). **O:** passage, extract; chapter, poem; letter. **o:** novel; anthology; newspaper: *Before the children went to bed, Father would* ***read from*** *their favourite book of stories.* ○ *Dickens* ***read*** *extracts* ***from*** *his novels before audiences in the theatre.*

read into [Vn.pr pass] find (meanings) in the words of a speaker or writer which he did not intend. **O:** implications, ideas; things. **o:** book, letter; statement, account: *'Now don't go* ***reading into*** *my letters things I didn't put there!'* ○ *He probably* ***read into*** *her not very complex emotions fine shades of sensibility.* BLCH

read off [Vn ⇆ p pass] read (sth) completely, aloud or to oneself. **O:** message; figure, measurement; temperature: *Frank tore open the envelope,* ***read off*** *the brief message it contained and picked up the telephone.* ○ *'I want you to sit down in front of those dials and* ***read off*** *any fluctuations that occur in oil pressure.'*

read out [Vn ⇆ p pass] read aloud to an audience (sth which is of interest to them, or of which they must take special notice). **O:** announcement, instruction; article: *'If it's a letter from Anna,* ***read*** *it* ***out*** *loud, Mum!'* ○ *After morning prayers, important notices are* ***read out*** *to the assembled school.*

read over [Vn ⇆ p pass] read (sth) carefully in order to check it. **O:** text, script, draft: *'****Read*** *the report* ***over*** *to yourself, and see if you can spot anything odd.'*

read through [Vn ⇆ p nom pass] read (sth) completely, from beginning to end. **O:** report, account; statement, evidence: *He lifted out the topmost two letters, and though he knew what he would see, he* ***read*** *them* ***through*** *again.* PW ○ *I never* ***read through*** *these notes, I simply wrote them in response to some blind impulse.* LIFE ○ *'Give them a quick* ***read-through****. What do you notice?*

read-through [nom (Vn.p)] reading of the whole text of a play by the actors in preparation for the stage performance: *At the end of the* ***read-throughs*** *the cast sat somewhat tensely.* ST ○ *There were expressionless* ***read-throughs*** *of a script with his cast.* NS

read oneself to sleep [Vn.pr] read with the aim or in the hope of falling asleep; read so much, or so late at night, that one falls asleep: *He felt wide-awake in bed — he'd drunk too much coffee — so he tried to* ***read himself to sleep****.*

read up [Vn ⇆ p pass] acquire a knowledge of (a subject) through reading. **O:** facts, details, elements: *There's no need to attend classes in theory: you can* ***read*** *it* ***up*** *for yourself in the library.* ○ *I knew nothing of the subject, but I could* ***read up*** *enough to pass a simple test.*

read up on [Vp.pr pass] improve one's knowledge of (sth) by reading; bring one's knowledge of (sth) up to date by reading. **o:** details, facts, events; what has happened: *I must* ***read up on*** *recent developments; I'm getting terribly out of touch.* ○ *There's so much to* ***read up on*** *in literary theory.*

realize

realize (from/on) [Vn.pr pass emph rel] get (sth) as a price for, or as a profit on (sth). **O:** (handsome) profit, return; sum, price. **o:** (the sale of) furniture, painting, jewellery: *We didn't* ***realize*** *as much as we'd hoped* ***on*** *the china.* ○ ***From*** *overseas sales he's* ***realized*** *as much in six months as in the whole of previous year.*

reap

reap (from) [Vn.pr pass emph rel] derive, obtain (benefit) (from sth). **O:** (a rich, poor) return; benefit, dividend. **o:** investments, savings: *He* ***reaped*** *handsome dividends* ***from*** *the hard work he'd put in earlier.* ○ *This is an investment* ***from*** *which we expect to* ***reap*** *a very good return.*

rear

rear up [Vp] rise high on its hind legs from fear and/or to attack an enemy. **S:** the horse, stallion; the beast: *For no apparent reason the horse* ***reared up****, almost unseating its rider.*

reason

reason into [Vn.pr pass rel] persuade (sb) by reasoned argument to do (sth). **o:** membership, participation; agreement, dissent; doing sth, behaving thus: *This is something he can be* ***reasoned into****, given time.* ○ *I'm afraid he can't be* ***reasoned into*** *making a public protest.* □ usu passive. ↔ reason out of.

reason out [Vn ⇆ p pass adj] obtain (an answer) through careful reasoning. **O:** solution, result; that this is the case: *How odd, she thought, that my mind can* ***reason*** *that* ***out*** *while my body seems to have given up.* TFD ○ *The police* ***reasoned out*** *that* *if the men had left by the midday train, it would be easy to pick them up at the terminus.* = figure out 2, work out 3.

reason out of [Vn.pr pass rel] persuade (sb) by reasoned argument not to do (sth), or to leave or abandon (sth). **o:** joining, taking part; black mood, bad temper, stubbornness: *We tried to* ***reason*** *him* ***out of*** *it, but without much success.* ○ *These were deeply held convictions and he couldn't be* ***reasoned out of*** *them very easily.* ↔ reason into.

reason with [Vpr pass rel] argue with (sb) reasonably in the hope of convincing him: *Have you tried* ***reasoning with*** *him?* ○ *She won't be* ***reasoned with*** (ie she won't listen to reasoned argument).

rebel

rebel (against) [Vpr pass emph rel] oppose (those in authority) vigorously. **S:** subject, follower, soldier. **o:** (established) authority; regime, system, government: *The Queen* ***rebelled against*** *the Romans because they had beaten her and been rude to her daughters.* BRH ○ ***Against*** *a system such as this anyone would* ***rebel***.

rebound

rebound (from) 1 [Vpr emph rel] bounce back (from sth). **S:** ball; stone, pebble: *The dart struck the board sideways on and* ***rebounded*** *(****from*** *it).*
2 [Vpr emph rel] (*finance*) recover suddenly from (a low level). **S:** price, shares, equities: *Shares* ***rebounded from*** *Friday's losses but ended below the day's highs.* IND

rebound on/upon [Vpr emph rel] affect the person responsible for the action or sb else for whom it was not intended. **S:** cruelty, harsh words, thoughtlessness. **o:** oneself; one's family, friends: *I shouldn't write that letter; it could* ***rebound*** *very badly* ***on*** *us.* ○ *If you make trouble, it'll* ***rebound upon*** *everyone.*

recall

recall (from) [Vn.pr pass emph rel] call (sb) back to the home country (from abroad). **O:** envoy, attaché, consul: *The Indian High Commissioner has been* ***recalled from*** *London.* ○ *A Foreign Office spokesman named the countries* ***from*** *which our missions were being* ***recalled***.

recall to mind [Vn.pr pass] remember, recollect (sth). **O:** face; words; what he looked like; his saying anything; that he did so: *After so many years I find it hard to* ***recall*** *all their names* ***to mind***. ○ *I* ***recalled to mind*** *many instances of personal kindness.* ⇨ call to mind.

recede

recede (from) [Vpr emph rel] (*formal*) move gradually away (from sth/sb); be lost (from). **S:** shore, coastline; face, voice; memory. **o:** sight, view; one's mind: *We gained height and the airport buildings* ***receded from*** *view.* ○ *As human contact seemed to* ***recede from*** *her grasp, she craved for it all the more.* MSAL

receive

receive back into [Vn.p.pr pass] admit (sb) again as a member of (a body which he has left). **o:** party, church; fold, bosom of society: *The party was prepared to* ***receive*** *Stevens* ***back into*** *the fold because of his wide contacts and influence in the City.* ○ *What if he were not* ***received back into*** *the bosom of society as freely as he had hoped and expected?* GIE

receive (from) [Vn.pr emph rel] have (sth) sent or given to one (by sb). **O:** gift; parcel, letter; kindness, insults; visit, envoy: *I expect to* ***receive*** *nothing but empty promises* ***from*** *him.* ○ ***From*** *his employers he* ***received*** *a less than generous pension.*

reckon

reckon among 1 [Vn.pr pass] include (sb) as one of (a certain category). **o:** (leading, expert) experts, judges, critics; (most) able, competent (people); one's acquaintances, friends: *I don't like him, but I wouldn't* ***reckon*** *him* ***among*** *my enemies.* ○ *We'd* ***reckon*** *these two correspondents* ***among*** *the best on the paper.* ○ *He can be* ***reckoned among*** *the best guides to form in racing.* = count among.
2 [Vn.pr pass emph rel] consider (particular person(s)) to be best, worst etc in their group. **o:** students; applicants, candidates: *I'd* ***reckon*** *him (to be) the least suitable* ***among*** *those coming forward for places.* ○ *He was* ***reckoned*** *best* ***among*** *the new recruits.* ○ ***Among*** *those applying I'd* ***reckon*** *him (the) least qualified to do research.* □ the Object is followed by an Object Complement — usu an adj eg *best, most able, least acceptable, best suited (to do sth).*

reckon (as) [Vn.pr pass] consider (sth) (to be sth). **O:** agriculture, industry; farm, factory; expenditure, saving. **o:** efficient, wasteful; (good) investment, security; declining, running to waste: *Investment in this area is* ***reckoned as*** (or: ***reckoned*** *to be) money poured down the drain.* ○ *We don't* ***reckon*** *this work* ***as*** *essential to the development of the department.* ○ *The garage was* ***reckoned as*** *forming* (or: ***reckoned*** *to form) part of his rateable property.* = regard as.

reckon in [Vn ⇆ p pass] include (sth) as part of a bill, estimate etc. **O:** cost, expense: *When you submit your claim, don't forget to* ***reckon in*** *the money spent on petrol.* ○ *'Don't bother to tip: the service charge has already been* ***reckoned in***.*'*

reckon on [Vpr] estimate or assume (sth). **o:** two drinks per guest, three ships per day, twenty miles to the gallon; demand staying at the present level: ***Reckoning on*** *an average of five letters to a word, this means that about fifteen of the . . . pulses are required per word.* TBC ○ ***Reckoning on*** *the same rate of increase this year, we should be in profit next year.* □ v is usu in the *-ing* form and begins the clause.

reckon on/upon [Vpr pass emph rel] make one's plans in the sure knowledge that sth will happen, or be the case. **o:** support, help; kindness, generosity: *The Bonn finance Minister said East German workers could* ***reckon on*** *a wages top-up of 200DM per month.* FT ○ *Tom would always back you in a crisis:* ***on*** *that you could safely* ***reckon***. = bank on 1, depend on/upon 2.

reckon up [Vn ⇆ p pass] find the total, amount, of (sth). **O:** expenses, outgoings, takings; losses, damage: *When she was handed change she found it impossible to* ***reckon up*** *quickly.* LM ○ *We've* ***reckoned up*** *the cost of repairing your car.*

reckon with 1 [Vpr pass emph rel] include (sth/sb) in one's plans or calculations. **o:** (possible, likely) difficulty, obstacle; cost, weight, size; manager, headmaster: *I had not* **reckoned with** *the facts of my temperament, training and habits.* DOP ○ *Sydney had to* **reckon with** *the rector of the parish, whose permission was essential.* SS ○ *The only person* **with** *whom you hadn't* **reckoned** *was Mad Jenny.* MOQ ↔ reckon without.
2 [Vpr pass emph rel] handle or tackle (sth) so as to remedy or reform it. **o:** problem, difficulty, danger, shortage: *When you consider all the delays and shortages they had to* **reckon with**, *it's a wonder they kept their sense of humour.* ○ *All these problems had to be* **reckoned with** *as they arose, before they grew large enough to hinder progress.* = deal with 2.
3 [Vpr pass] punish (sb), esp in an unpleasant way. **S:** police; authorities. **o:** enemy, dissenter, critic: *The secret police* **reckoned with** *anyone suspected of supporting the government in exile.* ○ *Anyone not obeying the decrees of the military junta could expect to be* **reckoned with**. = deal with 3.

reckon without [Vpr pass] not include (sth/sb) in one's plans or calculations. **o:** weather, climate; (chance of) slump, depression; help, intervention; director, administrator: *The organizers of the garden party had* **reckoned without** *the possibility of a freak thunderstorm.* ○ *Being by nature pessimistic, I'd* **reckoned without** *their willingness to lend me the money.* ↔ reckon with 1.

reclaim

reclaim (from) [Vn.pr pass emph rel] make (sth) available for use, or restore (sth) to use, by draining off water, using fertilizers etc. **O:** acres; flooded land, waste land. **o:** sea, flooding: *In Holland thousands of hectares have been* **reclaimed from** *the sea and turned over to arable land and pasture.*

recognize

recognize (as) 1 [Vn.pr pass] accept that (sb/sth) has the rank or importance that is claimed for him or it. **O:** son, brother; claimant, contender; government, regime. **o:** rightful heir, lawful descendant; legally constituted: *The break-away committee has not been properly constituted, and will not be* **recognized as** *such.* ○ *It is not certain that the Court will* **recognize** *him (***as** *his father's rightful heir).*
2 [Vn.pr pass] regard, consider (sb) (to be sth). **o:** an authority, the last word; authentic, genuine; eminent, distinguished: *In years to come they will* **recognize** *him* **as** (or: **recognize** *him to be) one of the great founding-fathers of our movement.* ○ *This has long been* **recognized as** *the standard work on the Napoleonic period.*

recoil

recoil (from) [Vpr pass emph rel] (*formal*) withdraw sharply and in fear or pain (from sth that appears suddenly, that one has to do etc). **o:** sight, prospect; action, deed: *The leading troops* **recoiled from** *the murderous barrage.* ○ *She* **recoils from** *the sight of blood.* = reel back (from).

recommend

recommend (to) [Vn.pr pass emph rel] say (to sb) that (sb/sth) is suitable for a post, for use etc. **S:** teacher, tutor; (previous) employer. **O:** applicant; model, pattern; item, ingredient: *I feel quite confident in* **recommending** *Sarah Jackson* **to** *you for the vacant post of research assistant.* ○ *A new man will be joining the project next October. He has been strongly* **recommended to** *us by the head of our Manchester office.* ○ *This model was* **recommended to** *me by one of your sales assistants.*

recompense

recompense (for) [Vn.pr pass emph rel] reward (sb) for some good he has done; repay (sb) for some loss he has suffered. **A:** amply, fully, richly. **o:** help, services, loyalty, support; damage, suffering: *You will be amply* **recompensed for** *your loyal support.* ○ *The company now presents itself as the innocent victim of the Second World War, and has been handsomely* **recompensed for** *its injuries.* OBS = compensate (for).

reconcile

reconcile to [Vn.pr pass emph rel] (cause sb to) accept (sth unpleasant). **o:** humble status, low wages; poverty, obscurity: *He had* **reconciled** *himself cheerfully* **to** *a modest livelihood in a small country town.* ○ *Even though his health had improved, Sydney was not entirely* **reconciled to** *the soft Somerset weather.* SS = resign (oneself) to.

reconcile (with) 1 [Vn.pr pass emph rel] bring (one person) and (another) together after a quarrel, an angry separation etc: *Friends managed to* **reconcile** *him* **with** *his wife after years of estrangement.* ○ *He was* **reconciled with** *his brothers* (or: *He and his brothers were* **reconciled**) *after a fierce family quarrel.*
2 [Vn.pr pass emph rel] make (one fact etc) be consistent (with another). **O:** action, event; decision, statement; principle, tenet. **o:** claim, profession (of goodwill); philosophy, theory: *I can't* **reconcile** *what he says here* **with** *statements in the earlier parts of the book.* ○ *How can their aggressive actions be* **reconciled with** *their talk of peace and brotherhood?* ○ *The two sets of figures can't be* **reconciled** *(***with** *each other).* □ with *can/could*; often neg. = square with.

record

record (from) (on/onto) [Vn.pr pass emph rel] make a sound or video recording (esp onto tape). **O:** broadcast; speech, music; interview, play. **o:** (**from**) radio, disc, TV; (**on/onto**) (audio-/video-) tape: *'We managed to* **record** *the whole of the concert* **from** *a live studio broadcast.'* ○ *Jack has a set of Duke Ellington numbers* **recorded from** *the original 78s* **onto** *tape.*

recover

recover (from) 1 [Vpr pass emph rel] get well again, improve, after some kind of set-back. **o:** illness, operation; depression, slump; shock, surprise: *She's still* **recovering from** *a bout of 'flu.* ○ *Isaiah was in bed* **recovering from** *a hangover.* SU ○ **From** *a prolonged depression such as this, industry is always slow to* **recover**. = get over 3.
2 [Vn.pr pass emph rel] regain (sth lent or lost) (from sb/sth): *Fabian* **recovered** *his cricket ball* **from** *the neighbours' lawn.* ○ *Several of the missing coins were* **recovered from** *the bed of the river.*

recruit

recruit (into) (from) [Vn.pr pass emph rel] enlist (sb) as a member (of a particular force or body) (from a particular source). **o:** (**into**) army, navy; (**from**) another service, industry: *Groups of managers regularly visit the universities to* ***recruit*** *graduates* ***into*** *traineeships in industry.* ○ *At first, the Government* ***recruited*** *men (****into*** *the forces)* ***from*** *non-essential industries.*

recur

recur to [Vpr rel] (*formal*) be recalled by (sb), come again into sb's mind. **S:** idea, thought; memory, recollection; experience, event: *The memory of those days often* ***recurs to*** *me.* ○ *The tune* ***recurred to*** *me while I was having my bath.* = come back 3.

redeem

redeem (from) 1 [Vn.pr pass emph rel] preserve, save (sth) (from falling to a low level). **O:** occasion; party, meal; performance, spectacle. **o:** (total) failure, disaster, ignominy; (outright) farce, comedy, tragedy: *It was John who* ***redeemed*** *the occasion* ***from*** *utter failure by telling some of his funny stories.* ○ *The second act was* ***redeemed from*** *total disaster by Lucy's performance.*

2 [Vn.pr pass rel] get back (an article) (from a pawnshop) by paying money. **O:** clothing, furniture, jewellery. **o:** ⚠ pawn, hock: *He* ***redeemed*** *his one and only suit* ***from*** *pawn to attend a wedding.*

3 [Vn.pr pass rel] (*religion*) make free (from sin) by sacrifice (esp the Sacrificial Atonement of Christ). **S:** Christ; Christ's sacrifice, blood. **O:** mortal; sinner. **o:** ⚠ sin, death, damnation: *We are* ***redeemed from*** *sin and shame by the blood of Jesus.*

redound

redound to [Vpr] (*rhetorical*) add to (sth); increase, enhance. **S:** action, deed; success, exploit. **o:** fame, honour, credit, reputation: *Her achievements will* ***redound to*** *the good name of the school.*

reduce

reduce (from) [Vn.pr pass emph rel] ⇨ reduce (to) (from).

reduce to 1 [Vn.pr pass emph rel] change (sth) into smaller pieces or into its chemical constituents. **O:** wood; cloth, paper; gas, liquid. **o:** pulp, splinter; rag, shred; atom, molecule: *A crushing machine* ***reduces*** *the logs* ***to*** *pulp.* ○ *Water can be* ***reduced to*** *oxygen and hydrogen by electrolysis.* = break down 7.

2 [Vn.pr pass] convert (a sum of money) in a calculation to (smaller units). **O:** amount, sum; dollars, pounds. **o:** cents, pence: *You can* ***reduce*** *the amount in pounds* ***to*** *new pence by simply multiplying by 100.*

3 [Vn.pr pass] make (sth) seem of no value or importance, by revealing its faults, inconsistencies etc. **O:** argument, case; claim, pretension. **o:** shreds, tatters; nothing: *Our case was argued by an able barrister, who* ***reduced*** *the prosecutor's submissions* ***to*** *nothing.*

4 [Vn.pr pass emph rel] bring (sb) to a low or undignified position or state. **o:** (pretty) pass, (parlous) state; such straits, indignities; beggary; begging, borrowing; mortgaging one's property: *A succession of bad harvests had* ***reduced*** *the small farmers* ***to*** *penury.* ○ *You apologize to the one who ought to apologize to you —* ***to*** *such straits does love* ***reduce*** *dignity and common sense.* SPL

5 [Vn.pr pass] seriously weaken the physical or nervous condition of (sb). **o:** ⚠ a (nervous, physical) wreck, a skeleton, skin and bones, a shadow: *Weeks in an open boat had* ***reduced*** *the surviving crew members* ***to*** *skin and bones.* ○ *Anxiety about the fate of his family* ***reduced*** *him* ***to*** *a nervous wreck.*

6 [Vn.pr pass emph rel] state or view (sth) in a more concise or simplified form; summarize as. **O:** chapter, book; paper, report; case, argument. **o:** notes, headings; (a few) pages; its essentials, the bare bones: *We can* ***reduce*** *his rather lengthy statement* ***to*** *one or two essential points.* ○ *Take the complications of modern marriage in your stride. Try and* ***reduce*** *it* ***to*** *its simplest essentials.* DIL

reduce to silence [Vn.pr pass] make (sb) stop talking, complaining etc, through one's moral authority or force of personality. **O:** crowd, audience; rabble, mob. **adj:** total, complete, absolute: *The moral force of his appeal* ***reduced*** *his critics* ***to silence.*** ○ *His appearance on a platform could* ***reduce*** *even professional hecklers* ***to silence.***

reduce to tears [Vn.pr pass] affect (sb) so deeply that he cries. **S:** performance, performer; anger, fit of temper; speech, appeal. **O:** audience, listener: *He often* ***reduced*** *the women* ***to tears*** *at their first lesson.* GJ ○ *Verlaine's poem … had the instant effect of* ***reducing*** *Fournier* ***to tears.*** AF

reduce (to) (from) [Vn.pr pass emph rel] lower, decrease (sth) (from one level to another). **O:** pressure, temperature, volume, weight, speed: ***Reduce*** *the speed of your car* ***to*** *30mph when entering a built-up area.* ○ *It was our opinion that we must* ***reduce*** *the tempo of our operations* (ie ***from*** its existing high level). MFM

reef

reef down [Vp] (*nautical*) reduce the area of a sail by gathering up part of it: *If you must* ***reef down*** *in an emergency always tend to reduce sail by too much than too little.* SAIL

reek

reek of 1 [Vpr] have the strong and unpleasant smell of (sth). **S:** room, house; food; breath. **o:** smoke; onion, garlic; whisky, beer: *'Open a window: the place* ***reeks of*** *stale cigarette smoke.'* ○ *It was stiflingly hot inside the bus, which* ***reeked of*** *petrol.* BM

2 [Vpr] strongly suggest (sth unpleasant, pretentious etc). **S:** atmosphere; talk. **o:** corruption, intrigue; snobbery, class: *His conversation* ***reeks of*** *the literary world.* HAA ○ *I'm stepping out, my dear,/ Into an atmosphere/ That simply* ***reeks of*** *class.* (IRVING BERLIN)

reel

reel back (from) [Vp, Vp.pr] move back out of control, esp after receiving a powerful blow or shock; stagger back. **S:** army; soldier, boxer: *Two other Armies* ***reeled back*** *in a state of accelerating disorder.* B ○ *I felt rather as though I had been kicked in the face by a horse, and* ***reeled back****, momentarily blinded by the pain.* DF = recoil (from).

reel in [Vn ⇆ p pass] wind (a fishing line) onto the reel fastened to the end of the rod, causing the line to rise from the water. **O:** line; fish: *'You've got something on the end of your line:* ***reel*** *it* ***in****.'*

reel off [Vn ⇆ p pass] say or repeat (sth) rapidly and smoothly. **O:** list, catalogue; (a string of) names, figures, facts: *Alun . . .* ***reeled off*** *a string of heartfelt appreciative expressions.* OD ○ *'I think your father's marvellous. Fancy being able to* ***reel*** *all that* ***off****!'* ASA

refer

refer back (to) [Vn ⇆ p pass, Vn.p.pr pass emph rel] send back (sth) for further examination (to sb who has already considered it). **O:** letter; application, claim. **o:** office, department: *Accounts Dept keep* ***referring*** *our travel claims* ***back****. We're claiming five pence a mile for official journeys, and they insist we're only entitled to three.* ○ *'I've had my application for a vacation grant* ***referred back to*** *the University. It seems I should have asked my tutor to write a few words in support.'* ⇨ refer to 4.

refer to 1 [Vpr pass emph rel] mention (sth). **o:** matter, question; need, importance, urgency: *I have already* ***referred to*** *our guest's distinguished record in local government.* ○ *The minister* ***referred to*** *the importance to the nation of increased exports.* SC ○ *The problem* ***to*** *which you* ***referred*** *has already been dealt with.* = allude to.

2 [Vpr emph rel] affect, concern (sb). **S:** remark, statement; rule, restriction: *'What I have to say* ***refers to*** *all of you.'* ○ *There are no categories of workers* ***to*** *whom this order does not* ***refer****.* = apply (to) 1.

3 [Vpr pass emph rel] look at (sth) to find sth out or refresh one's memory; consult. **S:** announcer, actor, student. **o:** notes, script, dictionary: *'You've all got copies of the script; but you shouldn't need to* ***refer to*** *them after the first week of rehearsals.'* ○ *He carried a sheaf of notes,* ***to*** *which he frequently* ***referred*** *during the course of the talk.*

4 [Vn.pr pass emph rel] hand or pass (sb/sth) (to another person or body) for help or a decision. **O:** customer, inquirer; matter, case; dispute; claim. **o:** (another) branch, department; tribunal, court of inquiry: *Somebody in reception* ***referred*** *me* ***to*** *the manager.* ○ *'If he gives any more trouble* ***refer*** *him* ***to*** *me.'* ○ *'Your claim has been* ***referred to*** *the Bursar's office.'*

reflect

reflect on/upon 1 [Vpr pass emph rel] think carefully about (sth). **o:** position, state; (next) move; reply, response; how to react, what to do: *He* ***reflected*** *carefully* ***on*** *the likely outcome of his action.* ○ *We have to* ***reflect upon*** *our share in the relationship of the human with the divine.* CF

2 [Vpr pass] indicate or suggest that (sb/sth) is sound, unsound etc. **S:** remark; report; recommendation. **o:** courtesy, efficiency; ability, skill. **A:** well, favourably; adversely, unfavourably: *This mysterious man asked questions and made recommendations which* ***reflected on*** *their efficiency.* DS ○ *People . . . assume that everyone has something to hide. I think it* ***reflects*** *rather badly* ***on*** *them.* SE ○ *The opening of assembly plants in Europe* ***reflects*** *very well* ***on*** *the vigour and enterprise of Japanese industry.* □ when no adv is present the implication is that events etc reflect *badly* on sb or sth.

reflect credit on/upon [Vn.pr emph rel] be good for the reputation of (sb). **S:** behaviour, conduct; success, achievement; result, outcome. **adj:** some; no (not) any/much, little; great. **o:** participant, member; player, competitor: *The success of the meeting* ***reflected*** *the greatest* ***credit on*** *all concerned.* ○ *The naturalness of this proceeding* ***reflected credit on*** *both parties.* AH

refrain

refrain from [Vpr pass emph rel] not begin to do, or stop doing (sth unpleasant or antisocial). **o:** bad language, anti-social behaviour; aggression, hostilities; smoking, drinking: *I wish he would* ***refrain from*** *scattering his ash all over the carpet.* ○ *Please* ***refrain from*** *smoking during the performance.*

refund

refund (to) [Vn.pr pass emph rel] return (to sb) money which he has already paid for goods or services, usu because those goods etc cannot be supplied or are unacceptable. **S:** shop, cinema; local authority, college. **O:** cost (of goods, of admission); payment, fee. **o:** customer, patron; student: *If patrons will kindly go to the booking office the cost of tickets will be* ***refunded to*** *them.* ○ *The University is unable to* ***refund*** *tuition fees* ***to*** *students who fail to complete the course.*

regain

regain (from) [Vn.pr pass emph rel] (*formal*) obtain (sth) once again (from sb). **O:** land, possessions; freedom, independence. **o:** the state; a colonial power: *The island was* ***regained from*** *the French during a minor eighteenth-century war.* ○ *Former colonies often maintain trading links with the countries* ***from*** *which they have* ***regained*** *their independence.*

regale

regale with [Vn.pr pass emph rel] (*formal* or *jocular*) persuade or oblige (sb) to accept, consume or listen to (sth). **o:** gift, present; food, drink; song, story: *Don't imagine that when you go on a trade mission overseas our customers will* ***regale*** *you* ***with*** *champagne and cigars.* ○ *I'm tired of being* ***regaled with*** *stories of little Michael's exploits.*

regard

regard as [Vn.pr pass] consider (sb) to be (sth). **O:** son, brother; addition, improvement; machine, process. **o:** rightful owner, legitimate heir; useful, valuable; inferior, a waste of time: *Freud himself* ***regarded*** *the essay* ***as*** *'the only truly beautiful thing I have ever written.'* F ○ *He is generally* ***regarded as*** *the leading authority on the subject.* = reckon (as).

regard with [Vn.pr pass emph rel] consider (sb/sth) with (a particular attitude or in a certain light). **o:** approval, favour; caution, hesitation; disapproval, disfavour: *If you would like to put in an application I am sure it will be* ***regarded with*** *sympathy.* ○ *His intervention at that point was* ***regarded with*** *some disfavour.* ○ ***With*** *such widespread hostility was the Poll Tax* ***regarded*** *that the Government was forced to abandon it.*

register

register (with) (as) 1 [Vpr rel, Vn.pr pass rel] be perceived or felt (as sth); perceive or feel (sth) (as sth). **S** [Vpr], **O** [Vn.pr]: sensation, feeling; noise, disturbance. **o:** (**as**) pain, ache; acute distress; high-pitched humming: *The sensation* ***registered with*** *me* ***as*** *an intermittent sharp pain.* ○ *A sense of guilt can be . . . experienced without perhaps being* ***registered as*** *such in the consciousness.* ESS □ [Vn.pr] pattern usu passive.

2 [Vpr rel, Vn.pr pass rel] (cause sb to) be included in a list or register (as a person for whom some service will be provided). **S** [Vpr], **O** [Vn.pr]: child, teenager; unemployed person. **o:** (**with**) doctor, dentist; clinic; job centre: *Lady Berowne then* ***registered with*** *me under the National Health Service* (ie as a patient). TFD ○ *No boy is interviewed . . . until he is sixteen, nor is he* ***registered as*** *a candidate for a vacancy until he is seventeen.* OBS

register with [Vpr rel, Vn.pr pass rel] leave a formal record of (one's name etc) (with the civil authorities). **O:** one's name; oneself, one's family. **o:** police, Home Office: *She suffered the usual humiliation of foreigners in time of war, being obliged to* ***register*** *herself as an alien* ***with*** *the police.* GJ

reign

reign (over) [Vpr emph rel] rule as the king or queen (over sb/sth). **o:** people, country: ***Over*** *these Edens* (ie homes that were like paradise) ***reigned*** *the gentle, indulgent, loving, angelic mother.* BRN ○ *He was forced to leave the country* ***over*** *which he had* ***reigned*** *since boyhood.*

reimburse

reimburse (for) [Vn.pr pass emph rel] repay to (sb) money spent for a particular purpose, or the value of sth lost. **o:** breakage, loss; moving, travelling: *We shall be glad to* ***reimburse*** *you* ***for*** *sending us the papers* (or: ***reimburse*** *you the cost of sending* etc). ○ *He thought himself amply* ***reimbursed for*** *the loss of his typewriter.*

rein

rein in 1 [Vn ⇆ p pass] check or restrain (a horse) by pulling on its reins. **O:** mount; horse, pony: *The scout* ***reined in*** *his horse, dismounted, and ran forward with a message.*

2 [Vp.n pass] check or restrain (feelings etc). **O:** impulse, inclination (to do sth); emotion; anger, temper: *She* ***reined in*** *a sudden urge to hit Peter over the head with her handbag.* ○ *His wilder flights of fancy are* ***reined in*** *by common sense.*

reissue

reissue (to) [Vn.pr pass emph rel] ⇨ next entry

reissue with [Vn.pr pass emph rel] issue again to (sb) (sth that was temporarily withdrawn). **S:** firm, office; clerk, storekeeper. **o:** document, pass; overall, apron: *The office will* ***reissue*** *you* ***with*** *your cards when the details have been checked.* ○ *The men were* ***reissued with*** *warm clothing after an unexpected change in the weather* (or: *Warm clothing was* ***reissued to*** *them* etc).

rejoice

rejoice at/over [Vpr pass emph rel] (*formal*) be very glad about (sth). **o:** news, announcement; success, victory: *He's not the kind of man to* ***rejoice at*** *other people's misfortunes.* ○ *The British* ***rejoiced over*** *the end of food rationing, which marked an important stage in the lifting of austerity.*

rejoice in 1 [Vpr rel] take great pleasure in (sb/sth). **o:** one's son, daughter; sb's achievements, success: *Although Thetis* ***rejoiced in*** *her little son she was anxious about his future.* GLEG ○ *He* ***rejoiced in*** *Jeffrey's growing personal reputation.* SS

2 [Vpr rel] (*jocular*) have the nickname or title of (sth). **o:** ⚠ the name, title, style of (sth): *'He is a comedy man to his toenails,' said Ern, . . . and Ammonds, who* ***rejoices in*** *the nickname 'Big A', agreed.* RT ○ *Our unpleasant friend* ***rejoices in*** *the name of Minister of Justice.* SC = glory in 2.

relapse

relapse (into) [Vpr rel] be overcome (by sth) again. **o:** illness, fever; crime, heresy; (bad) ways, (old) habits: *After a short burst of enthusiasm, he* ***relapsed into*** *his usual apathy.* ○ *'Here's to love!' she said and* ***relapsed into*** *unconsciousness.* GJ

relate

relate (to) [Vn.pr pass emph rel] connect, link (one thing) (to another). **O:** event, phenomenon, occurrence; fact, detail: *I find it hard to* ***relate*** *these events* ***to*** *the story as it has emerged so far.* ○ *The recent price increase is not* ***related to*** *the change in Value Added Tax* (cf *The increase and the change are not* ***related***). ⇨ connected (with).

relate to 1 [Vpr rel] be concerned with, have to do with (sth/sb). **S:** event, occurrence, development; remark, comment. **o:** desire, wish, intention; something he said earlier: *His remarks* ***relate to*** *something that happened at the Board meeting last week.* ○ *Most of the surviving anecdotes* ***relate to*** *his later years.* SS

2 [Vpr rel] form an easy and natural relationship with (sb). **o:** colleague, workmate; the opposite sex; doctor, analyst: *She finds it difficult to* ***relate to*** *her tutors and fellow-students.* ○ *It was not his kind of world: there were very few in his immediate circle* ***to*** *whom he could* ***relate***.

related (to) [pass (Vn.pr)] connected to (sb) by blood or marriage; belonging to the same species as (sth). **o:** family, house; order, species: *The present Queen is* ***related****, directly or by marriage,* ***to*** *most of the other royal families of Europe* (cf *She and they are* ***related***). ○ *The zoologist's classification by species, genera, and so on, shows how the animals known to man are* ***related to*** *each other.* □ also used with *appear, seem,* or after a noun.

relax

relax one's grip/hold (on) [Vn.pr pass emph rel] allow one's grip or control (on sb/sth) to become less tight or severe. **S:** dictator, tyrant; (strict) parent; weather. **o:** people, country; family; countryside: *Frank continued to talk quietly and soothingly to the girl until* ***her*** *frightened* ***grip on*** *his arm was* ***relaxed***. ○ *Winter had* ***relaxed its*** *iron* ***grip on*** *the landscape.* ○ *Better times ahead may persuade the Chancellor to* ***relax his hold on*** *the economy.*

relay

relay (to) [Vn.pr pass emph rel] pass (to sb) a message etc which originates from sb else. **S:** radio station, switchboard; messenger, secretary. **O:**

signal, message; order, instruction: *Sub-stations were asked to* **relay** *the message* **to** *all receivers tuned to their networks.* ○ *A standard procedure ensured that orders were* **relayed** *quickly* **to** *all sub-units in the division.*

release

release (from) 1 [Vn.pr pass emph rel] allow (sb) to leave (a place). **O:** captive, prisoner. **o:** detention, prison: *He was re-arrested on a fresh charge two days after being* **released from** *prison.*

2 [Vn.pr pass emph rel] set (sb) free from (sth). **O:** teacher, employee, servant. **o:** contract, bond; obligation, commitment: *She* (was) *busy and amused until darkness fell and* **released** *her* **from** *her obligations.* MSAL ○ *During study leave you will be* **released from** *all teaching and administrative commitments.*

relegate

relegate (to) [Vn.pr pass emph rel] place (sb) in a lower or inferior position. **O:** wife, servant, employee; team. **o:** (lower) status, rank; (third) division: *How is it that this ... enthusiastic but erroneous woman has not been* **relegated to** *the sidelines of English fiction?* JA ○ (League football) *Our local team is struggling to avoid being* **relegated** *(to the second division).* □ usu passive.

relieve

relieve of 1 [Vn.pr pass rel] take (sth) away from (sb), to help him, lighten his burden etc. **O:** traveller, visitor; colleague. **o:** luggage, load; responsibility, workload: *Bill* **relieved** *himself* **of** *his thick overcoat.* ○ *Dale* **relieved** *him* **of** *his suitcases.* GL ○ *He was glad to be* **relieved of** *some of the detailed paperwork of the project.*

2 [Vn.pr pass rel] (*formal*) dismiss (sb) from (a post). **O:** general; civil servant. **o:** command; post: *Generals were* **relieved of** *their commands on trumped-up political charges.* = remove (from) 2.

3 [Vn.pr pass] (*jocular*) steal (sth) (from sb). **o:** money, valuables: *Somebody in the crowd had* **relieved** *him* **of** *his wallet.*

rely

rely on/upon [Vpr pass emph rel] (be able to) trust (sb/sth) to behave or function in a particular way. **o:** him etc; help, aid, support; machine, instrument. **Inf:** to support you, not to let you down, to behave badly: *You can't* **rely on** *his assistance* (or: **on** *him for assistance;* or: **on** *him to assist you).* ○ *She had proved that she could be* **relied on** *in a crisis.* DC ○ *Most industry within Cornwall can be* **relied on** *to produce only modest growth.* OBS □ used with *can/could.* = bank on 2, depend on/upon 1.

remain

remain behind [Vp] stay where one is after others have left. **S:** student, participant; (several members of the) class, audience: *Some of the committee offered to* **remain behind** *after the meeting to help clear up.* ○ *'If you interrupt the lesson any more, you'll have to* **remain behind** *when the others have gone home.'* = stay behind, stop behind, wait behind.

remand

remand in custody [Vn.pr pass] (*legal*) order (sb) to be sent back to prison while further inquiries are made about him. **O:** accused, prisoner: *The accused was* **remanded in custody** *for a further week to await the outcome of police investigations.*

remark

remark upon [Vpr pass adj] notice and comment on (sth). **o:** absence, lateness; appearance, dress; conduct, habits: *The quality of his work has often been* **remarked upon** *by his superiors.* ○ *One of his most* **remarked-upon** *faults is a lack of tact and discretion.*

remember

remember to [Vn.pr pass emph rel] give one's greetings, best wishes, to (sb). **o:** the family; your wife; Nick and Lucy: **Remember** *me* **to** *everyone at home.* ○ *He asks to be* **remembered to** *all his friends in the department.* □ often imperative, and used as a conventional way of asking sb to give one's greetings to others.

remind

remind (of) [Vn.pr pass emph rel] make or help (sb) remember (sth). **S:** colleague, friend; letter, souvenir. **o:** date, appointment; holiday, happy time: *She had ... to* **remind** *him* **of** *her existence, tell him she needed his help.* MSAL ○ *'I keep the book in the drawer of my desk and look at it sometimes. It* **reminds** *me a bit* **of** *our talks.'* UTN □ note the alternative patterns: *Fortunately, he* **reminded** *me* **of** *my meeting with Jones* (or: **reminded** *me that I had to meet Jones).*

remind of [Vn.pr pass] make (sb) think that a person, place etc is like or looks like (sb/sth else). **S:** he etc; face, manner; place; food. **o:** father, sister; celebrity, actor; Paris; curry: *The way he behaves when he is angry* **reminds** *me* **of** *his father.* ○ *This town* **reminds** *me* **of** *York.* ○ *I am trying to think who she* **reminds** *me* **of**. = put in mind of.

remit

remit (to) [Vn.pr pass emph rel] (*banking*) send or transfer (money) (to sb), usu by regular instalments, and by arrangement with a bank etc. **O:** money; part, a proportion (of one's salary, one's pay); allowance: *Soldiers serving overseas arrange to* **remit** *part of their pay* **to** *their wives and families.* ○ *The Bank will be glad to* **remit** *your monthly repayments* **to** *the building society by Banker's Order.*

remonstrate

remonstrate (with) [Vpr emph rel] (*formal*) try to persuade (sb), by strong argument, that a course of action is wrong: *We tried* **remonstrating with** *him over his treatment of the children.* ○ *There's little point in* **remonstrating with** *John. He won't listen to reason.*

remove

remove (from) 1 [Vn.pr pass emph rel] make (sth) disappear (from sth) by cleaning. **O:** mark, stain; oil, grease. **o:** coat, table-cloth; paintwork: *Act promptly to* **remove** *spots* **from** *these delicate fabrics.* ○ *All traces of rust should be* **removed from** *the metal before you begin to apply paint.*

2 [Vn.pr pass emph rel] dismiss (sb) (from a post). **O:** officer; minister; manager. **o:** command; post, office; control, management (of a business): *Timoshenko was quietly* **removed from** *command and transferred to the north-western front.* B ○ *The* *new managing director* **removed** *Mrs Reid* **from** *her position as head of marketing.* = relieve of 2.

rend

rend to [Vn.pr pass] break (sth) to pieces with strong, tearing movements. **S:** tiger, eagle; machinery. **O:** deer, mouse; wood, metal. **o:** ⚠ pieces, shreds; matchwood, tatters: *Whole logs are fed into the jaws of the machine and* **rent to** *pieces in a matter of minutes.* = rip to 1.

render

render down [Vn ⇆ p pass adj] turn (a solid substance) into fat etc, usu by applying heat. **O:** lard, (solid) fat; carcass: *You can* **render** *the chicken carcass* **down** *to make stock* (for soup or gravy). ○ *The whale blubber is* **rendered down** *to make oil.*

render into [Vn.pr pass emph rel] (*formal*) put (sth) into (another language). **O:** text; play, novel. **o:** foreign tongue, present-day English: *Candidates were instructed to* **render** *the passage* **into** *clear, idiomatic English.* ○ *It was a collection of short stories, badly* **rendered into** *French.* = translate (from) (into).

render (to) [Vn.pr pass emph rel] (*dated* or *formal*) give (sth) (to sb), often in return for benefits one has received. **O:** thanks, tribute; help, assistance. **o:** God, Caesar; the aged; developing countries: *'***Rendering to** *Caesar the things that are Caesar's means meeting one's proper obligations as a citizen — for example, paying one's taxes.* ○ *Young volunteer workers* **render** *a valuable service* **to** *third-world countries* (or: **render** *third-world countries a valuable service*).

rent

rent out [Vn ⇆ p pass adj] allow sb to occupy or use (a building) in return for payment; let. **O:** flat, house, shop, hall: *The village hall is* **rented out** *for plays and dances.*

repay

repay by/with [Vn.pr pass emph rel] perform (a mean or ungenerous action) in return for (a generous one). **O:** hospitality, generosity, kindness; sacrifice, service. **o:** (**by**) behaving badly, acting meanly; (**with**) ingratitude; indifference: *'They* **repay** *our hospitality* **by** *drinking all my beer and playing the stereo at full blast!'* ○ *Their dedication and professionalism are* **repaid with** *very low wages.* ⇨ next entry

repay (for) [Vn.pr pass emph rel] give sth to (sb) in return (for help). **A:** handsomely, generously. **o:** generosity, kindness; effort, hard work: *Let's do something to* **repay** *him* **for** *his kindness.* ○ *I felt amply* **repaid for** *the extra hours I'd worked.* ⇨ previous entry

repel

repel (from) [Vn.pr pass emph rel] (*formal*) force (sb) to withdraw (from a place). **O:** enemy; invader. **o:** lines, trenches; island: *Assault troops were* **repelled from** *the west bank of the river before they could establish a firm bridgehead.*

replace

replace (by/with) [Vn.pr pass rel] put or use (sth/sb) in the place of (sth/sb else). **O:** coal, gas; horse; turbo-prop engine. **o:** electricity, nuclear power; motor-transport; jet engine: *They've* **replaced** *most of the old looms* **with** *brand-new ones imported from Japan.* ○ *The bailiffs were to be* **replaced** *later by a single magistrate* (cf *A magistrate was to* **replace** *the bailiffs* etc). SHOE ○ *There is nothing left in stock* (**with** *which*) *to* **replace** *the damaged machinery.*

reply

reply (to) [Vpr pass emph rel] speak or write in answer (to sb/sth); answer. **o:** questioner, prosecutor; accuser; correspondent; question, inquiry; letter: *The visiting speaker spent ten minutes* **replying to** *questions put to him by the audience.* ○ *I've written three times to complain about late deliveries of spare parts. None of my letters have been* **replied to**. ○ *The prisoner will have an opportunity to* **reply to** *these charges in due course.*

report

report for duty/work [Vpr] arrive at one's place of work etc, and tell the person in charge that one is ready to begin: *He* **reported for work** *a few minutes before the night shift went on.* ○ *'Corporal Smith* **reporting for duty**, *Sir!'* ⇨ report (to) 1.

report on/upon [Vpr pass adj emph rel] give news or information (about). **o:** event, development; crisis, disaster; meeting, gathering: *The local newspaper* **reported** *very unfavourably* **on** *the recommended route for the new by-pass.* ○ *There are few aspects of Far Eastern affairs* **on** *which he has not* **reported** *for our readers.*

report (to) 1 [Vpr rel] announce (to sb) that one has arrived and is ready for duty, work etc. **S:** newcomer; recruit; new boy. **o:** manager, duty clerk; orderly sergeant; head of year, school secretary: *On arrival, new recruits should* **report to** *the orderly room.* ⇨ report for duty/work.

2 [Vn.pr pass emph rel] inform (sb in authority) that sth serious has occurred. **O:** loss, breakage, discrepancy; that stocks were low. **o:** manager, domestic bursar: *You must* **report** *the disappearance of these keys* **to** *the hotel manager.* ○ *Any serious fluctuations in pressure should be* **reported** *at once* **to** *the engineer in charge.*

3 [Vn.pr pass emph rel] complain about (sb/sth) (to sb in authority). **O:** employee; trader, retailer; conduct, impertinence. **o:** management; Office of Fair Trading; head teacher; board, association: *'I'm* **reporting** *you* **to** *the police for dangerous driving.'* ○ *These serious errors of judgement were* **reported to** *the directors.*

report to [Vpr rel] be responsible to and controlled by (sb). **S:** salesman, executive. **o:** area manager, managing director: *'I'm sending you to the North on a fact-finding trip. Now, you won't have any dealings with the area managers: you* **report** *direct* **to** *me here in London.'*

report (upon) [Vpr pass adj emph rel] ⇨ report (on/upon).

repose

repose in [Vn.pr pass emph rel] (*formal*) trust (sb) to behave, or manage affairs, well. **O:** ⚠ (great, a good deal of) trust, faith, confidence. **o:** him etc; promises, good intentions; ability, powers: *We* **repose** *great confidence* **in** *his ability to handle the negotiations.* ○ **In** *his tact and discretion, especially, we had always* **reposed** *great trust.*

represent

represent (as) [Vn.pr] portray (sb/sth) make (sb/sth) appear, in a particular position or role, or as having certain qualities. **S:** painter, sculptor; writer; picture, report; leader, statesman. **O:** subject, patron; landscape; event, incident; oneself. **o:** youth, athlete, scholar; outline, blur; tragic, unavoidable; showing discretion, possessed of all the virtues: *In this early portrait the prince is* ***represented as*** *a young Grecian warrior.* ○ *How are these Victorian fathers* ***represented*** *to us? As rather terrifying figures of authority.* ○ *Tolstoy ...* ***represents*** *them* ***as*** *poor, misguided, feeble-witted creatures.* RTH

reproach

reproach (for) [Vn.pr pass emph rel] criticize (sb/oneself) (for some failing). **O:** colleague, husband; oneself. **o:** forgetfulness, laziness; neglecting one's family, spending too freely: *You've nothing to* ***reproach*** *yourself* ***for.*** ○ *'You shouldn't* ***reproach*** *the children* ***for*** *forgetting birthdays. You're pretty bad at remembering dates yourself.'* ⇨ next entry

reproach with [Vn.pr pass emph rel] name (a fault) as a reason for criticizing (sb). **O:** friend, colleague. **o:** fault, failing; neglect, laxness: *She's not mean or vindictive. That's the last thing you could* ***reproach*** *her* ***with.*** ○ *This Government cannot be* ***reproached with*** *neglect of the elderly.* ⇨ previous entry

reprove

reprove (for) [Vn.pr pass emph rel] (*formal*) criticize (sb) sternly (for sth); chide (for). **O:** people, flock; follower, member. **o:** indolence, backsliding, extravagance: *Southerners are* ***reproved*** *(by Northerners)* ***for*** *their indolence and moral laxity.* ○ ***For*** *all these shortcomings they should expect to be severely* ***reproved.***

request

request (from) [Vn.pr pass emph rel] (*formal*) ask (sb) for (sth) in a polite but formal way. **O:** fact, detail; help, advice. **o:** office, agency, department: *The sales manager* ***requested*** *up-to-date information* ***from*** *his sales force* (or: ***requested*** *them to provide up-to-date information).* ○ *The secretary listed the companies* ***from*** *which we had* ***requested*** *donations* (or: *which we had* ***requested*** *to provide donations).*

require

require (from/of) [Vn.pr pass rel] (*formal*) expect or demand (sth) (of sb) as a duty or obligation. **O:** obedience, conformity, good manners; that they should behave, that we should be punctual. **o:** employee, child, pupil: *All he* ***requires of*** *a class is that they should be clean, punctual and submissive.* ○ *Monty went on doing what was* ***required of*** *him officially.* MRJ

research

research into [Vpr pass emph rel] study or investigate (sth) to discover answers to problems, extend knowledge etc. **S:** (social, natural) scientist, linguist, historian. **o:** custom, habit; structure, system; period, reign: *She is* ***researching into*** *the reading difficulties of young school children.* ○ *This is an important problem* ***into*** *which few social scientists have* ***researched.***

reserve

reserve (for) 1 [Vn.pr pass emph rel] keep (sth) unused, for use later. **O:** food, drink; supplies. **o:** guests, visitors; emergency use: *We'd better* ***reserve*** *some of the wine* ***for*** *the weekend guests.* **2** [Vn.pr pass emph rel] book a place (for sb), or show that one is being kept free, eg in a theatre, stadium or restaurant. **O:** seat, place, table. **o:** passenger; latecomer, special guest: *'Try to* ***reserve*** *a seat* ***for*** *me* (or: ***reserve*** *me a seat) on the Saturday afternoon coach.'* ○ *'Do you mind if I sit here?' 'I'm sorry, I'm* ***reserving*** *the place* ***for*** *a friend.'* ○ *The front row is* ***reserved for*** *overseas visitors.*

reserve for [Vn.pr pass emph rel] aim or direct (sth) in an intense or concentrated way at (sb). **O:** scorn, anger; criticism; taunts, jibes. **o:** bureaucrats, politicians; hypocrites, parasites: *Tolstoy's bitterest taunts, his most corrosive irony, are* ***reserved for*** *those who pose as specialists.* RTH

reside

reside in [Vpr emph rel] (*formal*) exist in or be represented by (sth/sb). **S:** authority, power. **o:** legislative body, chamber; king, president; court: *The highest judicial authority* ***resides in*** *the Supreme Court.* ○ *'Immemorial wisdom' is said to* ***reside in*** *peasants and other 'simple folk'.* RTH ○ ***In*** *which of the two Chambers does the legislative power really* ***reside****?* = embodied in.

resign

resign (from) [Vpr emph rel] declare formally that one intends to leave (a post etc). **o:** post, seat, place; committee, panel, board; the civil service, magistrature: *He has* ***resigned*** *(****from****) his post as Permanent Secretary.* ○ *Mary intends to* ***resign from*** *the Liberal Democrats.* □ from is deletable before *post, job* etc, but not before *committee, panel* etc. = give up 2.

resign (oneself) to [Vn.pr pass emph rel] accept, though not happily, (sth which cannot be avoided). **o:** consequences, outcome; fate, destiny; not succeeding, losing sb: *He must* ***resign himself****, in fact,* ***to*** *the loss of a percentage.* PL ○ *With less than a week to go before I left, I had* ***resigned myself to*** *not being able to add a Golden Cat to the collection* (ie of wild animals). BB ○ *'There's no escaping death, it catches you in the end; my end is here and now, and now I'm* ***resigned to*** *it.'* HSG □ often passive (with *appear, be, become, feel, look, seem*).

resolve

resolve on/upon [Vpr pass emph rel] (*formal*) decide firmly to have or do (sth). **o:** action; attack, advance; success; expansion, growth: *By November 1828, Charles had* ***resolved upon*** *and taken a bold step.* CD ○ *A plan was* ***resolved on*** *which avoided a major restructuring of the school system.* = agree (on/upon).

resort

resort to [Vpr pass emph rel] adopt (a particular method, usu unpleasant,) to achieve one's aims. **o:** guile, trickery; force, violence: *Nearly all settlers carry guns, and are increasingly using them as the local people* ***resort to*** *firearms.* T ○ *Carson ... required constant amusement and, when it was not forthcoming,* ***resorted to*** *whisky.* EB = have recourse to.

resound

resound in/through [Vpr] ⇨ next entry

resound to/with [Vpr emph rel] echo loudly (with sth). **S:** hall, house, church. **o:** shouts, singing, music: *Stephen enrolled as a Volunteer and his rooms* ***resounded to*** *the crash of arms drill.* LS ○ *The streets* ***resounded with*** *the clamour of bells* (or: *The clamour* ***resounded through*** *the streets*). = ring (with).

respect

respect for [Vn.pr pass emph rel] think highly of (sb) for (sth). **o:** courage, integrity; not yielding to pressure, keeping one's word: *I* ***respect*** *her enormously* ***for*** *the way she nursed David through his long illness.* ○ *'There aren't many who would put their careers at risk, as he did, over an issue of principle.* ***For*** *this one must* ***respect*** *him.'*

respond

respond (to) [Vpr pass emph rel] behave in a certain way in answer (to sth). **S:** body; muscle, limb; livestock, pets; plane, car. **o:** exercise, fresh air, good food; careful handling: *The patient is* ***responding*** *well* ***to*** *the new course of drugs.* ○ *It is impossible to be certain how human beings will* ***respond to*** *events.* BRN = react (to).

rest

rest on one's laurels [Vpr] pause to enjoy the fame one has earned by one's work; usu the suggestion is that one should be going on to face new challenges: *It might be better for his reputation if he stopped writing and* ***rested on his laurels****, as some other novelists had.* PW ⇨ look to one's laurels.

rest on/upon [Vpr emph rel] have (sth) as its basis; be based on. **S:** case, argument, contention; fame, reputation. **o:** (sound, poor) evidence, hearsay; writing, speeches: *Her reputation* ***rests on*** *two novels and a volume of critical essays.* ○ *Miss Lewis's serious evangelicalism* (a form of Christian belief) ***rested on*** *diligent study of the Scriptures.* GE ○ ***Upon*** *such slender evidence as this did our case* ***rest****.* ⇨ base on/upon.

rest up [Vp] rest completely for some time, eg when recovering from an illness: *She had injections of various kinds,* ***rested up*** *at times, and finally was readmitted to hospital.* TBU ○ *We would move at night, to avoid detection, and* ***rest up*** *during the day.*

rest with [Vpr emph rel] be the personal responsibility of (sb). **S:** choice, decision; result, outcome; when to go, how to do it; it ... to arrange everything. **o:** elector; manager, doctor; consumer: *Whether the talks are successful or not now* ***rests with*** *the British.* ○ *It* ***rests with*** *you to settle your differences as best you can.*

restore

restore belief/confidence/faith in [Vn.pr pass emph rel] give back to people the belief that sb/sth is powerful, efficient etc: *These measures have helped to* ***restore*** *some* ***faith in*** *the Government's economic management.* ○ *The judicial inquiry ... has a task of the highest importance: to* ***restore*** *public* ***confidence in*** *the criminal justice system.* IND

restore (to) 1 [Vn.pr pass emph rel] let (sb) have (his property) back again. **O:** money, jewellery; book, picture. **o:** owner, trustee; collection: *The stolen paintings have been* ***restored to*** *their owners.* ○ *I'll see to it that your property is* ***restored*** *(****to*** *you).*

2 [Vn.pr pass emph rel] give back (to sb) (a post, honour etc which he has lost). **O:** title, honour; position, office; command, rank. **o:** (public) servant; minister; officer: *The official was acquitted by a higher court and his post was* ***restored to*** *him.* ○ ***To*** *those subjects who had remained loyal the king* ***restored*** *their former titles and lands.* ⇨ restore to.

3 [Vn.pr pass emph rel] establish (order etc) once again (in a place). **O:** calm, peace, (law and) order. **o:** country, city: *It may be some years before peace is finally* ***restored*** *(****to*** *the Gulf Region).* ○ *Stewards struggled to* ***restore*** *order* ***to*** *the meeting.*

4 [Vn.pr pass] bring (sth) to its former state by painting, repairing etc. **O:** building, quarter; painting, sculpture. **o:** (former, earlier) state, condition; splendour: *The palace gardens have been* ***restored to*** *their former splendour.* ○ *The portrait has been carefully* ***restored*** *(****to*** *its original state) by museum experts.*

5 [Vn.pr pass] treat (sb) skilfully so that he becomes healthy again. **O:** patient, (sick, disturbed) person. **o:** ⚠ (full, sound) health, sanity: *After a long period in hospital she now feels completely* ***restored*** *(****to*** *health).*

restore to [Vn.pr pass rel] put (sb) back in a place of responsibility (from which he was removed). **O:** employee, officer. **o:** post, command: *The officials freed under the amnesty have been* ***restored to*** *their posts.* ⇨ restore (to) 2.

restrain

restrain (from) [Vn.pr pass emph rel] prevent (sb) by firm control (from doing sth). **O:** spectator, crowd; follower; child. **o:** violence, mischief; doing harm, injuring oneself: *The police had difficulty* ***restraining*** *the crowd* ***from*** *rushing onto the pitch.* ○ *Sometimes children must be* ***restrained*** (eg ***from*** *touching things) in their own interests.*

restrict

restrict (to) 1 [Vn.pr pass emph rel] keep (sth) below a certain level, or within particular limits. **O:** traffic; output, intake; discussion, debate. **o:** 30mph; ten kilos, five litres; (certain) topics, questions: *The doctor has* ***restricted*** *my smoking* ***to*** *ten cigarettes a day.* ○ *'I'm afraid we shall have to* ***restrict*** *discussion* ***to*** *questions arising from the report.'* = limit (to).

2 [Vn.pr pass rel] ensure that only specified people see certain materials. **O:** document, paper, file; film, tape. **o:** (senior) officer, official, minister: *The information in that booklet is* ***restricted to*** *military personnel.*

result

result from [Vpr emph rel] happen as a consequence of (sth). **S:** accident, injury; loss, damage; improvement, success. **o:** inattention, neglect, absence; help, involvement: *He believed that all his sufferings had* ***resulted from*** *... a marriage contracted in his youth.* CD ○ *The first goal* ***resulted from*** *a misunderstanding between two defenders.* ⇨ next entry

result in [Vpr] have (sth) as an outcome or consequence. **S:** talks, negotiations; match; help, participation; failure, absence. **o:** agreement, stalemate; victory, draw; improvement; disaster, accident: *The talks have **resulted in** a lessening of suspicion.* ○ *The game **resulted in** a goalless draw.* ⇨ previous entry

retail

retail (to) [Vn.pr pass emph rel] repeat (sth) (to sb) in detail. **O:** story, tale; news, gossip. **o:** all and sundry, everyone who would listen; reporter, police: *Investigations showed that a senior executive had been **retailing** industrial secrets **to** a rival concern.* ○ *I'd learned not to share confidences with David. Before you know where you were they'd be **retailed to** half the department.* = pass on (to) 1.

retail (to) (at) [Vpr rel, Vn.pr pass rel] be sold from a shop direct (to the customer) (at a certain price); sell (sth) in this way. **S** [Vpr], **O** [Vn.pr]**:** goods, merchandise; article; soap, sugar. **o:** (**to**) customer, shopper; (**at**) (special, bargain) price; discount: *What do the family-size cartons **retail at**?* ○ *Supermarkets can afford to **retail** cigarettes **at** a lower price than small tobacconists.* ○ *The books should not be **retailed at** a discount of more than 10 per cent.* GE

retain

retain on/over/upon [Vn.pr pass emph rel] continue to influence or control (sb/sth). **O:** control, dominance, hold, influence. **o:** child, wife; public, electorate; game, match: *The generals struggled to **retain** their control **over** a very fluid battle.* ○ *This great player **retains** his strong hold **on** the affections of the crowd.*

retaliate

retaliate (against) [Vpr pass] hurt, punish (sb) in return for some offence or injury one has suffered. **o:** attack, incursion; bandit, hooligan, tough; conspiracy: *The regular forces **retaliated** swiftly **against** guerrilla attacks from across the border.* ○ *Gooch **retaliated against** the pugnacious attack by driving the next two balls past the bowler for four.*

retire

retire (from) [Vpr rel] leave (sth) because of age, fatigue etc. **o:** job; the civil service, business; fight, struggle: *He's thinking of **retiring from** his job several years before the normal age* (of retirement). ○ *Of course if we did **retire from** the field you would lose the benefit of our ... unique experience.* EHOW

retire (from) (to) [Vpr rel] (*military*) move back (from one position) (to another), usu in an orderly manner: *We **retired to** prepared positions behind the river line.* ○ *The enemy were careful to destroy the immensely strong fortifications **from** which they were **retiring**.*

retire to 1 [Vpr rel] (*formal*) go from one room etc to (another) esp to relax or rest. **o:** sitting room, sun lounge; bed: *After dinner the guests **retired to** the drawing room.* ○ *Peter **retired to** his study to finish a report.*

2 [Vpr rel] go to live in (a place) after leaving one's job permanently. **o:** the seaside, the country; Brighton, the Cotswolds: *He concentrated on business interests until ill health forced him to **retire to** Eastbourne.* IND

retrieve

retrieve (from) [Vn.pr pass emph rel] find (sth) which was believed lost. **O:** belongings, furniture; letter; valuables. **o:** fire; wreck, ruin: *Some of the passengers were able to **retrieve** their luggage **from** the wreck of the aircraft.* ○ *He **retrieved** his papers **from** the dusty files where they had lain for years.*

return

return to 1 [Vpr pass emph rel] consider (sth) again, in the course of an argument or presentation; go back to. **o:** theme, point, proposal: *In the course of my remarks I shall **return** several times **to** this statement.* ○ *'I wonder if we could **return** for a moment **to** what you were saying earlier.'*

2 [Vpr pass emph rel] go back again to (old ways). **o:** (former, old) ways, habits, style of life; tactics, methods: *After going straight for a bit, he will **return to** petty thieving.* ○ *The Chancellor has **returned to** tried and trusted methods of raising revenue.*

3 [Vpr rel] go back to (a previous state). **S:** farm, estate; arable land. **o:** desert, scrub, bush: *West African farmers may cut a new farm from the bush every one or two years, allowing the land previously cultivated to **return to** forest.*

rev

rev up [Vp, Vn ⇆ p pass adj] increase the speed of revolutions of (an engine), usu before moving off. **S** [Vp, Vn.p]**:** driver, motorist. **S** [Vp], **O** [Vn.p]**:** engine; car, lorry: *I could hear the cars of the soldiers and the diplomats **revving up**.* QA ○ *Soon we hear the sound of the lorry **revving up** and moving off.* ITAJ ○ *They were out there for an hour ... **revving up** their bikes.* OD

reveal

reveal (to) [Vn.pr pass emph rel] make known (to sb) sth that was previously hidden. **O:** fact, detail; truth, falsehood; hopelessness, inadequacy: *The death of Jesus **reveals to** us the true meaning of being human.* CF ○ *He is not the kind of person you **reveal** your closest personal secrets **to**.*

revel

revel in [Vpr pass rel] take great pleasure or delight in (sth). **o:** display, ceremony; mischief, gossip; poking fun, taking risks: *As a student, he **revelled in** dangerous escapades, such as climbing university buildings at night.* ○ *He wanted to go out on night patrol alone; that was the kind of situation of personal risk **in** which he **revelled**.*

revenge

revenge (oneself) on [Vn.pr emph rel] satisfy one's pride by hurting (sb) in return for an injury one has suffered: *In some societies it is a point of honour to **revenge oneself on*** (or: *be **revenged on***) *somebody who has insulted a member of one's family.* = take revenge (on) (for).

revert

revert to 1 [Vpr pass emph rel] (*formal*) consider (sth) again in the course of an argument or account. **o:** statement, argument; question, matter: *Later he **reverted to** the subject after Peel had mentioned the case in a speech.* SS ○ *'I must ask the Court's indulgence as I **revert** again **to** the events of that Friday evening.'* = return to 1.

2 [Vpr pass emph rel] (*formal*) adopt (sth) again; resume. **o:** (old, former) ways, habits; methods, policies: *The Province has **reverted to** a system of direct rule from London.* = return to 2.

3 [Vpr rel] (*formal*) go back to (a previous state). **S:** land, farm. **o:** desert, scrub: *The land which is unprofitable to farm will be allowed to* ***revert to*** *moorland.* = return to 3.

4 [Vpr rel] (*legal*) become the property of (sb) again at some time or under certain conditions. **S:** property; estate, land. **o:** original owner; State, Church, Crown: *If he dies without leaving an heir, his lands will* ***revert to*** *the Crown.* ○ *When the lease on your house runs out, the property will* ***revert to*** *Smith and Sons.*

revolt

revolt (against) [Vpr emph rel] oppose (authority) in a forceful and perhaps violent way. **S:** nation, people; youth, women. **o:** leader, government; tyranny, oppression: *Many responded to the call to* ***revolt against*** *the monarchy.* = rebel (against).

revolt against/from [Vpr emph rel] (*formal*) feel disgust or horror at (sth); be repulsed by. **S:** sensitive, decent, compassionate person. **o:** cruelty, violence, corruption: *My soul* ***revolted against*** *this way of doing business, and I made that very plain.* MFM

revolve

revolve about/around [Vpr emph rel] have (sth) as its chief topic or concern. **S:** one's life; argument, debate, discussion; dispute; struggle. **o:** family, work; question, matter; admission, exclusion (of sb); priority, method: *Mary has no outside interests at all. Her whole life* ***revolves around*** *her husband and children.* ○ *The argument at the moment* ***revolves around*** *whether other leaders should attend.* = centre on/round.

reward

reward (for) [Vn.pr pass emph rel] pay (sb) in return (for sth he has done). **O:** staff, employee; finder (of lost property). **o:** work, services; honesty, loyalty; giving sth back: *Teachers feel they are inadequately* ***rewarded for*** *the important work they do.* ○ *Anyone returning the necklace will be handsomely* ***rewarded*** *(****for*** *doing so).*

rhyme

rhyme (with) [Vpr rel, Vn.pr pass emph rel] (of words, or parts of words, at the ends of lines of verse) have the same sounds (as each other); set at the ends of lines words etc, which have the same sounds. **S** [Vpr], **O** [Vn.pr]**:** morn; striding; air. **o:** dawn; riding; there: *'Seen'* ***rhymes with*** *'been'* (or: *'Seen' and 'been'* ***rhyme****); they are also close in spelling.* ○ *In an early sonnet Keats* ***rhymes*** *'eyes'* ***with*** *'surmise'* (or: ***rhymes*** *'eyes' and 'surmise'*).

rid

rid of [Vn.pr pass rel] free (sth/sb) of (sth/sb). **O:** country, town, house; friend; oneself. **o:** pest, rodent; burden, illness; bandit, criminal: *They sat and watched the stripping. ... A girl went from table to table* ***ridding*** *herself* ***of*** *clothes.* OMIH ○ *What wouldn't we have given yesterday to have been* ***rid of*** *Kingsley. Perhaps you'd still like to be* ***rid of*** *him.* TBC □ usu passive. = get rid of.

riddle

riddle (with) [Vn.pr pass emph rel] make many holes in (sth), esp by shooting at it. **O:** building, fortification; vehicle, aircraft; body. **o:** shot, bullets, splinters: *The balloon was* ***riddled with*** *anti-aircraft fire and sank burning to the ground.* ○ *With his first burst he missed,* ***with*** *his second he* ***riddled*** *the target.*

riddled with 1 [pass (Vn.pr)] so full of (holes etc) that it is no longer sound. **S:** floor, panelling; curtain, carpet. **o:** holes; termites, woodworm, moth: *'Have you seen the joists under the bathroom floor? They're* ***riddled with*** *fine holes.'*

2 [pass (Vn.pr)] containing so many (flaws etc) that he or it cannot be depended on. **S:** document, case, argument; character. **o:** errors, mistakes, inconsistencies; flaws, faults: *'Yes, I've read the report and I don't think much of it. It's* ***riddled with*** *the most elementary errors.'* ○ *She didn't look up. She was* ***riddled*** *through* ***with*** *anger and depression.* SE

ride

ride down [Vn ⇆ p pass] direct one's car, horse etc at (sb) as if to knock him down. **S:** troops, police. **O:** spectator, onlooker: *Opponents of the Bill would try to break up meetings by threatening to* ***ride down*** *supporters of reform.*

ride for a fall [Vpr] act so recklessly that disaster is likely: *He has survived many escapades, but this will be his last: he's* ***riding for a fall.*** □ continuous tenses only.

ride out 1 [Vp.n pass] survive (bad weather) safely. **S:** ship, aircraft. **O:** storm, tempest, rough seas: *Is his boat strong enough to* ***ride out*** *the storms of the Cape?*

2 [Vp.n pass] survive (a crisis). **S:** country, government; economy. **O:** crisis, emergency; slump: *Is it* (the Government) *clever enough to exploit the present boom to the full? Is it strong enough to* ***ride out*** *the next recession?* ST ○ *That was the last time the executive* (in Northern Ireland) *felt it had the strength to* ***ride out*** *the Loyalist strike.* ST

ride to hounds [Vpr] (*sport*) go fox-hunting on horseback: *In the eighteenth century, the clergy, like the nobility and gentry, often* ***rode to hounds.*** ○ *He paid a subscription to the Hunt but never* ***rode to hounds****, though his daughter always did.* DBM

riffle

riffle through [Vpr nom pass] scan (a book, bundle of cards etc) by flicking the pages etc between one's thumb and forefinger. **o:** book, dictionary; card-index; papers, cards: *'Leary, Leary,' she said,* ***riffling through*** *a box of index cards.* AT = flick through, leaf through, thumb through.

rig

rig out (in) [Vn ⇆ p nom pass adj] provide (sb/oneself) (with clothes, kit etc); dress (sb/oneself) for a special occasion, or in a strange manner. **O:** crew, staff; oneself: *He'd* ***rigged*** *the children* ***out in*** *special boots and trousers for their climbing holiday.* ○ *She was* ***rigged out in*** *an ancient green skirt of her mother's.* ○ *Some of the crew were very oddly* ***rigged out*** (or: *had a very odd* ***rig-out***). = kit out (with).

rig up [Vn ⇆ p pass adj] place (sth) in position, ready for use; make (sth) from materials perhaps not intended for the purpose. **O:** record-player, stereo; camera, lights; shelter, hut, raft: *Then we got the recording machine and* ***rigged*** *it* ***up*** *near the rattlesnakes' lair.* DF ○ *On one side of the room they had* ***rigged up*** *a small bar.* SML = fix up 1.

ring

ring about/around/round [Vn.p pass] form a circle around (sb/sth), esp to defend or imprison him or it. **S:** bodyguard, security man; enemy, intriguer. **O:** president; palace; town, fortress: *Germany in 1914 was not* ***ringed about*** *with enemies, as Kaiser Wilhelm claimed, but it was faced with the possibility of war on two fronts.* ○ *The security services took care to ensure that the President was* ***ringed around*** *by a party of exceptionally tall policemen.*

ring around/round [Vp, Vpr] telephone (one address after another) esp to find which of a number of tradesmen can provide the cheapest or best service. **S:** householder, shopkeeper, motorist. **o:** shop, store; dealer: *Before you start ordering oil for the central heating* ***ring around*** *the suppliers to see who will offer you the best terms.* ○ *'Maybe we'd better have the party tomorrow, instead of on Saturday. I'll* ***ring round*** *to find out who's free to come.'* = phone around/round.

ring back 1 [Vp] telephone (sb) again, eg having failed to contact him a first time: *'I'm afraid Mr Thomson isn't in at the moment. Would you like to* ***ring back*** *later in the morning?'*

2 [Vp, Vn.p pass] after speaking to (sb) on the telephone, call him again later, eg to give him more information: *'I can't talk now: I've got Guy with me. I'll* ***ring back*** *in a couple of minutes.'* ○ *'I haven't got all the details with me at the moment, Peter. Can I* ***ring*** *you* ***back*** *in about ten minutes?'*

ring the curtain down/up 1 [Vn ⇆ p pass] (*theatre*) signal for the curtain to be lowered or raised: *When* ***the curtain*** *was* ***rung down*** *on the first act, the audience broke into enthusiastic applause.*

2 [Vn ⇆ p pass] mark the end or beginning: *He played the next hole* (at golf) *somewhat shakily, but handled the sixteenth and seventeenth confidently before* ***ringing down the curtain*** *with a suitable flourish.* OBS ○ *With the arrival of William of Orange,* ***the curtain*** *was* ***rung up*** *on a new epoch in our history.*

ring (for) [Vpr rel] summon (a servant etc) by ringing a bell or a telephone. **o:** maid, butler, waiter; service; tea, breakfast: *'Would you mind* ***ringing for*** *some more hot water?'* ○ *'If there's anything you need, all you have to do is* ***ring*** *(****for*** *it).'* = phone (for).

ring (in) [Vpr] ⇨ ring (with).

ring in [Vp] telephone one's place of work to give a message: *I* ***rang in*** *to say that my car had broken down and that I would be late.*

ring in one's ears [Vpr] (of words) still be remembered because of the force with which they are spoken. **S:** words; warning, curse: *Those words may have a hollow sound with his recent insults still* ***ringing in our ears.*** BM ○ *That motto of my Mama's would have been* ***ringing in my ears.*** GL

ring in the New (Year) (and) ring out the old (Year) [Vn ⇆ p pass] announce and celebrate the end of one year and the beginning of the next by ringing bells, giving a party etc: *I bought another whisky and put gloom out of my mind: I was* ***ringing a New Year in*** *as well as* ***an Old Year out.*** SML ○ *The subject of this week's cover* (of the 'Radio Times') *is the* ***ringing out*** *of* ***the Old*** *and the* ***ringing in*** *of* ***the New.*** RT

ring off [Vp] end a telephone conversation by replacing the receiver: *'I'll have to* ***ring off*** *now: I have a train to catch.'* ○ *'Damn your dinner,' I heard him howl as I* ***rang off.*** CON

ring the changes (on) [Vn.pr pass emph rel] keep varying one's choice (from a range of things). **o:** one's clothes, wardrobe; style, cut; act, performance: *After a week at the hotel I had* ***rung*** *all* ***the*** *possible* ***changes on*** *their limited menu.* ○ *They give cooks a whole range of interesting new flavours* ***on*** *which to* ***ring the changes.*** TO

ring out 1 [Vp] be uttered, sound, suddenly and sharply. **S:** shot, cry, scream; applause, cheers: *It was an area of London where . . . screams* ***rang out*** *day and night to no one's alarm.* GL ○ *A sudden report* ***rang out*** *— like the sound of a car backfiring.*

2 [Vp] (of a number that one is trying to call) give the 'ringing' tone. **S:** call; number: *'Hello, caller. The number you wanted is* ***ringing out*** *now.'* (Pause) *'I'm afraid they're not answering. Would you like to try again later?'*

ring out the Old (Year) [Vn ⇆ p pass] ⇨ ring in the New (Year) (and) ring out the Old (Year).

ring round 1 [Vn ⇆ p pass] form a circle round (sb/sth). ⇨ ring about/around/round.

2 [Vp, Vpr] telephone one address after another. ⇨ ring around/round.

ring up 1 [Vp, Vn ⇆ p pass] call (sb) on the telephone: *'I do wish he'd get out of the habit of* ***ringing*** *me* ***up*** *at mealtimes.'* ○ *'I'll* ***ring*** *(you)* ***up*** *some time during the week.'* = phone up.

2 [Vn ⇆ p pass] record (the amounts being paid for goods) by pressing keys or buttons on a cash register. **O:** sale, purchase; goods, groceries: *In the village store our weekend groceries were* ***rung up*** *on an old-fashioned cash register.*

ring the curtain up [Vn ⇆ p pass] ⇨ ring the curtain down/up.

ring (with) [Vpr] be filled with a ringing sound. **S:** hall, street; ears, head. **o:** shout, cry: *The children made Bird Grove* ***ring with*** *happy laughter.* GE ○ *Our ears* ***rang with*** *their cries* (cf *Their cries* ***rang in*** *our ears*). = resound to/with.

rinse

rinse out [Vn ⇆ p nom pass adj] wash (sth) thoroughly with clean water, in order to remove impurities etc. **O:** clothing; pot, basin; mouth: *Wash the tights in warm, soapy water, then* ***rinse*** *them* ***out*** *carefully.* ○ ***Rinse*** *your mouth* ***out*** *well* (or: *Give your mouth a good* ***rinse-out***) *to get rid of the taste.* ⇨ next entry

rinse out/out of [Vn ⇆ p pass, Vn.pr pass] remove (dirt etc) from (sth) by washing in clean water. **O:** dirt, impurities; soap; coffee-grounds. **o:** clothes; pan, cup: *Don't* ***rinse*** *the tea-leaves* ***out*** *into the sink: you'll clog the drain.* ○ *Be careful to* ***rinse*** *all the soap* ***out of*** *your hair.* ⇨ previous entry

rip

rip across 1 [Vn.p pass] divide (sth) in two by pulling at it sharply and with force. **O:** paper, letter; sheet, shirt: *Without a word he* ***ripped*** *the report* ***across*** *and threw the halves into the basket.* ○ *In a particularly fierce tackle one player had his shirt* ***ripped across.*** = tear across.

2 [Vpr] move across (the sky) making a tearing sound. **S:** lightning; flash, zigzag: *Lightning* *flashed, an enormous zigzag of it* ***ripping across*** *the sky, followed by a deep rumble of thunder.* MJ ○ *(figurative) Since then the markets have wobbled through the sequence of storms which have* ***ripped across*** *the political scene.* IND

rip apart [Vn.p pass] dismantle (sth) with sharp, forceful movements; disarrange (a place), esp when searching for sth. **O:** garment; book; room, flat: *'For Heaven's sake, get my paper away from the cats before they* ***rip*** *it* ***apart****.'* ○ *'The electrical wiring will all have to be replaced, and I dare say the house will be* ***ripped apart*** *in the process.'* = tear apart 1.

rip away (from) 1 [Vn ⇆ p pass, Vn.p.pr pass emph rel] take (sth) away (from sth) with sharp, forceful movements. **O:** curtain, cover. **o:** wall, bed: *He* ***ripped away*** *the faded curtains.* ○ *The light fittings had been* ***ripped away from*** *the walls.*
2 [Vn ⇆ p pass, Vn.p.pr pass emph rel] remove (sb/sth) forcibly and perhaps painfully (from sb/sth). **O:** mother, child; support, security: *Her childhood was ... painful, particularly after her nanny had been* ***ripped away from*** *her.* BRN

rip down [Vn ⇆ p pass adj] take (sth) down from a higher level with a sharp, forceful movement; cause (sth) to fall by pulling sharply at the base. **O:** curtain, picture; hut, fence; undergrowth, tree: *The crowd* ***ripped down*** *posters put up by the opposition.* ○ *The coarse grass and small shrubs were* ***ripped down*** *by the blades of the cultivator.* = tear down.

rip in half/two [Vn.pr pass] divide (sth) in two with a sharp tearing movement. **O:** paper, cloth; document, form; shirt: *John* ***ripped*** *the letter* ***in two*** *and threw the halves in the fire.* ○ *'That last tackle was a bit dirty. The winger nearly had his shirt* ***ripped in half****.'* = tear in half/two.

rip into [Vpr pass] make holes in (sth), with a vigorous, tearing movement; make a vigorous attack upon (sb/sth). **S:** saw, cutter; bulldozer; boxer. **o:** tree; plaster, wall; opponent: *The lion's teeth* ***ripped into*** *the meat.* ○ *Bullets from his wing guns* ***ripped into*** *the bomber's fuselage.* ○ *The champion* ***ripped into*** *his opponent with lefts and rights to the body.* = tear into 1.

rip off 1 [Vn ⇆ p pass adj] remove (sth) with a sharp tearing movement. **S:** gale, wind; saw. **O:** roof; branch; limb: *He* ***ripped off*** *one end of the thick envelope and pulled out the letter.* ○ *Both wings were* ***ripped off*** *the aircraft in the crash.*
2 [Vn ⇆ p nom pass adj] *(slang)* steal (property); rob (sb/sth); cheat or deceive (sb). **O:** money, car; bank, shop: *Isn't it extraordinary to find students* ***ripping off*** *books* (cf ***ripping off*** *a bookshop*)? ○ *Beware of the friendly operators* (ie builders etc) *who have 'just finished a job down the road' and so can offer you a cut price. Ten to one it's a* ***rip-off****.* ST = knock off 6.

rip out/out of [Vn ⇆ p pass adj, Vn.pr pass rel] remove (sth) from the centre of (sth) with a sharp tearing action. **O:** page, enclosure; middle, heart. **o:** magazine; city: *He* ***ripped out*** *and threw away any news items referring to his early years.* ○ *The planners have* ***ripped out*** *the maze of narrow streets which formed the centre of the old city.* = tear out/out of.

rip to 1 [Vn.pr pass] reduce (sth) to (pieces) with vigorous tearing movements. **O:** cloth, paper; wood; hut, shed. **o:** ⚠ pieces, shreds, matchwood, tatters: *Wooden buildings on the front were* ***ripped to*** *matchwood by the gale.* = rend to.
2 [Vn.pr pass] attack (sth) critically; demolish. **O:** account, story; evidence. **o:** pieces, shreds, tatters: *'His story doesn't stand up to close examination. Anyone could* ***rip*** *it* ***to*** *shreds.'*

rip up 1 [Vn ⇆ p pass adj] destroy (sth) by pulling vigorously. **O:** paper, document; cloth; wood; road-surface, tarmac: *The machine* ***rips up*** *old cloth to provide fibres for new material.* ○ *'Do you get free coupons for soap stuck through your letterbox?' 'Yes, and I* ***rip*** *them* ***up*** *and throw them in the waste-bin.'* = tear up 1.
2 [Vn ⇆ p pass] vigorously renounce (sth). **O:** treaty, agreement: *Very little faith can be placed in these bargaining processes if agreements can be* ***ripped up*** *with the ink hardly dry on the paper.* = tear up 3.

rise

rise above 1 [Vpr pass rel] move higher than (a particular level). **S:** water, oil; salary, income; recruitment; production, sales. **o:** level, mark; figure; standard: *Sales have* ***risen*** *way* ***above*** *last year's level.* ○ *Incomes will* ***rise above*** *the 4% set by employers in the industry.*
2 [Vpr pass rel] show that one is superior to (sth) and can ignore it; surmount, overcome. **o:** meanness, greed; strife, squabbling; difficulty, hardship: *Surely we can* ***rise above*** *petty personal jealousies.* ○ *It must be hoped that the MCC* (a famous London cricket club) *will* ***rise above*** *this anxiety.* G

rise from the ashes [Vpr] return to its former state after having been badly damaged or destroyed. **S:** country, city; industry, economy: *After a few years of active reconstruction, the city* ***rose from the ashes*** *of war.* ○ *New factories were everywhere* ***rising from the ashes*** *of the old.*

rise in the world [Vpr] reach a higher social and economic position in society: *The customs officer explained that he had once been a radio engineer, but it was difficult to understand whether he had* ***risen*** *or fallen* ***in the world*** *by local standards.* BM

rise to a/the bait [Vpr rel] respond to sth aimed at interesting, attracting or trapping one: *She could put on perfume and change her hair-style: she knew he'd* ***rise to that*** *kind of* ***bait****.* ○ *They left food and ammunition on the track — but would the enemy* ***rise to*** *so obvious* ***a bait****?*

rise to the challenge/occasion [Vpr rel] show the daring, imagination etc which fits a particular occasion: *Her breath was clean and fresh. I* ***rose to the occasion*** *like a shot. 'Kiss me, my sweet,' I said.* SPL ○ *She presented me with* ***the challenge*** *and I was man enough to* ***rise to*** *it.* GL

rise to one's feet [Vpr] stand up, usu to make a speech, propose a toast etc. **S:** chairman, member, guest: *Someone* ***rose to his feet*** *to question the chairman on a point of order.* ○ *He* ***rose*** *unsteadily* ***to his feet*** *to reply to the speech of welcome.*

rise to the surface 1 [Vpr] come to the surface of a lake, sea etc. **S:** fish, whale, submarine: *Great waves formed and spread as the hulk* ***rose to the surface****.* ⇨ raise to the surface.
2 [Vpr] become known after having been hidden for some time. **S:** fact, detail; information: *A num-*

ber of unsavoury details about his personal life are now ***rising to the surface****.*

rise up 1 [Vp] move upwards, eg from the surface of the sea: *Aphrodite, the goddess of love,* ***rose up*** *from the sea and came ashore at Cyprus.* GLEG

2 [Vp] begin to fight against an oppressive ruler, an occupying army etc. **S:** civilian population, oppressed people: *The French were* ***rising up*** *in arms against the retreating Germans.* HA □ the action of rising up *in arms* is an uprising.

rivet

rivet one's attention/eyes/gaze on [Vn.pr pass emph rel] give one's whole attention to (sth/sb). **o:** scene, spectacle: *She* ***riveted her eyes on*** *the gate through which Peters was expected to leave.* ○ ***Our*** *whole* ***attention*** *was* ***riveted on*** *this close-fought duel between batsman and bowler.*

rivet to the ground/spot [Vn.pr pass] cause (sb) to remain completely still. **S:** news; shock, explosion. **O:** spectator, onlooker: *The sudden roar of low-flying aircraft* ***riveted*** *us* ***to the spot****.* ○ *She stood as if* ***riveted to the ground****, unable to utter a word in reply.* □ usu passive. = root to the ground/spot.

roam

roam about/around [Vp, Vpr] move about in an aimless way. **S:** vagrant; explorer; cattle, sheep. **o:** country, world; plain, prairie: *He was always a rather footloose character,* ***roaming about*** *all over the place, picking up odd jobs, but never settling to anything.* ○ *Before the fencing of the open range the herds* ***roamed around*** *freely.*

roar

roar (at) [Vpr pass rel] shout or laugh at (sb) in a loud, deep voice like that of a lion. **S:** crowd, mob; sergeant, teacher. **o:** leader, speaker; squad, class: *The Liverpool manager waved to the crowd and the fans massed behind the goal* ***roared*** *back* ***at*** *him.* ○ *The first night audience were hushed for the telling moments and* ***roared at*** *the subtle humour.*

rob

rob of 1 [Vn.pr pass rel] steal (sth/sb) from (sb). **o:** money, watch, wallet; husband, daughter: *'It's a bit unfair to* ***rob*** *you* ***of*** *a cigar and then ask you personal questions into the bargain.'* HD ○ *Demeter* ***robbed of*** *her daughter would not be an enemy to take lightly.* GLEG

2 [Vn.pr pass rel] prevent (sb) from enjoying (sth that is within his grasp). **o:** success, victory; rest, sleep: *Arsenal were* ***robbed of*** *victory in the last few minutes of play.* ○ *'That damned cat* ***robbed*** *me* ***of*** *a good night's sleep.'*

roll

roll about [Vp] (*informal*) laugh hilariously. **S:** audience; spectator, listener. **A:** helplessly; in their seats: *The comedians of the silent movies don't seem to lose their appeal. They can still have an audience* ***rolling about*** *in their seats.* = roll in the aisles.

roll away [Vp] move away steadily; recede. **S:** cloud, fog, mist, smoke: *A stiff breeze got up and the thick smoke* ***rolled away****.*

roll back 1 [Vn ⇆ p pass adj] remove (sth) by bending and turning it over and over. **O:** cover, tarpaulin, carpet: *We had to* ***roll*** *the carpet* ***back*** *to get at a squeaky floorboard.* ○ *The car has a soft hood, which can be* ***rolled back*** *in fine weather.*

2 [Vp] move back in steady succession. **S:** ⚠ the tide, waves: *The waves* ***rolled back*** *to reveal a black wooden box, half embedded in the sand.*

3 [Vp, Vn ⇆ p pass] (make sth) move back, in a steady, uniform way. **S** [Vp], **O** [Vn.p]**:** enemy; tide, wave (of disaffection, unrest): *The battle* ***rolled back*** *and forth with neither side able to claim a clear victory.* ○ *The new administration is confident of* ***rolling back*** *the tide of unrest which is sweeping across the country.*

4 [Vp, Vp.n] (make the time between now and a past event) close up or disappear. **S** [Vp], **O** [Vp.n]**:** ⚠ the years, centuries: *As his father spoke, the years* ***rolled back*** *and John saw himself as a small boy again, playing on the beach at Sandgate.* ○ *History as well narrated as this can* ***roll back*** *the intervening centuries and set the period vividly in focus.*

roll by [Vp] pass in steady succession. **S:** time; (the) months, years: *Months and then years* ***rolled by*** *until the most optimistic of the prisoners gave up all hope of a reprieve.* ○ *Many years had* ***rolled by*** *since I last sat talking to her.*

tear(s) roll down [Vpr] fall in a steady stream. **o:** ⚠ cheeks, face: *As his voice rose the* ***tears*** *began to* ***roll down*** *her cheeks.*

roll in 1 [Vp] arrive steadily in great masses. **S:** waves, breakers; rain clouds; bad weather: *Big breakers were* ***rolling in*** *from the open Atlantic.* FL ○ *Now the storm clouds, forecast for the afternoon, were* ***rolling in*** *from the West.* TFD

2 [Vp] arrive in a steady stream. **S:** money, gift, donation; offer, promise (of help etc): *Since the appeal was launched, cheques, postal orders and cash have kept* ***rolling in****.* ○ *A flood of specimens* (of wild life) *would soon be* ***rolling*** *in.* BB

3 [Vpr] (*informal*) have a good deal of (sth). **o:** money; jewels, furs: *'What do the Americans want with £250? They're* ***rolling in*** *dollars.'* RM □ continuous tenses only.

roll in the aisles [Vpr, Vn.pr] (cause sb to) laugh uproariously: *'I* ***rolled in the aisles****,' he says. 'It was the funniest thing I heard — I've only been in the* (comedy) *business for fifty years.'* RT ○ *Over 38 years ago, Billy Dainty started* ***rolling*** *them* ***in the aisles****. Now this veteran comedian ... has his own variety show.* TVT = roll about.

rolled into one [pass (Vn.pr)] put together, all combined: *In my memory the last few pre-war years are all* ***rolled into one****.* CON ○ *The trouble in the docks is really three problems* ***rolled into one****.* OBS ○ *Even the humblest of us is received ... with the honour due to a Chaplin and a Garbo and a Dietrich* ***rolled into one****.* T □ may be used with *be, seem* (first example) or after a noun (examples two and three).

roll off 1 [Vn ⇆ p pass] print, duplicate (paper etc) by passing it through the rollers of a machine. **O:** copy, print, sheet: *You can quickly* ***roll off*** *some extra copies of the exercise on the duplicating machine.* ○ *'I'll* ***roll*** *you* ***off*** *a couple of dozen prints.'* □ note the Indirect Object (*you*) in the second example.

2 [Vpr] leave a production line as a finished product. **S:** washing machine, TV set, stereo; car, lorry, plane. **o:** ⚠ conveyer belt, track; assembly line, production line: *The seven millionth Zhigali car **rolled off** the assembly line not long ago.* LFM

roll on [Vp] (*jocular*) may that day etc come quickly! **S:** Tuesday; next year, next month; death: *If the next few months are going to be as tough as this, then all I can say is: **roll on** death!* ○ *'Cheers everybody,' he said, raising his glass. '**Roll on** Monday!'* DBM □ a jocular way of expressing a fervent hope or wish; subject placed after roll on.

roll-on/roll-off [nom (Vp)] kind of ferry onto which, and from which, fully laden lorries can be driven, thus saving the time and expense involved in transferring goods from a vehicle to an ordinary cargo vessel: *One alternative which has been suggested for the Eastern Wharf is the provision of a **roll-on/roll-off** ferry terminal.* SC ○ *Little has been heard of the **roll-on/roll-off** development since the question of North Sea oil arose.* SC □ used attrib, as in the examples; a hyphen or comma can be used instead of the oblique: *Another 7 per cent of exports and imports went by **roll-on, roll-off** ferries.* G

roll out [Vn ⇆ p pass adj] make (sth) flat and smooth by pressing it with a roller, or rolling-pin. **O:** dough, pastry: *Spread some flour on the board and **roll** the pastry **out** very thin.*

roll over [Vp] move to one side, esp in bed, by turning over: *Every time Stephen **rolled over** he pulled more of the bedclothes to his side.* ○ (children's song) *'There were ten in a bed and the little one said "**Roll over!**" They all **rolled over** and one fell out.'*

roll up 1 [Vn ⇆ p pass adj] form (a flat object) into a cylinder by bending and turning it. **O:** carpet, linoleum; map, chart: *The paintings were taken from their frames and **rolled up** for storage.* ○ *She was tapping me with her **rolled-up** napkin.* THH
2 [Vpr] move forward by turning over and over heavily. **S:** waves, breakers; tide; tanks, lorries: *At last the tide began to **roll up** the beach.* OBS ○ *A column of heavy tanks **rolled up** the hill to our observation post.*
3 [Vp emph] (*informal*) arrive in some numbers; arrive in an impressive or self-important way. **S:** crowd; dignitary, official: *The whole family **rolled up** to see Kate's first appearance on the stage.* ○ *They'll be putting up the price of food when they see us **roll up** in this car.* DBM

roll-up [nom (Vn.p)] cigarette that a smoker makes by rolling tobacco inside a piece of paper with a sticky edge: *The assistant director was smoking cigars between **roll-ups**.* ST

roll one's sleeves up [Vn ⇆ p pass] (*informal*) prepare oneself for serious work: *The girls **rolled their sleeves up** and got to work on her. 'You must get him out of your system,' they said.* RATT ○ *It's time he **rolled up his sleeves** and did an honest day's work.*

romp

romp home [Vp] (*racing*) win easily. **S:** horse; runner: *The favourite **romped home** several lengths clear of the rest of the field.*

romp through [Vp, Vpr pass] (*informal*) complete or pass (sth) with no difficulty. **o:** course; test, exam; paper: *It's a tough course: nobody **romps through**.* ○ *Patrick **romped through** his geography paper.* = sail through.

roof

roof over [Vn ⇆ p pass adj] put a roof over (sth). **O:** balcony, drive, approach: *They rolled through the neighbourhood, down streets **roofed over** with trees.* AT ○ *A walk **roofed over** with glass led to the greenhouse.*

root

root for [Vpr] (*informal*) strongly express one's support for (sb). **S:** crowd, spectators; family, friends. **o:** contender, underdog: *'Come on, Jeff, you know we're all **rooting for** you.'* ○ *In the last campaign, the young, the intellectuals and the racial minorities were **rooting for** Dukakis.*

root out [Vn ⇆ p pass] get rid of (sb); destroy, eliminate. **O:** slacker, parasite; (unreliable, dissenting) elements: *Agents were ordered to **root out** elements hostile to the regime.*

root to the ground/spot [Vn.pr pass] cause (sb) to stand fixed and unmoving. **S:** fear, shock; noise, explosion: *Persephone remained standing alone on the hillside, as though terror had **rooted** her white feet **to the ground**.* GLEG ○ *John was standing **rooted to the spot**, his expression stony.* MJ = rivet to the ground/spot.

root up [Vn ⇆ p pass] pull (sth) from the ground with the roots; uproot. **O:** tree, shrub, flower: *They cut down the big trees and **rooted up** the stumps.*

rope

rope in/into [Vn ⇆ p pass, Vn.pr pass] (*informal*) persuade (sb), often against his better judgement, to join or take part in (sth). **O:** member, follower. **o:** group, organization; joining sth, becoming a member: *She had **roped in** a recruit to the Women's Institute.* PW ○ *He tried to **rope** me **in** on that swindle.* DBM ○ *A syndicate is formed. Against his better judgement, Emmanuel Burden is **roped into** it.* HB

rope off [Vn ⇆ p pass adj] separate or enclose (an area) with a rope fence. **O:** field, pitch, paddock: *The judges' enclosure was **roped off** from the spectators.* ○ *The horses paraded in a small **roped-off** area.*

rope up [Vn ⇆ p pass adj] tie a rope around (sth), thus making it secure. **O:** bale, bundle, crate: *His cases and trunks were **roped up** for additional safety.*

rot

rot away [Vp] decay to the point where one or it breaks up completely. **S:** body, flesh; limb, branch, tree: *Slates had been dislodged, and the wood underneath was **rotting away**.* ○ *She would gradually **rot away** until she was as thin and dry as the boughs.* DC

rot off [Vp] separate from the main body because of decay. **S:** branch, limb: *The ground is covered with stiff, dry branches which have **rotted off** as the trees die.*

rough

rough in [Vn ⇆ p pass adj] enter (sth) roughly or in outline on a drawing. **O:** detail, shape, mass: *I **roughed in** one or two figures to give some idea of the finished drawing.* ○ *The plan showed a few **roughed-in** trees and buildings.*

rough out [Vn ⇆ p pass adj] make (a plan) roughly or in outline. **O:** scheme, plan; route, itinerary: *So they **roughed it*** (the future) ***out**: Ned was going* *into the army and Robert into the navy.* CON ○ *I've* ***roughed out*** *some arrangements for the move tomorrow.*

rough up [Vn ⇆ p pass adj] (*informal*) push (sb) about, tear and dirty his clothes etc, usu with the intention of frightening him, though not of hurting him badly. **S:** hooligan, ruffian: *A gang of youths set on him outside a pub and* ***roughed*** *him* ***up*** *a bit.* ○ *Keegan* (a footballer) *alleged that he had been* ***roughed up*** *by officials.* BBCR

round

round down [Vn ⇆ p pass] bring (a price etc) to a round figure by lowering it. **O:** figure; price, cost: *Shopkeepers don't like the small 5p coins and would even prefer to* ***round*** *their prices* ***down*** *if they can't round them up to the next 10 pence.* ○ *The figures are* ***rounded down*** *to the nearest whole number.* ↔ round up 2.

round off [Vn ⇆ p pass adj] make (sth) round and smooth. **O:** (sharp) edge, corner, angle: *Take a piece of sandpaper and* ***round off*** *the edges of the frame.*

round off (with) [Vn ⇆ p pass adj, Vn.p.pr pass rel] end, complete (sth) suitably or satisfactorily. **O:** remarks, speech, sentence; meal, feast; performance, show. **o:** reference (to sth), mention (of sth); port, brandy; speech, sing-song: *To* ***round off*** *the evening, a last snort* (ie drink) *may be taken at one of the thinly attended hotel discothèques.* G ○ *The affair was pleasantly* ***rounded off with*** *a surprising resolution of thanks.* SD ○ *This somewhat abstract description is* ***rounded off with*** *a number of examples.* SNP = finish off/up (with), top off (with).

round on/upon [Vpr pass emph rel] turn to (sb) in sudden anger or irritation. **o:** companion; guard, questioner: *Stanley was irritated and* ***rounded on*** *his son: 'Why were you so late last night?'* FFE ○ *He* ***rounded on*** *her with an exasperated cry: 'Do you have to keep following me everywhere?'*

round out [Vn ⇆ p pass adj] make (sth) fuller, more complete. **O:** story, narrative; sketch, painting: *These stories are exercises in observation,* ***rounded out*** *by guesswork.* EB ○ *The original scheme has been* ***rounded out*** *with ideas from close colleagues.*

round up 1 [Vn ⇆ p nom pass adj] collect together (people or animals who are scattered, or who have fled etc); assemble. **O:** cattle, herd; fugitive, escapee, enemy; team, panel, party: ***'Round up*** *the rest of the committee.'* WDM ○ *The enemy were still there, though they should have been* ***rounded up*** *by that time.* MFM ○ *I have ordered the whole squad to be* ***rounded up*** (or: *ordered a* ***round-up*** *of the whole squad*).

2 [Vn ⇆ p pass adj] bring (a price etc) to a round figure by raising it. **O:** price, cost; amount: *Suppose there's a 10% increase in costs. An existing price of, say, £1.30 is more likely to be* ***rounded up*** *to £1.50 than to £1.43.* ↔ round down.

round upon [Vpr pass emph rel] ⇨ round on/upon.

rouse to anger etc [Vn.pr pass] make (sb) extremely angry. **o:** ⚠ anger, fury, rage: *Of all the sins committed by mortal man, selfishness, greed and inhumanity were perhaps most quick to* ***rouse*** *great Zeus* ***to anger****.* GLEG ○ *He would fight when pushed far enough, and . . . he was dangerous with the danger of a quiet man* ***roused to fury****.* BRH

rout

rout out/out of [Vn ⇆ p pass, Vn.pr pass rel] drive, chase (sb) vigorously from (a place). **O:** children; fugitive; pest; rebels, infiltrators. **o:** house, hiding-place, lair; party, country: *The leader knew that she would have to* ***rout out*** *the extremists in her party if she wanted to be elected to the premiership.* ○ *We were* ***routed out of*** *our beds at three in the morning for a fire practice.*

rub

rub along (together/with) [Vp, Vp.pr] (*informal*) live (together/with sb) smoothly, without friction. **o:** wife, husband; children, neighbours: *Church and State* ***rub along together****.* LFM ○ *Most of them are* ***rubbing along*** *well enough* ***with*** *their neighbours.* F ○ *He prided himself on being able to* ***rub along*** *pretty easily* ***with*** *the other chaps.* FL

rub away [Vn ⇆ p pass adj] remove (sth) by continuous rubbing or friction. **O:** mark, letter; pain, stiffness: *The paint had been* ***rubbed away*** *from the arms of his chair.* ○ *You need a good course of massage to get the aches and pains* ***rubbed away****.*

rub down 1 [Vp, Vn ⇆ p nom pass adj] prepare (a surface) for painting etc, by rubbing it with sandpaper etc. **O:** surface; woodwork; door, wall: *Give the doors a coat of primer, and then* ***rub down*** *well before applying the top coat.* ○ *He* ***rubbed down*** *the old paintwork* (or: *He gave the old paintwork a* ***rub-down***) *before putting on a coat of gloss.*

2 [Vn ⇆ p nom pass adj] dry (sb/oneself) thoroughly, after a shower etc; dry a horse vigorously after exercise: *'****Rub*** *yourself* ***down*** *properly after your swim; I won't have you catching cold.'* ○ *The horses get a thorough* ***rub-down*** *after their morning gallop.*

rub in [Vn ⇆ p pass] (*informal*) constantly remind (sb) that he is unfortunate, inferior or dependent in some way. **O:** the fact, it; that he'd failed; how successful one is: *She first arranged to meet me and then changed her mind: I called that* ***rubbing*** *it* ***in*** *a little too far.* SPL ○ *There's no need to* ***rub in*** *the fact that we lost by three goals.*

rub sb's nose in it [Vn.pr pass] (*informal*) remind sb painfully of sth unpleasant he has done: *'I know that I let you down over fixing the meeting, but don't* ***rub my nose in it*** *in front of my friends.'*

rub in/into [Vn ⇆ p pass adj, Vn.pr pass emph rel] force (sth) into (a material) by rubbing it over the surface of the material. **O:** oil, polish, cream; ointment, linament. **o:** wood; furniture; skin, pores: *They gave me some linament to* ***rub in****.* INN ○ ***Rub*** *some of this cream* ***into*** *your skin to protect it from the sun.*

rub off 1 [Vn ⇆ p pass adj, Vn.pr pass] remove (sth) from (a surface) by rubbing. **O:** mark, letter, drawing; oil, paint; skin. **o:** blackboard, wall; table, shelf; knee, elbow: *The plating on the spoons was so thin that it easily* ***rubbed off*** (ie *one could easily* ***rub*** *it* ***off***). ○ *'You'd better* ***rub*** *those words* ***off*** *the blackboard before somebody sees them.'*

2 [Vp, Vpr, Vn ⇆ p pass, Vn.pr pass] (cause sb to) appear less bright, remarkable, praiseworthy etc. **S** [Vp Vpr], **O** [Vn.p Vn.pr]**:** gloss, glitter, shine. **o:** achievement, success: [Vp] *With the passing of time some of the glitter of the achievement has* ***rubbed off****.* ○ [Vn.pr] *The news of rigged ballots has* ***rubbed*** *some of the shine* ***off*** *their election victory.*

rub off on/onto/on to [Vp.pr] pass from one person or thing to (another) by contact or close association. **S:** quality; fame, success; nastiness, unpleasantness. **o:** family, associate, colleague: *The headmistress ... had an ironic manner, which* ***rubbed off on*** *the girls.* EB ○ *If he stays in the group, some of his warmth and outgoingness may* ***rub off onto*** *the shyer people.* ○ *Stay with him for a while, and let some of the glory* ***rub off on to*** *you.* TT

rub out 1 [Vn ⇆ p pass adj] remove, by rubbing, (sth which is deeply or firmly marked or embedded in a fabric etc). **O:** dirt, stain, mark: *If you spill coffee on the carpet try to* ***rub*** *it* ***out*** *immediately with a damp cloth.* ○ *She tried to remove the mark from his jacket with a cleansing fluid, but it wouldn't* ***rub out*** (ie *she couldn't* ***rub*** *it* ***out***).
2 [Vn ⇆ p pass] (*slang*) kill, murder. **O:** gangster, cop, boss: *A couple of mobsters were* ***rubbed out*** *in a fracas with the law.*

rub up 1 [Vn ⇆ p nom pass adj] polish (sth) until it is clean and shiny. **O:** silver; table, chair; leather: *'Dust the shelves and* ***rub up*** *the ornaments.'* ○ *Those chairs will look fine once they've been given a good* ***rub-up*** (or: *once they've been well* ***rubbed up***).
2 [Vn ⇆ p pass] (*informal*) refresh one's knowledge of a subject that has been neglected for some time. **O:** French, Polish; maths, statistics: *If I'm going to spend two weeks in Italy, I'd better* ***rub up*** *my knowledge of Italian.* ○ *Your shorthand is a bit rusty: you'd better* ***rub*** *it* ***up*** *a bit.* = brush up.

rub up the right way [Vn.p pass] (*informal*) handle (sb) in a careful, soothing way so as to get the best from him: *He was careful to* ***rub*** *Mason* ***up the right way****, saying how invaluable his services had been to the club, and so on.* ⇨ next entry

rub up the wrong way [Vn.p pass] (*informal*) treat (sb) clumsily or tactlessly so as to anger or offend him: *He's so easily* ***rubbed up the wrong way****: everything you say he seems to take offence at.* ○ *'Don't* ***rub*** *me* ***up the wrong way****: I'm in a foul mood this morning.'* ⇨ previous entry

rub shoulders (with) [Vn.pr rel] (*informal*) be on easy, intimate, terms (with sb), mix on terms of equality (with sb). **o:** professional people, working men; crooks, villains: *This is not the sort of club where the great* ***rub shoulders with*** *the humble* (or: *where the great and the humble* ***rub shoulders***). ○ *Duke Ellington ... also* ***rubbed shoulders with*** *conmen and card-sharpers at the poolroom and burlesque theatre.* □ also occasionally rub elbows with: *Expeditions from a dozen countries were* ***rubbing elbows with*** *each other there.* TBC

ruffle

ruffle up 1 [Vn ⇆ p pass adj] (*informal*) disturb (sth), making it untidy. **O:** hair, feathers: *'I've just had my hair set, Henry, and I can't bear you to* ***ruffle*** *it* ***up****.'*
2 [Vn ⇆ p pass adj] annoy, irritate (sb). **O:** friend, brother, colleague: *'You look rather* ***ruffled up****. Has anything happened to upset you?' 'I'm not in the least* ***ruffled up****. I've never felt better in my life.'*

rule

rule against [Vpr pass] (*legal*) make an official, or legally binding, decision that sth is not to be allowed. **S:** court, magistrate; council, committee. **o:** admitting evidence; allowing visitors: *The chairman* ***ruled against*** *admitting the press to the meeting.* ○ *He won't be allowed to make his submission: the court has* ***ruled against*** *it.*

rule off [Vp, Vn ⇆ p pass adj] separate (one part of a page etc) from another by drawing a line with a ruler. **O:** drawing, footnote, heading: *Write out the figures in a column and* ***rule off*** *neatly at the bottom where you want the total to go.* ○ *Put your name to one side of the page, leave a margin and then* ***rule*** *this* ***off****.*

rule out [Vn ⇆ p pass] treat (sth) as impossible or undesirable; dismiss; forbid. **O:** possibility, chance; performance, appearance; scheme, project: *The plan was eventually abandoned, presumably because circumstances, possibly financial,* ***ruled*** *it* ***out****.* F ○ *I'm sure that Dr Macgregor would* ***rule out*** *visits from you as much too exciting for the patient.* RM

rule with a rod of iron [Vn.pr pass emph] govern or manage (sb) with great firmness or severity. **O:** people; employee; family, children: *A small kingdom* ***ruled*** *by herself* ***with a rod of iron*** *was what she liked.* ASA ○ *The schoolteacher took control of the newly-formed Albanian Communist Party and ... has* ***ruled*** *the country* ***with a rod of iron*** *ever since.* L

rumour

rumour about/abroad [Vn.p pass] spread about news which is based on hearsay and not very accurate. **O:** news; report, story (that he is leaving); it ... that he has been dismissed: *It's being* ***rumoured about*** *that he's been offered a job in Scotland.* ○ *I suppose somebody in the Department first* ***rumoured*** *it* ***about*** *that Harry was leaving.* ○ *To stop the wrong sort of story being* ***rumoured abroad****, they've issued an official statement.*

run

runabout [nom (Vp)] (*informal*) small car, esp of the kind in which one can make short journeys easily in towns: *'We're getting rid of the station-wagon. We can never park it in town. What we need is a cheap little* ***runabout*** *that'll nip in and out of the traffic.'*

run across [Vpr] meet (sb), or discover (sth), by chance. **o:** (old) friend, acquaintance; reference, allusion; picture, record: *I* ***ran across*** *one of my former colleagues on a visit to London.* ○ *I* ***ran across*** *one of his earliest recordings in a second-hand shop.* = come across 1, run into 4.

run after 1 [Vpr] run to try to catch (sb/sth): *'Quick,* ***run after*** *him: he's left his wallet on the counter.'* ○ *'Don't bother* ***running after*** *the bus, you'll never catch it.'*
2 [Vpr pass] (*informal*) follow (sb) persistently in the hope of attracting that person; pursue. **o:** (attractive) girl, (eligible) man: *She had never before* ***run after*** *a man, and she was not very good at doing it seriously.* H ○ *I hate to feel I'm being* ***run after****: it makes me want to run hard in the opposite direction.*

run one's head against/into a brick wall [Vn.pr] (*informal*) attempt sth in the face of immovable opposition: *Trying to change the political views of these people is like* ***running your head into a brick wall****.* ○ *With any luck, you'll get your proposal ac-*

cepted next year; at the moment you're ***running your head against a brick wall****.* = bang one's head against a brick wall.

run aground [Vp, Vn ⇆ p pass] (*nautical*) (cause sb/sth to) touch and become fixed on rocks or, in shallow water, on the seabed. **S** [Vp], **O** [Vn.p]**:** ship; tanker, liner. **A:** in shallow water; on a rock, on a sandbank: *Oil is gushing from the tanker which* ***ran aground*** *on the Seven Stones (rocks).* OBS ○ *'Keep us out into the centre of the stream or you'll* ***run us aground****.'* ⇨ go aground (on).

run along [Vp] go away; be off with you: *'Be a good girl and* ***run along****: Daddy's busy.'* AITC ○ *'For God's sake* ***run along****,' Robert snapped. 'You're dissipating my creative mood.'* CON □ command to sb, usu a child or inferior, to go away — usu because that person is being tiresome or because one is busy.

run around [Vp] (*informal*) move restlessly from one companion or activity to another: *When is he going to stop* ***running around*** *and settle for one girl?* ○ (American blues song) *She treated me right, she didn't let me down. But I wasn't satisfied, I had to* ***run around****.* ○ *He sees today's kids as without ambition, 'just* ***running around*** *in circles'.* NS

run-around [nom (Vn.p)] (*informal*) behaving towards sb in a deceitful cunning, or skilful way, so upsetting him or putting him at a disadvantage: *He's been getting the* ***run-around*** *from Sheila. He doesn't know where he stands from one moment to the next.* ○ *Mogul is taking over the firm that is giving them the* ***run-around*** *in plastics production.* BBCTV □ used with the verbs *get, give*.

run rings around/round [Vn.pr] (*informal*) perform so skilfully that one's opponent looks clumsy or foolish. **o:** opposition, competition: *She had* ***run rings around*** *him in a debating competition.* TP ○ *In the second half the Forest winger* ***ran rings round*** *the Spurs defence.*

run at [Vpr] run towards (sb) as if to attack him, or towards (sth) with the aim of jumping over it. **o:** fellow, guy; fence, wall: *A big fellow* ***ran at*** *me with a knife.* ○ *He set his horse to* ***run at*** *the fence.*

runaway [nom Vp] happening or developing very quickly or uncontrollably: *We are faced with* ***runaway*** *inflation.* ○ *Unlike many of our competitors, we must contend with a* ***runaway*** *trade deficit.* □ a nom form which is always used as a noun modifier.

run away (from) 1 [Vp nom, Vp.pr emph rel] escape (from a place), usu because the life is unpleasant, frightening etc. **o:** school, home; front, battle: *He* ***ran away*** *twice* ***from*** *his boarding school; he hated being cooped up in an institution.* ○ *Uncle Leslie had* ***run away from*** *the war.* SATS □ nom form is runaway, often used before a noun: ***runaway*** *children, slaves.*

2 [Vp, Vp.pr pass emph rel] avoid (sb/sth) because one is shy, frightened, lacking confidence etc. **o:** teacher, father; difficulty, challenge: *'Don't* ***run away****. I shan't eat you!'* ○ *Difficulties shouldn't be* ***run away from****; they should be faced up to!* ↔ face up to.

run away (with) [Vp nom, Vp.pr rel] leave home (with sb) eg with the aim of marrying without one's parents' consent. **o:** daughter, girlfriend: *She was engaged to two men simultaneously and got out of the difficulty by* ***running away with*** *a third.* BLCH ○ *After making a* ***runaway*** *marriage, Elizabeth settled down to a conventional life as a suburban housewife.* □ runaway used only before a noun, as in the second example. = elope (with). ⇨ run off (with).

run away with 1 [Vp.pr] steal and carry (sth) away. **o:** cash, takings; jewels; papers: *Someone in the office* ***ran away with*** *the plans for the new engine.* = run off with.

2 [Vp.pr] consume a great deal of (sth). **S:** scheme, project; machine, appliance. **o:** money; energy, electricity: *Holidays abroad* ***run away with*** *a lot of money.* ○ *These new heaters* ***run away with*** *a lot of electricity.* = use up.

3 [Vp.pr] win (sth) clearly or easily. **o:** match, game, tournament; cup, prize: *The Italian team* ***ran away with*** *the first match in the series* (cf *The team scored a* ***runaway*** *win in the first match*). □ runaway used only before a noun.

4 [Vp.pr] gain complete control of (sb); dominate. **S:** feelings, emotion, imagination: *You tend to let your feelings* ***run away with*** *you.* TT ○ *He's not a good man for the job: he lets a fondness for intrigue* ***run away with*** *him.*

run away with the idea/notion [Vp.pr] be misled by an idea, accept an unfounded idea: *Don't ever* ***run away with the idea*** *that bankruptcy is a joke.* TGLY ○ *The audience could be forgiven for* ***running away with the idea*** *that economic recovery was close at hand.* □ often used in neg commands, as in the first example; usu followed by a *that*-clause.

run back [Vn ⇆ p pass] wind (a film etc) in reverse so that it can be shown or heard again. **O:** film, tape, film-strip: *'****Run*** *that sequence* ***back*** *to the beginning and replay it in slow motion.'* ○ *'Just wait a minute while we have that section* ***run back****.'* = play back 1.

run back over [Vp.pr rel] review (sth) in one's mind or when speaking to others. **o:** events; career; year, month: *'I should like to* ***run back over*** *the past term, singling out events of particular importance.'* ○ *If you* ***run back over*** *the season, you can't pick out a game in which he played badly.*

run behind [Vp, Vpr] not keep pace with (one's timetable) for a meeting, radio programme etc. **S:** interviews, oral examinations; programme. **m:** five minutes, half an hour. **o:** ⚠ schedule, time: *'Please tell Miss Williams to cancel my eleven o'clock appointment. We're* ***running*** *about fifteen minutes* ***behind*** *as it is.'* ○ *'If we* ***run*** *more than a few minutes* ***behind*** *schedule the whole evening's viewing will be thrown out of gear.'*

run counter to [Vp.pr pass] contradict, not match (sth). **S:** statement, behaviour, event. **o:** principle, professed belief, code: *This result* ***runs counter to*** *a very basic principle of human learning.* SNP ○ *The situation* ***runs counter to*** *ordinary logic.* SC = conflict (with).

run down 1 [Vp, Vn ⇆ p pass adj] (cause sth to) lose power, through neglect, age etc. **S** [Vp], **O** [Vn.p]**:** engine, motor; clock; battery: *The crusading spirit disappeared: there was the sensation of a machine that was* ***running down****.* MFM ○ *'If you leave the car lights on all night you'll* ***run*** *the battery* ***down****.'*

2 [Vp nom, Vn ⇆ p nom pass adj] (cause sth to) fall or decline in size, strength or effectiveness. **S** [Vp],

O [Vn.p]**:** strength, force; nuclear capability; nationalized industries; airline, railway; inner city areas; establishment, sales team: *The farm labour force is* ***running down*** *steadily* (cf: *There is a steady* ***run-down*** *of the farm labour force*). OBS ○ *We are* ***running down*** *our military presence in the region.* ○ *Environmental groups are fighting the* ***run-down*** *of the railway network.* ○ *Through the drying-up of capital investment, industry in the region was in a thoroughly* ***run-down*** *state.*

3 [Vn ⇆ p pass] damage (sth), injure (sb), by driving straight at him/it; collide with. **S:** car, bus; liner, tanker. **O:** pedestrian, bicycle; boat: *I didn't get to her before she died. She'd been* ***run down*** *by a lorry.* LLDR ○ *The destroyer was* ***run down*** *by an aircraft-carrier while manoeuvring across her bows.*

4 [Vn ⇆ p pass] find (sb) eventually after a long search; trace. **S:** search-party, police. **O:** missing person, escaped convict: *I had a bit of trouble* ***running*** *Anderson* ***down****.* AITC ○ *The suspect was finally* ***run down*** *at the home of one of his associates.* = track down.

5 [Vn ⇆ p pass] (*informal*) criticize (sb) unkindly; belittle, disparage. **O:** family, friend; attempt, achievement: *'The food had better be good after all that talk.' 'That's enough of* ***running down*** *my cooking,' she said.* TT ○ *She's always* ***running*** *her husband* ***down*** *in public. I'm surprised he puts up with it.* = do down.

6 [pass adj (Vn.p)] tired and in poor condition, because of overwork, lack of sleep etc: *He emerged from his ordeal in a completely* ***run-down*** *condition.* ○ *The doctor said he was* ***run down*** *and needed rest.* PPLA ○ *'You look thoroughly* ***run down****. Why don't you take a week's holiday?'* □ adj used before a noun and after *appear* etc. ⇨ run down 1.

run-down [nom (Vn.p)] (*informal*) information; a briefing: *'I've asked Mr Phillips to join us at this meeting because he can give us a* ***run-down*** *on the latest developments.'* ○ *'Go over to headquarters and try and get a* ***run-down*** *on the situation.'*

run down to [Vp.pr rel] stretch as far as (sth); extend to. **S:** garden, estate. **o:** river, road: *The grounds at Hampton Court* ***run down to*** *the water's edge.* ○ *A narrow row of predominantly wooden houses . . .* ***ran down to*** *the very centre of a hugely overcrowded . . . city.* MLT

run for [Vpr rel] (esp *US*) offer oneself as a candidate for (office). **o:** mayor, governor; office: *If he was* ***running for*** *the top office in the US, he would have had a planeload of flunkies* (= assistants). OBS ○ *It was for the sake of this . . . that he had first decided to* ***run for*** *the Presidency.* HHGG = stand (as) (for).

run for dear life/one's life [Vpr] escape quickly because one's life is in danger: *With pieces of burning masonry falling all around him, he* ***ran for dear life****.* ○ *Office workers* ***ran for their lives*** *as an earth tremor shook the centre of the city.*

run for it [Vpr] escape from danger by moving quickly: *At first he was a bit suspicious and ready to* ***run for it*** *should the animal attack him.* DF ○ *'Never mind your bloody boots.* ***Run for it****.'* UTN

run a mile (from) [Vn.pr] (*informal*) try hard to avoid (sb), because he is boring, conceited etc: *I could have been made into a boring, heartless* (social) *climber whom everyone* ***ran a mile from****.* HAA ○ *'She disliked hot water, abominated soap, and would* ***run a mile*** *from the sight of a scrubbing brush.'* SAMK □ often used with *would*.

run in 1 [Vn.p pass] (*informal*) arrest (sb) and take him to a police station. **O:** vagrant, hooligan; driver, drunk: *Trevor was* ***run in*** *for dangerous driving on Saturday night.* SPL ○ *If you throw eggs at the speaker, you're liable to get* ***run in*** *for causing a disturbance.* □ usu passive.

2 [Vn ⇆ p pass adj] prepare an engine, esp a motor car engine, for use by driving it slowly and carefully for a certain distance. **O:** car; engine: *'Don't expect me to get you home quickly—I'm still* ***running*** *my car* ***in****.'* ○ *The point of* ***running*** *your engine* ***in*** *carefully is to reduce friction between the new working parts.*

run in the family [Vpr] be a physical, moral etc feature which keeps appearing in successive generations of a family. **S:** hair, nose, eyes; temper, courage, obstinacy: *He was a big boy . . . but it* ***ran in the family****.* SE ○ *He refused to fill in personal details on some form. This idiosyncrasy appears to* ***run in the family****.* BM

run-in (with) [nom (Vp)] quarrel or unpleasant encounter (with sb): *She had a* ***run-in with*** *her landlady on her first day in London.* ○ *Aziz was shaken and bruised from yet another* ***run-in with*** *the playground bully.* BBCR

run into 1 [Vpr, Vn.pr pass] (cause sth to) strike, collide with (sth). **S** [Vpr], **O** [Vn.pr]**:** ship; bus, lorry, car. **S** [Vn.pr]**:** captain; driver. **o:** bank; wall, hedge: *The prow of the boat* ***ran into*** *a bank of soft mud and stuck fast.* ○ *Russian counter-attacks during the afternoon had* ***run into*** *the full strength of the 4th Panzer Army.* B ○ *He lost control of his car and* ***ran*** *it* ***into*** *a lamp-post.*

2 [Vpr] unexpectedly meet, encounter (sth). **S:** country, firm, department. **o:** trouble, difficulty, snag, problem: *President George Bush's latest peace efforts in the Gulf* ***ran into*** *trouble yesterday.* OBS ○ *We expect to* ***run into*** *a few snags before the machine is ready for production.*

3 [Vpr] enter (an area of bad weather). **S:** ship, plane. **o:** storm, blizzard: *The weather held good until they* ***ran into*** *one of these thick midsummer mists.* JUNG ○ *During the crossing, they* ***ran into*** *a tremendous hurricane.* BRN

4 [Vpr] meet (sb) by chance. **o:** (old) friend, acquaintance: *I* ***ran into*** *my old English teacher while on holiday in Scotland.* ○ *Malcolm* ***runs into*** *him in the pub occasionally.* OD = come across 1, run across.

5 [Vpr] reach (a certain figure or amount). **o:** six figures; thousands of francs; three editions: *'I don't know how much money we're talking about, exactly, but it must* ***run into*** *five figures.'* ○ *John Locke's 'Some Thoughts Concerning Education' . . .* ***running into*** *twenty-five editions by 1777.* JA

run into the ground [Vn.pr pass] (*informal*) cause (sb/sth) to move, work, play etc so energetically that he/it is near to exhaustion. **S:** captain, coach; general. **O:** team, player; troops, transport: *While the Germans were slowly* ***running*** *all their divisions* ***into the ground*** *with fatigue and casualties the Red Army was building up a formidable reserve.* B ○ *He is such a strong and willing player that in a key match he can be expected to* ***run*** *himself* ***into the*** *ground.* □ often reflex with *team, player* etc as Subject.

run one's head into a brick wall [Vn.pr] ⇨ run one's head against/into a brick wall.

run off 1 [Vp, Vn ⇆ p pass adj] (cause sth to) flow from a vessel etc. **S** [Vp], **O** [Vn.p]**:** liquid; wine, dye, fat: *'The oil in your engine looks very dirty—get the garage to* **run** *it* **off***.'* ○ *When the temperature reaches melting point, the metal* **runs off** *as a liquid and flows into special moulds.*

2 [Vn ⇆ p nom pass adj] print or duplicate (sth). **O:** copy, photocopy, print: *I have to* **run off** *a few hand-outs on the photocopier.* ○ *'***Run** *me* **off** *some copies of his electoral address* (or: *Do me a* **run-off** *of his address).'*

3 [Vn ⇆ p pass] cause (sth) to be run or contested, esp at an athletics meeting. **O:** race, heat; 100 metres: *The semi-finals of the 200 metres are being* **run off** *tomorrow.* ○ *The final of the 5 000 metres was* **run off** *in blazing heat.*

4 [Vpr, Vn.pr pass] (make sth) use a particular source of power. **S** [Vpr], **O** [Vn.pr]**:** cleaner, stereo, recorder; car, train. **o:** batteries, the mains: *His bedside radio* **runs off** *a couple of torch batteries.* ○ *We* **run** *all our domestic appliances* **off** *the mains.*

run off his feet [Vn.pr pass] (*informal*) make (sb) work hard and/or move about a lot, thus tiring him. **S:** customer; patient; child, pupil. **O:** assistant; nurse; parent, teacher: *'Polly needs a holiday: the children do* **run** *her* **off her feet***, you know.'* ○ *During the New Year sales rush, the staff in the fashion departments are* **run off their feet** *all day.*

run off the rails [Vpr] (*informal*) begin to lead a wild or unconventional life. **S:** son, daughter: *Since his son started at college, he's* **run** *completely* **off the rails***, dressing like a tramp and coming home at all hours.* = go off the rails.

run off (with) [Vp, Vp.pr rel] leave in the company of (sb), having left one's wife, husband, family etc. **o:** lover; (someone else's) wife, husband: *He decided that Art could only be some man or other that Rosemary had* **run off with***.* DBM ○ *Her mother had left her husband and* **run off with** *a Captain Christie.* TU □ also run off without: *'Oh yes, now your old man's* **run off without** *you, you come crying back.'* DPM ⇨ run away (with).

run off with [Vp.pr rel] steal (sth) and carry it away. **o:** receipts, takings; plan, secret: *'Someone's* **run off with** *the keys to my safe.'* ○ *If you leave your money lying about, somebody's sure to* **run off with** *it.* = run away with 1.

run on 1 [Vp emph] flow, continue, without a break, often monotonously or annoyingly. **S:** voice; words, speech, conversation; contact: *'How that woman's tongue does* **run on***!'* ○ *Jung's correspondence with Freud was to* **run on** *for ten years.* JUNG

2 [Vp, Vn ⇆ p pass adj] (cause sth to) continue, without indenting, to mark the beginning of a paragraph; (in verse) (allow a sentence to) continue from one line, stanza etc to another. **S** [Vp], **O** [Vn.p]**:** matter, text; sentence; sense: *'***Run on***' is an instruction to a printer to ignore a paragraph indentation.* ○ *In romantic poetry it becomes more normal to* **run** *the sense-groups* **on** *from one line to the beginning or middle of the next.*

3 [Vpr emph rel] have (sth) as its subject or chief concern; be concerned with. **S:** discussion, argument; thought, address. **o:** subject, theme, topic; event, occurrence; line, path: *His talk* **ran on** *recent developments in the industry.* ○ *His thinking* **runs on** *familiar lines.* ○ *Brigit's mind kept* **running** *foolishly* **on** *the same theme.* DC

run out 1 [Vp] be finished, exhausted. **S:** supply, stock (of wines, cigarettes etc); patience; time: *If his rice has* **run out** (or: *If he has* **run out of** *rice) he goes to the paddy-stores.* NDN ○ *Our time is* **running out** *and I think we ought to say something about the ending* (or: *We are* **running out of** *time* etc). ART ⇨ run out/out of.

2 [Vp] be no longer valid; expire. **S:** lease, contract, agreement: *The lease on their London flat* **runs out** *in a few months.* ○ *The foreign companies seem well protected, until their concessions* **run out** *towards the end of the century.* T

3 [Vn ⇆ p pass adj] (*cricket*) dismiss (a batsman) by striking his wicket while he is running; cause (a fellow batsman) to be dismissed in this way: *Jones was* **run out** *in the final over of play before lunch.* ○ *Peters* **ran** *his partner* **out** (ie caused him to be **run out** by the opposing side) *by calling for a run when there was none to be had.*

run out at [Vp.pr] (*informal*) reach (a certain amount). **S:** expenses, bill; cost, rent. **o:** £5 000; a good deal, more than we can pay: *What does the cost of converting the present building* **run out at***?* ○ *The actual bill* **runs out at** *considerably more than the original estimate.* = work out at.

run out/out of [Vp, Vpr] finish, exhaust (sth). **o:** supply, stock (of commodities); ideas; patience: *'There's been a tremendous demand for that brand. We've* **run out***.'* ○ *The Hogans were rapidly* **running out of** *what little money they had* (or: *Their money was rapidly* **running out**). HB ⇨ be out of 2, run out 1.

run out of [Vn.pr pass] (*informal*) force (sb) to leave (a place). **o:** ⚠ town, the country: *He'd only have to show his face once and the police would* **run** *him* **out of** *town.* ○ *You could have got him* **run out of** *this country. Maybe even got him hanged.* PP

run out of steam [Vpr] (*informal*) move more slowly, or halt, because the original driving force is lacking. **S:** campaign, advance; movement, crusade; marriage: *By March . . . the project had more or less* **run out of steam***.* RT ○ *The affair continued for another year or so, and . . . finally* **ran out of steam** *in the spring of 1905.* AF

run out (on) [Vp, Vp.pr pass] abandon (sb) who needs or expects one's support. **o:** friend, ally, associate; family, children: *If he refuses help, he will be accused of* **running out on** *the Federal Government, and of leaving the country's defences wide open.* OBS ○ *The aid did not arrive on the promised date, giving us the unpleasant feeling of having been* **run out on***.*

run over 1 [Vp] overflow. **S:** tank, barrel; jug, tankard: *'You'd better fetch the plumber: the cistern is* **running over***.'* ○ *'Don't fill the kettle too full: it'll* **run over***.'*

2 [Vn ⇆ p pass] knock (sb) down and possibly pass over his body. **S:** car, bus. **O:** pedestrian; animal: *Two children were* **run over** *at that road junction last month.*

3 [Vpr pass] read or say (sth) quickly, aloud or to oneself, in order to learn it or refresh one's memory. **o:** notes, minutes; script, part (in a play): *'Just* **run over** *my lines with me before the rehearsal* *begins.'* ○ *He* **ran over** *in his mind what he was going to say at the meeting.* EM

run an/one's eye over [Vn.pr emph rel] (*informal*) examine (sth/sb) closely in order to estimate its or his merits or value. **S:** dealer, buyer, critic. **o:** livestock, goods; applicant, newcomer: *'Just* **run your eye over** *these materials and tell me if there are any you like.'* ○ *I had the chance of* **running my eye over** *the new members of the company during rehearsal.* = pass an/one's eye over.

run over with [Vp.pr rel] show an abundance of (sth); overflow with. **o:** enthusiasm, joy; ideas, schemes: *The children are* **running over with** *energy and mischief—I can't keep them still for five minutes.*

run rings round [Vn.pr] ⇨ run rings around/round.

run through 1 [Vpr] pass quickly through (sth) or among (people). **S:** murmur, whisper; thought, tune. **o:** crowd, throng; head: *A snatch of their conversation kept* **running through** *his head.* ○ *An angry murmur* **ran through** *the audience.*
2 [Vn.p pass] play (a film etc) by passing it through a machine. **O:** film, tape; sequence, excerpt: *'Will you* **run** *that bit of tape* **through** *again? I didn't hear it the first time.'* ○ *'I'll* **run** *the whole of that sequence* **through** *again. Just watch the action carefully.'*
3 [Vpr nom pass] review, summarize (sth). **o:** argument, point, feature: *Let's* **run through** *the main points of the Budget so far* (or: *Let's have a* **run-through** *of the main points* etc). BBCTV ○ *'I think I've grasped the main proposals, but would you mind* **running through** *them once again?'* = pass in review, pass over 5.
4 [Vpr nom pass, Vn.pr pass] (cause sb to) act, perform (sth), esp at rehearsal. **S** [Vpr], **O** [Vn.pr]**:** actor, cast. **S** [Vn.pr]**:** producer, director. **o:** play, scene: *There'll be a* **run-through** *of the whole play at seven o'clock.* ○ *'I'd just like to* **run** *you* **through** *that scene you have with Paula.'*
5 [Vpr pass] spend (all one's money) quickly and foolishly. **o:** fortune, inheritance, allowance: *He* **ran through** *no end of money while he was at university.* ○ *The money inherited from his father was quickly* **run through**.
6 [Vpr] be present at all stages in (sth); pervade. **S:** pessimism, optimism; a concern for accuracy, close attention to detail: *This curious combination of idealism and scepticism . . .* **runs through** *all his writings.* RTH

run one's fingers/hand through one's hair [Vn.pr] pass one's fingers etc nervously through one's hair: *I could see from the way he kept* **running his fingers through his hair** *that the big occasion had tensed him up.* ○ (stage direction) *She winces as she feels the pain in her arm. She* **runs her hand through her hair**. LBA

run through (with) [Vn.p pass, Vn.p.pr pass emph rel] pierce (sb's body) (with a weapon). **O:** enemy, rival. **o:** sword, spear: *He attacked the post with grenades and* **ran** *the survivors* **through with** *the bayonet.* ○ *One soldier was* **run through with** *a spear* (or: *had a spear* **run through** *him*).

run to 1 [Vpr] be enough money to cover (sth); have enough money to cover (sth); afford. **S:** fund, allowance, budget; he etc; management, treasury. **o:** luxury, extras; holiday, outing; wine, cigar: *The budget would not* **run to** *champagne.* BFA ○ *I'm afraid we can't* **run to** *central heating in all rooms.*
2 [Vpr] be of (a certain size or extent). **S:** document, paper; book, report. **o:** ten pages, twenty typed sheets, two bound volumes: *A questionnaire devised by the Home Office . . . and* **running to** *some 96 questions is now being prepared.* NS ○ *It* (the paper) **ran to** *more than fifteen closely typed pages.* FL

run to earth/ground [Vn.pr pass] find (sb/sth) after a long and difficult search. **O:** quarry, (escaped) prisoner; book, document; house, shop: *Eventually, I was* **run to earth** *by a panting Ben, who reproached me for disappearing.* BB ○ *We* **ran** *the bird shop* **to earth** *eventually, on one side of an enormous square.* DF ○ *He was not in his office and I eventually* **ran him to ground** *in the lavatory.* MFM ⇨ go to earth/ground.

run to fat [Vpr] (tend to) become too fat, through neglect, overeating etc: *Her mother was wealthy and discontented,* **running to fat** *and losing her looks from idleness.* AITC ○ *After a year in a desk job, and only occasional weekend exercise, he was starting to* **run to fat**.

run to seed [Vpr] fall from a previously high level of attractiveness, efficiency etc; deteriorate. **S:** she etc; figure, looks; business, estate; economy: *Education is similar to the London public transport system which has also been allowed to* **run to seed**. IND ○ *It annoyed him that his daughter should let her looks* **run to seed** *in that sort of academic dowdiness.* ASA ○ *He should . . . make way for someone whose enthusiasm has not entirely* **run to seed**. RT

run together [Vp, Vn.p pass] (cause two or more separate things to) mix, combine or be confused. **S** [Vp], **O** [Vn.p]**:** colours; sounds, words; pictures: *'I shouldn't wash those shirts in the same water, or else the colours will* **run together**.*'* ○ *'Don't gabble, Lucy, I can't understand you when you* **run** *your words* **together**.*'*

run up 1 [Vn ⇆ p pass] hoist, raise (sth). **O:** flag, banner, standard: *The admiral* **ran up** *a signal ordering all ships to close with the enemy.* ○ *Then the white flag was* **run up**: *the post had surrendered.*
2 [Vp.n pass adj] make, construct (sth) quickly, and possibly from any materials that are near at hand. **O:** dress, fancy-dress costume; shed, shelter: *She hadn't been able to get a bathing-costume to fit her. She had consequently* **run up** *two for herself.* BFA ○ *To deal with the overcrowding problem, they were exhorting him to* **run up** *an annexe or lean-to.* ILIH
3 [Vn ⇆ p pass] cause (an account) to rise sharply; incur. **O:** bill, account; overdraft, deficit: *She's been* **running up** *accounts at half a dozen big stores.* ○ *On top of this, she* **ran up** *enormous bills.* BN ○ *The extra grant will only just cover the deficit that we've* **run up** *already.* OBS
4 [Vp nom] (*sport*) run towards a bowling-crease, or jumping-off point, so as to increase the speed of one's delivery or jump. **S:** bowler, (long-, high-) jumper: *Marshall is now* **running up** *to bowl the last ball before lunch.* ○ *The spin bowlers take quite a short* **run-up**. ⇨ next entry

run up to [Vp.pr] (*informal*) approach and prepare for (an important event). **o:** election, celebration, parade: *Because we are* **running up to** *the election,* *our panel comprises members of the three main political parties.* BBCR ○ *Labour must in the* **run-up** *to the election reawaken its supporters' loyalty.* OBS □ usu in the nom form run-up. ⇨ previous entry

run up against [Vp.pr pass] meet, encounter (sth); come face to face with. **o:** obstacle, difficulty, problem; misunderstanding, incomprehension: *These are only some of the problems we expect to* **run up against**. ○ *The same difficulties were* **run up against** *last year.*

rush

rush into [Vpr pass, Vn.pr pass rel] (cause sb to) undertake (sth) quickly, and without considering the consequences. **o:** buying, selling; partnership, take-over: *'Don't let anybody* **rush** *you* **into** *joining; think it over.'* ○ *We may eventually become members; but this isn't something that should be* **rushed into**. ○ *He didn't want to marry — she* **rushed** *him* **into** *it.*

rush into print [Vpr] publish sth too quickly in order to beat one's competitors, capture a ready market etc. **S:** author, writer; hack(-writer): *I deplore the writing of so-called military history by people concerned with* **rushing into print** *so as to catch a market that is still fresh.* MFM

rush through [Vn ⇆ p pass adj, Vn.pr pass] cause (sth) to become official policy, the law etc very quickly. **S:** government, assembly, committee. **O:** law, Bill: *The Chamber has* **rushed through** *legislation making the carrying of firearms a serious offence.* ○ *Two Private Members' Bills were* **rushed through** *Parliament before the end of the session.*

rush to conclusions [Vpr] form an opinion too quickly, ie without considering the evidence carefully: *'You were there last night. I saw your hat and coat.' 'Now don't start* **rushing to conclusions**.' ○ *'You were talking to Stevens at lunch. I wouldn't mind betting he offered you a job.' 'That would be* **rushing to conclusions**.' = jump to conclusions/the conclusion.

rush to [Vn.p pass] take (sb) to see (sb) very quickly, because of serious illness or injury. **O:** patient, casualty, animal. **o:** hospital; a doctor, the vet: *Two passengers were* **rushed to** *hospital suffering from severe head injuries.*

rustle

rustle up [Vn ⇆ p pass] (*informal*) find or prepare (sth/sb), eg for an unexpected guest or to meet a special need. **O:** meal, snack; support, help; friend, guest: *'Make yourself comfortable. I'll see if I can* **rustle up** *a few sandwiches.'* ○ *My list of girls, from whom I might have* **rustled up** *one for such an occasion, seemed to have dispersed.* SML

S

saddle

saddle up [Vp, Vp.n pass] put a saddle on (one's horse). **S:** jockey, rider; groom; trooper. **O:** horse, mount: *We went down to the stables early to* **saddle up**. ○ *The horses were* **saddled up** *and ready to move off.*

saddle with [Vn.pr pass rel] make (sb) accept a (burden). **O:** employee, colleague, husband; oneself. **o:** job, task; burden, responsibility; expense; family, child: *The government played some part in* **saddling** *industry* **with** *a heavier load.* SC ○ *The city, which declined to* **saddle** *itself* **with** *the cost of airport ownership, will still have an international airport.* SC ○ *I'm always being* **saddled with** *extra duties.* = land with, lumber (with).

sail

sail across, along, away etc [Vp emph, Vpr] move across etc in a stately or dignified way, like a ship under sail: *Mrs Vickers* **sailed** *majestically* **into** *the drawing room.*

sail through [Vp, Vpr] complete or pass (sth) with ease. **o:** audition, test, oral exam: *'Now stop worrying about your test: you'll* **sail through**.' ○ *Nick just* **sailed through** *his theory paper.* = romp through.

sally

sally forth [Vp] (*formal* or *jocular*) emerge suddenly, usu from a position where one is surrounded, and attack the enemy; suddenly leave a quiet, inactive state to do sth active and energetic. **S:** (besieged, beleaguered) army, force: *Few academics* **sally forth** *into the rough and tumble of the hustings* (ie active politics). OXTD ○ *An army of shoppers* **sally forth** *each year to do battle in the annual sales at the big stores.*

salt

salt away [Vn ⇆ p pass] (*informal*) save or invest (money) for the future. **O:** part of one's income, salary; profits, earnings: *Now's the time to* **salt** *something* **away** *for your old age.* ○ *Allegations have been made ... that 'millions of pounds are being* **salted away**' *illegally in the Channel Islands by speculators.* OBS

salvage

salvage (from) 1 [Vn.pr pass emph rel] recover sth which is undamaged and still usable (from a place which has suffered damage). **O:** cargo; furniture, machinery; box, bale. **o:** wreckage, debris; blaze, fire; (damaged) factory: *All that could be* **salvaged from** *the fire was a small metal box containing instruments.*

2 [Vn.pr pass emph rel] rescue or preserve (sth worthwhile) (from a situation that has grown worse). **O:** some shreds of respectability, one's self-respect. **o:** (collapse, failure of) one's marriage, business, career: *They smash the institution* (ie marriage) *and* **salvage** *some love* **from** *the wreckage.* ○ *The negotiators tried desperately to* **salvage** *something* **from** *the wrecked peace talks.*

sand

sand down [Vn ⇆ p pass adj] remove (rough parts of a surface) by rubbing it with sandpaper. **O:** paintwork; wall, door: *The surface should be thoroughly* **sanded down** *before you apply any paint.*

saturate

saturate (with) [Vn.pr pass emph rel] make (sth) absorb the maximum amount of (a liquid); soak (with). **O:** ground, soil; cloth, rag. **o:** water, oil: *Press the sponge into the liquid until it is* **saturated** (**with** *it*). ○ *We lay in the sun until our bodies felt* **saturated with** *the heat.*

save

save (from) [Vn.pr pass emph rel] make or keep (sb) safe (from sth). **o:** loss, injury; drowning, being burned: *By arriving when you did you* **saved** *her* **from** *more serious injury.* ○ *The sandwich would* **save** *him* **from** *going to bed on a completely empty stomach.* BFA

save up (for) [Vp, Vp.pr pass emph rel, Vn ⇆ p pass, Vn.p.pr pass emph rel] put (money) in reserve little by little (in order to obtain sth). **o:** car, bicycle, radio; holiday: [Vp] *'We're* **saving up** *to get married.'* TOH ○ [Vp.pr] *I told her I'd been* **saving up for** *her all my life.* KLT ○ [Vn.p.pr] *We had quite a bit* **saved up for** *a winter break in Italy.* □ in the second example there is a pun on saving oneself up, ie reserving oneself for sb/sth special.

savour

savour of [Vpr] (*formal*) suggest, indicate (an unpleasant feeling etc) on the part of the speaker. **S:** suggestion, plan, proposal. **o:** malice, mischief, ill-will: *The speaker's words* **savoured** *strongly* **of** *intolerance.* ○ *His remarks* **savour of** *ill-will.* = smack of.

saw

saw down [Vn ⇆ p pass] bring (sth) to the ground, using a saw. **O:** tree, post, mast: *Some of trees on the estate had to be* **sawn down** *and sold for their valuable timber.*

saw into [Vn.pr pass] divide (sth) in pieces using a saw. **O:** tree, timber. **o:** lengths, planks, battens: **Saw** *this board* **into** *pieces, each a foot long.* ○ *The trees are stripped of their bark and* **sawn into** *planks.*

saw off [Vn ⇆ p pass adj, Vn.pr pass] remove (part) of sth with a saw. **O:** branch; piece, length: *If you* **saw** *six inches* **off** *the legs of the table, you can use it to rest the television on.* ○ *'Would you* **saw** *me* **off** *a piece two metres by one?'* ○ *He* **sawed** *an inch* **off** *the barrel of his revolver to make it easier to draw* (cf *a* **sawn-off** *barrel*). ○ *He produced a* **sawn-off** *shotgun from a canvas bag.* BBCR □ note the Indirect Object (*me*) in the second example.

saw up [Vn ⇆ p pass adj] cut (sth) into pieces with a saw. **O:** tree, plank, board: *All the spare timber was* **sawn up** *to make logs for the fire.* ○ *Get the carpenter to* **saw** *the wood* **up** *to your requirements.*

say

say (about) [Vn.pr pass emph rel] make comments, observations (about sth/sb). **S:** reporter; newspaper, article; reference book. **O:** a lot, plenty; nothing, very little; what. **o:** event, accident, case; musician, painter: *What does the 'Times' leader* **say about** *the prospects of a settlement in the rail dispute?* ○ *'The science teacher tells me you've not been making much effort this term, Stephen. Now, what have you to* **say about** *that?'* ○ (film review) *It's a thriller from the John Le Carré novel, with plenty to* **say about** *people.* OBS

say for [Vn.pr] be a favourable/unfavourable comment or reflection on (sb/sth). **O:** ⚠ a lot, a great deal; not … much. **o:** sb's ability, wisdom, tact, maturity: *To play* (cricket) *to 75 000 Bengalis at Calcutta and keep them happy and amused for five days* **says** *a great deal* **for** *both teams.* BBCR ○ *He was late for his first interview and missed his second. It doesn't* **say** *much* **for** *his sense of commitment.*

never/not say no to [Vn.pr] (*informal*) never/not refuse (sth). **o:** drink, free meal, cigar: *'He would'***nt say no to** *a brandy.'* BFA ○ *He insisted on replacing my drink. I* **never say no to** *a drink.* JFTR ○ *'He's* **never said no to** *cake yet, and I don't suppose he'll start tonight.'* AITC

scale

scale down [Vn ⇆ p pass adj] reduce (sth) in size, value etc, sometimes in relation to sth else. **O:** wage, salary; investment, expenditure; output, production: *Their estimates have been* **scaled down** *every month since the turn of the year.* G ○ *The effect of all this* (ie inflation) *is to* **scale down** *people's spending plans.* BBCR ○ *Armies should be* **scaled down**, *but not if it meant giving one country an advantage over any other.* BBCR ↔ scale up.

scale up [Vn ⇆ p pass adj] increase (sth) in size, value etc, sometimes in relation to sth else. **O:** income, earnings; benefit, bonus: *The salaries of teachers should be* **scaled up** *to correspond to those of people in comparable professions.* ○ (statement of director after securing a large order) *'It is now a matter of* **scaling up** *production, of making 30 000 retort stands instead of 1 000.'* ST ↔ scale down.

scare

scare away/off 1 [Vn ⇆ p pass] cause (sb) to stay some distance away, or go away, by frightening him. **S:** security arrangements; guard-dog, police. **O:** burglar, intruder; visitor: *Intruders stay clear of his house. I think the bulldog* **scares** *them* **away**.
2 [Vn ⇆ p pass] make (sb) unwilling to buy, to invest, to stay somewhere etc. **S:** conditions; slump, recession; political unrest. **O:** investors, customers, tourists: *Small private investors* **scared away** *by the crash are reported to be returning in droves.* ○ *A lot of potential customers are* **scared off** *by the expensive look of the place.*

scare to death [Vn.pr pass] (*informal*) frighten (sb) very badly. **S:** noise, silence; film; flying, heights: *I'm afraid of my mother — and she's* **scared to death** *of me.* DPM ○ (fear of flying) *She had never been able to get over the tendency to be both airsick and* **scared to death**. DC

scatter

scatter about/around/round [Vn.p pass, Vn.pr pass] leave or throw (things) here and there in a haphazard or untidy manner. **O:** clothes, books, toys. **o:** place, room: *'It's clear the children have been playing here: there are toys* **scattered about** *all over the carpet.'* ○ *'I've* **scattered** *some ashtrays* **around** *the room so that cigarettes don't get trodden into the floor.'*

scheme

scheme (for) [Vpr pass emph rel] (*pejorative*) make plans, usu secret and dishonest ones, to achieve (some end). **S:** rival, rebel. **o:** downfall, overthrow; power, control: *He was* **scheming for** *a bigger share* (or: *to have a bigger share*) *in the running of the business.* ○ *They came perilously close to achieving the objectives* **for** *which they had been* **scheming**.

school

school (in) [Vn.pr pass emph rel] teach (sb) the elements or principles of (sth); usu the teaching is informal and by example; its purpose may be sinister or antisocial. **O:** child; follower, disciple. **o:** diplomacy, statecraft; cunning, double-dealing:

The young king was carefully **schooled in** *the art of balancing one force in the kingdom against another.* ○ *Movement at night, staying concealed, living off the land — these were all skills* **in** *which they had been well* **schooled**.

scoop

scoop out [Vn ⇆ p pass adj] remove (sth) using a deep, rounded shovel, one's hand shaped as one, or a paw; form (a hole) by removing soil etc in this manner. **S:** (burrowing) animal; badger, mole. **O:** soil, sand; hole, cavity, trench: *He* **scooped out** *a little of the earth, being careful not to disturb anything that was underneath.* ○ *This small rodent can* **scoop out** *a long, narrow tunnel in a very short time.*

scoop up [Vn ⇆ p pass adj] raise (sth) in a deep, rounded implement or vessel, or in one's hand shaped as one. **O:** liquid; dust; filings, shavings: *She cupped her hands and* **scooped up** *a little water.* ○ *He took a spoon and* **scooped up** *a few grains of the gold dust.*

score

score (for) [Vn.pr pass] (*music*) include parts (for particular instruments) in a musical composition. **S:** composer. **O:** piece; concerto, symphony. **o:** strings, woodwind, brass: *He* **scored** *one quintet* **for** *two violas and the other* **for** *two cellos.* ○ *Beethoven's Fifth is the first major symphony to be* **scored for** *trombones.*

score off 1 [Vpr pass rel, Vn.pr pass rel] (*cricket*) score (runs) by striking the deliveries of (a particular bowler). **S:** batsman. **O:** run; fifty. **o:** bowler; bowling: *Richards* **scored** *a quick thirty, mainly* **off** *a loose spell of medium-fast bowling.* ○ *'He made fifty before lunch, and as you know, the West Indies attack is never easy to* **score off**.*'*
2 [Vpr pass] (*informal*) make (sb) appear foolish, inadequate etc eg by a witty or unkind remark. **o:** friend, rival, opponent: *'You can cut out the cheap cracks. It's too easy to* **score off** *poor old Fred.'* ○ *If he had wanted to* **score off** *Robert, there were so many better ways than this.* CON

score out [Vn ⇆ p pass adj] cancel (sth) by drawing a line through it. **O:** line, mark, figure, letter: *Three of the names on the guest list had been* **scored out**. ○ *The paper was covered with untidy drawings and* **scored-out** *calculations.* = cross out.

scour

scour off [Vn ⇆ p pass, Vn.pr pass] remove (sth) by rubbing with a rough brush, wire pad etc. **O:** rust, grease, burnt food. **o:** pan, pot, stove: *See that all the burnt potato is* **scoured off** *the bottom of the pan.* ○ *If the bath is stained, don't try to* **scour** *the stain* **off**: *you'll only scratch the surface.*

scour out [Vn ⇆ p pass] rub the inside of (sth) with a rough brush etc, so as to remove dirt etc. **O:** (sauce)pan, pot, jar: *The boilers will have to be* **scoured out** *to remove the calcium deposits.* ○ *The heavy pans are regularly* **scoured out**.

scout

scout about/around (for) [Vp nom, Vp.pr rel] hunt, search, carefully (for sth). **o:** food, shelter, fuel: *'I know he's not here; go and have a* **scout-around** *in the garden (or: go and* **scout around** *in the garden).'* ○ *'***Scout around for** *a few bits of firewood.'*

scrabble

scrabble about/around (for) [Vp, Vp.pr rel] search, grope, in a blind, clumsy way (for sth): *He* **scrabbled about** *under the counter for a minute, and came up with a small green bottle.* ○ *Children* **scrabbled around** *on the pavement* **for** *coins that had been thrown down to them.*

scramble

scramble for [Vpr rel] struggle in rather a disorderly, undignified way to get more of sth than one's competitors. **S:** country, company, trader; spectator. **o:** possessions, market; seat, place: *The families that had enriched themselves in the previous generation now* **scrambled for** *official posts and honours.* ○ *The European powers* **scrambled for** *trading posts in the areas that had been opened up.*

scrape

scrape along (on) [Vp, Vp.pr emph rel] (*informal*) manage for some time to live (on very little money etc). **o:** a low wage, a few pounds (a week): *She spent three years at college,* **scraping along on** *an allowance from her parents.* ○ *They paid him a low salary,* **on** *which he was quite content to* **scrape along** *in the hope that something better would turn up.*

scrape by (on) [Vp, Vp.pr emph rel] (*informal*) manage to live, and esp to survive a difficult period (on very little money etc). **o:** small allowance, low grant; what one has saved: *The most difficult time was the winter, when we had the fuel bills to pay, but we managed to* **scrape by** *with a little money in hand.* ○ *The first year in the new house was the hardest, but they just* **scraped by on** *a loan from the bank.*

scrape in/into [Vp, Vpr] (*informal*) just manage to enter (a school etc) by getting the lowest acceptable marks. **o:** school, college, university; army, civil service: *'How on earth did he get into the Foreign Service?' 'He must have* **scraped in** *by the barest of margins.'* ○ *He* **scraped into** *the presidency by a single vote.*

scrape off [Vn ⇆ p pass adj, Vn.pr pass] remove (sth) from a surface eg by passing a blade between it and the surface, or by accidentally rubbing the surface against a rougher one. **O:** paint, tar; jam, butter; skin. **o:** wall, door; floor, table; hand, elbow: *'***Scrape** *those bits of putty* **off** *the window pane.'* ○ *He* **scraped** *the skin* **off** *his knee on a piece of corrugated iron.*

scrape out [Vn ⇆ p pass adj] empty, or clean, the inside of (a vessel) by passing sth along its surface. **O:** dish, bowl; pipe, channel: *'Would you like to* **scrape out** *the jam-jar? Here's a spoon.'* ○ *Once in a while the bowl of his pipe is thoroughly* **scraped out**.

scrape through [Vp, Vp.pr] just manage to pass (a test etc), pass it with the lowest acceptable mark. **S:** student, candidate. **o:** test, examination; selection board: *He got a comfortable pass in zoology, but barely* **scraped through** *in botany.* ○ *She just* **scraped through** *in the written papers, but may make up her marks in the oral.*

scrape together/up [Vn ⇆ p pass] (*informal*) save (money) with difficulty; collect together with difficulty (money from various sources) to meet an emergency. **O:** money; cash, funds, capital: *'Well, you'll have to* ***scrape*** *the money* ***up****. I'm not going to dip into my funds to save you from a scandal.'* HD ○ *'Couldn't we just try to* ***scrape together*** *a few pounds for a holiday?'*

scrape up an acquaintance (with) [Vp.n pass, Vn.p.pr pass rel] (*informal*) get to know (sb) with difficulty and/or superficially, because he is shy or aloof, or because you know no one in common etc. **adj:** some; slight, nodding, superficial: *He would nod over the garden wall once in a while and after a month we'd* ***scraped up*** *some kind of* ***an acquaintance****.* ○ *I managed to* ***scrape up an acquaintance with*** *some of the single passengers, but the married ones tended to keep to themselves.*

scratch

scratch about/around (for) [Vp, Vp.pr] dig here and there with sth sharp (in order to find sth). **S:** chicken, monkey; farmer, miner. **o:** corn, fleas; (signs, traces of) water, gold: *Sparrows were* ***scratching about*** *in the damp soil* ***for*** *worms.* ○ *'If you want to get through this rock, there's no sense in* ***scratching around*** *with a pick. You'll have to use explosive.'*

scratch (from) [Vpr emph rel, Vn.pr pass emph rel] (*sport*) (cause sth/sb to) withdraw from a sporting contest, eg because of illness. **S** [Vpr], **O** [Vn.pr]**:** horse; runner, long-jumper. **S** [Vn.pr]**:** owner; manager. **o:** race; event: *Two competitors have* ***scratched from*** *the 10 000 metres with torn leg muscles.* ○ *There will only be five runners in the 3.30 at Newbury as three horses have been* ***scratched*** *(****from*** *the race) at the last minute.*

scratch out [Vn ⇆ p pass adj] remove, cancel (sth) by making a deep, scoring mark with a sharp, narrow instrument. **O:** line, mark; name: *I looked at the list; somebody had* ***scratched*** *his name* ***out****.* ○ *His essay was disfigured by many blots and* ***scratchings-out****.* = cross out.

scratch sb's eyes out [Vn.p pass] (*informal*) (threaten to) make a violent physical attack on sb. **S:** wife, girlfriend: *'Be careful, Harry: she'll* ***scratch your eyes out*** *if you so much as glance at another woman.'* ○ *'You'll stop fooling around with Mike — unless you want to have* ***your eyes scratched out****!'* □ often with will/would; usu said by or about a possessive or jealous woman.

screen

screen (from) [Vn.pr pass rel] shelter, protect (sb) (from sth/sb). **O:** eyes, face; table, bed; ceremony, procession; child, pupil. **o:** sun, daylight; watcher; view, gaze; influence: *Use a hood to* ***screen*** *the lens of your camera* ***from*** *direct sunlight.* ○ *During her childhood she had been carefully* ***screened from*** *contact with 'undesirable' companions.*

screen off [Vn ⇆ p pass adj] separate (sth/sb), eg from the rest of a room, by means of a screen. **O:** bed, table; patient, invalid: *He would retire to his desk,* ***screened off*** *from the rest of the room by a heavy bookcase.* ○ *'****Screen off*** *her bed and make sure she's not disturbed.'*

screen out [Vn ⇆ p pass adj] make (sth/sb) invisible or inaudible by means of a screen, or sth resembling one. **O:** one's surroundings, the outside world; noise, light; intruders: *When you turn on a lamp after having been in a dark room, your irises contract to* ***screen out*** *some of the sudden light.* PVP ○ *I pulled a net around me to* ***screen out*** *the world. I stopped reading the papers and watching television. I was indifferent to the news.* LC

screw

screw down [Vn ⇆ p pass adj] fasten (a cover) to a box etc with screws; close (a box) by fastening a cover. **O:** lid, cover; hatch; coffin: *After the mourners have paid their last respects, the undertaker* ***screws down*** *the lid of the coffin.*

(have) one's head screwed on [pass (Vn.p)] (*informal*) (be) sensible and practical, of sound judgement: *'I'm sorry you're all so easy to fool. You ought to* ***have your heads screwed on*** *right, with all your experience of the trade.'* CON ○ *There's a lad with* ***his head screwed on*** *— he had the sense to buy in while the price was low.* ○ *The next time you go into partnership, make sure the other fellow****'s got his head screwed on*** *the right way.*

screw on/onto [Vn ⇆ p pass adj, Vn.pr pass rel] fasten (one thing) (to another), either with screws, or by a screw-thread cut into each. **O:** plate, board; top, lid; handle, knob. **o:** wall, door; jar, bottle; shaft: *The carpenter came along and* ***screwed on*** *a shining brass plate: C. R. JONES, M.B., B.Ch.* ○ *Don't forget to* ***screw*** *the lid back* ***onto*** *the jar.*

screw out of [Vn.pr pass] (*informal*) get money etc (from sb) by undue persuasion, pressure etc. **O:** money; cash, pound; promise, guarantee: *'Can't you manage to* ***screw*** *a bit extra* ***out of*** *your parents?'* ○ *He's so unscrupulous that he'd* ***screw*** *the last penny* ***out of*** *a pensioner.*

screw up 1 [Vn ⇆ p pass adj] make (sth) into a tight ball in the hands. **O:** paper; letter, bill: *With a muttered curse, Peter* ***screwed up*** *the second draft of his letter and threw it in the wastepaper basket.* ○ *At the end of a normal morning's work the study floor would be littered with* ***screwed-up*** *bits of paper.*

2 [Vn ⇆ p pass] tighten the muscles of the face, so shading one's eyes, expressing surprise etc. **O:** ⚠ one's eyes, features, face: *Even under the broad brim of my hat I had to* ***screw up*** *my eyes against the ferocious glare.* DF ○ *Janice* ***screwed*** *her face* ***up*** *into an expression of the utmost seriousness.* PW

3 [Vn ⇆ p pass adj] (*informal*) make (sb) nervous or tense. **S:** occasion; waiting; fear, anxiety. **O:** patient, examinee; soldier, prisoner: *The last few minutes before going on stage always* ***screw*** *him* ***up****, so he has a cigarette to help him relax.* ○ *'Flying never seems to bother my wife, but I get* ***screwed up*** *at the very thought.'* = tense up.

4 [Vp, Vn ⇆ p pass adj] (*informal*) mishandle, mismanage (sth). **S:** manager, organizer; agency, office. **O:** planning, arrangements; deal: *'We should never have left the arrangements to Smithers. He* ***screwed*** *the whole thing* ***up*** *from start to finish.'* ○ *The opening stage of the attack was badly* ***screwed up*** *and we suffered heavy casualties.* = mess up.

screw up one's courage [Vp.n] force oneself to be brave: *I've been* ***screwing up my courage*** *to tell you.* EHOW ○ *'Don't stand there —* ***screw up your courage*** *and jump.'*

scribble

scribble down [Vn ⇆ p pass] record (sth) in writing quickly and not very legibly. **O:** name, address, phone number: *I **scribbled down** his name on the back of an envelope.* ○ *'Hang on, I've got the details **scribbled down** somewhere.'*

scribble off [Vn ⇆ p pass] compose (sth) quickly and not very legibly. **O:** note, letter, message: *Letters he **scribbled off** after midnight, at the end of a long day.* HTS

scrub

scrub off [Vn ⇆ p pass, Vn.pr pass] remove (sth) from a surface etc by rubbing it with a stiff brush, soap and water etc. **O:** dirt, oil, glue, paint. **o:** hand; wall, floor: *'**Scrub** that mud **off** your fingers before you sit down to lunch.'* ○ *I got paint on my hands and it won't **scrub off*** (or: *I can't **scrub** it **off***).

scrub out 1 [Vn ⇆ p pass] remove (a mark) etc from fabric etc, by rubbing it with a stiff brush, soap and water. **O:** mark, stain; oil, tar; coffee: *When you spill ink on the carpet, remove it straight away; you won't be able to **scrub** it **out** later* (or: *it won't **scrub out** later*).

2 [Vn ⇆ p pass] clean (a place) by rubbing the surface with a stiff brush, soap and water. **O:** room, hall; cupboard: *As soon as they moved in, they started **scrubbing out** the rooms* (ie scrubbing the floors clean) *and washing down the walls.*

3 [Vn ⇆ p pass] (*informal*) cancel sth which is due to take place; treat sth which has taken place as invalid. **O:** instruction, order; arrangements, programme; practice, trial: *The whole exercise has been **scrubbed out**; you will receive fresh orders shortly.* ○ *We've **scrubbed out** event 1; move on to the next event.* ○ *The researchers had to **scrub out** the first set of results and start again.* □ scrub alone sometimes used in this sense: *We've **scrubbed** event 1* etc.

scrub round [Vpr pass] (*informal*) not apply or implement (sth); not follow or observe (sth). **o:** rule, regulation; difficulty, obstacle: *It says here that an applicant should have three years' experience, but I think we can **scrub round** that.* ○ *The entrance requirements are strictly applied: don't think you can **scrub round** them.* = get round 2.

scrunch

scrunch up 1 [Vn ⇆ p pass adj] (*informal*) make (sth) into a tight ball in the hands. **O:** paper, letter: *I woke stiff and cold, feeling as though I had been **scrunched up** like a paper bag.* AO = screw up 1.

2 [Vn ⇆ p pass] (*informal*) tighten the muscles of one's face to shade one's eyes etc. **O:** ⚠ one's eyes, features, face: *I **scrunch up** my face to stop myself from crying.* BB = screw up 2.

scuffle

scuffle (with) [Vpr rel] fight, struggle (with sb) in a confused way. **S:** spectator, demonstrator, marcher. **o:** police, troops: *One or two hecklers on the edge of the crowd **scuffled with** the stewards.*

scurry

scurry for [Vpr] hurry in a nervous, excited way towards (sth). **o:** ⚠ the door, exit; shelter, cover: *A sudden shower of rain sent the players **scurrying for** shelter.* ○ *As the plaster cascaded onto the tables, the guests **scurried for** the door.*

seal

seal off [Vn ⇆ p pass adj] close the entrance to (sth), so that nothing can move in or out. **O:** channel, passage; exit, entrance: *We reached the Baltic and thus **sealed off** the Danish peninsula with about six hours to spare.* MFM ○ *It did not seem to occur to the police to **seal off** the entrances or order nobody to leave.* OBS

seal up [Vn ⇆ p pass adj] fasten (sth) tightly. **O:** parcel, letter; hole, opening: *They **sealed up** the cracks in the window to stop the icy wind from blowing in.* ○ *Make sure the parcel of examination scripts is properly **sealed up**.*

search

search (for) [Vpr emph rel, Vn.pr pass emph rel] look carefully in or about (a place) (in order to find sb/sth). **S:** rescue party; plane, helicopter; detective. **O:** area, neighbourhood; house; drawer, cupboard; pockets. **o:** missing climber, airman; weapon; papers, keys: *Police and tracker dogs **searched** the woods **for** the missing boy.* ○ *'I've been **searching** everywhere **for** those scissors. Where did they get to?'* ○ *At last the evidence **for** which they had been **searching** came to light.*

search out [Vn ⇆ p pass] (try to) discover (sb/sth) by looking carefully for it. **O:** author, maker; culprit, one responsible; cause: *He went through drawer after drawer and eventually **searched out** a dusty portfolio.* = bring to light, hunt out.

search through [Vpr pass] look carefully for sth eg by moving steadily from one part of a room to another. **o:** drawer, cupboard; belongings; paper, book: *You can **search through** his autobiography without finding a single reference to his first wife.* ○ *There's no point in looking there: his personal papers have all been **searched through**.*

secede

secede (from) [Vpr emph rel] (*formal*) withdraw from membership (of sth). **S:** state, province, region. **o:** union, federation: *The problem is to stop the richer northern provinces **seceding from** a federation the greater part of which is poor.*

second

second (to) [Vn.pr pass rel] transfer (sb) from his normal post (to another) for special duties. **O:** soldier, officer; official. **o:** staff, research establishment: *Major Smith has been **seconded to** us to advise on the new signals procedure.* ○ *He enjoyed the small, up-country post **to** which he had been **seconded**.* □ note that the stress is on the second syllable: /sɪˈkɒnd/.

secure

secure (against) [Vn.pr pass rel] make (sth) safe (against sb/sth); strengthen (against). **O:** house; window, door; position, defences. **o:** intruder, thief; attack: *They **secured** the house **against** entry on either floor.* ○ *As Hancock had moved troops over to guard the left flank, he was **secured against** sudden attack from that quarter.*

see

see about [Vpr pass] act so as to achieve or correct (sth). **o:** cleaning, decorating; tax, insurance; damage, breakage: *That was how I got the idea of the* *market-garden, though I didn't get round to* **see-ing about** *it till now.* PW ○ (advertisement) *You're so pretty, Linda, it's a pity you neglect your breath. Why don't you* **see about** *it?* WI

see across [Vn.p pass, Vn.pr pass] guide, escort (sb) across (a road). **O:** child, old person. **o:** road, street: *'Ask a grown-up to* **see** *you* **across**.' ○ *I was there to make sure the children were* **seen** *safely* **across** *the road.*

see as [Vn.pr pass] consider (sth) to be (sth). **o:** dictatorship, bullying, interference: *He explicitly rejects what he* **sees as** *the centralizing tendencies of the British government.* G

see beyond [Vpr] (be able to) foresee and understand events etc which are at some distance in space or time; be far-sighted. **o:** the immediate present, the here and now, the next few hours/days; one's own family circle; one's own immediate concerns: *He's not the right man to put in charge of the food supply: he can't* **see beyond** *where the next meal's coming from.* ○ *A man responsible for a large business must be able to* **see beyond** *short-term goals. He may need to plan for several years ahead.* □ with can/could; often neg.

see beyond the end of one's nose [Vpr] (*informal*) (be able to) understand more than what is present and obvious: *'No one would think he's your son. You treat him abominably. Just because you can't* **see beyond the end of your** *stupid, commonplace* **nose**.' FFE ○ *'I've got an idea of offering Pelican a directorship,' Robin said. 'It'll be a bit tricky with my fellow directors. Pelican'd be the hell of an asset, but they can't* **see beyond the end of their noses**.' ASA □ with can/could and usu neg. ⇨ previous entry

see in a new etc light [Vn.pr pass] regard or understand (sth/sb) in a new or better way. **O:** things, conditions; problem, quarrel; brother, colleague. **adj:** new, fresh, different; best, more favourable, more flattering: *'We are all under somewhat of a strain, and in the morning we will probably* **see** *things* **in a** *totally* **different light**.' TT ○ *Most people want to be* **seen in the best light**. SNP

see of [Vn.pr pass pass(o) rel] meet, have contact with (sb) often, seldom etc. **O:** a lot, a good/great deal; more, less; (not) much, anything. **o:** each other, one another; friend, colleague, boss: *'We'll have to* **see** *more* **of** *each other, I can see.'* HAA ○ *Since Sadie had become so famous I had* **seen** *nothing* **of** *her.* UTN ○ *We expected Baker to move around the plant and talk to people. But for the first month, he wasn't* **seen** *much* **of** *outside his office.*

see an end of/to [Vn.pr] witness the ending of sth, usu sth unpleasant. **o:** event, development; conflict, dissention; squabbling, bickering: *All parties, surely, wish to* **see an end of** *violence in South Africa.* ○ *Perhaps with the appointment of a new chairman we would* **see an end to** *the jealousies and intrigue of the previous year.*

see off 1 [Vn.p pass] say goodbye to (sb), eg at a railway station. **O:** relative, friend: *A number of friends and well-wishers came to* **see** *me* **off** *at the airport.* = send off 2.

2 [Vn.p pass] drive, chase (sb) away. **S:** guard, dog; defence. **O:** intruder, prowler; attacker, opponent: *Some boys came round hoping to steal apples, but Dad* **saw** *them* **off** *with a few well-chosen words.* ○ *If the enemy failed to* **see** *us* **off** *on the beaches, he would try to rope us off* (= encircle us) *inland.* MFM

see out [Vn ⇆ p] (*informal*) not be eaten up, worn out etc, until the end of a period. **S:** supply, store; money; food, drink: *'That wine's not going to* **see out** *the weekend. We'd better stock up again.'* ○ *'The petrol I bought this morning should* **see** *the week* **out**.' = last out 1.

see out/out of [Vn.p pass, Vn.pr pass] lead, guide (sb) out of (a building): *'Don't bother to come down. I can* **see** *myself* **out**.' ○ *'Miss Jones will* **see** *you* **out of** *the building.'*

see over/round [Vpr] visit and examine (a place). **S:** visitor; prospective buyer. **o:** house; gardens; exhibition, show: *'I shall need to* **see over** *the house and grounds before I can make you any kind of offer.'* ○ *It took us two hours to* **see** *right* **round** *the Boat Show.* ⇨ show around/round, show over.

see through 1 [Vpr nom pass] (be able to) see from one side to the other of (sth), because it is transparent. **o:** window, partition; fabric, garment: *'Would you mind moving to one side? I can't* **see through** *your head, you know.'* ○ *Barbara was wearing one of those* **see-through** *blouses; in fact it was so* **see-through** *that she needn't have been wearing one at all.* □ see-through usu attrib, as in the first part of the second example.

2 [Vpr pass] understand the true nature of (sb) beneath a pleasant, deceptive appearance. **o:** him etc; act, show, manner; charm, glibness: *She has learnt to* **see through** *the smooth exterior to the real person underneath.* ○ *'Don't think you can fool me—I can* **see** *right* **through** *you!'*

3 [Vn.p, Vn.pr] ensure that (sb) passes safely through (a difficult time). **S:** friendship, support; skill, bravery. **o:** crisis, bad patch, troubled time: *She had known he might come back and trusted to him to* **see** *her* **through**. PW ○ *His courage and good humour have* **seen** *him* **through** *worse times than these.* ○ *'I shall need more than a couple of drinks to* **see** *me* **through** *one of their ghastly parties.'*

4 [Vn.p] (*informal*) handle a situation and bring events to a happy conclusion. **O:** it, the thing, things; project, job: *Together the whole team will* **see** *this thing* **through** *to the end.* MFM ○ *You can depend on James to* **see** *the job* **through**.

see to 1 [Vpr pass] take responsibility for (sth). **o:** food; room, bed; money, investments: *'Jo, go and* **see to** *that coffee!'* TOH ○ *Large sums of money would continue regularly to be moved, and their security must be* **seen to**. T = look after 2, take care (of) 2.

2 [Vpr pass] ensure that sb is properly received, helped etc. **o:** visitor, guest, customer; child, invalid: *'Now you go off and* **see to** *the visitors.'* ○ *'Are the guests being properly* **seen to**?'

see an end to [Vn.pr] ⇨ see an end of/to.

see to it (that) [Vpr] take care, ensure (that sth happens, is the case etc): *In later years Anne* **saw to it that** *Bill never drank again.* IND ○ *Here concealment was impossible. I simply had to hope that some kindly deity would* **see to it that** *I met nobody.* UTN ○ *'I promise to get everything finished on time.' 'Well,* **see to it** *you do!'* □ followed by finite (that) clause. ⇨ see to 1.

see eye to eye (with) (about/on) [Vpr emph rel] have the same views, sympathies etc (as sb) (about sth). **o:** (**with**) husband, child; employer; (**about/on**) money, housework, holidays; wages, hours (of work), conditions: *He never* ***saw eye to eye with*** *his father* (or: *He and his father never* ***saw eye to eye***). ○ *STANLEY: Clive, as you know, your mother and I didn't* ***see eye to eye about*** *sending you to University.* FFE ○ *'Patrick and I* ***see*** *pretty well* ***eye to eye on*** *most things.'* TGLY □ eye to eye is an adv phrase; often neg. = agree (with) 1.

seek

sought after [pass adj (Vpr)] wanted, desired; in demand. **S:** property, house; china, jewellery: *Houses in this area are very much* ***sought after***. ○ *Georgian silver teapots are much* ***sought-after*** *items these days.*

seek (for) [Vpr pass adj emph rel] try to find (sth). **o:** answer, solution; cause, explanation: *You should* ***seek (for)*** *a reason in the statements he has made over the past year.* ○ *The summit meeting has brought the results* ***(for)*** *which we were all* ***seeking***. ○ *Among the successes were some long* ***sought-for*** *changes in working conditions.* □ for may be omitted, except in the adj form: sought-for. = look for.

seek out [Vn ⇆ p pass] come looking for (sb), eg to ask for help, pass on news etc. **O:** friend, colleague, confidant: *Supposing he* ***sought*** *her* ***out*** *again and he asked her what she really did mean?* PW ○ *When Marlowe returned from lunch the secretary* ***sought*** *him* ***out***. *'Cable for you, Dr Marlowe.'* TBC

seethe

seethe (with) [Vpr] be restless (with sth), be agitated (by sth), like water in a kettle coming to the boil. **S:** country, town; population. **o:** discontent, unrest; anger, fury: *The square was now fully alight and* ***seething with*** *still more revellers converging on the cafés.* BM ○ *By now John was* ***seething with*** *indignation and we all gathered round trying to pacify him.*

seize

seize on/upon [Vpr pass emph rel] choose in a keen, alert way some aspect of (sth) for special comment or criticism. **o:** detail, feature; fault, flaw: *He quickly* ***seized on*** *a basic flaw in the argument I was developing.* ○ *Any weakness in their position will be* ***seized upon*** *and exploited.* = fasten on/upon.

seize up 1 [Vp] become fixed or jammed because of overheating etc. **S:** engine, motor; car: *'If you never bother to lubricate your engine of course it will* ***seize up****!'* = pack up 3.

2 [Vp nom] (*informal*) stop functioning well, because of fatigue, pressure etc. **S:** muscles, joints; back, shoulder; fridge: *I've been wagging my chin so fast these last months it'll* ***seize up*** *soon.* TGLY ○ *The extra parked cars could cause a complete* ***seize-up*** (ie of the traffic). BBCR

seize with both hands [Vn.pr pass] grasp (sth) eagerly, be quick to exploit (sth). **O:** opportunity, chance, opening; offer, invitation: *An opportunity is presented to each one of us; some of us are not aware of the full significance of what has happened, and the moment is lost. Others, alert and enthusiastic,* ***seize*** *the opportunity* ***with both hands*** *and turn it to good advantage.* MFM ○ *This offer was* ***seized*** *by Ernest Bevin* ***with both hands*** *and he organized a conference in Paris the next month.* MFM

sell

sell (at) [Vn.pr pass rel] give (sth) for money (at a particular price level). **o:** price, figure; gain, loss; discount; £100, ten dollars: *'What price are they being* ***sold at****?'* ○ *I can't afford to go on* ***selling*** *several of my lines* ***at*** *a loss.* ○ *He's* ***selling*** *his ties* ***at*** *ten per cent below the normal retail price.* □ one sells at a point on a scale (eg of loss or gain); one sells for a particular amount or sum of money. ⇨ sell (for).

sell down the river [Vn.pr pass] (*informal*) betray the interests of one's own people, of members of one's party, trade union etc. **S:** minister, leader; delegate, representative. **O:** country; union, member: (letter to Editor) *Sir: The phrase '****sold down the river****' is American, and refers to the Mississippi. Before the Civil War the treatment of slaves in the northern tier of slave States was generally better than that further south. Consequently, the practice of* ***selling*** *recalcitrant slaves '****down the river****' developed.* OBS ○ *At a mass meeting of car workers called by shop stewards the official leadership was accused of* ***selling*** *the rank and file* ***down the river***.

sell (for) [Vn.pr pass rel] give (sth) in exchange for a particular sum of money. **o:** £100; less than one gives, next to nothing: *'I'm thinking of* ***selling*** *the car.' 'Oh, how much* ***for****?'* ○ *I can't remember what I* ***sold*** *the collection* ***for***. ⇨ (note at) sell (at).

sell off [Vn ⇆ p nom pass] get rid of goods which have not sold well, or plant which is inefficient by selling them at a reduced price, so as to free the money invested in them. **O:** stock, line; holding, share; factory, store: *We are planning to* ***sell off*** (or: *planning a* ***sell-off*** *of*) *some of the lines which have been cluttering up our warehouses for so long.* ○ *Mogul have already undertaken to* ***sell off*** *Vornkind plastics* (a subsidiary company). BBCTV

sold on [pass Vn.pr] (*informal*) convinced that (sb/sth) is worthwhile; liking (sb/sth) very much. **o:** actor, singer, player; team; car, machine: *I'm really* ***sold on*** *this new computer!* ○ *He's completely* ***sold on*** *Lucy. You're wasting your time if you think he'll go out with you.*

sell-out/sold out [nom pass (Vn.p)] performance for which all the seats have been sold; with all the seats sold, and thus a great success. **S:** performance; concert, play, show; match, fight: *All the orchestra's Vienna concerts were* ***sell-outs***. ○ *Each of their seven home games is a virtual* ***sell-out***. OBS ○ *His London stage show was already* ***sold out***.

sell out/out of [Vp, Vpr pass] sell one's entire stock of (a particular article). **S:** shopkeeper; store. **o:** cigarettes; bread; petrol: *'I'm sorry, all the Sunday papers have gone: we've* ***sold out****.'* ○ *'We seem to have* ***sold out of*** *your size. Can you come back next week?'*

sell out (to) [Vp nom, Vp.pr, Vp.n] (*informal*) betray (one's side) (to sb). **O:** one's side, country; one's cause. **o:** enemy, opposition: [Vp] *The meeting broke up amidst cries of '****Sell-out****!'* BBCR ○ [Vp.pr] *They spoke of people who had* ***sold out to*** *the enemy.* NM ○ [Vp.pr] *The union leaders were* *accused of* **selling out to** *the employers* (or: *of a* **sell-out to** *the employers*).

sell up [Vp, Vp.n pass] sell a business, house etc to pay one's debts, or because one is moving or retiring. **O:** property; shop, factory; the family business: *We're* **selling up** *next week, so come round if there's anything you want to collect before the sale.* ○ *Before* **selling up** *their Clerkenwell place, they tried to borrow more money.* OBS

send

send about his business [Vn.pr pass] tell (sb) to stop interfering in the affairs of others, tell (sb) to mind his own business. **O:** onlooker, bystander; ghoul, busybody: *'I soon sent him packing. Soon* **sent** *him* **about his business**. *Now would you like to go and lie down for a while?'* TGLY ○ *Anybody taking too close an interest in what went on in the laboratories would soon be* **sent about his business**. ⇨ go about one's business.

send across (to) [Vn ⇆ p pass, Vn.pr pass, Vn.p.pr pass] send (sb/sth) from one side to the other of a road etc. **O:** messenger; delegate, salesman; freight, mail. **o:** (**across**) the road; the Channel; (**to**) shop, bank; France : [Vn.p] 'The evening paper hasn't come yet.' 'Oh, **send** *Michael* **across** *for it.'* ○ [Vn.pr] Reinforcements were **sent across** *the river under cover of darkness.* ○ [Vn.p.pr] The cross-Channel ferries are a quick and convenient means of **sending** *goods* **across to** *the Continent.* ⇨ get across 1, go/take across (to).

send after [Vpr, Vn.pr pass] ask (sb) to follow a person, to tell him he has left sth behind etc: *Mr Smith had left without his umbrella, so I* **sent** *one of the boys* **after** *him.* ○ *'Nobody told him to leave.* **Send after** *him and bring him back.'*

send ahead/ahead of [Vn ⇆ p pass, Vn.pr pass emph] dispatch (sb) in advance of a main party etc, to make inquiries, find lodgings etc; send (sth) so that it arrives sooner than one does oneself. **O:** patrol, scout; advance party; luggage, furniture. **o:** main force; the others, the rest: *Armoured cars were* **sent ahead of** *the main body of troops to spot and report on enemy movements.* ○ (holiday advertisement) *If you wish, we can arrange for your luggage to be* **sent** *on* **ahead** *to each of the overnight stops.* ⇨ go ahead/ahead of.

send away [Vn ⇆ p pass] make (sb) leave a place, often because he is not needed or is not welcome: *She* **sent away** *the physiotherapist who came to help her walk again.* ○ *'I wish you'd got home five minutes earlier. I had to* **send** *the milkman* **away** *without the money we owe him.'* ⇨ go away 1.

send away/off (for) [Vp, Vp.pr pass rel] post money, a coupon etc to a dealer (to obtain a special offer, free gift etc). **o:** wall chart, map; (set of) glasses, mats: (advertiser's blurb) *Have you* **sent off** *yet* **for** *your special guide to space-age exploration?* ○ *He* **sent away** *to one of the daily papers* **for** *a free fisherman's almanac.* = write away/off (for). ⇨ send for 2.

send back 1 [Vn ⇆ p pass] return (sth) to a shop or supplier, eg by post, because one is dissatisfied with it. **O:** dress, blouse; book: *'This coat is too short in one sleeve.* **Send** *it* **back** *to the shop.'*

2 [Vn ⇆ p pass] ask a waiter to take (food etc) back to the kitchen because it is unsatisfactory. **O:** soup, fish: *Don't accept poor service. If the wine is not at the right temperature,* **send** *it* **back**.

send down 1 [Vn.p pass] dismiss (sb) from a university, usu for misconduct. **O:** student, undergraduate: *Several students were* **sent down** *after incidents during the visit of a foreign Prime Minister.* ⇨ be/come down (from), go down 8.

2 [Vn.p pass] sentence (sb) to a term of imprisonment. **A:** for life, for several years; for fraud, for malicious wounding: *If he was convicted of armed robbery he could be* **sent down** *for ten years.*

send for 1 [Vpr pass, Vn.pr pass] send (sb) to fetch help etc, or (a message) to ask for help. **S:** parent, householder. **o:** police, fire brigade, doctor; help, assistance: *A doctor advises at what stage parents with ailing children should* **send for** *professional advice.* OBS ○ *'The plumber's been* **sent for**. *In the meantime help me mop up the water.'* ⇨ go for 2.

2 [Vpr pass] order (sth), usu through the post. **o:** catalogue, brochure; form; sample: *I'm going to* **send for** *that book on wild birds.* ○ *Don't delay.* **Send** *now* **for** *a free catalogue.* ⇨ send away/off (for).

send in 1 [Vn ⇆ p pass] submit (sth) to a judge or assessor, in the hope of winning a prize, being accepted etc. **S:** competitor. **O:** entry, coupon; answer, solution; manuscript, story: *Entries should be* **sent in** *to arrive by 1st August.* ○ *I shan't bother to* **send in** *the manuscript; it's sure to be rejected.*

2 [Vn ⇆ p pass] send (sth) to an official, or one's superior, to inform him or get his approval. **O:** application, claim; information; report, statement: *If you want a visa, be sure to* **send in** *your application in good time.* ○ *Situation reports were* **sent in** *three times a day, at 8am, 1pm and 6pm.* OBS

3 [Vn ⇆ p pass] dispatch (troops etc) to deal with a difficult situation. **O:** troops, armed police; bailiffs: *Mounted police were* **sent in** *to break up the demonstration.*

send off 1 [Vn ⇆ p pass] send (sth) by post; dispatch, post. **O:** letter, parcel; goods, consignment: *'Why haven't you got my letter? I* **sent** *it* **off** *last week.'* ○ *'Do make sure your application is* **sent off** *in good time.'*

2 [Vn ⇆ p pass] start (sb) moving to another place. **O:** child, husband: *Their younger daughter was* **sent off** *to stay with friends in France.* ○ *Mother always makes sure the children are* **sent off** *to school with a good breakfast inside them.*

send-off [nom (Vn.p)] (*informal*) party, or gathering at an airport etc, to bid farewell to a friend, relative etc: *'We must give old Leo a bit of a* **send-off**. *Nice little party. When we get back is best.'* ST ○ *He got a terrific* **send-off** *when he left for America.*

send off (the field) [Vn ⇆ p pass, Vn.pr pass] (*sport*) order (sb) to leave the field of play. **S:** referee. **O:** player: *'Now don't try arguing with the ref. You'll only get* **sent off**.*'* ○ *One player was* **sent off** *for a vicious late tackle on Platt.* = order off (the field).

send off (for) [Vp, Vp.pr pass rel] ⇨ send away/off (for).

send on 1 [Vn.pr pass rel] get (sb) to go somewhere to enjoy or experience (sth). **o:** holiday, vacation; tour, safari; course: *This year the school is* **sending** *a number of senior boys* **on** *an Outward Bound course.* ○ *Last year, when Tom was seriously ill,* *the firm* **sent** *him* **on** *a fortnight's convalescence.* ⇨ go on 1.

2 [Vn.p pass] ask or get (sb) to continue a journey ahead of others: *The marketing director had pressing business which kept him in Leeds, so he* **sent** *his deputy* **on** *to represent him in Edinburgh.* ○ *The damage to the truck would keep us busy for an hour, so we* **sent** *the others* **on** *to explain that we would be late back to camp.* ⇨ go on 3.

3 [Vn ⇆ p pass] dispatch (mail) after sb has left so that it reaches him at his new address; forward. **O:** mail, post; letter, bill: *'Would you be kind enough to* **send on** *any mail to my new address?'* ○ *Students are asked to leave their vacation addresses with the secretary so that examination results can be* **sent on**.

send out 1 [Vn ⇆ p pass] cause (light etc) to travel in a certain direction; radiate; emit. **S:** lamp, bulb; sun; stove; (signalling) station. **O:** light; heat; signal: *The oil-lamp* **sent out** *a gentle beam when you touched the knob.* THH ○ *Long disused antennae* **send out** *and receive all kinds of messages.* PW

2 [Vn ⇆ p pass] post or deliver to voters, possible customers etc: *We are still working on the wording of the letter we will* **send out**. IND ○ *There was never any discrepancy between the number of postal votes requested and the number of postal votes* **sent out**. G

send out (for) [Vp, Vpr, Vn ⇆ p pass, Vn.p.pr pass] ask (sb) to go from an office, shop etc (to fetch sth). **O:** secretary, messenger, office junior. **o:** newspaper; coffee, sandwiches : [Vp.pr] 'The coffee they make over the road is so much better than the foul stuff we brew up in the cupboard. Why don't we ***send out for*** *some?'* ○ [Vn.p] 'I forgot to pick up the flowers on my way in to the office. I suppose we could always **send** *Anne* **out** *to collect them?'*

send out/out of [Vn ⇆ p pass, Vn.pr pass] tell or ask (sb) to leave a place, eg as a punishment, at the start of a game etc. **O:** pupil, child. **o:** class; room, office: *'What are you doing out in the corridor, Mason?' 'Mr Naylor* **sent** *me* **out** *for throwing paper darts, sir.'* ○ *'Let's begin with a game of Hunt the Thimble, shall we? Now, who shall we* **send out of** *the room?'*

send to [Vn.pr pass rel] arrange for sb to attend (a particular school, college etc). **O:** son, daughter, ward. **o:** public school, State school; Oxford: *There was no question of* **sending** *the children* **to** *a public school. Paul disapproved, rather priggishly, of all forms of privilege in education.* ○ *Without the legacy, they wouldn't have been able to afford to* **send** *her* **to** *university.* ⇨ go to 1.

send to bed [Vn.pr pass] make (sb) go to bed eg because he is ill, as a punishment etc: *'John's been complaining of severe stomach pains all day. You'd better* **send him to bed** *and call the doctor.'* ○ *'If I get another cheep out of you two children you'll be* **sent to bed** *without any supper!'* ⇨ go to bed.

send to his death [Vn.pr pass] act in a way, whether consciously or not, that will cause sb's death. **O:** soldier, police officer; fireman, lifeboatman: *Incompetent generals* **sent** *thousands* **to a** *certain* **death** *in attacks on strongly fortified positions.* ○ *'You're looking pleased with yourself,' Beatrice said. 'Doesn't it occur to you that you may be* **sending** *a man* **to his death***?'* OMIH □ note pl forms in: *Men were* sent to their death/deaths.

send to sleep [Vn.pr pass] make (sb) fall asleep. **S:** (mother's) singing, cooing; rocking motion (of a cot, a boat); hot drink; (boring, tedious) speech, lecture; play, concert: *The gentle lapping of the waves against the side of the boat* **sent him to sleep**. ○ *If there's anything calculated to* **send** *me* **to sleep** *it's a party political broadcast on television.*

send up 1 [Vn ⇆ p pass] cause (sth) to rise. **S:** shortage, transport costs, strike; power failure, loss of oil. **O:** price, cost; temperature: *Any increase in production costs is bound to* **send** *prices* **up**. ○ *A rise in temperature will* **send up** *the pressure inside the casing.* ↔ bring down 5. ⇨ be up 1, go up 2, keep up 2, put up 4.

2 [Vn.p pass] destroy (sth), esp by fire or explosion. **S:** direct hit, salvo; bomber. **O:** building; ship; ammunition dump. **A:** in flames, in smoke; with a bang, with a roar: *A convoy of petrol lorries a mile to the rear was* **sent up** *in flames.* = blow up 4. ⇨ go up 5.

3 [Vn ⇆ p nom pass] (*informal*) imitate (sth/sb) in such a way that he/it seems ridiculous; satirize. **S:** cartoonist, singer, comedian. **O:** society, the monarchy; pop-singer, hippy: *In a recent satirical sketch they* **send up** *rich young women who work for charity appeals* (or: *do a* **send-up** *of rich young women* etc). ○ *'We'd never tell the other boys which school we went to because we'd have been* **sent up** *rotten* (ie unmercifully).' ST ○ *His amusement turned to delight when those* **send-up** *songs rocketed into the hit-parade.* H □ nom form may modify a noun, as shown.

send up the wall [Vn.pr pass] (*informal*) annoy (sb) unbearably; infuriate. **S:** noise, commotion; chatter, quarrelling: *'How much longer are the builders going to be blasting away with that damned drill? It's enough to* **send** *you* **up the wall***!'* = drive round the bend/up the wall. ⇨ go up the wall.

send up (to) [Vn.p pass, Vn.p.pr pass rel] cause (sb) to go to a university, or to London from the provinces, or towards the north: *Tom Trollope had ... been* **sent up to** *Oxford.* TRO ○ *We* **sent** *the children* **up to** *Leeds to stay with my sister.* ⇨ be up 2, come up 2,3, go up (to).

sentence

sentence (to) [Vn ⇆ p pass rel] (*legal*) declare that (sb) is to have (a certain punishment). **S:** court; judge, magistrate. **o:** six months, ten years; life (imprisonment); death: *The judge* **sentenced** *him* **to** *ten years' hard labour.* ○ *Those convicted of murder are no longer* **sentenced to** *death.*

separate

separate (off) (from) [Vn ⇆ p pass, Vn.pr pass emph rel, Vn.p.pr pass emph rel] set (one thing) apart (from another); put a barrier between persons or things. **O:** wheat; group, class; part, fraction; space. **o:** chaff; the main body; the whole; the total area: [Vn.p] *'See to it that the trouble-makers are* **separated off** *and given something special to do.'* ○ [Vn.pr] *He sat before the fire ...* **separating** *the grain* **from** *the husks.* KLT ○ [Vn.p.pr] *Two huts at the end of the camp were* **separated off from** *the rest by a wire fence.* = divide from 1.

separate out [Vp, Vn ⇆ p pass] (cause things to) become distinct from each other. **S** [Vp], **O** [Vn.p]: oil and water; cream and milk; elements, strands: (note in recipe) *This pudding* ***separates out*** *in the cooking into a custard layer with a sponge topping* (cf *The custard layer and the sponge topping* ***separate out***). ○ *I had trouble in* ***separating out*** *the two lengths of rope.*

serve

serve as/for [Vpr, Vn.pr] be suitable or useful (to sb) for (a particular purpose). **S:** stick, knife; weakness, absence. **o:** toothbrush, screwdriver; excuse, pretext: *His poor teaching record could* ***serve as*** *an excuse to get rid of him.* ○ *A hollowed-out stick* ***served*** *him* ***as*** *a spoon and a flat shell* ***as*** *a plate.* ○ *An old cardboard box* ***served for*** *a cat basket.* = do (as/for).

serve on 1 [Vpr emph rel] be a member of (sth). **S:** administrator, academic, councillor, judge. **o:** committee, board, tribunal: *Sir John* ***serves on*** *the boards of several companies.*

2 [Vn.pr pass emph rel] (*legal*) deliver (a legal document) to (sb). **O:** ⚠ a writ, summons, notice (to appear, to quit), warrant: *A summons was* ***served on*** *him to appear at the next Quarter Sessions.* ○ *They've* ***served*** *a writ* ***on*** *him* (or: *They've* ***served*** *him* ***with*** *a writ*).

serve under [Vpr emph rel] be a member of a force, organization etc under (the leadership of sb). **o:** (famous) leader, general, minister: *He's not the sort of man I'd like to* ***serve under***. ○ *There was a rumour that Forrest,* ***under*** *whose command we were* ***serving*** *at the time, was to be replaced by a younger general from England.*

serve up 1 [Vp, Vn ⇆ p pass] offer (food) to sb. **O:** soup, pasta, pudding: *Mother was just* ***serving up*** *the Sunday lunch as I walked in.* = dish up 1.

2 [Vn ⇆ p pass] offer (sth) to sb as entertainment etc. **O:** the same mixture (as before); nonsense, rubbish, tripe: *The new television networks* ***serve up*** *exactly the same diet of game shows, police serials and soap operas as the old ones.*

serve with [Vn.pr pass] ⇨ serve on 2.

set

set about 1 [Vpr] tackle (a task) purposefully and energetically. **o:** job, task; preparing, buying, selling: *We then* ***set about*** *the job of putting the animals into their travelling boxes.* DF ○ *How could she* ***set about*** *finding him when she was lying helpless in bed?* DC ⇨ go about 3.

2 [Vpr pass] (*informal*) attack (sb) with the fists or verbally: *'I'd* ***set about*** *them with this custard-ladle if we have any trouble,' said Mrs Fountain.* TT ○ *A gang of Manchester boys* ***set about*** *some of the Leeds supporters.*

set oneself above [Vn.pr] behave as though one is not governed by (the same laws, conventions etc as other people). **o:** law, convention, ordinary morality: *We have had a number of cases in which scientists have* ***set*** *themselves* ***above*** *the law and* ***above*** *public interest.* TBC

set against 1 [Vn.pr pass] cause people who may be related, or close friends, to become enemies or rivals. **S:** war, politics, business; ambition, greed. **O:** husband, brother. **o:** wife, brother: *Competing for the same well-paid job can* ***set*** *friend* ***against*** *friend.* ○ *In France, the Dreyfus Affair divided many families,* ***setting*** *father* ***against*** *son and brother* ***against*** *brother.*

2 [Vn.pr pass emph rel] balance or match (one thing) (against sth that has already been suggested). **O:** evidence, factor, consideration; cost, saving, economy. **o:** argument, case; expense, wastage: *I know it's dearer to buy than to rent a house, but you have to* ***set against*** *cost the solid benefits of home ownership.* ○ ***Against*** *the initial cost of buying a new car, you can* ***set*** *the considerable saving, in the first few years, on repairs and servicing.*

set one's face against [Vn.pr pass] oppose (sth) firmly. **o:** increased taxation, compulsory redundancies, cuts in defence spending: *Successive American Administrations have* ***set their face against*** *an increase in the gold price.* L ○ *Jane* ***sets her face against*** *the tension-forming, I-will-win attitude in sport as in everything else.* OBS □ note that, after a plural Subject, set their face or faces against are both possible.

set apart (for) [Vn ⇆ p pass, Vn.p.pr pass] reserve (sth) for a particular use. **O:** hour, day; period; building, room. **o:** work, recreation; visitors, games: *Several bedrooms were* ***set apart for*** *guests.* ○ *One area of the park was* ***set apart for*** *family picnics.* □ usu passive.

set apart (from) [Vn.p pass, Vn.p.pr pass emph rel] make (sb/sth) special or unusual. **S:** family, birth; distinction, (noble) character; intelligence, talent. **o:** others, ordinary people, the normal run of people: *His extraordinary talent* ***sets*** *him* ***apart from*** *other trumpet players of his generation.* ○ *For reasons he could not explain he was made to feel different,* ***set apart****,* ***from*** *the other boys.*

set aside 1 [Vn ⇆ p pass] place (sth) to one side. **O:** book, newspaper; task; knitting, sewing: *Peter* ***set aside*** *the papers he was marking and reached for his cigarettes and matches.* ○ *Work on the library extension had to be* ***set aside*** *while labour was diverted to more urgent projects.* = lay aside 1, put aside 1.

2 [Vn ⇆ p pass] (*legal*) cancel, annul, quash (a decision). **S:** higher court, court of appeal. **O:** decision, verdict, judgment: *The judge's verdict was quashed and their prison sentences* ***set aside***. BBCTV ○ (interview with trade union leader) *'There is a clause which says the Minister can* ***set aside*** *the decision of the Pay Board.'* BBCTV

3 [Vn ⇆ p pass] (*formal*) stop treating (sth) as important; suspend. **O:** difference; hostility, bitterness, strife; protocol: *In his dealings with his new boss, he tried to* ***set aside*** *his instinctive mistrust of the man.* ○ *In these discussions, all formality was* ***set aside***. = dispense with 2, put aside 4, put on one side 3.

4 [Vn ⇆ p pass] save (sth) for spending or use later. **O:** food, money; supplies, stores. **A:** to eat later; for an emergency, for use later: *We had to* ***set*** *some of the money* ***aside*** *to pay our next tax bill.* ○ *Some of the stores would have to be* ***set aside*** *for a possible emergency.* = put aside 2, put on one side 1.

5 [Vn ⇆ p pass] choose (sth) for a particular purpose; reserve, earmark. **O:** the time, moment; a particular day: *She tried to* ***set aside*** *a few minutes each day for her exercises.* ○ *This was the day* ***set aside*** *for his execution.* WI

set one's cap at [Vn.pr] (*dated*) (esp of a woman) try to interest (sb) sexually, esp with the aim of forming a lasting relationship. **o:** eligible bachelor, unattached male, new boss: *'She'll be jealous of you, you know, jealous of the good turns you've done me. She'll* **set her cap at** *you, I dare say.'* ⇨ get off with.

set sb's mind at ease/rest [Vn.pr pass] lessen or remove sb's anxieties about sth/sb. **S:** adviser; doctor, solicitor, tutor: *Robert could become a fashionable money-making artist, just another version of Ned, only more repulsive because of his greater pretensions. That ought to* **set Ned's mind at ease**. CON ○ *The specialist said Mrs Barnes need have no misgivings about her daughter's progress. In fact he could* **set her mind** *completely* **at rest**: *the new treatment was a total success.* □ note pl form in: *Let me* **set your minds at rest**.

set back 1 [Vn ⇆ p nom pass] hinder the progress of (sth), or reverse it by a certain amount. **O:** programme; progress, advance, development. **A:** (six) months, (three) weeks, (several) days: *Difficulties in raising money have* **set back** *our building programme.* ○ *Shortage of the right materials has* **set** *us* **back** (cf *We have suffered a* **setback** *because of the shortage* etc). ○ *Two years later, at the mid-term elections, his party suffered a very serious* **setback**. OBS ○ *Work on the new theatre has been* **set back** *three months.*
2 [Vn.p pass] (*informal*) cost (sb) a certain amount. **S:** house, car; party, celebration. **A:** quite a bit, a fair bit; £50, $200: *Their daughter's wedding must have* **set** *them* **back** *a bit.* ○ *A basic course costs . . . £318, and going through the entire curriculum can* **set** *the student* **back** *some £1500.* NS = knock back 2.
3 [Vn ⇆ p pass] build or position (sth) some distance away from a road etc. **O:** house, stables, greenhouse. **A:** some way, a fair distance; 100 yards: *They've* **set** *the workshops well* **back**, *out of sight of the house.* ○ *The house is* **set back** *some distance from the main road.* □ usu passive.

set great etc store by/on [Vn.pr pass emph rel] regard (sth) as having a particular value or importance. **adj:** great, little; much, more, less, no. **o:** (outward) show, manner, appearance, dress; efficiency, competence, originality; kindness, tolerance: *Martin* **set more store by** *official honours than I did.* NM ○ *It is odd that one so susceptible to the clash and glare of the theatre should* **set so much store by** *personal privacy.* RT ○ *'My wife, too,* **sets great store on** *the boys being at home.'* ASA = attach to 2.

set down 1 [Vn ⇆ p pass] allow (sb) to alight from a vehicle. **O:** passenger, fare: *'Would you mind* **setting** *me* **down** *at the next corner?'* ○ *The country buses will stop more or less anywhere to* **set down** *and pick up passengers.* ↔ pick up 4. ⇨ put down 4.
2 [Vn ⇆ p pass] record (sth) on paper. **O:** idea, thought, reflection: *I'll* **set down** *one or two points while they are fresh in my mind.* = note down, write down. ⇨ be down 3, get down 4, go down 9, put down 11, take down 3.
3 [Vp.n pass] (*legal*) choose, name (a day when a case is to be heard). **O:** day, date; trial, hearing: *The day* **set down** *for the trial has still to be announced.* ○ *'You knew the hearing was* **set down** *for today.'* BBCTV
4 [Vp.n pass] (*formal*) indicate (sth) as a law or requirement. **O:** law, rule, requirement; standard, norm: *The regulations governing postgraduate courses are* **set down** *in the University Calendar.* ○ *Any military court has to follow certain procedures, as* **set down** *in Queen's Regulations.* = lay down 2.

set down as [Vn.p.pr pass] consider (sb) to be a certain type of person, a member of a particular profession etc. **o:** sea captain, retired officer; rather intellectual, somewhat narrow: *Anyone would have* **set** *her* **down as** *an ordinary middle-class housewife.* ○ *People who trained in that department were* **set down as** *worthy but rather dull.* = put down as 2.

set sail (for) [Vn.pr rel] (*nautical*) begin a journey by sea (to a certain place). **o:** America, France; New York, Lagos: *The boat leaves Liverpool on the fifteenth, but before we* **set sail** *I have to spend a few days in Scotland.* ○ *My speculations were suddenly interrupted by recalling that Tom had postponed his* **setting sail for** *the land of liberty.* SPL

set the stage (for) [Vn.pr pass emph rel] get everything ready for (some event). **S:** government, minister; designer, inventor, planner. **o:** development, expansion; introduction, provision; discussion, argument, debate: *He was associated with the establishment of the blood transfusion service in the middle East, and* **set the stage for** *the application of chemotherapy to the wounded soldier as soon after wounding as possible.* T ○ *When the Bill came up for a second reading at the end of March* **the stage** *was* **set for** *a first-class row — which duly materialized.* MFM = prepare (for).

set forth 1 [Vp] (*formal*) leave home, base etc at the start of an expedition, campaign etc: *David* **set forth** *to do battle with Goliath.* ○ *We* **set forth** *on the last stage of our climb.* □ set out (on) is more usual.
2 [Vp.n pass] (*formal*) declare or explain (sth) clearly and systematically. **S:** document, manifesto; secretary, accountant. **O:** programme, aim, policy; figure, cost: *The Prime Minister* **set forth** *the aims of his government in a speech to party workers.* ○ *These figures are more clearly* **set forth** *in tabular form.* PL = set out 3.

set in 1 [Vp] begin and seem likely to continue; gain a hold and seem likely to spread. **S:** winter, autumn; freeze, thaw; decay, gangrene; doubt, depression: *The cold weather had* **set in**. HD ○ *The rails that remained looked as if the dry-rot had* **set in**. CON
2 [pass (Vn.pr)] having fixed, established ways of behaving, reacting etc. **o:** one's behaviour; one's habits, ways, customs; a way, method (of doing sth); one's reactions, responses: *I think I expected her to refuse. I just thought of her as* **set in** *her ways, and this sort of thing certainly wasn't among her habits.* CON ○ (He) *had got so* **set in** *this habit of drinking in the Grapes* (a public house) *every lunch-time that he would have been lost without it.* CON □ also used after *appear, be, become, seem* or after a noun.

set foot in [Vn.pr rel] enter, arrive in (a place). **o:** the place; France; her house: *She had never* **set foot in** *a place as grand as this before.* SML ○ *No sooner had Isabel* **set foot in** *the house than she felt her mother's influence seeping into her.* PW ○ *I had hardly* **set foot in** *England before somebody or other exclaimed, 'Oh, but you don't look in the least like your books!'* AH □ often in a subordinate clause introduced by *(from) the moment, as soon as, no sooner had she ... than, he had hardly ... before.*

set in motion [Vn.pr pass] make (sth) begin to move; initiate. **O:** procession, parade; avalanche; campaign, invasion; debate, meeting: *With efficient communications, armies at some distance from each other can be* **set in motion** *at the same time.* ○ *Suppose the Soviets lost control of the events they had* **set in motion**? OBS ○ *There followed a wave of selling on the Stock Market,* **set in motion** *by the rumour that the currency was to be devalued.*

set one's (own) house in order [Vn.pr] restore one's business, one's family life etc, to a proper state by removing disharmony, abuses etc: *People in the Finance Department should* **set their own house in order** *before venturing to criticize us.* ○ *The Press must* **set its own house in order** *before the ultimate disaster of having order imposed upon it.* SC □ often introduced by should/ought to/must and used as a recommendation to do sth; note pl form in: *They must* set their own houses in order. = put one's (own) house in order.

the rot set in [Vp] (*informal*) (of a decline or deterioration) begin: (cricket) *Smith made a few runs at number six and then* **the rot** *really* **set in** (ie wickets fell cheaply). ○ *Since Jones was made Managing Director,* **the rot** *has definitely* **set in**.

set off 1 [Vn ⇆ p pass] cause (sth) to explode. **O:** bomb, mine; charge, explosive: *The slightest spark can* **set off** *the explosive stored here.* ○ *All the beautiful seafront houses ... disintegrated as thousands of mines were* **set off**. G = spark off 1, touch off 1. ⇨ go off 5, let off 4.

2 [Vp.n pass] cause (sth) to happen or develop; prompt, stimulate. **S:** take-over, coup; news, report; discovery, invention. **O:** demonstration, rioting; rumours, speculation; investment, developments: *The threatened action by miners may* **set off** *sympathy strikes by transport workers.* ○ *The further decline of the pound as reported today has* **set off** *a fresh wave of selling in the City.* = spark off 2, touch off 2, trigger off.

3 [Vn ⇆ p pass] make (sth) appear more attractive by contrast; enhance. **S:** hair, lips; garden; carpet. **O:** complexion, pale skin; brick, stone; wall, curtain: *The outfit* **set off** *her dark red hair.* PP ○ *The formal beauty of the groves was* **set off** *by the perfection of the grey stonework.* HD

set off (against) [Vn ⇆ p pass, Vn.p.pr pass emph rel] balance or match (one thing) (against another). **O:** loss, expenditure; quick temper, shyness. **o:** (salary) increase, award; generosity, determination: *The withdrawals from your account can be* **set off** *by a refund of income tax.* ○ *You can* **set** *the expenses* **off against** *a probable increase in salary.* ○ *'I agree he can be difficult. But you have to* **set off against** *that his great kindness to the family when we really needed support.'* = set against 2.

set off (on) 1 [Vp, Vp.pr rel] start to move in a purposeful way; begin a journey. **S:** runner, cyclist, explorer. **o:** race, journey; lap, stage: *The cars* **set off** *in a cloud of dust.* BM ○ *The police* **set off** *in hot pursuit.* BB ○ *Look, education is like* **setting off on** *an expedition into the jungle.* FFE = set out (on), start out (on). ⇨ be off 3, get off 3.

2 [Vn.p pass, Vn.p.pr pass] start (sb) telling stories, laughing etc. **S:** remark, joke; reminiscence. **o:** tale, account: *That* **set** *all of them* **off** *laughing again.* EM ○ *The look on his face is enough to* **set** *you* **off**! ○ *'Don't say anything, John. You'll only* **set** *him* **off on** *one of his interminable war stories.'* = start off (on) 2. ⇨ be off (on).

set on 1 [Vpr pass] attack (sb) physically. **S:** gang, bully, tough: *I saw him* **set on** *a bloke once for no more than fixing him in a funny way with his eyes.* LLDR ○ *He was* **set on** *and beaten up on his way home from an evening class.*

2 [Vn.pr pass] cause (sb/sth) to make a physical attack on (sb). **O:** guard; dog: *We were always afraid he'd* **set** *that vicious dog* **on** *us.*

set eyes on [Vn.pr pass(o) rel] see (sb/sth). **o:** the man; each other; the place, his (new) home: *I was perfectly certain I had never* **set eyes on** *her before.* TST ○ *As soon as we* **set eyes on** *the place, we knew we would love it.* ○ *It seemed to me as if we'd done nothing but row and suffer like this from the moment we* **set eyes on** *each other.* LLDR □ often in a subordinate clause of time introduced by: *(from) the moment, as soon as, no sooner had he ... than, he had hardly ... before.* = lay eyes on.

set on his/its feet [Vn.pr pass] help (sb/sth) to be soundly established or to return to a sound state, prosperity etc. **S:** rest, holiday; doctor; loan, advance; bank: *You are aware of how much help you need to* **set** *you* **on your feet**. WI ○ *He became chairman of the club, and his business sense helped* **set** *it* **on its feet**. ○ *More than anything, the industry needs the creation of a highly-skilled workforce to* **set** *it back* **on its feet**. = put (back) on his/its feet.

set on fire [Vn.pr pass] cause (sth) to burn; set alight. **S:** tourist, picnicker; spark, heat; fire bomb: *'How many times have I got to warn you against* **setting** *the place* **on fire**?' HD ○ *The blaze was fanned by a stiff breeze and in a short time all the farm outbuildings were* **set on fire**. □ it is often things (not persons) which set sth on fire; if the action is caused by a person, it tends not to be a deliberate action: *'Stop emptying your pipe into the wastepaper basket: you'll* **set** *the house* **on fire**!' ⇨ set fire/light to.

set great etc store on [Vn.pr pass emph rel] ⇨ set great etc store by/on.

set one's heart on [Vn.pr pass emph rel] long deeply, with all one's heart, to do or achieve (sth). **S:** student; scientist; athlete. **o:** career, prize; discovery, achievement; record: *She was mad on show-jumping;* **her heart** *was* **set on** *horses.* DBM ○ *Isabel, Jeremy, and Janice would enjoy material benefits too, and Isabel,* **whose heart** *was* **set on** *bringing this about, would be appeased.* PW ○ *To compete at international level — this was the goal* **on** *which he'd* **set his heart**. □ note pl form: set their hearts on.

set the seal on [Vn.pr pass emph rel] mark in some appropriate way the high or final point of (a career etc). **S:** ceremony; formal reception, investiture (with a medal or honour); election, admission (to a society); marriage. **o:** career, life's work; progress, recovery: *Sir Francis Chichester's knighthood* **set the** *final* **seal on** *the remarkable career of this airman and lone yachtsman.* ○ *'Once a man marries a girl like you, I find it impossible to think of him as a fellow citizen. He's* **set the seal on** *his success today.'* CON

set one's sights on [Vn.pr pass emph rel] have (sth) as one's goal or objective. **o:** job, career; championship, gold medal; breaking the record, winning the geography prize: *It was not that Virginia had a consuming passion to work on a women's magazine. She had* **set her sights on** *it because there was a chance for her in this place.* AITC ○ ***John's sights*** *were* **set on** *acquiring the controlling interest in a group of stores.*

set sb's/the teeth on edge [Vn.pr pass] cause an unpleasant sensation in the teeth, as when one scrapes a fingernail on metal; annoy, irritate. **S:** the scrape of chalk on a blackboard; voice, accent; conversation, views: *'The man I killed — I know him. He was Russian and he was very thin. I scraped the bone when I pushed the steel in. It* **set my teeth on edge**.*'* OMIH ○ *'You say things that* **set these people's teeth on edge**. *You make them feel you're getting at them.'* SML

set the Thames on fire [Vn.pr] (*informal*) arouse considerable excitement; achieve a remarkable success. **S:** actor, singer, conductor; manager, executive: *She was a lady who once* **set** *the whole of the literary world (if not* **the Thames**) **on fire** (ie who achieved a limited, not a spectacular, success). MM ○ *'Take Jeffries. You wouldn't say he's the kind to* **set the Thames on fire**, *now would you?'* ⇨ next entry

set the world on fire [Vn.pr pass] arouse great interest and excitement in a place or among a group of people. **S:** actor, singer, writer; performance, appearance: *'Tomorrow is another day. Don't let's try to* **set the world on fire** *tonight.'* AITC ○ *She was a lady who once* **set the** *whole of the literary* **world** *(if not the Thames)* **on fire**. MM ○ *It is hard to see last week's statement* **setting the world on fire**. L ⇨ previous entry

set out 1 [Vp] begin work with the intention of achieving a particular goal. **Inf:** to climb Mt Everest, to win support for his scheme: *The Mexican peasant* **sets out** *to burn an acre of woodland in order to plant his maize.* HAH ○ *When I really* **set out** *to take care of somebody, I usually do the job properly.* TOH □ always followed by an inf.

2 [Vn ⇆ p pass adj] arrange (items) on a table, board etc. **O:** wares, goods; stall: *Michael* **set out** *the pieces on the chessboard.* ○ *The ties were attractively* **set out** *to draw in the customers.* = lay out 1.

3 [Vn ⇆ p pass adj] present (ideas etc) in an orderly manner. **O:** work; essay, dissertation; calculations, records: *The figures were clearly* **set out** *on a piece of squared paper.* ○ *I've seldom seen such a well* **set-out** *piece of work from a student.* = lay out 2.

4 [Vn ⇆ p pass adj] declare, state (sth). **S:** chairman, secretary; delegate; paper. **O:** conditions, terms; objection, criticism: *The staff side have already* **set out** *the safeguards which they think should be observed.* T ○ *Recent changes in personal taxation are* **set out** *in the enclosed booklet.*

set out (on) [Vp, Vp.pr rel] start to move in a purposeful way; begin a journey. **S:** traveller; convoy, procession. **o:** trip, tour; stage, circuit: *Vanity made you* **set out** *after the King, when you didn't care for him.* WI ○ *The reporters* **set out** *in high spirits.* TBC ○ *This morning, competitors* **set out on** *the last stage of the round-Britain cycle race.* = set off (on) 1, start out (on). ⇨ get off 3.

set to 1 [Vp] begin doing sth vigorously: *He is the fastest worker and* **sets to** *straight away, not stopping until his station is ready.* TK ○ *She* **set to** *to do all the housework.* UL ○ *The children* **set to** *and demolished the whole cake.* = go to work (on).

2 [Vp nom] (*dated*) begin to fight or argue. **S:** boxers; politicians: *When those two fellows* **set to** *(or: have a* **set-to**), *the fur will really fly.* ○ *What began as a mild discussion developed into a regular* **set-to**.

set fire/light to [Vn.pr pass(o) rel] apply a flame to (sth) to burn it. **S:** gardener; arsonist; bomb, explosive device. **o:** rubbish, dried leaves, wastepaper; house, factory; store, dump (of food); one's clothes: *The Dutch* **set fire to** *all their military installations.* TO ○ *In the retreat, wooden houses were* **set light to** *and stone buildings destroyed by explosives.* □ a person or a thing (hot ash, an incendiary bomb) may set fire/light to sth; the action may be deliberate or accidental; cf: *John* **set fire to** *the papers. Hot ash from John's pipe* **set fire to** *the papers.* ⇨ set on fire.

set one's mind to [Vn.pr pass] give one's full attention to (sth). **o:** task, job; finishing on time, repairing the damage: *JO: I can do anything when I* **set my mind to** *it.* TOH ○ *'Now just you* **set your mind to** *meeting these orders on time.'* = put one's mind to.

set to work [Vpr] begin working with a purpose. **A:** clearing a path, cleaning the swimming-pool; to make a cage, to remove the blockage: *After breakfast we* **set to work** *and made a cage for the armadillo.* DF ○ *The floor was so encumbered with objects that I had to* **set to work** *to clear myself a space.* UTN

set the world to rights [Vn.pr] discuss, argue about, important problems, perhaps in the belief that by doing so they will be solved. **S:** armchair critic, self-styled expert: *An intense-looking group had gathered at one end of the bar,* **setting the world to rights**, *no doubt.* ○ *'Do come round some time and talk about old times and,' she giggled slightly, '***set the world to rights** *again.'* HAHA

set up 1 [Vn ⇆ p pass adj] place (sth) in an upright position; erect. **O:** stall; mounting, tripod; telescope, range-finder; post, flag: *I* **set** *the camera* **up** *in a small patch of shade.* DF ○ *Nearby, he or one of his family* **set up** *an imposing Celtic cross.* SD

2 [Vp.n pass] establish, organize (sth). **S:** government, trades union, board of directors. **O:** office, centre; committee, commission; inquiry, investigation: *The Minister of Commerce* **set up** *an emergency committee today to ensure the maintenance of bread supplies.* OBS ○ *Back at the Heseltine country manor, his wife and three children act as campaign staff, filtering calls and* **setting up** *interviews.* OBS ○ *An operations room was* **set up** *in the Home Office with teleprinter links and weather charts.* OBS ⇨ set-up.

3 [Vp.n pass] begin to shout, protest etc, loudly. **S:** crowd; audience, class. **O:** ⚠ commotion, caterwauling, din: *As soon as he appeared on stage the crowd* **set up** *such a commotion that the show had to be stopped.*

4 [Vp.n pass] cause, produce (sth). **S:** diet, habit; climate. **O:** infection; swelling, rash: *Smoking* **sets up** *an irritation in the throat and bronchial passages.* ○ *The doctor has no idea how the condition was first* **set up**.

5 [Vp.n pass] (*sport*) achieve a new record speed, time, distance etc in a sporting event. **O:** ⚠ a record, a time (of 2hrs 8min 33.6 sec): *Stewart* **set up** *a new Commonwealth Games record in the 10 000 metres.*

6 [Vn.p nom pass] (*informal*) prepare (sb) carefully so that he can be tricked, swindled etc. **O:** partner, pal; sucker, punter: *'Have you noticed how pleasant Bill is being at the moment? I'm sure he's* **setting** *us* **up**.' ○ *'This is the* **set-up**. *Mabel finds some rich sucker who's interested in making a little easy money ....'*

set-up [nom (Vn.p)] organization, structuring of a business, government department, household etc: *The* **set-up** *in the business was far too hierarchical.* THH ○ *It took him some time to find out what the* **set-up** *was at head office.* ○ *By all accounts, this* **set-up** *has functioned with superbly improvised efficiency.* OBS ⇨ set up 2.

set up shop [Vp.n] start running a shop, large store, agency etc; begin practising a particular trade or profession: *Ackroyd* **set up shop** *as a retail tobacconist in the High Street.* ○ *Then eventually he* **set up shop** *as a freelance photographer.* ⇨ set up (in). ⇨ next entry

set up (as) 1 [Vp, Vp.pr, Vn ⇆ p pass, Vn.p.pr pass] establish (oneself/sb) in a business or trade. **O:** himself etc; her husband, his daughter. **o:** grocer, baker; locksmith, innkeeper: [Vp, Vp.pr] *His father moved to London and* **set up** *at the 'Golden Lion'* (ie **as** *an innkeeper*). ○ [Vn.p.pr] *There was enough money left to* **set** *the youngest boy* **up as** *a photographer.* ⇨ set up (in). ⇨ previous entry

2 [Vp, Vp.pr, Vn.p pass, Vn.p.pr pass] consider, reckon (oneself/sb) to be special or superior in some way. **O:** himself etc; his wife, her boss. **o:** authority, scholar; superior, something special : [Vp.pr] I didn't want to ***set up as*** *better than anyone else.* NM ○ [Vn.p.pr] Who was I to ***set*** *myself* ***up as*** *some sort of political expert?* OBS □ set up *to be* may be used instead of set up as: *He's not the great expert he* **sets** *himself* **up as** (or: **sets** *himself* **up** *to be*).

set up (in) [Vp, Vp.pr, Vn ⇆ p pass, Vn.p.pr pass rel] make it possible for (oneself/sb) to start a business, buy a house etc, by providing the money. **O:** himself etc; wife, brother; mistress. **o:** business, shop; flat, house: [Vp.pr] *In fact, few people do* **set up in** *hardware* (ie ironmongers' shops) *from scratch; they buy existing businesses or inherit them.* T ○ [Vn.p] *Perhaps he could take a flat for her in Downhaven, and* **set** *her* **up** *there.* PW ○ [Vn.p] *If I'm lucky enough to find a rich widow I shall be* **set up** *for the rest of my life!* ○ [Vn.p.pr] *One could do some things which otherwise could not be thought of, like* **setting up** *an unmarried daughter* **in** *a shop.* UL ⇨ set up (as) 1, set up shop.

set up house (together) [Vp.n] (*formal*) move into a house usu with the aim of remaining there for some time; begin to live together as man and wife, whether married or not: *He decided to settle in England,* **setting up house** *in London at Carlton Terrace.* NAP ○ *Military wives were not to be in the same area as their husbands, ie they were not to* **set up house together**. MFM

settle

settle back [Vp] lean comfortably back in one's chair: *The lights dimmed, the curtain went up, and we* **settled back** *to enjoy the play.* ○ *'Now, Mother, you're not to help with any of the housework. Just* **settle back** *in your armchair and read a magazine.'*

settle down 1 [Vp] grow less intense; subside, lessen. **S:** noise, hubbub; excitement, panic: *Don't come back for a day or two until the noise and commotion have* **settled down**.

2 [Vp, Vn.p pass] (cause sb/sth to) become calm and peaceful. **S** [Vp], **O** [Vn.p]**:** guest, child, patient; house, place; things: *It was two days after the attack. For the moment, things had* **settled down**. SD ○ *The baby seemed fractious and restless in her first weeks, but eventually she* **settled down**. ○ *'Go away a minute while I try to* **settle** *Mary* **down**.'

3 [Vp] seat oneself comfortably, usu for some quiet, prolonged activity. **A:** to discuss the match, to mend the chair; to a quiet read: *Then they came back to their positions and* **settled down** *to watch again.* TO ○ *We* **settled down** *to a quiet discussion of English slang.* EM

4 [Vp, Vn.p pass] (help sb to) marry, and begin the routine, stable life usu associated with marriage: *'He isn't married, you know. I don't know why, but writers often don't* **settle down** *like other people.'* PW ○ *He has no intention of* **settling down** *yet.* ○ *'I'll be the happiest man in Her Majesty's kingdom ... to see my girl* **settled down** *with the fellow of her choice.'* AITC

5 [Vp] establish oneself in a permanent job. **A:** in a steady job; as a schoolteacher; to being a mechanic: *Before you* **settle down** *to being an honest electrician, consider this offer.* EHOW ○ *He's a man whose one aim is to* **settle down** *in a safe job.* CON

settle for [Vpr emph rel] (be ready to) accept sth simple, undemanding, unrewarding etc, because one has modest tastes, or is lacking in ambition etc. **o:** the simple life, second best; low-paid work, a routine job; plain fare : *SAM: Don't* **settle for** *second best like your mother and I did. Marry a girl who shares your interests.* HSG ○ *'I'm not going to get the top price for these lambs; I'll just have to* **settle for** *whatever I can get.'*

settle in/into [Vp, Vpr rel, Vn.p pass, Vn.pr pass rel] (cause sb to) move into a new place and become comfortable or at home there. **S** [Vp, Vpr], **O** [Vn.p, Vn.pr]**:** family, child; pupil, student. **o:** district, area; house, flat; school : [Vp] 'We're still a bit disorganized after the move, but do come and see us when we've ***settled in***.' ○ [Vn.pr] We'd hardly ***settled*** *the children* ***into*** *their new school when we were posted to another district and had to uproot them again.*

settle on 1 [Vpr pass rel] decide or agree to use, take, buy etc (sth). **o:** date, rendezvous; meeting;

house, car: *After some discussion we* ***settled on*** *a date in early July.* ○ *'Now that the meeting-place has been* ***settled on****, can we talk about the agenda?'* = decide on.

2 [Vn.pr pass emph rel] give or leave (money etc) under the terms of a will etc. **O:** sum, amount; estate, fortune. **o:** wife, child: *The greater part of his fortune was* ***settled on*** *his three sons.* ○ *It ought to have been enough to* ***settle*** *a lump sum* ***on*** *her, even if that might have meant mortgaging the place.* WI

settle up (with) [Vp, Vp.pr pass] pay the money one owes before leaving a hotel, restaurant etc. **o:** manager; waiter, porter, doorman: *'I'm tired of this place: let's* ***settle up*** *and go.'* ○ *'I'm short of cash. Have you enough to* ***settle up with*** *the waiter?'* = square up (with).

settle accounts etc (with) [Vn.pr pass] punish (sb) for an injury one has suffered; get even with. **O:** ⚠ accounts, (old) scores; one's/an account, one's/a score: *He had several* ***scores*** *to* ***settle*** *in Singapore, and in Great Yarmouth, where he had also plied his dangerous trade.* NS ○ *'I hear Steve's back in town. It's just as well: I've got a* ***score*** *to* ***settle with*** *him.'* = square one's account/accounts with 2.

sew

sew down [Vn ⇆ p pass adj] using needle and thread, fasten to a surface (sth which is already partly attached to it). **O:** pocket, flap, lapel: *The flaps of his jacket pockets were* ***sewn down*** *so that they did not crease or wrinkle.*

sew on/onto [Vn ⇆ p pass, Vn.pr pass rel] attach (accessories etc) to a garment with needle and thread. **O:** button, zip-fastener; pocket, sleeve. **o:** coat, trousers; suit: *'The button has broken. Will you* ***sew*** *me a new one* ***on****?'* ○ *Medal ribbons are usually* ***sewn onto*** *a uniform above the top left pocket of the jacket.* □ note the Indirect Object (*me*) in the first example.

sew up 1 [Vn ⇆ p pass adj] seal or close (an opening) by drawing the edges together with thread etc. **O:** cut, slit; wound, incision: *The cut in his finger was* ***sewn up*** *with a piece of catgut.* = stitch up 1.

2 [Vn ⇆ p pass] (*informal*) organize an area etc, esp for purposes of trade. **S:** salesman, agent. **O:** region, district; market, trade: *Give me a good assistant and I'll have the area* ***sewn up*** *for you inside six months.* ○ *Superficially, the fat, glossy, advert-packed computer magazines would seem to have the market* ***sewn up****.* G □ usu passive.

3 [Vp.n pass] (*informal*) arrange (sth) so that the result is favourable. **O:** deal, contract; ballot, election: *We had time to* ***sew up*** *another deal before catching our plane back.* ○ *The contract was* ***sewn up*** *over drinks in the hotel bar.* □ usu passive. = tie up 2.

shackle

shackle with [Vn.pr pass rel] impose some control or check on (oneself/sb), so that he is not free to act. **O:** citizen, householder; trader, manufacturer. **o:** taxation, mortgage; control, regulation: *He's a bit young to* ***shackle*** *himself* ***with*** *the responsibilities of a family.* ○ *Family doctors are anxious to provide a proper service for their patients, but they can't give them the attention they need if they're* ***shackled with*** *paperwork.*

shade

shade (off) into [Vpr, Vp.pr] (of one colour adjoining another) merge gradually into that colour. **S:** red; blue. **o:** pink; green: *In the spectrum, what we regard as distinct colours* ***shade*** *imperceptibly* ***into*** *each other.*

shake

shake by the hand [Vn.pr pass] shake the hand of (sb), esp to thank or congratulate him. **O:** rescuer; winner; leader; winning team: *I should like to* ***shake*** *you and your men* ***by the hand****, and thank each one of you personally for all you have done.* MFM ○ *'Some day the world will know and acclaim, and then you, Virginia, will be able to say: ''I knew him before you did. I saw his works in manuscript,'' and people will* ***shake*** *you* ***by the hand****.'* AITC ⇨ shake hands (with).

shake down 1 [Vp nom] (*informal*) reach a state where things function smoothly and efficiently. **S:** (new) machinery, engine: *Following extensive modifications to the turbine blades, the liner underwent further trials at sea to ensure that everything* ***shook down*** *properly* (cf *underwent further* ***shake-down*** *trials*). □ shake-down used attrib, as in the example.

2 [Vp nom] reach the point where people are working harmoniously and well with their companions etc. **S:** staff, students; course-members, participants: *The delegates were from many different backgrounds, but they quickly* ***shook down*** *in their new surroundings.*

shake the dust (of sth) from/off one's feet/shoes [Vn.pr] leave an unpleasant place, trying consciously to rid oneself of its associations. **o:** (**of**) home, school, army life: *However, it was not very long before I was called up for military service, and I* ***shook the dust of*** *the school* ***off my shoes*** *for ever.* SPL ○ (of English writers living abroad) *But if they* ***shake the dust of*** *England* ***from their feet****, they can't so easily shake English from their pens.* L

shake off 1 [Vn ⇆ p pass] by taking avoiding action, escape from (pursuers etc). **S:** ship, aircraft; fugitive, escapee. **O:** attacker, pursuer: *The planes dived into a bank of cloud in an attempt to* ***shake off*** *their pursuers.* ○ *Walter* ***shook off*** *her unwelcome attentions and rushed into his room.* FFE

2 [Vn ⇆ p pass] get rid of or be cured of (sth). **O:** cold, fever; mood; image, reputation: *'I wish I could* ***shake*** *this cold* ***off****!'* ○ *He went out to the pub with a few friends, hoping to* ***shake off*** *the depression which had seized him.* ○ *Mr Major appears to be* ***shaking off*** *his colourless image now that he is seeking the limelight.* OBS

shake out [Vn ⇆ p pass] move (sth) about energetically, eg to get rid of sth; get rid of (sth) by acting in this way. **O:** cloth, bedspread, sheet; crumbs, dust: *Alex* ***shook out*** *the tablecloth and spread it on the grass.* ○ *We gathered up the napkins and* ***shook out*** *the crumbs.*

shake-out [nom (Vn.p)] (*industry*) a vigorous redistribution of staff, fresh use of resources etc, aimed at making an industry more efficient: *The store had got a little bit over-managed, a little top-heavy, and there was need of a* ***shake-out****.* G ○ *This* *week's announcement by Thomson Publishing that it is closing seven titles... means that the long-feared* ***shake-out*** *has arrived.* IND

shake out of [Vn.pr pass] make (sb) change (his normal behaviour etc) by means of a sharp shock. **o:** (set) ways, habits; complacency, apathy: *Perhaps this was the adventure that would* ***shake*** *him* ***out of*** *the neurosis of routine.* NM ○ *He hoped to be* ***shaken out of*** *the ruts of ordinary perception* (ie by taking drugs). DOP

shake up 1 [Vn ⇆ p nom pass] move (a bottle etc) to and fro vigorously, thus mixing the contents well. **O:** bottle; mixture, medicine, tonic: *The contents should be well* ***shaken up*** *until all the sediment disappears.* ○ *All the ingredients get a good* ***shake-up*** *in this new electric mixer.*

2 [Vn ⇆ p nom pass] shake (a cushion etc) after sb has been sitting or lying on it, to restore it to shape. **O:** cushion, pillow, bolster: *As soon as the visitor was announced, Liz bustled around,* ***shaking up*** *the cushions and tidying away the newspapers.* ○ *'Give the pillows a bit of a* ***shake-up*** *and smooth the sheets.'*

3 [Vn ⇆ p nom pass] unsettle (sb) with a physical and/or emotional shock. **S:** flight, ride; collision, impact; news; sb's death: *Neither driver was hurt in the collision but it had clearly* ***shaken*** *them* ***up*** *quite badly.* ○ *When the aircraft finally landed, most of us felt badly* ***shaken up***. ○ *Everyone was* ***shaken up*** *by the news of further redundancies at the Bedford plant.*

4 [Vn ⇆ p nom pass] rouse (lazy or apathetic people) by firm, vigorous action. **S:** teacher, officer. **O:** pupil, soldier: *'What these recruits need is half an hour's drill on the square — that'll* ***shake*** *them* ***up***.*'* ○ *After the lethargy of the last headmaster's rule, the place was ready for a vigorous* ***shake-up***.

5 [Vn ⇆ p nom pass] make, bring extensive and often drastic changes to (sth). **O:** methods; management structure, organization; force, establishment; ideas, notions: *Japanese successes have* ***shaken up*** *the manufacturing practices of our car makers.* ○ *The sales force has been* ***shaken up*** *in the hope of improving recent poor performance.* ○ *Primary schools are in the middle of a big* ***shake-up***. ECON

shake hands (with) [Vn.pr] grasp and shake sb's right hand, esp as a greeting or as a sign of peace after a quarrel or fight: *He was mobbed like a pop star in Boston and New York, and he and his wife* ***shook hands with*** *anything up to 500 people a day.* NS ○ *He very magnanimously said: 'Friendship is better,' or something like that, and we* ***shook hands*** *and got on very well together.* L □ cf: *I* ***shook hands with*** *John/John and I* ***shook hands***. ⇨ shake by the hand.

shame

shame into [Vn.pr pass rel] cause (sb) to behave well by making him feel ashamed of his earlier wrongdoing. **o:** apology, confession, admission; giving up his privileges, donating money: *Mary stared at him hard and eventually* ***shamed*** *him* ***into*** *giving up his seat to the old lady.* ○ *'Don't imagine that he can be* ***shamed into*** *admitting it was all his fault.'*

shape

shape (into) [Vn.pr pass rel] give to (material) a particular form or shape. **O:** metal, clay, stone, wood. **o:** figure, vessel: *The wet clay is patted onto the wire framework and* ***shaped into*** *the body of an animal.* ○ *You can* ***shape*** *the plastic* ***into*** *bowls or buckets by moulding it under pressure.*

shape up [Vp] (*informal*) develop, progress. **S:** pupil, student; musician; athlete; economy, industry, currency: *'How are the new boys in your team* ***shaping up****?'* ○ *I've been coaching two long-jumpers for the next meeting and they're* ***shaping up*** *very nicely.* ○ *The pound didn't* ***shape up*** *very well against other European currencies.* BBCR

share

share out (among) [Vn ⇆ p nom pass, Vn.p.pr pass rel] give a share of (sth) (to each of a group of people). **O:** money; food, clothing; booty, spoils: *At the end of each day, they met for a formal* ***sharing out*** *of the money they had earned.* HD ○ *After tonight's show, we'll have a* ***share-out*** *of the takings.* ○ ***Shared out among*** *five people, the food won't go very far.* = divide among/between.

share (with) 1 [Vn.pr pass emph rel] give a part of (what one has) (to one or more persons). **O:** food, tobacco, drink. **o:** relative, team-mate: *'****Share*** *the toffee* ***with*** *your brother and sister.'* ○ *'I'll* ***share*** *the last few peaches* ***with*** *Fabian.'*

2 [Vn.pr pass emph rel] use (facilities) in common with one or more other persons or things. **O:** bedroom, bathroom; garage, airfield. **o:** guest, visitor; car, plane: *'Met a fellow called Davis?' 'I don't think so.' '****Shared*** *digs* ***with*** *him at college.'* OMIH ○ *An American landing craft and a British destroyer* ***shared*** *the tiny harbour* ***with*** *a handful of smaller fry.* SD

sharpen

sharpen up [Vp, Vn ⇆ p pass adj] (cause sb/sth to) become more lively or keen. **S** [Vp], **O** [Vn.p]: player, contestant; wits, reflexes; game, contest: *The debate was* ***sharpening up*** *and drawing in leading speakers from both sides of the House.* ○ *Activities like this* ***sharpen up*** *the student's problem-solving skills.*

shave

shave off [Vn ⇆ p pass] remove with the razor a growth of hair that has been allowed to develop. **O:** moustache, sideburn(s), sideboard(s), beard: *It might be a good idea to* ***shave off*** *your beard before going to London for the interview.*

shear

shear off [Vp] (*technology*) break off because of structural strain. **S:** rivet, bolt; spout, rib; unit: *A piece of the plane's nose-cone* ***sheared off*** *and hurtled into the rear engine.* G ○ *The bolt joining the driveshaft to the rear axle* ***sheared off*** *as I was trying to overtake a tractor.* IND

shorn of [pass (Vn.pr)] with some parts removed or cut away. **S:** book, document; legislation, Bill; proposal, scheme. **o:** passage, section; clause; provision: *The story is* ***shorn of*** *its individualizing features, the descriptive passages lose most of what peculiarities of style and content they possess, and the original phrasing is replaced by current, commonplace clichés.* MFF ○ *In its passage* *through the House the Land Acquisition Bill was* ***shorn of*** *its most controversial provisions.*

shed

shed light on [Vn.pr pass emph rel] clarify or explain (sth). **adj:** no, (not) any/much, little; fresh, new, additional. **o:** event, incident; mystery, enigma; theft, disappearance: *The Israeli Attorney-General has flown to Paris to question persons who may* ***shed*** *new* ***light on*** *the 'Lavon Affair'.* T ○ *Considerable* ***light*** *was* ***shed on*** *events in Moscow by the interview he gave for BBC television.* = throw light on.

shed tears over [Vn.pr pass] express regrets, esp about a person or over an event that do not deserve them. **adj:** no, (not) any/much; few. **o:** ruffian, layabout, crook; failure, collapse (of an enterprise): *'You're not going to* ***shed*** *any* ***tears over*** *my Sandy, are you?'* EHOW ○ *'The famous Templar family is bankrupt.' 'I don't believe it.' 'I'm afraid it's true. The great and mighty Saunders wouldn't* ***shed tears over*** *anything but lack of money.'* DC □ usu neg or interr; occasionally, shed tears on sb's account: *Few* ***tears*** *are likely to be* ***shed on their account****.* NS

sheer

sheer away (from) [Vp, Vp.pr rel] move sharply away from sb or sth thought dangerous or unpleasant. **o:** bore, drunk, incessant talker; pitfall, trap: *If peers were unpopular, people would* ***sheer away from*** *them, would not want their daughters to marry them.* T ○ *This was a topic* ***from*** *which he always* ***sheered away****, as though unwilling to face the embarrassment it caused.*

sheet

sheet down [Vp] (of rain) fall heavily, in sheets. **S:** ⚠ the rain; it: *We sat gloomily by the hotel window, watching it* ***sheet down****.* ○ *The wind blew, the rain* ***sheeted down****, and we were all soaked.* = pour down.

shell

shell out [Vp, Vp.n pass] (*informal*) pay (sth), usu unwillingly. **S:** parent; firm, organization. **O:** full cost; money; subscription, donation: *I'm tired of* ***shelling out*** *on repairs to this car.* ○ *Northern consumers are less willing to* ***shell out*** *money to see the finished film.* ST = fork out.

shelter

shelter (from) [Vpr emph rel, Vn.pr pass emph rel] use sth as cover or protection (from sth); offer or afford cover (from sth). **S** [Vpr], **O** [Vn.pr]: child; soldier; animal. **S** [Vn.pr]: tree, porch; trench, bunker; hedge, shed. **o:** rain, storm; bombardment: *We huddled in a shop doorway to* ***shelter from*** *the rain.* ○ *The soldiers covered the roof with earth and rock, thick enough to* ***shelter*** *them* ***from*** *gunfire.*

shelve

shelve down (to) [Vp, Vp.pr rel] slope gently (towards sth). **S:** bank, cliff, shore. **o:** sea, water's edge: *At this point, the chalk cliffs* ***shelve down to*** *the beach.* = slope down (to).

shield

shield (from) [Vn.pr pass emph rel] give (sb) protection (from sth). **S:** metal plate, glass screen, spectacles; police; parent. **O:** eye, face; (dead) body; children. **o:** sun, glare; spectators; harmful influence: *You are not helping your children if you try to* ***shield*** *them* ***from*** *every danger.* ○ *In winter your eyes should be* ***shielded from*** *light reflected from the snow.*

shift

shift the blame/responsibility onto [Vn.pr pass emph rel] claim that sb else is to blame for sth unpleasant: *When his plans miscarry, he always looks around for somebody to* ***shift the blame onto****.* ○ *Much of* ***the responsibility*** *for the disaster was* ***shifted onto*** *Menzies, and that was quite undeserved.* = put the blame on.

shin

shin down [Vpr] (*informal*) climb down (sth) by gripping with the hands and legs. **O:** drainpipe, lamp-post, tree: *She* ***shinned down*** *the railing and dropped onto the pavement.* ⇨ next entry

shin up [Vpr] (*informal*) climb up (sth) by gripping with the hands and legs. **o:** wall, drainpipe, tree: *Thieves probably got into the house by* ***shinning up*** *a drainpipe and forcing open the window.* ⇨ previous entry

shine

shine out 1 [Vp] give out a bright light. **S:** sun, light: *The curtains were suddenly drawn and a bright light* ***shone out*** *across the lawn.*

2 [Vp] be clearly noticeable because of its moral quality. **S:** virtue, integrity, generosity: *Among so much backsliding and indecision his courage and resolution* ***shine out*** *like a beacon.*

shine through [Vp] appear clearly as a positive quality, esp against a negative background. **S:** essential humanity, goodness, kindness; intelligence, integrity: *Despite the appalling conditions of the refugee camps, her courage and humanity constantly* ***shone through****.*

ship

ship in [Vn.p pass] carry (sth) into a port etc as cargo. **O:** goods, materials, supplies; wheat, oil: *We'll have to* ***ship in*** *fresh supplies from Japan.* ○ *The wharves were piled with timber* ***shipped in*** *from the Baltic.* □ often passive. ↔ ship out.

ship off [Vn ⇆ p pass] send (people), dispatch (goods), esp by sea or air. **O:** reinforcements, convicts; load, consignment; goods, merchandise: *A younger son for whom there were no prospects at home might be* ***shipped off*** *abroad to make a career for himself.* ○ *A dozen crates were* ***shipped off*** *by air freight last week.* □ often passive.

ship out [Vn ⇆ p pass] carry (sth) from a port etc as cargo. **S:** maker, supplier; ferry, tanker; train, truck. **O:** cargo, load; cement, iron-ore, oil: *The oil company will* ***ship out*** *piping and heavy equipment* (ie to the oil rig). SC ○ *We have to suck in vast quantities of raw materials before we can convert them into exports and* ***ship*** *them* ***out*** *again.* ST □ often passive. ↔ ship in.

shock

shock into [Vn.pr pass] cause (sb) (to do sth) by shocking him. **o:** giving up drink, changing one's eating habits, making a donation: *She was* ***shocked into*** *giving up smoking by losing a close friend through lung cancer.*

shoot

shoot across, along, away etc [Vp, Vpr] move across etc very swiftly. **S:** motor-boat, sports car, plane: *A motor-boat towing a girl on water-skis* ***shot across*** *our bow.* ○ *Two more toboggans* ***shot down*** *the slope.* ○ *He* ***shot off*** *down the stairs before I could reply.*

shoot a glance (at) [Vn.pr] look quickly (at sb), and then away again. **adj:** curious, suspicious, hostile: ***The glance*** *he* ***shot at*** *Charles from beneath his straggling white eyebrows was, of all things, a slightly envious one.* HD ○ *The receptionist* ***shot an*** *inquisitive* ***glance at*** *the young man near the newspaper kiosk* (cf ***shot*** *the young man* ***an*** *inquisitive* ***glance***). = dart a glance/look at.

shoot down 1 [Vn ⇆ p pass adj] make (an aircraft) fall to the ground by shooting at it. **S:** fighter, anti-aircraft gun. **O:** bomber, transport; pilot: *Howes was ... with another Squadron and worried because he had as yet* ***shot*** *nothing* ***down***. TLE ○ *One sergeant pilot in 'A' Flight was* ***shot down*** *four times, but he seemed to bear a charmed life.* TLE = bring down 1.

2 [Vn ⇆ p pass] (*informal*) attack sb's ideas or arguments, and destroy them. **O:** idea, proposal, recommendation; him etc, speaker: *He got* ***shot down*** *for supporting an opposition motion on local government.* □ often passive; note the extended phrase shoot down in flames, and the link with the previous entry: *I'd be* ***shot down*** *in flames if I suggested anything of the kind.*

shoot one's mouth off [Vn.p] (*informal*) speak in a loud, and indiscreet or boastful, way: *'We were hoping to keep the party a secret—it was meant to be a surprise for Jane. What made you go and* ***shoot your mouth off*** *about it?'* ○ *'It's going to be one of those awful hearty evenings, with Bill swigging his beer and* ***shooting his mouth off****!'*

shoot out 1 [Vn ⇆ p pass] expel, evict (sb) from a house etc. **S:** landlord, owner. **O:** tenant, occupant: *Won't the Ministry of Agriculture people have something to say if they're* ***shot out*** *and we're moved in?* TBC

2 [Vn ⇆ p pass] (*cricket*) dismiss (a batsman) rapidly. **S:** bowler. **O:** team; batsman: *The Surrey team were* ***shot out*** *before lunch, thanks to a fine piece of spin bowling by Travers.*

shoot it out [Vn.p nom] fight to a conclusion, usu with hand-guns: *Since one man had no pistol, they agreed to* ***shoot it out*** *on horseback, with rifles.* ○ *There is always the risk of civilians being caught in the crossfire when terrorists and soldiers* ***shoot it out*** (or: *when there is a* ***shoot-out*** *between terrorists and soldiers).*

shoot out/out of [Vp emph, Vpr emph rel] emerge swiftly and suddenly (from a place). **S:** he etc; rabbit, snake. **o:** house; burrow, grass: *The lizard's tongue* ***shot out*** *and scooped up the fly.* ○ *The long and powerful arm* (of the monkey) *would* ***shoot out*** *through the bars.* BB ○ *The dog* ***shot out of*** *the gate and was half-way across the field before we knew it.*

shoot up 1 [Vp] (*informal*) grow, increase in size, quickly. **S:** plant, child: *'My word, you have* ***shot up*** *since I saw you last.'*

2 [Vp] rise, increase, sharply. **S:** price, cost, rent; temperature, pressure; applications, attendance: *We shall do what we can to stop prices* ***shooting up*** *still further.* ○ *My pulse rate would suddenly* ***shoot up*** *alarmingly.* DIL = race up (into/to).

3 [Vn ⇆ p pass] (*informal*) terrorize a place by moving through it and firing into the air, at houses etc. **S:** bandit, gangster. **O:** town; saloon: *'Nobody can scare them off: they'll come back and* ***shoot*** *the place* ***up***, *just for kicks.'*

shot up [pass adj (Vn.p)] (*military*) injured, damaged or reduced in numbers by enemy action. **S:** tank, plane; division, regiment: *John's regiment had been badly* ***shot up*** *in the last attack and was due to be relieved.* ○ *The area just inside the enemy perimeter was littered with* ***shot-up*** *tanks and trucks.* □ passive also with appear, get, seem, look.

shoot up (on) [Vp, Vp.pr] (*slang*) inject (a harmful drug) using a syringe. **S:** addict; teenager. **o:** cocaine, heroin: *At that time he was restless and bored,* ***shooting up on*** *coke and waiting for something to happen.*

shop

shop around [Vp nom] go from one shop, dealer etc to another until one finds the best value for money; examine claims, programmes, of various firms, colleges etc before deciding which to join: *It will pay you to* ***shop around*** *a bit before deciding which car to buy.* ○ *'Has Peter decided which universities he's going to apply to?' 'Not yet. He's* ***shopping around*** *for a course with a good choice of options.'* □ note the nom form in: *'Have a good* ***shop around*** *before making your mind up.'*

shore

shore up 1 [Vn ⇆ p pass adj] prevent (sth) from falling down, with props or pillars. **O:** house; wall, tree: *It only needs a heavy storm to bring the whole house down. We'll have to* ***shore*** *it* ***up***. BM

2 [Vn ⇆ p pass] support or strengthen (sth). **S:** government; Finance Minister; banks. **O:** economy; currency, the pound; company: *The nations reacted blindly in 1929,* ***shoring up*** *their national defences and then standing by helpless as the tide of demand ebbed away.* OBS

shoulder

shoulder aside [Vn ⇆ p pass] push (sb) to one side with the shoulder: *A big fellow rushed from the store,* ***shouldering aside*** *anyone who got in his way.*

shout

shout down [Vn ⇆ p pass] prevent (a speaker) from being heard by shouting while he is speaking. **S:** crowd; faction, claque. **O:** speaker; representative, leader: *Angry steel workers* ***shouted down*** *one of the committee as he tried to address them through a loud-hailer.* ○ *They all seem to be trying to* ***shout*** *us* ***down*** *before we have opened our mouths.* NS = howl down.

shout out [Vp, Vn ⇆ p pass] call (sth) in a loud clear voice. **O:** name, address; price; abuse: *'If you know the answer, don't* ***shout out****—wait till I ask you.'* ○ *The first person to complete a card* ***shouts out*** *'Bingo!' at the top of her voice.* = call out 2, yell out.

shove

shove about/around [Vn.p pass, Vn.pr pass] (*informal*) order (sb) to do things in an unpleasant, bullying tone: *DAVIES: I never see him, he comes in late, next thing I know he's* ***shoving*** *me* ***about*** *in the middle of the night.* TC = order about/around, push about/around.

shove down sb's throat [Vn.pr pass] (*informal*) repeat (sth) often in the hope that it will be learnt, accepted etc. **O:** lesson; history, Latin; view, opinion; merit, worth (of sth): *'You're always* ***shoving*** *it* ***down my throat*** *that you're the one with the job, but it's not so wonderful. I'm working far harder than you.'* AITC ○ *He'd had French* ***shoved down his throat*** *for five hours a week. No wonder he grew to hate it.* = ram down sb's throat.

shove off 1 [Vp] (*nautical*) move a boat away from the shore, by pushing the shore with a pole etc: *'Is everybody aboard? Right,* ***shove off****!'* = push off 1.
2 [Vp] (*informal*) go away, leave: *'Well, you've said your piece. Now why don't you* ***shove off*** *and leave us alone?'* ○ *'I can't stand his company any longer: let's* ***shove off*** *somewhere and have a drink.'* □ usu indicates boredom, irritation etc on the part of the person leaving or asking another to leave. = push off 2.

shove up [Vp] (*informal*) move along a bench etc to make room for sb else: *'****Shove up*** *a bit: there's no room for Peter!'* = move along/up.

show

show around/round [Vn ⇆ p pass, Vn.pr pass] take (visitors) on a tour of a place; guide round. **S:** guide, receptionist. **O:** party, delegation; visitor, tourist. **o:** house, garden; factory, site: *'Mr Jones is busy at the moment. He's* ***showing round*** *a party of visitors.'* ○ *If you are free at two o'clock on Friday, I shall be glad to* ***show*** *you* ***around*** *the department.* = show over. ⇨ see over/round.

show-down [nom (Vp)] (*informal*) moment, in a trial of strength, when one side reveals the weakness, pretensions etc of the other and/or its own strength: *There is too much easy talk in the press of the Government forcing a* ***show-down*** *with the unions.* ○ *If it comes to a* ***show-down*** *with the bank we can point to the encouraging trading forecast for the next six months.*

show in/into [Vn ⇆ p pass, Vn.pr pass rel] lead, conduct (sb) into a place. **S:** secretary, servant. **O:** caller, visitor; customer. **o:** waiting-room, drawing-room: *'Don't keep Mr Rodgers waiting.* ***Show*** *him* ***in****!'* ○ *'When the guests arrive please* ***show*** *them* ***into*** *the sitting-room.'* ↔ show out/out of.

show off 1 [Vn ⇆ p pass] make (sth) appear to the best advantage. **S:** setting; room; frame, mounting; clothes. **O:** jewel; furniture; painting; figure, shape. **A:** well, admirably; to advantage: *The room, very plain, formal and grey, was intended primarily to* ***show off*** *the drawings that were hung there.* ASA ○ *The cut of her dress* ***shows*** *her figure* ***off*** *to perfection.*
2 [Vn ⇆ p pass] draw people's attention to (sb/sth), esp out of pride or vanity. **O:** son, daughter; skill, trick; song, poem; clothes, car: *Her aunt liked to boast about her and* ***show*** *her* ***off*** *when she came home in uniform.* DC ○ *You'll have to practise that trick a little more before you can* ***show*** *it* ***off***. DC
3 [Vp nom] (often *pejorative*) display one's own abilities etc in order to impress people: *'Do stop* ***showing off****, Andrew. Nobody's impressed.'* ○ *He shows off tremendously* (or: *He's a tremendous* ***show-off****) in front of the ladies.* ○ *Mr Fielding is a* ***show-off*** *who has plenty to show.* ST

show out/out of [Vn ⇆ p pass, Vn.pr pass] lead, conduct (sb) from a place. **S:** butler, secretary. **O:** visitor, caller. **o:** house, office: *'I think that just about concludes our discussion. Miss Jones, will you please* ***show*** *Mr Hull* ***out****?'* ↔ show in/into.

show over [Vn.pr pass] take (visitors) on a tour of (a place). **O:** customer, buyer. **o:** plant, works: *'I'll get a guide to* ***show*** *you* ***over*** *the factory.'* = show around/round. ⇨ see over/round.

show round [Vn ⇆ p pass, Vn.pr pass] ⇨ show around/round.

show through [Vp, Vpr rel] be visible underneath (a covering). **S:** colour, texture; nature, character. **o:** paper, covering; façade, formal manner: *She has acquired a very good French accent, but her English speech habits still* ***show through****.* ○ *I've sprayed the bonnet, but the marks and scratches* ***show through*** *the paint.*

show up 1 [Vp, Vn ⇆ p pass] (cause sth to) be easily visible or apparent. **S** [Vp], **O** [Vn ⇆ p]**:** line, wrinkle; mistake, imperfection; poor workmanship; (true) nature, character. **S** [Vn ⇆ p]**:** light; (close) examination; stress, crisis: *Close study of the surface of the picture* ***shows up*** *a network of fine cracks.* ○ *At times like these the true character of the man* ***shows up****.*
2 [Vn.p pass] (*informal*) make (sb) feel embarrassed by behaving badly in his company. **S:** child; pupil; friend: *I can take the children anywhere. I'm never afraid that they're going to* ***show*** *me* ***up*** *in some restaurant.* ○ *'That's the last time you* ***show*** *me* ***up*** *in public!'*
3 [Vp] (*informal*) appear, arrive, often after some delay. **S:** guest, visitor: *Her place was laid for lunch and again for dinner. But she didn't* ***show up****.* PW ○ *'We've been waiting for hours for you to* ***show up****!'* = turn up 4.

show up (as/for) [Vn.p pass, Vn.p.pr pass] show (oneself/sb) to be inferior, morally weak, unpleasant etc. **o: (as)** weak, spineless; a coward, a crook; **(for)** the fool he is, what she is: *Should we expect him to tell the truth about himself if that truth would* ***show*** *him* ***up as*** *a rather poor sort of fish* (or: ***show*** *him* ***up*** *to be* etc). SNP ○ *Don't* ***show*** *yourself* ***up for*** *what you are!* TOH

shower

shower on/upon [Vpr emph rel, Vn.pr pass emph rel] be offered in abundance to (sb); offer (sth) in abundance to (sb). **S** [Vpr], **O** [Vn.pr]**:** gifts, presents; food, wine; compliments, praise. **o:** guest, visitor; hero, victor: *We were overwhelmed by people's generosity: offers of meals and shelter* ***showered upon*** *us.* ○ *From the moment we arrived, hospitality was* ***showered on*** *us.* = rain upon.

shrink

shrink back [Vp] move backwards or withdraw out of fear, sensitivity etc: *Nicky* ***shrank back****: he couldn't bear sharp voices.* DC

shrink from [Vpr] be unwilling to face or undertake (sth) out of fear, sensitivity etc. **o:** conflict, danger; physical contact; giving a sign of recognition, responding to the challenge: *Judy* ***shrank from*** *any close personal contact with her students.* ○ *I*

***shrank from** telling her the true cost of the damage.*

shrivel

shrivel up [Vp, Vn ⇆ p pass adj] (cause sth to) dry and curl up or wrinkle. **S** [Vp], **O** [Vn.p]**:** leaf, shoot, blade (of grass); skin; face. **S** [Vn.p]**:** heat, frost, age: *In the long drought, the leaves **shrivelled up** and died.* ○ *I looked down into her brown, **shrivelled-up** face and intense black eyes.*

shroud

shrouded in [pass (Vn.pr)] thickly covered by (sth), so that nothing is visible. **o:** fog; darkness; mystery: *The trees to either side of the lane were **shrouded in** thick fog.* ○ *(fig) The private lives of Stalin's relatives and close associates are **shrouded in** mystery.*

shrug

shrug off [Vn ⇆ p pass] dismiss (sth) as untrue, unimportant, not worthy of one's attention etc. **O:** protest, objection, complaint; whistles, catcalls: *He **shrugged off** suggestions that he was trailing in the leadership race.* OBS ○ *He has a way of **shrugging** criticism **off** as if it is somehow beneath his notice.*

shuffle

shuffle off (onto) [Vn ⇆ p pass, Vn.p.pr pass] (*informal*) in a furtive way, try to pass (one's responsibility) (onto sb else). **O:** ⚠ the blame, responsibility; (feelings of) guilt: (political broadcast) *He's running away because that is the only opportunity to **shuffle off** his responsibility.* BBCTV ○ (political broadcast) *He tried to **shuffle off** his own responsibility **onto** the men who dig the nation's coal.* BBCR

shut

shut away (in) [Vn.p pass, Vn.p.pr pass rel] enclose, confine (oneself/sb) in a secure or quiet place. **O:** himself etc; prisoner, hostage. **o:** country; castle: *Jennifer **shut** herself **away** for a month to catch up on her academic work.* ○ *'What made him **shut** himself **away in** the heart of the country?'* ○ *Important military prisoners were **shut away in** a remote mountain village.*

shut down [Vp nom, Vn ⇆ p nom pass adj] stop production at (a place) permanently or for a time. **S** [Vp], **O** [Vn.p]**:** plant, factory, workshop. **S** [Vn.p]**:** owner, manager: *Some businesses will have to **shut down** if there is a recession.* ○ *The threat of a **shut-down** in the newspaper industry has not been averted.* BBCR ○ *The commission has ordered two mines to be **shut down*** (or: *has ordered the **shut-down** of two mines*). = close down.

shut in 1 [Vn.p pass, Vn.pr pass] prevent (sb/oneself) from leaving (a place) by closing the door. **O:** child; dog; oneself. **o:** bedroom; shed; house: *We **shut** the dog **in** the garage.* ○ *She' s **shut** herself **in** the bedroom and won't come out.* ⇨ lock in 2.

2 [Vn ⇆ p pass adj] enclose, surround (sb/sth). **S:** mountain, forest; fog, snow: *For four months in the year the snow virtually isolates them and then they are **shut in** upon themselves.*

shut off [Vn ⇆ p pass] stop (sth) flowing; interrupt. **O:** supply; gas, water, steam: *'I haven't had a bath for days—they've **shut off** the hot water supply.'* ○ *Domestic supplies may be **shut off** at times of heavy demand.* = switch off 1, turn off 1.

shut off (from) [Vn.p pass, Vn.p.pr pass emph rel] prevent (oneself/sb) from having contact with others. **O:** himself etc; child: *He would **shut** himself **off** for days at a time to work on his book.* ○ *How can he possibly **shut** the children **off from** their mother in this way?* = cut off (from) 2.

shut out/out of [Vn ⇆ p pass, Vn.pr pass] prevent (sth/sb) from entering or being seen. **O:** light, sun, warmth; sound; view; visitor, spectator. **o:** room, studio; museum; ground: *The window was open, but the rain **shut out** the air as effectively as a curtain.* HOM ○ *Ticket-holders who arrive late may find themselves **shut out of** the stadium.* ○ *He tried hard to **shut** all thoughts of her **out of** his mind.*

shut one's eyes to [Vn.pr pass emph rel] pretend that one does not see (sth). **o:** suffering, distress; crime, corruption; infidelity: *In their heart of hearts, many scientists may still regard politics as an evil, but at any rate they no longer **shut their eyes to** it.* OBS ○ *This is one of the defects of modern society **to** which we complacently **shut our eyes**.* L = turn a blind eye (on/to).

shut up 1 [Vn ⇆ p pass adj] shut the windows and doors of (a building) securely, eg before leaving it, at night, for the summer etc. **O:** office, shop, house: *I **shut** my room **up** securely and left the key with the porter.* ○ *We detoured up side roads past **shut-up** holiday villas.* AM = close up 2.

2 [Vp, Vn ⇆ p pass] (*informal*) (cause sb to) stop talking, making a noise etc. **S** [Vp], **O** [Vn.p]**:** speaker, chatterbox; pest, nuisance: *Generals were in the greatest awe of him and **shut up** like an oyster in his presence.* MFM ○ *'For heaven's sake, **shut** him **up**: he's said quite enough already.'* = dry up 5.

shut up (in) [Vn ⇆ p pass, Vn.p.pr pass emph rel] hold or place (sb/sth) under lock and key. **O:** enemy, suspect; madman; valuables, jewellery. **o:** cell, dungeon; safe: *He's mad as a hatter, poor chap, and **shut up** somewhere.* PW ○ *So let Catherine lie **shut up in** Kimbolton Castle, where it's said you're having her poisoned.* WI

shy

shy away (from) [Vp, Vp.pr pass emph rel] avoid or move away (from sth) out of shyness, prudery, fear etc. **o:** contact, involvement, commitment; danger, threat: *Clive **shies away from** the thought of contact as Stanley makes to touch his shoulder.* FFE ○ *Modern English writers tend to **shy away from** using the stage for direct autobiographical expression.* ITAJ □ shy off [Vp, Vpr] can be used with the same meaning: *At the wedding they were both **shying off** each other like startled deer.* PPAP = shrink from.

sick

sick up [Vn ⇆ p pass] (*informal*) vomit (sth). **O:** food; meal; breakfast: *He can't keep anything down: he **sicked up** what little breakfast he had.* = bring up 6.

sicken

sicken of [Vpr pass emph rel] become weary of or disgusted with (sb/sth). **o:** old life, former companions; violence, cruelty; cant, hypocrisy: *After a few weeks working for him I* ***sickened of*** *his methods.* ○ *The casual violence of the gang — this was something* ***of*** *which we* ***sickened*** *early on.*

side

side against [Vpr] put oneself on the opposite side from (sb). **o:** one's own part, leadership: *He took the enemy's part and* ***sided against*** *his own people.* ⇨ next entry

side with [Vpr] put oneself on the same side as (sb); take sb's part. **o:** (weaker/stronger) faction, party; enemy, opposition: *She will always* ***side with*** *a minority against the official or established line.* ○ *They're careful to* ***side with*** *the party most likely to win.* ⇨ previous entry

sidle

sidle up (to) [Vp, Vp.pr pass] approach (sb/sth) in a nervous or furtive way: *If someone* ***sidles up*** *and offers to buy currency, pay no attention.* ○ *A small man* ***sidled up to*** *him and pressed a piece of paper into his hand.*

sift

sift through [Vpr pass] examine (sth) carefully and section by section, eg to obtain information. **o:** document, file; collection, archive: *Scientists are* ***sifting through*** *the evidence uncovered by the police.* ○ *There is still a great deal of material to be* ***sifted through***.

sign

sign away [Vn ⇆ p pass] surrender, abandon (sth) by signing a document etc. **O:** property, estate; livelihood, career; right, privilege: *Read the document carefully, so that you know what you are* ***signing away***. ○ *With one stroke of the pen he had* ***signed away*** *his country's independence for a decade.*

sign in (at) [Vp, Vp.pr rel] sign one's name in a register, on a form etc, on arriving at a hotel, conference etc; register. **S:** guest, visitor, delegate. **o:** hotel; reception: *'If you'll just* ***sign in****, I'll give you your room key and conference folder.'* ○ *What with the holdup at the airport, we didn't* ***sign in at*** *the hotel until after midnight.* = check in (at).

sign in/into [Vn ⇆ p pass, Vn.pr pass] by signing one's name as a member, enable (a non-member) to enter a club etc. **O:** friend, guest. **o:** club, discothèque: *'It's not worthwhile paying the membership fee for one evening. I'll* ***sign*** *you* ***in*** *on my card.'* ○ *Non-members must be* ***signed in*** *by a member.*

sign off [Vp] (*informal*) say or write one's name to mark the end of a letter or radio/TV programme. **S:** announcer, compère, disc-jockey (DJ): *'And this is your resident DJ, Jerry Miles,* ***signing off*** *till the same time tomorrow.'*

sign on 1 [Vp, Vn ⇆ p pass] (cause sb to) sign an agreement or undertaking to work for sb, or join a ship's company or the armed services for a specified period. **S** [Vp], **O** [Vn.p]**:** man; labourer; recruit; seaman; footballer. **S** [Vn.p]**:** employer; recruiting-sergeant; ship-owner; manager: *Men who came forward as volunteers agreed to* ***sign on*** *for the duration of hostilities.* ○ *We need to* ***sign on*** *some more deck-hands for the next trip.*
2 [Vp] register one's name, when unemployed, at the local unemployment benefit office. **S:** factory worker; machinist, redundant miner: *A lot of men* ***signed on*** *for the dole* (unemployment pay) *the week they closed the local steelworks.*

sign on the dotted line [Vpr] (*informal*) sign a document which legally binds one to work etc for sb, or which is a marriage certificate, a bill of sale etc: *'Now, Sir, if you will just* ***sign on the dotted line*** *the car becomes yours.'* ○ *'You have to give Liza credit for persistence. She's been trying to get James to* ***sign on the dotted line*** *for over three years.'*

sign out/out of [Vn ⇆ p pass, Vn.pr pass] show by signing one's name that one has left, or intends to leave, a place. **O:** oneself; friend, colleague. **o:** camp; college, hall of residence: *'I shan't be eating in college tonight. Would you mind* ***signing*** *me* ***out****?'* ○ *After basic training the soldiers were allowed to spend weekends at home, provided they* ***signed*** *themselves* ***out of*** *camp.*

sign over [Vn ⇆ p pass] transfer (property) by signing papers. **O:** goods; consignment, load; property, land: *A senior executive* ***signed over*** *a delivery of six aircraft on behalf of his company.* ○ *The top floor of the building was* ***signed over*** *for use as offices.*

sign up [Vp, Vn ⇆ p pass] (cause sb to) join a club, enrol for a course etc. **S** [Vp], **O** [Vn.p]**:** player; footballer, cricketer; member; student. **S** [Vn.p]**:** club; secretary; registrar: *Before you* ***sign up*** *for a course, make sure that the school is attached to an established employment agency.* H ○ *Arsenal have* ***signed up*** *a number of promising youngsters this season.*

silt

silt up [Vp, Vn ⇆ p pass adj] (cause sth to) become blocked with mud, sand etc. **S** [Vp], **O** [Vn.p]**:** mouth (of river), cove, bay, harbour. **S** [Vn.p]**:** sea; sand, shingle: *Places which were harbours in Roman times* ***silted up*** *long ago and are now some distance inland.* ○ *The drains got* ***silted up*** *with mud and bits of twigs.*

simmer

simmer down [Vp] become calm after being angry, excited, critical etc. **S:** excited, irascible man; situation; things: *'Give him a minute to* ***simmer down*** *— he's always like this when we discuss politics.'* ○ *When things have* ***simmered down*** *a bit more, talks can be started.* BBCTV = calm down 2, cool down.

sin

sin against [Vpr pass emph rel] break some moral or religious law; transgress. **o:** the Holy Ghost; decorum, propriety: *What is this unwritten law she is accused of* ***sinning against****?* ○ *He is a man more* ***sinned against*** *than sinning* (ie he does less harm to others than they do to him). = offend (against).

sing

sing out [Vp] greet sb, make a request etc, in a loud voice: *'Nice day,' Bill* ***sang out****. 'Do you feel like a walk?'* ○ *'If there's anything you need, just* ***sing out****.'* = call out 1.

sing to sleep [Vn.pr pass] make (a child) fall asleep by singing to him. **S:** mother, nurse. **O:** baby, infant: *If the child grew restless, she would take him out of his cot and* ***sing*** *him* ***to sleep***.

sing up [Vp] sing more loudly: ***'Sing up****, fellows, this is supposed to be a celebration, not a funeral!'*

○ *'Tell the people at the back to* **sing up**: *I can't hear them.'* □ usu direct or indirect command.

single

single out [Vn ⇆ p pass] choose, pick (one person/thing) from among several for special comment, treatment etc. **O:** assistant, companion; victim, prey; incident, event: *I imagine that to be* **singled out** *by the Captain for a farewell luncheon is indeed an honour.* WI ○ *He* **singles out** *in human nature the ugly elements — the elements that hurt him.* PW

sink

sink back [Vp] lean back in a chair etc or lie down on a bed etc from an upright sitting position. **A:** in an armchair, against the cushions, on the pillows: *He fixed himself a drink and* **sank back** *in an armchair.*

sink in 1 [Vp] be fully absorbed and understood. **S:** announcement, statement; idea, suggestion: *He said nothing; he stood without moving, while the news* **sank in**. WI ○ *Something good may result after all if the warnings* **sink in**. T

2 [Vn.pr pass emph rel] invest capital etc, usu heavily, in (some venture). **S:** investor, speculator. **O:** (a good deal of) capital, investment; personal savings, fortune. **o:** project; transport, the telecommunications industry: *A lot of their money had been* **sunk in** *mineral shares that everybody had warned them not to buy.* ○ **In** *this particular venture he'd* **sunk** *half the sum left him by his father.*

sink into 1 [Vpr emph rel] fall fast asleep; fall to a lower physical or moral level. **o:** (deep) sleep; trance, coma; depressed state, black mood: *For a moment, Yusef seemed about to* **sink** *again* **into** *drugged sleep.* HOM ○ *Nobody could rouse him from the mood of black depression* **into** *which he had* **sunk**.

2 [Vn.pr pass emph rel] press (sth sharp) into (sth). **O:** teeth, claws, nails. **o:** apple, peach; arm, leg, flesh: *The cat* **sank** *its sharp claws* **into** *my thigh.*

sink into/to one's boots [Vpr] (*informal*) become low, depressed. **S:** ⚠ one's heart; one's spirits, courage: *He got through his little scene with Jessica quite well till the moment for the song came, when his courage* **sank to his boots**. WDM ○ *Was this the place that she was going to have to live in for the next year? Her heart* **sank into her boots** *as she looked round the squalid little room.*

siphon

siphon off (from) (into) 1 [Vn ⇆ p pass adj, Vn.p.pr pass emph rel] draw (liquid) (from a tank) by sucking it through a tube. **O:** petrol, oil, water: *If you're short of petrol you can* **siphon off** *a gallon from my tank.*

2 [Vn ⇆ p pass adj, Vn.p.pr pass emph rel] (*informal*) transfer (sth) from one place or area of responsibility to another; (esp) transfer (funds) from one person to another for dishonest purposes. **O:** work, job; money, funds: *There is a lot of pressure now to* **siphon off** *the motoring cases* **into** *a court of their own.* TO ○ *A good deal of the money paid into the campaign fund has been* **siphoned off into** *private pockets.*

sit

sit about/around [Vp, Vpr] be seated in a relaxed or idle way in one place: *Passengers* **sat around** *waiting for their flight to be called.* ○ *He* **sits about** *the house all day, listening to his Walkman.*

sit at the feet of [Vpr rel] (*jocular*) go to learn from some real, or would-be, authority. **o:** (**of**) master, seer, guru: *'I was a Red (= communist) myself once. I even* **sat at the feet of** *Waterman and he was a phoney old prophet if you like.'* PP ○ *The talk was given by an elderly don* **at whose feet** *Peter had* **sat**, *many years before, at Cambridge.*

sit back 1 [Vp] relax, usu after strenuous activity: *He just* **sat back** *and let the waves break over him.* OBS ○ *Now it was all over, we could* **sit back** *with our feet up.* EHOW ○ *The bulk of investigative work has been done, and ... those detective reporters should* **sit back** *and let justice take its course.* L

2 [Vp] be idle and inactive when action is needed: *'When we needed your help, all you did was* **sit back** *and twiddle your thumbs.'* ○ *'But you can't just* **sit back** *and do nothing!'* □ note that sit by (next entry) suggests a lack of involvement; sit back suggests a lack of energy.

sit by [Vp] show a lack of concern and remain inactive when involvement and firm action are needed: *The Government will not* **sit** *idly* **by** *and let inflation wipe out the economic gains of the last ten years.* ○ *'I think,' Matthew began, 'that even I can hardly* **sit by** *and —.'* US □ often used in negative constructions to express a determination *not* to be inactive. = stand by 1.

sit down 1 [Vp nom, Vn.p pass] be seated, eg in an armchair; (cause sb to) take a seat: *When I came in, the others were already* **sitting down**. ○ *'I'll bandage your foot up and you can have a* **sit-down**.' ARG ○ *'***Sit** *your guests* **down** *and give them a drink.'* ○ *'***Sit** *yourself* **down**. *I shan't keep you waiting more than a minute.'* ↔ get up 2, stand up 1.

2 [Vp] settle down in a determined way, often with other people, to solve a problem, finish a task etc: *He urged that an Arab mediator be selected to* **sit down** *with both sides* (ie to negotiate). T ○ *We'll get nowhere until we have the various factions* **sitting down** *around the negotiating table.*

sit-down (demonstration/strike) [nom (Vp)] demonstration in which people sit down in the street, in the entrances to buildings etc, thus preventing others from passing; strike during which employees sit down in their place of work: *A* **sit-down** *in Trafalgar Square resulted in hundreds of arrests.* ○ *Groups attempted to organize* **sit-down demonstrations** *in Whitehall. These formed part of the wider movement against nuclear weapons.*

sit down under [Vp.pr] endure, suffer (sth) without protest or resistance. **o:** conditions; slight, insult, humiliation: *I couldn't* **sit down under** *things any longer.* NM ○ *He is a patient man, but not even he could* **sit down under** *that kind of provocation.*

sit for [Vpr rel] take an examination. **o:** examination, college entrance, scholarship: *A number of sixth-formers came up that week to* **sit for** *university entrance.*

sit in [Vp nom] occupy the building where one is employed etc, in protest against conditions, the action of authorities etc. **S:** worker, student, civil-rights campaigner: *A company admitted this week that it had passed information to the Special Branch on certain workers* **sitting in** *at its factory.*

ST ○ ***Sit-ins*** *were staged at lunch-counters known to have refused service to blacks.*

sit in judgement (on/over) [Vpr] judge the actions, character etc (of sb). **S:** parent, teacher; critic, pundit. **o:** charge, pupil; work, conduct: *Virginia imagined that the woman knew the whole story, and was* ***sitting*** *there* ***in judgement****.* AITC ○ *'Don't set yourself up as some great moral authority, Ben. You're in no position to* ***sit in judgement on*** *anyone.'*

sit on 1 [Vpr rel] serve as a member of (a body). **o:** committee, board, jury: *A number of distinguished academics and teachers* ***sat on*** *the committee which recommended the expansion of higher education.* ○ *This was only one of the many bodies* ***on*** *which he had* ***sat*** *during his life of public service.*

2 [Vpr pass] (*informal*) delay the processing of (sth) because of idleness, inefficiency, corruption etc. **S:** company, department; manager. **o:** letter; complaint, inquiry: *For weeks they did nothing about my case: they just* ***sat on*** *it.* ○ *Jenkins* ***sat on*** *those applications for a month. I suppose it fed his sense of power to think he could hold them up.*

3 [Vpr pass] (*informal*) handle firmly sb who behaves impertinently etc. **o:** impertinent, conceited, opinionated fellow: *I wish someone would* ***sit*** *hard* ***on*** *Rogers—he'll be telling me how to run my department next.* ○ *That young man is becoming insufferable: he needs to be* ***sat on*** *very firmly.* = put in his place.

sit on the fence [Vpr] hesitate between, not decide between, two opposite lines of action, sets of beliefs etc. **S:** council, committee; businessman, director: *It was my view that he always* ***sat on the fence****, never committed himself, and never gave a decision.* MFM ○ *COLONEL: I think you may take after me a little, my dear. You like to* ***sit on the fence*** *because it's more comfortable and more peaceful.* LBA

sit out 1 [Vp, Vn ⇆ p] (at a dance) leave the floor for the duration of one dance and sit down with one's partner. **O:** number; waltz, rumba: *'Let's* ***sit*** *this one* ***out****, shall we? I'm afraid I tango very badly.'*

2 [Vn ⇆ p pass] remain in one's seat till the end of a performance, even though one may find it unpleasant. **S:** audience, public. **O:** play, concert; match, bout: *I found the play terribly tedious—I don't know how I managed to* ***sit*** *it* ***out****.* ○ *'Let's just* ***sit*** *this bit* ***out****. The show may liven up later.'* ⇨ next entry

sit through [Vpr] remain in a theatre etc till the end of a performance, even though one may dislike it. **o:** play, film; concert; meeting: *'It was a dreadful film. I don't know how I managed to* ***sit through*** *it.'* ○ *'I had to leave before the end, but Bill* ***sat through*** *the entire debate. You'd better ask him how it went.'* ⇨ previous entry

sit up 1 [Vp] move into an upright position after lying flat; sit straight upright after lounging in one's seat: *I think the patient is well enough now to* ***sit up*** *in bed.* ○ *'Don't slouch over the table.* ***Sit up*** *straight!'*

2 [Vp] move to an upright position, in a tense, alert way, usu from fear or surprise: *She* ***sat up****, clapping her hands to her mouth, her eyes wide with fear.* DC

3 [Vp] stay awake and out of bed till past one's usual bedtime, to wait for sb to return, keep sb company etc: *They* ***sat up*** *till the small hours, exchanging gossip.* ○ *He had insisted on Nurse Ellen* ***sitting up*** *with her, although the need for a night nurse was past.* DC ○ *'I shall get back very late, so don't* ***sit up*** *for me.'* = stay up 2. ⇨ wait up (for).

sit up and take notice [Vp] (*informal*) become suddenly and keenly aware and interested. **S:** opponent, rival; critic, sceptic: *But when she married the delightful Colonial Bishop, now Canon Joram, the County and the Close suddenly* ***sat up and*** *began to* ***take notice*** *and now no party in Barchester was complete without her.* WDM ○ *We were at the point of war. I began, like most people to* ***sit up and take notice****.* PPAP

size

size up [Vn ⇆ p pass adj] form a judgement or opinion about (sb/sth). **O:** newcomer, stranger; situation; competition: *I was trying to* ***size*** *you* ***up****, and failing because you didn't fit into any type I knew.* HD ○ *He was trying to* ***size up*** *the reaction of the audience: how were they being received?*

skate

skate around/round [Vpr pass] fail to face and deal with (problems etc). **o:** real issues, difficult questions; difficulty, problem. **A:** nervously, warily, cautiously: *The government will not be able to* ***skate around*** *the issue of homelessness for very much longer.* ○ *Drafts of the Basic Law have* ***skated*** *awkwardly* ***around*** *the... political structure.* IND = skirt around/round.

skate on thin ice [Vpr] handle a delicate situation skilfully; venture into a situation where there are risks, and where therefore one has to act carefully: *The managing director had to explain that with the fall in demand we might be forced to lay people off, but of course he's used to* ***skating on thin ice*** *and managed the situation as well as could be hoped.* ○ *'If I were you, I shouldn't come in here telling my staff their business: you're* ***skating on*** *very* ***thin ice****.'* □ continuous tenses only.

skate over [Vpr pass] move over the surface of (sth), ie without really dealing with it or tackling it. **o:** surface; problem, difficulty, issue: *He's so cautious and evasive: always* ***skating over*** *the surface, never coming to grips with the issues underneath.* ○ *'This is not something that can be* ***skated over****—let's get down to brass tacks.'*

sketch

sketch in [Vn ⇆ p pass adj] add (sth) quickly, roughly and perhaps temporarily to a drawing. **O:** detail; figure, house, tree: *He* ***sketched in*** *the tail assembly of the plane very quickly to show colleagues how his ideas were developing.*

sketch out [Vn ⇆ p pass adj] give a rough, outline picture of (sth). **O:** plan, proposal, design; (housing) development, precinct, centre: *'Give me a pad and pencil and I'll* ***sketch out*** *what I have in mind.'* ○ *He showed me a hastily* ***sketched-out*** *plan of the road system.*

skim

skim off 1 [Vn ⇆ p pass] remove sth floating on the surface of a liquid. **O:** cream, clots; oil, fat; scum, slime: *The gravy is too greasy:* ***skim off*** *some of the fat before you serve it.*

2 [Vn ⇆ p pass] take the best, the most able, part of a group. **S:** special school, elite university; specialist arm, crack unit. **O:** cream; most able, best qualified: *In some areas, maintained grammar schools are still able to* **skim off** *the most able of the secondary school entry.* ○ *The cream of manpower was* **skimmed off** *into the 'workers' battalions'.* B = cream off.

skim through [Vpr nom pass adj] read quickly through (sth), getting a general impression of its contents. **o:** book, article; chapter, section; notes: *'Give me a moment to* **skim through** *these notes before the meeting.'* ○ *Don't read the book in detail:* **skim through** *it to get the general picture.* ○ *'Leave the essay with me: I'll give it a quick* **skim-through** *before lunch.'*

skimp

skimp on [Vpr pass] devote less time or money to (sth) than is needed for satisfactory results. **o:** building materials; wool, silk; meat, milk: *When you decorate your house, don't* **skimp on** *materials: buy the best paint and paper you can afford.*

skirt

skirt around/round [Vpr pass emph rel] go round the edge of (sth); avoid facing and dealing with (a problem). **o:** question, matter; problem, difficulty: *I think it's about time there was some truth and plain speaking for a change, instead of all this* **skirting round** *it.* TT ○ *He was glad that Robin had stepped over the border of personal privacy* **around** *which they had been* **skirting** *the whole evening.* ASA = skate around/round.

skittle

skittle out [Vn ⇆ p pass] (*cricket*) dismiss (the opposing batsmen) in quick succession. **O:** side, team; batsmen: *The tourists were* **skittled out** *for 161 runs.* ITV ○ *Kent* **skittled out** *Surrey on a green wicket that gave the ball plenty of lift.*

skive

skive off [Vp, Vpr] (*informal*) leave or stay away from (a place) furtively, esp to avoid some unpleasant task: *'Trust the men to* **skive off** *and leave us to do the clearing away.'* ○ *He spent most of his last term* **skiving off** *classes.*

slacken

slacken off [Vp] become less intense, less active; weaken. **S:** trade, commerce; student, athlete; drama, tension: *Business usually* **slackens off** *at this time of the year.* ○ *The one problem of the book is that the density and texture* **slacken off** *somewhat in the later pages.* G = ease off.

slag

slag off [Vn ⇆ p pass] (*informal*) attack (sb) verbally in a fierce and unsavoury way: *You keep disagreeing with each other violently ... and* **slagging** *each other* **off** *in the popular press.* HHGG

slam

slam down [Vn ⇆ p pass] put (sth) down violently and noisily. **O:** (telephone) receiver, window, hatch; money, paper: *Mr Gibbs was fighting a wild desire to* **slam down** *his receiver.* DF ○ *He* **slammed** *a dirty bundle of notes* **down** *on the table.*

slam the door in sb's face [Vn.pr pass] (*informal*) shut a door violently to prevent sb unwelcome from entering, or to show he is unwelcome; reject some approach or initiative in a hostile way. **o:** (**of**) salesman, pedlar, beggar; visitor; negotiator, delegate: *I used to hope that one day, somebody would have the guts to* **slam the door in our faces**, *but they didn't. They were too well-bred.* LBA ○ *He was a door-to-door salesman for a bit, but he soon got tired of having* **the door slammed in his face**. = bang the door in sb's face.

slam the brakes on [Vn ⇆ p pass] (*informal*) apply the brakes of a vehicle abruptly and strongly: *Peter made the mistake of* **slamming the brakes on** *as he entered a tight corner, and slid into the path of an oncoming car.* ○ *'If you find yourself losing control on a slippery surface don't, for Heaven's sake,* **slam on the brakes**.*'* = jam the brakes on.

slam to [Vn.p pass] close (sth) violently and noisily. **O:** door, gate, window: *At this point, he became speechless with anger,* **slammed** *the gate* **to**, *and strode away.* ○ *I didn't get a chance to speak to her — the door was* **slammed to** *in my face.*

slap

slap down 1 [Vn ⇆ p pass] put (sth) down firmly, with the sound of a flat palm striking a surface. **O:** envelope, packet; money, banknotes: *A boy in uniform came into the shop,* **slapped** *a telegram* **down** *on the counter, and went out without waiting for a reply.* ○ *The fishmonger picked up an enormous skate and* **slapped** *it* **down** *in front of me.*

2 [Vn ⇆ p pass] (*informal*) check or discourage a bold, venturesome, impudent etc person: *'Anyone who speaks out of turn in the Old Man's presence is liable to be* **slapped down**.*'* ○ *'Getting admitted to that club is likely to be tough for upstarts like you and me. You can try it if you don't mind being* **slapped down**.*'*

slap on/onto 1 [Vn ⇆ p pass, Vn.pr pass] (*informal*) apply (sth) vigorously or carelessly to a surface. **O:** paint, distemper; mud, clay; make-up. **o:** wall, fence; frame; cheeks: *'You'll need to* **slap** *a bit of creosote* **on** *those posts before you stick them in the ground.'* ○ *'The oil tank will rust unless you do something to protect it. So* **slap on** *a couple of coats of red lead.'*

2 [Vn ⇆ p pass, Vn.pr pass] (*informal*) add (sth) to (a price etc) in a way, or to an extent, that is unwelcome. **O:** tax, surcharge; levy; increase of 50 pence. **o:** beer, tobacco; betting; price, cost: *'Before we'd had time to recover from the last rise, the building societies* **slapped** *another one per cent* **on** *our mortgage interest.'* ○ *Tourists arriving at the airport for their charter flights found that the tour operators had* **slapped** *a £20 surcharge* **onto** *the cost of their holidays.* = clap on/onto.

slave

slave away [Vp] work continuously, like a slave. **S:** housewife, servant: *'Why should I* **slave away** *at a hot stove for half my life?'* ○ *'Look at them, we* **slave away** *and they play cards.'* DPM

sleep

sleep around [Vp] (*informal*) have one sexual partner after another without becoming seriously involved with any of them: *Nowadays there are compelling health reasons as well as moral ones for not* **sleeping around**.

sleep in 1 [Vp nom] sleep later than usual: *I'm going to **sleep in** tomorrow and generally have a lazy day.* ○ *We normally have a **sleep-in** on Sunday.*
2 [Vp nom] sleep on the premises where one works. **S:** porter, caretaker: *Most of the hotel staff **sleep in**.* ○ *They can afford a **sleep-in** nanny and cook.* □ nom form used only as modifier of a noun. = live in.

sleep off [Vn ⇆ p pass] get rid of (sth) by sleeping. **O:** indigestion, hangover, headache: *The clubroom seems to be used only by surgeons **sleeping off** official luncheons.* DIL ○ *'I know he's in an evil mood, but let's give him a night to **sleep** it **off**, shall we?'*

sleep on it [Vpr] have a night's sleep before making a difficult decision: *The thing to do with a problem is to **sleep on it**.* TGLY ○ *I went back ... to write a letter to Janet Prentice. I **slept on it**, tore it up, wrote it again, **slept on it** the next night, and wrote it a third time.* RFW

sleep together/with [Vp, Vpr] have sexual intercourse (with sth): *She's a very strictly brought-up girl; I doubt very much if she's **sleeping with** her boyfriend* (or: *I doubt if she and her boyfriend are **sleeping together***).

slew

slew around/round [Vp, Vn ⇆ p pass] (usu said of a heavy, awkward piece of machinery) turn around to face in a new direction. **S** [Vp], **O** [Vn.p]**:** crane, rig; gun, tank; car, lorry. **S** [Vn.p]**:** operator, driver: *It took time to **slew** the guns **around** to engage fresh targets.* ○ *The car **slewed round** in a complete circle on the icy road.*

slice

slice into [Vpr pass] insert a knife into (sth) to cut a slice from it. **o:** loaf, pie, sausage; arm, leg: *I like to **slice into** a loaf when it's fresh from the oven.* ○ *'Don't draw the knife towards you when you're carving: you might **slice into** your own finger.'*

slice off [Vn ⇆ p pass] remove (sth) as a slice from some larger object. **O:** end; crust, steak, cutlet; finger, toe: *The machine **sliced off** thin rounds of copper into a bin.* ○ *He **sliced off** a thick crust and bit into it hungrily.*

slice up [Vn ⇆ p pass adj] cut (sth) into slices. **O:** loaf, cake; sausage, side of bacon: *The long loaves were **sliced up** ready for making into sandwiches.*

slick

slick down [Vn ⇆ p pass adj] flatten down (one's hair) close to the head with oil etc. **O:** hair; wisp, lock: *Hair was drawn up from the side of his head and **slicked down** over the bald patch on top.* ○ *Hair thickly **slicked down** with grease suggests the rock-and-roll fashions of the 1950s.*

slip

slip across, along, away etc [Vp, Vpr] move across etc quickly, quietly and without attracting much attention: *Aunt Annabel had **slipped in** early with three cats playfully following the trailing cord of her dressing-gown.* DC ○ *He had suggested to Robert that they might **slip out** for a drink before lunch.* HD ○ *'I want to do a little shopping too. I'll **slip over** to Harrods.'* DC

slip away 1 [Vp] leave quickly and quietly, without attracting attention. **S:** guest, spectator, prisoner: *'If you want to **slip away**, now's a good time: everyone is dancing.'* ○ *Availing herself of the diversion caused by the landlord's appearance, the barmaid had **slipped away**.* PW
2 [Vp] pass quickly. **S:** weekend; afternoon, evening; days, weeks: *The last few days of August were **slipping away**; it would soon be time to pack up and return home.*

slip down [Vp] be swallowed smoothly and easily. **S:** drink; medicine; beer, liqueur; ice-cream, porridge: *John was handed a glass filled with a thick, green liquid. It **slipped down** pleasantly enough.*

slip in/into 1 [Vn ⇆ p pass, Vn.pr pass] put (sth) smoothly and without it being noticed into (sth). **O:** money, coins; note, letter; key. **o:** handbag; hand; lock: *Isabella Bennion had contrived to **slip in** presents for each of the five.* ILIH ○ *As he turned to leave, Uncle David **slipped** a five-pound note **into** my hand.*
2 [Vn ⇆ p pass, Vn.pr pass emph rel] mention (sth) important in conversation etc, so carefully that one does not appear to be drawing special attention to it. **O:** word, remark; reference, allusion. **o:** speech, address; conversation: *He liked to **slip in** the occasional reference to the important work he was doing.* ○ *One or two appeals for funds were **slipped into** the chairman's opening address.*

slip into [Vpr pass] put (sth) on, with a quick, easy movement. **o:** jacket, pair of trousers; dress, skirt: *She got up, **slipped into** a dressing-gown, and peered out of the window.* ○ *They're an old pair of shoes I can **slip into** to do the gardening.* slip off. ⇨ slip on.

slip off [Vn ⇆ p pass] take (sth) off, with a quick, easy movement. **O:** jacket, jumper; trousers; boots: *He **slipped off** his shoes and trousers and got into bed.* ○ *'**Slip** your jacket **off** and roll your sleeve up.'* ↔ slip into, slip on.

slip on [Vn ⇆ p pass] put (sth) on, with a quick, easy movement. **O:** jumper, shirt; slacks, trousers; shoes: *He **slipped on** a sweater and a pair of slacks and went down to open the door.* ○ *'**Slip** your overcoat **on**; it's getting chilly.'* ↔ slip off. ⇨ slip into. ⇨ previous entry

slip out [Vp] be said carelessly, through inattention. **S:** name, word, remark: *'I'm sorry—I didn't mean to give the game away—it just **slipped out**.*

slip over [Vn.pr pass] pass a garment over some protruding part of the body so that it covers that, or some other part. **O:** shirt, sweater; sash, armlet. **o:** head, shoulders, arm: *'It's a cool evening, so do **slip** a shawl **over** your shoulders.'* ○ *'You **slip** the life-jacket **over** your head, so that the parts which provide buoyancy rest on the chest and back.'*

slip past [Vp, Vpr, Vn ⇆ p pass, Vn.pr pass] (help or cause sb/sth to) pass sb who is watching or guarding a place, without him noticing. **S** [Vp Vpr], **O** [Vn.p Vn.pr]**:** prisoner, refugee, escapee; contraband; alcohol, tobacco; blow. **S** [Vn.p Vn.pr]**:** organization, gang; smuggler; boxer. **o:** guard; customs officer [Vpr] : *A well-staged diversion in the huts enabled two prisoners to **slip past** the men on the gate.* ○ [Vn.pr] . ○ *He managed to **slip** one or two good punches **past** his opponent's guard.*

slip through [Vp, Vpr, Vn ⇆ p pass, Vn.pr pass] (enable sth/sb to) pass through sth which is intended to control or check such movement. **S** [Vp Vpr], **O** [Vn.p Vn.pr]**:** article, product, specimen; money;

suspect, captive. **S** [Vn.p Vn.pr]: dealer, agent. **o:** checkpoint, control-point; customs; net, trap; sb's hands, fingers, clutches [Vp] : *We are unable to prevent a small number of defective parts* ***slipping through***. ○ [Vpr] . ○ *Some valuable information has* ***slipped through*** *the security network.* ○ [Vpr] *Money just* ***slips through*** *your fingers without your knowing what has become of it.* WI ○ [Vn.pr] *They are* ***slipping*** *very few aircraft* ***through*** *our defensive screen.*

slip up [Vp nom] make a mistake; blunder. **S:** manager, organizer: *Somebody must have* ***slipped up*** *badly* (or: *made a bad* ***slip-up***) *in your report. They seem to have left out her stage name.* EGD ○ *There is a slightly uncomfortable feeling of somebody having* ***slipped up*** (or: *of there having been a* ***slip-up*** *on somebody's part*). L

slobber

slobber over [Vpr pass] (*informal*) show too much sentimental feeling for (sb/sth). **o:** child, dog: *'I am always embarrassed by the way he* ***slobbers over*** *small children.* = drool over.

slog

slog away (at) [Vp, Vp.pr rel] (*informal*) work continuously, and in a hard, determined way (at sth). **o:** lesson, book; task, problem: *Nick's been* ***slogging away at*** *at that translation all morning.* ○ *'Keep* ***slogging away***! *You've nearly broken the back of the job.'*

slog it out [Vn.p] (*informal*) struggle, fight, until a conclusion is reached. **S:** contestants, opponents: *The fans were on the edge of their seats as champion and contender* ***slogged it out*** *in the final round.* ○ *I enjoy a good old intellectual rough and tumble, and I only wish I could stay and* ***slog it out*** *with the two of you.* EGD

slop

slop about/around 1 [Vp] (of a liquid) move about heavily, esp in a confined space. **S:** water, paint, petrol: *A couple of gallons of water were* ***slopping around*** *in the bottom of the boat.*
2 [Vp] (*informal*) move about in a lazy, casual way: *'I've tried to get the boy interested in decorating the house, but all he does is* ***slop around***, *picking at jobs and not settling to anything in particular.'* = slouch about/around.

slop out [Vp] (of prisoners) empty away dirty water, urine etc from vessels which have been kept overnight in the cells: *In the morning, prisoners in older jails have to take their basins and buckets to the latrine for* ***slopping out***.

slop over [Vp] (of liquids) spill heavily over the edge of a vessel etc. **S:** water; coffee, tea: *A saucepan fell into the basin, and dirty water* ***slopped over*** *onto the kitchen floor.*

slope

slope down (to) [Vp, Vp.pr rel] form a slope stretching down from one point to another. **S:** garden, lawn, field. **o:** river, road: *At the back, a flower garden* ***slopes down to*** *a line of poplar trees.* = shelve down (to).

slope off [Vp] (*informal*) go away rather furtively, usu to avoid doing sth unpleasant: *'Don't think that you can* ***slope off*** *just because my back's turned!'* ○ *'Let's* ***slope off*** *somewhere quiet and have a cigarette.'*

slosh

slosh on [Vn ⇆ p pass, Vn.pr pass] (*informal*) apply (paint etc) in a rough, vigorous way. **O:** paint, distemper; paste. **o:** wall; canvas; paper: *'Don't be afraid —* ***slosh on*** *plenty of bright colour.'* ○ *'Careful, you're* ***sloshing*** *paste* ***on*** *your shirt!'*

slot

slot in/into 1 [Vp, Vpr, Vn ⇆ p pass, Vn.pr] (cause sth to) fit smoothly and tightly into (a narrow space). **S** [Vp Vpr], **O** [Vn.p Vn.pr]: disc, cassette, cartridge, magazine: [Vp] *The twenty-round magazine* ***slots in*** *just in front of the trigger.* ○ [Vn.pr] *She* ***slotted*** *a Paul Simon cassette* ***into*** *the car stereo.*
2 [Vp, Vpr, Vn ⇆ p pass, Vn.pr pass] (cause sb/sth to) fit smoothly into (an organization etc). **S** [Vp Vpr], **O** [Vn.p Vn.pr]: salesman, executive, editor: [Vpr] *David has* ***slotted*** *very smoothly* ***into*** *our sales team.* ○ [Vn.p] *There was a vacancy in design, and we* ***slotted*** *her* ***in*** *there.*

slouch

slouch about/around [Vp, Vpr] move about in a lazy, slovenly way. **o:** the place, the house: *'I do wish the boy would stop* ***slouching about*** *with his hands in his pockets.'* = slop about/around 2.

slough

slough off [Vn ⇆ p pass] get rid of (sth); abandon. **O:** responsibility; worry, anxiety; habit, practice: *He had* ***sloughed off*** *all the petty cares of home and work.* RFW ○ *Magdalen* (has managed) *to* ***slough off*** *its image as the playground of the social upper crust.* OXTD □ literally, of a snake, discard its old skin.

slow

slow down 1 [Vp, Vn ⇆ p pass] (cause sth to) move more slowly; decelerate. **S** [Vp], **O** [Vn.p]: car, lorry; machine; pace, action. **S** [Vn.p]: driver, police; operator; director: *At first he drove rather fast and then* ***slowed down*** *to a silent crawl.* DBM ○ *'The motor's overheating. Can't you* ***slow*** *it* ***down***?' ○ *'Don't* ***slow down*** *the movement in this scene: it's tending to drag.'* ↔ speed up.
2 [Vp, Vn ⇆ p pass] (cause sb to) live, work etc in a less active and intense way, usu because one's health is in danger: *'You really ought to* ***slow down*** *— all these late nights are doing you no good.'* ○ *'If I could find some way of* ***slowing*** *my father* ***down***, *I would; he's taking on far too much work.'* ⇨ next entry

slow up [Vp] act, work etc less energetically or effectively because of age, poor health etc. **S:** worker, sportsman, writer: *I think he's beginning to* ***slow up*** *— his latest book is much weaker than the previous one.* ○ *He's over sixty, but he shows no signs of* ***slowing up***. ⇨ previous entry

sluice

sluice down [Vn ⇆ p pass adj] clear, clean (a surface) by using a heavy flow of water. **O:** wall, floor, street: *Moscow is a clean city. Huge water-carts* ***sluice down*** *the streets every day.* LFM

sluice out [Vn ⇆ p pass adj] clear, clean (an enclosed space or passage) by using a heavy flow of water. **O:** channel; drain, sink, gutter; one's mouth: *If the pipe gets blocked try **sluicing** it **out** with hot water.* ○ *The stables were **sluiced out** with water from a hose.*

smack

smack of [Vpr] indicate, suggest sth illegal or morally unacceptable. **S:** life; conduct, behaviour; language. **o:** corruption, immorality; treason, heresy: *I never went to race meetings, which to me always **smacked of** the idle rich.* SML ○ *To me, his suggestion **smacks of** underhand methods.* = savour of, smell of 2.

smarten

smarten up [Vp, Vn.p pass] (cause sb/sth to) become more smart, ie cleaner, better-dressed etc. **O:** oneself; place: *He's **smartened up** considerably since I last saw him.* ○ *'You'll spend the rest of your life in the ice-cream factory if you don't **smarten** yourself **up** a bit.'* ASA ○ *The shop will have to be **smartened up** a bit if you want to cater for the top end of the market.* = spruce up.

smash

smash down [Vn ⇆ p pass] knock (sth) down by striking it violently. **O:** wall, door, fence: *They could hear the door being **smashed down** with axes.* IND

smash in [Vn ⇆ p pass adj] make a hole, dent or wound in (sth) by striking it a violent blow. **O:** window, door; wing, boot (of car); ribs: *The explosion had **smashed in** all the ground-floor windows.* ○ *A single blow from an adult bear could **smash in** your rib-cage.*

smash sb's face in [Vn.p pass] (*informal*) make a violent physical attack on sb, eg to stop him interfering in one's affairs: *'If you mess my girl about, I'll **smash your face in**!'* ○ *Anyone trying to take over the gang's territory would get **his face smashed in**.* □ often uttered as a threat, as in the first example.

smash up [Vn ⇆ p nom pass adj] damage (sth) badly in a road accident etc, by striking it violently. **O:** car, lorry; train; furniture, crockery: *Stringfellows nightclub was **smashed up**, but the pub next door was left unscathed.* G ○ *There has been a serious **smash-up** on the motorway, involving a container lorry and three cars.*

smear

smear on [Vn ⇆ p pass, Vn.pr pass rel] apply a sticky or oily substance to (sth). **O:** grease, ointment; paint; butter. **o:** hand, face; wall: *'**Smear** some of this cream **on** your face before putting on the grease-paint.'* ○ *The children had **smeared** jam **on** the walls* (or: *had **smeared** the walls **with** jam*).

smear with [Vn.pr pass rel] ⇨ previous entry

smell

smell of 1 [Vpr] have or give out the smell of (sth). **S:** house, room; dinner, meat; breath. **o:** damp, decay; garlic; whisky: *The stew **smelt** deliciously **of** herbs and onion.* ○ *His breath **smelt** suspiciously **of** whisky.*

2 [Vpr] strongly suggest (sth). **S:** conduct, behaviour; suggestion, offer. **o:** intrigue, double-dealing; treason: *'If I were you, I should leave his offer alone. It **smells** strongly **of** shady dealing.'* = savour of, smack of.

smell out 1 [Vp.n pass] find (sth) by using one's sense of smell. **S:** dog. **O:** rat, rabbit; fugitive; explosive: *The police use dogs to **smell out** hidden explosive.* = sniff out 1.

2 [Vp.n pass] find (sth) by noticing and understanding certain clues. **S:** detective, investigator; traveller. **O:** corruption, rackets; excitement, adventure: *It's the committee's job to **smell out** corruption and abuse of privilege in the upper echelons of the party.* = sniff out 2.

smell to high heaven 1 [Vpr] (*informal*) have a strong, unpleasant smell. **S:** place; drains, cellar: *'When was the last time you cleaned out the cat's litter tray? It **smells to high heaven**.'* = stink to high heaven 1.

2 [Vpr] (*informal*) strongly suggest dishonesty, corruption etc. **S:** deal, business: *'There's been dirty dealing over the allocation of building permits. The whole thing **smells to high heaven**.'* = stink to high heaven 2.

smoke

smoke out/out of 1 [Vn ⇆ p pass, Vn.pr pass] drive (sth) from hiding by means of smoke. **O:** insect, snake, fox, rabbit. **o:** greenhouse, hole, lair, burrow: *We used a piece of pipe connected to the car exhaust to **smoke out** the rats.*

2 [Vn ⇆ p pass, Vn.pr pass] make (sb) emerge from hiding by cunning etc. **O:** terrorist, fugitive. **o:** hiding; lair: *'I came back too late,' he said. 'You wouldn't have come at all if I hadn't **smoked** you **out**.'* TLG

smooth

smooth down 1 [Vn ⇆ p pass adj] make sth flat which is standing up, esp by stroking downwards. **O:** fur, feathers; lapel, pocket (of a coat): *John straightened his tie, **smoothed down** his unruly hair, and went to welcome the first guest.*

2 [Vn ⇆ p pass adj] restore, with soothing words etc, sb whose feelings have been upset or disturbed; settle those feelings. **O:** angry boss, jealous husband; ruffled feelings, wounded pride: *'Father's in a dreadful temper, Sarah. Do what you can to **smooth** him **down**.'* ○ *The rooms allocated to the visitors were already occupied, and it took the intervention of the manager to **smooth down** injured national pride.*

smooth out 1 [Vn ⇆ p pass adj] make (a surface) smooth by removing irregularities. **O:** sheet, tablecloth; fold, wrinkle: *Mother brushed off the breadcrumbs and **smoothed out** the cloth.* ○ *His face was suddenly young again, the lines of strain and fear temporarily **smoothed out**.* DC

2 [Vn ⇆ p pass adj] remove (difficulties etc), thus making a situation easier for sb. **O:** obstacle, snag; problem, difficulty: *The office has **smoothed out** some of the formalities, so you will get your certificate as arranged.* ○ *There are some technical problems to be **smoothed out** before we can fly.*

smooth over [Vn ⇆ p pass adj] settle (a quarrel etc) by acting calmly and diplomatically. **O:** the thing, things; differences; disharmony: *This was a genuine attempt to placate him and **smooth** this thing **over**.* CON ○ *They were now arguing furiously, with*

James standing by and trying to **smooth** *things* **over**.

smother

smother (in/with) [Vn.pr pass rel] cover (sth) thickly (with sth). **O:** hall, table; fire; visitor, guest. **o:** flower, decoration; earth, ash; gift, present; kisses, praise: *The general's chest was* **smothered in** *medals* (or: *Medals* **smothered** *the general's chest*). ○ *The welcoming committee would* **smother** *him* **in** *compliments — always an embarrassing moment, which he tried to cut short.*

smuggle

smuggle in/into [Vn ⇆ p pass adj, Vn.pr pass] bring (sth) illegally into (a place). **O:** whisky; watch, camera; letter, tool. **o:** country; camp, prison: *A strict watch is kept to prevent the* **smuggling in** *of drugs.* ○ *Equipment was* **smuggled into** *the camp under the very noses of the guards.* ⇨ next entry

smuggle out/out of [Vn ⇆ p pass, Vn.pr pass] take (sb/sth) illegally out of (a place). **O:** prisoner; currency, goods; message. **o:** camp, gaol; country: *Information was* **smuggled out** *by a friendly guard.* ○ *The penalties are severe for people caught* **smuggling** *banknotes* **out of** *the country.* ⇨ previous entry

smuggle past [Vn ⇆ p pass, Vn.pr pass] take (sb/sth) illegally past (a checkpoint) without being detected. **O:** prisoner, illegal immigrant; wine, tobacco; message, food. **o:** guard, frontier post; customs: *'You'll be very lucky to* **smuggle** *that much wine* **past** *the customs.'* ○ *A couple of prisoners were* **smuggled past** *the sentries on the gate in empty swill bins.*

snap

snap at 1 [Vpr] try to grasp (sth) with the teeth by closing them sharply around it. **S:** dog, fish. **o:** leg, ankle; bait: *You must ask her to stop her dog* **snapping at** *visitors.*

2 [Vpr pass] speak sharply, irritably to (sb). **o:** wife, husband; child; employee: *We're both terribly tired at the end of the day. It's no wonder we* **snap at** *each other.*

3 [Vpr pass] try to grasp (sth) by accepting, agreeing etc, quickly. **S:** buyer, negotiator. **o:** bargain, offer: *'Give him half a chance to travel abroad for us and he'll* **snap at** *it.'*

snap one's fingers at [Vn.pr] (*informal*) treat (sb/sth) with contempt, derision etc. **o:** authorities, boss; rule, regulation; convention, established practices: *He* **snaps his fingers at** *his parents' most cherished beliefs.* ○ *Noone was going to stop Phil gatecrashing the party. He would just* **snap his fingers at** *them.*

snap sb's head off [Vn.p pass] (*informal*) react sharply and in bad humour to sth that sb has said: *I can't mention her boyfriend's name without her* **snapping my head off**. ○ (a tennis player) *He never smiled on court and anyone asking him a question the minute he came off court was likely to get* **their head snapped off**. G □ note the passive with *get* and the plural in: *If they spoke out of turn they would get* **their heads snapped off**. = bite sb's head off.

snap out [Vn ⇆ p pass adj] exclaim (sth) in a sharp, unpleasant tone. **O:** reply, retort; instruction: *The colonel suddenly* **snapped out** *the information.* QA ○ *'I don't see why I should tell you anything,' she* **snapped out** *in reply.*

snap out of it [Vpr, Vn.pr] (*informal*) (cause sb to) briskly get rid of a negative feeling: *'All that self-pity, my dear! He really ought to* **snap out of it**.*'* PW ○ *Quitting is a bad way to embark on life, and that young person had better* **snap out of it**. NY ○ (managing footballers) *'Shouting wouldn't* **snap** *them* **out of it**, *just reduce their chances of putting up any kind of show when the game started.'* IND ⇨ shake off 2.

snap to it [Vpr] (*informal*) get started, eg on a job; start moving quickly: *'I said I wanted that stuff moved. Now come on,* **snap to it**!*'* ○ *'We haven't got all day.* **Snap to it**!*'* □ usu direct or indirect command.

snap up 1 [Vn ⇆ p pass adj] take, buy etc (sth) quickly and eagerly. **O:** house, flat; drink, cigarettes; picture, antique: *The hit video was* **snapped up** *as soon as it reached the shops.*

2 [Vn ⇆ p pass adj] enrol, employ, marry etc (sb) before others can do so. **O:** candidate, applicant; skilled worker; eligible man: *The department was* **snapping up** *any applicant, however poorly qualified.* ○ *She'd stay with me rather than let herself be* **snapped up** *by a lousy provincial artist.* CON

snarl

snarl at [Vpr pass] make an unpleasant, growling sound at (sb). **S:** dog; boss, husband: *The dog has an unfortunate way of* **snarling at** *the postman.* ○ *'I'm not used to being* **snarled at** *— change your tone.'*

snarl up 1 [Vp nom, Vn ⇆ p nom pass adj] (*informal*) (cause sth to) become blocked or jammed. **S** [Vp], **O** [Vn.p]**:** traffic; car, lorry; communications; telephone/radio network, switchboard. **S** [Vn.p]**:** controller; operator: *Traffic had* **snarled up** *badly on the approach road to Dover harbour.* ○ *Extra demand at these times* **snarls up** *the whole system* (or: *causes a* **snarl-up** *of the whole system*).

2 [Vp nom, Vn ⇆ p nom pass adj] (*informal*) (cause people or things to) become confused or entangled. **S** [Vp], **O** [Vn.p]**:** colleague, partner; talks, discussions; affairs, relations: *They* (business people) *can plan in the knowledge that ministers and civil servants are not busy setting traps ... and looking for every chance to* **snarl up** *their affairs.* ST ○ *Against all the odds, he* (the Secretary for Trade) *has got Labour all* **snarled up** *in the referendum commitment on Europe* (ie confused over their commitment to hold a referendum). ST

snatch

snatch at 1 [Vpr pass] try to grasp (sth) by putting out one's hand suddenly. **o:** purse, handbag; hand; rope: *A man darted from a doorway and* **snatched at** *his briefcase.* ○ *He* **snatched at** *the rope ladder, but it swung tantalizingly out of reach.*

2 [Vpr pass] try quickly to seize or take advantage of (sth). **o:** opportunity, chance, opening: *There are a few vacancies on the production side each year. You have to* **snatch at** *them as they come along.* ○ *... another great swelling* (ie increase) *of the ranks of the displaced and hopeless, ready to* **snatch at** *any satisfaction.* HA

snatch away [Vn ⇆ p pass] remove (sth) quickly, out of discourtesy, fear, suspicion, dislike etc. **O:**

dish, tray; hand; child: *'I do wish the waiter wouldn't* ***snatch*** *our plates* ***away*** *before we've finished eating.'* ○ *In an uncontrollable nervous reaction, she* ***snatched*** *her hand* ***away***. DC

snatch from/out of [Vn.pr pass rel] remove (sth/sb) from (a place) quickly, out of fear, greed etc. **O:** paper, book; child; occupant, passenger. **o:** grasp, hand; fire, wreckage: *The letter was* ***snatched out of*** *my hand before I had a chance to read it.* ○ *He was one of the few in his family to be* ***snatched from*** *the Holocaust.*

snatch up [Vn ⇆ p pass] seize, grasp (sth) quickly. **O:** bag, weapon, phone, sheet of paper, pencil: *She* ***snatched up*** *a pencil and pad and ran out to the waiting car.*

sneak

sneak across, along, away etc [Vp, Vpr] move across etc quietly and furtively: *Her mother . . . has to* ***sneak off*** *when no one's looking.* FFE ○ *That was the summer when we used to* ***sneak out*** *and slide down haystacks.* REC

sneer

sneer at [Vpr pass] show that one thinks very little of (sb/sth) by smiling or talking in a mocking, superior way. **o:** effort, attempt; achievement, work: *He never gives praise for what we do. Half the time he seems to be* ***sneering at*** *us.* ○ *It's not exactly encouraging to have your efforts* ***sneered at***.

sneeze

not sneeze at [Vpr pass] (*informal*) not consider (sth) lightly or with contempt; take seriously. **o:** achievement, success; offer, proposal; chance, opening: *'When it* (my career) *leads up to this six-room house with a different coloured phone in each room it's* ***not*** *to be* ***sneezed at****.'* JFTR ○ *'It is a very remarkable achievement of your father's. . . . I do****n't*** *think it's glory to be* ***sneezed at****, you know.'* HAA □ usu passive, or active with *should/would*.

sniff

(not) sniff at [Vpr pass] (*informal*) (not) reject (sth) as unworthy of one's attention. **o:** offer; proposal, suggestion; idea: *'If someone made me an offer like that I certainly would****n't sniff at*** *it.'* ○ *There was as much to relish as to* ***sniff at***. IND □ usu passive, or active with*should/would*.

sniff out 1 [Vn ⇆ p pass] find (sth/sb) by using the sense of smell. **S:** dog. **O:** rat, rabbit; explosive; fugitive: *'If there's somebody hiding down there, the police dogs will soon* ***sniff*** *him* ***out****.'* = smell out 1.

2 [Vp.n pass] find (sth/sb) by noticing and understanding clues etc. **S:** investigator; traveller. **O:** crime, racket; danger, excitement; villain: *It's his job to* ***sniff out*** *abuses of power.* SC ○ *He's off on his travels again,* ***sniffing out*** *adventure in Tunisia.* THH ○ *And they have* ***sniffed out*** *the culprits.* OBS = smell out 2.

snip

snip off [Vn ⇆ p pass adj] cut off, separate (sth) with short, quick movements of scissors etc. **S:** tailor, cutter, dressmaker. **O:** (loose) thread, end, piece: *The seamstress runs over the finished garment with the scissors,* ***snipping off*** *the loose threads.*

snipe

snipe at 1 [Vpr pass] (of a concealed marksman) fire at (sb/sth). **o:** target; enemy; position: *Our position was being* ***sniped at*** *from some bushes to the right.*

2 [Vpr pass] make sudden, sharp attacks on (sb). **S:** rival, enemy; journalist; newspaper: *He's not too worried when he gets* ***sniped at*** *in the gossip columns.*

snoop

snoop about/around/round [Vp nom, Vpr] (*informal*) search in a persistent, irritating way for sth, esp signs that people are breaking rules, misbehaving etc. **S:** (prison) guard; inspector; prefect: *We've had the health and safety people* ***snooping around*** *again, counting the bars of soap in the kitchen.* ○ *Nobody is telling the truth, and least of all to. . . parliamentary private secretaries whose job it is to* ***snoop around*** *and sneak to their bosses about what is going on.* IND ○ *The manager's been in here again, having a bit of a* ***snoop-round***.

snort

snort at [Vpr pass emph rel] express contempt, annoyance etc at (sth), by puffing air sharply through the nose. **o:** interruption, delay; claim, conceit: *John* ***snorted*** *in disbelief* ***at*** *the doorman. 'What do you mean, we can't come in there?'* ○ ***At*** *the prospect of still further delays, Peter* ***snorted*** *in anger and frustration.*

snow

snowed in [pass adj (Vn.p)] prevented from moving or leaving a place by heavy snow. **S:** car, lorry; farmer: *Our train was* ***snowed in*** *by a terrible blizzard.* ○ *The roads were dotted with* ***snowed-in*** *cars.*

snowed off [pass adj (Vn.p)] (*sport*) cancelled or abandoned because of heavy snow. **S:** match, game; race: *Several fixtures in the League programme have been* ***snowed off****.* ○ *They are now playing the match which was* ***snowed off*** *at Manchester last Saturday.* BBCR

snowed under (with) [pass (Vn.p Vn.p.pr)] (*informal*) having a heavy load of (sth); overwhelmed (with). **S:** staff; business; office. **o:** work; order, commission; letter; appeal, application: *'Please don't give me any extra jobs: I'm* ***snowed under*** *as it is.'* ○ *In the weeks before Christmas they are* ***snowed under*** *with work.* ○ *At the time we were being* ***snowed under with*** *requests for medical aid.* □ passive also with *appear, get, look, seem*.

snowed up [pass adj (Vn.p)] isolated by heavy snow, unable to leave the house etc for this reason. **S:** house; occupant, traveller, guest: *This is the first time that I have actually been* ***snowed up****. And now this fog!* EM ○ *The staging camps higher up the mountain would be* ***snowed up*** *if this blizzard continued.* = snowed in.

snuff

snuff out 1 [Vn ⇆ p pass adj] extinguish (sth). **O:** candle, lamp: *The candles on the long dining table were* ***snuffed out****.* = put out 10.

2 [Vn ⇆ p pass adj] force (sth) to cease; suppress. **O:** hope, optimism; rising, revolt: *The authorities*

snuffed out *the radical movement as soon as it emerged into the open.* = put down 7.

snuggle

snuggle down [Vp] (*informal*) move under the bedclothes, to get warm and comfortable: *'Now, **snuggle** right **down** and I'll tuck you in.'* ○ *The child **snuggled down** with her doll and was quickly asleep.*

snuggle up (to) [Vp, Vp.pr pass] (*informal*) press up close (to another person) for warmth or comfort, or out of affection or desire. **S:** child; lover: *The children **snuggled up to** one another in the strange bed.* ○ *She **snuggled up to** her boyfriend in the darkened cinema.* = cuddle up (to).

soak

soak (oneself) in [Vn.pr] absorb as much as possible of (sth). **o:** history, lore, tradition: *During these long summer visits he had **soaked himself in** the traditions and customs of the place.* = steep (oneself) in.

soak off [Vn ⇆ p pass, Vn.pr pass] remove (sth) by soaking it in water. **O:** (postage-)stamp, transfer; wallpaper: *Rather than paint over the paper you'd do better to **soak** it **off**.* ○ (instruction in plastic model kit) ***Soak** the transfers carefully **off** the backing paper and slide them onto the model.*

soak through [Vn.p pass] make (sb's clothes) thoroughly wet. **S:** rain; storm, downpour: *'Don't stand out there: you'll be **soaked through**.'*

soak to the skin [Vn.pr pass] make sb's clothes wet right through. **S:** rain; downpour, cloudburst: *A passing bus swept through a large puddle and **soaked** us **to the skin**.* ○ *A storm burst over them as they slept in a field and they were **soaked to the skin**.* ASA

soak up 1 [Vn ⇆ p pass adj] absorb (sth). **S:** sponge, cloth; ground. **O:** water, tea: *If you spill ink on the carpet, **soak** it **up** straight away.* ○ *This sandy soil **soaks up** moisture very quickly.* = take up 2.

2 [Vp.n] allow one's body to absorb (sth). **O:** sun, sunshine; heat, warmth: *Alex lay by the edge of the pool, **soaking up** the sun.*

3 [Vn ⇆ p pass adj] assimilate, absorb (sth). **S:** student, class. **O:** information; figures, facts: *'Fred is very quick: he **soaks up** new information like a sponge.'*

soap

soap down [Vn.p pass] rub soap over (one's body): *After a hard game, it's refreshing to **soap** oneself **down** under a hot shower.*

sob

sob out [Vn ⇆ p pass] tell (a story etc) while crying bitterly. **O:** (sad) tale, story, account: *We listened sympathetically while she **sobbed out** the whole sorry tale.*

sob one's heart out [Vn.p] (*informal*) (from pain or distress) cry bitterly, drawing in the breath sharply and noisily: *When she heard her husband was leaving, Mary just **sobbed her heart out**.* ○ *There seemed no way of comforting the boy. He sat there **sobbing his heart out**.*

sober

sober down [Vp, Vn ⇆ p pass] (*informal*) (make sb) become calm and serious, esp after a period of lighthearted or irresponsible behaviour. **S** [Vp], **O** [Vn.p]: child; student; reveller, party. **S** [Vn.p]: parent; teacher: *'Now just **sober down**, everybody. I've important news for you.'* ○ *He doesn't take as many risks on the road as he used to. I suppose one bad crash and two near misses would **sober** most people **down**.* = sober up 2.

sober up 1 [Vp, Vn ⇆ p pass adj] (*informal*) (cause sb to) recover from a drunken state: *When he finally **sobered up**, he found that his wallet had been taken.* ○ *'Put his head under the cold tap — that'll **sober** him **up**.'*

2 [Vp, Vn ⇆ p pass] (*informal*) (cause sb to) become serious or thoughtful, esp after a period of lighthearted or irresponsible behaviour: *I stopped grinning, not out of politeness but because what he said really did **sober** me **up**.* = sober down.

sod

sod off [Vp] (*taboo*) leave, go away: *'Don't stand for any trouble from him. Just tell him to **sod off**.'* = clear off 1.

soften

soften up 1 [Vn ⇆ p pass] (*informal*) weaken (a place), by shelling etc, for later attack. **S:** bomber, artillery. **O:** position, trench system: *The beach defences were **softened up** before the landing craft went in.*

2 [Vn ⇆ p pass] (*informal*) weaken the resistance of sb whom one wishes to persuade, convert, seduce etc. **S:** salesman, preacher; lover. **O:** housewife, congregation, girl: *'She's **softening** me **up**, you see, so that I will be amenable by the time she gets here.'* AITC

soldier

soldier on [Vp] continue to work, despite discouragement, difficulties etc: *Diesel engines failed badly in the freeze-up while electrics and steam **soldiered on**.* OBS

sop

sop up [Vn ⇆ p pass] raise, remove (liquid) by pressing sth absorbent over it. **O:** water, milk, tea, ink: *'Get a towel and **sop up** the water before it runs over the floor.'* ○ *I dislike his habit of **sopping up** the gravy with a piece of bread.*

sort

sort out 1 [Vn ⇆ p pass adj] place, arrange (things or people) in groups, classes etc, according to size, shape etc. **S:** storekeeper, packer; teacher. **O:** part, fitting; box, tin; pupil, material: *She spent a happy afternoon **sorting out** her coins and stamps.* ○ *Members of the armed forces have been **sorted out** by trades and occupations.* MFM

2 [Vn ⇆ p pass] settle, resolve (sth). **O:** dispute, quarrel; matter, problem; tangle, muddle, confusion: *You'd better send somebody over to **sort** the situation **out**.* ○ *It's his job to **sort out** real grievances.* SC = straighten out 3.

3 [Vn ⇆ p pass] (*informal*) organize (people), making them behave in an orderly, disciplined way. **S:** leader, manager, teacher. **O:** force, unit; staff; class: *'I'll give you a week to **sort** your men **out**, then I expect things to run smoothly.'* ○ *I'll need time to **sort out** the office staff — they're hopelessly disorganized at the moment.*

4 [Vn ⇆ p pass] (*informal*) restrain or punish (sb). **S:** police, guard. **O:** trouble-maker, hooligan, bully: *'If you don't stop that din, I'll come in and*

*sort you **out**!' ○ He went after the bullies and really **sorted** them **out**.* = deal with 3.

sort oneself out [Vn.p pass] (informal) get organized, settle into a normal pattern. **S:** newcomer, trainee; situation, things; business, trade: *It's no good standing back and waiting for things to **sort themselves out**. ○ You can sleep here till you get yourself fixed up ... get **yourself sorted out**.* TC □ the passive is formed with get.

sort out from [Vn.p.pr pass] separate, distinguish (one thing) (from another). **O:** good, true, clever; truth, news. **o:** bad, false, stupid; falsehood, comment: *Her difficulty lies in **sorting out** what's 'right' **from** what's 'natural'.* H ○ *I have picked out a few fields of study in an attempt to **sort out** the chaff **from** the wheat* (ie sort things that are easily confused). SNP □ the Object, when it is a noun or a noun phrase, follows out.

sound

sound off [Vp] (*informal*) talk noisily and boastfully or pompously (about sth): *'I wish he'd stop **sounding off** about this fabulous house he's building.' ○ 'Please don't discuss the Budget: you'll start George **sounding off** on tax reform.'*

sound out [Vn ⇆ p pass] try to discover or elicit the feelings or opinions of (sb) on a question. **O:** colleague, partner; staff, employee; wife, family: *The Confederation of British Industry seems to have been frightened enough* (by inflation) *to start **sounding out** their members on a voluntary prices restraint.* OBS ○ *'Where does he stand on the issue?' 'I don't know; I shall have to **sound** him **out**.'*

soup

soup up [Vp.n pass adj] (*informal*) improve the performance of (a motor-car) by modifying its engine, body etc. **O:** production saloon; engine: *'If you **soup up** the engine, you'll have to do something to the suspension and brakes to take care of all the extra performance.' ○ 'The boy spends all his time racing around in a **souped-up** sports car.'*

souse

souse in/with [Vn.pr pass rel] put a lot of (sauce etc) on (sth) to give it flavour, preserve it etc. **O:** food, meal; herring, mackerel; cucumber. **o:** vinegar, (bottled) sauce; brine: *He **souses** everything he eats **in** tomato ketchup. ○ Roll-mops are raw herrings cleaned and boned and **soused in** brine. ○ ... a portion of chips ... well **soused with** salt and vinegar.* UL

space

space out [Vn ⇆ p pass adj] place, position (things or people) at intervals. **O:** post, pole; section, paragraph; output; children: *'You've put the figures in this sum too close together; **space** them **out** more.' ○ Birth control enables couples to **space out** their children and so spread the financial burden of bringing them up.*

spare

spare (for) [Vn.pr pass emph rel] manage to find or give (sth) (for some purpose). **O:** money, time; thought, look; any feeling. **o:** charity, activity; poor wretches, unfortunate people: *I'd like to join you in France, but I can't **spare** the time **for** a holiday. ○ The president did not **spare** a glance **for** the possibly mortal damage which many of the uses of science are doing to the living world.* NS ○ (child asking for money to buy fireworks for Guy Fawkes' night) *'**Spare** a penny **for** the guy, Mister!'*

spark

spark off 1 [Vn ⇆ p pass adj] cause (sth) to explode; detonate. **S:** stone, metal. **O:** charge; explosion: *The explosive was **sparked off** by someone striking the iron heel of his boot on the stone floor.* = set off 1, touch off 1.

2 [Vn ⇆ p pass adj] cause sth violent, disturbing etc to begin. **S:** action; appearance, intervention; remark, speech. **O:** war; argument, row; debate; trouble, controversy: *Local fighting might **spark off** a major war.* MFM ○ *The Government **sparked off** another row over its education reforms by doing nothing about modern language teacher shortages.* G ○ *A decent... pastor in Timisoara stood up to his supine bishop and unwittingly **sparked off** a revolution that brought a tyrant down in Romania.* HOC = set off 2, touch off 2, trigger off.

sparkle

sparkle (with) [Vpr rel] send out sudden, sharp flashes of light, intelligence etc. **S:** clothes, hair; eyes; conversation, writing. **o:** gem, ornament; mischief, excitement; wit, humour: *The dinner tables **sparkled with** silver and crystal. ○ This was the one dull interlude in a speech **sparkling with** witticisms.*

spatter

spatter on/onto [Vn.pr pass emph rel] cause (liquid) to scatter in drops on (sth). **S:** car, lorry; mechanic, painter. **O:** (drops of) water, mud, oil, paint. **o:** shoe, coat; floor: *A passing lorry **spattered** mud **onto** my new coat* (or: ***spattered** my new coat **with** mud*). ○ *Green paint was **spattered on** the tiles* (or: *The tiles were **spattered with** green paint*).

spatter with [Vn.pr pass rel] ⇨ previous entry

speak

speak about [Vpr pass emph rel] discuss (sth): *'What were you **speaking about** when I came into the room?' ○ There was a rule that her late husband should never be **spoken about*** (ie mentioned) *in her presence.* = talk about 1, talk of 1.

speak volumes about/for [Vn.pr] indicate a good deal about the nature of (sb/sth), be strong evidence that (sb/sth) is of a particular character. **S:** action, conduct; appearance, manners; absence, silence. **o:** character, courage, honesty; upbringing: *'They were mostly girls of impeccable morality. Mostly married in fact.' 'It **speaks volumes for** their husbands.'* TT ○ *It **speaks volumes for** his kind disposition that he did not go straight out of the room and bang the door.* WDM

speak against [Vpr rel] make a speech opposing (sth). **S:** member, councillor, delegate. **o:** motion, proposal: *Earlier he had **spoken against** bringing the law in; now he was inclined to support it. ○ This was a measure **against** which he had **spoken** and campaigned vigorously.* ↔ speak for.

speak for [Vpr rel] speak on behalf of (others); be a spokesman for others. **S:** delegate, representative. **o:** member, constituent; majority, few: *'I know I am **speaking for** all of us when I say how grateful* *we are to our hosts.' ○ 'Let's sit down,' Beatrice said. She **speak for** both of them.* OMIH ○ *The Minister asked whether the Opposition's record gave them any special right to **speak for** pensioners.*

speak for itself/themselves [Vpr] be so clear and self-evident that any further comment is unnecessary. **S:** record, report; figure, profit: *There is little need to comment on this record; it is true to say that it **speaks for itself**.* SNP ○ *'I think you will agree that the company's half-yearly figures **speak for themselves**.'*

speak for yourself/yourselves [Vpr] (*informal*) don't speak or make decisions on my/our behalf: *'I think we've done enough drinking for one evening.' '**Speak for yourself**, John!'* ○ *'Perhaps it's time we were leaving.' '**Speak for yourselves**, darlings.'* □ only imperative.

speaking for myself/ourselves [Vpr] in my/our view or opinion: *'**Speaking for myself**, I've got a feeling that you are in danger of oversimplifying things a bit.'* TBC □ only in the *-ing* form; note also the form only speak for oneself which means 'only expressing one's own opinion (when one says sth)': *'Sorry, I didn't mean to be offensive... **I only speak for myself**, and possibly Angela.'*

speak for/in favour of [Vpr rel] make a speech in support of (sth). **S:** member, councillor, delegate. **o:** motion, proposal: *Some members **spoke in favour of** the reintroduction of the death penalty for terrorist crimes.* ↔ speak against.

speak well etc of [Vpr pass emph rel] comment favourably etc on (sb/sth). **A:** well, favourably, glowingly; badly, unfavourably; with enthusiasm: *People **spoke well of** him because he was ... indifferent to worldly success.* LS ○ *She was always **spoken of enthusiastically** in the department.*

speak on [Vpr rel] give a talk, make a speech, on (a particular subject). **o:** topic, subject; education, sociology; Dickens, Victorian painting: *At our next meeting, Mr McDonald will be **speaking on** the early development of printing.* ○ *The lecturer has provided a list of topics **on** which he is prepared to **speak**.*

speak out (against) [Vp, Vp.pr pass] speak bravely and with conviction (on a particular question). **o:** corruption, scandal; immorality, vice; drugs, pornography: *We've been silent for too long: it's time to **speak out**.* ○ *I am glad that someone has had the courage to **speak out against** these abuses.*

speak to 1 [Vpr pass rel] address (sb) to exchange news etc: *'Have a word with grandmother — she doesn't often get the chance of **speaking to** young people.'* ○ *Don't speak until you're **spoken to**!'* = talk to 1.

2 [Vpr] have a word with (sb), with the aim of getting sth done, eg obtaining a favour for sb else. **o:** manager, director, producer: *'There's something wrong with the plumbing. I'll have to **speak to** the landlord about it.'* ○ *'Did you manage to **speak to** the Bursar about my salary?'*

3 [Vpr pass] scold, reproach (sb), with the aim of improving his conduct. **S:** father, teacher. **o:** child, pupil: *'You must **speak to** the children, Henry: they never listen to a word I say.'* ○ *'I'm not letting those boys trample over my garden again. They'll have to be **spoken to**.'* = talk to 2.

4 [Vpr] (*formal*) at a meeting of a committee, council etc, make a statement on (a particular question). **S:** member, councillor, deputy. **o:** question, item (on the agenda), matter: *'The next item is student accommodation. Mr Peters, could I ask you to **speak to** this?'* ○ *Patrick **spoke to** this question for some time, accommodating various points raised by Martha.* TGLY

speak up [Vp] speak in a loud, clear voice, so that one can be heard: *'Well, **speak up**!' Uncle Saunders demanded. 'Is he dead?'* DC ○ *I do wish he'd stop mumbling and learn to **speak up**.*

speak up (for) [Vp, Vp.pr] speak openly, publically, in favour of or in support of (sb/sth). **o:** change, reform; democracy; one's beliefs; what one believes in: *'I might just have managed to tip the balance, but unfortunately at that moment Ned **spoke up**.'* CON ○ (an obituary) *We shall remember the warmth of her voice and smile and the stalwart way she **spoke up for** everything that was good and true.* ESB

spoken for [pass adj (Vpr)] sexually or romantically tied to sb else; committed: *'Flattery will get you nowhere — I am, as you know, already **spoken for**.'* TT

specialize

specialize (in) [Vpr emph rel] study, or work in, one narrow part of a general field, eg logic within the more general field of philosophy. **S:** student, research worker, scientist. **o:** biophysics; paediatrics; criminal law: *In the second year of the degree course you can choose one of four areas to **specialize in**.* ○ *In the Sixth Form you can **specialize in** humanities or the natural sciences.*

speculate

speculate (about/on) [Vpr pass emph rel] form and state opinions (about sth), though with incomplete knowledge. **o:** future, fate, destiny; (possible) outcome, consequences: *At the moment all they can do is **speculate about** the future of the department — nothing is firm and definite.* ○ *We dare not **speculate on** the reactions of this fashionably dressed English girl to the nauseous brat.* TRO ○ ***About** such matters it is pointless to **speculate**; what we need is exact knowledge.*

speculate (in) [Vpr rel] buy and sell (shares etc) in the hope of profiting through changes in their market price. **S:** broker, investor. **o:** stock, share, bond; commodities, copper, rubber: *He made a fortune **speculating in** tin shares, and lost almost all of it in cocoa futures.*

speed

speed up [Vp nom, Vn ⇆ p nom pass adj] (cause sth to) go faster; accelerate. **S:** [Vp]. **O:** [Vn.p] train, engine; action, movement; process, procedure; production, delivery. **S:** [Vn.p] driver, operator; plant, factory; management: *The water **speeded up** and hit the back of the funnel.* PM ○ *There is now a system designed to **speed up** the work of factory inspection departments.* NS ○ *The new road will ensure a **speed-up** in the movement of traffic to the docks.* = quicken up. ↔ slow down 1.

spell

spell (for) [Vn.pr] indicate, mean, that (trouble etc) will follow (for sb). **S:** arrival, appearance (of sb); change, deterioration (in the weather); strike, lay-off. **O:** trouble, disaster, doom, ruin; suspension, delay; bad news, hard times: *His sight was now so bad that the line of each eye crossed and converged some distance in front of him. At the cinema he was forced down to the front row, and it* ***spelt*** *ruination* ***for*** *any football match.* LLDR ○ *The appointment of a new head* ***spelt*** *disaster* ***for*** *any pupil hoping for an easy passage through the middle school.*

spell out 1 [Vn ⇆ p pass adj] read (sth) slowly, going laboriously over each word. **O:** passage; page, chapter. **A:** in full, word by word, letter by letter: *It was painful to hear him* ***spelling out*** *a page of an elementary textbook.* ○ *'I want him to digest the contents of the letter fully, even if you have to* ***spell*** *it* ***out*** *word by word.'*

2 [Vn ⇆ p pass adj] make clear or explicit the full meaning or implications of (sth). **S:** speaker; article, book; statement, speech. **O:** policy, philosophy; intention, proposal; consequence. **A:** word for word, in detail: *His speech will* ***spell out*** *in some detail a short-term and a long term strategy for growth.* OBS ○ *The possible economic benefits of the treaty were* ***spelt out*** *in his recent book.*

spend

spend (on) [Vn.pr pass emph rel] pay (money) or give (time) to achieve (some object etc). **O:** money; fortune, pounds; time. **o:** house, car; family, girlfriend; mending his car, revising his lectures: *He has* ***spent*** *a small fortune* ***on*** *improving his property.* ○ *Every spare minute he gets is* ***spent on*** *the car.*

spew

spew out [Vp, Vn ⇆ p pass adj] (cause sth to) come out, issue, in a thick, unpleasant stream. **S** [Vp], **O** [Vn.p]**:** liquid; waste, effluent; gas. **S** [Vn.p]**:** factory; pipe, exhaust: *Several of our rivers have been polluted by factories* ***spewing out*** *their waste products into the water.* ○ *They heard nothing but government propaganda,* ***spewed out*** *over the air from state-controlled radio stations.*

spice

spice (with) [Vn.pr pass emph rel] add (sth) to (food etc) to give it a more interesting flavour; add (sth) to (a story) etc to make it more lively. **O:** dish; stew, gravy; story, conversation. **o:** herb; thyme, rosemary; joke, wit: *They ate a green salad, strongly* ***spiced with*** *garlic and pepper.* ○ *We had a long conversation,* ***spiced with*** *anecdotes.*

spice up [Vn ⇆ p pass adj] make (sth) more attractive, esp by adding sensational or pornographic details. **O:** story, book, film: *'You're not exactly going to get people fighting to see this movie, so why don't we* ***spice*** *it* ***up*** *a little?'*

spill

spill out/out of 1 [Vp, Vpr, Vn ⇆ p pass, Vn.pr pass rel] (allow sth to) overflow, run over the side (of a container). **S** [Vp Vpr], **O** [Vn.p Vn.pr]**:** water, oil, paint; flour, powder. **o:** tin, jar, bucket: [Vpr] *Seeds* ***spilled out of*** *the packet onto the floor.* ○ [Vn.p] *'Mind how you carry that pot: you'll* ***spill*** *some of the water* ***out****.'*

2 [Vp, Vpr] emerge suddenly, and in a scattered, disorganized way (from a place). **S:** passenger; audience, class: *The first of the football specials pulled in, and hundreds of fans* ***spilled out*** *onto the platform.*

spill over 1 [Vp, Vpr] flow over the edge of a (container), because it is too full or the container is moved. **S:** pot, jug, cup: *My cup was too full; some tea* ***spilled over*** *into the saucer.* = run over 1.

2 [Vp, Vpr] leave (a town etc) because there are too many people living there. **S:** population, inhabitants; district, region: *Great suburban estates were built to house the population* ***spilling over*** *from the crowded inner cities* (or: *to house the* ***overspill*** *from the inner cities*). ○ *New towns took the* ***overspill*** *from Greater London.* □ nom form is overspill.

spin

spin-off [nom (Vp, Vn.p)] (*economics*) the wider marketing of a product or material developed esp for a high technology project; general economic benefits resulting from the creation of new industries etc: *The defence and aerospace industries are obvious sources of* ***spin-off*** *because of their advanced technology.* T ○ *The need for facilities for oil rig service vessels could give Dundee some of the* ***spin-off*** *from the North Sea discoveries.* SC

spin out [Vn ⇆ p pass adj] make (sth) last as long as possible or seem as full and substantial as possible. **O:** story, tale; time, period, session; money, income: *Dorothea talked so, about nothing at all,* ***spinning*** *her phrases* ***out*** *and forever trying to win attention and applause.* GAL ○ *Robert couldn't think of any way of* ***spinning out*** *the conversation, so he called for the bill.* CON ○ *Cartoonists must carry out a daily exercise in* ***spinning out*** *the unimportant and insignificant.* UL

spiral

spiral up 1 [Vp emph] rise in a continuous spiral. **S:** smoke; aircraft, bird: *Smoke from the camp-fires* ***spiralled up*** *into a clear sky.*

2 [Vp] gain promotion, rise, in an organization. **S:** executive, trainee; teacher, functionary: *He was going to* ***spiral up*** *to being head of the design department as soon as he knew how things were run.* CON

spirit

spirit away/off [Vn ⇆ p pass] make (sb/sth) disappear quickly and mysteriously. **S:** host; porter, waiter. **O:** guest, visitor; coat, suitcase: *We were ushered smoothly to a table in the centre of the restaurant, and our coats and hats* ***spirited away****.* ○ *Johnny Mathis returns only for the finale and then he is* ***spirited way*** *by a member of his entourage.* ST

spit

spit at [Vpr pass rel] direct saliva from the mouth at (sb), as a sign of contempt or defiance. **S:** crowd, mob; prisoner. **o:** dignitary, leader; captor, tormentor: *A cat will* ***spit at*** *a snake as much out of fear as defiance.* ○ *He was* ***spat at*** *and reviled by the very people who had been his most ardent supporters.*

spit in sb's eye [Vpr] (*informal*) make a gesture of contempt or defiance towards sb, esp, though not necessarily, by spitting at him: *'Walk straight in, sit where you used to sit with him and* ***spit in his eye****.'* RATT ○ *With us it will be different, only* other *people make mistakes, we can* ***spit in the eye of*** *society.* TT

spit out 1 [Vn ⇆ p pass] send (sth) out sharply from the mouth. **O:** medicine; vinegar; pip, seed:

*He took one sip of the wine and **spat** it **out**. 'It's turned to vinegar,' he said.*
2 [Vn ⇆ p pass] say (sth) sharply and angrily, as if spitting. **O:** word; oath, curse; name: *'If I see you here again, I shall have you thrown out.' He **spat** the words **out** venomously.*

splash

splash about (in) [Vp, Vp.pr rel] sit or stand (in water) and make it fly about with one's hands or feet. **S:** child, swimmer. **o:** bath, swimming-pool: *A party of boys was **splashing about** at the shallow end of the pool.* ○ *I left the children happily **splashing about in** their bath.*

splash down [Vp nom] (*space technology*) (of a space capsule which has re-entered the earth's atmosphere) strike the surface of the sea. **S:** astronaut; module, capsule, vehicle: *The astronauts are scheduled to **splash down** at 3 pm local time* (cf ***Splashdown** is scheduled for 3 pm local time*).

splash on/onto 1 [Vn ⇆ p pass, Vn.pr pass rel] apply paint etc (to sth) with a brush in a vigorous or carefree way. **O:** paint, distemper. **o:** wall, fence; canvas: *Don't be timid. Take a big brush and **splash** the paint **on**.*
2 [Vpr rel, Vn.pr pass rel] (cause sth to) fall in heavy drops onto (sth). **S** [Vpr], **O** [Vn.pr]**:** water, (liquid) mud; oil, paint. **S** [Vn.pr]**:** bus, car; mechanic, decorator. **o:** clothes, table, floor: *A passing launch **splashed** water **onto** our deck.* ○ *Don't **splash** any paint **on** your clothes* (or: *Don't **splash** your clothes **with** paint*).

splash out (on) [Vp, Vp.pr] (*informal*) spend money (on sth) in an impulsive, carefree way. **o:** (new) clothes; furniture, equipment; entertainment: *'He's **splashing out** tonight, isn't he? First double whiskies, and now champagne all round.'* ○ *Before you start **splashing out on** books and records think of the money you already owe.* = lash out (on).

splash with [Vn.pr pass rel] ⇨ splash on/onto 2.

split

split away/off (from) [Vp, Vp.pr emph rel] separate, divide (from a larger body). **S:** twig, branch; section, faction, wing. **o:** tree; party, organization: *The wood is cracking in the heat, and pieces are **splitting away**.* ○ *Their problem is to prevent the more militant elements **splitting off from** the party organization.*

split (on) [Vpr pass] (*informal*) give information (about sb), eg of his breaking school rules, that will get him into trouble. **o:** friend, accomplice: *'Don't **split on** me, don't give me away!'* ○ *Somebody must have **split on** him to a teacher.* □ usu said of one child by another. = tell on.

split up [Vp] (*informal*) (of sexual partners in a stable relationship) end their relationship: *'Who told you that Jan and I had **split up**?'* ○ *There's nothing in the rumour that they're **splitting up**.* = break up 6.

split up (into) [Vp, Vp.pr rel, Vn ⇆ p pass, Vn.p.pr pass rel] (cause sb/sth to) divide into parts. **S** [Vp, Vp.pr], **O** [Vn.p, Vn.p.pr]**:** meeting, gathering, party; work, subject. **S** [Vn.p, Vn.p.pr]**:** host, organizer; teacher. **o:** committee, group; section: [Vp.pr] *The peons would **split up into** two groups, riding spread out into a long line.* DF ○ [Vp.pr] *About four-fifths of the boys leave school, the others **split up into** Science and Arts.* CON ○ [Vn.p.pr] *For art and craft lessons the class is **split up into** small groups.*

spoil

spoil for a fight [Vpr] (*informal*) be eager to fight. **S:** soldier, boxer: *We have well-trained troops, who **are spoiling for a fight**.* MFM □ in continuous tenses only.

sponge

sponge down [Vn ⇆ p pass] clean (sth/sb) by wiping with a wet sponge. **O:** patient; chest, legs; car, table: *I gave the car a hot shampoo from the jet, rinsed it off and **sponged** it **down**.*

sponge from/off [Vpr rel, Vn.pr pass rel] (*informal*) get money etc from (sb) without giving, or intending to give, anything in return. **O:** cash, a fiver; meal, drink: *In London he could stay with a friend **from** whom he'd **sponged** a meal from time to time.* ○ *'Don't keep **sponging off** your father! His money won't last for ever, and neither will his patience.'*

sponge on [Vpr pass rel] (*informal*) live at sb else's expense, taking money and assistance that one does not intend to return. **o:** family, friend: *He calculated that if things went badly and he was out of a job for six months he could always **sponge on** his parents.* ○ *We're getting a little tired of being **sponged on** by our relatives.*

spoon

spoon out [Vn ⇆ p pass] serve, distribute (sth), using a spoon. **S:** cook, hostess. **O:** potatoes, peas; plums; flour, sugar: *He **spooned out** a few mouthfuls of rice into each of the plates.* ○ *The relief supplies of beans and flour were **spooned out** from the back of a truck.*

spoon up [Vn ⇆ p pass] raise, take up (sth), esp to the mouth, with a spoon. **O:** food; dinner; soup, pudding: *He **spooned** his soup **up** hungrily and came back for more.* ○ *She tried to **spoon up** a blob of potato that had fallen on the floor.*

spout

spout (from) [Vpr emph rel] come (from sth) in a thick, powerful stream. **S:** water, oil, blood. **o:** rock, soil; pipe, tube, vein: *Dirty oil **spouted from** the damaged sump of his car* (or: *The damaged sump **spouted** dirty oil*). ○ ***From** a crack in the rocks **spouted** a stream of clear water.*

sprawl

sprawl about [Vp, Vpr] sit or lie (somewhere) in a casual, sloppy manner, eg with one's feet over the arms of a chair. **o:** the place, the house: *I wish I could teach the children not to **sprawl about** on the furniture.* ○ *He found his students **sprawling about** on the steps of the library.* = lie about/around/round 1, loll about/around, lounge about/around.

sprawl out [Vp] sit or lie with the arms and legs loosely and comfortably extended: *I just feel like **sprawling out** in the sun for a couple of weeks.* ⇨ next entry

sprawled out [pass adj (Vn.p)] lying with the arms and legs extended and relaxed: *We found him **sprawled out** on the lawn behind the house.* ○ *The feet of a **sprawled-out** figure appeared from beneath a large umbrella.* ⇨ previous entry

spray

spray on/onto [Vn.pr pass rel] send (liquid) in a stream of tiny drops (onto sth). **O:** paint, varnish;

perfume; disinfectant, weed-killer. **o:** wall; skin; plant: *The gardener* ***sprayed*** *insecticide* ***on*** *the rose-bushes* (or: ***sprayed*** *the rose-bushes* ***with*** *insecticide*). ○ *Insect repellent should be* ***sprayed onto*** *the skin to discourage mosquitoes* (or: *The skin should be* ***sprayed with*** *insect repellent* etc).

spray with [Vn.pr pass rel] ⇨ previous entry

spread

spread on [Vn.pr pass rel] place (sth) on (a surface) and extend it, eg by unfolding or pressing, thus covering the whole surface. **O:** cloth, rug; butter, jam. **o:** bed, table; bread, roll: *An embroidered blanket was* ***spread on*** *the sofa* (or: *The sofa was* ***spread with*** *an embroidered blanket*). ○ ***Spread*** *the butter thickly* ***on*** *the rolls* (or: ***Spread*** *the rolls thickly* ***with*** *butter*).

spread out 1 [Vn ⇆ p pass] open the hands or extend the arms, in a gesture of surprise, helplessness etc. **O:** one's arms, hands: *'I may possibly delay my departure.' He* ***spread out*** *his hands. 'Just by a fortnight.'* SPL ○ *He* ***spread*** *his arms* ***out*** *theatrically. 'What can I do about it?' he said.*
2 [Vn ⇆ p pass adj] open sth that is folded, or put sth down that is already open, so that it covers a surface. **O:** cloth, bedspread; documents, papers: *We took the picnic basket from the car, and* ***spread out*** *a cloth on the grass.*
3 [Vp, Vn ⇆ p pass adj] (cause people to) move away from each other, so as to cover a wider area; disperse. **S** [Vp], **O** [Vn.p]**:** soldiers, hunters; search-party: *The peons would split up into two groups, riding* ***spread out*** *into a long line.* DF ○ *'****Spread out*** *more. Don't bunch up at the centre.'* = fan out.

spread over [Vp, Vpr, Vn ⇆ p pass, Vn.pr pass] (cause sth to) extend over (a specified period of time). **S** [Vp Vpr], **O** [Vn.p Vn.pr]**:** course, studies, training; loan, mortgage: [Vp] *The grammar course will* ***spread over*** *into the Spring Term.* ○ [Vn.pr] *'I'll ask my bank manager if the repayments can be* ***spread over*** *two years.'*

spread (to) [Vpr rel, Vn.pr pass rel] (cause sth to) extend itself more widely, affecting other people and places. **S** [Vpr], **O** [Vn.pr]**:** fire, flood, epidemic; disturbance, riot; revolt, disaffection. **o:** area, district; tribe, class: *The strike is* ***spreading to*** *other groups of municipal workers.* ○ *What can we do to prevent the disease from being* ***spread to*** *other countries?*

spread with [Vn.pr pass rel] ⇨ spread on.

spring

spring back [Vp nom] return to its previous position after having been pushed, because it is attached to a spring or counterweight: *Be careful when somebody goes through the door in front of you that it doesn't* ***spring back*** *in your face.* ○ *The looseleaf binder* ***springs back*** *and grips the sheets of paper* (ie it is a ***spring-back*** *binder*). spring-back is usu attrib.

spring from 1 [Vpr] (*informal*) appear so suddenly and unexpectedly from (somewhere) that others do not know where one has come from. **o:** where (on earth); somewhere, anywhere, nowhere; I don't know where: *'Where on earth did you* ***spring from****?'*
2 [Vpr emph rel] have (sth) as its source or origin. **S:** curiosity, interest; restlessness, irritation. **o:** desire, wish; frustration, (thwarted) ambition: *Her interfering ways* ***spring from*** *a desire to see her daughters comfortably married.* ○ *The authorities failed to remedy the grievances* ***from*** *which these disorders* ***sprang****.*

spring into/to life [Vpr] suddenly begin to move or act vigorously: *Many dormant branches of our organization are now* ***springing*** *back* ***into*** *active* ***life****.* ○ *A bundly shape in the corner moved and* ***sprang to life****. . . . Nurse Ellen, blinking and full of alarm, rushed to the bedside.* DC

spring on [Vn.pr pass] (*informal*) present, introduce (sth) to (sb) suddenly, so that he is surprised, and not fully prepared. **S:** employer; government. **O:** (new, revised) arrangement, method, schedule; election, ballot. **o:** staff; electorate: *'Don't expect me to make the thing work immediately—I've just had the job* ***sprung on*** *me.'* ○ *The Headmaster* ***sprang*** *a revision of the timetable* ***on*** *us half-way through the term.*

spring out [Vp emph] appear suddenly from behind cover, with the intention or effect of frightening sb. **S:** thief, kidnapper: *'You did give me a fright,* ***springing out*** *at me like that!'* ○ *A masked man* ***sprang out*** *from a doorway.*

spring to attention [Vp] (*military*) suddenly adopt an alert, upright position, with the heels together and the arms pressed to the sides of the body. **S:** soldier; squad, platoon: *As the general's car reached the gate, the sentry* ***sprang*** *smartly* ***to attention****.* ⇨ be at/bring to/come to attention.

spring to sb's defence [Vpr rel] move quickly to defend sb from physical or verbal attack: *Till now he had ignored the lady* ***to whose defence*** *Mason had so gallantly* ***sprung****.* ○ *The stockbroker's wife* ***sprang to her husband's defence****.* HAA

spring to one's feet [Vpr] jump up quickly from where one is sitting or lying. **S:** class, squad; porter, sentry: *As the Headmaster entered the classroom, 4B* ***sprang*** *noisily* ***to its feet****.* ○ *Alex* ***sprang to his feet*** *to help bring the heavy dish to the table.*

spring to mind [Vpr] come suddenly into one's mind. **S:** thought, idea; consideration, argument: *One question* ***springs to mind*** *at once. Why should disillusion with one partner . . . lead to a sudden passion for a potential one?* NS = occur to.

spring up 1 [Vp emph] stand up suddenly: *'That's something Prissie is going to post for me. . . . It isn't too wet, is it?' Prissie* ***sprang up****. 'No, of course not.'* DC = jump up.
2 [Vp] arise, develop, grow, quickly. **S:** breeze, wind; weed, corn; factory, school, hospital; organization, relationship; suspicion, doubt: *Towards evening a cold wind* ***sprang up****.* ○ *Reform circles were* ***springing up*** *all over the place, calling for Mr Grosz's dismissal.* IND ○ *We may, in both global and domestic affairs, see a multiplicity of ideas* ***spring up****.* MARX

sprinkle

sprinkle on/onto [Vn.pr pass emph rel] throw a fine shower of (particles, drops etc) onto (a surface). **O:** water; sand; pepper, salt. **o:** flower; floor; food: *A cart went by* ***sprinkling*** *water* ***onto*** *the dusty streets* (or: ***sprinkling*** *the streets* ***with*** *water*). ○ *Ink was once dried by* ***sprinkling*** *fine sand* ***onto*** *the writing paper* (or: ***sprinkling*** *the paper* ***with*** *sand*).

sprinkle with [Vn.pr pass rel] ⇨ previous entry

spruce

spruce up [Vp, Vn ⇆ p pass adj] (*informal*) make (oneself/sth) clean and smart. **O:** oneself; department, house, hotel: (British Rail advertisement) *There's also a washroom where you can* ***spruce up****, ready to meet your client.* ST ○ *I decided to go home and* ***spruce*** *myself* ***up*** *— to let everyone know that life had not got me down.* SML ○ *The hotel was distinctly shabby these days, all incentive to keep it* ***spruced up*** *having long gone.* BRAZ

spur

spur (on) (to) [Vn ⇆ p pass adj, Vn.pr pass emph rel, Vn.p.pr pass emph rel] strongly encourage (sb) to do better, to achieve more. **S:** rider; teacher, coach; ambition, greed. **O:** horse; pupil, athlete; politician, businessman. **o:** greater success, higher things: [Vn.p] *He was constantly* ***spurred on*** *by a fear of failure.* ○ [Vn.pr] *Without these two* ***spurring*** *her enemies* ***to*** *action, and constantly reminding the King that ... his marriage to her was illegal, she might have found security.* WI ○ [Vn.p.pr] *James would have been content with a modest level of success, but his wife kept* ***spurring*** *him* ***on to*** *something 'higher' or 'better'.*

spurt

spurt (out) (from) [Vp emph, Vpr emph rel, Vp.pr emph rel] come out in a sudden burst. **S:** water; blood; flame. **o:** pipe; artery, wound; building: [Vp] *The surgeon lanced the boil and a mixture of pus and blood* ***spurted out****.* ○ [Vpr] *As we watched, flame and smoke* ***spurted from*** *an upstairs window.*

sputter

sputter out 1 [Vp] stop burning after making sharp, spitting sounds. **S:** flame; candle; fire, heater; engine: *The last candle* ***sputtered out****, leaving us in total darkness.*
2 [Vp] come to an end with gradually decreasing noise and activity. **S:** demonstration, rebellion, coup: *The demonstration* ***sputtered out*** *in a few half-hearted scuffles with the police.*

spy

spy on/upon [Vpr pass] watch the activities of (others) secretly, with the aim of informing the authorities, other governments etc. **S:** agent, informer. **o:** colleague, employer, fellow-worker: *He was paid by the secret service to* ***spy on*** *fellow students.* ○ *The research centre was so security conscious that we all ended up* ***spying on*** *each other.*

spy out [Vp.n pass] detect, identify (illegal activity etc), and report it to the authorities. **S:** agent, snooper. **O:** dissent, heresy, opposition: *These editors and writers have for years been ready to* ***spy out*** *dangerous novelty and deviation in works of art.* OBS

spy out the land [Vn ⇆ p] assess the situation, see how matters stand, eg in a battle, in industry, in the home: *He sent forward a few scouts to* ***spy out the land****.* ○ *I'm thinking of sending someone down to our Plymouth branch to* ***spy the land out****.*

squabble

squabble (with) [Vpr rel] have a petty, noisy quarrel (with sb). **o:** sister, wife; neighbour, workmate: *'I always arrive home to find you* ***squabbling with*** *your brother* (or: *you and your brother* ***squabbling****).'* ○ *'How like them: always* ***squabbling with*** *each other over nothing at all!'*

square

square off [Vn ⇆ p pass adj] give (sth) a square shape or outline; divide (a surface) into squares. **O:** piece, block (of wood, metal); pack, haversack; paper, page: *For inspections, soldiers used to* ***square off*** *their packs by fitting pieces of wood inside.* ○ ***Square*** *the page* ***off*** *with your ruler, then you'll by able to copy the drawing accurately.*

square up to [Vp.pr pass] (*informal*) prepare to fight (sb), ie by raising one's fists etc; confront (sb/sth) resolutely. **o:** opponent, attacker; problem, task: *He's not used to being* ***squared up to****: he may change his mind if you look fierce enough.* ○ *Opposition speakers accused the Chancellor of not* ***squaring up to*** *the realities of a major trade recession.*

square up (with) [Vp, Vp.pr] (*informal*) pay the money one owes before leaving a hotel, restaurant etc. **o:** waiter, tradesman; friend: *'Can I leave you to* ***square up*** *(****with*** *the waiter)?'* ○ *'It's high time I* ***squared up with*** *you.* = settle up (with).

square with [Vpr emph rel, Vn.pr pass emph rel] (make sth) be consistent with (sth). **S** [Vpr], **O** [Vn.pr]**:** account, story; action, practice. **o:** evidence, facts; principle, theory: *To think of himself as a lamb-gobbling wolf* (ie a highly successful seducer) *capable of leaping into any fold ... hardly* ***squared with*** *the facts.* TGLY ○ *There are many aspects of the case* ***with*** *which his statement does not* ***square****.* ○ *I wonder how he* ***squares*** *this attitude* ***with*** *his criticism of the government?* SC = reconcile (with) 2.

square one's accounts/accounts with 1 [Vn.pr pass rel] repay one's debts to (sb). **o:** creditor; bank, shop: *I should manage to* ***square my account with*** *the bank before the end of the quarter.*
2 [Vn.pr pass rel] punish (sb) for an injury one has suffered. **o:** spy, informer, traitor: *I've no further quarrel with Tom;* ***my account with*** *him is* ***squared****.* = settle accounts etc (with).

squash

squash in/into [Vp, Vpr, Vn ⇆ p pass, Vn.pr pass] (cause people/things to) press tightly against one another in a small space. **S** [Vp, Vpr], **O** [Vn.p, Vn.pr]**:** passengers, commuters; fruit, vegetables. **S** [Vn.p, Vn.pr]**:** driver, guard; packer. **o:** car, train; lift; box, case: [Vn.p] *'If you try to* ***squash in*** *any more peaches they'll get bruised.'* ○ [Vn.pr] *'I think we can* ***squash*** *a few more* ***into*** *the back of the van.'* ○ [Vn.pr] *We were* ***squashed into*** *the compartment like sardines in a tin.* = squeeze in/into.

squash up (against) [Vp, Vpr, Vn.p pass, Vn.p.pr pass] (cause sb to) press tightly and uncomfortably (against another person). **S** [Vp, Vp.pr], **O** [Vn.p, Vn.p.pr]**:** passenger, spectator: [Vp] *'You'll have to* ***squash up*** *to make room for the others.'* ○ [Vn.p.pr] *There were four of us* ***squashed up against*** *each other on one seat.* = squeeze up (against).

squat

squat down [Vp emph] sit on one's heels, or with the legs drawn up under or close to the body: *The porters* ***squatted down*** *with their loads at the edge of the road.* ○ ***Down*** *he* ***squatted*** *on the front porch, and defied anyone to move him.*

squeeze

squeeze in/into [Vp, Vpr, Vn ⇆ p pass, Vn.pr pass] force (oneself/sb) into a small space. **S** [Vp, Vpr], **O** [Vn.p, Vn.pr]**:** passenger, spectator. **S** [Vn.p, Vn.pr]**:** driver, manager. **o:** car, compartment; lift; theatre; ground: [Vp] *'**Squeeze in** and try to get a seat near the window.'* ○ [Vn.pr] *'If you **squeeze** any more **into** the back of the car you'll be stopped by the police.'* = squash in/into.

squeeze out/out of 1 [Vn.p pass, Vn.pr pass rel] by pressing, force (liquid etc) from (a container). **O:** water, juice; liquid soap, detergent; toothpaste. **o:** bottle, tube: *'The lemon looks dry to me, but you may be able to **squeeze out** a few drops.'* ○ *We have reached the point where cheese and meat-paste can be **squeezed out of** tubes.*
2 [Vn ⇆ p pass, Vn.pr pass rel] (*informal*) get money from (sb) by applying pressure of various kinds, eg threats or harsh legislation. **S:** blackmailer; government, Inland Revenue; party, association. **O:** money; tax, revenue; donation, levy. **o:** victim; tax-payer; member: *If you give in to the blackmailer, he will return later to **squeeze out** another couple of hundred.* ○ *The government will **squeeze** every penny it can **out of** the unfortunate tax-payer.*

squeeze through [Vp, Vpr pass rel] pass through (a narrow passage etc), by pressing in the sides of one's body. **o:** tunnel, passageway, shaft; door, entrance: *'Turn your shoulders round the other way and you'll manage to **squeeze through**.'* ○ *There was a small air-shaft **through** which he could just **squeeze** by lying flat on on his stomach.*

squeeze up (against) [Vp, Vp.pr, Vn ⇆ p pass, Vn.p.pr pass] (cause sb to) press tightly and uncomfortably (against sb else). **S** [Vp, Vp.pr], **O** [Vn.p, Vn.p.pr]**:** passenger, traveller; spectator, audience, crowd: [Vp] *'**Squeeze up** a bit more and let the others sit down.'* ○ [Vn.p.pr] *Several hundred spectators were **squeezed up against** each other in one corner of the stand.* = squash up (against).

squint

squint at [Vpr] look at (sb/sth) through half-shut eyes. **o:** sun, sunlight; arc lights, footlights: *He came out on the steps, **squinting** a little **at** the bright sunlight.*

squirm

squirm (with) [Vpr] twist or wriggle about (because of some unpleasant feeling). **S:** audience, listener, companion. **o:** shame, embarrassment, unease: *His remarks were so ill-judged that I **squirmed with** embarrassment.*

squirt

squirt out/out of [Vp emph, Vpr, Vn ⇆ p pass, V n.pr pass] (cause sth to) come out of (a container) with some force, and in a thin jet or stream. **S** [Vp, Vpr], **O** [Vn.p, Vn.pr]**:** soda, beer; liquid soap, detergent; foam. **o:** bottle, jar, can; extinguisher: [Vp] *He struck the can hard with the opener and juice **squirted out** all over his jacket.* ○ [Vn.pr] *You **squirt** foam **out of** a nozzle and direct it at the base of the fire.*

stab

stab at [Vpr pass] aim a blow with a knife at (sb), try to strike him with a knife: *The taller man **stabbed at** the security guard with a flick-knife.*

stab in the back [Vn.pr pass] (usu of sb who is known and trusted) attack sb's security, position, good name etc, while he is busy with sth else. **S:** friend, colleague, partner: *He has become the despair of comrades who can never be sure when he may . . . **stab** them **in the back**.* NS ○ *The Minister of Defence complained to his friends that he had been **stabbed in the back** by his Chiefs of Staff.* MFM

stack

stack against [Vn.pr pass] make it unlikely that (sb) will succeed. **S:** poor background, lack of family connections; behaviour, attitude. **O:** ⚠ the odds, chances, chips, cards: *'Making an enemy of the director will have **stacked** the cards **against** him getting his promotion.'* ○ *John always claimed that the odds were **stacked against** him from the start, but then he was the kind to blame everything on circumstances.*

stack up 1 [Vn ⇆ p pass adj] place (things) in a pile, one upon the other. **O:** plate, dish; chair, desk; record: *He was ushered into a dusty office, with files **stacked up** against the wall.* ○ *It's convenient to have chairs that will **stack up** (or: can be **stacked up**).*
2 [Vp nom, Vn ⇆ p pass adj] (*aviation*) (cause aircraft to) to circle one above the other near an airfield until the runway is clear for them to land: *With the added pressure of charter flights, aircraft are **stacking up** to an unacceptable extent at peak holiday times.* ○ *There are so many planes in the **stack-up** that there is always the possibility of two planes crashing into each other.* SC

staff

staff up [Vn ⇆ p pass adj] increase the number of staff in (a place). **O:** department, bureau: *'Of course they are understaffed and we are **staffing** them **up**.'* BBCR ○ *The project can't get under way without a fully **staffed-up** research section.*

stagger

stagger about/around [Vp] move about in an unsteady, uncontrolled way, because of illness, injury, drunkenness etc. **S:** patient, casualty; drunk: *He feels weak after his long illness, and is still **staggering about** a bit.*

stake

stake off (from) [Vn ⇆ p pass adj, Vn.p.pr pass rel] separate (one area) (from another) by means of stakes. **O:** vegetable patch, flower garden: *The men had **staked off** part of the yard as a cattle pen.* ⇨ fence off (from), wall off (from).

stake on [Vn.pr pass emph rel] place money with a bookmaker in the hope that a team, horse etc will win. **S:** racegoer, punter. **O:** money; fortune. **o:** horse, dog; team: *I'm not prepared to **stake** money **on** a horse that's lost three times in a season.* = put on 8, wager on 1.

stake one's life etc on [Vn.pr emph rel] be so confident that sth is the case, that one is prepared to sacrifice a good deal if one is wrong. **O:** ⚠ one's life, all, career, reputation. **o:** innocence, integrity, honesty; sb's being involved: *If old Philip had been honest, you wouldn't be living in a West End house, you can **stake your life on** that.* DC ○ *Decca can hardly be as inaccurate as the association makes it out to be, otherwise the British Govern-*

ment would not **stake its reputation on** *backing Decca in United Nations technical meetings.* NS ○ *It's absolutely genuine — on that I'd* **stake my life**. □ used figuratively.

stake out 1 [Vn ⇆ p pass adj] mark, with stakes, the boundaries of land etc in which one has a special interest. **O:** area, patch (of land); holding, farm: *He's* **staking out** *a farm at the top end of the valley.*

2 [Vp.n pass] appear to have reserved (an area of activity) as one's own, esp because of one's achievements in it. **O:** area, field (of study): *No one can emulate him in this field: it is as though he has* **staked out** *this bit of biology as his own.*

3 [Vn ⇆ p nom pass] (esp *US, informal*) watch and guard (a building) closely, esp one in which criminals are known or believed to be sheltering. **O:** house, office, farm: *'What are you going to do Lieutenant?* **Stake out** *my home?'* BBCTV ○ *'We need to know who's coming and who's going, so I want a 24-hour* **stake-out** *on the place.'*

stake (out) a/one's claim (on/to) 1 [Vp.n, Vn.pr, Vn.p.pr] mark, as one's own, the limits of (land where one wishes to farm, look for precious metals etc). **S:** farmer, miner, prospector. **o:** land, area, territory: *We'll go North and* **stake a claim**. *The great uranium fever is sweeping the world.* DPM

2 [Vp.n, Vn.pr, Vn.p.pr] declare a special interest in (sb/sth). **o:** girl, man; job, department; funds, resources: *He's* **staked out a claim to** *Susan.* RATT ○ *In the absence of the Inspector General, various subordinate departments began to* **stake out their claims on** *industrial production.* B

stake to [Vn.pr] (esp *US*) offer to buy (sth) for sb, esp when that person cannot afford to pay for it. **O:** meal, drink; ticket, bus fare: *It struck me as ... funny that Robert should ever have needed me to* **stake** *him* **to** *a plate of meat-and-potato pie.* CON

stamp

stamp on 1 [Vpr pass] bring one's foot down heavily on (sth), thus crushing or damaging it. **o:** beetle, spider, wasp; book, china: *In her rage, she would throw his papers on the floor and* **stamp on** *them.*

2 [Vpr pass] seek to control or suppress (sb/sth) by vigorous action. **o:** rebel, dissident; rebellion, dissent: *Anyone who stepped out of line in this period of minority government could expect to be* **stamped on** *by the party bosses.*

stamp on/onto [Vn.pr emph rel] print (sth) on (a surface) with ink, dye, paint etc. **O:** name, trademark, insignia; pattern, motif. **o:** box, bale, roll; cloth, paper: *A machine* **stamps** *the names and addresses of subscribers* **onto** *envelopes* (or: **stamps** *envelopes* **with** *the names etc*). ○ *His initials were* **stamped on** *the brief-case in black.*

stamp out [Vn ⇆ p pass] get rid of (sth) vigorously or by force; eliminate. **S:** government, police, army; fire brigade, health authorities. **O:** rebellion; dissent, heresy; malaria, cholera: *The police and the medical profession were trying to* **stamp out** *the increasing wave of drug addiction in young people.* SC ○ *The authorities are now trying, if not to* **stamp** *it* **out**, *then at least to control the black market.* LFM ○ *All opposition to the regime had been ruthlessly* **stamped out**.

stamp out/out of [Vn ⇆ p pass adj, Vn.pr pass rel] cut (pieces) from a sheet of metal etc, by striking it with a shaped tool. **O:** square, disc; coin, medal: *The older badges were shaped by hand; nowadays they are* **stamped out of** *gunmetal.* ○ *The machine can* **stamp out** *hundreds of components in an hour.* = punch out/out of.

stamp with [Vn.pr pass rel] ⇨ stamp on/onto.

stand

stand about/around [Vp] be still and inactive because one is relaxing or has nothing to do etc. **S:** visitor; passenger, commuter: *The guests were* **standing about** *after dinner, smoking and talking quietly.* ○ *'Don't just* **stand around** *doing nothing: give me a hand with the luggage!'*

stand head and shoulders above [Vpr] be much more able, gifted etc than (sb else). **o:** one's fellows, contempories, companions: *She knows there is still a long way to go before she* **stands head and shoulders above** *her rivals.* H ○ *'Of course we'll have to give her an interview. On paper, she* **stands head and shoulders above** *the other applicants.'* head and shoulders is an adv phrase of degree.

stand apart (from) [Vp, Vp.pr emph rel] place oneself, through shyness, arrogance etc, at a distance (from sb); hold aloof (from sb). **o:** one's fellow, other people: *Unlike Napoleon, Wellington tended to* **stand apart from** *his men, partly through natural reserve, and partly because he found it profoundly distasteful to court popularity.*

stand (as) (for) [Vpr rel] be a candidate (representing a particular party or interest) (for sth). **o: (as)** Liberal, Nationalist; executive nominee; **(for)** election; Parliament, local council; seat, place: *Is he prepared to* **stand for** *the vacant seat on the committee?* ○ *Mr Francis is* **standing as** *the official nominee* **for** *the post of District Secretary.*

stand aside 1 [Vp] move to one side, move out of the way, eg to let sb pass. **S:** crowd; onlooker, spectator: *People on the pavement were asked to* **stand aside** *to let the procession through.*

2 [Vp] remain at a distance from events, not be involved in them: *He* **stands aside** *and lets the current of events sweep past him.* ○ *Don't* **stand aside** *and let others make the important decisions.*

stand back (from) 1 [Vp, Vp.pr] be situated at a distance (from a place). **S:** building; house, church. **o:** road, street: *The school* **stands** *well* **back from** *a busy thoroughfare.* ○ *The big house* **stands back** *about half a mile* **from** *the main gates.*

2 [Vp, Vp.pr rel] distance oneself, esp mentally, from (sth) in order to understand or judge it better. **S:** writer; artist, teacher, organizer. **o:** work; painting; events, hurly-burly: *The painter* **stood back** *to get a better sense of he general balance of the composition.* ○ *Sometimes an administrator must* **stand back from** *day-to-day business to grasp the wider pattern of events.* = step back (from).

3 [Vp, Vp.pr rel] hesitate or be unwilling (to make decisions, influence events etc). **S:** leader; teacher, father. **o:** decision-making; argument, controversy; taking action, making decisions: *The leader of the Commons said that it was now time for him to speak out, for he had* **stood back** *and remained silent for too long.* ○ *These were vital discussions*

***from** which we couldn't afford to **stand back**.* = hang back (from).

stand between [Vpr emph] exist as an obstacle between (sb) and (a goal he wishes to achieve). **S:** hurdle, obstacle; examination, test. **o:** (sb and) success, triumph; successful career: *Only two men **stood between** him and a coveted place on the board.*

stand by 1 [Vp] observe events which require an active response without doing anything. **S:** country, government; army; partner, friend: *A man may not **stand by** and watch another destroy himself.* ARG ○ *We cannot **stand** idly **by** while children go hungry.*

2 [Vp nom] be ready to act; be on the alert. **S:** police, troops; fire services, ambulance crews: *The Government ordered the Guards to **stand by**.* AH ○ *Publishers of books **stand by**, ready to turn out a huge new edition.* UTN ○ *Troops are on **standby** alert tonight.* BBCTV □ standby may be used attrib, as shown, or thus: *Police and fire services were again on **standby** tonight.*

3 [Vpr] (be prepared to) support or help (sb). **o:** colleague, friend, family, ally; one another: *He's the sort of friend who will **stand by** you through thick and thin.* ○ *Our supporters continued to **stand by** us when the going was hardest.* = stick by.

4 [Vpr] be true or faithful to (sth). **o:** promise, undertaking, guarantee; principle, code; what one has promised: *'I'm sorry if you think my language is too strong, Donald, but I ... must **stand by** what I have said.'* RM ○ *I glowered. 'I **stand by** every word of it!' I said aloud.* SPL

stand down 1 [Vp] (*legal*) leave the witness box, ie after giving evidence. **S:** witness, prisoner: *'Unless you have any further questions for her, I think this witness may **stand down**.'*

2 [Vp, Vn.p] (*military*) end its life as an active unit; disband. **S** [Vp], **O** [Vn.p]: regiment, battalion: *A number of famous regiments have chosen to **stand down** rather than be amalgamated with other units.*

3 [Vp,Vn ⇆ p pass] (*military*) relax and return to other duties after having been alerted, esp at dawn or dusk. **S** [Vp], **O** [Vn.p]: troops; company, platoon. **S** [Vn.p]: officer: *The troops were **stood down** when it was clear that the warning of an attack was a false alarm.* ↔ stand to.

4 [Vp] withdraw one's application, resign one's position etc, esp in favour of sb else. **S:** candidate; chairman, member: *If Tony wants the job I'll **stand down**.* EHOW ○ *The company secretary has offered to **stand down** in favour of a younger person.* = step down.

stand (for) [Vpr rel] ⇨ stand (as) (for).

stand for 1 [Vpr] be an abbreviation of (sth). **S:** letter, initial; EC. **o:** John, Lisa; European Community: *'What does your second initial **stand for**?'*

2 [Vpr rel] support or represent (sth). **S:** church, party; faith; office, firm. **o:** values, principles; integrity, honesty: *'I detest the man and all he **stands for**.'* ○ *The values **for** which the party has always **stood** are now being challenged.*

3 [Vpr] (*informal*) tolerate or accept (sth). **S:** authorities; teacher, parent. **o:** nonsense, impertinence, rowdiness: *They had been wearing pyjamas until noon. Fiorella wouldn't **stand for** it.* ARG ○ *The Scottish Football Association might ask him to take the Holland game* (as manager) *and it would be surprising if he were to **stand for** that.* SC □ often used with *will/would*; usu neg or with neg implications. = put up with.

stand in good/better stead [Vn.pr pass] serve (sb) well, be of value to (sb). **S:** knowledge, experience; advice, tip; ability, gift; connection, relationship: *He had a pictorial imagination, which **stood** him **in good stead** in the first hasty shaping of the new museum.* SD ○ *This circle of people **stood** him **in** far **better stead** with his younger friends.* HAA

stand in need of [Vpr] (*formal*) require, need (sth). **S:** building, brickwork; machinery; painting, poetry. **o:** (**of**) attention; replacement, repair; reappraisal, re-evaluation: *No writer **stands** more **in need of** thorough reassessment than Kipling.* SC

stand in sb's way/in the way of sth [Vpr] prevent (sb) from doing sth; stop (sth) happening. **S:** employer, headmaster; tradition, precedent; difficulty: *'If you want to go overseas to teach, I certainly shan't **stand in your way**.'* ○ *No difficulty under heaven could **stand in the way of** that moment which he and Sonia so valued.* HAA

stand in (for) 1 [Vp nom, Vp.pr] take the place of (sb) on a given occasion. **S:** deputy, assistant: *During my trips abroad, Bill would **stand in for** me at Board meetings.* ○ *'If you can't make it to the inauguration, make sure you send a suitable **stand-in**.'* = fill in (for).

2 [Vp nom, Vp.pr] (*cinema, TV*) take the part of (a regular actor or actress) during certain sequences: *A professional stunt-man is **standing in for** the male lead during the car chase at the end of the film.* ○ *In some minor scenes, her part is played by a **stand-in**.*

stand in towards [Vp.pr] (*nautical*) move towards (the shore). **S:** ship; fleet. **o:** shore, coast, beach: *It was arranged that the MTB* (motor torpedo boat) *should lie there for two hours, and she would then **stand in towards** the town upon a certain bearing.* RFW

stand off 1 [Vn ⇆ p pass] discourage (sb who is taking an interest in one): *'Angela had told me she had had an affair with him, in fact he was the reason she **stood** me **off** a bit at first.'* DOAP □ note the form stand-offish which means 'discouraging' or 'distant': *The Association's **stand-offish** attitude towards Jesse Jackson's bid for the presidency in the last election hurt him.* G = put off 2.

2 [Vpr] (*nautical*) remain stationary at a distance from (the shore). **S:** ship; fleet, convoy. **o:** shore, beach; Dover, Beachy Head: *The bigger landing craft were forced to **stand off** the beaches until the tide turned.*

3 [nom (Vp)] (*rugby*) half-back who, with the scrum-half, forms a link between the forwards and the three-quarters: *The French **stand-off** gathered a bouncing ball and kicked deep for touch.* ○ *The Cardiff **stand-off** worked a dummy scissors with one of his centres and opened up a gap.* ST

4 [nom (Vp)] (*informal*) situation in which two people or groups confront each other without taking any hostile action: *How much have Britain and Argentina suffered from their prolonged **stand-off** over the Falklands/Malvinas?* G ○ *The long **stand-***

off *between UN and Iraqi forces in the Middle East forced a sudden rise in oil prices.*

stand on ceremony [Vpr] be too formal in one's behaviour, eg when entertaining sb: *I don't like too much* ***standing on ceremony*** *at a simple party like this.* ○ *'Now I'm going to kiss you too, just to show we don't* ***stand on ceremony*** *here.'* TGLY

stand on one's dignity [Vpr] insist that one should be treated with respect, that one's feelings, age, position etc should be taken into account. **S:** mayor, alderman; actor, singer: *Approachable and affable, he does not* ***stand on his dignity****, and I got the strong impression that horse racing will benefit for his four-year term of office.* G ○ *She was* ***standing on her dignity*** *as a promising young acress.* CON

stand on its head [Vn.pr pass] reverse the stated or expected order of (sth). **O:** case, argument, proposition; truth; course, order (of things): *John* ***stood*** *the curator's argument* ***on its head****, saying that charging admission to museums would attract more, not fewer, people to them.* ○ *In this, as in so many other ways, telepathy and clairvoyance seem to be intent on* ***standing*** *the ordinary, accepted and understandable course of nature* ***on its head****.* SNP

standing on one's head [Vpr] (*informal*) easily, without effort: *Mr Wickham, their agent for many years past, said if he kicked the bucket* (= died) *Mrs Merton could run the place* ***standing on her head****.* WDM □ a non-finite adv clause of manner; always in final position after a finite v.

stand on one's own (two) feet [Vpr] be independent, self-sufficient. **S:** child, pupil; (emergent) country, industry: *If he doesn't* ***stand on his own feet*** *at his age, he'll lose his self-respect.* HAA ○ *I* ***stood*** *squarely* ***on my own feet*** *— I became to a large extent financially independent of my father.* SD

stand out (a mile) [Vp] be striking, noticeable, prominent. **S:** fact, evidence; reason, explanation; remedy, answer; (it ...) what has to happen: *The first thing that* ***stands out*** *from the hold-up is that the routine precautions gave the bandits little trouble.* T ○ *It* ***stands out a mile*** *what has to be done.* NM = stick out a mile.

stand out against [Vp.pr pass] be firm, unmoved, in one's opposition to sth. **S:** employer, trade union; delegate. **o:** increase, reduction (in wages); change, modification (of terms of work): *The union leaders are* ***standing out against*** *the abolition of the piece-work system, which enables them to renegotiate wage-rates whenever a new job or process is introduced.* ○ *The Unionist Party in Northern Ireland has* ***stood out against*** *any policy which it feels might lead to the political unification of North and South.*

stand out (against/in contrast to) [Vp, Vp.pr emph rel] be clearly seen, because of a contrast of colour or tone (with sth else). **S:** figure, shape; tone, shade. **o:** background; sky, landscape: *The black smoke* ***stood out in*** *sharp* ***contrast to*** *the white fountains sent up by enemy shells.* SD ○ ***Against*** *a pale blue evening sky, the vapour trails* ***stood out*** *clearly.*

stand out for [Vp.pr pass] (*informal*) delay reaching an agreement in the hope of getting (sth one wants). **S:** negotiator; delegate; committee. **o:** increase (in wages), reduction (of working hours), removal (of grievances): *Our executive is* ***standing out for*** *the original claim of a ten per cent pay rise.* ○ *Students are* ***standing out for*** *a revision of the constitution.* = hold out for, stick out for.

stand out (from) [Vp, Vp.pr emph rel] be of high quality; be pre-eminent. **S:** school, college; scholar, scientist; factory. **o:** rest, others; fellow, contemporary: *Among modern universities some* ***stand out*** *with a special attractiveness.* TES ○ *In this list two names* ***stand out*** *in particular* (or: *are particularly* ***outstanding***). ○ *Even as a schoolboy player, he* ***stood out from*** *the rest of the team.* □ (*be*) outstanding is an adj equivalent in meaning to stand out [Vp].

one's eyes stand out of one's head [Vpr] (of the facial expression) show, express, extreme fear, surprise etc: *'Give him two double whiskies.'* ***My eyes stood out of my head****: I had never tasted whisky in my life before.* SD = one's eyes start out of one's head.

stand out to sea [Vp.pr] (*nautical*) move out from the shore towards the open sea. **S:** ship; fleet, convoy: *A destroyer, doubtless part of the local navy, was* ***standing out to sea****.* ILIH ○ *They were ordered to* ***stand*** *well* ***out to sea****, out of the range of shore batteries.*

stand outside [Vpr] not be sth which one wishes to consider, discuss etc. **S:** matter, question; compensation, re-housing. **o:** scope, range; (main) argument, discussion: *The issue of schools reorganization* ***stands outside*** *the scope of the present discussion.* ⇨ be/fall outside.

stand over 1 [Vpr pass] watch over (sb) closely; supervise. **S:** foreman, supervisor; teacher. **o:** worker, apprentice; pupil: *'You'll have to* ***stand over*** *the new man until he learns the routine.'* ○ *I hate being* ***stood over*** *when I'm trying to do a job of work.*

2 [Vp, Vn.p pass] be postponed, deferred; postpone, defer (sth). **S** [Vp], **O** [Vn.p]**:** business, matter, item; discussion, debate. **S** [Vn.p]**:** chairman, committee: *'There's no urgency about this matter: it can* ***stand over*** *till next week.'* ⇨ hold over.

stand to [Vp nom, Vn.p pass] (*military*) (cause sb to) be on the alert, with weapons ready, against enemy attack. **S** [Vp], **O** [Vn.p]**:** troops; company, squad. **S** [Vn.p]**:** officer, sergeant: *The men were* ***standing to*** (or: *were on* ***stand-to***) *half the night.* ○ *Units in the field are normally* ***stood to*** *just before dawn and dusk.* ↔ stand down 3.

stand to attention [Vpr] (*military*) stand in an alert posture, with the feet together; adopt this position. **S:** soldier; company, battalion: *Perhaps it was the absence of water which made one sweat vicariously, sweat for the troops* ***standing to attention*** *through the long speeches.* QA ○ ***'Stand to attention*** *when the officer speaks to you!'* ⇨ be at attention , come to attention.

it stands to reason [Vpr] it is only to be expected; it follows naturally, given that sth else is already the case: *'Delicate made he is, and only a boy.* ***Stands to reason*** *he couldn't rough it with the others.'* ASA ○ *DAVIES: All these big sports grounds,* ***it stands to reason*** *they need people, to keep the ground, that's what they want.* TC ○ ***It stands to reason*** *. . . that if a woman can expect no promotion she has no incentive to immerse herself* *in any one firm.* NS □ simple tenses only; often introduces a finite clause, as in these examples, but it can be in final position: *'Of course she was pleased.* ***It stands to reason****!'*

stand together [Vp] be united, eg in the face of some outside threat. **S:** family, firm, team: *Social classes whose interests usually conflict may respond to appeals to* ***stand together*** *if there is some danger from outside, which seems to threaten them all.* = stick together.

stand up 1 [Vp] rise to one's feet, possibly as a sign of respect. **S:** audience, public; employees, children: *He* (Mr Major) ***stood up*** *for his first Prime Minister's Questions in the Commons on Thursday.* OBS ○ *When the Headmaster entered the room, the class would* ***stand up*** *as a mark of respect.* ○ *I* ***stood up*** *to let my neighbour leave the theatre.* = get up 2.

2 [Vn.p pass] (*informal*) fail deliberately to keep an appointment with (sb). **O:** boyfriend, girlfriend; date: *As the minutes ticked on past eight o'clock, I began to suspect he'd* ***stood*** *me* ***up****.* ○ *Nobody likes to be* ***stood up*** *on their first big date.*

stand-up comedian/comic [nom (Vp)] comedian who appears on stage before a microphone and tells jokes and funny stories: *He worked for a while as a* ***stand-up comic*** *in the Northern Clubs.* RT

stand up and/to be counted [Vp] declare one's religious, political etc loyalties openly: *She ought to make more of it and declare herself more openly. Marxists, like Roman Catholics, should* ***stand up and be counted****.* NS ○ *A deep conviction or a deep need must ... be publically expressed. It is not enough to belong to a party; one must* ***stand up to be counted****.* ST □ often used with *must, should, ought to* as a strong recommendation to act.

stand-up fight [Vp] (*informal*) angry confrontation between people, usu involving physical violence: *Smouldering aggression can distort relationships into ugly scenes. Some parents and children never have such a* ***stand-up fight****, but others do.* OBS

stand up for [Vp.pr pass] support or champion (sb/sth) in a fight, or in a particular cause. **o:** (younger) brother; underdog, weaker side; oneself; rights, liberty: *Despite his dislike of Robin, he had always* ***stood up for*** *him if some other boy at school attacked him.* ASA ○ *Do you claim what is due to you and* ***stand up for*** *your rights?* WI = stick up for.

stand up (to) 1 [Vp, Vp.pr emph rel] last well, remain sound (despite severe treatment). **S:** metal, fibre; chassis, bodywork; cloth, garment; health, constitution. **o:** (rough) handling, (harsh) treatment; heat, pressure; exile, imprisonment: *Structurally the desks are sound, and will obviously* ***stand up to*** *a good deal of wear and tear.* TES ○ *How will his party's morale* ***stand up to*** *what could prove to be several years of bad news?* OBS

2 [Vp, Vp.pr] withstand, survive (examination). **S:** document; claim, argument, theory; acting, poetry. **o:** ⚠ a test; scrutiny, examination, analysis: *She knew that an hysterical letter from an old dying woman wouldn't* ***stand up*** *in a court of law.* DC ○ *I think this poem does* ***stand up*** *because this is brilliant descriptive writing.* BBCR ○ *Even if this possibility did not* ***stand up to*** *close scrutiny, Pavlov's theory would still be valid.* SNP

stand up to [Vp.pr pass] (be ready to) resist (sb/sth) boldly. **o:** (petty) dictator, officious person; pressure, threat, intimidation: *How will Sarah* ***stand up to*** *her partner's antagonism?* WI ○ *He thought of her as someone to be proud of, yet someone to be* ***stood up to*** *on occasion.* PW

stand (well) with [Vpr] (*formal*) have a good relationship with (sb), be on good terms with (sb). **o:** teacher, employer, bank manager: *What did she get out of it, why did she put up with so much vexation of spirit? Was it just to* ***stand well with*** *Jeremy, whom, though often defying, she really adored.* PW ○ *To move to the next phase of their programme they needed more capital. Whether they got the finance they needed would depend on how* ***well*** *they* ***stood with*** *their overseas backers.*

stare

stare (at) [Vpr pass adj rel] look intently (at sb/sth). **A:** intently, closely; critically. **o:** stranger, newcomer; spectacle, parade; clothes, jewels: *He looked round the room for support, but they* ***stared at*** *him stonily.* HD ○ *Dr Hasselbacher opened his eyes and* ***stared*** *straight* ***at*** *him.* OMIH ○ *If she wears that dress, she'll get* ***stared at*** *every time she goes out.*

stare down/out [Vn.p pass] look intently at a curious or ill-mannered person who is doing the same, and continue looking until he is forced to lower his eyes (often a playful trial of strength between two children): *An inquisitive small boy looked at us from one corner of the railway compartment. Our eldest son looked just as intently back at him, and did his best to* ***stare*** *him* ***down****.*

stare in the face [Vn.pr] be so clear, or so obvious, that one should not miss seeing or grasping it. **S:** building, monument; (lost) money, purse; truth, fact; disaster, crisis. **O:** scientist, politician: *'No wonder you woke up, with that piece of gold plate* ***staring*** *you* ***in the face****.'* DC ○ *This logic* ***stares*** *anyone* ***in the face*** *who knows the economic needs of this country.* ASA

stare out [Vn.p pass] ⇨ stare down/out.

start

start back [Vp] move back sharply in surprise, shock etc: *Jane* ***started back*** *in surprise and alarm as the firework was let off.* = step back.

start (for) [Vpr] leave one place to go (to another). **o:** home, work: *'What time do you usually* ***start for*** *school in the morning?'*

start from [Vpr] take as one's starting-point in an argument etc. **o:** assumption, premise, hypothesis, hunch, position: *'Your argument breaks down at the very beginning because you're* ***starting from*** *a false assumption.'* ○ *Every specialist who is urging the concert-goer to extend his horizons ... seems to* ***start from*** *the premise that his preference for the established classics is a symptom of ... delinquency.* T

start from scratch [Vpr, Vn.pr pass] start (sth) from the very beginning, esp when building or developing sth. **S:** industry, country; businessman, artisan, scientist. **O:** everything, the whole thing: *The company lost all its plant through enemy bombing, so that in 1945 they* ***started*** *absolutely* ***from scratch****.* ○ *If you tried to arrange social chaos in an inner city borough,* ***starting from scratch****, you couldn't* *outdo the present arrangements in London's Hackney and Shoreditch.* OBS ○ *JIMMY: I'll close that damned sweet-stall, and we'll* ***start*** *everything* ***from scratch****. What do you say? We'll get away from this place.* LBA

start in on 1 [Vp.pr] (*informal*) begin to do (sth). **o:** (one's) homework, research; (the) climb, search; cooking the meal, cleaning the yard: *Andy, one of the guides, . . . brought me a beer, and we* ***started in*** *to analyse the climb* (or: ***started in on*** *analysing the climb*). BM
2 [Vp.pr] (*informal*) begin to criticize, scold, harangue etc (sb). **S:** orator, preacher; father, boss. **o:** following, faithful; slacker, miscreant: *The team were hardly settled in the dressing-room before the manager* ***started in on*** *them for slovenly, unaggressive play.*

start off [Vp] begin, open one's remarks, or actions, by saying or doing sth special: *Our guide* ***started off*** *by pointing out the dangers involved in rock climbing.* ○ *They had* ***started off*** *saying that the accommodation wasn't as bad as we'd been told.*

start off (on) 1 [Vp, Vp.pr rel, Vn ⇆ p pass, Vn.p.pr pass rel] (cause sb to) begin working on sth. **S** [Vp, Vp.pr], **O** [Vn.p, Vn.p.pr]**:** class; pupil, athlete. **S** [Vn.p, Vn.p.pr]**:** teacher, coach. **o:** Latin, calculus; apparatus, simple climbs: [Vp.pr] *'What made him* ***start off on*** *this weekend cycling craze?'* ○ [Vn.p.pr] *It's a bright class: I can* ***start*** *them* ***off on*** *German in the second year.*
2 [Vp, Vp.pr pass, Vn ⇆ p pass, Vn.p.pr pass rel] (cause sb to) begin talking, story-telling etc, in a way that listeners find tedious. **S** [Vp, Vp.pr], **O** [Vn.p, Vn.p.pr]**:** bigot, bore, chatterbox. **o:** tirade, reminiscences, tale of woe: [Vn.p] *'You know that once she's been* ***started off****, it's almost impossible to stop her.'* ○ [Vn.p.pr] *'Don't for Heaven's sake* ***start*** *him* ***off on*** *one of his golfing stories.'* = set off (on) 2. ⇨ be off (on).

start on [Vpr pass rel, Vn.pr pass rel] (cause sb to) begin work on (sth), start dealing with (sth). **o:** preparations, invitations; flowers, meal; dresses, blouses; cleaning, sweeping; sorting out the cellar: *'The wedding's in a month, and I haven't even* ***started on*** *the guest list yet.'* ○ *'I'd better* ***start*** *her* ***on*** *the ironing now or we won't be ready for the morning.'*

start (off) on the right/wrong foot [Vpr, Vp.pr] (*informal*) begin sth, esp a relationship, in the right/wrong way. **S:** son-in-law, visitor, tenant; (new) student, recruit: *'It's not really very nice* ***starting on the wrong foot****, now is it?'* TT ○ *I want the girl to* ***start off on the right foot*** *with my mother.* RFW ○ *'Don't light a cigarette when you meet the boss: that'll really be* ***starting off on the wrong foot****.'* = get off on the right/wrong foot.

start out of [Vpr, Vn.pr pass] (cause sb to) awake suddenly, emerge quickly from a daydream etc. **S** [Vpr], **O** [Vn.pr]**:** listener, pupil. **S** [Vn.pr]**:** crash, explosion; pain. **o:** sleep, dream, reverie: *The appearance of the teacher at his side* ***started*** *John* ***out of*** *his happy daydream.* ○ *The audience was* ***started out of*** *its somnolence by a sudden crash on the drums.*

one's eyes start out of one's head [Vpr] (of the facial expression) show, express, extreme fear, surprise etc: *I'm sure Kenny thought he saw a monster. We were at the post office . . . when he arrived with the news, and* ***his eyes*** *were* ***starting out of his head****.* RM = one's eyes stand out of one's head.

start out (on) [Vp, Vp.pr] begin to move in a purposeful way; begin a journey. **S:** hiker, cyclist, car: *The small party of explorers* ***started out*** *with high hopes.* ○ *Ten machines* ***started out on*** *the last leg; only four finished.* = set off (on) 1, set out (on).

start up 1 [Vp, Vn ⇆ p pass] (cause a machine to) start running. **S** [Vp], **O** [Vn.p]**:** engine, plane, car: *I tried the ignition again. Still the car wouldn't* ***start up****.* ○ (order to aircraft mechanic) *'All right,* ***start*** *her* ***up****!'*
2 [Vp nom, Vn ⇆ p pass] (cause sth to) begin to operate; establish. **S** [Vp], **O** [Vn.p]**:** business, service: *He* ***started up*** *a successful car hire firm.* □ nom form usu attrib, as in: *. . .* ***start-up*** *capital, funds.* ⇨ start up (in).
3 [Vp.n pass] begin, initiate (sth). **O:** conversation, argument, debate; acquaintance: *There was no danger of* ***starting up*** *some stumbling conversation with them.* CON

start up (in) [Vp, Vp.pr rel] make a start (in a business etc). **o:** business, teaching, dentistry: *Twice he had raised the money and* ***started up in*** *engineering.* ARG ○ *They were thinking of* ***starting up in*** *the fruit and vegetable trade.* ⇨ start up 2.

to start with 1 [Vpr] at the beginning, initially: *I pulled hard* ***to start with****; but after a time I began to lose interest and I let go of the rope.* MFM ○ *The bottom of the atmosphere, the part where we live, will be cool* ***to start with****.* TBC □ an adv expression with no object; it may occur at the beginning or end of the sentence. = to begin with 1.
2 [Vpr] in the first place, first and foremost: ***'To start with****, Jones is a hopeless organizer. And as if that wasn't enough, he goes out of his way to annoy everybody.'* ○ *'Well,* ***to start with****, you can put out of your mind the notion that there's money to be made out of teaching.'* □ an adv expression with no object; usu occurs at the beginning of the sentence. = to begin with 2.

start with a clean sheet/slate [Vpr] begin afresh; make a fresh start: *It was just as well to* ***start with a clean sheet*** *about these things.* DBM ○ *All the wallpaper — layer on layer of it — and all the paint must go, so that we could* ***start with a clean slate****.* SC

starve

starve into [Vn.pr pass] force (sb) to surrender by cutting off his food supply. **O:** country, city; garrison. **o:** submission, surrender, capitulation: *They imagine that by blockading our ports they can* ***starve*** *us* ***into*** *submission.*

starve of [Vn.pr pass emph rel] keep (sb/sth) short of (sth). **O:** country, city; population; industry. **o:** essential foods; raw materials: *The Ministry had* ***starved*** *the workshops* ***of*** *vital components.* ○ *The railways are* ***starved of*** *first-class technical men.* NS ○ *In coronary thrombosis the coronary blood vessels supplying the heart are narrowed, . . . and so the organ is* ***starved of*** *blood.* NS □ often passive. = deprive of.

starve out/out of [Vn ⇆ p pass, Vn.pr pass] force (sb) to leave (a hiding-place etc), by cutting off his food. **S:** invader; hunter. **O:** population, army; rodent. **o:** city; lair, burrow: *Having failed to bomb* *the occupants out, the enemy resolved to* ***starve*** *them* ***out****.*

stash

stash away [Vn ⇆ p pass] (*informal*) store, deposit (sth) in a place where others are unlikely to find it. **O:** food, sweets; loot, contraband; money, profits: *Many rural dwellers still* ***stash*** *their money* ***away*** *in secret hiding places because they don't trust the banks.* ○ *'I suppose the Syndicate has a few millions* ***stashed away*** *in a numbered account somewhere.'*

stave

stave in [Vn ⇆ p pass adj] crush the side or covering of (sth), making a dent or hole in it. **S:** rock, pole; blow, impact. **O:** hull, body (of car); rib-cage: *Repeated batterings on the rocks had* ***staved in*** *one side of the craft.* ○ *He was admitted to hospital with two of his ribs* ***staved in****.*

stave off [Vn ⇆ p pass adj] prevent (sth) from overwhelming one. **S:** news, conversation, humour; ration, supply. **O:** misery, despair; defeat, disaster; criticism; hunger, thirst: *Only the sure prospect of relief* ***staved off*** *utter despair.* ○ *He stuffed down quantities of bread, trying to* ***stave off*** *increasing stabs of hunger.* BFA

stay

stay abreast of 1 [Vp.pr] remain level with (sb/sth), not slip behind (sb/sth). **S:** car, boat; runner, crew. **o:** competition, field: *Over the first five laps, Cram* ***stayed abreast of*** *the Moroccan runner.* ⇨ keep abreast of 1.

2 [Vp.pr, Vn.p.pr pass] stay well informed about (sth). **S:** scholar, scientist. **o:** (new) development, research: *With so much being published here and in the States, it's difficult* ***stay abreast of*** *all the new developments.* ⇨ keep abreast of 2.

stay ahead/ahead of [Vp, Vpr] not lose one's position in front (of others); keep the lead. **S:** horse, car; industry, manufacturer; thief. **o:** (rest of the) field; competitor, rival; police: *George is sometimes a few pounds down at the end of a week's gambling, but more often than not he* ***stays ahead*** *and goes into the next week several pounds in credit.* ○ *Initially, it won't be a matter of* ***staying ahead of*** *our European rivals: it'll be a question of catching them up.* ⇨ keep ahead/ahead of.

stay (at) [Vpr rel] take board and lodging (at a place). **o:** hotel, boarding house, hostel: *He travelled through the North,* ***staying*** *for a few nights at a time* ***at*** *small hotels.* ○ *'Where are you* ***staying****?' '****At*** *the Grand.'* = stop (at).

stay at home [Vpr] spend much of (one's time) at home: *SARAH: Hymie's all right. He's got a business. His children are married and he* ***stays at home*** *all the time.* CSWB ○ *The younger son* ***stays at home*** *and fiddles around with bits of machinery.* ○ *Kate's a quiet, conventional,* ***stay-at-home*** *sort of girl.* □ nom form stay-at-home may be attrib, as in the last example, and suggests that the person prefers a quiet, settled life at home.

stay away (from) 1 [Vp, Vp.pr rel] not be present (at a place), not appear (at a place). **S:** visitor, tourist; worker, student, child. **o:** resort; meeting, lecture, class; home: *If the visitors do* ***stay away*** *there is a very strong case for giving Cornwall some assistance.* OBS ○ *That term, John* ***stayed away from*** *school for weeks at a time.* = stop away (from). ⇨ keep away (from).

2 [Vp, Vp.pr] keep one's distance (from sth/sb). **S:** official, inspector; busybody; seducer, seductress. **o:** office, shop; wife, daughter, husband: *'I don't want men in bowler hats snooping around the place; tell them to* ***stay away****!'* ○ *We knew the kind of reputation the man had. If he knew what was good for him, he would* ***stay away from*** *Jessie.* ⇨ keep away (from).

stay behind [Vp] remain in a place after others have left. **S:** visitor, spectator, member (of a group or audience): *Several students* ***stayed behind*** *after the lecture to ask questions.* ○ *'Not everyone is trying to leave in a hurry. There will be those who* ***stay behind*** *for a few weeks, at least.'* T = remain behind, stop behind, wait behind.

stay down 1 [Vp] remain in a lowered position. **S:** handle, lever, switch: *'Both of these switches above the boiler have to* ***stay down*** *if you want the radiators to be on as well as the hot water cylinder.'* ○ *'Something's wrong with the gear lever. It won't* ***stay down*** *in fourth; it keeps shifting into neutral.'* ⇨ leave down.

2 [Vp] remain in the stomach, rather than be vomited. **S:** food; solids; medicine: *Ben had an upset stomach. His mother tried all kinds of special foods, but none of them would* ***stay down****.* ⇨ keep down 7.

stay for/to [Vpr] remain at sb's house to have (a meal). **S:** visitor, guest. **o:** meal; lunch, dinner: *They had decided to* ***stay to*** *lunch, and Brigit had fussed because there was not enough food.* DC ○ *'Catch the last train, and you can* ***stay for*** *supper.'* = stop for/to.

stay in 1 [Vp] remain at school after others have left, as a punishment. **S:** class, form; culprit: *'If this noise goes on for very much longer you'll all have to* ***stay in*** *after school!'* = stop in. ⇨ keep in 3.

2 [Vp, Vpr] remain in position, stay where it is. **S:** plunger, damper, peg; passage, note, reference: *The damper* ***stays in*** *and reduces the flow of air but does not put the fire out completely.* ○ *Gerald didn't very much care if the references to his old chief did offend his bosses in the Ministry. Whatever he cut from his book, those references would* ***stay in****.* ⇨ leave in.

3 [Vp] (*cricket*) remain at the wicket, not be dismissed. **S:** batsman; opening pair, last man. **A:** all afternoon, throughout the morning: *Turner* ***stayed in*** *all afternoon as the more aggressive member of two productive partnerships.* ⇨ be in 5, go in 4, put in 8.

stay in/indoors [Vp] remain in the house, because one is ill, the weather is bad etc. **S:** family, (hotel) guest: *We* ***stayed in*** *all that week, while the rain poured down outside.* ○ *'****Stay indoors*** *for a few days until your cold is better.'* = stop in/indoors. ⇨ keep in 1, keep indoors.

stay off [Vpr] not eat, drink, smoke etc, things which, if taken in excess, may be bad for one's health. **o:** beer, whisky; potatoes, sweet stuff; casual sex: *'Harry's wife would have had an easier time of it if he'd managed to* ***stay off*** *the bottle.'* ○ *'You'll have to* ***stay off*** *sweets and chocolates if you want to reduce weight.'* ⇨ keep off 4.

stay on 1 [Vp, Vpr] remain in position on top of (sth). **S:** lid, cover. **o:** pot, pan: *You shouldn't put* *large parcels on the roof rack. They won't* **stay on** *in a strong wind.* ⇨ leave on 1.

2 [Vp] remain alight, keep burning. **S:** light; fire; television: *'Our electricity bills are bound to be high if half the lights* **stay on** *after people go home at night.'* ⇨ be on 8, go on 15, leave on 2, turn on 1.

stay on (at) [Vp, Vp.pr] remain (at a place of study, with an employer etc) after others have left. **S:** pupil, student; employee. **o:** school, college; the works, bank; party, dance: *A medical student becomes a senior figure in college as he* **stays on** *year after year.* HD ○ *DAVIES: I'm* **staying on** *here as caretaker.* TC ○ *She's* **staying on at** *school to take her 'A' levels.* = stop on (at). ⇨ keep on 4.

stay on top (of) [Vp, Vpr] remain in a superior state with regard to one's health, work, colleagues etc. **o:** things; one's job; the opposition: (milk advertisement) *'Pick up a pinta* (= pint of milk). **Stay on top**!' ○ *You need to be lively and resourceful to* **stay on top of** *this job.* = keep on top (of).

stay out 1 [Vp] remain outside the house, esp after dark. **S:** child, husband: *'You* **stayed out** *after midnight last night. What happened?'* ○ *She lets the children* **stay out** *half the night.* = stop out 1.

2 [Vp] remain in the open. **S:** car, bicycle; washing: *'I'm sure it's laziness, but I just can't be bothered to put the car in the garage. It'll have to* **stay out** *tonight.'* ⇨ leave out.

3 [Vp] (*industrial relations*) remain on strike, continue a stoppage of work. **S:** worker; miner, postman. **A:** on strike; in sympathy: *The car-workers' leaders said the men were prepared to* **stay out** *until their grievances were remedied.* = stop out 2. ⇨ be out 1, bring out 1, come out 1.

stay out of [Vpr] remain at a point where sb can not reach one, or sth cannot affect one. **o:** range, reach; earshot; danger, harm's way, trouble: *I'd been looking for him for years, but always he managed to* **stay** *just* **out of** *reach.* ○ *Father hoped we'd* **stay out of** *trouble in the big city.* ⇨ be out of 1, keep out of.

stay to [Vpr] ⇨ stay for/to.

stay up 1 [Vp] not fall or sink. **S:** building; trousers; swimmer: *'I'm surprised that some of these houses* **stay up** *as long as they do.'* ○ *'If you do fall out of the boat, your lifejacket will help you to* **stay up** *until we can fish you out.'* ⇨ keep up 1.

2 [Vp] remain awake and out of bed, eg to wait for sb: *'Will you let us* **stay up** *till he comes?' 'Yes, if it's not too late.'* PW ○ *She liked listening to records and* **staying up** *half the night.* SPL = stop up 3. ⇨ be up 4, keep up 9.

3 [Vp] remain in a position where it has been mounted, hung etc. **S:** picture, decorations; curtain, hanging: *'Your notice can* **stay up** *for a week, but after that it'll have to come down to make room for others.'* ○ *Christmas decorations* **stay up** *until the sixth of January (Twelfth Night). Then, according to tradition, they have to be taken down.* ⇨ leave up, put up 2.

stay (with) [Vpr rel] be a guest (at sb's house). **o:** friend, relative: *At half-term we plan to* **stay with** *my sister near London.* ○ *The family* **with** *whom Michael was* **staying** *were old friends of his father's.*

stay with [Vpr] (*informal*) continue to listen to (sb), even though one may be tempted to go away etc, so giving him the chance to explain sth etc: *'Just* **stay with** *me a minute longer. I'm sure I can convince you that we have a reasonable case.'* ○ *'***Stay with** *me just one moment, ladies and gentlemen, while I tell you about our new rub-on rub-off carpet cleaner!'*

steady

steady on [Vp] be calm and reasonable in one's language or behaviour: *Frank became more and more excited as he put forward his theory.... Gerald was forced to turn round in his chair to speak to him. '***Steady on***,' he cried.* ASA □ imperative only. = calm down 2.

steal

steal a glance (at) [Vn.pr pass rel] take quick, secret looks at (sb/sth). **o:** visitor, suitor: *Toby* **stole a glance at** *Nick.* TP ○ *They* **stole** *covert* **glances at** *the picture high above the door.* TB ○ *The man's wife chattered on,* **stealing** *occasional* **glances at** *Peter.* CON

steal away [Vp] leave quietly, and possibly also furtively. **S:** guest, spectator; shy, embarrassed person. **A:** furtively, noiselessly; on tiptoe; like a thief in the night: *He* **stole away** *from his seat in the back row while the attention of the others was engaged.*

steal a march on [Vn.pr] do sth before (sb else), so gaining an advantage over him. **o:** neighbour, competitor, (business) rival: *Neither of you wants to look as if the other one had* **stolen a march on** *him.* CON ○ *The Tories have a unique opportunity to* **steal a march on** *their political opponents.* SC

steal over [Vpr] gradually fill or take possession of (sb). **S:** mood, feeling; depression, sadness; relief, liberation: *The party feeling, the community spirit, was beginning to* **steal over** *her.* PW ○ *A sense of futility* **stole over** *him.*

steal up on 1 [Vp.pr] advance quietly and carefully towards (sb), thus taking him by surprise. **S:** child; patrol, scout. **o:** him etc; position, camp: *'Don't* **steal up on** *me like that: you frighten the life out of me!'* ○ *A patrol* **stole up on** *the bridge under cover of darkness.*

2 [Vp.pr] come to (one) gradually, without one knowing. **S:** feeling; melancholy, depression; old age: *I must not let madness* **steal up on** *me and take me by surprise.* PM ○ *The deliciously lazy feeling that* **steals up on** *us when we sit in a garden acts like a tonic after a hard-working week.* WI

steam

steam across, along, away etc [Vp, Vpr] move across etc under steam power, and possibly emitting puffs of steam. **S:** ship, train: *Convoys carrying essential supplies and munitions* **steamed** *continuously* **across** *the Atlantic.* ○ *The London to Edinburgh express* **steamed into** *Newcastle right on time.* ○ *We arrived on Platform 10 just as the Rome train was* **steaming out**.

steam off [Vn ⇆ p pass, Vn.pr pass] remove (one piece of paper etc) from (another) by passing steam over them. **O:** (postage-)stamp, label. **o:** letter, box: *Before you can mount the stamps in your album, you must* **steam** *them* **off** *their envelopes.*

steam up [Vp] be covered with condensed steam. **S:** glass; window, mirror: *The insides of the car windows* **steam up** *very quickly in wet weather.* □ also used in the passive or as an adj of the [Vn.p] pattern:

The glass doors of the kitchen were ***steamed up****—a sure sign that the kettle had been boiling for a long time.* = mist up.

steamed up [pass adj (Vn.p)] (*informal*) excited, enthusiastic: *'You come on half-naked to get them all* ***steamed up*** *about you, so why grumble when you succeed?'* PE ○ *My mother came back all* ***steamed up*** *about modern decor, and painted the doors crimson.* RFW □ usu passive, with *appear* etc; note also: *in a* steamed-up *condition, state.*

steel

steel oneself (against/for/to) [Vn.pr emph rel] harden, toughen, oneself (to meet sth or to do sth). **o:** shock, blow, impact; disappointment, failure; (price) increase, (wage) cut, tax: *Citizens will probably* ***steel themselves for*** *a further levy.* SC ○ *It had taken me a long time . . . to* ***steel myself*** *to do it* (or: ***steel myself to*** *action*). *Now I was ready at last.* SPL ○ *The men around the Dowager Empress could never* ***steel themselves to*** *a policy of whole-hearted defiance.* BM

steep

steeped in [pass (Vn.pr)] (*formal*) having absorbed (sth) fully. **o:** tradition, lore, ritual: *Wednesday's Prom by the BBC Philharmonic Orchestra was* ***steeped in*** *nostalgia like it used to be.* G ○ *A trained soldier, who is* ***steeped in*** *all the rituals of kit inspections and parades, is put in charge of new recruits.* = soak (oneself) in.

stem

stem from [Vpr emph rel] have (sth) as its source or cause. **S:** (political) movement, agitation, unrest; dissatisfaction, anxiety; faith, hope, inspiration. **o:** (harsh) conditions, unemployment, hunger; statement, policy; tradition, (peasant) background: *The present wave of strikes* ***stems from*** *discontent among the lower-paid.* ○ *Significantly, he has not challenged my analysis of the Northern Ireland situation, only the solution that* ***stems from*** *it.* OBS = arise from.

step

step aside [Vp] move to one side, eg to let sb pass. **S:** passenger, pedestrian, spectator: *'Would you mind* ***stepping aside*** *to let this lady off the bus?'*

step back [Vp] move backwards, from surprise, shock, etc: *'Take her in your arms.' At that Nicky* ***stepped back****, his face stiff with distaste.* DC ○ *She* ***stepped back****, hardly able to believe her ears.* = start back.

step back (from) [Vp, Vp.pr rel] move away, distance oneself (from a problem etc) in order to understand it better. **o:** one's work, studies; problem, issue; events: *'****Step back*** *a bit and look at the problem from Tony's point of view.'* ○ *It would do you good to* ***step back from*** *the daily pressures and take a longer-term view of how the business is shaping.* = stand back (from) 2.

step down [Vp] resign, usu from a position of authority, often to let sb else take it. **S:** chairman, president, director: *If they disagreed seriously while I was chairman, I would at once* ***step down****.* MFM ○ *If the people want him to form a new party he will do so, or even* ***step down*** *if they say so.* T = stand down 4.

step forward [Vp] present oneself, eg to give information, to offer help. **S:** witness; volunteer, would-be helper: *When the appeal went out for volunteers to help with rescue work, several* ***stepped forward****.* = come forward (with).

step in [Vp] intervene, to help or hinder (sb/sth). **S:** government, ministry; owner, editor; (union) leader: *Seeing that I was lost for an answer, John* ***stepped in*** *to save the situation.* ○ *Our marriage was fine until she* ***stepped in*** *and broke us up.*

step inside [Vp, Vpr] enter a house, an office etc. **S:** visitor, caller: *'Would you care to* ***step inside*** *for a moment?'* ○ *He was invited to* ***step inside*** *the kitchen and take a seat.*

step into the breach [Vpr] help to run an organization, business etc, by filling the place of sb who is absent. **S:** (junior) colleague, assistant, understudy: *Douglas couldn't attend the meeting, but Martin* ***stepped into the breach*** *at the last minute.* ○ *Kathleen* ***stepped into the breach*** *with a generous devotion.* SD

step into sb else's shoes [Vpr] assume, take control of, a responsible task or post from sb else. **S:** son, nephew; assistant, deputy: *Then Father handed over control, and Geoffrey* ***stepped into the director's shoes*** *with the confidence of someone who had been measuring himself carefully for the responsibilities involved.*

step off 1 [Vp, Vpr] get off or out of (a vehicle etc). **o:** bus, train, boat; pier, dock: *As soon as she* ***stepped off*** *the plane, she was surrounded by a swarm of photographers.* ○ *He* ***stepped off*** *the store escalator on the ground floor.* OBS

2 [Vp] (*military*) begin to march. **S:** troops; company, squad: *'Now when you* ***step off****, take a full pace of thirty inches!'*

step off on the wrong foot [Vp.pr] (*informal*) begin a task, relationship etc, in the wrong way: *After all the care we took to prepare the ground, he has to* ***step off on the wrong foot****!* ○ *With girls, the first approach is all-important: don't* ***step off on the wrong foot****!* = start off on the right/wrong foot.

step on sb's toes [Vpr] (*informal*) behave, eg when taking up a new job, without proper regard for the feelings of others: *'As a newcomer to the department, I'm anxious not to* ***step on anyone's toes****, but it does seem to me that something needs to be done about the security of the building.'* = tread on sb's toes.

step on it/the gas [Vpr] (*informal*) press down the accelerator of a car to increase speed; hurry, go faster. **S:** driver, motorist: *'Tell the driver to* ***step on it****—we don't want to be late!'*

step out [Vp] lengthen one's stride so as to move more quickly: *'Tell the people at the front to* ***step out****—we'll never by back in time for supper.'*

step outside [Vp] (*informal*) leave a private party, bar etc to have a fight: *'****Step outside*** *and repeat what you've just said!'* ○ *Brother Nigel asked me to* ***step outside*** *when I told his mother she was evil-minded.* LBA □ often used in the imperative form to issue a threatening invitation.

step over [Vpr pass] raise one's feet to cross (an obstacle). **o:** rope, barrier; sb's feet: *We had to* ***step over*** *rows of outstretched legs to reach our seats in the stalls.*

step up 1 [Vp] come forward; approach: *'Will John Fisher please* ***step up*** *to receive his prize?'*

2 [Vn ⇆ p nom pass adj] increase, improve (sth). **S:** government, industry, information services, army.

O: effort, campaign; production, delivery; broadcast, propaganda; drive, offensive: *Resources allotted to these operations could be* **stepped up**. MFM ○ *We hope for a sharp* **step-up** *in production.* ○ *The social position of the Eastwoods had been much* **stepped up**. PW ○ *One side-effect of the lessons proved to be remarkably* **stepped-up** *attendance figures.* TES

stew

stew in one's own juice [Vpr] (*informal*) (leave sb to) bear the unpleasant consequences of his own actions: *His attitude was that, ready as he was to serve* (in a government), *he was also perfectly prepared to let Mr Bishweshwar* **stew in his own juice**. ST ○ *Let Ella* **stew in her own** *self-centered, neurotic* **juice**, *she thought.* HAA □ often preceded by *let someone ...*.

stick

stick about/around [Vp, Vpr] (*informal*) remain in a place waiting for sth to happen etc: *I didn't want to* **stick about** *waiting for the bomb to explode.* ○ *'***Stick around** *for a while — the boss will soon be back.'* = hang about/around, wait about/around.

stick at [Vpr pass] (*informal*) work steadily and persistently at (sth). **o:** work; task, job: *I* **stick at** *my painting five or six hours a day, but nothing much comes of it.* ○ *'You can get the report written inside a week, but you'll need to* **stick at** *it.'*

stick at nothing [Vpr] (*informal*) (be ready to) behave in an unscrupulous way to get what one wants: *'Like you? Of course he doesn't like you. He'll* **stick at nothing** *to get you out of the way!'* ○ *'If ruthlessness is the difference between staying in the middle and getting to the top, he'll* **stick at nothing**.*'* □ usu with *will/would*; often followed by an inf. = stop at nothing.

stick by [Vpr] (*informal*) support (sb) loyally. **o:** friend, colleague: *His wife has* **stuck by** *him in good times and bad.* ○ *The older staff would* **stick by** *the firm through thick and thin.* = stand by 3.

stick down 1 [Vn ⇆ p pass adj] fasten (the cover etc) of sth with glue, paste etc. **O:** flap, flange, edge; envelope: *'Don't forget to put the postal order in before you* **stick down** *the envelope.'* ○ *The corner of the page has been* **stuck down**; *I can't read what's written there.*

2 [Vn ⇆ p pass] (*informal*) place (sth) on the floor etc. **O:** bag, case; parcel; chair: *'You can* **stick** *the table* **down** *in a corner for the time being.'* ○ *'Where does the mail go?' 'Oh,* **stick** *it* **down** *over here.'* = put down 1.

3 [Vn ⇆ p pass] (*informal*) write (sth) on paper. **O:** name, address, phone number: *'***Stick** *your names* **down** *at the top of the form.'* ○ *He'd* **stuck** *the formula* **down** *on the back of an old envelope.* = put down 11, write down.

stuck for [pass (Vn.pr)] (*informal*) unable to say or write (words etc), because of ignorance, inexperience etc. **o:** ⚠ idea, word; answer, reply: *The questions will get harder as the* (TV quiz) *programme progresses, but Coxhead is not worried that the panellists will be* **stuck for** *answers.* TVT ○ *It's unlikely that* (the TV presenter) *will ever be* **stuck for** *words either, having had a rich experience as a free-lance broadcaster.* TVT

stick in [Vn ⇆ p pass, Vn.pr pass] fix, fasten (sth) into (a book etc) with glue, paste, etc. **O:** photograph, postcard, cutting. **o:** album, scrapbook: *The children spent a rainy morning* **sticking** *stamps* **in** *their albums.*

stuck in [pass (Vn.p)] (*informal*) really busy, fully involved in a task: *The painter got* **stuck in**: *nice firm strokes, no paint wasted, sure hands.* TT ○ *'Get* **stuck in**, *United!'* (encouragement to footballers to play hard). □ usu used after *get*.

stick in sb's craw [Vpr] (*informal*) be so unpleasant, painful etc that it cannot easily be borne or accepted. **S:** behaviour; treachery, deceit; rudeness, insensitivity: *When I thought about marrying Myrtle—yes, there were many, many moments when I did think of marrying her — this angry hurt recurred. I could not get over it. It* **stuck**, *as they say,* **in my craw**. SPL ○ *'What really* **sticks in my craw** *is hearing that odious man claim all the credit for himself.'*

stick one's heels in [Vn.p] (*informal*) resist, oppose, firmly sb's attempt to ignore one's rights, dictate to one etc. **S:** taxpayer, consumer, commuter: *The Education Authority wanted to move the school to new buildings, but parents and pupils* **stuck their heels in**. ○ *So many cases of our fighters being fired upon by friendly ships had occurred that we had* **stuck our heels in** *and demanded better aircraft recognition.* RFW = dig one's heels/toes in.

stick in sb's/the memory/mind [Vpr] be frequently recalled to the conscious mind; be vividly remembered. **S:** event; death, sacrifice; words, speech: *There are passages in that play which still* **stick in my mind** *twenty years after the first performance.* ○ *It is the unheroic sacrifices of ordinary people that chiefly* **stick in the mind**. ○ *His words on that day must have* **stuck in the memories of** *many people.*

stick in one's throat [Vpr] be difficult to express, because of nerves, strong feelings etc. **S:** word, name; line, verse: *The words almost* **stuck in her throat** *but she managed them.* WI

stick on [Vn ⇆ p nom pass, Vn.pr pass] fasten (sth) to (a surface) with paste, glue etc. **O:** label, picture, cut-out. **o:** trunk, case; wall: **Stick** *a few exotic labels* **on** *your suitcase if you want to make it look as though you're much travelled.* ○ *Pictures of football stars were* **stuck on** *the wall by his bed.* □ the kind of label one sticks on luggage is a stick-on label.

stick out 1 [Vp] project. **S:** rock, cliff; nose, chin: *I could see a pair of feet* **sticking out** *at the end of the blanket.* ○ *We parcelled up the material securely, without leaving any ends* **sticking out**. = jut out.

2 [Vn ⇆ p pass] cause (sth) to project; thrust forward. **O:** head, chest, tongue: *Someone* **stuck** *a foot* **out** *and tripped me up.* ○ *'Don't* **stick** *your tongue* **out** *at me — I'll tell your father.'*

stick it/this/that out [Vn.p] (*informal*) endure sth unpleasant: *He swore he'd* **stick it out**, *and stay unemployed, until he got something really worthwhile.* EGD ○ *He hated working in the City, but he would* **stick it out** *a bit longer for the sake of his family.*

stick out like a sore thumb [Vp.pr] be prominent or striking but in a ugly, unpleasant way. **S:** statue, monument; building; performance; remark, language: (luxury buildings in London) *There is one* *block that* **sticks out — like a sore thumb**, *some might say, although others find beauty in its austerity.* OBS ○ *Because of its sudden coarseness, one passage* (in the account) **sticks out like a sore thumb**. L

stick out (a mile) [Vp] (*informal*) be strikingly clear. **S:** motive, intention; origins, background; it ... that he intends to seize control: *He tried to disguise the purpose of his visit, but his real intentions* **stuck out a mile**. ○ *'It* **sticks out a mile** *that he's hoping to take over your job.'* = stand out (a mile).

stick one's neck out [Vn.p] (*informal*) behave in a bold, adventurous and possibly dangerous way, eg by expressing novel ideas, criticizing authority etc: *'I'm not sure of the answer myself, but I'll* **stick my neck out** *and say that John's solution is correct.'* ○ *'You can support the campaign if you want to, but I'm not* **sticking my neck out** *for anybody.'*

stick out for [Vp.pr] (*informal*) refuse to yield now, in the hope of getting sth better later on. **S:** worker, employee; union, striker. **o:** higher wage, bigger bonus: *The staff are in a fighting mood; they're* **sticking out for** *the full amount of their wage claim.* ○ *We're going to* **stick out for** *fuller representation on the Council.* = hold out for, stand out for.

stick to 1 [Vpr] not stray, wander, from (sth). **S:** speaker, lecturer. **o:** subject, facts; point (at issue), argument: *I find his lectures very confusing: he never* **sticks to** *the point.* ○ *The music pursued its course, never* **sticking to** *the same key for two bars together.* DOP ○ *'This is getting us nowhere. Let us* **stick to** *the facts. Mrs Carstairs has died — from cyanide poisoning.'* EM = keep to 1.

2 [Vpr pass] follow or observe (sth) closely. **o:** choice, decision; principle, belief. **A:** firmly, closely, faithfully: *'Once we've sorted out a programme of events, let's for Heaven's sake try to* **stick to** *it.'* ○ *Flying is simple if you* **stick to** *the rules.* DM = hold to 1, keep to 2. ↔ depart from.

stick to sb's fingers [Vpr] (*informal*) (of sb else's property) stay in one's possession; remain stolen. **S:** money, jewels, stones: *A million pounds went through his hands, and around forty thousand* **stuck to his fingers**. DS

stick to one's guns [Vpr] (*informal*) defend one's rights, point of view etc, stubbornly; refuse to change or give way on a matter of principle. **S:** speaker, author; politician, academic: ***I stuck to my guns*** *and refused to be overruled by my political masters.* MFM ○ *All the other musicians of his generation have gone their different ways but Steve Lane has* **stuck** *religiously* **to his guns**: *no selling out* (ie no giving in to commercial pressures). RT

stick to one's last [Vpr] confine oneself to the work one is trained to do: *Don't play around with jobs that are really outside your field:* **stick to your last**.

stick together [Vp] (*informal*) be united in the face of hostility or danger, in a strange environment etc. **S:** family, political party; old boys (of a school), members (of a club); (religious, racial) minority: *'We've been in worse situations that this before. If we keep calm and* **stick together**, *we shall be all right.'* ○ *'You can feel that Old Downhamians* (= former pupils of the same school) *even in this wild and distant part* **stick together**.*'* HOM ○ *New arrivals in a community are sometimes accused of* **sticking together**. *This may be because they are not given much encouragement to mix with their neighbours.* = stand together. ⇨ stick with.

stick up 1 [Vn ⇆ p pass] fasten (sth) with glue, nails etc to an upright surface, pole etc. **O:** picture, poster; effigy, statue; flag: *Supporters of the government* **stuck up** *pictures of the Prime Minister in their front windows.* ○ *The heads of traitors were once* **stuck up** *on London Bridge.*

2 [Vn ⇆ p nom pass] (*informal*) force (people) to hand over money or valuables by threatening them with a gun . **O:** train, stage-coach; bank, insurance office: *Masked bandits* **stuck up** *a bullion train yesterday.* ○ *'Nobody move — this is a* **stick-up**!*'* = hold up 2.

stuck up [pass adj (Vn.p)] (*informal*) full of (unwarranted) social pride; snobbish. **S:** social climber, the nouveaux riches: *'I don't know what they've got to be so* **stuck up** *about. Probably think they've done us a favour by moving in next door.'* ○ *The next customer was a very* **stuck-up** *lady with a terribly refined voice.* □ passive also with *appear, seem, sound.*

stick 'em/your hands up [Vn.p] (*informal*) hold your hands above your head: *'All of you,* ***stick 'em up*** *and get back against that wall!'* □ command used by bandits etc in thrillers and cowboy films. = put one's hands up.

stick up for [Vp.pr pass] (*informal*) take sb's side in a quarrel or fight; support a particular cause. **o:** brother, mate; oneself; rights: *'You don't need to be rough or tough to be a footballer but when you've got someone as big and well built as he is, the opposition try to get you so you just have to* **stick up for** *yourself.'* ST ○ *He's always* **stuck up for** *the lower-paid in industry and that's won him a lot of grass-roots support.* = stand up for.

stick with [Vpr] (*informal*) stay close to (sb), in the face of some danger or to ensure one's future wellbeing. **o:** the others; (the rest of the) group, party; Labour, the Liberals: ***Stick with*** *the gang on those beach parties. There's safety in numbers.* H ○ *'****Stick with*** *the Party you know you can trust!'* ⇨ stick together.

stuck with [pass (Vn.pr)] (*informal*) obliged to accept (sth/sb that is irksome, unpleasant etc). **o:** (onerous, tedious) job, task; handicap, disability; presence, company (of sb); (tiresome) guest, neighbour: *We were* **stuck with** *the job of addressing a thousand envelopes by the following morning.* ○ *'It's my face and I'm* **stuck with** *it!'* H ○ *Here the sites are leased by the Ministry for 50 years and we are* **stuck with** *some of these edifices until the end of the century.* OBS

sting

sting (for) [Vn.pr pass] (*informal*) collect money from (sb) which he is unwilling to give. **S:** club, society; treasurer; collector (for charity). **O:** public; member. **o:** subscription, donation, contribution: *Others seemed more concerned at being* **stung** *heavily* **for** *capital gains tax.* IND ○ *At the airport he got* **stung for** *a few quid for having excess luggage.* □ often passive.

stink

stink the place out [Vn.p] (*informal*) fill a room, house, laboratory etc with an unpleasant smell: *'You're* **stinking the place out**. *You don't belong in a nice place like this.'* TC ○ *Ever since he got that chemistry set for his birthday, he's been* **stinking the place out**.

stink to high heaven 1 [Vpr] (*informal*) have or give off a strong, unpleasant smell. **S:** place; garage, barn; yard deal: *'I'm sure the cats have messed in the small bedroom: it* **stinks to high heaven** *up there.'* = smell to high heaven 1.

2 [Vpr] strongly suggest dishonesty, intrigue, corruption etc. **S:** deal, sale; the whole thing: *'It's pretty certain that officials were bribed so that Phillips could get first claim on the land. The whole business* **stinks to high heaven**.*'* = smell to high heaven 2.

stir

stir in/into [Vn ⇆ p pass, Vn.pr pass emph rel] add (sth) to (a liquid etc), and mix everything together by stirring. **S:** cook; decorator. **O:** herb, stock, purée; water, turpentine. **o:** soup, stew; emulsion, paint: *Add a tin of chopped tomatoes to the mixture and* **stir** *them* **in** *well.* ○ *You can* **stir** *a small amount of thinner* **into** *the paint.*

stir to the depths [Vn.pr pass] move (sb) very deeply. **S:** address, speech; reception, demonstration of feeling; sight, spectacle: *It seemed to me incredible that I must constantly be passing quite ordinary men in the street whose natures were* **stirred to the depths** *by the sight of newly-born infants.* SML ○ *Still calm, still not* **stirred to any** *damaging or ennobling* **depths**, *he felt a tranquil and comforting sense of being welcome and in his right place.* HD □ often passive.

stir up [Vn ⇆ p pass] excite, stimulate, provoke (sth/sb). **S:** orator, agitator; teacher, leader, priest. **O:** hatred, unrest, trouble; it; follower, flock: *He is blamed for* **stirring up** *hatred between nations.* SC ○ *'Now, don't go in there* **stirring** *things* **up**!*'* ○ *The new priest had a quiet, placid parish — people badly in need of* **stirring up**. = whip up 4.

stitch

stitch on/onto [Vn ⇆ p pass adj, Vn.pr pass emph rel] attach (sth) to (a garment etc) with needle and thread. **O:** pocket, patch, button. **o:** blouse, coat: *One of the pockets of the jacket had been* **stitched on** *very badly.* ○ *Ask Mother to* **stitch** *the badge* **onto** *your blazer.* = sew on/onto.

stitch up 1 [Vn ⇆ p pass adj] close, seal (an opening) with needle and thread. **O:** seam; tear, rip; incision, wound: *The deep cut he'd made in his finger had to be* **stitched up**. ○ *'Don't mend the tear by hand —* **stitch** *it* **up** *on the machine.'* = sew up 1.

2 [Vn ⇆ p nom pass] (*informal*) by providing false evidence etc, make (sb) appear guilty of a crime: *A man from Kent claimed he had been* **stitched up** *on a robbery charge.* BBCR ○ *Several of the arrested men are complaining of a police* **stitch-up**. = fit up 2, frame up.

3 [Vn ⇆ p nom pass] (*informal*) settle, arrange (sth) without reference to others who have a right to be consulted. **O:** deal; treaty; election, contest: *It reeks of old style machine politics that the ... union barons* (most powerful union leaders) *should have already* **stitched up** *the race for the next leader.* ST ○ *The 40 per cent stake held by the trade unions in the leadership electoral college still gives the impression that* (they) *are* **stitching** *everything* **up** *over beer and sandwiches.* OBS ○ *What is the nation seeing? An old-fashioned union* **stitch-up**. ST

stock

stock up (with) (for) [Vp, Vp.pr rel] obtain or accumulate (supplies) (for some occasion or purpose). **S:** shop, store; housewife; garrison, expedition. **o:** (**with**) food, wine, fuel; (**for**) Christmas, New Year; weekend, holiday; siege, winter: *People started to* **stock up** *when a shortage of oranges was reported.* ○ *The power stations, anticipating a long strike, had* **stocked up with** *coal.* ○ *Jerry is* **stocking up with** *wine and brandy* **for** *the New Year party.*

stoke

stoke up (with) 1 [Vp, Vp.pr rel, Vn ⇆ p pass adj, Vn.p.pr pass rel] put (fuel) on (a stove etc). **O:** stove, furnace; boiler. **o:** coal, anthracite: [Vp] *'Check that all the ash has been raked through and then* **stoke up** *again.'* ○ [Vn.p] *It's his job to see that the boilers are* **stoked up** *last thing at night.*

2 [Vp, Vp.pr rel, Vn.p pass, Vn.p.pr pass rel] (*informal, dated*) fill (sb/oneself) with food. **o:** buns, hamburgers: [Vp] *She was* **stoking up** *as though this meal was going to be her last.* ○ [Vp.pr] *He would* **stoke up with** *food and drink for thirty-six hours.* CON

3 [Vn ⇆ p pass adj] encourage sb to feel (an emotion) more intensely; make (a situation) become more intense. **O:** anger, envy, jealousy; suspicions; feud, pressures: *I think her intervention would only* **stoke up** *emotions still further.* ○ *Ethnic hostility, which had died down, has been* **stoked up** *again by people in the government.*

stoop

stoop to [Vpr emph rel] act in a mean or contemptible way in (doing sth). **o:** intrigue, blackmail, forgery; cheating; anything: *He would* **stoop to** *anything to further his career.* ○ *There is no folly* **to** *which she would not* **stoop**. = descend to.

stop

stop (at) [Vpr rel] live, take board and lodging (at a place). **o:** hotel, inn; one's parents' house: *We* **stopped** *for a fortnight* **at** *a camping site on the southern shore of Lake Garda.* = stay (at).

stop at nothing [Vpr] behave in a ruthless, unscrupulous way (to get sth). **Inf:** to get ahead, to gain promotion, to win approval: *She'd* **stop at nothing** *to get a big part in the play.* ○ *'He wants to get to the top, and he'll* **stop at nothing**.*'* □ usu with *will/would*; often followed by inf. = stick at nothing.

stop away (from) [Vp, Vp.pr rel] not be present (at sth), be absent (from sth). **o:** lecture, seminar; school, home: *'What made you* **stop away from** *that particular lecture? It was one of the best he's given.'* = stay away (from) 1.

stop behind [Vp] remain after a meeting etc has ended, to ask questions etc. **S:** audience; member: *The audience was invited to* **stop behind** *to discuss the play with its author.* ○ *'Will a few of you* **stop behind** *to help clear the chairs away?'* = remain behind, stay behind, wait behind.

stop by [Vp, Vpr] (esp *US*) call at sb's house. **S:** friend, relative: *'Ask him to* **stop by** *and talk things* *over.'* ○ *'Why don't you* **stop by** *my hotel and say hello?'* = call (in) (at).

stop down [Vp] (*photography*) reduce the size of the aperture on a camera through which the light passes: *'The sun's just come out again: you'll have to* **stop down** *at bit.'*

stop for/to [Vpr] remain at sb's house to have (a meal). **o:** meal; lunch, dinner: *'Why don't you* **stop for** *supper? I dare say the pizzas will stretch to feed four.'* = stay for/to.

stop (from) [Vn.pr pass] prevent, hinder (sb) (from doing sth). **S:** authorities; parent, teacher; employer. **O:** public; child, ward, pupil; staff. **o:** trespassing, stealing; disturbing, playing; pilfering: *Someone tried to* **stop** *us* **from** *parking* (or: **stop** *us parking) in the square.* ○ *'I wish you'd* **stop** *him* **from** *playing that damned trumpet!'*

stop in [Vp] remain at school after others have left, as a punishment. **S:** child, pupil; trouble-maker: *'If I have any more of this nonsense the entire class will* **stop in** *after four o' clock.'* = stay in 1.

stop (dead) in one's/his tracks [Vpr, Vn.pr pass] (cause sb to) stop sharply, suddenly. **S** [Vpr], **O** [Vn.pr]**:** traveller, hunter; animal. **S** [Vn.pr]**:** sight, spectacle; shock, surprise: *I* **stopped in my tracks** *—for there was Tom kissing a girl.* H ○ *What I saw as I opened the door made me* **stop dead in my tracks**. UTN ○ *At most places the Ethiopians were* **stopped in their tracks** *by rifle fire.* BN

stop in/indoors [Vp] remain inside the building, eg because the weather is bad: *It poured with rain all day and we had to* **stop indoors**. ○ *I* **stopped in** *all weekend trying to shake off that damned cold.* = stay in/indoors.

stop off [Vp] break one's journey by car, rail etc, to rest, visit friends etc: *'We'll* **stop off** *for a few days in Paris to visit your cousins.'* ○ *David* **stopped off** *on his journey north to have a meal and a drink.*

stop on (at) [Vp, Vp.pr] remain (at a place of study etc) after others have left. **o:** school, college: *Jill* **stopped on** *for an extra year in the Sixth Form to take a University Scholarship.* ○ *Some of the senior boys won't* **stop on at** *school for a month later than they have to.* = stay on (at).

stop out 1 [Vp] remain out of doors, esp after dark. **S:** daughter, husband; guest: *'If you're going to* **stop out** *half the night there's really not much point in your living at home.'* = stay out 1.

2 [Vp] (*industrial relations*) remain on strike, continue a stoppage of work. **S:** worker; fitter, boilerman. **A:** on strike; in protest against sth: *The car workers decided to* **stop out** *until their demands were met.* = stay out 3.

stop (out of) [Vn.pr pass emph rel] (*informal*) deduct (money) (from sb's income). **S:** government, Inland Revenue, employer. **O:** tax, subscription, donation. **o:** pay, wages: *Students pay the college a deposit, and the cost of breakages is* **stopped out of** *that.* ○ *He's paid £300 pounds a week, but* **out of** *that a sizeable amount is* **stopped** *for tax and National Insurance.*

stop over [Vp nom] break one's journey by air for sightseeing etc, afterwards going on by another aircraft: *These are pictures of the Jumbo-jet passengers when they* **stopped over** *in Rome.* BBCTV ○ *I'm buying a* **stop-over** *ticket for the return journey* (ie *one which will enable me to* **stop over** *at one or more places*).

stop to [Vpr] ⇨ stop for/to.

stop up 1 [Vn ⇆ p pass adj] fill a (hole etc). **S:** carpenter, decorator. **O:** crack, nail-hole: *'Before you start painting, you'll have to* **stop up** *the holes you made in the skirting-board.'*

2 [Vn ⇆ p pass adj] block (a pipe etc) with waste matter so that water cannot pass through. **O:** pipe, drain; sink; lavatory: *If you don't clear the dead leaves away, the drains will get* **stopped up**. ○ *There were no . . .* **stopped-up** *sinks and dirty dishcloths.* RATT = block up.

3 [Vp] not go to bed until after the usual time: *We* **stopped up** *late to hear the midnight news.* ○ *'I shall be in late, but don't bother to* **stop up** *for me.'* = stay up 2.

store

store away [Vn ⇆ p pass adj] put away or keep (supplies) in a safe place for use later. **O:** food, water, ammunition; note, quotation: *He* **stored away** *everything for future use — every scrap of information that came his way.* ○ *Survival rations are* **stored away** *in waterproof boxes.*

store (in) [Vn.pr pass emph rel] keep as a stock (in a place). **O:** food, wine; information, fact. **o:** refrigerator, cellar; brain, computer: *The squirrel* **stores** *nuts* **in** *his burrow.* ○ *You can* **store** *a lot of kit* **in** *this locker* (cf *This locker will* **store** *a lot of kit*).

store up 1 [Vn ⇆ p pass adj] accumulate (supplies etc), eg for an emergency. **S:** dealer, shopkeeper, housewife: *Mother had* **stored up** *enough food to last through a siege.*

2 [Vn ⇆ p pass adj] allow (bad feelings) to develop, fester etc. **S:** rival, opponent. **O:** bitterness, resentment, hatred, jealousy: *'I know Bob's had more than his share of lucky breaks, but you're not doing yourself any good by* **storing up** *resentment.'*

storm

storm in/into [Vp emph, Vpr emph] enter (a room etc) noisily and aggressively: *Clare* **stormed into** *the meeting waving a piece of paper about.* ○ *Just when we thought we had the matter nicely settled,* **in stormed** *Alan, claiming that the vote was irregular.* ⇨ next entry

storm out /out of [Vp emph, Vpr emph] leave (a room etc) noisily and aggressively: *As soon as he saw he couldn't get his own way, he* **stormed out of** *the room.* ⇨ previous entry

stow

stow away 1 [Vn ⇆ p pass adj] pack (sth) away carefully. **O:** stores, kit, clothes; ammunition, weapons: *'As soon as you get to your quarters,* **stow** *your kit* **away** *in your lockers.'* ○ *'Get all the kitchen stuff neatly* **stowed away**.*'*

2 [Vp nom] hide aboard a ship or aircraft, with the aim of travelling free to another country: *At the age of sixteen, he* **stowed away** *on a cargo-boat bound for America.* ○ *The crew found three* **stowaways** (ie people who had **stowed away**) *in the hold.*

straighten

straighten out 1 [Vp, Vn ⇆ p pass adj] (cause sth to) lie in a straight line or form a straight line. **S** [Vp], **O** [Vn.p]**:** string, rope; tie, cloth: *After much tugging, the rope untangled itself and* **straightened out**. ○ *'Get all the wires* **straightened out**, *so that we know which is which.'*

2 [Vp, Vn.p] (cause an aircraft to) return to a level position after tilting, banking etc. **S** [Vp], **O** [Vn.p]: aircraft, plane, glider: *The plane banked and then* ***straightened out***. DF

3 [Vn ⇆ p pass] put (sth) in proper order; put right. **O:** house, room; mess, confusion; quarrel, misunderstanding: *Their flat certainly needs* ***straightening out***. ○ *We have inherited a very confused situation, which we are now trying to* ***straighten out***. ○ *The disagreement between them will not be* ***straightened out*** *overnight* (cf: *will not* ***straighten*** *itself* ***out*** *overnight*). = sort out 2.

4 [Vn ⇆ p pass] (*informal*) remove the doubt, ignorance etc in the mind of (sb); help (sb) solve his problems. **S:** adviser, parent, teacher. **O:** client, child, pupil: *I tried to* ***straighten*** *him* ***out***, *but it was no use. Those two weren't made to understand each other.* TC ○ *I'd have been up on a rape charge if Sheila hadn't* ***straightened*** *them* ***out*** (ie made them understand what really happened). JFTR ○ *'I wish she'd have a talk with Mother Clare. I'm sure it'd* ***straighten*** *her* ***out*** *a bit. That girl's just a great emotional mess at present.'* TB

straighten (oneself) up [Vp, Vn.p] make the body straight, eg after being in a crouching position: *The old man bent to pick up a piece of paper, and had some difficulty in* ***straightening up*** (or: ***straightening himself up***).

strain

strain after an effect [Vpr] try in a forced, unnatural way to make sth seem impressive. **S:** author, director, actor: *The playwright does something quite remarkable in this scene, but without any impression of* ***straining after an effect***. ○ *'Read the speech naturally: don't* ***strain after effects***.'

strain at [Vpr] exert effort or energy by pulling at (sth). **o:** rope, mooring; oar; lead, leash: *The crew* ***strained at*** *the oars to keep the boat clear of the rocks.* ○ *The dog is so powerful that every time it* ***strains at*** *its lead it nearly pulls me off my feet.* ⇨ next entry

strain at the leash [Vpr] (*informal*) pull against some restriction, eg of one's home background, in the desire to be free, make progress etc: *She was planning to go to England, and* ***straining at the leash*** *to get away.* RFW ○ *We'd like to keep these young scientists with us, but you can see they're* ***straining at the leash*** *to move to better-paid jobs.* ⇨ previous entry

strain away/off [Vn ⇆ p pass adj] separate (liquid) from solid matter by placing both together in a wire mesh, vessel with holes etc. **O:** water, gravy, juice: *When you've boiled the cabbage,* ***strain off*** *the water through a colander.*

strap

strap in/into [Vn.p pass, Vn.pr pass rel] fasten (sb/oneself) securely into (sth) with a belt. **O:** passenger, child; oneself. **o:** seat, pushchair, pram; glider: *'****Strap*** *yourselves* ***in*** *and we'll be off.'* ○ *There's a small seat at the back* ***into*** *which a child can be* ***strapped***.

strap on/onto [Vn ⇆ p pass, Vn.pr pass emph rel] fasten (one thing) to (another) by means of straps. **O:** equipment, pack, haversack; radio; watch. **o:** back, wrist: *The climbers* ***strapped on*** *a variety of equipment.* ○ *The soldiers' heavy coats were* ***strapped onto*** *their packs.*

strap up [Vn ⇆ p pass adj] keep (sth) closed, safe, clean etc by binding it with straps, bandages etc. **O:** case, trunk, bundle; arm, leg: *'Don't get dirt in that cut: ask somebody to* ***strap*** *it* ***up*** *for you.'* ○ *All the luggage was* ***strapped up*** *and waiting to go to the station.* ○ *George didn't play rugby that Saturday. He was sitting on the terraces with a heavily* ***strapped-up*** *shoulder.*

stray

stray from [Vpr pass emph rel] move from, abandon (sth) through inattention, moral slackness etc. **S:** speaker, writer; follower, adherent. **o:** point, issue; custom, accepted practice; the right path, the straight and narrow: *'We are* ***straying from*** *the subject, dear. The subject is what action is Maria likely to take.'* OMIH ○ *These regulations form the bedrock of our wages policy, and are not to be* ***strayed from***. = depart from, wander from/off.

stream

stream across, along, away etc [Vp, Vpr rel] move in a continuous stream across etc (sth). **S:** torrent, flood-waters; rain; tears, sweat; crowd, supporters: *Sweat* ***streamed down*** *the miners' bodies* (or: *Their bodies* ***streamed with*** *sweat*). ○ *Casualties were* ***streaming into*** *London's hospitals.* PPAP

stream with [Vpr rel] ⇨ previous entry

stretch

stretch away [Vp] extend to a great distance. **S:** plain, prairie, steppe; wood. **A:** into the distance, as far as the eye can see: *A day's journey brought them to the coastal plain, which* ***stretched away*** *to a distant blue haze.*

stretch out 1 [Vn ⇆ p pass] extend (the hand etc), eg to greet sb, or take sth. **S:** onlooker; beggar, suppliant. **O:** ⚠ a hand, an arm: *Sarah* ***stretched out*** *her hands. 'Me! Me!' 'No, not you, greedy.'* DC ○ *The officials walked coldly by, ignoring the* ***outstretched*** *hands of the crowd.* □ adj form is outstretched. = reach out (for) 1.

2 [Vp, Vn ⇆ p pass] (make sth) cover one's needs; (make sth) last. **S** [Vp], **O** [Vn.p]: money, housekeeping (allowance); food, fuel: *'Will the food* ***stretch out****? We've got two extra guests for dinner.'* ○ *I don't see how I can* ***stretch out*** *the housekeeping money to the end of the month.*

stretch (oneself) out [Vp, Vn.p pass] relax by lying at full length: *He* ***stretched himself out*** (or: ***stretched out***) *on the floor, and fell asleep.* ○ *A few holiday-makers were* ***stretched out*** *in the sun outside the window* (ie *they had* ***stretched themselves out*** *in the sun*).

strew

strew on/over [Vn.pr pass emph rel] throw (sth) down so that it forms a covering over (sth). **S:** crowd, onlooker; mourner. **O:** branches, leaves, flowers. **o:** route, path; grave: *Rubbish was* ***strewn*** *all* ***over*** *the back yard* (or: *The back yard was* ***strewn with*** *rubbish*). ○ *The villagers had* ***strewn*** *flowers* ***on*** *the simple grave* (or: *had* ***strewn*** *the simple grave* ***with*** *flowers*).

strew with [Vn.pr pass emph rel] ⇨ previous entry

strike

strike (against) [Vpr emph rel] (*industrial relations*) stop work in protest (against sth). **S:** miner, teacher, clerk. **o:** (bad) conditions, low wages: *The* *proposed change from piece-work arouses strong feelings and is certainly something* ***against*** *which the men are prepared to* ***strike****.* ○ *The nurses are* ***striking against*** *the Department of Health's refusal to grant an interim pay increase.* ↔ strike (for).

strike as [Vn.pr] appear or occur to (sb) as having certain qualities. **S:** idea, suggestion, proposal; voice, manner. **o:** excellent, ridiculous; the very thing, just what was wanted; strained, pretentious: *Long after the idea, whatever it was, had ceased to* ***strike*** *her* ***as*** *funny, she went on giving peal after peal, just for practice.* CON ○ *Mr King does not* ***strike*** *a stranger* ***as*** *a deeply religious man, but rather as a determined cleric preoccupied with social reform.* OBS

strike at [Vpr pass] (tend to) hurt or damage (sth). **S:** law; action; proposal. **o:** root, basis, foundation; principle, right: *By acting now, we hope to* ***strike at*** *the root cause of the trouble.* ○ *The Opposition's view has always been that the proposed Act* ***strikes at*** *the civil rights of the individual.*

strike back (at) [Vp, Vp.pr] counter-attack (sb/sth) vigorously; reply vigorously to (opponents); retaliate. **S:** aircraft, rockets; government, ministers. **o:** airfield, position; critic, opposition: *Bombers* ***struck back*** *at missile sites in the early hours of this morning.* ○ *In a radio interview, the Secretary of State* ***struck back*** *at critics of his transport strategy.* = hit back (at).

strike a/the balance between [Vn.pr] give equal attention to (two sets of demands). **adj:** right, true; nice, fine; fair, just. **o:** serious and frivolous comment, light and heavy touches, artistic and commercial considerations: *The treatment* (ie in a film) ***strikes a*** *nice* ***balance between*** *tongue-in-cheek melodrama and straightforward narrative.* TVT ○ *Their lives are shrouded in religious ritual and magic. It's a full-time job to be a good farmer and also to* ***strike the*** *right* ***balance between*** *good and bad spirits.* L

strike down 1 [Vn ⇆ p pass] make (sb) incapable of leading an active life; lay low. **S:** (serious) illness; thrombosis, paralysis: *TB, measles, polio, whooping cough, tetanus or diphtheria could* ***strike*** *Musa* ***down*** *tomorrow.* OBS ○ *Many active professional men at the peak of their careers have been* ***struck down*** *by heart disease.*

2 [Vn ⇆ p pass] kill, assassinate (sb). **O:** king, president: *The chancellor told them 'a cowardly and brutal murder' had* ***struck down*** *'one of our country's most outstanding businessmen'.* IND

strike (for) [Vpr emph rel] (*industrial relations*) stop work in order to gain (sth). **S:** miner, cleaner, doctor. **o:** higher wages, (better) conditions: *Assembly workers are* ***striking for*** *an improvement in their overtime earnings.* ○ *The technicians never expected to win all the concessions* ***for*** *which they were* ***striking****.* ↔ strike (against).

strike a blow for [Vn.pr pass emph rel] act firmly, decisively, in support of (sb/sth). **o:** voter, consumer; education, medicine; freedom of speech: *The play* ***strikes a blow for*** *literacy at a time when the word is increasingly challenged.* L ○ *The BBC have provided a great cultural service by screening* (the Marx Brothers' films), *so* ***striking another blow for*** *good-natured anarchy.* RT

strike home (to) [Vp, Vp.pr emph rel] strongly impress (sb) as being true, worthwhile etc. **S:** force, truth, validity (of sb's remark, argument, plea): *The full measure of his detachment had for the first time really* ***struck home to*** *me.* SML ○ ***To*** *cost-conscious managers the value of having a manufacturing base in Europe must surely* ***strike home*** *very forcibly.*

strike dread/fear/terror into [Vn.pr emph rel] make (sb) afraid, esp by sudden, vigorous action. **S:** arrival, appearance; attack, drive; prospect, outlook. **o:** enemy; hearts: *Meeting one's first class in a tough London school has* ***struck*** *cold* ***fear into*** *many young teachers.* ○ *'I can't talk about my driving test. The mere thought* ***strikes terror into*** *me!'*

strike off 1 [Vn ⇆ p pass] remove (sth) with a sharp blow. **O:** head, limb; branch, twig: *He* ***struck off*** *the head of the dandelion with a swish of his cane.* = knock off 1.

2 [Vn.p pass adj, Vn.pr pass] remove (sb) from membership of a professional body. **O:** doctor, solicitor, barrister. **o:** the Medical register, the Roll: *Before the law on abortion was changed, a British doctor might be* ***struck off*** *for terminating a pregnancy.* ○ *The Law Society ordered that their names be* ***struck off*** *the roll of solicitors.* T ○ *The* ***struck-off*** *solicitor must be 'Simon Pure'. His conduct will be examined. Any misdemeanour will be held against him after he applies for restoration to the Roll.* TVT □ usu passive.

strike out [Vn ⇆ p pass adj] remove (sth) by drawing a line through it. **O:** word, name; reference, mention: *The offending parts of the article have been* ***struck out****.* ○ (instructions on a form) ***Strike out*** *any questions which do not apply.* = cross out.

strike out (at) [Vp, Vp.pr pass] aim a blow suddenly and vigorously (at sb). **o:** friend, wife; captor, tormentor: *If the animal feels trapped he will* ***strike out*** *wildly.* ○ *My wife had* ***struck out at*** *me again.* QA

strike out for/towards [Vp.pr] move in a vigorous, determined way towards (a place). **S:** swimmer, oarsman; patrol, expedition. **o:** shore, bank; home: *Without hesitating, he* ***struck out*** *strongly* ***for*** *the beach.* ○ *She stood looking up and down before she* ***struck out for*** *the bus-stop.* AITC

strike through [Vn.p pass] draw a line through (sth), thus cancelling it. **O:** paragraph, sentence; word, name: *If you disagree with anything I have written,* ***strike*** *it* ***through****.* ○ *Their names had been* ***struck through*** *and made almost illegible.*

strike up [Vp, Vp.n pass] begin to play (sth). **S:** band, musicians. **O:** tune, march: *The Russian band would* ***strike up****, playing waltzes.* BM ○ *She* ***struck up*** *the first carol on the grand piano.* ASA

strike up (with) [Vp.n pass, Vn.p.pr pass emph rel] begin (a friendship etc) by casually meeting and talking (to sb). **O:** ⚠ a friendship, an acquaintance; a conversation: *I'd first* ***struck up*** *an acquaintance* ***with*** *him on Waterloo Station* (or: *We'd first* ***struck up*** *an acquaintance* etc). ○ *He'd* ***strike up*** *conversations* ***with people*** *just to hear them say something in the local accent.* CON

string

string along [Vn.p pass] (*informal*) mislead, deceive (sb) into doing sth he might not otherwise do. **O:** colleague, partner: *'I've a feeling that the young man is just* ***stringing*** *us* ***along****. Check his* *credentials.'* ○ *The governors felt that they were being* **strung along** *by their advisors.* T

string along (with) [Vp, Vp.pr pass] (*informal*) stay with, accompany (sb) in work, pleasure etc. **o:** (older) friend, (experienced) colleague: *'Can't you stop them* **stringing along** *— they're such dreadful bores!'* ○ *Take my advice —* **string along with** *me. I know this business inside out.* EGD ○ *If you're celebrating, what about* **stringing along with** *me?* TC

string out 1 [Vn.p pass adj] cause (people/things) to be widely separated from each other. **S:** leader, commander. **O:** (members of) team, squad; vehicles, ships; horses: *Russian armour was now* **strung out** *over seventy miles, without having brought the enemy to combat.* B ○ *On the night of August 13/14, with racing yachts* **strung out** *between the Isles of Scilly and Fastnet Rock, winds increased to hurricane force.* G □ usu passive.

2 [Vp.n pass] make (sth) last longer; prolong. **O:** dispute, conflict; trial, proceedings, hearing; slump: *American legal sources say that Mr Ward may be able to* **string out** *proceedings for up to two years.* IND ○ *A long and inconclusive stand-off in the Middle East ... would* **string out** *the recession but not deepen it greatly.* ECON

string together [Vn ⇆ p pass] combine (words etc) to form meaningful statements. **O:** words, phrases, sentences: *As for his French, it was as much as he could do to* **string** *a couple of words* **together**. ○ *His sentences were so badly* **strung together** *that it was difficult to grasp their meaning.*

string up 1 [Vn ⇆ p pass] hang (sth), eg as a decoration, from a line or cord. **O:** flag, banner, bunting, streamer: *Pop ... was helping the Brigadier to* **string up** *gay lines of square and triangular flags about and among the tents.* DBM ○ *A makeshift notice was* **strung up** *above the door.*

2 [Vn ⇆ p pass] (*informal*) put (sb) to death by hanging. **S:** executioner; mob. **O:** traitor, rebel; suspect: *'I didn't know then that I would soon see ... a real bloke* **stringing** *himself* **up**.*'* LLDR ○ *Count Tolstoy agreed he had written in a letter to Nigel Watts that Lord Adlington was an evil man who should have been* **strung up** *years ago.* IND

strung up [pass adj (Vn.p)] (*informal*) tense, nervous: *Surprisingly, he didn't seem at all* **strung up** *on the evening of his big speech.* ○ *The experience of working under this dreadful man has left her with a permanently* **strung-up** *expression.* □ passive also with *appear* etc. ⇨ tense up.

strip

strip away/off 1 [Vn ⇆ p pass] remove sth which has been attached to a surface. **O:** wallpaper; paint: *Using solvent and a palette knife John* **stripped** *four coats of paint* **off**. ○ *'***Strip away** *that awful patterned paper, fill the cracks with plaster, apply a couple of coats of emulsion and you might have a reasonable-looking room.'*

2 [Vn ⇆ p pass] remove sth which is hiding the true nature or intentions of sb. **O:** pretence; mask, facade; fine words: *'***Strip away** *the cheap political rhetoric and what are you left with?'*

strip down [Vn ⇆ p nom pass adj] take (an engine etc) to pieces; dismantle. **O:** motor; gearbox, carburettor; clock: *'I'll have to* **strip** *the mechanism right* **down** *to trace the fault.'* ○ *Any test of* (petrol) *consumption would entail a* **strip-down** *of the engine.* G ○ *Parts of a* **stripped-down** *gearbox were spread out on the bench.*

strip (down) (to) [Vp, Vpr, Vp.pr] take off all, or all but a few, of one's clothes. **o:** the skin, the buff; one's underclothes, one's pants and bra: [Vp] *Geoff* **stripped down** *and leaped into the stream.* ○ [Vpr] *When one is nearing a point of collapse ... there is only one way to sleep —* **strip to** *the buff and get in between the coldest sheets you can find.* ○ [Vp.pr] *Like the rest of the women she had* **stripped down to** *her brassière.* DBM

strip of [Vn.pr pass rel] take (sth of value) away from (sb). **O:** statesman, soldier, civil servant. **o:** honours, titles, rank: *Having been* **stripped of** *all his titles, he disappeared completely from public life.*

strip off 1 [Vp, Vn ⇆ p pass] remove one's clothing. **O:** clothes; shirt, pants: *The boys* **stripped off** *behind the bushes and dived naked into the river.* ○ *Patients were asked to* **strip off** *their clothes, put on dressing gowns and take a seat in the waiting room.*

2 [Vn ⇆ p pass adj, Vn.pr pass] remove, take off (the covering) from (sth). **O:** skin, peel, bark; lining, backing. **o:** fruit, tree; jacket: *Thieves had* **stripped** *the lead* **off** *the church roof.*

3 [Vn ⇆ p pass] remove sth which has been attached to surface. ⇨ strip away/off 1.

4 [Vn ⇆ p pass] remove sth which is hiding the true nature or intentions of sb. ⇨ strip away/off 2.

strive

strive after an effect [Vpr] ⇨ strain after an effect.

strive (against) [Vpr pass emph rel] (*formal*) fight to overcome or resist (sth). **o:** enemy, oppressor; adversity, hardship; ignorance, disease: *The crew* **strove against** *wind and tide to bring the ship to a safe anchorage.* ○ *The terms which the Government sought to impose should not have been accepted tamely but resolutely* **striven against**. ⇨ struggle (against). ⇨ next entry

strive (for) [Vpr pass emph rel] (*formal*) fight to obtain or achieve (sth). **o:** freedom, human rights; (better) standards, conditions: *The political freedoms which their fathers had long* **striven for** *had now been achieved.* ⇨ struggle (with) (for). ⇨ previous entry

struggle

struggle (against) [Vpr pass emph rel] fight to overcome or resist (sb/sth). **o:** tyrant, regime; system, conditions: *Troops moving through Burma had to* **struggle against** *appalling weather conditions, which could make the primitive roads impassable.*

struggle with [Vpr pass emph rel] fight inwardly with (sth). **o:** uncertainty, doubt; problem, question: *Matthews* **struggled** *briefly* **with** *his conscience before making the false entries in the accounts book.* ○ *The supply problems* **with** *which we'd* **struggled** *for so long were now a thing of the past.* = wrestle with.

struggle (with) (for) [Vpr pass emph rel] fight (with sb) to obtain or achieve (sth). **o:** (**with**) intruder, assailant; employer, government; (**for**) gun, knife; (higher) wages, (improved) conditions: *Two men were* **struggling** *(***with** *each other)* **for** *the possession of a small jewel box.* ○ *We're* **struggling for** *a bigger say in decision-making within the com-*

pany. ○ *She'd* **struggled for**, *and finally won, the right to appoint her own editorial staff.*

strut

strut about/around/round [Vp, Vpr] walk about in a pompous, self-important way; suggest pomposity, solemnity by one's style of walking. **S:** official, guard, leader; goose, cockerel: *I dread the effect of promotion on him: he'll be* **strutting about** *the place like a turkey-cock.*

stub

stub one's toe (against/on) [Vn.pr rel] catch, strike, one's foot (on sth which projects). **o:** stone; kerb, step: *I* **stubbed my toe on** *your front step: it was very painful.*

stub out [Vn ⇆ p pass adj] extinguish, put out (a cigarette) by pressing it hard against sth. **O:** cigarette, cigar: *'Don't* **stub** *your cigarettes* **out** *on my mantlepiece!'* ○ *The place was littered with empty glasses and* **stubbed-out** *cigarettes.* = put out 10.

study

study (for) [Vpr pass emph rel] give time and effort to learning sth (for a special purpose, eg passing an exam). **o:** qualification; diploma, degree; test, exam; the Bar: *She's* **studying for** *a degree in Economics in her spare time.* ○ *'The next stage is A-levels,* **for** *which he'll need to* **study** *very much harder.'*

stuff

stuff down sb's throat [Vn.pr pass] (*informal*) force sb, esp by tedious repetition, to accept or learn (sth). **O:** opinion, view; morality, religion; French, maths: *'For a start, he can stop* **stuffing** *his revolting views on race* **down people's throats.'** ○ TONY: *What are the words — don't say I've forgotten them, they've been* **stuffed down my throat** *all my life — liberty, democracy, brotherhood.* EHOW = force/ram sth down sb's throat.

stuff into [Vn.pr pass rel] press, pack (sth) tightly into (a space). **O:** kit, clothing; padding, lining; food. **o:** bag, sack; space, hole; child: *All kinds of gear have been* **stuffed into** *their kitbags* (or: *Their kitbags have been* **stuffed with** *all kinds of gear*). ○ *That child has been* **stuffing** *food* **into** *himself* (or: *He has been* **stuffing** *himself* **with** *food*) *all morning.*

stuff up [Vn ⇆ p pass adj] close, block (sth) by pushing material etc into it. **O:** ear, nose; vent, hatch, window: **'Stuff up** *your ears — there's going to be an almighty bang!'* ○ *We had to* **stuff** *the ventilator shafts* **up** *to stop the smoke entering the room.*

stuffed up [pass adj (Vn.p)] (of one's nose) full of mucus, because one has a bad cold: *'Don't come near me — my* **nose** *is terribly* **stuffed up** *today.'* ○ *'I shan't be coming to the party. You don't want to take along a girl with a* **stuffed-up** *nose!'*

stuff with [Vn.pr pass rel] ⇨ stuff into.

stuff sb's head with [Vn.pr pass] (*informal*) fill sb's mind (with information, esp of a useless or harmful kind). **o:** facts; nonsense, rubbish: *The press* **stuffed the people's heads with** *dreary and largely invented figures for industrial production.* ○ *'How can you expect these children to exercise their minds?* **Their heads** *have been* **stuffed with** *pap from the television.'*

stumble

stumble across/on/upon [Vpr pass] discover (sth/sb) by chance. **o:** evidence, clue; manuscript, remains; dealer, client: *They* **stumbled across** *the entrance to an underground passage, half covered by ivy.* ○ *Karl had* **stumbled on** *just the right contact, and arranged a series of fruitful meetings.* DS = come across 1, run across.

stumble over [Vpr pass emph rel] hesitate awkwardly when saying (sth). **o:** words, lines; speech, address: *The chairman must have felt embarrassed at reading out such an abnormally low set of figures, because he* **stumbled over** *that section of his report.*

stump

stump across, along, away etc [Vp, Vpr] move across etc heavily, and often in anger or irritation: *Throwing down his paper with a snort of impatience, Bill* **stumped across** *to the door.* ○ *Uncle Saunders went* **stumping up** *to bed at his usual time, followed by Aunt Annabel.* DC

stump up [Vp, Vp.n pass] (*informal*) pay a sum of money required; the suggestion is that the person finds it hard or irksome to pay. **S:** parent; taxpayer, debtor: *He's tired of* **stumping up** *for school fees, books and uniform.* ○ *'Every time you get into trouble I have to* **stump up** *the money to get you out of it!'* = cough up 2.

subject

subject to 1 [Vn.pr pass rel] (*formal*) make oneself the master of (sb/sth), eg by conquest. **S:** power, nation; aggressor; army. **O:** neighbour, (weaker) country. **o:** rule, control, sway, dominion, domination: *In two swift campaigns, the seasoned troops* **subjected** *the whole of the North* **to** *Roman control.*

2 [Vn.pr pass rel] apply (force etc) to (a substance etc). **S:** physicist, engineer. **O:** metal, wood, cloth; bar, strip. **o:** force, strain; temperature; pressure: *On this test-track, the makers* **subject** *standard production cars* **to** *extremely rough treatment.* ○ *The metal plate was* **subjected to** *intense pressure.*

3 [Vn.pr pass rel] make (sb) experience or undergo (sth). **O:** speaker, author; prisoner, victim; animal. **o:** criticism, questioning; humiliation; torture, grilling: *The last speaker was* **subjected to** *a bit of a grilling.* ○ *He was tough and determined enough to survive the harsh treatment* **to** *which he was* **subjected**.

submit

submit (to) 1 [Vn.pr pass emph rel] (*formal*) present (sth) (to sb) for discussion, decision etc. **S:** author; architect, engineer; union. **O:** manuscript; plan, proposal; claim. **o:** publisher; committee, panel; arbitration: *Some students have not yet* **submitted** *their essays* **to** *their tutors.* ○ *I eventually came face to face with the official* **to** *whom I had* **submitted** *my first application for planning permission.*

2 [Vpr pass emph rel] give way, yield (to pressure). **o:** pressure; bullying, intimidation; enemy: *Need a Church* **submit to** *a silence imposed by the State?* SC ○ **To** *pressure such as this we have no intention of* **submitting**.

submit oneself to [Vn.pr emph rel] place oneself under the control of (sth/sb). **S:** student, priest, disciple. **o:** discipline, rule; authority, master: *No one becomes a monk if he is not prepared to* ***submit himself to*** *the rules of his Order.*

subscribe

subscribe (to) 1 [Vpr pass emph rel, Vn.pr pass emph rel] give money (to a charity); donate (to). **S:** philanthropist, benefactor. **O:** sum, amount. **o:** charity, (good) cause, fund: *Two local businessmen have* ***subscribed*** *large sums* ***to*** *the rebuilding fund.* ○ *This is a cause* ***to*** *which he has* ***subscribed*** *generously in the past.*

2 [Vpr pass emph rel] pay in order to have (a newspaper etc) regularly and for some time. **o:** paper, (learned) journal, magazine: *He* ***subscribes to*** *a number of journals devoted to his subject.* ○ *The library committee decides whether the publications* ***to*** *which we* ***subscribe*** *are to be ordered for a further year.*

subscribe to [Vpr pass emph rel] (*formal*) support (sth). **o:** philosophy, code; belief, opinion: *How could anyone* ***subscribe to*** *such an inhuman code?* ○ *This is a deeply pessimistic view* ***to*** *which I have never* ***subscribed***. = agree (with) 1.

subsist

subsist (on) [Vpr emph rel] (*formal*) stay alive by eating (sth). **o:** bread, potato, rice: *There are whole villages* ***subsisting on*** *rice and a little milk supplied by the relief organizations.* ○ ***On*** *this diet a manual worker could hardly manage to* ***subsist***. = live off/on.

substitute

substitute (for) 1 [Vn.pr pass emph rel] put or use (sth) (in place of sth else). **O:** margarine, synthetic fibre; word, phrase. **o:** butter, natural wool; original text: *'The recipe specifies butter, but vegetable oil will do just as well. So* ***substitute*** *oil* ***for*** *butter at this stage.'* ○ *Copies have been* ***substituted for*** *the original manuscripts to save wear and tear on the latter.*

2 [Vpr, Vn.pr pass] (*sport*) (cause sb to) enter a game (in place of sb else). **S** [Vpr], **O** [Vn.pr]**:** player; striker, sweeper: *Beardsley* ***substituted for*** *Lineker just before half-time.* ○ *A striker was* ***substituted for*** *a midfield player in the hope that increased pressure on the Scottish defence would produce the winning goal.*

subsume

subsume under [Vn.pr pass emph rel] (*formal*) place (sth) (under a heading etc). **O:** item, article; example, instance. **o:** heading, rubric, rule: *These various trades may all be* ***subsumed under*** *the general heading of 'distributive'.*

subtract

subtract (from) [Vn.pr pass emph rel] take one number (from another). **O:** 20; 32 kilos; 13 cents. **o:** 29; 36 kilos; one dollar: *If you* ***subtract*** *75* ***from*** *100 you get 25.* ○ ***From*** *this amount you need to* ***subtract*** *something to cover fixed overheads.*

succeed

succeed (in) [Vpr emph rel] do what one sets out to do; fulfil (one's aim). **o:** passing (a test), climbing (a mountain); aim, objective, intention: *We'd ...* ***succeeded in*** *upsetting the whole underground diamond trading fraternity in Monrovia.* DS ○ *The new marketing team promised to push up sales, and* ***in*** *this they have certainly* ***succeeded***.

succeed (to) [Vpr rel] take (a title etc) on the death of its previous holder. **S:** heir; son, cousin. **o:** throne, title; estate: *The present Queen* ***succeeded to*** *the throne on the death of her father in 1952.*

succumb

succumb (to) 1 [Vpr emph rel] give way (to sth), without conscious intention but through weakness etc. **o:** pressure; flattery, persuasion, blandishments: *People still* ***succumb to*** *persuasion through TV advertising, but the approach now must be subtle and indirect.*

2 [Vpr emph rel] die from (physical strain, overexposure to the natural elements etc). **o:** injuries; (low) temperature: *The climbers would face exposure to extreme temperatures and biting winds,* ***to*** *which many had* ***succumbed*** *before.*

suck

suck down/under [Vn ⇆ p pass] pull (sb/sth) down below the surface of sth. **S:** undertow, current; bog, marsh: *The whirlpool* ***sucks down*** *everything floating on the surface.* ○ *We were able to pass a rope to him before the bog* ***sucked*** *him* ***under***.

suck up [Vn ⇆ p pass adj, Vn.pr pass] draw (liquid etc) up (a tube) by making a vacuum at its upper end. **O:** milk, juice; grain, flour. **o:** straw, pipe: *The chemist* ***sucked up*** *20 cc of acid into a pipette.* ○ *Great quantities of grain are* ***sucked up*** *into the elevators through flexible tubes.* ○ *The dredger in the middle of the channel was* ***sucking*** *gravel* ***up*** *huge pipes and discharging it into a barge moored alongside.*

suck up to [Vp.pr pass] (*pejorative*) try to please (sb important or influential) by praising him, doing favours etc. **S:** schoolboy, student; (ambitious) junior, (young) executive. **o:** teacher, professor; boss, manager: *'She was always trying to get Johnnie to her parties, but he saw pretty soon they were no use to him and then she tried to* ***suck up to*** *me.'* ASA ○ *While Jacques* ***sucked up to*** *Spinks with natural abandon, he did not in the least care for him as a man.* SML = butter up to.

sue

sue (for) [Vpr rel, Vn.pr pass rel] (*legal*) make a legal claim against (sb) for injury to oneself, neglect of one's interests etc. **S:** employee, customer; wife. **O:** firm, shop; husband. **o:** costs, damages, compensation; divorce: *If you broke your leg as a result of their negligence, you could* ***sue*** *them* ***for*** *damages.*

suffer

suffer from 1 [Vpr rel] be affected by (an illness). **S:** patient, inmate, prisoner. **o:** backache, gout, insomnia: *He* ***suffers*** *terribly* ***from*** *hay fever in the summer.* ○ *There were 140 sentenced prisoners and 189 on remand* ***suffering from*** *serious mental disorders.* OBS

2 [Vpr rel] have (sth) as a serious weakness. **S:** plan, proposal, production. **o:** (bad) execution, (faulty) planning: *His direction of the play* ***suffers from*** *over-attention to the small details of the text.*

suggest

suggest itself/themselves (to) [Vn.pr emph rel] come into one's mind. **S:** idea, thought; plan, scheme: *'Another possibility* ***suggests itself to*** *me, which is that he's been misleading us all along.'* ○ *A better way out of our difficulties then* ***suggested itself to*** *us.* = occur to.

suit

suit (down) to the ground [Vn.pr, Vn.p.pr] (*informal*) be perfectly suitable for (sb), be ideal for (sb). **S:** job, work; arrangement, schedule; room, flat: *'Terence,' he said, 'is battling at the bar* (ie to get a drink). *It* ***suits*** *him* ***to the ground****.'* HAA ○ *Joe had got himself a job as one of the gardeners. Literally and metaphorically it* ***suited*** *him* ***down to the ground****.* TBC ○ *I have a nice line in tin coffins that would* ***suit*** *you* ***down to the ground****.* DPM

suit to [Vn.pr pass] make (sth) suitable or appropriate for (sth/sb). **O:** language, dress, behaviour. **o:** topic, occasion; audience: *Take care to* ***suit*** *the punishment* ***to*** *the offence.* ○ *His approach was well* ***suited to*** *the sophistication of his audience.* ○ *'Do you really think this work is* ***suited to*** *a class of beginners?'* □ usu passive.

suited (to) [pass (Vn.pr)] (of a person) right in one's nature, suitable (for sb/sth). **S:** wife; partner, colleague. **o:** husband; life, routine: *'It's no surprise to me that Roger and Elaine are breaking up. I never felt they were particularly well* ***suited*** *(****to*** *one another).'* ○ *Robert was not temperamentally* ***suited to*** *the tedium of life in a small country town.* □ passive also with *appear, seem, feel, look.*

suit the action to the word/suit one's actions to one's words [Vn.pr pass] follow a threat, invitation, promise etc with suitable action: *'Politicians should learn to* ***suit their actions to their words****. Of course, I say this more in hope than expectation.'* ○ *'There's nothing we can do except give you a drink.' He* ***suited the action to the word****.* PW ○ *On this occasion* ***the action*** *was* ***suited to the word****. A cheque arrived by the next post.*

sum

sum up 1 [Vp, Vn ⇆ p pass] (at the end of a speech etc) give the main points of what has been said; state people's feelings in a few words. **S:** chairman, lecturer. **O:** debate, discussion; feelings: *I found it hard to* ***sum up*** *after such a wide-ranging debate.* ○ *Wendy* ***sums up*** *the way the members feel in a few words.* H

2 [Vp, Vn ⇆ p pass] (*legal*) review, and comment upon, the main points of (a legal case). **S:** judge, magistrate. **O:** case; evidence, arguments: *In a packed and silent court-room the judge began to* ***sum up*** (or: *began his* ***summing-up***).

3 [Vn ⇆ p pass] state the important features of (sth) in a few words; summarize. **O:** difference (between things), special character (of sth); plot, story: *He* ***sums up*** *the difference between the two jobs.* OBS ○ *'Let me try to* ***sum up*** *the story so far.'*

4 [Vn ⇆ p pass] form or pass a judgement or opinion on (sb). **O:** acquaintance, colleague: *A difficult fellow to* ***sum up*** *— you never know what he's thinking.* ○ *'A quiet American.' I* ***summed*** *him* ***up*** *as I might have said, 'A blue lizard'.* QA

summon

summon (to) [Vn.pr pass emph rel] (*formal*) call or require (sb) to be present officially (in a place). **S:** ruler, employer, (magistrates') clerk. **O:** subject, official, witness. **o:** court, office, law-court: *Ambassadors were* ***summoned*** *hastily* ***to*** *their home countries.* ○ *A message arrived* ***summoning*** *him* ***to*** *the director's office.*

summon up 1 [Vp.n pass adj] bring (sth) to mind; evoke. **O:** picture, souvenir, thought: *We find it hard to* ***summon up*** *thoughts of Venice at the sight of the lake today.* T

2 [Vp.n pass adj] gather (strength etc), eg to meet a crisis. **O:** energy; resolution, will-power: ***Summoning up*** *his last ounce of strength, he flung himself over the finishing line.*

superimpose

superimpose (on/upon) [Vn.pr pass emph rel] (*formal*) place (one thing) on top (of another). **O:** picture, slide, cut-out; (one) culture. **o:** another (picture etc), background; preceding (one): *The negative showed that one exposure had been* ***superimposed on*** *another.* ○ *From archaeological evidence it is clear that each group* ***superimposed*** *its ideas and culture* ***on*** *the previous one.*

supply

supply (to) [Vn.pr pass emph rel] give (sth) (to sb) for his use. **S:** school, firm, army. **O:** food, clothing, weapon. **o:** pupil, employee, soldier: *Schools* ***supply*** *the basic necessities* ***to*** *pupils (or:* ***supply*** *pupils* ***with*** *the basic necessities).* ○ *Overalls have been* ***supplied to*** *everyone (or: Everyone has been* ***supplied with*** *overalls).* = furnish (to).

supply (with) [Vn.pr pass emph rel] give (to sb) (an excuse etc). **O:** rival, enemy, critic. **o:** excuse, pretext, reason: *'You're* ***supplying*** *your enemies in the department* ***with*** *an excuse to get rid of you.'*

surge

surge up [Vp emph] rise up in a wave. **S:** feeling; anger, longing, frustration: *She felt the desire to burst into tears* ***surging up*** *within her.* ○ *These feelings* ***surged up*** *uncontrollably* (cf *an uncontrollable* ***upsurge*** *of feeling*). = well up.

surrender

surrender (to) 1 [Vpr emph rel, Vn.pr pass emph rel] (*military*) place oneself, one's soldiers etc, in the enemy's hands, in admission of defeat. **S** [Vpr], **O** [Vn.pr]**:** troops; army, force: *Through the interpreter the officer tried to persuade us to* ***surrender to*** *the 'heroic German army', as defence was useless and we would not be able to hold our positions any longer.* B

2 [Vn.pr emph rel] weaken, give way, in the face of some pressure. **o:** appeal, plea; argument, persuasion; (one's own) feelings: *'In an emergency, keep cool. Don't* ***surrender to*** *panic.'* ○ *Blackmail was one kind of pressure* ***to*** *which they were not prepared to* ***surrender****.*

suspect

suspect (of) [Vn.pr pass emph rel] feel, sense, that sb is guilty (of sth). **O:** colleague, employee. **o:** lying, cheating; treason, theft: *We* ***suspected*** *him* ***of*** *removing* (or: ***suspected*** *that he had removed*) *the cash-box.* ○ *He was* ***suspected****, and accused,* ***of*** *selling state secrets.*

suspend

suspend (from) 1 [Vn.pr pass emph rel] hang (sth) (from sth). **O:** lamp, ornament; rope, cord. **o:** ceiling, beam, hook: *We* ***suspended*** *a rope-ladder*

from *the rail of the ship.* ○ *The pot was attached to a chain* **suspended from** *the ceiling.*

2 [Vn.pr pass rel] remove (sb) usu temporarily (from a post etc). **O:** official; player. **o:** post, job; team: *Two tax officials were* **suspended** *(***from** *their posts) pending investigations into charges of corruption.*

suss

suss out [Vn ⇆ p pass] (*informal*) learn about (sth); learn how matters stand in (a place); learn what (sb) is like. **O:** situation, position; house, shop; neighbour: *They* **sussed out** *the situation in our house in no time at all.* PPAP ○ *Yachtsmen or dinghy sailors wanting to* **suss out** *the wind strengths in the Solent can ring the ... weather chart service.* RT ○ *He'd sussed out Ms Penumbra from the start.* HERM □ note the common expression *have (got) sb/sth* sussed out.

swab

swab down [Vn ⇆ p pass adj] clean (a floor) from one end to the other with water and a swab or mop. **S:** sailor, charwoman. **O:** deck, floor: *The crew were ordered to* **swab down** *the decks.*

swab out [Vn ⇆ p nom pass adj] remove dirt etc from the floor of (a place) with a mop and water. **O:** yard, stable: *The grooms have to* **swab out** *the stables* (or: *give them a* **swab(-)out**) *each morning.* ○ *The place was freshly* **swabbed out** *and disinfected.*

swallow

swallow up 1 [Vn ⇆ p pass] make (sb/sth) disappear, as if taking him/it in like food. **S:** earth, forest, jungle; crowd. **O:** expedition, traveller, vehicle: *There was no gaping dark hole that would* **swallow up** *bad people.* DC ○ *They had only to travel a short distance to be* **swallowed up** *by the dense vegetation.* ○ *She was so deeply embarrassed, she wished the earth would open and* **swallow** *her* **up**.

2 [Vn ⇆ p pass] use (things/people) till no more are left; consume. **S:** project, scheme; bill, debt; attack, offensive. **O:** resources, manpower; money, income; troops, divisions: *Pay increases are no good if they are instantly* **swallowed up** *by rising prices.* ○ *His reserves of men and tanks were soon* **swallowed up** *in the spring offensive.*

3 [Vn ⇆ p pass] absorb (sth) so that it loses its separate identity. **S:** conglomerate, multinational (company); metropolitan council, faculty. **O:** family concern, small business; borough council; department: *'This company will survive. Nobody is going to* **swallow** *us* **up**!' ○ *Many ancient boroughs were* **swallowed up** *in the reorganization of local government.*

swamp

swamp with [Vn.pr pass rel] send (sth) in a great volume to (sb). **O:** office, radio-station, school, factory. **o:** letter, request, application, order: *Indignant viewers* **swamped** *the TV studios* **with** *complaints.* ○ *Dealers have been* **swamped with** *orders for the new car.* □ usu passive.

swap

swap for [Vn.pr pass] exchange (one thing) for (another). **O:** car, flat; stamp, coin; seat, place; job. **o:** minibus, house; another, sb else's; a better one: *'Who wants to* **swap** *a ham sandwich* **for** *a cheese and tomato?'* ○ *I certainly wouldn't* **swap** *my life* **for** *his.* □ alt spelling: swop for.

swap over/round [Vp, Vn ⇆ p pass] (of two persons) change places with one another; put one thing in the place of another; change events so that one takes place at the time of the other. **O:** chair, plate; wire, plug; time, period; lecture, class: *'Go on,* **swap over** *and let Jane sit next to him!'* ○ *'David, I've given you the wrong plate. Do you mind* **swapping round** *with Daddy, please?'* ○ *'I want the chair with the hard seat, so let's* **swap** *them* **over**.' ○ *'No wonder the thing isn't working. Someone has* **swapped** *the wires* **round**!' □ alt spelling: swop over/round.

swap (with) [Vn.pr] give (sth) (to sb) in return for a similar thing. **O:** clothes; places; jobs. **o:** friend, colleague: *I* **swapped** *jackets* **with** *John to get a better fit.* (or: *John and I* **swapped** *jackets* etc). ○ *'Can you* **swap** *seats* **with** *Joan* (or: *Can you and Joan* **swap** *seats*)? *She can't see the screen.'* □ alt spelling: swop (with). = exchange (with/for) 1.

swarm

swarm over/through [Vpr] gather or move in large numbers throughout (a place), like a swarm of bees. **S:** reporter, photographer; rodent, pest. **o:** building, site; field, crop: *The crowd* **swarmed over** *the pavements, trying to catch a glimpse of the President's car.* ○ *Locusts* **swarmed over** *the fields* (or: *The fields* **swarmed with** *locusts*).

swarm with [Vpr] ➪ previous entry

swathe

swathe in [Vn.pr pass] wrap (sth) tightly around (sb). **O:** child; body, arm, leg. **o:** towel, blanket, bandage: *Michael emerged from the bathroom* **swathed in** *a towel.* ○ *'Don't* **swathe** *the poor chap* **in** *bandages. Just put on a dressing.'*

swear

swear at [Vpr pass] direct bad language or curses at (sb). **o:** wife, pupil, staff: *'There's no need to* **swear at** *me. Control your language!'* ○ *She resents being* **sworn at**, *even if she has made a mistake.*

swear (by) [Vn.pr emph] appeal (to sb/sth sacred) in saying (that sth is true etc). **O:** that one is innocent, that I am telling the truth; to tell the truth, to uphold the law. **o:** ⚠ Almighty God, all the gods, all that is holy/sacred, all one holds sacred: *He* **swore by** *all that was holy that he hadn't touched a hair of the child's head.* □ note the form of oath taken in court: *I* **swear by** *Almighty God that the evidence I shall give shall be the truth ....* ➪ swear (on).

swear by [Vpr] have great confidence in (sth) as a remedy, food, machine etc. **o:** medicine; pill, lotion; bread, cereal; razor: *'Why don't you try these pills for your hayfever? I* **swear by** *them.'* ○ *'Jill* **swears by** *these cordless phones, but I've always found them a damned nuisance.'*

swear in 1 [Vn ⇆ p pass] make (sb) take an oath to be truthful, fair etc in court. **O:** witness, jury (member): *The defendant objected to one member of the jury, so another had to be* **sworn in**.

2 [Vn ⇆ p pass] admit (a member) to a society by making him take an oath: *The full committee has to attend when a new member is* **sworn in** (or: *attend the* **swearing-in** *of a new member*).

swear off [Vpr pass] (*informal*) promise to stop doing or taking (sth). **o:** drink, smoking, gambling: *'I won't have a cigarette, thanks. I've **sworn off** them on doctor's orders.'* = cut out 4, give up 9.

swear (on) [Vn.pr emph] appeal (to sb/sth sacred) in claiming that sth is so. **O:** that he is lying, that I wasn't there. **o:** ⚠ the Bible, his son's head: *I'm sure he'd **swear on** a stack of Bibles that he was leading a blameless life.* □ object is a *that*-clause and is usu in final position. ⇨ swear (by).

swear to [Vpr] be certain about (sth). **o:** having seen sb, having heard sth; figure, sum; it: *Had there been a voice? Now, in the silence, she could not **swear to** it.* DC ○ *I wouldn't **swear to** any figure for smuggling — it's just grown with the industry.* DS □ with *can/could* or *will/would*; usu neg.

sweat

sweat off [Vn ⇆ p pass] remove, lose (weight) by making oneself sweat. **O:** three pounds, several kilos: *If he keeps up the road training, he'll **sweat off** quite a bit before the fight.* ○ *'Try the sauna for a change. You'll **sweat** pounds **off**.'*

sweat out [Vn ⇆ p pass] wrap up warmly, and by sweating try to get rid of (a cold etc). **O:** fever, cold, 'flu: *When you feel 'flu coming on, get into bed and **sweat** it **out**.*

sweat one's guts out [Vn.p] (*informal*) work extremely hard. **S:** miner, shopkeeper, athlete, boxer: *'Why should I **sweat my guts out** for sixty pounds a week?'* ○ *Normally, I **sweated my guts out** on a milling machine with the rest.* LLDR

sweat it out [Vn.p] (*informal*) keep going, persevere, in an unpleasant situation; suffer, endure, such a situation: *'Don't throw up your job; **sweat it out** just a bit longer.'* ○ *The climbers will just have to **sweat it out** till we can get a rescue team to them.* ○ *'The exam results won't be posted till six. We'll have to **sweat it out** for another hour.'*

sweep

sweep aside [Vn ⇆ p pass] dismiss (comments etc) and continue as if they had not been made. **S:** speaker, organizer, salesman. **O:** argument, criticism, objection: *He was so convinced of the value of these schemes, that he **swept aside** reasonable doubts.* ○ *Interruptions were **swept aside** with a wave of the hand.* = brush aside 2.

sweep away 1 [Vn ⇆ p pass] carry away, remove (sth) with great force. **S:** storm, flood, avalanche. **O:** bridge, dyke, dam: *The torrent **swept away** part of an embankment.* ○ *A bridge was **swept away** by the floodwaters.*

2 [Vn ⇆ p pass] remove, abolish (sth) by vigorous action. **S:** reformer, revolutionary. **O:** system, society; convention, practice; inequality, injustice: *Successive left-wing governments have promised to **sweep away** the last vestiges of privilege in education.* ○ *The press spoke of the need to **sweep away** corrupt practices in local government.* = make a clean sweep of.

sweep in/into 1 [Vp emph, Vpr emph] enter (a place) in a proud, lordly way. **S:** king, chief; bandit. **o:** hall, room: *Peter **swept in**, with his dignity and insolence.* DC ○ *The royal procession **swept into** the hall, preceded by trumpeters.*

2 [Vp, Vpr, Vn ⇆ p pass, Vn.pr pass] (cause sb to) return to office by a clear majority. **S** [Vp Vpr], **O** [Vn.p Vn.pr]**:** Labour, the Conservatives. **o:** ⚠ office, power: [Vp] *Labour **swept in** on a rising tide of discontent with high unemployment.* ○ [Vn.pr] *The government **swept into** power by the election of 1979 was to remain in office for over eleven years.*

sweep off his feet [Vn.pr pass] (*informal*) fill (sb) with enthusiasm, strong romantic feelings etc; captivate. **S:** orator, actor, hero. **O:** audience; girl: *His speeches were calculated to **sweep** uncommitted people **off their feet**.* ○ *After one meeting she was completely **swept off her feet**.* □ notice the pun in: *JASON:* (pinching her) *Lend me a broom and I'll **sweep** you **off your feet**.* DPM

sweep out [Vn ⇆ p nom pass] remove dirt from (a place) with a broom. **O:** hall, room, attic: *This room needs to be well **swept out*** (or: *needs a good **sweep-out***). ⇨ next entry

sweep out/out of 1 [Vn ⇆ p pass, Vn.pr pass] remove (dirt) from (a place) with a broom. **O:** dust, fluff; scraps, crumbs: *'**Sweep** the fluff **out** from under the bed.'* ○ *'Don't forget to **sweep** those leaves **out of** the garage.'* ⇨ previous entry

2 [Vp emph, Vpr emph] leave (a place) in a proud, lordly way. **S:** king, duchess; actor. **o:** room, house: *Without a word, she turned and **swept out of** the room.* = fling out/out of.

sweep under the carpet [Vn.pr pass] (*informal*) hide or avoid facing (sth) because it is difficult to resolve or because it might cause trouble for oneself etc. **O:** things; problems, issues; findings, evidence: *It's too easy to **sweep** things **under the carpet**: schools and parents have to learn how to deal with these problems.* RT ○ *But the ... intractable issues, which many politicians **sweep under the carpet**, are about economic management, public expenditure and taxation.* OBS

sweep up [Vp nom, Vn ⇆ p nom pass adj] lift, collect (dirt etc) with a broom. **S:** housewife, maid. **O:** mess; crumbs, cigarette-ends: *A cleaner found the missing part when he was **sweeping up**.* ○ *This place needs a bit of a **sweep-up**.*

swept up in [pass (Vn.p.pr)] fully involved in (sth), perhaps against one's will. **o:** revolution, war; movement; whirl, round (of activity): *The whole region had been **swept up in** the forced collectivization of the 1930s.* ○ *As students they were **swept up in** the national liberation movement.* □ also used with *get, become*. = caught up in 2.

sweeten

sweeten up [Vn ⇆ p pass adj] make (sb) cooperative by being pleasant, offering him sth etc: *'I'd like her to manage a bigger share of that market; of course, we'll have to **sweeten** her **up** a bit first.'*

swell

swell up 1 [Vp] rise to form a bulge on the skin. **S:** boil, blister; arm, leg: *'Don't prick that boil; allow it to **swell up** and burst.'* ○ *The flesh around the ankle had **swollen up**.*

2 [Vp] rise up strongly within sb. **S:** strong feelings; resentment, frustration; longing, desire: *This is the time when there must **swell up** in the nation every noble thought, every high ideal ...* MFM = surge up, well up.

swerve

swerve (from) [Vpr emph rel] change one's direction or aim. **S:** disciple, follower. **o:** way, path; purpose, aim: *He is a natural rebel who has often*

swerved from *the official line.* ○ *'She won't* ***swerve from*** *her course once her mind is made up.'*

swill

swill out [Vn ⇆ p nom pass adj] clean (a container etc) by pouring water in and out of it. **O:** tub, pot, basin; mouth: *The buckets have to be* ***swilled out*** *with disinfectant.* ○ *The tanks are given a good* ***swill-out*** (or: *are well* ***swilled out***) *before being refilled with fresh water.* = rinse (out).

swindle

swindle out of [Vn.pr pass emph rel] (*informal*) get money from (sb) by fraud or deceit. **O:** citizen, customer, heir. **o:** money; donation, investment; inheritance: *He's just the kind to* ***swindle*** *old people* ***out of*** *their pensions* (or: *to* ***swindle*** *pensions* ***out of*** *old people*). ○ *'Of course he's angry. You would be if you'd just been* ***swindled out of*** *three hundred pounds!'* = cheat out of.

swing

swing at [Vpr pass, Vn.pr pass] swing one's fist etc in an arc in an attempt to hit (sb/sth). **O:** fist; bat, club. **o:** chin, jaw; ball: *'I didn't want to start a fight. I made a harmless remark to some guy at the bar and he* ***swung at*** *me.'* ○ *He* ***swung*** *his bat* ***at*** *the next delivery, got an outside edge, and was well caught in the slips.*

swing round [Vp] turn round suddenly, eg to answer sb, argue etc: *He* ***swung round*** *to confront the man, and seized him by the collar.* ○ *Saunders* ***swung round*** *on his wife. 'I won't have those police in my house again,' he said.* DC

swing round (to) 1 [Vp, Vp.pr emph rel] change so that it blows from another direction. **S:** wind; weather-vane. **o:** east, south-west: *The wind had* ***swung round****, so that now instead of fighting against it we were being borne along by it.*

2 [Vp nom, Vp.pr emph rel] come to hold (quite different opinions etc). **S:** public, electorate; public opinion. **o:** contrary view, opposite position: *Since the last election public opinion has* ***swung round*** *completely* (or: *there has been a complete* ***swing-round***) *on this question.* ○ *She has now* ***swung round to*** *the exactly opposite view.*

swipe

swipe at [Vpr pass] (*informal*) aim a vigorous blow at (sth/sb). **S:** golfer, cricketer. **o:** ball; wasp, mouse: *'Every time you* ***swipe at*** *the flies you knock over the marmalade.'* ○ *He doesn't enjoy being* ***swiped at*** (= clumsily attacked) *in the local paper.*

swirl

swirl about [Vp, Vpr, Vn.p pass, Vn.pr pass] (cause sb/sth to) move about in thick masses, constantly changing speed and direction. **S** [Vp Vpr], **O** [Vn.p Vn.pr]**:** smoke, dust; crowd, dancers; leaves, clothes : [Vp] Thick clouds of dust ***swirled about****, getting into our food and water.* ○ [Vpr] Happy people linked arms and ***swirled about*** *the streets.* ○ [Vn.p] Inside the launderette old ladies dozed in front of their washing-machines or gazed vacantly through the glass windows at the drums ***swirling*** *their dirty washing* ***about****.*

swish

swish off [Vn ⇆ p pass] remove, cut off (sth) with a stick etc which makes a hissing sound. **S:** he etc; scythe, sword, cane. **O:** leaf, stalk, head (of plant): *He* ***swished off*** *the tops of the grasses with a neat flick of his cane.*

switch

switch around/round [Vn ⇆ p pass] alter the positions of (people or things) relative to each other. **O:** staff, managers, editors; furniture, dishes: *His parents are always redecorating the rooms and* ***switching*** *the furniture* ***around****. The flat is never the same for two months on end.* ○ *It's part of company policy to* ***switch*** *its young trainees* ***round*** *within and between departments.*

switch off 1 [Vp,Vn ⇆ p pass adj] disconnect (an appliance); disconnect a supply (of gas or electricity). **O:** (gas-)fire, (electric-)stove, radio; power; gas, electricity: *Television sets have the great advantage that they can be* ***switched off****.* OBS ○ *Make sure the electricity is* ***switched off*** *at the mains before you leave to go on holiday.* = turn off 1, put out 10. ↔ switch on.

2 [Vp] (*informal*) stop paying attention: *He's such a boring lecturer that I generally* ***switch off*** *after about five minutes.* ↔ switch on.

switched off [pass adj (Vn.p)] (*informal*) not aware of fashionable or up-to-date things: *I suppose you could call her* ***switched off****. She doesn't listen to pop music and she hates noisy parties.* ○ *He's the most* ***switched-off*** *guy you ever met. He shuts himself away and studies all the time.* ↔ switched on 1.

switch on [Vp, Vn ⇆ p pass adj] connect (an appliance); connect a supply of (gas or electricity). **O:** light, lamp; television, washing-machine; current, power: *Prissie had come to* ***switch on*** *the light, light the fire and make the room cheerful.* DC ○ *The transmitters were* ***switched on*** *during the first week of December.* TBC = turn on 1. ↔ switch off 1.

switched on 1 [pass adj (Vn.p)] (*informal*) aware of all that is fashionable and up-to-date: *Her parents just weren't* ***switched on****: they knew nothing about teenage fashion or pop music.* ↔ switched off.

2 [pass adj (Vn.p)] (*informal*) under the influence of drugs; excited. **S:** pop-music; alcohol, drugs; company, atmosphere: *At his all-night parties there are always plenty of* ***switched-on*** *teenagers.*

switch over (to) 1 [Vp nom, Vp.pr, Vn ⇆ p pass, Vn.p.pr pass] (cause sth to) use one kind of power etc rather than another. **S** [Vp, Vp.pr], **O** [Vn.p, Vn.p.pr]**:** industry, plant; household. **S** [Vn.p, Vn.p.pr]**:** Government, Board, Council. **o:** nuclear power; electricity, gas: [Vp] Several major industries now use nuclear power, but we have not yet ***switched over*** (or: *made the* ***switch-over***). ○ [Vn.p] All the petrol pumps on our forecourt have been ***switched over*** *to show decimal values.* ○ [Vn.p.pr] The aim is to ***switch*** *the whole country* ***over to*** *natural gas.*

2 [Vp, Vp.pr, Vn ⇆ p pass, Vn.p.pr pass] (cause sb to) do one job instead of another. **S** [Vp, Vp.pr], **O** [Vn.p, Vn.p.pr]**:** staff; teacher, craftsman, salesman: [Vp.pr] *Peter* ***switched over to*** *teaching* (or: *made a* ***switch-over to*** *teaching)in mid-career.* ○ [Vn.p.pr] *A lot of staff are being* ***switched over to*** *sales.*

3 [Vp, Vp.pr] change (to another channel) by pressing a switch etc on a TV set. **o:** BBC2, Channel 4: *'There's rugby on BBC1. Why don't you* ***switch over****?'* ○ *'Let's* ***switch over*** *to ITV for the news.'* = turn over (to) 2.

switch round [Vn ⇆ p pass] ⇨ switch around/round.

switch through (to) [Vn.p pass, Vn.pr pass] connect (an outside caller) to sb on an internal network; transfer (an incoming call) from one extension to another on the same network. **S:** operator; switchboard. **O:** call; caller: *'I've got a caller from London on the line, Mr Jeffries.' 'All right, Joan,* ***switch*** *him* ***through****.'* ○ *'Operator, would you* ***switch*** *this call* ***through to*** *Mr Martin on extension 7049?'* = put through (to) 1.

swoop

swoop down (on) 1 [Vp, Vp.pr pass] move downwards suddenly to seize or attack (sth/sb). **S:** vulture, bomber. **o:** prey, target: *Gulls* ***swooped down*** *and snatched the pieces of bread.*

2 [Vp, Vp.pr] suddenly approach (a place) and attack it. **S:** rustler, bandit; police. **o:** herd; ranch; club, hideout: *Detectives* ***swooped down on*** *a Leeds gambling club last night and made several arrests.*

swop

swop for [Vn.pr pass] ⇨ swap for.

swop over/round [Vn ⇆ p pass] ⇨ swap over/round.

swop (with) [Vn.pr] ⇨ swap (with).

swot

swot (for) [Vpr] (*informal*) study hard (for a particular purpose). **S:** pupil, student, apprentice. **o:** exam; Finals, GCE: *He's* ***swotting*** *every evening* ***for*** *his Bar exams.*

swot up [Vp, Vn ⇆ p pass] (*informal*) learn or revise (sth) by hard effort. **S:** student, candidate. **O:** maths, physics; table, formula: *'I seem to spend most of my time* ***swotting up****!'* ○ *'You'll need to* ***swot up*** *your irregular verbs during the holiday.'* = mug up.

T

tack

tack down [Vn ⇆ p pass adj] fasten (sth) with small nails, esp to a floor. **O:** carpet, mat; corner, edge: *'You'd better* ***tack down*** *the edge of the carpet: people keep tripping over it.'*

tack on/onto 1 [Vn ⇆ p pass adj, Vn.pr pass emph rel] attach (sth) with long, loose stitches, esp before finally assembling a garment with a sewing-machine. **O:** sleeve, collar. **o:** jacket, blouse: *The lining has been* ***tacked on*** *too loosely — it keeps coming unstitched.*

2 [Vn ⇆ p pass adj, Vn.pr pass emph rel] (*informal*) make (sb/oneself) a member or part (of sth larger). **O:** oneself; one's name. **o:** (end of the) line, queue; list: *John* ***tacked*** *himself* ***onto*** *the end of a long queue at the bus-stop.*

3 [Vn ⇆ p pass, Vn.p.pr pass emph rel] add (sth) to a document etc that is already complete. **O:** paragraph, appendix. **o:** document, report: *The Bill was not allowed to go forward without further modification. Another clause was* ***tacked on*** *at the last minute.*

tackle

tackle about/on/over [Vn.pr pass] speak to (sb) frankly and boldly (about sth that one is troubled by); confront about. **O:** neighbour; landlord; (school, local) authorities. **o:** disturbance, nuisance; (high) rents, repairs; (provision of) amenities: *'He's always playing his stereo at full blast: it's high time we* ***tackled*** *him* ***about*** *it.'* ○ *At the last meeting, the headteacher was* ***tackled over*** *the policy of treating GCSE English Literature as an optional subject.*

tag

tag along (after/behind) [Vp, Vp.pr] (*informal*) accompany or follow (sb) in a tame, dependent way. **S:** child; younger brother; personal assistant. **o:** parent; older brother; boss: *She gives these ghastly parties and poor Robin has to* ***tag along****.* ASA ○ *Some of these men — we used to knock about together sometimes. I used to* ***tag along*** *on some of their evenings.* TC ○ *Wherever the three Party leaders went in their election campaigning a gaggle of press and TV reporters was sure to* ***tag along behind****.*

tail

tail back [Vp nom] (of road traffic) form into a long, stationary or slowly moving line, because of road works or an accident ahead. **S:** cars, lorries: *Traffic is* ***tailing back*** *on the eastbound carriageway as far as the junction with the M1.* ○ *'There are long* ***tailbacks*** *on all routes into Manchester.'*

tail off 1 [Vp] decrease gradually. **S:** output, supply, demand; spending, investment: *We expect production to* ***tail off*** *at this time of the year. Ours is a seasonal business.* ○ *There's some* ***tailing off*** *in the demand for new cars at the end of the summer holidays.* = taper off 2.

2 [Vp] fade into silence, usu because the speaker is shy or embarrassed. **S:** speaker; voice, words: *John was clearly overwhelmed by the occasion. After a few sentences, his voice* ***tailed off*** *into complete silence.*

tailor

tailor to [Vn.pr pass rel] make or structure (sth) in such a way that it fits (particular needs). **O:** scheme, plan; product. **o:** need, requirement, purpose: *Our insurance policies are specially* ***tailored to*** *the earnings pattern of the insured at different stages in his or her career.* ○ *Experience has taught us to* ***tailor*** *our merchandise* ***to*** *the particular requirements of each overseas market.* = adapt to.

take

take aback [Vn.p pass] surprise, and upset or dismay (sb). **S:** criticism, reproof; answer, retort: *The reply* ***took*** *me* ***aback****, so that for a moment I was lost for words.* ○ *Looking back, I'm surprised I wasn't more* ***taken aback*** *by the whole thing.* TC ○ *He was somewhat* ***taken aback*** *by the news that the police intended to prosecute him.* □ usu passive or adj after *appear* etc.

take aboard [Vn ⇆ p pass, Vn.pr pass] take (sth) on board a ship or aircraft. **o:** lifeboat, fishing-vessel; plane: *The vessel had to jettison some of the cargo* ***taken aboard*** *at Liverpool.* ○ *Passengers may only* ***take*** *a single item of hand luggage* ***aboard*** *the aircraft.* = take on 1. ⇨ come/go aboard.

take umbrage (about/at) [Vn.pr] feel displeased, annoyed, offended (by sth). **o:** remark, comment; neglect, slight: *'He's like the rest of you, forever*

taking umbrage about *something.'* US ○ *Although Steve was given to lying, he never* ***took umbrage at*** *being accused of it.* SPL = take offence (at).

take abroad (with) [Vn ⇆ p pass, Vn.p.pr pass] take (sb/sth) to a foreign country (with one). **O:** family; car, caravan; money, foreign currency: *'Are you thinking of* ***taking*** *your car* ***abroad*** *again this year?'* ○ *Restrictions have been eased on the amount of currency holiday-makers may* ***take abroad with*** *them.* ⇨ go abroad.

take across (to) [Vn.p pass, Vn.pr pass, Vn.p.pr pass] take (sb/sth) from one side (to the other). **O:** child, blind person; vehicle; goods. **o:** (**across**) road, busy crossing; the Channel, the North Sea; (**to**) France, the Continent : [Vn.p] There ought to be someone posted at this point to ***take*** *the children* ***across*** *in the morning.* ○ [Vn.pr] 'Would you mind ***taking*** *me* ***across*** *the main road?'* ○ [Vn.p.pr] 'Have you tried ***taking*** *a caravan* ***across to*** *France yet?'* ⇨ get across 1, go/send across (to).

take after [Vpr] resemble (a parent) in looks and/or character. **o:** father, mother; grandfather: *'You must* ***take after*** *father. I don't. I long to have lashings of cash.'* DC ○ *HELEN: You're not fond of work, are you? JO: No. I* ***take after*** *you.* TOH

take against [Vpr] dislike (sb/sth): *'I'm sure he* ***took against*** *me from the start.'* ○ *For some reason, she* ***took against*** *the training programme immediately.* ↔ take to 4.

take aloft [Vn.p pass] take (sb/sth) into the air on board an aircraft. **S:** pilot; plane. **O:** passenger, stowaway; load: *There were at least two cases of soldiers being* ***taken aloft*** *hanging on to the undercarriage or tail wheel in desperation.* B

take apart 1 [Vn.p pass] reduce (sth) to its component parts; dismantle. **O:** car, radio, clock: *Nick had* ***taken*** *the fuel gauge* ***apart*** *and spread the bits all over the carpet.* = take to bits/pieces. ↔ put together.

2 [Vn.p pass] (*informal*) defeat (sb) utterly; punish (sb) severely; criticize (sth) harshly. **S:** team; bowler, forward, boxer; critic; the press. **O:** opponents, visitors; performer, artist: *He had a rough time in his first fight. He was drawn opposite a real old pro who* ***took*** *him* ***apart*** *inside two rounds.* ○ *Her first novel had rave notices; her second was* ***taken apart***. = pull apart 2.

take around/round (with) [Vn ⇆ p pass, Vn.p.pr pass] take (sb/sth) as a companion, wherever one goes. **O:** mother, younger brother; dog: *It's as though he can't let the girl out of his sight. He* ***takes*** *her* ***around*** *all over the place.* ○ *He's beginning to teach his son the business. He* ***takes*** *him* ***around with*** *him in the car when he calls on customers.* ⇨ go around/round (together/with).

take aside/to one side [Vn.p pass, Vn.pr pass] lead (sb) away from a group in order to talk privately to him: *I shall have to* ***take*** *Alex* ***aside*** *one of these days and warn him against the kind of company he's keeping.* ○ *'Will you* ***take*** *Mrs Stevens* ***to one side*** *and tell her that some important news has come through on the phone?'* = draw aside 2.

take at (his/its) face value [Vn.pr pass] treat or evaluate (sb/sth) according to what he or it appears to be on the surface. **O:** stranger, visitor; dealer, salesman; remark, statement; goods: *These people respect an artist. They* ***take*** *everybody* ***at his face value***. CON ○ *I can* ***take*** *nothing you say* ***at face value***. TC ○ *The truth is that few titles* (ie of nobility) *can be* ***taken at their face value***. T

take a look (at) [Vn.pr] examine (sth). **adj:** close, good, quick, careful. **o:** face, features; letter, report; evidence, signs, traces: *'Those drawings, did you examine them?' 'I sent them straight on.' 'Well,* ***take a*** *good* ***look at*** *them now.'* OMIH ○ *He* ***took a*** *quick* ***look at*** *his notes.* OMIH = look at 1.

take offence (at) [Vn.pr pass emph rel] be offended (by sth). **o:** manner, tone (of voice); remark, (supposed) insult: *If she was going to* ***take offence at*** *everything he said, she had got to be put right straight away.* AITC ○ *I couldn't* ***take offence at*** *his tone, but I resolved to be more careful in front of him in future.* RATT ○ *They then wrote a new version of the play* ***at*** *which no one could possibly* ***take offence***.

take umbrage (at) [Vn.pr] ⇨ take umbrage (about/at).

take at his word [Vn.pr pass] behave as though sb is speaking the truth. **O:** speaker, official, employer: *'Why not* ***take*** *him* ***at his word*** *and act accordingly? When has he ever given you any reason to doubt him?'* ○ *'Could you ...* ***take*** *him* ***at his word****, and see whether we can't all pull together as a team for once.'* TT

take sb's breath away [Vn ⇆ p pass] surprise, startle (sb). **S:** (sudden) arrival; (unkempt, tattered) appearance; injuries; expense, cost; it ... to find her in this state: *'Please don't come too close* (ie to kiss me). *You* ***take my breath away****, and you know how much I love talking.'* DPM ○ *The appetite with which he consumed, during these next few days, really* ***took my breath away***. CON ○ *It* ***takes one's breath away*** *to see how much the place has changed in a few years.*

take away (from) 1 [Vn ⇆ p pass, Vn.p.pr pass emph rel] cause (sb) to leave a place, or a person to whom he was entrusted etc. **O:** child, ward. **o:** school, children's home; foster parents: *Father was convinced that Peter was unhappy at boarding school, and made arrangements to* ***take*** *him* ***away***. ○ *He can't be accused of* ***taking*** *the baby* ***away from*** *its mother irresponsibly. For various reasons, she's unable to look after the child.*

2 [Vn ⇆ p pass, Vn.p.pr pass emph rel] remove (sth) (from sb), eg because it is dangerous, no longer deserved etc. **O:** gun, knife; plaything, sweets; privilege, office. **o:** intruder, bandit; child; official, prefect: *One unit of the army has had its firearms* ***taken away*** *following the recent mutiny.* ○ *He's always been a slave to women — who* ***take away*** *with one hand while they give with the other.* PW ↔ give back (to) 1. ⇨ get away (from).

3 [Vn ⇆ p pass, Vn.p.pr pass emph rel] make (a feeling etc) disappear (from sth). **O:** joy, fun; pain, distress. **o:** existence, life; experience; body, leg: *This queer worry and apprehension had* ***taken away*** *all her pleasure in her regained mobility.* DC ○ *'Now, I'll just give you some tablets to* ***take away*** *the pain.'*

4 [Vn ⇆ p pass, Vn.p.pr pass emph rel] (*mathematics*) subtract (a smaller sum) (from a larger). **O:** (smaller) number, digit. **o:** (larger) number, total: (a child is speaking) *'I can do adding up, but we haven't done any* ***taking away*** *yet.'* ○ *'****Take away*** *this number* ***from*** *that, and tell me how much you have left.'* ↔ add up 2.

take away/out [Vn ⇆ p nom pass] buy and carry away, from a special restaurant or shop, cooked dishes for consumption at home. **O:** meal, snack; curry, chop suey: *'They do a very good curry here, and you can* **take** *stuff* **out** *if you want.'* ○ *There's a small* **take-out** *on the corner, where you can get baked potatoes with various fillings.* ○ *'Incidentally, I hope nobody's eating Chinese* **take-aways** (or: **take-away** *meals) for breakfast.'* BBCR □ the nom forms take-away and take-out can refer to the meal etc and to the place where it is prepared; take-out is the more common nom-form in US English; both forms can modify another noun: *Those high-speed* **take-away** *foodshops—are they as hygienic as they should be?* BBCR

take back 1 [Vn ⇆ p pass] cause (sb/sth) to return. **O:** child; (stray) animal; (borrowed) book, record, camera: *'It's nearly time for afternoon school. Margaret, do you mind* **taking** *the children* **back** *in your car?'* ○ *'Some of these library books are long overdue. I really must* **take** *them* **back**.*'* ⇨ be back 1, ⇨ bring back 1, come back 1, get back 1, go back 1.
2 [Vn ⇆ p pass] agree to accept or receive sth which one has sold, or sb whom one has dismissed. **S:** shopkeeper, store; wife. **O:** (shoddy, defective) article; (errant) husband: *There's something seriously the matter with this car. Under their guarantee, the dealers are obliged to* **take** *it* **back**. ○ *After all his wife has gone through, I think Frank will be extremely lucky if she* **takes** *him* **back**. ⇨ have back 2.
3 [Vn ⇆ p pass] withdraw, retract (sth said). **O:** remark, statement; accusation; it all; what one has said: *I wanted you to ask me to marry you, and you did. Now* **take** *it* **back**, *if you want to.* H ○ *He would have given anything to be a small boy, who by saying '***Take back** *what I said' could erase a whole conversation.* ASA

take back (to) [Vn.p pass, Vn.p.pr pass] recall (earlier experiences) to (sb). **S:** conversation, reminiscences; music, voice; smell. **o:** his etc early days, childhood: *'Just chatting over a drink like this—it certainly* **takes** *you* **back**, *doesn't it?'* ○ *Seeing Mike again* **took** *me* **back to** *my first years as a teacher overseas.* = carry back (to). ⇨ bring back 2, come back 3.

take before [Vn.pr pass] make (sb) appear in a court etc to explain his actions, to be punished etc. **O:** offender, accused; child, pupil; soldier; case. **o:** magistrate; headteacher; company commander: *People who failed to pay their poll tax could be* **taken before** *the magistrates.* ⇨ be before 2, bring before, come before 2, go before 2, put before 2.

take below [Vn.p pass] (*nautical*) lead (sb), carry (sth), to a cabin etc from the deck of a ship. **O:** passenger, visitor; gear, tackle: *The rescued seamen were* **taken below** *and given some hot food and dry clothes.* ⇨ be below 3, go below (decks).

take the bit between the teeth [Vn.pr] (*informal*) settle to a hard task in a determined way. **S:** athlete; climber, swimmer; worker, student: *I wouldn't have given him much credit for determination, but he's* **taken the bit between the teeth**, *and there's no keeping him back.*

take by [Vn.pr pass] in grasping (sb/sth), take hold of (a certain limb, or part). **O:** him etc; pot, kettle, dish. **o:** hand, elbow; scruff of the neck, seat of the pants; handle: *He* **took** *Mary gently* **by** *the wrist, and drew her aside.* ○ *'I'll have you* **taken by** *the scruff of your neck and thrown out of the club.'* ○ *Don't* **take** *the knife* **by** *the blade;* **take** *it* **by** *the handle.*

take the bull by the horns [Vn.pr pass] handle a difficult, or dangerous, situation by facing it boldly and directly: *'You won't get the financial support you need by staying here.* **Take the bull by the horns**. *Go and speak to your bank manager.'*

take by storm [Vn.pr] fire (people) with great enthusiasm. **S:** actor, singer, dancer; boxer. **O:** audience, crowd; young people: *British rock bands have* **taken** *the world* **by storm**, *British computer games could do the same.* G ○ *The pop star the crowds were fighting to see was a 12-year old boy actor ... who had already* **taken** *the provinces* **by storm**. OBS

take by surprise [Vn.pr pass] come to (sb), happen to (sb), when he is quite unprepared for it. **S:** he etc; her arrival, marriage, divorce; news, announcement: *Helen had not announced the date of her arrival, and she* **took** *Virginia* **by surprise** *by arriving at Weston in a taxi.* AITC ○ *I must not let madness steal up on me and* **take** *me* **by surprise**. PM ○ *One day a publisher approached me directly with a proposal for its publication. This* **took** *me* **by surprise**. UTN

take down 1 [Vn ⇆ p pass] remove (sth) from a high level, eg on a wall or shelf; lower, drop. **O:** flag, bunting, streamer; picture, curtain rail; book, ornament: *An old tradition has it that Christmas decorations must be* **taken down** *before Twelfth Night.* ○ *I* **took down** *my copy of 'The Tibetan Book of the Dead' and opened it at random.* DOP ↔ put up 1.
2 [Vn ⇆ p pass] dismantle (sth). **O:** scaffolding; crane, derrick: *They've* **taken down** *the iron railings on this side of the park.* ○ *The ornamental gates have been* **taken down** *and sold as scrap.* ↔ put up 3. ⇨ come down 1.
3 [Vn ⇆ p pass] record (sth) in writing. **O:** lecture, speech; remarks, statement: *We were sitting about listlessly while the Bloater* (a teacher) *droned out some stuff we were supposed to be* **taking down**. CON ○ *These occasions are ghastly enough without feeling that what one says may be* **taken down** *and used against one.* ASA . □ cf the last example with the form of official caution used by the police when taking a statement: *Anything you say will be* **taken down**, *and may be used in evidence.* = write down. ⇨ be down 3, get down 4, go down 9, put down 11, set down 2.

take down a peg (or two) [Vn.p pass] (*informal*) humble an arrogant or conceited person: *'I've never heard such pretentious nonsense: he needs to be* **taken down a peg or two**.*'* □ a peg (or two) is an adv phrase (of degree).

take for 1 [Vn.pr pass] mistakenly assume that (sb) is (sb/sth else). **o:** his brother; (genuine) official, member of staff; local person, foreign visitor; fool, idiot: *'I'm sorry I spoke to you so familiarly: I* **took** *you* **for** *a close friend.'* ○ *He speaks English so well that he's often* **taken for** *a native.*
2 [Vn.pr] assume (sb) to be (a fool etc). **o:** fool, idiot, coward: *'So!' he said, in a surprised tone. 'And yet, Briggs, I should not have* **taken** *you* **for** *a coward.'* EM ○ *'What sort of idiot do you* **take** *me*

***for**?' ○ 'Of course I wouldn't walk out on you. What do you **take** me **for**?'*

take credit for [Vn.pr emph rel] be recognized and praised as the person who has acted well in a certain situation. **adj:** some (of the), all the, a lot of the; full, due. **o:** saving, rescuing (sb), restoring (sth); our success, its revival: *'He will also **take** the **credit for** getting rid of a dangerous agent.'* OMIH ○ *'Of course the exhibition was a tremendous success, and **for** that you must **take** full **credit**.'* ⇨ give credit for, give credit (to) (for).

take for granted 1 [Vn.pr pass] assume that (sth) is true, is the case, and act on that assumption. **O:** nothing, no facts; a lot, too much; his reliability, trustworthiness; his help, co-operation; it ... that he speaks the truth, it ... that the room is available: *Cyril Robertson was a stimulating, provocative man who **took** nothing whatever **for granted**.* OBS ○ *There are certain standards of civilized behaviour in international relations which it should be possible to **take for granted** in the family of nations.* SC ○ *'Then if it's **taken for granted**, let's get on with it. We might as well commit the crime if we're certain to receive the punishment.'* TBC
2 [Vn.pr pass] treat (sb) insensitively, without taking account of his wishes and feelings. **O:** wife, colleague, partner: *She knew that she was in danger of **taking** him too much **for granted**.* PW ○ *'You might consult me before making these arrangements: I do resent being **taken** so much **for granted**.'*

take revenge (for) [Vn.pr emph rel] ⇨ take revenge (on) (for).

take for a ride [Vn.pr pass] (*informal*) fool or outwit (sb) in a business deal, a legal transaction etc. **O:** customer, consumer; client; partner, shareholder: *'If you paid more than £2 000 for that car, you've been **taken for a ride**!'* ○ *Vin was the sharp, clever boy who wasn't to be **taken for a ride** by anybody, the boy who knew all the answers.* ASA

take sb's word for it/that [Vn.pr] accept on sb's authority that sth is the case: *'Oh, don't worry to explain, Gerrie, I'll **take your word for it** that it's important.'* ASA ○ *'They can do without you, **take my word for it**. But without them, you're lost — nothing.'* EGD ○ *'And as Ada says,' Mr Blearney went on, 'she's only a woman. I have to **take her word for that**, mind you.'* HD □ it introduces, or refers back to, a finite clause.

take from 1 [Vn.pr pass emph rel] choose (a text) from (a larger work). **S:** priest, preacher; student, scholar. **O:** reading, text, passage: *The vicar preached a short and effective sermon, **taking** his text **from** St Mark's Gospel.* ○ *'I am going to **take** an extract **from** some recordings I've made of bird songs, and play it over to you.'*
2 [Vn.pr emph rel] (*informal*) suffer (attacks etc) from (sb). **O:** abuse, insults; a lot, too much; not ... any more: *I've **taken** more than I can stand **from** those two.* ○ *For the sake of general harmony, he was someone **from** whom I was prepared to **take** a certain amount of sniping and petty jealousy.*
3 [Vpr] (*formal*) lessen or weaken the effect or value of (sth). **S:** scarcity, expense, poor quality (of labour, materials); voice, appearance. **o:** attractiveness, feasibility (of a project); success, effectiveness (of a speech): *His appearance in a shabby dressing-gown **took** somewhat **from** the impression of stern authority he wished to convey.* = detract from.

take heart (from) [Vn.pr emph rel] be encouraged or heartened (by sth), esp in difficult times. **o:** news; knowledge, realization (that ...); words, remarks: *Whenever I spoke of the Bushman a look of wonder would come into their eyes, and I **took heart from** that.* LWK ○ *But let them **take heart** (**from** this): it might have been worse. So far we have had neither frost nor snow.* T

take it from me/us [Vn.pr] (*informal*) (one may) believe, on the speaker's authority, that sth is true. **O:** it ... that the worst is over; it ... he won't be back: ***Take it from me**: your troubles are nearly over.* ○ *DAVIES: I might have been on the road* (ie a tramp) *a few years but you can **take it from me** I'm clean.* TC □ usu imperative, or after *can*.

take it from the top [Vn.pr] (*theatre*) (an instruction to) play, repeat, a scene from the beginning: *'Right, everybody. When you've settled down, can we **take it from the top**, please.'*

take one's pick (from/of) [Vn.pr emph rel] choose what one likes from (a selection). **o:** (**from**) range, assortment (of articles); variety, mixture; (**of**) ties, shirts; horses, dogs (in a race); partners, girls: *Ask the chemist for our product, and **take your pick from** eight romantic shades.* H ○ *He was handed a list, and told he could **take his pick of** the drinks available.*

take home [Vp.n nom pass] (*industry*) have as (net wages) after deductions have been made for tax, national insurance etc. **O:** wage; pay; £200: *Last month, Miss Silsby **took home** £507, including 18 hours overtime.* IND ○ *Because the married couple's new allowance is given to the husband, a woman's **take-home** pay will always be proportionally less.* WR □ take home usu used as a modifier of a noun: ***take home** pay, wage, earnings.*

take in 1 [Vp.n] receive, admit (lodgers) for payment. **O:** lodger, paying-guest; student, commercial traveller: *Many households in the neighbourhood of the University add to their income by **taking in** students.*
2 [Vn ⇆ p] accept (work) for payment to be done in one's own home. **O:** washing, sewing, mending: *Mrs Peters, who is a widow with young children, **takes in** machining and sewing to supplement her pension.*
3 [Vn ⇆ p pass] make (a garment) narrower to fit a thinner person. **O:** dress, trousers: *The dress is not a bad fit, but it needs **taking in** a little at the waist.* ○ *'I'll have the waistband **taken in** for you a couple of inches.'* ↔ let out 4.
4 [Vp.n pass] include, cover (sth). **S:** (field of) study, discipline; work, responsibilities; tour, journey. **O:** branch, speciality; teaching, research; region, area: *Forensic science **takes in** criminology, which covers the causes of crime.* NS ○ *These tours **took in** every part of the British Empire.* MFM ○ *Her accusation **took in** not only Mrs Curry, but Mrs Craddock also.* HAA
5 [Vp.n] include a visit to (a place) while travelling in or to the vicinity. **O:** show, musical; film, concert; museum: *Polly tries to **take in** a show or auction on one of her regular trips to London.*
6 [Vn ⇆ p] note (sth) visually; observe. **O:** surroundings; room; contents, occupants. **A:** at a

glance, at once: *Scrodd was* ***taking in*** *with his short-sighted glance the general area within which his interlocutor might be found.* HD ○ *Her eyes were* ***taking in*** *nothing but the telephone.* NM
7 [Vn ⇆ p pass] hear or read (sth) with understanding. **O:** talk, lecture; words, remarks; (difficult) material, subject; what was being said: *Isabel wondered how much Irma was* ***taking in*** *of what was said.* PW ○ *Halfway through the chapter I stopped. I wasn't* ***taking in*** *a single word.* RATT ○ *She couldn't* ***take in*** *this new situation or size up what Irma's revelation meant to her.* PW ⇨ go in 5.
8 [Vn ⇆ p pass] (*informal*) fool, trick (sb). **S:** salesman; quack doctor; magician; politician. **O:** customer; patient; audience: *I'm sorry you're all so easy to* ***take in****. You ought to know better with all your experience of the trade.* TC ○ *The public must be pretty gullible to be* ***taken in*** *so easily by TV advertisements.* □ usu passive.

take in hand 1 [Vn.pr pass] begin work on (sth); undertake. **O:** project, scheme, programme: *We are just now* ***taking in hand*** *a massive programme for the redevelopment of the city centre.* ○ *The plans which have been laid before you will be* ***taken in hand*** *by the autumn.* ⇨ be/have in hand.
2 [Vn.pr pass] (*informal*) assume responsibility for (sb), with the aim of training him, changing his character etc. **O:** (unruly, delinquent) child, youth; horse, dog. **A:** firmly, seriously: *'Why don't you go to a decent school?' 'I've never been to any school.' 'You need* ***taking in hand****.'* TOH ○ *Clearly somebody new had* ***taken*** *Madge* ***in hand****, somebody far more expert than Sammy.* UTN

take an interest in [Vn.pr pass emph rel] interest oneself in (sth), become interested in (sth). **S:** scientist, scholar; businessman; teacher; police. **adj:** (not) any/much, no, little; keen, lively, added. **o:** field, topic; developments, opportunities; organizing playgroups, studying the locality, reducing the accident-rate: *You never* ***took any interest in*** *what he did.* AITC ○ *Ex-Superintendent Williams was* ***taking a*** *keen* ***interest in*** *George's affairs.* PE ○ *Rock-climbing is an activity* ***in*** *which more and more young people are* ***taking an interest****.*

take one's life in one's hands [Vn.pr] (*informal*) run a serious risk of being killed. **S:** motorist, pilot, diver: *I reckon you* ***take your life in your hands*** *every time you move into the fast lane of a motorway.* ○ *The swimmers are conscious of* ***taking their lives in their hands*** *whenever they venture into these waters.*

take part (in) [Vn.pr emph rel] be involved (in sth), give one's support (to sth). **adj:** some; (not) any/much, no, little; (a) leading, prominent, decisive. **o:** festival, celebrations; demonstration, strike; contest, struggle; supporting sth, achieving sth: *It is not yet clear if all the coalition partners will* ***take part in*** *a government led by Mr Aylwin.* G ○ *They were asked to* ***take*** *a* ***part in*** *organizing the emergency preparations that were gaining momentum.* TBC ○ *The Scottish TUC have* ***taken*** *a leading* ***part in*** *efforts to strengthen the economy.* SC

take pride in [Vn.pr pass emph rel] be proud of (sth), get satisfaction from (sth). **adj:** such, some; (not) any/much, no; little, great, considerable. **o:** work; appearance; achievement, success; being fashionably dressed, looking smart: *Nurse Ellen sewed beautifully and* ***took*** *great* ***pride in*** *her work.* DC ○ *He seems to* ***take*** *a* ***pride in*** *being offensive to everyone he meets.* ○ *I can assure you: I* ***take*** *no* ***pride in*** *the way some of our employees have behaved.*

take refuge in [Vn.pr emph rel] use (sth) as a mask or cover for embarrassment, inefficiency etc. **o:** daydreams, fantasy; lies, excuses; silence; pretending not to understand: *Bill, feeling at a disadvantage,* ***took refuge in*** *words.* HAA ○ *Mrs Curry* ***took refuge*** *for a moment* ***in*** *licking her little lips.* HAA ○ *The fiction that there are 'foreign agitators' wishing to destroy the country, is one* ***in*** *which many governments have* ***taken refuge****.*

take in one's stride [Vn.pr pass] manage (a difficult situation) without effort or strain. **O:** obstacle, difficulty; examination; setback, failure; mood, temper; (difficult, unfamiliar) person: *She might not like to be the wife of a factory hand; but to his surprise she* ***took it in her stride.*** AITC ○ *This over-response to an emotional situation — St Clements* ***took*** *it all* ***in his stride****.* HAHA

take in/into [Vn ⇆ p pass, V n.pr pass] receive (sb) into one's house, offer shelter and hospitality to (sb). **O:** child, orphan; vagrant; stray animal. **o:** house, home: *You've been a good friend to me. You* ***took*** *me* ***in****.* TC ○ *Several families in the area have* ***taken*** *overseas students* ***into*** *their homes at Christmas.*

take into account/consideration [Vn.pr pass] include (sth) in one's study, calculations etc; consider. **O:** factor, circumstance; pressure, light; view, attitude: *The third reason why Birkhoff went wrong lies in his failure to* ***take into account*** *some additional complexities.* SNP ○ *In your proposals you haven't* ***taken into consideration*** *the special needs of old people.* ○ *In this case there are special features to be* ***taken into account****.* SC = make allowances (for), take account of.

take into one's confidence [Vn.pr pass] share with (sb), confidentially, one's plans, problems etc. **O:** colleague; staff, work-people: *He had contemplated* ***taking*** *Mr Mackay* ***into his confidence****, and asking his advice about his difficult position.* RM ○ *Much of the success of the project is due to the fact that the unions were* ***taken into the employers' confidence*** *from the outset.* = confide in.

take it into one's head that [Vn.pr] (*informal*) get the foolish idea, form the mistaken impression that (sth is happening). **O:** it ... that one is being watched, that money was to be made, that the law is one's vocation: *Somehow he'd* ***taken it into his head that*** *his wife was trying to poison him.* ○ *'Try to stop them* ***taking it into their heads that*** *we're planning any big organizational changes.'*

take it into one's head to do sth [Vn.pr] (*informal*) decide to do sth, form the intention of doing sth. **O:** it ... to move, change jobs; it ... to argue, disagree: *If I should* ***take it into my head to tell*** *what I had heard, tremendous mischief could result.* AH ○ *I watched a troop of little birds, which every so often* ***took it into their heads to move*** *on a few yards.* SPL

take the law into one's own hands [Vn.pr] start to act as a policeman, judge, etc because one believes that the machinery of law is slow or ineffective. **S:**

vigilante, Citizens' Defence Committee; (irate, intemperate) citizen: *Where troops and police have to operate against urban guerrilas, it may be hard to prevent sections of the public* ***taking the law into their own hands****.*

take matters into one's own hands [Vn.pr] act on one's own behalf when the people responsible do not act for one: *The head was plainly going to do nothing to ensure my allowance was paid, so I* ***took matters into my own hands*** *and went to see someone at the Education Office.* ○ *'What I hoped you could suggest is some way of apprehending the criminal. I see I must* ***take matters into my own hands****.'* MM

take account of [Vn.pr pass pass(o) emph rel] include (sth) when measuring or assessing sth etc. **adj:** (not) any/much, no; small, little; careful. **o:** factor, circumstances; speed, light; change, movement; economy, expenditure: *Have you* ***taken account of*** *possible shifts in demand?* ○ *No* ***account*** *was* ***taken of*** *potential increases of productivity per animal, especially in developing nations.* GLWM ○ *Future movements of population cannot always be* ***taken account of*** *when deciding what schools and hospitals we shall need in 20 years' time.* = make allowances (for), take into account/ consideration .

take advantage of 1 [Vn.pr pass pass(o) emph rel] use (the opportunities one has) well, properly etc. **adj:** (not) much/any, no; little; full, ample, proper. **o:** (social) service, benefit allowance; opening, opportunity: *The careers teacher urged girls who were leaving to* ***take*** *full* ***advantage of*** *facilities for further education.* ○ *Proper* ***advantage*** *is not being* ***taken of*** *this splendidly equipped sports hall.* ○ *The Headmistress hoped that the newly expanded library would be* ***taken*** *full* ***advantage of****.* = avail oneself of.

2 [Vn.pr pass(o)] use one's strength, or another person's weakness, to get money, sex etc from (that person): *'I don't like people who* ***take advantage of*** *me while my back is turned: hand back the money.'* ○ *In flirting with him she had gone to such lengths that three times he had wished to* ***take advantage of*** *her* (ie seduce her). SNP ○ *'Miss Elliott is much too nice a girl to be* ***taken advantage of*** *by you.'* TT

take care (of) 1 [Vn.pr pass(o)] make sure that sb is well and happy. **adj:** good, proper. **o:** children, elderly relatives; patient, invalid; oneself: *There had been no accident ... that afternoon and Guy said, 'Didn't I tell you? Nurse Ellen can* ***take care of*** *herself.'* DC ○ *Don't worry about the children while you're away: they'll be* ***taken*** *good* ***care of****.* □ take care of yourself (or take care) are used when saying goodbye to someone: *'G'bye,' he said huskily. '****Take care of*** *yourself.'* WI = attend to 1, care for 1, look after 1 .

2 [Vn.pr pass(o)] make oneself responsible for doing (sth). **o:** problem, difficulty; bill, tax: *'And what about our tax bill?' 'That's all right, I've already* ***taken care of*** *that.'* ○ *'I've* ***taken care of*** *the waiter* (ie tipped him).*'* = attend to 2, look after 2.

take charge (of) [Vn.pr emph rel] assume the leadership of (sth), or responsibility for (sth/doing sth). **S:** officer, executive; agency, ministry. **o:** campaign, project; planning, selling; district, area: *Eisenhower told me that he wanted me to* ***take*** *complete* ***charge of*** *the land battle.* MFM ○ *'Make sure that she's the right type. Someone capable of* ***taking charge of*** *the technical side.'* OMIH ⇨ be in charge (of).

take control (of) [Vn.pr emph rel] assume a position where one manages or controls (sb/sth). **S:** teacher, parent; pilot, skipper; director, manager. **o:** pupil, child; plane, vessel; operation, situation: *It's not the easiest task to* ***take control of*** *a class of young children.* ○ *Surely she would* ***take control of*** *the situation; after all she was a professional.* OMIH ⇨ be in control (of), have control of/over.

take heed (of) [Vn.pr pass pass(o) emph rel] (*formal*) note (sth) and draw from it any lesson it teaches. **adj:** (not) much/any, no; little; proper, sufficient. **o:** warning, threat; potent, sign; advice, recommendation: *Fog warnings are clearly displayed on motorways, but many drivers still* ***take*** *no* ***heed of*** *them.* ○ *Little* ***heed*** *was* ***taken of*** *the reminders sent about his overdue account.* ○ *There are indications, and I hope they are* ***taken heed of****, that we are heading for an economic recession.*

take (one's) leave of [Vn.pr rel] (*formal*) bid farewell to (sb/sth). **o:** host, guest; country: *The sound of drums, flutes and rattles heralded the arrival of the Fon to* ***take his leave of*** *me.* BB ○ *This was the end of our conversation and ... it was going to be very difficult to* ***take leave of*** *each other.* UTN

take leave of one's senses [Vn.pr] behave in a wild, irrational way: *'You have* ***taken leave of your senses****, Taylor,' said Dame Lettie, 'and I can do no more for you.'* MM ○ *'It's maddening. There was no need for it whatsoever. I just* ***took leave of my senses****.'* SPL ○ *He looked at me as though I had* ***taken leave of my senses****.* BB □ usu perfect tenses.

take note of [Vn.pr pass pass(o) emph rel] (*formal*) consider (sth) when making a decision or taking action; note, record. **o:** factor, circumstances; statement; request, submission; feelings; preference: *The Authority will* ***take note of*** *a teacher's stated preference for one posting rather than another, though it cannot undertake to send every teacher to the school of his first choice.* ○ *Your remarks have been* ***taken*** *careful* ***note of****, and I hope soon to give a detailed reply to each of them.*

take notice (of) [Vn.pr pass pass(o) emph rel] give one's attention to (sb/sth). **adj:** some, no, (not) any/much; not... a blind bit of. **o:** him etc; child, parent; advice, comment; appearance, dress: *Carry on ... with your own ideas and don't* ***take*** *any* ***notice of*** *your friends' criticism or advice.* WI ○ *'****Take*** *no* ***notice of*** *him, Nan. To hell with him and what he said to you.'* WI ○ *I am angry that so little* ***notice*** *is* ***taken of*** *these warnings.* ○ *She's a charming child, but she's never* ***taken*** *any* ***notice of*** *at home.* □ usu neg or interr.

take the/this opportunity (of) [Vn.pr pass] use a favourable chance offered to do (sth). **adj:** this; the first, the earliest. **o:** expressing one's views, challenging his decisions, making one's escape: *Mr Nehru may* ***take the opportunity of*** *pointing out* (or: ***take the opportunity*** *to point out*) *that the effect of China's conduct is to unite Asia, as well as the rest of the world.* SC ○ *The Government should* ***take the opportunity of*** *demanding a more forward-looking attitude from the British Transport Commission.* NS □ object is the *-ing* form of a v; take this opportunity (of), or more usu, take this opportunity to do sth, is used in formal speeches, tributes etc: *Could I* **take this opportunity of** *welcoming all our overseas visitors?* ○ *I want to* **take this opportunity** *to pay a public tribute to him.* MFM

take one's pick (of) [Vn.pr emph rel] ⇨ take one's pick (from/of).

take a poor etc view of [Vn.pr pass emph rel] (*informal*) regard, consider (sth) in a negative etc way. **adj:** poor, dim, sombre, pessimistic; optimistic, sanguine, bright. **o:** future; events, circumstances: *The federation* **takes a gloomy view of** *the prospects for the economy in the months to come.* ○ *Most other road-users* **take a stern view of** *the private motorist.* SC

take stock (of) [Vn.pr] after a period of activity, pause to weigh or assess (sth/sb/oneself). **adj:** careful. **o:** supplies, ammunition; situation, position; one's partner; oneself: *We had been out three days,* **taking stock of** *the huts in this valley and making them secure.* BM ○ *Dennis* **took stock of** *the odds. Though he had been under fire often enough, he had no experience of attack.* ARG ○ *While he had been away on this last trip to America, she had had a chance to* **take stock of herself**. WI

take a/its toll (of) [Vn.pr pass emph rel] reduce the strength or size of (sth); damage. **S:** crisis, shortage; fever, malnutrition; bomb, shell; attack. **adj:** severe, serious, heavy. **o:** business, trading; population; armour, transport: *Years of long hours were* **taking their toll** (ie of sb's health). OBS ○ *On the London Stock Exchange, the threat of a credit squeeze has been* **taking its toll of** *business.* SC ○ *He* (the enemy) *is now being 'written off', and heavy* **toll** *is being* **taken of** *his divisions by ground and air action.* MFM

take off 1 [Vn ⇆ p pass, Vn.pr pass] remove, detach (esp sth fastened to a surface or edge). **O:** fitting; knob, handle, knocker; door; paint. **o:** car; door, window; hinges; wall: *Before the body of the car can be properly repaired, all the external fittings must be* **taken off**. ○ *The intense heat* **took** *most of the paint* **off** *the doors.* ⇨ be off 2, come off 2.

2 [Vn ⇆ p pass, Vn.pr pass] remove (sth). **O:** coat, hat; tablecloth, bedspread. **o:** him etc; table, shelf, divan: *'***Take** *your shoes* **off** *and dry your feet.'* ○ *Mark noticed that while she had combed her hair and made up her face, she had also* **taken off** *her engagement ring.* AW ↔ put on 1. ⇨ get off 4.

3 [Vn ⇆ p pass] amputate. **O:** limb; leg, toe: *Gangrene was far advanced, and the leg had to be* **taken off** *above the knee.* = cut off 1.

4 [Vn ⇆ p pass, Vn.pr pass] remove (sth) from service. **O:** bus, train. **o:** route, run: *There is no night flight to Lisbon at this time. The service was* **taken off** *at the end of the summer.* ○ *They've had to* **take** *two of the evening buses* **off** *this route because of a shortage of crews.*

5 [Vn ⇆ p pass, Vn.pr pass] transfer (sb) to another vessel; rescue. **S:** lifeboat, helicopter. **O:** crew, passenger. **o:** (stranded, shipwrecked) vessel: *The crew of the tanker which ran aground last night were* **taken off** *by helicopter.*

6 [Vn.p pass, Vn.pr pass] ask or order (sb) to leave one job, usu to do another. **O:** executive, assistant; journalist; policeman. **o:** job, assignment; case: *Two detectives have been* **taken off** *the inquiry to help with a murder case.* ↔ put on to 4. ⇨ come off 7.

7 [Vn ⇆ p pass, Vn.pr pass] remove (excess weight). **O:** kilograms, pounds, stones: *At the Health Farm they guarantee to* **take off** *at least a stone in one course of treatment.* ○ *'She's slimming.* **Taken off** *pounds.'* BFA ○ *'We'll* **take** *a bit of surplus weight* **off** *you before you finish basic training.'* ↔ put on 3.

8 [Vn ⇆ p pass, Vn.pr pass] remove (sth) from (a price); remove (a tax etc). **O:** £10, fifty pence; tax, levy, surcharge. **o:** price, total; car, washing-machine; import: *It's not so much a case of what taxes will be* **taken off** *in the next Budget as what new taxes will be put on.* ○ *There is little prospect of the present levy being* **taken off** *betting.* ↔ put on 6. ⇨ come off 9.

9 [Vn ⇆ p pass, Vn.pr pass] remove (an item) from (a menu in a restaurant). **O:** fish, chicken. **o:** menu, bill of fare: *My favourite dish has usually been* **taken off** *just before I get to the restaurant.* ○ *'We're running low on steak: you'll have to* **take** *it* **off** *the menu.'* ⇨ be off 5.

10 [Vn.p] have (some period) as a break from work, or as a holiday. **O:** (a few) days, week, weekend; Easter, Bank Holiday: *'You need a break. Why not* **take** *a fortnight* **off** *from work?'* ○ *Everyone* **takes** *Christmas* **off**. FFE

11 [Vn ⇆ p pass] no longer perform (sth); withdraw. **O:** production; play, show, opera: *The play was* **taken off** *after libel charges had been laid against its author.* ↔ put on 11.

12 [Vp nom] (cause an aircraft to) leave the ground. **S:** pilot; plane, aircraft; passenger: *The Prime Minister's party* **takes off** *for Brussels this morning for the next round of economic discussions.* ○ *Another lot of tracks showed that the plane had started down the beach on its* **take-off** (or: *to* **take off**). DS ○ *The pilot made a smooth* **take-off** (or: **took off** *smoothly*). ○ *The pilot had turned short of the boundary line thereby diminishing the length of his* **take-off** *run.* G ↔ put down 3.

13 [Vp nom] (*commerce*) begin to improve economically, show a profit etc. **S:** economy; sales campaign; product, commodity: *Following a low-key launch with minimum advertising, the product suddenly* **took off** *and had soon captured a quarter of the market.* ○ *The Government is clearly reluctant to throttle down expansion now that the economy is reaching its* **take-off** *point.*

14 [Vp] (*informal*) move off, leave, hurriedly, eg to keep an appointment: *I grabbed my hat and* **took off** *for the Town Hall.* TST ○ *The moment he saw a police car turn the corner, Bloggs* **took off** *in the opposite direction.*

15 [Vn ⇆ p nom pass] (*informal*) mimic, imitate (sb), esp in an amusing or satirical way. **S:** comedian, satirist. **O:** politician, minister, actor: *Bill* **took off** *the Prime Minister to perfection* (or: *did a perfect* **take-off** *of him*).

take the edge off 1 [Vn.pr pass] make (a tool) blunt. **o:** blade, knife, axe: *'If you keep using that chisel as a screwdriver you'll* **take the edge** *right* **off** *it.'*

2 [Vn.pr pass] reduce the sharpness or force of (sth). **o:** blow, disappointment, criticism; pleasure; hunger, appetite: *There won't always be an adoring mother to* **take the edge off** *the blows. It's just* *one of the prices of growing up.* HAA ○ *Stocker was halfway through his lunch, and had* **taken the edge off** *his appetite sufficiently to talk.* CON

take one's eyes off [Vn.pr] stop looking at (sth/sb). **o:** stage, television screen; match, fight; pretty girl: *If you* **take your eyes off** *the dials for one instant, you may miss an important change in temperature.* ○ *'That dark girl in the corner — she's lovely. I can't* **take my eyes off** *her.'* □ usu neg and with *can/could.*

take the gilt off the gingerbread [Vn.pr] (of bad news or events following upon good) reduce or cancel the pleasant feelings aroused by good news: *It* **takes the gilt off the gingerbread** *when you arrive on holiday to find that the rooms you've booked have been allocated to someone else.* ○ *Increased mortgage payments coming on top of a salary rise — that's really* **taking the gilt off the gingerbread**.

take off (his) guard [Vn.pr pass] make (sb) less watchful or careful, so that he may make a mistake, reveal information etc. **S:** interrogator, detective; question, comment: *A sudden, unexpected question might* **take** *her* **off guard** *and startle her into an admission.* PE ○ *'But that's the other side of the world!' she gasped,* **taken off her guard**. WI ↔ put on his guard (against).

take off sb's hands [Vn.pr pass] (*informal*) remove from sb the responsibility or expense of looking after (sb/sth). **O:** daughter, elderly parent; guest; house, car: *With other girls, he had not cared whether they cheated him or not: it was a relief when another man* **took** *them* **off his hands**. AITC ○ *We've not let a single one of those flats in six months; I should be glad if a buyer* **took** *the entire block* **off our hands**. ⇨ be off one's hands.

take a load/weight off sb's mind [Vn.pr pass] (*informal*) relieve sb of his anxiety. **S:** news, announcement; reduction (in cost), cuts (in taxation); escape, rescue. **adj:** great, tremendous: *It* **took a load off my mind** *to know he was alive and well.* ○ *A reduction in the interest charged on bank loans* **took a weight off the minds of** *many small borrowers.*

take sb's mind/thoughts off [Vn.pr pass] help sb not to think about (sth worrying or distressing). **o:** himself; accident, illness, bereavement; examination, ordeal; law-suit, trial: *At least, wondering about Prissie's secret, real or imaginary,* **took Brigit's mind off** *herself.* DC ○ *He played cards, read, went for a walk — anything to* **take his thoughts off** *the decision he knew he must make.* ○ *'Let's put the radio on. It might* **take our minds off** *what's happening in the operating theatre.'*

take oneself off [Vn.p] (*informal*) remove oneself, leave; the suggestion often is that one is no longer needed, or in the way: *A quarrel was developing between husband and wife: it was high time I* **took myself off**. ○ *'Now, why don't you* **take yourself off** *to the pictures while I try and get through this correspondence?'*

take the smile off one's/sb's face [Vn.pr pass] (*informal*) make sb who is being frivolous suddenly become serious. **S:** (stern) teacher, parent; drill-sergeant; (spectacle, experience of) suffering, hardship: *'And you can* **take those smiles off your faces**, *or I'll take them off for you!'* ○ *'Yes,' she said, 'me and my unmarried mothers' hostel. Would you like to come with me one evening? It would* **take the smile off your face**.*'* TT

take the weight off one's feet [Vn.pr] (*informal*) sit down and relax after tiring work or exercise: *'Now here's the most comfortable chair. Sit down and* **take the weight off your feet**.*'* ○ *HELEN: Wouldn't she get on your nerves? Just when I was going to* **take the weight off my feet** *for five minutes.* TOH

take years off [Vn.pr] (*informal*) make (sb) appear younger. **S:** holiday; life abroad; diet, course of treatment, exercise; change of job: *I never imagined that an outdoor life could do so much for a man: it's* **taken years off** *him.* ○ *Moving to London may have* **taken** *five* **years off** *her, but it's put ten years on him.* ↔ put years on.

take off (to) [Vn.p pass, Vn.p.pr pass rel] lead, accompany (sb) away from one place to another. **O:** family, team, party; friend, relative; suspect, prisoner. **o:** seaside, mountains; France, London; police station: *The French teacher is planning to* **take** *a school party* **off to** *Paris at Easter.* ○ *One of the police officers* **took** *her* **off** *for questioning.* OBS ○ *Grandfather greatly resents being* **taken off to** *an Old People's Home.* ⇨ go off 1.

take one's hat off to [Vn.p.pr] (*informal*) express admiration for (sb), though without literally removing one's hat. **o:** rescue team, fire brigade; missionary, parish priest, doctor: *I* **take my hat off to** *anyone who is prepared to work underground for long hours.* ○ *He was doing important work for very little money, and I* **took my hat off to** *him.* □ usu first person; present or past simple tenses. = raise one's hat to.

take on 1 [Vn ⇆ p pass] take (sb) on board a ship or aircraft. **O:** fuel; stores, provisions; cargo; passengers: *The fuel oil we* **took on** *at Freetown will be enough to get us to Tilbury.* ○ *The pilot refuses to* **take** *any more passengers* **on**: *he's overweight for take-off as it is.* = take aboard.

2 [Vn ⇆ p pass] employ (sb) as staff; enrol (sb) as a student or pupil. **O:** staff, personnel; assistant, secretary: trainee, pupil: *They no longer have to* **take on** *large numbers of temporary staff to do the checking.* TES ○ *Six candidates were to be* **taken on** *for three months' trial, after which three of the six would be selected for permanent employment.* SD ○ *You come here recommending yourself as an interior decorator, whereupon I* **take** *you* **on**. TC

3 [Vn ⇆ p pass] undertake, assume (a burden etc). **O:** work; contract, engagement; patient, invalid, problem family: *He blamed his own weakness for letting her* **take on** *too much work.* ASA ○ *I'm beginning to regret that I* **took** *the job* **on**; *I'm working overtime every evening.*

4 [Vp.n] have a new (appearance, sound, form, meaning etc); assume. **S:** face, body; walk, posture; street, house, garden. **O:** look, appearance; suppleness, elegance; colour, fragrance: *Now her hair has* **taken on** *a healthy shine.* WI ○ *Our lives had* **taken on** *a certain regularity.* AH ○ *In this context the words of Socrates, in the Phaedo,* **take on** *a new significance.* HAH

5 [Vn ⇆ p pass] take (sb) as one's opponent; tackle. **S:** team; boxer, footballer; government, employer. **O:** tough opponents; a heavier man; union, shop steward: *In the third round of the FA Cup, several minor league teams will be* **taking on**

First Division sides. ○ *In* **taking on** *the miners the Government was faced with the toughest fight of its term of office.*

take action (on) [Vn.pr pass emph rel] act so as to achieve or settle (sth). **adj:** some; (not) any, no; swift; firm, resolute. **o:** recommendation, proposal; plan; matter, issue: *The Party would not be able to* **take action**, *in one Parliament,* **on** *all the proposals now before the annual Conference.* ○ *The Government has promised to* **take** *swift* **action on** *the energy crisis* (ie to settle the crisis).

take a chance (on) [Vn.pr emph rel] run the risk of sth unpleasant happening, but with the hope that this will be avoided and that all will be well. **o:** his not turning up, her not being willing to pay; his willingness to co-operate; the door being unlocked, the guard being asleep: *'Are you willing to* **take a chance on** *the petrol running out before the end of the journey?'* ○ *'He'll pay up all right. Anyway, I'm prepared to* **take a chance on** *it.'* PE □ object is usu the *-ing* form of a v.

take pity on [Vn.pr pass(o) rel] show kindly feeling, or sympathy, for (sb). **adj:** (not) any/much, no; (very) little, great. **o:** wife, child; poor, hungry, people; the homeless, the deprived: *She was so vexed with curiosity, that Virginia* **took pity on** *her and restored her peace of mind.* AITC ○ *She would bring into the house stray animals* **on** *whom she had* **taken pity**.

take (right) on the chin [Vn.pr pass] (*informal*) receive (a hard blow) without flinching or complaining. **O:** blow, punch, knock; it: *He felt dazed and groggy, like a boxer who has* **taken** *a hard one* **on the chin**. PE ○ (*figurative*) *Our industry has* **taken** *a few nasty ones* **on the chin** *since the bank borrowing rates were increased.* ○ (*figurative*) *He must have felt acutely disappointed when his job went to another man, but he never said a word: he* **took** *it* **right on the chin**.

take on (so) [Vp] (*informal*) express strong feelings, esp of sorrow or displeasure: *'Poor darling, you mustn't* **take on so**. *You don't see it now, but it* (his mistress's death) *was all for the best.'* RATT ○ *'It's no good your* **taking on**, *because the matter's settled, signed and sealed.'* PW

take on trust [Vn.pr pass] assume that (sb/sth) may be trusted, is reliable. **O:** him etc; statement, claim, version of the facts, report: *'Sarah* **takes** *everyone* **on trust**, *just like you do. Nicky is more like me.'* DC ○ *You don't have to* **take** *everything he says* **on trust**. *Do a little checking up occasionally.* ○ *He's wrong if he thinks a teacher's report on a child is to be* **taken** *more or less* **on trust**.

take on (at) [Vn ⇆ p pass, Vn.p.pr pass] accept (sb) as an opponent, esp in a sporting contest. **O:** anybody, everybody; the (whole) world; champion, record-holder. **o:** billiards, darts, chess: *With that amount of liquor in him he felt fit to* **take on** *the whole territory.* BM ○ *You can't expect to* **take** *a professional* **on at** *tennis the first time you go out on the court.*

take revenge (on) (for) [Vn.pr emph rel] act (against sb) in return for some injury, real or imagined, which one has suffered. **o:** (**on**) enemy, rival; neighbour; (**for**) offence, crime, injury; murder; insult, slight: *To* **take revenge for** *acts of revenge was merely to extend the horror and call it justice.* ARG ○ *The Medici* **took revenge on** *the Pazzi family by slaughtering as many as they could find and forcing the rest into exile.* = revenge (oneself) on .

take a (firm) stand (on/over) [Vn.pr pass emph rel] behave in a firm, unyielding way (over some issue). **S:** government, minister; employer, trades union; teacher, coach. **o:** question, matter, issue (of); inflation, incomes policy; productivity, redundancy; indiscipline, slackness: *The Government is forced to* **take a firm stand on** *the cost of living issue.* ○ **Over** *whether shipping can move freely through these waterways we shall of course* **take** *a very* **firm stand**.

take a (firm) grip/hold on/upon oneself [Vn.pr] (*informal*) control oneself, calm oneself, in a difficult situation: *'OK, let's just* **take a firm grip on ourselves**. *This road's not leading anywhere, so I suggest we turn back.'* ○ *Miss Murphy* (trapped in a phone box) **took a hold upon herself** *and tried to think. The thing to do was to stop someone. There did not seem to be any pedestrians. But there were cars.* ARG

take out 1 [Vn ⇆ p pass] obtain, by payment, a document that will ensure some kind of service in the future. **O:** subscription (to a journal); (personal, vehicle) insurance; (TV, driving) licence; permit: *It's more expensive, because of postage costs, to* **take out** *an annual subscription than to buy the periodical from a newsagent.* ○ *Road-fund licences may be* **taken out** *for four months or a whole year.*
2 [Vn ⇆ p pass] (*military*) destroy, neutralize (sth). **S:** artillery, rockets; tanks, aircraft. **O:** strong point, pillbox: *Had the initiative been Israel's, the Air Force would have spent the first 48 hours or so attacking air fields and* **taking out** *the missile screens.* OBS
3 [Vn ⇆ p nom pass] buy, from a special restaurant, cooked dishes for consumption at home. ⇨ take away/out.

take out (against) [Vp.n pass, Vn.p.pr pass] (*legal*) issue a document calling upon sb to appear in court. **S:** police; injured party. **O:** ⚠ a writ, summons, petition: *The police have decided to* **take out** *a summons* **against** *the drivers of both cars involved in the accident.*

take out (for/to) [Vn.p pass, Vn.p.pr pass] escort, accompany (sb) somewhere for exercise or recreation. **O:** wife, child; girlfriend; school party; dog. **o:** (**for**) drive, walk, ride; (**to**) cinema, theatre: *'I thought the nurse was looking after you.' 'No, she* **took** *the children* **out** *this afternoon.'* DC ○ *'***Take** *the dog* **out for** *a walk: he needs the exercise.'* ○ *I'll* **take** *her* **out to** *the pictures.* AH ⇨ be out (at), come/go out(for/to).

take it out in [Vn.p.pr pass] be given goods etc to the value of money which one is owed. **o:** goods; trading stamps, vouchers; savings certificates: *When I returned the appliance, the shop wouldn't refund the money, but they did let me* **take it out in** *vouchers redeemable at the shop.*

take out/out of 1 [Vn ⇆ p pass, Vn.pr pass] lead (sb) or carry (sth) from (a place). **O:** child; animal, pet; chair, carpet; car. **o:** house, room; garage: *'Will you* **take** *this dog* **out** *at once? It's chewing the carpet.'* ○ *As danger threatened, young children were* **taken out** *of the major cities into the country.* ⇨ be out/out of 1, bring out/out of, come out/out of 1, get out/out of 1, keep out/out of.

2 [Vn ⇆ p pass, Vn.pr pass] withdraw, extract (sth) from (an inner space). **O:** nail, screw; tooth; cup, plate; money. **o:** wall; gum; cupboard; bank, safe: *Then she unbuttoned her navy-blue coat and* **took out** *the ball from the pocket.* TT ○ *I* **took out** *a packet of cigarettes and offered the man one.* CON ○ *Cash was* **taken out of** *my account without my knowledge.* = draw out/out of 1. ↔ put in/into 1. ⇨ be out/out of 2, come out/out of 2, get out/out of 2.

take the easy etc way out/out of [Vn.p, Vn.pr] escape from (a difficult situation) by choosing a simple, painless solution. **adj:** easy; simplest, quickest; coward's; only, usual. **o:** difficulty, dilemma, crisis: *As Simons seemed to be waiting for him to say something, he* **took the simplest way out** *by pointing to the empty glasses and saying, 'Another?'* HD ○ *The one thing we* (ie British industry) *cannot afford is to* **take the usual way out** *— and cut investment.* OBS

take out of [Vn.pr pass] deduct (money owed etc) from (a particular source). **O:** cost; breakages; subscription, donation. **o:** expense account; pay, wages, salary: *'Don't you pay for the meal.* **Take** *it* **out of** *this* (ie a £20 note).*'* ○ *Contributions to a pension scheme are* **taken out of** *a teacher's monthly salary.*

take out of sb's hands [Vn.pr pass] remove from sb the responsibility for dealing with sth. **O:** matter, issue; responsibility; job, task; inquiry, investigation: *'I shall have to make a report to my office. Then if you don't co-operate, it'll be* **taken out of my hands**.*'* DBM ○ *As matters are developing, the CID will step in and* **take** *the inquiry* **out of our hands**.

take sb out of himself [Vn.pr pass] make sb forget his worries, problems etc. **S:** change (of scene), holiday; companionship, party: *One of the things about a surprise or shock is that it is said to* **take one out of oneself**. SML ○ *The experience meant an enlargement of the spirit that would* **take her out of** *and above* **herself**. PW

take it/a lot out of [Vn.pr] (*informal*) make (sb) physically or nervously tired. **S:** nursing, teaching; domestic crisis, accident: *Keeping on the alert* **took it out of** *him.* ILIH ○ *Getting turned down in marriage must have* **taken a lot out of** *you.* SML

take a leaf out of sb's book [Vn.pr pass] copy sb else in some respect: *The new teacher* **took a leaf out of his colleague's book**. *Instead of teaching anything fresh, he asked the boys to do silent revision.*

take the mickey/piss (out of) [Vn.pr pass] (*slang, taboo*) mock, ridicule (sb), in the hope, or with the effect, of irritating him: *Larrie's face flushed and his eyes blazed. 'You're not going to* **take the mickey out of** *me,' he cried.* ASA ○ *I can see perfectly well that you are trying to* **take the piss out of** *me. Only it won't work.* CON ○ *Every time a new teacher walks into the classroom she gets* **the mickey taken out of** *her.* □ the passive is usu formed with *have* or *get*.

take a/the rise out of [Vn.pr pass] (*informal*) make fun of (sb), with the aim of irritating him. **o:** brother, friend, colleague: *'He didn't seriously mean that you were a bad driver: he was just trying to* **take the rise out of** *you!'* ○ *'If there's one thing I can't stand, it's having* **the rise taken out of** *me by a pipsqueak like you!'* □ the passive is usu formed with *have* or *get*.

take the sting out of [Vn.pr pass] (*informal*) make (sth) seem more pleasant or bearable. **S:** kindness, sympathy; (pleasant) manner, tone. **o:** disappointment, setback; reproach, criticism: *Once you've resigned yourself to marriage you can* **take** *a lot of* **the sting out of** *it by grabbing one of the really good girls as she comes past.* TGLY ○ *The smile which accompanied it* **took the sting out of** *the reproof.* RATT ⇨ go out of.

take the wind out of sb's sails [Vn.pr pass] (*informal*) upset or disturb an overconfident or pompous person: *'I hope I shall see you and Kay at Marie Hélène's .... She's insisted on inviting brother John, but I hope to have a bit of news to* **take the wind out of his sails**.*'* ASA ○ **The wind** *was* **taken out of his sails**, *but he collected himself enough to ask: 'And may I call you Irma?'* PW

take out on [Vn.p.pr pass] (*informal*) make (sb else) the scapegoat for sth one has done or suffered. **O:** it, things; one's disappointment, frustration, irritation. **o:** wife, child; dog: *Feeling obscurely that she had better not* **take** *things* **out on** *Mrs Jones, she decided to* **take** *them* **out on** *Daniel.* US ○ *'I know how you must be feeling, but there's no need to* **take** *your disappointment* **out on me**.*'* = work off against/on, vent (on).

take out (to) [Vn.p pass, Vn.p.pr pass] ⇨ take out (for/to).

take (over) [Vn.pr pass emph rel] spend a certain length of time (in doing sth). **O:** ⚠ too long, a long time, ages. **o:** job, task; meal: *Would the doctorate ever be completed? He had already* **taken** *three years* **over** *it.* ○ *'Make your phone call, but don't* **take** *too long* **over** *it.'* ⇨ be over 3.

take over [Vp, Vn ⇆ p nom pass] (*commerce, industry*) acquire control of (a firm), esp by obtaining the support of a majority of its shareholders. **O:** business, company: *An Australian publisher is bidding to* **take over** (or: *is making a* **take-over** *bid for*) *an important national newspaper.* ○ *British industry should give as much status to the scientist as it does to the* **take-over** *bidder and advertising manager.* T ○ *The City pages are full of news of company mergers and* **take-overs**.

take a (firm) stand over [Vn.pr pass emph rel] ⇨ take a (firm) stand (on/over).

take pains/trouble over [Vn.pr pass emph rel] show great care in performing or completing (a task). **adj:** some, such; (not) any, no; great, considerable, enormous. **o:** arrangement, organization; project, essay; plan, drawing; finishing, preparing (sth): *It's worth* **taking** *some* **trouble over** *getting the two sections perfectly aligned.* ○ *He enjoyed the assembling and painting best.* **Over** *that part he'd really* **taken** *tremendous* **pains**. □ to take pains over sth is to be painstaking about it.

take one's time (over) [Vn.pr pass] (*informal*) not be in a hurry (to do sth), do (sth) at a leisurely pace. **o:** meal, drink; bath; getting ready to leave, finishing one's work: *I* **took my time over** *this book, with the result that I was able to shape it exactly as I wanted it.* AH ○ *'You* **took your time** *coming back from Vienna, Middleton,' said Sir Edgar gruffly* (cf *'You* **took your time over** *the journey'*). ASA ○

Much too much **time** *was* **taken over** *sorting out a very simple problem.*

take over (from) [Vp, Vp.pr pass rel, Vp.n pass, Vn.p.pr pass rel] assume the direction or control of sth (in place of sb else). **S:** (new, younger) man; pilot, skipper; specialist, expert; runner, car. **O:** management, direction; controls, helm; case, inquiry; lead, first place. **o:** (retiring) director; crew member; assistant; competitor: [Vp] *Some fellow has suddenly been taken ill, and I've got to* **take over**. WI ○ [Vp.pr] *Prissie was saying that she could* **take over** *very well* **from** *Nurse Ellen.* DC ○ [Vp.n] *My father was asked to* **take over** *the London office of his newspaper.* SD ○ [Vn.p.pr] *30 Corps had now* **taken over** *the lead* **from** *10 Corps.* MFM

take over (to) [Vn ⇆ p pass, Vn.p.pr pass] lead (sb) or carry (sth) to a place in another part of a large town etc, or across intervening water. **O:** family; passenger, fare; goods. **o:** one's parents' house; park, swimming pool, shops; island, mainland: *I was thinking of* **taking** *the children* **over to** *my mother's this weekend.* ○ *Prissie has* **taken** *them* **over to** *Harrods to shop.* DC ○ *'Ask the boatman what he charges to* **take** *passengers* **over to** *the island.'* ⇨ go over (to).

take round [Vn ⇆ p pass, Vn.pr pass] conduct (sb) on a tour of (a place). **O:** visitor; delegate, customer. **o:** building; college, factory: *When you arrive inside the gate an official guide is waiting to* **take** *you* **round**. ○ *The Press Secretary is* **taking** *a Chinese delegation* **round** *the University this afternoon.* ⇨ go round 2.

take the hat round [Vn ⇆ p pass] (*informal*) collect money, eg at work, for sb who is sick etc: *Union leaders appealed from the platform for contributions to the strike fund and a couple of stewards* **took the hat round**. = pass the hat round.

take round (with) [Vn ⇆ p pass, Vn.p.pr pass] ⇨ take around/round (with).

take through [Vn.pr pass] read (sth) with (sb), repeat it to him, so that its accuracy can be checked; (theatre) help (sb) to rehearse a scene etc. **S:** detective, official; director. **o:** story, statement; argument; scene, text: *'Now, I'll just* **take** *you* **through** *your application for benefit, to check the details, and then you can sign at the bottom.'* ○ *'I want to* **take** *you* **through** *your scene with Sheila again. There are one or two things that are not quite right.'* ⇨ go through 5.

take to 1 [Vpr] go away to (a place), esp to escape from an enemy. **S:** population; townspeople, villagers; guerrillas. **o:** hills, mountains; woods, forests: *He was Caodist Chief of Staff, but he's* **taken to** *the hills to fight both sides, the French and the Communists.* QA ○ *As the enemy advance continued, whole families would* **take to** *the forests carrying all their belongings.*
2 [Vpr] move towards and enter (sth). **o:** boat, car; the beach, sea: *When after tea the other guests* **took to** *their cars to leave, John Major stayed on.* OBS ○ *Families are* **taking to** *the water for bathing, boating, sailing, skin-diving in larger numbers than ever.* OBS
3 [Vpr] adopt (sth) as a habit, practice, pastime etc. **o:** drink(ing), drugs, smoking (a pipe); interrupting, waving one's hands; golf, bowls: *Some men would go off their heads. Others'd* **take to** *drink. My form of escapism is to roar at politicians.* TBC ○ *As Harold became more an acquaintance, almost a stranger, Isabel* **took to** *noticing him more.* PW
4 [Vpr pass] form a liking for (sb/sth). **o:** newcomer, visitor; place, house. **A:** right away; quickly, instantly: *It was embarrassing if the mother did not* **take to** *you. It looked as though it were your fault.* AITC ○ *I* **took to** *him immediately.* SML ○ *As Robert had reached the age of forty-four without getting married, it was obvious that he was not the sort of man who* **takes to** *matrimony like a duck to water.* SML ↔ take against.

take to (one's) bed [Vpr] go to bed, esp to recover from an illness: *Half the children in the class had* **taken to their beds** *with streaming colds.* ○ *If everybody with a disordered metabolism* **took to bed** *it would never do.* AH

take to bits/pieces [Vn.pr pass] reduce (a complex machine etc) to its parts. **O:** car; motor, gearbox, dynamo; radio, television; clock: *The gas-fitter* **took** *the stove* **to pieces** *before Virginia had a chance to cook supper.* AITC ○ *He's* **taken** *the television* **to bits**. *The question is: can he put it together again?* = take apart 1.

take to one's bosom [Vn.pr pass] (*jocular*) draw (sb) affectionately to oneself; embrace. **O:** (the) poor, needy, homeless: *Did he cherish wart-hogs and dote on hyenas, did he* **take** *the skunk* **to his bosom**? AH ○ *His Italian listeners were* **taken to his bosom**, *and their hearts beat with his.* SD

take to court [Vn.pr pass] (*legal*) begin legal proceedings against (sb) leading to a court action. **O:** dealer, tradesman; case: *If you have agreed specifications with the builder which he fails to carry out, you can* **take** *him* **to court**. TO ○ *'You can* **take** *me* **to court** *if you want to. There's nothing in writing.'* DM

take exception to [Vn.pr pass pass(o) emph rel] be much offended by (sth). **adj:** grave, serious, strong. **o:** remark, statement; smear, innuendo; accusation, charge; his being present: *This remarkable gift made us nickname her Dormouse, a name that she* **took** *grave* **exception to**, *but which nevertheless stuck.* DF ○ *We in Obaig* **take** *strong* **exception to** *the attack on Mr Mackay made by your anonymous correspondent.* RM ○ *The strongest* **exception** *is* **taken to** *the suggestion that our actions were politically motivated.*

take a fancy to [Vn.pr pass(o)] (*informal*) form a liking for (sb/sth), be attracted by (sb/sth). **adj:** big, great; decided. **o:** girl, man; house, ornament, car: *'I met this young man in the train, and I've* **taken a** *big* **fancy to** *him already.'* HD ○ *There's this new kind of pocket computer game that I've rather* **taken a fancy to**.

take to heart [Vn.pr pass] be greatly affected in one's feelings by (sth). **O:** disappointment, setback, loss; things; it, everything. **A:** very much, too much, so: *'Come now, we have been through much together. Do not* **take** *a little incident so much* **to heart**.' ARG ○ *'Have I upset you? . . . Don't* **take** *it* **to heart** *so, love.'* AITC

take to one's heart [Vn.pr pass] (*informal*) give a warm, enthusiastic reception to (sb); show affection for. **S:** crowd, audience; staff, membership. **O:** actor, comedian; (new) director, leader: *It was when the candidate began to talk about local problems, in language that the farmers could understand, that they* **took** *him* **to their hearts**. ○

The public, bless them, **took** *me* **to their hearts**, *right from the first.* HD

take to one's heels [Vpr] run away; flee. **S:** (shy, nervous) child, girl; animal: *Then I doubled back into Welbeck Street and* **took to my heels**. UTN ○ *A few of the antelope caught our scent, and in a matter of seconds the whole herd had* **taken to their heels**.

take to one side [Vn.pr pass] ⇨ take aside/to one side.

take a shine to [Vn.pr] (*informal*) come to like (sb), be attracted to (sb). **o:** stranger, visitor; girl, fellow: *In prison, a likeable rascal called Sammy* **took a shine to** *him.* DS

take to task [Vn.pr pass] criticize, reprimand (sb) for an error, failure etc. **O:** colleague, assistant; child, pupil: *We were sure that the gate had been left unlocked. We would* **take** *the night-watchman* **to task** *over it.* ○ *The Minister was* **taken** *severely* **to task** *about her decision to close two rural hospitals.*

take under one's wing [Vn.pr pass] behave protectively towards (sb), act as his patron or mentor. **S:** (older, more experienced) teacher, worker, sportsman. **O:** trainee, newcomer, novice: *The Bannions were resident in Portugal and had evidently* **taken** *the Marchants* **under their wing**. ILIH ○ *He took care to bring Ned into the conversation a good deal. But here he ran into another problem; Ned didn't need to be* **taken under anybody's wing**. CON ○ *He was* **taken under the** *diplomatic* **wing of** *the Swedish Embassy in Baghdad.* T

take up 1 [Vn ⇆ p pass] lift, raise (sth). **O:** pen, book; carpet, floorboard: *The electricians had to* **take up** *the skirting board to lay new electric wires.* ○ *She was expecting that Brigit, like the young man in the Bible, would* **take up** *her bed and walk.* DC

2 [Vn ⇆ p pass] absorb (sth). **S:** sponge, flannel; blotting-paper. **O:** liquid; milk, ink: *The cloth is saturated: it can't* **take up** *any more of the liquid.* = soak up 1.

3 [Vp.n pass] adopt (sth) as a pastime. **O:** gardening, golf, stamp-collecting: *I should have* **taken up** *singing—everybody used to tell me so.* TOH ○ *Why not* **take up** *some outdoor sport as a relaxation from office work?*

4 [Vp.n pass] start (a job), begin (work). **O:** office; work, employment; one's duties: *He effectively left showbusiness, in the early Thirties . . . and he* **took up** *various business ventures.* OBS ○ *Charley threw up his job to* **take up** *more respectable, more sensible employment.* BFA

5 [Vn ⇆ p pass] adopt (sb) as a protégé; patronize. **S:** impresario, actor-manager, conductor. **O:** (promising, young) singer, actor, soloist: *A young actor will find it hard to make his way on the London stage unless he is exceptionally talented or has someone established to* **take** *him* **up**.

6 [Vp.n pass] adopt (an attitude etc). **S:** speaker, writer, academic. **O:** attitude, position; line (of reasoning, of argument): *He always* **takes up** *this tough stance whenever anybody mentions reorganization.* ○ *'Sit back and I'll talk you out of any position you've decided to* **take up**.' CON

7 [Vn ⇆ p pass] add one's voice to (sth); join in. **O:** song, chant; chorus, refrain: *It was Pop who started the song, and everyone* **took** *it* **up** *in shrill voices.* DBM ○ *Someone started to sing 'For he's a jolly good fellow,' and the chorus was* **taken up** *by all the others.* PE

8 [Vp.n pass] continue a story which has been interrupted, or left unfinished by someone else. **O:** tale, story; (narrative) thread: *He* **takes up** *the tale at the outbreak of war in 1939.* NM ○ *We were back at our posts again and Ned was* **taking up** *the thread. Even Randall was listening.* CON = pick up 15.

9 [Vn ⇆ p pass] raise, mention (a topic) in order to consider or discuss it. **O:** question, matter, issue, point: *Much in the story has interesting parallels to the present time. I shall not* **take** *these* **up**, *however.* SNP ○ *There are one or two points of detail that should be* **taken up** *before we move on.*

10 [Vn.p pass] interrupt (sb) in order to disagree or criticize him. **A:** sharp(ly), short: *'I wonder if you'll find them likeable?' 'What's the difference?' he* **took** *me* **up** *sharply.* CON ○ *'Not hungry?' the old man* **took** *him* **up**. *'Are you ill or something?'* = pull up 2.

11 [Vn ⇆ p pass] occupy, fill (sth). **S:** desk, cupboard; work, study; question, matter. **O:** space, room; time, hours; attention: *'How can you move about in here? The bed* **takes up** *half the room.'* ○ *Some very important issue was* **taking up** *all his attention.* CON

12 [Vp nom, Vp.n nom pass] gather onto itself, by winding, a long thread or ribbon. **S:** spool, bobbin. **O:** thread; cotton, silk; (magnetic) tape, film: *The spool on my tape recorder isn't* **taking up** *very well: the tape's spiralling all over the floor.* ○ *The reel which* **takes up** *the film after it has been projected* (ie *the* **take-up** *reel*), *is below and behind the lamp.*

13 [Vp.n nom pass] apply for and receive (a cash benefit), esp from a government welfare department. **O:** rent allowance, free school dinners, low income support: *Poor families simply don't* **take up** *all they're entitled to.* ○ *Apart from free school meals . . .* **take-up** *of listed benefits is persistently and disappointingly low. Rent allowances have particularly poor* **take-up**. ECON

take up the challenge [Vp.n pass] accept a challenge. **S:** runner, boxer, golfer; industry, trade: *As one athlete after another* **took up the challenge** *of the front-runners, the pattern of the 5 000 metres race was constantly changing.* ○ *Some sections of the motor industry are complacent about the increase in foreign imports:* **the challenge** *is not being* **taken up**.

take up a position [Vp.n pass] (esp *military*) occupy ground suitable for defence, or from which an attack could be made. **S:** general; army, force: *The evening before the battle, Wellington* **took up a** *defensive* **position** *along, and just to the rear of, a long ridge.* ○ *'Now, while the fieldsmen are* **taking up their positions** *for the left-hander, I'll bring you up to date on the score-card.'*

take up residence [Vp.n] (*formal*) begin to live somewhere. **A:** overseas, in the country, at the palace: *For part of the year, the Queen* **takes up residence** *at Sandringham.* ○ *Snakes sometimes* **take up residence** *in the disused portions of the nest.* DF

take up the slack [Vp.n pass] (*industry*) make men and plant which are now idle or under-used active and productive again. **S:** industry; government, ministry; policy, decision: *Such a move would* ***take up the slack*** *which now exists in our economy.* BBCTV ○ *There's a good deal of* ***slack*** *to be* ***taken up*** *before we have reached full productive capacity.*

take up arms (against) [Vp.n, Vn.p.pr emph rel] go to war (with sb), begin to fight (against sb). **S:** nation, power; minority, peasantry. **o:** neighbour, invader; oppressor, tyrant: *The country would certainly* ***take up arms*** *in its own defence.* ○ *His people and the Emperor Charles would* ***take up arms against*** *him if he killed either the woman or her daughter.* WI

take up on [Vn.p.pr pass] (*informal*) get (sb) to prove or confirm sth which he has claimed or offered. **o:** it, that; claim, boast; offer: *'What's more I can drink as much beer as you.' 'I'll* ***take*** *you* ***up on*** *that.'* RATT ○ *The insurance company guarantees to replace any parts of the car which are stolen: you should* ***take*** *them* ***up on*** *their guarantee.*

take up with 1 [Vn.p.pr pass rel] raise (a matter), for critical comment, with the person(s) most involved or responsible. **O:** issue, question, matter, problem. **o:** authorities; manager, shopkeeper; official, teacher: *I* ***took*** *the matter* ***up*** *at once* ***with*** *M Coulet, and was informed that he had received no complaint.* MFM ○ *My son is being given too much homework; I shall have to* ***take*** *things* ***up with*** *his class-teacher.*

2 [Vp.pr] (*informal*) begin to keep company with (sb one should perhaps avoid). **o:** crank, half-wit; (disreputable) man, woman; gang, set: *His conventional parents were alarmed to find that he had* ***taken up with*** *a group of 'long-haired anarchists'.* ○ *She's* ***taken up with*** *a man old enough to be her father.*

taken up with [pass (Vn.p.pr)] occupied with (sth). **o:** discussion, debate; meeting; seminar, lecture: *The rest of the morning session was* ***taken up with*** *a row over procedure.*

take a (firm) grip/hold upon oneself [Vn.pr] ⇨ take a (firm) grip/hold on/upon oneself.

take liberties (with) [Vn.pr pass] behave in an over-familiar or presumptuous way (towards sb); handle too freely sth that belongs to, or has been made by, sb else. **adj:** such, many; (not) any, no; few; great. **o:** sb's sister, wife; one's friend, colleague; (original) work; text, score: *'Don't start* ***taking liberties with*** *my old mother, let's have a bit of respect.'* TC ○ *Cane rats would not hesitate to bury their large incisors in your hand if you tried to* ***take liberties with*** *them.* BB ○ *The film was a largely successful adaptation of the stage play, though there were times when one felt that the scriptwriter had* ***taken*** *too many* ***liberties with*** *the original text.*

take the rough with the smooth [Vn.pr pass] accept adversity along with good fortune: *If you want to enjoy the pleasure of living far from the maddening crowd* (ie far from cities) *you have to* ***take the rough with the smooth.*** RM ○ *She knew what the future would be like, and how different it would be from what she had hoped. She must learn to* ***take the rough with the smooth****, just like everybody else.* TGLY

take turns (with) [Vn.pr] share a task (with sb), working turn and turn about. **o:** (messy, unpleasant, tiring) job, chore; cleaning, washing; supervision, checking; keeping watch, steering: *We drove to the South of France in a day,* ***taking turns with*** *the driving.* ○ *Some working-class husbands will share the washing-up if their wives go out to work, or will* ***take turns with*** *the baby if their job releases them early and not too tired.* UL

talk

talk about 1 [Vpr pass adj rel] exchange thoughts about (sth); discuss. **o:** weather; trade, business; family: *He* ***talked*** *a great deal* ***about*** *these countries.* OBS ○ *He brought out a bottle of whisky, and began to* ***talk about*** *old times.* SPL ○ *The road-accident rate is a much* ***talked-about*** *topic; but how much good does talking do?* □ adj talked-about always preceded by *most, much, little* etc. = speak about, talk of 1.

2 [Vpr pass adj rel] discuss (sth) in an inquisitive, slightly shocked way. **S:** newspapers, gossip writers, fans. **o:** clothes, car; love life, affair: *'Why must she go about with that dreadful man? She's beginning to get herself* ***talked about****.'* ○ *What has made our new, candid series for adult readers the most* ***talked-about*** *event in Fleet Street?* □ adj talked-about always preceded by *most, much* etc.

3 [Vpr pass rel] propose or consider (possible action), though usu without acting in fact. **o:** going to live abroad, buying a larger house, decorating the kitchen: *'Of course, for years they'd* ***talked about*** *moving to the country, getting away from the stress of city life, but nothing ever came of it.'* = talk of 2.

4 [Vpr] (*informal*) an idiom which humorously reinforces or underlines a statement, either by exaggeration (first example) or by apparently denying what one has just said (second example): *At the first sign of trouble, my old headmaster used to haul boys into his study for a good caning —* ***talk about*** *a Reign of Terror* (ie he ruled through the fear of punishment)! ○ *First the Government promises to reduce prices, then it gives way to inflationary wage demands —* ***talk about*** *consistency* (ie the Government is not consistent)!

talk above/over sb's head [Vpr] (*informal*) talk of matters, or in a way, that others cannot understand. **S:** specialist, expert; lecturer, teacher: *'He really talked to us intelligibly ... he didn't* ***talk over our heads****.'* RT ○ *If only he had lived up to his philosophy of life, they would not have minded his* ***talking over their heads****.* HAA

talk around/round [Vpr pass] in conversation, avoid approaching (a subject) directly, eg through shyness, the wish to keep sth secret etc. **o:** subject, topic; issue, problem: *'With him, you never get a direct discussion of the thing that's bothering you. He'll always* ***talk around*** *it.'* ○ *'Don't try to put me off this time. I don't want to* ***talk round*** *the subject, I want to talk about it.'*

talk at [Vpr pass] (*informal*) address (sb) in a superior or pompous way. **S:** self-important bore, pompous ass: *'Don't* ***talk at*** *me, talk to me: you're not in the classroom now!'* ○ *There we were, being* *talked at for two solid hours by the great man, and quite unable to escape.*

talk back (to) [Vp, Vp.pr] answer, reply to (sb), esp in a questioning or critical way. **S:** audience, listener, student. **o:** speaker, director, teacher: *She **talked back** knowledgeably and with confidence, and they had to listen.* ○ *This weekly programme gives viewers the chance to **talk back to** producers on aspects of broadcasting that displease them.*

talk down [Vn.p pass] (*aeronautics*) bring (a plane) in to land by giving the pilot instructions over the radio. **S:** control tower, air traffic control. **O:** aircraft; pilot: *There is a particular need to **talk** aircraft **down** when visibility is poor or when several pilots are waiting to land.*

talk down (to) [Vp, Vp.pr pass] address (sb) as though he were a social or intellectual inferior; patronize. **S:** (office) manager, (shop) assistant, house agent; lecturer, teacher. **o:** customer, client; audience, class: *'Credit the child with some intelligence; try not to **talk down**.'* ○ *However poor their technical knowledge may be, adult students have a good deal of practical experience: they greatly resent being **talked down to**.*

talk-in [nom (Vp)] discussion, usu in a public place, or on radio or TV, of some important topical issue: *We sat through the Dimbleby* (a TV presenter) ***talk-in** on meat prices.* RT ○ *The marathon **talk-in** at no 10 Downing Street . . . finally broke up without agreement.* L ⇨ sit in.

talk into [Vn.pr pass] by talking, persuade (sb) to do sth. **O:** (prospective) buyer, member, recruit. **o:** selling, joining, signing on; membership, participation: *'I know you've got a smooth tongue, so don't even start to **talk** me **into** buying.'* ○ *He had better see the lawyer before anyone could say he had been **talked into** anything.* NM ↔ talk out of.

talk of 1 [Vpr pass adj rel] exchange thoughts about (sth); discuss. **o:** weather; business; crisis, disaster; this and that: *For weeks, the BBC's correspondents in the United States could **talk of** little else except the Gulf crisis.* ○ *At the time, he was very much **talked of** as a likely candidate for the Presidency.* = speak about, talk about 1.

2 [Vpr pass adj] consider or discuss (possible action), though usu without acting in fact. **o:** giving up one's job, emigrating to Canada, getting a divorce: *At one stage he **talked of** throwing up his job in advertising — but nothing much came of it.* ○ *Then there was the much **talked-of** plan to open a travel agency.* □ adj talked-of always preceded by *much, often, frequently* etc. = talk about 3.

talk one's/sb's head off [Vn.p] (*informal*) speak at great length; tire or irritate sb by speaking to him at great length: *'Don't expect me to sit here like a good boy while Smithers is up there **talking his** fat **head off**!'* ○ (a child is speaking) *'When me and Jeremy are by ourselves, he talks, he talks, he **talks my head off**.'* PW

talk out of [Vn.pr pass] by discussion, argument etc, persuade (sb) not to do (sth). **S:** adviser, agent; colleague; wife. **o:** buying, selling; resigning, leaving; (hasty) decision: *It's my own decision entirely. In fact, she's just been trying to **talk** me **out of** it.* LBA ○ *He's rather impulsive, but he can sometimes be **talked out of** making over-hasty moves.* ↔ talk into.

talk over sb's head [Vpr] ⇨ talk above/over sb's head.

talk over (with) [Vn.p pass, Vn.p.pr pass emph rel] discuss (sth) fully (with sb). **O:** things, the (whole) thing; matter, question; project, scheme: *I would suggest a line that you may care to consider and **talk over** at our next appointment.* RFW ○ *He **talked** things **over with** his wife* (or: *He and his wife **talked** things **over***). DS

talk round [Vn.p pass] persuade (sb) to do sth which he was at first opposed to. **O:** partner, colleague, associate: *He thought he could **talk** me **round** like last time, when he had me voting for some candidate who refused to stand.* ART ○ *He's not the easiest man to persuade; he'll need some **talking round**.*

talk through [Vn ⇆ p nom pass, Vn.pr pass] (*theatre, cinema, TV*) during rehearsal, guide (sb) through the movements he must make. **S:** director, floor manager. **O:** cast, actor. **o:** scene; bit: *'Stay on stage for a minute — I want to **talk** Jenny **through** her scene with Bill.'* ○ *After a few **talk-throughs**, a few rehearsals, she said, 'Let's make it an equal concert'* (ie one with two performers appearing together). BBCR

talk through (with) [Vn.p pass, Vn.p.pr pass emph rel] discuss (sth) thoroughly (with sb) until a conclusion is reached. **O:** plan, scheme; idea, proposal; problem, difficulty: *'All right, let's **talk** the various proposals **through**.'* ○ *'Try to **talk** things **through with** your husband first.'*

talk to 1 [Vpr pass rel] address (sb) to give or exchange news, gossip etc. **o:** friend, neighbour; oneself: *She always complains that there's nobody living near that she can **talk to**.* ○ *'I've called to **talk to** you about our latest product.'* ○ *Sarah is struggling to fill out an official form — she **talks** a lot **to** herself.* CSWB = speak to 1.

2 [Vpr pass] speak reproachfully to (sb); scold. **o:** child, pupil; tradesman, workman: *'There's something the matter with this television. I'll have to **talk to** the shop about it.'* ○ *'That child needs to be **talked to**, and you're the person to do it.'* ○ *He jumped from his chair, arms akimbo as though to deliver him a **talking-to**.* ASA □ note the nom form in: *give sb/get a (good)* talking-to. = speak to 3.

tally

tally (with) [Vpr emph rel] match (sth). **S:** figure, sum; account, version: *You'll be hard put to it to make this set of figures **tally with** that* (cf *make the two sets **tally***). ○ *'What you are now saying does not quite **tally with** your statement to the police officer.'* = correspond (to/with).

tamp

tamp down [Vn ⇆ p pass adj] drive (sth) down so that it is firmly packed, with repeated light blows. **O:** tobacco; packing, wadding: *Unless the tobacco is well **tamped down** in the pipe it will burn too quickly.*

tamper

tamper with [Vpr pass] handle (sth) which is not one's concern, so breaking or disturbing it. **o:** paper, document, letter; catch, lock, hinge; wiring, plumbing: *Don't let an untrained person **tamper with** the electrical circuits.* ○ *'You can see someone has tried to break into the flat; the lock's been **tampered with**.'*

tangle

tangle with [Vpr] (*informal*) come into conflict with (sb); be involved in a dispute with (sb). **S:** striker, demonstrator, marcher; consumer, customer. **o:** police, troops; supplier, manufacturer: *'Don't try and **tangle with** him — he's bigger and tougher than you are.'* ○ *This is not the first time he's **tangled with** the Gas Board over the size of his bills.*

tank

tank up [Vp, Vn ⇆ p pass adj] (*informal*) (make sb) drink a great deal of alcohol: *A couple of the fellows were already at the bar, **tanking up** on lager.* ○ *'Now don't for heaven's sake get me **tanked up**. Remember I've got to drive you home.'*

tap

tap (for) [Vn.pr pass] (*informal*) (try to) extract (sth) from (sb). **O:** friend, parent, employer. **o:** money; donation, loan; cost, capital: *I managed to **tap** Dad **for** a few pounds towards our holiday fund.* ○ *Congressmen by the dozen are demanding that Japan, Germany, Saudi Arabia... should be **tapped for** the costs of Desert Storm* (ie the Gulf war). ECON

tap in [Vn ⇆ p] enter (sth) in a machine by pressing keys etc. **O:** information; number, letter; code: *To withdraw cash, you put your bank card in the slot and **tap in** your personal number.* ○ *You have to **tap** the letters **in** in the right sequence.*

tap into [Vpr] obtain sth from (a source). **o:** source; resources, funds; data, information: *Dictionary-makers can now **tap into** computerized collections of texts for their examples.* ○ *As state support dries up, scientists are having to **tap into** private sector finance for research funding.*

tap off [Vn ⇆ p pass adj] draw (liquid) from a cask etc through a tap. **O:** beer, cider, wine; bottle(ful), jug(ful): *He keeps a barrel of the local red wine in his cellar and **taps off** a couple of bottles every day.*

tap (on) [Vpr emph rel] give a quick, sharp blow (on sth). **o:** door, window; shoulder, arm: *'Who's that **tapping on** the window?'* ○ *A policeman **tapped on** his shoulder* (or: ***tapped** him **on** the shoulder*).

tap out [Vn ⇆ p pass adj] produce a rhythmic succession of sounds with the fingers etc. **S:** signaller, telegraphist; drummer. **O:** message; beat, rhythm: *A trained signaller can **tap out** messages at great speed on the Morse key.*

taper

taper off 1 [Vp, Vn ⇆ p pass adj] (make sth) become narrower towards one end. **S** [Vp], **O** [Vn.p]: plank, batten, strut; boat, vehicle: *The stern of the vessel **tapers off** sharply.* ○ ***Taper** the plug **off** a bit with the chisel so that it will fit into the hole.*

2 [Vp, Vn ⇆ p pass adj] (allow or cause sth to) grow less intense, active, productive etc. **S** [Vp], **O** [Vn.p]: production, output; investment; unemployment: *There has been some **tapering off** in demand following the price increases.* ○ *Production of small vehicles was deliberately **tapered off** to allow for re-tooling of part of the works.* = tail off 1.

tart

tart up [Vn ⇆ p pass adj] (*informal*) make (a woman or a place) attractive in an obvious and vulgar way. **O:** oneself; appearance; cottage, pub; street: *'I didn't expect you to **tart** yourself **up*** (or: *get **tarted up***)*: we're going to an official reception, not a disco!'* ○ *Frank, John and Betty chat in the Cherry Tree Centre, a shopping precinct in Wallasey **tarted up** in pink and plastic so that it resembles a ropey ice-cream parlour.* OBS

taste

taste of [Vpr rel] have the flavour of (sth). **S:** soup, stew; pudding, pie. **o:** garlic, onion; vinegar: *The ice-cream **tasted of** soap. The plums were sour.* HD ○ *'The filling in the buns **tastes of** cream cheese.' 'It is cream cheese.'*

taunt

taunt (with) [Vn.pr pass emph rel] refer in a cruel and mocking way to (sth thought to be shameful) about (sb). **o:** cowardice, desertion; family background, illegitimacy: *Right-wing critics **taunted** him **with** his membership, earlier in life, of the Communist party.* ○ *Enemies on the Left **taunted** him **with** having become a safe, middle-aged liberal.*

teach

teach-in [nom (Vp)] teaching session consisting of contributions from experts and general discussion, and usu on a subject of topical interest or concern: *A **teach-in** on the food aid programme for Africa will be held in the Union on Wednesday next.* ○ *The Trust have organized a weekend **teach-in** on the preservation of the rural environment.* ⇨ sit-in, talk-in, work-in.

team

team up (together/with) [Vp, Vp.pr] join or form a group for a common purpose, eg business or leisure activities. **o:** relative, neighbour; singer, musician: *Very soon I found some other people to **team up with** and we began to write songs.* T ○ *John then **teamed up with** a boat builder* (cf *They **teamed up together***) *and began making cabin cruisers.*

tear

tear across, along away etc [Vp, Vpr] (*informal*) move across etc quickly, and with a sense of urgency: *'The next time you **tear across** the road like that you'll go under a bus!'* ○ *He discovered the scent of a skunk or racoon and went **tearing off**.* REC ○ *A sports car **tore past** without even bothering to signal that it was overtaking.*

tear across [Vn.p pass] divide (sth) into two by pulling sharply at both sides. **O:** paper, letter; circular, bill: *He was so furious with the tone of the letter that he **tore it across** and flung it in the fire.* ○ *The usherette in the cinema **tears** your ticket **across** and gives you back one half.*

tear apart 1 [Vn.p pass] dismantle (sth) using considerable force; completely disarrange (a place), esp when searching for sth. **O:** place; house, flat: *I cannot wait to get out before the workmen come and start **tearing** the place **apart**.* BM ○ *'I'll find the equipment even if we have to **tear** the whole house **apart**.'* = rip apart.

2 [Vn.p pass] divide (people) painfully; upset, disturb (sb) severely. **S:** strife, antagonisms; (religious, linguistic) differences; spectacle, experience (of suffering). **O:** state, society; (married) couple, onlooker: *The country was **torn apart** by fierce tribal hostilities.* ○ *Angela didn't think* *she could sit through the film again. It was so harrowing, it* **tore** *her* **apart***.*

tear at [Vpr pass emph rel] try to pull (sth) open, or pull (sth) to pieces, with the fingers etc. **o:** collar, jacket; fastening, catch; fruit, bread: *The irritation of his burns was so intense that Hugh kept* **tearing at** *the bandages.* ○ *Margaret* **tore** *hungrily* **at** *the grapes.*

tearaway [nom (Vp)] (*informal*) impetuous, reckless and sometimes violent young person: *'The people round here think that every kid on a motorbike is a* **tearaway***. But only one or two youngsters are ever in trouble with the police.'* ○ *Bus conductors have complained of* **tearaways** *getting on late at night and terrorizing the other passengers.*

tear away (from) [Vn.p pass, Vn.p.pr pass rel] (*informal*) abandon or stop doing (sth) with great unwillingness; make (sb) leave (sth) despite his reluctance to do so. **O:** oneself; child. **o:** work, pleasures; book, toy; meal; companion: *I found the programme so fascinating that I couldn't* **tear** *myself* **away** *— even to finish an urgent letter.* ○ *'If you could* **tear** *Patrick* **away from** *his game perhaps we could all go out for a drive.'*

tear away/off 1 [Vn ⇆ p pass] remove (sth) (from a surface) by pulling sharply. **O:** wallpaper, curtain; plaster; pocket, label: *You could* **tear away** *some of the panelling with your fingers — it was so badly eaten by woodworm.* ○ *'You must have caught the pocket of your coat on a nail: it's nearly* **torn off***.'*

2 [Vn ⇆ p pass] take away (the covering) from sb/ sth. **O:** front, facade; mask (of pretence), cloak, veil (of secrecy): *If you* **tore away** *the smooth façade he puts on for everybody, you wouldn't find much underneath.* ○ **Tear off** *the rhetorical top-dressing from his speech and you'll find there's very little solid substance.*

torn between [pass (Vn.pr)] mentally or emotionally divided (by conflicting thoughts, feelings, etc). **o:** (two, several) aims, purposes; opposing impulses, emotions: *You are* **torn between** *two tendencies — your wish to indulge your personal fancies, while at the same time keeping within your resources.* WI

tear down [Vn ⇆ p pass adj] bring (sth) to the ground by pulling etc; demolish. **O:** fence, barrier; wall, house: *Streets of terrace houses were* **torn down** *to make way for blocks of flats.* ○ *A heavy lorry skidded across the fast lane of the motorway and* **tore down** *a section of the crash barrier on the central reservation.* = pull down 2, rip down.

tear in half/two [Vn.pr pass] divide (sth) into two parts by pulling sharply. **O:** ticket, coupon; letter; coat: *The ticket-collector* **tore** *my ticket* **in two** *and handed back the return half.* ○ *Nick emerged from the fight with his shirt* **torn** *nearly* **in half***.* = rip in half/two.

tear into 1 [Vpr pass] make a hole in (sth) with a strong, tearing movement. **S:** saw; bulldozer. **o:** plank; bank, hill-side: *Explosive shells* **tore into** *the walls of the strong point.* ○ *The dog was half starved. He positively* **tore into** *the dish of meat.* = rip into.

2 [Vpr] make a vigorous attack, physical or verbal, on (sb/ sth). **S:** boxer, fighter; critic: *Joe* **tore into** *his opponent with fists flailing.* ○ *That night on television she* **tore into** *her critics with unconcealed venom.*

tear off 1 [Vn ⇆ p pass, Vn.pr pass] remove (a garment) with urgent movements. **O:** coat, shirt: *The policeman* **tore off** *his jacket and plunged into the river.*

2 [Vn ⇆ p pass] write or draw (sth) rapidly. **O:** note, letter; sketch: *He* **tore off** *a letter to his family while waiting in the airport lounge.* ○ *'Don't give me something you've* **torn off** *in an odd moment: I want a carefully considered plan.'* = dash off.

3 [Vn ⇆ p pass] remove (sth) (from a surface). ⇨ tear away/off 1.

4 [Vn ⇆ p pass] take away (the covering). ⇨ tear away/off 2.

tear sb off a strip; tear a strip/strips off sb [Vp.n pass, Vn.pr pass] (*informal*) reproach, admonish (sb) severely. **S:** boss; foreman, supervisor; sergeant; father. **O/o:** workman; soldier; son: *Why did she feel frightened of Anna, as if the other was going to start* **tearing a strip off** *Jenny's family* (or: **tearing** *them* **off a strip***)?* TGLY ○ *'You've been a long time with the boss. Hasn't been* **tearing** *you* **off a strip***, has he* (or: **tearing a strip off** *you)?'* RATT □ the passive forms are: [Vn.p] *He was* **torn off a strip***.* ○ [Vn.pr] ***A strip*** *was/****Strips*** *were* **torn off** *him*; or: *He had* ***a strip/strips torn off*** *him.*

tear out/out of [Vn ⇆ p pass adj, Vn.pr pass rel] remove, separate (sth) by pulling sharply. **O:** page, sheet; picture, diagram. **o:** book, magazine: *He scribbled the address down in his notebook,* **tore** *the page* **out***, and handed it to me.* ○ *Her bedroom walls were decorated with pictures* **torn out of** *colour magazines.* = rip out/out of.

tear to pieces/ribbons/shreds 1 [Vn.pr pass] reduce, destroy (sth) by strong or violent physical action. **O:** paper, letter, magazine; cloth, garment: *Slowly and deliberately he* **tore** *her letter* **to pieces***.* ○ *It was the same terrain over which the original Panzers had* **torn** *the Polish cavalry* **to ribbons** *four and a half years before.* B ○ *Material passed through this machine is* **torn to shreds** *by a set of powerful blades.* = tear up 1.

2 [Vn.pr pass] (*informal*) destroy, demolish (sth/ sb) by critical argument. **S:** teacher, tutor, critic. **O:** essay, thesis; argument, case; colleague, individual: *She had reached the point where she couldn't face having another piece of work* **torn to pieces** *by her tutor.* ○ *Two people were discussing someone they mutually knew. ... Then it dawned on me that I knew the person they were* **tearing to shreds***.* RT

tear up 1 [Vn ⇆ p pass adj] destroy (sth) by pulling across it sharply. **O:** letter, bill, ticket: *'Did you mean me to keep the receipt? I'm afraid I've* **torn** *it* **up***.'* ○ *'Daddy hasn't got your letter at all. I have. I took it and* **tore** *it* **up***.'* DC = rip up 1, tear to pieces/ shreds 1.

2 [Vn ⇆ p pass adj] remove (sth) by breaking and raising it. **O:** tarmac; road, runway; railway lines; garden, park: *Men were* **tearing up** *the road surface with pneumatic drills.* ○ *Railway lines have been* **torn up***.* T

3 [Vn ⇆ p pass] vigorously renounce (sth); abandon. **S:** state; employer, trades union. **O:** treaty, agreement: *The other side doesn't regard such agreements as binding: they can be* **torn up** *at will.* = rip up 2.

tease

tease out [Vn ⇆ p pass] reveal (sth) in a slow, careful and subtle way. **O:** meaning, sense; idea, thought; nuance: *She . . . has a daring quality, constantly **teasing out** new and startling thoughts.* HA

tee

tee off [Vp nom] (*golf*) drive the ball from the tee — the point from which a stage of the game begins: *The first player **teed off** into a strong cross-wind.*

tee up 1 [Vp, Vn ⇆ p pass adj] (*golf, football* etc) settle (the ball) in a good position before striking it: *Golfers usually **tee** the ball **up** on a small wooden or plastic peg before driving off.* ○ (discussion following a football match) *'You don't have time to **tee** the ball **up** and then hit it.'* BBCTV **2** [Vn ⇆ p pass adj] (*informal*) arrange, organize (sth). **O:** (sales) drive, campaign; (military) offensive; things, the (whole) thing: *While this reinforcement was moving to the left flank, we **teed up** the blitz attack which was to go in when it arrived.* MFM ○ *'Now is everything properly **teed up** for your trip to Holland?'*

teem

teem down [Vp] (of rain) fall very heavily. **S:** ⚠ the rain; it: *It was **teeming down**, and we took shelter in a shop entrance.* = pour down.

teem in [Vpr] be present in large numbers in (a place). **S:** wild life; fish, insects, bacteria; idea, image. **o:** forest, stream; head, brain: *Grubs and insects **teem in** the rich soil around the roots of the tree* (or: *The soil **teems with** grubs* etc). ○ *Ideas for new plays and short stories **teemed in** his head* (or: *His head **teemed with** ideas* etc). □ simple tenses are used with teem in; simple and continuous tenses with teem with.

teem with [Vpr rel] ⇨ previous entry

telescope

telescope (into) [Vn.pr pass emph rel] simplify or shorten (sth) so that it fits a limited time or space. **S:** lecturer; author, editor; speaker. **O:** course, syllabus; (series of) lectures, books; reflections. **o:** five days, half a term; single volume; brief interview: *The publishers have **telescoped** the dictionary **into** a paperback edition suitable for college students.* ○ *He had a lot to explain, and no time for more than a short meeting. Thus a lengthy briefing had to be **telescoped into** a half-hour presentation.*

tell

tell about [Vn.pr pass] give (sb) information concerning (sb/sth). **O:** wife, husband, family; reporter, interviewer; audience. **o:** success, loss; incident, occurrence; experience: *'There's something I've not **told** you **about** yet. I can't find the air tickets!'* ○ *'I could see the driver of the lorry was in difficulties.' 'Right. **Tell** us **about** that.'*

tell against [Vpr] prevent (sb) from achieving success; hinder, hamper. **S:** (one's own) height, weight; youth; inexperience, immaturity. **o:** him etc; survival, success: *He's a very brave, aggressive player, but his weight is bound to **tell against** him in a game against a heavy pack of forwards.* ○ *Martin tends to act impulsively, without consulting people higher up. That'll **tell against** him in a firm where they play everything by the rule-book.* = weigh against.

tell apart [Vn.p] (be able to) distinguish between (two similar persons or things). **O:** twins, (two) brothers; animals, birds; buildings; programmes, courses: *Every day is identical with the one before. I literally can't **tell** them **apart*** (or: *I literally can't **tell** one **from** the other*). HAHA ○ *Even when greatly magnified, the two organisms are difficult to **tell apart**.* □ with can/could. ⇨ tell from, ⇨ next entry

tell the difference (between) [Vn.pr] (be able to) distinguish between two similar persons or things. **o:** (two) people, animals; butter and margarine, burgundy and claret; one performance and another: *The twins' mother reminded me that Stephen had the darker hair, but for the life of me I still couldn't **tell the difference between** them.* ○ *'How can I **tell the difference between** Scotch* (ie Scotch whisky) *and Bourbon?'* OMIH □ with can/could. ⇨ tell from, ⇨ previous entry

tell (by/from) [Vpr emph rel Vn.pr emph rel] judge or deduce (sth) by watching, listening etc. **O:** (probable) result, outcome; reaction; that he's an honest man, how far they can be trusted. **o:** look, expression; remark, comment; listening, taking note: *You can **tell** just **from** looking at him that he's nobody's fool.* ○ *'He'll make enemies in this department.' 'How can you **tell**?' 'Oh, just **by** listening to what people say.'* ○ ***From** monitoring the radio traffic you could **tell** that heavy reinforcements were moving up behind the enemy lines.* □ with can/could.

tell from [Vn.pr] (be able to) distinguish (one person/thing) from another, which may be similar to, or different from, the first. **O:** truth; order, democracy; male, older (one). **o:** lying; anarchy, tyranny; female, younger (one): *I was less capable than Dominguez of **telling** truth **from** falsehood.* QA ○ *On the beach she could hardly **tell** him **from** the other fathers.* PW □ with can/could. ⇨ tell apart, tell the difference (between).

tell sb where he gets off/where to get off [Vp] ⇨ entry after get off 7.

tell off (for) [Vn ⇆ p pass, Vn.p.pr pass] (*informal*) reproach, reprimand (sb) (for sth he has done). **O:** employee; pupil; child, husband. **o:** being late, leaving work undone, making a fool of oneself; negligence, slovenliness: *I was ten minutes late and she **told** me **off** in front of everyone.* H ○ *That child needs a darned good **telling-off**.* ○ *He didn't like being **told off for** something he hadn't done.* □ nom form is telling(s)-off. = tick off 2.

tell on [Vpr] (*informal*) (esp among children) report (sb) for sth he has done wrong. **S:** brother, sister; form monitor; sneak, toady: *'I won't ever do it again. I swear. Please don't **tell on** me!'* RATT = split (on).

tell on/upon [Vpr emph rel] have an effect on the health or condition of (sb/sth). **S:** strain, tension; overwork, long hours; responsibility. **o:** health, nerves, temper: *He's looking distinctly run down. All those late nights are beginning to **tell on** him.* ○ *Hard driving over bad roads will soon **tell upon** the suspension of the car.*

temper

temper with [Vn.pr pass emph rel] (*formal*) modify or soften (an action etc) by doing (sth which contrasts with it). **O:** severity, harshness, rigour (of an action, mood). **o:** mercy, compassion, humour:

The academic rigour of his lectures is fortunately ***tempered with*** *wit.* ○ ***With*** *these few concessions to the tax-payer the government hopes to* ***temper*** *the bleakness of its new measures.*

tempt

tempt into [Vn.pr pass] (try to) persuade (sb) to (a certain course). **O:** rival, opponent, competitor. **o:** (making) a false move, (taking) the wrong decision: *By varying his pace and spin, the bowler tried to* ***tempt*** *Smith* ***into*** *an over-hasty stroke.* ○ *This was a course of action he was not* ***tempted into*** *following.*

tend

tend towards [Vpr rel] be inclined to favour (a certain policy). **S:** industry, retail trade, building; government, management. **o:** what is safe, conventional, profitable; (newer, different) form, framework: *As far as supermarkets are concerned, we are* ***tending towards*** *much larger units, usually on the edge of towns.* ○ *New private housing still* ***tends towards*** *the traditional. Few buyers want anything really unusual.*

tender

tender (for) [Vpr pass rel] (*industry, commerce*) make a formal offer to do work, or supply goods, at a stated price. **S:** contractor, supplier. **o:** construction, building, erection (of sth); supply, furnishing (of sth): *Several major firms are known to have* ***tendered for*** *the construction of the new airport.* ○ *Offers have been invited, but the work has not yet been* ***tendered for***.

tense

tense up [Vp, Vn ⇆ p pass adj] (*informal*) (cause sb's muscles to) become strained or stiff; (cause sb to) become nervous. **S** [Vp], **O** [Vn.p]**:** athlete, footballer; traveller; examinee: *A runner exercises before a race to prevent his muscles from* ***tensing up***. ○ *He dislikes oral exams most of all: they always* ***tense*** *him* ***up***. ○ *She is never* ***tensed up*** *or nervous before a big event.* H ⇨ keyed up.

terrify

terrify into [Vn.pr pass] drive (sb) through fear (to do sth). **S:** tyrant, bully; prospect, likelihood (of failure, of disaster). **o:** surrender, submission; giving way, granting sb's demands: *The thought that the children might be in danger had* ***terrified*** *her* ***into*** *handing over the safe keys.* ○ *Let's not be* ***terrified into*** *hasty action — their threats are probably a bluff.* = frighten into.

test

test out [Vn ⇆ p pass adj] find, by experiment or practical use, whether sth is sound or effective. **O:** idea, theory; process, mechanism; machine, device: *Now that he had a post as scientific adviser to the Air Ministry, James would be able to* ***test out*** *his theories under the stress of war.* ○ *'We're not ready to go into production yet. The new switch mechanism isn't fully* ***tested out***.*'*

testify

testify (to) [Vpr pass emph rel] (*formal*) give evidence (of sth). **o:** truth, reliability, genuineness; ability, talent; good character, sound moral qualities: *'I would be prepared to* ***testify to*** *the reliability of the witness* (cf ***testify*** *that he is reliable).'* ○ *Experts have* ***testified to*** *the machine's excellent performance at extremes of heat and cold.* = bear witness to.

thank

thank (for) [Vn.pr pass emph rel] express gratitude to sb (for sth). **O:** participant, helper, donor. **o:** help, co-operation; gift, subscription: *'I should like to* ***thank*** *all of you* ***for*** *your support at a difficult time.'* ○ *He's been* ***thanked*** *enough* ***for*** *an action that was, after all, in his own interests.*

thaw

thaw out 1 [Vp, Vn ⇆ p pass adj] (cause sth to) become warm, liquid or soft. **S** [Vp], **O** [Vn.p]**:** (frozen, icy) hand, foot; (frozen) chicken, vegetables: *'Just give me a minute to take my wet clothes off and* ***thaw out*** *— then we can talk.'* ○ *Deep-frozen meat or poultry needs to be* ***thawed out***, *preferably overnight, before it is cooked.*
2 [Vp, Vn ⇆ p pass adj] (*informal*) (help sb to) become more relaxed or friendly. **S** [Vp], **O** [Vn.p]**:** official, dignitary; (stern) father, teacher: *'Let's all sit down,' said Isabel, 'if Daddy's thoroughly* ***thawed out***.*'* PW ○ *'Offer the visitor a drink. That will* ***thaw*** *him* ***out***.*'*

theorize

theorize (about) [Vpr pass emph rel] discuss (sth) in theory, as opposed to practice; construct theories in an attempt to explain (sth). **o:** construction, development (of motorways, of railways); language, human development, the nature of living matter: *'We can't just* ***theorize about*** *a better transport system: circumstances force us to make some hard practical decisions.'* ○ *Linguists* ***theorize about*** *the relationship between the structure of language and the ways in which language is used.*

thin

thin down [Vn ⇆ p pass adj] make (a liquid) less dense. **S:** decorator; turpentine, water. **O:** paint; emulsion: *You can apply the emulsion in one thick coat, or* ***thin*** *it* ***down*** *with water and put on two coats.*

thin out [Vp, Vn ⇆ p pass adj] (cause sth/sb to) become fewer or more thinly spread, over an area. **S** [Vp], **O** [Vn.p]**:** hair; crop; crowd, traffic. **S** [Vn.p]**:** age, disease: *The traffic had* ***thinned out*** *by then — we were out of London.* CON ○ *Periodic major floods had* ***thinned out*** *the rural population.*

think

think about 1 [Vpr] consider in one's mind (a past event etc); contemplate. **o:** childhood, schooldays; holiday, work; (sb's) kindness, generosity: *I was just* ***thinking about*** *the time when old Fred fell into the river.* ○ *'What are you* ***thinking about****?' 'Oh, nothing in particular.'* □ usu continuous tenses.
2 [Vpr pass rel] consider or examine (sth) to see whether one should take action. **o:** offer, proposal; plan, scheme; resigning, moving: *I'm interested in buying your house, but I'd like more time to* ***think about*** *it before making a decision.* ○ *He'd* ***thought about*** *selling up and emigrating at one stage.* ○ *This is something that needs to be* ***thought about*** *very carefully.* = think of 2.

(not) think twice (about) [Vpr] (not) pause for long or careful reflection before (doing sth). **o:** informing, betraying, recommending (sb); selling, acquiring (sth): *'There's no need for you to* ***think***

***twice about** it, is there? There's nothing for you if you don't take the offer.'* RATT ○ *The day after Martin's piece of persuasion I did what, at any previous time, I should **not** have **thought twice about**.* NM ○ *'I'd **think twice about** entrusting my savings to that company.'*

what do you think (about sth)? [Vn.pr] what is your opinion (on sth)?, how do you react (to sth)?. **o:** statement, declaration; decision; action, move: *'You've heard that he's offered his resignation? Now, **what do you think about** that?'* ○ *I don't know **what to think about** their decision to close the school.* □ direct and indirect questions only.

think ahead (to) [Vp, Vp.pr] cast one's mind forward (to an event); anticipate. **A:** five weeks, ten hours; far, a long way. **o:** (possible, probable) outcome, consequence, result; event, contingency: *I carried out certain movements which were, at the time, merely precautions, ie, I was **thinking ahead**.* MFM ○ *In this business it's wise tactics to **think** some way **ahead**.* ○ *We're already **thinking ahead to** our next move.*

think back (to) [Vp, Vp.pr] recall and reconsider (sth in the past). **A:** a long way, some way. **o:** remark, statement; occurrence; change, development; time, moment: *'Do you remember when we first met?' 'That's **thinking back** a long way.'* ○ *I **thought back** a few years **to** the last occasion when the issue was discussed.*

think of 1 [Vpr pass] consider, weigh (sth). **o:** (likely, probable) effect, outcome; cost, expense; wife, family; oneself: *He's a wonderful organizer: he **thinks of** everything!* ○ *We'd like to go to Portugal this summer, but **think of** the cost!* ○ *He never **thinks of** anyone but himself.* ○ *'That sounds a good idea, but have all the possible snags been **thought of**?'* □ usu with the simple tenses.

2 [Vpr] consider or examine (sth) to see if one should take action. **o:** travelling, visiting; asking, inviting; trip, holiday: *'Margot, are you **thinking of** marrying Jim?'* H ○ *They were **thinking of** calling for a final bottle of champagne, when there came a new and disconcerting blow.* OBS ○ *'Why don't we buy that flat in town?' 'Oh, I was **thinking of** a little place in the country.'* □ often with the continuous tenses; object is often the -ing form of a v. = think about 2.

3 [Vpr] call (sth) to mind; recall. **o:** name, address; date, time. **A:** at the moment, at this precise/exact moment: *'I can't **think of** his name, but he was a tall chap with glasses.'* □ with *can(not)*.

4 [Vpr pass] propose, suggest (sth); invent, devise (sth). **o:** name, title; scheme, project: *We're still trying to **think of** a suitable title for the book.* ○ *'**Think of** a number, double it, and add your age.'* ○ *'I know the prospect is a little bleak at the moment, but don't worry, we'll **think of** something.'* □ not usu with the continuous tenses. = think up.

5 [Vpr pass adj rel, Vn.pr pass(o) rel] have a certain opinion of (sb/sth), regard (sb/sth) in a particular way. **A** [Vpr]**:** well, highly. **O** [Vn.pr]**:** a great deal; the world, (very) little, not much. **o:** colleague, associate; work, achievement; writing, poetry; design, craftsmanship: *I know my dear brother doesn't **think** so highly **of** me.* ASA ○ *He's well **thought of** in government circles.* ○ *In Wales we **think** a great deal **of** our bards.* PW ○ *'I know you don't **think** much **of** him, although you've hung around him for ages, but I **think** the world **of** him.'* AITC □ simple tenses only.

think better of [Vn.pr pass(o)] reconsider (a possible action) and decide not to take it. **o:** it; action, step; intervention; interfering, interrupting: *Whatever retort Dr Bottwink was about to make, he **thought better of it**.* EM ○ *He'd clearly **thought better of** intervening in a situation which was already highly charged.*

never/not think of [Vpr] not allow (a particular idea) as a possibility; not entertain. **o:** allowing, permitting; interfering; giving way: *'Why don't you let me pay for the meal?' 'I would**n't think of** it!'* ○ *He'd **never think of** letting the boy decide for himself.* □ with could/would.

think nothing of [Vn.pr] not regard (sth) as important, significant or unusual. **o:** friendship, affair, connection; working all night, walking twenty miles: *Some would have thought these large transfers of money highly suspicious, but at least his colleagues **thought nothing of** it.* ○ *During training, these athletes **think nothing of** running eighty miles a week.*

think nothing of it [Vn.pr] a politely reassuring remark to sb who feels he has behaved rudely: *'I'm sorry if I interrupted your meal.' 'Oh, that's all right. **Think nothing of it**.'* ○ *'**Think nothing of it**,' he said, when Virginia apologized for keeping him out of his bed.* AITC □ always imperative form.

think out 1 [Vn ⇆ p pass adj] plan (sth) carefully, stage by stage. **O:** scheme, project; play, novel; things, the (whole) thing: *A work* (of art) *may have been **thought out** in the medium or be a translation from a painting or a drawing.* G ○ *Mother and I had bought the dress together on one of our well-**thought-out** expeditions to the West End stores.* THH □ adj thought-out always preceded by *well, carefully, badly* etc. = work out 1. ⇨ think over.

2 [Vn ⇆ p pass] understand or perceive (sth) by thinking carefully. **O:** answer, solution; future: *There is little opportunity to **think out** what the long-term solution may be.* NS

think over [Vn.p pass adj] review (past events) in one's mind; consider carefully sth that may affect the future. **O:** events, happening; things, it all; offer, suggestion: *With the beginning of a new day he had to **think** things **over** again, reconsider his position, see where he was now.* PE ○ *She had **thought** the plan **over**; it was important that he would think it had been his idea.* H ⇨ think out 1.

think through [Vn ⇆ p pass] consider (sth) very carefully, taking account of all difficulties or obstacles. **O:** problem, question; project, scheme; proposal; the whole thing: *I'm grateful for your offer, but I shall need a day or two to **think** it **through**.* ○ *The whole scheme needs to be **thought through** very carefully before we agree to back it.*

think up [Vn ⇆ p pass adj] invent, devise (sth). **O:** idea, scheme, plan; story, tale; excuse, apology: *There were one or two fellows who **thought up** ideas of their own.* CON ○ *He would have to **think up** some more catchy names for these designs.* HD ○ *He offered some quickly **thought-up** pretext for not coming to the meeting.* = think of 4.

thirst

thirst for [Vpr rel] (usu *jocular*) desire (sth) strongly. **o:** chance, occasion; revenge, vengeance; knowledge, adventure: *He was surrounded by savages* **thirsting for** *his blood.* PE ○ *I suppose these army recruiting ads are designed to appeal to young men* **thirsting for** *adventure.* = long for.

thrash

thrash about 1 [Vpr] move about, stir, in an agitated, restless way; stir water etc violently with one's limbs: *Stephen was* **thrashing about** *in bed with a high temperature.* ○ *We left the children* **thrashing about** *happily in the shallow end of the pool.*

2 [Vp] act in a nervous, restless way, often without aim or success: *Alan was getting all worked up over his maths homework,* **thrashing about** *for an answer to a perfectly simple problem.*

thrash out [Vn ⇆ p pass adj] remove or solve (sth) by thorough discussion; find (a solution) in this way. **O:** difficulty, obstacle; problem, issue; answer, solution: *He was worried enough to call a meeting at the Windsor Hotel to* **thrash** *the problem* **out**. OBS ○ *The top level should now be brought in to* **thrash out** *the whole business.* MFM ○ *We can leave the second part to them, and lastly we can* **thrash out** *our conclusions.* TBC

thread

thread one's way through [Vn.p, Vn.pr rel] move with difficulty, and in an indirect way, through (sth). **o:** crowd, throng; trees, undergrowth: *I* **threaded my way through** *the crowd with the dog at my heels.* UTN

thrive

thrive on [Vpr emph rel] grow strong or prosper by taking or using sth. **S:** child, animal; business, industry. **o:** milk, eggs; competition, hard work: *He* **throve on** *a pure meat diet for some time.* DF ○ *This is the kind of routine* **on** *which the children seem to* **thrive**. ○ *'Say something nice to Muriel. She* **thrives on** *compliments.'*

throttle

throttle down 1 [Vp, Vn ⇆ p pass] make (a vehicle) move more slowly by supplying less petrol to the engine. **O:** engine; car: *'***Throttle down** *a bit on these sharp bends — the tail of the car is swinging out.'*

2 [Vp, Vn ⇆ p pass] reduce the rate of development of (an economy etc). **O:** economy; growth, development, expansion: *It is absurd that the United States should be compelled to* **throttle down** *economic growth.* T

throw

throw one's money about/around [Vn.p] (*informal*) spend (money) in a reckless and conspicuous way: *The pub is full of a Saturday night crowd who enjoy* **throwing their money about**. ○ *Sailors tend to* **throw their money around** *on their first night ashore.*

throw one's weight about [Vn.p] (*informal*) behave in an arrogant, overbearing way so that others are made to feel small and unimportant: *'You come in here,* **throwing your weight about** *as though you were the big boss himself.'* ○ *Tell him not to* **throw his weight about** *when he starts his new job. He can sit back quietly and pick up a few ideas from the others.*

throw around/round 1 [Vn.pr pass emph rel] put (a barrier) around (sth), to control movement in and out. **S:** police, army. **O:** cordon; ring (of troops, armour). **o:** area, zone, city: *The state government has* **thrown** *a cordon* **around** *the stricken area to contain the spread of the epidemic.* ○ *A tight security ring was* **thrown round** *those parts of Southern England where invasion troops were concentrated.*

2 [Vn.p pass, Vn.pr pass] mention (a word etc) frequently and casually in conversation. **O:** word, term, expression; name: *The term 'war' was being thrown around loosely.* IND

throw (at) [Vn.pr pass] direct (a missile) (at sth or sb) with a sharp movement of the arm. **O:** stone, brick, mud. **o:** window, car; police: *'He had a brick* **thrown at** *him at that meeting. He's got concussion.'* UTN

throw the book (of rules) at [Vn.pr pass] (*informal*) remind (sb) forcefully of the correct procedure to be followed in some task, and perhaps punish him for not following it. **S:** officer, superintendent, foreman. **o:** pilot, constable, worker: *'If you spend more than £200 on that account again without referring the matter to me, I'll* **throw the book at** *you.'* ○ *'I know I'm* **throwing the book of rules at** *you, as you call it, but, believe me, you're never going to be happy without it. I tried throwing it away all these months, but I know now it just doesn't work.'* LBA

throw oneself at [Vn.pr] (*informal*) (usu of a woman) make over eager advances to (sb). **o:** (any, every) man, the first man one meets: *'You couldn't wait, could you? You had to* **throw yourself at** *the first man you met, didn't you?'* TOH

throw away 1 [Vn ⇆ p nom pass] get rid of (sth); discard. **o:** carton, can, box, packet; ticket, receipt: *Beer is now often sold in* **throw-away** *cans* (ie *cans that can be* **thrown away**). ○ *Don't* **throw** *your bus ticket* **away** *— the inspector may want to see it.* □ throw-away is used attrib, as shown; note also: *. . . the instant,* **throw-away** *fashion styles which dominated the sixties.* G

2 [Vn ⇆ p pass adj] let (sth) slip, by foolishness or neglect; lose. **O:** lead, advantage; match, game; life, career: *The visiting team built up an impressive lead in the first half, then* **threw** *it* **away** *by loose defensive play in the second.* ○ *More was loyal to him* (ie Henry VIII)*, and incorruptible, but he surely was worldly enough not to* **throw** *his life* **away** *for nothing.* WI = give away 4.

3 [Vn ⇆ p nom pass] (*theatre, broadcasting*) speak (sth) casually, under-emphasize it, for deliberate effect. **O:** ⚠ a line; a word, remark: *'Something special is usually made of those lines. But don't play them up —* **throw** *them* **away**.*'* ○ *The minister replied with a neat* **throw-away** *remark which made his interviewer smile in admiration.* □ nom form is often attrib: throw-away *line* etc.

throw away on [Vn.p.pr pass rel] waste (sth/oneself) in foolish ventures, on undeserving people etc. **O:** money; capital, investment; oneself, one's life. **o:** (wild, madcap) scheme, project; (unsuitable, unworthy) partner, lover: *'Think carefully. You may be* **throwing** *your savings* **away on** *shares* *that will be worthless in a few years.'* ○ *Mrs Knighton thought that Isabel had* **thrown** *herself* **away on** *Harold.* PW ○ *Any advice you might give is clearly* **thrown away on** *Bill.*

throw back 1 [Vn ⇆ p pass] return (sth) with a sharp movement of the arm or wrist. **o:** ball; book, magazine; box, packet: *The official* **threw** *the bundle of papers* **back** *across the desk. 'Everything seems in order,' he said.* ○ *The ball was* **thrown back** *underarm to the bowler.*
2 [Vn ⇆ p pass] raise or pull aside (sth) with a sharp movement. **O:** bedclothes, bedspread; hangings, curtain: *She sat up in bed and* **threw back** *the bedclothes.* DC ○ *The curtains were* **thrown back** *to reveal a small boy cowering by the french windows.*
3 [Vn ⇆ p pass] swallow (sth) quickly. **O:** drink; whisky, gin; medicine: *Patrick* **threw back** *his half of bitter and asked the barman for another.* = knock back 1, toss off 1.
4 [Vn ⇆ p pass] repulse, repel (sb/sth) vigorously. **O:** enemy; infantry, armour; assault, attack: *The attackers were* **thrown back** *in a series of fierce engagements.* ⇨ beat off.
5 [Vn ⇆ p pass] reflect (light etc). **S:** screen, wall, pavement. **O:** light, dazzle, glare; heat: *The white-washed walls* **threw back** *the intense midday heat.*
6 [Vn.p nom pass] remind (sb) strikingly of an earlier event, occasion etc. **A:** several years, to one's childhood, to an earlier period: *Meeting Bob* **threw** *me* **back** *ten years to the time of my first job in London.* ○ *Some of the clothes young people are wearing seem to be a* **throw-back** *to Victorian styles.* □ a throw-back is a thing that recalls earlier events etc. = carry back (to), take back (to).

throw-back [nom (Vn.p)] person who recalls physically, or in his character, a generation earlier than his parents: *'Well, I suppose there's a* **throw-back** *in every family.'* DBM

throw one's head back [Vn ⇆ p pass] move one's head back sharply, esp when laughing, crying out etc: *When I told Bill how Martha had fallen flat on her backside, he just* **threw his head back** *and roared.* □ passive usu follows *with*: *She stood with her head* **thrown back**.

throw back at [Vn.p.pr pass] (*informal*) remind (sb) reproachfully of sth he has done or said, esp after he has been shown to be wrong. **O:** past record, previous history; loyalty, connection, affiliation; belief, conviction: *'Why should you of all people* **throw** *my decisions* **back at** *me? You agreed with me at the time.'* ○ *Now that things are not going so well, Peter is sure to have all his earlier slips and blunders* **thrown back at** *him.* = throw in sb's face.

throw back on [Vn.p.pr pass] force (sb) to use or resort to (sth) as a defence or support. **S:** change, shift (in events); (sb's) attitude, reaction. **o:** defence, excuse; stratagem, device; one's own resources: *The failure of this policy* **threw** *the party leaders* **back on** *various schemes which had been canvassed earlier.* ○ *John secretly enjoyed a situation in which he was* **thrown back on** *his own reserves of shrewdness and stamina.*

throw down the gauntlet [Vp.n pass] issue a challenge. **S:** enemy, rival; contender (for a championship): *The champion will soon have to defend his title again — a young South American contender has* **thrown down the gauntlet**.

throw in 1 [Vp.n pass] (*informal*) include (sth) as a free or unexpected extra. **O:** carpets, furniture; (cost of) fitting, installing; (musical) encore; (theatrical) act, turn: *'If you're set on buying the house, we'll* **throw in** *the carpets and curtains at no extra cost.'* ○ *There was all that, and Barbara impersonating her mother* **thrown in**. ILIH
2 (*informal*) abandon, resign (a job). **O:** post, job; directorship: *She took a job as a delivery van driver but* **threw** *it* **in** *after six months.* = throw up 1.

throw (the ball) in [Vn.p nom pass] (*football*) put the ball back into play after it has crossed the touch-line: *'And it's Parker to* **throw the ball in** (or: *to take the* **throw-in**) *near the corner flag.'* ○ *The linesman has given the* **throw-in** *to Leeds.*

throw in sb's face [Vn.pr pass] remind (sb) reproachfully or insultingly of sth he is or has done, esp when it seems to explain sth that is now going wrong. **O:** (past) action, decision; friend, associate; family background: *'The last thing I want to do is to* **throw** *a man's past* **in his face** *unless he's a double-dyed villain.'* DS ○ *'My education, which you* **throw in my face**, *was an education along humane lines that didn't leave me with any illusions about the division of human beings into classes.'* HD = throw back at.

throw one's hand in 1 [Vn ⇆ p] (*cards*) withdraw from a game : *After a run of bad cards, James decided he had lost enough money and* **threw in his hand**.
2 [Vn ⇆ p] (*informal*) abandon, give up, sth in which one is engaged: *'I warned you. I told you I was* **throwing my hand in**. *Now didn't I?'* TOH

throw in the sponge/towel 1 [Vp.n] (*boxing*) acknowledge defeat (by throwing a towel into the ring): *After Fred had been knocked to the floor twice for a count of eight, we decided he'd had enough, and* **threw in the towel**.
2 [Vp.n] (*informal*) abandon the struggle; admit defeat: *'I know you've been going through a tough time, but it's a bit early to* **throw in the towel** *yet, isn't it?'*

throw in one's lot with [Vn.p.pr rel] become a supporter, ally, partner etc, of (sb). **o:** government, opposition; Labour, the Conservatives; trader, dealer; venture, expedition: *After years in the political wilderness, Stephens has* **thrown in his lot with** *the new party leadership.* ○ *He was hoping to convey the impression that he had been encouraged to* **throw in his lot with** *Bunder, and was hesitating.* HD

throw in/into [Vn ⇆ p pass, Vn.pr pass emph rel] insert (a remark etc) into the course of (sth). **O:** remark, comment, suggestion. **o:** conversation, discussion, debate: *'Could I just* **throw in** *the reminder that all these arrangements must be firmly tied up by next week?'* ○ *'He could never take these formal meetings seriously — always* **throwing** *some outrageous comment* **into** *the proceedings.'*

throw into confusion/disarray/disorder [Vn.pr pass emph rel] confuse or disorganize (sth/sb) by sudden or violent action. **S:** (sudden) arrival, appearance; announcement, statement; change, development. **O:** place; office, department; staff; plan, scheme: *The unexpected change of plans* **threw** *everyone* **into confusion**. ○ *Our arrange-*

ments were **thrown into** *complete* **disarray** *by that interfering fool from head office.*

throw oneself into [Vn.pr rel] undertake (a task) with enthusiasm. **A:** vigorously, wholeheartedly, enthusiastically. **o:** work, job; arrangements, organization; rebuilding the department, developing the sales force: *She tried again to* **throw herself** *with a will* **into** *life.* PW ○ *The Bafutians had obviously* **thrown themselves** *wholeheartedly* **into** *the task.* BB

throw into relief [Vn.pr pass] through contrast, make (sth) appear sharp and clear. **S:** light; colour; background, setting. **O:** shape, form; carving, moulding; house; tree: *Skilfully placed lights* **throw** *the marble figures* **into** *clear* **relief**. ○ *The roofs of the city are* **thrown into** *sharp* **relief** *against the evening sky.* ○ *Details of private behaviour are* **thrown into** *high* **relief** *against backgrounds of doom and disaster.* AH

throw off 1 [Vn ⇆ p pass] remove (sth) with a quick movement. **O:** clothes; coat, scarf, hat: *He* **threw off** *his shirt and trousers and plunged into the cool water.*

2 [Vp.n pass] get rid of (sth which prevents others from seeing one as one really is). **O:** mask, disguise; manner, pretence: *I wish he'd* **throw off** *the long-suffering look and be a bit more cheerful and outgoing.*

3 [Vp.n pass] get rid of (sb who, or sth which, troubles or irritates one). **O:** pursuer; tout, beggar; cold, 'flu: *The visitor has to* **throw off** *the swarm of guides and hotel touts who cluster round the station entrance.* ○ *'I can't manage the meeting tonight. I'm still trying to* **throw off** *this wretched cold.'*

4 [Vp.n pass] compose (sth) quickly and without effort. **O:** poem, satire, epigram: *The two men sat down over a bottle of wine and* **threw off** *a few songs and sketches for the evening's concert.* = knock off 4, toss off 2.

throw off (his) balance [Vn.pr pass] make (sb) lose his mental composure; upset, disturb. **S:** news, announcement; realization, awareness (of sth); shock: *The news that someone else had been given the job* **threw** *him momentarily* **off balance**. ○ *Not even the shock of passing his final examinations had upset Grimsdyke. But Nikki seemed to* **throw** *him* **off his** *psychological* **balance**. DIL

throw off the scent/the track [Vn.pr pass] do sth that will prevent (a pursuer) from following one. **S:** fugitive; (escaped) convict, prisoner. **O:** pursuer; police, troops: *The gang broke up into four groups in the hope of* **throwing** *the police* **off the track**.

throw light on [Vn.pr pass emph rel] help to explain or clarify (sth); illuminate. **S:** discovery, findings; research, investigation. **adj:** no, (not) any/much; a lot of, little; fresh, new. **o:** problem, question; mystery, puzzle, riddle: *The real importance of the* (Dead Sea) *Scrolls lies in the* **light** *they* **throw on** *Palestinian history.* OBS ○ *The fresh* **light** *which modern archaeology is* **throwing on** *the shadowy figures of St Columba and St Ninian . . . is the subject of two articles.* SC ○ *Hugo's inquiries rarely failed to* **throw** *an extraordinary amount of* **light on** *whatever he concerned himself with.* UTN = shed light on.

throw doubt/suspicion on/upon [Vn.pr pass rel] make sb doubtful or suspicious of (sb/sth). **S:** counsel, witness; evidence, testimony; report, article: *The reference* **threw** *considerable* **doubt on** *his claim to be widely experienced in the field.* ○ *The enquiry* **threw suspicion upon** *two crime squad officers.*

throw oneself on/upon sb's mercy [Vn.pr] beg for kind or lenient treatment from sb. **S:** captive, prisoner; accused: *The accused was clearly guilty; all he could now do was* **throw himself upon the mercy of** *the court.*

throw out 1 [Vn ⇆ p nom pass] get rid of (sth) because it is no longer useful; discard. **O:** old clothes; book, toy: *There are some bundles of old magazines here that I want to* **throw out**. ○ *Not all your* **throw-outs** *are useless rubbish. The metal, paper and glass may be useful scrap.*

2 [Vn ⇆ p pass] reject, dismiss (sth). **S:** council, committee, board. **O:** bill; amendment; proposal, suggestion: *A proposal to extend the urban motorway into the city centre was* **thrown out** *in committee.* ○ *The idea was put up to the Faculty Board, but they* **threw** *it* **out**.

3 [Vp.n pass] (*military*) extend one's position by moving (men) to a flank; deepen it by placing (men) in front. **O:** wing, screen, line: *The commander* **threw out** *a thin screen of motorized troops to protect his exposed flank.* ○ *In Wellington's time a line of sharpshooters was usually* **thrown out** *in front of the main defensive position.*

4 [Vp.n pass] express (sth) in an indirect, tentative or casual way. **O:** threat, (dark) hint; suggestion; (possible) solution, answer: *When last I spoke to him, he was* **throwing out** *heavy hints of a financial crisis.* ○ *I wasn't offering a positive answer. All I was doing was* **throwing out** *a few suggestions as to how we might proceed.*

5 [Vp.n pass] be a source of (heat); radiate. **S:** sun; fire, radiator. **O:** heat, warmth: *The new gas central heating is very effective — it* **throws out** *a lot of heat.*

6 [Vn.p pass] cause (sb) to make an error in sth. **O:** student, pupil; scientist, research worker; result, sum: *'Go and play your guitar somewhere else. I've nearly got this sum right, and I don't want you to* **throw** *me* **out**.*'* ○ *A tiny variation in temperature can* **throw** *us* **out** *in our results.* ○ *It* **throws** *their calculations totally* **out**. BBCTV = put out 12.

throw out/out of [Vn.p pass, Vn.pr pass] (*informal*) remove (sb) by force; dismiss, expel. **O:** intruder, trespasser; drunk, troublemaker. **o:** park, gardens; club, pub: *'Now that you know why I'm here, am I to be allowed to stay or are you going to* **throw** *me* **out**?*'* TBC ○ *'You know that Bill got* **thrown out of** *university for failing his exams?'* = kick out/out of.

throw the baby out with the bath water [Vn.p.pr pass] when getting rid of sth undesirable or unpleasant also reject sth of real value: *We must be careful not to* **throw the baby out with the bath water**. *Out task now is to control technology, not to turn away from it.* ST ○ *The Government wants to reduce unemployment but, if it raises inflation in doing so, it will be* **throwing the baby out with the bath water**.

throw overboard [Vn.p pass] (*informal*) abandon, reject (sth). **O:** rule, regulation; principle, standard; procedure, protocol: *We were* **throwing over-**

board the principle of concentration of effort. MFM ○ *Nobody knows how to proceed in these discussions — the book of rules seems to have been* ***thrown overboard****.*

throw round [Vn.pr pass emph rel] ⇨ throw around/round.

throw together 1 [Vn ⇆ p pass] assemble (things) roughly or hurriedly. **O:** clothes, books; ingredients; brick, plank: *'Give me five minutes to* ***throw*** *a few clothes* ***together****, then we'll be off.'* ○ *They'd* ***thrown together*** *a few planks and bits of canvas to form a rough shelter.*

2 [Vn ⇆ p pass] compile or compose (sth) roughly or hurriedly. **O:** essay, exercise; meal: *It was a dreadful essay, just* ***thrown together*** *with no real thought or preparation.*

3 [Vn.p pass] cause (people) to meet: *A newspaper assignment in Rome in the late 60s* ***threw*** *us* ***together****.* ○ *Bogart and Bacall were* ***thrown together*** *during the filming of a Howard Hawkes movie.* □ usu passive.

throw up 1 [Vn ⇆ p pass] (*informal*) abandon, resign (a post). **O:** job, post; (military) commission; assignment: *Charley had enough sense to* ***throw up*** *his job at the tax inspector's office.* BFA ○ *She had planned to do a management course but since then she had* ***thrown*** *it* ***up****.* THH = throw in 2.

2 [Vp, Vn ⇆ p pass] (*informal*) vomit (one's food). **O:** meal; food: *Robert gorged like a man driven insane by hunger. I was afraid he'd* ***throw*** *it all* ***up*** *over the table-cloth, but he didn't.* CON ○ *'How horribly servile and ingratiating that man is. He makes me want to* ***throw up****!'* = bring up 6, heave up.

3 [Vp.n pass] build (sth) hastily, and perhaps shoddily. **O:** house, dwelling, block of flats: *Speculative builders* ***threw up*** *terraces of cheap dwellings around the main railway terminals.*

4 [Vp.n pass] produce the appearance or development of (sb). **S:** country, district; generation; movement, organization. **O:** leader, organizer; inventor, artist: *I was anxious the Unions should grow naturally; this policy would ensure that the right leaders would be* ***thrown up*** *gradually.* MFM ○ *Not every generation* ***throws up*** *a composer of his remarkable gifts.*

throw up one's hands [Vp.n] express surprise or disapproval, sometimes, though not necessarily, by suddenly raising one's hands in front of one's body: *Jim reacted to the news of Geoff's appointment by* ***throwing up his hands*** *in horror.* ○ *Sarah* ***threw up her hands*** *in astonishment. 'Do you mean you've agreed to pay them all this money?' she said.*

throw oneself upon sb's mercy [Vn.pr] ⇨ throw oneself on/upon sb's mercy.

thrust

thrust across, along, away etc [Vn ⇆ p pass, Vn.pr pass] move (sth) across etc suddenly and forcefully. **O:** parcel, box; plate, cup; knife, sword; hand: *With an impatient gesture he* ***thrust*** *the food* ***away*** *from him.* ○ *With his hands* ***thrust*** *deep* ***into*** *his pockets, he walked restlessly about the room.*

thrust at [Vpr rel, Vn.pr pass rel] aim or direct (oneself/sth) at (sb) by moving forward suddenly and forcefully. **O:** oneself; finger, hand; stick, sword; paper, parcel: *'Please don't* ***thrust at*** *me with that umbrella* (or: ***thrust*** *that umbrella* ***at*** *me); it's bad for my nerves.'* ○ *He had a printed form* ***thrust*** *at* ***him*** *by an unpleasant official.*

thrust upon [Vn.pr pass rel] oblige or force (sb) to accept or undertake (sth). **O:** oneself; (one's) presence, company; (extra) work, duties; visitor, guest: *It was clear she was trying to* ***thrust*** *herself* ***upon*** *him: her attentions were too insistent to mean anything else.* ○ *I hope it hasn't put your housekeeper out having three extra guests suddenly* ***thrust upon*** *her.* WI

thud

thud into [Vpr] strike and partially enter (sth), with a dull sound. **S:** fist; bullet, arrow, knife. **o:** body; wall, door; parapet, embankment: *Shell fragments* ***thudded into*** *the earth piled in front of their trench.*

thumb

thumb through [Vpr nom pass] scan (a book etc), turning the pages with a quick movement of the thumb. **o:** magazine, report; (pile of) photographs: *I was* ***thumbing through*** *an old copy of a colour supplement when a secretary came in to say that Mr Matthews was ready to see me.* ○ *He took down a standard textbook and had a quick* ***thumb-through*** *to get a general idea of the lay-out.* = flick through, leaf through.

thump

thump out (on) [Vn ⇆ p pass, Vn.p.pr pass rel] play (sth) by striking (an instrument) heavily. **O:** tune, rhythm; message. **o:** drum; table: *A man in the corner of the pub was* ***thumping out*** *a tune* ***on*** *an old piano.* = bang out (on), beat out (on), hammer out (on).

thunder

thunder across, along, away etc [Vp, Vpr rel] move across etc with a heavy, continuous rumbling noise. **S:** train, engine; aircraft; lorry, cart: *The London express* ***thundered across*** *an iron bridge.* ○ *A flight of jet fighters* ***thundered past****.*

thunder against [Vpr pass rel] (*formal* or *jocular*) speak in a loud and fierce voice to criticize or condemn (sth). **S:** preacher; church; politician. **o:** sin, vice; excess, laxity, corruption: *A back-bench MP* ***thundered against*** *what he regarded as extravagant spending on the social services.*

tick

tick away [Vp] make light, regularly repeated sounds, so indicating the passage of time. **S:** clock, watch; meter; bomb: *A grandfather clock* ***ticked*** *solemnly* ***away*** *in the hall.* ○ *The taxi driver had left his meter* ***ticking away*** *while I dashed into the house. When I emerged there was an extra pound to pay.*

tick away/by [Vp] pass, go by, esp to the sound of a clock or watch. **S:** hour, minute, second: *The minutes* ***ticked away*** *interminably. How much longer would we be held up at the frontier?* ○ *Half his life had* ***ticked by*** *with little happening to disturb its even course.*

tick off 1 [Vn ⇆ p pass] put a small mark against (sth written down), to show that sth has been dealt with, sb is present etc. **S:** clerk, storekeeper; receptionist, housekeeper. **O:** item, article; entry; name: *'You can **tick** Sarah's name **off**. She's just arrived.'* ○ *Those two jobs can be **ticked off**. I've already done them.* = cross off.

2 [Vn ⇆ p pass adj] (*informal*) rebuke, reprimand (sb). **S:** boss; parent; commander. **O:** employee; child; subordinate: *If I went too fast again, I was quite prepared to be sent for and **ticked off**.* MFM ○ *The Captain gave me a hell of a **ticking-off** for firing at all.* RFW □ nom form is ticking(s)-off. = tell off (for).

tick over 1 [Vp nom] (of an internal-combustion engine) turn relatively slowly, eg before the gears are engaged and the vehicle moves off. **S:** engine, motor; car, lorry: *Buses and taxis **tick over** rather noisily* (or: *have a rather noisy **tick-over***). ○ *If an engine **ticks over** too slowly or too fast an adjustment must be made to the carburettor.*

2 [Vp] (*informal*) live or function quietly, without achieving much success or making great progress. **S:** pupil, worker; shop, industry, department: *'How is business?' Isabel asked. 'Oh, not too bad, just **ticking over**.'* PW ○ *'How are you **ticking over** these days? How is the big bad world treating you?'* THH

tickle

tickle to death [Vn.pr pass] (*informal*) greatly please or amuse (sb). **S:** news, announcement; story, joke; it ... to see, to hear, to realize sth: *It **tickled** me **to death** to hear how his wife had locked him out all night to sober him up.* ○ *First he's in despair because she comes back, and now he's miserable because she's gone away. He should be **tickled to death** and yet he isn't.* PW

tide

tide over [Vn.p, Vn.pr] (*informal*) help (sb) to live through or manage (a difficult period). **S:** loan, grant, allowance; (temporary, part-time) work; lodging, flat. **o:** year, month; crisis, bad time; illness, convalescence: *'Give me something, just to **tide** me **over** till I can get a decent, steady job,' said Robert.* CON ○ *Sarah could have found work other than nursing, to **tide** them **over** the years till the children could support themselves.* WI

tidy

tidy away [Vn ⇆ p pass] put (sth) away, eg in a drawer or cupboard, so that a room etc appears neat and orderly. **O:** book, letter, paper; toy; clothes: *'Do **tidy** your papers **away**; your desk looks in a terrible mess.'* ○ *It was difficult to tell that anyone had stayed at the cottage. Plates, cups, knives and forks had been carefully **tidied away**.*

tidy out [Vn ⇆ p pass] remove things from (a place), so making it neat and orderly. **O:** drawer; desk, cupboard: *The boys spend part of the last day of term **tidying out** their desks and handing in their books.*

tidy up [Vp nom, Vn ⇆ p nom pass adj] make (sth/sb/oneself) neat. **O:** room, office; desk; oneself; child: *Rebecca got rather tired of constantly **tidying up** after the children.* ○ *We need to **tidy** the place **up** a bit* (or: *give the place a bit of a **tidy-up***) *before the guests start arriving.* ○ *I ought to have found a wash-room and **tidied** myself **up**, perhaps even had a shower and a shampoo.* CON

tie

tie back [Vn ⇆ p pass adj] draw back (sth that is free or loose) and attach it in place with rope, string etc. **O:** hair; plant; vine, rose: *The girl had her long blonde hair **tied back** in a neat bun.* ○ *'**Tie** the gate **back** — it keeps banging to and fro in the wind.'*

tie down 1 [Vn ⇆ p pass adj] fix (sth) in a low position with string, cord etc. **O:** branch; hand, foot; awning, cover: *There was such a gale blowing that we had to **tie** the caravan **down** to prevent it overturning.*

2 [Vn.p pass] limit, restrict, sb's freedom of action or movement. **S:** family; work; debt, mortgage: *I'd like to take a job overseas, but there are too many things **tying** me **down** here.* ○ *They were the rebellious few, the vagabonds, who were not **tied down** by a wife and family.* AITC

3 [Vn ⇆ p pass] (*military*) occupy sb's attention, so that he finds it difficult to move. **S:** forces, troops; artillery, air force. **O:** reserves, reinforcements: *Partisans operating from the mountains were able to **tie down** three enemy divisions.* ○ *Armour coming up in support was **tied down** by air strikes.*

tie down to [Vn.p.pr pass rel] oblige (sb) to follow or conform to (sth). **O:** employee, client; company, firm. **o:** terms, conditions; contract, agreement; text, script: *During the candidate's election tour, his agent found it impossible to **tie** him **down to** the pre-arranged programme of visits.* ○ *John hates being **tied down to** a regular work schedule.* ⇨ tie down 2.

tie in with [Vp.pr, Vn.p.pr pass] (make sth) match or fit (sth). **S** [Vp.pr], **O** [Vn.p.pr]**:** statement, story; plan, project. **A:** well, badly; scarcely, fully. **o:** our version; the overall design, existing proposals: *This evidence **ties in** very well (**with** the picture which detectives have already built up).* ○ *'Blind drunk, did you say? That doesn't **tie in with** what I know of him.'* ○ *We managed to **tie in** our holiday arrangements **with** my work programme for the early summer.* = correspond (to/with).

tie on [Vn ⇆ p nom pass adj, Vn.pr pass rel] attach (sth) with string, cord etc. **O:** flag, pennant; label, badge; basket, bag. **o:** mast, pole; case, box; jacket; bicycle: *His shoes were **tied on** with old bits of string.* ○ *Use stick-on labels for your trunk and **tie-on** labels* (or: ***tie-ons***) *for your hand luggage.*

tie up 1 [Vn ⇆ p pass adj] fasten, bind (sth) together with string, cord etc. **O:** parcel, packet, bundle; sticks, twigs: ***Tie** the paintbrushes **up** into bundles and put them away carefully.*

2 [Vn ⇆ p pass adj] (*informal*) complete the organization of (sth). **O:** things, the (whole) thing; trip, visit; business, deal: *I like it when all the holiday arrangements can be **tied up** a month in advance.* ○ *'I'm glad I got that all **tied up**, Sarah. I never did like to see any ends sticking out, I always liked to finish things.'* WI □ usu passive. ⇨ tie up the loose ends.

3 [Vn ⇆ p pass] (*informal*) keep (sb) busy or occupied. **S:** work; accounts, calculations; social engagements: *'As far as I can tell, this editing will **tie** me **up** for the next fortnight.'* ○ *'I'm sorry, I* *shan't be able to get to your party after all. I'm a bit **tied up** at the moment.'* □ usu passive.

tie-up/tied up [nom pass (Vn.p)] (*informal*) connection, relationship; connected, related (to sth). **S** [pass]**:** firm, company; government; army, process, development; idea: *A good deal of British car manufacture is closely **tied up** with the continental industry* (cf *There is a close **tie-up** between the one and the other*). ○ *We can now look forward to a much closer **tie-up** between the educational systems of Western Europe.*

tie up the loose ends [Vp.n pass] finally settle (a matter), so that no unexplained or unresolved parts remain: *The motive which had brought her here was a desire to see **the loose ends** of her father's story satisfactorily **tied up**.* AITC ○ *'What happens now?' 'Oh, there are lots of **loose ends** to **tie up**.'* NM ⇨ tie up 2.

tie up (in) [Vn ⇆ p pass, Vn.p.pr pass rel] have (money etc) invested (in sth), so that it is hard to draw on it for other purposes. **O:** capital, savings, reserves. **o:** property; long-dated stocks: *It's unwise to **tie up** all your capital **in** one enterprise.* ○ *Most of the family money is **tied up in** land.*

tighten

tighten up [Vn ⇆ p pass] make (sth) more strict or effective. **S:** government, local authority; manager, commander. **O:** law, regulation; control; system: *He should be responsible for reorganizing and **tightening up** the local administrations.* SD ○ *Vitaly Fedovchuk … introduced a new law* (in Russia) ***tightening up** regulations on the importing of films and video.* LFM

tilt

tilt against/at windmills [Vpr rel] attack imaginary enemies, supposing them to be real ones: *Knowing when to proclaim victory, rather than continue to **tilt against windmills**, is a skill we have yet to master.* IND ○ *'So let us stop bickering within our ranks. Stop **tilting at windmills**. Stop talking of victories over our colleagues and concentrate instead on winning victories over the Tories.'* OBS

tinker

tinker (with) [Vpr pass] work (on sth) in a casual way, often for pleasure and sometimes with the effect of making matters worse. **o:** car; engine, suspension; watch; radio: *'Have a look at the engine if you like, but don't **tinker with** it. If something is really the matter I'd rather take the car to a garage.'* ○ *'No wonder the lights don't work — Harry's been **tinkering with** the switches.'*

tip

tip into [Vn.pr pass emph rel] by tilting or overturning a vessel, empty (its contents) into (sth). **O:** contents; salt, flour; sand; water; passenger. **o:** dish, bowl, bucket; river: *The cook **tipped** the reminder of the flour **into** a mixing-bowl and added two eggs.* ○ *A sudden gust of wind overturned the dinghy, **tipping** the crew and their gear **into** the water.* ↔ tip out/out of.

tip off [Vn ⇆ p nom pass] (*informal*) inform, warn (sb) that sth is about to happen, esp that a crime is going to be committed. **S:** (police) informer; spy, agent. **O:** police; customs, inland revenue; bank: *Mr Bevins denied that the Post Office had been **tipped off** that a raid on the train was planned.* G ○ *We'd been **tipped off*** (or: *been given a **tip-off***) *by London that a man of this name was believed to have arrived in Nairobi.* DS

tip out/out of [Vn ⇆ p pass, Vn.pr pass] by tilting or overturning a vessel, remove (its contents). **O:** clothes; flour, salt; seed, grains; passenger. **o:** suitcase; tin, bowl; bucket; boat: *Buckets rise on a long chain from the well, and the water is **tipped out** into irrigation channels.* ○ *The train stopped with a violent jerk, nearly **tipping** me **out of** my bunk.* ↔ tip into.

tip up [Vp, Vn ⇆ p nom pass adj] (cause sth to) turn upwards around a hinge or pivot; tilt. **S** [Vp], **O** [Vn.p]**:** seat, shelf, table: *If you press this catch, the bunks will **tip up** and fold back into the wall.* ○ *Many theatres and cinemas have seats that can be **tipped up*** (ie *have **tip-up** seats*).

tire

tire of [Vpr emph rel] no longer be interested in or attracted by (sth/sb). **A:** soon, quickly, never. **o:** experience, activity; (city, country) life; friend, lover; company, conversation; living alone, being flattered: *He never seems to **tire of** the sound of his own voice.* ○ *The things **of** which he **tires** least are good company, gardening and music.* □ cf the adjective tired of ('weary of', 'irritated with'): *He finally got **tired of** sitting in an office all day. He longed for a more active life.* = weary of.

tire out [Vn ⇆ p pass adj] exhaust (sb) physically or mentally. **S:** task; walk, climb; question, discussion; neighbour, relative. **O:** staff; traveller; student; oneself: *By midnight Janet was **tired out**, but there was no respite for anyone.* RFW ○ *I'm thinking about the future. I won't be **tiring** myself **out** dodging trouble.* JFTR = wear out 2.

toddle

toddle along/off [Vp] (*jocular*) leave, go away, esp after talking to friends, being at their house, etc: *'It's eleven o'clock, time I was **toddling along**.'* ○ *'There's not much else we can do now, is there?' 'No, that's right.' 'Don't you think we ought to **toddle along**?'* YAA

tog

togged out [Vn.p pass] (*informal*) dressed in unusual clothes, eg for a party: *Joe was **togged out** in his cowboy suit.* ○ *'Tell the kids to get **togged out** in their party clothes.'* □ used with *be, get*.

tog up [Vp, Vn.p pass] (*informal*) dress (sb/oneself), esp in formal clothes, for a reception, dinner etc: *'I don't want to go to the party if it means **togging up** in a dinner jacket.'* ○ *'Get **togged up** — we're going out to celebrate.'* □ note the passive with get.

toil

toil over [Vpr pass rel] work hard and continuously at (sth). **o:** task, chore; manuscript; corrections, accounts: *'I feel that I've been **toiling over** these exam scripts for weeks. There seems to be no end to them.'* = labour over.

tone

tone down [Vn ⇆ p pass adj] make (sth) appear milder or less extreme; moderate. **S:** author, critic;

reporter, commentator. **O:** account, story; description; view, opinion; adjective: *Ian Fleming had to* ***tone down*** *a few of my rather critical opinions.* DS ○ *The censor eventually accepted a* ***toned-down*** *version of my dispatch.*

tone in (with) [Vp, Vp.pr emph rel] match or combine well in colour (with sth). **S:** curtains, walls, door. **o:** carpet, ceiling, surrounding woodwork: *The roof was ... a kind of greyish colour that* ***toned in*** *well* ***with*** *the yellow sandstone.* PPAP = blend in (with).

tone up [Vn ⇆ p pass adj] make (sb/sth) more vigorous, lively, alert etc. **S:** exercise; walk, swim; shower-bath, dip (in the sea). **O:** him etc; body, system, muscle: *More exercise and a change of diet—that's what's needed to* ***tone*** *you* ***up****.* ○ *After a quick dip and a brisk rub-down his whole system felt* ***toned up****.*

tool

tool up [Vp] (*industry*) equip (a factory) with new machine-tools, as when a new product or model is to be manufactured. **S:** industry; plant, factory: *The real cost in car-making isn't design or raw materials, but the expense of* ***tooling up****.* OBS

top

top off (with) [Vn ⇆ p pass, Vn.p.pr pass rel] complete (sth) suitably or satisfactorily. **O:** meeting, ceremony; meal, party; day, weekend. **o:** speeches, champagne; fruit, cheese; excursion, outing: *A programme of folk dancing* ***topped off*** *a memorable evening.* ○ *The conference was* ***topped off with*** *a one-day excursion to Granada.* □ usu passive. = round off (with).

top out [Vp, Vn ⇆ p pass] (*building*) perform a ceremony, with speeches, drinks etc, to mark the completion of a high building. **O:** tower-block, office-block, hotel: *The Minister was present at the* ***topping-out*** *of London's Post Office Tower.* ○ *When we* ***top out****, there will be beer for everyone who has worked on the site.*

top up 1 [Vn ⇆ p nom pass adj] fill (a glass etc) which has been partially emptied. **S:** host; waiter. **O:** him, you etc; glass, tankard: *'Can I* ***top*** *that drink* ***up*** *for you?'* ILIH ○ *The waiters were constantly on the move,* ***topping up*** *the guests' glasses.* ○ *'Let me* ***top*** *you* ***up*** (or: *Let me give you a* ***top-up****).'*

2 [Vp, Vn ⇆ p nom pass adj] fill a petrol tank which is partially empty; add water, oil etc, esp to part of a vehicle's engine, to bring the level back to what is normal. **O:** tank, battery, radiator, engine: *The cells of a car battery need to be* ***topped up*** *with distilled water.* ○ *Keep the engine* ***topped up*** *with the right grade of oil.* ○ *During the fuel crisis, it was common for motorists to call at a garage for quite a small* ***top-up****. Many drove with* ***topped-up*** *tanks from fear of imminent petrol rationing.*

topple

topple over [Vp] become unsteady and fall. **S:** he etc; statue; lamp, vase; pile of books: *Father's rather unsteady on his feet: he could* ***topple over*** *if you don't take his arm.* ○ *A small pile of dictionaries* ***toppled over*** *and crashed to the floor.*

toss

toss about/around [Vn ⇆ p pass] (*informal*) mention or discuss (sth) in a casual way. **O:** name; idea, suggestion, proposal; word: *George's name was* ***tossed about*** *for a bit, but nobody really thought he was a suitable choice for the job.* ○ *'Why don't we have lunch and* ***toss*** *a few ideas* ***around*** *for the next conference?'*

toss for [Vpr, Vn.pr] decide (sth) with sb by spinning a coin in the air. **o:** (best, most comfortable) place, position; double bed, armchair; ends (of the field, in football): *'Who's going to sleep on the top bunk?' 'Let's* ***toss for*** *it.'* ○ *'To prevent any argument, I'll* ***toss*** *you* ***for*** *who does the washing-up.'* ⇨ toss up.

toss off 1 [Vn ⇆ p pass] (*dated*) drink (sth) straight down. **O:** glass (of sth); beer, whisky: *I never met a man who could* ***toss off*** *so many drinks in so short a time.* = knock back 1, throw back 3.

2 [Vn ⇆ p pass] produce or compose (sth) with little thought or effort. **O:** remark, answer; poem, song, story, article: *It isn't enough in this job to be able to* ***toss off*** *a few bright remarks. It calls for real thought and application.* = knock off 4, throw off 4.

toss up [Vp] decide sth, esp in a sporting contest, by spinning a coin in the air: *At the start of a football match the referee* ***tosses up*** *to decide which team will kick off.* ○ *In cricket the two captains* ***toss up*** *to see who will bat first and who will field.* ⇨ toss for.

toss-up [nom (Vp)] (*informal*) a matter which could be decided either way, a matter of doubt: *It's a* ***toss-up*** *which of the two yachtsmen will cross the finishing-line first.* ○ *It was an absolute* ***toss-up*** *whether that book* (Das Kapital by Marx) *caught on or not. The communist manifesto on its own didn't.* IND

tot

tot up [Vn ⇆ p pass] (*informal*) find the total of (sth). **O:** figures, amounts; marks, scores: *Every fortnight the form-masters had to* ***tot up*** *the marks scored by each boy and write out their names in a competitive list.* CON ○ *He took a pencil and paper and started to* ***tot up*** *all the monies he presently held against expenses he had.* AW = add up 2.

tot up to [Vp.pr] (*informal*) be equal to (a certain sum). **S:** bill, account; debt, overdraft; assets, reserves. **o:** sum, total; a considerable amount; very little, practically nothing: *This* (money) *was said to* ***tot up to*** *the considerable aggregate of four hundred pounds a year.* TRO = add up to 1, amount to 1.

touch

touch down [Vp nom] land at an airfield etc after a flight; reach the shore after a journey at sea. **S:** aircraft; pilot, passenger; boat; landing-craft: *We* ***touched down*** *at Galena. We made as good a landing as could be expected.* BM ○ *The first of the assault divisions* ***touches down*** *on the beaches at 6 am* (cf ***Touch-down*** *for the first of the divisions is at 6 am*).

touch (the ball) down [Vp nom, Vn.p pass] (*Rugby football*) ground the ball behind one's opponent's goal line to score a try, or behind one's own to prevent an opponent from doing so. **S:** forward, three-quarter, full-back: *Andrews kicked the ball over the opposing full-back's head, calculating that he could beat him to the* ***touch-down****.* ○ *Underwood* *broke through the centre to* ***touch down*** *right between the goal-posts.*

touch for [Vn.pr pass] (*informal*) borrow (money) from sb, without necessarily intending to pay it back. **o:** loan; (a few) quid, bob: *He's a bit tight with his money; definitely not the sort of man you can* ***touch for*** *a few pounds.* ○ *John had been* ***touched for*** *'a small loan' before; he wasn't going to be caught a second time.*

touch in [Vn ⇆ p pass] add (small details) carefully, to improve or complete sth. **O:** line, shape, shading: *The small figure to the right of the painting seems to have been* ***touched in*** *at a later date.* ○ *You need to* ***touch in*** *a few patches of colour with a fine brush.*

touch off 1 [Vn ⇆ p pass] cause (sth) to explode; discharge. **O:** cannon; explosive charge; guncotton, dynamite; explosion: *The explosive needs to be handled very carefully: the slightest jolt will* ***touch*** *it* ***off.*** ○ *Field guns were formerly* ***touched off*** *by a flame being applied to a hole near the breech.* = set off 1.

2 [Vp.n pass] cause (violent action) to begin. **S:** speech, harangue; appearance, intervention (of police etc). **O:** riot, disturbance; (violent) quarrel, argument, conflict: *Fresh violence was* ***touched off*** *when police moved in to disperse the crowd.* ○ *Argument continues as to what exactly* ***touched off*** *the disturbances.* = set off 2, spark off 2, trigger off.

touch on the raw [Vn.pr pass] (*dated*) offend, upset (sb) by referring to sth about which he is sensitive: *I had* ***touched*** *him* ***on the raw*** *somewhere, so I got up and said I was sorry to have taken up his time.* PP ○ *He was teasing me out of kindness, but* ***touched*** *me so accurately* ***on the raw*** *that I barely held back any retort.* LWK

touch on/upon [Vpr pass] treat (a matter) briefly or superficially. **S:** writer, speaker; book, article; lecture, lesson. **o:** subject, topic, question: *Your correspondent had only* ***touched upon*** *the fringe of the matter.* NS ○ *Let me now try to deal more fully with the important question that was* ***touched on*** *earlier.*

touch up 1 [Vn ⇆ p pass adj] alter (sth) by adding, or removing, small details. **O:** painting, photograph; portrait, landscape; article, essay: *These photographs appeared on front pages of the dailies, in some cases after a generous degree of* ***touching up.*** TBC ○ *He has two short articles almost ready for publication; they just need to be* ***touched up.***

2 [Vn ⇆ p pass] (*informal*) excite (sb) by touching sexually sensitive parts of the body; touch (sb) in an improper and suggestive way: *'He says that Julia was* ***touching*** *him* ***up*** *under the dinner table but I don't believe a word of it.'* ○ *There was this boy in school. He kept* ***touching*** *me* ***up****, touching my breasts. It ended in a fight.* SHE

toughen

toughen up [Vp, Vn ⇆ p pass] (cause sb to) become tough. **S** [Vp], **O** [Vn.p]**:** athlete; swimmer, boxer; child: *He needs a meat diet and plenty of hard exercise to* ***toughen*** *him* ***up.***

tout

tout about/around [Vn ⇆ p pass] (*informal*) offer (sth) for sale or acceptance in a furtive, underhand manner, since what is offered may not have been honestly acquired. **O:** (football, theatre) tickets; currency; (scarce) components, spares; trinket, jewel; idea, scheme (for making money): *'I wouldn't* ***tout*** *those dollars* ***about*** *here. You're likely to be picked up by the police for black market dealing.'* ○ *'They've been* ***touting*** *their scheme* ***around*** *in the City in the hope of interesting a few bankers.'*

tow

tow away [Vn ⇆ p pass] remove a vehicle, esp one that is illegally parked, by attaching it by a rope to another vehicle. **O:** car, van: *Motorists who do not display a parking disc will have their cars* ***towed away*** *and impounded.*

tower

tower above/over 1 [Vpr emph rel] stand much taller or higher than (sb/sth). **o:** brother, colleague; house, street: *Tim* ***towers above*** *his two cousins.* ○ ***Above*** *the Victorian houses and shops* ***tower*** *the monster office blocks of the redeveloped centre.*

2 [Vpr emph rel] be of greater intellectual power, artistic ability etc, than (sb). **o:** one's fellow scientists, students, musicians; other politicians: *As an original contributor to socialist thinking, and as a spell-binding orator, he* ***towered above*** *other leading figures of his day.*

toy

toy with 1 [Vpr pass] handle (sth) in a casual, absent-minded way. **o:** chain, bracelet, key-ring, pen, pencil: *He sat with his feet on the desk,* ***toying with*** *a glass paperweight.* = play with 3.

2 [Vpr pass] treat (sb/sth) lightly or frivolously. **o:** her etc; feelings, affections: *'He makes a great show of being fond of her in front of other people —just to show he's not altogether heartless—but he's only* ***toying with*** *her really.'* = dally with 2, play with 4, trifle with.

3 [Vpr pass] consider (a course of action), though not in a serious way. **o:** idea, scheme, plan: *He* ***toyed with*** *the idea of going back to his university town and getting a contract from his college.* HD ○ *He could still go to Australia. That was something he'd often* ***toyed with*** *but never done anything positive about.* = dally with 1, play with 5.

trace

trace back (to) 1 [Vn.p pass, Vn.p.pr pass emph rel] find the source or cause of (sth) by going back over a series of events etc. **O:** story, rumour; incident, event; illness, fear, phobia. **o:** author, instigator; source, root; childhood, infancy: *The police have* ***traced*** *her disappearance* ***back*** *as far as a day in April.* ○ *She* ***traced*** *her irrational fear of birds* ***back to*** *something which had happened to her as a child.*

2 [Vn.p pass, Vn.p.pr pass] be able, going back in time, to name (one's ancestors in succession). **O:** ⚠ one's family; one's descent; one's (family) line, lineage. **o:** Norman conquest, Huguenot settlement; twelfth, sixteenth century: *'How far* ***back*** *can he* ***trace*** *his family?'* ○ *On his father's side, he can* ***trace*** *his descent* ***back*** *to Elizabethan times.*

track

track down [Vn ⇆ p pass] find, discover (sth), esp by following evidence that has been left behind. **O:** fugitive, runaway; (lost, escaped) animal; truth, facts: *'Mrs Templar is taking the children in the park. They might* **track down** *that starved cat.'* DC ○ *It was almost 48 hours before the Army* **tracked down** *the facts: there had been a series of brawls, involving 30 soldiers.* OBS

trade

trade down [Vp] buy a cheaper house, car etc than one has already: *Many home-owners unable to afford the mortgage repayments are* **trading down** *into cheaper properties.* ↔ trade up.

trade (for) [Vn.pr pass] give (sth) in exchange (for sth else); barter (for). **O:** salt, tobacco, hides. **o:** knife, gun, cloth: *Early European travellers to the North of Canada* **traded** *manufactured goods* **for** *furs and skins.* ○ *'I'll* **trade** *you five comic books* **for** *your scout knife.'* □ in the second example, trade for is American usage; British speakers would use swap for.

trade in 1 [Vpr rel] buy and sell (esp natural, untreated products). **o:** furs, skins; precious metals, stones; timber, rubber: *In West Africa there are a number of businesses* **trading** *on a large scale* **in** *palm products, cocoa and rubber.* ↔ deal in 2.

2 [Vn ⇆ p nom pass adj] hand to a dealer (a used article) in part payment for a new one. **O:** car, motorbike; television, washing-machine: *He keeps a car for two years, then he* **trades** *it* **in** (or: *does a* **trade-in**). ○ *'Did you get a good* **trade-in** *on your fridge-freezer?'* ○ *You could also find that VW* (Volkswagen) *dealers will be prepared to do better* **trade-in** *deals than elsewhere.* OBS □ in the second example, the trade-in is the amount of money realized.

trade off [Vn ⇆ p nom pass adj] obtain (some advantage) by offering sth similar in exchange, or by making an equivalent sacrifice: *He will take to Moscow some formula for* **trading** (Soviet withdrawal from) *Afghanistan* **off** *against arms control.* BBCR ○ *The principle of* **trade-off** *operates in book design. If you include lots of full-page diagrams, then for a given size and price, you may have to accept a cheaper binding.*

trade on/upon [Vpr pass rel] use, exploit (sth) unfairly to get sth for oneself. **o:** (one's) charm, beauty; weakness, illness; (sb else's) generosity, forgiveness: *When are you going to stop* **trading on** *your helplessness—offering yourself all day to be petted and stroked?* FFE ○ *His easy, forgiving nature was something she was only too ready to* **trade upon**.

trade up [Vp] buy a more expensive house, car etc than one has already: *Not nearly enough people will be* **trading up** *out of their existing houses.* ST ↔ trade down.

traffic

traffic in [Vpr] be a dealer in (usu sth illegal). **o:** drugs, heroin, marijuana; illicit alcohol; arms, explosives: *People* **trafficking in** *obsolete tanks and small arms can still find a market for them in developing countries.*

trail

trail across, along, away etc [Vp emph, Vpr emph rel] move in line, slowly and wearily, in a particular direction. **S:** procession, column; prisoner, refugee: *Miss Jeffries came first;* **behind** *her* **trailed** *a dismal crocodile of small girls in uniform.* ○ *The army* **trailed back** *from the front in complete disorder.*

trail away/off [Vp] fade into silence. **S:** voice, words, sounds: *'He happens to have fallen in love, and wants to ....' Her voice* **trailed away**. PW ○ *Before the intimidating glare of the headteacher, Peter's words* **trailed off** *into silence.*

train

train (for) [Vpr emph rel, Vn.pr pass emph rel] (cause sb to) study, exercise, do practical work etc, in preparation for (sth). **S** [Vpr], **O** [Vn.pr]**:** student, pupil; athlete. **o:** profession, calling; race, match, contest: *A number of older men are coming forward to* **train for** *the priesthood.* ○ *This was not work* **for** *which he had been* **trained**. ○ *The coach believes in* **training** *the team hard* **for** *every match.*

train on/upon [Vn.pr pass rel] point (sth) towards an object, so as to hit it, make it visible etc. **O:** howitzer, field-gun; telescope, binoculars. **o:** target; enemy; view: *Anti-tank weapons were* **trained upon** *all possible approaches to the bridge.* ○ *I prised the glasses from her reluctant grasp and* **trained** *them* **on** *the distant scene.* DF = aim at 1.

train up (to) [Vn ⇆ p pass, Vn.p.pr pass] raise (sb) (to a particular standard) by giving instruction and practice. **O:** child; pupil, apprentice; soldier. **o:** standard, level, pitch: *They are unable to* **train up** *their successors* **to** *any higher standard than their own.* SD ○ *All the technical staff are* **trained up to** *a high level of efficiency.*

traipse

traipse across, along, away etc [Vp emph, Vpr emph rel] (*informal*) walk slowly, heavily and wearily in a given direction. **S:** (tired) shopper, traveller: *She's been* **traipsing back and forth** *across the world.* EHOW ○ *'It means* **traipsing upstairs** *to the bar if you want anything stronger than fruit juice.'* HAA

tramp

tramp across, along, away etc [Vp emph, Vpr emph rel] walk across etc with heavy steps. **S:** soldier, policeman: *The bridge shook as the column of troops* **tramped across**. ○ *The delivery man* **tramped in** *with a sack of potatoes across his shoulders.*

trample

trample down [Vn ⇆ p pass adj] flatten, crush (sth) by moving about heavily on it. **S:** cattle, elephant. **O:** grass, corn, flowers: *A flock of sheep had got into the garden and* **trampled down** *his prize begonias.*

trample on/upon 1 [Vpr pass rel] move about heavily (on sth) so as to crush it. **o:** foot, flower feelings, sensibilities: *Avoid the London Underground in the rush hour—you'll be buffeted about and have your toes* **trampled on**.

2 [Vpr pass] behave in a clumsy, insensitive way so as to hurt (sb). **o:** feelings, sensibilities; toes: *You could publish whatever you liked—so long as you didn't* **trample on** *the toes of the Government, the Church, the monarchy, family life ....* ST ○ *You shouldn't let yourselves be* **trampled on** *by officials.*

transfer

transfer (from) (to) 1 [Vpr emph rel, Vn.pr pass emph rel] (cause sb to) move (from one place) (to another), esp to run a business, take up a post etc. **S** [Vpr], **O** [Vn.pr]: employee; manager; civil servant; office, branch, department; footballer, cricketer. **o:** city, provinces; club, county: *Many Inland Revenue employees have had to* ***transfer from*** *the South of England* ***to*** *offices in Glasgow.* ○ *After two years in one appointment, staff officers are usually* ***transferred to*** *another.* ○ *David Platt was* ***transferred from*** *Aston Villa* ***to*** *the Italian club Bari.*

2 [Vn.pr pass emph rel] take (sth) from one place and place or invest it elsewhere. **O:** interest, enthusiasm; loyalty, affection; (bank) account, investments; business, trade. **o:** issue, (good) cause; friend, lover; bank, company: *£300 has been* ***transferred from*** *my savings account* ***to*** *my current account.* ○ *The Department also underestimated the amount it would have to pay staff and it was hit by chaos after* ***transferring*** *some of its accounts* ***to*** *a new computer.* OBS

3 [Vn.pr pass emph rel] take (interest etc) from one cause or person and give it to another. **O:** interest, enthusiasm; loyalty, affection. **o:** (good) cause, issue; friend, lover: *She has* ***transferred*** *her attention* ***from*** *writing textbooks* ***to*** *editing dictionaries.* ○ *His wife suspects that he has* ***transferred*** *his affections* ***to*** *a younger woman.*

transform

transform (into) [Vn.pr pass rel] change the form, nature or quality of sth (into sth else). **S:** heat, stress, pressure; experience; ordeal, suffering. **O:** substance, material; character, personality: *The training centre* ***transforms*** *some rather unpromising material* ***into*** *skilled craftsmen.* ○ *Thirty three people were drowned, and the main street was* ***transformed*** *overnight* ***into*** *a dramatically boulder-strewn river bed.* TTF = make into.

translate

translate (from) (into) [Vpr rel, Vn.pr pass emph rel] put sth spoken or written in one language into another language. **O:** text; book, letter; poem, play; speech, address. **o:** English, French, Russian: *Interpreters employed by international agencies must be able to* ***translate*** *instantaneously* ***from*** *one language* ***into*** *another.* ○ *Do you feel that his poems can be* ***translated*** (or: *can* ***translate***) ***into*** *German?* ○ *The book . . . has sold more than 450 000 copies in the United States alone and has been* ***translated into*** *several languages.* T

transliterate

transliterate (into) [Vn.pr pass rel] write (sth) in the script of a different language. **O:** word, sentence, passage. **o:** (foreign) script, characters, letters: *'Sputnik' is an example of a Russian word which has been* ***transliterated into*** *Roman script.*

transmit

transmit (to) 1 [Vn.pr pass emph rel] (*radio*) send (a message) (to sb); signal (to). **O:** message, signal; news, information: *On board ship, telephone messages may be* ***transmitted to*** *the shore by radio.*

2 [Vn.pr pass emph rel] convey (sth) (to sth/sb). **O:** power; heat, electricity. **o:** house, consumer: *A special generator* ***transmits*** *electricity* ***to*** *all parts of the factory.*

3 [Vn.pr pass emph rel] pass on (a disease, quality etc) (to a descendant). **O:** infection, disease; quality, characteristic. **o:** child, offspring: *An illness such as German measles will not be* ***transmitted to*** *an unborn child, though it may affect its normal development.* ○ *None of his finer qualities seem to have been* ***transmitted to*** *his children.*

trap

trap into [Vn.pr pass] make (sb) act as one wishes by setting a trap. **o:** admission, confession; revealing sth, betraying sb: *'Think carefully before you answer his questions. You may be* ***trapped into*** *giving away vital information.'* = trick into.

travel

travel over [Vpr emph rel] survey, consider (people/things) one by one. **S:** eyes, gaze; mind; thoughts, speculations. **o:** audience, crowd; subject, topic, field (of study): *His eyes* ***travelled*** *slowly* ***over*** *the rows of faces in front of him.* ○ *There are few problems* ***over*** *which his mind has* ***travelled*** *more searchingly than this one.*

tread

tread down [Vn ⇆ p pass adj] flatten or crush (sth) by putting one's feet on it. **O:** flower, vegetable; earth: *The soil around the plants should be well* ***trodden down****, so that they are firmly rooted.* ○ *The floor of the hut was of* ***trodden-down*** *red earth.*

tread on [Vpr pass rel] put one's foot, or feet, down on (sth) so as to move, spoil or damage it. **o:** clean floor, loose plank; flower-bed, young plant; foot, toe: *John* ***trod on*** *the head of the broom and the handle flew up and hit him in the face.* ○ *'Don't* ***tread on*** *that part of the floor — I've just finished varnishing it.'*

tread on sb's toes [Vpr pass] (*informal*) behave insensitively towards (sb), so that he is offended: *Robert, of course, hated Baxter from the first. But Ned arranged it so that they didn't* ***tread on each other's toes.*** CON ○ *'I'm rather used to having my* ***toes trodden on*** *by now, so I don't get upset.'* = step on sb's toes.

treat

treat of [Vpr rel] (*formal*) have (sth) as its subject. **S:** book; essay, thesis; lecture. **o:** event; progress, development; incidence, distribution: *The second volume of the series* ***treats of*** *social changes between the wars.* ○ *His doctoral thesis* ***treated of*** *the kinship system in a Nigerian city.* = deal with 4.

treat to [Vn.pr pass] give or offer to (sb) sth that will give special pleasure, eg as a reward for hard work. **O:** child, pupil; audience, spectators; oneself. **o:** holiday, outing; drink, ice-cream; (fine) spectacle, performance: *The whole school was* ***treated to*** *an extra half holiday after the Governors' annual visit.* ○ *I remembered the second-hand Austin Seven which the Chief Treasurer had just* ***treated*** *himself* ***to.*** RATT

trespass

trespass on/upon [Vpr pass rel] (*formal*) interfere in activities which are sb else's concern. **o:** (sb's) privacy, preserves; ground, sphere (of interest): *Smithers said he had no wish to* ***trespass on*** *my ground, but he felt he ought to point out one or two omissions in my report.* ○ *No one's privacy is so* *sacred that it can't be* **trespassed upon** *occasionally.*

trick

trick into [Vn.pr pass rel] by deceit, make (sb) do as one wishes. **O:** customer, client; employee, servant; girl. **o:** buying shoddy goods, giving away one's money, accepting low wages: *Don't let anyone* **trick** *you* **into** *signing any legal papers. Check everything with me first.* ○ *She was* **tricked into** *a disastrous marriage with a charming but quite unscrupulous younger man.* = trap into.

trick out [Vn.p pass] decorate or ornament (sth). **O:** sideboard, dressing-table; dress, coat, suit: *They'd* **tricked out** *the beds and wardrobe with antique decorative strips in gilt plastic.* ○ *He was wearing an old uniform jacket,* **tricked out** *with brass buttons and medal ribbons.* □ usu passive.

trickle

trickle in/into [Vp, Vpr] enter (a place) slowly and gradually. **S:** audience, spectators; money; donations, gifts; letters. **o:** theatre, stadium; bank; office: *The vote-counters are now* **trickling in** *and waiting for the ballot boxes to arrive.* BBCTV ○ *Cancellations are* **trickling in** *at Newquay which takes about a quarter of Cornwall's 2.2 million holidaymakers.* OBS ⇨ next entry

trickle out/out of [Vp, Vpr] leave in a thin stream. **S:** blood, water, oil; spectators; news, information. **o:** wound, crack; theatre, cinema; agency, (government) department: *Blood was* **trickling out of** *a cut near his right ear.* ○ *Someone had cut a hole in the bottom of the bag and sugar was* **trickling out** *over the floor.* ⇨ previous entry

trifle

trifle with [Vpr pass] treat (sb/sth) in a light, frivolous or insincere way. **o:** her etc; feelings; love, affections; offer, proposal: *'Stop* **trifling with** *our affections.'* SC ○ *'I'm in no mood to be* **trifled with**!*'* = dally with 2, play with 4, toy with 2.

trigger

trigger off [Vn ⇆ p pass] cause (an action, or sequence of actions) to begin. **S:** disagreement, argument; remark, accusation; visit, journey. **O:** fight, strike; (angry) exchange, discussion; tale, poem: *The present dispute was* **triggered off** *by a rumour that some workers were to lose their jobs.* ○ *Most of his stories are* **triggered off** *by word associations, or some odd juxtaposition of ideas.* ARG = spark off 2, touch off 2.

trim

trim down [Vn ⇆ p pass adj] make (sb/sth) smaller, less bulky, by removing matter. **O:** bulk, size; figure, waistline; budget, expenditure: *Cathy was made aware of how much her figure needed* **trimming down** *when she tried on last year's winter suit.* ○ *At a time of economies and cutbacks, the department will have to* **trim down** *its spending on stationery and duplicating services.*

trim off [Vn ⇆ p pass adj] make (sth) smaller, or neat and trim, by cutting, clipping etc. **O:** hair, sideboards, fringe; fat, gristle; (ragged) edge, border: *'You'll have to get some of that hair* **trimmed off** *before you go for your interview.'* ○ *'Ask the butcher to* **trim** *the excess fat* **off** *the joint.'* ○ (*figurative*) *'The finance department has* **trimmed** *about £2 000* **off** *our travel budget for the year.'*

trip

trip across, along, away etc [Vp, Vpr] move with quick, light steps in a particular direction. **S:** child, girl, dancer: *She* **tripped out** *of the office looking considerably less harassed than when she had arrived.* DOAP

trip on/over [Vp, Vpr] stumble, and possibly fall, because of some obstacle near the ground. **o:** step, kerb; tree-root, low branch: *I* **tripped over** *someone's foot in the darkened cinema and almost fell.* ○ *I used to make sure he didn't* **trip over** *paving stones and that we got across the road safely.* OBS ⇨ next entry.

trip up 1 [Vp, Vn ⇆ p pass] (cause sb to) stumble and fall. **S** [Vp], **O** [Vn.p]**:** footballer, runner, wrestler: *'Would you mind getting that dog out of the way? That's twice it's nearly* **tripped** *me* **up**.*'* ○ *He went into the kitchen,* **tripping up** *twice over his own feet.* RATT ⇨ previous entry.

2 [Vp, Vn ⇆ p pass] be led by a deliberate action to make a mistake, reveal a secret etc; lead (sb) to do this. **S** [Vp], **O** [Vn.p]**:** examinee, candidate; prisoner, accused. **S** [Vn.p]**:** interviewer; counsel, prosecutor, police officer: *The witness* **tripped up** *rather badly under close cross-examination.* ○ *'Be careful — there may be questions in the paper designed to* **trip** *you* **up**.*'*

troop

troop across, along, away etc [Vp emph, Vpr emph rel] move across etc in a group. **S:** audience, crowd; children, pupils: *The door opened and* **in trooped** *his first class of the afternoon.* ○ *The cricketers* **trooped off** *the field at the end of a long day in the sun.*

trot

trot across, along, away etc 1 [Vp emph, Vpr emph rel] move across etc at a pace between a walk and a run or gallop. **S:** horse, dog, sheep: *Her husband always follows at a discreet distance, like a small round dog* **trotting after** *its mistress.* ○ *Illingworth is now* **trotting in** *to bowl the first ball of a new over.*

2 [Vp emph, Vpr emph rel] (*informal*) walk across, along, away etc: *Mrs Trollope would then* **trot out** *on to the lawn with basket and secateurs.* TRO ○ *I used to go job-hunting in the morning and when that came to naught, ... I* **trotted off** *to the Grand* (cinema). OBS □ here, the verb trot does not refer to speed of movement, but reflects the attitude of the speaker, which is gently humorous and playful.

trot out [Vp.n pass] (*informal*) say or write (sth) quickly and easily, and often without careful thought. **O:** idea, thought, theory; remark; comment; story: *I said that my theory seemed improbable when I first* **trotted** *it* **out**. TBC ○ *The accountant* **trotted out** *a few figures in support of his argument.*

trouble

trouble one's head about [Vn.pr] be concerned about (sb/sth). **o:** him etc; politics, world affairs; money, one's debts: *She owned up to the age of 66. ... Amid loud laughter, Nancy told her she was much too young and pretty to* **trouble her head about** *such things.* ST ○ *He felt that the Church shouldn't* **trouble its head about** *political oppression.* L = worry (oneself) about/over.

trouble (for) [Vn.pr] ask (sb) to do or give (sth). **o:** match, light; the (correct) time; score (in a game): *'Can I* ***trouble*** *you* ***for*** *the time? My watch seems to have stopped.'* □ always in questions with *can/could*.

truckle

truckle to [Vpr pass] (*formal*) accept sb's orders or leadership in a timid or cowardly way. **o:** boss, chief, director: *He's always* ***truckled to*** *people in authority, which I suppose is why he's never moved up the ladder himself.*

trudge

trudge across, along, away etc [Vp emph, Vpr emph rel] move across etc in a heavy, weary way. **S:** soldier, refugee; procession, column; expedition: *In the early afternoon the first of the casualties began to* ***trudge into*** *the dressing-stations.* ○ *Progress was slow, as we had to* ***trudge through*** *deep mud.* ○ *Joe marvelled at the picture of himself as a solid breadwinner,* ***trudging off*** *to the station in the morning light.* AITC

trump

trump up [Vp.n pass adj] invent, construct (a case) in order to make sb appear guilty.S: police; authorities. **O:** ⚠ a case; charge, evidence: *The case against the prisoner was blatantly* ***trumped up****; the authorities had clearly decided that an example should be made of a leading opposition figure.* ○ *Others believed to be involved in the conspiracy were arrested on* ***trumped-up*** *charges.* □ usu passive or adj.

truss

truss up [Vn ⇆ p pass adj] (pin and) bind the wings of a fowl to its body before cooking it; bind sb's arms and/or legs tightly to his body. **O:** chicken, duck, turkey; prisoner: *The poultry is sold* ***trussed-up*** *and ready for the oven.* ○ *The captives were* ***trussed up*** *hand and foot and dumped in the back of a lorry.*

trust

trust (for that) [Vpr] (*informal*) confidently expect, from what one knows of sb, that he will act shrewdly, do sth difficult etc: *Alec got the house rebuilt when licences were almost unprocurable —* ***trust*** *him* ***for that*** (or: ***trust*** *him to do that)!* PW ○ *'Last night's meeting just left a beastly taste of spite and malice.' 'Yes* ***trust*** *Sherman* ***for that****.'* HAA □ used in imperative sentences, as in the examples.

trust in [Vpr emph rel] have confidence in (sb/sth), feel sure that sb/sth will serve one well. **o:** God; leader, organizer; judgement, sense of values, integrity: *'I told you it didn't pay to* ***trust in*** *him — he's let us down again.'* ○ *We felt that we could* ***trust in*** *his wide experience of the property market.* = believe in 1.

trust to [Vpr] leave the result or progress of events to be decided by (chance or by the unreasoning part of one's mind). **o:** ⚠chance, luck, fate, fortune; instinct, intuition: *You must have the whole project carefully planned in advance — don't just* ***trust to*** *luck.* ○ *There's not much room for cold analysis in judging human character — you have to* ***trust to*** *intuition.*

trust with [Vn.pr pass rel] confidently allow (sb) to take care of, use or share (sth). **O:** employee; junior, child; pupil. **o:** money; key (to safe, house); car, bicycle; secret: *He's not the sort of man you can* ***trust with*** *large sums of money.* ○ *'Is Peter reliable enough to be* ***trusted with*** *the details of the scheme?'*

try

try for [Vpr] attempt to win or achieve (sth). **o:** prize, medal; record; scholarship, bursary; post, position: *She decided to* ***try for*** *a place at her mother's old college.* ○ *I don't think I've much of a chance of getting the job, but it's certainly worth* ***trying for****.*

try on [Vn ⇆ p nom pass] put (a garment) on to see if it fits, looks well etc. **O:** coat, suit, dress; necklace, bracelet: *She* ***tried on*** *ten pairs of shoes before she found any that suited her.* ○ *She gave a wonderful personality display while having her hair done and* ***trying on*** *her jewellery.* OBS ○ *'Would you like to* ***try*** *this jacket* ***on*** *for size* (ie to find out whether it is the right size)*?'*

try on (with) [Vn.p nom, Vn.p.pr emph] (*informal*) act in a bold or impudent way to see if one's conduct, attentions, advances etc will be welcomed. **O:** ⚠ it; anything, something. **o:** girl, woman; teacher, prefect; boss, foreman: *She was just waiting for you to* ***try it on*** *so she could slap your face.* ILIH ○ *'Don't* ***try*** *anything* ***on with*** *the new class-teacher: she's a strict disciplinarian.'* ○ *'I wouldn't pay any attention to the flattery. If I know him, it'll just be a* ***try-on*** (or: *he'll just be* ***trying*** *it* ***on***).*'*

try out 1 [Vn ⇆ p nom pass adj] use, handle (sth) to see if it functions well. **O:** car, lawn-mower, razor, typewriter: *'Is the microwave I gave you any good?' 'I don't know, I haven't had a chance to* ***try*** *it* ***out*** *yet.'* ○ *These products give good cooks a whole range of interesting new flavours.* ***Try*** *them* ***out*** *for yourself.* TO ○ *Give the machine a thorough* ***try-out*** *before you buy.*

2 [Vn ⇆ p nom pass] test (sb), before employing him, allowing him to play for a team etc. **O:** applicant, candidate; player, competitor: *Fisher was* ***tried out*** (or: *given a* ***try-out****) in the marketing section before being shifted to finance.* ○ *Two new players will get a* ***try-out*** *in Saturday's home game.*

try out on [Vn.p.pr pass rel] test the effectiveness of (sth) on (sb). **O:** song, trick; disguise; invention, gadget. **o:** family, friend: *'You've been waiting to* ***try out*** *the Beethoven Opus 106* ***on*** *us. Now's your chance.'* TBC ○ *The new washing-up liquid has already been* ***tried out on*** *a small sample of London shoppers.*

tuck

tuck away 1 [Vn ⇆ p pass] (*informal*) consume great quantities of (food). **O:** pie, cake; meat, vegetables: *Between them, the children* ***tucked away*** *a small Christmas pudding and a plate of mince pies.* = put away 4.

2 [Vn ⇆ p pass] put (sth) in a box, drawer etc, because one has finished using it or wants to hide or protect it. **O:** dress, clothes; doll, toy; jewellery: *She brought out the dress in which she had been christened and, after allowing us to examine the very fine lace, wrapped it carefully in its tissue* *paper and **tucked** it **away** in the bottom of the trunk again.* = put away 1. ⇨ next entry.

tucked away 1 [adj (Vn.p)] stored, hidden and perhaps difficult to find. **S:** (antique) furniture; village, house: *Art dealers are always hoping to find some forgotten masterpiece **tucked away** in someone's attic. Occasionally they are lucky.* ○ *One of the most popular Moscow shops is **tucked away** in a side street near Gorky park.* LFM ⇨ previous entry.

2 [adj (Vn.p)] (*informal*) having money saved in a secretive way. **S:** (a tidy bit of) money, a fortune: *He never seems to spend a penny on anything, but I suppose he must still have a fair bit **tucked away**.*

tuck in 1 [Vn.p pass] settle (sb) in bed by pushing the sheets and blankets tightly under the mattress. **O:** child; patient: *'Get into bed and I'll be up in a moment to **tuck** you **in**.'* ○ *She calmly went on with her task of smoothing the bed and **tucking** Bridget **in**.* DC ⇨ tuck in/into 1.

2 [Vn ⇆ p pass adj] draw in a part of one's body that is sticking out. **O:** chin, stomach, belly, bottom: *'Put your chest out and **tuck** your chin **in**.'* ○ *'Stand up straight. **Tuck in** your bottom!'*

tuck in/into 1 [Vn ⇆ p pass adj, Vn.pr pass] press, push (sth loose) into a narrow space. **O:** shirt, blouse; banknote, letter; pistol. **o:** trousers, skirt; wallet, pocket; belt, waistband: *'Your shirt's hanging out: **tuck** it **in**!'* ○ *He had a villainous looking knife **tucked into** his belt.* ○ ***Tuck** the sheets and blankets **in** well.* ⇨ tuck in 1.

2 [Vp, Vpr] (*informal*) (begin to) eat heartily. **o:** meal; breakfast, dinner; pie, stew: *'Food's on the table. **Tuck in**!'* ○ *He was often seen sitting on his own in a nearby hamburger joint, **tucking into** junk food.* OBS = dig in/into 2, dive in.

tuck up [Vn ⇆ p pass adj] raise (sth) loose and fold or roll it around itself. **O:** sleeve, trouser-bottom, skirt: *He **tucked up** his sleeves and reached down into the water.*

tuck up (in bed) [Vn.p pass, Vn.p.pr pass] make (sb) comfortable in bed by drawing the sheets etc up around him. **O:** child; patient, invalid: *Nurse Ellen had **tucked** her **up** and left her to sleep.* DC ○ *The children are all safely **tucked up in bed**.*

tug

tug across, along, away etc [Vn ⇆ p pass, Vn.pr pass] draw sth/sb that is heavy or resisting in a particular direction. **O:** cart, sledge, boat; (unwilling) child: *A day in town isn't much fun if you have to **tug** a couple of the children **around** with you.*

tumble

tumble across, along, back etc [Vp emph, Vpr emph rel] fall or collapse, in a sudden, uncontrolled way, and in a certain direction: *We **tumbled** gratefully **into** bed at the end of an exhausting day.* ○ *A large jar **tumbled off** the shelf, spilling its contents over the floor.* ○ *The coach came to a halt and **out tumbled** a party of schoolchildren.*

tumble to [Vpr] (*informal*) realize the true character of (sb); understand what is being done, planned etc. **o:** him etc; plan, scheme, trick; what is going on, what sb is up to: *'I'm not a very nice chap, I suppose. You **tumbled to** it about the phone call, didn't you?'* TGLY ○ *He tries to keep his intentions well hidden, but it doesn't take too long to **tumble to** him.*

tune

tune in/into 1 [Vp, Vpr rel, Vn ⇆ p pass, Vn.pr pass rel] (*radio*) adjust the controls of (a set) so that one receives a certain station. **O:** radio; set, receiver. **o:** London, Radio Luxemburg; Radio 3: [Vp] *'Don't forget to **tune in** next Sunday at the same time, when we present another programme of jazz favourites.'* ○ [Vpr] *'No wonder you can't get the cricket scores: you've **tuned into** the wrong wavelength!'*

2 [Vp, Vpr, Vn ⇆ p pass adj, Vn.pr pass] (*informal*) (cause sb to) become sympathetically aware of sb's feelings, reactions etc. **o:** class, audience; wife, friend: [Vpr] *He hasn't developed the knack of **tuning into** people.* ○ [Vn.p, Vn.pr] *The lecturer could see from the expressions on the faces of his audience which students were really **tuned in** (**into** what he was saying).* □ for [Vn.p] and [Vn.pr] the passive patterns are more usual than the active.

tune up [Vp, Vn.p] (*music*) adjust (musical instruments) so that they can play together in tune. **S** [Vp], **O** [Vn.p]**:** instruments; violins, oboes. **S** [Vp, Vn.p]**:** players, musicians; orchestra: *The orchestra were already **tuning up** when we reached the concert hall.* ○ *The string section **tuned up*** (or: ***tuned up** their instruments*).

turf

turf out/out of [Vn ⇆ p pass, Vn.pr pass] (*informal*) forcibly remove (sb) (from a place). **S:** steward, doorkeeper, bouncer. **O:** hooligan, troublemaker; intruder, gatecrasher. **o:** theatre, cinema, dance-hall: *'I was just looking, Miss,' he said. 'And then Mr Woodgate **turfed** us all **out**, and he was properly wild.'* TT ○ *The meeting was marred by a noisy disturbance in the course of which several hecklers were **turfed out of** the hall.* = chuck out/out of, throw out/out of.

turn

turn about [Vp emph, Vn ⇆ p pass] (*military*) (cause soldiers to) face in the opposite direction. **S** [Vp], **O** [Vn.p]**:** troops; company, platoon. **S** [Vn.p]**:** sergeant, corporal: *The company **turned about** and marched ten paces to the rear.* ○ *'Squad will retire. **About turn**!'* □ about turn is the form used in commands.

turnabout [nom (Vp)] (*informal*) sudden and complete change in attitude or approach: *MPs are surprised at what they see as a **turnabout** in the Government's attitude.* BBCR □ the form about-turn is used in the same meaning: *Last night the employers did an **about-turn** and withdrew their offer.*

turn against [Vpr, Vn.pr pass] (cause sb to) be hostile to (sb), to oppose (sb). **S** [Vpr], **O** [Vn.pr]**:** father, colleague, friend: *He had the distinct impression that everyone was **turning against** him.* ○ *'What **turned** her **against** me, do you think? The child I suppose, horrid little creature.'* DC

turn around/round 1 [Vp, Vn.p pass] (cause sb/sth to) face in the opposite direction. **S** [Vp], **O** [Vn.p]**:** car, aircraft; procession, parade: *He **turned around** to find a policeman eyeing him suspiciously.* ○ *'We've come too far; **turn** the car **round** and go back to the last village.'*

2 [Vp nom, Vn ⇆ p nom pass] (*finance, commerce*) (cause sth to) start to show an opposite trend or movement; reverse. **S** [Vp], **O** [Vn.p]**:** (money, stock) market; economy: *The American market* ***turned round*** *very sharply about a week ago.* BBCR ○ *It is already too late to expect a* ***turn-round*** *in the balance of payments in the first half of next year.* G ○ *We know now how the Government proposes to* ***turn*** *the ailing economy* ***around***. BBCR □ nom forms are turn-around and turn-round.

turn away (from) 1 [Vp, Vp.pr emph rel] stop facing or looking at (sb/sth), esp because one finds him or it unpleasant, painful etc. **S:** passer-by, onlooker; spectator. **o:** sight, spectacle: *As his voice rose, she* ***turned away*** *in distaste.* ○ *It would have been easy to* ***turn away from*** *such an uphill task.*

2 [Vn ⇆ p pass, Vn.p.pr pass emph rel] refuse (sb) entry (to a place). **S:** manager, organizer; police; hotel keeper. **O:** spectator, visitor; car, coach. **o:** theatre, concert-hall; show, festival: *All seats were sold out in advance; many people hoping for last-minute cancellations were* ***turned away***. ○ *The Salvation Army hate to* ***turn away from*** *their hostels anyone in need of food and shelter.*

turn back 1 [Vp] return, go back, the way one has come. **S:** car; climber, explorer: *One of the party* ***turned back*** *to help a friend who had sprained an ankle.* ○ *The sight of the Castle was the end of her walk, and meant she must* ***turn back***. ○ *We have come so far in our programme of reorganization that there can be no* ***turning back***.

2 [Vn ⇆ p pass adj] fold one smaller part of sth over another larger part. **O:** sheet, bedspread, cover; cuff; corner, edge: *He* ***turned back*** *the coverlet and slipped between the sheets.* ○ *'Don't* ***turn back*** *the corner of the page to mark your place.'* ⇨ turn down 2.

turn the clock back return to the practices, values etc of an earlier period. ⇨ put the clock back.

turn down 1 [Vpr] enter a road leading off from the one on which one is travelling. **S:** driver, pedestrian; car; procession. **o:** side street, alley, passage-way: *You go straight along the High Street for about a mile and* ***turn*** *left* ***down*** *a narrow side-street.*

2 [Vn ⇆ p pass adj] fold one part of sth over another part, esp sth which is lower down. **O:** collar, neck (of a garment); brim (of a hat); sheet; blanket; corner (of a page): *He* ***turned down*** *the brim of his straw hat to keep the sun out of his eyes.* ○ *A leaf* (= page of a book) ***turned down*** *showed that she was in the middle of 'Two Gentlemen of Verona'.* OMIH ↔ turn up 1.

3 [Vn ⇆ p pass adj] refuse (sb who applies, sth which is submitted etc). **S:** board, committee; school; company, publisher. **O:** applicant, candidate; offer, bid; manuscript: *'I'm always proposing to you and you always* ***turn me down***.*'* EHOW ○ *You'd had a couple of stories* ***turned down*** *by the highbrow magazines.* ASA ○ *Other ... journalists are disgruntled because space officials have ...* ***turned down*** *proposals for their space flights.* OBS

4 [Vn ⇆ p pass adj] make (sth) less bright, intense or loud. **O:** light, flame; fire; gas, electricity; radio, television; sound, volume: *I* ***turned down*** *the gas.* BM ○ *He* ***turned*** *the wireless* ***down***. UTN ↔ turn up 2.

5 [Vp nom] (*finance, commerce*) become weaker, decline. **S:** (stock, money) market; economy; investment: *The economy was* ***turning down*** *of its own accord.* BBCTV ○ *Wall Street reports a* ***turn-down*** *in the economy.* BBCTV ○ *The province was beginning to experience a* ***downturn*** *in industrial production and consumer spending.* ST □ note the two nom forms turndown and (more usu) downturn. ⇨ turn up 8.

turn from [Vpr emph rel] leave, abandon (sth). **o:** life, career; study, consideration; problem: *She'd* ***turned from*** *her old routine and joined a troupe of travelling actors.* ○ *At this point we* ***turn from*** *simple observation and enter the realm of speculation.*

turn in 1 [Vp, Vn.p pass adj] (cause sth to) face or curve inwards. **S** [Vp], **O** [Vn.p]**:** ⚠one's toes, feet, knees: *His big toe* ***turns in*** (ie towards the other toes on that foot). ○ *His feet* ***turn in*** (ie towards each other).

2 [Vn ⇆ p pass] return (sth) because it is no longer needed, serviceable etc. **O:** uniform, equipment, bedding; radio, washing-machine: *'I'll give the machine one more week to behave itself. And if it doesn't then I'll* ***turn*** *it* ***in*** *for another.'* DBM ○ *'Don't forget to* ***turn in*** *all your camping gear before you leave.'*

3 [Vn ⇆ p pass] hand, submit (sth) to sb, eg for study or publication; achieve, attain. **O:** essay, exercise; article, contribution; performance: *'That was a terrible piece of work you* ***turned in*** *the other day. I could hardly believe it was yours.'* ○ *At yesterday's athletics meeting, Peter Elliott* ***turned in*** *a personal best time which was only two seconds outside the European record set last year.*

4 [Vn ⇆ p pass] (*informal*) surrender (sb) to the police etc. **O:** prisoner; runaway; escapee; suspect: *'I know you think I probably deserve it, but please don't* ***turn me in***!*'* ○ *I was in two minds — whether to* ***turn*** *the kids* ***in*** *or let them go.* = turn over (to) 1.

5 [Vn ⇆ p pass] (*informal*) abandon, leave (sth); renounce. **O:** job; night work, early shift; smoking, drinking: *Peter had to* ***turn in*** *his evening paper-round: he found he had too much homework to do.* ○ *'All this travelling about the country is doing your health no good. Why don't you* ***turn*** *it* ***in***?*'* = give up 2.

6 [Vp] (*informal*) go to bed: *'It's late — time I was* ***turning in***.*'* ○ *A week from the date, you began refusing second helpings,* ***turning in*** *early, and the rest of it.* CON

turn in one's grave [Vpr] (of sb already dead) be likely to be offended or displeased. **S:** father, ancestor; founder (of a company); writer, composer: *'Whether I'm in this or any Conservative club,' I said, 'my father'd* ***turn in his grave*** *if he could see me.'* RATT □ often used with *would*.

turn it in [Vn.p] (*informal*) stop behaving in a way which irritates, annoys etc: *'Oh,* ***turn it in***, *Robert. Can't you see that these people aren't the least bit interested in what you're saying?'* = knock it off, pack it in, pack it up.

turn in upon oneself [Vp.pr, Vn.p.pr pass] move away from contact with others and become unhappily preoccupied with one's own problems. **S** [Vp.pr], **O** [Vn.p.pr]**:** (hospital) patient; prisoner; divorcee, widow. **S** [Vn.p.pr]**:** life, experience; illness, bereavement: *Nothing was built, every activity was delayed, and the villagers* ***turned*** *bitterly* ***in upon*** *themselves, hoping for nothing better than food and peace.* BN ○ *He's one of those bitter, disillusioned men who will* ***turn you in upon*** *yourself. Avoid him.*

turn inside out 1 [Vn.p pass] make the inside of (sth) face outwards. **O:** umbrella; sock, jumper; bag, sack: *'Are you quite sure you haven't got the key on you? **Turn** your pockets **inside out**.'*
2 [Vn.p] (*informal*) search (a place) thoroughly, with the result that things are in disorder. **O:** place; house, flat: *The police were determined to get the evidence they needed, even if it meant **turning** the place **inside out**.*
turn into 1 [Vpr] be changed into (sth); become. **S:** water; wine; milk; caterpillar; youth, girl. **o:** ice, steam; vinegar; cheese; butterfly; man, woman: *From an animal pacing within the area of his defended posts, the goalkeeper **turned into** a leaping ape.* LLDR ○ *The bird in my arms **turned** from a placid and well-behaved creature **into** a flapping, panic-stricken beast.* DF ⇨ next entry
2 [Vn.pr pass] cause (sb/sth) to become (sth). **S:** experience, hardship, suffering; travel; builder; magician; heat. **O:** boy, girl; recruit; room, house; pumpkin; water. **o:** man, woman; veteran; workshop; fairy, coach; steam: *She had thought that being happy would **turn** him **into** a normal confident person.* DC ○ *She bought two villas at Freshwater in 1860 and **turned** them **into** a mansion, named Dimbola Lodge.* OBS ○ *The magic spell **turned** the frogs and rats back **into** men.* HD = change (from) (into), make into. ⇨ previous entry
turn off 1 [Vn ⇆ p pass] stop the flow of (sth); disconnect. **O:** light, fire; radio, television; shower; supply; electricity, gas, water: *'Don't forget to **turn** all the lights **off** before you come up to bed.'* ○ *Sarah goes to **turn off** the music.* CSWB ○ *The electricity supply must be **turned off** at the mains before you alter the lighting circuit.* = switch off 1. ↔ turn on 1. ⇨ be off 6, go off 8.
2 [Vn.p nom pass, Vn.pr pass] (*informal*) make (sb) lose interest; make (sb) lose the desire for (sth). **S:** visit, journey; smell, sight; sound. **o:** cooking, drink; tobacco, drug; music: *Pop music may turn you on, but it **turns** me **off**!* ○ *Nothing is less erotic than a nudist colony: a complete **turn-off**.* BBCR ○ *One sniff of his breath was enough to **turn** you **off** drink for good.* ↔ turn on 2. ⇨ be off 8, go off 4, put off 5.
3 [Vp nom, Vpr] leave (one road) for another. **o:** road, motorway, track: ***Turn off** about a mile further on.* ○ *'You must have missed the **turn-off*** (ie the road which ***turns off***) *to Northampton. You'd better take the next exit.'* ○ *We **turned off** the motorway at exit 31.*
turn on 1 [Vn ⇆ p pass] start the flow of (sth); connect. **O:** light, fire; radio, record player; bath water; gas, electricity: *'I think we'll **turn on** the electric fire — it's a little chilly this evening.'* ○ *'I've **turned on** your bath.'* = switch on. ↔ put out 10, turn off 1. ⇨ be on 8, go on 15, keep on 6, leave on 2, put on 2.
2 [Vn.p nom pass] (*informal*) stimulate, excite (sb). **S:** singer, actor; girl; music; drug: *Her suggestive dancing on stage is designed purely to **turn** men **on**.* ○ *I still occasionally crew a boat for my brother. But sailing never really **turned** me **on**.* TVT ○ *By the time I was 30 I wanted to be a millionaire. Money replaced sex as the great **turn-on**.* G ↔ turn off 2.
3 [Vpr pass] become hostile towards (sb), verbally or physically, esp to blame or reproach him for sth. **o:** leader, organizer; wife, child: *I lost the son you wanted; what a fine excuse you have at last for **turning on** me.* WI ○ *'There's no need to **turn on** me just because rain spoiled the picnic.'*
4 [Vpr emph rel] be decided by (sth), follow logically from (sth). **S:** result, outcome, decision, verdict. **o:** factor, circumstance; (previous) record, convictions: *The question of a reprieve may **turn on** the age of the victim.* OBS = depend on/upon 4, hinge on/upon.
5 [Vpr rel] have (sth) as its main topic or concern. **S:** discussion, debate; mind, thoughts. **o:** what was to happen, how things were to be arranged: *Our conversation **turned** mainly **on** what was to be done when the battle was over.* MFM = centre in/on/upon.
turn one's back on [Vn.pr emph rel] not face or confront (sth/sb); reject, desert. **A:** firmly, finally, decisively, irrevocably. **o:** problem, difficulty; family, friend, ally: (horoscope) *You really haven't much business sense, and you **turn your back on** material problems.* WI ○ *Many industrialists have **turned their backs** firmly **on** the government's counter-inflation policy.* ○ *Britain must not **turn its back on** Europe.*
turn the key on [Vn.pr pass] lock a door behind (sb). **S:** guard, gaoler. **o:** captive, prisoner: *I was thrown into a cell and the sentry assured me, as he **turned the key on** me, that my head would be cut off in the morning.* LWK
turn the tables (on) [Vn.pr pass emph rel] gain an advantage (over sb) after having been at a disadvantage. **o:** rival, competitor, opponent: *He enjoyed matching his wits against hers, allowing her to think that she was fooling him, and **turning the tables on** her eventually.* PE ○ *If he were not expecting any attack, he would be at the mercy of a quick approach. But since he was expecting it, **the tables** were **turned on** the attacker.* ARG
turn a blind eye (on/to) [Vn.pr pass emph rel] pretend not to notice (sth); overlook. **S:** authorities; (school) staff; police. **o:** proceedings, goings-on; fault, error; misdemeanour, misconduct; rule, regulation: *The Liberians **turned a blind eye on** the diamond traffic.* DS ○ *By **turning a blind eye to** the small faults of juniors, your popularity and prestige should grow.* WI ○ *These are petty infringements, **to** which the officials usually **turn a blind eye**.* = shut one's eyes to.
turn on/upon [Vn.pr pass rel] direct (sth) at (sb/sth); keep (sth) pointing towards (sb/sth). **O:** hose; blow-torch; torch, spotlight: *Fred put a token in the jet-wash and **turned** the hose **on** the doors and roof of the car.* ○ *Whenever she **turns** those steely blue eyes **on** me I run for cover.*
turn out 1 [Vn ⇆ p pass] extinguish (sth). **O:** (electric) light, (gas, oil) lamp: *'Make sure all the lights are **turned out** before you come up to bed.'* ⇨ be out 10, go out 6, put out 10.
2 [Vp nom] be present at, attend (sth). **S:** crowd; supporter, follower, member; voter, elector: *A large crowd **turned out*** (or: *There was a large **turn-out***) *to welcome the royal visitors.* ○ *Poor weather prevented people from **turning out** in large numbers to attend the rally.* ○ *Only in Northern Ireland was the* (election) ***turn-out** healthy — more than 70 per cent in two of the three constituencies.* OBS

3 [Vp] develop, progress, in a certain way. **S:** events, things; child, pupil. **A:** well, all right, for the best; badly; how: *She realized that perhaps what they all said was true — that Margot wasn't* ***turning out*** *very well.* H ○ *I don't like it when I know from the start how things will* ***turn out****.* ○ *We needn't have worried. Everything* ***turned out*** *all right in the end.* □ adv or adv phrase is present.

4 [Vn ⇆ p nom pass] empty the contents from (sth), esp to find sth. **O:** pocket, wallet, briefcase, satchel, drawer: *'But you must have the tickets on you somewhere.* ***Turn out*** *your pockets again.'* ○ *I must give my files a good* ***turn-out*** (or: *have a good* ***turn-out*** *of my files*).

5 [Vp.n pass] produce, make (sth); develop, train (sb). **O:** goods; car, van; yarn, fabric; student, pupil; athlete: *Why go up to the manager in my own factory and tell him the stuff I'm* ***turning out*** *is shoddy and vulgar?* FFE ○ *The press is ready to* ***turn out*** *a huge new edition.* UTN ○ *A company's performance is influenced by the quality of the people* ***turned out*** *by the education system.* G

6 [Vn.p nom pass adj] dress (sb/oneself) smartly etc. **O:** child, pupil; oneself. **A:** smartly, elegantly, beautifully: *She always* ***turns*** *her children* ***out*** *beautifully.* ○ *The boys were complimented on their neat* ***turn-out****.* ○ *We were always 'well* ***turned out****', well darned throughout the year, and had new outfits at Whitsun.* UL ○ *A chic, well* ***turned-out*** *young lady of seventeen minced demurely towards us.* BM

as it/things turn(s) out [Vp] as is shown or proved by later events: ***As it turned out****, it was not snakes that disturbed us that evening.* DF ○ ***As things turned out****, he had to tone down a few of my rather critical opinions.* DS

turn out (that) [Vp] come to be known (that); transpire (that). **S:** it . . . (that) he knew all along, (that) he was already married, (that) there was no money left: *It* ***turned out*** *he was born in the Caledonian Road.* CON ○ *It* ***turns out that*** *this method does not work well* (or: *This method* ***turns out*** *not to work well*). NS ⇨ next entry.

turn out to be sb/sth [Vp] prove (eventually) to be. **S:** stranger, visitor, newcomer; message, warning. **Inf:** to be a cousin, to be false; to have lost his way: *The symptom she had taken to the doctor hadn't* ***turned out to be*** *a false alarm.* PW ○ *This* ***turned out to be*** *none other than the passport officer's respectable relative* (or: *It* ***turned out that*** *this was none other than* etc). BM ○ *The girls would probably* ***turn out to be*** *models already* (or: *It would probably* ***turn out that*** *the girls were* etc). H ⇨ previous entry.

turn out (the guard) [Vp, Vp.n pass] (*military*) (of the soldiers guarding the regimental prisoners, the entry to barracks etc) (cause them to) parade with rifles in front of the guard-room: *The visiting general complimented the duty officer on* ***the guard's*** *quickness in* ***turning out****.* ○ ***The guard*** *always dislikes being* ***turned out*** *in the middle of the night.* ○ *'****Turn out the guard****!'* □ the last example shows the form of command used on these occasions.

turn out/out of [Vn ⇆ p pass, Vn.pr pass] drive (sb) out (of a place) by force, threats etc. **O:** intruder, invader; resident; worker. **o:** country; house, chair; job, post: *She would be heart-broken to leave . . . you can't* ***turn*** *her* ***out*** *unless she expressly wants to go.* GOV ○ *I was* ***turned out of*** *my own office.* AITC

turn over 1 [Vp, Vn.p pass] (cause sb/sth to) face in another direction by rolling. **S** [Vp], **O** [Vn.p]**:** body; car, aircraft: *'You bet you weren't listening* (ie *to me*)*. Old Porter talks, and everyone* ***turns over*** *and goes to sleep.'* LBA ○ *Alex had been sleeping face down. His mother* ***turned*** *him* ***over*** *and tucked up the sheets.* ○ *The aircraft struck the ground nose first and* ***turned over*** *and* ***over****.*

2 [Vp.n nom pass] (*commerce, industry*) do business to a particular amount; sell and replace (all) one's stock. **S:** trader; business, shop. **O:** amount, sum; £500, £2 000; stock: *With my type of business the* ***turn-over*** *can vary considerably. One year I might* ***turn over*** *£1m — the next only £100 000.* OBS ○ *The two men argued as to what sum, in a first year of market gardening, could be considered a reasonable* ***turn-over****.* PW ○ *This supermarket chain* ***turns over*** *its stock very rapidly.*

3 [Vn ⇆ p pass adj] cause disorder to (a place) while searching for sth. **O:** house, flat; luggage; belongings: *The police really* ***turned*** *the place* ***over*** *but still didn't find any evidence of his involvement in the crime.* ○ *Their meagre belongings, the fruits of years of toil, were disdainfully* ***turned over*** *by Iraqi customs.* IND

turn-over [nom (Vn.p)] (*commerce, industry*) rate of movement of workers into and out of a job or industry: *The* ***turn-over*** *of labour is very rapid in some sections of the catering trade.* ○ *Industries which need a stable workforce try to discourage a high* ***turn-over*** *of staff.*

turn over a new leaf [Vp.n] change one's way of life for the better: *I want to settle down,* ***turn over a new leaf****.* DPM ○ *It is due to his protection and advice that I remained at Sandhurst,* ***turned over a new leaf****, and survived to make good.* MFM

turn over in one's mind [Vn.p.pr pass] consider, think about (sth) carefully and at length. **O:** offer, proposal; idea, scheme: *He had the air of a man who is* ***turning over*** *a number of things* ***in his mind****.* CON ○ *He had plenty of time before him to* ***turn*** *the idea* ***over in his mind.*** PW = reflect on/upon 1.

turn over (to) 1 [Vn ⇆ p pass, Vn.p.pr pass] hand (sb) to the authorities. **O:** captive, prisoner; (escaped) convict. **o:** authorities; police: *'How do you know he isn't wanted by the police.' 'Why should he be?' 'If he is we ought to* ***turn*** *him* ***over****.'* ART ○ *'I am quite sure that you have no intention of* ***turning*** *me* ***over*** *to any of them.'* T = turn in 4.

2 [Vp, Vp.pr] change to another television channel: *We* ***turned over*** *in time to catch the nine o'clock news.* ○ *'You know I can't stand game shows;* ***turn over to*** *Channel 4.'* = switch over (to) 3.

turn over to [Vn ⇆ p pass, Vn.p.pr pass] pass the control or running of (sth) (to sb else). **O:** control, direction, management; business, company. **o:** brother, partner, associate: *The day-to-day management of the firm has been* ***turned over to*** *someone appointed from outside the company.*

turn round 1 [Vp, Vn.p pass] (cause sb/sth to) face in the opposite direction. ⇨ turn around/round 1.

2 [Vp nom] (*finance, commerce*) begin to show an opposite trend. ⇨ turn around/round 2.

3 [Vn.p nom pass] discharge passengers and/or cargo and get ready to sail or fly again. **O:** ship; liner, tanker; aircraft: *One of the factors in the* *profitability of passenger ships is speed of* ***turn-round*** (ie how quickly they can be ***turned round***).

turn round and do sth [Vp] (*informal*) suddenly and perhaps unexpectedly turn to sb to challenge or criticize him: *I know that the interested parties — builders, speculators — can always* ***turn round and tell me*** *that I am too slow in the uptake* (ie too slow to react to an opportunity). SC ○ *'You bring them* (ie children) *up, and they* ***turn round and talk*** *to you like that.'* TOH

turn to 1 [Vpr pass emph rel] go to (sb/sth) for help, advice, information etc. **o:** father, teacher, priest; dictionary, guide, calendar: *The child felt there was no one she could* ***turn to*** *with her problems.* ○ *The parish priest was someone* ***to*** *whom you could* ***turn*** *in difficult times.* ○ *It would have taken hours to work the sum out, so I* ***turned to*** *my pocket calculator.* = look to for sth/to do sth.
2 [Vpr emph rel, Vn.pr pass emph rel] begin to consider (sth) when speaking or writing. **O:** ⚠ one's mind, attention, thoughts. **o:** question, matter, subject: *'I wonder if we could now* ***turn to*** *another subject?'* ○ *The delegates then* ***turned*** *their minds* ***to*** *the issue of reunification.* ○ *I* ***turned*** *my attention back* ***to*** *the various containers that littered the verandah.* BB

turn a blind eye (to) [Vn.pr pass emph rel] ⇨ turn a blind eye (on/to).

turn a deaf ear (to) [Vn.pr pass emph rel] try, or pretend, not to hear (sth). **o:** complaint, criticism; moaning, caterwauling, commotion: (horoscope) *Affairs should move extremely well provided that you* ***turn a deaf ear to*** *the chatter of a frustrated female.* WI ○ ***To*** *all these accusations of foul play the referee* ***turned a*** *resolutely* ***deaf ear***.

turn one's hand to [Vn.pr] (be able to) undertake (esp sth practical). **o:** task, job; carpentry, decorating; sewing, dressmaking: *I'm not an interior decorator, but I could always* ***turn my hand to*** *most things.* TC ○ *I know you've always thought that you could do anything you* ***turned your hand to****, and mostly you could.* AITC □ with *can/could*.

turn to one's (own) advantage [Vn.pr pass] use, exploit (sth) in a way which favours oneself. **O:** situation; crisis; shortage; misunderstanding: *The Minister saw how the quarrel between his two senior colleagues could be* ***turned to his own advantage***. ○ *The swift stream hampered bridge building, but we could* ***turn*** *it* ***to advantage*** *by floating men across from up-river.*

turn up 1 [Vn ⇆ p pass adj] cause (sth) to face or point upwards. **O:** collar, sleeve, hat-brim: *The collar of his overcoat was* ***turned up*** *against the bitter wind.* ↔ turn down 2.
2 [Vn ⇆ pass adj] make (sth) more bright, intense or loud. **O:** light; gas, flame; sound, volume: ***'Turn*** *the television* ***up*** *a shade; I can't hear.'* ○ *'You can* ***turn up*** *the gas a bit, but mind you don't burn the onions.'* ↔ turn down 4.
3 [Vn ⇆ p pass] make (sth) visible, esp by digging; expose. **S:** plough, spade, excavator. **O:** bone, pottery, ornament: *A tile from a Roman villa was* ***turned up*** *during the restoration work at York Minster.* ○ *Relics from the First World War are still being* ***turned up*** *by farmers in Northern France.*
4 [Vp] arrive, appear, often after some delay. **S:** guest, visitor; bus, taxi: *'Guy will* ***turn up****. If he isn't here by morning we can start some inquiries.'* DC ○ *'The young scoundrel never had any thought for anyone. He shall hear about this from me when he* ***turns up****.'* DC = show up 3.
5 [Vp] be found, esp by chance, after it has been lost. **S:** ring, watch, key; cat: *Her purse eventually* ***turned up****. The boy who took it had got scared and dropped it behind some lockers.*
6 [Vp] present itself, become available, without one doing anything to create it. **S:** opportunity, chance; job, vacancy; something: *I've been putting off a decision, and trying not to think about it, hoping that something would* ***turn up****.* RFW ○ *He stayed in the North, hoping that an opening would* ***turn up*** *in textiles.*
7 [Vn.p] (*informal*) make (sb) feel physically sick; repel (sb) morally or emotionally. **S:** sight, smell; blood; cruelty, neglect: *The mere thought of flying* ***turns*** *her* ***up***.
8 [Vp] (*finance, commerce*) rise, increase; improve. **S:** investment, savings; (stock-) market; economy: *Investment is* ***turning up*** *sharply, including a flood of new projects flowing into the regions on the back of the Industry Act.* ST ○ *We don't know what the* ***upturn*** *in prices is going to be in 1980.* BBCR ○ *But the real* ***upturn*** *in the firm's fortunes only came with the arrival of a Canadian manager.* BBCR □ nom form is upturn. ↔ turn down 5.

turn-up(s) [nom (Vn.p)] trouser bottom which is permanently folded up: ***Turn-ups*** *seem to be coming back into fashion.* ○ *'Watch it,' I said to Ned. 'If she gives you any coffee, pour it into your* ***turn-ups****.'* CON ⇨ turn up 1.

turn-up for the book(s) [nom (Vp)] (*informal*) sth unusual or unexpected: *'Fancy Jones getting a steady job after a lifetime of crime — now that's a* ***turn-up for the book****!'*

turn it up [Vn.p] (*informal*) abandon a job etc: *I wish I could* ***turn it*** *all* ***up*** *and get away abroad for a bit.* ILIH = give up 2.

turn up trumps [Vp] (*informal*) act in a helpful or dependable way in difficult times: *Trust John to* ***turn up trumps*** *when they're short of cash.* ○ *He can always be depended on to* ***turn up trumps*** *in a crisis.*

turn one's nose up (at) [Vn ⇆ p, Vn.p.pr] (*informal*) behave in a superior way (towards sb). **o:** (ordinary, working-class) people; tradesmen; (foreign, provincial) voice, manners: *I know it's only fish fingers and chips again, but there's no need to* ***turn your nose up at*** *it.* ○ *Some people will still* ***turn up their noses*** *if you say your father was a miner or a docker.*

tussle

tussle (with) [Vpr pass] fight, struggle (with sb/sth). **o:** solicitor, bank; problem, difficulty: *She had to* ***tussle with*** *the lawyers for years before she could win custody of her daughter.*

twiddle

twiddle (with) [Vpr] turn or handle (sth) aimlessly. **o:** control, knob, button; bracelet, necklace: *He could quite happily spend hours* ***twiddling with*** *the controls on his stereo.*

twine

twine around/round [Vn.pr pass emph rel] wind sth thin and supple around (sth). **O:** (cotton, woollen) thread, yarn. **o:** spool, bobbin, reel: *As she spoke, Susan idly* ***twined*** *a piece of wool* ***round*** *her finger.* ○ *The brambles were* ***twined around*** (cf *had* ***twined*** *themselves* ***around***) *the garden fence.*

twist

twist around/round [Vn.pr pass emph rel] wind sth thin and stiff around (sth). **O:** (piece of) grass, wire. **o:** branch; spool, coil; leg, finger: *A bamboo support was stuck in the pot alongside the sunflower and a piece of raffia* ***twisted around*** *them to support the stem.* ○ *A thin piece of wire had got* ***twisted round*** (or: *had* ***twisted*** *itself* ***round***) *his ankle.*

twist around/round one's (little) finger [Vn.pr] (*informal*) by charm and guile persuade (a man) to do what one wants. **S:** daughter, wife: *I believe, if she wanted to, she could* ***twist*** *anyone* ***round her little finger.*** DC ○ *'You could even* ***twist*** *my uncle* ***around your little finger.'*** WI = wind around/round one's (little) finger.

twist off [Vn ⇆ p pass, Vn.pr pass] remove (sth) by turning. **O:** top, cap, cover; knob; button. **o:** pot, jar, bottle; door; coat: *'You try to* ***twist*** *the cap* ***off*** *this jar. My hands are too slippery.'* ○ *The handles can be* ***twisted off*** (cf: *The handles* ***twist off***).

twist up [Vn ⇆ p pass adj] make (sb) become tense and bend or turn his body; contort. **S:** pain; disgust, contempt; envy, greed. **O:** him etc; expression; face, body; inside, character: *Every time he tried to move, a sudden stab of pain* ***twisted*** *him* ***up.*** ○ *'He's a rather pitiful character, really — all* ***twisted up*** *with fear and jealousy.'*

type

type in/into [Vn ⇆ p pass adj, Vn.pr pass] insert (sth) in (a text) by typing it. **O:** (omitted, additional) word, phrase. **o:** text, script; notice, report: *'Don't bother to do the notice over again. You can* ***type*** *the missing name* ***in*** *above the line.'* ○ *'You'll notice I've* ***typed*** *a few afterthoughts* ***into*** *the margin of this letter.'*

type out [Vn ⇆ p pass adj] produce (sth) on the typewriter, ie without having first written it by hand; make a typewritten copy of a handwritten text. **O:** list, notice, application; speech: *'If you wait a minute, I'll* ***type*** *you out a proper receipt.'* ○ *'Would you mind* ***typing out*** *a list of first-year students?'* ○ *A secretary was* ***typing out*** *the candidate's election address.* □ the first example contains an Indirect Object (*you*).

type up [Vn ⇆ p pass adj] make a 'fair' typed copy of (a handwritten text); make, in typescript, a fuller, better organized version of (rough notes etc): *The final draft of his thesis has been approved by his supervisor. Now he must take it to be* ***typed up*** *and bound.* ○ *Mary spent the evening* ***typing up*** *the notes of her laboratory experiment.*

U

unaccounted

unaccounted for 1 [pass adj (Vpr)] not properly or fully explained. **S:** sum, amount; loss, disappearance: *A discrepancy in the miscellaneous earnings column remains* ***unaccounted for.*** ○ *There is an* ***unaccounted-for*** *gap of several minutes on the tape-recording of his telephone conversation.* ⇨ account for 1.

2 [pass adj (Vpr)] missing (ie people are not sure about the survival or safety of sb/sth). **S:** mountaineer, swimmer; passenger; boat, plane, helicopter: *Serious concern that 'some' Sam-7 anti-aircraft missiles are '****unaccounted for****' in Europe was expressed here by Administration sources.* T ⇨ account for 2.

unburden

unburden oneself (to) [Vn.pr emph rel] (*formal*) reveal (to sb) anxieties, sorrows etc which are a burden to one's thoughts or conscience. **o:** friend, relative: *She longed for some sympathetic friend* ***to*** *whom she might* ***unburden herself.***

uncalled

uncalled for [pass adj (Vpr)] not desirable or necessary. **S:** remark, comment; insult, rudeness; intervention intrusion: *His remarks on that occasion were quite* ***uncalled for.*** ○ *His* ***uncalled-for*** *criticisms upset quite a number of people.*

uncared

uncared for [pass adj (Vpr)] not properly tended or looked after. **S:** house, garden; child; appearance, hair, clothes: *Since the break-up of his marriage he has looked distinctly haggard and* ***uncared for.*** ○ *The hall was dark and cold. Like the rest of the house, it appeared* ***uncared for.*** CTD □ passive also with *appear* etc. ⇨ care for 2.

undreamed/undreamt

undreamed/undreamt of [pass adj (Vpr)] unimaginable. **S:** sum, amount (of money); riches, fortune; success, fame: *Investment on that sort of scale was* ***undreamed of*** *when I first joined the company.* ○ *'£30 000 a year? That was* ***undreamt-of*** *wealth to his father's generation.'*

unfold

unfold (to) [Vn.pr pass emph rel] (*formal*) make (sth) known (to sb). **O:** plan, intention, scheme. **o:** colleague, associate: *The board listened in silence as the details of the scheme were* ***unfolded to*** *them.* = reveal (to).

unguessed

unguessed at [pass adj (Vpr)] unsuspected. **S:** presence, existence; threat, danger (of invasion, absorption); size, gravity (of the problem): *The presence of invasion forces along the frontier went* ***unguessed at*** *for several months.* ○ *The imminence of the oil embargo was* ***unguessed at*** *even in government circles.* □ passive also with *go, remain.*

unheard

unheard of 1 [pass adj (Vpr)] unknown. **S:** writer, composer, actor; work, music, books: *He was virtually* ***unheard of*** *before his appearance in this West-End hit musical.* ○ *With a young,* ***unheard-of*** *poet and a first book of verse, the publisher is taking a risk.* ⇨ hear of 1.

2 [pass adj (Vpr)] without previous example, without precedent. **S:** achievement, feat; (it . . .) for sb to achieve so much: *It's virtually **unheard of** for a boy of his age to gain university entrance.* ○ *Combining a career with the responsibilities of running a house — this was an almost **unheard-of** achievement fifty years ago.*

unite

unite (in) [Vpr, Vn.pr pass] join with others (in expressing particular feelings or views). **S** [Vpr], **O** [Vn.pr]**:** country, (political) party, association. **o:** praise (for); condemnation (of), opposition (to), protest (against): *Opposition groups and the government **united in** condemning the... regime.* G ○ *The people of Poland are **united in** their distrust of further statist solutions.* IND

unite (with) [Vpr emph rel, Vn.pr pass emph rel] join (with another) to form one unit. **S** [Vpr], **O** [Vn.pr]**:** country, province, region: *Scotland was **united with** England* (or: *Scotland and England were **united***) *in 1707.*

unleash

unleash (against/on/upon) [Vn.pr pass emph rel] release (sb/sth) in a powerful attack (on sb/sth). **O:** dog, hound; army, forces; tanks, aircraft. **o:** stranger, intruder; country, people: *'I'm not going anywhere near his front gate if it means having that great bulldog **unleashed on** me.'* ○ *When the enemy at the centre had spent themselves with hard fighting, our reserves would be **unleashed against** their flanks.*

unload

unload onto [Vn.pr pass emph rel] (*informal*) pass (sth unprofitable or unpleasant) onto (sb else). **O:** stock, share; work, responsibility: *'The value of your holdings is falling. Better try to **unload** them **onto** the market now.'* ○ *There is always somebody in the office **onto** whom the really unpleasant jobs are **unloaded**.*

unlooked

unlooked for [pass adj (Vpr)] unexpected because it has not been sought. **S:** opportunity, break, chance; benefit, bonus: *The payments were all the more welcome for being quite **unlooked for**.* ○ *Then came an **unlooked-for** blessing in the form of a salary increase.* = unsought for.

unprovided

unprovided for [pass adj (Vpr)] having no money intended for him or her by a parent, guardian or husband. **S:** widow, child; relative, dependent: *His two unmarried sisters were left quite **unprovided for** in his will.* ⇨ provide for 1.

unsought

unsought for [pass adj (Vpr)] unexpected because no effort has been made to get it. **S:** promotion, appointment; salary increase, bonus: *I congratulated him on the promotion, which was all the more deserved for being quite **unsought for**.* = unlooked for. ⇨ seek (for).

unthought

unthought of [pass adj (Vpr)] unthinkable, inconceivable, and thus likely to arouse disapproval. **S:** step, move, initiative; questioning decisions, criticizing (one's elders), choosing one's own wife; (it...) to act independently: *In Victorian times it was **unthought of** for a middle-class girl to seek a professional career, except perhaps as a governess or schoolmistress.*

urge

urge on [Vn ⇆ p pass] encourage (sb) strongly to do sth. **O:** consumer; follower; team, crew. **Inf:** to invest wisely; to support the campaign; to train hard: *The director's **urging** me **on** to take a more active part in planning new courses.* ○ *Three of the couples, **urged on** by their children, are going on cycling or canoeing holidays.*

urge on/upon [Vn.pr pass emph rel] (*formal*) recommend (sb) strongly to show or accept (sth). **O:** restraint, prudence, caution, patience; solution, formula. **o:** follower, colleague, child; delegate: *The leaders had to **urge** restraint **upon** their younger members, who wished to renew the armed struggle at once.*

use

used to [pass (Vn.pr)] having learned to accept or expect. **o:** heat, cold, damp; uninteresting food, poor service, royal treatment; being ignored, having the best of everything: *It was some time before my eyes got **used to** the gloom in Stanley's workshop.* ○ *'I'm not too upset by the news. By now, I'm more or less **used to** these sudden changes of plan.'* □ passive also with *appear, become, feel, get, seem.* = accustomed to.

use up [Vn ⇆ p pass adj] use (sth) until no more is left; exhaust. **O:** supply, stock; fuel; ink; strength, energy: *The Government **used up** 5% of its gold and foreign currency reserves last month.* G ○ *'There isn't any more bread: it's all been **used up**.'*

usher

usher in [Vn ⇆ p pass] signal the start of (sth); announce. **O:** time, period, epoch: *It is the happy custom for the Viennese to **usher in** the New Year with a concert of music by Strauss.* RT ○ *It would be unwise to assume that the July elections will **usher in** a new millennium.* OBS

usher in/into [Vn ⇆ p pass, Vn.pr pass rel] conduct, lead in (to a place). **S:** butler, maid: *We were **ushered into** a waiting room lined with uncomfortable-looking chairs.* ○ *The next room **into** which we were **ushered** looked out on the gardens.* ⇨ next entry

usher out/out of [Vn ⇆ p pass, Vn.pr pass rel] conduct, lead out (of a place). **S:** butler, maid: *And he opened the door and **ushered** her **out**.* TT ○ *He was **ushered out** to a waiting car by two detectives.*

vacillate

vacillate (between) 1 [Vpr emph rel] (*formal*) be unsure which of two courses to choose. **o:** leaving and staying put, action and inertia: *At the moment they're **vacillating between** positive action and total inertia.* = waver (between) 1.

2 [Vpr emph rel] (*formal*) move restlessly from one emotional extreme to another. **o:** hope and despair, greed and disgust: *Total gloom and foolish op-*

timism — these are the extremes ***between*** *which he constantly* ***vacillates***. = waver (between) 2.

value

value (at) [Vn.pr pass emph rel] set the money value of (sth) (at a particular figure). **S:** estate-agent, auctioneer. **O:** property, estate; house, farm. **o:** amount, sum: *The house has been* ***valued at*** *around £60 000.* ○ *I'm not prepared to sell below the price* ***at*** *which the flat has been* ***valued*** *by the agents.*

vamp

vamp up [Vn ⇆ p pass adj] (*informal*) make (sth) seem new and attractive without making any genuine changes underneath. **S:** owner, manager. **O:** appearance; presentation, packaging; décor: *The front office has been* ***vamped up*** *with strip lighting and a new coat of paint.* ○ *There's no real change in the content of his lecture course — he's* ***vamped*** *it* ***up*** *a bit with one or two tricks of presentation.*

vanish

vanish (from) [Vpr] suddenly cease to be visible or present. **o:** sight, view; our presence, midst; the face of the earth: *The horsemen seemed to have* ***vanished from*** *the face of the earth.* = disappear (from sight/view).

varnish

varnish over 1 [Vpr, Vn ⇆ p pass] cover (sth) with varnish. **o/O:** table, chair: *Scrape the old paint off, sand the surface down and then* ***varnish over*** *it* (or: ***varnish*** *it* ***over***).

2 [Vpr, Vn ⇆ p pass] cover (sth unpleasant or unsatisfactory) with a smooth surface. **o/O:** flaws, blemishes; presentation, style: *The cracks and flaws in their argument are skilfully* ***varnished over***. = gloss over.

vary

vary (between) [Vpr] ⇨ next entry.

vary from to [Vpr] move up and down (a scale); fluctuate between (certain limits). **S:** temperature, pressure; takings, profit; demand, expenditure; mood, response. **o:** (**from**) (maximum) level, point; one extreme; (**to**) (minimum) level; another extreme; rock bottom: *Consumption of domestic fuel oil* ***varies from*** *150 gallons a month at the height of winter* ***to*** *practically nothing in July-August* (or: ***varies between*** *150 gallons* etc *and practically nothing* etc). ○ *'You never know how you're going to find him. His moods can* ***vary from*** *black introspection* ***to*** *wild exuberance* (or: *can* ***vary between*** *black introspection and wild exuberance*).' = range from to.

vent

vent (on) [Vn.pr pass emph rel] (*formal*) get rid of, express, (the hostile emotion felt towards sb/sth) by attacking (sb else). **O:** anger, fury, temper; spite, spleen, bitterness. **o:** husband, wife, child; subordinate; dog: *He longed to* ***vent on*** *George all the spite he felt against his former associates.* PE = take out on, work off against/on.

venture

venture on/upon [Vpr pass emph rel] (*formal*) attempt, undertake (sth involving risk or danger). **o:** undertaking, operation; journey, expedition; explanation, criticism: *The hope of making further discoveries led them to* ***venture upon*** *a second voyage.* ○ *The company secretary, who had never liked the scheme, but who also knew that stronger voices would be raised in support of it,* ***ventured*** *cautiously* ***on*** *a statement of the risks involved.*

verge

verge on/upon [Vpr] come close to (sth); approach. **S:** company, trader; idea, proposal; behaviour, condition. **o:** ruin, bankruptcy; lunacy, foolhardiness: *He had taken over an old company* ***verging on*** *liquidation.* ○ *She was not in that state* ***verging on*** *hysteria all the time.* DC = border on.

vest

vest in [Vn.pr pass emph rel] (*formal, official*) legally confer rights etc (on a person or body). **S:** sovereign, legislature; constitution. **O:** right, power, authority. **o:** official, public servant; Senate: *In the United States, the power to declare war is* ***vested in*** *the Senate* (or: *the Senate is* ***vested with*** *the power* etc). ○ *'By the powers* ***vested in*** *me, I declare you duly elected.'* □ usu passive.

vest with [Vn.pr pass emph rel] ⇨ previous entry.

vie

vie with each other/one another [Vpr] try to surpass one another in doing sth. **S:** (two, several) firms, departments; comedians; sportsmen: *Two engineering companies are* ***vying with each other*** *to capture this valuable market.* ○ *The members of the Military Board* ***vied with one another*** *in telling me agreeable things, and I kept looking around at them in astonishment.* OBS □ usu followed by an inf or a prep + *-ing* form.

volunteer

volunteer (for) [Vpr emph rel] offer oneself as willing (to serve in the armed forces, or to do a particular task). **o:** infantry, tank corps; flying duty, overseas service; work on the land: *The arm of the service* ***for*** *which he'd* ***volunteered*** *already had its full complement of men.* ○ *'I can't get any of the children to* ***volunteer for*** *work in the garden.'*

vote

vote (against) [Vpr pass emph rel] show that one opposes (sb/sth) by a ballot or a show of hands. **S:** member, delegate; elector(ate), country. **o:** leadership; proposal, motion; Bill: *He* ***voted against*** *the government party at the last election.* ○ *The Chamber* ***voted*** *overwhelmingly* ***against*** *changing the law.* ○ *'Which way did you* ***vote***?' '***Against*** *the Bill.'* ↔ vote (for).

vote down [Vn ⇆ p pass] reject (sth), or defeat (the person proposing sth), by a ballot or a show of hands. **O:** motion, proposal; member: *Someone proposed that the proceedings of the meeting should be recorded on tape, but the suggestion was* ***voted down***.

vote (for) [Vpr pass emph rel] show one's support (for sb/sth) by a ballot or a show of hands. **S:** member, delegate; elector, country. **o:** leader; policy; proposal, motion; Bill: *The government are not implementing the policies* ***for*** *which we* ***voted*** *in the last election.* ○ *Whether you* ***vote for*** *or against the proposal doesn't seem to matter very much.* ↔ vote (against).

vote in/into [Vn ⇆ p pass, Vn.pr pass] elect (sb) to serve in Parliament, on a local council etc. **O:** Labour, the Conservatives; MP, councillor. **o:** ⚠ office, power: *Labour was **voted in** for a second term of office, though with a greatly reduced number of seats.* ○ *The Democrats were **voted into** power on a wide-ranging environmental programme.* = put in 7 .

vote (on) [Vpr pass emph rel] express one's support (of sth) or opposition (to sth) by a ballot or a show of hands. **S:** chamber, assembly; meeting. **o:** motion, proposal; Bill: *We are now **voting on** a motion to adjourn the meeting.* ○ ***On** this Bill every member is free to **vote** as his or her conscience dictates.*

vote on/onto [Vn.p pass, Vn.pr pass] make (sb) a member of (some official body) by a ballot or a show of hands. **O:** specialist, expert; (additional) member. **o:** committee, board, panel; council: *'He has more experience of fund-raising than anyone, so we'll **vote** him **on** for a start.'* ○ *An accountant and an architect were **voted onto** the committee in the hope that they would contribute their expertise at the planning stage.*

vote out/out of [Vn ⇆ p pass, Vn.pr pass] remove from (office) by casting one's vote at an election. **O:** Labour, the Republicans; minister; member, representative. **o:** ⚠ office, power: *If the present Government is **voted out** it will be on its general handling of the economy.* ○ *'If you don't like the way the Council are going about things, you can always **vote** them **out of** office.'*

vote through [Vn ⇆ p pass] make (sth) law by a ballot or a show of hands; enact. **S:** House, chamber; meeting. **O:** legislation, Bill, Act: *The Bill was **voted through** by both Houses with no further delay.*

vouch

vouch for 1 [Vpr pass] confirm the truth of (sth), by producing evidence, showing that one was present etc. **o:** soundness, truth (of sth); technique, process; the fact that ..., it that ...: *One application of 'primitive' medicine, **vouched for** by modern anthropologists, goes back beyond the reach of human memory.* SNP ○ *I can definitely **vouch for** it that Robert and his Italian girl are washed up* (ie no longer lovers). CON

2 [Vpr pass] express one's confidence in (a person): *'If you needed a reference, I'm sure he'd **vouch for** me.'* ○ *'Well, I'm sure about Martin, anyway: he's already been **vouched for**.'*

W

wade

wade in/into 1 [Vp, Vpr] (*informal*) attack (sb) vigorously. **o:** opponent, adversary: *Fred **waded into** his tormentor with both fists flying.*

2 [Vp, Vpr] (*informal*) begin tackling (a task) in a vigorous, determined way. **o:** task, job; packing, cleaning: *He didn't stand about looking at all the jobs needing to be done: he **waded** straight **in**.*

wade through 1 [Vp, Vpr] walk through some liquid substance which reaches some way up one's legs. **o:** mud, slush; grain; oil; pond: *Rescue teams **waded** knee-deep **through** the flooded streets.* ○ *Every time our youngest daughter, Sarah, comes to a deep, muddy puddle she has to **wade through** it.*

2 [Vp, Vpr] (*informal*) proceed slowly and with difficulty with (some task). **o:** paperwork, marking, accounts, files: *'I shan't be able to get away this weekend: I've got six sets of exam scripts to **wade through**.'* = plough through.

wage

wage war (against/on) 1 [Vn.pr pass emph rel] fight, conduct, a war (against sb). **o:** country, people: *For almost a year they had **waged** a **war** of nerves **on** their neighbours; now it was to be war in earnest.*

2 [Vn.pr pass emph rel] try to control (sth) by vigorous action. **o:** disease, hunger; inflation, unemployment; tax evasion, drug trafficking: *The government promised to **wage** a ceaseless **war against** inflation.*

wager

wager on 1 [Vn.pr pass] bet (money) on (a horse etc) hoping that it will win. **O:** a few pounds, a large sum, a fortune. **o:** horse, dog; boxer: *'There's nothing in this race I'd be prepared to **wager** more than a couple of pounds **on**.'* ○ *A lot of money was **wagered on** a good-looking Irish horse in the second race.* = gamble on 1, put on 8, stake on.

2 [Vpr, Vn.pr pass] (*informal*) (be prepared to) believe confidently that sth is the case, or will happen. **O:** ⚠ anything; too much, a lot. **o:** it, that; John arriving in time; prompt delivery, good response: *'I suppose he just might start behaving more responsibly, but it's not something I'd **wager on**.'* ○ *'He promised me this fabulous holiday in the Bahamas.' 'Well I wouldn't **wager** too much **on** that.'* □ usu neg, with *should/could*. = gamble on 2.

wait

wait about/around [Vp] stay in a place, usu idly and impatiently, eg because sb who is expected does not arrive: *'I'm furious: you've kept me **waiting about** here for a whole hour.'* ○ *'Show the visitor in as soon as he arrives. Don't make him **wait around** in the corridor.'* = hang about/around.

wait at table(s)/on tables [Vpr] bring food and drink to guests at their table(s), remove dishes etc: ***Waiting at table** is a skilled job, requiring proper training.* ○ *I got holiday jobs in guest-houses, washing dishes and **waiting on tables**.* DC ⇨ wait on.

wait behind [Vp] stay in a room etc after others have left: *'John, you can **wait behind** when the class is dismissed: I want to have a word with you.'* ○ *One or two students **waited behind** to put further questions to the lecturer.* = remain behind, stay behind, stop behind.

wait for [Vpr rel] stay where one is until the arrival of (sb/sth); await. **o:** train, bus; end, beginning; better things, improvement: *A queue of people were **waiting for** the last bus.* ○ *The climax of the film is something worth **waiting for**.* ○ *The birth of a child was an event **for** which they had **waited** and prayed.*

wait for it [Vpr] (*informal*) a warning not to speak, move, etc, before the proper moment has come:

'Yes, I know what happened then: Mike fell out of bed.' **'Wait for it**, *can't you? Who's telling the story, you or me?'* ○ *By her side the old Chief said quietly, '***Wait for it**. *Remember, don't look at the tracer, just keep looking at the sights* (ie of the gun), *and mind what I told you.* **Wait for it**.' RFW □ imperative only.

wait in [Vp] wait at home, eg because one is expecting sb to call: *I* **waited in** *all morning for the plumber, but he didn't turn up.*

wait on [Vpr pass] bring food and drink to (guests). **o:** guest, visitor, diner: *Nick got a job* **waiting on** *tourists in a small seaside hotel.* ○ *'I quite enjoy being* **waited on** *once in a while.'* ⇨ wait at table(s)/on tables.

wait on tables [Vpr] ⇨ wait at table(s)/on tables.

wait on/upon [Vpr] wait for sth to be done or said before acting. **o:** developments, events; reply, reaction: *We were in no hurry to make an offer: we would sit back and* **wait on** *developments in New York.*

wait on/upon sb hand and foot [Vpr pass] act as a servant to sb, answering to his every need: *At home the boys never lifted a finger. We girls had to* **wait on** *them* **hand and foot**. ○ *She lived in great style —* **waited on hand and foot**.

wait out [Vp.n] await the end of (an unpleasant period) calmly and patiently. **O:** it; storm; trial, crisis; discussion; half-hour, weekend: *The storm showed no sign of easing. We'd have to be patient and* **wait** *it* **out**. ○ *We settled down to* **wait out** *the afternoon.*

wait up (for) [Vp, Vp.pr pass] stay awake and out of bed (for sb to come home). **S:** parent, wife, husband: *'I shan't get in till after midnight, so don't bother to* **wait up**.' ○ *The old folks always go to bed about ten. They don't* **wait up for** *me.* TC

wake

wake up 1 [Vp, Vn ⇆ p nom pass] (cause sb to) cease to sleep; awake: *I drowsed off and* **woke up** *to hear Bob talking to some fellow who was new to the place.* BM ○ *'Don't make such a noise — you'll* **wake** *the baby* **up**.' □ nom form is used before a noun: *I phoned down to reception to ask for a seven o'clock* **wake-up** *call.*
2 [Vp, Vn ⇆ p pass] (cause sb to) become more lively and involved; (cause sth to) become more lively and interesting. **S** [Vp], **O** [Vn.p]: audience, class; guest; party, proceedings; things: *'The guests need* **waking up**. *How about opening a bottle?'* ○ *If we brought in a guest speaker or two, the literature course might* **wake up** *a little.* = liven up.

wake up to [Vp.pr] suddenly become aware (of sth critical). **o:** danger, threat; the fact that times have changed, the realization that one is no longer young; (an awareness of) oneself: *She should* **wake up to** *the problems she's got on her hands.* ○ *It's time I* **woke up to** *myself. I had a good look in the mirror just now, and it's not flattering.* RFW

walk

walkabout [nom (Vp)] a tour on foot, esp by a politician, or visiting dignitary, to meet and talk to people informally: (picture caption) *President Bush at a Warsaw* **walkabout** *yesterday following a wreath-laying at the ... memorial to Second World War victims.* G ○ *New Zealanders are understandably proud that the Queen chose their country for the first-ever* **walkabout**. BBCTV □ may be used before a noun, as in: ... *quiet* **walkabout** *chats in the High Street.* ST

walk abroad [Vp] (*rhetorical*) spread far and wide. **S:** disease, pestilence; murder, arson: *There death and destruction had already* **walked abroad**. SD

walk away from [Vp.pr pass] leave, turn from (a challenge etc) because of fear, indifference etc. **O:** challenge, opportunity; danger, crisis: *'If you* **walk away from** *this challenge, you'll live to regret it.'* ○ *'She's just* **walked away from** *the biggest offer anyone ever made to her.'*

walk away with [Vp.pr] (*informal*) win (a contest) easily. **S:** player, team; (political) party, candidate. **o:** game, match; election: *'It's no good — they've lost. They should have* **walked away with** *the game.'* LLDR ○ *The official Labour Party candidate* **walked away with** *the election: his majority went up by five thousand.*

walk in/into [Vp, Vpr] enter (a place) easily, because it is not properly locked or guarded. **o:** shop, office: *The security is so bad here that anyone could simply* **walk in** *and take what he wanted.*

walk into [Vpr] receive (a blow, shock, etc) because one is inattentive or careless. **o:** blow, punch; trap, ambush: *For a second the champion's attention wavered, and he* **walked** *straight* **into** *a right hook.* ○ *'He loves to set traps for the unwary: you wouldn't be the first to* **walk into** *one.'*

walk off [Vn ⇆ p pass] remove, reduce (sth) by walking. **O:** some weight, a few pounds; (the effects of) a heavy lunch, business dinner; mood: *I'll have to get out into the country more, and* **walk off** *some of this fat.* ○ *We started out in a mood of deep depression, but had* **walked** *it* **off** *before we got home.*

walk off his feet [Vn.pr pass] (*informal*) make (sb) walk so fast and so far that he is exhausted: *'Let me sit down for a moment: the children have been* **walking** *me* **off my feet**.' ○ *'If you want a leisurely stroll through the museum, don't take that guide — she'll* **walk** *you* **off your feet**.'

walk off with [Vp.pr] take, carry away (sb's property) either intentionally or by mistake. **o:** purse, bag, briefcase: coat, hat: *'This isn't my mac — some idiot must have* **walked off with** *it.'* ○ *'Don't leave your suitcases unguarded. Somebody may* **walk off with** *them.'*

walk on [Vp nom] (*theatre*) have a small part, appear briefly, in a play: *When he first joined the company, Christopher was happy just to be able to* **walk on** *— to play the butler or the policeman.* ○ *She's had a couple of* **walk-on** (or: **walking-on**) *parts in West End productions — and that's about all.* □ nom forms usu attrib, as here.

walk out [Vp nom] (*industrial relations*) leave one's place of work to protest, to obtain sth etc. **S:** worker; engineer, fitter: *Building workers* **walked out** (or: *staged a* **walk-out**) *during the morning in protest at the sacking of a bricklayer.* = come out 1.

walk out/out of [Vp nom, Vpr] leave (a meeting etc) as an expression of disapproval, protest etc. **S:** delegate, representative; delegation. **o:** conference, meeting; talks; committee: *The President's address was interrupted by a mass* **walk-out** *of*

Baltic delegates. ○ *At various times, both teams of nogotiators had* **walked out of** *disarmament talks.*

walk out on [Vp.pr pass] (*informal*) abandon (sb), esp when he is in difficulties and expecting help; leave (sb) because the relationship is at an end, or difficult to bear. **o:** friend, child, colleague; wife, boyfriend, girlfriend: *'You've got his baby; you can't just* **walk out on** *him because he doesn't get on with your family.'* ASA ○ *'So you're* **walking out on** *the job, are you? You're just a louse like the rest of them.'* HD ○ *'So things didn't work out then?' 'No, I've just* **walked out on** *him, for better or for worse.'* EGD

walk-over 1 [nom (Vp)] (*informal*) victory that is easily won, success that is easily achieved: *'It won't be a* **walk-over** *this time: the champion has a tough fight on his hands.'* ○ *'Now, stop worrying about those exams. You've revised well, so relax. It's going to be a* **walk-over**.*'*

2 [nom (Vp)] permission to proceed to the next stage of a competition because one's opponent at the present stage is unable to compete against one: *Mark Kratzman was given a* **walk-over** *against the Swede Anders Jarryd, who damaged a rib in a collision with his doubles partner.* G

walk (all) over [Vpr pass] (*informal*) defeat (sb) thoroughly in a contest, in a power struggle etc; overpower. **S:** boxer, team; boss, father. **o:** novice, opposition; staff, children: *The replay wasn't much of a contest: Liverpool* **walked all over** *them.* ○ *'I'm just not prepared to let myself be* **walked over** *by the School Governors.'*

walk through [Vn.p nom pass, Vn.pr pass] (*theatre*) show (sb) the movements he must make in a scene etc, and make him copy them. **S:** director. **O:** cast, actor. **o:** scene, act: *'Don't worry too much about lines. I just want to* **walk** *you* **through** *part of Act I.'* ○ *'After lunch I want to do a* **walk-through** *of the ghost scene.'*

wall

wall in 1 [Vn ⇆ p pass adj] enclose (sth) with a wall. **O:** garden, park, yard: *Behind the house was a neat* **walled-in** *garden.* ⇨ fence in 1, hedge in 1.

2 [Vn ⇆ p pass adj] surround (sb), as if with a wall, so that he is not free to move. **O:** fugitive, quarry, prey: *The mass of faces pressed closer,* **walling** *him* **in**. ○ *The fox was* **walled in** *by the pack of baying hounds.* = fence in 2, hedge in 2, hem in.

wall off (from) [Vn ⇆ p pass adj, Vn.p.pr pass emph rel] separate (one area) (from another) by means of a wall. **O:** area, playground; garden: *The rose-gardens were* **walled off** *to one side of a lawn running down to the river.* ⇨ fence off (from), rail off (from).

wall up [Vn ⇆ p pass adj] close or seal (sth) with a wall of brick, plaster etc. **O:** space; door(way), window: *When the central-heating was installed, the fireplaces were* **walled up**.

wallow

wallow in 1 [Vpr rel] roll about pleasurably in (sth), usu to get or stay cool. **S:** elephant, buffalo. **o:** water, mud, slime: *The rhinoceroses* **wallow in** *the soft mud at the edge of the river.*

2 [Vpr rel] sink oneself into a particular emotion, usu self-indulgently or perversely. **o:** self-pity, remorse; corruption, sensual delights: *The longer she* **wallows in** *feelings of guilt the harder it will be to make a fresh start.*

waltz

waltz off with Vp.pr] (*informal*) win a prize etc, esp by beating others easily. **S:** athlete; schoolboy. **o:** cup, medal; scholarship, prize: *Later in the week, the Kenyans* **waltzed off with** *gold medals in the 5 000 metres and the steeplechases.* ○ *The head prefect* **waltzed off with** *the maths and science prizes.* = run away with 3.

wander

wander about [Vp, Vpr] move about without any sense of where one is going. **S:** traveller, expedition; (lost) child: *'I was the one who found your little boy. He was* **wandering about** *on the edge of the crowd and I took him to the police station.'* ○ *The survivors* **wandered about** *the jungle for days before being picked up by a search party.*

wander from/off [Vpr] move, stray, in an absent-minded way (from the subject one is concerned with). **S:** speaker; mind, thoughts. **o:** the main point, the key issue; the subject under discussion, the matter at hand: *Don't let your mind* **wander off** *the crucial issue.* ○ *The member seated at the chairman's elbow brought him back to the subject —* **from** *which he'd all too easily* **wandered**. = stray from. ↔ keep to 1.

want

(not) want for [Vpr] (not) be lacking in money, or the things that make life comfortable and pleasant. **S:** family, wife, parents. **o:** ⚠ anything, nothing; very much: *His children do***n't want for** *anything — they're all well provided for.* ○ *He makes sure that his widowed mother* **wants for** *nothing.*

want in [Vp] (esp *US*, *informal*) wish to be involved in sth profitable, pleasurable etc: *'Tell Smith that if he's still interested in going ahead with the new company, then I* **want in** *too.'* ⇨ next entry

want out/out of [Vp, Vpr] (esp *US*, *informal*) wish to be freed from (sth unpleasant). **S:** husband, wife; partner; company, country. **o:** involvement, commitment; risk; war: *'Please don't think that you can depend on my support any longer; I* **want out**.*'* ○ *The ordinary people* **want out of** *any further involvement in the war.* ⇨ previous entry

ward

ward off 1 [Vp.n pass adj] defend, protect, oneself against (sth). **O:** attack; blow, thrust: *He flung up an arm to* **ward off** *the blow.* PE = fend off 1.

2 [Vp.n pass adj] keep (sth) from affecting one mentally or emotionally. **O:** feeling; depression, despair: *To* **ward off** *the feeling, I drank the whisky quickly.* SML = fend off 2.

warm

warm to [Vpr] become more lively about, enthusiastic about (sth) as one proceeds with it. **o:** work, task; subject, theme: *Sensing the mood of the audience, the chairman* **warmed to** *his topic, giving the most entertaining and persuasive speech of the evening.* ○ *Pierre grew ruder and louder as he* **warmed to** *his work.* BFA

warm to/towards [Vpr] begin to like (sb): *I felt myself* **warming to** *this big friendly man who had* *done so much to help us.* ○ *She's not the sort of girl one* **warms towards** *easily — rather cold and aloof.*

warm up 1 [Vp, Vn ⇆ p pass adj] (cause sth to) become warm or warmer. **S** [Vp], **O** [Vn.p]: house, room; food, liquid: *Why is it this room always takes so long to* **warm up**? ○ *We agreed about the port and whisky: it would* **warm** *them all* **up**. BFA ○ *'Don't serve me* **warmed-up** *food* (ie food which has been cooked, allowed to get cold and then reheated).' = heat up 1.

2 [Vp, Vp.n pass] (cause an engine to) reach the point, after its parts are warm and working smoothly, where it can run properly. **S** [Vp], **O** [Vp.n]: machine, motor; car; television (receiver), radio: *In cold weather pull the choke out half-way, and let the engine* **warm up**, *before you move off.* ○ *Joe* **warmed up** *the engines and taxied to the end of the runway.*

3 [Vp nom] (*sport*) take exercises to loosen one's muscles etc, before a game etc. **S:** athlete, footballer: *The German manager has one of his substitutes* **warming up** *on the touch-line now.* ○ *The runners are having a quick* **warm-up** *before the race.* □ nom form also used before a noun: **warm-up** *exercises.*

4 [Vp, Vn ⇆ p pass] (cause sb/sth to) become more lively and interested. **S** [Vp], **O** [Vn.p]: audience, spectator; contest, campaign, game; party, celebration: *The election campaign is* **warming up** *now, with both parties trying to score points over their opponents.* ○ *The comedian told a few quick jokes to get his audience* **warmed up**.

warn

warn about/against [Vn.pr pass emph rel] tell sb to be wary of, or avoid (sth harmful, unhealthy etc). **O:** public; consumer; child, pupil. **o:** (danger, risk of) infection, poisoning; (excessive) smoking, drinking; swimming out of one's depth, travelling without a guide: *Travellers to the tropics are generally* **warned against** *drinking water that has not been filtered or boiled.* ○ *A Government notice on each packet* **warns** *the public* **about** *the dangers of cigarette smoking.*

warn off [Vn.p pass, Vn.pr pass] order (sb) not to trespass, investigate, intrude etc. **S:** company, landowner; police. **o:** property, land; looking into the case: *'That's twice I've had to* **warn** *you* **off** *my land. The next time I'll report you for trespassing.'* ○ *A reporter had got hold of some new information about an old political scandal. He wanted to follow it up, but the editor* **warned** *him* **off**.

wash

wash away [Vn ⇆ p pass] remove (sth) by striking it repeatedly. **S:** sea; breaker, wave; flood. **O:** cliff; road, railway; hut: *The base of the cliff had been* **washed away** *in the continuous gales.* ○ *The river flooded its banks,* **washing away** *part of the main railway line.*

wash down (with) 1 [Vn ⇆ p nom pass adj, Vn.p.pr pass] clean dirt from a surface (using water etc). **O:** wall, door; paintwork; car; deck (of a ship). **o:** jet, spray (of water); hose, brush: *On Sundays, he* **washes** *his car* **down with** *the garden hose.* ○ **Wash** *the walls* **down** *well* (or: *Give the walls a good* **wash-down**) *before putting on the emulsion.*

2 [Vn ⇆ p pass, Vn.p.pr pass] drink (sth) after, or at the same time as, taking a (solid meal). **O:** meal; meat and potatoes; bread and cheese. **o:** beer, wine: *We ate sausage, and* **washed** *it* **down with** *a whisky.* TC

wash one's hands of [Vn.pr emph rel] say or show that one no longer wishes to be responsible for (sb) or involved in (sth). **S:** parent, teacher; manager; shop, department. **o:** one's children, dependants; (the whole) affair, matter, business: *'Very well,' John got up and looked out of the window, 'I* **wash my hands of** *it. If you and Larrie want to fuss over the wretched bird, do.'* ASA ○ *'If you're going to regard every suggestion I make as a criticism, then I must* **wash my hands of** *the whole matter.'* ASA

wash off 1 [Vn ⇆ p pass, Vn.pr pass] remove (sth) from the surface of a material etc, by using water etc. **O:** dirt, grime; mark; grease, paint: *I tried to remove the grease spots from the wall but they wouldn't* **wash off** (or: *I couldn't* **wash** *them* **off**). ○ *'***Wash** *that dirt* **off** *your fingers before coming to the table.'*

2 [Vn.p] remove dirt etc from (sb/oneself) using water. **O:** him etc; oneself: *'***Wash** *yourself* **off** *before you come to the table.'*

wash out 1 [Vn ⇆ p pass] wash the inside of (sth) so as to remove the dirt etc from it. **O:** pot, basin; mouth; shirt, towel: *When you've cleaned your teeth,* **wash** *your mouth* **out** *with clean water.* ○ *'I just want to* **wash out** *one or two dish-cloths.'* ⇨ wash out/out of.

2 [Vn ⇆ p pass adj] (*informal*) make (sb) feel very tired; exhaust: *Rushing around in this heat really* **washes** *you* **out**. ○ *'I thought Mike was looking a bit* **washed out**.' *'I'm not surprised, with all those late nights.'* ○ *Vicky was in very bad shape — a dreadful* **washed-out** *appearance, with none of the old sparkle.* □ passive also with *appear* etc.

3 [Vn ⇆ p nom pass adj] (*sport*) bring (play) to an end; prevent (play) from starting. **S:** rain; downpour, cloudburst; storm. **O:** game, match: *Heavy rain this weekend* **washed out** *five league fixtures.* ○ *Last year Edberg was the victim of a rescheduling caused by the* **wash-out** *of a day's play.* IND ⇨ next entry

wash-out [nom (Vn.p)] (*informal*) failure; disappointment. **S:** party; meeting; show, film. **adj:** total, complete, absolute: *If you launch a sales campaign now, when there's so little money about, it'll be a total* **wash-out**. ○ *'Did you enjoy the party?' 'Not much; I thought it was a bit of a* **wash-out**.' ⇨ previous entry

wash out/out of [Vn ⇆ p pass adj, Vn.pr pass] remove (dirt etc) (from sth) by washing it. **O:** dirt, impurities; grease, paint. **o:** clothes; brush: **Wash** *all the blue* **out of** *your brush before starting on another colour.* ○ *'If you'd* **wash** *the sleep* **out of** *your eyes, you might be able to see what was going on.'* ○ *He wore* **washed-out** *blue overalls* (ie from which some of the dye had been removed by repeated washing). ⇨ wash out 1.

wash over [Vpr] (*informal*) take place, occur, all around (sb), without greatly affecting him. **S:** noise, disturbance; quarrels, tensions; backbiting: *The kids were making a tremendous din, and he sat there quietly typing his report. It all* **washed over** *him.* ○ *'He doesn't seem to mind what people* *say, does he? All the recent criticism seems to have* ***washed*** *right* ***over*** *him.'* = flow over.

wash overboard [Vn.p pass] (*nautical*) sweep (sb) over the side of a ship into the sea. **S:** (heavy) sea, wave. **O:** passenger, crew; cargo: *A huge wave* ***washed*** *a deck hand* ***overboard****.* ○ *Some of the cargo lashed to the forward deck was* ***washed overboard*** *in a gale.*

wash up 1 [Vp, Vn ⇆ p pass adj] wash (the dishes etc) after a meal. **O:** dishes, knives and forks; tea/dinner things: *He had helped Edith with the* ***washing up*** *on the maid's day out.* HD ○ *After supper we'd* ***wash up*** *and she'd sit by the fire.* ITAJ ○ *He lunged across to the sink and snatched the* ***washing-up*** *bowl.* HD □ note the nom form in: *do the* washing up; attrib use in: washing-up *liquid* (ie liquid soap etc used for washing up).
2 [Vp, Vn ⇆ p pass adj] (cause floating objects etc to) come ashore. **S:** sea, tide, waves. **O:** survivor, body; debris, wreckage; driftwood; oil: *Bits of wreckage were now* ***washing up*** *all along the beach.* ○ *The incoming tide* ***washed up*** *cargo from the wrecked coaster.* ○ *The surveyor's department — with men switched from drawing boards to beaches — were coping deftly with any oil* ***washed up****.* OBS

washed up [pass adj (Vn.p)] (*informal*) finished, at an end; ruined, a failure. **S:** marriage, affair; couple, friends: *'Your marriage was* ***washed up*** *long before Gilbert left: you should never have married him.'* ASA ○ *'Robin and I aren't lovers any more. We're* ***washed up****, as they say in the movies.'* ASA

waste

waste away [Vp] grow unhealthily thin, through illness, poor feeding etc: *Matthew was looking dreadful the last time I saw him — he's* ***wasting away*** *to skin and bone.*

watch

watch out [Vp] be careful to avoid danger, not to upset others etc: *'You need to* ***watch out*** *here. The ground's a bit boggy on either side of the path.'* ○ *'You'll be in deep trouble if you don't* ***watch out****.'* □ often in the clause pattern: *if he doesn't/you don't* watch out. = look out 1, mind out.

watch out (for) [Vp nom, Vp.pr pass rel] be alert, so that one notices (sb/sth important). **S:** authorities; police, customs. **o:** intruder, trouble-maker, smuggler; movement, change, sign: *I said I should be sick, and that I must* ***watch out for*** *symptoms.* PM ○ *'Keep a sharp* ***watch-out for*** *anybody trying to come in this way.'* = look out (for).

watch over [Vpr pass adj] be responsible for (sth/sb). **S:** parent, teacher, doctor; policeman, security guard. **o:** safety, security; well-being; pupil, patient, passenger: *The security of passengers travelling on routes favoured by hijackers needs to be* ***watched over*** *more vigilantly.* ○ *A new minister has been appointed to* ***watch over*** *the welfare of disabled people.*

water

water down 1 [Vn ⇆ p pass adj] make (sth) weaker, by adding water; dilute. **O:** beer, brandy: *'If you want to give the children wine, you'd better* ***water it down*** *a bit.'* ○ *There was no more whisky left, not even a drop to* ***water down****.* DBM
2 [Vp.n pass adj] make (arguments etc) less forceful or extreme; weaken. **O:** idea, philosophy; policy, programme: *I have considerably* ***watered down*** *Blaize's criticisms of the guilty men.* DS ○ *The Democrats have presented a* ***watered-down*** *version of their Trades Union policy.*

wave

wave aside [Vn ⇆ p pass] show that one considers (sth) to be unimportant, irrelevant etc; dismiss. **O:** argument, idea, proposal; objection, criticism: *Jill* ***waved aside*** *my objections and took out her cheque-book.* ○ *Formalities were* ***waved aside*** *so that Stephen could be got aboard the aircraft without further delay.*

wave away/off [Vn ⇆ p pass] show (sb), with a motion of the hand, that he must move or stay away. **S:** policemen, bodyguard; doorman, butler. **O:** onlooker; reporter, photographer; tout, door-to-door salesman: *John wanted to take a closer look at the silver Rolls, but a uniformed chauffeur appeared, and* ***waved*** *him* ***off****.* ○ *Nobody was allowed near the wreckage of the plane. Even those with press cards were* ***waved away****.*

wave down [Vn ⇆ p pass] stop (sb/sth), esp on a road, by moving one's hand up and down. **S:** policeman, soldier, traffic warden, steward. **O:** motorist, visitor; car, van: *A man wearing a blue arm-band* ***waved*** *us* ***down*** *and checked our ferry tickets.* = flag down.

wave on [Vn ⇆ p pass] tell (sb/sth) to continue by waving one's hand backwards and forwards. **S:** policemen, soldier, sentry. **O:** motorist, driver; car, truck: *A bored-looking frontier guard* ***waved*** *us* ***on****, without even bothering to glance at our passports.*

waver

waver (between) 1 [Vpr emph rel] be unsure which of two alternative courses to choose. **o:** action and inaction; a house and a flat: *At the moment he's* ***wavering between*** *a smart coupé and a large family saloon.* = vacillate (between) 1.
2 [Vpr emph rel] move restlessly from one emotional state to another. **o:** attraction and revulsion, tolerance and bigotry: *You never know what mood you're going to find him in — always* ***wavering between*** *despair and elation.* = vacillate (between) 2.

wean

wean away (from) [Vn ⇆ p pass, Vn.p.pr pass emph rel] lead (sb) away gradually from sth which appears pleasant, but which is no longer suitable for him. **O:** pupil, student; follower. **o:** idea, belief; association: *These were ideas* ***from*** *which we were tactfully trying to* ***wean*** *him* ***away****.* ○ *His son needs to be* ***weaned away from*** *the notion that everything will come easily to him.*

wear

wear away [Vp, Vn ⇆ p pass adj]: (make sth) disappear through constant pressure, friction etc. **S** [Vp], **O** [Vn.p]: hill, cliff; step, pavement. **S** [Vn.p]: weather, elements: *With the passage of time, the finer detail of the carvings has almost* ***worn away****.* ○ *Wind and rain have* ***worn away*** *the sharp ridges of these mountains.* = eat away (at).

wear down 1 [Vp, Vn ⇆ p pass adj] (make sth) become shorter or lower, through continuous pressure, friction etc. **S** [Vp], **O** [Vn.p]: point (of instrument), tread (of tyre), heel (of shoe): *Get the cobbler to fit metal studs to your boots: they won't*

wear down so quickly. ○ *'Your back tyres are badly* ***worn down****: you should fit new ones.'*
2 [Vp, Vn ⇆ p pass adj] (cause sth to) become weaker by constant moral pressure or attack. **S** [Vp], **O** [Vn.p]: resistance, opposition; conviction, faith. **S** [Vn.p]: argument, speech, sermon: *Under so much pressure from her parents, her will to independence was slowly* ***wearing down****.* ○ *He might be* ***wearing down*** *her superstitious belief in the punishment by constantly belittling it.* ARG

wear off 1 [Vp, Vn ⇆ p pass] (cause a surface etc to) disappear through continuous pressure, friction etc. **S** [Vp], **O** [Vn.p]: nap, pile (of carpet); paint, plating (on cutlery). **S** [Vn.p]: (rough) use, rubbing: *'Don't polish those badges: the gilt will* ***wear off*** *if you do.'* ○ *Don't buy a cheap carpet; children running in and out will soon* ***wear*** *the pile* ***off****.*
2 [Vp] no longer affect one; gradually disappear. **S:** newness, novelty; feeling, sensation; tiredness, depression: *The children lingered among their presents, feeling the strangeness* ***wear off*** *and the thrill of ownership begin.* PW ○ *The drink inside them had* ***worn off****, leaving only a sour feeling in the stomach.* HD

wear on [Vp] proceed slowly or tediously. **S:** day, week, month; meeting, party: *The gloomy afternoon* ***wore on****.* LWK ○ *The fields were covered with ice and, as September* ***wore on****, the noisy rivers were gradually silenced.* TBC

wear out 1 [Vp, Vn ⇆ p pass adj] (cause sth to) become unusable through continuous wear, handling etc. **S** [Vp], **O** [Vn.p]: clothing, shoe; engine, motor: *Children's clothes* ***wear out*** *very quickly— they get so much rough treatment.* ○ *Existing aircraft will already be* ***worn out****.* SC
2 [Vn ⇆ p pass adj] exhaust (sb) physically or mentally. **S:** movement, excitement; tension, stress; company, conversation: *Anne,* ***worn out*** *with anxiety and strain, followed from one house to the next.* WI ○ *I've seen plenty of girls* ***wear*** *themselves* ***out*** *trying to run a home and a job.* AITC = tire out.

wear through [Vp, Vn.p pass] (make sth) develop a hole through continuous use. **S** [Vp], **O** [Vn.p]: shoe, sole; carpet, vinyl: *John's* ***worn*** *the soles of his slippers right* ***through****.* ○ *The carpet is* ***worn through*** *just inside the front door.*

weary

weary of [Vpr rel] (*formal*) no longer be interested in or attracted by (sb/sth); become irritated by (sb/sth). **o:** girl, companion; relationship, love-affair; job, experience, pastime; chatter, nagging: *He had spent too long in the same job, and was beginning to* ***weary of*** *it.* ○ *Eventually one* ***wearies of*** *this constant bickering between political leaders.* = tire of.

weave

weave in and out/out of [Vp, Vpr] advance by moving first to the left then to the right around obstacles. **S:** car, bicycle; procession. **o:** traffic; crowd: *He goes to work on a motor-bike,* ***weaving in and out*** *of the traffic jams.* ○ *The cart moved over the dew-soaked grass,* ***weaving in and out*** *among the giant thistles.* DF

weave (up) (from) [Vn ⇆ p pass, Vn.pr pass rel, Vn.p.pr pass rel] make (cloth) (from threads) by weaving them together. **O:** length, piece; (cotton, woollen) cloth. **o:** yarn, thread: [Vn.pr] *The curtains were* ***woven*** *on a hand loom* ***from*** *local cotton.* ○ [Vn.p.pr] *'I* ***wove*** *this length* ***up from*** *hanks of cotton which I dyed myself.'* ⇨ next entry

weave (up) (into) [Vn ⇆ p pass, Vn.pr pass rel, Vn.p.pr pass rel] make (threads) (into cloth) by weaving them together. **O:** yarn, thread; cotton, wool. **o:** cloth; blanket, covering: [Vn.p] *'I've no yarn left; it's all been* ***woven up****.'* ○ [Vn.pr] *Threads of different colours and textures were* ***woven into*** *an intricate pattern.* ⇨ previous entry

wed

wed (to) [Vn.pr pass emph rel] (*formal*) combine (one quality etc) (with another). **S:** author, designer, builder. **O:** simplicity, strength, utility. **o:** feeling, grace, spaciousness: *In the design for the church, he has* ***wedded*** *a traditional ground plan* ***to*** *(or: and) modern structural methods.*

wedded to [adj (Vn.pr)] so attached to, or absorbed in (sth) that one finds no room for anything else. **o:** work; studies, research; car, gardening; view, opinion: *He spends most evenings at the office. You could say he's* ***wedded to*** *the job.* ○ *She won't be shifted — she's* ***wedded to*** *her prejudices.* □ also used after *appear, become, get, seem* and after a noun: *... a woman* ***wedded to*** *her work.*

weed

weed out [Vn ⇆ p pass adj] get rid of parts which weaken or injure the whole; improve the whole by doing this. **S:** farmer, breeder; commander, manager. **O:** runt, weakling; malcontent, dissident; herd, flock; group, unit: *Officers who couldn't stand the strain were to be* ***weeded out*** *and replaced.* MFM ○ *'You'll have to* ***weed*** *this intake* ***out*** *pretty ruthlessly if you want a good group next year.'*

weep

weep over [Vpr pass] express regret at (sth) or for (sb). **o:** loss, misfortune; past failings; his resignation, embarrassment, disgrace: *There's not much point in* ***weeping over*** *what's past.* ○ *If they were to send Johnson packing tomorrow, I don't suppose his departure would be* ***wept over*** *very much.* = cry about/over.

weigh

weigh against [Vpr] prevent (sb) from succeeding or doing his best; hinder, hamper. **S:** age; immaturity, lack of experience; evidence, testimony; criticism. **o:** him etc; candidate, applicant; his being selected: *'The landlady's evidence will* ***weigh against*** *him. I'm not very optimistic about the verdict.'* ○ *The fact that a man has taught overseas for several years ought not to* ***weigh against*** *his getting a senior post in Britain.* = tell against.

weigh down 1 [Vn ⇆ p pass adj] (of a weight) make (sb/sth) bend or sag. **S:** load, burden; box, parcel; crop. **O:** porter, shopper; plant, tree: *'Get this bundle off my back; it's really* ***weighing*** *me* ***down****.'* ○ *The branches were* ***weighed down*** *almost to the ground with ripe fruit.* □ alt form: weight down.
2 [Vn.p pass adj] make (sb) sad and anxious; depress: lower sb's spirits. **S:** responsibility, charge; cares, hardships: *He doesn't let the cares of parenthood* ***weigh*** *him* ***down****.* ○ *John seems terribly* ***weighed down*** *by all the extra administration.*

weigh in (at) [Vp nom, Vp.pr] (*sport*) have one's weight measured before a race or boxing match. **S:** jockey; boxer. **o:** 45 kilos, 80 kilos; 98 lbs, 200 lbs; 7 stone, 12 stone 8 lbs: *The first fighter* **weighed in at** *more than the limit for his class and had to sweat off a few pounds.* ○ *A number of reporters were present at the* **weigh-in** (ie *the time of* **weighing in**).

weigh in (with) 1 [Vp, Vp.pr] (*informal*) give (one's support) to an undertaking. **S:** firm, bank; member, sponsor. **o:** donation, loan; offer of support: *All of us will* **weigh in** *one hundred per cent to do what you want.* MFM ○ *The whole family* **weighed in with** *offers of help.*
2 [Vp, Vp.pr] use (forceful arguments) in a discussion: *One man leapt to his feet and* **weighed in with** *a fierce denunciation of the party executive.*

weigh on sb/sb's mind [Vpr emph rel] make (sb) anxious; worry. **S:** responsibility, burden; loss, debt; disgrace, dismissal: *'Don't disturb your mother; she has so many things* **weighing on her mind**.' ○ *Didn't Nurse Ellen's accident* **weigh on her** *at all?* DC ○ *He's the sort of man* **on whom** *professional setbacks* **weigh** *very heavily.*

weigh out [Vn ⇆ p pass adj] measure a quantity of (sth) by weight. **S:** chemist, grocer, cook. **O:** substance; flour, sugar; gram, kilo, pound: *The ingredients for the cake had all been* **weighed out**. ○ *She* **weighed out** *small quantities of dye to make up a colour.*

weigh up 1 [Vn ⇆ p pass] consider (things) carefully and make a judgement; assess, judge. **O:** situation; prospects, chances; things: *In a split second Mr Charlton had everything* **weighed up**. BFA ○ *When you come to* **weigh** *things* **up**, *there isn't any practicable alternative to this Government.* ILIH
2 [Vn ⇆ p pass] form an opinion, make a judgement, of (sb's character). **O:** visitor, newcomer: *Father usually has someone* **weighed up** *within a few minutes of meeting him.* ○ *The children haven't* **weighed up** *their new teacher yet.* = size up.
3 [Vn ⇆ p pass] consider (alternatives) carefully before choosing one of them. **O:** alternatives, pros and cons; whether to go or stay: *He was* **weighing up** *whether to stay with us or not.* SML ○ *Parents can then* **weigh up** *whether their child should leave or try for an apprenticeship.* OBS

weigh with [Vpr emph rel] (*formal*) be regarded as important by (sb), be seriously considered by (sb). **S:** factor, element; output, efficiency; talent, industry; evidence, opinion. **o:** director, consumer; selector; judge: *Trade considerations in particular are bound to* **weigh** *heavily* **with** *us.* SC ○ *The social background of the applicants does not* **weigh** *at all* **with** *the interviewing panel.*

weight

weight down [Vn ⇆ p pass adj] ⇨ weigh down 1.

welcome

welcome back [Vn ⇆ p pass] greet (sb) enthusiastically on his return. **S:** crowd, supporter, fan. **O:** king, president; player, actor, singer: *A large crowd gathered at the airport to* **welcome back** *the national football team.*

welcome in/into [Vn ⇆ p pass, Vn.pr pass] greet a visitor (to one's home etc) warmly. **O:** (foreign) visitor, student; delegate, envoy. **o:** house, office: *The bride and groom stood by the door to* **welcome in** *their guests.* ○ *A number of families* **welcome** *overseas students* **into** *their homes at Christmas.*

weld

weld together [Vn ⇆ p pass] unify, combine (things/people) strongly or solidly. **S:** leader, movement. **O:** element, force; people, tribe: *The regime has succeeded in* **welding together** *many diverse elements — religious, racial and linguistic.* ○ *The nation has been* **welded together** *by the shared experience of exile and persecution.*

well

well up [Vpr] rise like water in a well. **S:** water, tears; passion, powerful feelings: *The bath has filters through which hot water* **wells up** *and the waste drains away.* WI ○ *Tears suddenly* **welled up** *in her eyes.* ○ *Strong feelings* **welled up** *within him.* = surge up, swell up 2.

welsh

welsh on [Vpr pass] (*racing*) leave a race-course without paying winnings to those who have placed bets with one; repudiate an obligation or agreement previously entered upon. **S:** book-maker ('bookie'); he etc; the Government. **o:** racegoer, punter; debts; deal; election programme: *'Don't lay bets with any of the small bookies on the course: they may* **welsh on** *you.'* ○ *At the very last moment his main backer* **welshed on** *the deal, leaving him high and dry with no money to pay his creditors.*

wheel

wheel in/into 1 [Vn ⇆ p pass, Vn.pr pass] push a wheeled truck etc, or sb/sth mounted on one, into (a place). **O:** truck, trolley; stretcher; patient; tea things: *The door opened and a waiter* **wheeled in** *the tea trolley.* ○ *The patient was anaesthetized before being* **wheeled into** *the theatre.*
2 [Vn ⇆ p pass, Vn.pr pass] (*informal, jocular*) conduct, escort (sb) into a place where he is to be interviewed, questioned etc. **O:** applicant, visitor; prisoner: *'Who's next on the list, Miss Jones?' 'A Mr Davis.' 'All right,* **wheel** *him* **in**.'

while

while away [Vn ⇆ p pass] (do sth to) make (the time) pass pleasantly. **S:** reading, sewing; radio, television. **O:** time; afternoon, evening; (few) days, hours: *He had a volume of Pascal open on his desk to* **while away** *the time.* QA ○ *I was glad of his company to* **while away** *an hour until the train came.*

whip

whip away [Vn ⇆ p pass] remove (sth), eg from a flat surface, with a sharp, snatching movement. **O:** cloth, cover; cup, plate; newspaper: *The conjuror* **whipped away** *the cover to reveal two live rabbits.* ○ *The waiter* **whipped** *my cup* **away** *before I'd finished my coffee.*

whip back [Vp] return sharply, with the action of a whip. **S:** branch; boom (of a sailing boat); swing door: *Stephen was pushing through the wood just* *ahead of me, and a thin branch* ***whipped back*** *and cut me just below the eye.*

whip off [Vn ⇆ p pass, Vn.pr pass] take off, remove (sth) with a sharp, snatching movement. **S:** wind, draught; intruder, thief. **O:** hat; paper, letter. **o:** desk, shelf: *'Get to it!' snapped Morgan as he* ***whipped off*** *his overcoat, refused refreshments and eased his bulk into an armchair.* SHCK ○ *Gales uprooted trees and* ***whipped*** *the slates* ***off*** *roofs.*

whip on 1 [Vn ⇆ p pass] make (an animal) go faster by striking it with a whip. **S:** rider, jockey. **O:** mount, horse: *The horses flashed past the post,* ***whipped on*** *furiously by their jockeys.*

2 [Vn ⇆ p pass] drive (sb) to go faster, work harder etc, by means of curses, threats etc. **S:** foreman; boss; warder; fear, hunger. **O:** gang, team; workforce; prisoners: *The fugitives wanted to rest up for the night, but the fear of capture* ***whipped*** *them* ***on***.

whip out/out of [Vn ⇆ p pass, Vn.pr pass] take out, produce (sth) with a sharp, snatching movement. **O:** gun; wallet, letter. **o:** holster; pocket, drawer: *How would you react if someone entered your shop and* ***whipped out*** *a revolver?* ○ *He* ***whipped*** *a piece of paper* ***out of*** *his pocket and waved it in our faces.*

whip-round [nom (Vp)] (*informal*) appeal to colleagues etc for money to help in a good cause. **S:** department, shop, office party: *He's suggesting a* ***whip-round*** *to subscribe to a new statue.* RM □ often used in the pattern *have a* whip-round.

whip up 1 [Vn ⇆ p pass adj] beat (ingredients) vigorously until they are solid, thoroughly mixed etc. **O:** mixture; eggs, cream: ***Whip up*** *the eggs and flour to the consistency of a smooth paste.* ○ *When the cream is well* ***whipped up****, it should stick to the fork.*

2 [Vn ⇆ p pass adj] cause (waves etc) to form and become agitated or turbulent. **S:** wind, gale, typhoon. **O:** sea; waves: *The gale* ***whipped up*** *huge waves that crashed against the sea-wall.*

3 [Vn ⇆ p pass] make (a horse etc) move faster by striking it with a whip. **O:** horse, mule, ox; team: *The coachman* ***whipped up*** *the horses and we moved off down the drive.*

4 [Vn ⇆ p pass adj] arouse, excite (sb) by vigorous action, public speaking etc. **S:** demagogue, rabble-rouser. **O:** crowd, audience; feeling; anger, support: *Competitive journalism had* ***whipped up*** *public interest in a rather strange stunt.* SD ○ *The endlessly repeated chorus* ***whipped*** *the teenage audience* ***up*** *to a state of frenzy.* = stir up, work up (into/to).

whisk

whisk away [Vn ⇆ p pass] brush (sth) quickly and lightly away as if with a whisk. **O:** fly, mosquito: *He* ***whisked*** *the flies* ***away*** *from his food with a flick of his hand.*

whisk away/off [Vn ⇆ p pass] take (sb/sth) away suddenly, as if by magic etc. **S:** car, ambulance; police; waiter, attendant. **O:** guest, patient; prisoner; dish. **A:** to hospital, jail: *Stop him* ***whisking away*** *the remains of the meal.* OMIH ○ *Our special holiday issue* ***whisks*** *you* ***off*** *on a magic carpet to Starland.* WI

whisk up [Vn ⇆ p pass adj] mix and change the thickness of (ingredients) by beating them with a whisk. **O:** eggs, cream. **A:** to a smooth paste, creamy consistency: *To make meringues, you first take the whites of several eggs and* ***whisk*** *them* ***up***.

whisper

whisper about/around [Vn ⇆ p pass, Vn.pr pass] secretly pass around (stories which damage a person's good name or position); circulate. **S:** neighbour, gossip. **O:** tale, rumour, scandal; it . . . that sb has been in prison, that he is divorced: *It was* ***whispered about*** *that he had a conviction for drunken driving.* ○ *It doesn't take long for a bit of gossip to be* ***whispered around*** *this neighbourhood.* □ usu passive.

whistle

whistle for [Vpr] (*informal*) hope in vain for (sth). **S:** creditor, tradesman. **o:** money, loan: *John borrowed two of my favourite books, and as far as he is concerned, I can* ***whistle for*** *them.* □ with *can/could; may/might.*

whittle

whittle away 1 [Vn ⇆ p pass] remove the outer part of (sth) in small pieces, using a knife. **O:** bark, veneer: *'Make this plug smaller for me, but don't* ***whittle away*** *too much wood.'*

2 [Vn ⇆ p pass] remove, take away (sth) one by one or little by little. **S:** Chancellor, the Inland Revenue; inflation, escalating costs; legislation. **o:** gain, increase (in wages, profits); rights, privileges: *They put up our pay in October but a rise in the cost of food has* ***whittled away*** *the increase, so we're back where we started.*

whittle down 1 [Vn ⇆ p pass adj] make (sth) thinner by removing fine slices with a knife. **O:** stick, post; branch, twig: *He took a square block of wood and* ***whittled*** *it* ***down*** *to form the hull of a model boat.*

2 [Vn ⇆ p pass adj] reduce the size or importance of (sth) by degrees. **S:** employer, department; investigator. **O:** staff, work force; privilege, benefit; field, suspects: *The research team has been* ***whittled down*** *considerably to staff other projects.* ○ *The detective couldn't be expected to fool the smuggler unless his status was* ***whittled down***. DS ○ *We've* ***whittled down*** *a mass of evidence and produced two clear leads.*

whiz

whiz across, along, away etc [Vp, Vpr] go across etc quickly and esp making a high whistling noise. **S:** shell, bullet; car, aircraft. **o:** head, ear; house: *Bullets* ***whizzed towards*** *us and thudded into the sandbags.* ○ *All these cars* ***whizzing past*** *my front window keep me awake at night.*

whoop

whoop it up [Vn.p] (*informal*) celebrate in a cheerful, noisy way: *The bar stayed open late and groups of holidaymakers were still* ***whooping it up*** *after midnight.*

win

win back [Vn ⇆ p pass] get back (sth) after a struggle; recover, regain. **S:** country, industry; boxer, sprinter. **O:** territory, market; title, cup: *As a result of the 1914-18 war, France* ***won back*** *Alsace and Lorraine.* ○ *We have not* ***won back*** *the orders lost to our competitors.*

win (from/off) [Vn.pr pass emph rel] get (sth) (from sb) as a result of a contest, game etc. **O:** money;

bracelet, watch; title, crown. **o:** bookmaker, tote; opponent: *He* **won** *a gold watch* **off** *someone he met in a pub.* ○ *Douglas* **won** *the heavyweight title* **from** *Tyson and then promptly lost it to Holyfield.*

win out [Vp] (*informal*) be successful, defeat sb/sth, after a struggle. **S:** patient, invalid; applicant, student; army, expedition: *He fought his trouble down and I thought he was going to* **win out**. TBC ○ *Do you look business-like? If so you may* **win out** *over some more experienced applicant.* H

win over (to) [Vn ⇆ p pass, Vn.p.pr pass rel] persuade (sb) to agree to be on one's side etc. **O:** parent, colleague; rival, rebel. **o:** sb's cause, persuasion; way of thinking: *She wanted to marry, but her mother could never be* **won over**. ARG ○ *After some discussion, they were* **won over to** *our side.* ○ *This is a specious theory* **to** *which too many have been* **won over**.

win through [Vp] overcome an obstacle or difficulty: *He settled to his task with a good will, and with his help we* **won through**. SD ○ *The home side* **won through** *to the last eight of the competition by beating Derbyshire by 38 runs.* G

wind

wind around/round [Vn.pr pass emph rel] twist or fold (thread etc) round (sth/sb). **O:** string, wool; blanket, towel. **o:** spool, bobbin; post; waist, neck: *She was absent-mindedly* **winding** *a length of thread* **around** *her finger.* ○ *A strip of bandage was* **wound round** *his ankle.*

wind itself around/round [Vn.pr pass emph rel] become twisted or entangled around (sth/sb). **S:** cable, wire; hair, thread; creeper. **o:** engine; spindle, cog; post, tree: *When your car is being towed, keep the tow-rope taut, otherwise it may* **wind itself around** *your front wheels.* ○ *Pieces of wool had got* **themselves wound round** *the spindle of the machine.* □ passive with *get*, as in the second example.

wind around/round one's (little) finger [Vn.pr] (*informal*) through feminine charm, flattery etc, persuade (sb) to do what one wants. **S:** wife, girlfriend, daughter: *He almost admired her for the way she had succeeded in* **winding** *Utterson* **round her** *cunning* **fingers**. US ○ *She knows very well she can* **wind** *her father* **round her little finger**. = twist around/ round one's (little) finger, wrap around/round one's (little) finger.

wind back [Vp, Vn ⇆ p pass] bring back (a section of film etc) for re-showing, by turning the spool on which it is mounted; rewind. **S:** operator, projectionist. **O:** film, film-strip, tape: *'***Wind** *the film* **back** *a few frames. I want to see that sequence again.'*

wind down 1 [Vn ⇆ p pass adj] lower, bring down (sth) by turning a handle or wheel. **O:** window, shutter, screen: *He* **wound down** *the window of his car and leant out to ask the way.* ↔ wind up 1.

2 [Vp] (of a clock-spring) become slack, causing the clock to lose time and stop. **S:** clock, watch: *It's a one-day clock; the spring* **winds down** *in 24 hours.* ↔ wind up 2.

3 [Vp, Vn ⇆ p pass] (cause sth to) cease production or activity gradually, by reducing staff etc. **S** [Vp], **O** [Vn.p]**:** factory, industry; operation, programme: *The department is* **winding down** *as a centre for innovative research.* ○ *The plant is being* **wound down** *with the probable loss of 500 jobs.* = run down 1.

4 [Vp] relax gradually, eg after a working day: *In the evening she* **winds down** *by listening to classical music.*

wind in [Vn ⇆ p pass] draw (a fishing-line) from the water and coil it around a reel attached to the rod; bring (a fish) to land by doing this. **O:** line; fish, catch: *You play a fish by letting it have a bit of line, and then* **winding** *the line* **in** *sharply.*

wind on [Vp, Vn ⇆ p pass adj] move (a film etc) forward, so as to expose, or show, the next portion. **S:** photographer, cameraman. **O:** film, film-strip, tape: *If you don't* **wind on** *after taking a picture, your negative will be double-exposed.*

wind round [Vn.pr pass emph rel] ⇨ wind around/round.

wind itself round [Vn.pr pass emph rel] ⇨ wind itself around/round.

wind round one's (little) finger [Vn.pr] ⇨ wind around/round one's (little) finger.

wind up 1 [Vn ⇆ p pass adj] bring up, raise (sth) by turning a handle, wheel etc. **O:** bucket; window, roller-blind: *They drove along with all the car windows* **wound up**. ↔ wind down 1.

2 [Vn ⇆ p pass adj] tighten the spring of (a watch etc), to make it function. **O:** watch, clock; (clockwork) motor; spring: *She* **wound up** *the toy mouse and set it running across the carpet.* ○ *These old-fashioned watches only keep good time if you* **wind** *them* **up** *every morning.* ↔ wind down 2.

3 [Vn ⇆ p pass adj] raise (sb) to a pitch of excitement. **S:** orator, agitator. **O:** audience, follower: *By this time, he had* **wound** *the crowd* **up** *to fever pitch.* ○ *In any political discussion he always gets terribly* **wound up**. □ usu passive.

4 [Vn.p nom pass] (*informal*) annoy, irritate (sb): *'Why don't you stop* **winding** *me* **up***?'* ○ *'Are you* **winding** *your sister* **up** *again, Fred?'* □ note nom form wind-up used esp with the meaning of 'joke': *When you told me that she'd died her hair pink I thought it was a* **wind-up**.

5 [Vp, Vp.n pass] (of a speech or meeting) close, terminate. **S:** speaker, chairman. **O:** remarks, address; debate, discussion; session: *'This is the way I see it, in a nutshell,' said Ned,* **winding up**. CON ○ *As we walked along, Blaize* **wound up** *his story.* DS ○ *The charge was not denied by the Minister for the Armed Forces, as he* **wound up** *a two-day debate on defence spending.* IND

6 [Vp, Vn ⇆ p pass adj] (cause sth to) stop functioning, cease its activities; stop, cease. **S** [Vp], **O** [Vn.p]**:** department, firm; business; exercise, project, scheme. **S** [Vn.p]**:** director, manager: *We hope that when the campaign* **winds up** *officially its educational service will carry on.* TES ○ *The smuggling organization* **wound up** *its activities and prepared to disband.* DS ○ *Lawyers presided over the* **winding-up** *of the bank's affairs.* ⇨ wind up one's affairs.

7 [Vp] (*informal*) get or experience (sth unusual, and usu unpleasant) as a result of one's work, manner of life etc. **A:** with an ulcer; dead, exhausted; in charge: *'Don't carry on living at this pace: you'll* **wind up** *with nervous exhaustion.'* ○ *'You'll keep your nose out of my affairs, unless you want to* **wind up** *in hospital.'* ○ *'Mark my words, one day he'll* **wind up** *running the company.'* = end up.

wind up one's affairs [Vp.n pass] finally settle one's business or personal affairs before leaving, retiring etc: *In the last month I was* ***winding up my affairs*** *in England and saying goodbye to all my friends.* RFW ○ *I can't go on holiday until* ***my affairs*** *are properly* ***wound up****.* ⇨ wind up 6.

wink

wink (at) [Vpr pass] close and open one eye as a sign of friendship or invitation, eg to a girl, or as as a secret signal at some shared joke: *After making some outrageous remark, which no one except George would understand, he would turn to George and* ***wink*** *broadly* ***at*** *him.*

winkle

winkle out/out of 1 [Vn ⇆ p pass, Vn.pr pass] (*informal*) remove, dislodge (sb/sth) slowly and with difficulty. **S:** soldier; farmer. **O:** sniper, pocket of resistance; rabbit, rat: *Enemy troops hiding in the cellars had to be* ***winkled out*** *one by one.* ○ *'I've dropped a coin between the floorboards; try to* ***winkle*** *it* ***out of*** *there.'*

2 [Vn ⇆ p pass, Vn.pr pass] (*informal*) extract (information etc) with difficulty from (sb). **O:** news, story; gossip, scandal. **o:** witness, interviewee: *'See if you can* ***winkle*** *anything* ***out of*** *the wife; I'll question the husband.'*

wipe

wipe away [Vn ⇆ p pass] remove (sth) by rubbing with the hand or a cloth etc. **O:** tear, sweat; mark, spot: *He* ***wiped*** *the sweat* ***away*** *from his brow with his handkerchief.*

wipe down [Vn ⇆ p nom pass] clean (sth) from top to bottom, or from end to end, by rubbing it with a cloth. **O:** window, shop-front; table, dresser: *When you've washed the car,* ***wipe*** *it* ***down*** *well* (or: *give it a good* ***wipe-down***) *with a shammy leather.* ○ ***Wipe down*** *the walls with a soapy cloth.*

wipe off 1 [Vn ⇆ p pass, Vn.pr pass] take off, remove (sth) by rubbing it with a cloth etc. **O:** drawing, sentence, formula. **o:** blackboard; door, wall: *'****Wipe*** *that drawing* ***off*** *the board before the teacher sees it.'* ○ *Paint won't* ***wipe off*** (ie can't be ***wiped off***).

2 [Vn ⇆ p pass] (*finance, commerce*) accept that (sth) is a loss, cannot be got back etc. **O:** deficit, debt, loss; £10m: *There were banks forced to* ***wipe off*** *millions of pounds of bad debts.* = write off 1.

wipe off the face of the earth/off the map [Vn.pr pass] remove (sth) by violent action; obliterate. **O:** town, village; competitor, opponent: *'We'll* ***wipe*** *that company* ***off the face of the earth****.' She spoke with cruel satisfaction.* UTN ○ *Whole villages were* ***wiped off the map*** *as a reprisal for alleged atrocities.*

wipe the smile etc off one's/sb's face [Vn.pr pass] (*informal*) cause sb to stop smiling or grinning in a self-satisfied way. **O:** ⚠ smile, grin, smirk: *'I'd be glad if you'd* ***wipe that*** *silly* ***grin off your face****.'* ○ ***The smile*** *could be* ***wiped off the Government's face*** *if the economic winds changed for the worse.* OBS

wipe out 1 [Vn ⇆ p pass] clean the inside of (a container) by rubbing it with a cloth. **O:** bath, basin; dish, cup: *'Make sure the inside of the coffee pot is thoroughly* ***wiped out****.'*

2 [Vn ⇆ p pass] clear, repay (sth). **S:** borrower; company; theatre, club. **O:** debt, liability: *The museum's financial debt had been* ***wiped out****.* SD

3 [Vn ⇆ p pass] reduce (sth) to nothing; nullify. **S:** counter-attack, thrust; price increase, rising costs. **O:** gain, benefit, advantage: *An offensive on the central front* ***wiped out*** *the gains of the previous winter's fighting.* ○ *Escalating costs will almost certainly* ***wipe out*** *within a year the benefits of the latest salary increases.* = cancel out.

4 [Vn ⇆ p pass adj] destroy (sth) completely. **S:** fire, disease, drought; bombing. **O:** village, farm; stock, crop; population: *A summer fire can* ***wipe out*** *all the pasture feed.* RFW ○ *The whole of life on earth might be* ***wiped out*** *with little compunction.* TBC

5 [Vn ⇆ p pass] cleanse society of (sth). **S:** government, system; science, technology. **O:** crime, disease, poverty: *Many people still believe that wars, strikes and crime could be* ***wiped out*** *as if by some magic wand.* SNP ○ *In many areas once infested by mosquitoes, men have* ***wiped out*** *malaria.*

wipe over [Vn.p nom pass] pass a cloth etc over (sth), so cleaning it, but not thoroughly. **O:** table, shelf; wall, window: *There wasn't time to clean the windows properly, so Jane just* ***wiped*** *them* ***over*** *with a damp cloth.* ○ *'The table's a bit sticky. I'll give it a quick* ***wipe-over*** *before we lay the cloth.'*

wipe up 1 [Vn ⇆ p pass] pick up, remove (sth) with a cloth, esp sth that has fallen or been spilled on a table or floor. **O:** mess; beer, milk; food, gravy: *'Don't let the coffee sink into the carpet:* ***wipe*** *it* ***up****!'* ○ *'You can just go and* ***wipe up*** *the mess you've made in the kitchen.'*

2 [Vp, Vn ⇆ p pass] dry (crockery etc) after it has been washed. **S:** children, kitchen staff. **O:** dishes; plate, knife: *'Would you mind helping me to* ***wipe up*** (or: *helping me with the* ***wiping-up***)*?'* ○ *'Don't bother to* ***wipe up*** *the dishes; stack them on the draining-board.'* = dry up 2.

wire

wire up [Vn ⇆ p pass] connect (sth) with wires to sth else, so that current can pass between them; fit (sth) with wires. **O:** TV, video; plug, fitting; house, room: *'Get professional advice on* ***wiring up*** *these appliances.'* ○ *'Has the studio been* ***wired up*** *yet?'*

wise

wise up (to) [Vp, Vp.pr pass, Vn.p pass adj, Vn.p.pr pass] (*informal*) (make sb) become aware of the true nature (of sb/sth). **o:** intrigue, game, plan, tactics; newcomer, neighbour: [Vp.pr] *He was new to the company, but it didn't take him long to* ***wise up to*** *what was going on.* ○ [Vn.p] *By this time, I was fully* ***wised up****.* ○ [Vn.p.pr] *The new store detective was quickly* ***wised up to*** *the shoplifters' favourite methods.*

wish

wish away [Vn ⇆ p pass] (try to) get rid of (sth) by wishing it did not exist. **O:** problem, difficulty; increase, deficit: *The rising numbers seeking places in higher education cannot simply be ignored or* ***wished away****.* UL

wish (for) [Vpr pass] long to have, desire, sth which is difficult to obtain, or can only be had by extreme good fortune. **o:** opportunity, opening; wealth, success: *'Why should the children want to leave home? They have everything they could possibly* **wish for**.' ○ *'I couldn't* **wish for** (or: **wish** *to have) a better wife than I've got.'*

withdraw

withdraw (from) 1 [Vpr emph rel, Vn.pr pass emph rel] (*military*) (cause sb to) move back, esp in a controlled way, from (a position). **S** [Vpr], **O** [Vn.pr]**:** troops; division, regiment. **S** [Vn.pr]**:** general; the high command. **o:** front line, trench, outpost: *Our men were* **withdrawn from** *a position near the front line.*

2 [Vpr emph rel, Vn.pr pass emph rel] no longer (allow sb to) take part in (sth). **S** [Vpr], **O** [Vn.pr]**:** athlete, player; team. **S** [Vn.pr]**:** manager, organizer. **o:** contest, games: *Dunstable have* **withdrawn from** *the FA Cup following the abandonment of their game against Staines.* IND

withhold

withhold (from) [Vn.pr pass emph rel] (*formal*) not allow (sb) to know or have (sth). **O:** news, information; promotion, privilege; passport: *Visas have been* **withheld from** *some members of the delegation.* ○ *Teachers* **from** *whom salaries have been* **withheld** *are organizing a protest.* = keep back (from) 2.

wobble

wobble about [Vp] move unsteadily from side to side, from weakness or lack of skill: *John came into sight,* **wobbling about** *on an old bicycle.* ○ *He still* **wobbles about** *a bit after his recent fall.*

wolf

wolf down [Vn ⇆ p pass] (*informal*) eat (sth) hungrily or greedily. **O:** food; supper: *He went down to the kitchen in search of food and* **wolfed down** *a pie.*

wonder

wonder about [Vpr] ask oneself questions about (sb/sth). **o:** (absent) friend, relation; her marriage, their life together; how they are getting on; where they should go next: *'Have you seen the agenda for tomorrow's meeting?' 'No—in fact, I was just* **wondering about** *it myself.'* ○ *Warnie was now 12 years old and his parents were starting to* **wonder about** *where he should be educated.* CSL

wonder at [Vpr pass] (not) be surprised (if/that . . .). **o:** his resigning, her refusal to cooperate; it . . . if he resigns, it . . . that she refuses: *Can you* **wonder at** *it that people get angry about having to live in these conditions?* ○ *'So she's finally left him? I don't* **wonder at** *it.'* □ in neg or interr sentences.

work

work one's way across, along, back etc [Vn.p, Vn.pr] move, progress, usu in the face of obstacles, in a given direction: *Porters laden with stores were now* **working their way** *slowly* **across** *a rope bridge.* ○ *He managed to* **work his way back** *through the crowd of guests with two glasses of champagne.*

work against [Vpr] affect (sth/sb) negatively; impede. **S:** attitude; prejudice, ignorance; conditions; climate, disease. **o:** change; progress; any improvement in standards; student, pupil: *More than anything, it's the lack of investment in plant and training that* **works against** *real improvement in industrial performance.* ○ *'He has a poor grasp of the basic processes, and that's bound to* **work against** *him.'*

work among [Vpr rel] practise a profession or provide a service, in and for (a community). **S:** priest, doctor, teacher. **o:** people; the homeless, the poor; outcasts: *She has been* **working among** *immigrant families in the East End of London.* ○ *His early life was spent* **working among** *lepers.*

work around/round to [Vp.pr pass] (*informal*) eventually tackle (sth) some time after one has begun talking. **o:** problem, topic, discussion: *It was a long time before he finally* **worked around to** *what he wanted to say.*

work at [Vpr pass] give thought, energy etc to getting rid of or solving (sth). **o:** problem, task; sums, tables: *'You'll crack this problem if you really* **work at** *it.'* ○ *'There's no easy way round the difficulty: you'll have to* **work at** *it.'* ⇨ work on 1.

work away (at) [Vp, Vp.pr pass] give continuous effort, thought etc (to sth). **o:** maths, German; carpentry, decorating: *I found him* **working away** *in the library.* ○ *Chemistry was a subject he didn't mind* **working away at**.

work-in [nom (Vp)] (*industry*) form of industrial action in which workers occupy and run a factory etc, often one which is threatened with closure during a trade recession: *During the* **work-in** *a committee elected by the workforce made the day-to-day management decisions.* ○ *They* (a group of factory workers) *organized a* **work-in** *and enlisted the support of the powerful left wing in France.* BBCTV

work in/into 1 [Vn ⇆ p pass, Vn.pr pass] insert (sth) gradually, by moving it from side to side etc. **O:** bolt, shaft, key. **o:** socket, hole: *She* **worked in** *the key and opened up the classroom.* TT

2 [Vn ⇆ p pass, Vn.pr pass] add (sth) slowly and carefully to (sth). **O:** margarine, butter; oil, paint; cream. **o:** flour, mixture; surface; skin: *Take a little of the ointment and* **work** *it* **into** *the skin.*

3 [Vn ⇆ p pass, Vn.pr pass] include (sth) (in sth) by showing special care or cunning. **O:** bit, section; humour, romance, liveliness. **o:** account, story: *You won't get the story published unless you* **work in** *a bit of human interest.* ○ *He always contrives to* **work** *his war experiences* **into** *the conversation.*

work off 1 [Vn ⇆ p pass] get rid of an excess of (sth) by exercise etc. **O:** energy; fat; a few kilos, a pot-belly: *'If you feel like* **working off** *some energy, go and dig the garden.'* ○ *Boxers are constantly gaining weight and then* **working** *it* **off** *with gruelling training regimes.*

2 [Vn ⇆ p pass adj] settle (a debt) with earnings from paid work. **O:** loan, debt, overdraft; sum, amount: *It would take me a couple of years to* **work off** *a debt of that size.* ○ *Many students fear that it will take a long time to* **work off** *their loans.*

3 [Vn ⇆ p pass] get rid of (an unpleasant feeling) by doing sth. **O:** frustration, anger, bad mood: *'I'll give you a hand with the clearing up.' 'No thanks, I'll do it on my own, it's just what I need to* **work off** *my temper.'* FOLK ○ *The ethologists view is that young men are fighting animals who need to* **work off** *their aggression in sport.* SPTB ⇨ next entry

work off against/on [Vn ⇆ p pass, Vn.p.pr pass] get rid of (an unpleasant feeling) at sb else's expense. **O:** frustration, irritation; anger, spleen. **o:**

wife, child; junior; cat: *One generally has to* ***work off*** *one's irritation* ***on*** *somebody.* MFM ○ *'There's no need to* ***work*** *your frustration* ***off on*** *me.'* = take out on, vent (on). ⇨ previous entry

work on 1 [Vpr pass] give thought, effort etc to making or discovering (sth). **o:** book, play; Milton, Tolstoy; radio, rocket-motor; improvement: *For his doctorate, he's* ***working on*** *the use of dialect speech in the Victorian novel.* ○ *The manufacturers are* ***working on*** *a modification to the steering.* ⇨ work at.

2 [Vpr pass] (*informal*) try for some time to persuade (sb) to do sth: *'You speak to the mother; I'll try* ***working on*** *the father.'* ○ *'Perhaps they could be* ***worked on****; anyway, I don't mind giving it a try.'*

work on/onto [Vn ⇆ p pass, Vn.pr pass] place (one thing) gradually around (another), by moving it from side to side etc. **O:** ring; nut, washer. **o:** finger; bolt, spindle: *When he tried to* ***work*** *the nut* ***onto*** *the spindle, he broke the threads.*

work out 1 [Vn ⇆ p pass adj] plan, devise (sth). **S:** committee, team; engineer, architect; artist, philosopher. **O:** scheme, programme; theory: *A subcommittee has been appointed to* ***work out*** *a new constitution for the club.* ○ *Religious thinkers may* ***work out*** *a new interpretation of life.* AH ○ *Staff officers presented a fully* ***worked-out*** *plan of attack.*

2 [Vn ⇆ p pass adj] calculate, reckon (sth). **S:** accountant, bursar. **O:** pay, allowance, pension; cost; that it will cost £100, how much to pay him: *We have computers to* ***work*** *our salaries* ***out*** *these days.* ○ ***Work out*** *how much one needs to spend in shops to earn these 'free gifts'.* T ○ *Have you* ***worked out*** *the number of man-hours lost through illness?* = figure out 1. ⇨ work out at.

3 [Vn ⇆ p pass adj] find the answer to (sth); solve. **O:** problem, sum; riddle, code: *You seem to have the problem nicely* ***worked out****. All the details are in place.* CON ○ *See if you can* ***work*** *this puzzle* ***out****.* = figure out 2, puzzle out.

4 [Vn.p] understand the nature of (sb). **O:** relative, colleague; Peter: *'You are funny: I shall never* ***work*** *you* ***out****.'* ILIH ○ *For as long as I've known him, I've never been able to* ***work*** *Martin* ***out****.* □ usu with *can/could + not.* = make out 4.

5 [Vp] develop well/badly, prove successful/a failure. **S:** arrangement, relationship; things, it. **A:** all right, well; badly, unhappily; that way: *I hoped that you'd get married. But it doesn't seem to be* ***working out*** *that way.* RFW ○ *I'm glad that things are* ***working out*** *so well for them in Australia.* = pan out, turn out 3.

6 [Vp nom] (*sport*) (esp of a boxer) train for a contest by skipping, sparring etc. **S:** champion, heavyweight: *Frank Bruno spoke to reporters after* ***working out*** *at the gym this morning.* ○ *After breakfast, he had an intensive* ***work-out****.*

7 [Vp.n pass] complete the period which one is legally obliged to spend in training, or with an employer etc. **O:** ⚠ contract, apprenticeship, notice, service: *I'd rather give Joan her money now than have her* ***work out*** *a week's notice.*

work things out [Vn.p] settle personal problems. **S:** (married) couple, family: *'I wish their parents would leave them to* ***work things out*** *for themselves. You know how young people hate interference from their elders.'* ○ *'Have you managed to* ***work things out*** *with your wife, or is she still unhappy about the extra work you've taken on?'* ⇨ next entry.

things work themselves out [Vn.p] (*informal*) (of personal problems) be resolved, settled: *These* ***things*** *have a way of* ***working themselves out*** *in time.* ○ *'These* ***things work themselves out****, you know.'* SPL □ a remark meant to comfort sb who is anxious, upset etc. ⇨ previous entry.

work out at [Vp.pr] be equal to (sth), be calculated as (sth). **S:** pay, pension, contribution. **o:** ten pounds, fifty dollars: *His take-home pay* ***works out at*** *£250 a week.* ○ *What does his share of the bonus* ***work out at****?* = run out at, come out at. ⇨ work out 2.

work over [Vn.p pass] (*informal*) beat (sb) violently to extract information, or as a punishment etc. **S:** thug, gangster. **O:** informer, prisoner: *A couple of the boys* ***worked*** *him* ***over*** (or: *gave him a* ***working-over****) in a dark alleyway.* = beat up.

work round to [Vp.pr pass] ⇨ work around/round to.

work (one's way) through [Vpr pass rel, Vn.p rel] complete, finish (sth) by giving steady attention to it. **S:** student, class. **o:** exercise, problem; course, text; meal: *He* ***worked through*** *the theorems of Euclid when still quite young.* ○ *He was* ***working his way*** *steadily* ***through*** *an enormous steak.*

work to [Vpr pass rel] be guided, governed, by (a plan etc) when doing sth. **S:** builder, student. **o:** blueprint, pattern; timetable, deadline: *See that you are careful with money and* ***work to*** *a budget.* WI ○ *Magazine, photographers and dress houses* ***work to*** *tight schedules.* H

work to rule [Vpr] (*industrial relations*) follow strictly the rules laid down for a job, refuse to work overtime etc, as a form of protest, or in order to obtain higher wages. **S:** railwayman, docker, electrician: *The national executive of the union has ordered its members to* ***work to rule*** (or: *ordered a* ***work-to-rule***).

work towards [Vpr rel] strive to reach or achieve (sth). **S:** delegate, negotiator; trades union, church; student. **o:** settlement, agreement; understanding, amity; degree: *We have been* ***working towards*** *a new wages structure in the industry.* ○ *'There's no reason why we shouldn't reach a settlement. After all, we're* ***working towards*** *common objectives.'*

work under [Vpr rel] do a job under (sb's direction or guidance). **S:** scientist, engineer; student. **o:** (able) director, head, professor; direction: *The new headmaster's a very good man to* ***work under****.* ○ *'He's always been a lone wolf, you know — he hates to* ***work under*** *supervision.'*

work up 1 [Vn ⇆ p pass] develop, extend (sth) gradually. **S:** trader, shopkeeper. **O:** trade, business, market: *It took Sarah some years to* ***work up*** *a market for her products.* ○ *The retail side of the business was* ***worked up*** *by his father.*

2 [Vn ⇆ p pass] increase (sth) in numbers or strength. **S:** movement, union, party. **O:** support; a following, the membership level: *Local organizations are trying to* ***work up*** *more support for the party before the election.*

3 [Vn ⇆ p pass] make (sth) more keen; stimulate. **O:** appetite, thirst; interest: *I went out for a brisk walk to* ***work up*** *an appetite for lunch.* ○ *He doesn't seem to be able to* ***work up*** *any enthusiasm for his studies.*

work oneself/one's way up (from) [Vn.p, Vn.p.pr] (*informal*) rise (from a low level) to more responsible positions by one's own efforts. **S:** director, manager, officer. **o:** office-boy, private soldier; the shop-floor, the bottom: [Vn.p] *Major Burton joined the army as a boy recruit and* ***worked himself up***. ○ [Vn.p.pr] *The chairman of the company claims to have* ***worked his way up from*** *delivery boy.* □ also [Vp.pr]: *She* ***worked up from*** *a low level in the company.*

work up (into) [Vn ⇆ p pass adj, Vn.p.pr pass] gradually change the shape or nature of (sth), by effort, thought etc. **O:** wood, metal, stone; idea, note. **o:** figure, trinket; book, thesis: *The mass of clay was* ***worked up into*** *a reclining figure.* ○ *He's* ***working up*** *his notes on child language* ***into*** *a dissertation.*

work up (into/to) [Vn ⇆ p pass adj, Vn.p.pr pass rel] raise (sb/oneself) to a high level of excitement about sth. **S:** orator, agitator. **O:** crowd, follower; oneself. **o:** (**into**) state, frenzy; (**to**) (such an) extent, pitch, point: *She didn't say when she was coming back. Alec got quite* ***worked up*** *about it.* PW ○ *Don't get yourself all* ***worked up*** *over something which can easily be put right.* TT ○ *She's* ***working*** *herself* ***up into*** *a dreadful state over nothing.* □ note the passive with *get* in the first and second example.

work up to [Vp.pr] develop what one is doing or saying to (a high point). **S:** orchestra, singer, orator. **o:** crescendo, high note, climax: *I felt, as he* ***worked up to*** *a climax, an impulse to stand up and shout.* CON ○ *He took her out, all over the place. He was* ***working up to*** *a proposal of marriage.* YAA

worm

worm one's way into [Vn.pr rel] (*informal*) move gradually and cunningly into (sth). **S:** adventurer, careerist. **o:** position; favour, prominence; (sb's) confidence: *He was a plausible type who'd* ***wormed his way into*** *a position of trust in the department.* ○ *To ensure the success of his plans, Brown needed to* ***worm his way into*** *the director's confidence.*

worm out of [Vn.pr pass emph rel] (*informal*) extract (sth) from sb slowly and cunningly. **S:** wife, girlfriend. **O:** information; story, secret: *She was* ***worming out of*** *him shameful secrets about the Templar family.* DC ○ *All these personal details were* ***wormed out of*** *him eventually.*

worry

worry (oneself) about/over [Vpr emph rel, Vn.pr emph rel] cause oneself anxiety over (sb/sth), trouble oneself about (sb/sth). **A:** sick, silly; to death. **o:** family; work, health: *'Look after yourself, my dear, and don't* ***worry about me****.'* HOM ○ *He* ***worries about*** *the slightest thing* (cf: *The slightest thing* ***worries*** *him*). ○ *He* ***worries himself*** *sick* ***over*** *his eldest daughter.* □ *sick, silly* etc only present after *himself, herself* etc.

wrangle

wrangle (about/over) [Vpr pass emph rel] argue, dispute, noisily and keenly over (sb/sth). **S:** brother, partner, wife. **o:** rights, money; children: *In that family they are always* ***wrangling about*** *something.* ○ *'This business is not so crucial that it needs to be* ***wrangled over*** *endlessly.'*

wrap

wrap around/round [Vn.pr pass emph rel] wind (sth) in thick folds around (sth/sb). **O:** bandage, dressing; towel, blanket. **o:** finger, wound; baby: *He* ***wrapped*** *a clean rag* ***around*** *his ankle.* ○ *The mayor had a tricolour sash* ***wrapped around*** *his waist.*

wrap around/round/ one's (little) finger [Vn.pr] (*informal*) through feminine charm, wiles etc persuade (sb) to do what one wants. **S:** wife, girlfriend, daughter: *She could* ***wrap*** *the chairman of the board* ***round her little finger****.* = twist around/round one's (little) finger, wind around/round one's (little) finger.

wrapped in [pass (Vn.pr)] thickly covered by (sth), so that nothing is visible. **o:** fog, mist; darkness, obscurity: *The signposts along the route were* ***wrapped in*** *fog.* ○ (*figurative*) *The events of those days are* ***wrapped in*** *mystery.* = enveloped in, shrouded in.

wrap up 1 [Vn ⇆ p pass adj] (*informal*) close, conclude (sth). **S:** chairman, announcer. **O:** programme, meeting: *'Well, I think that just about* ***wraps up*** *our business for this evening.'* = wind up 5.

2 [Vn ⇆ p pass] (*informal*) conclude (sth) successfully. **S:** salesman, executive; firm. **O:** business, deal; sale, merger: *The sales team flew in at ten o'clock,* ***wrapped up*** *a couple of deals before lunch, and caught the afternoon plane back to Stuttgart.*

wrap (it) up [Vp, Vn.p] (*slang*) be quiet. **S:** speaker, musician: ***'Wrap up****, Dad.' he said, 'you'll bust a gut!'* ○ ***'Wrap it up****, will you, stop ringing those bells!'* LBA = shut up 2.

wrap (up) (in) 1 [Vn ⇆ p pass adj, Vn.pr pass rel, Vn.p.pr pass rel] cover (sth) with paper etc for presenting to sb or sending through the post. **O:** gift; book, dress; parcel. **o:** paper, foil: [Vn.p] *Teresa* ***wraps up*** *the children's presents on Christmas Eve.* ○ [Vn.pr] *'If the packet isn't* ***wrapped in*** *strong paper and sealed, it'll come open in the post.'*

2 [Vp, Vn ⇆ p pass adj, Vn.pr pass rel, Vn.p.pr pass rel] put on warm clothing so that it covers one completely. **o:** scarf, blanket: [Vp] *'Now* ***wrap up*** *warm: it's freezing outside.'* ○ [Vn.pr] *The nurse carried in a baby* ***wrapped in*** *a thick shawl.* ○ [Vn.p.pr] *The children were warmly* ***wrapped up in*** *scarves and anoraks.*

wrapped up in [pass (Vn.p.pr)] completely absorbed by (sb/sth), closely involved in (sb/sth). **o:** each other; his own little world; friendship, love; reflections; work, reading: *Annabel became* ***wrapped up in*** *a society dedicated to the welfare of animals.* DC ○ *I must have been* ***wrapped up in*** *my thoughts.* TC ○ *I got* ***wrapped up in*** *the book.* JFTR □ passive with *be, become, get, remain, seem.*

wrap (up) in cotton wool [Vn.pr pass, Vn.p.pr pass] (*informal*) overprotect (sb) from danger or risk. **S:** mother, nurse. **O:** child, pupil: *Charles hated feeling that he was being* ***wrapped in cotton wool****; he felt cheated when he was not allowed to do what other men did.* CHDI ○ *'Don't* ***wrap*** *the boy* ***in cotton wool*** *— let him play with the others!'* ⇨ wrap (up) (in).

wreathe

wreathe (itself) around/round [Vn.pr pass emph rel] wind (itself) in a coil or wavy line around (sth). **S:** smoke, mist; ivy, rose-bush; snake. **o:** house, tree; window: *A large snake had **wreathed itself round** the base of the tree.* ○ *Creeping plants were **wreathed around** the trellis* (cf: *The trellis was **wreathed in** creeping plants*).

wrench

wrench off [Vn ⇆ p pass adj, Vn.pr pass] take off, remove (sth) with a powerful, twisting movement. **O:** door; handle, grip. **o:** hinges, frame; door: *By placing a piece of steel pipe over the handle, the thief was able to **wrench** it **off**.* ○ *The house was a shambles, with windows broken and doors **wrenched off** their hinges.*

wrest

wrest from [Vn.pr pass emph rel] (*formal*) obtain, win (sth) from (sth/sb) by a hard struggle. **S:** worker, farmer; invader; interrogator. **O:** living, livelihood; city, castle; admission, secret. **o:** job, land; owner, inhabitant; prisoner: *Here you still find a few small farmers, **wresting** a poor living **from** the harsh soil.* ○ *The citadel was **wrested from** its defenders only after a hard struggle.*

wrestle

wrestle with [Vpr pass emph rel] fight inwardly, morally, with (sth). **o:** doubt, dilemma, problem; conscience: *Linguists are still **wrestling with** this problem.* ○ *These doubts, long **wrestled with**, were now resolved.* = struggle with.

wriggle

wriggle out of [Vpr pass] (*informal*) avoid (sth unpleasant) by careful or cunning movements. **o:** responsibility, task; being present, giving help: *'I notice that he's **wriggled out of** his share of the washing-up.'* ○ *Eventually, Bill was asked to supervise the exam, but of course he **wriggled out of** it.* = get out of 1.

wring

wring from/out of [Vn.pr pass emph rel] get (sth) from (sb) by applying moral or physical pressure. **O:** story, account; confession, secret: *'Have you ever tried **wringing** a donation **out of** him? It's like getting blood from a stone.'* ○ *An admission was **wrung from** the bank messenger that he had prior knowledge of the raid.* = extract from.

wring out [Vn ⇆ p pass adj] force water from (clothing), by twisting it or passing it through rollers. **O:** clothes; skirt, towel: *She has a few shirts to **wring out** and hang on the line.* ○ *Charles dipped the wash-leather in the pail and then **wrung** it **out**.* HD

write

write (about/on) [Vpr pass emph rel, Vn.pr pass emph rel] produce (books etc) (on a particular subject). **S:** author, playwright. **O:** novel, play; much, a good deal. **o:** childhood, home, family; love, war; Spain, Africa: *These events have been argued about and **written about** so much that I know them pretty much by heart.* ○ *He's an expert on breeding dogs—he's **written** several books **on** the subject.* ○ *This was a topic **on** which he'd **written** a number of articles.*

write away/off (for) [Vp, Vp.pr] send an order (for sth offered as a free gift, for sale etc) by post. **S:** reader, customer. **o:** catalogue, list; sample; map, book: ***Write away** now, enclosing the coupon in this week's Radio Times.* ○ *I've **written off for** the new edition of his grammar.* = send away/off (for).

write back (to) [Vp, Vp.pr rel] write, and send, a letter in reply (to sb). **S:** relative, customer. **o:** office, shop, factory: *I **wrote back** straight away to thank John for his kind invitation.* ○ *If the supplier sends you the wrong goods, **write back to** them at once.*

write down [Vn ⇆ p pass adj] record (sth) on paper, often as an aid to memory. **O:** name, address; detail, particular: ***'Write down** my phone number in your diary before you forget it.'* ○ *I **wrote** a few figures **down** on the back of an envelope.* = note down, put down 11, take down 3.

write in [Vn ⇆ p nom pass] (*politics*, esp *US*) add to the ballot paper the name of a candidate not already printed there. **O:** name; candidate: *British voting procedure does not normally provide for the **writing in** of candidates' names.* ○ *There was a heavy **write-in** vote for a candidate not officially sponsored by the Republicans.*

write in/into 1 [Vn ⇆ p pass adj, Vn.pr pass] include, insert (sth) in (a written text). **O:** correction, amendment, comment; line, word, passage. **o:** article, book: *Any alterations should be **written in** neatly to one side.* ○ *The editor had **written** numerous amendments **into** the text.*

2 [Vn ⇆ p pass adj, Vn.pr pass] make (sth) part of a legal document. **O:** provisions, terms; guarantee. **o:** Bill; contract, agreement: *A guarantee to protect pension rights has been **written into** their contracts.* ○ *The agreement would not be signed unless it contained **written-in** assurances that the work force would not be further reduced.* = build in/into 2.

write in (to) [Vp, Vp.pr rel] address an inquiry, complaint etc (to some central office). **S:** listener, viewer; motorist, consumer. **o:** BBC, newspaper office, advice bureau: *Indignant viewers have been **writing in** to complain of the moral content of plays.* ○ *To qualify for your free sample, all you do is **write in to** this address.*

write off 1 [Vn ⇆ p nom pass] recognize that (sth) is a loss, that (sth) cannot be recovered etc. **S:** creditor, bank, accountant. **O:** sum, amount; debt, loss: *The firm has **written off** two thousand pounds' worth of bad debts.* ○ *The Government have agreed to a **write-off** of* (or: *have agreed to **write off***) *£20m.* ○ *It is inevitable that losses should have to be **written off**.* SC = wipe off 2.

2 [Vn ⇆ p nom pass adj] damage (sth) so badly that it has no value; recognize that (sth) is so badly damaged that it is no longer economic to pay for its repair. **S:** motorist, pilot; insurance company. **O:** car, plane: *The car was completely **written off*** (or: *was a complete **write-off***) *and the driver seriously injured.* □ the write-off value of a vehicle is the amount paid by its insurer when it is written off.

3 [Vn ⇆ p nom pass adj] regard (sth) as a failure, beyond recovery etc. **O:** friendship, partnership, marriage; meeting, party, dance: *Everyone they spoke to had **written off** the marriage before it began.* ○ *It looks as though tonight's going to be a complete **write-off**.* TBC

write off as [Vn.p.pr pass] regard (sb/sth) as (unimportant, not worth listening to etc), because he or it is thought to be wild, foolish etc. **O:** speaker, author, preacher; opinion, statement, claim. **o:** simpleton, charlatan; absurd, nonsensical; hysteria, propaganda: *He can't just be* ***written off as*** *an eccentric recluse*. AH ○ *His political philosophy tends to be* ***written off as*** *an outmoded fantasy*. AH

write off (for) [Vp, Vp.pr] ⇨ write away/off (for).

write (on) [Vpr pass emph rel, Vn.pr pass emph rel] ⇨ write (about/on).

write out [Vn ⇆ p pass adj] write (sth) in full; complete. **O:** cheque, claim; statement, confession; imposition: *'I haven't got cash, but I can* ***write*** *you* ***out*** *a cheque.'* ○ *'****Write out*** *a receipt on this piece of paper.'* □ note the Indirect Object (*you*) in the first example. = make out 1.

write (oneself) out [Vn.p pass] reach the point where one is no longer original or creative. **S:** novelist, playwright: *He was still comparatively young and there was no reason to think he had* ***written himself out***. PW ○ *What were the critics saying about him? '****Written out*** *at the age of thirty'*.

write out/out of [Vn.p pass, Vn.pr pass] remove (a character) from a dramatic series on radio or TV, eg by arranging for him to 'die'. **S:** author, scriptwriter. **O:** character, part. **o:** script, story: *An actor who has been booked for a long series on television may be alarmed to hear that his part is being* ***written out of*** *the script*.

write up 1 [Vn ⇆ p pass adj] rewrite (sth) in a fuller, better organized way; give a full, written account of (sth). **S:** student, research-worker. **O:** note, observation; experiment, project: *'For homework you can* ***write up*** *the rough notes you made in class.'* ○ *The basic experimental work has been done; what I have to do now is* ***write*** *it all* ***up***.
2 [Vn ⇆ p nom pass adj] write a review of (a play etc), usu for a newspaper. **S:** critic, reviewer. **O:** play, film; novel: *You can go home afterwards and* ***write*** *the film* ***up*** *in the paper*. CON ○ *His latest book got* (or: *was given*) *an enthusiastic* ***write-up*** *in the press*.

wrought

wrought up [pass adj (Vn.p)] nervously strained; tense: *'Calm down, you're getting terribly* ***wrought up*** *over nothing.'* ○ *Spreading rumours would merely get people* ***wrought up*** *to no purpose*. TGLY ○ *He came in with a deadly serious,* ***wrought-up*** *look on his face*. □ passive with appear, be, become, get, look, seem. ⇨ work up (into/to).

yank

yank off [Vn ⇆ p pass, Vn.pr pass] (*informal*) remove (sth) with a sharp pull. **O:** handle, lock; cupboard. **o:** door, wall: *He seized my hand in his great clasp and nearly* ***yanked*** *it* ***off***. ○ *Lids had been* ***yanked off*** *desks and lay scattered about the floor*. = pull off 1.

yank out/out of [Vn ⇆ p pass, Vn.pr pass] (*informal*) extract (sth) with a sharp tug. **O:** tooth; nail, screw, bolt. **o:** jaw; plank: *I have to go to the dentist to have a few teeth* ***yanked out***. ○ *Tap the nails up from the back, and* ***yank*** *them* ***out*** *with pincers*. = pull out 1.

yearn

yearn (for) [Vpr pass adj emph rel] (*formal*) desire strongly sb/sth from which one is separated. **o:** lover, family; sight, touch, smell: *How he* ***yearned for*** *her whenever they were separated*. ○ *She* ***yearned for*** *a sight of* (or: ***yearned*** *to see*) *her dear ones*. = long for.

yell

yell out [Vp, Vn ⇆ p pass] cry or shout (sth) aloud, to attract attention, show pain etc. **O:** name; order: *'Don't squeeze his hand: it makes him* ***yell out*** *in pain.'* ○ *When the sergeant* ***yelled out*** *my number, I had to rush forward*. = shout out.

yield

yield to 1 [Vpr emph rel] (*formal*) allow oneself to be overcome (by pressure). **S:** shopper, tenant, striker. **o:** (sales, economic) pressure, argument, persuasion; force; emotion, anger: *'If they won't* ***yield to*** *reason we shall have to try other methods.'* ○ *Blackmail was a weapon* ***to*** *which she was never prepared to* ***yield***. ○ ***To*** *pressures such as these any government would have to* ***yield*** *eventually*. = give in (to), give way (to).
2 [Vpr] (*formal*) be replaced or succeeded by (sth). **S:** streets, terraces; heavy industry; traditional crafts. **o:** open countryside; small electronics plants; mass production: *As the train gathered speed, suburban streets* ***yielded to*** *green fields*. ○ *Quality entertainment films are* ***yielding to*** *slickly packaged video comedies and thrillers*.

yield up 1 [Vn ⇆ p pass] (*formal*) hand (sth) to the enemy in admission of defeat. **S:** governor, garrison. **O:** fortress, citadel; town; oneself, one's prisoner: *The city would only be* ***yielded up*** *when ammunition and food supplies were exhausted*. ○ *Did Calais* ***yield up*** *the burghers to the English?* = surrender (to)1.
2 [Vn ⇆ p pass adj] (*formal*) deliver or reveal (sth). **S:** earth, sea; rock, soil. **O:** wealth, treasure; secret: *In that year of plenty, the seas* ***yielded up*** *a rich harvest of fish*. ○ *What new mysteries will be* ***yielded up*** *by exploration of these underwater caves?* = give up 4.

Z

zero

zero in (on) 1 [Vp, Vp.pr pass] (*military*) find the exact range from one's guns to (an enemy position). **o:** position, emplacement; crossroads, bridge: *With first light, the artillery* ***zeroed in on*** *the road junctions, making it a nerve-testing journey for the men who had to bring through the barges*. ST = range in (on).
2 [Vp, Vp.pr pass] (*informal*) act quickly to grasp (sth) or profit from (sth). **S:** banker, investor, industrialist. **o:** opportunity, opening; market: *The City of London is never slow to* ***zero in on*** *an opportunity of this magnitude, and already certain parties are positioning themselves to get in on the act*. T

3 [Vp, Vp.pr pass] (*informal*) fix attention on (sb/sth). **S:** minister, chairman. **o:** issue, question, matter: *'Let's **zero in on** one or two of the key issues.'*

zip

zip along [Vp] progress, move along, at a fast, lively pace. **S:** car, train; (action of a) play, film; game. **A:** really, fairly: *'The car **zips along**, all right, but have you noticed how bad the bodywork is?'* ○ *The game got off to a sluggish start, but after half-time it fairly **zipped along**.*

zip up [Vn ⇆ p nom pass adj] close (sth) by means of a zip-fastener. **O:** pocket, fly-front; purse, bag: *He packed his books into his briefcase and **zipped** it **up**.* ○ *His flying jacket **zips up*** (ie can be ***zipped up***) *at the front.* □ nom used attrib as in: *a **zip-up** jacket, cardigan.*

zone

zone off [Vn ⇆ p pass adj] separate (an area) so that it can be used for a specific purpose, eg an area for shoppers where traffic is restricted, esp in a town or city. **O:** city centre, shopping precinct: *The business and commercial centre has now been **zoned off**: private cars are prohibited, and delivery vans may only enter and leave at specified times.*

zoom

zoom across, along, away etc [Vp emph, Vpr emph] move across etc swiftly, with engine(s) roaring. **S:** aircraft; jet, bomber; car, bus: *A flight of fighter aircraft **zoomed** low **over** the saluting base.* ○ *A heavily-laden minibus **zoomed past** in a cloud of dust.*

zoom in (on) [Vp, Vp.pr] (*cinema*, *TV*) by adjusting the 'zoom' lens on a camera, gradually change from a distant shot to a close-up (of sb/sth). **S:** cameraman; camera. **o:** table, bed; face, hand: *'Camera 3, **zoom in** a bit more. That's fine — hold it there.'* ○ *After an 'establishing' shot of a waiter carrying drinks on a tray, the camera **zooms in on** a couple seated at the bar.*

zoom out [Vp] (*cinema*, *TV*) by adjusting the 'zoom' lens on a camera, move gradually from a close-up to a longer shot: *'Camera 2. I want you to **zoom out** until you've got a head-and-shoulders shot of John and the girl.'*

The Scope and Aims of the Dictionary

Knowledge of a wide range of idiomatic expressions, and the ability to use them appropriately in speech and writing, are among the distinguishing features of a native-like command of English. Part of the great range consists of the two-word combinations usually known as phrasal verbs, e.g. **step up** (supplies), **lay on** (transport) and **take up** (the story). Phrasal verbs are commonly used by native speakers but constitute a well-known stumbling block for foreign learners, who because of the associated problems of structure or meaning may fall back on a more formal one-word equivalent – **increase**, **provide**, **continue**.

In dealing with phrasal verbs, the most serious difficulties are those of meaning. A French speaker would surely understand **continue** more readily than **take up**, while a native speaker might have difficulty in explaining the sense of the combination in terms of its constituent parts. In fact, a close study of phrasal verbs (and of more complex idioms containing phrasal verbs, such as **make up one's mind**) brings to light many curious anomalies of form and meaning. While we can equally well talk of **angling for** or **fishing for** compliments, where the verbs are as freely interchangeable as when they are used in a literal sense, we would not say of a friend that he had difficulty in **making up his thoughts** (as distinct from **his mind**). And while we might want to say of him that he found it hard to **hit the nail on the head**, we would not substitute **strike** for **hit** unless we were thinking literally of his skill with the hammer rather than figuratively of his inability to say precisely what he meant. Among collocational pitfalls of this kind the mature speaker of the language picks his way with unconscious ease. The foreign student, though, looks for clear guidance on many hundreds of phrasal verbs in current use, often in considerable detail. It was with a view to meeting that need that this volume was originally compiled and is now issued in a completely revised and updated edition.

With its companion volume *English Idioms*, completed in 1983 and dealing with a much broader and more heterogeneous range of expressions, *Phrasal Verbs* makes up the *Oxford Dictionary of Current Idiomatic English*, Vols. 1 and 2.

An important feature of the whole work was (and is) the illustrative use of citations from a variety of contemporary sources. For the first edition of Volume 1, the bulk of the examples were drawn from an analysis of works of fiction, history, biography etc, specially undertaken to provide illustrations for the dictionary. As the drafting of entries for that volume got under way, this collection of over 30000 excerpts was added to from such sources as the daily and weekly press and radio and television broadcasts. For the revision of Volume 1, this data has been diversified and brought up to date by additions from three new sources: the collection made by Isabel McCaig, one of the compilers of *English Idioms*, in the late 1970s and early 1980s; the slips illustrating phrasal verbs supplied from the Archive held at Oxford for the continuous updating of the *Oxford English Dictionary*; and a computerized corpus of 30 million words, also compiled at OUP, and covering the period 1989 to 1992.

The scope of this volume is explained in some detail below (0.1). We set out the grammatical patterns in which phrasal verbs occur, describe the approach to idiomaticity which is followed throughout the dictionary, and indicate the criteria used to decide which combinations to include. We also explain the sense in which the familiar term 'phrasal verb' is used. The second part of the Introduction (0.2) touches upon some features of the entries which are specifically designed to encourage the use of the dictionary as a learning and teaching aid.

The scope of the dictionary

0.1 One feature of idiomatic English which creates difficulties for the foreign student is that idioms correspond to a wide range of grammatical patterns. Idioms are found for example in the phrase patterns 'article + adj + noun' – *the last straw*, *a live wire*, *a lame duck*; 'article + present participle + noun' – *a parting shot, a sitting duck*; and 'article + past participle + noun' – *a foregone conclusion, a close-run thing*. Idioms also span sentences of various structural types, as in *break the bank, fill the bill, make sb's day, jump the gun*; *give him an inch and he'll take a mile, spare the rod and spoil the child*. This is only a small sample of the great diversity of grammatical patterns in which idiomatic expressions may occur. The spread is enormous but there is one outstandingly large category that does allow coverage in depth and uniformity of treatment within a single volume, and that is the subject of this part of the dictionary.

The basic requirement that expressions have to meet for inclusion in this volume is a simple one: all consist of, or include, a verb and a particle or preposition (ie one of the words **down**, **for**, **in**, **off**, **on**, **up**, **with**, etc). Most entries consist of simple combinations of verb + particle or verb + preposition, eg **back down**, **fall through**, **clog up**, **puzzle out**; **abide by**, **come across**, **run into**, **take to**; but there is a sizeable group containing both a particle and a preposition – **put up with**, **set down as**, **take out on**. A considerable number of entries, too, deal with more complex types, many with a noun, and sometimes also an adjective, as fixed elements in addition to the verb and preposition or particle: **get access to**, **give scope for**, **let off steam**, **lose track of**, **make a mental note of**.

Not all combinations in these various categories cause difficulties of understanding or construction. The two-word combinations are frequently used to express movement in a particular direction, as **fall through** does in the example

Be careful: you could easily **fall through** *into the room below.*

Or they may be used to express a process, as **clog up** does in the sentence

The grease has **clogged up** *the drain-pipe.*

(where **up** simply indicates the completeness of the clogging process). On the other hand, there are numerous combinations which pose severe problems for the foreign student. In the example

I'm afraid the deal has **fallen through**.

fall through no longer has a literal meaning. Instead, it has a far from straightforward idiomatic one ('fail' or 'miscarry'). Clearly, the fact that very many verbs with particles or prepositions are used like this (ie idiomatically) is the central problem that learners have to deal with in mastering this important area of the vocabulary.

In addressing the crucial question of idiomaticity some complex issues are raised, and it will be best to consider these under separate headings:

1 How in practice do we determine whether a given expression is idiomatic or not? We may sense for example that **put up** as used in the sentence

They're having a memorial **put up** *to him by public subscription.*

is not idiomatic, whereas **put up** in

A well-wisher had **put up** *the money (for the scheme).*

is idiomatic. What kinds of criteria can we call upon in support of our intuitions?

2 Is the distinction between non-idioms and idioms clear-cut, or does the one type shade off gradually into the other?

3 What criteria in particular determine the inclusion of some items in the dictionary and the exclusion of others?

4 Finally, how should the conclusions we reach affect the grammatical labelling of the idiomatic combinations? If a combination such as **put up** (in the second example at 1) is shown to be a unit of meaning, should we not reflect this in the name we give to the combination? (The term 'phrasal verb' is already available for this purpose.)

In considering these questions, unnecessary complications will be avoided if the complex items (eg **pass one's eye over**) are considered separately from the simple two-word combinations (eg **pass over**). The immediate discussion will centre particularly on combinations of transitive verb + particle; we shall return later to the more complex cases.

Discussions of idiomaticity are sometimes confused by introducing inappropriate grammatical criteria into an area where considerations of meaning carry particular weight. A question which is often raised in treatments of the verb + particle combination, but from the discussion of which the wrong conclusions are sometimes drawn, has to do with the different grammatical functions of **over** in such pairs of sentences as

An aircraft **passed** ('flew') **over** *our heads.*
We shan't **pass over** ('disregard') *any detail.*

There is certainly a difference of function here: we cannot shift the final noun phrase to precede **over** in the first sentence, but we can in the second:

An aircraft* **passed *our heads* **over**.
We shan't **pass** *any detail* **over**.

Further evidence of the difference is the contrastive positioning of 'us' and 'it' (as replacements for the noun phrases) in the two sentences

An aircraft **passed over** *us.*
We shan't **pass** *it* **over**.

It is on the basis of these criteria that **over** can be said to function as a *preposition* in the first example and as a *particle* (or adverbial particle) in the second. At the same time, we cannot use this grammatical evidence of contrastiveness in support of a claim that **pass over** ('disregard') is a unit of meaning, and thus an idiom. If we did, we should have to explain why it is that **pass over** as used in the sentence

Bill **passed over** *the bread.*

appears, and can be shown to be, *less* idiomatic, while at the same time displaying the *same* characteristics with regard to the particle. Compare:

Bill **passed** *the bread* **over**.
Bill **passed** *it* **over**.

We should also have to account for the fact that, whereas **pass over** (verb + preposition) in

An aircraft **passed over** *our heads.*

is intuitively less idiomatic than its homonym in the following sentence, **over** is equally 'prepositional' in both cases:

The chairman **passed over** ('reviewed') *the first few items.*

The evidence of such examples indicates that whereas the particle/preposition contrast is a valid and important one, it has no bearing on whether expressions are idiomatic or not. The idiom/non-idiom distinction *cuts across* this contrast and is established largely by semantic tests of deletion and substitution. Some grammatical tests are relevant too, but they are quite different from those used to make clear the contrast between particles and prepositions.

We can begin the discussion of idiomaticity with a simple and familiar assumption: an idiom is a combination of two or more words which function as a unit of meaning. This assumption can be tested: if a verb + particle expression (for instance) is a semantic unit we should be able to substitute for it a number of single words (in this case verbs) of equivalent meaning. By this criterion, **step up** as used in the sentence

His promotion has **stepped up** *their social status.*

is clearly idiomatic, since it is synonymous with 'improve', 'enhance'. By the same token, **take off** is an idiom in the sentence

*marks sentences that are considered unacceptable.

Bill **took off** *the Prime Minister to perfection.*

since it is equivalent in meaning to 'mimic', 'imitate'.

We can test our intuitions about idiomaticity in another way. If **step up** and **take off** are units of meaning, it should not be possible to break that unity either by removing the particle component or by replacing the verb component with other verbs of like meaning. The 'particle deletion' test shows both expressions to be idiomatic: the effect of applying it is to make nonsense of the example sentences:

His promotion has* **stepped *their social status.*

Bill* **took *the Prime Minister to perfection.*

'Verb replacement' also applies negatively in both cases: there are no precise equivalents to **step** and **take** as they are used here:

His promotion has **stepped up** *their social status.*

?**pushed**

?**bumped**

Bill **took off** *the Prime Minister to perfection.*

***grabbed**

***snatched**

(?marks choices which some speakers might find acceptable, and * marks choices that are totally unacceptable.)

The semantic unity which is characteristic of idioms tends to make them behave as single *grammatical* words also. This tendency is reflected in the fact that some verb + particle expressions which are idiomatic can be converted into *nouns*. So **to make up** (one's face) has a corresponding noun **make-up**, and **to break down** (the accounts, the figures) has the corresponding form **breakdown**. This characteristic suggests a further test – of 'noun formation' – which applies positively to both our examples. In parallel with the cases just cited, we find that **to step up** (someone's status) can be changed into **a step-up** (in someone's status) and **to take off** (the Prime Minister) into **a take-off** (of the Prime Minister).

Idiomatic expressions are units of meaning; non-idiomatic expressions, conversely, are made-up of distinct meaningful parts. We should expect this assumption about non-idioms to be borne out when they are tested in the same ways as idioms. This time however the tests should apply in reverse. Consider the item **draw out**, as in the example

Robert **drew out** *twenty pounds from his savings account.*

We note first that there is no corresponding noun in this case: we shall not find ***a draw-out** (of twenty pounds) to parallel **a step-up** (in status). We find too that we can equally well use **take** or **draw** in this context: the verbs are synonymous here. Again, the particle **out** can be deleted without affecting sense or acceptability:

Robert **drew** *twenty pounds from his savings account.*

The examples we have been looking at tend to suggest that there is a sharp contrast between idioms and non-idioms – that there are items like **take off** (a politician) to which all the tests apply, positively or negatively as appropriate, and other combinations like **draw out** (money) to which the same tests apply in reverse. In reality, the picture is not so clear-cut: even **draw out**, which on most counts seems unidiomatic enough, has a one-word equivalent in **withdraw** (suggesting semantic unity):

Robert **withdrew** *twenty pounds from his savings account.*

In fact, the more individual cases we examine the more it seems that the boundary between highly idiomatic items and the rest is not sharply drawn but hazy and imprecise. We would do better to think in terms of a *scale* of idiomaticity, with the 'true' idioms (**step up**, **take off**) clearly positioned at the upper end and **draw out** appearing near the bottom, but with many items representing varying degrees of semantic and grammatical unity spaced out in between. Among the intermediate types, or 'semi-idioms', we find items like **put up**, as used in the sentence

Increased transport costs will ***put up*** *the prices.*

and **muck up**, as in the example

The weather really ***mucked up*** *our weekend.*

What gives such items their special status is that when the tests used to identify idioms (or non-idioms) are applied, the results are not conclusive either way. We find for example that whereas **put up** and **muck up** are unitary according to one criterion ('raise' or 'increase' can be substituted for the first expression and 'spoil' or 'ruin' for the second), they are separable according to another criterion (replacement of the verb component by a verb, or verbs, of equivalent meaning). Thus we can say

Increased transport costs will ***send up*** *the prices* (or: *cause the prices to* ***go up***).

where **send** and **go** replace **put** in the original sentence; and we can also say

The weather really ***messed up*** *our weekend.*

where the synonymous **mess** has replaced **muck**.

What has been said about the nature of the relationship between idioms and non-idioms applies also to more complex expressions – those containing a noun and an adjective, for example. Here too there is a gradual shading-off from absolutely fixed expressions, such as **make an honest woman of** or **make a mental note of**, through those which allow the replacement of certain words by others of related meaning – **put the final/finishing touches to**, **put a bold/brave/good face on it/things** – down to expressions of which an adjective (etc) is not an essential part – **keep a (careful, professional, watchful) eye on, take (strong, instant, particular etc) exception to**. As these examples suggest, the special character of each complex expression (as more or less idiomatic) is brought out by applying the same simple tests of replacement and deletion that were demonstrated earlier.

We have discussed the nature of idiomaticity chiefly to show what criteria were used in deciding what to include in a dictionary which has 'idiomatic' as part of its title. Clearly all those items which are units of form and meaning must be recorded. Equally, there are expressions at the lower end of the scale which have to be left out. But as regards the central area – the semi-idioms – where is the line to be drawn? On the whole we have tended to include the marginal cases, drawing the line low rather than high. There are certain criteria, too, to which we have given special weight. These we explain below with reference to a number of common types of semi-idiom.

1 We have tended to include any expression, simple or complex, from which the preposition(s) or particle(s) cannot be deleted (ie without making nonsense of, or changing the sense of, the wider context in which the expression is used). This tendency explains the inclusion of pairs such as the following, which in terms of meaningful links between their verbs are less than idiomatic:

angle for	**fasten on/upon**	**jack in** (= abandon)
fish for	**seize on/upon**	**pack in**

2 The weighting given to this criterion also in part explains the inclusion of many semi-idiomatic expressions containing one of the major verbs **come**, **go**, **put**, **take**, etc. Because of the relationship of 'intransitive' to 'transitive' which exists between **come down** (for example) in certain of its senses and **bring down**, these expressions are often not full idioms. The fixity of the particle ensures their inclusion. In many such cases, we have also been guided by the need to include items which, while not idioms themselves, may throw light on the meanings of items which are. So **put aside** (a book, one's knitting) is included because it is related in sense to **put aside** (money, cash) and **put aside** (a grievance, one's differences).

3 Even when an expression contains a preposition which can be removed without affecting the meaning of the sentence in which the whole item appears, it may none

the less be recorded, provided that the preposition has a strong tendency to co-occur with the verb. Similarly, if a verb combines in a predictable way with two particles (or prepositions), such a combination is also included. The decision to deal with such expressions in the dictionary explains the presence of many verbs of Romance origin, whose meanings are often understood in isolation:

abstain (from) | **develop (from) (into)**
agitate (for) | **transfer (from) (to)**

4 As noted earlier, verbs of motion such as **march**, **run**, **walk** combine with a wide range of particles and prepositions of direction to form sets of expressions – **march through**, **march up**; **run across**, **run back**; **walk away**, **walk in**, **walk out** – whose meanings can be easily grasped. We have not attempted to account for these many possibilities in the dictionary. But when any such combination is used in a specialized way – as **march past** is when it means 'move ceremonially past sb' (ie on parade), or as **walk on** is when it means 'have a small part, appear briefly, in a play' – then that expression is recorded, even though the specialized meaning may sometimes be easily understood.

5 Verbs such as **puff**, **steam** and **zoom** also combine freely with particles and prepositions to form such expressions as **puff across**, **puff past**; **steam along**, **steam into**; **zoom down**, **zoom out**, etc. Such combinations have a different status from those containing **walk**, **run** or **march**, however. Since **steam**, for example, in combination with a particle of direction is interpreted as a verb of motion (**steam across** = 'move across under steam power', etc) the particle cannot be removed without changing the sense of the verb. Compare:

The train ***steamed out*** *noisily.*
The train ***steamed*** *noisily.*

It is for this reason that we have indicated in the dictionary the possible combinations in which verbs such as **steam** can occur (though in a special kind of entry; ⇨ *The headphrase*, 1.5, for fuller details).

Finally, we can take up the question of grammatical labelling that was raised earlier. We have seen that idiomatic combinations tend to function in certain ways as grammatical units (ie as single words). Should this unity decide how entries are classified and labelled in the dictionary?

One approach would be to use the familiar term 'phrasal verb' (itself indicating unity) to refer to idiomatic combinations of the various types covered by this volume (though not to the non-idiomatic ones). However, 'phrasal verb' is understood in different ways by different grammarians and teachers, and must be used with some care. The approach adopted in this dictionary is as follows:

1 'Phrasal verb' is used throughout these introductory sections, interchangeably with 'idiomatic combination of verb + particle/preposition', to refer to the following types of combination *provided they are idioms or semi-idioms*:

verb + particle (with no object following the verb):

(of a witness) **come forward**
(of an aircraft) **take off**

verb + preposition (with no object following the verb):

come across (an old friend)
run into (difficulties)

verb + particle + preposition (with no object following the verb):

face up to (one's responsibilities)
put up with (interruptions)

verb + particle (with an object following the verb):

make (one's face) **up**
take (a politician) **off**

verb + preposition (with an object following the verb):
hold (someone's past failings) **against** (him or her)
put (someone) **off** (driving)
verb + particle + preposition (with an object following the verb):
bring (someone) **up against** (a problem)
take (one's anger) **out on** (someone)

2 The relatively few non-idiomatic combinations of verb + particle, verb + preposition, etc, included in this dictionary are not referred to as phrasal verbs. It should be noted, though, that they are assigned to the same scheme of six sentence patterns (and given the same grammatical codes Vp, Vpr, etc) as the corresponding phrasal verbs. For example, the non-idiom **take off** (the table-cloth) is allocated to the 'transitive pattern with a particle', with the code [Vn⇆p], but so too is the phrasal verb **take off** (the Prime Minister) (⇨ *The dictionary – a detailed description*, 3.4).

3 As already shown, the dictionary treats many complex items (**push the boat out** and **make an honest woman of**, for instance) which though they contain a verb and a particle or preposition also incorporate a fixed noun (and possibly also a fixed adjective). These will be referred to as 'complex idioms', not as phrasal verbs. Note, however, that these too are allocated to the scheme of six sentence patterns just referred to. This approach to the grammatical treatment of complex idioms has the practical advantage of keeping to the minimum the number of distinct structural types in the overall scheme for the dictionary. All the expressions recorded, whether idiom or non-idiom, simple or complex, are accounted for by a system of six basic patterns (⇨ 3.1).

The dictionary and the practical needs of the learner

0.2 The dictionary is intended chiefly as a practical work of reference for students of English, and we have taken special account of their needs in deciding what information to include in the entries and how best to arrange it. In particular, we have incorporated certain special features which are designed to encourage the confident use of phrasal verbs and other idioms in grammatical patterns and lexical contexts which may be quite new to students. It is in this sense that the dictionary is designed as a practical learning and teaching aid.

Three related features are singled out for special mention here: the design of the *headphrases* (which sometimes indicate a limited number of alternative words); the inclusion in most entries of the habitual *collocations* in which headphrases occur; and the extensive *cross-reference system* by means of which intransitive verbs (for example) are explicitly linked to their appropriate transitives.

A problem commonly facing the would-be user of a phrasal verb or larger idiom is that of deciding how fixed it is. Take, for example, the complex expression **buck one's ideas up**. How invariable is this? Can **up** be deleted? Is **thoughts**, say, freely substitutable for **ideas**? Students need clear guidance on fine points of lexical detail such as those, as also on the question whether singular **idea** is as acceptable as plural **ideas**, since without it they may produce such variants as ***buck one's idea** or ***buck one's notions up**. When the lexical shape of an expression is perfectly fixed, as it is here, the help can be given simply and straightforwardly through the headphrase itself (ie the form in which the expression is conventionally represented in **bold type** at the head of the entry). Examples of headphrases which represent *fixed* expressions are:

buck one's ideas up **put on the back burner**
let the side down

Sometimes a very limited range of options is available: we can say, for example, either **drag** (sb's name, etc) **through the mire**, or **drag** (sb's name, etc) **through**

the mud, where **mire** and **mud** are possible alternatives, but ***slime** is not. This restricted range of choice can again be conveyed through the headphrase, by the use of the oblique. The single oblique in the following headphrases shows that the choice of noun in each case is limited to two:

drag through the mire/mud **take sb's mind/thoughts off**
make a bolt/dash for

As the examples show, there is often a clear relationship of meaning between the words marked off by the oblique in this kind of headphrase: **bolt** and **dash** both express rapid movement. But this awareness does not help us to decide what the acceptable choices are in any particular case.

The problems which learners face in handling the meanings of such complex expressions (and those of the more numerous two-word combinations) are well known. They may have difficulties of understanding or interpretation (especially when the form of an expression is a poor guide to its meaning). They may have trouble in discriminating accurately between various meanings of the 'same' item – those of **put out**, for example, or **take in**. And again, they may need help in distinguishing between phrasal verbs which are related in form (cf **level off** and **level up**) though not necessarily in meaning. Among the features we have included in the dictionary to help students deal with such problems is the regular listing in entries of 'collocating' words. We can consider briefly the special advantages of this guidance here.

The collocates of a phrasal verb are the words which, in the judgement of native speakers, normally and naturally combine with it to form sentences. Among the words which can be used (as subjects) in the same sentence as **bring to blows**, for example, are disagreement, difference and rivalry, and among those associated (as direct objects) with **bring to attention** are troops, platoon, company. Information about acceptable collocates comes from two sources: we can examine in written or spoken texts collocates already produced by native speakers, or we can elicit from native speakers – including ourselves – collocates that they and we would regard as suitable in a particular context. Both methods are used in this dictionary. Learners normally become aware of the collocations of phrasal verb + noun etc one by one through meeting them in books or hearing them in conversation, and as one association builds upon another they gradually develop a firm understanding of the meanings of **bring to blows** and **bring to attention**. The advantage of bringing together a number of these associated words in one place – as in the entries shown below – is that students are made aware of several at the same time. As a result the learning process can be greatly speeded up.

bring to attention ... **S:** sergeant, officer. **O:** troops; platoon, company ...
bring to blows ... **S:** disagreement, difference (of opinion): rivalry, enmity. **O:** (two) sides, parties ...

Another advantage is that students can make up sentences of their own on the basis of the collocates recorded in such entries, so strengthening still more their grasp on the meanings of the headphrases themselves.

Example sentences in dictionary entries can serve much the same purpose as lists of collocates. If the examples are carefully chosen, they too will contain words that are characteristically and unambiguously associated with the headphrase, and which help to develop the learner's understanding of its meaning. But collocates and examples have different and complementary parts to play in the definition of meaning. In a list of collocates some of the more important clues to our understanding of an expression are abstracted from their real contexts and presented in a highly condensed form. In examples, various kinds of information – grammatical and stylistic as well as lexical – are combined in actual instances of language use, though the most important clues to meaning may be rather thinly spread.

A further advantage of indicating the collocates of headphrases, and it is related to the first, is that it enables learners to distinguish, more precisely than they might otherwise be able to do, between phrasal verbs that are pronounced or spelt alike but which differ in meaning. Take for example the two items entered and defined in the dictionary as:

come down 1 [Vp emph] collapse, drop; fall.
3 [Vp emph] fall, be reduced.

These entries have the same grammatical patterns, and their definitions are related, but their *collocations* are quite unalike, and indicate clearly and economically the difference in sense between 1 and 3:

come down 1 . . . **S:** ceiling, wall; curtain, picture; rain, sleet . . .
3 . . . **S:** prices, costs, expenditure . . .

(where **S** in each case indicates that the collocates function as subjects.)

Yet another practical application of collocate lists is to indicate and suggest to the student fresh contexts in which a partially known item can be acceptably used. Take for example the sets of words shown to function as Direct Objects (**O**) and prepositional objects (**o**) in the following entry:

put to 1 . . . convey, express, communicate (sth) to (sb). **O:** point, suggestion, proposal; situation; it . . . that there were better times coming, it . . . that inflation will fall. **o:** meeting, audience; board, committee . . .

Students may already partly know this sense of **put to**, in that they can confidently use the expression in some of the collocations indicated, eg

The chairman . . . **put** *. . . this point . . .* **to** *. . . the meeting.*

The list of other likely collocates extends this capacity, so that for example they can now also construct the sentence:

I'll **put** *your proposal* **to** *the board.*

But as well as being directly available for use in this way, the collocates meeting, audience; board, committee (for example) can also suggest – perhaps to more advanced students – the area in which other suitable choices can be found (assembly, conference; cabinet, government).

Lists of likely or probable collocates are in an important way linked to the special cross-references which are given at the end of many entries, especially those where the verb in the headphrase is one of the 'heavy-duty' group **come, go, bring, take**, etc. Consider the collocates and cross-references in:

bring to fruition . . . cause sth to be fulfilled or realized. . . . **O:** hope, dream, ambition; plan . . . ⇨ come to fruition.

The cross-reference to **come to fruition** indicates that the latter is the 'intransitive' equivalent of the 'transitive' headphrase, a correspondence which is reflected in the tendency for the *same* words to collocate with both expressions. The matching collocates appear in the **come to fruition** entry, as follows:

come to fruition . . . be realized, fulfilled. . . . **S:** hope, dream, ambition; plan, scheme . . . ⇨ bring to fruition.

How can students make use of this information in a productive way? First of all, they can be sure that when a **bring** entry is cross-referenced to a **come** entry the two normally correspond as transitive to intransitive. They can check that there is a close correspondence in particular cases by comparing collocates and definitions. Having grasped the relationship between the expressions, they can practise it systematically, drawing on their awareness of the shared collocates:

Their hopes were never **brought to fruition.**
Their hopes never **came to fruition.**

Once again, the illustrative sentences in the entries are a further source of clarification and practice. Since the **bring/come** correspondence applies to many pairs of phrasal verbs or complex idioms recorded in the dictionary (cf **bring to the ground/come to the ground**), the learner's exploitation of it in one case can be extended to the many parallel cases.

The dictionary – a detailed description

In the following set of entries, the user is referred from a number of features which are often found in the dictionary itself to the detailed explanations provided in sections 1–9 of *The dictionary – a detailed description*.

Keyword – 2.1.1

alternative preps in headphrase – 1.1.2

basic patterns – 3.1

codes repeated before collocates – 6.3.1

centre

centre on/round [Vpr emph rel, Vn.pr pass emph rel] have or fix (sth) as its centre. **S** [Vpr], **O** [Vn.pr]: movement, activity; commerce, industry. **o:** (key) figure, personality; port, capital city: *The town's activities were* **centred on** *the main square.* F ○ *She became involved in the whirlpool of activity which* **centred round** *Joe.* AITC ○ *To give access to markets, the new industries had been* **centred on** *a motorway junction.* □ some purists object to the use of round with the v centre. = revolve about/around.

usage note – 8

cross-reference to synonyms – 9

alternative nouns in headphrase – 1.1.3

transforms – 3.2

dart a glance/look at [Vn.pr pass emph rel] look suddenly, sharply, at (sb sth). **adj:** furtive, anxious, hostile. **o:** stranger, visitor; watch, clock: *She* **darted an** *interested* **glance at** *the visitor from under lowered eyelids.* ○ *I* **darted a glance at** *the speedometer. We were doing over eighty miles an hour.* = shoot a glance (at).

transformations with no basic pattern – 3.3

technical field label – 4.3

flashback [nom (Vp)] *(cinema)* a return during a film either to events that have already been shown, or to events that occurred before the main action of the film began: *The main action of the film portrayed the hero's adult life; scenes from his boyhood were shown in* **flashback**.

headphrase picked out in an example – 7.2

go across (to) [Vp emph, Vpr, Vp.pr] pass from one side (of sth) (to the other). **o: (across)** road, bridge; river; Channel; **(to)** shop; other bank; France: [Vpr] Planks were laid so that the villagers could ***go across*** *the marshy area.* ○ [Vp.pr] 'I'm just ***going across to*** *the pub for half an hour.*' = go over (to). ⇨ get across 1, send across (to), take across (to).

make a good etc job of [Vn.pr pass rel] (*informal*) perform (a task) well, badly etc. **adj:** good, excellent, satisfactory; poor, dreadful. **o:** car, cooker; bathroom, kitchen; report, revision: *Many machines wash, rinse, spin-dry — but the new Acme Twin Speed Combination* ***makes a better job of*** *all three.* DM ○ *You can hand over to her any rewriting that needs to be done, knowing that a* ***first-class job*** *will be* ***made of*** *it.*

spray on/onto [Vn.pr pass rel] send (liquid) in a stream of tiny drops (onto sth). **O:** paint, varnish; perfume; disinfectant, weed-killer. **o:** wall; skin; plant: *The gardener* ***sprayed*** *insecticide* ***on*** *the rose-bushes* (or: ***sprayed*** *the rose-bushes* ***with*** *insecticide*). ○ *Insect repellent should be* ***sprayed onto*** *the skin to discourage mosquitoes* (or: *The skin should be* ***sprayed with*** *insect repellent* etc).

spray with [Vn.pr pass rel] ⇨ previous entry

turn in 1 [Vp, Vn.p pass adj] (cause sth to) face or curve inwards. **S** [Vp], **O** [Vn.p]: △one's toes, feet, knees: *His big toe* ***turns in*** (ie towards the other toes on that foot). ○ *His feet* ***turn in*** (ie towards each other).

- **optional prep in headphrase – 1.2**
- **preps repeated before collocates – 6.2.2**
- **codes preceding each example – 3.1.2**
- **cross-references to related verbs – 9.3**
- **reference to set of adjs – 1.4, 7.2.5**
- **style label – 4.1**
- **grammatical function of collocates – 6.2**
- **source of quotation – 7.1**
- **internal arrangement of collocate lists – 6.4**
- **transform shown in examples – 7.4**
- **dummy entry – 9.5**
- **sense number: order of entries – 2**
- **restricted set of collocates – 6.5**

The headphrase

1 The headphrase of an entry (ie the phrasal verb or longer idiom which the entry defines and illustrates) is printed in **bold type** and set slightly to the left of the column of text. We explain and illustrate here the *forms* in which verbs, nouns, adjectives etc appear in the headphrase as they are an indication of how those words can actually be inflected in speech and writing.

The form of the verb normally given in the headphrase is the 'base' form – the infinitive without *to*:

blow down **get one's eye in** **take up the slack**

The use of the base form indicates that the verb has its full range of inflected forms, finite and non-finite. Expressions in which the verb is restricted to the *to*-infinitive, the present tense, etc, appear in those forms in the headphrase:

to begin with 1 **pride goes before a fall**
to start with 1 **money doesn't grow on trees**

A few complex idioms correspond to subordinate clauses of time, condition, etc. In their headphrases the verb is given in the present tense to indicate the possible use of this tense *and* the past simple:

when it comes down to **when one's ship comes in**

In those few cases in which a phrasal verb is part of a longer idiom containing another verb, the *first* verb is given in the base form:

(have) one's head screwed on
tell sb where he gets off/where to get off

When a noun, pronoun, etc forms an integral part of a complex idiom and functions as Subject, it is placed before the verb in the headphrase. If the verb in such expressions has the normal range of tense forms, it is entered in the base form:

one's blood be up **it fall on/upon sb to do sth**
the game be up

Phrasal verbs and more complex expressions which are irregular in that they exist as passive forms or nominalized forms etc, but not the actives from which such forms are normally derived, are given appropriate headphrases (for a fuller treatment of this topic, ⇨ 3.3):

accustomed to **washed up** **hangover/hung over**
used to **wash-out** **spin-off**

In many complex expressions of which a *noun* is an integral part, the noun may be used in both the singular and plural forms. In other cases, the form of the noun cannot be varied. The different possibilities are dealt with in the following ways:

◆ When the noun can only be singular, it appears in the singular form in the headphrase and illustration(s):

come into season ... *Tomatoes* **come into season** *much earlier in Italy than in Northern Europe.*

◆ When the noun can only be used in the plural form, it appears in that form in the headphrase and illustration(s):

get to grips with ... *It's time you* ... **got to grips with** *the basic trouble* ...

◆ When the noun can function in both the singular and plural forms, the singular form is given in the headphrase, and both forms are illustrated:

bring a charge against ... *you might feel justified in* **bringing charges against** *him.* ○ *'You could* **bring a charge** *of dangerous driving* **against** *him* ... .'

◆ When the noun tends to occur more frequently in the plural form, but is sometimes met in the singular, the headphrase and example(s) show the noun in the plural, while a note at the end of the entry explains that the singular may also be used:

make allowances (for) ... *Now that I had seen this attitude abroad, I was even less ready to* ***make allowances for*** *it.* AH ... □ allowances occasionally sing, as in: *When every* ***allowance*** *has been* ***made for*** *his inexperience* ...

◆ Where special circumstances require it, the headphrase may include singular *and* plural forms:

keep a tab/tabs/a tag on

(where **tab** can be either singular or plural, while **tag** must be singular).

The possessive adjectives *my*, *his*, *her*, *one's*, *its*, *our*, *your* and *their* are usually represented in headphrases by one of the forms **one's**, **his**, **sb's** (⇨ *Examples* 7.2.1). These three headphrase forms are used to indicate differences in the way the possessive in *examples* is related to other parts of the sentence:

make one's way in the world ... *If he hasn't* ***made his way in the world*** *by now, he never will.* MM

Here **one's** is used in the headphrase because the possessive in the example (*his*) refers to the same person as the Subject (*he*).

bring to his feet ... *A jolt nearly threw me from the bed, and a second jolt* ***brought*** *me* ***to my feet.*** SD

Here **his** is used (rather than **one's** or **sb's**) because the possessive in the example (*my*) refers to the same person as the Object (*me*).

take off sb's hands ... *I should be glad if a buyer* ***took*** *the entire block* (ie of flats) ***off our hands.***

In this headphrase, the form **sb's** is used because in the example the person referred to by the possessive (*our*) is different from either the Subject (*a buyer*) or the Object (*the entire block*).

1.1 An oblique / is used to separate parts of a headphrase which can be substituted for each other. In many cases, though not in all, the use of the oblique also indicates that the substitutable words, etc have the same sense (ie are synonyms) so that they can be used in place of each other without affecting the meaning of the headphrase as a whole:

come into sight/view

(where **come into sight** has the same meaning as **come into view**).

The use of the oblique always indicates a *limited* range of alternative words, etc; it usually occurs once, and seldom more than twice, at a given point in the headphrase:

carry all/everything before one
fall on/upon evil days/hard times
scatter about/around/round

In the notes which follow, the kinds of alternatives most frequently recorded in the headphrases are dealt with in turn.

1.1.1 The particle **in** and the preposition **into** which are similar in meaning as well as form, often alternate after a verb. Similarly, **on** alternates with **onto** and **out** with **out of**. So we have **break in** ... (or: ***into*** *a house*, etc). In such cases, the particle and preposition are placed after the verb in the same entry, with an oblique separating the alternatives in the headphrase:

break in/into **dab on/onto** **opt out/out of**

1.1.2 When two or more synonymous particles (eg **about**, **around**, **round**) or prepositions (eg **on**, **over**, **upon**) alternate after a particular verb, they are given in one entry with that verb, and are separated from each other by an oblique in the headphrase:

look about/around/round **dote on/upon**
muck about/around **muse on/over/upon**

The same convention is used when particles (or prepositions) which are not generally equivalent in meaning are equivalent in a given expression:

brick in/up **centre in/on/upon**
fill in/out/up **hanker after/for**

1.1.3 In some longer expressions one or more *nouns* can be substituted for another without affecting the meaning of the whole. In such cases, the alternatives are marked off by the oblique in the headphrase:

come into being/existence **run to earth/ground**
tear to pieces/ribbons/shreds

The same convention has been adopted for expressions containing alternative equivalent *articles*, *adjectives* or *adverbs*:

run an/one's eye over **never/not think of**
have a soft/weak spot for

Adjectives, adverbs, etc which are alternatives but *opposite* in meaning are indicated in the same way:

get off on the right/wrong foot **do badly/well for**

Note, however, that when two *particles* (or *prepositions*) which are opposite in meaning can combine with a verb used in a particular sense, they are regarded as forming parts of different expressions and treated in separate entries:

leave down ie allow (sth) to remain in a lowered position
leave up ie allow (sth) to remain in a raised position
put back 2 ie move the hands of a clock back
put forward 3 ie move the hands of a clock forward

1.2 Parentheses **(in)** are used to enclose a part or parts of a headphrase which, though closely related to the whole, may under certain conditions be deleted. The classes of word, phrase, etc most commonly marked as deletable (or 'optional') in the headphrases will be considered in turn.

1.2.1 *Prepositions* are frequently enclosed by parentheses:

cope (with) **come home (to)** **take out (against)**

Each preposition here is closely tied to the verb (or verb + particle) in the sense that when **cope**, **come home** or **take out** occurs at the end of a piece of text, one can confidently predict that, if a preposition is to follow, it will be **with**, **to** and **against** respectively, rather than any other:

Our collection (of wild animals) *had reached such proportions that it took us all our time to* ***cope*** *...* ***with*** it. DF

You have to look at it carefully, then its meaning will ***come home*** *...* ***to*** you. CF

The police have decided to ***take out*** *a summons ...* ***against*** *the drivers of both cars involved in the accident.*

At the same time, it is possible to *omit* the prepositions (and their objects) altogether and still be left with correct sentences which are related in meaning to the fuller ones.

In headphrases such as

strike up (with)

the preposition **with** is deletable under different conditions. From a sentence such as

I'd first ***struck up*** *an acquaintance* ***with*** *him on Waterloo Station.*

the preposition + object (***with*** *him*) is not normally deleted. However, the sentence can be paraphrased as:

We'd first ***struck up*** *an acquaintance on Waterloo Station.*

The dictionary contains many entries with the same characteristics as **strike up (with)**, e.g.:

agree (with) **fall in love (with)** **make (it) up (with)**

The paraphrase relationship referred to above is illustrated in many of the entries for such expressions (usually in parentheses after one or more of the example sentences).

1.2.2 From some phrasal verbs and longer idioms a particle, adjective, adverbial phrase, etc can be deleted in the same way as the preposition from **cope (with)**, etc (⇨ 1.2.1). The optional item is highly predictable in the context; it can be removed without making nonsense of the remainder; the meanings of the expression with and without the particle, etc are closely linked. In these cases too, the optional part is placed in parentheses in the headphrases. Consider these headphrases and the examples given below them:

foist (off) on ... *He* ***foisted off*** *a few cases of inferior scotch* ***on*** *a too eager customer.* □ *I'm sorry all this has been* ***foisted on*** *you.* EHOW
make up a four (at bridge) ... *Ask Geoffrey if he'd mind* ***making up a four.***

and compare with those examples these possible variants:

He ***foisted*** *a few cases of inferior scotch* ***on*** *a too eager customer.*
I'm sorry all this has been ***foisted off on*** *you.*
Ask Geoffrey if he'd mind ***making up a four at bridge.***

1.2.3 A reflexive pronoun or phrase is sometimes placed in parentheses in the headphrase:

adjust (oneself) to **edge (one's way) across, along, back etc**

The reflexive item can be omitted from these combinations under the conditions outlined above (⇨ 1.2.1 and 1.2.2). Thus one meets:

I don't think I shall ever ***adjust to*** *life in this remote place.*
The climber ***edged*** *warily* ***along*** *the narrow shelf.*

as well as:

I don't think I shall ever ***adjust myself to*** *life in this remote place.*
The climber ***edged his way*** *warily* ***along*** *the narrow shelf.*

A different case is represented by the headphrases:

write (oneself) out **content (oneself) with**

The reflexive pronoun may not be deleted from these combinations in *active* sentences. We cannot say:

There was no reason to think he had ***written out*** *(cf* ***written himself out****).* PW

It is however deleted in *passive* sentences. One says (in the active):

We can't go abroad this year so we'll have to ***content ourselves with*** *a family holiday in London.*

but in the passive:

We can't go abroad this year so we'll have to be ***contented with****,* etc.

Note that in the appropriate entries (as here) this active/passive relationship is often clarified by means of examples.

1.2.4 In the headphrase

change over (from) (to)

two prepositions are put in separate sets of parentheses. Each preposition is related to the verb + particle in much the same way as **to** is related to **come home** in **come home (to)** (⇨ 1.2.1). The following example, for instance, can be complete as it stands:

We don't like the cooking arrangements in the flat. We want to **change over**.

though we can predict these possible continuations:

... ***from*** *gas.* or: *...* ***to*** *electricity.*

We could, however, continue by using *both* prepositions:

... ***from*** *gas* ***to*** *electricity.*

This is what is meant by placing prepositions in separate pairs of brackets.

1.3 In some headphrases parentheses and the oblique are used together. In all these cases, the words, etc marked as alternatives by the oblique are *enclosed* by the parentheses:

congratulate (on/upon)
make a song and dance (about/over)
tackle (about/on/over)

The use of *parentheses* here indicates that everything enclosed by them may be left out and that, if this is done, the meaning of the rest of the expression is unaffected (⇨ 1.2). The oblique is used to mark off words – in these examples prepositions with the same meaning (⇨ 1.1.2) – from which a choice can be made.

In the case of **tackle (about/on/over)** for instance, the conventions mean that the following variations on a single sentence are all acceptable, and all related in meaning:

'He's always playing his stereo at full blast: it's time we ***tackled*** *him.'*
...we ***tackled*** *him* ***about*** *it.'*
...we ***tackled*** *him* ***on*** *it.'*
...we ***tackled*** *him* ***over*** *it.'*

1.4 In some complex idioms in which a noun is a fixed element, the noun *must* be modified by one from a small selection of adjectives. When the number of alternative adjectives is limited to two or three, they can be shown in the headphrase and marked off by the oblique (as explained above, 1.1.3):

have a soft/weak spot for **hold in high/low esteem/regard**

Sometimes, however, the list of adjectives from which a choice must be made is longer:

make effective, good, proper use of
take the easy, simplest, quickest, coward's way out/out of

To put so much information in the headphrase might make the user lose sight of the *fixed* elements in each expression – **make ... use of** and **take the ... way out/out of** respectively. So one commonly occurring adjective (+ **etc**) is included in the headphrase:

make effective etc use of **take the easy etc way out/out of**

and this adjective is repeated, and other possible choices indicated, in the body of the entry:

adj: ⚠ effective, good, proper.
adj: easy, simplest, quickest, coward's; only, usual.

The use of the ⚠ in the first entry indicates that the number of options, while more than three, is still *limited* (though it may not be exhausted by the words listed). The absence of this sign from the entry **take the easy etc way out/out of** indicates a more open range of choice (⇨ also *Collocations*, 6.5). The same conventions are used when a *particle* must be modified by one of a small set of adverbs of degree:

be well etc off (for). ***m:*** ⚠ (very, fairly) well, comfortably, badly.

(where **m** = adverbial modifier. For a detailed treatment of words listed after **adj, m** etc in dictionary entries, ⇨ *Collocations*, 6.2)

1.5 Verbs such as **puff**, **steam**, **stump** and **zoom** combine freely with a number of particles and prepositions of *direction* (eg **across**, **along**, **back**) to form **puff across** (the bridge), **puff along** (the track), **steam into** (Newcastle), **steam through** (the tunnel) etc. Characteristically, these combinations are equivalent in meaning to a verb of *motion* + a particle of *direction* + an adverbial phrase of *manner*. Thus

puff across = move across sending out smoke, etc and/or panting noisily.

These special features of structure and meaning are dealt with in the dictionary, though no attempt is made to list *in separate entries* all the possible combinations of particles with any *one* verb. Each verb is generally entered once, with the possible choice of particles etc indicated after it, while the definition states the meaning shared by the various combinations:

stump across, **along**, **away etc** ... move across etc heavily, and often in anger or irritation.

zoom across, **along**, **away etc** ... move across etc swiftly, with engine(s) roaring.

In the form of headphrase used here, **across**, **along**, **away etc** refer to the following list of directional particles and prepositions which, because of their frequency, the user can with reasonable confidence combine with the verbs in question. The exclusion of one item from the list does not, of course, imply that it cannot combine with one or several of the verbs (for a full list, ⇨ *Alphabetical list of prepositions and particles*, p. vii):

across, along, away, back, behind, by, down, from, in, into, off, on, onto, out, out of, over, past, through, to, towards, under, up.

Note, finally, that when **zoom** etc is part of a verb + particle combination with a specialized or idiomatic meaning (ie a phrasal verb), this expression is dealt with in an entry of its own:

zoom out ... (*cinema, TV*) by adjusting the 'zoom' lens on a camera, move gradually from a close-up to a longer shot.

1.6 Phrasal verbs etc which have the same written form but quite different meanings are given separate numbered entries under one common headphrase:

be over 1 ... be ended, be finished. ... *work* ***was over*** *for the weekend.* HD
2 ... remain, be left. ... *A small piece of flannel* ***was over*** *when the tailor had finished cutting out my suit.*
3 ... spend a long time having or doing (sth) ... '*Don't* ***be*** *too long* ***over*** *breakfast* ...'

Where there is a lengthy series of numbered entries, the headphrases are arranged in an order which reflects differences and similarities of meaning:

pick up 1 ... take hold of and raise (sth) ...
2 ... collect (sth) ...
3 ... (*informal*) collect (sth) as wages; earn. ...
4 ... take (sb) on board; ...
5 ... rescue (sb) from the sea. ...

Order of entries

The arrangement of entries in this dictionary is guided by three basic principles:

◆ Headphrases are first listed according to the alphabetical position of the *verb* (Thus, **call** precedes **catch**.)

◆ They are then ordered according to the alphabetical position of the *particle* or *preposition* (Thus, **call in** precedes **call up** and **catch in** precedes **catch out**).

◆ In the lists of headphrases arranged according to these rules, some entries contain a noun, an adjective etc. Those entries are ordered according to the alphabetical position of the noun etc. (Thus **call to account** precedes **call to order**, and **take charge (of)** precedes **take control (of)**.)

This approach to arrangement brings together many complex entries (eg **take charge (of), take control (of)**) that are related in meaning, and is partly aimed at helping the student to understand and learn one entry by comparing it with others. In the following sequence, for instance, the meaning of **rub up 1**, which is literal, throws light on that of **rub up 2**, while the meaning of **rub up the right way** can also be understood as a figurative extension of the first literal sense:

rub up 1 ... polish (sth) until it is clean and shiny.

2 ... refresh one's knowledge of a subject which has been neglected for some time.

rub up the right way ... handle (sb) in a careful, soothing way ...

Though much importance is attached to semantic links in the dictionary, the need to ensure quick access to individual entries has not been overlooked. The following notes are intended to help the user locate both the simpler, phrasal verb entries and those which contain a noun and/or adjective in addition. Special help is also given in the *Index of nouns etc used in headphrases*, the first of two indexes provided at the end of the dictionary. Here, users can locate entries via the various nouns, adjectives etc which they contain, thus:

blow/blows ... bring to ~ s
right (*adj, adv*) ... rub up the ~ way
way ... rub up the right ~.

2.1 The alphabetical position of *verbs* takes precedence in deciding the order of headphrases:

chew over
check out/out of
chime in (with)

pick an argument/a quarrel/a fight (with) ...
picture to oneself ...
piece out ...

This rule is followed even when a noun, adverb, etc comes *before* the verb in a headphrase:

the sky cloud over
club together

2.1.1. To speed up access to individual entries, all entries beginning with the *same* verb are preceded by a keyword in a larger print size:

carry
carry about (with one)
carry along
carry away 1

2.2 The sequence of headphrases is *next* decided by the alphabetical order of the *particle* or *preposition*:

hand in
hand off
hand on (to) 1

talk at
talk back (to)
talk down

work towards
work under
work up

2.2.1 The location of headphrases consisting of a 'regular' past participle form of the verb (plus a particle or preposition) depends first on the alphabetical order of the verb:

enrol in
ensconce (oneself) in
enshrined in

indulge in
infatuated (with)
infect with

When two forms of the same verb are followed by a different particle etc, the particle determines the order:

deceived in
deceive into

used to
use up

When the verbs and particles in two headphrases are the same, except that the verb form in one is the (regular) past participle, the headphrase with past participle is placed *second*:

button up
buttoned up

tuck away 2
tucked away 1

wash up 2
washed up

Irregular past participles, eg **caught, fed** are positioned below the 'base' forms from which they are derived (ie they are *not* given in strict alphabetical order):

catch up in
caught up in 1. . . 2
catch up (on) 2

feed up
fed up (with)
feel for 1

In the alphabetical sequence, 'nominalized' forms such as **come-hither, flash-back, runabout** are generally treated like normal combinations of verb + particle:

come from/of 2
come-hither
come home (to)

flash (at)
flashback
flash back (to)

rumour about/ abroad
runabout
run across

2.2.2 When a headphrase contains a particle *and* a preposition, eg **live up to**, **muck in (with), throw away on**, the *particle* decides whether it comes after or before headphrases containing the same verb and a *single* particle (or preposition):

live it up
live up to

muck in (with)
muck out

throw away on
throw back 1

Similarly, when a headphrase contains *two prepositions*, the alphabetical order of the *first* preposition decides whether the headphrase follows or precedes one containing the same verb and *one* preposition:

answer (to)
answer (to) (for)

convert (from) (to)
convert (into)

gaze on/upon
gaze round

When a number of headphrases contain a particle and a preposition, and the particle and the verb are the same in each case, sequencing is determined by the alphabetical order of the *prepositions*:

build up (from)
build (up) into
build up to 1

line up (against)
line up alongside/with
line up behind

let in for
let in/into
let in/on

As these examples show, the use of parentheses or the oblique in a headphrase does not affect the ordering of headphrases when they are *in any case* different by virtue of the particles, etc which they contain. When two headphrases have the *same* form apart from parentheses, the headphrase with parentheses precedes:

agree (with)
agree with

bring round (to) 2
bring round to

2.3 The alphabetical order of noun(s), adjective(s), etc is taken into account *after* the headphrases have been placed in sequence according to the verb and particle/preposition:

be out of 4
be out of action

draw from 2
draw a conclusion (from)

keep in 6
keep in check 1

Several headphrases containing the *same* verb and particle/preposition but *different* nouns, etc are placed in sequence according to the alphabetical order of the nouns:

bring into focus 2	**get into the act**
bring into force	**get into sb's black books**
bring into the open	**get into deep water**

As these examples show, the indefinite and definite articles and the possessives (**one's**, **sb's**, **his**) are ignored when deciding which noun is to precede which.

However, when the article or possessive helps to distinguish two headphrases which are otherwise the same, the article, etc determines their order:

go out of one's mind	**make (a) peace (with)**
go out of sb's mind	**make one's peace with**

None of the parts of speech, noun, adjective, adverb, etc is given priority over the others when establishing the order of entries. Alphabetical order *alone* governs the location of a headphrase containing (say) a noun before or after one containing an adverb. When a headphrase contains *two* nouns (or an adjective + noun, etc) the *first* of these words decides the location of the headphrase:

	order determined by:
be at attention	**attention** (noun)
be at a dead end	**dead** (adjective)
be at an end	**end** (noun)
be at a halt/standstill	**halt** (noun)
be (hard) at it/work	**hard** (adverb)
be at it	**it** (pronoun)
be at pains to do sth	**pains** (noun)
what be at	**what** (interrog pronoun)

The relative positions in a headphrase of the noun, etc and the preposition/particle do not affect alphabetical placement of that headphrase. Neither does the use of parentheses (when the headphrases are in other respects different):

take at (his/its) face value
take a look (at)
take offence (at)
take umbrage (at)

2.3.1 Except for the articles and possessives, 'grammatical' words are given the same weight as 'lexical' words in determining the order of headphrases. The grammatical classes most frequently met with are *negative adverbs* and *indefinite adjectives*, especially **never**, **not**; **no** and *indefinite* and *personal pronouns*, especially **anything**, **nothing**, **something**; **it**, **me**, **us**, **you**. Note the order of headphrases in:

have a flair/gift for
have no fears/terrors for

(where **flair** and **no** decide the order)

lay (one's) hands on 3
never/not lay a finger/hand on

(where **hands** and **never** decide the order)

make a note of
make nothing of
make a nuisance of oneself

(where **note**, **nothing** and **nuisance** decide the order).

2.3.2 Since particles or prepositions take precedence over nouns, pronouns, etc in determining overall arrangements, such headphrases as

be in fashion/vogue
be in focus 1 . . . 2
be in force

form part of a series which is placed *above*

be in at the finish/kill

since **in** precedes **in at**. In the same way, the headphrases

be in charge (of)
be in control (of)

are placed earlier in the general arrangement than

be in accord/harmony/tune (with)
be in collision (with)
be in collusion (with)

because **in (of)** precedes **in (with)**.

Grammatical codes and tables

3 Verbs and particles/prepositions are elements in the structure of sentences. They are preceded, interrupted and followed by other elements – Subject, Direct Object, prepositional object, and so on – which may not themselves form part of the phrasal verb or longer idiom. As we show with reference to the particle/preposition contrast itself (⇨ *The Scope and Aims of the Dictionary*, 0.1, and 3.1.1) important differences of *function* cannot be made clear except by placing a combination in the sentence pattern (or patterns) in which it is regularly used. Again, we cannot indicate the 'transformational' possibilities of such phrasal verbs as **bring up** (children), **try out** (a machine), **fill in** (an application), etc except by reference to the wider pattern. It is for these reasons that each entry recorded in the dictionary is described in terms of the sentence pattern (or patterns) in which it normally appears.

These patterns (and their transformations) are not fully described in the entries themselves. Instead, we make use of a small set of abbreviations which for each entry make up a *grammatical code*. The code refers the user to a full treatment in tabular form (below, 3.4) of the appropriate pattern or patterns. The guidance provided by the codes is of two kinds:

◆ Capital 'V', with or without a following 'n', shows whether the verb is transitive or intransitive (ie used with or without a Direct Object); 'p' or 'pr' indicates whether **in, up, into** etc function as particles or prepositions:

cave in 1 [Vp ...] **blow up 6** [Vn⇄p ...]
run into [Vpr, Vn.p ...]

◆ One or more abbreviations, positioned after [Vp], [Vn⇄p] etc, show which of the structural transformations associated with that pattern can be applied to the entry in question:

cave in 1 [Vp nom] **blow up 6** [Vn⇄p nom pass adj]
run into [Vpr, Vn.pr pass]

Basic patterns

3.1 With very few exceptions, the phrasal verbs, etc treated in the dictionary can be shown to function in one or more of six simple, active sentence patterns. These 'basic' patterns can be divided into two groups according to *transitivity* (ie according to whether or not they contain a Direct Object). Intransitive sentences are labelled [V] and transitive sentences [Vn]. Within each of [V] and [Vn] the sentence patterns are further subdivided into [p], [pr] and [p.pr] according to whether they contain a particle, a preposition, or a particle *and* a preposition. The whole system of basic patterns can be represented schematically, and illustrated, as follows:

	Intransitive	Transitive
Particle	[Vp]	[Vn.p]
Preposition	[Vpr]	[Vn.pr]
Particle + Preposition	[Vp.pr]	[Vn.p.pr]

[Vp] *The electricity supply* **went off**.
[Vpr] *We were* **banking on** *a change of heart.*
[Vp.pr] *The committee* **fell back on** *an earlier plan.*
[Vn.p] *The awful food* **turns** *people* **off**.
[Vn.pr] *Peter* **foists** *all his problems* **on** *his unfortunate friends.*
[Vn.p.pr] *You can* **put** *the shortage* **down to** *bad planning.*
([Vn.p] is one of three subtypes, as will be shown, but these finer distinctions do not affect the others made in the scheme.)

3.1.1 This simple scheme of sentence patterns embodies the contrast between 'particles' (sometimes called adverbial particles) and 'prepositions'. The terms particle and preposition are used throughout the dictionary to reflect the ways in which words such as **away**, **back**, **off**, **on**, **with**, etc are used in sentences (ie their syntactic functions). In other words 'particle' and 'preposition' refer to use and not to form. We can see that in the sentences

[Vp] *The electricity* **went off**.
[Vn.p] *The awful food* **turns** *people* **off** / **turns** *them* **off**.

the word **off** does not introduce a noun phrase, noun or pronoun. It functions independently – as a *particle*. We can contrast

[Vpr] *John* **went off** *his food.*
[Vn.pr] *The instructor* **put** *me* **off** *driving.*

where **off** does introduce a noun phrase or noun – 'his food' and 'driving' respectively. In these sentences **off** functions as a *preposition* (the noun phrases themselves are prepositional *objects*). Or consider again the sentences

[Vp.pr] *The committee* **fell back on** *an earlier plan.*
[Vn.p.pr] *You can* **put** *the shortage* **down to** *bad planning.*

In the first of these, **back** has the function of a particle (no dependent noun phrase), while **on** has that of a preposition (it introduces the phrase 'an earlier plan'). In the same way, **down** is used as a particle in the second example, and **to** as a preposition.

This whole question is complicated by the fact that certain words (**on**, **off**, **up**, for example) are at times used as particles and at others as prepositions. Other words function only as particles (**away**, **back**, etc) while others again are used only as prepositions (**into**, **with**, etc). The fact that some words may have a *double* function, however, does not affect the way they are described in the dictionary. The user may find it helpful to remember that the way a word such as **off** or **on** is labelled in a particular context depends entirely on its use *in that context*, and not on its potentiality of use.

3.1.2 When a headphrase functions in two or more basic patterns (eg in a transitive as well as an intransitive one) these differences of use are indicated in the grammatical code, and often exemplified as well:

turn against [Vpr, Vn.pr] (cause sb to) be hostile to (sb). ... *He had the distinct impression that everyone was* **turning against** *him.* ○ *'What* **turned** *her* **against** *me, do you think? The child, I suppose, horrid little creature.'* DC

When a grammatical code refers to *four* basic patterns, the headphrase will often contain an optional preposition (⇨ *The headphrase*, 1.2), and the headphrase form *without* the preposition will function in two of the patterns, while the form *with* the preposition will function in the other two. In such complex entries, each example is preceded by the appropriate code (or codes):

keep away (from) [Vp, Vp.pr, Vn.p pass, Vn.p.pr] not go near, touch, use etc (sth/sb); prevent (sb) from going near, touching, using sth (sth/sb). ... ○ [Vp, Vp.pr] *The spectators have to* **keep away** (**from** *the players*). ○ [Vn.p] *'What's been* **keeping**

you ***away****?'* . . . ○ [Vn.p.pr] *You know you can't expect to* **keep** *Arthur* **away from** *women.* BLCH

3.1.3 The headphrases of a few entries do not conform to *any* of the basic patterns. Examples of such headphrases are:

bring to grips with **fall in love (with)**

If these headphrases did not contain the preposition **with** they would fit the [Vn.pr] and [Vpr] patterns respectively; as it is, they do not correspond directly with *any* of the six patterns. Nevertheless, the principle is followed of describing as [Vpr], [Vn.p], [Vn.pr] or [Vp.pr] all headphrases which would exactly match those patterns if it were not for an additional preposition. The codes allocated to the two example headphrases are therefore:

bring to grips with [Vn.pr pass] **fall in love (with)** [Vpr]

Transforms

3.2 A good deal of grammatical information about headphrases can be stated quite economically if some patterns are regarded as being 'transformationally' related to others. But what precisely is meant by grammatical transformation? In a sentence such as:

The prices **came down***.*

the order of words can be rearranged to give

Down came *the prices.*

This structural rearrangement is a 'transformation' (or 'transform') of the original sentence. Transformations may involve not simply a change of word order but also the corresponding replacement of one word (or phrase) by another. Compare the last sentence with:

Down *they* **came***.*

They may also include corresponding changes in the *form* of a word or phrase, as when an active sentence is transformed into a passive one. Compare:

The travel agent **messed up** *our bookings completely.*
Our bookings were **messed up** *completely (by the travel agent).*

(where **messed**→ *were* **messed**). Transformation, then, is a matter of structural change, and the changes may be of various kinds.

Sentences which are transformationally related are often closely related in *meaning* also. As a general rule the transforms which are referred to and illustrated in the dictionary are close in meaning to the sentences from which they derive. Again, it is usual to regard some sentences as more 'basic' or fundamental than others for purposes of describing transformations. As has already been suggested when introducing the simple, active patterns referred to as [Vp], [Vpr], etc, this is the procedure which we adopt here. It should perhaps be added that the decision to treat some kinds of sentence pattern as being derived from others has been made for reasons of descriptive convenience. It does not imply a commitment to the view that some patterns are more abstract, or 'deeper' than others, nor does it require a technical understanding of the rules of transformational grammar.

3.2.1 Whether or not a particular transformation can be applied to the sentence pattern of any given headphrase is shown by including the appropriate abbreviation in the code for that entry. The code in the entry for

make room for [Vn.pr pass . . .]

shows, for example, that a *passive* sentence can be formed from an *active* sentence in which that headphrase appears. Compare:

We need to **make** *more* **room** *on TV schedules* **for** *serious drama.*
More **room** *needs to be* **made** *on TV schedules* **for** *serious drama.*

Information about the transformational *restrictions* of idioms is of special importance to foreign learners, who might otherwise change the structure of sentences in ways regarded by the native speaker as unacceptable. In any given entry, this guidance of course takes the form of omitting from the grammatical code any reference to a transformation which is *not* applied to that entry.

3.2.2 A transform that is difficult to describe by means of a table alone is the so-called 'nominalized form' (abbreviated in the notes which accompany the tables to 'nom form'). A nominalized form is a noun derived from a verb + particle combination – **break-in**, **flypast**, **upkeep**, **outpouring** – or from a combination of verb + preposition – **glance-through**, **skim-through**. As the examples show, however, nouns formed from verbs with particles may have quite different internal patterns (cf **flypast**, **upkeep**, **outpouring**): there is a variety of nominalized *forms*, rather than a single *form*. Secondly, nouns which are composed of the same elements occurring in the same order may be hyphenated or not (cf **break-in**, **flypast**). Thirdly, two nouns which are formed on the same model (and are both hyphenated) may function in different sentence patterns. While a sentence such as

She gave the place a thorough **clean-out**.

is acceptable, the sentence

He gave the arrangements a thorough* **mess-up.

is certainly unacceptable. We deal with these questions in turn below, beginning with a simple classification of nominalized forms on the basis of differences in their internal structure. At this stage we disregard differences of spelling and stress.

We start with the class that includes **break-in**, **flypast**, **holdup**, **mess-up**, etc. This is the class most frequently recorded in the dictionary (as can be seen by referring to the *Index of nominalized forms* at the end of the dictionary). Most members of the class are derived from verb + particle combinations functioning in the [Vp] and [Vn⇄p] patterns and have the structure 'base form (of verb) + particle'. It should be noted that most nouns derived from combinations of verb + preposition (ie the [Vpr] basic pattern) have a similar structure, thus: **glance-through**, **look-over**, **look-through**, and are treated as part of the same major class. Whatever their source (ie as verb + particle or verb + preposition) all nouns of this type are pluralized in the same way: (two) **break-ins**, (several) **mess-ups**, (a couple of quick) **flick-throughs**, etc. Only nouns of this commonly occurring and highly productive class are identified in the appropriate grammatical codes as [... nom], though other types are illustrated, and listed in the *Index*.

A second category includes such examples as **'downpour**, **'offprint**, **'outbreak**, **'upkeep**, derived in all cases from verb + particle combinations and having the structure 'particle + base form'. The plural is formed in the same way as for the major class: (two successive) **downpours**, (three) **offprints**, etc. A small number of nouns formed on this pattern are paired with 'standard' forms originating in the same verb and particle (cf **print-off/offprint**; **turndown/downturn**).

A third type, of which the dictionary records very few examples, is represented by **outpouring** and **upbringing**. Both are derived from verb + particle combinations and have the pattern 'particle + *-ing* form'. Their plurals parallel those of the other classes: **outpourings**, **upbringings**.

It is possible to give firm guidance on how nouns in the two *minor* categories are regularly written or printed. British and American practice is to write them fully joined, as in **downturn**, **offprint**; **outpouring**, **upbringing**, and they appear in that form in the dictionary. As regards the major class, some uncertainty is inevitable in making recommendations to users. The difficulty arises from the fact that many of the nouns exist in two written forms (fully linked and hypenated) in British

English, and individual users and printing houses differ in the conventions that they favour. On the whole, we have tended to prefer the hyphenated forms in the examples we provide ourselves, though where citations are used we record the authors' own usage (and in some cases where this differs from our own, add an explanatory note: ⇨ **black out 2, 4**).

Nominalized forms of all three types carry principal stress on the *first* element. In the major class the placement of stress does not vary with the choice of the solid as distinct from the hyphenated form:

'downpour, 'offprint, 'upkeep
'outpouring, 'upbringing
'break-in, 'flypast, 'glance-through

This general rule is departed from only in cases such as the following, where an *unlinked* form exists side by side with, and may sometimes be preferred to, a *hyphenated* one:

a quick **look 'round** (cf a quick **'look-round**)
a quick **thumb 'through** (cf a quick **'thumb-through**)

Such unlinked alternatives, in which principal stress falls on the final element (particle/preposition) are recorded in the *Index* and often illustrated in the entries themselves.

Finally, we can consider the various sentence (and other) patterns in which nouns formed from (finite) verb + particle, etc are used. Many nominalized forms have a range of syntactic functions. The form **make-up** (in one of its senses) can be used attributively – as in **make-up** box, **make-up** girl – or as direct object – You're using too much **make-up** – or as Subject – Your **make-up**'s running. In certain cases, the noun may be associated with a particular sentence pattern which is a paraphrase of the 'basic' pattern in which the corresponding finite verb + particle operates. Compare, for example:

The pilot ***took off*** *smoothly / The pilot made a smooth* ***take-off****.*
Building workers ***walked out*** */ Building workers staged a* ***walk-out****.*

Each paraphrase of this kind may be regarded as a transform of the whole of the corresponding 'basic' sentence. Where a particular type of paraphrase occurs sufficiently often in relation to a basic pattern we explain and illustrate it in the form of a table (⇨ 3.4, [Vp nom], [Vn⇄p nom]).

However, not all the 'basic' sentences in which individual verb + particle combinations occur are paraphrased in the same way. We shall not find

Violence made/staged a sudden* ***flare-up**.*

to parallel the sentence

The pilot made a smooth ***take-off****.*

We have not attempted to deal with these complexities through the grammatical code (which indicates simply whether the noun itself – **take-off**, **flare-up** – occurs). As far as space allows, however, the characteristic syntactic uses of particular nouns are displayed in the examples.

3.2.3 In practice it is difficult to draw a sharp line between *passive* sentences and those in which a participial adjective follows a 'copula' or 'linking verb'. While a sentence such as:

John is being ***worn out*** *by an over-demanding boss.*

clearly falls into the first category and:

John seems utterly ***worn out****.*

into the second, there are various intermediate possibilities. A sentence in which there is no explicit reference to a human agent such as:

John is being progressively ***worn out****.*

may none the less indicate a process, or activity, rather than a state, while a sentence which appears to indicate John's condition may contain a reference to its cause (or causer):

John seems thoroughly **worn out** *by all the demands being made of him.*

It is the difficulty of separating sentences which are partially passive from those which are fully so, and also the need to keep the grammatical indications in entries simple and manageable for the user, which have prompted us to use the *one* abbreviation [... pass] to refer to a range of different (though related) 'passive' constructions. This variety is reflected in the following examples from the dictionary. It will be noted that only the first contains an agentive phrase ('by the Foreign Secretary') as well as indicating a process. The third is ambiguous. Is it an instruction to someone to ensure (i) that he seals the parcel up (action), or (ii) that it is already sealed up (state)?

[Vn.pr pass] *This offer was* **seized** *by the Foreign Secretary* **with both hands**.
[Vpr pass] *His personal papers have all been* **searched through**.
[Vn⇄p pass] *Make sure the parcel of examination scripts is properly* **sealed up**.

Transformations with no basic pattern

3.3 There are several nominalized forms, passive forms etc in everyday use which are abnormal in that there are no corresponding *active* phrasal verbs from which they can be derived in the normal way. While we can say, for example

John is suffering from a bad **hangover** *this morning.*
(or: *John is badly* **hung over** *this morning*).

there is no active sentence – such as

Drinking all those double whiskies* **hung *John* **over** *badly this morning.*

to which those two sentences could be transformationally related. In the same way, there is no acceptable active sentence such as

Mary has been* **running *John* **around**.

that the perfectly normal

Mary has been giving John the **run-around** (= making life difficult for him).

can be said to derive from.

A certain number of these apparent transforms have come into existence indirectly as figurative extensions of the meaning of an existing, 'regular' transform. The item **wash-out** ('failure', 'disappointment') is a case in point, as its meaning is recognizably related to that of a noun with the same spoken and written form (**wash-out**, in the sense 'an end to play, brought about by rain, etc'). The latter is however derived from a finite verb + particle, as is shown in this example:

Heavy rain completely **washed out** *today's play* (or: *caused a complete* **wash-out** of today's play).

In all such cases the grammatical code for the 'anomalous' entry is made to reflect its own special character and the connection with the 'regular' entry:

wash out 3 [Vn⇄p nom ...] (*sport*) bring (play) to an end ...
wash-out [nom (Vn⇄p)] ... (*informal*) failure; disappointment.

Anomalous transforms that are not related in this way are given codes which (i) identify the transform itself (as 'nom', 'pass', etc) and (ii) indicate the active pattern (eg 'Vp', 'Vn.p') that it would derive from if 'regular':

come-back 1 [nom (Vp)]
hangover/hung over [nom pass (Vn.p)]

Tables of patterns

3.4 The tables of basic patterns and transforms have been arranged below in the same order as the abbreviations ('grammatical codes') used to refer to them in the entries themselves. The arrangement can be compared with codes for the following entries:

compensate (for) [Vpr pass emph rel, Vn.pr pass emph rel]
fade out [Vp nom, Vn⇄p pass adj]
welcome in/into [Vn⇄p pass, Vn.pr pass]

When referring to the various tables set out below, users will notice that the examples appear in the same printed form as in the entries themselves, with the headphrase picked out in each example sentence in ***bold italic***. They should note especially that when an example illustrates a 'complex' headphrase such as **get off to a good start**, where the adjective and the noun are integral parts of an idiomatic whole, the full headphrase is printed in bold italic:

*The match **got off to a good start**.*

[Vp] intransitive pattern with a particle

subject	verb phrase verb	particle	(adv phrase etc)
1 *A gang of thieves*	***broke***	***in***	*last night.*
2 *A squadron of jet fighters*	***flew***	***past.***	
3 *Anthony Sher*	***makes***	***up***	*for the part of Richard III.*
4 *Students*	*are* ***sitting***	***in***	*at the university.*
5 *The astronauts*	***splashed***	***down***	*perfectly at 3pm local time.*
6 *The pilot*	***took***	***off***	*smoothly.*
7 *Parker*	***throws***	***in***	*near the half-way line.*
8 *The runners*	*are* ***warming***	***up***	*quickly before the race.*
9 *Building workers*	***walked***	***out***	*during the morning.*
10 *The snow*	***came***	***down***	*thick and fast.*
11 *The water*	***went***	***off***	*for a couple of hours.*
12 *The sun*	***went***	***in.***	
13 *The prices*	***came***	***down.***	
14 *He was*	***waiting***	***about***	*here for a whole hour.*

Notes

(a) There is a relationship of intransitive to transitive between this pattern and [Vn⇄p], [Vn.p] and [Vp.n], as is shown by the many correspondences between individual items:

[Vp] *Parker* ***throws in*** *near the half-way line.*
[Vn.p] *Parker* ***throws the ball in*** *near the half-way line.*

(b) An adverb is not normally inserted between the verb and particle, especially when the combination is idiomatic. But note:

12 *The sun* ***went*** *right* ***in.***
13 *The prices* ***came*** *right* ***down*** *(when people started buying elsewhere).*

[Vp nom] nominalized form of verb + particle

	subject	do/make	object	(adv phrase etc)
1	*A gang of thieves*	*did*	*a* **break-in**	*last night.*
2	*A squadron of jet fighters*	*did/staged*	*a* **flypast.**	
3	*Anthony Sher*	*does*	*his* **make-up**	*for the part of Richard III*
4	*Students*	*are staging*	*a* **sit-in**	*at the university.*
5	*The astronauts*	*made*	*a perfect* **splashdown**.	*at 3pm local time.*
6	*The pilot*	*made*	*a smooth* **take-off**.	
7	*Parker*	*takes*	*a* **throw-in**	*near the half-way line.*
8	*The runners*	*are having*	*a quick* **warm-up**	*before the race.*
9	*Building workers*	*staged*	*a* **walk-out**	*during the morning.*

Notes

(a) Various 'nominalized' forms are derived from verbs with particles used in the [Vp] basic pattern. The form referred to as [Vp nom] in the code consists of the base form of the verb plus the particle, which in writing may be hyphenated, thus: **break-in**, **make-up**, **sit-in**, **take-off**, or fully linked, thus: **flypast**, **splashdown**. The nouns are pronounced with principal stress on the verbal element: **ˈbreak-in**, **ˈmake-up**, **ˈflypast**, **ˈsplashdown**

(b) Nominalized forms often function in sentence types which stand in a paraphrase relationship to the basic [Vp] pattern. In the type shown in the above table, the nom form occurs as Direct Object, while the verb is one of a small set which includes 'do', 'make', and 'take'.

(c) The nominalized form also functions as the complement of the verb 'to be' in a sentence introduced by 'there':

1 *There was a* **break-in** *last night.*
2 *There was a* **flypast** *(by jet fighters).*
4 *There is a* **sit-in** *(by students) at the university.*
7 *There is a* **throw-in** *(by Parker) near the half-way line.*
9 *There was a* **walk-out** *(by building workers) during the morning.*

(d) This transformation is normally confined to idiomatic combinations (ie phrasal verbs), though not all of those allow it.

[Vp emph] emphatic transform

	particle	verb phrase	subject	(adv phrase etc)
10	***Down***	**came**	*the snow*	*thick and fast.*
11	***Off***	**went**	*the water.*	
12	***In***	**went**	*the sun.*	
13	***Down***	**came**	*the prices.*	

Notes

(a) In this transform, the particle precedes the verb (or verb phrase) and the subject follows. Compare:

[Vp] *The prices* **came down.**
[Vp emph] ***Down came*** *the prices.*

In this transform the particle may be stressed; stress combined with initial position gives the particle special prominence.

(b) In some sentences in which the subject is a noun phrase, it may precede the verb:

13 ***Down** the prices **came**.*

(c) When the subject of the 'emphatic' sentence is a *pronoun*, however, it *must* precede the verb:

13 ***Down** they **came**.*

(d) The verbs and particles in sentences 1–9 of the [Vp] table are not normally transposed:

5 ?***Down splashed** the astronauts perfectly.*

6 ****Off took** the pilot smoothly.*

In fact, it is generally the case that when combinations are idiomatic (phrasal verbs), as in these two cases, the emphatic transformation cannot be applied.

[Vpr] intransitive pattern with a preposition

	subject		verb phrase	prepositional phrase		(adv phrase etc)
			verb	prep	object	
1	*He*		***glanced***	***through***	*the article*	*quickly.*
2	*He*		***ran***	***through***	*the main points*	*briefly.*
3	*We*	*were*	***banking***	***on***	*a change of heart.*	
4	*You*	*can*	***cope***	***with***	*these few extra people*	*easily.*
5	*He*	*has*	***provided***	***for***	*his family*	*well.*
6	*We*	*'ve*	***talked***	***about***	*this topic*	*endlessly.*
7	*A gang of thieves*		***broke***	***into***	*Smith's warehouse*	*last night.*
8	*Olive*		***gets***	***at***	*her husband*	*frequently.*
9	*The Chancellor*	*would*	***go***	***into***	*these proposals*	*very carefully.*
10	*He*	*can*	***reckon***	***on***	*a safe political future*	*with some confidence.*
11	*I*		***got***	***through***	*the written papers*	*with special coaching.*
12	*The question of a reprieve*	*may*	***turn***	***on***	*the age of the victim.*	
13	*All our hopes*		***rested***	***upon***	*this venture.*	
14	*He*		***went***	***off***	*driving*	*altogether.*
15	*The company*	*has*	***fallen***	***into***	***disrepute***	*in recent years.*

Notes

(a) Some of the expressions appearing here have transitive equivalents (compare nos 11 and 14 in this table with nos 8 and 10, [Vn.pr] table).

(b) In many cases, an adverb or adverbial phrase can be inserted between the verb phrase and the prepositional phrase:

4 *You can **cope** easily **with** these few extra people.*

10 *He can **reckon** with some confidence **on** a safe political future.*

There may be restrictions when the combination is highly idiomatic, though not in every case. Compare:

8 **Olive **gets** frequently **at** her husband.*

9 *The Chancellor would **go** very carefully **into** these proposals.*

[Vpr nom] nominalized form of verb + preposition

Notes

(a) Nouns referred to in grammatical codes as [Vpr nom] have the internal pattern 'base form + preposition'. The dictionary does not record any case where they are written as fully joined. The hyphenated form corresponds to the stressing in speech of the verb element:

'glance-through, 'run-through

The user should note that hyphenated nouns derived from some verb + preposition items have a corresponding unlinked form, with principal stress falling on the final element. Compare:

a quick ***'flick-through****/a quick* ***flick 'through***
another ***'skim-through****/another* ***skim 'through***

It is also worth noting that none of these examples are highly idiomatic.

(b) These 'nom' forms occur in a number of sentence patterns, some of which are paraphrases of the basic [Vpr] pattern:

1 *He gave the article a quick* ***glance-through****.*
2 *He did a brief* ***run-through*** *of the main points.*

[Vpr pass] passive transform

subject	verb phrase			(adv phrase etc)
		verb	prep	
1 *The article*	*was*	**glanced**	**through**	*quickly.*
2 *The main points*	*were*	**run**	**through**	*briefly.*
3 *A change of heart*	*was being*	**banked**	**on.**	
4 *These few extra people*	*can be*	**coped**	**with**	*easily.*
5 *His family*	*has been*	**provided**	**for**	*well.*
6 *This topic*	*has been*	**talked**	**about**	*endlessly.*
7 *Smith's warehouse*	*was*	**broken**	**into**	*last night.*
8 *Her husband*	*is*	**got**	**at**	*frequently.*
9 *These proposals*	*would be*	**gone**	**into**	*very carefully.*
10 *A safe political future*	*can be*	**reckoned**	**on**	*with some confidence.*

Notes

(a) The transform is derived from the active pattern by moving the prepositional object to initial position (with corresponding modification of the verb phrase). Compare:

[Vpr] *The Chancellor would* ***go into*** *these proposals very carefully.*
[Vpr pass] *These proposals would be* ***gone into*** *very carefully.*

An 'agentive' prepositional phrase – 'by the Chancellor' – is an optional constituent:

[Vpr pass] *These proposals would be* ***gone into*** *very carefully (by the Chancellor).*

(b) There is no simple one-to-one correspondence between idiomaticity and the application of this transform. Some sentences containing an idiomatic combination (phrasal verb) may be passivized:

8 *Olive* ***gets at*** *her husband frequently.*
Her husband is ***got at*** *frequently.*

but the same is true of many sentences containing less idiomatic items:

1 *He* ***glanced through*** *the article quickly.*
The article was ***glanced through*** *quickly.*

(c) Sentences in which the prepositional object is part of a complex idiom are generally not passivized:

15 ****Disrepute*** *has been* ***fallen into*** *in recent years.*

(d) Some expressions are recorded in the dictionary which function in *passive* sentences of the [Vpr] type though not in the corresponding *active* patterns. (For a more detailed treatment of this topic ⇨ 3.3.) A highly irregular group is made up of such items as **unaccounted for**, **uncalled for**, and **unguessed at**. Certain of these combinations have a corresponding finite form without the negative prefix, thus **account for**, **call for**, **guess at**, and this can be used in both active and passive sentences. Compare:

These missiles are ***unaccounted for*** *by the authorities.*
These missiles are ***accounted for*** *by the authorities.*
The authorities have ***accounted for*** *these missiles.*

However, there is no such sentence as

The authorities have* ***unaccounted for* *these missiles.*

to correspond, as active, to the first of the set of three.

[Vpr pass(o)] passive transform, with the object of a second preposition becoming the subject of the passive sentence

Notes

(a) A small number of idiomatic expressions, such as **get to the bottom of** or **get to grips with**, form their passives in a special way. It will be seen that the expressions contain a verb and *two* prepositions, and that the object of the first preposition is an integral part of the idiom.

(b) In this special passive transform, the object of the *second* preposition is transposed to front position in the sentence (where it functions as Subject of the passive construction):

[Vpr] *I'll* ***get to the bottom of*** *this whole business.*
[Vpr pass(o)] *This whole business will be* ***got to the bottom of.***
[Vpr] *You* ***got to grips with*** *the basic trouble inside an hour.*
[Vpr pass(o)] *The basic trouble was* ***got to grips with*** *inside an hour.*

[Vpr adj] noun phrase with a participial adjective

noun phrase			
article	(adv)	participial adj	noun etc
1 *The*	*quickly*	**glanced-through**	*article ...*
3 *A*		**banked-on**	*change of heart ...*
4 *These*	*easily*	**coped-with**	*extra people ...*
5 *His*	*well*	**provided-for**	*family ...*
6 *This*	*endlessly*	**talked-about**	*topic ...*
7 *A (An)*	*(easily)*	**broken-into**	*warehouse ...*
9 *These*	*carefully*	**gone-into**	*proposals ...*

Notes

(a) Here, the noun phrase is drawn from the basic sentence as a whole and the participial adjective from the verb and preposition which function in that sentence. The grammatical link between the sentence and the phrase is most clearly shown by relating both to the passive:

[Vpr] *He* ***glanced through*** *the article quickly.*
[Vpr pass] *The article was quickly* ***glanced through.***
[Vpr adj] *The quickly* ***glanced-through*** *article*

(b) The connection of meaning between this transform and the passive is particularly close when the latter indicates a *state* (not a process). Compare:

His family seems well **provided for**.

His seems a well **provided-for** *family*.

(c) It is often essential to place an adverb before the participial adj, as in most of the examples here. When an adverb *must* be placed before the adj in any [Vpr] entry, this is pointed out in a footnote.

[Vpr emph] emphatic transform

	prepositional phrase		subject	verb phrase		(adv phrase etc)
	prep	object			verb	
4	**With**	*these few extra people*	*you*	*can*	**cope**	*easily.*
5	**For**	*his family*	*he*	*has*	**provided**	*well.*
10	**On**	*a safe political future*	*he*	*can*	**reckon**	*with some confidence.*
12	**On**	*the age of the victim*	*the question of a reprieve*	*may*	**turn.**	
13	**Upon**	*this venture*	*all our hopes*		**rested.**	

Notes

(a) This transform involves a simple change of order: the prepositional phrase of the basic pattern is transposed to initial position (cf [Vn.pr emph]):

[Vpr] *He can* **reckon on** *a safe political future with some confidence.*

[Vpr emph] **On** *a safe political future he can* **reckon** *with some confidence.*

(b) When the subject is a *pronoun* it must precede the verb phrase in this transform (cf [Vp emph]). The following sentence is unacceptable:

5 ***For** *his family has* **provided** *he well.*

When the subject is a noun, or noun phrase, it will precede the verb phrase in some sentences (as it would in nos 4, 5 and 10 above) but may precede *or* follow in others (nos 12 and 13). Compare the following sentences with the corresponding ones in the table:

12 **On** *the age of the victim may* **turn** *the question of a reprieve.*

13 **Upon** *this venture* **rested** *all our hopes.*

The expressions in both these examples, it should be noted, represent formal usage.

(c) In some examples of this transform, a contrast is implied between the noun in the prepositional phrase and another unspecified noun. This noun may be made explicit, as follows:

5 **For** *his family he has* **provided** *well (but not* **for** *his employees).*

(d) When the verb + preposition forms an idiomatic whole (phrasal verb), as in nos. 7, 8, 9 and 11, this transformation cannot usually be applied.

[Vp rel] relative transform

	noun phrase		relative clause					
	article	noun	prep	rel pron	subject	verb	phrase	(adv phrase etc)
1	*The*	*article*	**through**	*which*	*he*		**glanced**	*(so) quickly . . .*
3	*A*	*change of heart*	**on**	*which*	*we*	*were*	**banking . . .**	
4	*These*	*people*	**with**	*whom*	*you*	*can*	**cope**	*easily . . .*
5	*The*	*family*	**for**	*which*	*he*	*has*	**provided**	*well . . .*
6	*This*	*topic*	**about**	*which*	*we*	*'ve*	**talked**	*endlessly . . .*
10	*A*	*safe political future*	**on**	*which*	*he*	*can*	**reckon**	*with some confidence . . .*
12	*The*	*factor*	**on**	*which*	*the question of a reprieve*		**turns . . .**	
13	*This*	*venture*	**upon**	*which*	*all our hopes*		**rested . . .**	

Notes

(a) In this transform a noun (etc) originating in the *prepositional object* of the basic pattern is modified by a relative clause (part of which derives from the subject and verb phrase of the same basic pattern):

[Vpr] *We were* **banking on** *a change of heart.*

[Vpr rel] *A change of heart* **on** *which we were* **banking**

(b) Sentences in which the verb + preposition is highly idiomatic are not relativized as shown above. This sentence is unacceptable:

8 **The husband* **at** *whom Olive* **gets** *regularly . . .*

(c) As the transform is normally associated with formal, written English, items marked *informal* in the dictionary tend not to be used in this transform, even when they are not idiomatic. A relative construction that can safely be used with formal and informal items is:

7 *A warehouse which a gang of thieves* **broke into** *. . .*

[Vp.pr] intransitive pattern with a particle and preposition

	subject	verb phrase		particle	prepositional phrase		(adv phrase etc)
			verb		prep	object	
1	*The coaster*		**went**	**aground**	**on**	*a sandbank.*	
2	*He*		**scraped**	**along**	**on**	*a low salary.*	
3	*He*		**sent**	**away**	**for**	*a free fisherman's almanac.*	
4	*The office staff*	*are*	**looking**	**forward**	**to**	*his retirement*	*very much.*
5	*They*	*had*	**done**	**away**	**with**	*this piece of legislation*	*reluctantly.*
6	*She*	*is*	**facing**	**up**	**to**	*her responsibilities*	*badly.*
7	*We*		**put**	**up**	**with**	*these interruptions*	*cheerfully.*
8	*An outsider*	*had*	**come**	**in**	**on**	*our private arrangement.*	
9	*The family*		**came**	**up**	**against**	*fresh problems.*	
10	*The match*		**got**	**off**	**to**	**a good start.**	

Notes

(a) Here we must distinguish between the combinations **go aground (on), scrape along (on)**, and **send away (for)** (nos 1, 2, 3), from which the preposition (and its object) can be deleted, and the remaining combinations, where the preposition is a fixed element. Whether or not the preposition is removable tends to affect the transformational possibilities of the whole.

(b) This pattern is the intransitive equivalent of [Vn.p.pr], in terms of the correspondences of particular examples. Compare:

[Vp.pr] *The family* **came up against** *fresh problems.*

[Vn.p.pr] *The move* **brought** *the family* **up against** *fresh problems.*

(c) In some cases, an adverb or adverbial phrase may be inserted between the particle and the prepositional phrase. As the following examples show, it is possible to separate particle and preposition in this way even when the latter cannot be removed:

5 *They had* **done away** *reluctantly* **with** *this piece of legislation.*

7 *We* **put up** *cheerfully* **with** *these interruptions.*

(d) The verb may sometimes be divided from the particle, though generally only by the adverbs 'right' or 'straight':

5 *They had* **done** *right* **away with** *this piece of legislation.*

9 *The family* **came** *straight* **up against** *fresh problems.*

(Occasionally, we find such adverbs of degree as 'completely', 'totally', 'entirely' in the position of 'right' in no 5.)

[Vp.pr pass] passive transform

subject	verb phrase		particle		(adv phrase etc)
		verb		prep	
3 *A free fisherman's almanac*	*was*	**sent**	**away**	**for.**	
4 *His retirement*	*is being*	**looked**	**forward**	**to**	*very much.*
5 *This piece of legislation*	*had been*	**done**	**away**	**with**	*reluctantly.*
6 *Her responsibilities*	*are being*	**faced**	**up**	**to**	*badly.*
7 *These interruptions*	*were*	**put**	**up**	**with**	*cheerfully.*

Notes

(a) In this transform the object of the preposition is transposed forward (cf [Vpr pass]), and the form of the verb phrase modified:

[Vp.pr] *We* **put up with** *these interruptions cheerfully.*

[Vp.pr pass] *These interruptions were* **put up with** *cheerfully.*

(b) This transform tends to be restricted to cases where the preposition + object are *not* deletable (though see no 3 in the table above).

(c) Sentences in which the prepositional object is part of a complex idiom are generally not passivized:

10 ?***A good start*** *was* ***got off to.***

(d) Note the placing of stress in the passive transform:

. . . ***looked 'forward to***

. . . ***done 'away with***

. . . ***faced 'up to***

[Vp.pr adj] noun phrase with a participial adjective

noun phrase			
article etc	adv	participial adj	noun
4 *His*	*very much*	***looked-forward-to***	*retirement* ...
5 *This*	*reluctantly*	***done-away-with***	*piece of legislation* ...
6 *Her*	*badly*	***faced-up-to***	*responsibilities* ...
7 *These*	*cheerfully*	***put-up-with***	*interruptions* ...

Notes

(a) This noun-phrase transform derives from the basic [Vp.pr] pattern as a whole, and the adjective from the verb + particle + preposition which functions as part of that basic pattern. Note the connection provided by the passive between the basic pattern and this transform:

[Vp.pr] *She is **facing up to** her responsibilities badly.*

[Vp.pr pass] *Her responsibilities are being badly **faced up to**.*

[Vp.pr adj] *Her badly **faced-up-to** responsibilities* ...

(b) This transform is generally restricted to verb + particle + preposition items from which the last element is not removable. The following is an unusual (though possible) phrase:

2 ?*His* barely ***scraped-along-on*** *salary* ...

[Vp.pr emph] emphatic transform

prepositional phrase		subject	verb phrase	particle	(adv phrase etc)
prep	object		verb		
1 ***On***	*a sandbank*	*the coaster*	***went***	***aground.***	
2 ***On***	*a low salary*	*he*	*just* ***scraped***	***along.***	

Notes

(a) In this transform, the prepositional phrase of the basic pattern has been moved to the front (cf [Vpr emph]).

(b) Sentences from which the preposition + object are *not* removable are less likely to be transformed in this way than those (like 1 and 2 above) in which they are, though some speakers may find the following acceptable:

7 ?***With*** *these interruptions we* ***put up*** *cheerfully.*

8 ?***On*** *our private arrangement an outsider had* ***come in.***

[Vpr rel] relative transform

noun phrase						
		relative clause				
article	noun	prep	rel pron	subject	verb phrase	particle
1 *A*	*sandbank*	***on***	*which*	*the coaster*	***went***	***aground*** ...
2 *A*	*low salary*	***on***	*which*	*he*	***scraped***	***along*** ...
3 *A*	*free fisherman's almanac*	***for***	*which*	*he*	***sent***	***away*** ...

Notes

(a) Here, a noun (etc) derived from the *prepositional object* of the basic pattern is modified by a relative clause (part of which derives from the subject, verb phrase and particle of the same basic pattern (cf [Vpr rel])):

[Vp.pr] *The coaster* **went aground on** *a sandbank.*

[Vp.pr rel] *A sandbank* **on** *which the coaster* **went aground** ...

(b) Sentences from which preposition + object cannot be removed (ie without affecting the meaning of the whole) are less likely to be relativized, though we may hear, or read:

5 *This piece of legislation* **with** *which they had* **done away** ...

(c) Since this transform (like [Vpr rel]) is generally associated with formal styles, combinations normally found in colloquial use – whether the preposition is fixed or not – will tend not to be relativized in this way. Instead, a relative pattern will be used in which the preposition is *final*.

2 *A low salary which he* **scraped along on** ...

5 *This piece of legislation which they had* **done away with** ...

[Vn⇄p, Vn.p and Vp.n] Transitive patterns with a particle

General note

Verb + particle combinations which are used in transitive sentences can be subclassified according to whether (i) a short noun phrase Object can be placed on either side of the particle; (ii) such an Object must appear between the (main) verb and the particle; (iii) it must be placed after the particle. To account for these differences in Object placement, we recognize three types of transitive verb + particle pattern, identified in the grammatical codes at [Vn⇄p], [Vn.p] and [Vp.n]. We deal with these below, beginning with two tables for [Vn⇄p]:

[Vn⇄p] transitive pattern with a particle type (i) *Table A*

	subject	verb phrase		object	particle	(adv phrase etc)
			verb	noun phrase/pronoun		
1	*The studio*	*will*	**blow**	*your photographs (them)*	**up**	*well.*
2	*The accountant*		**broke**	*expenditure (it)*	**down**	*as follows* ...
3	*The travel agent*		**messed**	*our bookings (them)*	**up**	*completely.*
4	*We*	*can*	**play**	*the recorded programmes (them)*	**back.**	
5	*Bill*		**took**	*the premier (him)*	**off**	*to perfection.*
6	*The daily help*		**cleaned**	*the whole place (it)*	**out.**	
7	*Fred*		**tipped**	*the police (them)*	**off.**	
8	*I*	*will*	**try**	*the machine (it)*	**out**	*thoroughly.*
9	*You*	*have*	**brought**	*your children (them)*	**up**	*well.*
10	*You*	*have*	**filled**	*the application (it)*	**in**	*incorrectly.*
11	*These entertainers*		**make**	*their stories (them)*	**up.**	
12	*You*		**thought**	*the scheme (it)*	**out**	*carefully.*
13	*The shops*		**put**	*the prices (them)*	**up.**	

[Vn⇄p] transitive pattern with a particle type (i) *Table B*

	subject	verb phrase		particle	object	(adv phrase etc)
			verb		noun phrase	
1	*The studio*	*will*	**blow**	**up**	*your photographs*	*well.*
2	*The accountant*		**broke**	**down**	*expenditure*	*as follows . . .*
3	*The travel agent*		**messed**	**up**	*our bookings*	*completely.*
4	*We*	*can*	**play**	**back**	*the recorded programmes.*	
5	*Bill*		**took**	**off**	*the premier*	*to perfection.*
6	*The daily help*		**cleaned**	**out**	*the whole place.*	
7	*Fred*		**tipped**	**off**	*the police.*	
8	*I*	*will*	**try**	**out**	*the machine*	*thoroughly.*
9	*You*	*have*	**brought**	**up**	*your children*	*well.*
10	*You*	*have*	**filled**	**in**	*the application*	*incorrectly.*
11	*These entertainers*		**make**	**up**	*their stories.*	
12	*You*		**thought**	**out**	*the scheme*	*carefully.*
13	*The shops*		**put**	**up**	*the prices.*	

Notes

(a) This sub-pattern accounts for the great majority of verb + particle combinations (whether idiomatic or not) which are used transitively. It is thus the standard or 'regular' sub-pattern.

(b) A combination of verb + particle is classified as [Vn⇄p] when a noun or short noun phrase functioning as Object can either precede the particle (as in Table A) or follow it (as in Table B). A personal pronoun substituted for such an Object will always *precede* the particle (note the pronouns in parentheses in Table A).

(c) If a short Object (as illustrated in Tables A and B) is *extended* there are two possibilities: either the *extension* of the Object follows the particle:

We can **play** *the programmes* **back** *that you recorded last week.*

or the *whole* of the extended Object follows:

We can **play back** *the programmes that you recorded last week.*

(d) A verb + particle combination whose Object is a *clause* is classified as [Vn⇄p] if it can also be used with noun phrase Objects that function as in Tables A and B.

An expression of this kind is **work out** (meaning 'calculate'). Compare the examples:

We have computers to **work out** *what we earn, these days.*

We have computers to **work** *our salaries* **out***, these days.*

We have computers to **work out** *our salaries, these days.*

(e) Expressions such as **sew on** or **saw off**, which can take an Indirect as well as a Direct Object, are assigned to this sub-pattern when a short Direct Object, as shown in the following examples, can be placed on either side of the particle:

'The zip has broken. Will you **sew** *me a new one* **on***?'*

. . . **sew** *a new one* **on** *(for me)?'*

. . . **sew on** *a new one (for me)?'*

(Here the Direct Object is 'a new one'.) Compare:

'Would you **saw** *me a piece* **off***?'*

. . . **saw** *a piece* **off** *(for me)?'*

. . . **saw off** *a piece (for me)?'*

(Here the Direct Object is 'a piece'.)

(f) Adverbs other than 'straight' or 'right' seldom appear between the verb and the particle even when the combination is not idiomatic (cf [Vp]). This sentence is therefore unacceptable:

The daily help* ***cleaned* *the whole place quickly* ***out****.*

'Straight' and 'right' are themselves not usually inserted when the verb + particle combination is idiomatic (ie a phrasal verb):

Bill* ***took* *the premier right* ***off****.*

This rule is relaxed when the combination is not highly idiomatic:

The shops ***put*** *the prices straight* ***up****.*
The daily help ***cleaned*** *the place right* ***out****.*

But note that in these examples the order is (main) verb + object + adverb + particle; this order is invariable and the following is unacceptable:

The daily help* ***cleaned* *right* ***out*** *the place.*

[Vn⇄p nom] nominalized form of verb + particle

Notes

(a) Nouns referred to as [Vn⇄p nom] are formed on the 'base form + particle' model and may be written as fully joined or hyphenated (occasionally as two separate words). The verbal element carries principal stress:

ˈbreakdown, ˈmess-up, ˈtake-off

(b) These nominalized forms are often in sentence patterns which are paraphrases of the basic [Vn⇄p] pattern. In one type of paraphrase, the 'nom' form functions as (part of) the Direct Object of the verb 'do' (or 'make'), as in this table:

subject	do/make	object
1 *The studio*	*will do*	*a good* ***blow-up*** *of your photographs.*
2 *The accountant*	*did*	*a* ***breakdown*** *of expenditure as follows . . .*
3 *The travel agent*	*made*	*a complete* ***mess-up*** *of our bookings.*
4 *We*	*can do*	*a* ***play-back*** *of the recorded programmes.*

(c) In some cases, an Indirect Object pattern with 'give' is used, as in this table:

subject	give	indirect object	direct object
5 *The daily help*	*gave*	*the whole place*	*a* ***clean-out****.*
6 *Fred*	*gave*	*the police*	*the* ***tip-off****.*
7 *I will*	*give*	*the machine*	*a thorough* ***try-out****.*

(d) This sentence type can in turn be related to one containing 'get':

5 *The whole place got a* ***clean-out****.*
6 *The police got the* ***tip-off*** *from Fred.*
7 *The machine will get a thorough* ***try-out****.*

[Vn⇄p pass] passive transform

	subject	verb phrase		particle	(adv phrase etc)
			verb		
1	*Your photographs*	*will be*	**blown**	**up**	*well.*
2	*Expenditure*	*was*	**broken**	**down**	*as follows . . .*
3	*Our bookings*	*were*	**messed**	**up**	*completely.*
4	*The recorded programmes*	*can be*	**played**	**back.**	
5	*The premier*	*was*	**taken**	**off**	*to perfection.*
6	*The whole place*	*was*	**cleaned**	**out.**	
7	*The police*	*were*	**tipped**	**off.**	
8	*The machine*	*will be*	**tried**	**out**	*thoroughly.*
9	*Your children*	*have been*	**brought**	**up**	*well.*
10	*The application*	*has been*	**filled**	**in**	*incorrectly.*
11	*Their stories*	*are*	**made**	**up.**	
12	*The scheme*	*was*	**thought**	**out**	*carefully.*
13	*The prices*	*were*	**put**	**up.**	

Notes

(a) The passive pattern is derived from the active by transposing the Direct Object to the front position and by changing the form of the verb phrase (*will* **blow** → *will be* **blown**; *can* **play** → *can be* **played**). The particle now immediately follows the (main) verb. Compare:

[Vn⇄p] *Fred* **tipped off** *the police.*

[Vn⇄p pass] *The police were* **tipped off**.

A prepositional phrase, 'by Fred', originating as the subject of the active sentence, is optional in the passive:

[Vn⇄p pass] *The police were* **tipped off** *(by Fred).*

(b) When the Object of the active sentence is a *clause*, it remains in the final position in the transform and 'it' is introduced initially. Compare:

We **worked out** *that we should need £100.*
It was **worked out** *that we should need £100.*

(c) There may be two types of passive sentence when the active pattern contains an Indirect (as well as a Direct) Object. Compare these acceptable transforms:

I was **sent down** *a list of missing stock.*
A list of missing stock was **sent down** *to me.*

with the unacceptable

A list of missing stock was* **sent down *me.*

(d) There is a close similarity (in terms of word order) between the passive transform and that of the [Vpr] pattern. However, the transforms are in most cases differentiated by stress placement. Compare:

[Vpr pass] *The doctor's been* **'sent for**.

[Vn⇄p pass] *The student's been* **sent 'down** (ie from a university).

(e) This transform applies to the great majority of combinations in this pattern. The fact that a combination is idiomatic does not normally affect transformation to the passive.

(f) Several transitive phrasal verbs listed in the dictionary (eg **frosted over**, **run down 6**) are used in a passive form but not in the actives from which such passives are normally derived. We find examples such as these:

After the severe cold of last night, all the windows are **frosted over**.
The doctor said he was **run down** *and needed rest.*

but not all the corresponding 'actives':
?*The severe cold of last night has* **frosted** all the windows **over**.
The doctor said all those late nights had* **run him **down** and he needed rest.

[Vn⇄p adj] noun phrase with a participial adjective

noun phrase			
article	(adv)	participial adj	noun
1 *Your*	*well*	**blown-up**	*photographs . . .*
3 *Our*	*completely*	**messed-up**	*bookings . . .*
4 *The*		**played-back**	*programmes . . .*
8 *The*	*thoroughly*	**tried-out**	*machine . . .*
9 *Your*	*well*	**brought-up**	*children . . .*
10 *Your*	*incorrectly*	**filled-in**	*application . . .*
11 *Their*		**made-up**	*stories . . .*
12 *Your*	*carefully*	**thought-out**	*scheme . . .*

Notes

(a) The noun phrase of this transform is derived from the basic pattern as a whole, and the participial adjective from the verb + particle (eg **blow up**, **mess up**) which functions in it. Note the link between the basic pattern and this transform provided by the *passive*:

[Vn⇄p] *You* **thought** *the scheme* **out** *carefully*.
[Vn⇄p pass] *The scheme was carefully* **thought out**.
[Vn⇄p adj] *Your carefully* **thought-out** *scheme . . .*

(b) The pattern indicates 'completed action' and not 'action in progress':

Those **played-back** *programmes are not a success.*
(implying that they have already been **played back**).

A close connection of meaning between this transform and the passive can be shown when the latter expresses a state also. Compare:

[Vn⇄p pass] *Your children have been* **brought up** *well.*
[Vn⇄p pass] *Your children are well* **brought up**.
[Vn⇄p adj] *Yours are well* **brought-up** *children.*

(c) Idiomaticity appears to have no bearing on whether this transform is possible or not.

(d) Several combinations listed in the dictionary (eg **played out**, **run down 6**) are used in the adj form but not in the active pattern from which the adj is normally derived. Examples like these occur:

She drifted from one affair to another, eventually setting up house with a **played-out** *opera singer.*
He emerged from his ordeal in a completely **run-down** *condition.*

But neither of these are acceptable:

His fondness for drink had* **played *him* **out**.
His ordeal had* **run *him* **down** *completely.*

[Vn.p] transitive pattern with a particle type (ii)

	subject	verb phrase		object	particle	(adv phrase etc)
			verb	noun/pronoun		
1	*The comedian*	*doesn't*	**get**	*his jokes* (*them*)	**across.**	
2	*The police*		**moved**	*the spectators* (*them*)	**along.**	
3	*The technician*	*will*	**run**	*that bit of tape* (*it*)	**through**	*again.*
4	*The government*	*will*	**see**	*the thing* (ie crisis) (*it*)	**through.**	
5	*I*	*'ll*	**knock**	**his block**	**off.**	
6	*Parker*		**throws**	**the ball** (*it*)	**in**	*near the half-way line.*

Notes

(a) In this sub-pattern there is a restriction on the positioning of an Object consisting of a short noun phrase. This must *precede* the particle, as is shown in the table. A personal pronoun substituted for the noun phrase also precedes, as is the general rule for the whole [Vn⇄p], [Vn.p] and [Vp.n] pattern.

(b) If a short Object is lengthened (say, by the addition of a clause) the *extension* may follow the particle, or the *whole* Object may:

The comedian doesn't **get** *the jokes* **across** *that he prepares in advance.*
The comedian doesn't **get across** *the jokes that he prepares in advance.*
(though the second pattern is more unusual: see the next note).

(c) This sub-pattern is often preferred for such verbs as **move**, **run**, **get**, **see** and such particles as **across**, **over**, **through** because if a short Object were free to *follow* those particles, the particle might, in particular cases, be mistaken for a preposition, and the combination as a whole misinterpreted. Compare the examples:

[Vn.p] *He* **saw** *the crisis* **through** (ie he survived it).
[Vpr] *He* **saw through** *the crisis* (ie he didn't really believe there was one).

(d) Combinations such as **burn (oneself) out** (= 'ruin one's health through overwork etc') belong to this sub-pattern because the only Object possible is a *reflexive pronoun*, and such pronouns must precede the particle. The headphrase and grammatical code for this item are therefore:

burn (oneself) out [Vn.p ...]

We can compare in this respect:

fix up (with) [Vn⇄p ...] ... arrange for (sb) to have ...

Here, **fix up** is described as [Vn⇄p] because, although the combination can be used reflexively, it can also be used with short Objects which either precede or follow the particle. Compare:

He's **fixed** *the whole family* **up** *(***with** *good jobs).*
He's **fixed up** *the whole family (***with** *good jobs).*
He's **fixed** *himself* **up** *(***with** *a good job).*

[Vn.p nom] nominalized form of verb + particle

Note

Though only one example has been given in the main [Vn.p] table above of a verb + particle combination from which a noun can be derived (ie **throw in**, yielding **throw-in**), there is no general restriction on noun formation for combinations used in this sub-pattern. The following entry provides a further example:

walk through [Vn.p nom pass] (*theatre*) show (sb) the movements he must make in a scene etc ... '*After lunch I want to do a* **walk-through** *of the ghost scene.*'

and several others are recorded. The code [Vn.p nom] should be taken to mean – as here – that the noun is of the 'base-form + particle' type (for fuller details see the notes and tables at [Vn⇄p nom], above).

[Vn.p pass] passive transform

subject	verb phrase		particle	(adv phrase etc)
		verb		
1 *His jokes*	*aren't*	**got**	**across.**	
2 *The spectators*	*were*	**moved**	**along.**	
3 *That bit of tape*	*will be*	**run**	**through**	*again.*
6 ***The ball***	*is*	**thrown**	**in**	*near the half-way line.*

Notes

(a) This passive transform and that of the 'major' [Vn⇄p] sub-pattern are in all respects – word-order, form of the verb phrase, treatment of clause Objects, stress placement – exactly the same, and users needing a fuller explanation of those features are referred to the notes at [Vn⇄p pass].

(b) Since some of the words functioning as particles in the [Vn.p] pattern (eg **across**, **over**, **through**) can also be used as prepositions, the passive treated here and the [Vpr] passive may resemble each other in individual cases to the point where misinterpretation is possible. In speech, however, the two types are often (though not always) differentiated by the placing of nuclear stress. Compare:

[Vn.p pass] *The video tape needs to be carefully* **run 'through** (i.e. through the recorder).

[Vpr pass] *The money he'd inherited was quickly* **'run through.**

(c) When the Direct Object of this sub-pattern is a reflexive pronoun (and no other kind of Direct Object is possible), we shall not find:

He had been* **written out *by the age of thirty.*

as a passive of:

He had **written himself out** (= had nothing new to write) *by the age of thirty.*

though the following passive-like construction is acceptable:

He was/seemed **written out** *by the age of thirty.*

[Vp.n] transitive pattern with a particle type (iii)

subject	verb phrase	particle	object
	verb		
1 *The cavalry*	*will* **bring**	**up**	**the rear.**
2 *The search party*	*has* **given**	**up**	**all hope** *of finding the missing aircraft.*
3 *Jeremy*	**put**	**in**	*a brief* **appearance.**
4 *The hedgerows*	**put**	**forth**	*new buds.*
5 *Many households*	**take**	**in**	*lodgers.*
6 *The authorities*	**trumped**	**up**	*a case against Smith.*

Notes

(a) In this sub-pattern an Object consisting of a noun, or short noun phrase, is placed *after* the particle.

(b) Following the general rule for types (i), (ii) and (iii), a substituted pronoun Object, if there is one, *precedes* the particle. Compare:

Many households **take in** *lodgers.*
Many households **take** *them* **in**.

(c) Combinations of verb + particle whose Object is a *clause* but which cannot have a noun or noun phrase Object are classified as [Vp.n] because the clause must, following the general rule, be placed *after* the particle. Consider:

find out 2 [... Vp.n] discover a mistake, a loss, sb's dishonesty etc ... *One day someone will start asking questions and* **find out** *precisely why we've been losing so much money.*

If a combination can take a clause or a short noun phrase as Object, and the latter *must* follow the particle, the item will also be described as [Vp.n]:

find out 1 [... Vp.n pass] learn (sth) by study, calculation or inquiry. *Do you feel a need to* **find out** *what you have done with it?* (cf *Do you feel a need to* **find out** *its whereabouts?)*

[Vp.n nom] nominalized form of verb + particle

Note

Though we provide no example in the table just above of a verb + particle combination from which a 'nom' form derives, there is no general restriction on the transform here, provided that the expression is not complex (as **bring up the rear** and **put in an appearance** are). When an entry has the code [Vp.n nom], as in the following entry, this is to be taken to mean that the noun in question is of the 'base form + particle' type (for further details see the notes and tables at [Vn⇄p nom], above).

make up 4 [Vp.n nom ...] form, compose (sth larger) ... *There are plans to change the* **make-up** (= composition) *of the Board.* ○ *There is something in his* **make-up** (= nature, character) *that repels people.*

[Vp.n pass] passive transform

	subject	verb phrase		particle	(agentive prep phrase)
			verb		
1	***The rear***	*will be*	**brought**	**up**	*(by the cavalry).*
2	***All hope*** *of finding the missing aircraft*	*has been*	**given**	**up**	*(by the search party).*
3	***A*** *brief* ***appearance***	*was*	**put**	**in**	*(by Jeremy).*
4	*New buds*	*are*	**put**	**forth**	*(by the hedgerows).*
5	*Lodgers*	*are*	**taken**	**in**	*(by many households).*
6	*A case against Smith*	*was*	**trumped**	**up**	*(by the authorities).*

Note

As regards word order, the form of the verb phrase, the treatment of clause Objects and the placing of stress, the passives of the sub-patterns [Vn⇄p] and [Vp.n] are alike. The user is referred to the notes at [Vn⇄p pass] for an explanation of these features.

[Vn.pr] transitive pattern with a preposition

	subject	verb phrase		object	prepositional phrase	
			verb		prep	object
1	*He*		**makes**	*rather too* **much**	**of**	*his aristocratic connections.*
2	*The governor*		**made**	**an example**	**of**	*these prisoners.*
3	*I*	*have*	**taken**	*careful* **note**	**of**	*your remarks.*
4	*We*		**take**	*strong* **exception**	**to**	*the attack on Mr Mackay.*
5	*Peter*		**foists**	*all his problems*	**on**	*his unfortunate friends.*
6	*Some*		**pinned**	**their faith**	**on**	*a religious revival.*
7	*Warning cries*		**cheated**	*the cat*	**of**	*its prey.*
8	*Special coaching*		**got**	*me*	**through**	*the written papers.*
9	*I*	*don't*	**hold**	*his past failings*	**against**	*him.*
10	*The instructor*		**put**	*him*	**off**	*driving altogether.*

Notes

(a) Some of the phrasal verbs and longer idioms classified as [Vn.pr] – and illustrated here – are related to [Vpr] items in terms of the transitive/intransitive contrast. Compare:

[Vn.pr] *Special coaching* **got** *me* **through** *the written papers.*
[Vpr] *I* **got through** *the written papers with special coaching.*
[Vn.pr] *The instructor* **put** *him* **off** *driving altogether.*
[Vpr] *He* **went off** *driving altogether.*
(see examples 11 and 14 in the [Vpr] table).

(b) In many cases, an adverb or adverbial phrase can be placed between the Direct Object and the prepositional phrase. This may be possible even when the combination is idiomatic:

2 *The governor* **made an example**, *only last week,* **of** *these prisoners.*
5 *Peter* **foists** *all his problems, year in and year out,* **on** *his unfortunate friends.*

(c) When the Object is relatively long and the prepositional phrase relatively short, they are often transposable, as follows:

10 *The instructor* **put off** *driving every student who came his way.*

When the Object – or part of it – is an element in a complex expression, however, this kind of transposition is usually not possible:

4 ?*We* **take to** *this attack the strongest possible* **exception**.

though we do sometimes meet acceptable transpositions of this kind as in:

1 *He* **makes of** *these connections rather too* **much**, *I feel.*

(d) Sometimes a long Object can be *divided*, with part of it – usually a relative clause – following the prepositional phrase:

9 *I don't* **hold** *past failings* **against** *him for which he can't really be held responsible.*

[Vn.pr pass] passive transform

	subject	verb phrase		prepositional phrase	
			verb	prep	object
1	*Rather too* **much**	*is*	**made**	**of**	*his aristocratic connections.*
2	**An example**	*was*	**made**	**of**	*these prisoners.*
3	*Careful* **note**	*has been*	**taken**	**of**	*your remarks.*
4	*Strong* **exception**	*is*	**taken**	**to**	*the attack on Mr Mackay.*
5	*All his problems*	*are*	**foisted**	**on**	*his unfortunate friends.*
6	**Their faith**	*was*	**pinned**	**on**	*a religious revival.*
7	*The cat*	*was*	**cheated**	**of**	*its prey.*
8	*I*	*was*	**got**	**through**	*the written papers.*
9	*His past failings*	*are not*	**held**	**against**	*him.*
10	*He*	*was*	**put**	**off**	*driving altogether.*

Notes

(a) This passive pattern is derived from the active by transposing the Direct Object of the latter to front position and by changing the form of the verb phrase. The prepositional phrase remains in final position. Compare:

[Vn.pr] *Warning cries* **cheated** *the cat* **of** *its prey.*
[Vn.pr pass) *The cat was* **cheated of** *its prey.*

A prepositional phrase, 'by warning cries', which originates from the subject of the active pattern, is optional:

[Vn.pr pass] *The cat was* **cheated of** *its prey (by warning cries).*

(b) There is a general parallel between this passive and those of the sub-patterns [Vn⇄p], [Vn.p] and [Vp.n]. This is particularly evident when the *same* combination of words functions in the [Vn.pr] pattern and, say, the [Vn.p] pattern. Compare

[Vn.pr] *I was* **got through** *the written papers (by special coaching).*
[Vn.p] *I was* **got through** *(by special coaching).*

(c) A [Vn.pr] expression may take as Object a clause introduced by 'that', 'how', etc:

You should **bear in mind** *that he wasn't present*
(cf *You should* **bear** *that fact* **in mind**).

The passive of a [Vn.pr] sentence with a clause as Object is:

It should be **borne in mind** *that he wasn't present.*

though the following alternative construction is found:

That he wasn't present (at the time) should be **borne in mind.**

(d) A number of [Vn.pr] items listed in the dictionary (eg **embroiled in, used to**) occur in the passive form but not in the active form from which passives are normally derived. These examples are quite normal:

Members became **embroiled in** *heated debate over the issue of political union.*
I'm **used to** *these sudden changes of plan.*

but the following active patterns are unacceptable:

The issue of political union* **embroiled *members* **in** *heated debate.*
Experience has* **used *me* **to** *these sudden changes of plan.*

(For a fuller treatment of this topic, ⇨ 3.3.)

[Vn.pr pass(o)] passive transform, with the prepositional object of the active pattern becoming the subject of the passive

subject	verb phrase		object	
		verb		prep
1 *His aristocratic connections*	*are*	***made***	*rather too* ***much***	***of.***
2 *These prisoners*	*were*	***made***	***an example***	***of.***
3 *Your remarks*	*have been*	***taken***	*careful* ***note***	***of.***
4 *The attack on Mr Mackay*	*is*	***taken***	*strong* ***exception***	***to.***

Notes

(a) This transformation only applies when there is a close idiomatic link between parts of a complex expression functioning as (main) verb, Direct Object and preposition. It will be noted, for example, that nothing can be removed from **make an example of** or **take exception to** without making the remainder unacceptable. In the [pass(o)] transform these parts remain together and a subject is introduced originating in the *prepositional object* of the active pattern:

[Vn.pr] *The governor* ***made an example of*** *these prisoners.*

[Vn.pr pass(o)] *These prisoners were* ***made an example of*** *(by the governor).*

(b) Note that in this transform it is the pronoun or noun forming (part of) the Direct Object which bears principal stress, and not the main verb:

1 *His aristocratic connections are* ***made*** *rather too* **'much of.**

3 *Your remarks have been* ***taken*** *careful* **'note of.**

[Vn.pr emph] emphatic transform

prepositional phrase		subject	verb phrase		object
prep	object			verb	
1 ***Of***	*his aristocratic connections*	*he*		***makes***	*rather too* ***much.***
2 ***Of***	*these prisoners*	*the governor*		***made***	***an example.***
3 ***Of***	*your remarks*	*I*	*have*	***taken***	*careful* ***note.***
4 ***To***	*the attack on Mr Mackay*	*we*		***take***	*strong* ***exception.***
5 ***On***	*his unfortunate friends*	*Peter*		***foists***	*all his problems.*
6 ***On***	*a religious revival*	*some*		***pinned***	***their faith.***

Notes

(a) This transform results from a simple change of order, with the prepositional phrase shifted to initial position (cf [Vpr emph]):

[Vn.pr] *Peter* ***foists*** *all his problems* ***on*** *his unfortunate friends.*

[Vn.pr emph] ***On*** *his unfortunate friends Peter* ***foists*** *all his problems.*

(b) In some of the examples, a contrast may be implied between a noun, etc in the prepositional phrase and other unspecified words. These words may be made explicit. Consider:

4 ***To*** *the attack on Mr Mackay we* ***take*** *strong* ***exception*** *(though not* ***to*** *your other remarks).*

(c) In some cases adjustments in vocabulary and style will affect the extent to which the emphatic transform can be acceptably applied. Compare:

Of** *its prey warning cries* ***cheated *the cat.*

Of *all these benefits a sudden fall in share values* ***cheated*** *the hopeful investors.*

However, highly idiomatic combinations of verb + preposition (eg nos 9 and 10) are generally nor transformed in this way, whether the vocabulary is changed or not.

[Vn.pr rel] relative transform

noun phrase					
	relative clause				
(article) + noun	prep	rel pron	subject	verb phrase	object
1 *Aristocratic connections*	**of**	*which*	*he*	**makes**	*rather too* **much** ...
2 *These prisoners*	**of**	*whom*	*the governor*	**made**	**an example** ...
3 *Remarks*	**of**	*which*	*I*	*have* **taken**	*careful* **note** ...
4 *The attack*	**to**	*which*	*we*	**take**	*strong* **exception** ...
5 *The friends*	**on**	*whom*	*Peter*	**foists**	*all his problems* ...
6 *A religious revival*	**on**	*which*	*some*	**pinned**	**their faith** ...

Notes

(a) In this transform the article + noun (etc), which originates in the prepositional object of the basic pattern, is modified by a relative clause (which itself contains the subject, verb phrase and Object of that same pattern):

[Vn.pr] *The governor* **made an example of** *these prisoners.*
[Vn.pr rel] *These prisoners* **of** *whom the governor* **made an example** ...

(b) Sentences containing idiomatic combinations (phrasal verbs) are not normally made into relative clauses. Consider:

9 **A man* **against** *whom I don't* **hold** *his past failings* ...

(c) Whether a relative transform is possible often has to do with the formality of the combination. Even an unidiomatic combination would not be relativized if it was at the same time informal in style:

8 **The written papers* **through** *which special coaching* **got** *me* ...

though it might be used as follows:

The written papers which special coaching **got** *me* **through** ...

[Vn.p.pr] transitive pattern with a particle and preposition

subject	verb phrase		object	particle	prepositional phrase	
		verb			prep	object
1 *We*		**brought**	*them*	**around**	**to**	*a different way of thinking.*
2 *The women*	*had*	**decked**	*themselves*	**out**	**in**	*satin frocks.*
3 *They*		**filled**	*me*	**in**	**on**	*the latest developments.*
4 *Some trickster*	*had*	**fobbed**	*him*	**off**	**with**	*this story.*
5 *Someone*	*had*	**let**	*an outsider*	**in**	**on**	*our private arrangement.*
6 *The move*		**brought**	*the family*	**up**	**against**	*fresh problems.*
7 *The referee*		**got**	*the match*	**off**	**to**	***a good start.***
8 *You*	*can*	**put**	*the shortage*	**down**	**to**	*bad planning.*
9 *They*		**put**	*him*	**up**	**to**	*some mad escapade.*
10 *You*	*shouldn't*	**take**	*your resentment*	**out**	**on**	*me.*

Notes

(a) In each of nos 1–4 the preposition (and its object) can be removed without changing the meaning of the remainder of the sentence. To some extent this affects possibilities of transformation.

(b) The pattern has an intransitive equivalent in [Vp.pr]. Compares nos 5, 6 and 7 here with nos 8, 9, 10 in the [Vp.pr] table.

(c) In the table, the Direct Object is placed before the particle. In some cases it can, when it is a short noun phrase, follow the particle:

3 *They* ***filled in*** *their colleagues* ***on*** *the latest developments.*
10 *You shouldn't* ***take out*** *your resentment* ***on*** *me.*

(d) In most of the examples here, an adverb or adverbial phrase may be placed between the particle and the prepositional phrase:

2 *The women had* ***decked*** *themselves* ***out*** *gaudily* ***in*** *satin frocks.*
7 *The referee* ***got*** *the match* ***off****, despite the incident on the terraces,* ***to a good start.***

(The idiomaticity of items does not appear to affect adverb insertion in a general way.)

[Vn.p.pr pass] passive transform

subject	verb phrase		particle	prepositional phrase	
		verb		prep	object
1 *They*	*were*	**brought**	**around**	**to**	*a different way of thinking.*
2 *The women*	*were*	**decked**	**out**	**in**	*satin frocks.*
3 *I*	*was*	**filled**	**in**	**on**	*the latest developments.*
4 *He*	*had been*	**fobbed**	**off**	**with**	*this story.*
5 *An outsider*	*had been*	**let**	**in**	**on**	*our private arrangement.*
6 *The family*	*was*	**brought**	**up**	**against**	*fresh problems.*
7 *The match*	*was*	**got**	**off**	**to**	**a good start.**
8 *The shortage*	*can be*	**put**	**down**	**to**	*bad planning.*
9 *He*	*was*	**put**	**up**	**to**	*some mad escapade.*
10 *Your resentment*	*shouldn't be*	**taken**	**out**	**on**	*me.*

Notes

(a) In transforming an active [Vn.p.pr] sentence into the passive, the same general rule applies as to sentences in the [Vn⇄p] and [Vn.pr] categories: the Direct Object (noun, noun phrase or pronoun) of the basic pattern shifts to front position and becomes the subject of the passive construction:

[Vn.p.pr] *Someone had* **let** *an outsider* **in on** *our private arrangement.*
[Vn.p.pr pass] *An outsider had been* **let in on** *our private arrangement.*

(b) A *clause* is occasionally found as Object of a [Vn.p.pr] sentence:

[Vn.p.pr] *We* **put** *it* **up to** *the committee* (ie proposed to them) *that Frank should be made secretary.*

This sentence is transformed as follows:

[Vn.p.pr pass] *It was* **put up to** *the committee that Frank should be made secretary.*

(c) When a combination functioning in the [Vn.p.pr] pattern has a *deletable* preposition + object (eg **bring around (to), deck out (in)**), and those constituents are removed, the passive is of the [Vn⇄p] type. Compare these passive sentences:

[Vn.p.pr pass] *They were* **brought around to** *our way of thinking (eventually).*
[Vn⇄p pass] *They were* **brought around** *(eventually).*

[Vn.p.pr emph] emphatic transform

prepositional phrase		subject	verb phrase	object	particle
prep	object		verb		
4 **With**	*this story*	*some trickster*	*had* **fobbed**	*him*	**off.**
5 **On**	*our private arrangement*	*someone*	*had* **let**	*an outsider*	**in.**

Notes

(a) The transform results from a simple change of order, with the prepositional phrase being shifted to front position (cf [Vn.pr emph]):

[Vn.p.pr] *Someone had* **let** *an outsider* **in on** *our private arrangement.*
[Vn.p.pr emph] **On** *our private arrangement someone had* **let** *an outsider* **in**.

(b) In some cases, there may be an implied contrast between part of the prepositional phrase and other unspecified words. These words may on the other hand be specified in the context:

4 **With** *that kind of excuse you could* **fob** *her* **off** *(but don't pretend that your mother was ill).*

[Vn.p.pr rel] relative transform

noun phrase	relative clause					
article + noun	prep	rel pron	subject	verb phrase	object	particle
1 *A different way of thinking*	**to**	*which*	*we*	***brought***	*them*	**around** . . .
4 *This story*	**with**	*which*	*some trickster*	*had* **fobbed**	*him*	**off** . . .
5 *The private arrangement*	**on**	*which*	*someone*	*had* **let**	*an outsider*	**in** . . .

Notes

(a) The 'article + noun' of this transform is derived from the prepositional phrase of the basic pattern. The relative clause itself contains the subject, verb phrase, Object and particle of the original pattern (cf [Vn.pr rel]):

[Vn.p.pr] *Some trickster had* **fobbed** *him* **off with** *this story* . . .

[Vn.p.pr rel] *This story* **with** *which some trickster had* **fobbed** *him* **off** . . .

(b) This transform, in common with other relative transforms, is often associated with formal styles, and expressions commonly found in colloquial use will *tend* not to be relativized on this model. A common alternative in everyday informal use is as follows (note the preposition in *final* position):

4 *This story which some trickster had* **fobbed** *him* **off with** . . .

Style, Evaluation and Technical Field

4 The phrasal verbs and more complex idioms recorded in this dictionary represent the usage[1] of educated British speakers in the latter part of the twentieth century. This is not to say that the dictionary confines itself to usages which are not found outside Great Britain – to British English, in the narrow sense. Very many of the entries are also readily understood, and commonly used, in other countries where English is spoken as a mother tongue or second language. Thus the dictionary describes idiomatic items which are peculiarly British and those which, while also British, are widely used throughout the English-speaking world.

While no attempt has been made to list and describe expressions which are solely, or largely, American, the dictionary does include a few items – marked (*US*) or (esp *US*) – which have a marginal status in British English. These are items which though not fully established among British speakers, and still regarded as 'American' by some, are none the less used sufficiently often to merit inclusion in a dictionary of British usage. Examples are:

get to first base with. . . (esp *US informal*) make significant progress towards achieving an objective . . .

run for . . . (esp *US*) offer oneself as a candidate for (office) . . .

want out/out of . . . (esp *US informal*) wish to be freed from (sth unpleasant).

Not all the phrasal verbs etc treated in this dictionary are used across the entire age range. Some items (eg **stoke up**, **blow up 2**, **chivvy along** are used by older speakers but not by the majority of younger ones. These items are clearly passing

[1] By usage we mean not only those expressions which educated speakers may 'produce' in speech or writing, in a variety of styles, but those which they may readily understand when used by others, though they themselves might never use them. For example, the taboo expressions given in the Dictionary would never be used by many people who nevertheless must often hear or read them with understanding.

out of use, and are marked (*dated*). No items are included which have passed out of use altogether.

stoke up . . . 2 (*dated*) *He could* **stoke up** *with food and drink for thirty-six hours.* CON

From the total range of phrasal verbs and longer idioms covered by the dictionary, some can be singled out as being associated with particular *styles* of use, or as belonging to specific occupational groups or specialized fields of activity. The native speaker knows, for instance, that items such as:

ascribe to **give credence to** **make application (to)**

are more likely to be found in an official document or a set speech than to crop up during relaxed conversation among friends. In a similar way, the expressions

find against (the prisoner) **set aside** (a decision, verdict)
pass sentence (on the accused)

unmistakably suggest the specialized language, or register, of court proceedings.

Since foreign learners often finds it difficult to identify, or use in the right contexts, items which are restricted in style, evaluation or technical field, a scheme of markings has been devised to help them. When an expression can be clearly identified as having a restricted use, the appropriate marking is entered in parentheses after the grammatical code:

ascribe to [Vn.pr. . .] (*formal*) **find against** [Vpr] (*legal*)

Style labels: formal, informal, slang, taboo

4.1 The *style* markings given to phrasal verbs or more complex idioms in this dictionary reflect various factors in the situations in which they are normally used. The most important of these factors are:

◆ the relationship between the speakers, or correspondents (remote or official, or intimate and relaxed).

◆ whether one is speaking or writing (compare a spoken commentary on a football match with a newspaper report of it).

◆ the level of seriousness, detachment, etc suggested or imposed by the occasion (compare a speech at an official banquet with one given at a farewell party for a personal friend).

Four categories are set up to indicate differences of style in the dictionary: *formal*, *informal*, *slang* and *taboo*. Each category places a different emphasis on aspects of the factors outlined just above.

4.1.1 *formal* – reflecting a distant rather than a close relationship; used when speaking or writing in a serious or official context (eg in a letter to a civil servant or a bank manager):

accrues (to) (from) . . . (*formal*) . . . *Interest at 8.5%* **accrues to** *us from a building society account.*

4.1.2 *informal* – intimate rather than distant; spoken rather than written; relaxed and casual rather than grand or imposing:

pass out . . . 3 . . . (*informal*) *'I'd only have to point a gun at him and say bang, bang, and the little twerp would* **pass out** *cold from fright.'* AITC

4.1.3 *slang* – usually met in (and invariably derived from) the spoken language; suggesting an easy and intimate relationship between the speakers; serving to establish and reinforce the 'togetherness' of particular sub-groups in society, eg the police, criminals, schoolboys, etc, and their distinctness from other groups; tending to date quickly, and therefore needing to be used with care by foreign speakers:

bang up... (*slang*) ... *He said sex was no fun if you couldn't get a girl* ***banged up*** ORRF

4.1.4 *taboo* – 'swear words'; highly informal; generally avoided by educated male speakers when in the company of women and children, though conventions vary greatly from speaker to speaker, as well as from one social group to another; often expressing tension, irritation, anger, etc; best avoided by foreign speakers:

bugger off ... (*taboo*) ... *If you're going to be rude you can* ***bugger off!'*** UNXL

The user should note that it is impossible to assign fixed stylistic values to most items which call for a marking of some kind. The boundary between 'formal' and 'informal' usage is constantly shifting, and the conventions observed by individual speakers and writers differ very considerably. We can only attempt to give general guidance here.

Evaluative labels: pejorative, euphemistic, figurative, jocular

4.2 The use of certain phrasal verbs indicates a particular attitude (disapproving, humorous etc) towards the person or thing denoted. The following evaluative categories are used here:

4.2.1 *pejorative* – applied to items which express a strongly disapproving attitude to an action and the person performing it:

suck up to ... (*pejorative*) try to please (sb important or influential) by praising him, doing favours etc. ... *While Jacques* ***sucked up to*** *Spinks ... he did not in the least care for him as a man.* SML

4.2.2 *euphemistic* – used of items which refer to something painful or unpleasant in a pleasant (because indirect) way:

pass away/on/over ... (*euphemistic*) die. ... *'You'll be sorry to hear that Mr Barker's* ***passed over'*** *she said.* ASA

4.2.3 *figurative* – this label is applied in the dictionary to examples which illustrate a relatively fresh and unfamiliar non-literal (usually metaphorical) sense which has developed from a well-established one:

open up ... **4** ... make (a gap) appear in sth by cutting etc. ... (*figurative*) *They* ***open up*** *a chink in the armour of the Exchequer.* SC

4.2.4 *jocular* – applied to items which are intended to be funny, whether grim or innocent humour is meant:

put one's foot in it ... (*jocular*) say sth embarrassing or hurtful ... *I just said what came into my head, and there I go,* ***putting my foot in it*** as usual. AITC

Technical field labels

4.3 The occupations or specialized fields with which certain expressions are particularly associated are much more numerous than the stylistic and evaluative categories, and more clearly separated from each other. The following examples show a selection of the markings used in the dictionary. As will be seen, the labels are largely self-explanatory:

blast off [Vp ..., Vn⇄p ...] (*space technology*)
fold in/into [Vn⇄p ..., Vn.pr ...] (*cooking*)
cut back 1 [Vn⇄p ...] (*horticulture*)
turn around/round 2 [Vp ..., Vn⇄p ...] (*finance, commerce*)

convict (of) [Vn.pr . . .] (*legal*)
come to attention [Vpr] (*military*)
cast off 1 [Vp . . .] (*nautical*)

Definitions

5 In general, the definitions in this dictionary are concise and easily understandable phrases which do not assume a knowledge of – and do not contain – phrasal verbs listed elsewhere in the dictionary. Single words which are synonyms of the headphrase are placed immediately *after* the definition proper:

come to rest [Vpr] reach a final position; stop. . . .

Note, though, that when *another headphrase* is a synonym, opposite, etc of the one being defined, an appropriate cross-reference to it is given *at the end* of the entry (⇨ 9).

5.1 In entries where the headphrase takes a Direct Object and/or prepositional object, the abbreviations (sb) (= 'somebody'), (sth) (= 'something') or (sb/sth) (= 'somebody or something') are included to show the nature of the object(s):

answer back 1 . . . speak or interrupt (sb) rudely when being scolded. . . .
patch up 1 . . . repair (sth) roughly or temporarily. . . .
fight off 2 . . . prevent (sb/sth) from approaching one or gaining control. . . .

When the Direct Object or the object of a preposition refers to a place (as in: *I packed them off to the appropriate hospitals*), (a place) is included in the definition:

pack off to . . . send (sb) away briskly or urgently to (a place). . . .

Collocations

6 As has already been explained (⇨ 0.2), an important aim of the dictionary is to help the user produce new and acceptable sentences by listing words which regularly *collocate* with the headphrases. Information about collocating words is set out in the entries in a way which makes clear the relationship between collocations on the one hand and grammatical patterns (and their transforms) on the other.

Position of the collocates in entries

6.1 Words which collocate with the headphrase of an entry are arranged in sets preceded by an abbreviation in **bold type** and are placed immediately after the definition:

curl up 1 . . . turn up into a curl or sth like a curl . . . **S:** paper, leaves, material . . .
fade up . . . gradually make (sth/sb) louder, esp in a radio or TV studio). **S:** technician, sound effects man. **O:** music, voice; announcer . . .

The words given in the sets may be repeated lower down in the examples, but if the range of possible collocates is large, those used in one or more illustrations are often chosen to extend the list(s) already given:

add up to 2. . . mean (sth) overall or in total. **S:** refusal, statement, attitude. **o:** what (in initial position); the fact that: *'What your statement* **adds up to** *is that you helped to plan the break-in'*. ○ *'Your evidence, then, really* **adds up to** *this – that you were nowhere near the scene of the crime?'* . . .

Abbreviations used

6.2 The abbreviations which introduce sets of collocates are generally single letters standing for the main elements of the basic sentence patterns set out in the tables in Section 3.4. The letters are printed in **bold type**:

S = Subject (all basic patterns)
O = (Direct) Object ([Vn⇄p], [Vn.p], [Vp.n], [Vn.pr], [Vn.p.pr])
o = object of a preposition ([Vpr], [Vp.pr], [Vn.pr], [Vn.p.pr])
A = Adverbial phrase or clause, adverb (all basic patterns)

When **S** introduces a set of collocating words in an entry, this means that any of the words can function as (part of) the Subject in a sentence formed on the pattern given in the grammatical code for that entry:

break down 4 [Vp nom] stop through some mechanical or electrical failure. **S:** train, car, lorry, crane, lift: ... *Ed's car had broken down.* AITC

The same principle governs the use of the other letters introducing collocates:

act on/upon 2 [Vpr emph rel] have an effect on (sb); affect. **o:** organ; heart, liver, spleen, gland: *These pills* ***act on*** *the liver.*

6.2.1 The following abbreviations refer to parts of sentences (or parts of phrases) which are not dealt with in the tables of basic patterns:

Inf=Infinitive (either standing alone or introducing a non-finite clause)
adj=adjective (usu modifying the noun in an expression of which the noun is a fixed part)
m=adverbial modifier of a particle

The usual grammatical functions of the collocates introduced by these abbreviations are shown in the examples in the following entries:

bring up to do sth ... lead or persuade (sb) by deliberate training to do sth. ... **Inf:** to scorn convention, to respect his parents wishes: *He had always been* ***brought up to think*** *that his parents knew best.*

make a mockery of ... treat (sth) with no seriousness or respect; flout, mock. ... **adj:** complete, total. ...: *The conduct of the elections* ***made an*** *absolute* ***mockery of*** *democratic procedures.*

be out 12 ... be inaccurate, be wrong. ... **m:** (some) way, well, not far; five minutes, several miles. ...: *His forecast of rapid growth in the public sector of industry* ***was*** *some way* ***out.***

In a few entries (especially entries whose headphrases are 'nominalized forms') the word **Verb** introduces a set of collocating verbs:

look-in [nom [Vp] (informal) a chance to take part or be involved. **Verb:** get, have; give sb: *I wanted to talk to her but with all those guys around I didn't get a* ***look-in.*** ...

6.2.2 Some headphrases contain *two prepositions* and therefore do not exactly fit any of the basic patterns, though in practice they are given the codes [Vpr] and/or [Vn.pr] (⇨ *Grammatical codes and tables*, 3.1.3):

develop (from) (into) [Vpr ... Vn.pr ...]
lodge (against) (with) [Vn.pr ...]

To help the user to distinguish between the words collocating with *each* preposition in such entries, the preposition is placed (in ***bold italic***) in front of its particular collocates:

develop (from) (into)... **o:** (***from***) village; small-holding, family firm; obscure centre. (***into***) metropolis; estate, vast complex; multi-national company; the best, most advanced of its kind ...

Collocations and grammatical patterns

6.3 Collocating items always have grammatical functions (eg as Subject, Object, etc, as indicated above), and those functions may alter when the pattern of a sentence is changed (eg from 'active' to 'passive'). Consider the example:

write up 1 [Vn⇄p pass adj] rewrite (sth) in a fuller, better organized way; . . . **O:** note, observation; experiment, project . . .

Here, the words 'note, observation', etc can function in the *active* pattern [Vn⇄p] as *Objects*, as in the example:

'*For homework you can* **write up** *your rough notes.*'

When this sentence is transformed into the *passive*, however, 'notes' functions as (part of) the *Subject*:

'*For homework, your rough notes can be* **written up**.'

Awareness of these changes of function will help dictionary users who wish to construct sentences of their own. They can safely assume that when a grammatical code shows that a passive transform (for instance) is possible, they can use the *same* set of collocating words *twice* – as the Object (or prepositional object) in active sentences, and as the Subject in passive ones. (For a description of the transforms themselves, ⇨ the appropriate tables in 3: *Grammatical codes and tables*.)

6.3.1 In entries with two *basic* patterns, a single set of collocates may have different functions in the two patterns. The set of collocating words is introduced in a special way to show this:

close down [Vp nom, Vn⇄p pass adj] (cause production to) end or cease, permanently or for a time. **S** [Vp] **O** [Vn.pr]: school; plant, factory; theatre, broadcasting. **S** [Vn.p]: governor; owner, management. . . .

Here two capital letters and two codes are placed together before 'school; plant, factory' etc to show that those words can be used both as the Subject of the intransitive *and* the Object of the transitive, thus:

[Vp] *The factory had to* **close down** *through lack of orders.*
[Vn⇄p] *The owner had to* **close** *the factory* **down** *through lack of orders.*

On the other hand, 'governor; owner, management' can function only in a transitive pattern. Hence, **S** [Vn.p]. The same kind of 'causative' relationship is shown in the following entry, even though there are *four* basic patterns:

build (up) into [Vp, Vp.pr, Vn.pr, Vn.p.pr pass] (of parts) come together to form a whole; put (parts) together to form a whole. **S** [Vpr, Vp.pr] **O** [Vn.pr, Vn.p.pr]: piece, scrap; stamp, medal, book. . . . Compare the examples:

[Vp.pr] *Eventually, these books will* **build up into** *a fine library.*
[Vn.pr] *The sculptor has* **built** *these scraps of metal* **into** *a fine composition.*

In other entries with two (or more) basic patterns, the Subject of an intransitive pattern [Vp] may *also* be the Subject of a transitive one [Vn⇄p]. Compare:

[Vp] *If you don't* **wind on** *after taking a picture, your negative will be double-exposed.*

[Vn⇄p] *If you don't* **wind** *the film* **on** *after taking a picture . . . .*

In such entries the Subject and Object collocates are kept separate, and there is no reference before those lists to sentence patterns. The user can assume that what are Subject collocates for the [Vp] pattern are also Subject collocates for the [Vn⇄p] pattern:

wind on [Vp, Vn⇄p . . .] move (a film etc) forward so as to expose, or show, the next portion. **S:** photographer, cameraman. **O:** film, film-strip, tape. . . .

Internal arrangement of lists of collocates

6.4 Collocates are arranged within their lists so as to reflect similarities and differences of grammar and meaning. Grouping like with like is designed to help users grasp the *shared* meaning of collocates, so enabling them to make lexical choices of their own. Note especially:

◆ Nouns of the same type (eg common, abstract, proper) are put together:

engrave on ... **o:** presentation cup, plate; memory, mind. ...

work on 1 ... **o:** book, play; Milton, Tolstoy; radio, rocket motor; improvement. ...

◆ General terms precede and are separated from particular terms:

chug across, along, away etc ... **S:** (old) ship, boat; steamer, tug, tramp (-steamer). ...

act on/upon 2 ... **o:** organ; heart, liver, spleen, gland. ...

◆ Words which are closely related in sense are placed together and divided by a semi-colon from others which are more remote in meaning:

prepare (for)... **O:** oneself; pupil, class; follower, subject; article, book; room. ...

saturate (with) ... **O:** ground, soil; cloth, rag. ...

◆ When one part of a set of words, etc collocates closely with one part of another set, the semi-colon is used in each set to mark this part off. In certain entries, a set of words may be divided into several groups according to the relations which those groups have with parts of other sets:

take over (from) ... **S:** (new, younger) man; pilot, skipper; specialist, expert; runner, car. **O:** management, direction; controls, helm; case, inquiry; lead, first place. **o:** (retiring) director; crew member; assistant; competitor. ...

The particular lay-out of this entry indicates that (among other collocations) 'skipper' collocates with 'helm' and 'crew member', to give the sentence:

The skipper **took over** *the helm* **from** *a crew member.*

'Open' and 'restricted' sets of collocates

6.5 A distinction can be drawn between sets of collocates to which other words can be added freely, and sets which virtually exhaust all the possibilities of choice open to the speaker. The difference between the first, or *open* kind of set and the second, or *restricted*, kind is not clear-cut but a gradual progression. An example of the first kind is found in the entry:

come in 1 ... become fashionable. **S:** long hair, whiskers; short skirts, full sleeves. ...

Since a wide variety of styles of dress, ways of wearing one's hair, and so on, can become the fashion, the suggested collocates far from exhaust the range of suitable items, but simply indicate the general areas in which *many* appropriate choices can be made.

The kind of set which represents a severely *limited* range of choice is marked in a special way – with the sign ⚠:

keep an/one's eye on ... observe (sb/sth) and if necessary take appropriate action. **adj:** ⚠ (a) careful, professional, sharp, watchful, ...

Here this sign warns the users that the set is highly restricted: other adjectives are unlikely to collocate with the headphrase. This set, like similarly marked sets in other entries, does not *exhaust* our options: we might, for special effect, choose 'vigilant' or 'amateurish'. But these are unusual choices, and foreign learners would be wise to regard this sign as a warning to confine themselves for some time to the choices indicated.

All such restricted sets of collocates marked with this sign are listed, together with collocates used in headphrases, in the *Index of nouns etc used in headphrases* at the end of the dictionary, and referred back to the entry or entries in which they occur.

Examples

Position of examples

7.1 Examples are placed after the collocations, or where there are no collocations, after the definition, and preceded by a colon : thus:

dive (one's hand) into ... **o:** pocket, purse, handbag: *He* ***dived into*** *his jacket pocket to make sure his wallet was still there.*

Where two or more examples are given they are divided from each other by a small circle ○:

care about ... **o:** outcome, result; the homeless, the less able: *Arendt constantly avoids that question and does not seem to* ***care about*** *the answer.* HA ○ *He doesn't appear to* ***care*** very much ***about*** *the future of the company.*

When an example is quoted from a text, the title of the book, newspaper, etc is given in abbreviated form at the end of the example:

usher in ...: *It is the happy custom for the Viennese to* ***usher in*** *the New Year with a concert of music by Strauss.* RT ○ *It would be unwise to assume that the July elections will* ***usher in*** *a new millennium.* OBS

(where RT = *Radio Times* and OBS = *The Observer*; ⇨ *List of Sources*, pp 488–493.)

Examples and the headphrase

7.2 Examples are printed in *italic*. To help the user to pick out the headphrase in example sentences, it is printed there in ***bold italic***. In most entries, when allowance has been made for inflection of the verb, there is a close similarity between the headphrase as it appears at the top of the entry and the particular form it takes in the example(s).

start up (in) ... *Twice he had raised the money and* ***started up in*** *engineering.* ARG ○ *They were thinking of* ***starting up in*** *the fruit and vegetable trade.*

In certain entries there are differences between the *forms* of adjectives, nouns, etc given in the headphrase and those appearing lower down in the example(s). In some entries it is a matter of the choice of different words. The user should note in particular the following conventions.

7.2.1 Generally speaking, the use of **one's**, **sb's** or **his** in a headphrase represents the full set of possessive adjectives – **my**, **his**, **her**, **its**, **one's**, **our**, **your**, **their**. The appropriate choice from this set is given, according to context, in the examples, and printed there in bold italic (for the difference between **one's**, **sb's**, **his**, ⇨ 1, *The headphrase*):

come into one's own ... *he only* ***came into his own*** *after the age of 30.* NSC

get on sb's nerves ... *She* ***gets on your nerves****, doesn't she, the way she never stops talking about her brilliant son.*

bring to his feet ... *A jolt nearly threw me from the bed, and a second jolt* ***brought*** *me* ***to my feet.*** SD

The use of **sb's** in a headphrase can also represent the possessive form of nouns and possessive phrases introduced by 'of'. In order to avoid typographical complexity the whole of the possessive noun is printed in bold italic, but only the 'of' introducing the possessive phrase is. Compare:

follow in sb's footsteps ... *One of my passes was in Maths, so my old lady decided that I should* ***follow in*** *my poor* ***father's footsteps.*** JFTR

bring to sb's attention/notice ... *An inspector first* ***brought*** *these deficiencies* ***to the attention of*** *the management.*

7.2.2 In general, the use in headphrases of the reflexive forms, **himself** or **oneself** represents the following set of reflexive pronouns:

myself, himself, herself, itself, oneself, ourselves, yourself, yourselves, themselves.

Again, the appropriate choice from this list is made, according to context, in the examples:

come to oneself ... *I didn't realize how ill I had been ... till I* ***came to myself*** *in that pretty, sunny sitting-room* ... PW

draw oneself up ... *He* ***drew himself up*** *portentously, walked stiff-legged over to the table, and sat down.* DC

A headphrase may contain the phrase **one's way**, with or without parentheses. If the phrase is picked up in an example, **one's** may be replaced by **my**, **his** etc as already shown:

work one's way across, along, back etc ... *He managed to* ***work his way back*** *through the crowd ... with two glasses of champagne.*

7.2.3 A noun given in the singular form in the headphrase often means that both the singular *and* plural forms may be used. In such cases both forms are illustrated (⇨ 1, *The headphrase*).

7.2.4 When **a/an** or **the**, or an indefinite adjective (eg **any**, **no**) appears in the headphrase, and other similar words are listed as collocates (after **adj**), then *whichever* indefinite adjective, etc appears in the examples is treated as part of the headphrase, and printed in bold italic:

make a fuss of ... **adj:** much, a lot of; (not) any. ... *We* ***made*** *such a* ***fuss of*** *them. Give them cigarettes and cups of tea.* CSWB ○ *Too* ***much fuss*** *can be* ***made of*** *very young children.*

7.2.5 When a selection of adjectives (or particles) is indicated in the headphrase, then whichever adjective(s) or particle(s) are chosen as example(s) are treated as part of the headphrase, and printed in bold italic:

take a poor etc view of... **adj:** poor, dim, sombre, pessimistic; optimistic, sanguine, bright ... *The federation* ***takes a gloomy view of*** *the prospects for the economy in the months to come.* T ○ *Most other road-users* ***take a stern view of*** *the private motorist.* SC

file across, along, away etc ... *The men* ***filed across*** *a narrow footbridge.* ○ *The staff* ***filed into*** *the canteen for their mid-morning break.*

Coverage of various patterns in the examples

7.3 When the grammatical code in an entry refers to two or more basic patterns, both or all will normally be illustrated by means of separate example sentences.

draw in/into [Vp, Vpr] ...: *As I reached the ticket barrier the London train was just* ***drawing in.*** ○ *The 'Cornish Riviera'* ***drew into*** *Plymouth a few minutes ahead of schedule.*

When an entry has three or four patterns, the various examples illustrating them are preceded by the appropriate code, or codes:

move in (with) [Vp, Vp.pr, Vn.p pass, Vn.p.pr pass] ... [Vp] *The new lodger is* ***moving in*** *on the first of the month.* ○ [Vp.pr] *She had to suffer the humiliation of* ***moving in with*** *the parents of the man who had jilted her.* GJ ○ [Vn.p] *'Won't the agricultural people have something to say if ... we're* ***moved in****?'* TBC

Treatment of related patterns in examples

7.4 Sometimes the relationship between two basic patterns (and possibly two alternative forms of the headphrase) is shown by adding illustrative material in parenthesis. This is done, for instance, when a pattern with a singular subject + **with** corresponds to one with a plural subject + **together**:

team up (together/with) [Vp, Vp.pr] ... *John then* ***teamed up with*** *a boat builder (*cf *They* ***teamed up*** *(****together****)) and began making cabin cruisers.*

The same convention is used when a basic pattern containing a verb with a preposition alternates with one containing the same verb + an infinitive:

yearn (for) [Vpr ...] ... *She* ***yearned for*** *a sight of* (or: ***yearned*** *to see) her dear ones.*

Note that when alternatives are given inside examples from recorded sources, the abbreviation indicating the source is given last:

trust (for that) [Vpr ...] ...: *Alec got the house rebuilt when licences were almost unprocurable –* ***trust*** *him* ***for that*** (or: ***trust*** *him to do that)!* PW

Sometimes a basic pattern containing a verb + a preposition **on** or **to** (eg **spread on**, **supply to**) is equivalent to a construction with the same verb + **with** (here, **spread with**, **supply with**). In such cases, the alternative patterns are given in the entry for **spread on** etc:

spread on ... *An embroidered blanket was* ***spread on*** *the sofa* (or: *The sofa was* ***spread with*** *an embroidered blanket).* ○ ***Spread*** *the butter thickly* ***on*** *the rolls* (or: ***Spread*** *the rolls thickly* ***with*** *butter).*

In all such cases, the same verb + **with** is also listed as a headphrase and referred back to the main entry:

spread with ... ⇨ spread on.

In the entry **fill up 1**, there are two related meanings: 'become completely full' and 'cause (sth) to become completely full'. There are many similar 'causative' entries in the dictionary (⇨ 6.3.1). In such entries, the two meanings are combined, but there are separate codes and separate examples:

fill up 1 [Vp, Vn⇄p pass] (cause sth to) become completely full ... *the storage tanks are* ***filling up*** *again.* ○ *I've* ***filled up*** *all the buckets I can lay my hands on.*

In some entries, the connection is different. Compare:

The grease spots wouldn't ***wash off.***
I couldn't ***wash off*** *the grease spots.*

In the first example, a certain quality is being ascribed to the Subject, ie the grease spots were so bad, so ingrained, that I couldn't wash them off. In other words, the [Vp] pattern, which in this meaning usually contains *not/n't* and/or an adverb such as *easily, quickly* is the equivalent of a [Vn⇄p] pattern. Only that pattern is given in the code, while the meaning connection is shown by linked examples:

wash off 1 [Vn⇄p pass ...] remove (sth) from the surface of a material etc ...: *I tried to remove the grease spots from the wall but they wouldn't* ***wash off*** (or: *I couldn't* ***wash*** *them* ***off***).

All nominalized forms (eg **breakdown**, **mess-up**, **walk-out**) are illustrated and the relationship is often shown between a basic pattern containing a phrasal verb and a pattern incorporating the nom form:

walk out [Vp nom] ...: *Building workers* ***walked out*** (or: *staged a* ***walk out***) *during the morning ...*

Notes on grammar, meaning and use

8 When there are special features of grammar, meaning or use which cannot be dealt with conveniently elsewhere in the entry, they are explained (and often illustrated) in a note placed after the examples, and separated from them by a box – □ :

accustom to ... □ often preceded by *find it difficult/easy/hard to.*

make allowances (for) ... ▫ allowances occasionally sing, as in: *When every* ***allowance*** *has been* ***made for*** *his inexperience....*

Among the special features which the notes are used to point out and explain are the following:

◆ special restrictions of *tense* or *aspect* are shown:

finish with 3 ...: *'No, he can't go. I haven't* ***finished with*** *him yet.'* ▫ usu with perfect tenses.

◆ use of the headphrase with one or more modal verbs is indicated thus:

do with ...: *'I could* ***do with*** *two weeks away from the children and the washing-up.'* ... ▫ used only with *can/could*.

◆ when one pattern which is indicated by means of a code alternates with another which is not, the alternative is pointed out and usually illustrated:

be in progress [Vpr] ... ▫ also used after a noun: *Discussions now* ***in progress*** *are covering a wide range of issues.*

have doubts about [Vn.pr ...] ... ▫ note the pattern with *with*: *She was a woman* ***with*** *no serious* ***doubts about*** *her role in the enterprise.*

◆ when a particular non-finite form of the verb always (or usually) follows the headphrase, this is indicated:

set out 1 [Vp] ...: *The Mexican peasant* ***sets out*** *to burn an acre of woodland* ... ▫ always followed by an inf.

◆ when one or more of the transforms of a phrasal verb etc are used more often than the basic pattern, these restrictions are pointed out:

call away [Vn.p pass] ...: *'I'm afraid the doctor isn't in. He was* ***called away*** *a few minutes ago.'* ▫ very often passive, with no agent mentioned.

◆ some headphrases which include the verb **be** can also be used with the 'copula' verbs **appear**, **feel**, **look**, **seem**, **sound**. The same is true of some 'fixed' passive forms (eg **embroiled in**). When this full range of copula verbs can be used, the following note appears in the entry:

be at one (with) [Vpr] .... ▫ also used with *appear* etc ...
embroiled in [pass (Vn.pr)] ... ▫ used with *appear* etc.

When, however, there is some restriction on the choice of copula verb, the permitted choices are listed:

enamoured of [pass (Vn.pr)] ... ▫ also used with *become, appear, seem.*

◆ when a phrasal verb (or more complex idiom) can be the Direct Object etc of a larger construction, this possibility is explained in a note:

what (to) do with oneself [Vn.pr] ...: *Now that Jenny's retired, she doesn't know* ***what to do with herself.*** ▫ what do with etc may be the Object of a larger sentence ...

The cross-reference system

9 The cross-references used in this edition of the dictionary are of three main types:

◆ one entry may be cross-referred to another *synonymous* entry (cf **brim over with** and **overflow with**);

◆ one entry may be cross-referred to another which is *opposite* in meaning (cf **put down 1** and **pick up 1**);

◆ one entry may be cross-referred to another which has a more *inclusive* meaning (cf **come to light** and **bring to light**).

Cross-reference to synonyms

9.1 An entry may contain a cross-reference to one or more headphrases which are *synonyms* of the headphrase being defined. The cross-reference (or cross-references) are placed at the end of the entry after the sign '=':

talk about 3 ... propose or consider (possible action), though usu without acting in fact. ... = talk of 2.

Phrasal verbs etc are close synonyms when they can be substituted for each other in various sentences without the cognitive and stylistic meaning of those sentences being affected as a result. When entries in the dictionary are synonyms in this strict sense, they are cross-referred to each other. Compare the entry just given with:

talk of 2 ... consider or discuss (possible action), though usu without acting in fact. ... = talk about 3.

Note also the following pair of entries, and how each of the headphrases can be used in the examples provided for the other:

adapt (oneself) to ... change one's outlook or behaviour to suit (sth). ...: *The new teacher was very slow to* **adapt to** *the unusual rules of the school.* ○ *I don't think I shall ever* **adapt myself to** *this hot climate.* = adjust (oneself) to.

adjust (oneself to) ... change one's outlook or behaviour to suit (sth). ...: *I don't think I shall ever be able to* **adjust myself to** *life in this remote place.* ○ *Jenkins was well* **adjusted to** *the community in which he lived.* = adapt (oneself) to.

Many entries are related in this way. Sometimes, though, the user will find that while two phrasal verbs may express 'the same ideas', one has a transform that is not shared by the other, ie the two items are not fully interchangeable. Compare in this respect:

pour down ... *It was* **pouring down** *non-stop* ... = teem down.

teem down ... *It was* **teeming down**, *and we took shelter in a shop entrance.* = pour down.

These entries have the same *meaning*, as the examples demonstrate. However, the first entry has a nom form (**downpour**) while the second does not. We can say:

There was a steady **downpour** *all afternoon.*

but not:

There was a steady* **downteem *all afternoon.*

The user should watch out for such grammatical differences, which are always pointed out and usually illustrated.

In other cases, two or more headphrases will have the same meaning but not the same stylistic or emotive overtones. For example, the phrasal verbs **balls up**, **cock up** and **mess up** can all be given the same general definition – 'mishandle, mismanage, spoil, ruin (sth)' – but the contexts in which they would be used are quite different. While **mess up** is neutral in style, **balls up** and **cock up** are taboo items. In cases like these, the entries with stylistic markings are cross-referred to the neutral entry (in this case **mess up**):

balls up ... *(taboo)* ruin, mishandle (sth). ... ⇨ mess up.

cock up ... *(informal)* spoil or ruin (sth). ... ⇨ mess up.

mess up ... spoil, ruin (sth). ...

Note, though, that when two or more entries have the same meaning and are at the *same* stylistic level they are cross-referred to each other:

admit of ... *(formal)* leave room for (sth) ... = allow of, permit of.

allow of ... *(formal)* leave room for (sth). ... = admit of, permit of.

permit of ... *(formal)* leave room for (sth). ... = admit of, allow of.

Cross-references to opposites

9.2 When two headwords are opposite in meaning, their entries are cross-referred to each other. The cross-reference in each case is placed at the end of the entry, introduced by the sign '↔':

change down ... (in driving a car) move to a lower gear. ... ↔ change up.
change up ... (in driving a car) move to a higher gear. ... ↔ change down.
bring down 5 ... reduce, lower (sth). ... ↔ send up 1.
send up 1 ... cause (sth) to rise. ... ↔ bring down 5.

Cross-references between entries for the 'major' verbs

9.3 The major verbs (eg **come**, **go**, **bring**, **put**, **send**, **take**) are those which show the strongest tendency to combine with particles and prepositions to form phrasal verbs and related idioms. The verb **put** is a highly productive member of this group. Not only do we find **put in**, **put off**, **put out** and **put up**, but also **put at a premium** and **put in a nutshell**. Another important common feature is that these verbs, in combination with particles and prepositions (and sometimes also nouns), often correspond to each other in meaning. Consider:

be up for auction/sale ... be available or offered for purchase ...
come up for auction/sale ... become available for purchase ...
put up for auction/sale ... offer (sth) for sale ...

Here, the meaning of the **come** entry is 'included' in that of the **put** entry, since 'offer something for sale' means '*cause it to become* available' etc. Similarly, the **be** entry is related to the **come** entry: if something *is up* for sale it *has come up* for sale.

The same kinds of relationships exists between very many sets of entries in which there is an entry with **be**, one with an intransitive verb (eg **come**, **go**) and one with a 'causative' verb (eg **bring**, **put**, **send**, **take**). Whenever such links are found, the entries concerned are cross-referenced to each other. Relevant cross-references, preceded by the sign '⇨', are placed at the end of each member of the group of entries. Note that when reference is made to two or more entries which are alike except for their verbs, their headphrases are combined, as here:

be out of action ... ⇨ go/put out of action.
go out of action ... ⇨ be/put out of action.
put out of action ... ⇨ be/go out of action.

In some cases, a grouping of related phrasal verbs etc will contain two or more intransitive verbs (eg **come**, **go**) and/or causative verbs (eg **bring**, **put**). These will all be indicated, as in this entry:

take before ... ⇨ be before 2, bring before, come before 2, go before 2, put before 2.

9.3.1 There is a strong tendency for **come**, **go**, **get** and **stay** (to name only the most common of the major intransitives) to be associated with some causative verbs rather than others. Those intransitives, and the causatives with which they tend to be linked, are dealt with below. It is important to note that these connections (signalled by cross-references) are a *productive* feature of the dictionary. Users referring to an intransitive entry will be made aware of the related causative phrasal verb, and by referring to the appropriate entry will be able to construct parallel causative sentences.

◆ In very many of the phrasal verbs etc in which it occurs, **come**, as intransitive verb, corresponds to **bring** as causative:

come back 3 ... return (to the memory). ... ⇨ bring back 2.
come in 6 ... be received as income. ... ⇨ bring in 2.

There is also an important connection between **come** and **take** (in the general sense 'cause (sth) to come towards one':

take off 1 ... remove, detach (esp sth fastened to a surface ...) ... ⇨ be off 2, come off 2.
take off 6 ... ask or order (sb) to leave one job ... ⇨ come off 7.

◆ For phrasal verbs etc with **go**, the most common corresponding causatives recorded in the dictionary contain the verb **put**:

go in 3 ... fit; enter. ... ⇨ put in 4.
go up 4 ... be constructed. ... ⇨ put up 3.
go out of action ... ⇨ be/put out of action.

Other links (less frequently recorded in the dictionary) are with **send** and **take**, especially in the general sense 'move (sb/sth) *away* from the speaker':

go up 5 ... be destroyed ... ⇨ send up 2.
go around/round (together/with) ... keep company with (sb) ... ⇨ take around/round (with).

◆ When **get** is used as a verb of motion (as distinct from a 'possessive' verb) it can, in various combinations, have both an intransitive and a transitive (causative) function. These two functions are normally handled in the same entry with no need for a cross-reference:

get off on the right/wrong foot [Vp.pr, Vn.p.pr ...] (cause sb to) make a good/bad start. ...

When **get** is used as a possessive verb (ie in the senses 'receive', 'recover' etc) it may have links with **give** and **have**. Such connections are shown as follows:

get back 4 ... recover sth which belongs to one. ... ⇨ give back (to) 1, have back 1.

◆ Several combinations of intransitive **stay** + particle/preposition are matched by combinations of transitive **keep** (= 'cause to stay'), etc:

stay in 1 ... remain at school after others have left, as a punishment ... ⇨ keep in 3.

An important transitive equivalent of **stay**, though less commonly found in the dictionary than **keep**, is **leave**:

stay down 1 ... remain in a lowered position. ... ⇨ leave down.

Other cross-references

9.4 Cross-references between entries whose headphrases do *not* include a major verb serve a variety of purposes. The commonest of these are as follows.

9.4.1 Combinations which are close in meaning (and possibly also in form) but which need to be carefully distinguished are usually cross-referenced to each other, with additional explanatory notes where necessary:

sell (at) ... give (at a particular price level). ... □ one sells at a point on a scale (eg of loss or gain); one sells for a particular amount or sum of money.
sell (for) ... give in exchange for a particular sum of money. ... ⇨ (footnote at) sell (at).
work at ... give thought, energy etc to getting rid of or solving (sth). ... ⇨ work on 1.
work on 1 ... give thought, effort etc to making or discovering (sth). ... ⇨ work at.

9.4.2 When a complex idiom (ie one containing a noun or nouns) is related in meaning to a phrasal verb, and it is helpful to point to this connection, the entry for the complex expression is cross-referenced to the entry for the simpler one, as follows:

see beyond ... (be able to) foresee and understand events etc which are at some distance in space or time; be farsighted. ...
see beyond the end of one's nose ... (be able to) understand more than is present and obvious ... ⇨ previous entry.

9.4.3 When two combinations are related in such a way that the Subject of one corresponds to the prepositional object of the other (and perhaps vice-versa), the entries for the combinations are cross-referenced to each other:

break out in 1 .. suddenly become covered in (sth). **S:** patient; face, body. **o:** spots, pimples, sores; rash ... ⇨ break out on.

break out on ... appear suddenly upon (sth). **S:** spots; rash. **o:** face, arm ... ⇨ break out in 1.

run out 1 ... be finished, exhausted. **S:** supply, stock (of wines, cigarettes etc); patience; time ... ⇨ run out/out of.

run out/out of ... finish, exhaust (sth). **o:** supply, stock (of commodities); ideas; patience ... ⇨ run out 1.

9.4.4 If two expressions ending with a preposition are related in such a way that the Direct Object of each one corresponds to the prepositional object of the other the connection is shown by means of a cross-reference in each entry:

weave (up) (from) ... make (cloth) (from threads) by weaving them together. **O:** length, piece; (cotton, woollen) cloth. **o:** yard, thread ... ⇨ next entry.

weave (up) (into) ... make (threads) (into cloth) by weaving them together. **O:** yarn, thread; cotton, wool. **o:** cloth; blanket, covering ... ⇨ previous entry

9.4.5 Some phrasal verbs and longer idioms containing a transitive verb (such as **raise**) are closely matched by others containing the corresponding intransitive verb (thus, **rise**). The matching entries are cross-referenced, as follows:

raise to the surface ... ⇨ rise to the surface 1
rise to the surface 1 ... ⇨ raise to the surface

(For transitive/intransitive correspondences between the heavy-duty verbs, ⇨ 9.3, above.)

Cross-references from 'dummy' entries

9.5 Entries such as

spatter with [Vn.pr pass rel] ⇨ previous entry.

contain a minimum of information about the headphrase. They are empty or 'dummy' entries, designed simply to direct the user to a main entry – in this case the immediately preceding one – where fuller information is provided. Dummy entries perform two main functions in the dictionary. In the case of the entry just quoted and also of

splash with [Vn.pr pass rel] ⇨ splash on/onto 2.
spread with [Vn.pr pass rel] ⇨ spread on.

their purpose is to refer the user to main entries in which the verb + **with** pattern is illustrated side by side with the verb + **on** (or **onto**) pattern. (This relationship is dealt with in more detail in *Examples*, 7.5.)

Many headphrases in the dictionary contain two or more alternative prepositions or particles, divided by the oblique. Others contain two optional prepositions or particles, within separate sets of parentheses:

come along/on ... **2** ... make progress. ...
take around/round (with) ... take (sb/sth) as a companion. ...
stand (as) (for) ... be a candidate ... (for sth). ...

Each of these headphrases introduces a main entry, with a definition and examples. However, users meeting **come on**, **take round (with)** or **stand (for)** – in the senses indicated – for the first time in speech or writing, who are not aware that there are alternative prepositions, might have difficulty in locating the main entries they need. To help them, the following dummy entries are provided (at the appropriate alphabetical places):

come on 2 . . . make progress. ⇨ come along/on 2.
take round (with) . . . ⇨ take around/round (with).
stand (for) . . . ⇨ stand (as) (for).

Users will notice that the numbered entry **come on 2** (like the main entry **come along/on 2**) contains the definition 'make progress'. The additional information is given so that this dummy entry can be distinguished from other members of a **come on** series (some of which are not dummy entries).

LIST OF SOURCES

This list records the original texts used as the basis for some of the example sentences. It is arranged in alphabetical order according to the reference initials of the title that are used in the text of the dictionary to identify the source. The author's name, if known, follows after the source abbreviation and the full title of the work is then indicated in italic type. Finally, the name of the original publisher and the date of publication are indicated.

50MH R Lindner *The Fifty-Minute Hour: A Collection of True Psychoanalytic Tales* Free Association Books 1986

50S Peter Lewis *The Fifties: Portrait of a Period* Herbert Press 1989

AE Alice Thomas Ellis *The Sin Eater* Duckworth 1977

AF David Arkell *Alain-Fournier: A Brief Life* Carcanet 1986

AH William Plomer *At Home* Jonathan Cape 1958

AITC Monica Dickens *The Angel in the Corner* Michael Joseph 1956

AM Sue Townsend *The True Confessions of Adrian Albert Mole* Methuen 1989

AO T Oliver and R Sale *Arctic Odyssey: Travelling Arctic Europe* Crowood Press 1991

AP7 Miriam Waddington *Apartment Seven: Essays Selected and New* Oxford University Press 1989

ARG *Argosy Magazine* September 1958

ART N F Simpson *A Resounding Tinkle* (in *New English Dramatists 2*) Penguin 1960

ASA Angus Wilson *Anglo-Saxon Attitudes* Secker & Warburg 1956

AT Anne Tyler *The Accidental Tourist* Chatto & Windus 1985

AUG *Amstrad Personal Computer Word Processor Guide* Amsoft 1985

AV *Audio Visual* (magazine) 1988-91

AW J McGahern *Amongst Women* Faber 1990

B Alan Clark *Barbarossa* Hutchinson 1965

BB Gerald Durrell *The Bafut Beagles* Rupert Hart-Davis 1954

BBCR BBC Radio programmes 1973-92

BBCTV BBC Television programmes 1967-92

BCIN James Park *British Cinema: The Lights that Failed* Batsford 1990

BDD General Sir William Jackson *Britain's Defence Dilemma* – Batsford 1990

BEST *Best* (magazine) April-June 1991

BFA H E Bates *A Breath of French Air* Michael Joseph 1959

BID Alec Guinness & Christopher Sinclair-Stevenson (Ed) *Blessings in Disguise* Hamish Hamilton 1985

BLCH Howard Sturgis *Belchamber* Oxford University Press 1986

BM *Blackwood's Magazine* July 1960

BMTD Ruth Rendell *The Best Man To Die* Hutchinson 1969

BN Alan Moorhead *The Blue Nile* Hamish Hamilton 1962

BONE Keri Hulme *The Bone People* Hodder & Stoughton 1985

BOOK *The Bookseller* (magazine) 1988-91

BP Harold Pinter *The Birthday Party* Eyre Methuen 1965

BRAZ William Boyd *Brazzaville Beach* Sinclair-Stevenson 1990

BRH R Sutcliff *Blue Remembered Hills: A Recollection* Oxford University Press 1984

BRN Jonathan Gathorne-Hardy *The Rise and Fall of the British Nanny* Hodder & Stoughton 1972

BV Angela Carter *Black Venus* Chatto & Windus 1985

CD E Johnson *Charles Dickens* Penguin 1986

CED Richard Cobb *A Classical Education* Chatto & Windus 1985

CF Roderick Strange *The Catholic Faith* Oxford University Press 1986

CH Jack Higgins *Cold Harbour* Heinemann 1990

CHAL *Challenger Enquiry* Transcript of proceedings concerning USA shuttle disaster

CHDI Penny Junor *Charles and Diana* Headline Book Publishing 1991

CHGG Denis Pagen *Complete Hang-gliding Guide* Sport Aviation Publications 1991

CL *Community Librarian* (journal) The Library Association 1986-91

CLSH	Sedley Sweeny *The Challenge of Smallholding* Oxford University Press 1985
COAA	Laurence Olivier *Confessions of an Actor* Hodder & Stoughton 1984
CON	John Wain *The Contenders* Macmillan 1958
COS	Ian McEwan *The Comfort of Strangers* Jonathan Cape 1981
CR	Nicholas Humphrey *Consciousness Regained* Oxford University Press 1984
CSWB	Arnold Wesker *Chicken Soup with Barley* Penguin 1959
CTD	Lesley Grant-Adamson *Curse The Darkness* Faber 1990
D	Os Guinness *Doubt: Faith in two minds* Lion Publishing 1976
DBM	H E Bates *The Darling Buds of May* Michael Joseph 1958
DC	Dorothy Eden *Darling Clementine* Macdonald 1955
DELI	Rosemary Moon *Delicatessen: A Celebration and Cookbook* David and Charles 1989
DF	Gerald Durrell *The Drunken Forest* Rupert Hart-Davis 1956
DIL	Richard Gordon *Doctor in Love* Michael Joseph 1958
DL	Donald Metzer *Dream Life* Clunie 1984
DM	*Daily Mirror* (newspaper) June 1960
DOAP	Janet Neel *Death of a Partner* Constable 1991
DOP	Aldous Huxley *The Doors of Perception* Chatto & Windus 1954
DPM	Bernard Kops *The Dream of Peter Mann* Penguin 1960
DS	Ian Fleming *The Diamond Smugglers* Jonathan Cape 1957
DT	*The Daily Telegraph* (newspaper) 1988-91
DTW	David Adamson *Defending the World: The Politics and Diplomacy of the Environment* I B Tauris 1990
E	Samuel Beckett *Embers* Faber 1959
EB	Patricia Craig *Elizabeth Bowen* Penguin 1986
EC	Ursula Holden *Eric's Choice* Methuen 1984
ECON	*The Economist* (magazine) March-June 1990
EDTH	R George Thomas *Edward Thomas: A Portrait* Oxford University Press 1987
EFLG	*EFL Gazette* 1988-1991
EGD	J Osborne and A Creighton *Epitaph for George Dillon* Faber 1958
EH	A J P Taylor *English History 1914-45* Oxford University Press 1965
EHOW	Doris Lessing *Each His Own Wilderness* Penguin 1959
EM	Cyril Hare *An English Murder* Faber 1951
ESB	*English Speaking Board* (journal) 1988-91
ESS	D W Winnicott *Home is Where We Start From: Essays by a Psychoanalyst* Penguin 1986
EXP	*Daily Express* (newspaper) 1988-91
F	R W Clark *Freud: The Man and The Cause* Weidenfeld & Nicholson 1980
FAE	Jeffrey Archer *First Among Equals* Hodder & Stoughton 1984
FFE	Peter Shaffer *Five Finger Exercise* Hamish Hamilton 1958
FIB	Anthony Burgess *Flame into Being: The Life and Work of D H Lawrence* Heinemann 1985
FL	Jonathan Raban *Foreign Land* Collins 1985
FOLK	Kingsley Amis *The Folks that Live on the Hill* Hutchinson 1990
FOX	Fox FM (Oxford local radio) station news reports February-November 1990
FT	*Financial Times* (newspaper) 1990
FUNB	Len Deighton *Funeral in Berlin* Jonathan Cape 1964
FV	Clive James *Flying Visits* Jonathan Cape 1984
G	*The Guardian* (newspaper) 1967-1990
GA	Iris Murdoch *The Good Apprentice* Chatto & Windus 1985
GAL	Susan Hill *Gentleman and Ladies* Hamish Hamilton 1976
GBART	Frances Spalding *British Art since 1900* Thames & Hudson 1987
GC	*Good Cookery* (magazine)1990
GE	G S Haight *George Eliot: A Biography* Oxford University Press 1968
GF	*Good Food* (magazine) March, April 1991
GIE	A N Wilson *Gentlemen in England* Hamish Hamilton 1985
GJ	Susan Chitty *Gwen John* Hodder & Stoughton 1981
GL	Paul Bailey *Gabriel's Lament* Jonathan Cape 1986

List of Sources

GLEG K Lines *Greek Legends* Faber 1986

GLWM Jeremy Legget (Ed) *Global Warming: The Greenpeace Report* Oxford University Press 1990

GS Malcolm Muggeridge *Chronicles of Wasted Time : Vol 1 "The Green Stick"* Fontana 1975

GSG P F Gura *A Glimpse of Sion's Glory: Puritan Radicalism in New England* Wesleyan UP 1986

GT Doris Lessing *The Good Terrorist* Jonathan Cape 1985

GW *Gardener's World* (magazine) August 1991

H *Honey* (magazine) August 1960

HA Derwent James May *Hannah Arendt* Penguin 1986

HAA Angus Wilson *Hemlock and After* Secker & Warburg 1952

HAH Aldous Huxley *Heaven and Hell* Penguin 1960

HAHA Jennifer Dawson *The Ha-Ha* Blond 1961

HB A N Wilson *Hilaire Belloc* Hamish Hamilton 1984

HD John Wain *Hurry on Down* Secker & Warburg 1953

HERM Storm Constantine *Hermetech* Headline Book Publishing 1991

HHGG Douglas Adams *The Hitch Hiker's Guide to the Galaxy* Pan 1979

HOC John McManners (Ed) *The History of Christianity* Oxford University Press 1990

HOM Graham Greene *The Heart of the Matter* William Heinemann 1948

HOTC Shiva Naipaul *A Hot Country* Hamish Hamilton 1983

HQ *Harpers and Queen* (magazine) April 1990

HSG Bernard Kops *The Hamlet of Stepney Green* Penguin 1959

HTS John Updike *Hugging the Shore: Essays and Criticism* Deutsch 1984

HWKM P Ackroyd *Hawksmoor* Hamish Hamilton 1985

ILIH Kingsley Amis *I Like It Here* Gollancz 1958

IND *The Independent* (newspaper) 1989-1990

INN P Fitzgerald *Innocence* Collins 1986

IRANCN Anne Wroe *Lives, Lies and the Iran-Contra Affair* I B Tauris 1991

ISOH John Houston *In Search of Happiness* Lion Publishing 1990

ITAJ Arnold Wesker *I'm Talking about Jerusalem* Penguin 1960

ITFL Alexandre Jardin *In The Fast Lane* Quartet 1989

ITV Independent Television programmes 1967

JA Tony Tanner *Jane Austen* MacMillan Editions 1986

JFTR Stanley Price *Just for the Record* Michael Joseph 1961

JUNG A Storr *Jung* Fontana 1986

KLT Samuel Beckett *Krapp's Last Tape* Faber 1959

L *The Listener* (magazine) February-April 1963

LA Claire Rayner *Long Acre* Weidenfield & Nicholson 1982

LBA John Osborne *Look Back in Anger* Faber 1960

LC Sara Davidson *Loose Change* Fontana 1978

LFM Jim Weir *Letters from Moscow* Hodder & Stoughton 1989

LIFE Joanna Field *A Life of One's Own* Virago 1986 (orig. published 1934)

LLDR Alan Sillitoe *The Loneliness of the Long Distance Runner* W H Allen 1959

LM Margaret Forster *Lady's Maid* Chatto & Windus 1990

LPOL John Davis *Libyan Politics: Tribe and Revolution* I B Tauris 1987

LS Noel Annan *Leslie Stephen* University of Chicago Press 1979

LTOW Peter Ackroyd *The Last Testament of Oscar Wilde* Hamish Hamilton 1983

LWK Laurens van der Post *The Lost World of the Kalahari* Hogarth Press 1958

MAA Mary Gordon *Men and Angels* Cape 1985

MARX *Marxism Today* (magazine) June 1990 & March 1991

MBNK Midland Bank information leaflets 1989-90

MEF Eugene Forsey *A Life on the Fringe: Memoirs of Eugene Forsey* OUP (Canada) 1990

MFF Ian L Hunter *Memory: Fact and Fancies* Pelican 1961

MFM Field-Marshall Montgomery *The Memoirs of Field-Marshall Montgomery* Collins 1958

MJ Emma Blair *Maggie Jordan* Bantam 1990

MLT A.N. Wilson *The Life of John Milton* Oxford University Press 1983

MM	Muriel Spark *Memento Mori* Macmillan 1959
MOB	Melvyn Bragg *The Maid of Buttermere* Hodder & Stoughton 1987
MOQ	John Le Carré *A Murder of Quality* Penguin 1964
MP	D W Winnicott *The Maturational Processes and the Facilitating Environment* Hogarth Press 1965
MR	Peter Ustinov *My Russia* Macmillan 1983
MRJ	M Cox *M R James: An Informal Portrait* Oxford University Press 1983
MSAL	Anita Brookner *A Misalliance* Jonathan Cape 1986
NAP	William H C Smith *Napoleon III: The Pursuit of Prestige* Collins & Brown 1991
NATC	Angela Carter *Nights at the Circus* Chatto & Windus 1984
NDN	W R Geddes *Nine Dayak Nights* Oxford University Press 1957
NL	Rosalind Dymond Cartwright *Night Life: Explorations in Dreaming* Prentice-Hall 1977
NM	C P Snow *The New Men* Macmillan 1959
NS	*The New Scientist* (magazine) 1959-1991
NTG	Andrew Sinclair *The Need To Give* Sinclair-Stevenson 1990
NW	David Lodge *Nice Work* Secker & Warburg 1988
NY	*New Yorker* (magazine) 1988-1991
OBS	*The Observer* (newspaper) 1960-1992
OD	Kingsley Amis *The Old Devils* Hutchinson 1986
OI	Marghanita Laski *The Offshore Island* Cresset Press 1959
OMIH	Graham Greene *Our Man in Havana* William Heinemann 1958
ORRF	E Fairweather *Only The Rivers Run Free* Pluto Press 1984
OSOF	Alice Thomas Ellis *The Other Side of the Fire* Duckworth 1983
OXST	*Oxford Star* (newspaper) 1988-91
OXTD	*Oxford Today* (magazine) 1989-90
OXTM	*Oxford Times* (newspaper) 1988-91
PATM	Ray Harrison *Patently Murder* Constable 1991
PE	Hugh Clevely *Public Enemy* Cassell 1953
PL	C Northcote-Parkinson *Parkinson's Law* John Murray 1958
PM	William Golding *Pincher Martin* Faber 1956
POL	Bob Purdie *Politics in the Streets* Blackstaff Press 1990
POS	A S Byatt *Possession* Chatto & Windus 1990
PP	Robert Harling *The Paper Palace* Chatto & Windus 1951
PPAP	Margaret Forster *Private Papers* Chatto & Windus 1986
PPLA	Anthony Burgess *The Piano Players* Hutchinson 1986
PS	H Guntrip *Personality Structure and Human Interaction* Hogarth Press 1961
PTLB	André Maurois *Prometheus: The Life of Balzac* Bodley Head 1965
PTN	Robert Fisk *Pity The Nation: Lebanon at War* Oxford University Press 1990
PTTP	Martha Gellhorn *Pretty Tales for Tired People* Michael Joseph 1965
PVOH	Kazuo Ishiguro *A Pale View of Hills* Penguin 1983
PVP	Carolyn Bloomer *Principles of Visual Perception* Herbert Press 1990
PW	L P Hartley *A Perfect Woman* Penguin 1959
QA	Graham Greene *The Quiet American* William Heinemann 1955
R	Arnold Wesker *Roots* Penguin 1959
RAEU	Douglas Adams *The Restaurant at the End of the Universe* Pan 1980
RATT	John Braine *Room at the Top* Eyre & Spottiswoode 1957
REC	M Sarton *A Reckoning* Women's Press 1984
RFW	Neville Shute *Requiem for a Wren* William Heinemann 1955
RI	Michael Gilsenan *Recognizing Islam* I B Tauris 1990
RM	Compton McKenzie *The Rival Monster* Chatto & Windus 1952
RT	*Radio Times* (magazine) December 1960
RTH	Isaiah Berlin *Russian Thinkers* Hogarth Press 1978
RUN	*Running* (magazine) April 1991
RW	*Rugby World and Post* (magazine) March 1991
SAIL	P Copley *Sailing* Hamlyn 1976
SAMK	Frank O'Connor *The Saint and Mary Kate* Blackstaff Press 1990
SAS	*Sight and Sound* (magazine) 1988-91

SATS	Julian Barnes *Staring at the Sun* Jonathan Cape 1986
SC	*The Scotsman* (newspaper) 1960-72
SCIT	Jonathan Raban *Soft City* Collins Harvill 1988
SD	Sir Mortimer Wheeler *Still Digging* Michael Joseph 1955
SHCK	Colin Forbes *Shockwave* Pan 1990
SHE	*She* (magazine) October 1989, August 1990
SHOE	Asa Briggs *A Social History of England* Penguin 1987
SKIS	*Ski Survey* (magazine) February, March 1991
SML	William Cooper *Scenes from Married Life* MacMillan 1961
SNP	H J Eysenck *Sense and Nonsense in Psychology* Pelican 1961
SPL	William Cooper *Scenes from Provincial Life* Jonathan Cape 1950
SPTB	Richard Holt *Sport and the British* Oxford University Press 1990
SS	A Bell *Sydney Smith* Oxford University Press 1980
ST	*Sunday Times* (newspaper) 1967-1992
STDIY	B Cater & S Crabtree (Eds) *Sunday Times Book of D.I.Y.* Sphere books 1976
SU	Gerald Priestland *Something Understood* Deutsch 1988
SWIA	Shirley Conran *Superwoman in Action* Penguin 1979
T	*The Times* (newspaper) 1960-1992
TB	Iris Murdoch *The Bell* Chatto & Windus 1990
TBC	Fred Hoyle *The Black Cloud* William Heinemann 1957
TBU	M I Little *Transference Neurosis and Transference Psychosis: Toward Basic Unity* J Aronson, U.S. 1981
TC	Harold Pinter *The Caretaker* Methuen 1960
TCB	Agatha Christie *They Came to Baghdad* Collins 1951
TES	*The Times Educational Supplement* February, March 1963
TFD	P D James – *A Taste For Death* Faber 1986
TGLY	Kingsley Amis *Take a Girl Like You* Gollancz 1960
THES	*The Times Higher Education Supplement* 1988-91
THH	John Arden *The Happy Haven* Penguin 1962
THMAN	Oliver Sacks *The Man who Mistook his Wife for a Hat* Duckworth 1985
TK	Arnold Wesker *The Kitchen* Penguin 1960
TLE	Richard Hilary *The Last Enemy* Macmillan 1942
TLG	Raymond Chandler *The Long Goodbye* Hamish Hamilton 1953
TMB	Thomas Moore *The Minstrel Boy* (poem) 1834
TO	*Today* (magazine) June 1960
TOH	Shelagh Delaney *A Taste of Honey* Methuen 1960
TP	Celia Brayfield *The Prince* Chatto & Windus 1990
TRO	James Pope Hennessy *Anthony Trollope* Penguin 1986
TSE	R Bush (Ed.) *T.S. Eliot: A Study in Character and Style* Oxford University Press 1984
TSMP	Margaret Forster *The Seduction of Mrs Pendlebury* Secker & Warburg 1974
TST	John Wyndham *The Seeds of Time* Michael Joseph 1956
TT	G W Target *The Teachers* Penguin 1962
TTF	Jeremy Purseglove *Taming The Flood* Oxford University Press 1989
TTRIB	*Tampa Tribune* (newspaper) 1988-91
TU	Catherine Peters *Thackeray's Universe: Shifting Worlds of Imagination and Reality* Faber 1987
TVT	*T V Times* (magazine) 1975-78
TWL	Emma Tennant *Two Women of London* Faber 1989
UL	Richard Hoggart *The Uses of Literacy* Chatto & Windus 1954
UNXL	Alice Thomas Ellis *Unexplained Laughter* Duckworth 1985
US	Pamela Hansford Johnson *The Unspeakable Skipton* Macmillan 1959
UTN	Iris Murdoch *Under the Net* Chatto & Windus 1954
W	Graham Swift *Waterland* Heinemann 1983
WC	*Which Computer* (magazine) 1988-91
WDM	Angela Thirkell *What Did It Mean?* Hamish Hamilton 1954
WI	*Woman's Illustrated* (magazine) July 1960
WR	*Women: A Cultural Review* (journal of women's studies) Oxford University Press 1991

WTR Bruce Michael Cooper *Writing Technical Reports* Penguin 1964
YAA Michael Hastings *Yes, and After* Penguin 1962
YP *Yorkshire Post* (newspaper) 1988-91

Index of nouns etc used in headphrases

This index lists the nouns, adjectives and adverbs which appear in the headphrases in the dictionary, whether as part of an entirely fixed expression (eg *candle* in *not hold a candle to*), or as an optional part of an expression which is otherwise fixed (eg *right* in *take (right) on the chin*), or as alternative elements in an expression (eg *ease, rest* in *set sb's mind at ease/rest*). Also listed are the less fixed, but still restricted, elements of an expression which, though not included in the headphrase itself, are marked with the sign ⚠ in the group of collocating words of an entry (those listed after **S:**, **O:**, **o:** etc), eg **o:** ⚠ *the opportunity, the chance, the offer* at the entry *leap at*.

In addition some verbs are included in this index because they are not in the normal alphabetical sequence in the dictionary (eg *done* in *be over and done with*) or because they are subordinate to the main verb + particle/preposition entry (eg *take* in *sit up and take notice*).

The index will help users to find an entry by means of the non-verbal elements of the idiomatic expression, when they are unsure of the verb or of the construction in which it is used. Thus users may also explore the relationship of a noun with different verbs (eg *chance* with *jump at*, *leap at*, *leave to* etc).

The arrangement of the index is as follows:

1 Each index word (printed in **bold** type) is listed alphabetically and followed by the headphrase(s) (printed in light type) in the form in which it appears in the dictionary, a tilde (~) being used for the indexed word:

fun

make ~ of

poke ~ at

The headphrases themselves are arranged in the order in which they appear in the dictionary, and users will be able to find the main entries by their verb + preposition elements (*make + of*; *poke + at*).

2 When the indexed word does not appear in the headphrase but is one of the collocates in the dictionary entry, the tilde representing the indexed word is shown inside square brackets to mark it off clearly from the actual headphrase entry:

blazes

blow to 2 [~]

confidence

repose [~] in

The actual headphrases here are *blow to 2* and *repose in*. In some cases, when the collated word is (part of) a complex variation on the original headphrase, perhaps replacing one word in it or extending the idiom, this is shown by giving the variation in full, followed by a colon and the actual headphrase to which it is linked:

blazes

go to ~: go to hell etc

much

not amount to very ~: amount to 3

3 In some entries particular meanings (printed in *italic* type) of parts of speech are recorded for the sake of greater clarity

bed

put to ~ (*printing*)

right (*adj, adv*)

come out on the ~/wrong side

right/rights (*n*)

be within one's ~

Index of nouns etc used in headphrases

Index of nouns etc used in headphrases

Index of nouns etc used in headphrases

Index of nouns etc used in headphrases

Index of nouns etc used in headphrases

Index of nouns etc used in headphrases

Index of Nominalized Forms

This index covers all the nominalized forms (ie nouns derived from verbs + particles/prepositions) recorded in the main part of the dictionary (usually but not always the base form of the verb + particle/preposition, with or without a hyphen). For a full treatment of these forms, see *The Student's Guide to the Dictionary*.

Nominalized forms sometimes consist of the -ing form of the verb + particle/preposition (eg *(a) dressing-down, (a) summing-up, (a) telling-off*). The more common examples are recorded here.

Each nominal form is listed alphabetically and is followed by the headphrase(s) of the entry (or entries) in which it appears in the main text:

change-over change over (from) (to); change round/over

output put out 7

When the nominalized form is the headphrase itself, the fact is noted as follows:

fall-out *(main entry)*

(There is no finite verb + particle expression in regular use from which *fall-out* derives: a sentence such as **The nuclear tests fell out over a large area* is unacceptable.)

When a nominalized form is generally used attributively, a noun with which it commonly occurs is given in parentheses after it:

(a) see-through (blouse) see through 1

start-up (capital) start up 2

Whether a nominalized form appears as one word, as one word with a hyphen, or as two words, is often a matter of printing convention or individual usage. The entries in the dictionary and in this index generally show the most accepted form in British usage, but variations are recorded where appropriate, eg *(a) poke(-)about/around*.

Verb patterns and their transforms

[Vp] Verb + particle
The pilot ***took off*** *smoothly.*
The snow ***came down*** *thick and fast.*

[Vp nom] nominalized form
The pilot made a smooth ***take-off****.*
[Vp emph] emphatic transform
Down came *the snow thick and fast.*

[Vpr] Verb + prepositional phrase
He ***glanced through*** *the article quickly.*
You can ***cope with*** *these few extra people easily.*

[Vpr nom] nominalized form
He gave the article a quick ***glance-through****.*
[Vpr pass] passive transform
The article was ***glanced through*** *quickly.*
[Vpr adj] adjective transform
The quickly ***glanced-through*** *article …*
[Vpr emph] emphatic transform
With *these few extra people you can* ***cope*** *easily.*
[Vpr rel] relative transform
These people ***with*** *whom you can* ***cope*** *easily …*

[Vp.pr] Verb + particle + prepositional phrase
He eagerly ***looked forward to*** *his retirement.*
He just ***scraped along on*** *this low salary.*

[Vp.pr pass] passive transform
His retirement was eagerly ***looked forward to****.*
[Vp.pr adj] adjective transform
His eagerly ***looked-forward-to*** *retirement …*
[Vp.pr emph] emphatic transform
On *this low salary he just* ***scraped along****.*
[Vp.pr rel] relative transform
This low salary ***on*** *which he just* ***scraped along*** *…*

[Vn⇄p] Verb + object noun + particle
We can ***play*** *the recorded programmes (them)* ***back****/*
We can ***play back*** *the recorded programmes.*

[Vn⇄p nom] nominalized form
We can do a ***play-back*** *of the recorded programmes.*
[Vn⇄p pass] passive transform
The recorded programmes can be ***played back****.*
[Vn⇄p adj] adjective transform
The ***played-back*** *programmes …*